RESPONSES

Photograph by Ken Laffal Photography

University of Nebraska Press: Lincoln and London

Edited by Werner Hamacher, Neil Hertz, and Thomas Keenan

Responses

On Paul de Man's

Wartime Journalism

The paper in this book meets the minimum require-
ments of American National Standard for Information
Sciences—Permanence of Paper for Printed Library
Materials, ANSI Z39.48-1984.

In the interests of timeliness this book has been set
in type and printed from computer disks provided by the
editors and authors, without benefit of the editing and
proofreading normally provided by the publisher.

Library of Congress Cataloging-in-Publication Data
Responses: on Paul de Man's Wartime journalism / edited
by Werner Hamacher, Neil Hertz, and Thomas Keenan.
     p.   cm.
     ISBN 0-8032-2352-8 (alk. paper).   ISBN 0-8032-7243-X
(pbk.: alk. paper).
     1. Journalism, Military—Belgium—History—20th cen-
tury.   2. World War, 1939–1945—Journalism, Military—
Belgium—History.   3. De Man, Paul.   I. Hamacher,
Werner, 1948–   .   II. Hertz, Neil.   III. Keenan,
Thomas, 1959–   .
PN5267.M5R47   2989   88-29979
070.4'33—dc19   CIP

Contents

Preface

The publication of these *Responses,* a companion volume to Paul de Man's *Wartime Journalism, 1939–1943,* requires some explanation.

When Paul de Man's early writings came to light last year, the news that he had written a great deal before his emigration to America, and the discovery that much of the writing was for collaborationist journals in occupied Belgium, took most of his readers by surprise. The news was provocative, and it provoked, in the first instance, hasty gestures of explanation, condemnation or defense. It very soon became clear that if the questions raised by the existence of these writings —questions about the historical, ideological, and biographical contexts in which they were written, questions about their relations to de Man's later work as a literary critic and theorist—were to be taken seriously, the writings needed to be widely and rapidly disseminated. The editors of the *Oxford Literary Review* agreed to bring out a special issue which would reprint the articles—it was unclear at the time just how much writing was involved —along with, as an introductory text, the transcript of a round-table discussion that had taken place at the University of Alabama in early October, when Jacques Derrida had brought a selection of the articles to the attention of the participants in a colloquium there. On reflection, however, the transcript of their remarks— the first reactions of people who had had little time to consider some, but not all, of the articles—was judged inappropriate as an introduction.

After a month of discussions, we decided to undertake two projects: first, to collect and make available the entirety of de Man's Belgian writings; second, to open a forum for the publication of more studied responses from a larger group of scholars. It seemed to us that the public acts of a public figure could not simply be addressed as a matter of individual conscience; they demanded critical, public responses. In November, we wrote to fifty or so people here and abroad whose acquaintance with Paul de Man's writings from the 1950s on, with the theoretical issues they raised, or with the cultural and political history of occupied Europe, seemed to us to qualify them to produce particularly cogent and informed commentary. In order to initiate the process of responsible assessment, we addressed both critics and friends of Paul de Man's later work, as well as those without a clear *parti pris,* and offered to provide copies of all of de Man's wartime writings and "an opportunity for those who have something to say about these texts to publish their views." Many, but not all, responded with essays; others, learning of the projected volume, submitted unsolicited essays, which we have also included. We made clear to our contributors that we had no interest in monitoring what they wrote; they were told that they could write on any aspect of the subject, at any length, and that their texts would be printed as they were received, without editorial intervention on our part. We have kept to that principle, and the result is the present ungainly volume. It is considerably longer than it would have been had we not promised to print whatever was sent to us; there are more overlaps and redundancies in it than we would have liked; the articles themselves vary not only in the positions they take up—which was what we had anticipated—but also in their quality. We offer them as they are—a not unrepresentative sampling of the research and thinking, interpretive and polemical, that the discovery of Paul de Man's Belgian writings has elicited.

One further consequence of the size of this volume is noticeable on the title page: our publisher is the University of Nebraska Press. As the full extent of de Man's wartime journalism became clear, and as more responses, many of them lengthy, came in, our manuscripts grew. It became impossible for the small editorial staff of the *Oxford Literary Review* to handle the preparation of the volumes, and the task was turned over to Nebraska, which had already been involved as our American distributor. We are grateful to the editors of the *OLR* for their early help and encouragement, and to the staff of the University of Nebraska Press for their willingness to take on a demanding project late in the day.

One of our texts has been previously published: Jacques Derrida's essay first appeared in *Critical Inquiry* (March 1988), and it has since been slightly revised for *Mémoires: pour Paul de Man* (Paris: Galilée, 1988). We print the revised version.

With the assistance of some of our contributors, a number of Belgian historians (in particular, Chantal Kesteloot of the Centre de Recherches et d'Etudes Historiques de la Seconde Guerre Mondiale in Brussels), and some of Paul de Man's contemporaries, we have collected the historical and biographical material to be found in the Chronology. The other contributions by the editors have, for reasons of timing, been located at the end of this volume. The names of those who helped us are listed in the acknowledgements, but we wish to express our gratitude to them here as well.

WH, NH, TK
Baltimore, October 1988

Acknowledgements

Many people have helped in the preparation of the chronology, the notes added to Edouard Colinet's letter, and the collection of documents and information for this book. The editors would like to thank: Myriam Abramowicz, Frank Albers, David Braybrooke, Bruno Bernaerts, Edouard Colinet, Alain Dantoing, Els de Bens, Ortwin de Graef, Pierre de Ligne, Jan R. de Man, Marc de Man, Patricia de Man, Jacques Derrida, F. K. De Vos, Charles Dosogne, Georges Goriely, José Gotovich, Anne (Baraghian) Ipsen, Shaun Irlam, Gilbert Jaeger, Peggy Kamuf, Adella Englert Kay, Chantal Kesteloot, Georges Lambrichs, Christian Lepoivre, Erik Leroy, Jean Lescure, Sura Levine, Marie-Rose Logan, Christie McDonald, Philippe Muret, Mme. Chaim Perelman, Georges Poulet, Raymond Rifflet, Moshe Ron, Hilda (Rosner) Pomerantz, Francis Sartorius, Esther Sluszny, Marcel Slusny, Maxime Steinberg, Jean Stengers, Allan Stoekl, Frida Vandervelden, Walter Van Glabbeek, Andrzej Warminski, Paul Willems, Hendrik Woods.

We have also relied on a number of printed sources. Thanks particularly to Chantal Kesteloot of the Centre de Recherches et d'Etudes Historiques de la Seconde Guerre Mondiale (CREHSGM), Brussels, and to Ortwin de Graef, we were able to examine unpublished material including reports from the Belgian Auditorat Général on *Le Soir,* the Agence/Agentschap Dechenne, and the Editions de la Toison d'Or; the dossier in the Fonds Union Nationale de la Presse Clandestine on *L'Insoumis*; files on the Propaganda Abteilung Belgien, Raymond de Becker, and the press during the occupation of Belgium; copies of *Galerie des Traitres, L'Etudiant,* and *Debout*; and Paul de Man's birth and educational records. Thanks to the Bibliothèque Royale Albert I in Brussels, the Service des Archives at the Université Libre de Bruxelles, and the Library of the Hoover Institution at Stanford University, we consulted *Jeudi, Les Cahiers du Libre Examen, Le Soir, Het Vlaamsche Land,* and the *Bibliographie Dechenne,* as well as the *Bulletin des Lettres,* the *Bulletin de la Toison d'Or,* and *Messages.* Among the books and articles we found most useful are: Jean-Marie Apostolidès, *Les métamorphoses de Tintin* (Paris; Seghers, 1984); Els de Bens, *De Belgische dagbladpers onder Duitse censuur (1940–1944)* (Antwerp/Utrecht: Nederlandsche Boekhandel, 1973), and "La Presse au Temps de l'Occupation de la Belgique (1940–1944)," in *Revue d'histoire de la deuxième guerre mondiale* 80 (October 1970), 1–28; Walter De Bock, *Les plus belles années d'une génération* (Berchem [Belgium]: EPO, 1983), 63–76; Paul Delandsheere and Alphonse Ooms, *La Belgique sous les Nazis,* four volumes (Brussels: L'Edition Universelle, [1946–47]); Bernard Delcord, "A propos de quelques 'chapelles' politico-littéraires en Belgique (1919–1945)," in *Cahiers du CREHSGM* 10 (November 1986),

153–205; Hendrik de Man, *Cavalier seul: 45 années de socialisme européen* (Geneva: Cheval Ailé, 1948) and *Gegen den Strom: Memoiren eines europäischen Sozialisten* (Stuttgart: Deutsche Verlags-Anstalt, 1953); Peter Dodge, *Beyond Marxism: The Faith and Works of Hendrik de Man* (The Hague: Martinus Nijhoff, 1966) and *A Documentary Study of Hendrik de Man, Socialist Critic of Marxism* (Princeton: Princeton University Press, 1979); Jean Dujardin, "Belgique," in Hélène Eck, ed. *La guerre des ondes: Histoire des radios de langue française pendant la Deuxième Guerre mondiale* (Paris: Armand Colin, 1985), 157–225; Michel Fauré, *Histoire du surréalisme sous l'Occupation* (Paris: Table Ronde, 1982); Jules Gérard-Libois and José Gotovitch, *L'An 40: La Belgique occupée* (Brussels: CRISP, 1971); Pascal Fouché, *L'édition française sous l'occupation 1940–1944* (Paris: Bibliothèque de Littérature française contemporaine, 1987); Philip Friedman, *Roads to Extinction: Essays on the Holocaust* (New York and Philadelphia: Jewish Pub. Soc., 1980), 34–58; Jo Gérard, *La Belgique sous l'occupation 1940–1944* (Brussels: Meddens, 1974); Jan-Albert Goris, ed. and trans., *Belgium under occupation* (New York: Moretus Press and Belgian Government Information Center, 1947); Gerhard Heller, *Un Allemand à Paris 1940–1944* (Paris: Seuil, 1981); Raul Hilberg, *The Destruction of the European Jews,* revised definitive edition (New York and London: Holmes and Meier, 1985); Jacques de Launay and Jacques Offergeld, *La vie quotidienne des belges sous l'occupation (1940–1945)* (Brussels: Paul Legrain, 1982); Nora Levin, *The Holocaust* (New York: Schocken, 1973); Gérard Loiseaux, *La littérature de la défaite et de la collaboration* (Paris: Publications de la Sorbonne, 1984); Marcel Liebman, *Né juif: Une enfance juive pendant la guerre* (Paris-Gembloux: Duculot, 1977); Henri Neuman, *Avant qu'il ne soit trop tard: portraits de résistants* (Paris-Gembloux: Duculot, 1985); Pascal Ory, *Les collaborateurs 1940–1945* (Paris: Seuil, 1976); Boris Rousseeuw, *Van hier tot Peking: Over Willem Elsschot* (Antwerp: Dedalus, 1983); Robert Paxton, *Vichy France: Old Guard and New Order, 1940–1944* (New York: Alfred A. Knopf, 1972); Anne Somerhausen, *Written in Darkness: A Belgian Woman's Record of the Occupation, 1940–1945* (New York: Alfred A. Knopf, 1946); Georgette Smolski, "L'U.L.B. devant la guerre d'Espagne," in *Revue belge d'histoire contemporaine* 18: 1–2 (1987), 419–446; Maxime Steinberg, *Le Dossier Bruxelles-Auschwitz* (Brussels: Comité Belge de Soutien . . . , 1980); Maxime Steinberg and Serge Klarsfeld, *Mémorial de la déportation des Juifs de Belgique* (Brussels: Union des Déportés Juifs en Belgique, 1982); Zeev Sternhell, *Neither Right nor Left: Fascist Ideology in France* (Berkeley: University of California Press, 1986); Paul Struye, *L'évolution du sentiment publique en Belgique sous l'occupation allemande* (Brussels: Editions Lumière, 1945); George K.

Tanham, *Contribution à l'histoire de la résistance belge 1940–1944* (Brussels: Presses Universitaires de Bruxelles, 1971); Jacques Willequet, *La Belgique sous la botte: résistances et collaborations* (Paris: Editions Universitaires, 1986); Robert Wistrich, *Who's Who in Nazi Germany* (New York: Macmillan, 1982); Joseph Wulf, *Literatur und Dichtung im III Reich: Eine Dokumentation* (Frankfurt-Berlin-Wien: Ullstein, 1983) and *Presse und Rundfunk im III Reich* (Gütersloh: Mohn, 1964); L. Yahil, "Madagascar: Phantom of a Solution for the Jewish Question," in Bela Vago and George Mosse, eds., *Jews and non-Jews in Eastern Europe* (New York: John Wiley and Sons, 1974), 315–334; and *Quarantième Anniversaire de la Fermeture de l'Université Libre de Bruxelles (25 novembre 1941),* U.L.B. *Etudes et monographies* 2 (1987).

Paul de Man: A Chronology, 1919–1949

1919

6 December: Paul Adolph Michel Deman born in Antwerp, son of Jan Robert de Man (b. 1890) and Magdalena Maria Adolphina de Braey (b. 1893). Father, known as Robert (Bob), grandson of the Flemish poet Jan van Beers, is manufacturer of medical instruments and x-ray equipment, accomplished amateur musician. Uncle, Robert's brother, is politician and socialist theorist Hendrik (Henri) de Man (b. 1885). PDM has one sibling, Hendrik, born 1915. Family lives in Antwerp, with summer house in countryside north of city at Kalmthout.

1933

30 January: Hitler chancellor of German Reich.

April: Hendrik de Man leaves University of Frankfurt, where he held chair in social psychology and was involved in socialist and anti-Nazi political activities, and returns to Brussels; teaches at Université Libre de Bruxelles (ULB), leader in Belgian socialist party, Parti Ouvrier Belge (POB).

24–25 December: Meeting in Brussels, POB Congress elects Hendrik de Man vice-president and adopts his "Plan du travail," program to end mass unemployment by public works and structural changes including nationalized control of credit, banking, and some monopolies.

1935

29 March: POB, breaking with tradition, joins coalition Van Zeeland government; Hendrik de Man named Minister of Public Works and Unemployment Reduction.

3 October: Italian troops invade Ethiopia.

1936

7 March: Hitler dissolves Treaty of Locarno, remilitarizes Rhineland.

3 May: Popular Front wins majority in French elections; Léon Blum heads government.

20 June: Death of PDM's brother Hendrik in bicycle accident at railroad crossing.

24 June: Second Van Zeeland government; Hendrik de Man is Minister of Finance.

16 July: Outbreak of Spanish Civil War.

19 August: Moscow purge trials begin; within eighteen months, almost 100 Soviet Central Committee members elected in 1934 tried and executed.

Fall: PDM's last year of high school at Koninklijke Athenaeum, Antwerp, begins.

1937

1 March: First issue of *Les Cahiers du Libre Examen,* monthly journal of Cercle du Libre Examen, left-liberal student group at Université Libre de Bruxelles (ULB). Founded by student Charles Dosogne, *Cahiers'* second issue (April) states its position: "libre-exameniste, democratic, anticlerical, antidogmagtic, and antifascist."

May: Stalinist suppression of anarchist and POUM forces in Barcelona.

20 June: Suicide of PDM's mother.

July: PDM graduates from Athenaeum magna cum laude, passes entrance exam for Ecole Polytechnique at ULB.

October: PDM enters Ecole Polytechnique to study engineering, and soon joins Cercle du Libre Examen. While at ULB, PDM lunches weekly with his uncle Hendrik and Hendrik's son Jan; for first three years at ULB (1937–8 through 1939–40), PDM continues to live with his father in Antwerp and commutes to Brussels, sometimes staying in Jan's apartment.

Hendrik de Man is regular guest of Edouard and Lucienne Didier, whose Brussels salon is meeting place in prewar years for various Belgian politicians and intellectuals—right- and left-wing—as well as German diplomats such as Otto Abetz and Max Liebe, members of Ribbentrop's circle. Other visitors include French intellectuals Brasillach, Fabre-Luce, and Montherlant, Belgian writers Louis Carette and Raymond de Becker, and, infrequently, socialist politician P.-H. Spaak and writer Robert Poulet.

1938

March: Hendrik de Man resigns from post as Minister of Finance.

13 March: Annexation (Anschluss) of Austria by Germany.

July: PDM finishes year of engineering studies at ULB but does not take examinations leading to a degree.

Meeting in Evian, France, at Roosevelt's initiative, representatives of 32 nations consider international refugee problems, especially fate of German Jewry. No immigration policies changed, and no plans adopted, but talks concern plans to re-settle German Jews in Madagascar, British Guinea, Kenya, or Alaska. From 1938 on, such proposals are frequent topic of high-level diplomatic discussions between, a.o., Hitler, Chamberlain, Mussolini, Rosenberg, Pope Pius XII, and French government.

September: Defeat of Popular Front in France.

29–30 September: Munich Pact signed, authorizes ceding to Germany of German-speaking provinces in Czechoslovakia (Sudetenland).

October: PDM transfers to Faculty of Sciences (ULB), begins studies in chemistry. Wide reading in philosophy and literature (English novels, German romanticism); weekly literary discussions bring together PDM, Georges Lambrichs, Dosogne, Frida Vandervelden, Marcel Sluszny, other members of Cercle du Libre Examen.

Fall: Socialist and communist members of the ULB's Etudiants Socialistes Unifiés threaten to split over Moscow Trials; unity maintained by appeal to importance of efforts to aid Republican Spain.

9 November: "Kristallnacht": Jews, their stores, homes, and synagogues across Germany are attacked.

December: Hendrik de Man undertakes peace mission, aimed at second Munich conference, on behalf of Belgian King Leopold III and neutral "Oslo nations." Abandoned after three months.

1939

27 January: ULB students call for lifting of embargo on arms to Republican Spain; after street demonstration, student leaders (including Edouard Colinet, Louis Fonsny, Marcel Sluszny of Libre Examen) meet with minister P.-H. Spaak.

Winter-Spring: PDM meets future wife, Anaïde Baraghian (AB); recently arrived from Romania, she is married to Gilbert Jaeger (GJ); both enrolled at ULB, involved in literary and political discussions within Libre Examen.

15–16 March: German troops occupy Czechoslovakia; establishment of "Reichs-Protektorat" in Böhmen and Mähren (Sudetenland).

23 March: First issue of *Jeudi,* weekly (later biweekly) newspaper of Cercle du Libre Examen. PDM writes on "L'examen médical des étudiants"; publishes four more articles in *Jeudi* during spring of 1939.

27 March: Fall of Madrid to Franco's forces, final defeat of Spanish Republicans.

May: Hendrik de Man elected president of POB.

Spring–Summer: ULB's Etudiants Socialistes (anti-Stalinist socialists, including PDM, Dosogne, Fonsny, Georges Goriely, Sluszny) split from Etudiants Socialistes Unifiés.

23 August: Hitler-Stalin non-aggression pact.

1 September: Germany invades Poland.

3 September: France and Great Britain declare war on Germany. Official policy of Belgian government had been and remains one of strict neutrality. Hendrik de Man enters new "government of national union" as Minister without portfolio.

17 September: Red Army enters eastern Poland.

October: PDM passes his 1ère candidature en sciences chimiques, "with distinction." Joins editorial boards of *Cahiers du Libre Examen* (including Pierre de Ligne, Dosogne, Jaeger, Youra Livchitz, Sluszny) and *Jeudi* (including Jean Burgers, Colinet, Lambrichs, Sluszny).

November: Cercle du Libre Examen votes to expel Stalinist members. Anti-German and anti-Soviet demonstrations at ULB.

30 November: Russia attacks Finland.

1940

January: Hendrik de Man leaves government, serves in military as captain attached directly to King's Service.

Winter: As "drôle de guerre" intensifies, student protests against German and Soviet aggressions continue in Brussels. Debates within Cercle du Libre Examen between "socialist interventionists" (favoring Belgian military alliance with France and Britain) and "socialist neutralists" (anti-war antifascists). PDM, in latter group, publishes three articles in *Jeudi*, including two in defense of Belgian neutrality. Writes two articles on literature in *Cahiers* (issues of January and February).

February: PDM takes over from Dosogne as "directeur" of *Cahiers du Libre Examen*: edits its final two issues (on "Civilisation Occidentale" and "Totalitarisme") before CLE ceases publication during German occupation. Probably writes unsigned editorial for issue on "Civilisation Occidentale."

9 April: German army enters Denmark and Norway.

10 April: Belgian government rejects offers of preventive intervention from France and Britain, reaffirms policy of neutrality.

10 May: Blitzkrieg invasion of (neutral) Belgium by German army. Some Belgian ministers leave Brussels to set up government in exile in France. Exodus of about two million Belgians south through France. PDM and AB flee Belgium by train as far as Bagnères de Luchon, in French Pyrénées, where they spend summer months waiting, unsuccessfully, for permission to cross into Spain.

28 May: King Leopold III, following advice of Hendrik de Man and against that of government in France, surrenders Belgian army unconditionally; chooses to remain in Belgium as "prisoner of war" rather than join government. Belgium governed by Militärverwaltung, German military administration, not civilian (SS) regime as in Holland; General Alexander von Falkenhausen is Militärbefehlshaber für Belgien und Nord-Frankreich. Belgian state bureaucracy left gener-

ally intact; ministerial "secretaries general" direct state apparatus in absence of government ministers.

10 June: Appropriation by German military authorities of Agence/Agentschap Dechenne, Brussels, distribution firm for newspapers, periodicals, and books. Placed under control of German director Lothar von Balluseck from Reichsverband deutscher Zeitungsverleger; seizure given quasilegal form when principal shareholder Hachette required to sell stock to Reichsverband. Agency used to centralize German control over newspaper distribution.

14 June: First issue of *Le Soir* under occupation. Published in Brussels, *Le Soir* had been Belgium's largest newspaper; in absence of its owners (fled to France), its name and facilities have been appropriated by German authorities, and it is turned over to new editorial staff. Widely read during occupation; derisively known as *Le Soir volé*. Among its 25 full-time editors are Raymond de Becker, "Tintin et Milou" cartoonist Georges Remy (Hergé), as well as de Ligne and Fonsny from Cercle du Libre Examen.

14 and 18 June: German military administration decrees that prior approval required for all Belgian newspapers and journals started or re-started at this time, and imposes strict preventive censorship. *Le Soir*, like all other publications, censored by Militärverwaltung's Propaganda Abteilung. *Cahiers du Libre Examen* and *Jeudi* do not resume publication.

16 June: Maréchal Philippe Pétain, president of council of IIIe Republic.

19 June: Capitulation of France.

25 June: France signs armistice with Germany, dividing country into two zones: north, including Paris, occupied by German troops; south, including Vichy, unoccupied. Legal French government at Vichy, led by Pétain, maintains nominal sovereignty over entire nation, "except for the rights of the occupying power." Although German military administration in effect governs, significant differences do remain between zones; e.g., Vichy regime imposes strict censorship rules, while Germans in Paris do not.

3 July: Hendrik de Man, acting as president of POB, publishes "Manifeste aux membres du POB," dated 28 June: "do not believe it is necessary to resist the occupant; accept the fact of his victory and try rather to draw lessons from it"; "for the working classes and for socialism, this collapse of a decrepit world, far from being a disaster, is a deliverance . . . Consider the political role of POB as finished."

9–10 July: French National Assembly at Vichy votes to abandon 1875 Constitution and give full powers to Pétain.

14 July: Hitler's orders for occupation of Belgium: "The Führer has not reached a definite decision concerning the future of the Belgian state. For the time being, he wishes all possible consideration for the Flemish, incl. the return of the Flemish prisoners of war to their homeland. No favor should be accorded to the Walloons."

August: PDM and AB return to Brussels from "exodus" in France, live at Square des Latins near ULB.

13 August: Occupation authorities decree removal from Belgian bookstores of "all aggressive ["anti-German"] literature of French, English, and Dutch origin."

20 August: Occupation authorities in Belgium require that all new books treating political and military affairs (including race, Judaism, and free-masonry) be submitted to censors in advance. 100 of 600 books reviewed in 1940 rejected.

29 August: Creation of SS concentration camp at Breendonck, between Brussels and Antwerp. During occupation, 3860 people interned there; more than 300 killed.

August–September: German authorities in Paris and Brussels conduct "épuration" or purging of bookstores, based on preliminary "Liste Bernhard" of banned books.

3 September: Belgian administration decrees provisional suspension of unemployment benefits to those refusing to accept work in Germany; later withdrawn. German authorities set weekly quota of 5600 "voluntary" Belgian workers for German industry, to be recruited with cooperation of Belgian officials.

28 September: "Convention de censure" between German occupation authorities and French publishers signed. No German censorship in occupied zone (Vichy maintains strict censorship in unoccupied zone). Publishers agree to auto-censorship: no works by Jews, free-masons, or "anti-German" writers; can ask for advice from German officials if seizure feared; allowed to take chances and publish without clearance, at own risk. At same time, first "Liste Otto" published, naming French "Ouvrages retirés de la vente par les éditeurs ou interdits par les autorités allemands." Targets are books of an "esprit mensonger et tendancieux," and "in particular, publications of political refugees or Jewish writers," including works by Aragon, Benda, Franz Boas, Claudel, Duhamel, Einstein, Freud, Heine, Herzl, Jung, Kracauer, Lefebvre, Rosa Luxemburg, Malraux, Heinrich and Thomas Mann, Maurois, Nizan, Trotsky, Wells, Arnold and Stefan Zweig, and *Zeitschrift für Sozialforschung*.

October: PDM passes his 2ème candidature in chemical sciences, roughly equivalent to bachelor's degree, "with distinction"; transfers to ULB program in social sciences, reading philosophy and preparing for examinations leading to 1ère license. Cousin Jan de Man leaves Brussels to work in Wallonia. *Le Soir* circulation at more than 275,000 copies.

1 October: Paul Colin, extreme right-wing editor of weekly *Cassandre*, publishes first issue of *Le Nouveau Journal*, Brussels' other major francophone collaborationist newspaper besides *Le Soir*; its editor-in-chief is Robert Poulet.

10 October: Lacking staff to practice rigorous pre-publication censorship of newspapers and periodicals, German Propaganda Abteilung in Belgium adopts policy of a posteriori control: only important political articles censored in advance; after-the-fact penalties and sanctions for transgressive articles; PA supplies ready-made articles and illustrations, as well as regular directives on stories and their interpretations, provided in weekly press conferences and on Belgapress wire.

28 October: German military command in Belgium issues first major Jewish ordinance, defining "Jews" and requiring them to register and have identity cards marked (43,000 people are registered in Belgium). Bans Jews from civil service, law, teaching, press and radio, effective 31 December.

31 October: Four Belgian cabinet ministers officially reconstitute government in exile in London. (Unlike France, Belgium has no collaborationist national government under occupation.)

November: Gestapo "perquisition" at apartment of PDM, AB, and GJ; day of interrogation by Germans about PDM's involvement in Cercle du Libre Examen.

19 November: King Leopold III and Hitler meet at Berchtesgaden.

21 November: German authorities require all Belgian publishers and bookstores to join professional associations: Cercle belge de la Librairie, or Vereening ter Bevordering van het Vlaamsche Boekwezen.

22 November: Founding of Union des Travailleurs Manuels et Intellectuels (UTMI), single central federation of Belgian labor unions, organized by Hendrik de Man and others.

December: First issue under occupation of *Nouvelle Revue Française* appears in Paris, with texts by Alain, Eluard, Gide, Valéry; new director, installed by Germans, is Pierre Drieu la Rochelle.

5 December: Raymond de Becker named editor-in-chief of *Le Soir*.

17 December: Approximately 90,000 Belgian "voluntary" workers have gone to work in German economy.

24 December: PDM's first article, on "Audition d'élèves au Conservatoire," appears in *Le Soir*. PDM possibly introduced to de Becker by Hendrik de Man. First articles primarily on musical and cultural events; as free-lance contributor, publishes 170 signed articles, including regular "chronique littéraire," over next two years. PDM, still a student at ULB, is not an editor, rarely at *Soir* offices; given "carte blanche" to submit articles directly.

1941

January: Birth of Hendrik, first son of AB and PDM. Sometime in 1941, family moves from Square des Latins to Boulevard Saint-Michel in Brussels. Friends during occupation are politically heterogenous: including Goriely, de Lignes, Slusznys, Dosogne and Vandervelden, Lambrichs, Jaeger, from ULB; author-broadcaster Louis Carette; Flemish nationalist Lode Claes; author Paul Willems and Elsa de Groodt; musician-composers Oscar Espla and André Souris. PDM's literary society is "perhaps a café at the Porte Louise in Brussels where, on occasion, writers like Lambrichs, [Paul] Colinet, [Marcel] Lecomte, and perhaps Souris and [Camille] Goemans, used sometimes to meet" (Willems). Vacations during summer chez Dosogne/Vandervelden, in Villers-la-Ville, and at family house in Kalmthout. "He does not seem to have had any political affiliations, neither with resistance groups nor with collaborators" (Frank Albers).

1 January: *Het Vlaamsche Land,* small Flemish-language daily, begins publication in Antwerp, sponsored by the German authorities and printed on presses of what had been the *Gazet van Antwerpen.*

20 January: German authorities require 10,000 Belgian workers for Todt Organization; "work centers for recalcitrant unemployed people will be organized."

28 January: After ULB students boycott classes by German professor, Gestapo arrests and questions many former student activists, including leaders of Cercle du Libre Examen. Marcel Sluszny jailed for three months.

1 February: Opening in Brussels of exhibition on "La Vérité sur la franc-maçonnerie." Period of most extensive anti-semitic and anti-masonic propaganda in *Le Soir* (roughly November 1940 to April 1941), including front-page articles by editor Léon Van Huffel, working for SD: "Pour un antisémitisme racial" (29 Jan.), "Y a-t-il une race juive?" (10 Feb.), "Vers une solution européenne du problème juif" (9 Apr.).

9 February: First anti-Jewish riot in Amsterdam, organized by Germans. Answered by strikes of several thousand workers.

25 February: PDM begins regular "chronique littéraire" in Tuesday issues of *Le Soir.*

4 March: PDM writes "Les Juifs dans la Littérature actuelle," "under pressure" (AB) of "demand" (GJ) by de Becker; published on back page of *Le Soir* titled "Les Juifs et Nous: Les Aspects Culturels," organized by Van Huffel.

12 March: Severe food shortages in Belgium: almost two million people, or about a fifth of the population, require aid from welfare organization "Secours d'Hiver." Hunger drives many Belgians to accept work in German industry.

15 March: Agence Dechenne given monopoly over distribution of all newspapers in Belgium.

25 March: Publishing house Editions de la Toisin d'Or founded; directed by Raymond de Becker, Pierre Daye, and Edouard Didier, backed by Ribbentrop's Foreign Office through its Mundus publishing group. With offices in Brussels and Paris, Toison d'Or plans extensive list of political and literary publications, especially translations from German and Flemish, with aim of "giving Belgian authors the chance to be published in their country, and . . . putting the Belgian public in contact with the most remarkable works of nordic and germanic culture." Toison d'Or and *Le Soir,* both run by de Becker, have close ties.

28 March: Reichsleiter Alfred Rosenberg, in inaugural address at Frankfurt "Institute for Study of the Jewish Problem," calls for creation of extra-European "Jewish Reserve": "For Europe, the Jewish problem will not have found its solution until the last Jew has left the European continent" (quoted in *Le Soir*).

14 April: Two synagogues sacked in Antwerp anti-Jewish riot.

7 May: Hendrik de Man's memoirs, titled *Après Coup,* first book published by Editions de la Toison d'Or; extensively excerpted in *Le Soir* during May.

June: Propaganda Abteilung Frankreich in Paris draws up "Gesamtliste des fördernswerten Schrifttums bis 31.12.42," list of about 200 French books, political and literary, to be promoted by German propaganda officials; includes sections on "Neues Deutschland" and "Aktiv-Schrifttum" (anti-democratic, -American, -English, -communist, -gaullist, -semitic, and -masonic writings), as well as works of history and literature by, a.o., Benoist-Méchin, Bonnard, Brasillach, Chardonne, de Jouvenel, Drieu, Fabre-Luce, Fallada, Giono, Goethe, Grimm, Jünger, Montherlant, Sieburg, and Stehr.

2 June: First act of armed resistance in Brussels: shooting of a German officer.

7–8 June: PDM publishes interview with Abel Bonnard in *Le Soir,* following Bonnard's Brussels lecture on "La constitution d'une élite dans l'Europe nouvelle."

13 June: German military decree requires that trilingual sign marking "Jewish Enterprise" be placed on all businesses in Belgium owned by Jews, and that Jews make declarations of wealth.

21–22 June: Announcement of "concours littéraire" in *Le Soir*: contest for best new novel about the war, conducted by PDM, concluded 19 September 1942.

22 June: Operation Barbarossa: Germany invades Russia.

July: Hendrik de Man prohibited by German authorities from speaking in public in Belgium.

6 July: Military administration in Belgium announces that "all unemployed fit for work must present themselves daily at the Werbstelle [German hiring offices]. Those who refuse work will be considered asocial and subjected to disciplinary measures of forced labor."

9 July: Publication in Brussels of list of books banned by occupation authorities in Belgium, titled "Tegen ophitsing en wanorder" or "Contre l'excitation à la haine et au désordre." Based on Otto list, it includes about 1500 books, "above all, works whose authors, political emigrés and Jewish writers, have abused the hospitality provided them and led their hosts . . . to the edge of the abyss."

August: First issue of monthly *Bibliographie* of Agence Dechenne, containing detailed listing and brief reviews of new books published in Belgium, Germany, France, and Holland. Dechenne also distributes newspapers, periodicals, books, and paper; sells books and art reproductions; and runs literary and publishing information service.

18 August: Public ceremony marking 200,000th Belgian worker departing for "voluntary labor service in Germany."

23 August: 6000 Jews in Paris rounded up for internment at Drancy, in what *Le Soir* reports as "a vast anti-Jewish operation." 3600 Polish Jews had already been interned in May.

September: PDM, along with three other former members of Cercle du Libre Examen, denounced for working at *Le Soir*, in *L'Etudiant*, clandestine "Journal des Etudiants Socialistes Unifiés" at ULB.

5 September: Jews in Belgium restricted to living in Brussels, Antwerp, Liège, or Charleroi; 8:00 pm to 7:00 am curfew imposed.

October: PDM does not take examinations for 1ère license en sciences sociales.

Le Soir circulation figures show 270,000 readers daily.

24 October: Founding at Weimar of Nazi-sponsored European Society of Writers. Hans Carossa is president; Belgian delegates to "Congress of European Writers" are Filip de Pillecijn, Félix Timmermans, and F. Vercnocke; French delegates include Bonnard, Brasillach, Chardonne, Drieu, and Jouhandeau.

November: Hendrik de Man leaves Belgium for France, where for the next year he lives in Paris and Haute Savoie, engages in public activities acceptable to occupation authorities, but is also in contact with French resistants and informed about plot to kill Hitler. Returns to Belgium infrequently.

25 November: ULB closes, refusing to accept attempted interference by German authorities; PDM has received only candidature in chemistry.

Occupation authorities found "Association des Juifs en Belgique," Belgian "Judenrat"; membership obligatory for all Jews living in Belgium.

7 December: United States enters the war.

1942

10–11 January: PDM publishes interview with Paul Valéry in *Le Soir*, following Valéry's Brussels lecture on "Souvenirs poétiques."

20 January: At Wannsee conference in Berlin, plans for extermination of European Jews are discussed and agreed upon: 43,000 Jews in Belgium included.

27 January: Militärverwaltung decree prevents Jews from leaving Belgium.

February: PDM's first contribution to *Bibliographie Dechenne*, essay on "Ontwikkeling der Zuid-Nederlandsche Letterkunde." Publishes 7 essays and 93 short book reviews over next thirteen months, most of them in French. PDM's job at Agence Dechenne involves considerable work on *Bibliographie*, allowing him to obtain job for Georges Lambrichs there, and trips to Paris to import new books.

25 February: Brussels opening of major propaganda exposition on German books, runs for two weeks at Palais des Beaux-Arts. Reviewed by PDM in *Le Soir* 2 March.

March: Editions de la Toison d'Or publishes *Le double visage*, PDM's French translation of Paul Alverdes' *Das Zwiegesicht* (München: Langen und Müller, 1937). PDM holds job as "lecteur" at Toison d'Or, with some responsibility for selecting works and hiring translators (including Lambrichs, Goriely, H. Rosner).

6 March: German military authorities in Belgium institute obligatory labor service for some categories of workers. In 1941, more than 212,000 workers had gone to work "voluntarily" in Germany; in 1942, another 131,000 will go.

15 March: First issue under occupation of *Messages: Cahiers de la poésie française*, published in Paris by Jean Lescure; "une sorte d'anti-NRF" (Heller), "nettement résistant" (Lescure).

Because published in occupied zone, uncensored, but writers and editors at some risk.

24 March: First meeting of Association of Belgian Journalists. President is Paul Colin. All full-time journalists must be members of association; Jews and members of clandestine organizations are not permitted. PDM was not a member.

29 March: Hendrik de Man dissociates himself from UTMI after appointment of militant pro-Nazi as its head; letter of protest publicly circulated.

29–30 March: First of ten articles by PDM in *Het Vlaamsche Land*, on "Kunst als spiegel van het wezen der volkeren: Beschouwingen over *Geist der Nationen* van A. E. Brinckmann."

31 March: Average daily circulation figures for Belgian newspapers show: *Le Soir,* at 255,000 copies each afternoon, is most widely read paper in Belgium; *Het Vlaamsche Land,* 21,000 copies; *Le Nouveau Journal,* 35,000; *Cassandre,* 30,000 weekly.

26 April: New Vichy government formed, under prime minister Pierre Laval (Abel Bonnard named Minister of National Education). Pres. Roosevelt recalls American ambassador Leahy in protest, leaving only US chargé d'affaires at Vichy for remainder of occupation.

27 April: German authorities in Paris (occupied zone), on pretext of paper shortage, institute de facto censorship, requiring that all publications be submitted in advance to Propaganda Abteilung for approval and assignment of authorization number. Now both zones are subject to censorship.

June: Editions de la Toison d'Or publishes *Le soldat Johan,* PDM's French translation of Filip de Pillecijn's Flemish novel *De Soldaat Johan* (Amsterdam: Van Kampen, 1941). Hendrik de Man's *Reflexions sur la paix,* also published by Toison d'Or, seized and banned by military authorities, in spite of pre-publication approval by censors.

Belgian industries required to submit lists of workers at their factories to German labor officials. Many refuse.

1 June: Jews in Belgium and France required by order of German military command to begin wearing yellow Star-of-David on their outer clothing this week, and banned from medical and pharmaceutical professions. Belgian Conférence des Bourgmestres (mayors) protests and refuses to cooperate.

11 June: Himmler sets quotas for deportations of Jews from occupied territories: 15,000 from Holland, 10,000 from Belgium, 100,000 from France ("including the unoccupied zone").

16–17 June: Vélodrome d'Hiver: mass arrests of Jews in Paris; some 20,000 interned at Drancy for deportation.

June-July: Second issue of *Messages,* "Dramatique de l'espoir," published in Paris without required German approval but backdated to "Spring 1942." Contains texts by, a.o., Ponge ("14 Juillet") and Eluard.

8 July: Photo of PDM published in front page *Le Soir* article naming committee to judge "concours littéraire du *Soir.*" Photo later used in *Galerie des traitres,* clandestine denunciation of journalists at *Soir volé.*

Second "Otto list" published in Paris: bans all works by Jewish authors (except some science books), biographies of Jews, and translations of English authors (except "classics"); works by Gide added to list of "undesirables."

13 July: *Le Soir* announces that due to paper shortages it will publish issues of only four pages. By fall, three of each week's six issues are reduced to two pages (front and back of one sheet).

14 July: PDM publishes "Continuité de la poésie française: à propos de la revue *Messages*" in *Le Soir.*

Late July: Plans for deportation of Jews to death camps are put into operation in Belgium. Non-Belgian Jews living in Belgium—Belgian citizens are initially exempted—required by military authorities to report for "work duty." Many comply. Some are sent to Todt Organization work camps in Northern France; others are concentrated at Caserne Dossin in Malines, between Antwerp and Brussels, beginning on 27 July.

Belgians forbidden to shelter Jews outside their legal residence. Later in 1942 or 1943, PDM and AB's friends Nahum and Esther Sluszny, accidentally locked out of apartment where hiding after curfew, take refuge with them for several days until they can return to apartment; PDM and AB shelter others on other occasions as well.

28 July: PDM publishes over his signature article on Dutch novelist Mme. Neel Doff, in large part written by his friend Georges Goriely.

August: Third issue of *Messages,* "Exercice de la pureté," with text by Lescure and photographs by Belgian surrealist Raoul Ubac, published in Paris, again without required approval and hence dated "pour l'equinoxe de printemps."

4 August: First convoy of Belgian deportations, carrying about 1000 Jews, leaves concentration center at Malines for Auschwitz. Twenty-five more convoys over next two years.

12 August: Propaganda Abteilung Belgien tightens restrictions on newspapers, reimposing requirement that all articles be censored before publication and prohibiting any discussion of future form of Belgian state.

15 August: As number of Jews voluntarily responding to "ordre de prestation du travail" falls off, Germans begin full-scale raids in Antwerp (repeated on 28 August).

19 August: Allied commando attack on Dieppe, though repulsed, raises Belgians' hopes of invasion of Continent in near future.

3 September: First German raids to arrest Jews in Brussels.

4 September: Imposition in France of "service de travail obligatoire" in Germany; workers conscripted by German authorities on case by case basis.

19 September: Announcement of winner in *Le Soir*'s concours littéraire: Pierre Peyel's war novel *Hohenmoor*, later published by Editions de la Toison d'Or.

28 September: Creation of new administrative unit of "Grand-Bruxelles." PDM's cousin Jan de Man, economist, son of Hendrik, returns from Wallonia to take post on new board of aldermen.

Fall: In broadcast from London, Belgian government-in-exile offers amnesty to all journalists working for collaborationist newspapers who cease writing by year's end.

October: Second "Congress of European Writers" at Weimar. *Le Soir* circulation at about 260,000 copies daily.

6 October: German authorities require all able-bodied Belgian men to furnish proof of employment or be subject to drafting as laborers in Germany.

20 October: PDM's last article appears in *Het Vlaamsche Land*.

23 October: Tank battle at El Alamein begins.

7–8 November: Allied troops land in Morocco and Algiers.

11 November: German army overruns line of demarcation between occupied and Vichy France. Troops remain throughout rest of war, although Vichy government continues to administer its territory.

November: Hendrik de Man, on visit to Brussels, learns that his name is on list of potential German hostages; returns illegally to France. After lecturing in Paris (20 November, "Au delà du nationalisme"), held and questioned by Gestapo, but released on intervention of Otto Abetz and on implicit condition that he abandon all political activity; leaves Paris to spend rest of war in Haute Savoie, French Alps. (Does not leave retreat except for rare clandestine personal trips within France and "sauf trois voyages à Bruxelles en catimini, le temps d'aller dire bonjour à mes enfants et deux ou trois amis.")

27 November: First retaliatory execution of Belgian hostages by German military; eight civilians killed after resistance assassinates mayor of Charleroi.

28–29 November: PDM's last article published in *Le Soir*.

10 December: Publication in Brussels of fourth issue of *Messages, Exercice du silence*, after it had been refused authorization by German censor in Paris. PDM, at request of Lescure's Belgian "correspondant" Georges Lambrichs, arranges through Agence Dechenne for its printing in Brussels. Includes texts by, a.o., Bataille, Eluard, Frénaud, Lambrichs, Lecomte, Leiris, Lescure, Queneau, Sartre, Ubac.

1943

17 January: Léon Degrelle, head of Belgian fascist party Rex, calls in Brussels speech for Belgians to recognize themselves as "children of the Germanic race," and supports plans for annexation of Belgium to a greater German Reich. Opposed by Belgicists like Raymond de Becker, who resigns from "conseil politique" of Rex in protest. Robert Poulet's articles attacking Degrelle are censored; he resigns and leaves Belgium for occupied Luxembourg.

17 and 24 January: *Exercice du silence* reviewed in two issues of *Cassandre*, right-wing weekly edited by Paul Colin and known to specialize in political denunciations. First article singles out Georges Lambrichs for criticism. Second, after noting in Lescure's preface "certain rather transparent allusions and insinuations" about "persecution" and "inquisition," comments "we have understood," and mockingly concludes: "On 'résiste' comme on peut. . ."

27 January: Louis Fonsny, former member of Cercle du Libre Examen and politico-literary contributor to *Le Soir*, shot and killed by resistant Jean Coppens at Brussels tram stop. Fonsny had supported "travail obligatoire" in November 1942 article "Il y a trop d'étudiants en Belgique." Coppens later arrested and executed.

2 February: Surrender of German army at Stalingrad.

15 February: Obligatory work service in Germany put into full-scale practice in France; first conscription of workers by age groups ("classes" of 1940–42).

March: Last reviews signed by PDM appear in *Bibliographie Dechenne*. Lambrichs, for whom PDM has obtained work, and PDM are fired from Agence Dechenne because of participation in publication of *Exercice du silence*.

April: Snoeck-Ducaju, Ghent, publishes Gerard Walschap's *Genezing door aspirine* and French version, *Cure d'Aspirine*, said to be translated by Willem Elsschot but in fact done by PDM; illustrations by René de Pauw.

2 April: Propaganda Abteilung Belgien closes numerous print-ing firms and seizes paper stocks.

14 April: Paul Colin, director of *Cassandre* and *Le Nouveau jour-nal,* shot and killed by resistant Arnaud Fraiteur (later ar-rested and executed).

19 April: Youra Livchitz (of Cercle du Libre Examen) and two other resistants intercept twentieth Brussels-Auschwitz con-voy (carrying 1600 people) and during ensuing fire fight, open doors to three cars, allowing some deportees to escape. (Clandestine Comité de défense des Juifs had learned of real-ity of exterminations in November 1942.) Livschitz soon ar-rested, held at Breendonck, executed there 17 February 1944.

30 April: German labor recruitment authorities in Belgium de-cree penalties against families of, and people aiding, those evading obligatory work in Germany.

1 May: Trotskyist surrealists in Paris "La Main à Plume" criticize *Exercice du silence* for mysticism, neo-religiosity, and desire to 'go beyond' surrealism, in tract *Nom de Dieu!* Group had earlier tried to join with *Messages* but split over its eclecti-cism.

10 May: Third "Otto list" published in Paris, includes appendix with "list of Jewish authors in French"; bans work by nearly 1600 writers, almost 750 of them Jewish.

May–June: In *Poésie* 43, French review from unoccupied zone which published "poets of the resistance," editor Pierre Seghers reports on recent trip to Brussels: "A palace revolu-tion has removed from the directorship of certain publishing houses Georges Lambrichs and Paul de Man, who had de-fended new currents in French literature [la jeune littérature française]," alluding to their role in the publication of *Exer-cice du silence.*

June: *Nouvelle Revue Française* under Drieu la Rochelle folds.

28 June: German military administration requires Belgians to carry 'work cards' as documentation of employment; raids conducted to discover those lacking cards and hence subject to conscription for work in Germany.

9–10 July: Allied landings in Sicily.

24–25 July: Mussolini deposed and imprisoned. Italy out of war.

September: German military authorities in Belgium institute forced labor draft by age groups for "service de travail oblig-atoire en Allemagne."

3 September: Gestapo raids begin systematic deportation to death camps of Jewish Belgian citizens.

At *Le Soir* editors' meeting, editor-in-chief Raymond de Becker contests the idea of a "New Europe" under German leadership. "European unity is in the process of being acheived, but against Germany."

8 September: Announcement of armistice between Italy and Al-lies; Allied troops land.

Fall: Book-length issue of *Messages* for 1943 published in Ge-neva, titled *Domaine français.* Includes, a.o., Aragon, Benda, Eluard, Lambrichs, Jean Paulhan, Valéry, Elsa Triolet.

September–October: Editions de la Toison d'Or publishes A.E. Brinckmann's *Esprit des Nations,* translated by PDM and Jean-Jacques Etienne from *Geist der Nationen: Italiener-Franzosen-Deutsche* (Hamburg: Hoffman und Campe, 1938).

October: PDM and 43 other journalists of *Le Soir (volé)* de-nounced in pamphlet published by resistance newspaper *L'Insoumis,* entitled "*Galerie des Traitres.* ière série. Dans l'an-tre du *Soir-Erzatz.*" Assassination of Fonsny celebrated: "Abattu! Justice est faite!"

4 October: Raymond de Becker removed from editorship of *Le Soir* and placed under house arrest in Bavaria; Pierre de Ligne and two other editors also expelled from *Le Soir.*

9 November: Belgian resistants in Front de l'Indépendance score major propaganda victory with publication and distribution of 50,000 copies of satiric imitation *Le Soir.* Although its edi-tors are not discovered, clandestine newspaper printer Ferdi-nand Wellens arrested and executed for role in printing it.

December: PDM leaves Brussels with family for Antwerp, where they will live with his father for remainder of war (much of this time probably spent in translating *Moby Dick*).

1944

16 January: Resistance sabotage unit Groupe G, led by Jean Bur-gers (Libre Examen), destroys thirty high-tension pylons. Sabotage actions in Belgium were increasingly effective dur-ing 1943–44.

Spring: Gestapo arrests increase to 500–600 per month. Climate of terror and counter terror reigns: in eight weeks, 33 collab-orating mayors are killed by resistance, dozens of Belgian hostages executed by Germans in reprisal.

17 May: PDM and AB married.

6 June: D-Day, Allied beachhead in Normandy.

9 June: King Leopold III and family transferred from Laecken palace to house arrest at Hirschheim in Germany.

June: Hendrik de Man's *Cahiers de ma montagne* published, in Belgium only, by Editions de la Toison d'Or.

18 July: Military administration of occupied Belgium ends, re-placed by political (SS) Zivilverwaltung. General von Fal-kenhausen removed, Gauleiter Grohé installed.

20 July: Bomb attack on Hitler inside East Prussian "Wolfs-schanze" headquarters fails to kill him. In aftermath, hundreds of German officers, politicians, and clergy involved in conspiracy are arrested, many killed.

31 July: 26th and final Brussels-to-Auschwitz convoy leaves Malines. Out of total of approximately 66,000 Jews in Belgium, almost 35,000 will have been deported or interned, more than 25,000 of them from Malines, and nearly 29,000 killed by war's end.

August: As German troops retreat, Hendrik de Man escapes to Switzerland where after some time he is allowed to remain and live in exile.

26 August: Liberation of Paris.

3 September: Liberation of Brussels.

4 September: Liberation of Antwerp. Fighting continues north of city where German army still controls approaches to port. PDM and family are staying at Kalmthout, north of liberated sector, where they have spent summer.

6 September: First legal issue of *Debout,* journal of Fédération Bruxelloise des Etudiants Socialistes Unifiés, includes denunciation of PDM and others from pre-war ULB left who had worked in occupation press and publishing.

18 September: Pierlot government returns to Belgium from London exile.

20 September: Leopold III's brother Prince Charles installed as regent; Leopold still held in Germany.

26 November: After fierce fighting north of Antwerp, approaches to port secured and first Allied ships able to enter.

Winter: PDM and family return to Antwerp; PDM finishing translation of *Moby Dick.* City, now Allied debarkation port, under heavy German V-1 and V-2 rocket attacks.

1945

6 February: Robert Brasillach executed in Paris.

11 February: First postwar Belgian government formed.

March: Robert, second son of AB and PDM, born. Sometime in 1945, PDM and AB and their two children move into own apartment in Antwerp. PDM occupied with starting publishing house, Editions Hermès, to produce art books, using recent inheritance and borrowed money to finance it. PDM is "managing director" with three other partners, including his uncle Jan Buschmann, printer; two of three have been resistants; meets and employs as Hermès translator David Braybrooke, stationed with U.S. Army in Antwerp.

15 March: Suicide of Drieu la Rochelle in Paris.

8 May: V-E Day.

May: PDM called before Auditeur Général, military prosecutor, at Palais de Justice in Antwerp, for day of questioning about his activities during occupation; released without charges being filed: "Paul de Man was not the object of charges brought before the Conseil de Guerre for his attitude or his activity during the war" (Auditeur Général, 23 June 88*)*.

July: Robert Poulet sentenced to life in prison, increased to death sentence on appeal, for "high treason" during occupation. Later commuted to life and then to exile in 1951.

Fall: Publication of PDM's Flemish translation of Herman Melville's *Moby Dick,* illustrated by René de Pauw, by Editions Helicon, small publishing house in Antwerp. Helicon also publishes *Les plus belles images du cinéma,* bearing Georges Lambrichs' name but assembled by PDM, prefaced by Jacques Kupissonoff, friend from Cercle du Libre Examen. PDM's exact relation to Helicon is uncertain; Jan Buschmann was printer.

1946

First books published by Editions Hermès, in Brussels: Jean de Beucken, *Vincent van Gogh, un portrait* and *Vincent van Gogh, een portet.* Firm specializes in deluxe illustrated art books, printing several editions with identical plates but text in different languages; also publishes art reproductions. PDM travels to arrange co-publications; while in Paris attends university lectures, associates with literary figures such as Lambrichs, Bataille, Blanchot, and Michaux.

21 February: José Streel, journalist for *Le Soir* and other occupation papers, executed for wartime activities.

1 May: Brussels Auditeur Général's "résumé des faits" in case against 28 editors and writers for wartime *Le Soir* does not charge or name PDM. Others receive jail terms, including de Ligne.

24 July: Raymond de Becker sentenced to death for wartime work at *Le Soir*; sentence commuted to life imprisonment 14 June 1947, then to exile in France 22 February 1951.

12 September: Hendrik de Man sentenced in absentia to twenty years in prison; continues to live and write in Switzerland. On 20 June 1953, he and wife killed when car is hit by train at unguarded crossing.

November: Marc, third son of AB and PDM, born. PDM travelling in Sweden for Hermès.

29 November: Edouard Didier sentenced to death in absentia for wartime work at Editions de la Toison d'Or; later pardoned.

1947

Summer: PDM makes two-month trip to New York and else-
 where in US to arrange for American co-publishers of
 Hermès books. Editions Hermès publishes Paul Haesaerts,
 Renoir sculpteur and *Renoir beeldhouwer* in Antwerp (after
 PDM trip, Reynal & Hitchcock in New York publishes *Renoir, sculptor*; Swedish edition, *Renoir som bildhuggare,* published by P.A. Norstedt in Stockholm). Hermès apparently
 in financial difficulties, in part due to competition from
 French art publishers and English import restrictions. Other
 Hermès projects, unpublished, include book on Goya by
 Paul Willems and translation of V.L. Parrington's *Main Currents of Western Thought*. PDM returns from US intending to
 emigrate there.

1948

Winter: PDM and AB seek visas for family to emigrate to United
 States. American Consul in Antwerp, dubious of their
 means of support, refuses visas to AB and children, but offers
 tourist visa to PDM.

Spring: PDM and AB sell all possessions; he leaves first for New
 York, then AB and children sail for Argentina, where they
 will stay with her parents, recently settled in Buenos Aires.
 PDM plans to establish himself in United States, then send
 for family.

May: PDM arrives in New York, takes job in Doubleday bookstore at Grand Central Station; deals with editors of literary-
 political reviews in New York (Dwight Macdonald, William
 Phillips) and in Paris (Bataille) seeking to arrange for exchanges of articles and overseas distribution; socializes in
 New York intellectual-artistic circles (e.g., Mary McCarthy,
 Guggenheims, Greenberg, Calder, Vidal). Maintains position in Editions Hermès, but apparently has no active role
 (firm collapses, and is sued by creditors in 1949).

1949

September: With help of Mary McCarthy, PDM takes job as Instructor in French at Bard College, Annandale-on-Hudson,
 N.Y.

WH, NH, TK   October 1988

Telephonic Crossroads: The Reversal and the Double Cross

TIMOTHY BAHTI

There is a children's language-game: "telephone." The rule of this game is that error must occur as a voice is transferred, from afar, to yet another distance. With each repetition of the voice, the message is increasingly—"immer wieder potenziert"—distorted. Among children, this can give rise to hysterical laughter. Paul de Man would have understood the irony of this "game." What happens when an error "begins" the game, when there is nothing "right" from the start? The telephonics may claim, at its end, a discovery about history and ethical behavior, and another about the project of de Man's theory. It may be worthwhile to try to hear the distortion that is behind the production of the chain.

* * *

The most infamous piece of de Man's journalism for *Le Soir* is also his single antisemitic piece. Many have seized on its notorious last paragraph, with its inexcusable gesture toward an evacuation of Jews from European literature by way of its mention of plans to expel Jews from Europe altogether. I have nothing to say in exculpation of such expressions, and there is little further that needs to be added by me about the pain they have caused, above all to de Man's friends. The best evidence available today suggests that de Man refused several times the editorial demand that he write for the special page of anti-Jewish slander, and that he acquiesced only under the threat of not being allowed to continue to publish in *Le Soir*. This may already be, as has been suggested, to have accepted the unacceptable. There is also the evidence of his later wartime assistance with the publication of an issue of the French resistance journal, *Messages*, an issue called *Exercice du Silence*. Independently of the testimonies of those who knew him, and who attest that he was not to the slightest degree an antisemite, these historical circumstances suggest, then, that the article in question is weirdly encoded in and determined by a tactics and perhaps a strategy of wartime publication in occupied Belgium and France.

Much of this has already been carefully and sensitively analyzed, notably by Jacques Derrida. The context will continue to need careful research, and I don't pretend to understand it yet. But something may already be observed about part of the message of this article, "Les Juifs dans la littérature actuelle."

In the middle of the article, on his way to arguing that literature's "basic nature is healthy," de Man invokes its stability amidst the momentous times of the war: "La guerre mondiale a provoqué un bouleversement profond dans le monde politique et économique. Mais la vie artistique a été relativement peu remuée, et les formes que nous connaissons actuellement sont des suites logiques et normales de ce qu'il y avait en avant . . . Les formes [de la poésie] qui nous semblent les plus révolutionaires . . . ont, en réalité, des ascendances orthodoxes dont on ne peut les détacher." And in the middle of this set of claims for the "normal orthodoxy" of literature, where his privileged example is the contemporary novel, he produces this list of names: "Gide, Kafka, Hemingway, Lawrence—on pourrait allonger indéfiniment la liste." The full paragraph reads:

Gide, Kafka, Hemingway, Lawrence—on pourrait allonger indéfiniment la liste—ne font tous que tenter de pénétrer, selon des méthodes propres à leur personnalité, dans les secrets de la vie intérieure. Par cette caractéristique, ils se montrent, non comme des novateurs ayant brisé avec toutes les traditions du passé, mais comme de simples continuateurs qui ne font qu'approfondir davantage l'esthétique réaliste, vieille de plus d'un siècle.

As a friend of mine said when first remarking on this list in the imagined voice of a shocked Nazi censor or propagandist: "A homosexual, a Jew, an anti-fascist, and a pornographer." Where does this list come from?

It comes from Aldous Huxley, and for Paul de Man—as well as for our reading of his wartime writings—it also comes from what is probably his very first article of literary journalism, "Le Roman anglais contemporain," published in *Les Cahiers du Libre Examen* 4:4 (January 1940), pp. 16–19. The sentences there, quoted from Huxley's "Music at Night," read (in de Man's French): "Proust, D.H. Lawrence, A. Gide, Kafka, Hemingway—voici cinq auteurs contemporains significatifs et importants. Cinq auteurs aussi différents les uns des autres que possible. Ils n'ont que ceci en commun, c'est qu'ils respectent tous la *complète vérité* (the Whole Truth)" [emphasis and English in de Man's text].

In "Les Juifs dans la littérature actuelle," the list of contemporary novelists was supposed to represent a *continuous* development in the genre, from "scrupulously respect[ing] exterior reality" to "exploring psychological reality," "search[ing] even the most secret corners of the souls of characters," "penetrat[ing] . . . into the secrets of interior life." All this "constitutes the one and only terrain of investigation of the novelist," and the "list" comprises "not innovators who have broken with all past traditions, but mere continuers who are only pursuing further the realist aesthetic that is more than a century old." It's worth noticing that as literature is made hyperbolically continuous (that "indefinite" list) and exclusive ("the one and only"), de Man's language also condescends or belittles ("mere continuers who are only pursuing"). What argument, however, does the same "list" serve in "Le Roman anglais contemporain"?

This article contrasts the novel in pre– and post-1914 England. After asserting a continuity between pre-1914 novelists and their predecessors in Victorian fiction (and a calm of reading: "Aucune inquiétude, aucun bouleversement intérieur n'assaille le lecteur après les avoir lus"), it says: "Et brusquement, après la guerre mondiale, tout change . . . Plus trace de cette mesure, de cet ordre, de cette dignité. Au contraire, on se permet les pires excès." If the drama of sudden and total reversal is hyperbolic enough, the tone of outraged taste is sheer melodrama. Rather, it covers

un bouleversement radical et profond. Car, pour le lecteur, il n'est plus question de se laisser vivre confortablement en suivant sans effort un récit bien construit. On lui en fait voir de toutes les couleurs; il sort de sa lecture harassé par un effort cérébral continuel et avec ses préjugés et croyances remus de fond en comble.

There are at least four key words here: the introduction of a "*bouleversement*" into reading, and the "effort *cérébral continuel*" as one's preconceptions and beliefs are "*remus*" from top to bottom. And a fifth word—a name—is immediately added by de Man: he invites consideration of "cet abîme" felt to open between Galsworthy's *Forsythe Saga* and Joyce's *Ulysses,* between Bourget's *Démon du Midi* and Proust's *Du côté de chez Swann,* between Mann's *Buddenbrooks* and . . . *Kafka's The Castle.*

"Les Juifs dans la littérature actuelle," at its center and perhaps at its core, appears to be a rewriting of "Le Roman anglais contemporain." In the obviousness of its reversals of key terms and names *and arguments,* "Les Juifs . . ." may be understood as itself a reversal. But what might this mean?

The claims in the later piece reverse the direction and the quality of the flow of time as it was presented in the earlier one: not from calm (pre-1914) to disturbance (post-1914) within a modern literary tradition, but from disturbance outside of literature ("La guerre mondiale a provoqué un bouleversement profond") to a calm inside art ("Mais la vie artistique a été relativement peu remue"). There's no "abyss" between novels in the second article, but "the one and only terrain of investigation of the novelist." There's not a break with a tradition ("non comme des novateurs ayant brisé avec toutes les traditions du passé"), but a (reestablished) continuity ("mais comme de simples continuateurs"). Where, in the earlier piece, one had to respond to this disturbing flow, abyss, break with a "continuous cerebration" while reading, here, in the later piece, the calm flow, solid ground, and continuous tradition of literature are safe from the "cerebralism" of the Jews. It is as if there is no longer any reading, any need for it.

"Le Roman anglais contemporain" goes on to sketch the

shift in the genre from the novel of "character, . . . born of observation," made of "types" that are "vraisemblable," and self-consistent or self-identical, to the "contemporary" novel which displays "a more penetrating and more lucid attention to the observation of the human being." Even as this appears to be a *continuity* from "observation" to "observation," it rapidly reaches a breaking-point: the next sentence has the contemporary novelists "inspect[ing] as completely as possible all the aspects of the soul [d'inspecter aussi complètement que possible tous les aspects de l'âme; recall "il entreprend des recherches jusque dans les recoins les plus secrets de l'âme des personnages"]," and "obeying only that thirst to tell the whole truth about man [dire l'entière vérité sur l'homme]." This is where the quotation from Aldous Huxley appears, followed by this sentence: "The novelists are thus transformed into pitiless psychologists, enemies of all simplification that would falsify the truth about human nature."

What de Man went on to say, in "Le Roman anglais contemporain," about this "new discipline" was that it "is in reality perfectly revolutionary and will tear down the solid edifice that was the novel of the 19th century in order to replace it with an anarchic chaos." Already in this earliest article, de Man's irony emerges: this revolutionary, anarchic, chaotic novel of pitiless psychological truth *is* the truth. "It is in effect manifestly false that man is an immovable and rigid composition. He is on the contrary essentially mobile, continually overturned or bowled over [*continuellement bouleversé*: those words again] by new aspirations, always in search of an equilibrium or in the course of losing the one that one has provisionally acquired." After brief, superficial discussions of Joyce, Woolf, Huxley and Lawrence, the positive conclusions de Man would draw stand out clearly:

Never has the novel been so reasoning, so hair-splitting as in this [contemporary] period. Never has it had such respect for the form and the beauty of expression, either. This is normal enough. For to avoid the boredom that risks being released by these quasi-scientific exposés, one is indeed obliged to make recourse to the resources of a purely aesthetic order. All those who are not true artists have no possibility of shining among the great writers of the hour. The English seem to have understood this better than anybody. [The prose of Lawrence, Charles Morgan, Huxley] are all, in their own way, successes of style. It is doubtless for this reason as well that the contemporary English novel seems so particularly attractive [attachant] to us.

The "revolution" and its "truth" are calming into—combining with—form, beauty, expression, style: "a purely aesthetic order." Call this literature. The end of this article is already, then,

the beginning of "Les Juifs . . . ," with its calm and safe *and normal* literary traditions. Notice especially the absence already of that disturbing reading described at the beginning of the article.

But this is a continuity instated by a reversal, a violent reversal—a *bouleversement,* a revolution—which continues, then, as an inversion: the inversion of inside (literature's post-1914 revolution) into outside ("the political and economic world"), outsider (Jew) into insider (Kafka), reader (cerebral) into writer *manqué* ("Their cerebralness . . . seemed to be [a] very precious quality for the work of lucid analysis that the novel demands"). Most thematically (most banally), it is the inversion of revolution into tradition, and of "pitiless psychology" into "health." This *cure* is, not surprisingly, the other side of a "continual *bouleversement*," of an imbalance always seeking its other, only to lose it as quickly as it's found.

That the later article is specifically an ironic rewriting and re-reading of the first would probably have been known by de Man's friends from *Les Cahiers du Libre Examen,* in its own words "democratic, anti-clerical, anti-dogmatic and anti-fascist." Under the code of *Le Soir*'s antisemitic "special page" ("Les Juifs et nous: Les aspects culturels"), under its specific form of censorship, de Man wrote the *resistance* of literature and its reading. Literature is made to resist a violence that had been internal to it and its reading, but that had then been rejected or expelled in the name of an artistic, aesthetic calm. But the "external world" into which literature's violent order—its *bouleversement continuel*—has been ejected, then returns to haunt literature, as an "other" that has to be expelled again, and this time not only from literature: those "cerebral ones," who neither need any longer to exert that effort of reading, nor are acknowledged as writing, can be "expelled" from European life as well.

Literature resists one-sidedness because it is two-sided, double-crossed: one side is its writing as disturbed, and disturbing of reading; the other—the reversal—its rereading as artificially (aesthetically) calm. Together, in this writing about reading, and then this rewriting and rereading, it is "toujours à la recherche d'un équilibre ou occupé à perdre celui qu'il a provisoirement acquis."

This is irony, as de Man taught us to recognize it in its vertiginously maddening instantaneity of incessantly self-re-presenting reversals. *Our* question is whether we can read de Man, and specifically this juncture of two articles from his wartime journalism. When we read his reversal of one text into another, of one code (democratic, anti-fascist) into another (occupied, censored, collaborationist), we are reading the work of a literary reader and writer. Precisely because he reads and writes of literature's reversals, we are already at the crossroads. No turning back, which means no easy undoing of the reversal into a simple (one-fold), single "fact" or "life" of Paul de Man. Literature doesn't *simply* turn back into life; no, never. Rather, it turns and turns, always at least twice, allegorically. Irony can only be read allegorically. One reversal, of literature into the life of pre– and post-1914 Europe, will of necessity be met by its counterpart, its *double* cross, of life into literature—of European life in 1941 into a discussion of its literature, and today, of the afterlife of that wartime into a discussion of literary theory. As de Man wrote much later about Rousseau, the rhetoric of allegorical misreading also accounts for his own double cross:

Accounting for the "rhetoricity" of its own mode, the text also postulates the necessity of its own misreading. It knows and asserts that it will be misunderstood. It tells the story, the allegory of its misunderstanding . . . In accordance with its own language, it can only tell this story as a fiction, knowing full well that the fiction will be taken for fact and the fact for fiction; such is the necessarily ambivalent nature of literary language. ("The Rhetoric of Blindness," *Blindness and Insight,* pp.135, 136)

De Man's fatal error, between the first and the second articles in question, was, in artificially withdrawing literature from a life he had first inserted it in, paradoxically to turn literature's violence toward and into life: as a resistance to reading, as an expulsion of "the Jew," the cerebral one. We—I, you, de Man, literature, life—are double-crossed, from the start.

The knowledge of the double cross is what remains and what matters. If we think we can uncross the reversal, flatten literature—its writing, its reading—into the "simple" (the *pharmakon*) of life, we would pretend to claim unironic knowledge of irony, a detached cognition of the disjunction between an empirical and a linguistic self. We would be waiting for a fall, and the ironist could await his laughter. If, on the other hand, we know that we can't uncross the reversals, we remain entwined in the reversible relations of writing and reading that literature is. Can we know *this* knowledge? No, strictly speaking. Is this any comfort? Probably not. Generosity is called for nonetheless. We can know that Paul de Man was not a Nazi, or a fascist, even if he was able to write and sign a piece of literary antisemitism and erring reading.

* * *

There will be much more to say and think about "Les Juifs dans la littérature actuelle," especially after the immensely clarifying analysis provided by Jacques Derrida. Here, I want only to say a few things about some of the rest of de Man's wartime journalism, before returning to the recent journalism about it.

In *Le Soir,* de Man could praise Paul Eluard, a well-known communist, in the summer of 1942. He could favorably review Ernst Jünger after the Nazi propaganda office had forbidden reviews of his work in Germany. He could praise Ernst Wiechert after this German author had already done time in Buchenwald. He could praise Charles Péguy's aggressive engagement as a Dreyfusard.

In late 1942, he could write these two phrases in two of his last articles in *Het Vlaamsche Land*: "the common ground of the whole of humanity" (6–7 September 1942) and "the dominant bad taste of the broad masses" (20 October 1942), the first while reviewing Max Dauthendey, the second a propos of popular editions of books in Flemish. The latter phrase is certainly not populist, or egalitarian; it is written from a stance of aesthetic elitism. But it could be uttered for *many* purposes, even directed against the aesthetic politics of the Germans of the day. "The common ground of the whole of humanity" could never be affirmatively uttered as a Nazi utterance.

This journalism, then, is not the gung-ho collaboration and plugging of the Nazi hit-parade that one enthusiastic misreading is quoted as having it be. (Be watchful also for the morally shady—and self-righteous—claims of "common Nazi hack work" and "moral shabbiness.")

But given that this, and much, much more, *is* being said about de Man's wartime journalism, what are we to make of it? I suggest two things, in two steps. First, that these further occasions for telephonic error, for misreading, and, indeed, for *resistance to reading,* will be occasions once again to test and confirm the truth of de Man's theories. "What is the truth? A mobile army of metaphors, metonymies, anthropomorphisms . . ." The tropological governance and production of discourse will be readable in every trope that is turned around these texts:

Metaphor ("an academic Waldheim," *The Nation,* 9 January 1988; "the young de Man became a Fascist," *The Nation,* ibid.; "a Nazi, a convinced antisemite," *Basler Zeitung,* 12 February 1988);

Metonymy ("There was also the matter of de Man's relationship to the German literary critic Hans Robert Jauss . . . now known to have served in the S.S.," *The Nation,* ibid.);

Hyperbole ("De Man's early love for fascism," *Tages-Anzeiger* [Zürich], 1 March 1988; "de Man . . . expressed a virulent strain of anti-Semitism," *Newsweek,* 15 February 1988);

Synecdoche ("he wrote anti-Semitic essays for a pro-Nazi newspaper," *Newsweek,* ibid. [my emphasis]);

Comparison ("The 'deconstructionist' Paul de Man did not behave any differently than a Joseph Goebbels," *Frankfurter Allgemeine Zeitung,* 16 March 1988);

Metalepsis ("In Mehlman's view, there are even 'grounds for viewing the whole of deconstruction as a vast amnesty project for the politics of collaboration during World War II,'" *Newsweek,* ibid.; "Suddenly one sees in each argument and each thesis that it is supposed to serve an illusionary flight from factual remembrance, a neurotic consolidation of a well-practiced loss of memory," *Frankfurter Allgemeine Zeitung,* 10 February 1988);

Diminutio ("the ninety-two articles in French will not be translated . . . that will discourage anyone but experts from examining the documents," *The Nation,* ibid.);

Allegory ("As one Ivy League professor gleefully exclaims, 'deconstruction turned out to be the thousand-year Reich that lasted 12 years,'" *Newsweek,* ibid.);

Irony [with two metaphors] ("Ironically enough, the articles appear to go to the heart of the ethical debates still raging over Dr. de Man's work," *New York Times,* 1 December 1987).

The more one encounters this sort of stuff (it would be unkind to extend the evidence), the more one's inclination is to forget it. That was, in fact, my initial response to de Man's wartime journalism; upon reading in the *Le Soir* articles, I penned this note to myself: "One or two things—juvenile, offensive. To admit anything else is perfidy. Things which he forgot with a ruthlessness that he analyzes persistently elsewhere. We should be grateful that our culture forgets so much." But I now believe not only that there *is* something ugly worth remembering in these writings (Jacques Derrida's analysis has helped persuade me of this: even one article by Paul de Man that may be antisemitic—*and,* simultaneously, may *not* be antisemitic—is worth remembering). I also believe that the recent journalism about de Man's journalism will prove de Man right. This leads to my last point.

Heinrich Heine wrote that when you begin by burning books, you end up burning people. Some hysterical association notwithstanding—triggered, perhaps, by the alliteration (another trope) of burning books and babies—Paul de Man did neither. He burned bridges. The bridges he burned, like all those in the metaphor, were textual ones. Those wartime text-bridges, and the firestorm of ire and spite now raging around them, confirm de Man's claim that "the bases for historical knowledge are not empirical facts but written texts; even if

these texts masquerade in the guise of wars and revolutions" ("Literary History and Literary Modernity," *Blindness and Insight,* p.165). This statement—infamous, or just famously applicable?—predicts the present retrospect of resentment. De Man's wartime journalism masqueraded literature in the talk of world war and revolution, with disastrous consequences. Today, journalism masquerades in the guise of talk of *that* war, *that* "revolution." Which war? Paul de Man's scholarship and teaching were always textual events of great power with, as he knew, enormous stakes. *Those* events—texts—are the basis for the "war" today over de Man's past history. The journalistic accusations and invective are not about a young Paul de Man, 1940 to 1943, Belgium and Germany, "collaboration" and resistance. Their war is a textual one, in which their hit-and-run tactics have heretofore never left a dent in the theoretical arguments and exegetical readings of Paul de Man. What a find, these "wartime" articles: like other wars and revolutions, if they hadn't already come to exist, they would have had to be invented.

What time is "wartime"? The time is the textual now.

University of Michigan, Ann Arbor

"Difficult Reading": De Man's Itineraries

IAN BALFOUR

L'erreur est à tout instant possible.—*Jean Paulhan*

There is a moment in a late essay by Paul de Man when he confronts the matter of certain racial and national stereotypes in an early work of Kant. The text in question is Kant's *Observations on the Sentiment of the Beautiful and the Sublime,* one that hardly belongs to Kant's "juvenilia," though de Man can with reason refer to it as "early" and "precritical" in relation to the rest of the Kantian corpus.[1] Recalling some of the absurdities of Kant's early typologies of the aesthetic in terms of nation and gender, de Man notes how a number of disturbing remarks by Kant "make for . . . difficult reading."[2] De Man is not expansive on this point, since his main interest in the text lies elsewhere, but his comment seems to convey dismay at the spectacle of an otherwise enlightened and critical thinker resorting to what he calls "distressing commonplaces." In what way are these commonplaces of Kant's patriarchal and Eurocentric text "difficult" to read? Not foremost in the sense of being hard to decipher: it is not with regard to propositions like those in Kant's *Observations* that de Man sometimes pondered the impossibility and necessity of reading. The distressing commonplaces of an unthought prejudice are often all too easy to comprehend: they are difficult to read because difficult to accept. In the essay on Kant the presence of such "difficulties" in no way obviates the task of reading, the most categorical of de Man's imperatives. De Man here implies something that he made clear in his teaching: that the notation of ideologically suspect moments in a text does not in itself constitute a "reading." In encountering the disturbing pronouncements of Kant's early text on aesthetics it is easy to feel momentarily more enlightened than the pre-eminent spokesman for the Enlightenment. But a reading of Kant's text—or any other—demands something more.

The question of Kant's itinerary has never posed much of a problem for his commentators: Kant himself established the terms with talk of his Copernican revolution, such that scholars do not hesitate to divide the corpus into pre-critical and critical writings. De Man too seems to see a certain progression in Kant from the pre-critical to the critical, a change fortuitously accompanied by the absence in the later work of some of the commonplaces that marred the former. But the break is not an absolute one, neither in content nor in argument. Indeed de Man is concerned to link Kant's early remarks in the *Observations* on the absence of affect to the later argument of *The Critique of Judgment,* even if Kant's "judgment" on a number of matters changed substantially in the interim.[3]

De Man's itinerary is more enigmatic than Kant's: it is more "difficult" to read in a sense which has to do with the complexities of understanding texts and relations between texts whose significance is not at all self-evident. This was the case even before the recent discovery of de Man's writings from the early 1940's and now the problem is greatly exacerbated. At the very least, however, de Man's wartime articles for *Le Soir* and *Het Vlaamsche Land* appear "pre-critical" in a sense other than the technical one of Kant's philosophy. What is more, if one posits that for de Man rhetorical analysis corresponds to what is called "critique" in Kant, then the early texts of de Man's tenure at *Le Soir* appear massively "pre-rhetorical" as well. Rhetorical reading in de Man does indeed parallel Kantian critique to the extent that the focus in both is on the modalities of discourse and cognition, as well as the conditions of their possibility, prior to a concern with the content of meaning or knowledge as such. The problem with the early, "pre-rhetorical" texts from *Le Soir* is at least double: not only do they at times propound abhorrent political sentiments, but they often betray as well a certain aestheticism which, as Walter Benjamin recognized, was not one among other aspects of fascist ideology.

A number of the common and uncommonplaces that one encounters in reading de Man's articles from *Le Soir* and *Het Vlaamsche Land* are more than difficult to accept: they are impossible to accept. What is most "distressing" of all is the simple fact of their existence, inscribed in the political and cultural agendas of publications under the control of the Nazi occupants of Belgium. Even if a patient reading of de Man's texts of this period reveals a contradictory and sometimes subversive program, their inclusion in *Le Soir* and *Het Vlaamsche Land* signals participation in a heinous political program for which there can be no good excuse. Not only are the contents of de Man's own texts sometimes shocking, they gain an additional force by virtue of their metonymic relation to the rest of the collaborationist and propagandistic output of *Le Soir* and *Het Vlaamsche Land*.

It is surely the fact and the forum of the articles rather than a reading of the texts themselves that gave rise to the initial journalistic responses to the de Man "revelations," the inaccuracies of which were numerous and sometimes egregious. Quickly labelled in global fashion pro-Nazi and anti-Semitic, these texts of a young man in his early twenties are reputed to lead "to the heart of the ethical debates" surrounding de Man's later work, and further to the ethics of deconstruction *in general*.[4] There are thus two historical problematics at stake in the reading of these texts: one about the status of de Man's efforts in ideological collaboration, and another about the status of 'deconstruction' in contemporary thought. What then is the itinerary—if there is one—that could lead from one to the other?

* * * * *

In a late essay on Bakhtin, de Man draws attention to the phenomenon of "double-talk, the necessary obliqueness of any persecuted speech that cannot, at the risk of survival, openly say what it means to say."[5] He cites Leo Strauss from a singular work on *Persecution and the Art of Writing,* where the latter enumerates the markers of such doubly-encoded discourse: "obscurity of the plan, contradictions, pseudonyms, inexact repetitions of earlier statements, strange expressions, etc."[6] Hence the demand, congenial to de Man's criticism from the 1950s onward, for reading that would take account of such rhetorical complications.[7] To consider de Man's texts provisionally under the rubric of "persecution and the art of writing" is not to equate his situation with the persecution of a Bakhtin, much less with the infinitely graver persecution of the Jews, with which some of de Man's early writings were complicit. As a writer for *Le Soir* de Man was, of course, acting on the side of the Nazi persecutors, even though Belgium as a whole was "persecuted" by the occupants. Yet the proposals Strauss makes for a hermeneutic that accounts for the double-encoding of writing under political pressure may help in deciphering de Man's wartime writings. Simply in order to comprehend, much less judge, de Man's early texts, it is important to bear in mind that he was writing in an *occupied* country with considerable constraints on what could be said or done. A conspicuous lack thus far in the responses to the de Man revelations has been a consideration of what it is to live, work, and write in an occupied country, as if one were simply free to choose between resistance and the path of least resistance much as one chooses between different political parties in a democratic state. (None of the early journalistic accounts of de Man's wartime activity mentioned his unsuccessful attempt to flee Belgium.) The fact that de Man's writings during the occupation contain certain disturbing statements and positions with no parallel in his other writings before or after the occupation makes it difficult to read his newspaper articles as straightforward expressions of deeply held beliefs. His work for the *Cahiers du Libre Examen* and *Jeudi* in the period before the occupation as well as one current of his writing for *Le Soir* and *Het Vlaamsche Land* suggest a political profile at odds with the ideology of the Nazi occupants. Such complications do not lessen the gravity of de Man's work for collaborationist publications: political and ideological effects do not depend on authorial sincerity or the lack of it. The discrepancies, however, that mark the totality of the early writings might give pause to those who have labelled de Man an "ardent anti-Semite" and "a gung-ho collaborator," the latter a word that some associated with the resistance refuse to employ with regard to de Man.[8] A reading of the entire range of de Man's writings from 1939–43 reveals two anti-Semitic references. Would not an "extreme" or even moderate anti-Semite have taken more advantage of the position at *Le Soir* to promote an anti-Semitic agenda?

The most disturbing of all de Man's wartime writings, the article on "The Jews in Contemporary Literature," does seem to have been written under some pressure for inclusion in a group of feature articles on anti-Jewish topics. That is not to say it was written under censorship in the strict sense, which at the time seems to have applied primarily to articles of directly political import.[9] Whatever the conditions of the article's production, the text as it stands complete with de Man's by-line is an outrageous article with a deeply disturbing conclusion. But the contradictory impulses of the article—the hypothesis of a Europe free of Jewish writers together with an attack on vulgar anti-Semitism and a canonization of Kafka—suggest a scene of writing not unlike those analyzed by Strauss in the light of the hermeneutic he proposed for the reading of philosophical texts written under political pressure.[10]

The vast majority of de Man's wartime writings were reviews of books and concerts. The genre is not a matter of indifference, especially since one thing at stake in these texts is a certain aestheticism. To be sure, the review as a genre virtually demands aesthetic judgments: a review typically cannot afford the elaboration necessary for literary scholarship, much less for a "reading" of the texts in question. Moreover, the fact that reviews are taken up by a good deal of expository writing makes it sometimes difficult to locate precisely the reviewer's own stance. Often praise will be merely ritualistic or of a damning, faint sort, a mere prelude to severe criticism to come. Jeffrey Mehlman has been quoted as saying that de Man's chronicling of literary publications "plugged the Nazi hit parade."[11] This is certainly true to the extent that writings of Brasillach, Drieu la Rochelle, Chardonne and others are taken seriously and often praised for this or that quality.[12] There is no doubt that the tenor and topics of many of de Man's articles are in line with what one would expect of collaborationist publications. But it also true that de Man "plugged" the Nazi hit parade full of holes in a remarkable way, given what one imagines as the constraints of his position.[13] A good many references in de Man's chronicling of this canon seem to fly in the face of Nazi ideology: praise of Eluard, Proust, Kafka, a number of surrealists, and, perhaps most notably of all, praise of Charles Péguy as a Dreyfusard.

In the article on Péguy de Man recounts at considerable length the itinerary of his subject's life, especially his championing of Dreyfus. Indeed, the text on Péguy is singular in de Man's wartime writings for its attention to an author's *life,* a life held up as exemplary. De Man begins by noting that in discussing the life and times of Péguy "we are far from the pacific serenity of an intellectual not participating in action."[14] Péguy, we are told, is imbued with "ideas of socialism and egalitarian justice," (two things that did not necessarily go hand in hand, as the example of 'National Socialism' demonstrates). "He would be a Dreyfusard forever," de Man proclaims.[15] He goes on to characterize the notorious independence that got Péguy into trouble with his superiors in a socialist publishing concern. Then follows a remarkable sequence of sentences, *almost* all of which pertain as much to de Man's life as to Péguy's: "He has to leave his job as editor. A dangerous move for someone who had abandoned his studies in order to take up a career, someone, moreover, who is married and the father of a child. Here he is: without money, without friends, without a job. Not entirely without friends, however, because he will be able to surround himself with several faithful ones, keeping them up to date on the project he is contemplating. He wants to start a journal, not one subject to any party, but one which would appear freely, defending again socializing ideas (*idées socialisantes*), but not under any control. The title? The Notebooks (*Les Cahiers*), recalling, says Halévy, his school notebooks, so neat, so well kept."[16] De Man himself had been director of a journal, *Les Cahiers du Libre Examen,* whose title parallels Péguy's. (De Man's journal ceased publication with the coming of the Nazi occupation. Prior to the invasion, the journal had plainly declared itself "anti-fascist": special issues had been devoted to the most contemporary problems of politics and the arts, with clear polemics against the "totalitarian mystique," for example). De Man, like Péguy, found himself with a wife and child but without a job, before the offer to write the literary chronicle for *Le Soir* was extended, with or without the influence of his uncle, Henri de Man.[17] No one would now want to liken de Man's action writing for *Le Soir* with Péguy's writing for his *Cahiers.* Neither it seems would de Man, who, by holding up Péguy's life as exemplary, offers an implicit contrast to his own position. The numerous parallels bring out all the more clearly the points at which the two itineraries diverge. But they do not diverge altogether and de Man's article on Péguy is itself one instance of their convergence.

One of the two texts under discussion in de Man's review is the study of Péguy by the Jewish historian Daniel Halévy, another champion of Dreyfus, and Halévy's text receives not a word of negative comment from de Man.[18] More remarkable perhaps is the mention of the group who helped Péguy with his *Cahiers*: "Romain Rolland, Halévy, Sorel, Benda." That Julien Benda appears here in what is for de Man such a praiseworthy cause runs exactly counter to the tenor of the grotesque hypothesis of two months earlier in "The Jews in Contemporary Literature," where Benda had been named as one of the authors whose absence would not detract from the literary scene in Europe if Jewish writers were to live in a colony elsewhere.[19] Can the author of "The Jews in Contemporary Literature," be reconciled with the author of the article on Péguy? And where in this ideological spectrum from an aestheticized anti-Semitism to praise of Dreyfusards does one locate other texts such as de Man's numerous favorable reviews of Ernst Jünger's *On the Marble Cliffs,* a novel—ultimately banned by the Nazis—that has often been read as a thinly veiled attack on the Hitler regime?[20] The reading of de Man's articles becomes difficult indeed if one is trying to form a composite psychological and political profile, for not only does de Man have several "pasts" even as a young man (the *Cahiers du Libre Examen* as well as *Le Soir*), he has different pasts *at the same time*. This complexity should at least disable summary judgments that label de Man an "ardent anti-Semite" and a "pro-Nazi." Even in the restricted context of de Man's writings for *Le Soir,* to say nothing of his work before and after the occupation, the anti-Semitism of "The Jews in Contemporary Literature" cannot help but appear as an aberration. His silence—his exercise of silence—on the "Jewish question" throughout his other writing for publications like *Le Soir* and *Het Vlaamsche Land* is remarkable, though even a resistance of silence remains complicit with the dominant ideology of the occupiers. Gestures such as de Man's praise of Péguy and his denigration of Brasillach and other Nazi ideologues for their bad political judgment cannot undo all the damage done by the disturbing articles, indeed by their very forum regardless of their content.[21]

Perhaps the strongest impression one takes from the writings of the early 40s, for all their contradictions, is that of a certain aestheticism—a qualified aestheticism, since de Man will not hesitate to accuse some authors of an aestheticist position that he himself seems to take up.[22] De Man was employed as a reviewer and the genre of the journalistic review, again, virtually demands evaluation of aesthetic merit. In a programmatic article in *Le Soir* on "The Possibilities of Criticism," the young de Man claimed that the "most fundamental mission" for criticism "consists in defining the value of a literary work," a statement that finds no echo in de Man's later work.[23] To judge by de Man's concert reviews from 1941 and 1942 one would think that scarcely a false note or a lackluster performance had unsettled a Brussels concert hall. By contrast, his judgments of literary works are more variegated: kudos are much less routine and denigrations of style and faulty political judgment mark the re-

views of many authors favored by the Nazi ideologues. Nonetheless, whether dutifully submitting to a party line or going against the grain, aesthetic judgment is the primary mode of the early essays. Indeed, even the most troubling of all the passages is no exception to the rule, for the sinister concluding hypothesis of "The Jews in Contemporary Literature," takes the form of an *aesthetic* judgment.

It is in part due to their aestheticism that de Man's texts from *Le Soir, Het Vlaamsche Land,* and *Les Cahiers du Libre Examen* are not, it should go without saying, examples of deconstruction. The paradigmatic form of deconstruction is that of a 'reading.'[24] Even in the lengthiest of de Man's journalistic pieces from the wartime period, there is little that resembles what in the later de Man would be called a reading, a detailed engagement with the rhetoric of exemplary passages. Instead one finds grandiloquent claims about vast topics, judgments of style and politics, aperçus about literature and life: nothing like the rhetorical analysis of de Man's postwar essays. And a good many of de Man's pronouncements are made in a mode of literary criticism and literary history (organic, totalizing, teleological) that would be the explicit and implicit object of his criticism from the 1950s onward, as the example of his judgment of Marcel Raymond's *De Baudelaire au surréalisme* demonstrates.[25] What then is the relation—or are the relations—between the early de Man and the late? What itinerary leads from the one to the other, from the ambiguous, suspect journalism of the early 40s to the 'deconstructive' essays of his later life?

De Man's own sense of the itinerary of his career is set out in an interview conducted in the year of his death, 1983. While one need not consider de Man's self-presentation as authoritative, it does seem to make good sense of the transition from "early" to "late" de Man. "I have always maintained," de Man observes, "that one could approach the problems of ideology and by extension the problems of politics only on the basis of critical-linguistic analysis, which had to be done in its own terms, in the medium of language, and I felt I could approach those problems only after having achieved a certain control over those questions. . . . It was in working on Rousseau that I felt I was able to progress from purely linguistic analysis to questions which are really already of a political and ideological nature."[26]

At the time of his death, de Man was about to teach a seminar on Marx and Kierkegaard (via Adorno) in which the question of ideology, German and otherwise, would be taken up most directly. But de Man is certainly right, as Michael Sprinker among others confirms, to point out that these issues already preoccupied him from his essays of the early 1970s onwards.[27] The articulation of language, aesthetics, and politics, became a prominent project in the last, foreshortened phase of de Man's work. Many of relevant essays are already published; others are forthcoming in a volume, *Aesthetic Ideology,* which names their insistent concern. In a series of seminars and essays, de Man examined the category of the aesthetic primarily through a reading of German Idealist philosophy, demonstrating how especially in Kant the aesthetic constituted the articulation between the cognitive and the practical (ethics, morals, politics) rather than their suspension in some self-enclosed realm. Beyond this analytical movement, located in Hegel as well as Kant, de Man went on to question via a reading of Schiller the seemingly unassailable *value* of the aesthetic, especially as a solution for more properly social and political problems. That Nazi ideology was one of the targets of this critique was made clear by his alignment of a passage from a novel by Joseph Goebbels with the politico-aesthetic program of Schiller.[28] Though the signs of de Man's critique of aesthetic ideology can be read in his essays from the 1950s onward, the explicit, sustained attention to ideology in relation to aesthetics came relatively late. Why the delay?

One of the key terms with which de Man conducted his rhetorical and linguistic analysis was "impersonality," at its most explicit in his essay on Blanchot but present in a numerous texts taken up with the critique of the subject and the primacy of language over the self. Some might say that such a rhetoric of impersonality was precisely an attempt to evade the very particular self who authored the wartime writings. But de Man's theoretical and practical concern with impersonality is much less an evasion than an attempt to situate what appear to be simply matters of the self in a larger framework, most notably, that of language.[29] Indeed language, for de Man, was one name for that impersonality. Does such a concern with language necessarily bypass issues of history, ethics, and politics? Not unless one has an impoverished conception of language to begin with. There are, of course, degrees of emphasis: the essays prior to the ones on Rousseau are indeed more "purely linguistic," as de Man characterizes them. But de Man insisted that the critical analysis of language was one step in an itinerary that would lead to considerations of historical and political issues, "a reemergence of history at the far side of rhetoric."[30] Again and again, de Man argued against certain forms of pseudo-historical investigation, maintaining, for example, that periodizing terms such as "romanticism" and "classicism" stand at "the furthest remove from the materiality of actual history."[31] What may seem like a long "detour" through the aridity of rhetorical and linguistic analyses was a prerequisite for de Man to return to an investigation of history, ideology, and politics. The path that leads from the writings of *Le Soir* to *Aesthetic Ideology* is, then, a negative one, for the final moment in the itinerary consists, among other things, in an implicit condemnation of the immense false step he took in writing for *Le Soir* and *Het Vlaamsche Land*. One can well imagine that for de Man the questioning of aesthetic ideology—the ideology *of* the aesthetic — would have to be founded on "impersonal" criteria.

For it was by no means only the early de Man who had to be "buried" but also aesthetic ideology in general, and the particular aesthetico-political ideology with which he had once complied. Was this "burial" a hiding, an immensely mediated cover-up for de Man's sinister past? Why was the critique of aesthetic ideology not accompanied by an explicit auto-critique? Despite numerous charges that de Man never owned up to his past, the evidence thus far suggests that in his later life the one and only time de Man was publicly accused, he admitted, in a letter to the Director of the Harvard Society of Fellows, having written for *Le Soir*. Was it a gesture that should in some way have been reiterated, staged again at a later moment when de Man was no longer an unknown graduate student but a well-known professor?

What de Man had to say and to teach was singular but it did not depend for its value on his merely personal experience. Whatever authority de Man achieved came as a reader of texts and a teacher of reading, not as a source of moral or political wisdom. Now whatever authority the works de Man may retain in the future will depend even less on de Man the man: no longer will his name be able to function as kind of talisman, or as intellectual shorthand for some body of truths or practice of reading. And this will be entirely in line with one lesson de Man taught: there is no substitute for the work of reading.

* * * * *

"Penser," de Man remarked in his last seminar with more than a note of irony, "c'est trouver la bonne citation." ("To think is to find the right quotation.") Are there any "right" quotations that one could cite now, from the early or the late de Man? Perhaps it will never again be possible to cite a passage from "de Man" and imagine a single voice, if there ever was only one. The current debates over the texts of de Man turn to a considerable degree on how the texts are reconstructed and staged through a practice of (necessarily) selective citation. The initial journalistic accounts of de Man's wartime journalism limited quotation to a small number of passages—usually phrases rather than complete sentences—including, understandably, the most troubling ones. These phrases constituted all of what one could know of the texts in the first phase of their reception. Will things change substantially now that all the texts are available to be read? The fact that there are fewer than a handful of anti-Semitic passages from nearly three hundred articles and reviews does not minimize their gravity but it does raise a question about their exemplarity. Would the same image of de Man have been created if recent newspaper accounts had set the more sensational passages alongside the one about Péguy cited above? What would the effect have been if the *New York Times* had given the same historical information but cited representative passages from his concert reviews of the time?

Every quotation is a quotation out of context: only the degree of violence changes from case to case. Quotations tend to function as synecdoches, parts that are taken to represent a whole. Thus in the present instance journalists and scholars could pass with apparent ease from a number of phrases from *one* article by de Man to characterizations of his wartime writing as "anti-Semitic" in general.[32] In the journalistic responses as well as the more recent essayistic accounts of the de Man affair, a number of quotations from de Man's later writings have surfaced repeatedly in attempts to work out the relations between the disparate moments of de Man's career. The passages that emerge most frequently are predictable and familiar, though that is not to say well understood.

The status of "history" in de Man's work had been much debated well before the discovery of his wartime writings. One passage in particular has surfaced repeatedly, usually as evidence of de Man's "hostility" to history and his perverse textualization of non-linguistic events. The scandalous lines in question come from de Man's essay "Literary History and Literary Modernity" and read as follows: "To become good literary historians, we must remember that what we usually call literary history has little or nothing to do with literature and that what we call literary interpretation—provided only it is good interpretation—is in fact literary history. If we extend this notion beyond literature, it merely confirms that the bases for historical knowledge are not empirical facts but written texts, even if these texts masquerade in the guise of wars and revolutions."[33] This no doubt provocative passage has often been attacked for its presumed opposition to action, even though the Nietzsche text on which de Man comments, *On the Use and Abuse of History,* is in large measure about the possibility and desirability of action that would not be debilitated by a merely monumentalizing relation to the past. Frank Lentricchia, for example, reads this passage as evidence of de Man's "fundamental hostility toward the political, a stacking of the cards against action's political efficacy."[34] Even more pointed is Terry Eagleton's verdict on the passage: "A text which starts out with a problem in literary history ends

up as an assault on Marxism. For it is of course Marxism above all which has insisted that actions may be theoretically informed and histories emancipatory. It is only by virtue of an initial Nietzschean dogmatism—practice is necessarily self-blinded, tradition necessarily impeding—that de Man can arrive at his politically quietistic aporias."[35] Why Eagleton reads this as an assault on Marxism is unclear, since revolutions and wars can be bourgeois, populist, or fascist, as well as Marxist. But the more serious and symptomatic misreading, in Eagleton and Lentricchia, is the unmotivated translation from de Man's remarks about *knowledge* to the question of *action,* political or otherwise. Nothing in de Man's passage addresses the question of political action, much less cautions against it. The text's principal message, which approaches something of a structuralist truism, is that history comes to us linguistically mediated. This by no means implies that a war or a revolution is *merely* a text: numerous passages from elsewhere in de Man could be summoned to contradict such a claim.[36] History is only "reduced" to (literal) language if one begins with a reductive notion of language. The late de Man's understanding of language—with its attention to performatives, persuasion, and the arbitrary imposition of meaning—is anything but reductive. Moreover, to argue that the bases for historical knowledge are textual is not to suspend altogether notions of representation and reference. Indeed, de Man is capable of invoking precisely those concepts even in the most unlikely of places, as in his discussion of a hermetic sonnet by Mallarmé.[37]

It is no wonder that the passage which seems to trivialize history by transforming wars and revolutions into mere texts should be unearthed again in the debates provoked by the discovery of de Man's wartime writings. The most vehement objection has been voiced by David Hirsch in an article in the *Sewanee Review* entitled, significantly, "Paul de Man and the Politics of Deconstruction." There de Man is said to attack, in his notorious essay "Literary History and Literary Modernity," nothing less than "the concept of 'the past.'" Hirsch has some difficulty is staging quotations to support his argument about de Man's "will to obliterate the past,"[38] though to his credit he does cite passages that go directly against his thesis. He quotes de Man's gloss on Nietzsche's description of life as follows: "It is a temporal experience of human mutability, historical in the deepest sense of the term in that it implies the necessary experience of any present as a *passing* experience that makes the past irrevocable and unforgettable, because it is inseparable from any past or future."[39] For Hirsch this last phrase implies the following: "But it is soon clear that 'the past' that must be remembered has melted into an eternal present," quoting as proof the phrase "because it is inseparable from any past or future." Hirsch cannot quote the words "eternal present" because neither the words nor the concept occur in de Man's essay. Indeed it is difficult to imagine a concept that de Man would find more mystified than that of the eternal present. One can look almost anywhere in de Man to find refutations of the possibility of an eternal present, in "The Rhetoric of Temporality," for example, or perhaps most tellingly in "The Temptation of Permanence," one of the first articles de Man published after resuming a writing career in the 1950s.[40] There, at the close of a consideration of certain texts by Heidegger, de Man warns "it is a question of putting oneself on guard against the possibility of letting oneself be seduced by promises of permanence that these texts suggest, and which can support the mind in a state of beatitude which properly speaking is a lethargy."[41] One could go on to catalogue the passages where de Man thinks through and employs notions of history and temporality, as in the closing passage of "Anthropomorphism and Trope in the Lyric" where de Man recognizes the lyric as a historical mode of language power, and sees one task of criticism —there called "mourning"—as the enumeration of those historical modes.[42] This aspect of de Man's writing has yet to find much reception, though work along these lines is underway and will continue as criticism comes to terms with the difficult texts of Paul de Man.[43]

A second passage has surfaced often in the initial responses to de Man's wartime writing, one from a text that intersects with the ethical and linguistic issues raised by such activity: the essay from *Allegories of Reading* entitled "Excuses." I quote the passage in question first in abbreviated fashion, as it has most often been cited: "it is always possible to face up to any experience (to excuse any guilt), because the experience always exists simultaneously as fictional discourse and as empirical event and it is never possible to decide which of the two possibilities is the right one. The indecision makes it possible to excuse the bleakest of crimes because, as a fiction, it escapes from the constraints of guilt and innocence."[44] These lines have been cited numerous times by professors and journalists as an example of moral irresponsibility, indeed of "moral idiocy."[45] The quotation—almost always broken off at a strategic point—may seem to imply the abdication of all moral standards. What else is suggested by the notion that any guilt can be excused?

The most rudimentary complication of this passage when read in the context of de Man's essay on Rousseau's *Confessions* and the *Reveries* has to do with what an excuse is. It is, first of all, a performative speech-act: unlike the confession, which can be verified in relation to an extra-linguistic event, an excuse is a performative, persuasive utterance. As de Man notes earlier in

the essay: "No such possibility of verification exists for the excuse, which is verbal in its utterance, in its effect and its authority: its purpose is not to state but to convince, itself an 'inner' process to which only words can bear witness."[46] The controversial passage does not say and does not imply that a *good* or morally upright excuse can be offered with regard to any guilt whatsoever: it means quite simply that such performative utterances can be pronounced. That excuses are offered for the bleakest of crimes is empirically verifiable, as a whole range of excuses from Nazis, among others, confirms.[47] The crime continues to be bleak no matter what excuse is or is not enunciated. And if we read back from de Man's theoretical statement to the example from Rousseau in question, we can see that de Man by no means believes that the excuse in question "excuses" (absolves, whitewashes) the guilt. Rousseau, as the reader of the *Confessions* and the *Reveries* will recall, in effect blames "Marion" for the theft of a ribbon by uttering her name as the first thing that comes into his mind. The excuse in this instance not only fails to absolve the guilt, it exacerbates it. As de Man observes of the ultimate effect of the incident: "This is truly shameful, for it suggests that Marion was destroyed, not for the sake of Rousseau's saving face, nor for the sake of his desire for her, but merely in order to provide him with a stage on which to parade his disgrace or, what amounts to the same thing, to furnish him with a good ending for Book II of his *Confessions*."[48] Though the excuse *qua* performative speech act (and in contrast to the constative statement of a confession) is free from the constraints of truth and falsity, it may still have unjust effects and be judged accordingly. The performative as such is not necessarily free of the constraints of guilt and innocence but the excuse as *fiction* may be. But what then is fiction? Is it simply a linguistic world apart where the categories of guilt and innocence do not obtain? If one returns to the controversial passage from de Man in question and picks up the citation where it is usually interrupted, one can read the other side of the coin: "The indecision makes it possible to excuse the bleakest of crimes because, as a fiction, it escapes the constraints of guilt and innocence. On the other hand, it makes it equally possible to accuse fiction-making, which, in Hölderlin's words, is 'the most innocent of all activities,' of being the most cruel. The knowledge of radical innocence also performs the harshest mutilations. Excuses not only accuse but they carry out the verdict implicit in their accusation."[49] Thus the suspension of reference that separates fiction from non-fictional discourse does not imply that fiction is confined to the pseudo-cognitive sphere of non-reference: it can *perform* as knowledge the harshest mutilations, a phrase that signals the undoing of the performative/constative distinction in this regard. When read in full and in the context of its enunci-ation de Man's controversial statement does not suggest that there are morally cogent or compelling excuses available for any crime whatsoever, much less does it provide a grand theoretical "excuse" for the bleak injustices to which some of de Man's early writings gave ideological support.

A number of those who have commented so far on the de Man "affair" have demanded, as far as it is possible of someone who is dead, an excuse. Richard King in a letter to the *London Review of Books* comes close to the demand for an excuse proper when he writes: "George Steiner said that Heidegger's great flaw was not that he flirted with, and even actually courted, the Nazis, but that after 1945 he never deigned explain himself, much less admit that he had been wrong. It seems to me that the same sort of charge can be brought against de Man."[50] It is unclear why those justly suspicious of the young de Man would trust the excuse of an older de Man. Moreover, it seems odd to be more concerned (the "great flaw") with the *text* of an excuse rather than with the wartime texts that did the grave damage, and doubly so when some of the demands for the excuse come from those who accuse de Man of textualizing history to such an extent that language displaces it. Indeed, there is in a number of responses to the de Man "affair" an oddly skewed view to the effect de Man did more damage in his later life—when he did not publicly excuse himself—than in his collaborationist past. Consider, for example, the sense of betrayal attested by two writers whose work is avowedly indebted to de Man's: "He cer-tainly withheld from us the most important lesson he could have taught us."[51] What was the most important lesson de Man could have taught? If it was that Nazi fascism and anti-Semitism are abhorrent, there are better sources than de Man from whom to learn that simple but infinitely repeatable lesson. The same writers greatly exaggerate the naiveté and star-struck character of even de Man's most ardent admirers, finding it possible to personify such an imaginary de Manian and put these words in his or her mouth: "Well, if *de Man* thought fascism was OK I guess it was OK."[52] Has anyone thought—much less enunci-ated—anything positive about fascism because de Man in his young twenties complied with the Nazi occupiers? Already a number of responses from journalists and professors have di-vided the literary critical world into two camps, de Man's "critics" and de Man's "defenders," as if there could be no more differentiated position on a very complex matter. The situation was of course aggravated before the texts of the wartime writ-ings were generally available, when there seemed to be a neces-sity to have a "position" on the de Man affair, regardless of whether or not one had read the texts in question. Now there

should be no question of defending "de Man" in general, as if everything he did and wrote from 1939 to 1983 were of a piece.

* * * * *

From the very first newspaper account of de Man's wartime writing the debate has often been allegorical, that is to say, about "something other" than those early texts. That some-thing other has, for the most part, gone under the name of de-construction. One can understand why the specter of decon-struction might be raised in such a context, since Paul de Man's has so been named as one of its foremost practitioners. Yet 'de-construction'—a mode of thinking, reading, and writing that attempts to come to terms with the problematic of the proper name—itself bears a problematic relationship to the proper names with which it is most often associated. How does one pass from the name of the young Paul de Man to deconstruc-tion in general and from there to other proper names, such as Jacques Derrida's? No doubt, by way of a certain totalizing rhetoric, manifest in a good many of the early responses to the discovery of de Man's wartime texts. One could have expected glib generalizations from journalists who knew nothing about deconstruction and were suddenly called upon to say some-thing about it.[53] But the most spectacular instance of totaliz-ing—and hence historically misleading—rhetoric comes from a professor of literature well acquainted with the texts of Derrida and de Man. Jeffrey Mehlman is quoted in *Newsweek* as claiming that there are "grounds for viewing the *whole* of deconstruction as a vast amnesty project for the politics of collaboration during World War II" (my emphasis).[54] Perhaps Mehlman, like many others, has been misquoted here, though to the best of my knowledge *Newsweek* printed no letter of protest. As a matter of intellectual history Mehlman's judgment is absurd, to say noth-ing of insulting to all those implicated by his statement.

In Mehlman's defense one could say that his charge against deconstruction was not a casual, offhand remark. Indeed Mehl-man is in the singular position of having linked deconstruction to collaboration well before the revelations about de Man's war-time writings. His 1984 essay "Deconstruction, Literature, His-tory: The Case of *L'Arrêt de mort*" charged Derrida with "a strange act of piety" for his failure to account for the political reality of the novel's setting (partly in Munich, October 1938).[55] This essay, drawing upon his previous work on Blanchot in-cluded in *Legacies: Of Anti-Semitism in France,* was a mild-man-nered prelude to a much more vituperative article in *Repre-sentations* entitled "Writing and Deference: The Politics of Lit-erary Adulation." In the first essay of the sequence, Mehlman offers a sometimes ingenious analysis of a series of Blanchot's works, from the dubious *Combat* essays to numerous fictional narratives of the 1940s and beyond to statements on the May '68 uprising. But Mehlman's object of study is the relation between various Blanchot texts of very different periods; Derrida's focus in the target essay, "Living On / Borderlines," is on a certain problematic of life and the suspension of death in part dictated by the original organization of *Deconstruction and Criticism* around Shelley's *The Triumph of Life*. Derrida notes the setting of part of the novel in the Munich of October 1938 but that aspect of the *récit* is not elaborated in his text. Neither is it in Blanchot's. Laudable as is Mehlman's attempt to point out what is omitted in Derrida's reading (a strategy regrettably not widespread in the widespread critiques of deconstruction) Mehlman does not succeed in showing how Derrida's essay is disabled by this omission or "failure," if it is one.[56] Mehlman argues for a "historical" reading of *L'Arret de mort* primarily through its intertextual status, its relation to a good many other Blanchot texts and his embedding of the *récit* in its historical setting is only accomplished through a baroquely allegorical reading.[57] Is Derrida's essay guilty as charged because he chose to address certain narrative and thematic concerns not limited by the setting of one part of the *récit* and thus did not follow the same path as Mehlman?[58]

In the subsequent *Representations* essay, "Writing and Deference, "Mehlman elaborates an extraordinarily attenuated series of analogies that enable him ultimately to speak of "Derrida's opus as the textual instantiation of the amnesty or radical forgetting that seemed to constitute the horizon of Paulhan's writings on postwar politics in France."[59] Mehlman invokes the gray eminence Jean Paulhan, the resistance figure who after the war "resisted" the attempts of the *Comité national des écrivains* to purify or purge French writing of those authors with fascist or collaborationist credentials.[60] Derrida is linked by analogy to Paulhan as a postwar collaborator with ex-collaborators, based primarily on the facts that 1) both Derrida and Paulhan are interested in language and etymology; 2) both Derrida and Paulhan are the objects of adulation (Derrida by naive, domesticating Americans, Paulhan by the sycophantic Gerhard Heller, a German literary attaché in wartime Paris). Beyond these minimal structural similarities (is everyone interested in etymology and everyone who is the object of adulation something like a collaborator?), Mehlman's argument is carried by innuendo that hardly meets the requirements of historical or hermeneutic responsibility. For example, we are informed that Ezra Pound is "one of the tutelary figures of *Grammatology*," a phrase embedded in a discussion of Pound's *Jefferson and/or Mussolini,* a text Mehlman with reason calls "wrong, risky, and juridically soon

to be judged crazy."[61] Not only it is a great exaggeration to describe Pound as a "tutelary figure" of *Grammatology* just because his fascination with the Chinese ideogram is mentioned as marking a break with western tradition, but that aspect of Pound surely has little to do with his support of Mussolini's (thoroughly western) fascism. And yet it is those two aspects of Pound that are yoked together in the same paragraph of Mehlman's essay and linked to Derrida. Is there no difference?

Between Paulhan and Derrida there are differences, Mehlman assures us, but, he says, "the differences are too great to need rehearsing." His own procedure, which he acknowledges required "a few particularly vigorous intertextual leaps," rehearses only certain similarities of the sketchiest sort. Mehlman closes his essay in this way: "My sense is that the discourse of difference will be able to make good its claims to heterogeneity only on the condition of running such interpretive risks." But what sort of "discourse of difference" is it that enumerates tenuous similarities and leaves the admittedly great differences unspoken? Especially when a good deal of the historical and political "background" of his other subject matter has been elided, not to say forgotten: Derrida as a victim of anti-Semitism, critic of ethnocentrism from the first page of *Grammatology*—facts that make the analogy of collaboration all the more suspect.[62] Such arguments by analogy and innuendo have been taken up again and again in the responses to deconstruction since the revelation of de Man's wartime writings, for they could hardly be made in a more substantive fashion.[63]

In reviewing some of the early responses to the discovery of de Man's wartime texts, one encounters numerous instances of egregious errors, outrageous and scandalous in their circumscribed way. Many of them are conducted—or committed —in the name of historical, hermeneutic, and ethical responsibility at the moment that de Man, young and old, as well as deconstruction in general is accused of patent irresponsibility on just those counts. These contemporary "errors" hardly correspond to those of the young de Man: the former do not come close to the latter in gravity. It is the infinite gravity of the stakes involved in collaboration that makes any attempt to defend (any aspect of) de Man a difficult, even a perilous task. But one should be able to distinguish between works of utterly different character (e.g. the *Le Soir* writings versus the essays on aesthetic ideology) even if they were all written by Paul de Man, much as one might distinguish between a music review Adorno wrote for a Hitler Youth publication and his later, radically different works.[64]

For some even the attempt to consider de Man's early and late work in the light of each other seems suspect. Roger Kimball, a staff writer for the *New Criterion,* readily admitted he had not read the texts from *Le Soir* and *Het Vlaamsche Land.* Nonetheless he felt capable of attacking not just de Man's early (unread) writings but also Geoffrey Hartman's essay "Blindness and Insight" (*New Republic,* March 7), primarily because Hartman persists in seeing something valuable in the later de Man's work. The hermeneutic errors of Kimball's article are many, the most telling of which is his characterization of Hartman's procedure as "an apologia for Paul de Man's *early* writings" (my emphasis).[65] Hartman is unequivocal in his condemnation of the *Le Soir* texts, especially as his focus is on the most troubling article, "The Jews in Contemporary Literature." When Hartman, trying to convey the character of de Man's texts to those who had not read them, assesses them within the spectrum of anti-Semitic writings of the day, he determines that they stand out "by their refusal to engage directly with political matters."[66] Hartman's judgment is entirely correct, for one of the remarkable aspects of de Man's texts is the sustained argument for the autonomy of literature, which seems such an unlikely position for a supposed Nazi ideologue to take. But Kimball is not content with this assessment of the texts he has not read. He concludes: "The idea is, I suppose, that simply not descending to the vicious racial slurs of a Goebbels merits some sort of commendation."[67] Hartman, however, says not one word of commendation on behalf of de Man's *Le Soir* articles. Like the Belgian authorities after the war who imposed no punishment on the young de Man, Hartman is able to distinguish between degrees of violence, between a Goebbels and a young and ambiguous chronicler of literature. Why is it so difficult for Kimball to accept an attempt to weigh the suspect journalism of a man in his early twenties against three decades of essays of an utterly different character? Hartman is persuasive in arguing that one thrust of those essays is, in his words, "a deepening reflection on the rhetoric of totalitarianism." The debate, again, takes on an allegorical character, for the real quarrel is with deconstruction and the later de Man. Kimball takes every opportunity to trivialize the project of deconstruction as Hartman outlines it for a broad, non-specialist audience. To Hartman's general characterization that for de Man "we are always encountering epistemological instabilities, the incompatibility or disjunction between meaning and intent, or between what is stated and the rhetoric or mode of stating it," Kimball has only this to say: "But this is an insight that any well-educated high school student should have when reflecting for the first time on the way language works."[68] And indeed, Kimball has little patience with matters of language: what he finds "most troubling" is that Hartman in his article quickly "transforms the entire discussion into debate about language."[69] Is this so strange when de Man's work was preoccupied with the question from beginning to end? And not only were de Man's late essays always focused on linguistic problems, the scandal of surrounding his early politics is based solely upon *texts* he wrote, largely literary reviews. But lest one think that Kimball is jettisoning all of deconstruction for the sins of de Man's past, he also provides a critique of de Man's "reading" of Husserl set out in the "Criticism and Crisis" essay. In response to de Man's remarks on Husserl's characterization of the European spirit, where de Man had wondered why Husserl's vision of geographical expansion should have stopped at the Atlantic Ocean and the Caucasus, Kimball quite rightly quotes (part of) the appropriate passage from Husserl where it is clear that the "spirit" of Europe extends beyond its geographical boundaries.[70] Kimball's corrective to de Man he himself terms "a small point" but adds that "it gives one a good indication of the kind of 'close reading' from our premier deconstructionists." De Man's discussion of Husserl's text runs less than two pages in *Blindness and Insight* and is hardly exemplary of "close reading," understood as a technique or methodological procedure. Readers can decide for themselves how representative the passage from de Man is and how his skill in reading stands up against, say, Kimball's failure to understand Hartman's condemnation of de Man's collaborationist writing. Some of these details of reading are indeed "small points" but it is on the basis of Kimball's "reading" (or the lack of it) that he comes to his concluding denunciation of Hartman's essay and the *New Republic*'s decision to publish it as "a stunningly blunt failure of moral and intellectual conscience."[71]

It is perhaps the allegorical character of the current debates—that their object is really deconstruction and not de Man's writings in his early twenties—which in part accounts for conspicuous lack of historical and hermeneutic responsibility in some of the texts considered here. Perhaps it also helps explain the precipitous character of the debates—the rush to judgement in advance of reading the texts—for the real target of hostility was deconstruction, linked together with two other known and despised quantities, fascism and anti-Semitism. That deconstruction—if there is such a thing—has nothing to do with the latter should be clear to anyone who has read more than a few pages of Derrida or the later de Man.

De Man's earliest work on the *Cahiers de Libre Examen,* his thwarted attempt to flee occupied Belgium, and his work in publishing resistance material in Brussels, suggest that he was by no means a committed supporter of the heinous agendas of the Nazi occupiers. But how exactly does one weigh whatever good de Man did before and sometimes during the occupation with the damage done by writing for collaborationist publications? In reading the responses to the de Man affair so far, one might be struck by a discrepancy between the comments of some who worked on behalf of the resistance (admittedly those who knew de Man) and those who had no experience of the war, especially of what life was like in an occupied country. The former refuse even the name of collaborator to characterize de Man's wartime action while many of the latter, like Kimball, express their moral outrage at any attempt to consider his wartime writing in the more positive light of de Man's long career as a critic and teacher. Is it because those who lived in an occupied country knew the pressures and the difficult decisions one had to make in matters of life and death? Surely everyone now would like to think that if faced with a similar situation he or she would resist rather than collaborate with the occupying forces. And yet, for whatever complex of political, economic, and psychological reasons, collaboration was massive. We like to distance ourselves as completely as possible from fascists and collaborators by calling them "inhuman," even when we know otherwise: that they were—they are—all too human.

The resistance de Man's writing manifests in the Péguy article and elsewhere, even as he is officially enlisted in a collaborationist agenda, suggests that he was aware of his wrongdoing even as he was engaged in it. His struggle against the forces he was working for may seem meager in comparison to the support he gave to them simply by writing for *Le Soir* and *Het Vlaamsche Land*. But this immense false step, I believe, was recognized as such, and the later de Man in a circumscribed and modest way worked against the circumscribed and immodest legacy of his wartime writings. The only reason there is any interest in de Man's texts from 1939–43 lies in the significance of his later achievements. From his writings for *Le Soir* and *Het Vlaamsche Land* there is only a negative lesson to be learned. If de Man's later writings have anything valuable to say, they do so in spite of and against the now scandalous texts of his youth. There is no need to privilege the late de Man, the critic of aesthetic ideology, as a reader of the early de Man, though that is one way for the dead to bury the dead. The texts from *Le Soir* cannot and should not be forgotten, but it is the texts from *Blindness and Insight* to *Aesthetic Ideology* from which we may continue to learn, even if we must now read them in a colder, a harsher light.

York University

NOTES

1. "Phenomenality and Materiality in Kant," in *Hermeneutics, Questions and Prospects,* ed. Gary Shapiro and Alan Sica (Amherst: University of Massachusetts Press, 1984), p. 138. A somewhat different version of this same material is found in de Man's "Kant's Materialism," forthcoming in *Aesthetic Ideology,* to be published by the University of Minnesota Press.

I am grateful to Deborah Esch and Tom Keenan for helpful commentaries on an earlier draft of this essay.

2. Ibid., p. 136.

3. This aspect of de Man's reading of Kant was clearer in the more elaborate seminar version of this material.

4. For this quotation see "Yale Scholar Wrote for pro-Nazi Newspaper," *New York Times,* 1 December 1987 (late edition, corrected), p. B6.

5. "Dialogue and Dialogism" in *The Resistance to Theory* (Minneapolis: University of Minnesota Press, 1986), p. 107.

6. This is de Man quoting Strauss, *Persecution and the Art of Writing* (Westport, Conn: Greenwood, 1973 [1952]), p. 36.

7. Strauss notes in the programmatic opening chapter of his study: "One may say without fear of being presently convicted of grave exaggeration that almost the only preparatory work to guide the explorer in this field is buried in the writers of the rhetoricians of antiquity." Ibid., p. 24.

8. See, for example, the testimonies recorded at the end of Jacques Derrida's "Like the Sound of the Sea Deep Within a Shell: Paul de Man's War," *Critical Inquiry* 14: 3 (Spring 1988), pp. 651–652.

9. On censorship in occupied Belgium, see Els de Bens, "La presse au temps de l'occupation de la Belgique," *Revue d'histoire de la deuxième guerre mondiale* 80 (October 1970), pp. 1–28. Aside from auto-censorship and peer pressure, there was at *Le Soir* a system of after-the-fact penalties that could be levied on articles not conforming to a certain agenda.

10. For a painstaking reading of the article, I refer the reader to Derrida's "Like the Sound of the Sea Deep Within a Shell: Paul de Man's War," especially pp. 621–632. (Derrida's essay outlines much that needs to be said and is an excellent point of departure for future thinking about these matters.) It may well be argued that in attacking vulgar anti-Semitism, de Man was writing on behalf of a more "refined" one. That is one way to read the substance and the rhythm of the article on Jewish literature. Yet the dismissal of vulgar anti-Semitism reads like a dismissal of anti-Semitism *tout court*.

That does not excuse the sinister character of the hypothesis of a Europe deprived of its Jewish writers, but it suggests a tension between two opposing movements in the text.

11. Quoted in Jon Wiener, "Deconstructing de Man," *The Nation*, 9 January 1988 p. 22.

12. For a valuable study of especially the French-language canon in particular, see Alice Yaeger Kaplan, *Reproductions of Banality: Fascism, Literature, and French Intellectual Life* (Minneapolis: University of Minnesota Press, 1986). Especially helpful for rethinking the categories by which fascism can best be understood is the section of Chapter 1 entitled "The Polarity Machine," pp. 25–35.

13. Here it would be helpful to know the extent of Henri de Man's influence in obtaining a position for his nephew or in persuading him that it was a viable option, given the prospect of continuing Nazi hegemony. Thus far no documentary evidence has emerged to shed light on the matter.

14. *Le Soir,* 6 May 1941. Translations from this and other articles from *Le Soir* are my own.

15. For a brief but suggestive account of Péguy's stand on the Dreyfus affair and of his relation to Judaism in general, see Jean-Michel Rey, *Colère de Péguy* (Paris: Hachette, 1987), especially pp. 102–116.

16. *Le Soir,* 6 May 1941 (my translation).

17. On the theory and practice of Henri de Man, I am indebted to the excellent study by Zeev Sternhell, *Neither Right nor Left: Fascist Ideology in France* (Berkeley: University of California Press, 1986). The text is a revised and expanded version of the author's *Ni droite ni gauche: L'idéologie fasciste en France* (Paris: Seuil, 1983). See especially Chapter 4 (The Ethical Socialism of Henri de Man). More generally, Sternhell's study helps illuminate the relations among Marxism, socialism, and fascism in the pre-war period and shows how the itinerary from a leftist socialism to fascist collaboration was by no means atypical; Henri de Man's trajectory in this regard was only the most notable. One might also want to reread, in this light, the sobering section on "Leftist Anti-semitism" in Hannah Arendt's *The Origins of Totalitarianism* for an account of the historical roots of that conjunction.

18. On Halévy's career and particularly his championing role in the Dreyfus affair, see the informative study by Alain Silvera, *Daniel Halévy and his Times* (Ithaca: Cornell University Press, 1966), especially Chapter 3. Halévy was of Jewish extraction on his father's side. A good deal of his early work was in collaboration with and under the shadow of Péguy. His politics until roughly 1930 were in

an egalitarian socialist mold whereupon he turned to a more elitist and anti-democratic socialism characteristic of some of the remarkable conjunctures of left and right wing ideology in the thirties. That his books were available to be reviewed by de Man is one index of his political acceptability to the right. The final section of Halévy's *Trois Epreuves* is quite sympathetic to Pétain, at whose trial he would speak after the war. Thus Halévy was no political saint, but de Man's emphasis in his review of Halévy is on Péguy as a Dreyfusard and egalitarian socialist.

19. One might recall here that the *Cahiers du Libre Examen* under de Man's directorship featured many Jewish authors writing on topics such as totalitarianism and racism. In the copy at the Bibliothèque Royal in Brussels, the table of contents for the *Cahiers du Libre Examen* issue on "Totalitarisme" (April 1940) features the hand-written designation "juif" beside the names of six of the eight authors.

20. In his reviews of the novel de Man does not speak explicitly of it as an allegory. But he does seem to draw attention to its allegorical character when he writes in the *Bibliographie Dechenne* for January 1943: "It is not in a first reading that one will be able to grasp the full riches of this book, the meaning of which is expressed on different, separate planes." The novel has been read, by Jewish exiles among others, as a critique of the Hitler regime. See, for example, Gerhardt Loose's *Ernst Jünger* (New York, Twayne, 1974), Chapter 5. Some useful articles on the text as political allegory are Peter Uwe Hohendahl, "The Text as Cipher: Ernst Jünger's Novel: *On the Marble Cliffs*," *Yearbook of Contemporary Criticism* 1 (University Park and London: Pennsylvania State University Press, 1968), pp.129–69; Helmut J. Gutmann, "Politisches Parabel und mystisches Modell: Ernst Jünger's *Auf den Marmorklippen*," *Colloquia Germanica* 20: 1 (1987), pp.53–72. De Man's several reviews of the novel bear comparison with Maurice Blanchot's essay, "Une oeuvre d'Ernst Jünger" in *Faux Pas* (Paris: Gallimard, 1943), pp.287–292. Blanchot cautions that the text resists "une interprétation allégorique trop simple."

21. In addition to the opposing tendencies that are clearly marked in the articles for *Le Soir,* there are also numerous passages whose political referent is difficult to decipher. For example, when de Man writes in *Le Soir* (26 August, 1941) of the "decomposition and degeneracy" of things and speaks of the present as a most propitious time for a renewal (*renouveau*) of institutions at the moment they are being replaced, is he speaking of the degeneracy of the occupying forces or of the pre-occupation regime?

22. A full reading of the *Le Soir* texts would attend to all the arguments for and against aestheticism to determine as precisely as possible when and where de Man was strategically invoking the very

thing that he would elsewhere argue against. Why, for example, is Theo Léger praised for his pure poetry (*Le Soir* 31 March 1942) and others castigated for their aestheticism? What can it mean for de Man to term "très pure" the work of Eluard whose politics were anathema to the Nazis? (See *Le Soir*, 14 July 1942.) When is the resistance to the political to be understood as a resistance to a certain politics?

23. *Le Soir,* 2 December 1941.

24. It is partly because deconstruction typically takes the form of a "reading"—readings that are not at all limited to merely textual matters—that it resists definition. I cannot take up here the problems with a definition of deconstruction but I refer the reader to one of Derrida's recent "definitions" for it: *"plus d'une langue—* both more than a language and no more of *a* language." *Mémoires: for Paul de Man* (New York: Columbia University Press, 1986), p. 15.

25. See the young de Man's "Critiek en literatuurgeschiednis" ("Criticism and Literary History"), *Het Vlaamsche Land,* 7–8 June 1942, p. 3.

26. "An Interview with Paul de Man," *The Resistance To Theory* (Minneapolis: University of Minnesota Press, 1986), p. 121.

27. If one wanted to date the appearance of this interest in de Man, it might be conveniently located as the publication of "Theory of Metaphor in Rousseau's *Second Discourse,*" *Studies in Romanticism* 12:2, Spring 1973, pp. 475–98. The "interest" of course predates the publication. For a discussion of the importance of de Man's thought in this regard, see Michael Sprinker, *Imaginary Relations: Aesthetics and Ideology in the Theory of Historical Materialism* (London: Verso, 1987), especially Chapter 9: "Politics and Language: Paul de Man and the Permanence of Ideology."

28. The point was not to read Schiller's "aesthetic state" as proto-fascist, but rather to show one form the unquestioning valorization of the aesthetic could take. The juxtaposition of Schiller and Goebbels was particularly chilling when this material was presented in seminar form, as de Man first read the "Schillerian" passage aloud and then identified its author as Goebbels.

29. Even in the essay on Blanchot where the "theory" of impersonality is most elaborated, de Man can write the following: "In the askesis of depersonalization, [Blanchot] tries to conceive of the literary work, not as if it were a thing, but as an autonomous conscious entity, a 'consciousness without a subject.' This is not an easy undertaking. Blanchot must eliminate from his work all elements derived from everyday experience, from involvement with others, all reifying tendencies that tend to equate the work with natural ob-

jects. Only when this extreme purification has been achieved, can he turn toward the truly temporal dimensions of the text. This reversal implies a return toward *a subject* that, in fact, *never ceased to be present*" (my emphasis). *Blindness and Insight* (Minneapolis; University of Minnesota Press, 1983), p. 78.

30. "Introduction" to "The Rhetoric of Romanticism" issue of *Studies in Romanticism* 18:4 (Winter 1979), p. 499.

31. "Anthropomorphism and Trope in the Lyric," *The Rhetoric of Romanticism* (New York: Columbia University Press, 1984), p. 262.

32. Jon Wiener's article in *The Nation* paraphrased and cited from a single article as if it were more than one.

33. "Literary History and Literary Modernity," *Blindness and Insight,* 2nd rev. ed. (Minneapolis: University of Minnesota Press, 1983), p. 165.

34. Frank Lentricchia, *Criticism and Social Change* (Chicago: University of Chicago Press, 1983), p. 44.

35. *Against the Grain* (London: Verso, 1986), pp. 137–38.

36. See, for example, the passage on the French Revolution in "Wordsworth and Hölderlin," *The Rhetoric of Romanticism* (New York: Columbia University Press, 1984), p. 55.

37. See de Man's reading of Mallarmé's *Tombeau de Verlaine* in *Blindness and Insight,* p. 175.

38. David Hirsch, "Paul de Man and the Politics of Deconstruction," *Sewanee Review* 96:2 (Spring 1988), pp. 330–338. Professor Hirsch argues for historical and hermeneutic responsibility but his own text rarely displays it. He muses: "One suspects that those same scholars who were shocked to learn about de Man's unsavory past would be equally surprised to learn about the existence of German death camps" (p.330). How can Hirsch equate perhaps the most widely-known fact of modern European history with something that hardly anyone knew about? De Man's "American graduate students" and "academic peers" are all termed "naive" (p. 331) because they did not know something there was scarcely any way of knowing.

39. *Blindness and Insight,* pp. 148–49.

40. Professor Hirsch refers the reader to an earlier article of his which is his own words "questioned the worship lavished on the Nazi Martin Heidegger by de Man and his followers." Does Hirsch also find it a sign of worship when de Man in another essay claims that Hölderlin says exactly the opposite of what Heidegger makes him say? Hirsch, a teacher of Holocaust literature, is justifiably sus-

picious of Heidegger's politics and de Man's collaborationist writing but there seems little justification for making such statements about the later de Man whose texts he does not seem to have read with any care. The reduction of Heidegger's thought to Nazi philosophy is also enlisted in a critique of de Man by Tzvetan Todorov in the *Times Literary Supplement* (June 17–23, 1988) who after reviewing the charges of Heidegger's Nazism goes on to call de Man "an influential propagator of Heidegger's philosophy" (p. 676). Is that an accurate description of de Man, who could much more justifiably be called a propagator of Rousseauean philosophy or Benjaminian criticism? Rousseau is certainly more highly valorized in the de Manian canon than Heidegger, to whom de Man devotes only two essays in the 1950s that are often critical of his object of study. De Man also learned much about allegory from Benjamin and wrote with great sympathy about his essay on translation but to align his name with de Man would disrupt Todorov's politico-critical agenda.

41. "The Temptation of Permanence," in *Southern Humanities Review* 17:3 (Summer 1983), p. 220.

42. *The Rhetoric of Romanticism*, p. 262.

43. See, for example, essays by Kevin Newmark and Werner Hamacher forthcoming in *Reading de Man Reading* (Minneapolis: University of Minnesota Press, 1988).

44. *Allegories of Reading* (New Haven and London: Yale University Press, 1979), p. 293.

45. See, for example, David Lehman "Deconstructing de Man's Life," *Newsweek,* February 15, 1988, p. 63.

46. *Allegories of Reading*, p. 281.

47. In this regard it is of interest to read the interview with Maurice Bardèche at the end of Alice Kaplan's *Reproductions of Banality* where Bardèche can still defend "rational" anti-Semitism.

48. *Allegories of Reading*, pp. 285–286.

49. Ibid., p. 293.

50. "Letters," *London Review of Books* 10:7, 31 March 1988, p. 4.

51. Dean MacCannell and Juliet Flower MacCannell, "News and Notes," *American Journal of Semiotics* 5:1 (1987), p. 184.

52. Ibid.

53 . See, for example, Jon Wiener's caricature: "Deconstruction claims not only are books 'texts,' but that everything is at some level a text and thus 'undecidable'…" (*The Nation,* 9 January 1988, p. 22).

Does de Man ever say or imply that *everything* is undecidable? The words "undecidable" and "undecidability" occur perhaps half a dozen times in the complete works of de Man, and always in the course of a reading. When de Man decides, for example, that Yeats' line "How can we know the dancer from the dance?" is undecidable because of the impossibility of determining whether it is a real or a rhetorical question, that by no means suggests that *everything* is undecidable. De Man's essays are riddled with decisions of many kinds, indeed much to the consternation of critics like Frank Lentricchia whose critique of de Man comes under the rubric of "The Rhetoric of Authority" for the way in which de Man decides too many things. Lentricchia, as quoted by Wiener, also succumbs to totalizing caricature as when he says, for example, that for de Man "every linguistic act is duplicitous" (p. 24).

54. *Newsweek,* February 15, 1988, p. 63.

55. *Proceedings of the Northeastern University Center for Literary Studies,* Vol. 2 (1984), pp. 33–53.

56. For a brief, suggestive critique of Mehlman's essay, see Naomi Schor's "Response" printed in the same volume, pp. 53–57.

57. See, for example, the ingenious but tenuous passages elaborated from the mention of "the perfect rose," which leads Mehlman on a complicated itinerary that takes in Paulhan's *Les Fleurs de Tarbe*. If Mehlman believes the major problematics of the text can be restricted to—and are only intelligible in the light of—its historical setting, he has yet to demonstrate it.

58. In a postscript to his essay, Mehlman reflects back on his own earlier writing on Blanchot, writing which did not take account of Blanchot's texts from *Combat* in the 30s. Would readers of that essay accuse Mehlman of a "radical forgetting," tantamount to a retroactive complicity in collaboration, as he has accused Derrida?

59. "Writing and Deference: The Politics of Literary Adulation," *Representations* 15 (Summer 1986), p. 12.

60. Among the many relevant texts see especially the *Lettre aux directeurs de la résistance* and *De la paille et du grain,* both collected in *Oeuvres completes de Jean Paulhan* (Paris: Cercle du Livre Precieux, 1970).

61. Ibid., p. 3.

62. I refer the reader to the subsequent exchange in *Representations* 18 (Spring 1987) between Ann Smock and Jeffrey Mehlman. Mehlman resists Smock's objections to what she rightly reads as the sinister and unfounded insinuations of the article. Mehlman replies that he "would like to disassociate himself" from any conclusions

that are "abusive toward the person of Derrida" and then shifts the terrain to "American academic deconstruction," which had indeed been one object of his attack. But in the explicit analogy of the article it is Derrida (not American deconstruction) who is set up as analogue of Paulhan in his role as provider of the amnesty for collaborationist and fascist writing that Mehlman terms, with an ethical rather than an epistemological charge, "radical forgetting." Even as a denunciation of "American academic deconstruction," Mehlman's attack leaves much to be desired, for the reception of Derrida in America has led to some very productive and politically responsible work, as the cases of Gayatri Spivak and Samuel Weber demonstrate.

63. One might note here one other outrageous linking of fascism and deconstruction, somewhat apart from the controversy now surrounding de Man. Manfred Frank in a programmatic essay ("Kleiner (Tübinger) Programmentwurf," *Frankfurter Rundschau*, 5 March 1988, p. zb 3) attacks the "new French criticism of 'logocentrism,'" which he associates with Derrida, Deleuze, and Lyotard. These names are in turn linked with the "prefascist" writers Klages, Spengler, and Bäumler based on the notion that the badmouthing (*Schimpfe*) of logocentrism originates (*herrührt*) with Klages. Frank further inscribes the designated French thinkers into an "unbroken irrationalistic tradition since the Third Reich." Like Mehlman, Frank loses sight of all the important differences between the two groups of thinkers he violently yokes together. Is every criticism of rationalism, or a certain form of rationalism, fascistic or proto-fascistic? On the minimal criteria Frank provides, a thinker like Hamann, for example, might as well be considered a fascist.

64. On this review and Adorno's letter acknowledging his authorship, see Philippe Lacoue-Labarthĕ, *La fiction du politique* (Paris: Christian Bourgeois, 1987), pp. 150–51n.

65. Roger Kimball, "Professor Hartman reconstructs Paul de Man," *The New Criterion* (May 1988), p. 36.

66. As quoted in Ibid., p. 38.

67. Ibid., p. 38.

68. Ibid., p. 39.

69. Ibid., p. 42.

70. Kimball breaks off Husserl's sentence before its final phrase, citing it thus: "in the spiritual sense it is clear that to Europe belong the English dominions, the United States, etc. but not, however, the Eskimos or Indians of the country fairs, or the Gypsies. . . ." Kimball omits the last phrase which reads, "or the Gypsies, who constantly wander around in Europe (*die dauernd in Europa herumvagabondieren*)." The phrase implies that not everyone in Europe is European; not every European partakes of the European "spirit." How then is it decided who is a real, who is a phony European? For the full passage, see Edmund Husserl, *The Crisis of European Sciences and Transcendental Phenomenology,* trans. David Carr (Evanston: Northwestern University Press, 1970), p. 273. See also Jacques Derrida's brief commentary on this "sinistre passage" in *De l'esprit: Heidegger et la question* (Paris: Galilée, 1987), p. 95.

71. "Professor Hartman reconstructs Paul de Man," p. 43.

Fascist Commitments

JOHN BRENKMAN

The articles Paul de Man wrote for *Le Soir* in 1941–42 furnish the evidence, beyond a reasonable doubt, that he was at that time a fascist and an anti-Semite as well as an active collaborator with the Nazi occupation of Belgium.

A juridical stance and prosecutorial attitude respond to the circumstances of the controversy that has begun to unfold since these articles were discovered and made known. De Man eschewed any acknowledged reflection on his writing and activity during the war. He participated in fascism publicly, but did not abandon it publicly. Those of us concerned with his work and career—ourselves participants in an intellectual culture he helped shape—are obligated to investigate his involvement with fascism as thoroughly as possible. The prosecutorial stance establishes the aggressiveness required of such an inquiry. By the same token, I have demanded of myself the limiting standard of being convinced beyond a reasonable doubt before drawing conclusions as to de Man's positions, beliefs, and actions.

PUBLICIST AND PROPAGANDIST

From December 1940 until November 1942 de Man wrote book reviews and cultural criticism for the Brussels daily *Le Soir*. The paper was published under the censorship of the German military authority which administered Belgium after the German invasion of May 1940. Its owners' power was abrogated by the occupying power. The Germans made Raymond de Becker editor-in-chief. De Becker and many other members of the editorial staff belonged to the Rexist party, a fascist organization that originated in the 1930s from the ultra-right youth movements and split from the Catholic party in the 1930s. *Le Soir* had a circulation of 230,000, making it the largest publication in Belgium during the occupation.[1]

De Man regularly performed the duties of publicist and propagandist. During the first several months of his tenure at *Le Soir* he frequently reported—always uncritically, often enthusiastically—cultural events designed to foster fascist ideology.

He praised lectures by a scholar named Luigi Pareti on Italian history for "reveal[ing] fundamental aspects of the current revolution," from "the suppression of the struggle among classes" to a colonial and racial policy which "sends colonists into conquered territories to organize the social life of the natives without any intermingling with them, assures the solidity of the empire and the maintaining of the race."[2] In Pareti's second lecture he saw a "lesson. . . important for Belgians wanting to see their country reconstructed," in particular, a greater reliance on their own native qualities. The lecture had been a refutation of the influence of the French Revolution on the Risorgimento. The real key to Italian unification had been "a philosophy of the meek. . . in which labor and earth were exalted and where the necessity of an amelioration of the relations between classes was noted" (3/17/41).

De Man reported the publication of four pamphlets in Flemish on the Third Reich. He found they provided "precious clarifications and important data" on Nazi policies and reforms. One pamphlet explained worker support for Hitler. Another revealed "how the attitude of the German victors was more worthy, more just, and more humane than that of the French in 1918" (4/14/41).

De Man interviewed Abel Bonnard, Vichy Minister of Education and member of the governing committee of Groupe "Collaboration,"[3] just before the latter's lecture on "the constitution of an elite in the new Europe." The idea that "'the collapse of democracy is not alien to this reviving of the mind'" is among the views approvingly quoted by de Man as "some of the principles that must lead to this regrouping of forces which, in Belgium, as in France, is a necessary condition for the nation to be able to revive" (6/7–8/41).[4]

He reported, with apparent approval, the words of the burgomaster-commissioner of Ghent. Hendrick Elias was an activist and theoretician of the Vlaamsch Nationaal Verbond (VNV), a fascist party within the Flemish nationalist movement; the Nazis had designated the VNV the one political organization permitted in Flanders (its counterpart in Wallony being the Rexist party) and installed Elias in his governmental position. During a German-Flemish cultural event in Ghent, "M. Elias indicated how the current war had given birth to an immense hope for definitive emancipation, a hope which will be realized when this people [that is, Flemings], who live from Dunkerque all the way to Dollart, with its own spiritual unity, its language and its own culture, will have firmly established its collaboration with the German Reich" (8/16–17/41).

FASCIST COMMITMENT

De Man's more active contribution to fascist ideology and right wing opinion came in the book reviews and cultural commentaries. There emerges from those writings a constellation of social and cultural ideas, political values, and historical interpretations that places de Man's thinking squarely within radical right wing doctrine of the times. Particularly attuned to the intellectual currents of Italian fascism and the anti-bourgeois strains of Nazism, de Man looked to the fascist revolution as the promise of an anti-democratic, anti-individualistic era that

would replace class antagonisms with class cooperation; that would stabilize social hierarchies and educate youth to assume roles within a disciplined, highly centralized social order; and that would couple authoritarian political rule with an expanded role for managerial and intellectual elites entrusted with the task of reviving the economy and renewing national cultural traditions within a harmonious rather than conflictual environment of European spiritual values.

De Man consistently emphasized the popular basis of Nazism. Reviewing Jacques Chardonne's *Voir la figure,* he praised the author's grasp of the situation in Germany. Others had mistakenly assumed that there was

an integral dualism between Germany on the one hand and Hitlerism on the other. The latter was considered a strange phenomenon unrelated to the historical evolution of the German people. . . . It is not merely a matter of a series of reforms but of the definitive emancipation of a people who in turn find themselves called to exercise hegemony in Europe (10/28/41).

De Man asserted that German actions had been "systematically and knowingly deformed by a tendentious propaganda" and a "policy based on incomprehension and lying" (10/28/41). And he decried a situation in which, "by dint of undergoing long years of brain-washing by French and British propaganda, the Belgian reader is unaware of all that has been done in Germany from the social and political point of view" (4/12–14/41).

An extremely favorable review of a book by Bertrand de Jouvenal—a supporter of Jacques Doriot's pro-Hitler Parti Populaire Français—established the central theme of de Man's view of Nazi Germany:

Thanks to his feeling for the psychology of crowds he is able to provide a very pertinent analysis of the moral evolution that leads German youth to become the most furious enemies of the triumphant democratic bourgeoisie of 1914–18. Up until now this inner evolution has not been taken seriously enough. Fascism was considered a kind of passing madness, whereas it is on the contrary an extremely normal and lasting reaction in the face of the circumstance created by world politics; de Jouvenal is eager to explain its depth. (3/18/41)

He found similar merits in a book by Pierre Daye, a Rexist journalist and political correspondent for *Le Nouveau Journal,* a significant collaborationist periodical edited by Robert Poulet. De Man found especially "pertinent and judicious . . . the paragraphs that demonstrate that the present war is, beyond an economic and national struggle, the beginning of a revolution that aims at organizing European society in a more equitable manner" (8/26/41).

What de Man expected of the fascist revolution was a hierarchical social order that would overcome the individualism of the pre-fascist era:

For a long while . . . a certain form of individualism claimed that everyone had to choose for himself what kind of person he desired to become and to resolve with his own consciousness the difficulties born with that effort. . . . It is not the least innovation of the totalitarian regimes to have substituted for this imprecise anarchy a framework of definite obligations and duties to which everyone must adapt his talents. (10/28/41)

Overcoming bourgeois individualism, particularly its risks of alienation, held the promise of ending a situation that had created "a large number of unstable people unable to adapt to any of the norms in fashion and forced to search in solitude for the realization of their stability and happiness" (10/28/41).

This kind of lament, coupled with the hope that new, more collective ideals were emerging, also became a motif of the literary criticism de Man wrote for *Le Soir*. He developed the idea that over against the preoccupation of pre-war, especially French writers with the psychological ordeals of the individual, an emergent trend—sometimes associated directly with fascism, sometimes more generally with what he considered the Germanic resurgence in European culture—was "in search of a perhaps simpler, but more energetic, more productive, and happier kind of man" (6/30/42).

The rejection of individualism did not stop at the critique of bourgeois culture. It extended to a condemnation of workers' pursuit of class interests over national interests. And de Man was willing to lend legitimacy to the Nazis' social disciplining of labor. In March 1942, he contributed directly to a highly controlled public discussion designed to justify compulsory labor and, potentially, the deportation of Belgian workers to Germany. A crisis gripped Belgium beginning March 9, when the German authorities announced their intention to establish a policy of compulsory work, supposedly in response to "the fact that a shortage in the labor force is making itself felt in certain branches of the economy."[5] *Le Soir* carried the announcement on the front page. Widely interpreted with alarm as the signal that Belgians would be forced to work in Germany to sustain the war effort, the policy was quickly explained by officials in the following terms by March 13:

The ordinance is related to the Belgian market in order to combat certain forms of "visible" and "invisible" unemployment and to repress abuses. It is with this aim that the Office of Labor will be able to make those asocial elements take a job who are often simply professionally unemployed, living to the detriment of the collectivity. The authorities will also be concerned with unemployed people who are sponging off their families, or living by some less blameless expedient, instead of devoting themselves to a useful job. The constraints will only have to be exercised on elements refractory to all social discipline.[6]

De Man entered the discussion on March 17, with a review of a book entitled *L'Emotion Sociale,* by Charles Dekeukeleire. He again sounded the theme that the current era was far more than "a simple conflict of political powers. . . . The military events, as gigantic and full of consequence as they are, cannot make us forget that a crisis of a spiritual order is proceeding at the same time." He then approvingly summarized Dekeukeleire's contention that

the mentality of the worker is warped at its base. He has completely lost the notion of the collective and does not realize that through his action he collaborates in a task from which the whole community profits. If he could succeed in recovering this sentiment he would soon be led back to a more joyous and more harmonious state of mind. (3/17/42)

The rhetorical strategy of this review followed a pattern de Man had begun to perfect. The high-toned, visionary announcement of imminent social renewal—of "a more joyous and more harmonious state of mind"—was used to justify repressive measures. In this instance, his vision of workers' participation in harmonious social cooperation entailed more immediately the abolition of workers' most basic rights. And his laments against selfishness and individualism served the call for discipline in the service of the German war effort. Indeed workers were eventually forced, first, into mines in Belgium, and later into German factories.

De Man's anti-individualism was a nodal point in his social thought. On the one hand, it furnished a means of legitimating the assault on workers' rights, including the imposition of compulsory labor and potential deportation. On the other hand, anti-individualism voiced a reaction against the alienation and solitude of bourgeois forms of maturation. Through this doubly charged anti-individualism de Man's writings participated directly in fascist ideology. Beginning with what George L. Mosse has examined as the Volkish "search for a 'third way,' an alternative to capitalism and Marxism,"[7] fascism combined the repression of workers' rights with the rejection of bourgeois values. The anti-Marxist, anti-bourgeois synthesis was accomplished through the notion of a hierarchical social order cemented with popular nationalist feeling on the one hand and political authoritarianism on the other. It was just this synthesis that informed de Man's social and political outlook.

Moreover, de Man ably articulated the cultural critique of bourgeois values to the political dimension of fascist ideology and Nazi practice. His commitment is especially apparent in an article devoted to several French fascist intellectuals. He looked to the works of de Jouvenal, Robert Brasillach, Alfred Fabre-Luce, Drieu la Rochelle, and others, as a means of achieving self-understanding as an intellectual in the Belgian situation:

The best evidence that [their] recapitulative sentiment corresponds to a genuine necessity of the moment—at least for us, inhabitants of a country that has not yet made its revolution and for whom the war years are like a moment of meditation in the face of future tasks—is the very particular pleasure one feels in reading these books in which a part of our experience turns out to be reflected. (1/20/42)

Not only did de Man underscore his commitment to the fascist revolution he thought lay ahead for his own country but he also criticized his French counterparts for a mentality that he thought inhibited their commitment. They continued to adhere to the "individualist French spirit," just when the times required that one be able to "abandon oneself without second thoughts to the intoxication of common efforts" (1/20/42). De Man chastised these writers for seeking in individualism an "inoffensive loophole" through which to escape the political exigencies of the era:

Paradoxically, at a moment when all energies are bent toward collective accomplishments, the idea that predominates in the mind of these French men of letters is the protection of the individual. . . . Here then is a group of authors all of whom are preoccupied with saving man before saving the world. . . . (1/20/42)

De Man presented himself as ready to envision the new social order that writers like Brasillach and Drieu glimpsed but did not fully accept. The terms in which he framed his critique rejected the very notion that the rights of individuals could take precedence over the power of rulers. De Man's critique of individualism took the form of a wholesale rejection of the ideological heritage of 1789:

The problem that presents itself is no longer that of knowing what political forms the sacred laws of the individual will dictate to the reigning power, but indeed of elucidating the considerably more modest question: how to insert the human person into a highly centralized and disciplined order. (1/20/42)

The article of January 20, counts against the hypothesis that de Man's interest in 1941–42 lay exclusively in his practice and career as a literary critic, as though the political context had been a circumstance he adapted to more out of ambition than conviction. In fact, it was de Man who pictured his French counterparts as mere "men of letters" who did not fully appreciate the political needs of the age.

Similarly, de Man's first extended discussion of Brasillach's *Notre avant-guerre,* on August 12, 1941, stressed "how much the members of that generation lacked political sense" (8/12/41). When writing of the student life in Paris, Brasillach, according to de Man,

writes excellent pages filled with poetry and freshness. But when he gets down to circumstances relating to political upheaval (the failure of the Popular Front, war in Spain, the triumph of National-Socialism in Germany), one feels him losing his way in a domain that is not his own. . . . Without wanting to rush into too risky a generalization, one can nevertheless underscore that this kind of apolitical life, turned toward aesthetic and poetic delights, fits the French mentality particularly well. Unhappily for the French, the demands of the moment come from just the opposite direction. (8/12/41)

What was the political sense Brasillach lacked? The key example de Man presented illuminates much about his own attitudes. In 1937, Brasillach attended one of the weeklong celebrations of the Nazi Party held at Nuremberg. His account—along with Leni Riefenstahl's film *Triumph of the Will* and the post-war memoir of Nazi architect Albert Speer, *Inside the Third Reich*—remains a significant historical source because of its descriptions of the liturgy and rituals of the Nuremberg rallies. Even though Brasillach's narrative is shot through with expressions of awe and envy regarding these Nazi rites of political participation, de Man emphasized those moments where Brasillach expresses some reserve or admits a lack of understanding. There de Man saw signs of the Frenchman's lack of political commitment:

Brasillach's reaction before a spectacle like that of the Nazi Party congress at Nuremberg, when he expresses horror before that "strange" [or: "foreign"] demonstration, is that of someone for whom this sudden importance of the political in the life of a people is an inexplicable phenomenon. (8/12/41)

Brasillach hesitates when it comes to those inventions of symbol and ritual which seem, on the one hand, to make political participation a virtually religious experience and, on the other hand, are such a departure from traditional forms of political expression as to make him doubt their effectiveness outside Germany. His most explicit concerns—couched as a reminder to his French readers that fascism in France need not conform exactly to its German model—are expressed in reflections on the ceremony he witnessed Hitler perform. The Führer, holding in one hand the "flag of blood" commemorating the failed *putsch* of 1923, blesses new flags with the other hand—as though the power of the bloody flag were being transmitted through him to the "new symbols of the German fatherland." I will quote Brasillach at some length in order to give a feel for what de Man found compellingly present, and what unfortunately absent, in Brasillach's account of Nazism:

A purely symbolic ceremony? I don't think so. There really is in Hitler's thinking, as in that of the Germans, the idea of a kind of mystical transfusion analogous to that of the priest's blessing of the water—if not, dare say, to that of the Eucharist. Whoever does not see in the consecration of the flags the analogues of the consecration of the bread, a kind of German sacrament, risks understanding nothing of Hitlerism.

And it is then that we are uneasy. Faced with these solemn and delightful scenes of ancient romanticism, this immense flowering of flags, these flags of Oriental origin, I asked myself on the last day if indeed everything were possible. One can give a people more strength. But can one expect to transform everything, to the point of inventing new rites that penetrate the life and heart of the citizens to this degree? The Frenchman, who understands the foreigner poorly, begins, before understanding, by being amazed. . . .

In many aspects of this new politics—one wants to say, instead, this poetry—not everything assuredly is for us, and one need not dwell on that point. But what is for us, what is a constant call to order, and undoubtedly a kind of regret, is that unfailing preaching to the youth on behalf of faith, sacrifice and honor.[8]

De Man's allusions to this discussion in Brasillach establish that he found the new politics appealing rather than "foreign" or "strange," and that he saw in the rituals and symbols of the Nazi Party the inauguration of a new, and valued, form of political participation. It may well have been Brasillach's descriptions themselves—always vivid, frequently insightful—of "the incontestable novelty of the Third Reich" that inspired de Man in the first place. Brasillach describes the anti-Marxist and anti-Semitic exhibits, the cathedral of light that turned the *Zeppelinfeld* into "the sacred site of the national mystery," the ceremonies over which Hitler presided, and the torchlight parades of S.A. groups. And Brasillach's own enthusiasms are by no means slight. He emphasizes in particular the importance of the Hitler Youth and the fact that Nazism addressed itself so much to the nation's youth: "It is the character of their discipline that is striking to us. The militarization of children in Germany is not

at all what one would think. Those who speak with us approach us joyously, without fear, and on their own."[9]

Brasillach's reserve—the sense of estrangement at "the astonishing mythology of a new religion"[10]—provoked de Man's criticism because it diminished the scope and stake of Nazism's innovation in *political* life. The focus of de Man's critique of Brasillach clearly indicates that his commitments to fascism were deeply ideological and political, rather than merely opportunistic; that his cultural critique of bourgeois values had become linked to a program of social change and political reconstruction; and that his political hopes included the spread of the new politics inaugurated by the Nazis, not merely the stability and peace of his own country.

THE YOUNG DE MAN'S INTELLECTUAL SELF-PORTRAIT

A self-portrait of the radical young intellectual emerges from de Man's review of Brasillach and from a later article on representations of adolescence in the pre-war novel. That self-portrait confirms that de Man, at the time in his early twenties, saw his work at *Le Soir* as a participation in a larger political movement and a reflection of political choices and intellectual commitments made at a historical crossroads. These implicit self-reflections center on the stresses and opportunities peculiar to his own generation.

De Man's chastising of Brasillach's generation may well have concealed envy of their aesthetic life, their carefree student days in Paris, their devotion to style. He may well have begrudged Brasillach his pre-war. In any case, the predicament and the possibility of his own generation he located in the political as distinct from the aesthetic realm:

Since 1935, young people coming out of adolescence have no longer known this sweetness. Upon their first contact with an independent life they found themselves face-to-face with political realities—in the form of a threatening war—and social realities—in the form of a nearly always uncertain material future. This is why their mentality has a completely different orientation. And things will be even sharper for those who will come immediately after them. Instead of seeing in political activity a mere exciting and lively game, they will consider it an inevitable necessity that demands all their attention and devotion. For the tasks that will assert themselves will be so urgent that no one will be able to ignore them. This does not mean that artistic creation will be suspended, but that indeed literature will not hold the same place in the life of those we call intellectuals. An attitude that will better suit those peoples who have a very developed sense of the collective and have spontaneously reached less individualist lifestyles. (8/12/41)

This kind of oblique autobiography was continued in an article the next year on the "problem of adolescence." De Man was again concerned to define the generational difference that distinguished pre-war literature and culture from his own period. The varying treatment of adolescence in novels was his key. Before the war, "the adolescent's mentality had become in some way the symbol of the spirit of an entire era that found the image of its troubles and its restlessness in the torments of young people" (6/30/42). The portrait that de Man painted of the ordeal of adolescence—"that particularly delicate crisis that man goes through around his twentieth year"—crystallized his sense of the life experience to which fascism's anti-individualistic, hierarchical, and authoritarian elements appealed:

If one had to characterize the state of mind of the man on the threshold of maturity in one word, I would choose the term "indecision." . . . Being indecisive means not only that one proves incapable of making a choice in the world of ideas, consolidating the political, philosophical and religious doctrines to which one intends to adhere, but also—and moreover—that one does not succeed in having a stable opinion of oneself. This constant doubt about one's own value, about one's possibilities for happiness or greatness, literally poisons the adolescent's existence. There results a sterile inactivity, a deep instability, an incessant inner tumult in which, disordered and unrestrained, the best mixes with the worst. There results especially a strong feeling of solitude, for only the person who has successfully stabilized his inner orientation proves capable of living with his fellows on a plane of equality. The relations of the undecided with the rest of humanity are always marred by incomprehension, misunderstandings, even quarrels. (6/30/42)

This experience was no longer, in de Man's view, a symbol of the spirit of the age. The life crisis undergone at the end of one's teens had ceased to be a valid figure of social life as a whole as it had been for Gide and others. A new set of values was emerging. They glorified, as we have seen in other of de Man's articles, conformity rather than individualism, action rather than contemplation, established hierarchy rather than endless searching, social discipline rather than inner turmoil. In a very rare use of the first-person singular, de Man expressed his utter distaste for the adolescent hero of a recent novel under review; his remarks indicate how thoroughly he sided with the transformation of values associated with fascism, even as the poignancy of his account of adolescence reveals that those values went in part against the grain of his own recent experience:

For my part, I found that his hero—is it intentional?—was perfectly odious. Incapable of doing anything with simplicity and feeling himself obliged to accompany action as natural as loving with a multitude of abstract and profound considerations, this reasoner seems the very incarnation of what is artificial in intellectualized youth. (6/30/42)

The autobiographical resonance of these passages suggests that de Man, having recently crossed the threshold of maturity, having chosen his "political, philosophical, and religious" doctrines, and having passed from confusing solitude to "the moral solidity that is the index of an authentic maturity," invested fascism with the power not only to provide the psychological solution to his individual crisis but also the cultural alternative to the individualism and alienation of the pre-war era. Fascism had become for de Man the grid through which to interpret the pattern of his own experience and to connect it with an ongoing historical process. He did not take on fascist ideology lightly. As ideology, it linked private with public experience, personal with historic choices.

COLLABORATION

Likewise, de Man's collaboration—his active participation through his intellectual practice as critic and commentator in the aims of the Nazis—was not a casual choice. It was a commitment renewed and extended many times in the writings published between 1940 and 1942.

To reconstruct the meaning of de Man's collaboration several questions need to be answered. What purposes and intents underlay his own cooperation with the Nazi occupation? What arguments did he marshall in appealing to *Le Soir*'s readership to accept collaboration? Where did he situate himself within the array of ideological and political stances held by those who cooperated with the Nazis? How did his intellectual practice enter into the processes of discipline and punishment, obedience and acquiescence, complicity and common cause exacted by Nazi policy in occupied Europe?

Reference to the French situation—including de Man's own understanding of it—helps to clarify the sorts of choices collaborators of differing intentions, assumptions, and ideologies made.

In France, collaborators fell initially into two quite distinct camps. David Littlejohn has termed the positions, respectively, "French survival" collaboration and "German victory" collaboration. Proponents of the former dominated the scene at Vichy; proponents of the latter were concentrated in Paris in loosely affiliated fascist organizations and included several journalists with strong, often longstanding ideological commitments to fascism. In the wake of France's military defeat, the Paris groups pushed for an alliance with the Nazi regime and a German victory over France's erstwhile ally Great Britain. From the armistice in June 1940 until Vichy moved decidedly into the German war effort in April 1942, the Paris group was agitating for a closer alliance.

The "French survival" collaborationists hoped to steer France back to sovereignty along a path of neutrality in the war, combined with economic cooperation with Germany and controlled acquiescence to German demands for anti-Jewish measures. They were, however, gradually pulled toward positions that were less and less distinct from those of "German victory" collaborators. Littlejohn describes the process as follows:

The two meanings of the word "collaboration" were these. To the majority of "collaborators" it signalled only that degree of cooperation with the occupying power necessary to secure for France a tolerable life in the "New Order." To another, and much smaller group, it meant actively working, and if necessary, *fighting* for German victory. . . . [B]ut fine distinctions between working *for* and working *with* the enemy tended to become progressively more blurred until, in the end, the two were virtually indistinguishable. The tragedy of those who collaborated because they felt that it was in the best interest of France is that they were driven more and more into the camp of those who collaborated because they thought it was in the best interests of Germany.[11]

Important documentation of this process comes from the second volume of Alfred Fabre-Luce's *Journal de la France,* published in 1942. Fabre-Luce had been an early recruit to the Parti Populaire Français (PPF),[12] founded by Jacques Doriot in 1936 and one of the most influential pro-German organizations in occupied Paris. The book was reviewed enthusiastically by de Man on July 21, 1942. And his response to Fabre-Luce's narrative and arguments reveals where he stood along this spectrum of collaboration—and how he read, or wanted to read, the historical processes in which collaborators participated.

De Man was, to use Littlejohn's terminology, a "German victory" collaborator who most often made his arguments for collaboration through more modest proposals for "survival" collaboration. He began his review by lamenting "a certain indifference on the part of the public toward political problems of France." He urged his readers to recognize the "genuine parallelism" between Belgium and France, and to see the stakes in France's ordeal with Germany: "the clash of two complementary but often hostile civilizations, the birth of a new spirit on the ruins of past errors, the agonizing problem of knowing if one of the pillars of Western culture will successfully adapt to the exigencies of a new era" (7/21/42).

Addressing himself to "every man desirous of finding his bearings in the present chaos," de Man recommended Fabre-Luce's book for its objectivity. Collaboration was here shown to be a necessity of the times, an adaptation to the irreversible direction of history, in short a means of survival, that would be vindicated by the ultimate outcome of events:

One could not, at first sight, point out a tendency in this book, so scrupulously does it maintain the tone of perfect objectivity, detached above reality to the point of averting any personal reaction. However, a line of argument does unfold without ever relying on ideological considerations, but by sticking jealously to the necessities inscribed in the facts. What emerges is a demonstration of that ineluctable historical truth according to which, at certain moments, the weight of events reaches the point where it drags nations in a particular direction even though their will seems to go against it. That is what happens in this case: the policy of collaboration results from the present situation not as an ideal desired by the whole of the people, but as an irresistible necessity from which no one can escape even if he believes he must go in another direction. *Attentisme* is thus condemned not from the moral viewpoint, but from the viewpoint of the overbearing reality: it is untenable because contrary to the current of history, which continues to flow without bothering about the reticence of a few individuals who persist in not understanding its power. Those rare perspicacious minds who have grasped it appear at present isolated, alone to combat the inertia and the hostility of the masses. Later it will turn out that they were the precursors of a unanimous will. There is no better demonstration of this phenomenon of belatedness in the reaction of the masses—and of the leadership—than this "Journal de la France." (7/21/41)

Attentisme—meaning a "wait-and-see" attitude—was the label "German victory" collaborators pinned on "French survival" collaborators. The term had been coined by Marcel Déat, founder of the Rassemblement National Populaire (RNP), another significant fascist organization centered in Paris.[13] Fabre-Luce builds to the conclusion of his account by citing a speech Déat gave on April 13, 1942, in which he "undertakes to formulate the ultimatum that has not yet been delivered to us: 'Either we will have a French government whose policies will correspond to the necessities of the hour, or French sovereignty in the occupied zone will be put back in question by the direct administration of the conqueror.' "[14]

Déat, and then Fabre-Luce, evoked the superior might of

Germany to justify the course of action—obedience to the Nazis—they wanted all along. De Man repeated the gesture. By subscribing to Fabre-Luce's critique of *attentisme* de Man associated himself with the more radical and pro-German elements in France. At the same time, he addressed his argument to a reluctant Belgian public whose passivity, even recalcitrance toward the occupying power had to be overcome.

De Man admired the "tone of perfect objectivity" that enabled Fabre-Luce to demonstrate the need for collaboration "without ever relying on ideological considerations." Fabre-Luce's narrative and argumentative strategies are worth examining as a way of illuminating the political and intellectual values embedded in de Man's admiration of his French counterpart. Moreover, we can glimpse in the more evolved political rhetoric of Fabre-Luce the sort of intellectual practice that de Man was striving to attain.

The narrative of *Journal de la France* is crafted to make the culminating event appear the only rational outcome of the nation's struggle for survival. That event was Pierre Laval's return to power as the Chief of Government in April 1942. Laval had been the Vice-Premier at the beginning of the Vichy regime. Pétain ousted him in December 1940 under pressure from those who thought he was pushing France into the war as a German ally. Vichy had reached a new crisis in the spring of 1942. The crisis had several elements. Since the German invasion of Russia on July 22, 1941, internal and external pressure had built on Vichy to support Germany. On the one hand, Paris fascists fanned enthusiasm for the war against the Soviet Union and began forming the Legion of French Volunteers Against Bolshevism; Pétain himself began to speak of the Germans' "defense of civilization in the East" and "the crusade against Bolshevism." And, on the other hand, Germany increased its demands for economic and military support. Meanwhile, Vichy staged a trial at Riom in 1941–42 accusing several figures from the Third Republic of "political responsibility for the war." The defendants were so successful in turning the trial into an indictment of the Vichy regime's leaders' role in the defeat that Hitler himself ordered the embarrassing trial stopped. Still unable to control the degree or the form of his government's collaboration with the Nazis, Pétain reinstated Laval.[15]

Fabre-Luce's narrative does indeed achieve an appearance of objectivity. The story he tells recasts the *actions* of the Nazis as merely the *condition* of France. The actions are therefore never evaluated, or even open to evaluation. The story's only significant actor is "France." But this "France" is an ideal emptied of all particular values, traditions, and institutions. Actions are evaluated on one basis alone. Do they enhance or do they threaten the survival of this mythical entity? The nation has no purpose other than to persist, and it is given no identity other than being that which has persisted. And, finally, Fabre-Luce can, as de Man put it, "avert any personal reaction" in telling this story because he always identifies himself with "France." With this posture he acknowledges no interests other than those that enhance the survival of "France." The formula *we = France* runs throughout the book, and even the ambiguity in the title, Journal *of* France, signals this same identification.

What results—"without ever relying on ideological considerations"—is an argument in the guise of chronicle, a political testament in the guise of survival manual, values in the guise of "necessities." Fabre-Luce's stratagem and style are evident in the following excerpt from his concluding argument; his stylistic powers are stretched to their limit, for he is advocating, by means of appeals to necessity and survival, that France become Germany's co-belligerent at a point when the war's likely duration and the hardships to be suffered had increased with the entry of the Soviet Union and the United States:

The choice offered us is simple. A new Europe is being built. We are invited to participate in its construction. If we refuse, slavery is kept in store for us. Our response can no longer be held back. . . . If we tergiversate again, there will be a sanction. . . . To keep from being overwhelmed by domestic and foreign events, Pétain has to recall the man who, in the eyes of Germany as in the eyes of France, incarnates collaboration: Pierre Laval. Sixteen months earlier the news would have been the sign of an assuagement of our misfortune. That possibility (limited from the beginning) has disappeared. Germany loyally warns us, and Laval is careful not to raise false hopes. . . . To begin with, France will have to impose new efforts on itself. . . . But at least we have avoided the worst: a rupture with Germany, a putting in question of national unity.[16]

While Fabre-Luce speaks of a national unity to be saved, he was actually aiming at a national identity yet to be fully constructed. He wanted to see Vichy—already flying the banner of Work, Family, Fatherland—replicate the Nazis' ability to forge a link in popular consciousness between the deaths inflicted or suffered on behalf of the State and the symbolization of collectivity and tradition as the Fatherland. He relished what he considered the beginning of just that process. In June 1941, Vichy forces gathered in Syria at the behest of the Germans went into combat against a British-led force that included Free French troops. The fact that the Vichy forces were overrun at the cost of 1,038 lives did not mean for Fabre-Luce military defeat, or the tragedy of Frenchmen killing Frenchmen, or the consequences of fighting proxy wars for Germany.[17] Rather, it meant that national identity could be refashioned in the imagery of blood and soil: "The army has fought. Vichy has been died for! Impossible, henceforth, to maintain that the government of Marshal Pétain does not represent France."[18]

De Man's other articles dealing with collaboration suggest how he viewed his own relation to the occupying power. As regarded the prospects for social revolution in Belgium and elsewhere, he considered collaboration a rare opportunity and a duty. As regarded the fact of occupation and Belgium's loss of sovereignty, he regarded collaboration as a harsh necessity that had to be undergone to restore national sovereignty on a new, justifiable basis.

On March 25, 1941, de Man reviewed a book by the right wing French author Jacques Benoist-Méchin. Entitled *La Moisson de Quarante,* the book chronicles the author's months as a prisoner of war. Having fallen into German hands shortly after the armistice was signed in June 1940, Benoist-Méchin and his fellow prisoners were required to harvest the crop. De Man, presumably picking up on Benoist-Méchin's own message, drew out the fable contained in the Frenchman's account of his role in helping to organize his fellow prisoners' forced participation in the harvest. The prisoner of war is transfigured into the very image of the good citizen:

In the cooperation between Germans and Frenchmen, in the purifying solidarity that is created between men who endure the same hardships and overcome the same ordeals, he has sought out signs of what the future might hold. His experience was hardly disappointing: it turns out that, when strictly controlled and rationally administered, this fragment of the French people, in which all social ranks were represented, courageously did their duty. (3/25/41)

Besides representing collaboration as a cooperation based on common experience, de Man also sounded the theme that necessity was bringing out the commonality between the Germans and the French. Despite "the very different mentalities of the two peoples," he argued, "no abyss separates them in reality, and when a common task has arisen, understanding has been perfect. That is the principal lesson to be drawn from this lovely book" (3/25/41).

Five months later—two weeks after the review of Brasillach—de Man again discussed collaboration. His review of Pierre Daye's *Guerre et révolution* praised the right wing Belgian journalist's commentary on the current situation. Subscribing to Daye's view that the war had in fact opened the possibility of sweeping social changes, de Man chastised those Belgians "who remain blinded by nationalist passions." The war was in fact "the beginning of a revolution." Collaboration was pitted against resistance as good will to ill.

Resistance to the Nazis was, in de Man's view, a stubborn refusal to fulfill a social duty, whereas collaboration offered active involvement in revolutionizing an inequitable society. De Man crafted an indictment of resistance and a praise of collaboration designed to reverse the identification of resistance with patriotism, collaboration with treason. His call for collaboration was an appeal for social transformation. He relegated the Nazis' invasion and occupation of Belgium to "secondary" significance:

Leaving aside questions of supremacy, which are in fact secondary, the situation creates a certain quantity of practical possibilities for replacing a political apparatus that has become harmful with an organism that would assure a distribution of goods more in keeping with justice. For whomever has thought that such achievements are possible and necessary, it is his duty not to absent himself under current conditions. For undoubtedly he will never again find circumstances so favorable for a renewal as at this moment when all institutions are in the process of being replaced. And even if this new program does not yet happen to be established with precision, things had come to such a point of decomposition and degeneration that the will to change must exist before everything else.

Pierre Daye's "Guerre et révolution" recalls in clear and simple terms just such fundamental truths which must guide the action of men of good will. (8/26/41)

De Man's comments, published in August 1941, appeared in the context of a multi-leveled struggle between resistance and collaboration. Several incidents occurred in July and August.

In mid-July, the Germans organized a trade exposition, but attendance was very poor. *Le Soir* editorialized against this "passive resistance" of the population. The editorial's tone differs from de Man's as that of the "bad cop" to the "good cop," but it contains the same double appeal to survival and uprightness:

This exposition offered to small and large manufactures, as well as to artisans, a means of getting work and of creating jobs. At this moment when English generosity has placed the barrier of its blockade between us and our overseas customers, only one market is open, the continental market. Germany comes to us as a buyer, and what's more as a peaceful buyer. And the Belgian economic world sulks. Waiting with arms crossed for an English victory, taking refuge behind the pretext of a false patriotism, in a passive resistance whose only victim is Belgium, is not only absurd but criminal.[19]

Active resistance too occurred during the summer of 1941. Moreover, the choice between resistance and collaboration entailed significant consequences, especially as the Nazis intensified their response to acts of sabotage and of defiance.

Journalists were targeted. Franz Peeters, director of the Belgian wire service, had been arrested at the end of February and charged with having done a disservice to Germany through a "lack of neutrality." He fell into a coma during his detention and interrogation by the Gestapo. He died at his home on May 29, 1941, without having regained consciousness.[20]

On June 2, the Nazis announced their policy of taking revenge on hostages when the perpetrator of some "crime" could not be found. In response to the fatal shooting of a German soldier, the authorities incarcerated one hundred male residents of the Laeken quarter, where the attack had occurred.[21]

The German authorities had also cracked down on Belgians who assisted English pilots downed over Belgium. While the reporting of acts of resistance was tightly controlled, some incidents were reported. Thus, on August 11, the papers reported—presumably as warning and example—the trial of a woman and her parents who had aided a British pilot after he had crash-landed and been brought to their home. All three were sentenced to death.

Citizens had several confrontations with German soldiers and with Belgian units of the S.S.

In the Flemish town of Hasselt, "black brigades" of the Vlaamsch Nationaal Verbond (VNV, Flemish National League) had been harassing residents who wore the national colors of Belgium on their lapels. In response, a crowd attacked a group of the black brigades on June 15, injuring as many as thirty, including a VNV deputy.[23]

On the national holiday, July 21, crowds in Brussels jeered German officers and soldiers, setting off several physical confrontations. The next day the authorities condemned such "anti-German demonstrations" and tightened the curfew. On July 23, similar incidents outside Brussels led to several arrests and detentions. The next day the authorities announced the widening of its policy of taking hostages in retaliation for anti-Nazi activity. On August 12, an altercation broke out at a tavern between a group of uniformed black brigades and residents of the Marolles quarter of Brussels. The fighting spread into the streets, and several pro-Nazi soldiers were seriously beaten.[24]

When *Le Soir* editorialized against "false patriotism" on July 16, and when de Man intoned against "nationalist passions" on August 26, they spoke against these kinds of acts of sabotage, protest, and resistance. The struggle for public opinion —collaboration vs. resistance—complemented the Gestapo's methods of guaranteeing acquiescence to the new order: unwarranted detentions, retaliatory arrests and hostage takings,

torture, and executions. De Man, as well as his paper, was actively complicit in the process of bringing a subjugated population to obedience. As an intellectual practice, de Man's writing responded to the surrounding context in general and in specific. Beyond his willingness to propagandize for the Nazis and beyond his general contribution to fascist ideology, he carried out the orders of the day and actively furnished the required justifications for an entire range of measures taken by the

One more episode from the summer of 1941 will illustrate how de Man's choices stood in sharp contrast to those of others who directly faced the pressures of the occupying power. It involves another act of conscience and resistance of the kind de Man condemned in August. Throughout the month of June a crisis unfolded between the burgomaster of Brussels, a man named Van de Meulebroeck, and the man whom the Nazis had installed as general secretary of the Interior, a VNV activist named Gerard Romsée. Romsée tried to force on Van de Meulebroeck a new slate of aldermen, all Rexists and Flemish nationalists; Van de Meulebroeck refused and protested Romsée's usurpation of powers that lawfully belonged to the burgomaster himself. On June 26, the German authorities dismissed Van de Meulebroeck. In defiance, he first convened a meeting to appoint a successor and then made a visit to the hundred hostages being held in retaliation for the killing of the German soldier. On June 29, he had a letter posted all through the city informing the population that he was being unlawfully removed from office: "I am, I continue to be, and I will continue to be the only legitimate burgomaster of Brussels." He called his refusal to obey Romsée a matter of "honor and duty." On July 1, Van de Meulebroeck was arrested, along with the printer who prepared the posters of his letter. In addition, the city of Brussels was fined five million francs in the form of a "Van de Meulebroeck tax" to be paid by the residents.[25]

Circumstances gave even de Man's most empty phrases very precise and concrete meanings. The intellectual's participation in fascism was carried out in the struggle over the meaning of keywords and the interpretations to be given to specific forms of conflict and action. Over against Van de Meulebroeck's sense of his duty not to obey the orders given him, de Man spoke of "one's duty not to absent oneself under present conditions." Over against Van de Meulebroeck's protest against the illegitimacy of Nazi rule and appeal to the legitimacy of Brussels' civic government, de Man welcomed the replacement of a "harmful political apparatus" with a new and more just "organism" for governing the society. And over against those who took to the streets against the presence and the emblems of

Nazi power, de Man elevated the collaborator as the image of those "men of good will" who could transcend "nationalist passions."

ANTI-SEMITISM

On March 4, 1941, *Le Soir* published a special page under the banner "The Jews and Us." It included several articles, one of which, entitled "The Jews in Contemporary Literature," was written by de Man.

He advanced three sets of claims in the article:

(1) He challenged the idea that European literature and culture since 1920 were "degenerate and decadent because Judaized." That idea, he argued, reflected a "vulgar anti-Semitism" that accepted "the myth of Jewish dominion" in modern culture, a myth that "the Jews themselves have helped spread."

(2) He advanced the idea that European literature possessed an evolutionary continuity that linked even the "most revolutionary" trends in modern literature to the longer span of the tradition. That continuity refuted the notion that the "particular mentality of the 1920s" could have been responsible for the development of modern literature. "So too, the Jews could not claim to have been the creators of it, nor even to have exercised a preponderant influence on its evolution."

(3) On the basis of this challenge to "vulgar anti-Semitism" and this view of literary tradition, de Man drew his conclusion: If the Jews were "isolated" from Europe and its cultural life, the contemporary European literature and its ongoing evolution would not be significantly affected.

The article is rhetorically complex. But it is not ambiguous. The complexity derives from the fact that it was aimed at two radically distinct audiences. On the one hand, de Man was engaged in an ongoing discussion conducted by fascist intellectuals, within earshot of the occupying power, about the evaluation of modern culture and the role of Jews within it. On the other hand, he was contributing directly to an anti-Semitic campaign addressed to the Belgian public and designed to legitimate the anti-Jewish measures of the Nazis.

Within the first of these contexts, de Man's position can be sharply distinguished from the other contributors to the March 4 issue. Indeed, his charge of *vulgar* anti-Semitism could easily have been directed at them. He did not explicitly evoke the specifically racial ideology of Nazism, whereas the lead editorial declared, "Our anti-Semitism is racial. . . . We are resolved to forbid all cross-breeding with [Jews] and to rid ourselves of their destructive influence in the domain of thought, literature, and the arts." And, de Man's whole line of aesthetic argument concerning the continuity of modern art with the European tradition directly contradicts the view presented in Georges Marlier's attack on modern painting, particularly expressionism, cubism, and surrealism, as caught in "the grip of Jewish nihilism."[26]

De Man's argument was designed to contain anti-Semitism. But he did not object to the repression of Jews; he was objecting to the repudiation of modernism. He in fact used the prevailing stereotype of the soulless Jew to turn the tables on the anti-modernists:

On closer examination, this influence would even appear extraordinarily slight, for one might well have expected, considering the specific characteristics of the Jewish mind, that they would have played a more shining role in this artistic output. Their cerebralness, their ability to assimilate doctrines while maintaining a certain coldness toward them, would seem quite precious qualities for the lucid analytical work that the novel requires. . . . That [Western intellectuals] have been capable of protecting themselves from Jewish influence in so representative a domain of culture as literature attests to their vitality. We could not entertain many hopes for our civilization if it had let itself be invaded without resistance by a foreign force.

De Man's response conforms to a pattern that was fairly typical among non-German fascist intellectuals. Mosse has shown that many French fascists initially rejected the philosophical and scientific underpinnings of the racial doctrines, yet actively fostered cultural and religious anti-Semitism. Brasillach, for example, in 1938 "criticized the Nazis for making race into a metaphysical doctrine (whatever that meant) while he himself considered all Jews as an alien people with undesirable characteristics."[27] Doriot's Parti Populaire Français did not become racist until the German victory and occupation. The pattern Mosse discerns is that of a gradual adaptation to, and then adoption of, Nazi doctrine on the part of other fascist movements.

It is really the shape and scope of that adaptation on de Man's part that needs to be interpreted. The article should not necessarily be considered a centerpiece of de Man's thinking at the time. It was his one sustained foray into openly anti-Semitic writing, and he managed before and after its publication to develop his ideas about literary trends and traditions without explicit recourse to anti-Semitism. The fact that it appeared as part of a special page of *Le Soir* suggests the possibility that de Man did not initiate the article but responded to an editor's request. I propose, therefore, to approach the question of de Man's relation to anti-Semitism through a more narrowly focused question:

How could he have come to the point of writing this particular article?

Let us assume that anti-Semitism had not been part of de Man's intellectual-moral makeup before the war. The article would then lie somewhere along a path of decisions taken in the wake of the invasion and occupation. Indeed, de Man had to have crossed several thresholds to write the particular article he contributed to *Le Soir*'s anti-Semitic supplement.

First, he had to have already found that the advantages of association with the Nazis outweighed the moral, intellectual, and personal costs of acquiescing to their anti-Semitism. His own convictions must not have obligated him to contest the racial doctrines, even if he did not subscribe to them. And he must have found that his ideological commitments and intellectual ambitions could tolerate, even adapt to, the anti-Jewish measures the German military authority had already undertaken by March 1941. According to Holocaust historian Raul Hilberg, those measures began with two decrees issued in October 1940, "which ran the whole gamut of the preliminary steps of the destruction process. The concept of 'Jew' was defined; Jewish lawyers and civil servants were ousted from their positions; Jewish enterprises and stocks were subjected to registration; and all transactions were made subject to official approval. Finally, the Jewish population was also ordered to register for future surveillance."[28] These policies encountered opposition from Belgian officials. Several officials in the judiciary and bar protested that the decrees were "in opposition to our constitutional rights and our laws."[29] The country's secretaries general likewise protested to the German military authority against the order to dismiss all Jewish public employees: "The principle of the eligibility of all Belgians for employment means that everyone, without distinction based on birth or religious or political opinion, has an equal right to obtain public employment."[30]

De Man crossed a second threshold when he reached the point of being able to make a written contribution to the anti-Semitic campaign. Minimally, he must have deemed the contribution a means of demonstrating his loyalty to the occupying power. He may well have been instructed by an editor to write something on literature and the "Jewish problem" which would satisfy the German overseers. But the skill with which he evoked key anti-Semitic themes went beyond merely fulfilling his assignment. He fashioned an argument that not only might have been a convincing performance for his superiors but also aimed at convincing his readership that the anti-Semitism of the Nazis need not become an assault on highly esteemed cultural values and institutions.

De Man subordinated the anti-Semitic themes to his focal argument about modern literature and tradition. Does that argumentative structure indicate a reserve on his part toward anti-Semitism, perhaps even the core of a disguised critique? To the contrary, the argumentative structure of the article shows that de Man had crossed a third threshold in his complicity with Nazi anti-Semitism. He had become willing to voice a whole cluster of anti-Semitic ideas in order to enhance the acceptability of his own cultural criticism. He had taken up anti-Semitism as an instrument of persuasion. He thus reproduced an essential procedure of Nazi propaganda; anti-Semitism had long served Nazism as a means of articulating other features of its ideology and program: for example, the Jew as figure of capitalistic greed and of communist conspiracy.

The *way* de Man made the linkage between anti-Semitism and his own defense of modern literature, especially in his article's final remark, marks the crossing of a fourth threshold. For he passed from an ideological association with Nazi policies toward Jews over to an overt acceptance of further acts of repression. He presented the prospect of deporting and colonizing the European Jews as a means of underscoring his notion that the long continuities of the cultural tradition proved the "resistance" of "our civilization" to the "foreign force" of "Jewish influence." De Man thus made the absence of the Jews an image for the vitality of European literature:

By keeping its originality and character intact despite the Semitic meddling in every aspect of European life, [our civilization] has shown that its deep nature was healthy. Moreover, one thus sees that a solution of the Jewish problem which would aim at the creation of a Jewish colony isolated from Europe, would not entail deplorable consequences for the literary life of the West. The latter would altogether lose some personalities of mediocre value and would continue, as in the past, to develop in accordance with its greater evolutionary laws.

Between 1938 and 1941 the idea of forcibly removing the European Jews to a colony was the prevailing proposal for a "solution of the Jewish problem." Various schemes were discussed by the leadership of the Third Reich, both among themselves and in diplomatic contacts with foreign governments. The idea had also been publicly presented in terms that made clear that the Nazis' intention was to remove the Jews from all of Europe, denying them citizenship rights and expropriating their property to pay for the scheme. The Berlin government held a news conference for foreign journalists on February 7, 1939. Alfred Rosenberg, author of the Nazis' key racial doctrines, presided and challenged the Western governments to help solve the "Jewish problem":

What territories are the democracies willing to provide for the purposes of settling some fifteen million Jews? The Jewish millionaires and multi-millionaires will have to place their means at the disposal of, let us say, the office of the Evian Conference. If millions of Jews are to be settled, elementary humanity toward the Jews demands that they shall not be left to themselves, but that the colony be placed under administrators trained in police work. There is no question of establishing a Jewish State, but only of a Jewish Reserve.[31]

By 1940–41 the Reich leaders were exhausting the last of the "emigration" plans, the so-called Madagascar plan. The plan called for France to cede the African island to Germany. But the diplomatic requirements could not be met. According to Hilberg's account, the plan "hinged on the conclusion of a peace treaty with France, and such a treaty depended on an end of hostilities with England. . . . When the project collapsed, the entire machinery of destruction was permeated with a feeling of uncertainty. No one could take the decisive step on his own, for this decision could be made only by one man: Adolph Hitler."[32] It is a very grim coincidence that in March 1941, even as de Man was promoting the idea of deportation and colonization in the pages of *Le Soir,* the leadership of the Third Reich was deciding that the "emigration" plans were unrealizable. The decisive turn toward the Final Solution followed.

Even though the Final Solution was probably unfathomable to de Man early in 1941, he was asking his readers to imagine that their society could be emptied of the Jews and yet remain unchanged in all its essentials. As a message crafted for a public that was proving uncooperative with German policies, his brief discourse evidences an acute sense of what might be required to transform that resistance into acquiescence. It was a question of maximizing the sense of the foreignness of Jews while minimizing the sense of their importance to the common life of the country. De Man may also have been looking to strike some chord of resentment toward the 30,000 Jewish refugees who had fled into Belgium beginning in 1939, increasing Belgium's Jewish population to 90,000. By trying to use the deportation and colonization of European Jewry as an image of the harmony and continuity of Western culture, de Man was experimenting with the most virulent form of anti-Semitism within his political culture.

That he backed away from it after the article on "The Jews in Contemporary Literature" may indicate that he found that step morally untenable. It may, however, merely indicate that thereafter he abandoned the attempt to connect his cultural criticism to anti-Semitism—either because of the nonreceptiveness of the Belgian population to anti-Semitic propaganda or because of an inability to find a systematic connection. The question cannot be answered based on the evidence at our disposal. What the evidence does show is that he did not, at least through August 1942, repudiate the notion and image of the absence of Jews. The theme recurred twice more in his writings. On March 16, 1942, in his role of publicist, de Man reported, in glowing terms, on a History of Germany exhibition in Brussels. He praised the unity of the exhibition:

That's the first element that will interest the visitors: to have a clearer vision of the very complex history of a people whose importance is fundamental for the destiny of Europe. It will be seen that the historical evolution of Germany is governed by a fundamental factor: the will to unify a set of regions that have one and the same racial structure, but which its enemies ceaselessly endeavor to divide. (3/16/42)

And then on August 20, 1942, de Man published an article on contemporary German fiction in the Flemish journal *Het Vlaamsche Land.* By this time, the anti-Jewish measures had extended to the "Aryanization" of Jewish property, the requirement that Jews wear the yellow star, roundups, forced labor, and the first deportation of Jews from Belgium to Auschwitz. It is extremely unlikely that de Man would have failed to feel the magnitude of the possible complete deportation of Jews from Belgium. Of the 90,000 Jews in the country at the time of the German invasion in May 1940, nearly all lived in Antwerp and Brussels. There had been 50,000 Jews in Antwerp, a city of 273,000 (the Antwerp agglomeration being 493,000); there were 30,000 Jews in Brussels, a city of 192,000 (the agglomeration 912,000.)[33] Raised in Antwerp and working in Brussels, de Man could not have been unaware of the presence of the vulnerable population whose absence he was so ready to imagine. Nonetheless, the pattern of his thinking had not changed since March 1941:

When we investigate the post-war literary production in Germany, we are immediately struck by the contrast between two groups, which moreover were also materially separated by the events of 1933. The first of these groups celebrates an art with a strongly cerebral disposition, founded upon some abstract principles and very remote from all naturalness. The in themselves very remarkable theses of expressionism were used in this group as tricks, as skilful artifices calculated [for] easy effects. The very legitimate basic rule of artistic transformation, inspired by the personal vision of the creator, served here as a pretext for a forced, caricatured representation of reality. Thus, [the artists of this group] came into open conflict with the proper traditions of German art which had always and before everything else clung to a deep spiritual sincerity. Small wonder, then, that it [was] mainly non-Germans, and in specific Jews, that went in this direction.[34]

The consistency in de Man's thinking lay in the absence of the Jews as an image of some valued unity or harmony. Their absence from Europe a sign of cultural vitality and literary continuity; their absence from Germany the realization of a national and racial destiny; their exile, imprisonment, and deportation after 1933 a sign of German literature's recovery of the true tradition of German art.

There is a pointed lack of evidence that de Man undertook any moral reassessment of his relation to anti-Semitism during the occupation. Moreover, there is significant, though indirect evidence that his moral commitments included a detached acceptance that innocent people had to die. On September 1, 1942, he reviewed Hubert Dubois' *Le Massacre des Innocents*—a poem I have not been able to locate in order to comment more precisely on de Man's interpretation—and used it to present a moral vision of the ongoing war:

One could readily call this *Massacre des Innocents* a meditation on the culpability that has led humanity to the frightful state in which it finds itself at the moment. Complaint and lamentation cannot be justified, even in so pitiful a situation. For all that is now happening is not the blind and pitiless action of destiny, but the consequence of a misdeed [*faute*], an accumulation of moral misdeeds committed in the course of the ages. The utility of such an ordeal is to force an awareness of this culpability, to make the masses [*les foules*] see that they have acted badly. Consequently, the harsher the punishment the greater the hope of seeing arise, at last, the true values which must permit harmonious living instead of the false indulgences that have led to the catastrophe. (9/1/42)

This particular moral vision cast the Nazi war machine and police state as instruments of moral renewal. It envisioned the specific crimes of Nazism as, instead, the response of the moral universe to unspecified historical crimes committed by the masses. By adopting that vision, de Man intricated himself in a web of self-justification from which he never did disintricate himself.

I have set out to make the case that Paul de Man was a fascist, an anti-Semite, and an active collaborator with the Nazis during the German occupation of Belgium.

I have reconstructed the various levels of de Man's intellectual practice in order to disclose the precise degree and nature of his commitment to fascism. The results of the inquiry are incontrovertible. De Man responded, consistently and actively, to an entire range of ideological imperatives associated with European fascism and political imperatives specifically dictated by the Third Reich.

He reported uncritically on cultural events that the Nazis and the Belgian fascist parties staged to foster fascist ideology. In a context defined by continual confrontations between Nazi rule and Belgian resistance, de Man also supplied rationalizations and legitimations for the repressive measures the Nazis took against armed and unarmed acts of resistance, against journalists and civic leaders, against workers, and against Jews.

Fascism provided de Man with a means of interpreting his private experience, including the psychological-cultural crisis of maturation, and of connecting that experience to values that would orient his active participation in a public world. He placed himself within, and measured himself against, the intellectual and political culture of French fascism. The writers who actively collaborated with the Nazis and pressed the Vichy regime toward stronger alliances with Germany in the war served as models for his own intellectual practice. He actually saw his own political commitment to fascism as more informed and less restrained than theirs.

De Man went beyond merely voicing anti-democratic, anti-bourgeois, and anti-communist sentiments. The intellectual project he pursued aimed at synthesizing a critique of bourgeois culture and an authoritarian politics that would cement a hierarchical society through totalitarian discipline and mass ritual. In striving to articulate that synthesis, de Man tested the usefulness of anti-Semitism as a means of persuasion in the struggle over the cultural values of fascism. In the process he promoted the image of a Europe without Jews as a fitting symbol of the new order he anticipated and the new values he desired.

I have dwelt on de Man's writings of 1941–42. Two questions that have great relevance today—By what path did he arrive at his post-war intellectual identity? And how do his later writings respond to the earlier?—cannot really be addressed until, and unless, we come to grips with his fascist commitments. Otherwise critique and apology alike will ring false.

Northwestern University

NOTES

1. Paul Delandsheere and Alphonse Ooms, *La Belgique sous les nazis* (Bruxelles: Edition Universelle, 1953), II, 155; 412; III, 317–319.

2. *Le Soir,* March 31, 1941. Hereafter I will cite, by date, de Man's writings in *Le Soir* in the text.

3. David Littlejohn, *The Patriotic Traitors: A History of Collaboration in German-Occupied Europe, 1940–45* (London: Heinemann, 1972), p.222.

4. In addition to other works cited, I have found the following works extremely helpful:

Geographical Handbook Belgium, B. R. 521 (Restricted), Naval Intelligence Division (Great Britain, February 1944).

G. Carpelli, "Belgium," in S. J. Woolf (ed.), *Fascism in Europe* (London and New York: Methuen, 1981), pp.283–306.

Jean Stengers, "Belgium," in Hans Rogger and Eugen Weber (eds.), *The European Right: A Historical Profile* (Berkeley and Los Angeles: University of California Press, 1965).

Jacques Willequet, "Les fascismes belges et la seconde guerre mondiale," *Revue d'histoire de la Deuxième Guerre Mondiale* 66 (avril 1967), pp.85–109.

5. Quoted in Delandsheere and Ooms, II, 105.

6. Ibid., II, 110.

7. George L. Mosse, *The Crisis of German Ideology: Intellectual Origins of the Third Reich* (New York: Grosset & Dunlap, 1964), p.280. See also his *Germans and Jews: The Right, the Left, and the Search for a "Third Force" in Pre-Nazi Germany* (New York: Grosset & Dunlap, 1970), esp. pp. 3–33, and pp.144–170.

8. Robert Brasillach, *Notre avant-guerre* (Paris: Plon, 1941), pp. 276–277.

9. Ibid., p.272.

10. Ibid., p.278.

11. Littlejohn, pp.210–211.

12. Eugen Weber, "France," in Rogger and Weber, p.109.

13. Littlejohn, pp.213–215, 222–223.

14. Alfred Fabre-Luce, *Journal de la France: 1939–1944* (Paris: Fayard, 1969), p.443. In this edition, "Part III: Vichy"—pp. 281–444—corresponds to the original second volume.

15. Littlejohn, pp.239–246; and Fabre-Luce, pp.340–352; 424–444.

16. Fabre-Luce, pp.432–444.

17. Littlejohn, pp.225–226.

18. Fabre-Luce, p.362.

19. Quoted in Delandsheere and Ooms, I, 397.

20. Ibid., I, 342–343.

21. Ibid., I, 345–346.

22. Ibid., I, 419–420.

23. Ibid., I, 361–362.

24. Ibid., I, 399–406; 422–423.

25. Ibid., I, 359–360; 368–376; 381–383.

26. De Man renewed his polemic with Marlier in a review of the latter's book on Belgian painting (8/4/42). Though respectful in tone, de Man clearly rejected Marlier's judgments of French surrealism and German expression. According to Delandsheere and Ooms, I, 150, Marlier was on the editorial board of the Rexist daily, the *Nouveau Journal.*

27. George L. Mosse, *Toward the Final Solution: A History of European Racism* (New York: Howard Fertig, 1978), p.195.

28. Raul Hilberg, *The Destruction of the European Jews* (Chicago: Quadrangle Books, 1961), p.384.

29. Cited in Lucien Steinberg, *Le Comité de défense des Juifs en Belgique 1942–1944* (Bruxelles: Editions de l'Université de Bruxelles, 1973), p.32.

30. Cited in Delandsheere and Ooms, I, 159.

31. Cited in Gerard Reitlinger, *The Final Solution: The Attempt to Exterminate the Jews of Europe, 1939–1945* (London: Vallentine, Mitchell, 1953), pp.21–22.

32. Hilberg, p.261.

33. The population figures are from *Geographical Handbook Belgium,* p.217. The figures are 1939 estimates, based on the 1930 census. The figures for the number of Jews in Belgium are from Hilberg, p.383.

34. Paul de Man, "Blik op de huidige Duitsche romanliteratuur," *Het Vlaamsche Land,* August 20, 1942, p.2. Text and translation supplied by Ortwin de Graef.

Synchronic Theory and Absolutism: *Et tu, Brute?* De Man's Wartime Writings

STEPHEN BRETZIUS

Antony and Cleopatra offers a useful reference for an important debate currently surrounding the work of Paul de Man. In recent years, a number of critics of de Man have referred to a tacit but deep conservatism in his "Hamlet-like detachment from the world of practical affairs."[1] For such readers, de Man's radical reduction of history and psychology to "truth's inability to coincide with itself" (AR, p.78), to an aporia inherent in representation, neutralizes from the beginning any possibility for motivated political action. Marx, of course, had made similar claims in *The German Ideology* regarding the Young Hegelians, and, much more recently, critics like John Fekete had written related and important critiques of American New Criticism, substituting "agrarianism" for the "idealism" attacked by Marx, and for what would later become the "quietism" associated with de Man.[2] The principal source for this reading of de Man, however, is Adorno, whose work is regularly concerned with detailing the deep investment of ahistoric theory in the totalizing powers it claims to obviate or undo. In the terms of this debate, the de Man of trope and Nietzschean forgetting is the de Man of imperative and Nietzschean power; in the terms of the play, Egypt is Rome—or rather, the more Egypt, the more Rome.

This is a reasonable thesis, and one Shakespeare seems to share. The play works like a grand deconstruction of the two worlds, and if Caesar rules Rome like a logos, Cleopatra governs Egypt according to all the deconstructive paradoxes— "makes hungry where most she satisfies," "and what they undid did," "bless her when she is riggish," and so on. Without suggesting that *différance* represents the punning Cleopatra for which an entire school of American literary theory has given the world, it is worth emphasizing that all the Shakespearean paradoxes that "make defect perfection" in Cleopatra represent for the play a similar deconstructive non-center, but one which has itself been deeply politicized. "It goes without saying that it cannot be *exposed,*" Derrida remarks of *différance,* but gone is the extraordinary class metaphor of Enobarbus' "For her person, / It beggar'd all description" (2.2.197–98).[3] Such juxtapositions might suggest that the terms of contemporary literary theory closely parallel those of Shakespearean drama, but what the comparison really suggests is that the plays themselves are already scenes of interpretation, and that the subject, as we will determine, is their own relation to power. In this they most resemble the literary theory to which they will be referred here, increasingly powerful figurations of a progressive internalization of figure's own relation to power—what we will call, after Adorno, the figure-power dialectic.

To better see this dialectic as it functions in criticism, we need to consider in a little more detail the precise relation of synchronic theory and absolutism. The earliest essay to juxtapose on a large scale synchronic linguistics and literary theory was Roman Jakobson's "Linguistics and Poetics." The essay, first delivered at Indiana University in 1958, exerted a strong influence on de Man, for whom "contemporary literary theory comes into its own in such events as the application of Saussurean linguistics to literary texts" (RT, p.8). Where Saussure had developed a model for synchronic linguistics, Jakobson's goal in the essay is to translate that model into a "synchronic poetics" (LP, p.89). I do not want to rehearse his argument here, but move directly to his concluding example. This is a careful grammatical and lexical unfolding of Antony's funeral oration for Caesar in *Julius Caesar,* which Jakobson condenses to the following:

> The noble Brutus
> Hath told you Caesar was ambitious. . .
> For Brutus is an honorable man. . .
> But Brutus says he was ambitious,
> And Brutus is an honorable man. . .
> Yet Brutus says he was ambitious,
> And Brutus is an honorable man. . .
> Yet Brutus says he was ambitious,
> And, sure, he is an honorable man.

Jakobson emphasizes the way grammar functions to convey irony, turning reported facts into reported speech. Our concern now is not with the correctness of his grammatical method—de Man himself takes this up in "Semiology and Rhetoric"—but rather to follow in a little more detail the relation of synchronic theory and absolutism implicit in the *selection* of this passage and not another. The essay's more famous "I like Ike" example is a primitive enough assertion of support for the status quo, but one which suspends identification between resemblance ("I" *sounds* like "Ike") and desire, between an authority in the world and the seemingly separate authority of a language that makes "Ike" like "I"—and, more powerfully, "like" like "like." The essay as a transitional mode between synchronic linguistics and synchronic poetics is useful for the way it suggests the necessarily complex relation of both to historical process, and to related questions of influence and tradition. When, early in the essay, Jakobson illustrates the meta-lingual function of language with "'I don't follow you—what do you mean?'. . . or in Shakespearean diction, 'What is't thou say'st?'" (LP, p.93), he labors the point but only to bring in the Shakespearean context which Antony will ultimately bring to fruition. When, even earlier, he illustrates what he calls the phatic function with "'Are you lis-

tening?' or in Shakespearean diction, 'Lend me your ears'" (LP, p.92), he is not only borrowing directly from the oration but setting up a relation with his audience modeled explicitly on Antony's relation to his. Of course, even given his first name, Roman, the Jakobson of "Linguistics and Poetics" is not exclusively Antony, or Brutus, for that matter, "the noblest Roman of them all." Nor has he come to bury Saussure, but to praise him. On the other hand, a juxtaposition of proper names—in which Saussure himself attempted to inscribe the subject of Latin poetry from within synchrony—suggests how a succession from Caesar to Antony is being laid over a succession from Saussure to Roman Jakobson. In the essay's closing remarks, the two subjects converge, the synchronic theorist and the Roman (and ultimately Jacobean) hero, just at the moment where identity itself is conferred:

My attempt to vindicate the right and duty of linguistics to direct the investigation of verbal art in all its compass and extent can come to a conclusion with the same burden which summarized my report to the 1953 conference here at Indiana University: '*Linguista sum: linguistici nihil a me alienum puto*.' (LP, p.120)

Saussure is vindicated, but in the language of Antony—or Caesar, we may assume, given Jakobson's earlier "the symmetry of the three disyllabic verbs with an identical initial consonant and identical final vowel added splendor to the laconic victory message of Caesar: '*Veni, vidi, vici*'" (LP, p.96). The essay ends by making explicit, and explicitly personal, the synchronic dispersal of historical power in a pattern of images which underwrites the essay's claims to, if not "vindication," succession.

These are preliminary remarks which may guide us as we turn now directly to de Man's recently discovered wartime writings. What makes these writings so important is that they bring to the surface the complicitous relation to established power—and to an absolutist ideology—which his later work had already been said to repress, or hide, or excuse, or allegorize, but always draw on. "Absolutism" will name here an authority that, answering only to itself, rules *by* the power it rules *with,* a performative-constative difference developed most fully by de Man in his reading of autobiography, a genre which shares the textual logic of absolutism (as Hitler's *Mein Kampf,* or Caesar's *Bellum Gallicum,* might suggest).[4] It is this difference which every mandate or imperative seeks to close, but necessarily deepens, occasioning a stronger imperative. Absolutism in this sense is absolute not because it reaches everywhere, but because it can't stop. Or start. It can't stop because it can't start—this we will refer to as its properly *historical* power.

The questions raised by de Man's early association with this imperative, however one understands it, are deeply complicated: in part by reason of his own biography, by the vexed question of Flemish autonomy, and by the no doubt powerful influence of his uncle, Henri de Man. The association with absolutism is also complicated by the writings themselves. In their most extended discussion of the subject, the report of a lecture at the Institute of Italian Culture entitled "Les systèmes impériaux de la Rome antique" (13 March 1941), de Man follows the editorial line when he notes how modern Italy impressively combines the Romes of Caesar and Augustus, but here and elsewhere it is never clear if this is the lecturer's opinion or de Man's. Nor is this the only opinion. In his article four days later on a second lecture entitled "Le 'Risorgimento' italien" (17 March 1941), the moral drawn from the resurgence of Rome almost seems to dangerously step across that same editorial line: "Et la leçon est importante pour les Belges qui desirent voir leur pays se reconstruire: ils verront comment il faut trouver ses forces régénératrices, non pas en regardant au delà des frontières, mais en tirant parti de qualités spécifiques qui s'étalent tout au long de l'histoire du pays."

No text, of course, joins de Man's early writings to the later work, and no reading can ever ultimately develop their moments of connection, or disprove them. One of the meanings of absolute power for theory may be that its relation to the figural can never be more than felt, nor merely felt in readings like de Man's that develop the absolute power of figure. I want to suggest now: 1) that a thoroughly synchronic theory can only begin by inscribing the unmediated relation to authority played out, in Jakobson's essay, at the level of the proper name (and coextensive, however complicated their complicity, with de Man's wartime writings); and 2) that it can move forward (or constitute a movement) only with reference to an end that is no longer historically absolute but, by contrast, absolutely historical. This last is more than a tautology, as if the end of theory were praxis. In the first place, theory as de Man represents it "never quite reaches its mark" (AR, p.130). Nor is the relation of early to late as specular or circular as the above juxtaposition of terms might suggest. The opposition late-early may be undermined in de Man's later writings, but we will see that it is only because the end of theory is perpetually undermined by something like a founding relation to power that it becomes "impossible to decide. . . whether [its] flourishing is a triumph or a fall" (RT, p.20).

The return of the wartime writings *in* the later work is explicitly at issue in de Man's essay "Excuses"—at least if we are to take seriously its opening footnote to Michel Leiris' "De la littérature considerée comme une tauromachie," to which de

Man attaches "The essay dates from 1945, immediately after the war" (AR, p.278). The reference is perhaps too arbitrary for anything beyond de Man's own wartime writings to really explain it, but it is also autobiographical by default, since de Man praises Leiris' essay *because* it appears in "a text that is indeed as political as it is autobiographical" (and here de Man attaches the note). In these terms, "Excuses" is autobiographical because it never pretended to be, sentencing de Man for the same failure to reveal it uncovers in Rousseau, for keeping what he gives away, the exposure of a desire to expose. The essay ends the second part of *Allegories of Reading* on just these terms, reserving its harshest judgment ("what is truly shameful") for what may be its own worst crime, that the slander of the innocent Marion was committed "not for the sake of Rousseau's saving face, nor for the sake of his desire for her, but merely in order . . . to furnish him with a good ending for Book II of his *Confessions*" (AR, p.286). Viewed against the wartime writings (and "Confiteor" is the last chapter of Henri de Man's autobiography *Après coup*),[5] "Excuses" develops its own "implicit shift from reported guilt to the guilt of reporting" (AR, p.290), setting in motion the repetition compulsion it describes, and which Freud in fact first notes in cases of war trauma. What makes the essay transitional to work after *Allegories of Reading* is that it thereby interiorizes the very relation to responsibility it continues to undermine, at which point, we will need to consider, its power to undermine is virtually limitless.

In his essay "Rhetoric of Tropes," and again in "Anthropomorphism and Trope in the Lyric," de Man develops a specific but crucial convergence of figure and power when he considers Nietzsche's influential definition of truth as "a mobile army of metaphors" ("ein bewegliches Heer von Metaphern"). In the earlier essay, Nietzsche's definition serves to underscore the figural displacement of philosophical "truth"; in the later essay, de Man develops the metaphor itself:

Truth, says Nietzsche, is a mobile *army* of tropes. Mobility is coextensive with any trope, but the connotations introduced by "army" are not so obvious, for to say that truth is an army (of tropes) is again to say something odd and possibly misleading. It can certainly not imply, in *On Truth and Lie,* that truth is a kind of commander who enlists tropes in the battle against error. (RR, p.242)

The wit of the last sentence is the pun on "enlists troops"; truth is a trope, but de Man's own rhetoric suggests that a trope is a troop. It also makes a trope (paronomasia) of "tropes," which is no longer the power described by the pun but an image of the power it describes by—the way Nietzsche's "army of metaphors" is no longer a metaphor the moment it becomes a kind of standard for the avant-garde. "Tropes" marks a momentary convergence of performance and paraphrase, a momentary troping of trope, but the same relation is increasingly at issue in de Man's later writing. This can be seen most easily by juxtaposing a relatively early essay like "Literary History and Literary Modernity," where a troop is unabashedly a trope (BI, p.165), with a later essay like "The Resistance to Theory." In the earlier essay, de Man considers how, "the more radical the rejection of anything that came before, the greater the dependence on the past" (BI, p.161); in "The Resistance to Theory," the same dialectic has been internalized, and "the more [literary theory] is resisted, the more it flourishes, since the language it speaks is the language of self-resistance" (RT, pp.19–20). In the earlier essay, "literature, which is inconceivable without a passion for modernity, also seems to oppose *from the inside* a subtle resistance to this passion" (BI, p.154, my emphasis); in the second essay, "theory *is* itself this resistance" (RT, p.19). Most of the terms are the same from one essay to the other, but the background has shifted. Thus while Keats' *The Fall of Hyperion* serves as an image of the theorist in "Literary History and Literary Modernity" (BI, p.149), in the later essay it appears instead as an image of theory (RT, p.16). The earlier essay develops the way literature opposes the very passion for modernity it exemplifies; in "The Resistance to Theory" the same dynamic is at work with respect to the essay itself, with respect to theory. The power to which the later essay refers is absolute power but only because that power is, strictly speaking, its own.

Perhaps. It may still be the case that the self-determination of figure's relation to power responds just as radically to an absolutist agenda equally its own. In Jakobson's "Linguistics and Poetics," Shakespeare mediates between the universalizing claims of synchronic theory and the absolutism represented by Caesar, and it may be useful to develop this relation more carefully now from within Shakespeare. If *Antony and Cleopatra* (1607) stages the civil war, and the rise of Caesar, which followed events portrayed in *Julius Caesar* (1599), so, in their own ways, do the intervening tragedies. This is especially true in *Hamlet,* where the ghost of Old Hamlet is explicitly a theatrical echo of Caesar's ghost in *Julius Caesar* ("*Hic et ubique?*" [1.5.156]), and where Hamlet dies against Horatio's "I am more an antique Roman than a Dane" (5.2.341— Polonius' "I did enact Julius Caesar. I was kill'd i' th' Capitol; Brutus kill'd me" [3.2.103–04]). Macbeth himself draws the comparison to Antony when he says of Banquo, "under him / My Genius is rebuk'd, as it is said / Mark Antony's was by Caesar" (3.1.54–56). At the end of *Othello,* to cite one last example, "Cassio rules in Cyprus" (5.2.332), "a soldier," Iago observes early in the play, "fit

to stand by Caesar / And give direction" (2.3.122–23). In these terms each of the major tragedies represents a resistance to the coming order of Caesar on which they end, one by one and as a group.[6] The relation of figure to power is no doubt as problematic in theater as it is in theory, and I want to consider for a moment only one aspect of its functioning in *Antony and Cleopatra,* but one with important—if still unresolved—implications for literary theory. This is the relation of the dialectic to sexual difference. When Cleopatra, reflecting on Antony in a famous passage, remarks how "I drunk him to his bed; / Then put my tires and mantles on him, whilst / I wore his sword Philippan" (2.4.21–23), the surrendering of the sword turns Antony into Cleopatra but it also turns history—in this case, the ghosting of Brutus at Philippi— into theater. This is a momentary association, but the later "boying" of Cleopatra's "greatness" establishes it for the entire play. Both references suggest that figure's difference from history is sexual difference, but they also imply that the more sexual difference is undermined by figure, the closer to a thoroughly historical imperative the representation. In these terms, if *Macbeth* precedes *Antony and Cleopatra* because the undoing of sexual difference in the Witches' "none of woman born / Shall harm Macbeth" (4.1.80–81) speaks directly to the Caesarean Macduff, "untimely ripp'd" from his mother's womb, *Coriolanus* follows because the hero's mother Volumnia *is,* in a very real sense, Rome. In each of these plays the figure-power dialectic is pushed to its absolute limit, but I want to suggest now that the relation of the dialectic itself to sexual difference is, in every case, the same: as long as the title character (or characters, in the relevant case of *Antony and Cleopatra*) remains the locus of unstable gender identifications, the struggle for historical power a given play chronicles is, again, its own. "Caesar's will?" (3.13.46), Cleopatra demands of an incoming messenger, and one doesn't need to be Shakespeare to read through this to "Caesar is Will," or "Will is Caesar's." At the least it must be referred back to the clamor for "Caesar's will" in *Julius Caesar,* which Antony reads to the citizens among a chorus of "will's," "well's," and "we'll's." This in turn can be referred back to the extended play on "will" in sonnets 135–36. Whether or not "Caesar's will" actually *names* Shakespeare—and this is not just our question I am suggesting but his—it is worth adding in the context of the play's own struggle for authority that, excluding the history plays, there are two William's in Shakespeare, both of whom are equally suggestive of their author, and both of whom appear just after *Julius Caesar.* In *The Merry Wives of Windsor* (1600?), William Page, son of George Page, enters for a comic Latin lesson (4.1.). His proper names speak for themselves, and Page and author are brought together in a further reference to William Lily, author of Lily's *Grammar*. The other William is the rustic William in *As You Like It* (1599), who enters just as briefly to woo Audrey. Undone by Touchstone, he withdraws into the forest of Arden. This proper name—Arden, Shakespeare's mother's—situates the forest's difference from the court in terms of Cleopatra's difference from patriarchy, but with this obvious and important difference: *As You Like It* is not a tragedy. Duke Frederick invades for his brother in the final act with all the determination of Caesar, but is converted by the forest rather than the reverse. The sexual difference revealed by Rosalind's disguise is, moreover, stable, a disguise. Shakespeare's comedies push the figure-power dialectic to its same absolute limits, but only to mock or subvert them. The Pageant of the Nine Worthies in the closing scene of *Love's Labor's Lost*—Costard's "Pompey the Big"—is only the most famous example. Rosalind herself draws the distinction when she likens the suddenness of her sister's wedding to "Caesar's thrasonical brag of 'I came, saw, and overcame'" (5.2.31–32—Falstaff's "Caesar, Keiser, and Pheazar," *The Merry Wives of Windsor*, 1.3.9–10).

When I juxtapose Jakobson on Saussure with Shakespeare on Caesar, I want to underscore the specular or obverse relation joining theory to theater, but I also want to emphasize the way Shakespeare's function in Jakobson's essay is similar to Caesar's function in *Julius Caesar*. I want to suggest now that the same relation is in fact true for a wide range of literary theory, that the figure-power dialectic internalized by Shakespeare's plays is, as such, a feature of their reading as well, only in reverse. In the play's composition, the dialectic accounts for its particular figuration of power; in its reading, the same dialectic accounts for the (consequently) illimitable power of its figuration. This is Shakespeare's importance for criticism, but also his danger. His danger—and Marx in his own unlimited enthusiasm for Shakespeare probably understood this better than anyone—is also his importance. Both are in evidence when Jakobson remarks how "the trope becomes a part of poetic reality" in Antony's

My heart is in the coffin there with Caesar,
And I must pause till it come back to me.

Antony's "pause" takes the "heart" metonymy literally, but there is another trope governing the lines, and governing the pause itself. This is the figure of prosopopeia, the "*sta viator*" or "voice-from-beyond-the-grave," as de Man characterizes the term in "Autobiography as De-Facement" (*The Rhetoric of Romanticism*). I mention the trope now because it is along this figure that authority is transferred in Jakobson's essay, from Saussure to Jakobson but also from Shakespeare to structural

linguistics. I mention de Man's essay on autobiography because in it, too, Shakespeare functions as a kind of limit, as de Man suggests during a discussion of Milton's memorial lines to Shakespeare,

Then thou our fancy of itself bereaving,
Dost make us marble with too much conceiving.

Shakespeare represents a subjective limit for the essay at a particular moment in it, when "Milton speaks of the burden that Shakespeare's 'easy numbers' represent for those who are, like all of us, capable only of 'slow endeavoring art'" (AD, p.78). Prosopopeia is "the-voice-from-beyond-the-grave," but behind or containing that, de Man implies, and issuing from the subject of autobiography itself, are Shakespeare's "easy numbers." Jakobson's identification with Antony indicates for "synchronic poetics" how an increase in autobiography converges on an increased presence of the Shakespearean subject, as de Man's essay on autobiography converges on Shakespeare, but the same relation could, again, be developed across a wide range of literary theory. "Is it I," Hélène Cixous writes in the closing pages of her "Sorties" in *The Newly Born Woman*, "when at the thought of Octavia—because she kept you far from our bed, had all the governments and thrones been thrown at my feet, and all Asia added to Egypt to spread my power. . . Is that me? . . . O my husband-mother. . . I no longer recognize myself! But now I know myself."[7] More tentatively, perhaps, Freud also comes immediately to mind, whose comments in *The Interpretation of Dreams* make clear the extent to which Shakespeare was the authority from whom his own Oedipal theory was wrestled. *Hamlet* instantiates the archetypal Oedipus myth, but Freud's own theory, continuing that tradition, holds the mirror up to *Hamlet,* uncovering the origin of its guilt in a repetition which has all the earmarks of the play's own dumb show ("the image of a murther done in Vienna" [3.2.238–39]). Marx in *The Eighteenth Brumaire of Louis Bonaparte* wrestles with the same authority, one who precedes or subsumes class difference in the way Freud's pre-Oedipal subject precedes sexual difference. Hence the book's exuberant vision of the revolution, now submerged and "making its way through purgatory," surfacing one day victorious, when "Europe will leap from its seat and cry in triumph, 'Well burrowed, old mole!'" (EB, p.128), but hence, too, its image of the nephew-turned-Emperor "behind the iron death mask of Napoleon" while "the old dates rise up again, the old chronology, the old names, the old edicts" (EB, p.21).

In *Antony and Cleopatra,* Shakespeare *stages* the play's own difference from the history, ancient and contemporary, it brings to expression, and the play itself regularly suggests how Egypt's difference from Rome rehearses the play's own difference from the historical and cultural imperatives of its day. Cleopatra's "I shall see / Some squeaking Cleopatra boy my greatness / I' th' posture of a whore" (5.2.219–21) resembles nothing in the play so nearly as her earlier "Shall they hoist me up, / And show me to the shouting varlotry / Of censuring Rome?" (55–57). When the ghost of Hercules departs Antony on the eve of battle, a sentry remarks, "It signs well, does it not?" (5.3.14), and the reference is to the sign of Hercules outside the Globe theater, "Hercules and his load," as Rosencrantz remarks in a corresponding allusion from *Hamlet* (Cleopatra's "little O, the earth"). In the play's opening scene, the lovers jest while Caesar's messenger stands idly by:

Antony	What sport to-night?
Cleopatra	Hear the ambassadors.
Antony	Fie, wrangling queen! (47–48)

The suggestion that "the ambassadors" constitute a kind of theater is largely a joke at Caesar's expense, but it also makes explicit the purely formal relation to an audience which brings together Caesar's messengers and Shakespeare's company, the King's Men. The excessive theatricality of Cleopatra needs to be read against the London stage, and the domestic Rome of Fulvia, and finally Octavia, against Stratford. Such juxtapositions make Shakespeare important for an investigation of theory's relation to power, or figure's relation to structures of domination, but they also complicate any perspective, Shakespeare's included, on the power shaping the relations themselves. In Antony's reference to Caesar's "all-obeying" power it is impossible to determine whether the ambiguity of "all-obeying / obeying all" results from a fondness for wordplay or from a profound engagement with the paradoxes of absolute power. When the elder Caesar is assassinated in *Julius Caesar,* the magnificent shout of Cinna, "Liberty! Freedom! Tyranny is dead!" (3.1.78), could sound to the ears of an audience and not the eyes of a reader like "Liberty, Freedom, Tyranny is dead!" The reading which these and other such moments give way to—that Shakespeare believed the strong rule of a single mastermind was the only hope for civilization—has in fact been regularly offered,[8] but does it spring on Shakespeare's part from a commitment to rhetoric—the delayed-fuse effect of "Liberty. . . is dead" functions in thousands of lines by Shakespeare—or from an engagement with power? The difference is easily overlooked, as the confusion of Cinna the poet and Cinna the conspirator makes clear ("Tear him for his bad verses, tear him for his bad verses" [3.3.30–31]).

What makes the difference so difficult to read, even unreadable, is that the violence it provokes is itself produced as a reading. This at least is de Man's position in later essays, but also Shakespeare's position, or Brutus's, at a crucial juncture late in *Julius Caesar:*

Let me see, let me see; is not the leaf turn'd down
Where I left reading? Here it is, I think.
　　　Enter the Ghost of Caesar (4.3.273–74)

Three things are possible here: Caesar's ghost returns when reading is resumed; the ghost returns when reading is left off; the ghost returns when reading is both resumed and left off. It is this last position which brings the play closest to theory, at least as de Man represents it. "The leaf" brings Caesar to life, but that is only because it was a failure to read which killed him in the first place ("If thou read this, O Caesar, thou mayest live" [2.2.15]).[9] Where the history it describes ends and the one it performs begins is a difference any text necessarily obscures, especially a text like *Julius Caesar,* which performs history. What starts out as a question ends as an exclamation when Cassius cries: "How many ages hence / Shall this our lofty scene be acted over / In states unborn and accents yet unknown!" (3.1.111–13)— this is the shift which sets the performance at odds with the struggle for historical power it brings to expression, in the play but also in any radically performative theory. This is why Marxist critics of de Man are correct to develop in his later work the close relation to established power made explicit in the early writings, but this is also why, we need to consider now, they may be wrong to stop there.

The importance of Adorno for the controversy surrounding de Man is that he seems to condemn de Man's criticism, but to validate his art.[10] Obviously the opposition of criticism to art is not an opposition to be deployed casually in a discussion of either Adorno or de Man, since so much of their work both questions and insists on the difference. But while Adorno regularly undermines the professed detachment of ahistoric criticism, he is much less prepared than many of his followers to collapse the ostensibly apolitical works of the avant-garde into the reigning imperatives, categorical or otherwise, of this totalizing power. If ideology, by definition, hides where it is least expected, it doesn't necessarily appear where it seems most inevitable. What it does by design it need not do by default. In a very late essay entitled "Commitment" (1962), Adorno juxtaposes directly political art with "Art for Art's Sake" in terms as close to de Man as to those of his Marxist critics:

Each of the two alternatives negates itself with the other. Committed art, necessarily detached as art from reality, cancels the distance between the two. 'Art for Art's Sake' denies by its absolute claims [*Verabsolutierung*] that ineradicable connection with reality which is the polemical *a priori* of the very attempt to make art autonomous from the real. Between these two poles, the tension in which art has lived in every age till now, is dissolved. (CM, p.301)

The authentically political work of art doesn't trumpet its commitment to activism, nor does it simply hold the mirror up to nations, as one of de Man's early articles would have it (*Het Vlaamsche Land,* 30 March 1942). In an era of radical reification, the historical expresses itself as the negative determinant of either extreme. For Adorno, one test of a work's authenticity is that it be attacked with equal intensity by both the left and the right, and here the terms are even closer to de Man:

Cultural conservatives who demand that a work of art should say something, join forces with their political opponents against atelic, hermetic works of art. Eulogists of 'relevance' are more likely to find Sartre's *Huis Clos* profound, than to listen patiently to a text whose language jolts signification and by its very distance from 'meaning' revolts in advance against positivist subordination of meaning. (CM, p.302)

Adorno has no doubts about the strong reliance of authentically political art on the totalizing powers that be, but Picasso's supposed reply to the Nazi officer who had pointed to *Guernica* and asked, "Did you do that?"—"No, you did"—problematizes rather than proves his involvement. It is hardly a confession but neither is it an alibi. The line is a fine one, but Adorno attempts to draw it in his conclusion:

Paul Klee too belongs to any debate about committed and autonomous art: for his work, *écriture par excellence,* has roots in literature and would not have been what it is without them—or if it had not consumed them. During the First World War, or shortly after, Klee drew cartoons of Kaiser Wilhelm as an inhuman iron eater. Later, in 1920, these became—the development can be shown quite clearly—the *Angelus Novus,* the machine angel, who though he no longer bears any emblem of caricature or commitment, flies far beyond both. The machine angel's enigmatic eyes force the onlooker to try to decide whether he is announcing the culmination of disaster or salvation hidden within it. But, as Walter Benjamin, who owned the drawing, said, he is the angel who does not give but takes. (CM, p.318)

For de Man, of course, it is hardly a question of "flying far beyond both." Nor could it ever be so for Adorno, whose descrip-

tion doesn't merely emphasize the flight but its grounding in absolutism. It is in these terms that I intend the drawing as an image, too, for the relation of de Man's later work to the early writings, but with an important and necessary qualification. If there is an allegory here for de Man's development from Klee's "inhuman iron eater" to M. H. Abrams' "deconstructive angel," it is immediately more complicated in the case of de Man's later work. For by this time the "machine angel" made from the same iron that feeds power has become "the textual machine of its own constitution *and* performance, its own textual allegory" (AR, p.278)—and that, early and late, for better or worse, is *its* power.

Klee's drawing, as Adorno represents it, is the perspective of two perspectives, one of criticism and art, one of both of these and their relation to power. Klee's *Angelus Novus* "no longer bears any emblem of caricature or commitment," but "the development can be shown quite clearly." It is this contradiction which brings the drawing closest to de Man's own *écriture.* The internalization of the figure-power dialectic may make the later work look and feel like the early writings written out so far into the margins that the newspaper is no longer readable, but what is harder to decide is whether the newspaper has disappeared from view because absolutely present, as critics like Terry Eagleton and Frank Lentricchia might suggest, or finally erased, as critics like Andrew Parker have argued, for whom de Man's later work is politically enabling, even revolutionary.[11] Andrzej Warminski has commented how de Man's picture in the *New York Times* article on the wartime writings seemed to a student of his as potentially sinister as the same photograph on the cover of *The Lesson of Paul de Man* looked benign. It is, again, a difficult difference: de Man's later work is still probably far more reactionary than we know, and far more radical. The wartime writings, by deepening the perspective, further blur the distinction. They make explicit the collusion of figure with power submerged or resisted in the later writing, but they also make explicit the resistance.

Harvard University

ABBREVIATIONS

AR *Allegories of Reading* (New Haven: Yale University Press, 1979)
BI *Blindness and Insight* [1971] (Minneapolis: University of Minnesota Press, 1983)
CM "Commitment," in *The Essential Frankfurt School Reader,* eds. Andrew Arato and Eike Gebhardt (New York: The Continuum Publishing Company, 1987)

EB *Der achtzehnte Brumaire des Louis Bonaparte* (Leipzig: Dietz Verlag, 1984), my translation.

LP "Linguistics and Poetics," in *Style in Language,* ed. Thomas A. Sebeok (Cambridge, MA: The MIT Press, 1960)

RR *The Rhetoric of Romanticism* (New York: Columbia University Press, 1984)

RT *The Resistance to Theory* (Minneapolis: University of Minnesota Press, 1986)

NOTES

1. Christopher Norris, "Allegories of Disenchantment: Poetry and Politics in De Man's Early Essays," forthcoming in *Reading de Man Reading,* eds. Wlad Godzich and Lindsay Waters (Minneapolis: University of Minnesota Press, 1988).

2. John Fekete, *The Critical Twilight: Explorations in the Ideology of Anglo-American Literary Theory from Eliot to McLuhan* (London: Routledge, 1977). For de Man's "quietism," see Frank Lentricchia, *Criticism and Social Change* (Chicago: University of Chicago Press, 1983), p.51.

3. Jacques Derrida, *Margins of Philosophy,* tr. Alan Bass (Chicago: University of Chicago Press, 1982), p.5. All citations to Shakespeare are from the *Riverside Shakespeare,* ed. G. Blakemore Evans (Boston: Houghton Mifflin, 1974).

4. It is interesting to note that the title of both of these autobiographies is seldom translated. This is in fact one effect of the textual authority we are considering here.

5. *Après coup* was completed early in 1941, when Henri de Man was still in Belgium, and still vaguely optimistic about his vision of a socialist Europe: "Maintenant, à la fin de l'hiver de guerre où j'ai écrit ce livre, je puis dire, comme le spectre de Hamlet: 'Il me semble que je hume l'air du matin'—même sans être sûr si je verrai encore se dissiper les ténèbres" (Brussels: Editions de la Toison d'Or, 1941, p.322).

6. The exception of course is *King Lear,* both regarding Caesar, whom the action of the play precedes, and its conspicuous lack of closure.

7. Hélène Cixous, and Catherine Clément, *The Newly Born Woman,* tr. Betsy Wing (Minneapolis: University of Minnesota Press, 1986), pp. 124–25.

8. See Ernest Schanzar's "The Problem of *Julius Caesar,*" *Shakespeare Quarterly* VI (Summer 1955), for an interesting account of variant readings given Shakespeare's Caesar.

9. This warning is spoken in soliloquy by Artemidorus of Cnidos, identified in the *dramatis personae* of the First Folio as "a teacher of rhetoric."

10. An interesting parallel to de Man's wartime writings is provided by the discovery of a pro-Nazi review published by Adorno in June of 1934 in *Die Musik,* "the official journal for the direction of the youth of the Reich." In a note in *La Fiction du politique* (Paris: Christian Bourgois, 1987, pp.150–151), Philippe Lacoue-Labarthe summarizes the events surrounding an open letter to Adorno published in the Frankfurt student journal in January of 1963, inquiring whether he was the author of the review, and asking how he could thus condemn all those complicitous in the development of Germany beginning from 1934, particularly Heidegger. In response, Adorno acknowledged authorship, and expressed his regret. But he also asked whether, in the scales of an "equitable justice," the review presented "a very great weight in comparison to my work and to my life." On the question of Heidegger, he writes: "Concerning the continuity of my work, it should not be permitted to compare me to Heidegger, whose philosophy is fascist down to its innermost cells [*dessen Philosophie bis in ihre innersten Zellen faschistisch ist*]." Of this response, Lacoue-Labarthe notes, "Hannah Arendt wrote to Karl Jaspers on July 4, 1966 that she found it "'indescribably distressing.'"

Adorno's letter is reprinted in an afterword to *Musikalische Schriften* VI (Frankfurt: Suhrkamp, 1984), pp.637–38.—My thanks to Jonathan Culler for drawing this to my attention, and for many helpful suggestions elsewhere.

11. I develop this question in much more detail in my review of Frank Lentricchia's *Criticism and Social Change,* "'By Heaven, Thou Echoest Me': Lentricchia, *Othello,* de Man" (*Diacritics,* Spring 1987).

Trappings of an Education
toward what we do not yet have.

CYNTHIA CHASE

How to take the measure of a certain kind of trap.

After the emergence of de Man's 1940–42 articles, one necessarily writes about his writings differently than before—insofar as one writes about a subject they do not as such address, about an occurrence they do not see. The reappearance of those abandoned texts is something that happens to de Man's writing from the outside, which thus strikes it with blindness with regard to what is nevertheless its own situation, or rather ours, that of his students, readers. Here for the first time indubitably is an occurrence pertinent to his writing which it cannot see and about which it has nothing to say.

But at the same time it says a great deal about just that predicament—the blindness of writing; and also—but why is it only now that one learns to read this?—about the implication of thought and writing in the violence of history, and particularly that European 20th-century violence, Nazism—its essence (as Lacoue-Labarthe argues in *La Fiction du politique*) a "national aestheticism" in which "the aesthetic ideology" finds realization. What is the economy, or the mechanism of waste, by which the writings that fail to speak of Nazism, fail to speak or inscribe the word "Nazism" (or several others, comparably specific), more than other writing make it possible for Nazism to be read? (not mistaken, that is, for the personal experience of individual guilt; nor for the sheerly aberrant event of absolute evil quite outside any history that could be "ours"). For my claim will be not only that de Man's writings on the violence of "the aesthetic state" analyze the complicities of modes of education and models of history with the fascist totalitarian state. But also that these writings' not knowing, not seeing, their circumstances—which is not a matter of repressing or concealing—is a key dimension of what they give us to read.

This means therefore that one has (I have) not the possibility of writing differently about this very situation than in the ways that de Man's own writings suggest—since they both perform, acknowledge, and analyze the blindness and the violence of writing. And this (too) is the trap de Man called "aesthetic education"; as thus in the closing paragraphs of *The Rhetoric of Romanticism* (1985, his first posthumous book):

As we know from another narrative text of Kleist, the memorable tropes that have the most success (*Beifall*) occur as mere random improvisation (*Einfall*) at the moment when the author has completely relinquished any control over his meaning and has relapsed (*Zurückfall*) into the extreme formalization, the mechanical predictability of grammatical declensions (*Fälle*).

But *Fälle,* of course, also means in German "trap," the trap which is the ultimate textual model of this and of all texts, the trap

of an aesthetic education which inevitably confuses dismemberment of language by the power of the letter with the gracefulness of
a dance. This dance, regardless of whether it occurs as mirror, as
imitation, as history, as the fencing match of interpretation, or as
the anamorphic transformations of tropes, is the ultimate trap, as
unavoidable as it is deadly. [RR, p.290]

*

There is an effect of blinding in the very precision, rigor, and intricacy of the final chapter of *Allegories of Reading,* "Excuses
(*Confessions*)." This chapter and the preceding one, "Promises
(*Social Contract*)," are de Man's most sustained analysis of texts
that are speech acts or performatives; of texts that, in particular,
perform political or social acts—legislating, promising, confessing, denouncing, excusing. In the intricacy of the details of this
analysis, something is obscured, such that in one's reading of
"Excuses (*Confessions*)" it tends to become elided or buried, or
missed, despite the fact that it is explicitly written out: that the
random or mechanical violence of language, of what Rousseau
calls "fiction," is *inexcusable,* even if it has proved to be inevitable. This conclusion of both de Man and Rousseau is obscured
not only by the complexity of its context but also by the radical-
ness of the preceding move in the argument, which bears the
brunt of one's attention and resistance: the counter-intuitive
claim that Rousseau's slander of Marion, his uttering the sound
marion, was sheer accident. Or rather, what de Man argues is
that this possibility has to be seriously considered: with the
abrupt anacoluthon "je m'excusai sur le premier objet qui s'of-
rit," de Man observes, Rousseau's text interrupts its psychological explanation of his theft and slander in terms of his desire and
shame, with an assertion of the gesture's sheer contingency.
That a random or mechanical dimension of language exists that
cannot be assimilated to a system of intentions, desires, or motives—this claim, the culmination of de Man's reading of the
"purloined ribbon" passage in the *Confessions,* takes such strong
arguing that the subsequent moves of the argument are diminished. Moreover the subsequent argument is indeed obscure—
difficult and enigmatic: that the random arbitrary functioning
of language as "fiction"—that is, "in the absence of any link between utterance and a referent, . . . governed by any . . . conceivable relationship that could lend itself to systematization" [AR,
p.292]—is mechanical, is the functioning of a machine (". . .
l'effet machinal de mon embarras," writes Rousseau of his white
lies); and that this very mechanical functioning is "inexcusable."
What is the nature of this argument and what is the significance
of this conclusion?

Another essay helps, I think, determine them: "Aesthetic

Formalization: Kleist's "'Über das Marionettentheater'" illuminates the stakes and the contexts of the argument in "Excuses
(*Confessions*)"—by way of offering, as I shall argue, an incisive
diagnosis of the conditions of possibility of Nazism.

That bend of the argument of the essay on Rousseau's autobiographical texts reappears in a more visible and indeed more
lurid form in de Man's essay on "Über das Marionettentheater."[1] Something obscured in the denser text of the previous essay comes through in the rapid and looser articulations of the
later one; here a single sentence suffices to make the connection
that in the reading of Rousseau's *Confessions* and *Rêveries* took
several pages: between the arbitrary, mechanical functioning of
language and the wounding of a body. It was the connection, in
the previous essay, between the lies that are the "mechanical effect" of being in a situation where one is compelled to speak
and the mutilation of a hand by a too admiringly regarded machine ("I looked at the metal rolls, my eyes were attracted by
their polish. I was tempted to touch them with my fingers and I
moved them with pleasure over the polished surface of the cyl-
inder. . .'") (AR, p. 298). The connection recurs in his Kleist essay where de Man has been discussing one of three anecdotes or
scenes within the text: a young man is stricken with embarrassment and loses his youthful grace when he fails to reproduce at
will, challenged by the older man who tells the story, a graceful
pose, a gesture (lifting his foot to dry it after bathing) in which
he had observed his resemblance to the pose of the celebrated
classical statue the Spinario.

In the Kleist essay as in the Rousseau essay, the reading begins with a psychological interpretation. De Man unravels how
the *Confessions* explain and excuse Rousseau's theft and slander
in terms of his desire and shame, and ultimately, his desire for
shame, for the exposure of the desire for self-exposure. Such is
the utter bad faith of the excuse, of making the excuse "I feared
to be ashamed" for not confessing a misdeed: Rousseau's desire
had been not so much the desire to possess (the ribbon) but to
express, expose, his desire (for Marion); "One is more ashamed
of the desire to expose oneself than of the desire to possess. . . .
since the crime is exposure, the excuse consists in recapitulating
the exposure in the guise of concealment":

The excuse is a ruse which permits exposure in the name of hiding,
not unlike Being, in the later Heidegger, reveals itself by hiding.
Or, put differently, shame used as excuse permits repression to
function as revelation and thus to make pleasure and guilt interchangeable. Guilt is forgiven because it allows for the pleasure of
revealing its repression. (AR, pp.285–6)

So much for "Being, in the later Heidegger"; and for gestures of excuse for not having confessed and for having spoken awry in words whose interpretation was a cause of harm to others. Such excuses effect an effacement of guilt and appropriate and offer a form of understanding inseparable from pleasure. It is right, I think, to read this passage as a reflection on the gesture of excuse that de Man declined to make (and in particular, of excuse for his article "Les juifs dans la littérature actuelle" of 4 March 1941) and not only on the speech act of Rousseau's *Confessions*. But what I take to be ultimately still more important or revealing here is something else: the position of this interpretive moment in a particular structure of argument. It recurs in the Kleist essay, where the ephebe's loss of gracefulness is ascribed to "the loss of control, the confusion caused by shame"—shame at "the exposure of his desire for self-recognition." After one more paragraph comes the same shift carried out to stunning effect in the Rousseau reading: from a psychological interpretation of utterances and gestures, to a reading focused on a mechanical action or repetition—and in the Kleist essay, simultaneously on its implications for a body:

Up till now, we have read the young man's blushing ("er errötete. . .") as mere shame, a wound of the ego, but it now appears that the redness may well be the blood of an injured body. The white, colorless world of statues is suddenly reddened by a flow of blood, however understated. What is not more than the pinprick of a splinter will soon enough grow to a very different order of magnitude. (RR, p.279, my italics)

Here the shift away from interpretation of a scenario in psychological terms to an interpretation stressing the role of mechanical repetition (just as in Rousseau) coincides with the evocation of "actual, bodily mutilations" (AR, p. 298). The strangeness of the final sentence comes from the unexpected temporal allusion in which a vast and sinister historical trajectory abruptly makes its appearance. "Soon enough": in the space of the century and a half that separates German Classicism, its aesthetic model for the self and the state, from Nazism; in the space of the twenty-four centuries that separate Greece and classical art from the aestheticist totalitarian state, from the ultimate machine of Nazism as "national aestheticism." The Kleist essay makes plain what the Rousseau essay taken alone does not: that the sheerly mechanical dimension of language is a violence that takes place not only at the level of individual texts (such as Rousseau's autobiographies) but at the level of the state, of culture and of politics.

In the sentences preceding those above, de Man has been commenting on the aesthetic ideology, in particular the idealization of Greece in Germany after Winckelmann, exemplified by the canonization of the Spinario:

Maybe the delusion was to believe that the model was graceful in the first place. The statue, we are reminded, represents the figure of a young boy who is extracting a splinter from his foot, an action very unlikely to be the least bit graceful or requiring, at the very least, a considerable amount of idealization to be made to appear so. More important still is the fact that the original perfection, the exemplary wholeness of the aesthetic model is itself, however slightly yet unquestionably, impaired. . . . What is not more than the pinprick of a splinter will soon enough grow to a very different order of magnitude. (RR, p.279)

For much of European history classical art is idealized in a way that prevents the idealization *performed* by classical art from coming into question. "Few commentators, if any, have hinted at the potential ridicule of trying to imitate gracefully someone engaged in minor repairs on his own body" (RR, p.280)—perhaps not even Nietzsche, though it is the famous optical metaphor in *The Birth of Tragedy* that comes to mind with this allusion to carrying out repairs on one's own body: the Apollinian "lucidity" and "precision" of Sophoclean tragedy described as "luminous spots to heal the look wounded by gruesome night."[2] This is part of what it would mean to say that "the original perfection, the exemplary wholeness of the aesthetic model is . . . however slightly yet unquestionably, impaired": that Greek art "itself" is split, fissured, in Nietzsche's account between "Apollinian" and "Dionysian" elements or imperatives, such that one can only try to "heal" the other. The slight displacement from tragedy as catharsis to prosthesis stands behind the principal premise depicted in Kleist's text: the affirmation by the narrator's interlocutor, the lead dancer of the opera, Herr C., of the superiority of a ballet of marionettes to one of living dancers—if only the puppets be constructed with sufficient skill, the possibility of which is proven, he maintains, by the excellence of the mechanical legs created by English craftsmen for those who have lost a limb, which enable them actually to dance. The idea of a mutilation for the sake of the prosthesis ensuring gracefulness is not far from the surface. Kleist's text brings together, de Man shows, to deeply disquieting effect, the idea of a fall from grace, the loss of a state of nature or paradise which ultimately can be recovered, and the conception of art as prosthesis, for art, skill, or "aesthetic education" as the means of such a recovery. This notion, this project, is a second referent of that allusion to "the aesthetic model . . . however slightly yet unquestionably, impaired": the model of the work, and of the work as model for the state, reflecting as de Man puts it "the carelessness of classical aestheticians who misread Kant," preeminently Schiller (RR, p.279). The impaired aesthetic model instituted in Schiller's *On the Aesthetic Education of Mankind* is the aesthetic as *not impaired,* as an ideal wholeness and harmony offering the model for an ideal human society—rather than, as from a reading of Kant, framed, fragmented, contradictory; an aesthetic ideology overlooking and concealing the *failure* of aesthetic judgment in fact to articulate theoretical with practical reason and ethics (de Man argues in essays on Kant).[3] The Schillerian aesthetic and political ideal is that of society as "a well-executed *dance*." It is one of total form, of total, and incipiently totalitarian, control. Kleist's text offers de Man a narrative and set of figures that bring this ideal into question.

De Man begins his essay on "Über das Marionettentheater" with a quotation from a 1793 letter of Schiller, cited in Wilkinson and Willoughby's English translation "as a fitting description of Schiller's main theoretical text, the *Letters on the Aesthetic Education of Mankind,*" a passage which begins, "I know no better image for the ideal of a beautiful society than a well-executed English dance, composed of many complicated figures and turns" (RR, p.263). In borrowing Schiller's metaphor and model for the ideal society for their description of his own text, Wilkinson and Willoughby carry out a Schillerian gesture, conceiving the work on the model of its own model for society and for the state: an artistic work, a dance. Schiller on "the aesthetic education of mankind" and Kleist's "Über das Marionettentheater" ought to be read together, de Man suggests, for key themes and statements of Schiller's text and its commentary appear also in Kleist's text, but there—presented as the assertions of Herr C. who affirms the gracefulness of a dance of marionettes, of puppets—they "reveal some of what is hidden behind Schiller's ideology of the aesthetic" (RR, p.265). De Man is not alone in noticing the proximity of the two texts. In a passage often quoted by critics and interpreted as if it were Kleist's own statement (and an aphorism of deep wisdom), Herr C. remarks, "Paradise is bolted and the Angel behind us; we must journey round the world and see if perhaps it is open somewhere from behind. . . . To return to the state of innocence, we must eat again from the tree of knowledge." As Lacoue-Labarthe observes, "This is exactly what Schiller, in his own words, had wanted to say, and what he had said: 'We have been nature . . . and our culture must lead us back to nature by the path of reason and liberty'" (HG, p.467). Schiller's metaphor of the dance singled out by Wilkinson and Willoughby, and redeployed by Kleist, brings to the fore the fundamental roles of imitation and formalization in the educational process envisaged by Schiller's

Letters. De Man will read in Kleist's text the political as well as cognitive mutilations entailed in such a process.

As he begins analyzing Wilkinson and Willoughby's celebration of what they call "the tautology of essential art," de Man indicates the scope of the inquiry. "The Schiller text, with its commentary, condenses the complex ideology of the aesthetic in a suggestive concatenation of concepts that achieve the commonplace, not by their banality but by the universality of their stated aspirations." To social harmony, but also to knowledge, which is indeed the stake of the aesthetic in the Kantian tradition, in which it is "a principle of *articulation* between various known faculties, activities, and modes of cognition" (RR, p.265, my italics). (Kleist's text plays out the pun available from the German word for "articulation," *Gliederung.* Herr C. locates gracefulness "in dem Gliedermann, oder in dem Gott" (UM, p. 342); *Gliedermann* is the word for marionette or puppet.) De Man writes:

The aesthetic, as is clear from Schiller's formulation, is primarily a social and political model, ethically grounded in an assumedly Kantian notion of freedom; despite repeated attempts by commentators, alarmed by its possible implications, to relativize and soften the ideal of the aesthetic state (*Aesthetischer Staat*) that figures so prominently at the end of the *Letters on Aesthetic Education,* it should be preserved as the radical assertion that it is. The "state" that is here being advocated is not just a state of mind or of soul, but a principle of political value and authority that has its own claims on the shape and the limits of our freedom. It would lose all interest if this were not the case. For it is as a political force that the aesthetic still concerns us as one of the most powerful ideological drives to act upon the reality of history. (RR, p.264)

Certainly this passage concerns the emergence of fascism (for Brecht and Benjamin, famously, the aesthetification of politics) and the rise of Nazism. It addresses at the same time a problem said to be one that "still concerns us": the conditions of the possibility of those historical events in the history of thought, in ways of thinking about art and literature. The implied historical context of the ideas and events this essay concerns has become more legible, I think, in the wake of our knowledge of de Man's participation in currents of thought about literature, history, and politics during the forties. I want to interpret the judgment in this essay, made also in the Rousseau essay but obscured, as to the inexcusableness of the violence attendant upon the formal, mechanical dimension of language; and to clarify what I find to be this essay's penetrating analysis of essential conditions of Nazism. Yet this will be in some important respects an interpretation that cannot credit de Man's essay with communicating its results; for my claim is that it is by way of the auto-biographical dimension marked, but not filled in, in the essay that—after becoming aware of de Man's wartime writing—we have access to the historical dimension of the argument within which alone its resources as critique and counter-proposal become fully intelligible.

It would appear that de Man's Kleist essay does not know, or "ignores," the historical conditions of its reading, at least that is to say the current conditions of its reading now. This question of the essay's knowledge or acknowledgment of its historical conditions is a tricky one, however. It could not be said of any text that it knows or masters its contexts or conditions. And yet precisely *this* essay of de Man's could be said to anticipate upon and invite the intertextual reading only now made possible: that of this text with de Man's articles on literature and criticism of 1940–2. For what this essay does is to analyze models of the literary work—notions of what a text is and what one should do about it—as aspects of an aesthetic ideology related, in diverse but fundamental ways, to authoritarian and totalitarian forms of the modern state. If the object-lesson of the Kleist essay is one we fail to take in until we have de Man's own earliest writings to practice on, that is a measure of our own conditioned obtuseness (that of supposing, for instance—and even when we thought we knew better—that discussion of literary texts was not discussion of the "world") rather than of de Man's failure to consider one of his essay's most obvious points of reference. Moreover, the essay is at the same time, and most explicitly, an analysis of the conditions and suppositions of the intertextual reading we practice precisely now: these models of the text as imitation, as object and subject of a hermeneutic process, and as "system of tropes" are those of our current critical practice, not only the protocols of literary criticism in the thirties and forties. Can there be any doubt, furthermore, that the following passage, for instance, refers among other things to the situation of precisely this text, on "aesthetic education" ("the articulation of history with formally arrived-at truth" [RR, p. 276])?

If the author knows that he produces meaning, and knows the meaning he produces, his mastery is established. But if this is not the case, if meaning is produced that he did not intend and if, on the other hand, the intended meaning fails to hit the mark, then he is in difficulty. *One consequence of such loss of control over meaning will be that he is no longer able to feign it* ["it"="the loss of control over meaning," as well as "control over meaning"]. For this is indeed the best and perhaps the only proof of his mastery over meaning, that he is free to decree it, at his own will, as genuine or as fake; it takes a stolid realist to believe in the existence of pure, unfeigned fiction.

Hence the need to mislead the reader by constantly alternating feints with genuine thrusts: the author depends on the bewilderment and confusion of his reader to assert his control. *Reading is comparable to a battle of wits in which both parties are fighting over the reality or fictionality of their discourse, over the ability to decide whether the text is a fiction or an (auto)biography, narrative or history, playful or serious.* (RR, p.282, my italics)

Could we hazard this formulation for de Man's situation in this particular text—that of a loss of control over meaning such that he is unable to feign the loss of control? And declines to feign, indeed, that this text is not at the same time autobiography—and history—as well as fiction and theory?

De Man begins his essay on "Aesthetic Formalization" by quoting a quotation of Schiller and commentary by his English translators and focusing his opening analysis on the commentary rather than on the initial passage (from a letter to Körner of 1793). This establishes the focus of his argument: not Schiller's text but its reception, and more particularly, conceptions of art and of the literary work which may be seen to derive from Schiller's notion of the aesthetic and which continue to predominate—in the translation with commentary of the well-meaning Wilkinson and Willoughby (published 1967), and in literary criticism and theory generally, as well as in notions of history with which they are solidary. Schiller's misreading of Kant is treated by de Man in another lecture that was part of the same series (the Messenger Lectures) delivered at Cornell in 1983. "Kant and Schiller" makes plain that Schiller's misreading of Kant's *Third Critique* is indeed seen by de Man as the first drastic error in a history of fatal misreadings of which he alludes only to the most fatal, Goebbels' misreading of Schiller.[4] In comparison with that allusion, the Kleist essay's gesture is less welcome and more stringent. Autobiographical and historical, this is also a profoundly pedagogical text, instructing, warning, even as it warns against the principal conceivable models of instruction.

De Man chooses Kleist's text as one that makes legible "the possible tension between the two functions" of art or what Wilkinson and Willoughby call "the tautology of essential art," unregistered in their commentary or in Schiller. It is the tension between the dimension of formality making the dance (model for the work and for society) susceptible of repetition or inscription—thus they write, "The perpetually repeated figures—so highly formalized that they can easily be recorded in notation—admit of only as much individuality in their successive execution by the different dancers as can be expressed through the grace of bodily movement"; and what Wilkinson and Willoughby call "the tautology of essential art," their expression for art's universality: "its inherent tendency to offer a hundred different treatments of the same subject, to find a thousand different forms of expression for the thoughts and feelings common to all men" (RR, p.264). De Man unpacks: "As the privileged and infinitely varied mode of expression of this universality, art is in fact what defines humanity in the broadest sense. . . On the other hand, as a principle of formalization rigorous enough to produce its own codes and systems of inscription, tautology functions as a restrictive coercion that allows only for the reproduction of its own system, at the exclusion of all others" (RR, p.265).

The tension defined here—between universality and exclusion—is an observable paradox of Western democratic states, universalist in their principles since the seventeenth century or the Enlightenment, but exclusionist in their principle of operation (whether the exclusion be of religious minorities, women, or on the basis of "race"). This is not unrelated, one could infer from de Man's commentary, to the ways in which modern states instantiate the aspiration to "the aesthetic state," the very tension between the inclusiveness and the repetitiveness (and thus exclusiveness) of *form* as a model. That model is a measure of how in certain fundamental respects, the modern national state remains modeled on the idea of the ancient state, conceived as one with, and as a form of, artistic achievement. Lacoue-Labarthe pursues such an argument in *La Fiction du politique*, bringing it to bear on the logic of racism ("Racism is an aestheticism . . . ") and on the tendency to totalitarianism. It is that signification that one now can read in the passage that links the Rousseau essay with the essay on "Aesthetic Formalization": "By saying that the excuse is not only a fiction but a machine" ["l'effet machinal de mon embarras"], writes de Man,

one adds to the connotation of referential detachment, of gratuitous improvisation, that of the implacable repetition of a preordained pattern. Like Kleist's marionettes, the machine is both "anti-grav," the anamorphosis of a form detached from meaning and capable of taking on any structure whatever, yet entirely ruthless in its inability to modify its own structural design for nonstructural reasons. The machine is like the grammar of the text when it is isolated from its rhetoric, the merely formal element without which no text can be generated. (AR, p.294)

What is the significance of the doubly given subject of these sentences, language and "the machine"?

The passage designates a performative function of language unconstrained by a cognitive or referential dimension, the non-referential and non-intentional status of grammar having come

into play without check, in a performance that in itself is violent in sundering the connection between action and cognition (like the gracefulness Herr C. describes as increasing precisely as consciousness is dimmed). The sundering of that connection is also an exclusion of the other: of any other—including a signified or an intention—than the performing, functioning, structure itself. That the totalitarian state, with the limitless destructive power of its technical and technological function, is related to the performative power of language, of grammar, is the difficult thought being offered by this description of "the machine." It will help to understand it to bring together de Man's return to this topic in the Kleist essay—where the model of language as a functioning "system of tropes" holds a particular position differentiated from two others—with Lacoue-Labarthe's discussion of Nazism as a certain realization of the logic of *technè* we inherit from Greek thought. This will also make it possible to read the final sentence of this paragraph as something other than an aporia: "There can be no use of language which is not, within a certain perspective thus radically formal, i.e. mechanical, no matter how deeply this aspect may be concealed by aesthetic, formalistic delusions" (AR, p.294). For the two-part conclusion condensed in this sentence (its own syntactical structure lopped or disarticulated by the omission of a comma after "perspective") will reappear in the Kleist text in the double judgment that consists, as here, in ascribing this radically formal and violent dimension to any discourse—thus the Kleist essay will speak of how the "next textual model . . . will *have to be* that of the text as a system of turns and deviations, as a system of tropes" (AR, p.285, my italics)—and differentiating modes of engagement with this formal dimension, this machine, different stances with regard to this "certain perspective." To anticipate: the Kleist essay differentiates between admiration of the machine's performance, such as Herr C.'s celebration of the marionette's dance, and a contest with that performance, such as the fencing match recounted by the narrator, a contest with an apparently infallible machine-like opponent, a trained bear. Two ways of coping with a totalizing, totalitarian tendency always incipient (like the repetitive formal element here: *t*'s), if precisely because—totalization being impossible—this tendency cannot be recognized and reduced once and for all to a program, be it called variously totalitarianism, antisemitism, fascism, racism, nazism.

*

De Man analyses "the aesthetic ideology"; Lacoue-Labarthe, analyzing Heidegger's identification with, then rupture and distantiation from what he called "the essence of national socialism," diagnoses "national aestheticism." How does nationalism or the nation come into play in "aesthetic ideology"? The question is enormous, one in which that of "language" and that of languages meet and which would need to be addressed through a reading of philosophical as well as political discourse from at least the late 18th century. I want however to take the risk here of sketching only the elements of an answer to that question that seem to me most revealing with regard to an intertextual reading of de Man's 1983 essay on "Aesthetic Formalization" and the writing that marks his first "aesthetic education," the book reviews in *Le Soir* of 1941–2 where he is teaching himself *Vergleichende Literaturwissenschaft*, "comparing" "the literatures." One of the motifs of these texts is the characterization of French versus German national temperament or "genius": "the virtues of clarity, logic, harmony" that are "the constants of the latin spirit," versus the "sense of greatness and the infinite" that are German ("Le Problème français. *Dieu est-il français?* de F. Sieburg," *Le Soir,* 28 April 1942). I draw those quotations from an article reviewing a book specifically about the problem of nationalism; in reviews of literary or literary-critical works, the characterizations become more complex and differentiated. But the very carry-over of those national stereotypes into the discussions of particular literary works is a significant ideological aspect of these early articles.

The presence in the articles of such national stereotyping by no means amounts to celebration of German nationality or the German nation; the characteristic qualities of at least three nations, France, Belgium, and Germany, are being identified and valued, in terms exerting some check or pressure upon the design of German domination. But while the stereotyping thus lacks a direct and pro-Nazi political significance, its deeper ideological significance persists, and how and whether the texts diverge from that "national aestheticism" is an important question. A significant divergence would not be located, I think, in the fact that the reviewer's strongest interest or enthusiasm is elicited by the co-presence of these qualities or the circumvention of their opposition. Goethe's *Elective Affinities,* for example, is praised for attaining true universality through "the synthesis of these two national temperaments," French and German, namely "the eternal leit motiv of French prose, the primacy of the psychological motive," and "the introduction of the time factor, of the *duration* [*durée*; de Man's italics] of the events"—"these characteristics that one could call the 'French' virtues of the *Elective Affinities* [de Man's quotation marks]," as well as "a glimpse of the unfathomable depths, a metaphysical feeling of the infinite, proper to German thought," from which point of view, "the novel remains a reflection of the nationality

of its author" ("Universalisme de Goethe. *Les Affinités Electives,*" *Le Soir,* 26 May 1942).

National categories are not inevitably a feature of the articles' practical criticism, and they do not appear in the articles or passages (such as "Sur les possibilités de la critique," *Le Soir,* 2 Dec. 1941, and "Le Renouveau du roman," 27 Jan. 1942) in which theoretical or methodological principles are enunciated. These consist in a combination of formalism and historicism made to cohere in the notion that a history of literary forms offers an overview of "the way humanity changes and develops," a sort of Hegelianism almost as familiar in literary criticism of the past thirty years as of the previous thirty. Neither nationalism nor aestheticism can be imputed to these pieces, though the totalizing effect of such a program, and the correspondence it establishes between being and form, could well be linked with the identification with wholeness which Lacoue-Labarthe, when it is vested in the nation and the work of art, terms "national aestheticism."

A divergence of another sort from nationalist and from aestheticist thinking comes in what looks to be within it: in the reviews' analysis of and commitment to works described as drawing their characteristic excellence from the disparity and tension between conflicting norms and the infiltration or incorporation of one set of norms by another—as in discussions of the modern German novel and modern French poetry where the very stereotypicality of notions of national tradition makes them function in almost sheerly formal terms, as shorthand for recurrent combinations of generic elements and, at the same time, it is the mutual interference of these norms or combinations, in a structure that is mixed, that the review praises. De Man is interested in the novels of Ernst Jünger as bringing something new, symbol and myth, to the genre he identifies with psychological realism, with the French and with Stendhal; in the difficulty posed for German novelists of having to adapt to the genre's "reigning norms . . . very distant" from what in their own national temperament is of most significance; and above all in the "adventure" undertaken in French poetry, where symbolism and surrealism have attained to "that romantic spirit, entirely opposed to the consecrated French norms."[5] We will come back to this. Also important is to give some genealogy of the national stereotyping that acquires such sinister ideological import. (To indict it, to point only where one could say, "That's Nazism," is not enough.)

The notion of distinctive national identities and the habitual distinction between French clarity and German sense of the infinite, between French classicism and German romanticism, is embedded in just the tradition of thought that the 1983 essay on

Kleist concerns, an educational and philosophical tradition dating back to before 1800, when Schiller held out a solution to the problem of imitation that troubled Enlightenment thought, how (not) to (merely) imitate the works of classical antiquity. "On Naive and Sentimental Poetry" proposes that while the Greeks' nature is the natural, or "naive," "our" nature is cultural, or "sentimental," and has the ultimate value, Schiller's *Letters on Aesthetic Education* suggest, of enabling us to regain paradise, or nature, as it were from the far side: roughly speaking, such is the ideal of "aesthetic education" and the "aesthetic state." This new theoretical "solution" to the problem of imitation comes down at bottom, "and this no doubt was the decisive gesture of Schiller," writes Lacoue-Labarthe, "to translating historically or 'historicizing' the Aristotelian definition of art" (HG, p.467).

Schiller's gesture of historicization emerges at the same time as the question of Germany's national identity is posed by the emergence, with the French Revolution, of France as a modern national state, and it provides the terms for the assertion of a distinctively German achievement of the solution to the problem of modernity, unlike the French imitation of antiquity in the adoption of a neo-classical form of government (a republic). The definition common in de Man's early articles of the German spirit as romantic and the French as classical can be traced back to this period. For the writers we significantly designate as German "Classicism and Romanticism," it was high culture, art, above all literature, poetry—the selfproduction of the German language—that were conceived as the realm in which the achievement of Greek antiquity was to be rivaled. "Generally," says in fact a canonical text of the *Physics*, "on the one hand *technè* accomplishes that which *physis* is incapable of accomplishing, on the other hand it imitates it" (HG, p.467). Lacoue-Labarthe goes on,

Interpreted in historical terms, this double postulate can give this result: art, inasmuch as it imitates nature, is specifically—and in conformity with Winckelmann—Greek art: mimesis is Greek. It belongs on the other hand to the Moderns to accomplish, to accomplish, bring to term, achieve, what nature cannot effectuate. It belongs in consequence to the Moderns to take a step beyond the Greeks—and to accomplish them.

Which is to say also to surpass them or surmount them. (HG, p.467)

This artistic and philosophical rivalry with "Greece," displaced onto a political and national rivalry with France, is reflected in the nationalist stereotypes of literary critical writing of the thirties and forties. The aspiration to "universality" (as in de Man's review of Goethe's *Elective Affinities*)—or, usually indistinguishably, to the authentically "European"—has the same source; universality is conceived along the (pseudo-dialectical) lines of the reconciliation of art and nature: of the "intuitive and speculative, objective and subjective, . . . finite and infinite, necessary and free or, to abbreviate the list," writes Lacoue-Labarthe, "for it's all of metaphysics itself that comes to range itself in this set of oppositions, body and spirit" (HG, p.467): that "reconciliation" rendered possible, in theory (or rather: in rhetoric), by the symmetrical chiasmus implicit in the pseudo-historical scheme distinguishing Greek culture, which is "nature," from Western nature, which is "culture."[6]

De Man's reading of the narrative concerning the young man who glimpses his resemblance to the Spinario provides an allegorical history and interpretation of the role of this relationship to "Greece" in modern thought about art, education, and the state. It is as "aesthetic education" rather than according to the concept of imitation or the principle of resemblance that that relationship is structured and that it needs to be conceptualized. De Man's reading observes the non-specular, non-mirroring structure of this narrative first in the discrepancy between the example—the story of the young man—and the general truth is is supposed to illustrate, the proposition asserted by C, that grace is recovered after an experience of infinite self-consciousness: instead "the young man remains frozen in deadly self-alienation" (RR, p.277). Rather than exemplifying the recovery of a state of nature or grace after the passage through its extreme opposite, rather than being a "parable of consciousness" in which the self comes to recognize itself, this narrative or this history—in which the ephebe confronts or imagines his resemblance to the Spinario, the West its resemblance to Greece—is an aesthetic education: "what the young man confronts in the mirror is not himself but his resemblance to another" (RR, p.278). The young man is enmeshed in a relationship not simply "specular," de Man observes, but triangular: the narrative involves not simply the question of a self's resemblance to itself or to a specular double (the young man's ability to reproduce or mirror his own initial gesture), but that of the self's power to resemble an other of a different order, (the classical, the "natural" statue, the Spinario, and the Spinario's classical, "natural" gesture), and to achieve its recognition (the recognition by another, the older man, the narrator, of the young man's achievement of this power).

This triangular structure of "aesthetic education" has mediated the relationship between the (Aristotelian) definition of art and the trajectory of modern political history, in which "the essential has been played out, and is probably being played out still, in the process of national identification" (FP, p.122). It is the process of national identification as effected through identification with the work of art, as well as the self's undoing through the "desire for self-recognition" (RR, p.278), that de Man's reading of Kleist's narrative of the ephebe evokes and diagnoses. At stake for the ephebe is not successful imitation of the beautiful work of art so much as identification with an authoritative model, a model (the classical statue) of naturalness, self-identity, autonomy. The ephebe's predicament as read by de Man emblematizes the singular and exemplary predicament taken to itself by Germany—or at least, and at first, by certain German writers, Hölderlin, Nietzsche: that the very logic of imitation, of mimesis, requires that imitation as such efface itself; that imitation, as the imitation of nature, attain to originality—to the self-engendering status of nature or *physis*. I quote at length Lacoue-Labarthe:

. . . the constraint that governs *imitatio,* the mimetological law, requires that *imitatio* rid itself precisely of *imitatio,* or that it address itself, in what it erects . . . as a model, to that which does not derive from an imitation: *What the German imitatio seeks in Greece is the model—and thus the possibility—of a pure Entstehung [surgissement], of a pure originality: the model of an auto-formation. Whence . . . the implacable contradiction that inhabits the imitatio radicalized to this point. . . . the requirement of the imitation of an auto-formation, which is precisely the exigency of the heritage or transmission of genius according to Kant, entails a pure double bind.* Germany, in sum, in its attempt to accede to historical existence . . . , quite simply aspired to genius. But genius is by definition inimitable. And it is in the impossibility of that imitation of genius that Germany literally exhausted itself, succumbing to a kind of spiritual-historical psychosis or schizophrenia, of which some of its most outstanding geniuses, from Hölderlin to Nietzsche, were the premonitory signs (and victims). Only moreover a schizophrenic logic could authorize the unthinkable that is the Extermination; and the actual division of Germany is as if symbolically the result of this process. Germany still does not exist. If not in the distress at not existing. (FP, p.122)

That it is only the ephebe "frozen in self-alienation" who suffers the consequences of this structure in K's anecdote should not conceal from us that it is the exigency of auto-formation which is dramatized in this scenario, nor allow us to miss its implications. De Man has this to say about the actual stakes of the ostensible concern, for gracefulness:

Gracefulness was clearly not an end in itself but a device to impress his teacher. When the device fails, he at once loses his talent, not because he has grown self-conscious but because he cannot endure the critical gaze of another in whom his desire for selfhood has been invested. The work of art is only a displaced version of the true model, the judgment of authority. . . . The ensuing clumsiness is the loss of control, the confusion caused by shame. And what the young man is ashamed of is not his lack of grace but the exposure of his desire for self-recognition. (RR, p.278)

That *shame* be provoked by the exposure of a desire for selfhood vested in the identification with another would have to do with its incompatibility with the demand to be autonomous, self-engendering, original: the tension of the "desire for self-recognition."

In de Man's reading of Kleist's text, the aspiration to gracefulness, to that "aesthetic state," is demystified as in fact the aspiration to authority, to the authority of that which is self-engendered, self-authoring. The imitation of the work of art is motivated by and conceals the work's idealization as just such a self-engendering whole. Imitation, and grace, art, supposedly a process of reflection or of unconcealment and a matter of truth (the truth of nature), is rather a performance of idealization. "The imitation conceals the idealization it performs" (RR, p.291). That process is cognitively aberrant and performatively violent (what detracts from the form as whole will have to be eliminated). "Up till now, we have read the young man's blushing ('er errötete') as mere shame, a wound of the ego, but now it appears that the redness may well be the blood of an injured body" (RR, p.279).

Lacoue-Labarthe, like de Man, links the specific structure of Germany's aspiration to national identity and to genius with the general structure connecting imitation, politics, and education. "Schematizing excessively," he writes,

one can say that at least since Plato, education, or political formation, *Bildung,* is thought *on the basis of* [*à partir de*] the mimetic process. Plato draws on it, dreaming precisely of a (philosophical) auto-foundation of the political. . . . Inversely, in the realm of the accomplishment [the drawing to an end] of the philosophical— and, what's initially indissociable, of the reversal of Platonism—the program is drawn up, according to the terms of Schiller, of an "aesthetic education" of humanity. Of little consequence, here, the inversion of "values." The essential is that *Bildung* is always thought on the basis [*sur le fond*] of the archaic mythic *paideia*, that is to say on the basis of what the Romans will understand as *exemplarity*. . . . Identification or appropriation—the becoming-itself of the Self— will always have been thought as the appropriation of a model, that is to say as the appropriation of a model of appropriation, if the model (the example) is the always paradoxical imperative of propriation: imitate me to be what you are. (FP, pp.123–4)

Such is the double bind of the young man in K's anecdote, of whom de Man writes:

It is easy enough for the ephebe to be one more cast, one more *Abguss* in the long series of reproductions of the Spinario figure which, as the text tells us, "are to be found in German collections." If aesthetic education is the imitation of works of art considered as models of beauty or moral excellence, then it is a rather mechanical process that does not involve a deeper problematization of the self.

This however is not what happens in this case. . . . (RR, p.278)

Nor in another: that of modern literature as it is conceived by the young man writing in *Le Soir* in 1941–2. For whom the aesthetic education of mankind entailed in reading and writing about literature is emphatically not a matter of "the imitation of works of art considered as models of beauty or moral excellence":

La littérature est une domaine indépendente qui a une vie, des lois, des obligations qui n'appartiennent qu'à lui et ne dépendent en aucune manière des contingences philosophiques et éthiques qui se meuvent à ses côtés. Le moins qu'on puisse dire est que les valeurs artistiques qui régissent le monde des lettres ne se confondent pas avec celles du Vrai et du Beau. . . . On n'a pas le droit de condamner Gide en tant que romancier parce que sa morale a été discutable ou d'en vouloir à Henri de Montherland [sic] parce que son caractère ne vous plaît pas. ("Sur les possibilités de la critique." *Le Soir,* 2 Dec. 1941)

Literature is not a matter of imitating the True and the Good, nor is criticism a matter of imitating, according to the opening paragraphs of this text—whether moral teaching or literature. For criticism is an "autonomous discipline," as literature is an independent domain.

The young man who wrote "On the Possibilities of Criticism'" makes a judgment similar to the older de Man's about another ephebe: that the relevant relationship to works of art is not one of imitation. "The least that one can say" is that in Belgium in 1941 this is a claim that goes against the current: the refusal of political tests for literature. Its bearing is similar to that of de Man's judgment in the Kleist essay, where what is the relevant relationship to the work of art in "aesthetic education"— the *identification* with the work as a model of the original and natural self as which the ephebe seeks recognition from a figure of authority—is charged in effect with maintaining a law of imitation that commits violence, both to the work and to bodies. But its critical bearing does not prevent the early text from at the same time participating in that process of identification or in the double bind described by Lacoue-Labarthe. For the *for-*

mal (as opposed to imitative) character of literature does indeed function in this text as a means of authority, not only for the ephebe but for the discipline of criticism as the study of the development of forms—which is claimed to become by this process "a philosophy of literary history not less rich than the philosophy of history," disclosing an aspect of humanity no less revealing than its political history. Formalism thus issues in a historicism whereby the initially rejected structure of imitation is restored. Nor does this aesthetic education—by no means only Paul de Man's in 1941—take its course without doing violence. In this text however the movement is not one of identification with the autonomy or "auto-formation" of the work of genius; authority or meaning is vested in a construction without that kind of closure, in the self-engendering form of a historical process rather than of an individual work. The "formalization" of the historical will be addressed by de Man in a culminating critique in his Kleist essay.

The imitation of the work of art, and indeed the work, or art, as imitation, performs an idealization of the text or work as self-engendered, whole work or being. There never was such a work, nor being. Art—or the being of a people, or of "man"— will always have been rather a matter of "making minor repairs on one's own body," de Man's description of the classical art of the Spinario. "The original perfection . . . is itself, however slightly. . . , impaired." What is deadly is that that process of "making repairs" can take the form, precisely, of idealization; this takes place already in classical art. "The white, colorless world of statues is suddenly reddened by a flow of blood." It takes place as well in the institution of pedagogy, one that coincides with the institution of philosophy, again Greek. Such are some of the reflections to be read out of the brashly off-handed indictments concluding the previous paragraph: "As for the teacher's motives in accepting to enter into these displacements of identity, they are even more suspect than those of the younger person, to the precise extent that sadism is morally and socially more suspect than masochism. Socrates (or, for that matter, Winckelmann) certainly had it coming to him" (RR, p.279).

De Man's essay has at times a quality of unleashed improvisation and blithe unselfcautious aggressiveness akin to that evoked in the Kleist text alluded to toward the end of the essay, "Über die allmählige Verfertigung der Gedanken beim Reden." One recognizes it too in the brashness of certain moves of the pieces in *Le Soir*: for instance, the chastising of Brasillach and Montherlant for their weak grasp of the importance of collective political life to the Germans or of the economic and social dimensions of historical change; the apodictic assertion that far from being decadent, surrealism, in contemporary French poetry, is the source of "the sole poetic manifestations worthy of that name"; or the attack, quoted earlier, on moralizing criticism of literature.[7] Like the Kleist text, de Man's essay treats of the significance of a mechanical factor in such effects, the way in which the boldness of judgments relates to a certain formalization, to their deriving from the commitment to a formal, mechanical process generating the capacity for improvisation. The mechanical effect, "l'effet machinal," of the commitment to speak (or write): such is the topic of texts of Kleist and Rousseau that de Man singles out and such is the topic posed by his own performance, as well as the question the essay pursues, under the heading of "formalization" and the ways it may be both requisite and ruinous to pedagogy and to truth. De Man's performance suggests that effects of daring are not definitively separable from the formal commitment, the mechanical process, that occasions them. The commitment to produce weekly reviews for a newspaper is not definitively separable in kind or in effect from the commitment to conceiving literature as primarily form or to conceiving history as intelligible: each of these, insofar as it is systematic, has a generative mechanical element. It is not the content of the two latter conceptions I am remarking (at the moment) but rather their status as not strictly distinguishable from the former insofar as they all entail a process of formalization. Materialism means, I take it, just such a dissolving of hierarchy between conditions of production and "ideas." It will have been through the performance of his writing, more than through the cognitive content of its statements, perhaps, that de Man's work will have taught us most about "the materiality of actual history" (RR, p.262).

The zany feats of improvisation one registers repeatedly in the Kleist essay are inseparable from unexpected intensifications and swerves of interrogation whereby the performance is continually checked. The essay recurrently turns back to its primary pedagogical gesture: the question, addressed to the text in the place or the voice, if not in the name of, the reader—the other, the student. Thus after the sentence on Socrates and throwaway afterthought for Winckelmann the essay commences a new paragraph: "But is all this bad faith not precisely what the aesthetic, as opposed to the mimetic, specular education, is supposed to avoid?" (RR, p.279). Yet my point would be that it is not alone from the inquiry and argument deliberately pursued that this writing acquires its pedagogical effectiveness; that also comes from the effects of meaning generated by the improvisational element I have described. And indubitably and strangely, the element of uncontrol, of the mechanical, in those moments, constitutes a sense in which they do not essentially differ from

the effects of a contingency that seems to impinge on the text from the outside: the nonintentional process of the maintenance of the archive—the discovery of the *Le Soir* articles, with the possibility for further effects of meaning that it sets up. A confessional element some might wish now to discover in de Man's work is not what I have in mind; the confessional dimension some will impute to de Man's writing is an effect of displacements of identity and authority in which they themselves (as "ephebe" and as "teacher") are caught up, not a component of the essays. Rather there is an autobiographical and a historical dimension to this writing that knowledge of the contexts of one of its intertexts merely extends and exacerbates.

The temptation and the possibility thus arises, for instance, of reading the three successive models of the work that de Man identifies in the Kleist text's three scenarios or anecdotes as successive models of the work *and of the state* actually succeeding one another in the course of German intellectual and political history. The conception of the literary work first as imitation, then as a locus of hidden or transcendental meaning requiring a hermeneutic process of uncovering, and finally as a formal pattern, "a system of tropes," could indeed be considered to have succeeded one another not only logically, but historically: this is, roughly, the trajectory of aesthetics and of literary theory between about 1800 and about 1980. It can be demonstrated—such will be one of my aims here—that such an account entails a penetrating diagnosis and critique of authoritarian and totalitarian politics. At the same time, we are called upon to recognize in such a schema once again "aesthetic education as the articulation of history with formally arrived-at truth" (RR, p.276). Aesthetic education so defined is not a project or habit we could lightly abandon. But neither is it one we can embrace, given the disclosure of its contingencies and consequences (like the dance that entails its participants' mutilation) that is the thrust of de Man's pedagogical argument.

The sense of the historical dimension of the problem impels one to notice how de Man's discussion of the concept of the aesthetic—and more particularly of the mimetic and hermeneutic models of the work—stresses the decisive function of the structure of authority, and indeed of a certain authoritarian pedagogy. The discussion thereby converges with an interpretation according to quite different premises of this same intellectual tradition: an account of the failure of humanistic *Germanistik* and classics to function as "oppositional criticism," during and after the Second World War. In a recent article for GRIP (Group for Research on Institutionalization and Professionalization), Henry J. Schmidt, examining German literary criticism from the 1930's through the 1960's, argues that the celebration of the eternal values of art and poetry may have seemed a defense of human values against Nazi domination, but instead perpetuated assumptions and attitudes that were among the conditions that made Nazism possible, since the discourse asserting an opposition between spiritual values and the state "obscured the possibility of the appropriation of *Geist* by *Staat*." Schmidt argues that the oppositional potential of literary study under Nazism "was further diminished by the traditional attitudes of its practitioners toward their subject and their students": "Students were taught to view great art—and its sanctioned interpreters—with reverence. Thus conventions were sustained which . . . exactly reproduced the political behavior models of an authoritarian state."[8] De Man writes, "The work of art is only a displaced version of the true model, the judgment of authority" (RR, p.278).[9] So much for one of our most cherished severe pieties?—rendered by a much-trusted teacher and critic, Jacques Ehrmann, long of the French Department at Yale, in the formulation, "Trust the text." Which de Man, with his trace of accent, would have pronounced, "Truss de text." "The politics of the aesthetic state are the politics of education" (RR, p.273), de Man writes, and thus it is that various models of the literary work and the procedures of imitation or interpretation linked with them have to be critically examined.

If the identification of the two possible meanings of the expression "the aesthetic state" is a hallmark of the aesthetic ideology that de Man's essay analyzes and indicts, then his critique would forbid direct identification between various models of the work and forms of the state. But the correlation[10] between an authoritarian state and a model of imitation concealing a hermeneutic struggle, and between a totalitarian state and a model of the text as a formal "system of tropes" (RR, p.285), is more than an impression and other than an analogy. Just what it is, according to this essay, can be figured out only through the process of examining de Man's text's own articulations, the hinges whereby the three successive models of the work de Man describes are logically and narratively connected. To anticipate: the first of these resembles *aletheia*, a coming to light of what was truly going on all along; such is the disclosure, behind the ideal of "gracefulness" or the imitation of the work of art (as imitation of nature), of the desire and demand for authority, ultimately for the authority of authorship as self-authorization or of a "transcendental locus of signification." The second of these transitions is rendered in a sort of *style indirect libre*. It will have been found intolerable, de Man's essay suggests—an intolerable disorder and waste of energy—to persist in the futile combat for mastery of meaning; whence, the shift to conceptualization

of the text as a sheerly formal process, like the puppet ballet, "a system of turns and deviations" (RR, p.285).

Why is not aesthetic detachment the solution to the scenario of desire and humiliation that proved (in K's anecdote of the ephebe) to be the content of an intersubjective pedagogical structure associated with conceiving the work as imitation? Schiller's purpose seems to be "to fix the attention on the free integrity of the work in order to turn it away from the inevitable lack of integrity in the self. . . . Kleist's story," de Man remarks, "has less to do with self-deluded and self-deluding villains than with the carelessness of classical aestheticians who misread Kant. Their motives are open to the worst of suspicions as well as to the most convincing of excuses, thus making the entire question of intents and motivations a great deal less compelling than the philosophical question from which it derives: the assumed integrity, not of the self, but of the work" (RR, p.279).

That assumption informs the notion of the work of art or imitation as one that substitutes "the spectacle of pain for the pain itself," "the pleasures of imitation" for "the pains of experience." But "the neoclassical trust in the power of imitation to draw sharp and decisive borderlines between reality and imitation . . . depends, in the last analysis, on an equally sharp ability to distinguish the work of art from reality." And the concept of the aesthetic, the concept of imitation or the fictional, escapes such determinability, has an illimitable potential applicability: "None of the connotations associated with reality can invade art without being neutralized by aesthetic distance." This very fact suggests a flaw in the original assumption, that of "the power of *imitation* to draw" a distinct borderline between reality and imitation, "which, in aesthetic education, becomes the . . . ability to distinguish clearly between interested and disinterested acts, between desire and play" (RR, p.280, my italics). "None of the connotations associated with reality can invade art without being neutralized by aesthetic distance. Kleist's story suggests however that this may be a ruse to hide the flaw that marred aesthetic perfection from the start or, in a more perverse reading, to enjoy, under the cover of aesthetic distance, pleasures that have to do with the inflicting of wounds rather than with gracefulness" (RR, p.280). A *ruse* to hide the imperfection of the original.

The aesthetic is being indicted for something other, here, than concealing (or "turning the attention away from") the lack of integrity of a self. It relates in another way to another kind of "original." The original is a work, is an art; and Kleist's text makes the point of how it differs from the imitation (another process performed on a body): "the imitator is merely drying himself off whereas the original is curing a wound." The terms of this distinction (de Man's and Kleist's) are no longer those of neoclassical aesthetics, since the distinction is not between a self and a representation nor nature and an imitation but between one art or work and another: between a work having to do with wounds and cures and a work having to do with restoring a surface (in the example, the dry surface of the body). The *ruse* is designed to conceal the wound or fracture in the original and in the relationship between them—the fracture "between actual meaning and the process of signification" (RR, p.281). De Man makes a similar distinction, drawing it from Benjamin, in his essay introducing Timothy Bahti's translation of H. R. Jauss, *Toward an Aesthetic of Reception*: "The conflict is stated, in most general terms, between what language means (*das Gemeinte*) and the manner in which it produces meaning (*die Art des Meinens*)." This distinction arises within Benjamin's reflection on the task of translation, which de Man with Benjamin is invoking, "rather than the reception or even the reading of a work," as "the proper analogon for its understanding."[11] (De Man's introductory essay is incidentally attributing to the translator, Bahti, and not to the author, Jauss, commitment to a valid cognitive activity). It is once again translation that becomes the frame of reference in de Man's reading of the Kleist text, insofar as the difference between the ephebe's imitation and the Spinario's care, between drying oneself off and curing a wound, figures the difference between "the process of signification" and the "actual meaning," the conflict (in the words of the other essay) "between one linguistic function and another." Such is the imperfection of the original, "the flaw that marred aesthetic perfection from the start"—the disparity between the intentional, meaningful dimension of the work and its sheerly mechanical, formal component or grammar.

But that the frame of reference is an intralinguistic process does not prevent this passage from introducing a question of intent or more exactly the question of a "ruse," linked with an ethical question, about cruelty. I quote once again: "None of the connotations associated with reality can invade art without being neutralized by aesthetic distance. Kleist's story suggests however that this may be a ruse to hide the flaw that marred aesthetic perfection from the start or, in a more perverse reading, to enjoy, under the cover of aesthetic distance, pleasures that have to do with the inflicting of wounds rather than with gracefulness" (RR, p.280).

How does this reflection on "aesthetic distance" as "ruse" relate to the reflection in the Rousseau essay on "fiction" as "excuse"? There de Man stressed that Rousseau's claim to have produced a pure "fiction," to have spoken sheerly at random, had to be taken seriously, that is to say, not simply assimilated

to an interpretation of his actions in terms of their concealed desires and motives and thus ignored or understood as a claim offered in bad faith, a rhetorical expediency. De Man's point here would appear to be the reverse: that the claim of aesthetic distance or "play" can be seen as motivated by the concealed desire to conceal desire or indeed to inflict pain. But these sentences are saying something slightly different and much more radical. "Kleist's story however suggests that *this* may be a ruse to hide the flaw . . .": "this" refers to, not a claim or speech-act of an individual (or of several or many individuals), but a speech-act of another order: the effect of the aesthetic. This effect is real. "None of the connotations associated with reality can invade art without being neutralized by aesthetic distance." It is precisely in this respect—a different matter from the bad or good faith, and the correctness or error, of "classical aestheticians who misread Kant" as well as their sometime ephebes (such as the *Le Soir* columnist Paul de Man)—that the aesthetic is a "ruse," serving to conceal a flaw or a violence. Not the fictitiousness of aesthetic distance, but precisely the reality of its neutralizing power, constitutes the "ruse" which is deadly. The very illimitableness of the possibility of the aesthetic—of the hypothesis of "imitation," play, "fiction"—constitutes (not the deplorable bad faith or error, but) the deadly ruse that "hide(s) the flaw" and enables the untrammeled enjoyment of "the original," or, violence. Such is what de Man is saying here.

This is also the argument of the Rousseau essay, where de Man goes on to discuss the violence of the primacy of language as machine. The "ruse," the aesthetic, makes possible the enjoyment of sheer performance, of the aesthetic or fiction as machine—what appears in Kleist's story as the dance of marionettes celebrated by Herr C. In Rousseau's autobiographies, the excuse precisely as "fiction," as "play" inassimilable to the logic of interested actions or desire and its concealment, de Man argues, is what prevents the seemingly exhaustive discussion of Rousseau's guilt in the "Marion" passage in the *Confessions* from being closed off and generates the reopening of the issue in the *Fourth Rêverie*, where ultimately there emerges the enjoyment of the machine. The fact that an actual machine (in fact, a machine for printing—cloth) appears as enticing in one of the episodes of the autobiographical text merely substantiates that the motive of the discourse was simply the text, as machine: e.g. the mechanical generating of the *Fourth Rêverie* by the fiction of the *Confessions,* but further, the mechanical generating of the very slander of Marion, for instance, by the motive of generating a text, or more exactly: by the machine's enjoyment. The mechanical functioning of the work is the enjoyment concealed and practiced by the ruse of the aesthetic—by the mechanical coming into play of "fiction," of the "excuse" that a signifying structure or event is the coming into play of the mechanical. The Rousseau essay evokes and indicts this enjoyment. De Man observes that the self-aggrandizing or defensive narratives of Rousseau's generosity to others (the manifest dimension of "confession" as "excuse") are scenes of injury to Rousseau's body (his head split open, his fingers crushed, by the unwitting gestures of childhood friends). De Man comments, "They seem to exist primarily for the sake of the mutilations they describe," and continues, "But these actual, bodily mutilations seem, in their turn, to be there more for the sake of allowing the evocation of the machine that causes them than for their own shock value; Rousseau lingers complacently over the description of the machine that seduces him into dangerously close contact. . . . In the general economy of the *Rêverie,* the machine displaces all other significations and becomes the raison d'être of the text" (RR, p.298). What comes to the fore is the pleasure of the text as machine. At the origin of the work, or art, would be the flaw of the mechanical, the disjuncture of performance from an intention or meaning. That primacy of the mechanical does violence both to meaning and to the body and language; the Rousseau essay, like the Kleist essay, describes both mutilations.

We had been examining the first articulation between the three successive models of the work that that reading identifies: how the model of the work as imitation (in the anecdote of the ephebe) gives place to the work as struggle for authority over meaning ("The work of art . . . is a displaced version of . . . the judgment of authority") and thus gives way to the hermeneutic model, of the work as a "transcendental locus of signification" (RR, p.281). With the critique of the aesthetic model through the reading of Kleist's anecdote of the ephebe, "the theoretical problem has been displaced: from the specular model of the text as imitation, we have moved on to the question of reading . . . The problem is no longer graceful imitation but the ability to distinguish between actual *meaning* and the *process* of signification" (RR, pp.280–1, my italics). The process of reading the text on the ephebe has entailed encountering a performative dimension of the text at odds with its stated cognition. "The imitation *conceals* the idealization it *performs.*" This implies the introduction of a new model of the work: "The technique of imitation becomes the hermeneutics of signification"; the work as imitation is replaced by the "labor of decoding and interpretation," the work as "reading." "This progression (if it is one)," writes de Man, "occurs between the stories of the ephebe and of the bear, between the story of text as a specular model and text as the locus of transcendental signification" (RR, p.281). The for-

mulation of that crucial articulation or rather disjunction between the work as imitation and as reading has to be stated so suspiciously—leaving in doubt whether this difference is an improvement, as well as whether it is temporally successive—because the hermeneutic ideal, the conception of the text as such a transcendental locus, is the very idealization that was uncovered and disqualified in the critique of the aesthetic model, where the aesthetic was found to be a ruse to hide the imperfection of an aesthetic process consisting of making "minor repairs on [the] body" or of the enjoyment of the machine.

Kleist's text about K's fencing match with a bear who infallibly parries this thrusts and ignores his feints has the signal virtue of making legible that idealization of the text, as well as figuring the conditions that disqualify it as an error. De Man points out that the bear is cast as a super-reader—as a reading consistently able to determine which moves count and which do not, which gestures or elements are literal or meaningful and which are rhetorical or gratuitous. Such would be the mastery of the author totally in control of his text; able, like the ideal hermeneutic process or a reading that would be total, to *determine* its meaning; K. recounts:

The seriousness of the bear robbed me of my presence of mind, thrusts and feints succeeded one another, I was running with sweat; in vain! Not only did the bear, as if he had been the first fencer of the world, parry all my thrusts; by my feints he never once (and in this, no fencer in the world resembles him) was taken in: eye to eye [*Aug in Auge*], as if he could read my soul in them, he stood, his paw raised ready for a blow, and if my thrust was not seriously intended, then he never moved.

Do you believe this story?

Perfectly! cried I; from any stranger, it is so plausible; how much the more coming from you! (UM, p.342; my translation)

The scenario of infallibility is staged and framed by Kleist's text as a scene of credulity.

De Man's gusto in writing about this passage—very different from the steely demystification and indictment of the other two scenes or models—may have several sources. It responds to the *prima facie* absurdity, marked by Kleist's framing, of vesting the ideal of infallibility or gracefulness in a bear. De Man is happy that the bear does not really win, that there is no such bear, as well as in the fact that there is no winning out over him by the attainment of some truly graceful, unbearlike, fencing strategy like "a well-executed . . . dance." Who, or what, is this bear? Whom its opponent conceives as facing him "eye to eye, as if he could read my soul there"?

The *sujet supposé savoir* in Kleist's book (life, that is) is Kant, and so too in de Man: Kant is the super-text, Schiller ("or, for that matter," Longinus, or Neil Hertz[12]) the never-failing mis-reader of the sublime. Such is the scenario (of "Kant and Schiller" and of "Phenomenality and Materiality in Kant") that Kleist, and de Man, *reads* here, where imaginative involvement in the scenario modulates into recollection of a significance vested in the scene's implausibility:

No one is hurt, for the bear never attacks, except for the game itself, forever slain in the unequal contest between seriousness and play. Thus Kant would have forever ended the play of philosophy, let alone the play of art, if the project of transcendental philosophy had succeeded in determining once and forever the limits of our faculties and of our freedom. If it were not for the mess of the *Critique of Judgment* and the breakdown of aesthetic theory, we would all be fighting this transcendental bear in vain. (RR, p. 283)

This passage is making both a connection and a distinction, which the surrounding passages contrasting the fencing match with the puppet dance will clarify, between the success of transcendental philosophy and the success of totalitarianism. "Determining once and for all the limits of our faculties and of our freedom" evokes the latter as well as the former. The phrase thereby evokes a contingency of philosophy and history, an occurrence—that aesthetic theory, the ruse of reason, did inspire Schiller's claims for the "aesthetic state." But to take the next step—to identify in transcendental philosophy already the fatality of national aestheticism, of Nazism—would be to make the move that Kleist's text and de Man's alerts us not to make, that of believing in the bear. It would be to believe that history was determined by philosophy.

De Man both draws attention to the jeopardy of "the game itself" and recalls that the notion of its definitive undoing is an illusion. What is jeopardized by the effect of the bear's infallibility is the model of the work as, and of, reading—none other than, in de Man's words, *"the question of reading as the necessity to decide between signified and referent, between violence on the stage and violence in the streets"* (RR, p.280): the necessity and the possibility to practice politics as a process of interpretation and decision, rather than conceding victory in advance to History, as Herr C. would be inclined to do in imagining that the bear can anticipate his every move. Herr C's experience provokes impatience with the fencing match, the tricky process of alternating feint with thrust, trying to score, while keeping the thrusts (and the feints) from becoming actual blows. Confronting an infallible opponent, even one who provokes no wounds but only exhaustion, is no game at all, and Herr C. will be glad to give it up, in favor of another experience altogether, that of the dance,

or, better still (as he tells K), the dance of marionettes, where the "soul" resides in the puppeteer, who lifts the puppet from its center of gravity, while "all its other members [are] what they should be, dead, mere pendula." Having encountered, as he sees it, an infallible opponent in a contest of skill and for authority, Herr C. will be glad to move on—from the futilities of politics, to the consummate apparatus of totalitarianism, of the ultimate aesthetic state. Such is de Man's interpretation of the link between the second and the third model of the work and of the state in which Kleist's text educates us. "We have traveled some way from the original Schiller quotation to this mechanical dance, which is also a dance of death and mutilation. The violence which existed as a latent background in the stories of the ephebe and of the bear now moves into full sight" (RR, p.288).

Thus de Man is telling us that all is not lost in the fencing match with the bear, for all is never lost: there is no infallible bear, no infallible reader or all-knowing text of history; or, put another way, the opponent is not the bear: reading, and politics, do not find themselves engaged with transcendence. But he is also giving us to understand that through the imaginary confrontation with an infallible opponent, all could indeed be lost, as the impulsion arises to close the gap between the one art and the other, between the thwarted skill of the fencer and the unfailing power of the bear—to merge them in a single infallible motion, replacing the difference between "violence on the stage and violence in the streets" with politics as art.

Fascism involves the predomination of the Imaginary in (or over) politics, as Lacoue-Labarthe's book recalls where he discusses the "process of national identification" that both "veils and unveils the essence of the political" (FP, p.122). So the imaginary match with infallible power *unveils* the struggle for authority which would be of the essence of politics (the dimension disclosed in the unveiling of the work of imitation as the hermeneutic struggle for mastery) and *veils* the struggle for authority as a struggle—(not History, but) the essence of the political as persistent conflict over its very conditions, as a contest in distinguishing between thrust and feint: the tension maintained in the work of reading, the contestatory exercise of the "ability to distinguish between actual meaning and the process of signification"(RR, p.281).

The fencing match with a seemingly inexhaustible opponent is an apt metaphor for the ongoing ambiguity of politics, of gestures and actions whose status, effect, consistency, are decided within an ongoing temporal and historical process—determining their status, effect, import, being precisely its stakes. Thus the historical, the political, is a situation in which it is not possible to decide, as it were, unilaterally, only to thrust; what counts as a thrust that could score is always in the course of being decided in the conflict *between* the opponents: the decision to take only direct, effective action does not make its action on history direct or effective. The opponent, in some sense, is "history" as resistance to the possibility of change, to "the game itself" as the power to determine what is through the exercise of freedom rather than encountering reality as given. In de Man's reading, Kleist's anecdote of the fencing match with a bear becomes an account of the precariousness of politics due to its exercise in historical conditions, where the indeterminableness of the impact of acts can create the image of an inexorable enemy. Thus he raises the question of why Herr C. did not cease trying to feint and decide to only thrust, forcing the bear at least to further exertions to counter his movements. "Such a common-sensical notion however is logically possible only if one concedes that C is free to choose between a direct and an oblique attack. But this is precisely what has to be proven. It is only a hypothesis, and as long as it has not been verified, C can never unambiguously attack" (RR, p.285). In history, or in "the social," there is no *non*-discursive practice, no *non*-symbolic action; only more and less compelling or effective ones—from the point of view of Herr C, who narrates this situation as a face-off with inexhaustibleness, invariably *less*: "From the point of view of the bear, who knows everything, he [C] always feints. . ." (RR, p.285).

From C's own point of view, which is deluded, no thrust ever goes where it is supposed to go. His blows are always off the mark, displaced, deviant, in error, off-target. Such is language: it always thrusts but never scores. It always refers but never to the right referent. The next textual model—actually the first in the order of narration—will have to be that of the text as a system of turns and deviations, as a system of tropes. (RR, p.285).

Thus we come to the dance of the marionette.

Kleist's figure of the infallible bear is that of an infallible reader of almost supernatural powers: "by my feints he never once (and in this no fencer in the world resembles him) was taken in: eye to eye [*Aug in Auge*], as if he could read my soul in them, he stood, his paw raised ready for a blow, and if my thrust was not seriously intended, then he never moved" (UM, p.342). One finds a stunning example of just such an idealized figure of a super-reader in one of Paul de Man's book reviews from 1942, billed as "L'Histoire Vivante: *Journal de la France* (volume 2) by Alfred Fabre-Luce" (*Le Soir*, 21 July 1942). Here is no fascination with history as cinema, but, just as delusive, fascination with "living history" as living legible text. Maximum delusion and maximum sense of certainty, through an idealiza-

tion of powers of perception and interpretation, coincide in this dazzled review. To the point of bathos approaching or exceeding that of Herr C's description of the bear: Fabre-Luce is

capable, moreover, of grasping facts where they are barely apparent, in a hardly perceptible psychological nuance, in a circumstance which, beneath a banal surface, hides definitive revelations and opens perspectives without end. This special talent shows through in the almost supernatural manner of informing us about what is happening in inaccessible countries, like America, or in regions as secret as the offices of statesmen. Such exploits suggest a superiorly organized information service but they result above all from the faculty of discerning in a scene lived or testimony heard, the telling sign that will illuminate the whole [*le trait marquant qui éclairera le tout*], as well as of a lucidity akin to coldness which entails that never is reality being distorted in favor of defending a thesis.

The illusion of objectivity the book sustains is of a piece with a vision of history, as an inexorable process almost gratuitous to approve and futile to contest; thence an untypical, but unerasable, moment in these articles of de Man's in *Le Soir*—this evocation of "a necessity inscribed in the facts":

There thus comes clear [*Il s'en degage*] the demonstration of that ineluctable truth of history according to which, at certain moments, the weight of events becomes such that it draws nations in a certain direction, even when their will seems to oppose it. That is what has produced itself in this case: the politics of collaboration results from the present situation not as an ideal desired by all of the people but as an irresistible necessity which none can escape, even if he thinks he ought to head in the other direction. Wait-and-see-ism [*L'attentisme*] is thus condemned, not from a moral point of view, but from that of the imperious reality: it is untenable because contrary to the current of history that continues to flow, without concerning itself with the reticence of a few individuals persisting in not understanding its power.

There is a terrific irony in this conjuncture, which de Man may have appreciated afterward; he got it most wrong, at the point when he thought he—or the author, super-reader he is merging with in this passage—was most lucid: in perceiving the conflict between *intents* and the *action* of history. Thus appears the worst illusion: that of seeing, and mastering, the discrepancy between "cognition" and "performance," by dint of reading what is "inscribed," of the faculty of "discerning . . . the telling sign" or feature, "le *trait* marquant," that will explain the whole thing, "qui éclairera le tout."

The error is in deciding or "resolving" the question (the conflict between intent, or cognition, and performance) in favor of the cognition *of* performance. That is also the *aesthetifying* move: to perceive an arbitrary process as a recognizable, and in that measure a satisfying, formal whole, its temporal aspect only making it more compelling. It is the move that consists in the imaginary experience of beholding, and valorizing—as a single shape or "current"—an overdetermined, nondetermined, insolubly dual, contradictory and conflictual process. The very conviction of identifying such a moment, however, or such a structure of error, ought, radicalizing this principle, to make me wary of supposing that the content of this error is manifestly and determinably an error, that it has been proven, once and for all, that history was *not* going in that direction. The direction, after all, was not merely of German hegemony, but of totalitarianism, and fascism. One would have to be able to entertain the possibility that in some respect "Fabre-Luce" (if not the particular big-time collaborator, then *faber-lux,* or the light-fabricator) was right, that history might still be about to go inexorably in the direction of formalization. That it *is indeed not settled* whether history is going where it seemed then to be going, is in one respect the point of the Kleist essay; the point of saying, "The only place where infallible bears like this one can exist is in stories written by Heinrich von Kleist" (RR, p.285).

The mastery of history, that achievement by the Germans that impelled collaboration, did not as it turns out occur. How it happened that it didn't happen would also be overdetermined and indeterminable. What happens in texts, including texts of philosophy, cannot be excluded from, no more than it can simply be conflated with, the process. If "this transcendental bear" (mastery, History), at least, is a bugbear, de Man suggests, we might have, still, "the mess of the *Critique of Judgment* and the breakdown of aesthetic theory" to thank for it; no triumph of the West. No triumph of the West, thank Kant . . . A Triumph of Life in which would be forever slain "the game itself," with "no one . . . hurt" since all become moments in the dance of the *Gliedermann* of which Kleist writes, "all its other members (are) what they should be, dead, mere pendula, and they follow the law of pure gravity" (RR, p.288).

De Man's evocation of frustration with the exercise of contestatory, conflictual discursive practices as the prelude to a totalitarian solution corresponds with social historians' analysis of the advent of National Socialism, the social revolution that finally effected the modernization of Germany. For example, Ralf Dahrendorf, writing of the lack of widespread resistance to, and in that sense the legitimacy of, the Nazi regime, comments,

In respect to the structure of society, the Weimar Republic marked a phase of hardly bearable stagnation. Moving to and fro between old regime and modernity, people found no point of orientation for their behavior; the parties with whom they sought such points of orientation usually disappointed them. In that sense the mere fact that something happened under the new rules seemed a relief. That this involved rigid forms of organization, strengthened the new feeling of security, although it was precisely this basis of security that was precarious and would hardly have withstood a longer period of peace. (SDG, pp. 393–4)

(The dance will be "also a dance of death and mutilation.") De Man interprets the fencing match scenario, which he reads as figuring both the hermeneutic and the rhetorical models of the work (a contest for a "transcendental locus of signification," or a contest in distinguishing "meaning and the *process* of signification") in terms of a tension between authoritarian and conflictual models of discursive practice. His construal of a logically successive relation between the three scenarios of Kleist's text, the ephebe's humiliation, the fencing match with the bear, and the puppet dance, points to the continuity between authoritarian and totalitarian structures. Dahrendorf, similarly, describes the conflict in the period of Germany's belated social revolution as deferral of the totalitarian structure by the authoritarian:

In terms of our thesis, the German resistance must indeed be understood as largely a reaction; in this we encounter one of the most difficult and tragic chapters of recent German history. If it is true that, in order to establish its total rule, the Nazi regime had to bring about a social revolution, then resistance against the regime may be described as counterrevolutionary. Given the premise, the substance of resistance is the attempt to resurrect the prerevolutionary state. Where the National Socialist revolution promoted, however reluctantly, modernity, the counterrevolution aimed at the conservation of traditional ties to family and class, region and religion. While the social revolution of National Socialism was an instrument in the establishment of totalitarian forms, by the same token it had to create the basis of liberal modernity; the counterrevolution on the other hand can be understood only as a revolt of tradition, and thus of illiberalism and of the authoritarianism of a surviving past. (SDG, pp.390–1)

De Man does not share Dahrendorf's belief in "liberal modernity," or in modernization (meaning capitalism, as the centralization and homogenization of social institutions, their rationalization in the terms of a market economy) as the "basis" for liberal democracy. Dahrendorf evokes the necessity and the risk of modernization, a matter of economy; de Man, that of "the question of reading as the necessity to decide between violence on the stage and violence in the streets"—which perhaps proves to be an irredeemably uneconomical process.

In de Man's Kleist essay, in Dahrendorf's *Society and Democracy in Germany,* and in the social historian Norbert Elias' *The History of Manners* (treating, more broadly, the social transformation of modern Europe), one finds a sense of the necessity or inevitability of the process of modernization, of "formalization," of the emergence of the model of social life or the state as a "figuration" (Elias's term) or "system of tropes"; but this sense of inevitability has a different status in the three analyses.[13] In de Man's, it is itself a component of the process on trial, the ideal of aesthetic education, of "the articulation of history with formally arrived-at truth." That de Man's allegorical history of Germany (from Schiller to Goebbels and Hitler) is a *construction* through the reading of a text that stages a prominent classical-romantic theme and thesis (*Anmut* and *Grazie,* the reentry into paradise or nature) is crucial to the conception of history it seeks to get across: of an overdetermined process wherein the intelligible is incommensurable with the real. As construction from elements of a fiction, de Man's narrative points both at the compelling *logical* necessity of its sequence and at the *non*-determining character of the logical structure. The sense that the transition from the fencing match to the dance *has to* take place, that the rationalization and aesthetification of the seemingly "wasteful" movements of the fencer is inevitable or necessary, is framed, thematized, as an *imaginary* necessity. Through its literary-historical mode de Man's essay accomplished a difficult double gesture: to diagnose and analyze the totalitarian state, to render its occurrence intelligible, its components recognizable, without according it status as *determined*.

How, where, does a progression from imitation, to contest for authority, to total formalization—the last, abruptly, unmistakably totalitarianism—logically and ineluctably proceed? Via the progression of the aesthetic education of mankind: via the process of interpreting the work as such—the inquiry that takes us from the model of the work as imitation, to the work as contest for authority, to the formal, total model. The aesthetic illusion—the illusion of the aesthetic education—is precisely to believe that this process is determining; that it describes or determines, cognizes or causes, what happens, history.

To produce this construction *and to believe in it as what is, as what must be,* is deadly. To dwell in this construction . . . (Strictures bearing upon a Heideggerian topos, "building, dwelling," such as in de Man's 1955 essay "Tentation de la permanence,"

would have this awareness as their source).[14] What is ultimately diagnosed and condemned as deadly, in the Kleist as in the Rousseau essay, is the *valorization* of the construction—which is not simply a dwelling, but a machine. What is condemned by de Man as deadly is precisely its *aesthetification*: its construction or construal as a whole, total, form, a non-referential, because all-encompassing, self-sufficient system. For the mechanics of the process of signification to be conceived (idealized) as a pure form is for both the possibility of meaning and the possibility of difference (and this has concrete concomitants) to be eliminated, as the ambiguous, conflictual process in which meaning is continually being decided gives way to one in which, as de Man writes of the marionette ballet, "seriousness and play" has been resolved into the sheerly formal "synthesis of rising and falling" (RR, p.287). The status of the aesthetic *as* political, as in Schiller's notion of the "aesthetic state," is a model that ultimately consists in none other than the modeling of the state, of the polis, on *the aesthetic work, of which the integrity is presumed—* the polis being a non-referential work of art, a dance. The concept involves an idealization that is present from the start in the model of imitation, the notion of a nature to be imitated by art; the expectation and assumption that that model brings with it, the neoclassical conception of a fixed boundary line between the ideal and the real, between the realm of art and reality (and the notion of aesthetic distance), participates in, defers and prolongs, the disaster rather than alleviating it. For what counts as mere discourse, mere "process of signification," as distinct from reality, or "actual meaning," is then fixed, is in principle determined, in advance; what is, is a code, with variations, but non-negotiable. De Man invokes instead the continual renegotiation of the conditions of signification—participatory process. (Thus his text evokes "the problem [of] the ability to distinguish between actual meaning and the process of signification" (RR, p.280), as a persisting *problem*—one resolved and unresolved through conflict or struggle, that of the *reading* process.) That it is conflictual, "wasteful," incipiently chaotic, is not for him a motive for its replacement by the "mechanical dance" (RR, p.288).

Thus though it is through the process of reading that one moves from the work as imitation to the contest for authority to the total and totalitarian model, the reading of the Kleist text is a "*problematization* of reading conceived as the *determination* of meaning" (RR, p.273, my italics). The reading undercuts precisely the claim that its content or sequence *determines* (decides and knows) nontextual events, such as Germany's or Europe's political history. (Thus de Man will write: "Aesthetic education . . . succeeds all too well, to the point of hiding the violence that makes it possible. But one should avoid the pathos of an imagery of bodily mutilation and not forget that we are dealing with textual models, not with the historical and political systems that are their correlate" [RR, p.289].) We saw this undoing of the claim to determination occur with the emergence of the work as a process of reading, as the model of imitation gave way to the work of interpretation. Therewith the prospect of "the determination of meaning" does not remain intact: instead of to be found, uncovered, determined, meaning has to be decided, in an interminable process of deciding between the *meaning* and *process* of signification. Though the compelling logic of the process of reading the work as such leads from the model of imitation to the model of "a system of tropes"—and of the deadly dance of the puppet—the text (Kleist's as well as de Man's) signals that progression—the status of which is the status of the aesthetic—to be neither an uncovery of meaning, nor determining.

It might come as a surprise, especially to readers of de Man's text who are "opposed to deconstruction" (but one may wonder, do those two groups at all overlap?), to find that this essay reserves its most intense indictment for the conception of the work "as a system of tropes," a formal pattern of turns and figures. De Man's deadliest irony is reserved for the aesthetification of the formal, mechanical aspect of language, the model of the work "as a system of turns and deviations, as a system of tropes," that this essay conveys as being also a conception of the state or of the social order (RR, p.284). De Man's critique of "formalization"—the aesthetification, as a satisfying, recognizable form, of the formal, mechanical, arbitrary, and contradictory process of language—gets at both aspects of Nazism the combination of which has bemused political analysts: the Nazis' romantic aestheticism, an ideology of organic form, and at the same time unparalleled total commitment to sheer mechanical technological power.

(Thus Dahrendorf, for instance, writes:

One can . . . indicate . . . the contradiction between the ideology and practice of National Socialism by saying that the Nazi regime tried everywhere to replace organic social structures by mechanical formations. Instead of an interdependence of a diversity of institutions with a degree of autonomy, and often their own historical dimensions, National Socialism needed the uniform orientation of all institutions to one purpose. . . . The contrast to an ideology dominated by organic notions—if in a primitive or vulgar version— could hardly be more acute. But then a view of state and society as an organic system of interdependent elements could not be in the interest of the claim to total power. The organic theory of the state

is an authoritarian notion. It concedes to the constituent elements a life of their own, so long as this does not affect the claim to certainty advanced by the leading stratum. . . . The contrast between the National Socialist ideology of the organic and the mechanical practice of co-ordination remains so striking that one is almost tempted to believe that the ideology was not simply an instrument to mislead people deliberately. Possibly some of the National Socialist leaders themselves believed in some of their sentimental traditionalisms . . . But even if this was so, their wishes had to remain unfulfilled. . . . [They] had the choice of either disappearing as such or setting in motion a social revolution in Germany with all brutality. (SDG, pp.385–6))

An interpretation of the emergence of totalitarianism that focuses on the concept of the aesthetic, such as de Man's analysis of "aesthetic formalization" or Lacoue-Labarthe's of "la *fiction* du politique," provides an account of the continuity between the ideology of organicism and the commitment to mechanical formations and technological power.

It is the notion of art, in the originary sense of *technè,* or skill, that gives the full range of the sense in which the essence of totalitarianism is the conception of the political as "organic." De Man's analysis parallels Lacoue-Labarthe's, who writes—of the dream of the *Cité* as a work of art important in German thought since the Enlightenment, and generated out of a two thousand year tradition—"In its essence the political is *organic.* Here one has to sound the word two times and hear, beneath *organon, ergon* [work]. *It's there that is dissimulated the truth of what one calls 'totalitarianism'* " (FP, p.108, my italics). The organicity of the political consists not simply in organic ideologies or organic metaphors of the state or nation but in a certain relation to the technical or technological. As technè, skill, art, these are conceived as an outgrowth of being or nature. The totalitarian state is instantiated not simply as an infra-political order, through the organic metaphors of a natural community, but, in a motif going back to Plato's *Republic,* through the conception of the political as a forming, a making (*fiction,* notes Lacoue-Labarthe, in the strict sense of the word): as arising through "*technè* in the highest sense of the term, the sense in which *technè* is conceived as the accomplishment and revelation of *physis* itself" (FP, pp.102–3).

If *technè* can be defined as the outgrowth [*sur-croît*] of *physis,* by which *physis* "decrypts" itself and presents itself—if then one can describe *technè* as *apophantic,* in the Aristotelian-Heideggerian sense of the word—political *organicity* is the outgrowth [*surcroît*] necessary to the presentation and the self-recognition of a nation. (FP, pp.108–9)

Such is the political function of art, Lacoue-Labarthe concludes, and more, such is the status of the state's commitment to technological power. Once the aesthetification of the mechanical, technical, processes or devices of production and signification has taken place—once they are conceived as the vital surplus of *form,* in the sense of original or model—nothing checks their performative power. This is de Man's point, and the point implied in Lacoue-Labarthe's observation about anti-Semitism and the Extermination, his statement that it is *because racism is an aestheticism* that it is allied, not less fundamentally, with a massive unleashing of technological power (FP, p.110).

A formal, that is to say a mechanical process, seen as a formal, i.e. an aesthetic one: such is the effect de Man finds evoked in Kleist's Herr C's praise of the puppet ballet. The self-referential or non-referential character of the movement is its crucial feature. In the example of the puppet ballet or the marionette theater, as de Man observes, the aesthetic effect lies not in the beauty of the movements of either the puppet or the puppeteer, not in the relation the movement maintains to something outside it (albeit only a graceful abstract shape), but in its sheer formality, "in the text that spins itself *between* them" (my italics). "This text is the transformational system, the anamorphosis of the line as it twists and turns into the tropes of ellipsis, parabola, and hyperbole. Tropes are quantified systems of motion. The indeterminations of imitation and of hermeneutics have at last been quantified into a mathematics that no longer depends on role models or on semantic intentions" (RR, p.286). One has left behind the problem of meaning, the element of *intention* at odds with *performance,* the tension between what the text is doing and what it may have meant to say; and this elision or solution is deadly. Far from conceiving literature or language or the text as non-referential or purely self-referential, may I reiterate again, de Man (and "deconstruction") conceives these as the tension, the conflict, between referential and formal, between cognitive and performative dimensions, through which the process of signification takes place. Not only literature but language as such (and "the game itself") is lost should one of these dimensions be eliminated. The elimination of the referential and the cognitive dimensions of discourse is what Kleist's figure of the puppet ballet evokes, in de Man's reading, and evokes, not only as a success, but as a process of mutilation, via the allusion to the "dead" limbs of the puppets and the severing of the limb of the cripple who will dance gracefully fitted with an artificial leg. De Man goes on, with measured irony, to describe the "success" ("Aesthetic education by no means fails; it succeeds all too well, to the point of hiding the violence that makes it possible" (RR, p.289)):

The benefits of this formalization are considerable. They guarantee, among other things, the continuity and the balance that are a necessary condition for beautiful lines and shapes. This is possible because they are *once and for all cleansed from the pathos of self-consciousness as well as from the disruptions and ironies of imitation.* Unlike drama, the dance, is truly aesthetic because it is not expressive. . . . The great merit of the puppets, "the outstanding quality one looks for in vain in the large majority of our dancers" is that they follow "the pure law of gravity". . . . Their motion exists only for the sake of the trope, not the reverse, and this guarantees the consistency and predictability of truly graceful patterns of motion. (RR, p.286, my italics)

The next paragraph describes this graceful pattern as one indifferent to death, and moreover, as it happens, to "dead." It is, de Man's reading makes plain, precisely a function of the "freeing of the tropes of their semantic function"; of the fact that (as Herr C explains) the puppets are "anti-grav"—unlike human dancers who need the ground, "in order to *rest* on it," marionettes are free of the need to touch the ground except "to skirt it." De Man's reading of this point constitutes an interpretation of the deadly character of totalitarianisms as the culmination of aesthetic ideology or "aesthetic formalization": performance unchecked by "self-consciousness," by a tension with an intent or re-cognition. This it is that makes the unthinkable performable; the power of the technical become an end in itself. So Lacoue-Labarthe writes, "There is as it were a 'lethal' essence of the technical, by dint of which its 'anything is possible' brings about in fact, that is to say *operates* [opère], if not the impossible, at least the unthinkable (the Extermination, or genetic manipulation—which is still on the agenda)" (FP, pp.110–111). Not altogether fortuitously, the aesthetic ideal attained by the puppets recognizably belongs to, among others, Christian Europe. De Man, on the marionette dance: "By falling (in all the senses of the term, including the theological Fall) gracefully, one prepares the ascent, the turn from parabola to hyperbole, which is also a rebirth" (RR, p.287). It would be impossible to *determine* whether the oddity of expression in the next sentences is the mark of a deliberate intention, an accident of mechanical transcription, or a meaningful slip (whose meanings, plural, we would be in a position only to guess, thinking not only of those dead through genocide and war but of other dead met with by Paul de Man). It *can* be said that, explicating what subsequent paragraphs call "also a dance of death and mutilation," these statements are neither incomprehensible nor indifferent:

Caught in the power of gravity, the articulated puppets can rightly be said to be dead, hanging and suspended like dead bodies:

gracefulness is directly associated with *dead,* albeit a *dead* cleansed of pathos. But it is also equated with a levity, an un-seriousness which is itself based on the impossibility of distinguishing between *dead* and play. Rather than speaking of a synthesis of rising and falling one should speak of a continuity of the aesthetic form that does not allow itself to be disrupted by the borderlines that separate life from death, pathos from levity, rising from falling. (RR, p.287, my italics)

What is *readable* (in a double sense: printed and intelligible, indeed the warning of this paragraph) is that this ultimate formalization has crucially to do not alone with life and death but with "dead," with "dead"—with the dead whose death is no stay to the operation of sheer mechanical performance.

This total performance is not without "effects," or figures, of self-consciousness: interiorization, dialogue.

Such a dialogue occurs as the visible motions of the puppets are linked to the inner, mental imaginings of the puppeteer by what Kleist calls "the way of the dancer's soul—*der Weg der Seele des Tanzers.*" The "soul" results from the substitution of the machinist's consciousness for the movement of the marionettes, one more substitution added to the transformations that keep the system going. (RR, p.286)

It is no stay whatever to the total or the totalitarian system that there come into play the dynamics of inwardness and expression. For all its pathos and prestige, *Erinnerung,* "recollection," "inwardizing," is no stay against the mechanical function of memory, *Gedächtnis*:

As an affective exchange between subjects, dialogism is the most mechanical of figures; nothing is more mechanical than the overpowering romantic figure of interiorization and self-consciousness. Hegel will say the same thing in a crucial passage from the *Encyclopedia* when he defines thought (*Denken*) as the substitution of *Gedächtnis* (the learning by rote of a conventional code) for *Erinnerung* (interiorization, represented in Kleist's text as the affective response of a consciousness to a mechanically formalized motion). (RR, p.288)

And yet the alternative or check to the mechanical dance, evoked by de Man toward the close of the essay, has much to do with Romantic figures and self-consciousness. We have seen that the model the dance displaces is the exhausting and ludicrous match with the bear, and more generally the precarious game of fencing, interpreted as the work of reading, of deciding between literal and figurative, thrust and feint, evoked in terms that describe the contest of politics. This struggle is evoked

once again in a passage identifying the differences between the deadly marionette ballet and a human motion. I want to point not only to the explicit statement of this passage, but to the way in which it reads like a list, a re-marking one after another of the features that have been associated for de Man, in this essay and elsewhere, with the texts of Romanticism (Hölderlin, Rousseau, Schlegel, Baudelaire, Hegel, Wordsworth):

The text indeed evokes the puppet's dance as a *continuous* motion. A non-formalized, still self-reflexive consciousness—a human dancer as opposed to a puppet—constantly has to interrupt its motions by brief periods of repose that are not part of the dance itself. They are like the parabases of the ironic consciousness which has to recover its energy after each failure by reinscribing the failure into the ongoing process of a dialectic. But a dialectic, segmented by repeated negations, can never be a dance; at the very most, it can be a funeral march. And although a march can resemble a minuet in its structure—theme, trio, theme da capo—it can never come near it in the gracefulness which, in this text, is the necessary condition for aesthetic form. By freeing the tropes of their semantic function, one eliminates the discontinuities of dialectical irony and the teleology of a meaning grounded in the weightiness of conceptual understanding. The aesthetic form "needs the ground only . . . in order to skirt it, to recharge the elasticity of the limbs by momentary friction; we [dancers, that is, that are not puppets] need it in order to *rest* on it." (RR, p.287)

In the course of describing the mechanical dance, the ultimate formalization, the textual model "of the text as a . . . system of tropes," de Man interrupts the description with names of the model or motion it superceded. He evokes a turn back from performance to the referential and cognitive dimension of language, and to the temporal structures composed of their mutual interference; he does so, rather than by making claims for them (valorizing them, or even affirming their existence; they are being invoked here as what the dance is *not*), by literally figuratively "turning" to them, alluding "back" to them. All those words, "repose," "dialectic," "ironic consciousness," inscribe a turning back performed, in his own wording, to what "by freeing the tropes from their semantic function, one *eliminates.* . . ." The essay carries out a turning back from that "freeing"—from the "insight" into the formal, the arbitrary, the mechanical, "nature" of our language.

Though this is a thesis I cannot fully defend here,[15] that turning back is also one to the Romantic writing that records, along with "repose" (that of Rousseau's *Cinquième Rêverie*), a turning back—a turning back from, or forgetting of, the blinding lucidity as to the freedom, the arbitrariness, of language and of consciousness. It is evoked in the close of the essay on "The Image of Rousseau in the Poetry of Hölderlin" earlier in the same volume (*The Rhetoric of Romanticism*). And it is invoked with precision in an essay of 1956, "Le Devenir, la poésie," where de Man has this to say about "process" (*le devenir*: becoming) and "poetry": "For Hölderlin, the ultimate truth of poetry resides neither in the eternal nor in the temporal, but in the *turning back* through which a poetry of the sensuous *tears itself away* from its need to become selfconsciousness, or a poetry of process tears itself away from its desire to get back to the object" (DP, p.121). A "turning back" that is a tearing away from a seemingly ineluctable trajectory: such is the gesture recorded also by this passage of de Man's essay on aesthetic formalization.

It is in Hölderlin's poetry and poetic theory that de Man's essay of 1956 (as well as essays of 1954, 1960, and 1966: "Heidegger's Exegeses of Hölderlin," "The Intentional Structure of the Romantic Image," and "Wordsworth and Hölderlin") locates the resource for a conceptualization of the historical character of literature, for what he terms, in "The Dead-End of Formalist Criticism" (1966), a "historical poetics" as opposed to the "salvational poetics" and "naive poetics" that continue to dominate literary criticism in the United States.[16] Significantly, de Man's reference, for his own historical poetics, is to the idea in Hölderlin's work that complicates and dismantles the ideal of an aesthetic state and the potential for national cultural stereotypes in Schiller and other texts of Idealist aesthetics. Hölderlin's thought has been interpreted, notably by Lacoue-Labarthe, as that divergence within speculative idealism in the Romantic period that disqualifies the concept of the aesthetic for assimilation to aesthetic ideology or "national aestheticism" (Lacoue-Labarthe's term for the aesthetic ideology he argues was the essence of Nazism (in FP and HG)). In "Le Devenir, la poésie," de Man refers the power of Hölderlin's vision of poetry's historicality to "the profoundly original idea that what is inborn appears to us as what is most difficult, whereas spirit finds it easy to thrive in what is most foreign to it" (FP, p.122), and he goes on to locate its significance in its having arisen in the context of Hölderlin's translations of Sophocles' tragedies, an intra- and interlinguistic process. Hölderlin radically rethinks the relation between Greece and the Occident posed by Schiller: the Greeks' most successful achievement ("clarity") was what was *not* "native" to them ("sacred pathos"); Hölderlin redefines what is one's "own" as that which is most difficult to accomplish, which one is least likely to achieve. The notion of a proper national cultural identity is thereby dismantled, and with it the notion of historical process (whether of poetry or society) as an imitation

or return, as well as the possibility of modeling a modern state or culture on a harmonious aesthetic whole.

In his 1956 essay De Man alludes to the "historical symbolism" by which Hölderlin expresses, through reference to the difference between as well as within the Occidental and the Greek, his conception of the conflictual character of any historical situation or any consciousness—the thesis of de Man's critique of eternalist humanism. The essay's starting point is a critique of "eternalist poetics" as it appears in contemporary thought about poetry—a matter of "conferring on it a power of eternity that makes it either distinct from or superior to a process of becoming." While it "remains historical in appearance, since it situates poetry with regard to a certain temporal destiny. . . . This kind of meta-temporality coincides at bottom with a belief that poetry founds Being immediately." This way of thinking's effect and function is to allay anxiety about the relation of poetry and history. It does so by conceiving any historical threat to poetry as coming from the outside, such as for instance the demand of utility or function implied in the notion of historical efficacy.[17] This view—and this is its own very function—evades and conceals the genuine historical threat, which is the threat to and of the process of becoming that poetry, as "the most disembodied of all the arts," has as its task, one which "finds in the past no guarantee that it will be possible for it to come into being" (DP, p.124).

"Every meta-temporal poetics is reassuring," de Man writes, for "it knows that no matter how strong the historical process that would assimilate poetry to its own movement, it is always possible for poetry to elude this pull since it is not bound to it essentially." De Man quotes Blanchot asking the reason for the prevalence of such a conception of art in the wartime and postwar period—"Why is it that at the point where history contests and subordinates it, art becomes essential presence?" —and continues,

Such a question contains its own answer since it is obvious that if art (or poetry) can be essential presence, that is, grounded and preserved, then history can have no hold on it; its permanence and power remain secure despite the hollows and chasms it contains. Moreover, this explains how it then becomes possible to speak of these chasms in an even and balanced tone which changes what are often terms of terror into an atmosphere of serenity that leaves open the question of whether it has been earned. (DP, p.112)

Whence the conclusion, which opens onto the main subject of the essay: "There is reason to question the validity of this assurance to the precise extent that it is possible to see poetry as indeed being threatened, not by a historical process of becoming that acts on it from without, but from within the very process of becoming" (DP, p.112). (The argument of the essay becomes more complex as the critique of "eternalist poetics" with which it opens is succeeded by a validation of a certain "poetic eternalism," namely the "poetry of being" of Baudelaire, differentiated from the "poetry of becoming" of Mallarmé, both of which de Man validates, and both of which are described as combining, but in different ways, a mode of performance at odds with its intention, a tension between performative and cognitive dimensions. After writing that in such a poetry as Baudelaire's, "poetry becomes a mask," "trying to imprint, on its true face [that of 'becoming'], the mask of the eternal," de Man continues, "However, this undoubtedly goes counter to the process of becoming. For becoming is not oriented toward what we no longer have, but *toward what we do not yet have.* . . . *Becoming is of the order of being other and not of having been.* . . ." (DP, p.123, my italics).) This threat to *and of* the work, within the very process of its becoming, we have seen de Man trace in the three logically successive models of the work in "Über das Marionettentheater." Or so we would be warranted to think—despite the difference between genuine and illusory historical process, between the process of becoming, and the process of "aesthetic education" or of the reading of the status of the work as such—by de Man's attention to "the historical destiny of the created object that poetry *becomes* [devient], and which generations of readers will use for various purposes" (my italics). From "uses"—be they only of wounding and curing—the work has never been exempt. That other "becoming"—the work's appropriation for the work of *Bildung*—is indeed a threat, from within, to "the game itself": the seemingly inexorable operation of aesthetic formalization—formalization requisite, from the start, for pedagogy, not alone for the work of art—culminating in the inexorable performance of the machine.

As the process of the work compounds with the becoming of the member of the "aesthetic state," so the radically arbitrary utterance, "fiction," compounds with the operation of "excuse." Precisely the sheerly mechanical operation of that excuse is deadly. We may understand now why the arbitrary functioning of language as fiction is mechanical, and why de Man like Rousseau deems this very mechanical functioning "inexcusable." Its deadliness is not only a matter of its potentially deadly effects, such as Rousseau's employers' dismissal of Marion or other consequences of a misreading of a fictional utterance or figure. De Man considers, in reading the Marion episode, why the excuse of fiction or accident is buried in an interrupted syntactical structure and all but suppressed, why "Rousseau's own

text, against its author's interests, prefers being suspected of lie and slander rather than of innocently lacking sense." "It seems to be impossible to isolate the moment in which the fiction stands free of any signification; in the very moment at which it is posited, it gets at once misinterpreted into a determination which is, *ipso facto*, overdetermined. *Yet without this moment, never allowed to exist as such, no such thing as a text is conceivable*" (AR, p.293, my italics). This very necessity—this necessity for the text—is violent. The close of the paragraph describes the total character of that violence; that which in providing instead of the excuse of mere mechanical "random error," a (re)*cognition* of his theft and slander, Rousseau would seek to avoid.

We know this to be the case from empirical experience as well: it is always possible to face up to any experience (to excuse any guilt), because the experience always exists simultaneously as fictional discourse and as empirical event and it is never possible to decide which one of the two possibilities is the right one. The indecision makes it possible to excuse the bleakest of crimes because, as a fiction, it escapes from the constraints of guilt and innocence. On the other hand, it [the indecision] makes it equally possible to accuse fiction-making, which, in Hölderlin's words, is "the most innocent of all activities," of being the most cruel. The knowledge of radical innocence also performs the harshest mutilations. *Excuses not only accuse but they carry out the verdict implicit in their accusations.* (AR, p.293, my italics)

Qui s'excuse, s'accuse. The verdict the excuse not only hands down, but carries out, is that of exclusion from a system of meaning. Which means, of elimination from a social order and from language.

The mutilations of totalitarianism are total. They include the dead limbs of the dancing puppet, as well as those dead through the aesthetic operation of the machine.

But this loss means, also, something else.

The text as body, with all its implications of substitutive tropes ultimately always retraceable to metaphor, is displaced by the text as machine and, in the process, it suffers the loss of the illusion of meaning. . . . This threatens the autobiographical subject not as the loss of something that once was present and that it once possessed, but as *a radical estrangement between the meaning and the performance of any text.* (AR, p.298, my italics)

That "radical estrangement" implies—the *conflict* between the performative and cognitive dimensions of language implies—that, as this text goes on to say, "the linguistic model cannot be reduced to a mere system of tropes" (AR, p.300). Language, the text, is indeed mechanical. *Inefficacious* mechanical processes, however, insofar as they are persistently susceptible to mutual interference; persistently susceptible to checking, interruption. The clumsy and precarious conflict of *deciding* meaning, rather than either its presence, or the infallible performance of an ideal machine.

*

What is the nature of the autobiographical dimension of de Man's Kleist essay?

In one quite specific respect, here it is not a matter of "deciding." If we give an ear (not to say, an arm and a leg) to the implication of this passage:

To decide whether Kleist knew his text to be autobiographical or pure fiction is like deciding whether or not Kleist's destiny, as a person and as a writer, was sealed by the fact that a certain doctor of philosophy happened to bear the ridiculous name of Krug.[18] A story that has so many K's in it (Kant, Kleist, Krug, Kierkegaard, Kafka) is bound to be suspicious no matter how one interprets it. Not even Kleist could have dominated such randomly overdetermined confusion. *The only place where infallible bears like this one can exist is in stories written by Heinrich von Kleist* (RR, pp. 284–5, my italics)

It is difficult not to read this as addressed to de Man's students; a gesture of admonition and (effectively unreassuring) reassurance. The passage says that what he knows about this question is not the point.

De Man's Kleist essay has a bearing on his own "aesthetic education," writing articles on literature for *Les Cahiers du libre examen, Het Vlaamsche Land,* and most of all, *Le Soir,* the newspaper of widest circulation in Belgium, which was taken over by collaborationists after the German invasion in May 1940. One finds in those articles the models of the literary work, as imitation, transcendental locus of meaning, and system of tropes that de Man analyzes in his Kleist essay. What sort of "correlation" is there between those "textual models [and] the historical and political systems that are their correlate" (RR, p.289)? And in what ways do those early articles participate in the social and political history of Europe in the period of the Belgian and the French defeat and the Nazi occupation of Belgium? The second question is not the same as the first, and properly answering it would involve a labor of interpretation reconstructing their reception and the circumstances of their production in addition to the interpretive reading focused on models of the text that I am doing here. Properly answering the first question would involve in the first place maintaining it as a question with regard to "systems," in the plural; it is not alone the political history of

Germany culminating in Nazi totalitarianism that involves the hegemony of those textual models. I will take up here only the more limited question of how de Man's articles of 1940–2 assume and use those models and what sort of organicism one finds in them.

Certainly there appears in the articles the conception of artistic achievement as the self-revelation of a people that we have followed Lacoue-Labarthe in seeing as a condition of totalitarianism. Sometimes this conception appears in the form of an immediate identification between a people and a national art distinctively theirs (eg. in "Le destin de la Flandre," *Le Soir,* 1 Sept. 1941, and passages of "A propos de *Quelques visages du romantisme* par Paul Colin," *Le Soir,* 21–2 Nov. 1942); more often, in some relation to an effort to describe a literary tradition (and thus an internally differentiated and mediated relationship between a nation and an art). The articles seem to me to demonstrate that neither formalism nor historicism provides effective defense against that conception of art, the ineluctably political organicism described in *La Fiction du politique* and in the Kleist essay. In this they reveal something important about literary-critical writing generally. The habitual recourse to the notion of national characteristics in de Man's early articles is typical of historical and literary-critical discourse since the early modern period. It would be found I think to differ rather little from other criticism of the thirties and forties that only an ideology-critique tracing the conditions of totalitarianism in the fundamentals of Western thought, a critique such as de Man's or Lacoue-Labarthe's, can implicate. It would differ in a way predictable from de Man's early pieces being reviews and short articles written for a daily newspaper—by greater simplification (and incoherence). Of course the very involvement in producing under those circumstances, and for this particular newspaper, is itself ideologically charged. Their writer's illusion of being able to control the limits of his involvement would be a truly delusive "autonomy."

One would have to consider as well connections between the enthusiasm for German romanticism evinced in some articles (such as "A propos de *Quelques visages du romantisme* par Paul Colin") and the notion of literature as an autonomous realm with its own rules and laws. In the context of these articles such connections would load the latter idea with the notion of the auto-formation of a subject, a self or a people, in short with "national aestheticism." But we have seen the claim for the "independent domain" of literature function in the articles in another way, as a defense of works and writers against political attack. The political context which can be invoked to condemn de Man's early writing is the same context in which some of his statements can be seen as a critique of the political apparatus in place. In other contexts—in other texts—the concept of the autonomy of the literary, or of the "rhetorical," has proved a powerful critical and analytical instrument (one thinks of François Furet's interpretation of the French Revolution, for instance, as well as the literary theory of Paul de Man). As for German romanticism, its texts' theorization and practices of literature, that history is still to be unravelled.[19] There can be read, in German romantic texts (what do we call Kleist's? but also in texts of Friedrich Schlegel and Novalis), a conception of literature identified with the disjunction between cognition and performance whose ramifications are still being distinguished and decided.

There is one place in the *Le Soir* articles where the notion of the relative autonomy of literature breaks down into or combines with that of the distinctive cultural characteristics of a people to distastrous ideological effect: the March 4, 1941 article "Les juifs dans la littérature actuelle." Ostensibly essential traits of Jews as such are evoked, "les caractères spécifiques de l'esprit juif"—"their cerebrality, their capacity to assimilate doctrines while maintaining toward them a certain coldness." It is in addition asserted that these are qualities crucial to the "work of lucid analysis required by the novel," the cultural achievement being affirmed and defended in the middle portion of the article. However, it is further asserted: Jews have *not* been important in the development of the contemporary novel, which emerges, rather, out of a long literary tradition not affected by the "artificial and disordered existence" of recent social and political history, in which Jews "have, in fact, played an important role."

The invidious and damaging cast of these assertions is hardly disputable. One notices also, however, that they entail a disconnection between a people's qualities and those of a genre or work which is evidently overdetermined. It functions in accomodating the article's account of contemporary literature to the assignment to write something anti-Semitic. It functions also in an account of literature as evolving according to its own laws which are those of a history of forms, as is stressed in other articles on this theme of literature's autonomous evolution (such as "Sur les possibilités de la critique," *Le Soir* 2 Dec. 1941, "Le Renouveau du roman," *Le Soir* 27 Jan. 1942, "A propos de la revue *Messages*," *Le Soir* 14 July 1942). It functions also in composing an argument *contradicting* that of the current anti-Semitic view, which held that contemporary literature had been corrupted by the Jews, a view that the article identifies as an "error" that brings with it "rather dangerous consequences."

This article *is* unbearable; for the gesture of exclusion of the Jews, even if it is undercut; for the connection, thereby—circumstantial as it is and marked as our sense of it is by the blind-

ing hindsight of what was going to happen—with the genocide of the Jews. These factors make it difficult to figure out what in addition makes this article's existence, or arguments, intolerable; and perhaps that hardly matters.[20] What I am trying to approach, though, is how this article's arguments repeat stances and ideas we meet with elsewhere, in contexts where they form part of what it is hard not to see as a *good* political position; and how just that, perhaps, is almost intolerable.

Ironically but not surprisingly perhaps, the article which states an argument in light of which the argument of the "Les juifs" article seems most disastrous is the single one unconcealedly political in its topic and aim, the aim of defending the national autonomy of Belgium against absorption into a greater German state. "Le destin de la Flandre" (*Le Soir* 1 Sept. 1941) begins:

Among the criteria by which one can determine whether a certain geographic area deserves the name of nation, one of the most important is the existence of a culture proper to it, or, more particularly, of an art which belongs only to the inhabitants of that country. That is a prime factor—itself resulting in a multitude of historical, racial [*racique*; there is another word *raciale*], etc. components —among those that allow one to designate whether a people as, yes or no, a nationality worthy of being respected.

The word "*race*" appears once in this article on "the destiny of Flanders," not at all, or rarely, in any others; it is used here to refer to the Flemish and the German "races," the similarity between them: ". . . the danger of assimilation exists and all the more clearly in that affinities link the two races." This article presses uncharacteristically the notion of an immediate identification between people and a national art that is distinctively theirs: the immediate response of a Flemish visitor to "the museum of Florence or Madrid" on entering the rooms hung with Flemish painting, "an unforgettable impression of entering a world that is familiar to him, that belongs to him, where he feels at home"; namely with an art manifesting "attachment to exterior forms rather than to cerebral analysis" and distinguished from French art by attention to "aspects of shape and color" rather to "abstract content." This account is explicitly being mobilized for a defense of the relative national autonomy of Belgium in the wake of German domination. One finds here a conception of art as entirely determined by a people's shared experiences as qualities immediately present in them. The emphatic political motive of this article presumably contributes to generating a position considerably different from the articles' usual position, that art has its own autonomous laws. De Man writes here, "It is in the name of these values that one can require that the line of frontiers and interior administrative powers be so conditioned that the continuity of the national spirit be ensured. If not, the *elective virtues* [voluntary virtues, *vertues électives*] that belong solely to the Flemish will be eliminated."

The thesis of the central part of the "Les juifs" article is a defense of the modern novel, of "Gide, Kafka, Hemingway, Lawrence—one could extend the list indefinitely"; the thesis of "A propos de la revue *Messages*"—a journal of contemporary French poetry by surrealist writers and writers in the Resistance in France, such as Jean Lescure and Eluard—is a defense of modern French poetry, of surrealism and Symbolism; invoking, as the other article invokes the continuity of the novelistic tradition (from Stendhal and the examination of "exterior reality" to contemporary writers' exploration of "psychological reality," of "the interior life"), the "continuity of French poetry" ("Continuité de la poésie française. A propos de la revue *Messages*," *Le Soir*, 14 July 1942).[21] This article is dated 14 July, 1942, and resoundingly asserts the greatness of French surrealist poetry and the independence of literature from the demands of the "totalitarian" "revolution." Both those positions, in the circumstances of 1942, have to be seen as bold and good ones. Yet there are further judgments to make as one distinguishes more closely.

A first distinction would consist in very plainly separating artistic evolution from what is qualified justifiably as the present revolution. On the pretext that this revolution is totalitarian, that is to say that it intends to modify all aspects of individual and collective life, some have brutally included art among its objectives. It would prove, then, to be dependent on the ideologies that arise in the political and social world, ideologies that are all in absolute reaction against those that dominated a past forever gone by. In other terms, art, and more particularly literature, finds itself transformed into a tool, an instrument, destined to combat by every means an outdated worldview and to impose another.

Certainly, it is doubtless that the profound changes being accomplished in the general way of proceeding [*allure*] of our civilization cannot leave writers and poets indifferent. Their work will carry the imprint of the cares that weigh on the humanity of our day. It expresses its anxieties and hopes, its revolts and enthusiasms. But this interference of events of the moment [*l'ingérence de l'actualité*] does not determine the course of literary history proper. The only effect it can have is to make certain themes of inspiration dominate that were overlooked at other moments. It's to that that its influence is restricted.

Alongside these modifications imposed by the revolutionary cli-

ate of the period other factors orient creation, factors which are determining for the evaluation and even the mere historical description of poetry. As an example let us cite that of form. Poetic forms—the same as plastic or musical forms—are not born arbitrarily from an individual will. They are much rather imposed unconsciously on each individual, for they live like free organisms having an infancy, a maturity, and a decadence. Their vital process must unroll itself in a continuous manner, without letting itself be checked or stopped by extra-formal considerations. And in the case of French poetry, we find ourselves at the beginning of an ascent and hence all systematic taking of control [*emprise systématique*] would be in the highest degree nefarious.

Is there not the gesture, here, of setting a totalizing conception of "artistic evolution" against the claims of the totalitarian revolution or state? And an organicism of artistic form against the claim to absolute rupture, of fascist politics? One sees how readily the description of forms as organic slides into the description of a "continuous" inexorable process, the metaphor of growth ("they live like free organisms") into the description of sheer performance, that of a machine, unchecked "by extra-formal considerations." At the same time the word "must" (in the assertion that poetic forms" "vital process must allowed to unroll") is not merely descriptive (of an invulnerable eternal order); it is addressed, descriptively, both to poets and writers (implicitly) and to those in charge of policy; the next paragraph spells explicitly spells this out ("It would be then at the very least premature to submit art to revolutionary imperatives linked to passing conditions"); there follows an affirmation of the outstanding poetic value of surrealism, as exemplified in such poetry as (the communist) Eluard's.

The following paragraph, rather than describing an inexorable historical evolution of literature, evokes for literature a fraught, eventful, unpredictable, historical existence. It ascribes to French poetry an authenticity having to do with a "shock" and a "second wave" of unfamiliar aspirations, surrealism being the second, Symbolism the first. This paragraph argues: contemporary French poetry is not a decadence but "une naissance,"

the beginnings of a great adventure in which the French artistic soul has launched itself, and which cannot be impeded by the political and military failures of the country. The beginning of this adventure is represented by symbolism; there, for the first time, there manifested itself that romantic spirit, entirely opposed to the consecrated French norms, or opening[22] wide the doors onto the infinite plains of the irrational . . . a second wave, consecutive to the first, soon broke upon the country: that was surrealism. And the effects of this shock are far from being over [. . . *une seconde vague, consécu-tive à la première, déferla bientôt sur le pays: ce fut le surréalisme. Et les effets de ce choc sont loin d'être terminés.*]. . . The current poetry is, from the point of view of form, at the dawn of its splendor . . . As for the "spirit" of this art, it is an admirable thing to see French po-etry detach itself from the precepts in which it ran the danger of fi-nally smothering. Already the surrealists, after the symbolists, affirmed with force the necessity of annexing the world of dream and myth and of setting out in it on dazzling adventures. Will one see, finally, succeeding upon this theoretical intention [*volonté théo-rique*] a real creation, worthy of the proposed objectives?

How is one to read the metaphor of "annexation" in the next to last sentence? An earlier allusion to the political and historical context is explicit: the triumph of French poetry cannot be im-peded by the country's political and military defeat. In the fur-ther sentence, the political and military is implicitly linked with Germany, the poetic and artistic with France; the sentence im-plicitly evokes, as rivals, politics and art, Germany and France.

This paragraph evokes a rivalry dating back to Plato, bet-ween the artistic and the political, between the poets and the governors. De Man's metaphor of "annexing" belongs to that tradition. To match the French against the Germans, it appro-priates as trope the political and military action marking a pe-riod of national imperialism. One "fiction" ("making") is pitted against another, the power of French poetry is upheld against the claims of German politics. It is within the tradition of this conception of the political, of the polis, not only more locally and specifically, that the possibility of the Nazi state has to be located. Lacoue-Labarthe has written indispensably on the thought of politics as making or fiction in *La Fiction du politique* (FP, pp. 92–102). A propos of the searching indictment in Hans Jürgen Syberberg's "Hitler: un film d'Allemagne," Lacoue-La-barthe writes,

the intuition of Syberberg goes deeper, and in a certain way takes literally and radicalizes the Brechto-Bejaminian verdict [indicting fascism as the aestheticification of politics]: the *political* model of na-tional-socialism is the *Gesamtkunstwerk* [total art work] because, as Dr. Goebbels knew very well, the *Gesamtkunstwerk* is a political project, the *Festspiel* of Bayreuth was supposed to be for Germany what the great Dionysiads were supposed to be for Athens and all Greece: the place where the people, gathered in its State, gives to it-self the representation of what it is, and of what founds it, as such. Which does not mean simply that the work of art (tragedy, musical drama) offers the truth of the *polis* or of the State, but that the polit-ical itself institutes and constitutes itself (and re-founds itself regu-larly) in and as the work of art. . . . Behind this setting at issue of

the becoming-cinema of the world and of politics, and behind the emphatic declarations of Goebbels and some others, Syberberg does not fail to be aware, either, that there lies an entire tradition, two millennia long in fact, or at least the dream that this tradition will have engendered in German thought since the end of the En-lightenment. And this dream is, in effect, that of the *Cité* as work of art. (FP, pp.97–8, 102)

This tradition is that of the ideal of the "aesthetic state" targeted in de Man's Kleist essay.

The sentence in "A propos de la revue *Messages*" has simul-taneously another significance. It evokes a sort of symmetrical chiasmus: while the German state is "affirming with force the necessity of annexing" the territory of France, French poetry is "affirming with force the necessity of annexing" the territory of dream and myth that in other articles Paul de Man associates with German literature and German romanticism. The date of the article, *le quatorze juillet*. . . , belongs to the "message": French aspirations are being revindicated—but in a particular ambiguous form. It is a form that consists of the appropriation of a spirit not French but "romantic"; in a form that consists of French poetry precisely not simply *being itself*. . . .

That perhaps is the crucial difference between the view of the autonomy of literature in this piece and in "Les juifs dans la littérature actuelle"; despite the subtitle, "Continuité de la poésie française," this article speaks in fact of the *dis*continuity within a poetic tradition; the other, of the continuity of a genre, the novel (albeit, again, in order to defend it). Clashing with the intense responsiveness to a radical literary-historical change within this piece is its reassertion of the "eternal" character of literature. "The danger of a revolution is that, in its inevitable destructive work, it risks eliminating the eternal values which, subsequently, it could not itself do without." There one hears an embattled variant of the "eternalist poetics" de Man will crit-icize, as an inadequate response to totalitarian pressures, in 1955. But in the previous paragraph, something else is apparent, in the element that strains the national frame of reference for the subject matter, as well as the claim of organicism: in the rupture and internal conflict being deemed the vitality of contemporary poetry; in the word "shock" (for the impact of surrealism), in the phrase "And the effects of this shock are far from being over."

It might have been a practice of "historical poetics." It nearly describes an achieved tension (in Eluard's poetry) between cog-nition and performance, certainly, at least, between intention and form ("to annex the world of dream and myth," a poetry of "crystalline clarity"). But its author was, or had been, much invested in something else: in "the possibilities of criticism," notably those coincident with the potentialities of formalization.

The commitment to the formalization of the study of literature is most manifest, significantly, in an article of late 1941 that begins by taking issue with the statement, "Le critique n'est pas historien." In this 1,400 word essay, "Sur les possibilités de la critique," de Man defends the claim of criticism to be "an autonomous discipline," neither a form of creative writing using literature for inspiration nor a lesson in morality. "Its most fundamental mission . . . consists in defining the value of a literary work," and this involves "a liberation from all prejudices and extra-literary inclinations." I alluded earlier to the unselfregarding boldness of the attack here on moralizing criticism, in a time when art's conformity to a dominant set of values was the order of the day ("One has no right," asserts Paul de Man, "to condemn Gide as a novelist because his moral life was dubious [*discutable*] or to hold it against Henri de Montherland [sic] because you don't like his character"). Nor has that line of argument lost its pertinence:

The most beautiful pages of the world literatures are often those that express a failure, an abandonment, a capitulation. And the worst platitudes have been written to exalt the noblest sentiments. All that is perfectly evident and it would be useless to repeat it if one did not hear reaffirmed that criticism must be ". . . an ensemble of deductions, attached to a philosophy of broad humanism, or better of a moral responsibility, linked to the supernatural fidelity of man."

(Indeed. How long has it been since we last heard that song?) But—having read, precisely, Paul de Man—one has also to make another judgment about this text, about the critical project it goes on to propose: a formalist historicist poetics and literary history.

Thus divested of his individual opinions and prejudices, there remains to the critic to seek out the laws of the genres and to draw up a sort of code that will be his touchstone. The difficulty of this enterprise results from the extreme mobility of aesthetic precepts and formulas. It is not a matter of an eternal and immutable Beauty, but of *a series of movements that superpose and intersect with, influence and combat one another,* and have, all of them, their own law. But an attentive examination will reveal beneath this anarchic appearance a certain order, and a mind in the least capable of synthesis will be able to indicate that *these motions move about several points of reference that mark the different stages of cyclical and coherent evolutions.* To each one of these evolutionary stages corresponds an ensemble of criteria which will modify themselves as another level of the progression is

attained. It will therefore be necessary continually to reverify the methods of evaluation and to adapt them to the modalities of the period. And that cannot be done without applying methods that come directly from the domain of history. That is to say that *it is fitting to base oneself on that ensemble of experiences and of symptoms that the examination of the past furnishes.* In devoting oneself to the comparison of these phenomena in time and space, it will be possible to disentangle their true significance.

And the [critical] judgments properly speaking will appear only as almost a secondary operation, a practical application based on a theoretical apparatus which, in fact, surpasses it in interest—just as certain applications of mathematics are effaced before the grandeur and rigor of the abstract deductions that made them possible. It isn't, at bottom, very important to know whether Mr. X . . . has respected all the rules of the game when he wrote his last novel. But it can be extremely instructive to formulate those rules and to observe the way in which they change over the course of the centuries. For this examination is as revelatory as that of the political behavior of peoples to which history gives such a preponderant place. It permits one to acquire an overview [*vue d'ensemble*] of the way in which humanity modifies itself and develops, for just as revealing a part of its mentality reflects itself in the work of its artists as in the unrolling of its wars and its conquests. ("Sur les possibilités de la critique," *Le Soir,* 2 Dec. 1941)

These expectations and assumptions continue to be those of most practice of comparative literature and of the study of literary history. The study of shifting generic conventions as a study of an aspect of the history of humanity: this project and premise informs modes of criticism as apparently diverse as structuralism, marxism, and in its original form the New Criticism. It takes a critique such as de Man's in his writing of 1956 or 1983, or other critical projects or reading practices ("poststructuralist," "postmarxist") focused on the conflictual character of literary and other discourse, to reveal the flaw and threat in that engaging aspiration. The passage quoted above is imagining language "as a system of turns and deviations, a system of tropes," with a movement as determined and determinable as history's—as that of "history" conceived as the unfolding of an "evolution" like that of a self-referential motion or a system of tropes. (That "série de mouvements qui se superposent et s'entrecroisent," in which the attentive mind can distinguish beyond the visible awkwardness "un certain ordre," resembles, even more than a dance, the marionette theater, its aesthetic effect residing in the intricate pattern of connections between the visible and invisible parts.) Implicit in that conception of history as determined is a conception of history as the past and as an ensemble of effects directly available as meaning: "experiences and symptoms." The notion of the possibility of deducing a code is complicated, but only momentarily, by the prompt appeal to the historical or temporal character of the phenomenon, to literature's existence as a process of change, for the model of history that surfaces is closest to that of an object of the natural sciences. At the same time, the passage reflects a powerful aspiration to theory, which is also a commitment to abstraction and formalization. Although this pitches the critical project at a different level than that of deciding how far an individual work conforms to a generic code, the pretension to totalization inherent in the model identifies it with a totalizing conception of history stressing works' conformity within a larger whole, though its closure is deferred, and as it were displaced onto the critical model:

If this conception of criticism may appear hardly brilliant and hardly useful, then, and resemble at first sight a sterile mental exercise, it nonetheless would permit the establishment of a philosophy of literary history which is not less rich than the philosophy of history as such [*tout court*].

. . . . What is above all important, is to seek out in the tendency of a work or of a writer *the aspect by which it integrates itself into the tendencies of its era and the support that its production brings to future developments*. Any criticism that would deny either of these studies will be no more than vain and fragmentary work [*ne fera qu'oeuvre vaine et fragmentaire*].

It is in rather similar terms that de Man's essays written between 1960 and 1983 are described in the Preface of *The Rhetoric of Romanticism*: "Such massive evidence of the failure to make the various individual readings coalesce is a somewhat melancholy spectacle. . . . they do not evolve in a manner that easily allows for dialectical progression, or, ultimately, historical totalization. Rather, it seems they always start again from scratch. . . ." (RR, p. viii). Juxtaposing these passages one also hears the monumental absence of irony that marks the initial dismissal of "vain and fragmentary" accomplishment. The Kleist essay gives the reasons for relinquishing the determination not to engage in such vain exercise as criticism that produces no account of a work's or writer's contribution to his or her or the next era in history. The formalization of literature and of history brings with it the power of systematization and a force of momentum. But it implies the exclusion and elimination of all but the constituents of one universal performance. Yet his alternative to contributing to ultimate historical totalization cannot, by de Man, be described with complacency. For instance, this is the unreassuring model offered in the reading of Kleist:

More often than not the diversity that becomes manifest in the successive readings of a text permits one to determine a central crux that works as a particularly productive challenge to interpretation. Not so with the *Marionettentheater*; this brief narrative engenders a confusion all the more debilitating because it arises from the cumulative effect produced by the readings. Each of the essays (including the bad ones) is quite convincing in itself, until one reads the next one, equally persuasive yet entirely incompatible with its predecessors. The outcome, seen from the perspective of literary scholarship, is anything but graceful. The collective body of interpreters resembles the harassed fencer of the final story rather than the self-assured teacher. C. and his interlocutor maintain a measure of composure, but the dance performed by the commentators offers only chaos. Far from finding, as in Schiller's description of the aesthetic dance, that the spot toward which one directs one's steps had been vacated, one finds oneself bumping clumsily into various intruders or getting entangled in one own's limbs and motions. One is left speculating on what it is, in this text, that compels one, despite clearly perceived warnings, to enter upon this unpromising scene. For it would appear that anyone still willing to engage a bear in a fencing match after having read *Über das Marionettentheater* should have his head examined. (RR, pp.271–2)

There is an unmistakable amusement and even delight in this passage, along with its irony, nevertheless, which marks a specular moment; it is indeed de Man's sense of his own project that is being evoked here.

The mood and the balance shifts significantly in the very next paragraph, which turns to the question of what happens when—"increased formalization" via "the salutary influence of contemporary methodology"[23] having brought within reach "the true aesthetic dimension of the text" and a formal control or mastery, "at the expense of stable and determined meaning," "a fair enough price to pay for mastery over form"—what happens when, "after the possibility of assertion has been decanonized by means of a systematic poetics . . . this poetics threatens to become, in its turn, canonized as exemplary." The question is being asked by de Man both about semiotics, about the pedagogical success of that formalized study of sign systems, and about his own work. Not simply the mistaking of literary theory and rhetorical reading for the theory of the formal status of literature is involved, but the tendency to "aesthetic formalization" involved in teaching itself: in education, pedagogy, as requiring formalization, while nevertheless formalization, or aestheticization, is irremediably at odds with the pedagogical. This paragraph continues toward its close with a genuinely disequilibrated and disequilibrating set of questions, unevenly rhetorical and unrhetorical, ones that the writing of the essay is undertaken to meet.

What remains problematic is whether the pedagogical function can remain compatible with aesthetic effect. Formalization inevitably produces aesthetic effects; on the other hand, it just as compulsively engenders pedagogical discourse. It produces education, but can this education still be called *aesthetic* education? It produces a special kind of grace, but can this elegance be taught? Is there such a thing as a graceful teacher or, rather, is a teacher who manages to be graceful still a teacher? And if he is not, what then will he *do* to those who, perhaps under false pretenses, have been put in the position of being his pupils? The problem is not entirely trivial or self-centered, for the political power of the aesthetic, the measure of its impact on reality, necessarily travels by ways of its didactic manifestations. The politics of the aesthetic state are the politics of education. (RR, p.273)

*

If the closing paragraph of de Man's Kleist essay that I began this essay by quoting evokes aesthetic education as a "trap, as unavoidable as it is deadly," it maintains, even as it warns against the inevitability of mistaking, the difference between an arbitrary and violent process and a dance. And if the final paragraph elides—in best, most sinister, most negative de Manian style—the differences between proceedings all deemed fatal: aesthetic education "as mirror, as imitation, as history, as the fencing match of interpretation, or as the anamorphic transformations of tropes"—the reading, as we have read, differentiates between a conflictual and cumbersome process, which focuses and defers violence—the process of reading as the necessity "to distinguish between actual meaning and the process of signification" and "to decide between . . . violence on the stage and violence on the streets"—and a compelling though not necessarily visibly unified process which unleashes or incarnates it: aesthetic formalization—the aesthetification, as a recognizable form, of the formal, mechanical, and contradictory processes of signification; a formalization that potentially takes in not only the work of art, but of the state, not only the literary, but the social, in a total aesthetification; as a dance.

The resource for the swerve in de Man's own aesthetic education, from formalization to "the question of reading," after the war, is the very historical valuation present in his articles from 1940–2, the significance accorded to Romanticism. The decisiveness of the new interpretation of that judgment (not its abandonment), and the exact content of the new interpretation, are plain in the polemical pointedness as well as the unremitting

complexity of the lecture de Man delivered at the Ecole des Hautes Etudes in 1955, "Le Devenir, la poésie," where a crucial factor in the difference between his earliest and his later writing stands out unmistakably: the reading, with and against Heidegger, of the poetry and poetic theory of Hölderlin. De Man's critique here of "poetic eternalism" leads into a counter-proposal specifically derived from Hölderlin, a reading of modern poetry (here of Mallarmé and Baudelaire) as performing the "task of poetic consciousness" in coming to terms with its historicality, its non-essentiality, the impossibility of being (something single, proper, whole). Hölderlin's detailed theorization of his translations of Sophocles that de Man discusses here manifestly inspires the practice of deconstructive or "rhetorical reading" which this lecture as well as later essays carries out, though without a linguistic or rhetorical vocabulary.

The distinctive complication of Hölderlin's distinction between what is one's "own" ("*eigen*") from what is strange or foreign ("*fremd*"), his idea that what is strange to us comes more "naturally" while what is our own is hardest or impossible to achieve, provides de Man with the idea of a disparity between the "intent" and the mode of existence of a work, and of a distinction between irreducible, incompatible and yet inseparable, dimensions of a work and of language—which can be conceptualized as its cognitive and performative dimensions, as its rhetoric and its grammar, or in other ways. There are causes for locating an emergence or exacerbation of that disparity in Romantic literature, as an intensification both of the demand for the freedom of consciousness or language from the given (from imitation) and of the demand of cognition.[24] It is something like that conflict and disparity that is identified by Paul de Man in his book reviews of 1941–2 as the factor that intrigues him most, or that elicits unconditional assertions of its significance and importance. He locates it in the poetry of Symbolism and surrealism and novels of Novalis (*Heinrich von Ofterdingen*) and (though with considerably less enthusiasm) Ernst Jünger (*Die Marmorklippen*)—in which the tension between (according to the reviewer) *le roman* and *le romantique,* and between the romantic character of the authentically poetic and the classical character of the French poetic tradition, makes for powerful and unpredictable writing.[25] One finds other romanticisms too among de Man's book reviews, sometimes their evaluation, sometimes their celebration, in discussion ranging from Jean Giono's novels to the "aesthetic of childhood" in Alain Fournier and Marcel Delhaye.[26] What the reviews explicitly associate with romanticism, however—and accord utmost significance—is German romanticism as exemplified by Novalis and the complex and contradictory achievement of a "romantic" poetry in

France by Symbolism and surrealism, its conditions described in these terms: "We have there the example of a struggle between a movement overturning from top to bottom the mentality of the West, on the one hand, and the fundamental qualities of a people, opposed to that current" ("A propos de *Quelques visages du Romantisme* par Paul Colin," *Le Soir,* 21–2 November 1942).

The ambiguity of the ideological implications of this valuation would be roughly the following. If romanticism is simply identified with the German nation presently winning victories under Nazism, then stress on the significance of its winning out in literary movements in France would open the "perspective" of a German hegemony embracing both literature and politics. If romanticism is identified as an artistic movement contrasting with a classical respect for limits, a "sense of measure" predominant in French literature, then stress on the significance of its winning out in literary movements in France would imply the perspective of a gain for modern literature and culture from precisely the interplay and combination of ostensibly incompatible national norms. The dangers and also the potential promise of the valuation of romanticism are apparent in a review of *Quelques visages du Romantisme* ("Some faces (or "aspects") of Romanticism"), one of the last articles de Man wrote for *Le Soir.* The attraction exercised by the romantic phenomenon on certain theoreticians, he writes, is "the indication of a very important turning point in the preoccupations and, hence, of the creation of French writers." One is in the presence of "an essential change in sensibility and thought, a change of which the effect is only beginning to be felt, but which will not be long in opening unsuspected perspectives [*des perspectives insoupçonnées*]." What these are, one is told at the end of the article: if further accomplishments confirm the achievement of surrealism, "One will have to revise the generally held judgment about the artistic nature of the French and concede that it is not incompatible with creations that are profoundly and veritably romantic."

In other words, that national cultural identities are more complex or different than one had thought. Or even—that the notion of such identities is fatally simplistic and mistaken. (And more: are not the "perspectives insoupçonnés" that this reading of contemporary French poetry opens, also the notion of the work that Blanchot articulates in 1955 in *L'Espace littéraire?*— "that profound distance of the work from itself by which it eludes, always, what it is [*cette profonde distance de l'oeuvre à l'égard d'elle-même par laquelle celle-ci échappe toujours à ce qu'elle est*]." But if the article seems on the verge of this idea—brought to it by the reading of a Romantic tradition, in diverse genres

and languages—it by no means reaches it. The review relapses instead into the commonplace that the Germans were naturally better at romantic writing than the French, because it was their national character, whereas the French to write romantically had to overcome their national character, which is classical. This degraded post-Schillerian, pre-dialectical not to say pre-critical version of a certain idea about the Occident and the Greeks is at its worst in passages of this text: crude national stereotypes plus the identification between a national artisitc tradition and the "specific nature" of that "people"; in the service of a literary-historical argument that runs, "If one accepts that the very idea of romanticism is equivalent to the rupture of certain barriers, the suppression of certain intellectual constraints," it would make sense that the French have been the most timid in developing it, their tradition consisting in (qualities valorized, both here and more emphatically in other articles) "the sense of measure, the primacy of reason."[27] Yet for the flicker of an instant or rather the wavering of a clause one is on the verge of another idea: that of the necessity of negating what comes most easily, as the crucial means of an albeit precarious achievement: "Incontestably, the effort of *furnishing in order to eliminate* the formal and spiritual rules of classicism is much greater for it [the French people], than, for example, for the Germans" (my italics). It doesn't last: what follows is the predictable—that what follows is that "the romanticism of that country [the French] remained inferior to that which affirmed itself elsewhere" (in England and Germany). Nor *could* a consideration of literary history operating with the assumption of national cultural identities arrive at a dialectical conception of the poetic process, or the process of consciousness.

Perhaps because he is inventing an argument rather than reviewing one, in "A propos de la revue *Messages,*" the journal he helped to publish an issue of in Belgium when its publication was prevented in occupied Paris, de Man writes differently and better of poetry and history, evoking, despite the rhetoric of organicism that still predominates here, an ineffaceable yet ruptured historicality of literature. Just at the point of "shock" there is a continuity between the Messenger Lectures (at Cornell in 1983) and "A propos de la revue *Messages,*" between its rhetoric and *The Rhetoric of Romanticism.* In describing the conflict between "cet esprit romantique" and "des contre-courants classiques, issus de la tradition ancestrale de la nation," this article is describing a conflict inherent in language and consciousness that "Le Devenir, la poésie" (1956) will describe as the process of becoming, and "Aesthetic Formalization: Kleist's 'Über das Marionettentheater'" (1983) will describe as the conflict between cognition and performance, or "the question of reading as the necessity to decide between violence on the stage and violence in the streets." And the effects of that shock are far from being over.

Cornell University

ABBREVIATIONS

AR Paul de Man, *Allegories of Reading* (New Haven: Yale University Press, 1979)

DP De Man, "Le devenir, la poésie," *Monde nouveau* 105 (November 1956), pp.110–24; forthcoming as "Process and Poetry" in Paul de Man, *Critical Writings, 1953–70,* ed. Lindsay Waters (Minneapolis: University of Minnesota Press, 1988)

HG Philippe Lacoue-Labarthe, "Hölderlin et les grecs," *Poètique* 40 (1979). pp.465–74

FP Lacoue-Labarthe, *La Fiction du politique* (Paris: Christian Bourgois, 1987)

RR De Man, *The Rhetoric of Romanticism* (New York: Columbia University Press, 1984.)

SDG Ralf Dahrendorf, *Society and Democracy in Germany* (New York: Norton, 1967)

UM Heinrich von Kleist, "Über das Marionettentheater," *Samtliche Werke und Briefe* (Munich: Hanser, 1961), vol. 2, p.335–42. English translations appear in *Salmagundi* 33–4 (Spring-Summer, 1976), by Beryl de Zoete, and *Times Literary Supplement,* 20 October 1978, by Idris Parry

NOTES

1. On the connection between Rousseau's autobiographies and another Kleist text, see Cynthia Chase, "Mechanical Doll, Exploding Machine," *Decomposing Figures: Rhetorical Readings in the Romantic Tradition* (Baltimore: Johns Hopkins University Press, 1986), p.221, note 12.

2. Friedrich Nietzsche, *Geburt der Tragoedie,* section ix, paragraph 1, in *Werke,* vol. 1 (Munich: Hanser, 1969).

3. See Paul de Man, "The Epistemology of Metaphor," *Critical Inquiry* 5:1 (1978), pp.13–30; "Phenomenality and Materiality in Kant," in *Hermeneutics: Questions and Prospects,* ed. Gary Shapiro and Alan Sica (Amherst: University of Massachusetts Press, 1984), pp.121–44; and "Kant's Materialism" and "Kant and Schiller," forthcoming in de Man, *Aesthetic Ideology* (Minneapolis: University of Minnesota Press, 1988).

4. "Kant and Schiller" is included in *Aesthetic Ideology* (Minneapolis: University of Minnesota Press, forthcoming).

5. "Sur *Les Falaises de marbre,* par Ernst Jünger," *Le Soir,* 31 March 1942; "En marge de l'Exposition du livre allemand: Introduction à la littérature allemande contemporaine," *Le Soir,* 2 March 1942; "Continuité de la poésie française: A propos de la revue *Messages,*" *Le Soir,* 14 July 1942.

6. De Man evokes the constant repetition of symmetrical chiasmus in Schiller's texts in "Kant and Schiller" in *Aesthetic Ideology.* On this configuration, see also "Autobiography as De-facement" (RR, p.78) and Andrzej Warminski, *Readings in Interpretation: Hölderlin, Hegel, Heidegger* (Minneapolis: University of Minnesota Press, 1987), especially pp. xxiv–lxi, and "Facing Language: Wordsworth's First Poetic Spirits," *Diacritics,* Winter 1987.

7. "Notre Chronique littéraire. *Notre Avant-Guerre* de Robert Brasillach," *Le Soir,* 12 August 1941; "Chronique littéraire. Le *Solstice de juin,* par Henri de Montherlant," *Le Soir,* 11 November 1941; "Continuité de la poésie française. A propos de la revue *Messages,*" *Le Soir,* 14 July 1942; "Sur les possibilités de la critique," *Le Soir,* 2 December 1941.

8. Henry J. Schmidt, "What is Oppositional Criticism? Politics and German Literary Criticism from Fascism to the Cold War," *Poetics Today,* 9:4 (1988).

9. Early in the Kleist essay de Man links authoritarian pedagogy to the process of aesthetic education. He observes that this text, which has been received principally for the Schillerian precepts uttered by one of its characters, in fact stages this dogma as the assertion of professional authority: namely Herr C's authority, as the lead dancer of the opera, to speak about the ballet of the marionettes, and, emulating him, K's authority in the role of instructor to the ephebe, in the episode of the young man's loss of gracefulness. "The ephebe, as well as K, are being educated in the art of gracefulness, *Anmut*"; "Their education is clearly an *aesthetic* education that is to earn them citizenship in Schiller's aesthetic state" (RR, p.270); and since the Kantian conception of the aesthetic that is involved here entails the aesthetic as the articulation of theoretical reason with "the practical judgment of the ethical world," the "possibility arises that the postulate of ethical authority is posited for the sake of maintaining the undisputed authority of teachers in their relationship to their pupils" (RR, p.270).

10. Cf. RR, p.289: "But one should avoid the pathos of an imagery of bodily mutilation and not forget that we are dealing with textual models, not with the historical and political systems that are their correlate." For an analysis of the gesture whereby de Man intro-

duces and disqualifies such images, see Neil Hertz, "Lurid Figures," in *Reading de Man Reading* (Minneapolis: University of Minnesota Press, 1988).

11. De Man, "Introduction," *Toward an Aesthetics of Reception,* by Hans Robert Jauss, trans. Timothy Bahti (Minneapolis: University of Minnesota Press, 1982), pp. xv–xvi.

12. See the preceding Messenger lecture, "Hegel on the Sublime" in *Displacement: Derrida and After,* ed. Mark Krupnik (Bloomington: Indiana University Press, 1983), p.144.

13. Elias's *History of Manners* (New York: Urizen, 1978), originally published as *Wandlungen des Verhaltens in den weltlichen Oberschichten des Abendlandes,* volume one of *Über den Prozess der Civilization,* in Switzerland by Haus zum Falken, 1939 is a study of "the civilizing process," focused on the extension of "manners," of less spontaneous, more inhibited modes of behavior, originating in court life, from the middle ages to the modern period. As Elias' essay of introduction dated "Leicester, 1968" (included as an appendix in the 1978 edition) makes plain, his book seeks to explain the history of ideas with reference to social history, and in this sense, to explain philosophy with reference to sociology. In Elias this is not an unphilosophical (or unthoughtful) gesture. It entails a critique of the epistemology of certain positivisms (including Talcott Parsons' sociology) and, generally, of "more object-related than self-related conceptual instruments"; it entails a putting into question of the supposed split between "subject" and "object," a critique of the "inside" versus "outside" metaphor as inadequate for the conceptualization of an individual inhabiting a social order (p.256). Elias observes the performative effect of the ideal of objectivity evidently demanded by scientific observation: "The act of conceptual distancing from the objects of thought that any more emotionally controlled reflection involves . . . appears to self-perception at this stage as a distance actually existing between the thinking subject and the objects of his thought." It is a hypostatization of "an *act* of distancing" coincident with the civilizing process, as both the spread of manners and the emergence of modern science (p.256).

For Elias, however, this constitutes the entire and sufficient explanation of the tension and difference experienced illusively as that of the "individual" versus "society" and that of "subject" versus "object." For Elias the experience and the concept of a difference or gap can be fully accounted for—and insofar as it is understood, alleviated—as an effect of the social history of Europe or "the civilizing process." As his essay of introduction continues this explanation its sociobiological premise becomes apparent. Thus there merge, in this summation of Elias' argument, explanation in terms of a single ineluctable historical process or "civilizational shift" and explanation in terms of a biological apparatus it affects directly:

The firmer, more comprehensive and uniform restraint of the affects characteristic of this civilizational shift, together with the increased internal compulsions that, more implacably than before, prevent all spontaneous impulses from manifesting themselves directly and motorically in action, without the intervention of control mechanisms—these are what is experienced as the capsule, the invisible wall dividing the "inner world" of the individual from the "external world" or, in different versions, the subject of cognition from its object, the "ego" from the "other," the "individual" from "society." What is encapsulated are the restrained instinctual and affective impulses denied direct access to the motor apparatus. They appear in self-perception as what is hidden from all others, and often as the true self, the core of individuality. The term "the inner man" is a convenient metaphor, but it is a metaphor that misleads. (p.258)

It must be replaced by a metaphor that does not mislead (so Elias implies): not surprisingly (although it is a shock to come upon it after reading de Man on Kleist), that of a "social dance." Elias' essay repeats the logic of the shift from a hermeneutic to a formal tropological model (of the work, that is of man and man's creation of himself in his "society," his state, his politics) diagnosed by de Man via his reading of Kleist's rewriting of Schiller.

The point I would make is that, while Elias' critique of the traditional model of inside versus outside (and indeed of the ideal of the "inner self") is altogether valid—that model being conceptually inadequate and in fact solidary with the fundamentally monistic concept of "nature"—his critique would dispense not only with the inadequate metaphor but with *any* conceptualization of *irreducible* disparity or conflict—as well as with the problem (or conceptualization) of metaphor—and that this makes for an inadequate notion of the social, as well as of the text. Instead of an alternative conceptualization of discontinuity or difference, what follows is a model—at once operative (it is Elias' methodology) and ideal (it is the "image of man" on which "work [should] begin" (p.259))—of society as a "figuration," as an (aesthetic) whole made up of interdependent parts. Like C's conception of the puppet theater, this model realizes the Schillerian ideal: culture once again becomes nature: "an image of numerous interdependent people forming figurations (i.e., groups or societies of different kinds) with each other. Seen from this basic standpoint, the rift in the traditional image of man disappears" (p.261).

Elias repeats the exemplary "modern" gesture of positing "the civilizing process," or modernization, as both a reality (of which phenomena of a conceptual order, such as scientific and philosophical epistemologies, are derived effects) and an ideal (to which man or society ought to conform). Classically "modern" too is this gesture's taking the form of a will to depart from an earlier and illusive version of the "modern": ". . . the theory of civilization which the following study attempts to develop helps us to see the misleading image of man in what we call the modern age as less self-evident, and to detach ourselves from it, so that work can begin on an image of man oriented less by one's own feelings and the value-judgments attached to them than by men as the actual objects of thought and observation" (p.259). This then is the culminating passage:

The concept of figuration has been introduced precisely because it expresses what we call "society" more clearly and unambiguously than the existing conceptual tools of sociology, as neither an abstraction of attributes of individuals existing without a society, nor a "system" or "totality" beyond individuals, but the network of interdependencies formed by individuals. . . . What is meant by the concept of figuration can be conveniently explained by reference to social dances. They are, in fact, the simplest example that could be chosen. One should think of a mazurka, a minuet, a polonaise, a tango, or rock 'n' roll. The image of the mobile figurations of interdependent people on a dance floor perhaps makes it easier to imagine states, cities, families, and also capitalist, communist, and feudal systems as figurations. By using this concept we can eliminate the antithesis, resting finally on different values and ideals, immanent today in the use of the words "individual" and "society." One can certainly speak of a dance in general, but no one will imagine a dance as a structure outside the individual or as a mere abstraction. The same dance figurations can certainly be danced by different people; but without a plurality of reciprocally oriented and dependent individuals, there is no dance. . . . Just as the small dance figurations change—becoming now slower, now quicker—so too, gradually or more suddenly, do the large figurations which we call societies. The following study is concerned with such changes. Thus, the starting point of the study of the process of state formation is a figuration made up of numerous relatively small social units existing in free competition with one another. The investigation shows how and why this figuration changes. It demonstrates at the same time that there are explanations which do not have the character of causal explanations. For a change in a figuration is explained partly by the endogenous dynamic of the figuration itself, the immanent tendency of a figuration of freely competing units to form monopolies. . . . At the same time, it indicates how the personality structure of human beings also change in conjunction with such figurational changes. (pp.262–3)

Two questions that do not come into play in such an account: Yeats's question, or de Man's:

*O body swayed to music, O brightening glance,
How can we know the dancer from the dance?*

(From chapter one of *Allegories of Reading*: "It is equally possible . . . to read the last line literally rather than figuratively, as asking

with some urgency the question . . . since the two essentially different elements, sign and meaning, are so intricately intertwined in the imagined 'presence' that the poem addresses [as in the symbol of the dance elaborated by Elias], how can we possibly make the distinctions that would shelter us from the error of identifying what cannot be identified?" (AR, p.11)—a question in which "the game itself" (RR, p.283) —politics, and language—is at stake.)

And Marx's question (or in another way, Freud's; and in another way, variously related to them both, one's question as a feminist): what about the *conflict* of ideals and interests involved in that "antithesis, resting finally on different values and ideals," which Elias supposes can be "eliminated"? Elias' text closes with the wish that the ideas introduced will afford his reader (aesthetic) "pleasure" in serving to "facilitate and deepen the understanding" offered by his book (p.263).

Elias' investment in modernization and "the civilizing process" may have to do with the historical circumstances of the writing of his book, which was first published in 1939. It may be related to a certain understanding of Nazism—via a distinction evoked in the opening chapters between "Civilization" and "Kultur," which seems to be carrying with it an implicit interpretation of Nazism, viz., as succeeding upon the German ideal of *Kultur,* rather than the French and English one of "civilization." I am led to hazard this inference not only by the way in which Elias' historical and philological distinction becomes a value judgment informing his choice of subject and methodology, but by my sense that the discrepancy through which Dahrendorf (in *Society and Democracy in Germany*) seeks to discuss the possibility of Nazi domination is essentially congruent with or derivative from Elias' distinction between *Kultur* and *Civilization*. To try to describe and understand the conditions and qualities that may have contributed to the possibility of the death camps, Dahrendorf (in a chapter entitled "Humanistic Theory and Practical Inhumanity: An Excursus") has recourse to a distinction between Germans' sense of "private values"—all too highly developed—and their practice of "public virtues"—traditionally, for the Germans in contrast to the British, according to Dahrendorf, minimal or nil. Dahrendorf and Elias would have in common, then, a conception of Nazism as a barbarism to be understood in terms of the insufficient development in Germany of the civilizing process or the process of modernization, and of the inability of the ideal of "Kultur" (a form of "humanistic theory," to quote from Dahrendorf's title) to defend against political and social barbarism ("practical inhumanity"). If de Man cannot follow Elias or Dahrendorf in this line of thought, it is because of the incisive critique, not only of the ideal of culture, but of the ideal of civilization (of the process of aesthetic formalization) he derives through a reading of the speculative philosophical tradition including Kleist and Hölderlin; and because of the fact that it is texts of that tradition—precisely that of *Kultur,* not simply of "civilization"—that provide the critique and an alternative conceptual framework: that of a difference or disparity situated, not between subject and object or the individual and society, but within discourse, within texts, within the process of reading, between "meaning and the *process* of signification."

14. De Man, "Tentation de la permanence," *Monde nouveau* 93 (October 1955), pp.49–61; translated by Dan Latimer as "The Temptation of Permanence," *Southern Humanities Review* 17:3 (1983), pp.209–21.

15. I argue the significance of de Man's relation to romanticism in "Remembering Forgetting: De Man's Romanticism," paper for Center for Literary Studies, Harvard University, March 1988, part of a projected book, *Romantic Theory.*

16. De Man, *Blindness and Insight,* pp.241–3, 245.

17. Once again, then, *a certain* separation of poetry from history, as in the July 14, 1942 review "A propos de la revue *Messages.*" History in one sense—the demands of the present, including the demand to be of the present or of history: to be "efficacious"—does not impinge upon poetry; poetry exists historically in another way. Cf. Maurice Blanchot, in a passage toward the end of one of the chapters of *L'Espace littéraire* ("La Communication") which de Man cites in his lecture:

La distance qui met l'oeuvre hors de notre portée et hors des atteintes du temps—là où elle périt dans l'immobilité de la gloire—l'expose aussi à toutes les aventures du temps, la montrant sans cesse en quête d'une nouvelle forme, d'un autre achèvement, complaisante à toutes les métamorphoses qui, la rattachant à l'histoire, semblent faire de son propre éloignement la promesse d'un avenir illimité. . . . ce qui se projettait dans l'intimité de l'oeuvre, tombant hors d'elle pour la maintenir et la figer dans une immobilité monumentale, se projette, à la fin, au dehors et fait de la vie intime de l'oeuvre ce qui ne peut plus s'accomplir qu'en s'étalant dans le monde et en se remplissant de la vie du monde et de l'histoire. (L'Espace littéraire *(Paris: Gallimard, 1955), pp.214–5)*

18. "Dr. Wilhelm Traugott Krug was Kant's successor in the latter's chair in philosophy" and married Kleist's fiancée Wilhelmine. "What could Kleist do but finish writing, in the same year 1805, a play to be called—what else could it have been—*Der zerbrochene Krug*?" (RR, pp.284–5).

19. A crucial discussion is Philippe Lacoue-Labarthe and Jean-Luc Nancy, *L'Absolu littéraire: Théorie de la littérature du romantisme allemand* (Paris: Seuil, 1978), translated by Philip Barnard and Cheryl

Lester as *The Literary Absolute* (Albany: SUNY Press, 1988). The theorization and practices of literature in the texts of Friedrich Schlegel, Novalis, Tieck, do not necessarily lead to German romantic ideology. The notion of "absolute irony," for instance, is not that of the autonomy of the subject.

20. It does matter, I think, that on the occasion of being offered a professorship in Comparative Literature at Yale, de Man told the delegate sent to make that offer of the existence of this article. De Man told Harold Bloom, in the course of their discussion, in Baltimore, in 1969, of his moving from Johns Hopkins to Yale, that during the war, in Belgium, he had written reviews and articles for a collaborationist newspaper, and that one of them was patently anti-Semitic. He said: Do you want to read it? I don't have a copy, but I could probably get you one if you want to read it. Bloom said: No, I don't want to read it. They then went on to other things.

On October 14, 1987, told of the existence of the articles in *Le Soir* by Carol Jacobs, who had been at the conference in Alabama that weekend where Derrida had made them known, Jonathan Culler and I saw Harold Bloom in Cambridge, where he was delivering the Norton Lectures. I said: "Harold, we have some bad news to share with you." He (leaning up against a wall for support): "My dear, what is it?" I said: "Nobody's died," then drew him into my office, and said: "It's emerged that in 1941 and '42, during the war, in Belgium, de Man wrote articles for a collaborationist newspaper." That single sentence; to which *he* said: "My God! I knew it. *He told me.* He was a baby; it was the poppa and the uncle." I stress that mine was the only statement of the facts that Bloom had heard—apart from de Man's own, therefore—at the point at which, shortly after the exchange I have quoted, he recounted to us de Man's having stated to him what he did, including, what I had said nothing of, the existence of an anti-Semitic article. I stress the point because I take it as significant—what this sequence proves— that de Man indeed said to Harold Bloom as the delegate of Yale: one of them was patently anti-Semitic. (I take it that de Man referred to precisely that article's existence, and not to any others in particular, as to the gravest fact.)

21. For a thesis about the novel similar to that in "Les juifs dans la littérature actuelle," see "Le Renouveau du roman, *Que votre volonté soit faite,* de Jacques Perrin et *Les Copains de la belle étoile,* de Marc Augier" (*Le Soir,* 27 January 1942), a more elaborated and complex argument which includes a consideration of Jean-Paul Sartre's position on the modern novel.

22. The text reads "ou ouvrant," a misprint for "où ouvraient," "in which there opened"?

23. So de Man writes with an irony connected with the argument spelled out in "The Resistance to Theory," roughly: theory, as formalization, is the resistance to theory as reading. See *The Resistance to Theory* (Minneapolis: University of Minnesota Press, 1985), pp.3–20.

24. See Lacoue-Labarthe and Nancy, *L'Absolu littéraire: Théorie de la littérature du romantisme allemand,* and Maurice Blanchot, "L'Athenaeum," in *L'Entretien infini* (Paris: Gallimard, 1969), translated by Deborah Esch and Ian Balfour, in *Des allemagnes,* ed. Jeffrey Mehlman, MLN 22:2, 163–72 (Summer 1983). Blanchot's text describes with extraordinary precision the stakes of Romanticism to which it seems to me de Man was responsive, beginning in the late thirties and early forties. "Romanticism in Germany and secondarily in France has been a political investment," Blanchot begins, "with extremely diverse vicissitdes": in Germany, claimed at different times by the most reactionary regimes and contrastingly, eg. by Dilthey, "as a demand for renovation"; after the war, condemned by Lukács as obscurantist, it meets with "similar abhorrence in France only among critics linked to an extreme right-wing school"; "Surrealism, by contrast, recognizes itself in its great poetic figures, and recognizes in them what it then discovers on its own: poetry, the power of absolute freedom." Such is the surrealism celebrated in "A propos de la revue *Messages*" and the genealogy asserted in "A propos de *Quelques visages du romantisme* par Paul Colin." Blanchot identifies with a certain early Romanticism, the brief existence of the *Athenaeum,* in six issues published between 1798 and 1800, the emergence of the consciousness of literature: the moment at which "literature (understood as the totality of forms of expression, including forces of dissolution as well) suddenly becomes conscious of itself." De Man's essay "Aesthetic Formalization" is a critical engagement with the Romanticism described by Blanchot thus: Hegel, he writes, "recognizes in romanticism proper only the dissolution of a movement, its mortal triumph, the moment of decline when art, turning against itself the principle of destruction at its center, coincides with its interminable and pitiful end." "Let us acknowledge that, from its beginning and well before Hegel's *Lectures on Aesthetics,* romanticism—and this is its greatest merit—is not unaware that this is its truth." And again (Blanchot's conclusion): "Literature, nonetheless, beginning to manifest itself to itself thanks to the romantic declaration, will henceforth entail this question—*discontinuity or difference as form*—a question and a task that German romanticism, particularly that of the *Athenaeum,* not only adumbrated but already clearly formulated before passing them on to Nietzsche and, beyond Nietzsche, to the future" (my italics).

25. "Novalis: Henri d'Ofterdingen," *Le Soir,* 9 June 1942; "Sur *Les Falaises de marbre* par Ernst Jünger," 31 March 1942 (cf. "*Jardins et routes,* par Ernst Jünger," 23 June 1942); "A propos de la revue *Messages,*" 14 July 1942; "A propos de *Quelques visages du romantisme* par Paul Colin," 21–2 November 1942.

26. "Le Roman française et le sentiment de la nature," *Le Soir,* 22 April 1941; "*Le Triomphe de la vie,* par Jean Giono," 24 March 1942; "Magie de l'enfance, *Hopje l'insaisissable,*" 19 May 1942; "*Philippe Doriot,* par Camille Melloy et *Par le monde qui change* de Pierre Daye," 3 February 1942.

27. One finds a nuanced discussion of how these qualities appear in Valéry, and a sober passion for their persistence, in "Paul Valéry et la poésie symboliste," *Le Soir,* 10–11 January 1942.

On Paul de Man's Collaborationist Writings

STANLEY CORNGOLD

"You have not enough respect for the written word and you are altering the story." . . . "You are the prison chaplain," said K.

I commend Werner Hamacher, Neil Hertz, and Tom Keenan for circulating the newspaper articles that Paul de Man wrote in 1941 and 1942. There is, however, something about the way they characterize these articles that I must reject immediately. They speak of "texts, chiefly on literary and cultural topics, [which] at times take up the themes and idiom of the discourse promulgated during the Occupation by the Nazis and their collaborators."[1] But it isn't "texts" that are at stake. Nor do texts by themselves enigmatically "take up" "themes and idioms." Such a way of putting things can only serve to veil rhetorically a moral event.[2]

In the perspective of Hamacher-Hertz-Keenan, de Man's texts in 1941–1942 merely repeated certain phrases from the speeches of Nazi hacks. But such a view of de Man's collaborationist writings takes for granted the very thing to be proved. It assumes the position that now needs most defending: namely, de Man's conception of the mere contingency of the personal intention vis-à-vis the literary work, and his way of endowing texts with the attributes of persons even while undertaking to unmask all anthropomorphizing strategies elsewhere.

It is this very claim of the irresponsibility of textual production that is jeopardized by the early pieces, which were written by an actual person, Paul de Man, and flow from a moral choice. That an authorial personality needs to vanish in order for texts to come about is a familiar article of de Man's theory. But in Belgium and in post-War America, de Man evidently did not want to vanish. He was determined to constitute and preserve himself as the moral personality he had been, by writing. If anything was supposed to vanish, it would have been his wartime journalism, since its public disclosure would have given his "second birth" a quick quietus.

The evidence of de Man's collaboration urgently raises two questions. The first is a matter of historical reconstruction. What were de Man's intentions at the time he wrote his anti-Semitic and collaborationist articles? The second is the question concerning de Man's subsequent literary-critical writings and the change which these disclosures will produce in the way readers will read his work.

We should know from the start the kind of work we are dealing with. I quote from an article in *Le Soir* published on March 4, 1941; it is entitled "The Jews in Contemporary Literature." In the matter of the novel, writes de Man,

Jewish writers [in France] have always been second rate. . . . This finding (*constation*) is comforting for Western intellectuals: that they have been able to safeguard themselves from Jewish influence in a domain as representative of culture as literature proves their vitality. There would not have been much hope for the future of our civilization if it had allowed itself to be invaded without resistance by a foreign force. In keeping its originality and character intact, despite the Semitic meddling into all aspects of European life, it has shown that its nature was healthy at the core. Furthermore, one sees therefore that a solution to the Jewish question which envisages the creation of a Jewish colony isolated from Europe would not lead to deplorable consequences for the literary life of the West. It would lose, all told, a few personalities of mediocre value and would continue, as in the past, to develop according to its own great evolutionary principles.[3]

In *The London Review of Books* of February 4, 1988, Christopher Norris explained that de Man's articles "contain many passages that can be read as endorsing what amounts to a collaborationist line" (my italics). This is a plain enfeeblement of passages like the one quoted above, and Geoffrey Hartman's piece in *The New Republic* (March 7, 1988) does not do much better in this respect. For example, Hartman singles out an essay in which de Man describes Hitler as bringing about a "definite emancipation of a people called upon to exercise, in its turn, a hegemony in Europe." The article, says Hartman, shows de Man moving "closer to being explicitly collaborationist" (28). This could prompt one to ask what it would take to occupy an *explicitly* collaborationist position.[4] According to Norris, one should "read Paul de Man's earliest essays as a *search for some conceivable way forward* from the stark and appalling reality of the Nazi occupation" (my italics.) Yet de Man refers acquiescently to the Nazi occupation as "the contemporary revolution" (*Het Vlaamsche Land,* March 29-30, 1942) and asserts that "the necessity of action which is present in the form of immediate collaboration is obvious to every objective mind." Furthermore, what de Man literally wrote about the occupation was not that it was "appalling" but that it "creates a troubled climate in which the best and the worst, the noblest commitments and the worst forms of *arrivisme,* go together" (*Le Soir,* October 14, 1941).

De Man's position in his pieces is not "perhaps" readable as a position "amounting to" collaborationist; however suavely put, it is collaborationist. He invites from the public an informed reading of Nazi political tracts to counterbalance French and English propaganda; discusses the "decency, justice, and humanity" of the Nazi attitude toward France after its capitulation (*Le Soir,* April 12, 13, and 14, 1941); finds "a very beautiful and original poetry" flourishing "in the fascist climate" in Italy, in accord with the wishes of Mussolini (*Le Soir,* February 11, 1941); and identifies the German soul with the "Hitlerian," lest there be any doubt on this point. This particular description

of the German spirit, which Geoffrey Hartman referred to above, deserves fuller citation:

Germany is a *Volk* (*peuple*) . . . heavy with a host of aspirations, values, and claims coming to it from an ancestral culture and civilization. The War will only bring about a tighter union of these two things—the Hitlerian soul and the German soul which, from the start, were so close together—until they have been made one single and unique power. This is an important phenomenon, because it means that one cannot judge the fact of Hitler without judging at the same time the fact of Germany and that the future of Europe can be envisioned only in the frame of the needs and possibilities of the German spirit. It is not a matter only of a series of reforms but of the definitive emancipation of a *Volk* (*peuple*) which finds itself called upon to exercise, in its turn, a hegemony in Europe. (*Le Soir,* October 28, 1941)

For this "cause . . . an entire *Volk* (*peuple*) is sacrificing itself" (*Le Soir,* August 20, 1942).

To the all-important second question, "Ought knowledge of de Man's political past bear on our understanding of his literary-critical writings?" the answer, practically speaking, is that it is no longer possible not to think so. That is, at least in part, because Christopher Norris and Geoffrey Hartman have produced apologetic theories about the connection between de Man's earlier and later writings. For Norris, one could "view the entire subsequent production as an attempt to exorcise the bad memory, to adopt a critical standpoint squarely opposed to that mystified philosophy of language, tradition, and organic national culture." Hartman says, "De Man's critique of every tendency to totalize literature or language, to see unity where there is no unity, looks like a belated, but still powerful, act of conscience."

Anything in de Man's later writing could look the way these critics want it to, but too much in it looks different to me. Rather than a definitive change suggested by concepts like exorcism or renunciation, I see in the later works certain elaborations of de Man's beginnings. In the following remarks, I shall discuss a few possible connections between the earlier and the later works.

* * *

The late work is marked by a recurrent and major tone of arbitrary violence. De Man's essay on Rousseau's *Confessions* in *Allegories of Reading* (his wildest essay, and now we may be able to understand why) declares: "Writing always includes the moment of dispossession in favor of the arbitrary power play of the signifier; and from the point of view of the subject, this can only be experienced as a dismemberment, a beheading, or a castra-tion" (AR 296). This sentence is so much simply an instance of a habit and preoccupation, of a subject matter and an intellectual procedure, that I believe it represents a fascination or even com-plicity with violence. Another passage: "With the threatening loss of control [of the signifier], the possibility arises of the en-tirely gratuitous and irresponsible text, not just . . . as an inten-tional denial of paternity for the sake of self-protection, but as the radical annihilation of the metaphor of selfhood and of the will" (AR 296). This idea reappears in his and his students' studies of Romantic poetry, which profile "defaced" and "de-composing" figures of selfhood and of the will.

It is best, perhaps, for de Man's later critical work (in light of his article supporting the deportation of Jews) if readers have not seen Lanzmann's film *Shoah.* The surviving Jews of Chelmno, who were made to disinter the decomposing corpses of other Jews gassed by the Nazis, were beaten while doing so by Nazi guards because they called these bodies "Menschen" (human beings) or "Opfer" (sacrifices). Their guards insisted they refer to the corpses as *Dreck* ("filth") or *Figuren* ("pup-pets," "shapes," also "figures of speech"). In *Blindness and In-sight* de Man wrote the notorious epigram: "texts masquerade in the guise of wars or revolutions" (BI 165)—meaning that rev-olutions are, for all that we can know of them, basically texts. Genocide, too, could basically be a text, and the persons rotting beneath the ground, for all we could know of them, basically figures.

I stress that the persons whose real decomposition de Man's early hackwork may have helped bring about appear in his later writing as only the masks of a rigorous literary operation—ob-jects of "coercive displacements" that occur, to be sure, only "tropologically" (AR 163). What Nazis and their collaborators once accomplished in fact, literature is seen as accomplishing figuratively. But the figurative text also displaces fact, so that "death," for example, becomes "a displaced name for a linguis-tic predicament" (RR 81) and textual events become essential historical occurrences. "Things happen in the world . . . and they always happen in linguistic terms. . . . To account for them historically, *to account for them in any sense,* a certain initial dis-crepancy in language has to be examined" (RT 101, my italics).

What de Man went on to write about figures in *Allegories of Reading* did not make it easier for Nazis to torment their vic-tims. And yet he consistently taught that the reality of persons is found in the "disarticula-tion" of rhetoric and emphasized the obligatory "dismemberment of the aesthetic whole into the un-predictable play of the literary letter" (RT 70). De Man's later theory submits so-called persons to the coercions of rhetoric

with the same effect produced by his literary judgments when they smoothed out the moral obstacles in the way of eliminat-ing Jewish personalities. Early and late, De Man has no stake whatsoever in the survival of persons—figurative or authorial. And the analogy is more than figurative when de Man literally displaces figures onto the world of real persons. This is the con-sequence of his steadfast belief in the necessity of a superself called "poetic consciousness" or "literary language" or "text" to develop or occur according to its own great laws independent of its effect on the moral relations between persons and the lives of persons.

In his later work, de Man's rare acts of attention to the rela-tion of literature and empirical reality continue to put the mat-ter in terms of a one-way effect. For example, "literature has had an immense impact on life. . . . Fictional narratives are . . . part of the world and of reality; their impact upon the world may well be all too strong for comfort" (RT 11). But there is no sug-gestion that literary texts arise or could arise responsibly out of the experience of their makers. What "characterizes the work of literature in its essence" is "its separation from empirical reality" (BI 17). "Considerations of the actual and historical existence of writers are a waste of time from a critical viewpoint" (BI 35). "Mimesis becomes just one trope among others. . . ." (RT 10).

Hence, for that fragile environment in which persons live and work and have their experience—what is called empirical reality—de Man usually reserves scorn or irony. I will give a few examples. In *Blindness and Insight,* de Man speaks of "the du-plicity, the confusion, the untruth *that we take for granted* in the everyday use of language" (my italics, BI 9). Quite forgetting Tolstoi's sense of "the miraculousness of the ordinary," we are required to define the everyday as a domain of irremediable fal-sity. Here, for example, "the direct expression of desire" is im-possible. Here, too, the associated question of articulating and interpreting "ethically shameful desires" is by contrast an only "very simple problem." That is because it arises, presumably, from the categorical confusion of ineluctable error with mere shortcoming or mistake. What produces the distorted expres-sion of any human desire is always the radical falseness of an empirical reality that can never be the source of a literature wor-thy of its name. Hence, the pointlessness of attempting to elab-orate or explain personal experience in autobiographical writing, for "autobiography veils a defacement of the mind of which it is itself the cause" (RR 81)—note well: *it,* and not the mind's experience. The ethical issue is not properly one of cour-age and rigor but rather of unavoidable error. The expression of shameful desires could never acquire the truthful status of a his-torical "occurrence," which consists only in "the recognition of the true nature of that error"—namely, the primordial error of an inhuman linguistic predicament (RT 104).

I conclude from the remarks above and many like them that de Man is a great philosopher of the inhuman condition. This is, as he tirelessly repeats, a condition in which the important relations are necessarily inhuman. It is no individual poet but "poetic language" that engages "in its highest intent, . . . tending toward the fullest possible self-understanding." "Poetic language names this void [of empirical reality] with ever-renewed understanding and . . . never tires of naming it again" (BI, 31). Not the writer but "the text imposes its own understanding and shapes the reader's evasions" (DH 5). Here, the viewpoint and rhetoric is entirely in keeping with de Man's in 1942, when he wrote that "the development [of literary style] does not depend on arbitrary, personal decisions but is connected to forces which perform their relentless operations across the doings of individuals" (*Het Vlaamsche Land,* June 7–8, 1942).

All these rigorous and relentless texts and mechanisms suggest the "unconscious artist," the artist-type who has "the ability to organize." The source for this way of thinking is Nietzsche: "Wherever [such artists] appear, something new soon arises, a ruling structure that lives, in which parts and functions are delimited and co-ordinated, in which nothing whatever finds a place that has not first been assigned a 'meaning' in relation to the whole."[5] This is Nietzsche's description of that "creation and imposition of forms" instituting the first "state," which happens to be the work of "the blond beasts." In assigning to texts the properties of persons who kill, disfigure, mutilate, entrap, and constrain readers, no doubt for their own good, de Man conjures an heroic personality beyond Good and Evil of the type of Nietzsche's New Man as he was received in de Man's youth by George, by d'Annunzio, by Benn. Though literature is supposed to originate from the non-empirical transcendental poetic consciousness (*Blindness and Insight,* 1971) and the non-empirical mechanisms of literary language (*Allegories of Reading,* 1979), it operates like a type of reckless person or implacable machine. Moreover, its attributes will be recognizeable as those of the Nietzschean self of which, in his youth, de Man believed "the Hitlerian soul" and its collaborators to be the avatar.

A final word about the ethical implications of the deconstructive view in De Man. If it were indeed as bare of moral implication as some people have held it to be—if, in alleging the inhumanity of language (in poetry and even in its own system), the deconstructionist view proved the impossibility of representing moral intentions and drove out moral awareness from

literary criticism—then the disclosure of de Man's collaborationist writings in 1941–1942 would be only trivially upsetting. De Man's theory of language would have been revealed as unconsciously self-serving, because designed to exculpate him in advance. As a writer, he could then be charged with ignorance as to his real intentions; but by the same token he would be excused as one who after all had never excluded himself—*as a writer, as a being constituted through acts of writing*—from ignorance of his empirical interests and from the possibility, entirely contingent for an author, that his text might turn out to be personally useful. After all: "Far from [our] seeing language as an instrument in the service of a psychic energy, the possibility . . . arises that the entire construction of drives, substitutions, repressions, and representations is the aberrant, metaphorical correlative of the absolute randomness of language, prior to any figuration or meaning." (AR 299)

But all this is contrary to fact. For de Man's deconstructionist discourse has always itself employed a moralizing rhetoric: if language is unreliable, it is at once the "highest," the most "rigorous" of powers. To understand the deconstructionist perspective is necessarily to rise to a consciousness of rigor not even hinted at in intersubjective experience. It is to consent to live with an unheard-of minimum of wishful thinking.

At the same time, it is hard to escape the conclusion that, throughout his life in the United States, de Man was thinking wishfully that he would not be called into the open forum to defend his politics; and all that time he was hiding—as the rigorous literary sensibility never hides—the experience of a frustrated and defeated consciousness in the mask of the beautiful soul. De Man knew that he was asking of literary language or of criticism a rigor from which he had exempted himself. In light of the "contingent" findings of soldiers breaking open the gates of Auschwitz and Bergen-Belsen in 1945, de Man could not own up that his work might have contributed in whatever degree to all the forces at work in Europe which, if they could have gone their way without opposition, would have prevented such disclosures forever.

In speaking of de Man's consciousness as "frustrated and defeated," I use words which he himself assigned to the deluded projections of critics for whom "the so-called 'idealism' of literature is . . . an idolatry, a fascination with a false image that mimics the presumed attributes of authenticity when it is in fact just the hollow mask with which a frustrated, defeated consciousness tries to cover up its own negativity" (BI 12). I believe that just because of his political frustrations, de Man, too, was subject to the temptations of idolatry. He saw fit to say of Heidegger's misreadings of Hölderlin as a religious thinker that

Heidegger had to invent this Hölderlin who had experienced Being because he needed at least one other witness-bearer to justify his own enterprise as ontologist. Similarly, de Man appears to have required at least one other witness-bearer of the possibility of a moral heroism Beyond Good and Evil—and that hero is "literature." So he invests the text-personality with the morally distinctive attributes of the Nietzschean hero and moralist, the "new philosopher," whose goal is "to prepare great ventures and over-all attempts of discipline and cultivation by way of putting an end to that gruesome dominion of nonsense and accident that has so far been called 'history'. . . ."[6] Here, too, I believe, is one focus of de Man's appeal to students: he was inviting into existence, among souls chained to the workbench of paper-writing, matter-of-fact rhetorical moods of violence, superiority, and dismissiveness.

It must have been ironical for de Man to find himself publicly under attack, on trial, at the end of his life, not for his former politics but for a radical doctrine of "deconstruction." Indeed, the situation must have been strangely gratifying, because it was made up of many elements of the very scene he had dreaded all along. But whereas in that situation he would have been on trial without excuse, in this instance he could evoke the truth, the difficult truth, the rigorous and unavoidable truth of nihilism. "Understand by nihilism," he wrote, claiming to paraphrase Walter Benjamin, "a certain kind of critical awareness which will not allow you to make certain affirmative statements when those affirmative statements go against the way things are" (RT 104). But de Man's life, as it has come to light, succeeds in destroying his right to such a position. For when he allowed himself to affirm "a distinctively literary mode of totalization" (BI 33) as well as "the estrangement and falsification of everyday existence" (BI 45), he was hiding from his readers the knowledge that these statements did not go against "the way things are" but actually helped protect his past. To repeat them keeps alive features of the very idolatry which had once inspired his delusions.

Princeton University

ABBREVIATIONS

AR   *Allegories of Reading: Figural Language in Rousseau, Nietzsche, Rilke, and Proust* (New Haven: Yale University Press, 1979).

BI   *Blindness and Insight: Essays in the Rhetoric of Contemporary Criticism*, 2nd ed. rev. (Minneapolis, Minn.: University of Minnesota Press, 1983).

DH   "Introduction," Carol Jacobs, *The Dissimulating Harmony: The Image of Interpretation in Nietzsche, Rilke, Artaud, and Benjamin* (Baltimore: Johns Hopkins University Press, 1978).

RR   *The Rhetoric of Romanticism* (New York: Columbia University Press, 1984).

RT   *The Resistance of Theory* (Minneapolis, Minn.: University of Minnesota Press, 1986).

NOTES

1. Letter dated November 24, 1987.

2. Here we can see the enigma being *created*. The "taking up" of Nazi idioms by texts is offered as an irreducible catachresis—an expression that, like "the eye" of a needle, seems figurative although it is actually literal because no other term exists for it that is any more literal. With regard to de Man's work, or anyone else's, this view is false. Paul de Man wrote these articles.

3. Some commentators have attempted to mollify the ugliness of this essay because it contains a remark favorable to a writer called "Kafha." In this piece, de Man undertakes to distinguish the contribution of second-rate Jewish novelists from a genuine modern tradition based on the curious reading list "Gide, Kafha, D.H. Lawrence, Hemingway." Yes, it is true that all the names are in some sense deviant, and if de Man had preferred to write literary history in the manner of a Julius Peterson or a Hermann Pongs, he could have selected writers more obviously racially pure. But de Man's essay "Le Roman anglais contemporain," written a year before, makes clear the source of this quartet. It is taken from a list in Aldous Huxley's *Music at Night* that cites as the modern masters "Proust, D.H. Lawrence, A. Gide, Kafka, Hemingway." In his article in *Le Soir,* de Man is truly "taking up" Huxley's reading list in a way that is neither inventive nor subversive.

I emphasize, furthermore, that Huxley's list of the genuine makers of modern literature contains a name which de Man has not bothered to cite—that is "Proust."

4. This way of framing the matter I borrow from David Bromwich.

5. *Basic Writings of Nietzsche,* Walter Kaufmann, tr. and ed. (New York: Modern Library, 1966), pp.522–523.

6. Ibid., p.203.

Paul de Man and the Collaborationist Press

ELS DE BENS

If an assessment of the role that Paul de Man played is to be founded on a scientific basis, one will have to give an outline of the Belgian press during the German occupation. In consequence, the present paper, which draws on the author's doctoral dissertation *De Belgische dagbladpers onder Duitse censuur 1940–1944* (*The Belgian daily press under German censorship 1940–1944*) (Antwerp, 1973, 564 pp.), will successively deal with the press regime imposed by the German occupiers, the way the censorship operated, the variety of Belgian papers, the varying degrees in which the different press organs collaborated with the Germans, and finally a detailed account will be given of the contribution that de Man made to two newspapers, *Le Soir* and *Het Vlaamsche Land*.

1.1 *The German institutions involved in the "Lenkung" of the Belgian press*

As soon as the Germans invaded Belgium, they sought to reorganize the news media as quickly as possible. Even before the capitulation of the Belgian army, two prewar newspapers received the Germans' backing to re-enter the market. Since Belgium had a military administration (*Militärverwaltung* or MV) until July 1944, the organization and control of the press was left to the *Wehrmacht,* not to the SS. Within the *Militärverwaltung,* it was the *Propaganda Abteilung* (PA) which controlled the media and the cultural sector.

Goebbels was very much displeased that the mass media in occupied Belgium came under the Wehrmacht instead of under the *Promi* (the usual name given to the *Propagandaministerium*), itself an abbreviation for *Reichsministerium für Volksaufklärung und Propaganda*). Still, Goebbels's people managed to interfere in various ways, so much so that the press system as a whole was increasingly influenced by Promi. Besides, the structure and the operation of the PA was copied from that of Promi. The directives given by Goebbels to the press in the form of his *Tagesparole* were passed on by the PA to the mass media. Promi also took in hand the restructuring of *Belga,* the prewar news agency. Towards the end of the occupation, Promi became increasingly obtrusive as the SS was extending its power at the expense of the Wehrmacht. Eventually, when Belgium came under civilian (i.e. SS) administration (the so-called *Zivilverwaltung,* July 1944), the Wehrmacht lost what power it had and the PA became an integral part of Promi.

It was not Goebbels alone who strove for a position of power within the PA: the *Ministry for Foreign Affairs* too felt that it should have a say in setting the media policy in occupied territories. Moreover, the Foreign Minister, von Ribbentrop, claimed for his own ministry the right to cover any news relating to foreign affairs. Hitler complied, adopting as always the divide-and-rule principle. The feud between Goebbels and von Ribbentrop over the control of foreign news coverage in the media of the occupied countries was re-enacted in Belgium, with the press department of the German embassy claiming a say in the PA's press policy.

From Berlin, the PA came under pressure, and the head of the press department of the German embassy in Brussels, Dr. Liebe, was able to obtain the permission for a representative of the Ministry of Foreign Affairs to also issue directives at the PA's daily press conference (where journalists were given directives, as will be explained below).

Furthermore, the editorial staff of the newspapers were the beneficiaries of a steady flow of miscellaneous material from the German embassy: ready-made articles, pictures, drawings, etc. Also, a number of newspapers (e.g. *Le Soir*) were given financial support by the Ministry of Foreign Affairs.

Other bodies that tried to encroach on the PA's territory were the *Germanische Leitstelle* (SS) and the *Abteilung III* of the *Sicherheitsdienst*; however, as things turned out their activities remained confined to a small number of newspapers. The Germanische Leitstelle used its abundant financial resources to win certain press organs over to the SS cause. The Abteilung III mainly focussed on spying on a number of journalists, and during the postwar press trials some journalists were found to have been in the pay of the Abteilung III of the Sicherheitsdienst.

Yet, in spite of all the meddling from Promi, Foreign Affairs, Abteilung III of the SD, and the Germanische Leitstelle of the SS, the PA still played a crucial role in the media and in setting cultural policy. In fact, the PA had three chief assignments: to organize information (daily and weekly papers, radio and film news), to design and implement an active propaganda strategy (brochures, leaflets, posters, etc.), and to redirect (*lenken*) cultural and social life as a whole, i.e. to sensitize public opinion to what the "new order" stood for.

In view of the subject of the present paper, it is mainly the PA's actions with regard to the daily and weekly press which are of primary importance. It was the PA which granted publication licenses, which set up the censorship system, which determined the distribution system, which allocated newsprint and which imposed sanctions on the "disobedient" press.

1.2 *The press regime in occupied Belgium*

The media policy as adopted by the PA followed in the main the strategies laid down by Goebbels, which were based on the concept of *Gleichschaltung*: the content of the media was to be made as uniform as possible in order to promulgate in all places and at all times one invariable message, that of national socialism. Goebbels thought, quite rightly, that "repetition" of the national socialist beliefs and slogans would have a cumulative effect in the long run. Of course, the concept of *Gleichschaltung* implied that no media could function uncontrolled. Indeed, Hitler had stamped all forms of freedom of the press as *eine tödliche Gefahr für jeden Staat* (a mortal danger for any state).[1] Every line in the newspaper, the political, business, cultural and regional news, the sports coverage, even the advertisements were to be imbued with the new teachings.[2] Furthermore, the national socialists held firmly that the media should be keyed to the level of the masses, in other words that they should use black-and-white techniques and be brief, simple and emotional. Hitler had pointed out in *Mein Kampf* that the intellectual level of the average citizen is very limited, so that *aus diesen Tatsachen heraus hat sich jede wirkungsvolle Propaganda auf nur sehr wenigen Punkte zu beschränken* (it follows that effective propaganda must confine itself to a very small number of issues).[3]

And indeed, the national socialists were masters at "simplification." Goebbels noted in his diary that "propaganda must always be extremely simple and repetitive. In the long run, only he will achieve a fundamental impact on public opinion who knows how to reduce problems to their simplest forms, and who has the courage of repeating them in these simplified forms in the face of the objections voiced by the intellectuals."[4]

Analyses of the newspapers published in Belgium under the German occupation confirm this trend towards "oversimplification".

The pursuit of *Gleichschaltung* and the attempt to convince public opinion meant that the censor's instructions were used to paint a rosy picture of events in the Third Reich. However, glossing over, and often hiding the truth, also resulted in the decreased credibility of the censored press, particularly in the occupied countries. There it was hard indeed to cut off the clandestine information flowing in from the allied camp. As a result the PA found it very difficult to achieve *Gleichschaltung* in Belgium.

The first important step was to issue a decree or *Verordnung* (14 June 1940) that all papers and periodicals were to apply for an official permission to be published. The purpose of this measure, according to the *Tätigkeitsbericht* of the MV, was "not to lose a comprehensive view" (*um den Überblick nicht zu verlieren*),[5] and hence it was a convenient means for implementing a policy of *centralization*. More applications were sent in than had been expected, and the PA was forced to refuse about half of them. Eventually, 27 dailies (before the occupation: 62) and 600 periodicals (before the occupation: 2,500) were given a publication licence.[6] The application was mandatory, and the assertion made by certain publishers that they came on the market without the Germans' official permission is completely unfounded.

In the course of 1943 the PA was to issue two more decrees, under the pretext of paper shortage, seizing the opportunity to impose a publication ban on recalcitrant newspapers.

But *Gleichschaltung* was achieved much more efficiently by means of *censorship*.

Initially, the Germans had imposed a particularly rigid censorship system, notably *preventive censorship,* which implied that everything that was going to be published had to be submitted to the PA censors first. Such a system proved to be unworkable in the 20th century, because the censors were not able to check the huge mass of information in time. The passages deleted by them often could not be replaced with new copy, and blank spaces would constantly remind the reader of the presence of censorship. As early as 10 October, 1940, the Germans switched to a more practical formula: *a-posteriori censorship.* The editors were now snowed under with the German instructions coming from *Belgapress,* a news agency controlled by the occupying forces. In addition, the PA organized a weekly press conference, to which all the newspapers were required to send a representative and where the Germans made their wishes and demands clear to the assembled press. A journalist who went against the German instructions was punished with sanctions ranging from a mere warning to a fine, suspension from his work or imprisonment.

However it may be, the switchover to a-posteriori censorship entailed more freedom of action for the Belgian journalists.[7] The press now presented a livelier picture, since more variation became possible. Some newspapers actually engaged in hot debates on delicate issues, such as the future destiny of Belgium, of Flanders and of Wallonia. These were precisely the subjects that the Germans had put under taboo, because Berlin had prohibited any discussion of what the future had in store for Belgium. In the end, the PA was forced to reintroduce preventive censorship on all matters relating to domestic affairs (August 1942).[8] Journalists who contributed articles to the censored press after August 1942 must have realized that the Germans no longer allowed them any freedom of action. It is important, therefore, to note here that Paul de Man did not write any articles after the end of 1942!

In brief, the bulk of the *censorship instructions* consisted of "directives" and a set of sanctions if the directives were disobeyed.

The instructions were issued by two different ways: the PA press conferences and the news agency. The PA press conferences were held twice a week and were to be attended by a journalist representing his newspaper[9] and by the radio services.

The directives issued at the press conference were drawn up in the same invariable order: first the PA directives, next the *Tagesparole* of Promi, and finally the instructions from the German embassy. Moreover, the whole press conference was transmitted to all media institutions via the telexes of Belgapress.[10]

Indeed, Belgapress played a crucial role in the policy of *Gleichschaltung.* The PA had seized the news agency Belga, and thanks to the material and technical assistance of DNB and a number of Belgians who were willing to work for the Germans the agency could resume its activities very quickly. The PA found the news agency an indispensable instrument, because its telexes provided the best way of transmitting the daily instructions. In addition, it enabled the Germans to achieve full control of the flow of information, for no other foreign agency (apart from DNB, of course) could provide information.

As to the instructions that the PA transmitted via Belgapress, four groups can be distinguished:
— a request or an order for insertion or for comment;
— a ban on insertion or comment;
— a request to publish fully completed articles;
— extra-directives from the economic service.[11]

Many of these directives were lost at the end of the occupation because the PA ordered everything to be burnt. Still, the remaining material does point out clearly that the PA sometimes went as far as to insist on even the slightest detail. Instructions were given, for example, on the place where a particular article was to be printed (page, title and typeface to be used, position of the picture, etc.), the descriptive words to be used, and so on. The negative result of this kind of *Gleichschaltung* is homogeneous and monotonous uniformity.

By and large, the journalists complied with these instructions (self-censorship!), for few sanctions had to be imposed. Such sanctions as were given were mainly confined to admonitions, fines and brief suspension from work; very rarely were journalists sent to prison.

Besides, the PA could also resort to *indirect pressure.* The allocation of newsprint, for example, was a very practical means for exercising pressure. Newspapers which did not prove to be very docile were put on a very meager ration of newsprint. Such a measure was not only disastrous from the editorial point of view, it also affected the paper's revenue from advertising.[12]

The PA was also instrumental in restructuring the former *Algemene Belgische Persbond* (General Belgian Press League) into the *Vereniging van Belgische Journalisten* (Association of Belgian Journalists) in March 1942. The new Association's structure was copied from that of the *Reichsverband Deutscher Journalisten*. The publishers were obliged by the PA to employ as full-time journalists only those who were members of the Association.[13]

At the ceremony marking the foundation of the Association, P. Colin made a speech to the journalists present, stating unambiguously that the new professional association backed the national socialist cause: "Vous êtes le Front de l'Intérieur, vous combattez comme nos frères qui combattent au Front de l'Est . . . (You constitute the Home Front, you fight the enemy just like our brothers who are fighting on the Eastern Front)."[14] Being a casual contributor, Paul de Man was never a member of the Association.

In order to facilitate its control over the circulation, the sale and the distribution of the papers, the PA gave a distribution monopoly to the Dechenne agency, which was in charge of the distribution of newspapers throughout the occupation.[15] The papers were forbidden to use their own channels of distribution.[16] A letter from the PA to the distribution agency states in no uncertain terms that "the agency has a propagandist function . . . and the general management must look after the interest of the Third Reich."[17] After discontinuing his journalistic activities Paul de Man worked in this distribution agency (see below).

2. Survey of the Belgian "collaborator press"[18]

2.1 The re-introduction of the daily press

After issuing its *Verordnung* of 14 June 1940, the PA received many applications. As early as October 1940 24 dailies were on the market, i.e. about one third of the prewar number, but their overall circulation equalled that of before the war: in 1939 the overall number of copies stood at 1,560,000, and in November-December 1940 it was 1,472,290.[19] Considering that the number of papers had been reduced to one third and that the overall circulation remained roughly the same as before the war, most newspaper publishers must have made a handsome profit during the war.

2.2 Belgian journalists and their motives for contributing to the "collaborator press"

That the dailies could be published again so soon after the Germans had taken over, was largely due to the great willingness of Belgian journalists to contribute to the wartime press.

There is a variety of motives which made the journalists "collaborate" with the occupying forces. The German victory of May 1940, the King's appeal for general resumption of work, and the fear of being out of a job were no doubt the major incentives for many journalists to return to their work.

Yet quite a number of them hesitated to do so and first sought the advice of eminent personalities from aristocratic, political, judicial and clerical circles. Among these dignitaries there were several who recommended a policy of attendance: they felt it was preferable to resume work as a journalist rather than leave the newspaper to extremists, who would then put it on the market as a "stolen" publication.

There were also opportunists among those who were willing to resume work, as well as confirmed advocates of the new order. But it is a fact that the phenomenon of collaborating with the enemy emerged in all ideological and political groups. Not only were collaborating journalists found in the prewar antiparliamentary movements such as VNV, Verdinaso, and Rex, but also the traditional catholic, liberal and socialist camps proved to have journalists who were willing to contribute to the censored press.

Because of his background (his studies at the Université Libre de Bruxelles and his relationship with his uncle Hendrik de Man) Paul de Man belonged to the socialist intellectual circles which were found to be ready to collaborate with the wartime press.

2.3 "Old," "New" and "Stolen" Newspapers

As a rule, the newspapers published in Belgium during the occupation are classified in three groups: old, new, and stolen papers. However, this classification is rather rudimentary. Indeed, the term "old" newspapers includes not only those papers which continued to be published on the grounds of their ideological convictions, being adherents of the new order (for example *Volk en Staat* and *Le Pays Réel*), but also those papers which had adopted the policy of attendance (amongst others *Het Algemeen Belang*, alias *De Standaard*, *Het Nieuws van den Dag*, *De Dag*, *De Gentenaar-De Landwacht*). This category therefore comprises two extremes, adherents of collaborating groups as well as those who did not want to have anything to do with collaboration with the enemy.

In the category of "new" newspapers we find, of course, a very clear situation : the papers founded during the occupation could only be published in close cooperation with the Germans (*Het Vlaamsche Land*, *De Gazet*, *Le Nouveau Journal*, *Le Travail*, *La Légia* and *L'Avenir*).

"Stolen" newspapers, finally, refers to those newspapers which were published during the occupation against the wishes of their owners or managers. But again the situation is somewhat blurred: in the final analysis some of these "stolen" newspapers do turn out to have been published with the tacit or at least partial approval of their owners/managers.

In view of the confused situation within two of the three traditional categories, we shall characterize the newspapers according to the degree of their involvement in active collaboration with the Germans.

2.4 *Essentials of the evolution of the dailies during the four years of the occupation*

The number of dailies hardly changed during the four years of the occupation.[20] From 1941 onward, the circulation of most newspapers was marked by a downward trend. Several factors account for this recession, for example the compulsory scaling back of the circulation because of newsprint shortage. In addition, a degree of apathy had seized the readers, mainly in 1943 or thereabouts, due to the long drawn-out war and the increasing lack of money. And the PA itself stamped as one of the major causes of the fall in the circulation the campaigns that the clergy was waging against the censored press.

Among the Belgian journalists themselves a malaise was noticeable towards the middle of 1943. It was stimulated, on the one hand, by the gradual decline of German military supremacy, and, on the other, by the growing rigidity of the Germans' press policy after August 1942 (return to a system of partial preventive censorship). The editors-in-chief of the two biggest French-speaking newspapers, *Le Soir* and *Le Nouveau Journal,* left their papers in 1943.

As for the Flemish newspapers, the chief editors of the two biggest dailies were removed by the PA: the chief editor of *De Standaard* in March 1944, and of *Het Laatste Nieuws* in June 1943. *De Gentenaar* and *Het Nieuws van den Dag* were suppressed at the beginning of May 1944.

It is obviously not possible to deal extensively with all the wartime newspapers. The following will be confined to the two dailies to which Paul de Man contributed articles, *Le Soir* and *Het Vlaamsche Land.* These two newspapers will be analyzed with regard to their relation to the PA and to the major collaborating groups.

3. *The "stolen" Le Soir*

3.1 *Events surrounding the publication of the "stolen" Le Soir*

After the German invasion the owners of *Le Soir,* the Rossel sisters, and the then editor-in-chief had left Belgium. The paper was seized by the Germans, and as early as 13 June 1940, a so-called "stolen" issue was printed. The PA had appointed Mauromati, a second-rate journalist, interim editor-in-chief. Later, R. de Becker, a former journalist of *L'Indépendance,* was made editor-in-chief through the agency of the German embassy, with which he had had contacts before the war. From December 1940 on, A. Schraenen became the manager (*Verwalter*). His appointment had been a long time coming because the Rossel family, on their return to Belgium, had lodged a complaint with the Germans against the use of the paper's name, saying that they were the legitimate owners. They declared that they were willing to enter into negotiations that might lead to their managing the paper themselves. But the negotiations broke down over the issue of the editor-in-chief: the Rossels demanded that R. de Becker should go. However, at the press trial after the war several witnesses stated that this issue was merely the crystallization of the various points of contention.[21] The Rossels were said to have been prepared to make certain concessions, but most of the former editors stubbornly refused their cooperation. Besides, the anti-German reputation of the prewar *Le Soir* must have made the Germans suspicious.

In the end, 25 full-time journalists were recruited, none of whom belonged to the prewar team. In addition, dozens of part-time contributors were taken on, among whom Paul de Man and the prewar cartoonist P. Jamin (alias Alidor).

At his trial, R. de Becker insisted that he had been given the moral backing of the royal palace and of various dignitaries, and in the course of the trial a number of the eminent personalities cited did not deny this. Later, de Becker's alleged contacts with the Palace, by way of the King's secretary, Count Capelle, were to fan the postwar Royal Question in Belgium.

There is no doubt that such contacts did take place. Having shown the King an issue of *Le Soir* that he had been sent by R. de Becker, Count Capelle wrote to de Becker: "J'ai eu l'honneur de remettre au Roi votre message ainsi que l'exemplaire d'honneur du numéro spécial du *Soir* consacré à l'unité belge. Sa Majesté a été sensible à cet hommage et me charge de vous en remercier . . . (I have had the honor of submitting to the King your message and the honorary copy of the special issue of *Le Soir* devoted to the unity of Belgium. His Majesty accepts this homage and asks me to thank you)."[22] De Becker had a personal meeting with Count Capelle in March 1941. The occasion was the PA's ban on articles about the royal family. De Becker later declared that the Count gave him an article to be published in *Le Soir*.[23]

De Becker had no personal contacts with Capelle later than 1941. In June 1943 he wrote him a last letter, asking him again for moral support.[24] The reply to his letter was negative; the King's silence was to be seen as "une prise de position vis-à-vis des problèmes actuels (taking a position with regard to the current problems)."[25] After the war de Becker was to say that this particular letter had greatly contributed to his decision to leave *Le Soir,* and had also persuaded other journalists to do so.

The precise extent to which the backing given by certain dignitaries and by the Palace was important can only be assessed roughly, of course. But it is a fact that R. de Becker used this "moral support" as an argument to explain his "collaboration." And it is obvious that he told his journalist colleagues about his contacts with the Palace.

3.2 *Characterization of the "stolen" Le Soir*

Le Soir was the most widely read daily paper in occupied Belgium. Until the end of 1943 its circulation exceeded the number of 200,000: 278,855 in October 1940,[26] 270,000 in October 1941,[27] 260,297 in October 1942,[28] and 225,000 in October 1943[29]. From 1944 on the circulation began to fall, and in July 1944 it stood at 157,335.[30]

The success of the "stolen" *Le Soir* was largely due to the use of the prewar title. Moreover, during the occupation there were 12 French-speaking dailies less in Brussels than before the war, which obviously greatly benefited the market position of the "stolen" *Le Soir*.

Actually, the "stolen" daily was a fine product, journalistically speaking. Also, it consistently took a belgicistic point of view. De Becker tried to find a new destiny for the country in the new Europe: "sauver de la Belgique tout ce qui peut être sauvé, construire une Belgique régénérée dans une Europe unifieé (save all that can be saved of Belgium, build a regenerated Belgium in a unified Europe)."[31] He did state explicitly and repeatedly, however, that the destiny of the "new" Belgium was in the hands of the Germans.

It is probably under the influence of Count Capelle that de Becker published two articles in 1943 with a defiantly "belgicistic" content.[32] They caused the PA acute embarrassment, and when de Becker organized a press conference on 3 September 1943, where he declared that the idea of a new Europe under German rule had proved to be an illusion because the Germans did not understand other peoples and therefore were not able to

lead Europe,[33] he cut himself off from the PA. He was removed in October 1943 and the Germans had him take up residence in the Bavarian Alps.

The relationship of *Le Soir* with the most important group of collaborators, Rex, was at first cautious and detached. But after the leader of Rex, L. Degrelle, had made his notorious speech of 17 January 1943, in which he called the Walloons a Germanic people, the relation cooled down completely.

The removal of de Becker from *Le Soir* soon gave rise to rumors that L. Degrelle wanted to obtain control over the paper. But by that time Degrelle had lost much of the credit that he had once had with the Germans. The military administration regarded Degrelle as a political charlatan.[34] Even the SS despised him, and Heydrich, the head of the Sicherheitsdienst, wrote to Degrelle saying that he was unsuited for a political role because of his " . . . unpolitischer und eitler Character sowie seine mangelnde Menschenkenntnis (his unpolitical and vain nature as well as his lack of insight into human nature)."[35] Thanks to the Germans' antipathy to Degrelle, his repeated attempts to lay his hands on *Le Soir* eventually miscarried.

3.3 *Paul de Man and Le Soir volé*

Paul de Man had contacts with the regular visitors to the "salon Didier" even before the war, and in all likelihood it is these relations that brought him to *Le Soir*. In prewar days, the salon of Mr. and Mrs. Didier was a fashionable meeting-place for intellectuals and artists. E. Didier was the founder of the club of "Jeune Europe" and the editor-in-chief of the periodical of the same name. In his salon eminent politicians, journalists and writers assembled. Hendrik de Man, Paul de Man's uncle, was one of the regular guests. So were the journalists R. de Becker (who was to be the editor-in-chief of "*Le Soir*" volé") and R. Poulet (the editor-in-chief of *Le Nouveau Journal*, which was founded during the occupation).

The salon Didier is often described as an embryonic pre-collaboration group. Though they were a politically very heterogeneous company, its frequenters shared an aversion to Belgium's "decadent" political establishment. They dreamt of a "new Europe", and for Belgium they claimed the status of a neutral country. It is obvious enough that some of the visitors to the salon Didier dabbled in fascism and national socialism. Indeed, Dr. M. Liebe and Dr. O. Abetz of the German embassy in Brussels were among the salon's habitués.

During the occupation the Didiers, together with R. de Becker and D. Daye, founded the publishing house of *La Toison d'Or* (March 1941). Actually, the firm was a subsidiary of the

Mundus group, which was controlled by von Ribbentrop's services![36]

Paul de Man's introduction to *Le Soir* dates from the period when La Toison d'Or was founded. His uncle Hendrik de Man put him in touch with the group of intellectuals meeting at the Didiers'. He was recruited by R. de Becker to write a weekly "Chronique littéraire" and he was also to report various cultural activities (concerts, exhibitions, theatre, etc).

The reader of Paul de Man's weekly literary chronicle is struck by his focus on the publications of La Toison d'Or. This publishing house selected mainly authors whose work had much ground in common with the ideology of the new order. Examples are the works of Hendrik de Man (the founder of the united trade union), P. Colin (the founder of the daily *Le Nouveau Journal*, which sympathized with Rex), R. Poulet (the editor-in-chief of *Le Nouveau Journal*) and P. Daye (journalist of the same newspaper); all these authors were published by *La Toison d'Or* and consequently reviewed extensively by Paul de Man.

Foreign authors too, who sided with the new order, were published by *La Toison d'Or*: for example, R. Brasillach, J. Chardonne, Drieu la Rochelle, E. Jünger, H. Fallada.

Paul de Man's reviews and reports of cultural events will not be discussed in detail since other papers in the present volume give an analysis of his articles (for example Ortwin de Graef). However, a number of topics will be dealt with in order to point out where de Man adheres to the ideas of the new order. The analysis is a qualitative one, and hence subjective. We feel that the traditional methods of content analysis are inadequate here because de Man's significant pronouncements are to be found in occasional subtle and carefully balanced passages.

A topic that recurs frequently in Paul de Man's articles is the concept of the *new Europe* which is being achieved. The precise content of the term remains vague, but it concerns a Europe which has shed off the old decadence and which promises a better world, with more solidarity, more real values, a greater sense of duty and greater soundness: ". . . et que la guerre présente est, en dehors d'une lutte économique et nationale, le début d'une révolution qui vise à organiser la societé européenne d'une manière plus équitable . . . (the current war, apart from being an economic and national war, is the beginning of a revolution which seeks to reorganize European society in a more equitable fashion)."[37]

Repeatedly, Paul de Man points to the *role of Germany* in the new Europe: "Il y a une raison pour laquelle le destin historique passé et futur de l'Allemagne ne peut nous laisser indifférents: c'est que nous en dépendons directement . . . En outre, parce que nul ne peut nier la signification fondamentale de l'Allemagne pour la vie de l'Occident tout entier (There is one good reason why Germany's past and future historical destiny should not leave us indifferent: we depend upon it directly. . . . Moreover, nobody can deny the fundamental significance of Germany for the West as a whole)."[38]

His reviews often show up his admiration for the German victors and his contempt of the old Europe: "L'impression qui se dégage de ces observations est le manque de discipline et d'esprit civique dont firent preuve les soldats des démocraties, par contraste avec la mentalité de leurs vainqueurs. Un sérieux effort de rééducation s'impose si ces pays veulent jouer un rôle constructif dans l'Europe future (The picture that becomes clear from these remarks shows the lack of discipline and civic virtue characteristic of the soldiers of the democracies, by comparison with the mentality of their victors. If these countries are to play a constructive role in the future Europe, a serious effort towards re-education will have to be made)."[39]

As a result of the year-long brainwashing by English and French propaganda, de Man writes, we neglected everything that Germany accomplished in the social and political fields.[40]

Paul de Man sometimes displays a naive faith in the artistic freedom that fascism and national socialism grant artists. On the occasion of a lecture by Prof. Donini on Italian poetry, de Man writes that "le régime fasciste laisse entière liberté au poète pour chercher sa source d'inspiration où il veut (the fascist regime leaves the poet entirely free to find his inspiration wherever he wants to)." He concludes by pointing out that poetry "se développe en Italie et qui semble réaliser avec le plus grand bonheur, le souhait exprimé par Mussolini lorsqu'il déclara que c'est surtout dans les temps présents que la poésie est nécessaire à la vie des peuples (poetry is in full development in Italy ; it appears to make come true to the full the wish expressed by Mussolini that particularly in these days poetry should be of the utmost importance in the life of the peoples)."[41]

National socialism too extends the desired freedom of action to novelists, at least in de Man's opinion: "Le véritable nationalisme artistique n'est jamais synonyme de petitesse ou d'étroitesse d'esprit . . . C'est ce qu'on a parfaitement compris en Allemagne . . . (True artistic nationalism is never synonymous with littleness or narrow-mindedness . . . This is what has been fully understood in Germany . . .)."[42] Paul de Man contends that art must find an intermediate way in between individualism and commitment to solidarity. In a comment on *Das innere Reich,* the periodical edited by P. Alverdes, de Man argues that here this intermediate way has been found: no isolation in the ivory tower of poetry, away from what Germany has accomplished, but neither the uncritical and blind acceptance of German propaganda: "En parvenant à établir une attitude intermédiaire, les rédacteurs de *Das innere Reich,* et en particulier leur directeur P. Alverdes servent à la fois la cause pour laquelle un peuple entier se sacrifie et garantissent la continuité artistique, sans laquelle toute grandeur future serait impossible (By finding this intermediate way, the editors of *Das innere Reich,* and particularly its director P. Alverdes, achieve two things: they serve the cause for which an entire people is sacrificing itself, and they safeguard the artistic continuity without which it would not be possible to achieve future greatness)."[43] In another article de Man says: "Il est possible qu'alors l'art deviendra l'expression de cette solidarité (Perhaps art will then grow into the expression of that solidarity)."[44]

In Paul de Man's reviews of a number of French literary works, the following topic recurs frequently: France will have to understand that a new age has begun, and that it will have to side with the German victors in building up a new Europe. In reviewing Brasillach's *Notre Avant-Guerre,* de Man writes: "Je m'imagine que pour un Français cultivé *Notre avant-guerre* évoque encore un paradis perdu. Mais il faudra bien qu'il se résigne à parachever une révolution politique et sociale avant de pouvoir espérer retrouver un paradis semblable mais basé sur des fondements plus solides et, pourtant, moins éphémères (I can very well imagine that a cultivated Frenchman will find another paradise lost in *Notre avant-guerre.* But he will have to resign himself to the completion of a political and social revolution; only then will he find back a similar paradise, based on more solid foundations and therefore less ephemeral)."[45]

In his discussion of J. Chardonne's *Voir la figure,* de Man has the comment that the individualism typical of the French will have to yield to duty, discipline and order: "Ce n'est pas une des moindres innovations des régimes totalitaires que d'avoir substitué à cette imprécise anarchie un cadre d'obligations et de devoirs définis auxquels chacun doit adapter ses talents (It is not one of the lesser achievements of the totalitarian regimes that they have substituted for this blurred anarchy a set of precise obligations and duties to which everybody must adapt their talents)."[46]

Quite often de Man criticized in his literary chronicle "le bavardage superficiel (the superficial tittle-tattle)"[47] of which he feels the French in particular are guilty. It comes as no surprise therefore that he praises Drieu la Rochelle's *Notes pour comprendre le siècle,* as this book seeks to create a new type of man: ". . . d'autant plus prometteur dans un pays qui était tombé si bas que la France (so very promising in a country that had fallen as low as France)."[48]

It will be clear from the notes above that Paul de Man had, at least to some extent, taken to the ideology of the new order. One must bear in mind, however, that he was very young at the time, and that he must have been taken along by those he had met in the Didier circle and in particular by the fascinating personality of his uncle.

Paul de Man's main interests were art and literature; therefore the question arises if we ought not to characterize his "politically committed" views as merely political naivety. However, can one attribute his article "Les Juifs dans la littérature actuelle" (4 March 1941) to political naivete?[49] The reader of the article has the uneasy feeling that Paul de Man shows a leaning towards the anti-semitic aspect of national socialism. De Man argues that Jewish writers have remained "au second plan (second-rate)," and that authors like A. Maurois, H. Duvernois, H. Bernstein, T. Bernard and others "ne sont pas parmi les figures les plus importantes, ni surtout parmi elles qui ont dirigé de quelque façon les genres littéraires (are not among the most important figures, and particularly not among those who have, in whatever way, given new directions to the literary genres)."

The final remarks of the article are particularly disconcerting. Here de Man claim that it would not be a disaster for literature if Europe's Jews were to be isolated in a Jewish colony: "En plus, on voit donc qu'une solution du problème juif qui viserait à la création d'une colonie juive isolée de l'Europe, n'entraînerait pas, pour la vie littéraire de l'Occident, de conséquences déplorables (One finds, moreover, that a solution to the Jewish problem consisting in setting up a Jewish colony isolated from Europe, would not entail any deplorable consequences for literary life in the West)."

Although Paul de Man does not refer to the extermination camps, yet he does hint at the idea of isolating the Jews. He must have been aware of the anti-semitic witch hunt of the national socialists, and with the quotation above he appears to approve of their anti-semitic stand. We also feel that the anti-semitic tones of the article are reinforced by the editorial layout, which inserts a vehement anti-Jewish quotation from Benjamin Franklin after de Man's text and name. Paul de Man himself cannot have overlooked this; at the same time it is a blemish on the editorial policy adopted by *Le Soir.*

Before drawing a final conclusion, it is appropriate to have a brief look at Paul de Man's contributions to *Het Vlaamsche Land,* the second newspaper that he wrote for.

4. *Het Vlaamsche Land*

This section will be much more succinct than the one on de Man's contributions to *Le Soir* because he wrote only ten articles for *Het Vlaamsche Land.*

4.1 *Characterization of Het Vlaamsche Land*

The daily was founded in January 1941 and printed on the "stolen" presses of the well-known Flemish newspaper *Gazet van Antwerpen.* This made many people think that the new paper was the continuation of *Gazet van Antwerpen,* but this was totally wrong.

Het Vlaamsche Land was founded during the occupation, which implies that it benefited from German financial assistance. It is often considered to have been the unofficial spokesman of Devlag, a politically active group collaborating with the Germans and among the most extreme groups in Flanders: it was backed by the ss, and its leader, Jef Van de Wiele, advocated the annexation of Flanders into the Third Reich. Indeed, the members of Devlag repeatedly took part in Gestapo raids against Jews and resistance fighters.

However, a content analysis of *Het Vlaamsche Land*[50] shows that the newspaper did not put itself forward as the mouthpiece of Devlag. The newspaper owed this bad reputation to its so-called Reich edition, which was circulated among Flemish workers employed in Germany itself and which explicitly adhered to the Devlag principles. The following quotation from a circular letter by ss-Sturmbannführer Wim Fret leaves no doubt as to the import of the Reich edition of *Het Vlaamsche Land*: "The Reich edition of the daily *Het Vlaamsche Land* is published with the approval of the Reich Ministry of Propaganda and is the only Flemish newspaper which is fully at the disposal of Devlag; . . . it is moreover the only newspaper which rests squarely on national socialist foundations and fully adheres to the Reich idea" (our translation).[51]

But the domestic, i.e. Belgian, edition of *Het Vlaamsche Land* shows hardly any traces of Devlag influence. Very exceptionally, an article by the Devlag leader Jef Van de Wiele was printed.[52] Devlag had no great liking for *Het Vlaamsche Land,* which explains why a new Devlag paper was founded in 1943, *De Gazet.*

4.2 *Paul de Man and Het Vlaamsche Land*

De Man wrote only ten articles for *Het Vlaamsche Land.* We have been unable to go through the Reich edition of the paper,

but we are practically certain that his articles were printed in the Belgian edition alone. It is possible that Paul de Man was not aware of the link between the paper and Devlag. It has proved to be impossible to find out in what circumstances de Man began to contribute to this paper.

De Man's ten articles concern literary reviews and reports of cultural events. The topics that betray a certain affinity with the ideology of the new order are the same as in the *Le Soir* articles. Again we find references to a new and better Europe: "One of the more striking, and at first sight more paradoxical phenomena of our age, is the gradual growth of the concept of European unity at the very moment when the most important peoples of the continent are waging war among themselves" (our translation).[53]

And again we hear de Man's views on the twofold role of literature: aesthetic experience as well as commitment.[54] He claims that it is never possible for an artist to renounce his own nature, i.e. his blood and soil (compare the *Blut und Boden* concept!), but that he should nevertheless also find inspiration in other "great" cultures.[55]

In an article "The present-day German novel" de Man looks upon a number of writers as "renegades," because they have no interest in what is going on in Germany: "This is degeneracy" (compare *Entartung*!); and de Man concludes by saying that it comes as no surprise that "it is mainly non-Germans, in particular Jews, in whom this development can be seen."[56]

Towards the end of 1942 silence fell around de Man and his contributions to the daily press. His decision to stop writing for the dailies is probably due to a concurrence of circumstances: embittered, his uncle had renounced active collaboration as early as March 1942; the War was dragging on; and the climate of terror was growing worse. Of even greater importance is that, in August 1942, preventive censorship was imposed again on everything relating to domestic affairs. The journalists saw their freedom of action curtailed and the climate in which the press had to work was becoming increasingly rigid. Therefore Paul de Man's disappearance from the daily press at the end of 1942 is an important fact: during the postwar press trials those journalists who had gone on working after 1942 had severe charges pressed against them.

* * * * *

Paul de Man, looking for a livelihood, worked in the Dechenne agency until the middle of 1943. The agency, as pointed out above, had been granted by the Germans the monopoly of the distribution of dailies and weeklies. It was also producing a bibliography, and this is where de Man found work: he wrote seven essays and 93 bibliographic notes for this bibliography.[57]

He must have known that the Dechenne agency was supervised by Lothar von Balluseck, who was working for the *Reichsverband Deutscher Zeitungsverleger,* the association of German newspaper publishers.[58] Why de Man left the Dechenne agency, and where he went afterwards, are questions which we cannot answer.

To what extent are these war years significant for the status of Paul de Man as a scholar of literature? Are these years not to be considered a brief, isolated period of his life, one about which he himself was actually always anxious to keep silent? Perhaps his attitudes at the time can be explained as the ill-considered, youthful *Schwärmerei* or zealotry of a young man well-versed in cultural affairs but lacking in political insight. In any case, the links so far proposed between his wartime activities and his later career and theories remain rather vague and speculative.

University of Ghent, Belgium

NOTES

1. H. Picker, *Hitler's Tischgespräche im Führerhauptquartier,* 14.5.1941, Stuttgart, 1963, 343.

2. H. W., *Die Presse steht im Kampf,* in "Zeitungsverlag," 1.2.1941, nr. 5, 1ff.

3. A. Hitler, *Mein Kampf,* Vol. I, Ch. VI, 198.

4. L. P. Lochner, *Goebbels Tagebücher,* 29.1.1942, Zürich, 1948, 62.

5. *Tätigkeitsbericht der MV,* nr. 3, 19 June 1940, National Archives, Washington, German Records Microfilmed at Alexandria (GRMA), T501, R102.

6. *Jahresbericht der PA,* 1941, National Archives, Washington, T77, R982.

7. *Tätigkeitsbericht der MV,* 6 July 1940, National Archives, Washington, GRMA, T501, R102.

8. Doc. Jans, nr. 1S7, Advocate General, Brussels.

9. *Tätigkeitsbericht der PA,* 1–15 February 1941, National Archives, Washington, GRMA, T77, 982.

10. Interview with Dr. Gerhardus, in charge of the PA Brussels, Gemünd, February 3, 1968.

11. Belgapress File, Experts' report, Advocate General, Brussels, Documentation.

12. Newsprint center File, Doc. nr. 278, File F, Advocate General, Brussels.

13. F. Cannivez, "La Presse et les journalistes en Belgique sous le régime allemand," File F, Doc. nr. 17, Advocate General, Brussels.

14. Ibidem.

15. *Jahresbericht der PA,* 1941, National Archives, Washington, GRMA, T77, R982 ; see also: Telegram from von Bargen, nr. 430, 9 April 1941, Politisches Archiv Bonn, Büro Staatssekretär Belgien, Vol. 2.

16. Letter PA from Gerhardus to Dechenne, 18 January 1941, File Dechenne, Doc. Advocate General, Brussels.

17. Letter PA to Dechenne, 9 September 1942, ibidem.

18. Sections 2 and 3 use material mainly from E. De Bens, *De Belgische dagbladpers onder Duitse censuur* 1940–44, Antwerp, 1973, 564.

19. *Tätigkeitsbericht der PA,* 1–15 February 1941, op. cit., T77, R982.

20. E. De Bens, *Inventaris van de gecensureerde informatiepers* 1940–44, Brussels, 1–26. In October 1940: 27; in October 1941: 23; in October 1943: 25; in September 1944: 21.

21. Press trial, *Le Soir,* Experts' report, Advocate general, Brussels.

22. Appendixes to the statement of R. de Becker, press trial, file 3, appendix 17, 17 July 1946. Copy made available by G. Beatse.

23. Statement of R. de Becker during the *Le Soir* trial, 10 July 1946. Copy made available by G. Beatse.

24. Ibidem.

25. R. Capelle, *Au service du roi,* 132.

26. Summons R. de Becker, archives of G. Beatse.

27. Doc. Jans, nr. 97, Circulation tables, Doc. Advocate General, Brussels.

28. F. Baudhuin, *L'économie belge sous l'occupation,* Brussels, 1945, 226.

29. Doc. Jans, op. cit., nr. 97.

30. Dechenne File, Accounting, 1944, Doc. Advocate General, Brussels.

31. *Le Soir,* 5 August 1940, 1.

32. *Le Soir,* 21 July 1943: "L'oeuvre du Congrès de 1830 doit être maintenue"; and 3 August 1943: "Espace, Peuple et Etat."

33. *Le Soir* File, Doc. Advocate General, Brussels.

34. Compare for example *Tätigkeitsbericht der MV,* nr. 15, March 1941, GRMA, National Archives, Washington, T501, 2104. See also *Tätigkeitsbericht,* nr. 26, October 1943.

35. Heydrich to Ribbentrop, 3 February 1941, Politisches Archiv Bonn, Contents IIg, Vol. I.

36. E. De Bens, op. cit., 239.

37. "Notre chronique littéraire. Dans nos murs," *Le Soir,* 26 August 1941, 2.

38. "L'exposition 'Histoire d'Allemagne,'" *Le Soir,* 16 March 1942, 2.

39. "L'actualité littéraire", *Le Soir,* 11 August 1941, 2.

40. "Brochures flamandes sur le IIIe Reich," *Le Soir,* 12 April 1941, 2.

41. "La troisième conférence du Prof. Donini," *Le Soir,* 18 February 1941, 2.

42. "Introduction à la littérature allemande contemporaine," *Le Soir,* 2 March 1942, 1.

43. "Paul Alverdes et sa revue *Das innere Reich,*" *Le Soir,* 20 April 1942, 1.

44. "A la recherche d'un nouveau mode d'expression. *L'émotion sociale* de Ch. Dekeukelaire," *Le Soir,* 17 March 1942, 2.

45. "Notre avant-guerre," *Le Soir,* 12 August 1941, 2.

46. "*Voir la figure* de J. Chardonne," *Le Soir,* 28 October 1941, 2.

47. "*L'Homme pressé* par P. Morand," *Le Soir,* 7 October 1941, 2.

48. "Notes pour comprendre le siècle," *Le Soir,* 9 December 1941, 2.

49. "Les Juifs dans la littérature actuelle," *Le Soir,* 4 March 1941, 10.

50. The history and a content analysis of *Het Vlaamsche Land* are to be found in E. De Bens, op. cit., 228–235.

51. Circular nr. 28, 25 October 1943, Hildesheim, signed Wim Fret, Doc. Advocate General, Brussels.

52. See *Het Vlaamsche Land,* 20 February 1943, 1; 27 February 1943, 1; 13 March 1943, 1.

53. "Inhoud der Europeesche Gedachte," *Het Vlaamsche Land,* 31 May 1942, 3.

54. "Kunst als spiegel van het wezen der volkeren. Beschouwingen over *Geist der Nationen* van A. E. Brinckmann," *Het Vlaamsche Land,* 29 March 1942, 3.

55. "Duitsche Letteren. Een groot schrijver: E. Jünger," *Het Vlaamsche Land,* 26–27 July 1942, 3.

56. "Blik op de huidige Duitsche romanliteratuur," *Het Vlaamsche Land,* 20 August 1942, 2.

57. Research by O. de Graef, T. Keenan, and C. Kesteloot.

58. Letter PA to RVDZ, 19 June 1940, Doc. Advocate General, Brussels.

Aspects of the Context of Paul de Man's Earliest Publications

followed by Notes on Paul de Man's Flemish Writings

ORTWIN DE GRAEF

Et rien n'est plus crispant que ces biographies superficiellement romantiques qui visent à démontrer qu'à chaque instant, l'activité des élus portait l'empreinte de leur destin exceptionnel. Il n'en est pas ainsi, puisque les élans admirables se cachent le plus souvent sous une individualité normale, c'est-à-dire mélangeant le meilleur au pire. Le génie n'est qu'une façon momentanée et épisodique de se surpasser. Une fois l'éclair éteint, tout devient usuel et médiocre.—*Paul de Man, "Chronique littéraire," 7 octobre 1941*

Dans une ordre d'idees plus abstrait je tiens quand-même à revenir brièvement sur les remarques que vous m'avez communiquées, en me mettant en garde contre ce que vous appelez assez justement la solitude morale. C'est une erreur de croire que cet état d'esprit pour lequel je marque en effet une préférence consciente, doit nécessairement être dangereux et apte à entrainer des catastrophes intérieures. Au contraire, je suis souvent forcé à le préferer à n'importe quel autre. Si je marque une telle réticence à me livrer ce n'est pas en premier lieu, comme vous semblez le croire par peur d'être dupé. C'est plutôt par crainte de m'attacher, alors que je sais que ma mobilité d'esprit me mènera nécessairement dans d'autres voies, me forçant à abandonner ce qui m'était utile avant. Je ne tiens pas à enfreindre cette mobilité ni à imposer à un(e) ami(e) et à moi-même le déchirement que comporte une telle separation. Dès lors il y a avantage à apprendre à rester seul, à se passer des autres c.a.d. à rester dans les rapports avec eux aussi objectif et détaché que possible.

Evidemment, la question est complexe et digne de discussion approfondie. Ce n'est pas par ce vague schema d'argumentation que je puis réfuter le grand nombre de raisons qu'on sait opposer à l'attitude choisie. Enfin, c'est un problème qui vaut la peine d'être pris au sérieux.—*Paul de Man, Spring-Summer, 1938*

[. . .] ce que je ressens envers [. . .] les gens qui croient sincèrement qu'il y a des causes bonnes et des causes mauvaises, qui ont fait le choix ou la construction d'une doctrine déterminée et qui se sont fixés comme but de vivre pour la défendre et l'imposer. [. . .] Tout d'abord, dans le domaine purement cérébral, j'éprouve une certaine hostilité à ce qu'une attitude semblable comporte de manque d'objectivité et de souplesse, avec en plus un certain naïveté, un manque de sens critique qui n'est pas sans ridicule. [. . .] D'autre part, je suis cependant prêt à reconnaitre tout ce qu'il y a en ce type d'homme de force agissante, à l'influence de laquelle je suis loin d'être insensible—sans toutefois y céder. D'où ma gêne, je dirais même ma timidité en présence d'un caractère de cette espèce. En outre, je ne puis m'empêcher de ressentir une envie allant jusqu'à la jalousie pour la fixité d'orientation qui met à l'abri des angoisses d'irresolution. Je sais fort bien qu'en ce qui me concerne, je suis, par définition, en continuel état d'instabilité, d'inconséquence—fut-ce par rapport aux idées, aux personnes ou à moi-meme. Je ne crois pas [. . .] que cela provient du manque de formation et de la jeunesse—mais il est bien possible que ce n'est qu'étant jeune que parfois on en souffre.—*Paul de Man, 15 décembre 1938*

Je puis vous donner tous vos apaisements à ce sujet, car j'évolue à peu pres dans le sens que vous me préconiser. C.a.d. que si, depuis un certain temps dejà, j'ai abandonné l'espoir de m'appuyer sur une théorie, doctrine quelconque pour vaincre l'angoisse du doute je ne compte plus guère non plus sur un individu pour prouver la fixité d'orientation intérieure. Ou, plus simplement, en cct instant je puis me passer de cet individu; plus que cela, il me gène et me dérange. C'est affirmer, assez prétentieusement, que je suis en état de supporter, de braver le doute en me contentant uniquement des plaisirs élémentaires (c.a.d. matériels, esthétiques et cérébraux). [. . .] Une chose vous déplaira peut-être dans ceci, c'est le détachement humain qu'un tel état d'esprit comporte inévitablement. Intéressez-vous d'avantage aux hommes, me dites vous. Comment donc, si je m'y interesse; ils me passionnent—mais uniquement aussi longtemps que je reste detaché, non lié, non polarisé. La solitude morale que vous semblez tellement craindre devient, pour moi, inévitable dès que je m'oriente tel que je le fais en ce moment—et je sais que je m'y expose et que je la supporterai.—*Paul de Man, 3 janvier 1939*

1. Introduction

In a short essay on Mikhail Bakhtin, published in 1983, Paul de Man considered some of the meanings that can be given to the notion of "dialogism" which figures so prominently in this Russian theoretician's writings. First of all, he says, it can "[. . .] simply mean double-talk, the necessary obliqueness of any persecuted speech that cannot, at the risk of survival, openly say what it means to say [. . .]."[1] Quoting from Leo Strauss's *Persecution and the Art of Writing,* he then lists some characteristic features of such discourse—"obscurity of the plan, contradictions, pseudonyms, inexact repetitions of earlier statements, strange expressions, etc."—after which he adds one more "salient feature" of his own:

[. . .] the circulation of more or less clandestine class or seminar notes by initiated disciples, or, even more symptomatic, the rumored (and often confirmed) existence of unpublished manuscripts made available only to an enterprising or privileged researcher and which will decisively seal one mode of interpretation at the expense of all rival modes—at least until one of the rivals will, in his turn, discover the real or imaginary counter-manuscript on which to base his counterclaim.

Already in 1983, it was difficult to fail to recognize the tongue-in-cheek applicability of this observation to de Man's own case. After all, it was he himself who kept referring to as yet un-published (and even largely unwritten) manuscripts that dealt (or were going to deal) rather more explicitly with questions of a political and ideological nature than had formerly been the case, while it was (and is) indeed over the issue of politics and ideology that the main quarrels in de Man interpretation took (and still take) place.[2] Now, in 1988, with the discovery of de Man's previously unknown—albeit not unpublished—earliest texts, we are only beginning to realize how much more was at stake in these lines of apparently unproblematic wit and self-irony.

According to some arguments, the upshot of the recent discoveries just alluded to is that the ironic reticence and sometimes obscure wit characteristic of de Man's style are now being forced to face the facts, to shed their masks, and to reveal themselves for the deceit and duplicity they really are. The present introduction, on the contrary, proposes to offer some fairly factual information and a hopefully not inordinate amount of corroboration by quotation which may enable readers of de Man puzzled by these early texts to judge the extent to which the self-congratulatory simplicity of this conclusion fails to appreciate the intricacy of the matter at hand.

Before moving on to this task, however, and at the risk of adding a fatal, because seemingly circular and self-defeatingly hermetic, turn to the screw already annoying those detractors of deconstruction intent upon using de Man's past in order to invalidate the entirety of his work, I would like to refer to one more, rather more complex, instance of what can now perhaps be construed as de Man's ironic encounter with his own 'history':

Rather than putting it in terms that suggest deceit and duplicity, one could say that the poet, like the philosopher, must forget what he knows about his undertaking in order to accede to the discourse to which he is committed. Like all writers who happen to think wittily of some figure of language and then keep it embalmed, so to speak, in the coffin of their memory (or, in some cases, in an actual wooden box) until the day they will compose the text that proclaims to discover what they themselves had buried, poets know their figures only by rote and can use them only when they no longer remember or understand them. No actual bad faith is involved in such a process unless, of course, one claims transcendental merits for a move that pertains to the ethics of survival rather than of heroic conquest.[3]

To unpack this and similar passages in de Man's later work as veiled comments—if that is indeed what they are—upon his personal predicament is, as was said, not the purpose of this paper. I only hope to have succeeded in concisely conveying an impression of the fascinating complexity these new texts may add to the rereading of one of the most eminently readable writers of the century. It is, then, as a kind of anticipatory footnote to such rereading that the present text will try to sketch a context for de Man's earliest publications.

2. Les Cahiers du Libre Examen (*1939–40*)

So far as has been established to date, Paul de Man published his first texts in 1940, at the age of 20, in *Les Cahiers du Libre Examen,* a francophone Belgian journal issued by the Cercle du Libre Examen, a *cercle d'étude* of the Université Libre de Bruxelles.[4] Being a student at this university since 1937,[5] de Man had joined the editorial staff of *Les Cahiers* towards the end of 1939. Already in February 1940, he was promoted to the position of director, a function which, however, he was only to hold for some three months, as the *cercle d'étude* saw itself forced to interrupt its activities when Germany invaded Belgium in May 1940. The reasons for this abrupt hartal are fairly obvious, as the following sketchy survey of the journal's early history will show.

When the first issue of *Les Cahiers du Libre Examen* appeared, in March 1937, the editors tried to make it quite clear what their intention with this initiative was: first, to offer a forum for students (and professors) on which to vent their opinions about the most diverse topics, "[. . .] conformement à notre principe du LIBRE EXAMEN, base de toute étude et raison d'être de notre Université";[7] second, to further the understanding and appreciation of this principle itself, and of the stakes involved in the clash between dogmatism and freedom which they felt to be more acute now than ever before. Politically speaking, this declaration of intent was clearly designed as a confirmation of the often vehement opposition between the liberal enlightened doctrine of the Université Libre (*Scientia vincere tenebras* was, and still is, its telling motto) and the catholic tradition in university policy which found its most important embodiment in the prestigious Université Catholique de Louvain. At the same time, however, the editors of *Les Cahiers* did not wish their journal to become too explicitly involved in the rivalries of a more concrete party politics: "[. . .] notre revue sera une revue d'opinions, d'idées, de culture générale [. . .] Elle ne sera jamais une organe politique, ce qui ne veut pas dire que nous n'y ferons pas place aux questions politiques et sociologiques."[8]

One month later, in the journal's second issue, the editors repeated their previous statement in a rather more shrill tone than before, which may already serve as an indication of the mounting pressure on the Belgian, and European, political landscape of the pre-war period:

[. . .] nous voulons que cesse l'invasion de notre Université par des fascistes et cléricaux cherchant à y faire des adeptes. [. . .] Rappelons-le donc: l'UNIVERSITE DE BRUXELLES EST LIBRE-EXAMINISTE, DEMOCRATIQUE, ANTICLERICALE, ANTI-DOGMATIQUE ET ANTIFASCISTE. Le devoir de tous les etudiants, et principalement le nôtre, sera de le faire savoir tant à l'intérieur qu'à l'extérieur de l'Université, dans tous les milieux. Aucune équivoque n'est possible, notre position est claire, et nous sommes decidés à la maintenir.[9]

If the increased tension of this second declaration already betrays a narrowing of the initial distance the editors had wished to keep from practical politics in a stricter sense, the events of the years that were to follow could not but be conducive to a fortification of this tendency.

Thus, when Czechoslawakia, Poland, and Finland were attacked towards the end of 1939, *Les Cahiers du Libre Examen* was quick to express its profound disapproval of these German and Russian aggressions. At the same time, however, the editors also drew attention to the weakness of the European democracies and the "moral decadence" of the period which had, in fact, enabled the "nationalist and belligerent totalitarian mystiques" that lay at the roots of these conflicts to flourish into unprecedented prominence. In a country that at the time was still able to maintain a neutralist policy, *Les Cahiers* saw its mission now modified but not yet, as the editors believed, rendered impossible:

Il nous est inutile de nous lamenter sur nos espoirs perdus. Nous devons examiner froidement les problèmes qui se posent à l'heure actuelle. Nous souhaitons la victoire de la cause démocratique, car tout en nous assurant le maintien de nos libertés essentielles, elle nous donne plus de latitude pour l'établissement d'une situation juste et équitable pour toutes les nations européennes sans exception.[10]

The next issue of *Les Cahiers,* devoted to "l'organisation de la paix", repeated this intention, now with a marked stress on the specific responsibility resting on the shoulders of the intellectuals:

Comme la guerre n'est plus actuellement un but en soi, on ne peut l'envisager qu'en fonction de certains objectifs, qu'il est nécessaire de préciser. Car, si les masses peuvent se contenter de quelques formules lapidaires, il serait inadmissible que les intellectuels en fassent autant. Il convient au contraire qu'ils définissent et discussent aussi rigoureusement que possible les diverses solutions proposées, afin de préparer une paix raisonnable et juste [. . .], il convient de se mettre d'accord dès à présent sur certaines principes fondamentaux qui devront présider à une ordre nouveau, et qui resteront les mêmes quelles que soient les modalités matérielles existantes lorsque la guerre prendra fin. [. . .] Nous croyons [. . .], que c'est en faisant ces efforts de pensée que nous contribuons, dans la mésure de nos moyens, à établir un monde meilleur.[11]

We may wish to stress already at this stage a prominent feature of this mode of argument that will prove to be of primary importance for an assessment of de Man's later involvements: notably, the conviction that the war is in some ways almost a side-issue, precisely because it is not to be avoided anymore—that is to say, the belief that the war is a passing evil which "in itself" should not be allowed to detract "intellectuals" from already contemplating the "new order" (a phrase not as heavily burdened then as it is now) that should arise from the ruins it will leave in its wake. An awareness of this state of mind—an aversion to violence patterned with an acceptance of its inevitability —, presented as it is here in a decidedly anti-German context, is indispensable for any just appreciation of the data we will encounter later on.

In January 1940, de Man makes his first appearance as contributor to the pages of *Les Cahiers,* in a special issue devoted to art and literature. It is not, the editors hasten to assure their public, the desire to evade the harrowing troubles of the period which has motivated this shift of focus from politics to art, but rather their conviction that it is precisely through a study of art that one can come to comprehend a civilization and hence, it is suggested, its discontents.[12] However it may be, de Man's own essay, "Le roman anglais contemporain," a sweeping scan of "modern" English literature, stops short of any explicit extrapolations to the concrete circumstances at the time of its composition, for which reason we may be allowed to defer further discussion of its content for the time being in order to move on to the next issue of *Les Cahiers.*[13]

As we have mentioned before, this penultimate pre-occupation *Cahier* was the first to be published under de Man's chairmanship, which means that its editorial is perhaps of an even greater relevance to our attempt to evoke the context of his early work. In this short editorial, the journal justifies its option to present a number of essays on "western civilization" by claiming that in a period of which it has become a commonplace to say that it is decadent, an analysis of the norms of this civilization has become an urgent necessity. If one wishes to defend the values of western culture, it is argued, such an analysis,

which in tranquil times might even be qualified as "un vain jeu de théoricien," becomes, once these values have come to stand under threat, "une nécessité tactique." The editors then go on to say that,

Aussi incomplète que soit notre exploration de cette immense domaine, il se dégage néanmoins une certaine unité des quelques essais publiés. Les principes éthiques occidentaux semblent, pour presque tous les auteurs, se réduire en dernière analyse à l'idée de la libération de l'individu, grace à laquelle nous nous différentions des civilisations voisines. Et si nous nous croyons supérieures à elles c'est à ce concept que nous le devons.

Il n'a pas été explicitement parlé de la guerre dans ce numéro. On sent cependant sa présence diriger l'état d'esprit de tous nos collaborateurs et ce n'est certes pas effet du hasard que deux d'entre eux aient choisi la France comme symbôle de la culture occidentale. Mais on ne pourrait dire, sans simplifier dangereusement la question, que la guerre présent est une lutte de l'occident contre la barbarie. Les facteurs de décadence se trouvent dans toutes les nations, dans tous les individus, et la victoire des démocraties ne sera une victoire de l'occident que dans la mésure où on parviendra à établir un ordre dans lequel peut revivre une civilisation comme celle qui nous est chère.[14]

It should be noted, for the sake of accuracy, that de Man's own contribution to this issue—his second and final publication in *Les Cahiers*—does not strictly speaking pertain to the "quelques essais" referred to above, but appears as one of a series of *notes* presented in a separate section. Nevertheless, the concluding paragraph of this piece on French literature—more particularly, on Jules Romains—expresses a view quite similar to that of the editorial just quoted. One could, de Man writes in this conclusion, reproach Romains for the fact that the exaltation of the easy life in the most recent installment of *Les hommes de bonne volonté* clashes rather unpleasantly with the contemporary scene of conflict, but, he immediately continues, in fact, Romains' depiction of the ideals of sweetness and gentleness, as opposed to "les grandes formules catastrophiques de fausse grandeur et d'héroisme de parade" can come to play a useful edifying role upon this very scene: "[. . .] s'il nous décrit cet état de choses qui est tellement éloigné de notre condition presente, c'est un peu pour nous en donner envie, dans l'espoir que notre désir de vivre dans un monde semblable devienne si impérieux que nous ne puissions plus en concevoir un autre."[15]

Two months later, the *cercle d'étude* made a last concerted attempt to defend its point of view in the face of the now towering threat of German aggression by publishing a special issue devoted to a critique of totalitarianism. It took the Germans only a few more weeks to claim Belgium as occupied territory.

3. Le Soir "volé" (*1941–42*)

That the drastic alteration in political possibilities effected by the German victory confronted contemporary Belgian intellectuals with a rather more urgently material necessity to decide upon a future course of action than had been the case beforehand, needs little demonstration. Previously, the official neutrality of the country's government vis-à-vis the international conflicts had ensured a climate of communication in which highly divergent opinions could be publicly expounded without this necessarily involving great personal risk. After the invasion, however,—the government effectively having taken sides by going into exile in London, thus leaving the remaining adherents of a neutralist policy in an obviously unenviable position—the almost immediately operational Nazi propaganda and censorship machinery made it perfectly clear that from now on anyone unreservedly critical of the Germans would have to face dire consequences.

To judge from our sketch of the stance taken by *Les Cahiers du Libre Examen* before the occupation, one might be led to assume that those among its editors and contributors who were not willing to embrace instant martyrdom could not reasonably do anything but emigrate, go underground, or retreat into political silence, which is indeed what most of them did. Some members of the former *cercle d'étude,* however, among whom Paul de Man, chose to follow a rather different path, commonly and conveniently referred to as that of "moderate collaboration" with the occupant. As the extant testimony to this phase in de Man's intellectual career—if a phase it can indeed be called, which, given the presuppositions underlying such classifications, is by no means self-evident—as this testimony, then, consists almost exclusively in his contributions to *Le Soir,* the most widely distributed Belgian newspaper of the period, it is to this journal that we shall presently turn.

3.1 Recalcitrant collaboration and internal division: the circumstances of publication

As we have already indicated, one of the more eminently tangible consequences of the invasion was the German usurpation of the Belgian press.[16] In order to ensure the lasting success of this appropriation, the *Militärverwaltung*—a supervising organism installed by the Germans after the Belgian capitulation on May 28—put one of its sections, the so-called *Propaganda*

Abteilung (PA), in charge of the media. As it was the intention of the *Militärverwaltung* (consisting as it did—as opposed to a *Zivilverwaltung*—of a relatively small number of expert members of the military entrusted with the task to harness a maximum of the occupied territory's potential to the German enterprise) to have most of the work done by citizens of the defeated nation, the PA understandably devoted most of its energy to attempts at goading the leading pre-war papers into resuming publication under foreign control. The difficulty it saw itself confronted with was, however, that the majority of these newspapers had, previous to the invasion, expressed opinions unfavorable to the Nazi warmongers, so that a mere authorization to start up publication anew could not be expected to be highly efficient. Therefore, after having banned the more radically anti-German journals which obviously did not qualify for such ventures, the PA decided to lease a number of other leading papers to third persons sympathetic to the occupant.

Such was the case with *Le Soir,* which had been sequestered by the Germans after its owners had left the country. Despite *Le Soir*'s former anti-German reputation, the PA was anxious to profit from this journal's prestige and popularity and consequently saw to it that already on June 13 1940 its first war-time edition—the first issue of what would come to be known as *Le Soir* "volé"—was made available to the public. The paper's editorial staff had been entirely replaced (none of its previous editors had been found willing even to consider continuing their work under the new rule) and consisted, in the words of a PA *Tätigkeitsbericht* of August 1940, of "die zur Verfügung stehenden besten Journalisten", almost all of them Belgian, for "Es kam darauf an dafür zu sorgen, dass sie von den Belgiern als eine von ihren Kreisen geschriebene Zeitung anerkannt wurde."[17]

It would, however, be wrong to conclude from all this that henceforth *Le Soir* could be seen as a mouthpiece for the official Nazi doctrine. For one thing, this 'official Nazi doctrine' was not by any means as solid and universally accepted by all German officials as we are sometimes led to believe: quarrels between the two authorities under which the PA resorted, to wit, General Reeder of the *Militärverwaltung* in Brussels and the Third Reich's Minister of Information and Propaganda, Dr. Goebbels, as well as intrigues between the PA and the German Embassy's press agency—to name only a few of the conflicting parties—made it very difficult to maintain a truly official policy. In addition to this, and arguably more importantly, there was always a significant margin of recalcitrance to a number of German decrees among the journal's editors and contributors to be reckoned with. Especially the issue of the future of the Belgian nation proved to be a very sensitive one: many of *Le Soir*'s principal figures, among whom the editor in chief, Raymond de Becker, and one of his close colleagues, Pierre de Ligne (the latter a personal acquaintance of Paul de Man and like him a member of the board of *Les Cahiers du Libre Examen* before the occupation), were confirmed "Belgicists," which did not agree with the considerable number of proponents of a downright abolition of the Belgian nation as such among the Germans.[18] Another inevitable source of conflict was the fact that, as a francophone publication, *Le Soir* could not but show evidence of the cultural influence of France which the Germans' had intended to break by taking recourse to what they referred to as "an ethnical hygiene, derived from the laws of race and place."[19] Both of these issues, we shall see, are of crucial importance for an understanding of de Man's thoughts on politics and culture as they appeared in the columns of *Le Soir*.

Thus, notwithstanding the fact that the PA was theoretically supposed to be capable of making certain that *Le Soir* fulfilled its function in the German propaganda scheme, the physical impossibility of a persistent regime of pre-publication censorship, combined with the unwillingness of the paper's contributors to meekly follow all the occupant's stipulations, caused this journal to be a less than ideal representative of 'loyal collaboration.' Still, even while the preceding remarks should suffice to give at least some impression of the considerable heterogeneity of opinion the Germans both elicited and wished to reduce, as well as a rudimentary notion of the extent to which *Le Soir* could certainly not be labelled a mere bearer of the Third Reich ideology, this should not keep us from appreciating the rather puzzling difference in outlook between the two publications Paul de Man chose to contribute his earliest writings to. In doing this we should however not neglect the important point that de Man's non-editorial position in *Le Soir* as writer of, predominantly, literary reviews is not wholly comparable to his activities as editor and editor in chief of *Les Cahiers du Libre Examen*.

The precise nature of de Man's position in *Le Soir* is, in fact, not very clear. Indeed, about the only data we can be certain of are those we can deduce from the collection of texts itself: that he started contributing in the Christmas 1940 issue; that he eventually got to be in charge of a weekly *chronique littéraire* in which he reviewed recent publications or discussed general topics of contemporary literature; that he infrequently wrote a front page article on a literary subject important at the time; and that he published a number of journalistic pieces on cultural events (concerts, manifestations, exhibitions. . .)—all this until the end of November 1942 when, for reasons we can only guess at, he disappeared from the columns of *Le Soir*.[20] In the following pages we shall consider some central topics he addresses in the various writings just mentioned, but before we do so, I wish to point out that, prior to any further interpretation of this involvement, we should, I believe, appreciate the 'simple' fact that for an intellectual in his early twenties, who did not have any usable university degree, writing for Belgium's most prominent newspaper must have been a very desirable way to earn a living in a country crippled by the war. And while this observation ought not to be used to completely relativise the extent of de Man's collaboration, the latter should, conversely, not be allowed to totally override the issue of material necessity just alluded to.

3.2 Aspects of complementary nationalism: de Man's contributions to Le Soir

A first major difficulty that confronts us in the task to present a survey of de Man's writings for *Le Soir* is, inevitably, the problem of selection. On the one hand, the nature of our undertaking requires that we highlight those moments in these texts which most explicitly bear witness to his awareness of the political tensions riddling the contemporary context, while, on the other hand, such a focus all too easily leads to a heavily distorted perspective, blind to the oscillations, uncertainties, and complexities characteristic of any period of political upheaval, as well as to the more strictly literary-critical aspects of the material studied. The rather unfortunate and at times even ludicrously inaccurate newspaper reports on the discovery of de Man's 'collaborationist' texts are only an extreme instance of such historical myopia.[21] As a possibly sadly ineffectual *caveat*, then, I wish to stress that the following survey cannot by any means be considered to be an exhaustive presentation of the wealth of material involved, but should rather be taken as a circumstance-bound and relatively single-minded account of his more evident public politico-ideological pronouncements in the first years of the Second World War.

3.2.1 The Order of the Golden Fleece

Already in one of his first contributions (13 February 1941) to *Le Soir*, de Man gives evidence of a marked concern about the future of Europe and its nations. This text, although presented as a review of René Benjamin's *Le Printemps tragique* (one of the earliest novels dealing with the French campaign), also discusses two other books, the second of which, a work about Philip the Good—*Conditor Belgii*—enables de Man to approach the contemporary difficulties via a historical detour. It is not very difficult to understand this move: the wishful similarity between, on the one hand, the greatest Duke of Burgundy's impressive contributions towards a unification of the Low Countries in the fifteenth century—one of the peaks of western European civilization—and, on the other hand, twentieth century attempts to level intra-European discordances, could indeed hardly avoid becoming some sort of ideological topos in the early nineteen forties. As de Man puts it in the conclusion of his review

Grâce à la ténacité de Philippe, et grâce surtout à ses extraordinaires facultés d'organisateur, il fut possible de maintenir une paix relative entre des sujets jaloux l'un de l'autre et attachés à leurs privilèges. En réussissant cette tâche, il parvient à créer un des premiers Etats modernes et à jeter les bases d'une organisation politique nouvelle. A notre époque, où il faudra réorganiser l'Europe d'une façon plus rationnelle et plus équitable, il est particulièrement utile d'étudier comment de grandes figures du passé ont résolu des problèmes analogues.[22]

In itself, this conclusion is, significantly, vague enough to allow for its being interpreted in widely divergent ways, i.e. either as critical of or as sympathetic to the German enterprise—indeed, it will be readily seen that a statement such as the above would not have looked incongruous in the pages of, for instance, *Les Cahiers du Libre Examen*. Nevertheless, it should be pointed out here that the analogy here proposed—between the struggles for (re-)organization in the early years of the war and the feats performed by Philip the Good—was not merely, as has already been said, an ideological topos at the time, but that it was also a topos clearly preferred by those who were not averse to the idea of successfully ending these struggles in cooperation with the German occupant. Two months after the text just quoted, de Man published an other review which shows him to have been rather sympathetic to this interpretation of the historical parallel in question as well.

In this second text, a review of a monograph by Paul Colin, *Les Ducs de Bourgogne*, de Man once again points to the acute significance of the Burgundian epoch for the present, but the general European perspective of the previous article has now been superseded by an explicitly Belgian one:

Le sujet est à l'ordre du jour, car c'est vers cette période historique qu'on doit se tourner pour prouver la possibilité d'un Etat belge indépendant vis-à-vis de ses deux puissants voisins, la France et l'Allemagne.[23]

Evidently, given the PA's emphatical prohibition to write about the future of Belgium as a nation (some two months before the publication of this review, *Le Soir* had been fined 500 Reichsmark for its several transgressions of this decree), a statement such as the above cannot, at first sight, be construed as evidence of a collaborationist tendency in de Man's writings. Still, the context in which it figures may shed a rather different light on the matter, for the author of the book de Man sympathetically comments upon here, Paul Colin, was a renowned right-wing collaborationist, director of the German-controlled *Le Nouveau Journal*, and, in the words of a contemporary, "the cleverest, meanest, most unscrupulous and most influential of the quisling newspapermen in Belgium."[24] What is important to us in this respect is that on the basis of this observation, we can formulate as an admissible hypothesis that by giving a favorable account of this work, de Man effectively aligns himself with a group of intellectuals who looked upon the occupant as a potential ally in the struggle towards a new future for a Europe that was believed to be heading for disaster. At the same time, however, this alignment should not make us lose sight of the considerable heterogeneity characterizing the collaborationist milieu in occupied Belgium: even while de Man's approval of a work by Colin can be rightly said to indicate his sympathy for this milieu, this does not entail that he fully endorsed Colin's opinions. Indeed, his praise for the latter's decision not to vent his personal views in his portrayal of the Dukes of Burgundy already suggests, albeit in a roundabout way, his distance from Colin's perspectives, while, in fact, the notion of an independent Belgian state de Man advocates in the passage just quoted was one which Colin himself did emphatically not subscribe to. This distinction is particularly interesting as it allows us to briefly turn to another 'quisling,' extremely important at the time, whose views are much more akin to those underlying de Man's remarks: Robert Poulet, brother of the famous literary critic Georges Poulet, whom de Man was to encounter in very different circumstances later on.[25]

Robert Poulet ranks undoubtedly among the strongest of those Belgian intellectuals who had explicitly expressed themselves in favor of a collaboration of principle with the Reich once a consistent neutralist policy had been rendered impossible. Next to his activities as literary critic and creative writer, he also held the function of editor in chief of Colin's *Le Nouveau Journal*, which provided him with a fairly prestigious platform from which to promulgate his political views. As was suggested, however, Poulet's stance was very much different from that taken by Colin: an incomparably more subtle thinker than this latter (who, it may be recalled, was an adherent of the doctrines expounded by the hard-nosed collaborator and leader of the extremist party Rex, Léon Degrelle), Poulet envisaged a future for Belgium as an independent state centered around the three complementary principles of respect for the existing dynasty, respect for the Christian spirit he considered to be the indispensable basis of western civilization, and respect for social justice. Importantly, Poulet's proposals also exceeded the boundaries of the German New Order, in so far as he—heavily influenced as he was by people like Charles Maurras—defended the upholding of a 'Latinate' spirit over and against the pan-Germanic crudities advocated by people like Degrelle and, notably, Colin. Nevertheless, Poulet was at the same time fairly convinced that, given the circumstances, it was only through a moderate and conditional collaboration with the occupant that the said goals could be attained—a view which cannot but recall that held by Poulet's 'left-wing counterpart,' Hendrik de Man, the latter, as is well known, being Paul de Man's uncle.[26]

It is this Belgicism, then, which makes a *rapprochement* between Paul de Man and Robert Poulet—notwithstanding their substantial differences, not the least of which was their respective age—far more plausible and revelatory than one between de Man and Colin. Admittedly, the mere fact that de Man favorably reviewed a historical study written by the owner of the newspaper Poulet was politically speaking in charge of, would in itself be a rather tenuous link for the construal of such an affiliation—especially as Poulet was quite often explicitly at loggerheads with Colin over the issue just mentioned, a conflict which even led him, like Raymond de Becker in *Le Soir* after him, to resign from his function as editor in chief in January 1943—, but it is nonetheless a viable circumstantial confirmation of a tendency otherwise also noticeable in de Man's writings at the time. All this, provided we do not stretch the point too far beyond the observation that, like Poulet, albeit less explicitly, de Man chose to argue for a Belgian independence within channels controlled by the *Militärverwaltung*. Like Poulet's, too, de Man's attitude towards the German regime was not by far as slavishly celebratory as that of, for instance, Colin or Degrelle, but this did not preserve him from becoming, like these last, a despicable collaborator in the eyes of the underground resistance.

The case of Poulet is, of course, instructive in other respects too, in that it refers us once more to the existence of an impressive section of the Belgian intelligentsia of the thirties which could be said to have prepared, in one way or another, a discursive climate that would prove to be all too vulnerably congenial to some of the more respectable aspects of authoritarian and Eurocentric thought that were also to be found—alongside the crass stupidities we can now all too comfortably discern—in various doctrinary expositions of the German ideologues. It is not my intention here to give an adequate survey of the numerous leagues, salons, groups and reviews in which this climate prevailed (Bernard Delcord's study of the "'chapelles' politico-littéraires en Belgique (1919–1945)" considers the most prominent ones),[27] but I do wish to emphasize the fact that any appreciation of de Man's collaborationist activities will have to take into account that such involvements cannot be seen as instances of a sudden and simple complicity with a violently introduced new style of thinking, but should, on the contrary, be assessed in connection with what can almost be deemed to be a proto-collaborationist *tradition* which featured some of the finest minds of his time.

Particularly interesting in this respect is the so-called "salon Didier," which, during the interbellum, served as a meeting-place for intellectuals from often widely divergent backgrounds—catholics and liberals, left-wing and right-wing 'socialists' alike—who found a common denominator in their dismissal of the system of party-politics then institutionalized in Belgium, in their adherence to a neutralist policy without concessions to the French and the British, and in their understanding and at times even admiring attitude vis-à-vis *some* phenomena of national-socialism and fascism.[28] It was in this salon, most notably, that Hendrik de Man found a sympathetic audience with which to discuss the post-Marxist socialist theories which were to direct him eventually towards an admittedly grudging acceptance of a loyal collaboration of principle with the occupant. Notwithstanding the fact, however, that the salon Didier could consequently be considered to be, in some ways and for some of its patrons, a breeding-ground of pre-collaboration, the immediate aftermath of the German invasion witnessed the termination of its habitual gatherings and even the short imprisonment of its hosts Edouard and Lucienne Didier—another instance of the often confused and contradictory policies of the aggressor. After their release, and this is of a more immediate relevance to our purpose, the Didiers did nevertheless not hesitate long before resuming their activities in a different format, and in March 1941 they founded a publishing house, *Les Editions de la Toison d'Or*, which was supported and controlled by the press group *Mundus*, itself an instrument at the hands of one of Hitler's most servile admirers, the German Foreign Minister von Ribbentrop.

What is important for us, then, is that there is ample evidence that Paul de Man entertained fairly intimate relations with this enterprise, whose list of publications comprised works by Robert Poulet, Raymond de Becker, Robert Brasillach,

Bertrand de Jouvenel, Alfred Fabre-Luce, Henry de Montherlant, and, of course, Hendrik de Man. Not only did he review a large number of the books published by *La Toison d'Or,* but he also attended the "intimate reunions" it organized[29] and even published three of his own translations in its collection of Flemish and Foreign Literature.[30] And we may add that, as is well known, the Golden Fleece proudly carried in the name of this publishing house is none other than the symbol of the order of chivalry with which Philip the Good had ensured the allegiance of nobles and landowners to the House of Burgundy in the fifteenth century, which brings us back to the issue of the new European unity we have taken our cue from.

3.2.2 Collaborating for national independence: a future for Belgium

What, then, we must ask ourselves at this juncture, did de Man exactly have in mind when he indulged in prophesying the advent of a regenerated Europe? We have already quoted a passage to the effect that such a new Europe would have to preserve the independence of Belgium as a nation, which is to say that, for de Man, the various annexation-schemes that were being drawn up at the time, were unacceptable. As is (perhaps not very) well-known, this issue was rather more complicated in Belgium than it was in some other occupied countries, owing to its constitutional division into two different speech-areas, Flanders and Wallonia.[31] Given the shared Germanic roots of Flanders and Germany, it is not surprising to see that'during the occupation several groups advocated an annexation of Flanders to the Reich, leaving Wallonia to merge with France, to which it was linguistically, culturally and historically more closely connected. On the other hand, however, there were also a considerable number of francophone pan-Germanic ideologues—such as Degrelle—who argued that Wallonia, too, had its Germanic substrata and should thus, by rights, become part of Germany as well. De Man, as we have already stressed, left no doubt as to his opinion regarding this matter: as both 'solutions' would effectively abolish the Belgian nation, both had to be rejected.

Thus, in a brief reflection on some linguistic studies, he takes issue with those who would exploit the internal division of the country in order to attain their separatist goals. Himself a native speaker of Dutch (Flemish) raised and educated among the French-speaking bourgeoisie of Antwerp, he refused to accept this linguistic division as an absolute scission and found a (not altogether convincing) confirmation of this view in two idiotica attesting to "a veritable interpenetration of the Germanic and the Romance" dialects in Belgium. For reasons that will be readily apparent, one can hardly resist the temptation to quote the following lines from this short review, de Man's first focussed encounter with linguistics:

Entre le flamand officiel et le français, il y a donc bien une intégrale différence. Mais ce n'est pas en considérant les langues écrites qu'on peut se faire une idée de l'âme populaire. Le langage littéraire est une norme conventionnelle, parfois—comme en France—née d'un dialecte, mais qui est à cent lieues de correspondre au mode d'expression de l'homme du peuple. Celui-ci ne se traduit fidèlement que dans la langue parlée et le philologue qui désire acquérir des lumières sur l'état d'esprit d'une population devra tout d'abord s'attacher a l'étude de la dialecte vulgaire.

Unfortunately, we cannot afford to dwell on these logocentric wild oats here; for our present purpose, the conclusion of the argument, which, it should be stressed, is by no means unrelated to the linguistic mystification just referred to, is of more immediate relevance:

Il ressort de tout ceci qu'il est faux de croire que Flamands et Wallons se sont, au cours de temps, toujours considérés comme des étrangers ou même commes des ennemis. Aux endroits où ils vivraient l'un près de l'autre ils ont enduré les mêmes souffrances, subi les mêmes guerres et savouré les mêmes joies. Il en est résulté une grande solidarité. Et, en même temps que le spécifique flamand se mélangeait avec le spécifique Wallon, la langue, élément sensible entre tous, a pris l'empreinte de cette fraternité.[32]

Similarly, in a leading article on the occasion of "les journées culturelles germano-flamandes," de Man writes that from the time a balance was struck between the rights of the linguistic communities, the Belgian state has always guaranteed a cultural autonomy for Flanders, thus eliminating all motives for the latter's courting absorption by its German neighbor. Wedged between two major cultures, Flanders must remain "[. . .] ce noyau qui a pu donner à l'humanité des produits admirables d'un génie indépendant. C'est conformément à ce dessein que le statut politique de la Flandre doit être etabli dans l'Europe nouvelle."[33]

But what role was Germany to play in this new Europe of nations, according to de Man? This, too, is clearly stated in a number of his writings at the time; most straightforwardly, perhaps, in a report on the exhibition "Greatness of ermany" which was held in Brussels in March 1942:

Toute la continuité de la civilisation occidentale dépend de l'unité du peuple qui en est le centre. C'est pourquoi les faits qui déterminent le cours de son histoire nous touchent doublement: en tant que Belges, puisqu'ils agissent sur des valeurs que nous partageons avec lui; et en tant qu'Européens, puisque la force de l'Europe en dépend. L'ignorance factice des choses de l'Allemagne dans laquelle nous sommes restés durant ces dernières années nous à détourné d'une source vivante de notre civilisation: on peut espérer qu'une manifestation comme celle-ci orientera le regard de plusieurs de nos compatriotes vers des réalisations qui leur sont très proches.

To gauge the import of de Man's words here, we may perhaps refer to the speech held by General Reeder, head of the *Militär-verwaltung* in Brussels, at the inauguration of this exhibition, as this speech clearly expresses the occupant's interpretation of the state of affairs presented in the preceding passage:

La Belgique remplira à l'avenir le role de pays intermédiaire européen que la nature lui a imposé. Cependant, du bastion de l'Occident qu'elle était et pour lequel tant de sang a déjà coulé, elle redeviendra le glacis pacifique du centre germanique de ce continent.

Puisse une victoire rapide de nos armées combler le voeu de ce pays de voir s'instaurer une longue paix en collaboration harmonieuse avec la chère patrie allemande, du sein de laquelle est issu notre libérateur, le fondateur et le Fuehrer du nouveau Reich allemand: Adolf Hitler.[35]

It would, however, show a deplorable lack of discernment to conclude from this that de Man can be comfortably pigeonholed as a staunch proponent of Nazi foreign politics and a fervent admirer of Hitler. Indeed, it should be understood that, in itself, the dream of a united Europe of nations, even while it was relayed through a collaboration of principle with the powerful occupant, did not necessarily entail an allegiance to the perpetuation of expansionist violence contained in the strategies of Hitler and his executive entourage. Consider, for instance, as an appropriate illustration of this point, the following entry, dated May 20 1940, from the diaries of Hendrik de Man:

Cette guerre est en réalité une révolution. Le vieil ordre social, le vieux régime politique sont en train de s'écouler. Hitler est une espèce de force élémentaire ou démoniaque, qui fait une besogne de déstruction probablement devenue nécessaire. Je ne sais si Hitler fera l'unité politique européenne; je crois qu'il est surtout un déstructeur, mais il est probablement en train d'enlever les obstacles.[36]

These doubts and insights of the uncle do not in themselves 'exculpate' the nephew, of course, but they may help us to attain a more adequate understanding of a passage like the following, taken from a review by the latter of *Guerre et Révolution,* a book written by another collaborator, Pierre Daye. Daye's work, de Man comments, written as it is in the format of letters to a French friend, not only contains passages relevant to this foreign correspondent, but also reflections that are equally pertinent and judicious for Belgian readers:

Et plus particulièrement les paragraphes qui démontrent que la guerre présente est, en dehors d'une lutte économique et nationale, le début d'une révolution qui vise à organiser la societé européenne d'une manière plus équitable. C'est une vérité que ceux qui demeurent aveuglés par des passions nationalistes devraient souvent se repeter. A côté des questions de suprématie, *qui sont en fait sécondaires,* la situation crée une certaine quantité de possibilités pratiques afin de mettre à la place d'un appareil politique, devenue néfaste un organisme qui assurerait une répartition des biens plus conforme à la justice. Pour celni qui a cru que de telles réalisations sont possibles et nécessaires, il est de son devoir *de ne pas s'abstenir dans les conditions présents.* Car il ne trouvera sans doute plus jamais des conditions si propices à un renouveau qu'en ce moment où toutes les institutions sont en voie d'être remplacées. Et même si ce nouveau programme ne se trouve pas encore fixé avec précision, les choses en étaient venues à un tel degré de décomposition et de dégénérescence que, avant tout, la volonté de modification doit exister.[37]

"Le devoir de ne pas s'abstenir"—in another text of the same period de Man speaks of "la nécessité d'action qui se présente sous la forme d'une collaboration immediate [et qui] s'impose à tout esprit objectif"[38]—: like his uncle, Paul de Man evidently hoped that collaboration would remove the obstacles formed by decaying, decadent democracies and would thus lead to a better world. Not at all evident, on the contrary, is the *practical* course such collaboration should follow according to de Man. This wariness of *concrete* hortatory rhetoric becomes most apparent when de Man considers the situation in France (which he frequently does), and it is to this topic that we shall presently turn.

3.2.3 The French Problem

In one of his first contributions to *Le Soir,* de Man directs his attention to the first reactions to the national defeat in literary France, more in particular to Bertrand de Jouvenel's *Après la défaite* and to some statements made by André Gide and Pierre Drieu la Rochelle. What is important in these writings, de Man comments, is their common denunciation of a political climate that had become uninhabitable and could not but invite the victory of the German aggressor. Speaking of de Jouvenel's analysis, de Man singles out an additional merit, notably its awareness of the importance of the rise of fascism in Germany, as opposed to the previous cavalier dismissal of this "internal revolution" by the French as "une espèce de folie passagère." For de Jouvenel—and de Man appears to subscribe to this view— German fascism is "une réaction extrèmement normale et durable devant des circonstances crées par la politique mondiale," but, and this is of primary importance, this recognition does not lead him, de Man, to advocate an imitation of German fascism in France. What he on the contrary repeatedly insists upon is the necessity to abstain from attaching value judgements to the "objective observations" that have to be made regarding world politics—a rule which he takes de Jouvenel to task for not having observed. Thus, in the absence of the sense of moral confidence any sanguine judgement inevitably inspires, de Man's final comments on the state of affairs are extremely reticent:

Les conclusions de l'ouvrage [i.e., *Après la défaite*] et les vues qu'il ouvre pour l'attitude future peuvent paraître asses minces. C'est que les Français ne se sont pas encore habitués à l'idée que la création de l'organisation mondiale nouvelle ne dépend plus d'eux. Ce que de Jouvenel leur demande est le maximum qu'ils peuvent fournir: création d'un noyau chargé de constituer une pensée nationale. [. . .]

La lucidité de quelques écrivains dans leur condamnation d'une régime néfaste et leur détermination de se lancer sur des voies nouvelles est certes un symptome reconfortant. . . . Mais tant que cette volonté ne s'exprime pas unanimement dans l'opinion publique il est pour le moins prématuré de parler d'un redressement national.[39]

For our purpose, two of the most salient features of this commentary are, first, its denunciation of a certain French complacency, and, second, its concomitant call to abandon this lassitude for a concerted effort in the domain of national political thought. The same structure recurs in several other reviews of French literature de Man produced at the time. In his reading of Robert Brasillach's *Notre avant-guerre,* for instance, he comments upon the lack of political insight characteristic of French intellectual life in the interbellum, which he finds illustrated in this writer's incomprehending attitude with respect to the Nazi congress in Nurnberg. Indeed, for Brasillach, at the time of this event, "[. . .] Cette importance soudaine du politique dans la vie d'une peuple est un phenomène inexplicable."[40] At present, however, de Man continues, such an attitude of bemused distantiation is no longer tenable, and politics has become an inevitable necessity which requires any contemporary intellectual to accept the urgent tasks imposed upon him by a fundamentally changed perspective.[41]

Still in the same vein, de Man applauds one of Bernard Grasset's publishing ventures, "A la recherche de la France" (a collection which contained works by the communist-turned-fascist leader of the Parti Populaire Français, Jacques Doriot, pamphlets by Drieu la Rochelle, as well as essays such as Georges Marez's *Pétain ou la démocratie? Il faut choisir*):

C'est la première tentative d'effectuer une regroupement des forces spirituelles de la France après que celles-ci eussent été dispersées par la catastrophe. Il y a, dans ce pays, un certain nombre d'hommes qui ont compris qu'il fallait définitivement rompre avec le passé si on voulait que la France joue encore un certain rôle en Europe. Semblable en cela aux révolutionnaires du 18e siècle, ils tentent de formuler des principes politiques nouveaux et d'établir, en se basant sur les qualités héréditaires de la race française, quel sera le rôle et le régime de leur pays lorsqu'il s'agira de se partager les charges après la guerre.[42]

We could quote several other instances of this type of argument in de Man's 1941–42 writings,[43] but the general tenor should be clear by now: France has to face up to its defeat and embrace the task of political reflection and tentative reconstruction inside the channels the occupant has designated to this purpose. This, of course, can hardly be called an unequivocal attitude, especially as de Man never uncritically praises any of the collaborationist books he reviews, but characteristically preserves a tellingly indeterminate margin of disagreement (usually along the lines of "The initiative behind this book is in itself laudable, but there are some things I cannot agree with, although I unfortunately cannot discuss and refute them within the framework of this review."). Still, there are some instances where he risks some rather more substantial observations, as we shall presently see.

One of the most striking texts in this respect is his review of Jacques Chardonne's *Voir la figure.* Chardonne, who, it may be recalled, was a close friend of Robert Poulet (as were, for that matter, Brasillach, Drieu la Rochelle, and, to a lesser extent, Céline), wrote this book in some ways as a reaction to Gide's reproach that his previous works were rather too vague and equivocal—*Voir la figure* certainly redresses this wrong. Like Poulet, Chardonne advocated a collaboration of principle with the conqueror in order to establish a unified Europe; and unlike the 'early' Brasillach, de Man asserts, he thoroughly understood the true import of the rise of Hitler in Germany:

La guerre n'aurait fait qu'unir plus étroitement ces deux choses si voisines qu'étaient dès l'origine l'âme hitlerienne et l'âme allemande, jusqu'à en faire une seule et unique puissance. C'est un phénomène important, car il signifie qu'on ne peut juger le fait hitlerien sans juger en même temps le fait allemand et que l'avenir de l'Europe ne peut être prévu que dans le cadre des possibilités et des besoins du génie allemand. Il ne s'agit pas seulement d'une série de réformes, mais de l'émancipation définitive d'un peuple qui se trouve à son tour appelé à exercer une hégemonie en Europe.[44]

Chardonne does not hesitate to draw these arguments to their 'logical' conclusion, and here too, de Man implicitly follows his example. If Germany is to be the center, and if France is to collaborate with Germany, this will have to entail a profound change in the traditional French outlook. More particularly, the inbred individualism de Man detects in French intellectual life in the twentieth century will have to be superseded by a new type of human existence:

Une certaine forme d'individualisme prétendait que chacun avait à choisir soi-même le genre de personne qu'il désirait devenir et résoudre les difficultés qui naissent de cette tentative avec sa propre conscience. [. . .] Ce n'est pas une des moindres innovations des régimes totalitaires que d'avoir substitué à cette imprécise anarchie un cadre d'obligations et de devoirs définis auxquels chacun doit adapter ses talents.

As could be expected, de Man immediately qualifies this by saying that the advent of this new "personnalité-type" will not at all result in a complete egalization of all human beings, and that the present manifestations of this novel state of mind cannot yet be deemed to be accomplished representatives of this spiritual revolution, which, moreover, he warns will always bring with it "dangerous temptations"[45]—but these qualifications do not alter the fact that the kind of statements we encounter here go rather further in the way of ideological involvement than those we have considered before. Nor is this the only locus where de Man enlarges upon the dubious matter of the creation of a new type of social behavior, variously described as a "new collectivism," "new solidarity", and a new organizing power in answer to the question "[. . .] comment insérer la personne humaine dans un ordre fortement centralisé et discipliné."[46]

At the same time, however, he deliberately refuses to let these notions carry him towards a form of pan-Germanic idolatry—an attitude which was not without its risks in occupied Belgium, witness the quarrels between people like Poulet and de Becker on the one hand, and those who actively supported annexation to the Reich such as Colin and Degrelle on the other. Indeed, as we remarked earlier on, de Man's insistence upon the extraordinary importance of the rise of German fascism as a natural and normal evolution did not therefore imply a proposal for European fascism in a German mould, and, all appearances notwithstanding, the spiritual renewal rhetoric we have given a succinct impression of just now does not invalidate this. A key text here is his review of *Dieu est-il français?*, the French translation of a book by F. Sieburg, tellingly presented under the title "Le problème français." After having given a short exposition of the various modes in which there can be said to be "une incompatibilité foncière entre les normes culturelles et politiques orientant la révolution actuelle et les traditions françaises," de Man takes pains to drive home the point that this does not necessarily have to result in a wholesale rejection of these latter. Rather on the contrary, for even while France will have to abandon its mistaken sense of superiority and its exclusivist nationalism,

Le maintien de la continuité de l'esprit français est une condition inhérente de la grandeur de l'Europe. Particulièrement lorsque l'orientation générale conduit vers les forces profondes, obscures, naturelles, la mission française qui consiste à modérer les excès, à maintenir les liens indispensables avec le passé, à équilibrer les poussées erratiques, s'avère de première nécessité. C'est bien pourquoi il serait néfaste et inepte de détruire, en voulant les modifier par la force, les constantes de l'esprit latin. Et c'est également pourquoi nous commettrions une erreur impardonnable en rompant les liens avec les manifestations de cette culture.

Thus, just as was the case in de Man's conception of a future for Belgium, we find here an expressly articulated defense of what is called a "complementary nationalism," which would ensure a peaceful and balanced European unity. Given this, and keeping in mind the observations on persecuted speech with which we began this essay, we might already venture to ask whether it would be too rash a move to suggest a latent irony in de Man's indignant rejection of the expansionist nationalism characteristic of French politics before the defeat of the nation in 1940. Is it indeed possible that his scorn for "le besoin d'exporter, d'imposer ses lois aux autres" did not find a ridiculously sitting duck in the German scorn for and violent suppression of French culture in Belgium as well?

These, however, are interpretive gestures we will have to suspend for the time being—what matters now is de Man's conception of complementary nationalism as it is being defended here, in a paragraph which, as it sums up some of the major points we have come across so far, deserves to be quoted by way of conclusion to this section:

Le nationalisme actuel est tout le contraire d'exclusif: il est complémentaire. Son objet est de découvrir les vertues nationales, de les cultiver et de les honorer, mais de les adapter à celles des peuples voisines, pour parvenir ainsi en sommant les dons particuliers, à une réele unification de la culture occidentale. Chaque nation tend, en premier lieu, a être soi-même; elle est fière de son originalité mais, parce qu'elle conçoit que les autres pays ont le même sentiment, elle respecte leur charactère et ne songe pas un instant à imposer ses vues propres. Au lieu d'une dénationalisation artificielle et forcée, qui conduit à une considérable appauvrissement—comme nous avons vu se produire en Flandre et en Wallonie sous l'effet de l'attraction française—une libre contact entre des peuples qui se savent différents et qui tiennent à cette différence, mais qui s'estiment réciproquement, garantit la paix politique et la stabilité culturelle.[47]

3.2.4 Literary nationalism in a European frame

In the preceding sections of this chapter on de Man's *Soir* writings, we have focussed our attention upon statements relative to the organization of a peaceful Europe, which, as we already indicated, has led us to bracket to a considerable extent the literary preoccupations which are in actual fact the main component of the texts studied. In an attempt to partially make up for this, to all practical purposes inevitable, shortcoming, we will now endeavour to present a more immediate articulation of literature and politics as it appears in de Man's contributions.

In this respect, one constant feature of de Man's writings of this period is of primary importance, to wit, his insistent claim that, as far as literature in a strict sense is concerned, the events of war have not in themselves effected any marked changes. That is to say, apart from a number of essayistic works that immediately address the question of contemporary politics (by writers such as Drieu la Rochelle, Pierre Daye, Alfred Fabre Luce, Robert Brasillach, Jacques Chardonne and Jacques Benoist Mechin), and apart from those books that present themselves as eye-witness accounts of the military operations at the beginning of the hostilities (such as René Benjamin's *Le Printemps tragique,* Jacques Chardonne's *Chronique privée de l'an* 1940, André l'Hoïst's *La Guerre* 1940 et le rôle de l'armée belge and F. Rouuseaux's *Ma deuxième guerre*), the main "literary" output of the period remains, in de Man's opinion, unaffected by the fierce struggles in its context of production. A review written towards the end of 1941, in which he surveys the year's work in literature, puts this as clearly as possible: "Une première constatation, si nous observons la création artistique par rapport aux événements politiques, est l'influence extraordinairement minime de la guerre."[48]

This, to be sure, does not mean that no changes have occurred at all—it is just that they cannot legitimately be seen as issuing from the changed social, cultural and political structures established by the violence of the war. In fact, de Man argues, there is undeniably an urgent need for change, and changes are indeed being made, but this could already be observed well before 1940 ("[. . .] on peut se rappeler que Marcel Arland médisait du 'Grand Meaulnes' et que Jean-Paul Sartre malmenait François Mauriac bien avant que le premier coup de fusil ait été tiré en Europe."). Admittedly, the revolutionary and iconoclastic spirit characteristic of a period of political upheaval tends to speed up the process of renovation, but there are no simple and absolute determining forces to be detected, let be harnessed:

Ce serait se faire de dangereuses illusions que de croire que parce que quelques-uns le souhaitent, ce renouveau va surgir du jour au lendemain. Ou même de supposer que la guerre, bien qu'elle ait remue les esprits jusque dans leurs fondements, aura creusé un fossé si profond entre le passé et le présent que, nécessairement, tout écrivain digne de ce nom tentera de régénerer et de modifier son art. En réalité, ce jeu d'influences est plus complexe et les résultats, pour autant qu'il y en ait, sont moins tangibles et immédiats.

In the same vein, de Man takes issue with what he designates as "une hérésie de politicien," notably, the tendency to either accuse literature of having not been sufficiently aware of international conflicts during the interbellum and of consequently having caused a great deal of the misery of war, or, alternatively, to demand of literature that it transform itself into a vehicle for social edification and political reform, into "un moyen utilitaire."[49] These two aberrations are most explicitly denounced in de Man's review of Charles Dekeukeleire's *L'Emotion Sociale,* a book which, among other things, proposes to remedy the spiritual poverty supposedly characteristic of the twentieth century by modifying the means of artistic expression. De Man's remarks here deserve to be extensively quoted, as they concisely rehearse most of the aesthetic principles he pledges allegiance to elsewhere:

C'est une affirmation pour le moins discutable que de considérer l'émotion esthétique comme identifiable à l'émotion sociale et de croire que les deux puissent s'interinfluencer profondement. [. . .] Non pas qu'on doive complètement nier cette efficacité sociale de l'art. [. . .] Mais ce qui n'est pas légitime c'est de la considérer comme le but ultime de l'art et de juger celui-ci en fonction de l'efficacité qu'il atteint dans ce domaine. Je songe plus particulièrement aux passages où Dekeukeleire adresse des reproches à la production artistique de ces dernières siècles et prétend que, en s'isolant dans une spécialisation individualiste, elle a manqué à ses devoirs essentiels. On peut aller jusqu'à exprimer ses regrets lorsque rien dans le style régnant ne se prête à une tâche organisatrice. Mais jamais on ne pourrait conclure de ce fait à une infériorité de l'art et condamner celle-ci parce qu'il ne se plie pas aux exigences sociales. Les lois puissantes qui régissent l'évolution des genres ne se soucient guère de ces objectifs. [. . .] la grandeur de l'art dépend en premier lieu de constituants éternels, et ce n'est qu'en fonction de ceux-ci qu'on pourra le juger. Toute tentative de le transformer en un moyen utilitaire, même dans un but grandiose et respectable, risque de mener aux pires déformations. Les théories de l'art pour l'art étaient funestes parce qu'elles limitaient arbitrairement le champ d'investigations et les sujets possibles. Mais il semble bien que l'excès contraire [. . .] est une attitude également dangereuse, sinon plus.

As indicated, this passage offers us, in addition to the aesthetic anti-utilitarianism we have already underscored, an impression of de Man's views on literature and literary evolution in general as he developed them at this early stage in his critical career. For convenience sake, we can, I think, qualify these views as pertaining to an aesthetics of impersonal eternalism—that is to say, an aesthetics which proposes to argue for the existence of powerful transindividual laws which govern the creation of literature, only to be called thus because it is infused with grand and eternal qualities that cannot be attributed to the discretion of the writer alone. This however, is but a crude, overly generalized characterization: while what we have called "impersonal eternalism" is clearly the foundation of de Man's critical judgement, his allegiance to a complementary nationalism in a European frame greatly modifies this aesthetics by relocating it inside the realm of contemporary cultural politics. Indeed, as a counterpoint to his explicitly stated eternalism, there is in his critical reflections an equally marked attention to the local and temporal *differentiae specificae* of a work of art—which sometimes leads to puzzling but not therefore irresolvable contradictions.

Thus, in contrast to the previously quoted decree that the greatness of art is primarily a function of eternal constituents, we also find sentences such as the following, which seem to assert the opposite: "Ce qu'il importe avant-tout, c'est de rechercher dans la tendance d'une oeuvre ou d'un écrivain le côté par lequel il s'intègre aux tendances de son ère et l'apport que sa production apporte aux développements ultérieurs."[50] The opposition is, however, indeed only apparent, for the upshot of these statements is, precisely, that it is through its integration in its context that the work of art fits inside the "cyclical and coherent evolutions" of an eternal order of literature, the study of which, de Man proclaims, is just as revealing as that of the political history of mankind. What is important for us, then, is to grasp that it is on the basis of this aesthetics that de Man can si-

multaneously uphold notions of universal literariness and precepts of national specificity, a not undesirable faculty for an advocate of complementary nationalism in a Europe of nations.

Practically speaking, this means that, here too, de Man opposes the pan-Germanic violence attendant upon the triumphant exploits of the Nazis and, it may be recalled, particularly in evidence in a country which quite literally balanced on the dividing line between Germanic and Latin culture. The following passage, in which de Man draws an implicit distinction between national specificity and the Germanic version of nationalist sensibility, leaves little to be desired in the way of clarity as to this issue:

Un des bons auteurs flamands remarquait récemment qu'il n'existe pas d'équivalent français du mot flamand "volksch" ou allemand "völkish." Il s'agit de l'ensemble des qualités qui font qu'une oeuvre d'art n'est pas seulement le produit d'une imagination individuelle mais possède également des vertus qui appartiennent à un peuple tout entier. En fait, le problème est plus complexe et plus profond. L'art s'inspire de certains valeurs, qu'il choisit au hasard des tempéraments. Il se peut que ces valuers soient proches de celles que le peuple honore. On distingue assez clairement des nations qui élisent des thèmes et honorent des formes qui sont populaires tandis que d'autres s'éloignent volontiers de ces normes. Grosso modo, on peut dire que les nations germaniques pratiquent ainsi un art plus "völkish" que les nations latines, que la France en particulier. C'est là un caractère inhérent, qui n'est pas qualitatif. On aurait tort d'en faire un argument en faveur d'une prétendue supériorité. Il s'agit d'une différence, sans plus, qui fixe à la majorité des artistes ressortissant de ces deux contrées des buts et des intentions différents mais qui n'établit aucune hiérarchie entre eux. Les deux mentalités ouvrent des perspectives grandioses, chacune dans leur domaine.[51]

In the light of the German condemnation of the "francité" or "latinité" lingering on among many of those otherwise willing to collaborate, under certain conditions, with the occupant, statements such as the above are perhaps rather more audacious than we are inclined to conclude at first sight. In any event, it should be more than clear from the preceding that de Man had but little in common with the bigoted imperialism inherent in any successfully deployed nationalist revolution, such as that of the Nazis at the time. This, however, did not prevent him from praising those German authors who expressly supported the national cause—indeed, by his own argument, he could hardly do otherwise. But here, too, de Man is careful to stress some crucial distinctions.

A significant instance of this prudence is his front page article of April 20 1942, "Guerre et littérature: Paul Alverdes et sa revue 'Das innere Reich'." Alverdes, whose novel *Das Zwie-gesicht* de Man translated and had published by *Les Editions de la Toison d'Or,* was one of those who tried to preserve a margin of literary culture inside the Third Reich—as opposed to those who, like Thomas Mann, fled the country, and as distinct from those who totally surrendered themselves to the violent mythologies of blood and soil propagated by the Nazi ideologues. Thus, while he did align himself with the German struggle for a restoration of national grandeur, he at the same time refused to become a puppet at the beck and call of masters of propaganda like the notorious Goebbels. The journal *Das innere Reich,* a joint venture of Alverdes and Benno von Mechow which functioned, among other things, as a forum for what would come to be known as the "innere Emigration," and which was the most important literary review officially published in Germany under Nazi rule, stands as lasting testimony to this ambivalent attitude of reserved implication.[52] De Man's comments go straight to the heart of the matter here:

La façon dont *Das innere Reich* concilie harmonieusement, par un choix habile et des exigences sévères, la valeur esthétique et la valeur pratique des textes qu'elle publie est suffisament remarquable pour qu'on la cite en exemple. Il était fort malaisé de trouver une formule établissant un juste milieu entre les exigences temporelles et éternelles. S'isoler complètement de l'énorme effort militaire qu'entreprend l'Allemagne pour se cantonner dans une tour d'ivoire poétique aurait été une véritable trahison du sentiment national. Par contre, dédaigner du jour au lendemain des valeurs de style établies par le génie de plusieurs générations pour ne plus servir que le présent signifierait s'égarer dans le pire excès de la propagande. En parvenant à établir une attitude intermédiaire, les rédacteurs du *Das innere Reich,* et en particulier leur directeur Paul Alverdes, servent à la fois la cause pour laquelle une peuple entier se sacrifie et garantissent la continuité artistique, sans laquelle toute grandeur future serait impossible.[53]

The point is sufficiently clear: Alverdes's attitude is, de Man argues, laudable precisely because it is consistent with both the national identity of his country and the evolutionary laws of literature. We find this theme repeated again and again in de Man's writings of the period, under different guises and with different local implications, but always with the same stress on the necessity of a middle way, negotiating between the literary and the national.

It is consequently not to be wondered at—to offer a final example of this attitude—that de Man frequently singles out for praise those German authors who, like Ernst Jünger and Hans Fallada—to name but two very different examples —, have suc-ceeded in retaining a national identity even while they open themselves up to literary principles and artistic sensibilities originating in other nations, most notable of which is, of course, France. Similarly, de Man's advice to contemporary French authors is that they break out of their pretentious isolation and allow foreign (i.e. German) influences to enrich their literature. In itself, a certain incompatibility between the German and the French "artistic spirit" is not problematic—it is even felicitous, as it is a token of the national identity de Man wishes to see preserved —, but the real challenge is to embrace this difference and exploit it in order to attain the highest peak of literary maturity, a universal particularity. "Car de nombreux examples [. . .] empruntés à l'histoire de la philosophie, de la littérature et des arts plastiques, indiquent que c'est lorsqu'un pays utilise des formules venant au delà de ses frontières et les transforme conformément à son temperament national, qu'il réussit ses plus durables performances."[54]

Up to now, we have considered the perspective of complementary nationalism characteristic of de Man's critical judgments at the time by turning to the various internal constituents of this nationalism (French and German in particular); at this stage, it is necessary to devote some attention to the unity supposedly arising from such complementarity, the specificity of Europe—or Western civilization—as a whole.

Such questions of wholeness are indeed always marked by a fairly complicated doubleness: inside that which is affirmed to be a whole, a balance has to be struck between the differences proper to its various constituents (in this case the European nations); at the same time, however, this "positive" identification of unity borrows its legitimation from a negative opposition to whatever is deemed to be outside of, and hence alien to, the proposed oneness and sameness of the whole (in this case European civilization). It is in this second move, then, that the flexibility of the doctrine of complementary nationalism de Man adheres to runs to its limit and risks turning into a rigid and potentially hostile ideology, becoming, in fact, an enlarged version of the exclusivist nationalism it set out to denounce. The positive rationale of this solidification is, of course, the historical and cultural bond between the different European nations (a bond which is, however, more often taken for granted in exalting rhetoric than actually demonstrated); while the inevitable negative counterpart of this rationale—and here we at last encounter an aspect of de Man's collaboration which looks rather more grim than the ones we have considered so far —is a firm belief in the irreducible difference and *therefore* unacceptability of non-European cultures. In so far as a politics of nations is concerned, this attitude is practically translated in a defense of European independence over and against latent and manifest imperialist moves on the part of, most notably, Russia and America.[55] What must concern us here, however, are the consequences of such views in the domain of internal European culture politics—in short: the Jewish problem.

On March 4, 1941, *Le Soir* devoted an entire page to the Jewish question. Under the heading "Les Juifs et nous: les aspects culturels," four writers turned their attention to the influence of semitic artists and intellectuals on Western civilization. In the introductory article, "Les deux faces du judaïsme", Léon Van Huffel proposes to underscore, "En tête de cette page consacrée à l'étude de quelques aspects de la question juive, [. . .] les éléments essentiels de notre antisémitisme"; the second text, by Georges Marlier, discusses "La peinture juive et ses répercussions"; thirdly, V.d.A. offers some reflections on "Une doctrine juive: le Freudisme"; finally, Paul de Man contributes a short text entitled "Les Juifs dans la Littérature actuelle."

It will be clear that with this text we are confronted with the most directly embarrassing aspect of de Man's wartime involvements but it would be wise not to jump to conclusions by giving in to the sentiment of moral indignation it has already elicited, without carefully consulting what is actually written. At the risk of being accused of devious strategies of denegation, I would like to stress here that it is by no means my intention to minimize the issue or to exempt this text from the charges of antisemitism which have already been levelled at it, partly because these charges are to a certain extent self-supporting and consequently difficult to enter into a dialogue with. What I do wish to point out, however, is that a closer examination of its contents may considerably facilitate the future discussion of this short reflection, if I may be allowed this unfortunately not altogether superfluous truism.[56]

De Man begins his text by taking issue with a "myth" he ascribes to "l'antisémitisme vulgaire" which consists in looking upon the culture of the interbellum in Europe as degenerate and decadent, because "enjuivé." Such a conception is, he argues, doubly dangerous: first, because it condemns the whole literary production of the period, which this literature does not deserve; and second, because, in the event that one does grant some merit to contemporary literature, "[. . .] ce serait une peu flatteuse appréciation pour les écrivains occidentaux que de les réduire à être de simples imitateurs d'une culture juive qui leur est étrangère." The point should be well-taken: it is not that de Man rejects antisemitic tendencies as such here, but rather that he refuses to accept that the people these tendencies take as their target are indeed as formidable an influence (that is to say,

an enemy) as a vulgar antisemitism—which is, more than incidentally, the *only* antisemitism de Man refers to—would have us believe. The Jews themselves, he continues, have contributed their share to fostering this mistaken view by frequently glorifying themselves as leading figures in contemporary literary movements, but the real source of this "myth"—of "la thèse de mainmise juive"—is, he contends, a faulty understanding of the relation of literature to its political environment. More in particular: the relation of literature to "l'existence factice et désordonnée de l'Europe depuis 1920." It is a fact, de Man writes, that the Jews have played an important role in bringing about this disorder, but this does not therefore entail that "[. . .] un roman né de cette atmosphère mériterait, jusqu'à un certain point, le qualificatif d'enjuivé."

This view is, in fact, perfectly consistent with the general notions of literature and literary evolution we have said to be characteristic of de Man's writings of the period. Indeed, he himself furnishes us with the explicit link in the text under scrutiny:

Il semble que les évolutions esthétiques obéissent à des lois très puissants qui continuent leur action alors même que l'humanité est sécouée par des événements considérables. La guerre mondiale a provoqué un bouleversement profond dans le monde politique et économique. Mais la vie artistique a été rélativement peu remuée, et les formes que nous connaissons actuellement sont des suites logiques et normales de ce qu'il y avait en avant.

That is to say: the eternal impersonal logic of literary evolution which, as we saw, comprises national specificity as well as universal literariness, is, for de Man, invulnerable to the factitious influence of the political and economic chaos for which the Jews are deemed to have been responsible to a considerable extent.

De Man illustrates this by giving a very brief rendition of what he takes to be the evolution of the novel since Stendhal famously defined it as "un miroir qui se promène sur une grande route." In this definition, the law of the genre is established as "l'obligation de respecter scrupuleusement la réalité extérieure." The subsequent step in the evolution—the turn towards interior or psychological reality—is nothing but a logical consequence of this initial aesthetics:

Gide, Kafka, Hemingway, Lawrence—on pourrait alonger indéfiniment la liste—ne font tous que tenter de pénétrer selon des méthodes propres à leur personnalité, dans les sécrets de la vie intérieure. Par cette caractéristique, ils se montrent, non comme des novateurs ayant brisé avec toutes les traditions du passé, mais comme des simples continuateurs qui ne font qu'approfondir l'esthétique réaliste, vieille de plus d'un siècle.

It is undoubtedly superfluous to remind the reader that Kafka was, after all, a Jew (de Man, significantly perhaps, does not do so), but the foursome listed here is remarkable in other respects too. For one thing, there is no German among them; for another, Hemingway can hardly be called a representative of the European culture referred to elsewhere in the article; and thirdly, Lawrence, despite any crypto-fascist substrata one may want to detect in his work, is sufficiently English (as well as depraved) not to be the best example one could choose, given the anti-British sentiment officially sponsored at the time. Admittedly, these may seem to be trivial remarks, but considering the context, they at least deserve to be reflected upon. Whatever Gide, Kafka, Hemingway, and Lawrence may be, they are not the first ones one would think of as leading contemporary illustrations of the thesis that European literature has not been profoundly influenced by the Jews, and in the absence of other major names, de Man's choice is undeniably slightly puzzling. But let us return to the argument at hand.

We saw that, for de Man, the erroneous thesis of massive jewification was a corollary of an oblivion to the fact that literature is governed by powerful laws possessing a logic of their own. Moreover, he continues, Jews have not only not *created* contemporary literature, they have not even played a very prominent role in it either. This, he says, is actually somewhat surprising, as the specific characteristics of the Jewish spirit—to wit, "leur cérébralité, leur capacité d'assimiler les doctrines en gardant vis-à-vis d'elles une certaine froideur"— would seem to be eminently suited for the lucid analysis required by the modern novel. Despite this asset, then, Jewish authors have always occupied a second place in European literature only and this, de Man asserts, is a reassuring observation for Western intellectuals. For indeed, the fact that "our" civilization has managed to affirm itself over and against the "force étrangère" of Jewish culture, notwithstanding the lingering presence of semitism in all aspects of European life, is proof of its vitality and of the health of its profound nature. De Man then formulates his conclusion:

En plus, on voit donc qu'une solution du problème juif qui viserait à la création d'une colonie juive isolée de l'Europe, n'entraînerait pas, pour la vie littéraire de l'Occident, de conséquences déplorables. Celle-ci perdrait, en tout et pour tout, quelques personnalités de médiocre valeur et continuerait, comme par le passé, à se développer selon ses grandes lois évolutives.

Sentences such as these evidently cannot but invite charges of antisemitism, but before we lump together de Man's views here with the unspeakable—or, perhaps, all too speakable—ideological stupidity of the Nazi creed and the horrible consequences of this stupidity—for stupidity it is, that I believe must be insisted upon —, we might be well advised to emphasize certain peculiarities of de Man's argument which differentiate it from the rabid racism of many of his contemporaries.

First, it is interesting to note that de Man quite straightforwardly challenges the paranoid scapegoat stratagems characteristic of Nazi ideology. While he does subscribe to the view that Jewish interests lay to a considerable extent at the root of the crisis Europe undeniably lived through during the interbellum, he does not see any major nuisance in their cultural influence, for the simple reason that he does not believe this influence to be very perceptible. If we compare this to statements such as the following, taken from the article by Léon Van Huffel on the same page on which de Man's text appeared, we may appreciate the import of de Man's deviation from hardboiled antisemitic doctrine:

En gros, les Juifs nous apparaissent comme d'une essence foncièrement étrangère et radicalement opposée à notre sang et à notre mentalité.

Nous croyons à l'existence d'un type juif, d'une génie juif. Nous sommes résolus à nous interdire tout métissage avec eux et à nous affranchir spirituellement de leur influence dissolvante dans la domaine de la pensée, de la littérature et des arts.

[. . .] Et que surtout dans nos pensées, dans nos actes et dans nos créations, nous nous débarrassions du vieux ferment judaique qui s'est infiltré imperceptiblement dans nos esprits, tout au long de vingt siècles de christianisme.[57]

Nowhere in de Man's texts do we find such crude exhortations to a concerted expulsion of "judaism" from European culture— what we do find is the remark that it would not in any important way affect this culture if it would lose the Jews living within its boundaries, which is another matter altogether.

In addition to this, and closely related to it, we should remark that de Man gives no negative definition of Jewishness whatsoever. This, again, in contrast to someone like Van Huffel who speaks of "un racisme étroit, exclusif, fondé sur une réligion peu humaine et formaliste" and of "un internationalisme apparamment détaché de tout atavisme racique, mais qui, dans le fond, puise le plus clair de ses énergies dans le rêve de puissance millénaire du peuple 'élu'." On the contrary, the only substantial qualification de Man offers his readers with respect to "l'esprit juif" is that it would appear to be extremely well suited for the creation of novels, as we remarked earlier on.

A final remark that should perhaps be made is that de Man's suggestion for a "solution of the Jewish problem" should, all first appearances notwithstanding, not be confused with the Nazi *Endlösung,* prepared as the latter was in concentration camps that may seem to be grim realizations of the colonies in de Man's text. It should indeed not be forgotten that the idea of a Jewish colony isolated from Europe is by no means an invention of antisemites—the state of Israel is there to prove it. The fact that de Man's suggestion has led some to see in it an oblique and disconcerting prefiguration of the deportation of the Jews in Europe, should, moreover, not blind us to the fact that, in Belgium, such deportations began only in the summer of 1942— the text under discussion was written, it may be recalled, more than a year earlier.[58]

All this is, again, decidedly not to say that de Man is not guilty of some involvement with antisemitism here: the mere fact that he wrote a piece for an unmistakably antisemitic special section of *Le Soir* is already sufficient evidence to the contrary. And while it is extremely doubtful that he had any precise notion of what the Germans envisaged in the way of a "solution to the Jewish problem," this does not alter the fact that he must have been aware of local acts of racist violence that were approved of by the occupant. It should be clear, nevertheless, that the antisemitism that may thus be held against him was by no means articulate or even coherent. Any just appreciation of this involvement should be sensitive to the important difference between an ideology of extermination such as that supporting the Nazi creed and an allegiance to European tradition which flatters itself by denying the "adulteration" of this tradition by the presence of "foreign" races. The historical fact—established, as is so often the case with historical facts, in an easygoing retrospect—that the latter almost inevitably breeds the former, or at least gives some fallacious justification to it, cannot, I believe be adduced as an argument for their having to be valorized in identical ways. There is, in other words, a distinction between affirmative Eurocentrism and reactive xenophobia which ought not to be too easily discarded, and while the one may typically imply the other, the fact that de Man does not give expression to racial hostility (a racial hostility which, according to everybody who knew him at the time, was totally alien to his thought anyway) should warn us that, once more, matters were—and are—not as simple as they may seem.

4. *The retreat (1942–1947)*

On 6 September 1944, shortly after the liberation of Brussels, the first legal issue of *Debout: Organe de la Fédération Bruxelloise des Etudiants Socialistes Unifiés,* a bi-monthly publication which had its basis at the Université Libre de Bruxelles, printed an extremely angry article aimed at what the editors sarcastically referred to as the "elite" of the U.L.B.

Vous ne connaissez pas l'Elite des Etudiants de l'U.L.B.? Vous ne connaissez pas les purs défenseurs du Libre-Examen? Ils l'ont défendu pendant l'occupation, eux. Et pas pour rire. Pas à moitié comme vous et nous. Eux, leur canard n'était pas un pauvre format de papier jauni, mal ronéotypé, qui se vendait sous le manteau. Eux, ils ont défendu le libre-examen de concert avec la Gestapo, avec la petite torture caline pour ceux qui ne pensaient pas fasciste, de concert avec Rex, avec le V.N.V., avec De Vlag. . . Pour eux, le paradis c'était six billets (grand format) par mois et un ravitaillement inépuisable. Oh, vous pouvez être surs qu'ils ont fui ou qu'ils se sont terré. Mais nous saurons les retrouver où qu'ils aillent et quoiqu'ils fassent!

Mais sans doute désirez-vous qu'on vous parle un peu de ces messieurs. Une ultime fois. Avant de laisser leur nom tomber dans l'oubli méprisant.

The article then lists the names of seven ex-students of the U.L.B. who, in one way or another, collaborated with the occupant—five of them wrote for *Le Soir,* the second in line is Paul de Man:

PAUL DE MAN—neveu d'Henri. Chef des de Mannistes (évidemment) de l'Université. Introduit par son très cher oncle au soi-disant "Soir" de Schranen-de Becker, il dissèque les romans et essais en de chroniques littéraires aussi peu lisibles que celles qu'il écrivait dans les Cahiers du Libre Examen. Au bout d'un moment, il sent que cela tourne mal et fait une retraite très prudente. Son nom ne parait plus dans les colonnes du soi-disant "Soir." Sa pauvre petite carcasse de petit homme blond et malingre, à la mèche à la Hitler, déserte la place de Louvain. Mais en compensation, le neveu d'Henri reçoit de ses amis fascistes un poste de rédacteur à la "Belgapresse."[59]

What must interest us here is, of course, the "retraite très prudente" this accusation refers to. Indeed, toward the end of 1942 de Man puts an end to his regular contributions to *Le Soir*[60].

It is extremely difficult to trace his precise motives in this decision, since, as the previous quote already indicates, any account of this move immediately involves the ambiguities of evaluative judgement: to say that de Man stopped writing for a collaborationist paper because he, like his uncle some months before him, at last recognized the occupant for what he was, is at the same time to invite the retort that he did it only to save his own skin—and vice versa. It may be better, therefore, once more to restrict ourselves to a presentation of the factual information—however scanty it may be—on de Man's activities after 1942[61].

After having left *Le Soir,* de Man found a congenial job in the publishing trade, as an employee of the Agence Dechenne.[62] This latter was primarily a distribution agency, founded in 1908, whose services were being made use of before the war by a large number of the smaller Belgian newspapers, i.e. those that did not have a distribution service of their own. At the onset of the German aggression, however, the agency decided to suspend its activities, but, in keeping with the *Militärverwaltung*'s policy, the occupant soon succeeded in re-establishing it as a Belgian German-controlled enterprise (the strategy, it will be noticed, was exactly the same as that used for *Le Soir*), after which he proceeded to ensure a monopoly for the agency by forcing all Belgian newspapers to surrender all initiatives of distribution and sale to Dechenne's agents. The rationale for this centralizing move was obvious: to put it in the words of the German officials, "auf das Verteilungsgebiet wesentlichen Einfluss zu nehmen" and "um die immer mehr um sich greifenden Flüsterpropaganda wirksam entgegen treten zu können."[63]

Dechenne's responsibilities were, however, rather larger than those of a mere distribution agency. Indeed, apart from this function, it also operated a service of book reprint and sale, and, later on, a "German Bookstore" and a bibliographical review. As its German director, Lothar von Balluseck, a representative of the *Reichsverband deutscher Zeitungsverleger,* put it in 1941, "Die Agence Dechenne hat [. . .] vom Reichsverband den Auftrag erhalten, eine kulturpolitische Aktion entsprechend den von der PA angegeben Richtlinien durchzuführen."[64] Practically speaking, this meant for instance, that Dechenne made available to the reading public cheap editions of novels approved of by the German regime, and it is probably in this department that de Man was active.

Already in his *Soir* days, de Man actively supported the initiatives of the Agence Dechenne by publishing extremely favorable reviews of their reprints and popular editions. Thus, in 1941, at the occasion of the publication of Felix Timmermans' *Pallieter,* a Flemish classic alternatively described by de Man as a mirror in which the Flemish soul could recognize its own qualities and as a hymn to the Flemish earth, he stresses the importance of such popularizing publishing ventures.

[. . .] l'initiative de l'Agence Dechenne [. . .] est extrêmement louable. Venant à un moment où le besoin de lire est très grand, elle profite de l'occasion pour améliorer le niveau spirituel du peuple, en lui offrant, non pas de vulgaires romans d'amour ou d'aventures, mais une littérature saine et joyeuses, grace à laquelle il peut s'améliorer en s'amusant. Et un fois ce contact avec la culture établi, un grand pas est fait et l'on peut croire qu'à ce premier achat d'un livre succéderont d'autres.[65]

Referring to similar enterprises in Scandinavia and Germany, de Man concludes by venting his high hopes for the future, "pour le grand bien de chacun." Nine months later, he touches upon the same note when commenting upon the "völkishe" quality of Germanic art we have discussed earlier on:

Une des heureuses conséquences, découlant directement de cette particularité des germaniques, est la possibilité de répandre des livres dans toutes les classes de la population. En Allemagne, en Scandinavie, en Hollande, on trouve des livres dans toutes les maisons. On n'avait jamais cru qu'un résultat semblable eût été possible en Flandre. L'initiative de l'Agence Dechenne, qui lance sur le marché des éditions populaires à bon marché, a permis de constater qu'il existe un réel besoin de lecture et que même des auteurs comme Stijn Streuvels—dont on vient de publier "De Vlaschaard"—ou Filip de Pillecyn—dont on édite "De Soldaat Johan"— peuvent apporter au peuple la richesse de leur imagination. La littérature flamande ne pourra que puiser une vigueur renouvelée dans ce contact avec ses sources.[66]

Finally, less than a month later, de Man devotes a front page article to, again, "les initiatives de l'Agence Dechenne," significantly entitled "Pour que le peuple lise," in which he rehearses the same points in a more elaborate and systematic fashion. An interesting element in this text is his remark that such initiatives are more likely to be successful for a Flemish reading public than they are for a Walloon one, "[. . .] car la littérature d'expression française est ou bien trop purement régionaliste pour representer un intérêt général, ou bien influencé à tel point par les mouvements littéraires français qu'elle en a perdue tout contact avec sa souche populaire primitive."[67] Still, he adds, there are works, such as Charles de Coster's *Thyl Ulenspiegel,* which the entire people can profit from, and it is to be applauded that Dechenne, in collaboration with *Les Editions de la Toison d'Or,* is going to issue a popular edition of this novel, as this may have a considerable influence "sur la régénerescence d'un véritable sens culturel wallon."

Given this attitude—a crusade against ignorance among the masses, as well as against aesthetic exclusivism among the intellectuals—it is not surprising to find de Man joining Dechenne during 1942. Since, however, it is not yet clear what exactly was his function in this agency, it would be premature to speculate more extensively upon this involvement here.[68]

Consequently, the story of de Man's earliest years begins to draw to a close. Sometime during 1943, he moved back to his family's house in the vicinity of Antwerp, and as that part of Belgium was liberated later than the capital, he managed to evade the first violent waves of post-war "purification" and re-pression—after all, many have been prosecuted and imprisoned for lesser involvements than those he had been 'guilty' of. In 1946, he left this relatively secluded 'hiding place'—where he is reported to have spent much of his time reading American liter-ary journals—and went to Paris, where he occasionally fol-lowed university courses (without, however, taking any exams). Around the same time, he set up a publishing house specialized in art books, which was based in Antwerp. This rather shady business—appropriately called *Hermès*—led only an ephemeral existence and appears to have gotten him into some unpleasant financial legal problems, which made it necessary for him to em-igrate in 1948.

It appears that after his arrival in the United States, de Man quite rapidly established contacts with a number of New York intellectuals, possibly through introductions by Hugh Gibson, a former American ambassador in Belgium and a close acquain-tance of Hendrik de Man. Presumably as a result of his working in a bookstore, he also met literary people such as Dwight Mac-donald and Mary McCarthy, the latter of whom eventually ob-tained him a position as instructor in French at Bard College in 1949. De Man's American period, however, lies outside the scope of this paper, the primary purpose of which has been, as was said, to present a relatively factual account of the earliest stages in the critical career of arguably the most challenging writer on literature to have emerged in the past few decades.

Notes on Paul de Man's Flemish Writings

Certes, j'ai vécu à une époque où le mouvement auquel je m'étais donner a traversé une phase de régression, de décadence, de décom-position. Qu'importe, puisque la douleur que j'en ai ressentie m'a poussé à repenser toutes mes pensees, au point de me sentir au-jourd'hui en contact plus réel avec les faits que quand j'ai commencé à vouloir agir sur eux.—*Henri de Man,* Après coup (Mémoires)

. . . as if the impossibility of distinguishing Paul de Man from the name "Paul de Man" conferred a power of resurrection on naming itself. . . .—*Jacques Derrida,* Mémoires: trois lectures pour Paul de Man

0. In November 1986, while doing some research in the Archief en Museum voor het Vlaamse Cultuurleven (Archives and Mu-seum for Flemish Cultural Life) in Antwerp (intent upon gath-ering materials on Hendrik de Man and his family by way of background for a dissertation on the work of his nephew, Paul de Man), I came across five articles signed "Paul de Man" which were published in the Flemish newspaper *Het Vlaamsche Land* (The Flemish Land) in the course of 1942. Further research soon yielded another five articles published in the same paper. After that the material seemed to be exhausted, and I proceeded to translate the ten articles I had found into English and to write an introduction for them, which I tried to get published, alongside four of the translations, in a number of literary jour-nals.

A few months later, an old friend of de Man pointed out to me that Paul de Man had also written for another Belgian news-paper, the francophone *Le Soir*. This time, the amount of texts I discovered was rather more substantial,[69] and due to the efforts of a number of distinguished academics, the interest of de Man's earliest writings began to be recognised (albeit not al-ways in a very responsible fashion).

A format of publication was soon decided upon: all the *Le Soir* texts would be published in their original form in the *Ox-ford Literary Review* and a volume of historical and critical con-tributions and reflections would soon follow in the same journal. (Later both volumes of the project would be taken up by the University of Nebraska Press after their size made the OLR's participation technically impossible.) For this latter vol-ume, I wrote a paper considering the context of de Man's French writings.[70] My earlier typescript, on his Flemish texts, was still being discussed for publication by the board of editors of another journal, so I decided not to deal with the materials it covered again. Subsequently, however, suggestions were made to publish all of de Man's wartime journalism, including the texts in *Het Vlaamsche Land,* in one volume, which entailed that it would be advisable to include some context for *Het Vlaamsche Land* in the accompanying volume of responses as well. As there was no time to rewrite my paper on de Man's writings in *Le Soir,* I suggested submitting a modified version of my earliest introduction, to which the editors of the volume and those of the journal which had already agreed to publish this introduction readily agreed.

The following pages, then, contain some contextual notes for de Man's Flemish writings, as well as some additional information which I could not use, lest I repeated myself, at the time when I wrote the contextual notes for his French texts. Needless to say that both contributions are meant to be read alongside each other.

* * *

1. Shortly after Paul de Man's death in December 1983, Minae Mizumura rightly remarked that "We possess not even a vague overview of de Man's work in the way we do of other important writers whose recognitions came early in their lives."[71] Admittedly, since then a considerable number of data have been established which appear to allow us to move towards the construction of such a "vague overview," but, with respect to (and for) a thinker like de Man, who, once he had come into his 'own,' has quite consistently expressed his distrust of the sequential narrativisation of history, such an enterprise will always remain particularly precarious (*particularly*: because, ironically, one does not so easily escape from the constraints of consistency and unity, even when (or even especially when) these entail a distrust of what is often uncritically accepted as the self-evidence of the consistent, and the whole). I hope that, nevertheless, the information presented here will at least help us to responsibly begin "to guess whose statue these fragments have composed" with all that this entails.[72]

2. Paul Adolf Michel de Man was born in Antwerp, on the 6th of December 1919, as the second son of a well-to-do Flemish bourgeois family. His great-grandfather, both on the paternal and on the maternal side, was the popular Belgian poet Jan van Beers (1821–1881), who has gone down in canonical Flemish literary history as "the poet whose romantic sensitivity and eye disease caused him to write lachrymose and melancholic verse." The de Man family was pre-dominantly liberal and non-religious (some of Paul de Man's ancestors were freemasons)— with, in the field of politics, the notable exception of Hendrik

de Man, Paul de Man's uncle, who was an extremely active socialist theorist and politician.

Like so many born into the Flemish upper classes of Antwerp in the first half of this century, Paul de Man received an important part of his education in French. Given this, and considering his family background, it is not surprising that, in 1937, he began his academic studies at the francophone Université Libre de Bruxelles, which, at the time, was the bulwark of anticlerical and liberal enlightened freethinkers. Although a student of science, de Man was evidently already seriously involved in literature at this early stage, as can be derived from the considerable erudition displayed in two short essays he published, in 1940, in *Les Cahiers du Libre Examen,* the journal of the Cercle du Libre Examen, a 'cercle d'étude' at the Université Libre.[73]

After the German invasion of Belgium, in May 1940, de Man found a new forum for his thoughts on literature and culture in *Le Soir,* Belgium's leading newspaper, which was published under German supervision; *Les Cahiers du Libre Examen,* politically unacceptable to the occupant, had been forced to suspend its activities.

As indicated above, I have documented this aspect of de Man's wartime involvements elsewhere; what concerns us here is his engagement with the Flemish side of what is known as 'moderate collaboration' with the occupant, that is to say, his 1942 writings in *Het Vlaamsche Land,* a journal which can to a certain extent be seen as the Flemish pendant of the francophone *Le Soir.*[74]

3. Like *Le Soir, Het Vlaamsche Land* was one of the Belgian newspapers existing already before the war that was re-modelled according to the directives of the Propaganda Abteilung (PA), a German apparatus in charge of the diffusion of the Nazi ideology among the general reading public. It should be noted that, again like *Le Soir, Het Vlaamsche Land* was certainly not a mere collaborator's journal. Nevertheless, for various reasons, the PA, in its report of March 1941, deemed it to be "an extremely useful instrument for propaganda purposes" (DB, 208), and praised it as one of the two Flemish daily papers that had developed the most positive attitude towards National Socialist Germany (DB, 234).

Unlike some other, more radically pro-German publications, *Het Vlaamsche Land* did not plead for the abolishment of democratic principles, but it did support the Germans as the brave defenders of the European (Christian) heritage against the "red terror" of the Bolshevik "monster" (DB, 449, 421–3, 489). The people of Flanders, according to this paper, should join the "new crusade" and engage in the war between "Western

Christian civilization and the godless barbarians" (DB, 492). From 1941 onwards, the journal also published some rather straightforward attacks on the Jews, whose dominion in the world of culture and finance would now at last be broken by the Nazi "revolution" (DB, 474). This, moreover, would end the war, as *Het Vlaamsche Land* argued that one of the main causes of the conflicts was to be found in the Jewish interests in the military industry, while a supposed Jewish lobby, together with the Jewish Bolsheviks, was to be held responsible for an important part of the actual confrontations (DB, 477).[75] In addition to this, the 'New Order' (which received only a very vague definition) was hailed as the answer to the problem of a decreasing sense of unity in a Europe menaced by Marxism, and the German system was praised as the only feasible passage to a 'real' socialist Europe (DB, 475, 462). Even the idea of an annexation of Flanders to Germany was favorably received in some articles published towards the end of 1942 (DB, 445).[76]

4. It will be clear that in the preceding characterization of *Het Vlaamsche Land* I have presented as a fairly homogeneous ideology what was in fact a much more confused set of ideas and beliefs, some of which were not necessarily shared by all those who contributed to the newspaper. In fact, *Het Vlaamsche Land* was on the whole a rather unprofiled publication which, at least editorially, kept its distance from the more controversial issues (this in contradistinction to *Le Soir,* which had a much more stormy existence, especially in so far as its editorial core was deeply divided over the issue of Belgian independence).

With regard to de Man's publications, then, we should not forget that most of them were not directly concerned with political but with cultural (mainly literary) subjects—although he himself did not see this as a very inhibiting distinction at the time, as we shall have the occasion to observe later on.In addition, it deserves to be mentioned that de Man was not a member of the paper's editorial staff, and that his contributions were limited to ten texts, published with irregular intervals over a period of some seven months. What exactly was de Man's position in this Antwerp newspaper is extremely difficult to ascertain: the files of *Het Vlaamsche Land,* which published its final issue on September 9, 1944, were all destroyed, and people who might be in possession of more specific information are very reluctant to co-operate. However this may be, to all appearances, de Man was only a free-lance contributor, and we should be extremely careful not to formulate easy identifications of de Man with the paper he wrote in, all the more so as the identity of the latter is not to be described in any clear-cut way either.

This notwithstanding, some of the notions and ideas dealt with by de Man in these early texts can hardly be called innocent in their historical context, and I believe that it is one of the requirements of the lesson in reading he has taught us that we, perhaps somewhat impertinently, apply some critical pressure to these pre-texts of his writings. In the following pages, I will therefore briefly turn to some of the central themes informing these ten Flemish texts.[77]

5. One of the most prominent ideologemes in de Man's Flemish articles, as in his *Le Soir* texts, is the combination of a nationalistic sentiment with a desire for European unity—or, to use one of his own phrases, "complementary nationalism." In his review of *Geist der Nationen* (1938) by the German art historian Albert Erich Brinckmann and in his essay on the content of the European idea, for instance, de Man insists that a future for Europe and its various countries can only be secured when a "sober faith" in "national personality as a valuable condition and a precious possession" (AM) is allowed to co-exist with attempts to "[. . .] unite the creative forces of all European states" (CE). Such notions, which were quite common at the time, evidently cannot in themselves suffice to conclude that de Man had marked pro-German sympathies. Indeed, a concern for the future of Europe and its different countries could also be found, be it without the nationalistic overtones, in *Les Cahiers du Libre Examen,* which was anything but a pro-German publication. Neither can, for that matter, professor Brinckmann himself be pigeon-holed as a prime example of the Nazi doctrine in the field of the history of art. Still, one can understand that Brinckmann's views on the evolutionary interaction of an Italian "hedonism," a French "humanity," and a German "vitality" could easily lend themselves to appropriation by the Third Reich ideologues when one comes across sentences like: "Neben das hedonistische und die Humanität tritt ins Reich der Geister als heiligstarke Schöpferkraft der Kampf!"[78] But while Brinckmann's work (which, incidentally, was partially translated into French by de Man and published in 1943) remains relatively aloof from the concrete political situation at the time of its composition, de Man explicitly connects its outcomes to what he calls "a great stream of thought" which has been born out of the tendency "[. . .] to consider the national essence of a nation as one of the foundations of all civilization" (AM). And when, some two months later, he speaks of the task of "the present revolution" to defend not only the national values "[. . .] to which it, owes its existence and vitality [. . .]"; but also "[. . .] the spiritual (but how very important!) European values without which a peaceful and flourishing future is unthinkable," one is tempted to draw certain conclusions regarding de Man's sym-

pathies at the time. Evidently, these sympathies were never with a pan-Germanic doctrine which would seek to destroy all other European cultures (among which, most notable, the French), but some sort of vague faith in the beneficial consequences of the German enterprise for the future undeniably informs his thought—and this in so far as this enterprise profiled itself as a vigorous new affirmation of national identity and European unity, which was, however, only one, and not the most prominent, of its manifestations.

Perhaps the clearest instance of this complementary nationalism is to be found in the following passage, taken from a short essay on the German novelist Ernst Jünger:

A sincere artist can never renounce his proper regional [character], destined by blood and soil [*bloed en bodem,* the exact counterpart of the notorious German *Blut und Boden*], since it is an integrating part of his essence, which he has to utter. But he systematically impoverishes himself, he refuses to make use of that which constitutes the vital force of our European culture, if he, allegedly in order to remain true to his own people, does not want to become acquainted with that which comes into being elsewhere.(EJ)

De Man repeatedly stresses this double task: national literatures (and the German and the French in particular) should remain true to their national heritage whilst simultaneously sustaining the possibility of cross-fertilization. A rather heady instance of this view can be found in his assessment of contemporary German fiction, "Blik op de huidige Duitsche Romanliteratuur." In this article, he distinguishes two groups, "[. . .] which moreover were also materially separated by the events of 1933" (GF). The first of these is explicitly denounced for having betrayed "[. . .] the proper traditions of German art which had always and before everything else clung to a deep spiritual sincerity." The artists of this group are said to have abused the "in themselves very remarkable theses of expressionism" and "the very legitimate basic rule of artistic transformation" as pretexts for a "forced, caricatured representation of reality." In this case, de Man ordains, one can justifiedly speak of a "degeneration" (*ontaarding,* the Dutch translation of the German *Entartung*), of an aberrant fashion", and he continues that it is not to be wondered at that "[. . .] it was mainly non-Germans, and in specific Jews, that went in this direction."

The second group, on the contrary, has "[. . .] remained true to the proper norms of the country, which does not at all mean that they felt and wrote regionally." As examples of this 'school,' de Man appreciatively lists Hans Carossa, Ernst Jünger, Herman Stehr, Erwin Guido Kolbenheyer, Benno von Mechow, and Paul Alverdes, all of whom were, at least initially, accepted by the Nazis and *some* of whom were definitely 'politically suspect.' De Man then concludes that by not giving in to the temptation of "[. . .] scoring cheap successes by using imported formulas," the authors of this 'second group' "[. . .] have not only succeeded in producing an art of abiding value, but they have also secured the artistic future of their country."

Some twenty-four years later, de Man was to write that the Nazi movement

[. . .] was, if anything, notable for its profound anti-intellectualism and the crude but effective manner in which it played on the most primitive mass instincts, as well as on the short-sighted economic interests of social classes that considered themselves underprivileged. The Nazis received little support from German writers and intellectuals and were not very eager to enlist them in their ranks.[80]

It is difficult not to suspect that this apparent about-face is due to the insight characteristic of those who, in de Man's famous phrase, have "[. . .] very extensively partaken of the danger and failure [. . .]"[81] attendant upon any revolutionary projection into the future. Still, can we be absolutely certain that there is indeed a complete reversal at work here? De Man's 1942 texts never mention the name of National Socialism—they merely speak of a "German tradition", a nationalistic "revolution" and an anonymous European future, and although it is not always easy to tell the difference, we certainly have to allow for its existence. Moreover, people like Carossa, von Mechow, Alverdes, and, in particular, Jünger (unlike Stehr and Kolbenheyer) did not at all fit the Nazi programme as smoothly as Goebbels c.s. might have wished them to. In short, there is the commonsensical truth that we should be aware of the fact that our comfortable position of retrospection also breeds a tendency to level more subtle distinctions (as well as, alternatively, attitudes that have "another and a finer connection than that of contrast"), and matters are certainly not as simple as they might appear at first sight.

In keeping with his professed views on literature, the fact that de Man's sympathies in the field of German literature were certainly not in any overt disagreement with those of the official cultural machinery of the occupant, did not prevent him from appreciating French literature as well. And here too, his insistence on the importance of a national specificity is strongly in evidence. Thus, he points to the advent of Baudelaire as the moment at which a profound break with "the traditional French artistic essence" (FP) had taken place, a break which brought French literature closer to German Romanticism than ever before. And although he gives a positive evaluation of symbolism and of the "theoretical insights" of surrealism (which he compares to the "[. . .] spiritual attitude, out of which Germany has drawn the invaluable wealth of its art for centuries" (FP), he feels forced to ask whether, with surrealism as it is actually practiced in literature (and in painting), the "deviation" from the "national, rational tradition" has not gone too far.

6. It should have become clear by now that de Man's conception of literature and literary language at this stage of his career is radically different from his later views on the matter. In 1942, de Man sees literature as an expression of a specific national disposition, which can profitably be used as one kind of reliable historical material for the deduction of "a general idea about the destiny of mankind" (CL). In combination with sociology (which, it may be recalled, was one of the subjects de Man had studied at the Université Libre), literature can "[. . .] open horizons and offer possibilities which otherwise would never have even been suspected" (LS). The study of literature and of art enables one to make extrapolations to "the terrain of the major cultural and political problems" and consequently ought to be undertaken in an attempt "[. . .] to ensure the future of Western civilization in all its aspects" (AM). The task of the literary critic and historian, then, is to satisfy "our natural urge for logical consistency" in offering us a "faithful reproduction of what is recognised as reality," i.e. in allowing "the organizing evolutionary laws" at work in history and literary history to speak out clearly (CL). And all this, finally, is part of the important mission of the "intellectual elite" to preserve European civilization, "[. . .] a task which cannot be accomplished by the will of the people but only by the knowledge and study of the few" (CE).[82]

Again, twenty-four years later, de Man would turn this creed upside down and write that "it is not in the power of philosophy or literature to prevent the degradation of the human spirit, nor is its main function to warn against this degradation."[83] And again, the topos of the restored awareness on the far side of failure forces itself upon us.

But perhaps we should not too eagerly jump to such reassuring conclusions which tend to confirm our hopes that every cloud has a silver lining, that there is a causal link between the obscure 'mistakes' or 'errors'—if that is indeed what they are—of the early de Man and the lucidity of the later de Man. Can we actually see a comprehensible (dialectical) continuity, a genetic development, an organic growth, in de Man's work, taken 'as a whole'? Or should we only "allow for non-comprehension," in the " true 'mourning' " de Man was to allude to so enigmatically towards the end of his life?[84] And what does this mean?

And how are we to counter that other reassuring conclusion, the one that confirms the conviction of those who have always resented de Man's work, that any 'obscurantist nihilist' is bound to have a dirty secret stacked away somewhere, an explanatory sin which will restore healthy intelligibility to its rightful place of prominence once it is brought out into the open?

How are we to account for the displacements from *Les Cahiers du Libre Examen,* to *Le Soir* "volé," to *Het Vlaamsche Land,* to *Critique,* to deconstruction, to de Man? Should we compare Heidegger's self-avowed "stupidity" of 1933 to de Man's ambivalent attitude to the German occupant? And would it be too cynical to apply de Man's statement about Husserl's claim to European supremacy to the writer of "Inhoud der Europeesche gedachte"? Can we say that, "Since we are speaking of a man of superior good will, it suffices to point to the pathos of such a claim at the moment when Europe was about to destroy itself as center in the name of its unwarranted claim to be the center"?[85]

All these questions—which have a distressing tendency to maximalize gossip and rhetoric of self-righteousness at the expense of attentive, sustained reading—have to remain suspended here.

Katholieke Universiteit Leuven

Note: I wish to express my gratitude to Mme. Frida Vandervelden, Mr. et Mme. Pierre de Ligne-Blockx, Dr. Charles Dosogne, Dr. Georges Goriely, Dr. Louis Dupré, Ms. Mary McCarthy, Dr. Artine Artinian and de Heer Lode Claes for their indispensable memories of the late Paul de Man. I am also indebted to Mme. A. Despy-Meyer, Archiviste de l'Université Libre de Bruxelles, for her generous support during my research into de Man's U.L.B.-years. Finally, credits are due to Erik Leroy, whose advice and research assistance have been extremely helpful.

This study forms part of a Ph.D. project I am engaged in as a research assistant of the National Fund for Scientific Research (Belgium) at the Katholieke Universiteit Leuven, under the supervision of Prof. Dr. Herman Servotte.

NOTES

1. Paul de Man, "Dialogue and Dialogism," *The Resistance to Theory* (Foreword by Wlad Godzich), Minneapolis, University of Minnesota Press, 1986, 106–114; 107.

2. For one instance of de Man's referring to these unpublished texts or thoughts, cf. Stefano Rosso, "An Interview with Paul de Man," *The Resistance to Theory,* 115–121, 121. For the political quarrels over de Man's work, see, for instance, Christopher Norris' forthcoming monograph on de Man.

3. Paul de Man, "Hegel on the Sublime," in Mark Krupnick, (ed.), *Displacement: Derrida and After,* Bloomington, Indiana University Press, 1983, 139–153; 152.

4. After the composition of this paper, a still earlier set of texts by Paul de Man has been found by Tom Keenan—seven articles about student life, literature, and politics in *Jeudi,* a (generally weekly) newspaper published in 1939 and 1940 by the same Cercle du Libre Examen at the Université Libre de Bruxelles. Paul de Man contributed to the first issue, of 23 March 1939, and wrote regularly in the issues of the spring semester 1939, and then again in the fall through January 1940. These articles, along with the rest of Paul de Man's presently-known wartime journalism, are reprinted in the companion volume to this one, published by the University of Nebraska Press, 1988.

5. In 1937–38, de Man was enrolled in the department of civil engineering, but never took exams there; in 1938–39 and 1939–40 he completed his first and second year of chemistry, which obtained him a degree of *candidat* (roughly comparable to a bachelor's degree); finally, in 1940–41, he followed courses in the first licence (i.e. the third year) of social sciences, but did not finish this programme either (partially due to the circumstances leading to the University's enforced closure in November 1941, as we shall see later on).

6. As the editors of the first post-liberation issue of the journal put it: "[. . .]—le cercle 'Le Libre-Examen' ne pouvait, ni ne devait avoir la moindre activité légale sous l'occupation—[. . .]." "Editorial," *Les Cahiers du Libre Examen,* 8:1, Juin 1945, 3. Henceforth, we shall refer to this journal by means of the abbreviation LCLE.

7. La Rédaction, "Editorial," LCLE 1:1, Mars 1937, 1–2; 1.

8. La Rédaction, "Précisons," ibid., 2.

9. Le Libre Examen, "A Louvain. Le congrès annuel de la Fédération Belge des étudiants catholiques (le 14 mars 1937)," LCLE 1:2, Avril 1937, 3–5; 5.

10. La Direction, "Editorial," LCLE 4:1–2, Octobre-Novembre 1939, 1–2; 1. It may be useful to recall here that this is the first issue of LCLE in which de Man participated as member of the editorial staff. Hence, it should be legitimate to assume that he has to a certain extent co-signed the sentences just quoted.

11. Les Cahiers du Libre Examen, "Editorial," LCLE 4:3, Décembre 1939, 1–2.

12. Les Cahiers du Libre Examen, "Editorial," LCLE 4:4, Janvier 1940, 1.

13. Paul de Man, "Le roman anglais contemporain," LCLE 4:4, Janvier 1940, 16–19. This, of course, is decidedly not to say that such extrapolations cannot be reasonably made on the basis of the aesthetics underlying this short essay in criticism, but such interpretations are not our main objective in the present paper.

14. "Editorial," LCLE 4:5, Février 1940, 1–2.

15. Paul de Man, "Littérature française," LCLE 4:5, Février 1940, 34–35; 35.

16. For detailed accounts of this aspect of Belgium under German rule, see J. Gérard-Libois et José Gotovitch, *L'An 40: La Belgique occupée,* Bruxelles, CRISP, 1971, esp. the chapter "Presse et Propagande, 306–325; and Els de Bens, *De Belgische dagbladpers onder Duitse censuur (1940–1944),* Antwerpen, De Nederlandsche Boekhandel, 1973. A small part of the latter book is also available in an earlier French version as Els de Bens, "La presse au temps de l'occupation de la Belgique," *Revue d'histoire de la deuxième guerre mondiale,* 80, 1970, 1–28. A concise account of the war-time history of *Le Soir* in particular can be found in the special edition of this paper, on the occasion of its 100th year of publication, a 96-page study by Désiré Denuit, "Une siècle d'histoire," *Le Soir,* 17 Décembre 1987, 2ième cahier. The following survey, drawing almost exclusively on the sources just mentioned, can of course not pretend to offer much more than a highlighting of the more obviously relevant aspects of this matter, at the inevitable expense of some of the complications and subtleties related to it which de Bens, Gérard-Libois and Gotovitch have taken pains to disentangle.

17. Quoted in de Bens, *De Belgische dagbladpers. . . .,* 339, 333.

18. This conflict was eventually to lead to de Becker's and de Ligne's rupture with the occupant in the second half of 1943 and their attendant dismissal as editors of *Le Soir,* an event which Robert Poulet—another 'collaborator' to whom we shall have the occasion to return—considered to be "le dernier épisode de la liquidation de la collaboration modérée en Belgique" (quoted from Poulet's *Mémoires* in de Bens, op. cit., 342). The PA's prohibition to write about a future for Belgium is referred to in de Bens, op. cit., 346.

19. Quoted in French translation from the PA's *Jahresbericht* of August 1941 in Gérard-Libois et Gotovitch, op. cit., 307. This latter issue, of course, became even more complicated when it was brought to bear on figures like Robert Brasillach, Pierre Drieu la Rochelle, Alfred Fabre-Luce and the inevitable Charles Maurras, as we shall see later on.

20. For a complete collection of these texts, see the companion volume to the one in which this essay appears, also published by the

University of Nebraska Press, 1988. I am grateful to Tom Keenan for having pointed out to me a large number of lacunae in my initial list, which were due to my not having been able to gain access to a complete collection of *Le Soir 'volé.'*

21. See, for instance, "Yale Scholar's Articles Found in Pro-Nazi Paper," *The New York Times,* 1 December 1987; and "Yale Scholar wrote for Pro-Nazi Paper: Belgian Discovery of Articles Shocks Colleagues of the Late Paul de Man," *The International Herald Tribune,* 2 December 1987.

22. Paul de Man, "'Le printemps tragique,' de René Benjamin," *Le Soir,* 13 Février 1941, 1. Henceforth, this newspaper shall be referred to by means of the abbreviation LS.

23. Paul de Man, "Récentes publications des lettres belges," LS, 15 Avril 1941, 6.

24. From the diary of A. Somerhausen, quoted in de Bens, op. cit., 358. Further data on Colin can be found in Gérard-Libois et Gotovitch, op. cit.; and in Bernard Delcord, "A propos de quelques 'chapelles' politico-littéraires en Belgique (1919–1945)," *Cahiers du Centre de Recherches et d'Etudes Historiques de la Seconde Guerre Mondiale,* 10, Novembre 1986, 153–205.

25. Information on the fascinating career of Robert Poulet can be profitably gleaned from Bernard Delcord, art. cit. This essay is accompanied by an annex which comprises, among other items, an instructive appreciation of the extent of Poulet's collaboration by Jacques Willequet, "Le cas Robert Poulet. Un historien rélit le *Nouveau Journal*," 200–204, in which the author, after having given a brief sketch of Poulet's "New Order" and his "fascism" —which are entirely different from what we customarily understand by these terms —, makes the following appropriate remark: "Et il est vrai que de nombreux jeunes, dans les années trente, ont été exaltés par cette sorte de syncrétisme généreux. Faut-il citer des noms aujourd'hui respectés, le président d'une grande république voisine, des hommes politiques de gauche, tel éditorialist influent du *Monde?* Remettons, s'il vous plaît, les choses à leur place et dans leur époque!" (202)

26. On the career of Hendrik de Man, see: Peter Dodge, *Beyond Marxism: The Faith and Works of Hendrik de Man,* The Hague, Martinus Nijhoff, 1966; id., *A Documentary Study of Hendrik de Man, Socialist Critic of Marxism* (Compiled, edited, and largely translated by Peter Dodge), Princeton, Princeton University Press, 1979; and Mieke Claeys-Van Haegendoren, *Hendrik de Man: Biografie,* Antwerpen, De Nederlandsche Boekhandel, 1972. Notwithstanding their differences, Poulet and de Man had a great deal in common: both were confirmed Belgicists, both had initially believed in a poli-

tics of presence under the occupation, and both—de Man towards the end of 1941, Poulet in the first half of 1943—terminated their collaborationist activities well before the end of the occupation. Both were nevertheless convicted for high treason during the repression trials.

27. Delcord, art. cit.

28. A helpful account of the history of this salon can be found in Gérard-Libois et Gotovitch, op. cit., 43–47. It may be useful to stress here that the "understanding" attitude referred to just now was not by any means incompatible with the neutralist stance we have said to be predominant among the visitors of the Salon Didier: before the war, there was a difference between taking sides with the Germans and refusing to take sides with the English and the French, although such a distinction was not always granted at the time, as was observed by Raymond de Becker when he wrote that "[. . .] les hommes sincèrement ralliés à la neutralité et à une politique européenne fussent déjà considéré à cette époque comme des hors la loi [. . .]" (quoted in de Bens, op. cit., 284–285). It is, nevertheless, in 'subtleties' such as this that an account can be found for de Man's 'shift' from *Les Cahiers du Libre Examen* to *Le Soir,* the former having expressed itself in explicitly neutralist terms as late as the end of 1939 (cf. La Direction, "Editorial," LCLE, Octobre-Novembre 1939, 2), the latter having always preserved traces of a neutralist tendency in its upholding a Belgicist stance up until the conflict which led to de Becker's dismissal in 1943.

29. Cf. Paul de Man, "Chronique littéraire. Quand l'auteur se transforme en critique," LS, 18 Novembre 1941, 2.

30. To wit, *Le double visage,* a translation of Paul Alverdes' *Das Zwiegesicht,* and *Le soldat Johan,* a translation of Filip de Pillecijn's *De soldaat Johan,* both published in 1942. Tom Keenan has moreover discovered that de Man, together with Jean-Jacques Etienne, translated the German art historian A. E. Brinckmann's *Geist der Nationen* into French as *Esprit des Nations,* a work also published by Les Editions de la Toison d'Or, in 1943. De Man published a review of this study in *Het Vlaamsche Land* in March 1942 (see my "Notes on Paul de Man's Flemish Writings," which follows this article). According to various informants, de Man also produced a French or Flemish translation of *Moby Dick* around this time, which Keenan believes is the unsigned Flemish edition published in Antwerp by Editions Helicon in 1945.

31. As a matter of fact, Belgium is a tri-lingual country, comprising a Dutch-speaking, a French-speaking, and a German-speaking community, but for our present purpose this latter is of lesser importance.

32. Paul de Man, "En marge du dialecte liégeois," LS, 22 Avril 1941, 10. A challenging suggestion on the importance of linguistic nationalism such as it is presented here can be found in a lecture delivered by Michael Holquist at the Politics or Poetics symposium at the Katholieke Universiteit Leuven in August 1987 ("The Pit of Babel: Minority Discourse and Profession Formation").

33. Paul de Man, "Après les journées culturelles germano-flamandes: Le destin de la Flandre," LS, 1 Septembre 1941, 1.

34. P.d.M., "L'Exposition 'Histoire de l'Allemagne' au Cinquentenaire," LS, 16 Mars 1942, 2. Passages such as this one, with their stress on sources and the alienation from them, cannot but evoke the Hölderlinian thematics de Man was to investigate so intensively later on, albeit with very different intentions.

35. Quoted in an anonymous report on "L'inauguration de l'Exposition 'Grandeur de l'Allemagne,'" LS, 17 Mars 1942, 2.

36. Quoted in Mieke Claeys-Van Haegendoren, op. cit., 316–317.

37. Paul de Man, "Notre chronique littéraire. Dans nos murs," LS, 26 Août 1941, 2 (italics mine).

38. Paul de Man, "Chronique littéraire. 'Trois épreuves' par Daniel Halévy," LS, 14 Octobre 1941, 2.

39. Paul de Man, "Chronique littéraire. Premières réactions de la France littéraire," LS, 18 Mars 1941, 6.

40. Paul de Man, "Notre chronique littéraire. *Notre avant-guerre* de Robert Brasillach," LS, 12 Août 1941, 2.

41. In fact, it is slightly ironic to see de Man reprimand in this fashion someone who played a prominent part in the preparation of a philofascistic climate in France—Brasillach, after all, was editor in chief of *Je suis partout,* the main political publication propagating fascist ideologemes already before the French defeat in 1940, expressly affirmed himself to be "germanophile et français," and was executed for his collaborationist activities in 1945. Information on Brasillach, as well as on the other French collaborators de Man singles out for discussion—such as Jacques Benoist-Mechin, Jacques Chardonne, Bertrand de Jouvenel, Bernard Grasset, and, of course, Pierre Drieu la Rochelle—can be profitably gleaned from Pascal Ory, *Les collaborateurs 1940–1945,* Paris, Seuil (Points), 1976.

42. Paul de Man, "Notre chronique littéraire. Tour d'Horizon," LS, 13 Mai 1941, 2.

43. See, for instance, Paul de Man, "Notre chronique littéraire. Le testament politique de Richelieu," LS, 19 Août 1941, 2; "Chronique littéraire. 'Voir la figure' de Jacques Chardonne," LS, 28 Octobre

1941, 2; and "Chronique littéraire. 'Trois épreuves' par Daniel Halévy, LS, 14 Octobre 1941, 2.

44. Paul de Man, "Chronique littéraire. 'Voir la figure' de Jacques Chardonne," LS, 28 Octobre 1941, 2.

45. Here, as elsewhere, a comparison with de Man's later reflections on revolutionary thought promises to be highly rewarding (see, for instance, his "Wordsworth und Hölderlin," *Schweizer Monatshefte* 45:12, März 1966, 1141–1155).

46. Paul de Man, "Chronique littéraire. La littérature française devant les événements," LS, 20 Janvier 1942. See also "Chronique littéraire. A la recherche d'un nouveau mode d'expression: *L'Emotion sociale,* par Charles Dekeukeleire," LS, 17 Mars 1942, 2.

47. Paul de Man, "Chronique littéraire. Le problème français: 'Dieu est-il français?' de F. Sieburg," LS, 28 Avril 1942, 2.

48. Paul de Man, "Chronique littéraire. Bilan d'une année," LS, 30 Septembre 1941, 2.

49. See, for instance, Paul de Man, "Chronique littéraire. A la recherche d'un nouveau mode d'expression: *L'Emotion sociale,* par Charles Dekeukeleire," LS, 17 Mars 1942, 2; and "Chronique littéraire. Premières réactions de la France littéraire," LS, 18 Mars 1942, 6. In another context, de Man speaks of "[. . .] la tendance que nous avons de voir actuellement en tout livre un côté politique—tendance bien excusable, vu les circonstances— [. . .]," but a tendency which, however, he explicitly asserts *not* to wish to give in to ("Chronique littéraire. Deux traductions de l'anglais," LS, 1 Avril 1941, 6).

50. Paul de Man, " Chronique littéraire. Sur les possibilités de la critique," LS, 2 Décembre 1941, 2.

51. Paul de Man, "Chronique littéraire. Regard sur la Flandre," LS, 30 Décembre 1941, 2.

52. For an excellent account of the ambiguous position of *Das innere Reich* in Nazi Germany, see Horst Denkler, "Janusköpfig. Zur ideologischem Physiognomie der Zeitschrift 'Das Innere Reich' (1934–1944)," Horst Denkler und Karl Prumm (Hg.), *Die deutsche Literatur im Dritten Reich: Themen Traditionen Wirkungen,* Stuttgart, Reclam, 1976, 382–405. The whole of this collection is an extremely useful source of information on the German authors chosen for review by de Man.

53. Paul de Man, "Guerre et littérature: Paul Alverdes et sa revue 'Das innere Reich,'" LS, 20 Avril 1942, 1.

54. Paul de Man, "Chronique littéraire. Le problème français: 'Dieu est-il français?' de F. Sieburg," LS, 28 Avril 1942, 2. See also, for instance, de Man's review of recent books by Herman Stehr and Hans Fallada, where he pleads for a synthesis of "un courant de fond" and "un style qui a subi des influences du dehors" ("Chronique littéraire. Romans allemands," LS, 10 Février 1942, 2.)

55. On this score, de Man rarely expresses himself directly. By way of illustration, the following quote from, again, his review of Sieburg's *Dieu est-il français?* may suffice: "L'américanisme nous offre le spectacle édifiant du danger qu'il y a à tout soumettre aux impératifs techniques. En 1929, Sieburg pouvait laisser supposer que l'Allemagne était en voie de suivre un exemple analogue. Il ne pourrait plus le dire maintenant, car il est manifeste que, tout en conservant et en développant même les principes d'organisation à outrance, un fort courant spirituel, rattaché aux origines du génie germanique et glorifiant les constantes de cet esprit, a donné à ces termes d'organisation extérieure le fondement profond sans lequel elles ne sont qu'enveloppe stérile et paralysante." For a remarkable modification of this view in de Man's later work, see Paul de Man, "Tentation de la permanence," *Monde Nouveau* 93, Octobre 1955, 49–61; 49–50.

56. In addition to this, it is perhaps useful to point out that, contrary to what the New York Times Service saw fit to publicize, there is no "[. . .] caricature of Jews with horns and claws who, wearing prayer shawls, pray that 'Jehovah will confound the gentiles,'" next to the essay (cf. note 21). The supposed 'caricature' is in fact nothing but a photograph of Jews engaged in an act of religious worship, admittedly rather blurred on the low-quality photocopy the NYT had at its disposal—what are taken to be "horns and claws" are merely hands raised in prayer. The American newspapers have been rather more quick in making this sensational mistake than in reporting that under de Man's article, Benjamin Franklin is quoted as saying that "Un léopard ne saurait changer ses taches. Les Juifs sont des Asiatiques; ils sont une menace pour le pays qui les admet, et ils devaient être exclus par la Constitution." For the sake of accuracy, I wish to add that neither quote nor picture are to be ascribed to de Man, who was not responsible for the lay out of the page, and that the Franklin quotation has been established, by Geoffrey Hartman with the help of Yale University's Benjamin Franklin Papers project, to be a forgery, one widely circulated in Nazi anti-semitic propaganda material (Hartman, "Blindness and Insight," *The New Republic,* 7 March 1988, 26). This is as good as any place to point out that, furthermore, contrary to what the New York Times Service reports, Hendrik de Man was never a member of the Belgian collaborationist government, for the simple reason that there never was such a government.

57. Léon Van Huffel, "Les deux faces du judaïsme," LS, 4 Mars 1941, 10.

58. See, for instance, Marcel Liebman, *Né juif: une enfance juive pendant la guerre,* Paris, Duculot, 1977; a personal account of the Nazi horrors by a Brussels Jew.

59. "Et voici, l'élite'" de l'U. L. B.," *Debout: Organe de la Fédération Bruxelloise des Etudiants Socialistes Unifiés,* 1er no. légal, 6 Septembre 1944, 3.

Perhaps some factual elucidations may be necessary here: *Rex,* Léon Degrelle's francophone pan-Germanic collaborationist party; v.n.v. (Vlaams Nationaal Verbond), a Flemish nationalist party which supported the German enterprise but which was opposed to the pan-Germanic annexation schemes propagated by Rex and Devlag; *Devlag* (Duits-Vlaamsche Arbeidsgemeenschap /Deutsch-Flämische Arbeitsgemeinschaft), an initially cultural society which rapidly turned explicitly political when its intention to solidify the cultural link between Germany and Flanders found new vigor in the proposed political unification of both communities; *Schranen* (actually A. Schraenen) the PA's representative in charge of *Le Soir; place de Louvain,* the address of the offices of *Le Soir.* We need not concern ourselves much with the indignant and self-righteous tone pervading this article; factually, however, it may be interesting to underscore the typical gesture of reactive amalgamation we witness here: Rex, Devlag, v.n.v., *Le Soir,* worlds apart as they were, are all being lumped together on the basis of their one common denominator, the fact of their collaboration. A move which is all too understandable, to be sure, but which must nevertheless be recognized for the error it is.

Finally, I wish to point out that none of de Man's contemporaries whom I have been able to contact confirm that he was the "chef des de Mannistes à l'Université." Hendrik de Man was undoubtedly a formidable character then, and it is only to be expected that the nephew was thought to be a representative of the uncle, but this does not seem to have been the case. Which is not to say that Paul de Man opposed his uncle, but only that his primary interests did not lie in the spheres of direct political action and socialist theory the latter commanded at the time. Indeed, there is at least one instance where we find Paul de Man obliquely defending his uncle's decision to refuse to join the government in exile and to remain at the side of the King (in fact advising the latter not to leave his country), notably when he denounces the "campagne mensongère" of the French premier Reynaud who, before the defeat of France, accused Leopold III of having betrayed the constitution of his country by having negotiated with the enemy (Paul de Man, "Notre chronique littéraire. Dans nos murs," LS, 26 Août 1941, 2).

60. We may want to recall here that around the same time, de Man also stopped writing for the Flemish newspaper *Het Vlaamsche Land,* a journal in many ways comparable to *Le Soir*—to which he contributed some ten texts in the course of 1942. See my "Notes on Paul de Man's Flemish Writings," which follows this essay, and note /68/below.

61. Some data nevertheless deserve to be mentioned in this respect. One is that in August 1942, the PA decided to reinstate the policy of pre-publication censorship it had abandoned in October 1940. Even while such censorship was only aimed at explicitly political contributions, the PA's decision undoubtedly narrowed the margin of disobedience *Le Soir* had seen fit to make use of previously. Closely related to this increased pressure is, of course, the quarrel between de Becker and the German officials over the future of Belgium as an independent nation which was to lead, as was said, to the former's forced retirement in October 1943. We may recall that people like Hendrik de Man and Robert Poulet also decided to publicly disengage themselves from the occupant.

62. The statement in the *Debout* article that de Man joined the press-agency Belgapress (not "Belgapresse"), an organization under the supervision of the PA and dependent on the *Deutsches Nachrichten-Büro,* has not been verified.

63. Quoted in de Bens, op. cit., 99.

64. Ibid., 97.

65. Paul de Man, "Chronique littéraire. Deux traductions de l'anglais /Une édition populaire de *Pallieter* de F. Timmermans," LS, 1 Avril 1941, 6.

66. Paul de Man, "Chronique littéraire. Regard sur la Flandre," LS, 30 Décembre 1941, 2. We may recall here that *Les Editions de la Toison d'Or* published a translation of *De soldaat Johan* by de Man in 1942; its author, Filip de Pillecijn, was convicted for collaboration after the war. As for Stijn Streuvels' *De Vlaschaard,* it might be mentioned that this Flemish classic, too, was exploited by the Germans for ideological purposes, witness its being adapted for the German cinema by Boleslav Barlog in 1943.

67. Paul de Man, "Les initiatives de l'Agence Dechenne: Pour que le peuple lise," LS, 20 Janvier 1942, 1.

68. Research carried out by Chantal Kesteloot (of the Centre de Recherches et d'Etudes Historiques de la Seconde Guerre Mondiale in Brussels) and myself, on a suggestion from Tom Keenan, after the composition of this paper has yielded more information on Paul de Man's position at the Agence Dechenne.

From August 1941 until July 1944, this organization published a monthly bibliographical review (as was mentioned earlier on) entitled *Bibliographie.* This review contained a survey of the new books in print, a number of which were presented in brief notices, some of them signed, others anonymous. Apart from this, most issues of the *Bibliographie Dechenne* contained a short essay commenting upon the contemporary literary scene and a usually unsigned section presenting additional information relative to the publishing trade. From February 1942 until March 1943, de Man published seven short essays and 93 bibliographical notices in this review, most of them in French, sometimes in French and in Dutch, and on a few occasions in Dutch only. A large part of these notices present publications he had already discussed or was to discuss in his chronicles in *Le Soir* and *Het Vlaamsche Land,* while the essays, too, develop arguments very similar, if not identical, to those developed in his journalism. It is very likely that in the period mentioned de Man published more notices than the 93 signed ones, but it is difficult to ascertain this. It seems on the other hand improbable that he continued to write anonymously for the *Bibliographie Dechenne* after March 1943: previous to this date, the large majority of the signed notices were written by G[uido] E[eckels] or P.d.M.; from April 1943 onwards, no sign of these initials is to be found, but the notices one would have expected to be signed by one of them now bear the initials J[ean] d[e] B[ackere], in later months replaced in turn by one K. and, finally, by one A. R. These data, then, only allow us to establish that Paul de Man was one of the editors of the *Bibliographie Dechenne* from February 1942 until March 1943. Exactly when and why he left this position is not yet clear.

All of de Man's texts in the *Bibliographie Dechenne* are reprinted in the companion volume to this one.

69. I initially found 92 articles—I was convinced that there had to be more, but due to practical circumstances and the inaccessibility of a number of sources, I could not complete my list. Since then, Tom Keenan, de Man's excellent bibliographer, has added 78 more articles to the list, thus bringing it to a total of 170.

70. "Aspects of the context of Paul de Man's earliest publications" (henceforth "Aspects"), above.

71. Minae Mizumura, "Renunciation," in *Yale French Studies* 69, 1985, 81–97: 82.

72. Paul de Man, "Shelley Disfigured," in *The Rhetoric of Romanticism,* New York, Columbia University Press, 1984, 93–123; 123. De Man's discussion of this quote from Hardy with respect to Shelley's 'biography' of Rousseau should at least put us on our guards against the construction of the sort of hasty interpretations of 'The Life of Paul de Man' the media have seen fit to offer us since De-

cember 1987 (and which, adding insult to injury, they glibly present as 'deconstructions').

73. For a detailed account of de Man's activities in this journal, see my "Aspects."

74. A difference between *Het Vlaamsche Land* and *Le Soir* was that the former was not, strictly speaking, a "stolen" newspaper (i.e. a journal which, like *Le Soir,* was published under the same name as a pre-war paper printed by the same press, even though the editors had all been replaced under German supervision). In fact, *Het Vlaamsche Land* was the 'continuation' of the *Gazet van Antwerpen,* and, as opposed to *Le Soir* "volé," its editorial staff was largely composed of employees of that pre-war journal. *Het Vlaamsche Land* was not by far as popular as *Le Soir,* but it was not a negligeable publication either. To avoid misunderstandings, it should be stressed that there were two very different newspapers called *Het Vlaamsche Land,* one of which was the extremely collaborationist organism of the *Devlag* (the *Deutsch-Flämische Arbeitsgemeinschaft*). The paper de Man wrote in was the other one.

My presentation of the position of *Het Vlaamsche Land* in occupied Belgium is fully indebted to Els de Bens' monograph on the Belgian daily press under German censorship during the war (Els de Bens, *De Belgische dagbladpers onder Duitse censuur (1940–1944).* Antwerpen, De Nederlandsche Boekhandel, 1973.) References to this study will henceforth be included in the text (DB, plus page number).

75. This is probably as good a place as any to point out that similar views were fairly widespread before and during the first years of the war. In retrospect, it is almost impossible (and often deemed to be cynical) not to label all manifestations of such an opinion as instances of simple anti-Semitism, but in fact in many cases there was no overt racial prejudice involved in such views. Thus, before the invasion, some of the most distinguished proponents of a neutralist policy and staunch opponents of the Nazi ideology also accused the Jews of unduly provoking the German warmongers into acts of military aggression, thereby rendering a diplomatic solution (which was still believed to be a feasible way out) impossible.

76. This last issue—the annexation of Flanders to the German Reich—perhaps stands in need of some elucidation. From its very foundation in 1830, Belgium has been a divided kingdom, consisting of two large communities, one francophone (Wallonia), the other Dutch-speaking (Flanders). Throughout the 19th century, and well into the 20th, French was the language of power, in Wallonia as well as in Flanders, which led to a number of discriminations against Flemish culture. The rebellious state of mind that grew out of such iniquities turned out to be very germane to Ger-

man expansionist interests, both in the First and in the Second World War. Indeed, the German propaganda machinery succeeded in gaining considerable support from a fairly large proportion of the Flemish community by promising Flanders a release from Walloon domination in a germanic Empire. However this may be, and running ahead a little, it is important to stress that Paul de Man, for one, very explicitly rejected such separatism-cum-annexation (see "Aspects").

77. For my translations of these ten texts, see the volume of de Man's *Wartime Journalism*. Regarding these translations, I wish to draw attention to a particular linguistic difficulty, notably, the fact that de Man's bilingual education brought with it a rather poor mastery of standard Dutch. This was a recurrent phenomenon at the time: many of those who spoke Flemish (which is a 'dialect' of Dutch) as their native language, were not always able to fully master the standard variety of this language in formal circumstances (such as the composition of critical texts), and ended up by using either French, or, if necessary, a rather uneasy language which might be called 'standard Flemish.' We do not need to consider this complicated form of pseudo-diglossia —which I have grossly oversimplified—in more detail here; I have only mentioned it in order to account for the sometimes awkward phrasing of my translations, an awkwardness which is a more or less faithful rendition of that of the originals.

For the sake of convenience, I will here list the ten texts in question, with English translations of their titles. The abbreviations preceding each entry are added for the purpose of reference in the subsequent discussion.

AM "Kunst als spiegel van het wezen der volkeren: Beschouwingen over 'Geist der Nationen' van A.E. Brinckmann ("Art as mirror of the essence of nations: Considerations on 'Geist der Nationen' by A.E. Brinckmann"), 29–30 March 1942, 3.

FL "Huidige strekkingen der Fransche Literatuur" ("Contemporary trends in French Literature"), 17–18 May 1942, 3.

CE "Inhoud der Europeesche gedachte" ("Content of the European idea"), 31 May 1 June 1942, 3.

CL "Critiek en literatuurgeschiedenis" ("Criticism and literary history"), 7–8 June 1942, 3.

FP "Hedendaagsche strekkingen in de Fransche Poëzie" ("Contemporary trends in French Poetry"), 6–7 July 1942, 3.

EJ   "Duitsche Letteren. Een groot schrijver: Ernst Jünger" ("German Literature. A great writer: Ernst Jünger"), 26–27 July 1942, 2.

GF   "Blik op de huidige Duitsche Romanliteratuur" ("A view on contemporary German Fiction"), 20 August 1942, 2.

MD   "Duitsche Letteren. Een groot Duitsch lyricus: Max Dauthendey" ("German Literature. A great German lyrist: Max Dauthendey"), 6–7 September 1942, 2.

LS   "Literatuur en sociologie" ("Literature and sociology"), 27–28 September 1942, 2.

PE   "Vooren nadeelen van de volksuitgaven" ("Advantages and disadvantages of the popular editions"), 20 October 1942, 2.

78. A.E. Brinckmann, *Geist der Nationen: Italiener Franzosen-Deutsche*. Hamburg: Hoffman und Campe, 1938, 260.

79. Hans Carossa (1878–1956), extremely popular during the Weimar years, managed to remain aloof from the official Nazi policies after 1933, but unwittingly served the purpose of a facade apologist of the regime by virtue of his appointment as President of the European Writers' Union in 1942 (cf. Robert Wistrich, *Who's Who in Nazi Germany*. London: Weidenfeld and Nicholson,1982, p.37); Erwin Guido Kolbenheyer (1878–1962) was a leading apologist of the Third Reich" who "[. . .] defended the Nazi burning of the books as a necessary act of 'purification' and wrote a poem in honor of Hitler, praising 'the man who won a way towards the light for his people.' [. . .] His work was a prime example of the genre of Nazi literature which enabled naked violence and political cynicism to be dissolved into a fog of idealistic mysticism" (Wistrich, 177–8); Herman Stehr (1864–1940), too, explicitly endorsed the National Socialist movement, in which he found a doctrine congenial to his dislike of democratic civilizations and Jewish intellectualism. He received the *Adlershild des Deutschen Reiches* in 1934 and was praised for his expressions of a "volkischer Erdverbundenheit"; the editors of *Das Innere Reich,* Paul Alverdes (1897–1979) and Benno von Mechow (1897–1960) were of lesser immediate prominence, and their attitude towards the regime was highly ambivalent (see also "Aspects"); the case of Ernst Jünger (1895), finally, is extremely complex—suffice it to say here that while Jünger "[. . .] helped foster a mental climate in which Nazism could flourish [. . .]" (Wistrich, 164), he grew more and more averse to National Socialism from the late Thirties onwards and frequently came into conflict with several Nazi officials (see also Noel O'Sullivan, *Fascism*. London, Dent (Modern Ideologies), 1983; 147–8). For extensive discussions of all these authors, cf. Horst Denkler und Karl Prümm(Hg.), *Die deutsche Literatur im Dritten Reich: Themen Traditionen Wirkungen*. Stuttgart, Reclam, 1976.

80. Paul de Man, "The Literature of Nihilism," in *The New York Review of Books,* June 23, 1966, 16–20; 17.

81. Paul de Man, "Wordsworth and Hölderlin" (translated from the German by Timothy Bahti), in *The Rhetoric of Romanticism,* 47–65; 58.

82. Here, as elsewhere, motifs of Hendrik de Man's work crop up in his nephew's journalism: in his notorious 1940 "Manifesto", Hendrik de Man had already proclaimed that the German victory was to lead to "[. . .] an era in which an elite—preferring a lively and dangerous life to a torpid and easy one, and seeking responsibility instead of fleeing it—will build a new world." (Quoted in Peter Dodge, *A Documentary Study of Hendrik de Man, Socialist Critic of Marxism* (Compiled, edited, and largely translated by Peter Dodge). Princeton, Princeton University Press, 1979, 327–328.)

83. Paul de Man, "The Literature of Nihilism", 17.

84. Paul de Man, "Anthropomorphism and Trope in the Lyric,"in *The Rhetoric of Romanticism,* 239–262; 262.

85. Paul de Man, "Criticism and Crisis", in *Blindness and Insight: Essays in the Rhetoric of Contemporary Criticism* (Second Edition, Revised, with an introduction by Wlad Godzich). London, Methuen, 1983, 3–19; 16.

Like the Sound of the Sea Deep Within a Shell: Paul de Man's War

JACQUES DERRIDA

Translated by Peggy Kamuf

Unable to respond to the questions, to all the questions, I will ask myself instead *whether responding is possible* and what that would mean in such a situation. And I will risk in turn several questions *prior to* the definition of a *responsibility.* But is it not an act to assume in theory the concept of a responsibility? Is that not already to take a responsibility? One's own as well as the responsibility to which one believes one ought to summon others?

The title names a war. Which war?

Do not think only of the war that broke out several months ago around some articles signed by a certain Paul de Man, in Belgium between 1940 and 1942. Later you will understand why it is important to situate the beginning of things *public,* that is the publications, early in 1940 at the latest, during the war but before the occupation of Belgium by the Nazis, and not in December 1940, the date of the first article that appeared in *Le Soir,* the major Brussels newspaper that was then controlled, more or less strictly, by the occupiers. For several months, in the United States, the phenomena of this war "around" Paul de Man have been limited to newspaper articles. War, a public act, is by rights something declared. So we will not count in the category of war the private phenomena—meetings, discussions, correspondences, or telephonic conclaves—however intense they may have been in recent days, and already well beyond the American academic milieu.

To my knowledge, at the moment I write, this war presents itself as such, it is *declared* in newspapers *and nowhere else,* on the subject of arguments made in newspapers, *and nowhere else,* in the course of the last world war, during two years almost a half century ago. That is why my title alludes to the passage from Montherlant quoted by de Man in *Le Soir* in 1941. I will come back to it, but the double edge of its irony already seems cruel: "When I open the newspapers and journals of today, I hear the indifference of the future rolling over them, just as one hears the sound of the sea when one holds certain seashells up to the ear."

The future will not have been indifferent, not for long, just barely a half century, to what de Man wrote one day in the "newspapers and journals of today." One may draw from this many contradictory lessons. But in the several months to follow, the very young journalist that he will have been during less than two years will be read more intensely than the theoretician, the thinker, the writer, the professor, the author of great books that he was during forty years. Is this unfair? Yes, no. But what about later? Here is a prediction and a hope: without ever forgetting the journalist, people will relearn how to read "*all*" of the work (which is to say so many others as well) *toward that which opens itself up there.* People will learn to reread the books, and *once again* the newspapers, and *once again toward that which opens itself up there.* To do so, one will need in the first place, and more than ever *in the future,* the lessons of Paul de Man.

Elsewhere, having more time and more space, one will also analyze from every angle the significance of the press in the modernity of a history like this one, in the course of a war like this one: the one and the other would be impossible and inconceivable without journalism. Yet, whatever one may think of the ignorance, the simplism, the sensationalist flurry full of hatred which certain American newspapers displayed in this case, we will not engage in any negative evaluation of the press *in general.* Such an evaluation belongs to a code that one must always mistrust. It is not far removed from what we are going to talk about. What is more, I think it is only normal that the American press does not remain silent about the emotion aroused by, I quote, the "pro-Nazi articles" or the "anti-Semitic articles" published in a "pro-Nazi newspaper" by a "Yale scholar," a "revered" professor, "Sterling Professor of Humanities" who "died in 1983 while chairman of Yale's Comparative Literature Department." Incidentally, what would have happened if Paul de Man had not been a great American professor or if, as a professor, he had not been at Yale? And what if one also did a history of Yale, or of the great Eastern universities, a history of certain of their past (just barely, very recently) ideologico-institutional practices having to do with certain themes that we are going to talk about?[1] Well, after having had to set aside the question "What is the press in the culture and politics of this century?" I will also have to postpone this other question: "What is Yale, for example, in American culture."

If newspapers have the duty to inform and the right to interpret, would it not have been better if they had done so with caution, rigor, honesty? There was little of that. And the press' most serious lapses from its elementary duties cannot be imputed to the newspapers or to the professional journalists themselves, but to certain academics.

The fact is there: at the point at which I take the risk of writing on this subject, I have the sense of being the first, thus so far the only one to do so, still too quickly to be sure, but without journalistic haste, which is to say without the excuses it sometimes gives the journalist but should never give the academic. It is a formidable privilege, one not designed to alleviate the feeling of my responsibility. For this deadly war (and fear, hatred, which is to say sometimes love, also dream of killing the dead in order to get at the living) has already recruited some combatants, while others are sharpening their weapons in preparation for it. In the evaluations of journalists or of certain professors,

one can make out strategies or stratagems, movements of attack or defense, sometimes the two at once. Although this war no doubt began in the newspapers, it will be carried on for a long time elsewhere, in the most diverse forms. There will be many of us who will have to take our responsibilities and who, at the same time, will have to say, in the face of what is happening to us today, what *responding* and taking a *responsibility* can mean. For what is happening with these "revelations" (I am quoting the word from a newspaper) is happening *to us.*

It is *happening* to all those for whom this event ought to have a meaning, even if that meaning is difficult to decipher and even if, for many, the person and the work of de Man still remain not well known. Let those in this latter category be reassured or still more troubled: even for his admirers and his friends, especially for them, if I may be allowed to testify to this, the work and the person of Paul de Man were enigmatic. Perhaps they are becoming more enigmatic than ever. Do you believe friendship or admiration ought to reduce everything about this enigma? I believe just the opposite.

Why do I now underscore that expression: "*what is happening*"? Because for me this belongs to the order of the absolutely unforeseeable, which is always the condition of any event. Even when it seems to go back to a buried past, what comes about always comes from the future. And it is especially about the future that I will be talking. Something *happens* only on the condition that one is not expecting it. Here of course I am speaking the language of consciousness. But there would also be no event *identifiable as such* if some repetition did not come along to cushion the surprise by preparing its effect on the basis of some experience of the unconscious. If the word "unconscious" has any meaning, then it stems from this necessity.

With or without a *recognition of the unconscious,* today this is *happening to us.* I name thereby, in utter darkness, many people. But it is also the darkness of a blinding light: *us,* we are still the living and the survivors, however uncertain and incomprehensible such a phrase may remain. The said war, then, could only take place, if that is what certain people want, *among us.* For we must never forget this cold and pitiless light: Paul de Man *himself* is dead. If there are some who want to organize a trial in order to judge him, de Man, they must remember that he, de Man, is dead and will not answer in the present. This thing will always be difficult to think and perhaps it will become more and more difficult. He, *himself, he is dead,* and yet, through the specters of memory and of the text, he lives *among us* and, as one says in French, *il nous regarde*—he looks at us, but also he is our concern, we have concerns regarding him, more than ever without his being here. He speaks (to) us among us. He makes us or allows us to speak of us, *to speak to us. He speaks (to) us* [Il nous parle]. The equivocality of the French expression, because it is barely translatable, translates well the murkiness of the question. What do we mean, what do *us* and *among us* mean in this case?

However obscure this may remain, we have to register it: we still have responsibilities toward him, and they are more alive than ever, even as he is dead. That is, we have responsibilities regarding Paul de Man *himself* but *in us and for us*. Yes, it remains difficult to think that he is dead and what that can mean. How are we to know about what or whom one is speaking when there are some who venture to exploit *what is happening* against others and for ends that no longer concern Paul de Man *himself*, that in any case will never reach him, while others will still try to protect *themselves* by pretending to protect Paul de Man against *what is happening*?

Is it possible to assume here one's own responsibility without doing one or the other, without using *what happens to us* in order to attack or to protect oneself? Without war, therefore? I do not know yet, but I would like to try to get there, to say at least something about it, and, this I do know, no matter what may happen.

So we have to answer [*répondre*] for what is happening to us. It will not be a matter only of the responsibility of a writer, a theoretician, a professor, or an intellectual. The act of responding and the definition of what "responding" means carry our commitment well beyond, no doubt, what may look like a circumscribed example, well beyond the limits of the literary and artistic column that a very young man wrote for a newspaper, almost a half century ago, for less than two years, in very singular private and political circumstances which we are far from fully understanding, before leaving his country and undertaking, in another country and another language, the story that we know, the only one that we knew something about until a few months ago: that of a great professor whose teaching and influence spread well beyond the United States, a fact that no one denies, whose work as a philosopher and as a theoretician of literature is admired or put to work by many scholars and students throughout the world, discussed or attacked by others, but dismissed by no one; that also of a man whose many friends, colleagues, students recognized what they owe to his lucidity, his rigor, his tireless generosity. We will come back to this.

Which war, then? Paul de Man's war, in another sense, is also the Second World War. He began to publish during the war. As far as I know, none of the incriminated articles was written after 1942, that is, well before the end of the war and of the German occupation. The reconstitution and the analysis of what his experience was of that war and that occupation will require patient, careful, minute, and difficult research. Any conclusion that does not rely on such research would be unjust, abusive, and irresponsible—I would even say, given the gravity of these things, indecent. And will it ever be necessary to conclude? Is that what this is about? Is a measure, a fair measure, possible? We will come back to this.

Which war, then? Paul de Man's war is finally, in a third sense, the one that this man must have lived and endured *in himself*. He *was* this war. And for almost a half century, this ordeal was a war because it could not remain a merely private torment. It has to have marked his public gestures, his teaching and writing. It remains a secret, a hive of secrets, but no one can seriously imagine, today, that in the course of such a history, this man would not have been torn apart by the tragedies, ruptures, dissociations, "disjunctions" (here I am using one of his favorite words and a concept that plays a major role in his thought). How did he undergo or assume on the outside these internal conflicts? How did he live this unlivable discord between worlds, histories, memories, discourses, languages? Do we have the means to testify to this? Who has the right to judge it, to condemn or to absolve? We will come back to this as well.

If it is now a matter of *responding* and of taking *responsibilities,* then we do so necessarily, as always, in situations we neither choose nor control, by responding to *unforeseeable* appeals, that is to appeals *from/of the other* that are addressed to us even before we decide on them. Permit me to say a few words about certain recent appeals to which I thought I ought to respond and without which I would not be writing what you are reading here.

Two of them took the allegorical form of the telephone call. One took me by surprise in August, the other in December.

So this time I will have to tell. "Have I anything *to tell*?" is a question I have often asked myself in English during these last months. Do I have anything to tell that those interested in these things do not already know, those who discovered these "early writings," as the newspapers put it, at the same time I did? Do I have anything to analyze in a pertinent fashion, to discern, to distinguish (to tell) in the tangled fabric of this enigma, in order to account for it? I am not sure, I still cannot tell. At least I will have been obliged to recall the first words of the *Mémoires* that I dedicated four years ago to the one who was and remains my friend. (May I be forgiven these "self-centered" references; I will not overdo them.) "I have never known how to tell a story"; those were its first words.[2] How could I have then imagined that it would be from the friend, from him alone, singularly from him, that would one day come the obligation to tell a story? And that this injunction would come to me from the one who always associated narrative structure with allegory, that discourse of the other, which always says something still other than what it says?

Mémoires speak especially, and often, of the future, that is, of that which cannot be anticipated and which always marks the memory of the past as experience of the promise. I claimed to know what a future should be *in general*: the unforeseeable itself. But without foreseeing as yet, and precisely for that reason, *what* it would be, I named in effect a future that it was absolutely impossible for me to see coming. And what a future! And the future of what a past! A future and a past about which I have at least, consciously, this absolute certainty: I never shared them and will never share them with Paul de Man, *himself,* whether one is talking about what *he* might have written a long time before I knew him, or about what is happening *to us* after his death.

I have just quoted the first words of a book. I believed I was chancing them in utter darkness. The last words of the same book resonate no less strangely, uncannily for me today. Forgive me once again this last and long quotation:

A promise has meaning and gravity only with the death of the other. When the friend is no longer *there,* the promise is still not tenable, it will not have been made, but as a trace of the future it can still be *renewed.* You could call this an act of memory or a given word, even an act of faith; I prefer to take the risk of a singular and more equivocal word. I prefer to call this an *act,* only an act, quite simply an act. An impossible act, therefore the only one worthy of its name, or rather which, in order to be worthy of its name, must be worthy of the name of the other, made in the name of the other. Try and translate, in all of its syntactical equivocity, a syntagm such as "donner au nom de l'autre" or "une parole donne au nom de l'au-tre." In a single sentence, it could mean in French, or rather in English: "to give to the name of the other" and "to give in the name of the other." Who knows what we are doing when we *donnons au nom de l'autre?* [*M,* p.150]

"*Who knows. . . ?*" Who can tell? Not only did I not know it myself, neither this nor the ordeal the future held in store for my bereaved friendship, for that promise that friendship always is—a promise and a grief which are never over. I also did not know *what* I was promising. Yet, what was I saying about this non-knowledge? That it is the very thing that makes of the promise to the other a true promise, the only true promise, if there is any, an excessive and unconditional promise, an impossible promise. One can never promise in a halfway fashion, one always has to promise too much, more than one can keep. I could not know that one day, the experience of such a wound would have to include responding for Paul de Man: not responding *in his place* or in his name, that will always be impossible and unjustifiable (the promise or friendship even supposes the respect of this impossibility or the irreplaceable singularity of the other). Nor do I mean judging, and certainly not approving of everything he did, but speaking once again, of-him-for-him, at a moment when his memory or his legacy risk being accused and he is no longer there to speak in his own name. To speak in one's own name, moreover, is that ever possible? Would he have done it, would he have been able to do it if he were alive? What would have happened? Would all this have happened if he were still alive today? What does that mean "to be alive today"? These are just so many questions that I will also have to leave unanswered, like that of a responsibility which would never be cancelled, but on the contrary provoked by the experience of prosopopeia, such as de Man seems to understand it.

Well, when I received, in December, the telephone call from *Critical Inquiry* which proposed, singular generosity, that I be the first to speak, when a friendly voice said to me: "it has to be you, we thought that it was up to you to do this before anyone else," I believed I had to accept a warm invitation that also resonated like a summons. Unable not to accept, I nevertheless wondered: why me? why me first? Why me who, by birth, history, inclination, philosophical, political, or ideological choice, have never had anything but a radically, explicitly, mistrustful relation to everything that is being incriminated with such haste about these texts? Why me, who did not even know of their existence until a few months ago? Why me, who knew nothing about the dark time spent between 1940–42 by the Paul de Man I later read, knew, admired, loved? I will have to try to explain the reasons for which I nevertheless accepted to respond *yes* to this appeal and thus to take such a responsibility.

But my account will begin with an earlier telephone call. In August, Samuel Weber calls me upon his return from Belgium. During a conference, he has met a young Belgian researcher, Ortwin de Graef, who informed him of a disturbing discovery: articles written by Paul de Man under the German occupation, between 1941 and 1942, in two newspapers, the French language *Le Soir* and the Flemish language *Het Vlaamsche Land.* This research assistant of the Belgian National Fund for Scientific Research at the Katholieke Universiteit Leuven is preparing a doctoral dissertation on Paul de Man. Sam Weber describes him over the phone: an intelligent young man who admires and knows well the work of Paul de Man. He can also foresee, therefore, what effects will result, especially in the United States, from the publication of his discovery. That is why he talked to Sam Weber about it and also hopes, the latter tells me, to get my advice. But—to an extent, under conditions, and in a form that I still today do not know—he has already communicated, by that time, his research and discovery, as well as his desire to make them public, to several persons in the United States, notably at Yale. Likewise, he has already sent to the British journal *Textual Practice,* along with the translation of four Flemish texts published by Paul de Man in 1942,[3] an introduction[4] that, he will subsequently tell me in a letter, "is not really to his satisfaction" but "he does not have the time" to write another text as he is about to begin his military service. All of this gives me the sense that this young man, whom I have yet to meet, is as worried about handling a dangerous and spectacular explosive as he is careful, for this very reason of course, not to let it get out of his hands (analysis interrupted).

After discussing it on the phone, we decide, Sam Weber and myself, to ask Ortwin de Graef to send us, if possible, copies of the articles published in French, which were the more numerous. Then we could advise him from a more informed position. Sam Weber writes to him to this effect on our behalf. A short while later, we receive copies of 25 articles in French, accompanied by a bibliographical notice concerning 92 articles published in *Le Soir* between February 1941 and June 1942. In a handwritten note, De Graef adds: "plus probably another 20–30 in the period July-December 1942."

I specify this point for two reasons. (1) First of all, I have still not understood why and how this selection of 25 articles was made from a set of about 125. But I have no reason to suspect the intention of he who wrote the following to me, in a letter accompanying the package and in order to forestall my anxiety: "Yesterday I received a letter from Mr. Samuel Weber in which he tells me that you are prepared to give me your opinion on the texts of Paul de Man that I have found. In this envelope, you will find a bibliographical list as well as a not altogether arbitrary selection of these texts (it is difficult, for practical reasons, to send you all the articles now, but if you wish to see them, I will try to find a way—in any case, the present selection can give an impression of the general content of the first writings of Paul de Man as concerns the events of the war)."[5] However neutral and honest the principle of this selection, however indispensable it may have seemed for technical reasons I know nothing about, it has perhaps privileged the texts that are politically and ideologically significant. Thus perhaps it has distorted a general configuration that would be better respected by an integral reading. It is for this reason, and I will come to this point

later, that we decided to pursue systematically the research—which De Graef by that time had to interrupt for reasons of military service—and to publish *all* the accessible articles. (2) For the same reason, at the moment of this writing, I have still been able to read, besides the twenty-five articles from *Le Soir,* only the four articles translated from Flemish into English and introduced by the translator. I cannot even evaluate the effects of this limitation on what I may say here, but I do not want to exclude them. The important thing is not only the limitation on my reading at the moment in which I must write, whatever meaning that may have, but the fact that all the sensationalist "information" delivered in great haste by the newspapers and by those who fed them their information remains marked by this same limitation that was generally *undeclared,* just as there was no mention made of the as yet very insufficient state of our most elementary knowledge concerning the essentials of this affair. I insist on heavily underscoring this point. To be sure, in the course of the research and debates that will undoubtedly continue, I will perhaps be lead to complete or correct the first impressions that I am delivering here as such. I would have waited to do a more systematic job if the press had not pressed us to hurry.

What were these impressions after a first reading toward the end of the August? As I said to Sam Weber, during the first phone call (and one may easily imagine this), I had first hoped to read less profoundly marked articles. I had hoped that the concessions to the occupier or the ideological contagion (which I already expected: one did not accept to publish in that context without paying the price, that is, without accepting what we know today to be unacceptable) would take minimal and some sort of negative forms: more those of omission or of abstention. This hope disappointed, I had to give in to this first appearance at least: things seemed serious and complicated. Paul de Man's discourse appeared to me right off to be clearly more engaged than I had hoped, but also more differentiated and no doubt more heterogeneous. The form of the engagement was even rather disconcerting. One could recognize very quickly in the writing, along with the traits of a certain juvenility, those of an extraordinary culture—a culture that was especially literary or artistic, already very international (French and German, especially, but also Anglo-American and Flemish), open to the great politico-philosophical problems that everything then made more dramatic and more pressing: the destiny of Europe, the essence and future of nations, the individual and democracy, war, science and technology, and most particularly the political meanings and importance of literature.

Rightly or wrongly, I believed I had to accept what could be in itself *contradictory* about this double impression. On the one hand, I perceived an intellectual maturity and a cultivation which were uncommon at that age, and thus an exceptional sense of historical, philosophical, political responsibilities. There can be no doubt about this; it forms, rather, the theme, so to speak, of all these texts. To a very great extent, Paul de Man knew what he was doing, as they say, and he constantly posed questions of responsibility, which does not mean that his response to his questions was ever simple. Nonetheless, on the other hand, this extraordinary precociousness was sometimes paid for (it is not so surprising) by some confusion, perhaps as well a certain haste. Especially when they go together, youth and journalism are not the best protections against such confusion. No doubt flattered to see himself entrusted with the literary and artistic column of a major newspaper, even if he owed this fortune (or misfortune) to his uncle Henri de Man, a young man of 22 did not resist the temptation. All the more so since, as we now know, this former student of the sciences dreamed of nothing but literature. I will also come back to what was no doubt the determining role of that uncommon man, Henri de Man, and to the question of age in this story.

I believed I could acknowledge something right away: the relative heterogeneity of these writings, due in part to the often careful articulation of the argument, to the skill, indeed the cunning of the ideologico-political rhetoric, was also to be explained, to an extent that I still cannot measure, by other factors. On the one hand, it was no doubt necessary to take into consideration a personal inability to give to the argument all its coherence, but there was also the structural impossibility that prevented this argument (I am talking about the fund of coded and stereotyped arguments from which Paul de Man had to draw) from attaining coherence. On the other hand, how can one avoid taking into account the mobility of a situation that, during this beginning of the occupation and however brief may be the period we are talking about, must have made things evolve quickly from one day to the next? The diachronic overdetermination of the context demanded that one proceed carefully in the reading of this series of articles. I will later spell out other necessary precautions, but first of all I want to go on with a story.

From the first reading, I thought I recognized, alas, what I will call roughly an *ideological configuration,* discursive schemas, a logic and a stock of highly marked arguments. By my situation and by training, I had learned from childhood to detect them easily. A strange coincidence: it so happens, on top of it all, that these themes are the subject of seminars I have been giving for four years as well as of my last book, on Heidegger

and Nazism.[6] My feelings were first of all that of a wound, a stupor, and a sadness that I want neither to dissimulate nor exhibit. They have not altogether gone away since, even if they are joined now by others, which I will talk about as well. To begin, a few words about what I thought I was able to identify at first glance but a glance that right away gave me to see, as one should always suspect, that a single glance will never suffice— nor even a brief series of glances.

And already, when I speak of a painful surprise, I must right away differentiate things.

A painful surprise, yes, of course, for *three reasons* at least: (1) some of these articles or certain phrases in them seemed to manifest, in a certain way, an alliance with what has always been for me the very worst; (2) for almost twenty years, I had never had the least reason to suspect my friend could be the author of such articles (I will come back again to this fact); (3) I had read, a short while earlier, the only text that was accessible to me up until then and that was written and signed by Paul de Man in Belgium during the war. Thomas Keenan, a young researcher and a friend from Yale who was preparing, among other things, a bibliography of de Man, had in fact communicated to me, as soon as he had found it in Belgium, the table of contents and the editorial of an issue from the fourth volume of a Brussels journal in which de Man had published his first writings. He had been a member of the editorial committee, then director of this journal, *Les Cahiers du Libre Examen, Revue du cercle d'étude de l'Université Libre de Bruxelles,* founded in 1937. Now, what did this editorial say in February 1940, at the point at which de Man had just taken over the editorship, *in the middle of the war but right before the defeat*? Without equivocation, it took sides *against* Germany and *for* democracy, for "the victory of the democracies" in a war defined as a "struggle . . . against barbarity."[7] This journal, moreover, had always presented itself as "democratic, anticlerical, antidogmatic, and antifascist."[8] Here then are three reasons to be surprised by the texts dating from the following year and that I discovered with consternation.

But I said that right away I had to complicate and differentiate things, as I will have to do regularly. My surprise did not come all at once. Even as I reassured myself ("good, during his Belgian youth that I know nothing about Paul was, in any case, on the 'good side' during the war!"), what I had quickly read of this editorial left me with an uneasy feeling and an aftertaste. In passing, but in a clearly thematic fashion, I was able to identify their source. And here we approach the heart of the problems we have to talk about. They are not only Paul de Man's problems, but those of the equivocal structure of all the politico-philosophical discourses at play in this story, the discourses from all sides. Today, yesterday, and tomorrow—let the dispensers of justice not forget that!

What, then, had already disturbed me in this editorial, in its opting so resolutely for democracy, and in its call for a struggle against barbarity in 1940?

1. First of all, an insistent reference to the West and to "Western civilization," a theme or lexicon whose careless manipulation has often slid over into rather undemocratic theses, as we know now from experience, especially when it is a question of the "decadence" of the said Western civilization. As soon as anyone talks about a "decadence of Western civilization," I am on my guard. We know that this kind of talk can sometimes (not always) lead to restorations or installations of an authoritarian, even totalitarian *order*. Now, the decadence of Western civilization was indeed the central theme of the editorial. It spoke vigorously of the necessity of lucidly going beyond a "commonplace," not in order to overturn it but to clarify its presuppositions, to "render account" of it and "to take account," with "lucidity," thus *to answer for it* [en répondre]—not only as a "theoretician," but in practical, ethical, political terms.

But since it has become a *commonplace* to say that Western civilization is in a state of decadence and that it is crumbling everywhere, it is indispensable to take account of what exactly these values are that are being so directly threatened. And if one wishes to present oneself as a champion ready to defend them, this lucidity no longer remains a pointless theoretician's game, but becomes a truly tactical necessity. [p.1, my emphasis; on which side is the *commonplace* to be found?]

2. I was also disturbed by a discreetly marked suspicion on the subject of the "individual" and the idea of the "liberation of the individual." We also know the constraints that this suspicion sometimes (not always) exercises whenever the program to which it belongs is not carefully engaged. Presenting the unity of this issue of *Les Cahiers,* the editorial of this resolutely democratic journal in fact said:

Western ethical principles seem, for almost all the authors, to come down in the final analysis to the idea of the liberation of the individual, thanks to which we are differentiated from neighboring civilizations. And if we think we are superior to them, we owe the belief to this concept. (p. 1)

This was a way once again of problematizing a "commonplace" at the same time as one seemed to be assuming it. The strategy of this brief editorial is thus already overdetermined, distanced, gravely ironic. It sets out at once positions of value (democracy, individual, Western civilization that must be saved from deca-

dence) and the necessity of not simplifying, of not giving in to *doxa,* to orthodox and conformist opinion, to the "commonplace," to the feeling of superiority, at least as long as it remains unjustified or unanalyzed: "if we think we are superior to them [neighboring civilizations], we owe the belief to this concept," that is, to this concept of the individual which must be analyzed and of which an account must be rendered, an account taken. The author of this editorial, then, has no taste for simplification or received ideas, for commonplaces and easy consensus. Good democratic conscience and the ideology of the "liberation of the individual" can sometimes give in to such facileness. Nothing permits us to imagine that the editorial was written by anyone other than the journal's editor, that is by Paul de Man who, as editor, would in any case have to be the first to answer for it.

3. But that was not all. Aware of the manner in which, discreetly but surely (perhaps not yet surely enough), it de-simplified consensus and good conscience, I clearly saw already that, in order to avoid "simplifying dangerously," this calmly insolent editorial ran the risk of other dangers. It called for a new "order." This word is perhaps not diabolical in itself. No word means anything by itself, out of all context, and the same word appears sometimes in discourses that many, perhaps, would never think of suspecting today. But it was then, in 1940, known to be too often, too regularly associated with antidemocratic ideologies. An order to come, a new order is not necessarily the extreme right that we know under the name of "ordre nouveau,"[9] (an expression which, moreover, appears elsewhere), but the resemblance ought to have been cause for more vigilance. On the other hand, the paragraph I am going to cite refuses, precisely in order not to "simplify dangerously," to draw a simple line there where the war was, nonetheless, simplifying it in fact. It is as if it were causing the fronts to proliferate and asking the reader not to forget that war could cross over "to the inside" onto other fronts. And that finally there were always several wars going on at once. The editorial suggests that decadence is not only on the side of the enemy, and that the expression "struggle of the West against barbarity" comes down precisely to "dangerously simplifying the question." Here then is the passage that left me perplexed and that explains why, a little while later, my surprise may have been painful, as I said a moment ago, but was not an absolute surprise. Up to a certain point, it had been prepared or cushioned; let us say rather it was divided by a kind of internal partition:

It has not explicitly been a question of the war in this issue. One senses, however, that its presence guides the thinking of all our contributors and it is certainly not by chance that two of them have chosen France as symbol of Western culture. But one could not say, *without dangerously simplifying the question,* that the present war is a *struggle of the West against barbarity. Factors of decadence are to be found in all nations, all individuals, and the victory of the democracies will be a victory of the West only to the extent it succeeds in establishing an order in which a civilization like the one we cherish can live again.* [p.2, my emphasis]

We can glimpse a certain "logic." It lies in wait for the calculation or the political consequence of political or rather any discourse. It is as if the possibility of its own overturning were ventriloquizing the discourse in advance, as if that possibility installed in it a quasi-internal war, or still more serious, an endless war, that is, both infinite and unconfined, a war that can never be totally internalized nor externalized. It consists, in effect, of multiple fronts and frontiers. A finite strategy can never formalize them totally, still less master them. Whence the effect produced by the incessant passage of these fronts or frontiers. It is a paradoxical effect because the very possibility of the passage seems to forbid any advance, it seems aporetic *in itself*. Now, it is precisely in this place and at this moment, I will even go so far as to say on this condition, that all decisions, if there are any, must be taken, and that responsibilities *are taken*.

Halfway reassured by this editorial in the *Cahiers,* but my ears still tuned to the uneasy rumblings within me, it is then that I discovered, several months later in 1987, a series of articles also written several months later, after February 1940, in *Le Soir* and *Het Vlaamsche Land*: this time, therefore, after the defeat and under the occupation. What had happened in those few months? What was it I thought I could identify on a first reading, through the sadness and consternation I have mentioned? First of all, this massive and irreducible fact: whatever may be the overdetermination of the content or the internal strategy, a "literary and artistic column" had been regularly supplied between 1940 and 1942. A rather large number of texts had been published in newspapers accepted by the Nazi occupiers. If anyone still had any doubts about this, it sufficed, even before reading de Man's articles, to look at what surrounded them, sometimes framing them immediately on the same page. The subjection of this newspaper[10] cannot have escaped de Man for very long, even if the latter, let us suppose hypothetically, had let himself be blinded for several days or several weeks; even if, let us suppose hypothetically, he had thought he ought to benefit from the authority of a famous and influential uncle, Henri de Man, to whom he was very attached and whom he no doubt admired a lot;[11] and even if, let us also suppose hypothetically, de Man initially took advantage of things so as to see his un-

questionable talent exercised and recognized—since the awarding of a prestigious literary and artistic column in a major newspaper cannot leave a young man of twenty-two indifferent, a young man who has things to say and who is longing to write once again, as he has already been doing in a brilliant way for several years, on all subjects: philosophy, sociology, politics, music, and especially literature.

Beyond this grave and undeniable fact, I would like to try to analyze now what I thought I was able to detect at the moment of that first, painful reading. It will be difficult, I prefer to say that right away, and for a number of reasons. The first has to do with the hypothesis of a general law that I believed I was able to form, then verify, at least in a first analysis. Like any law, this law supposes a sort of invariant, that in this case takes the form of a recurrent alternation, according to the disjunctive partition of an "on the one hand . . . on the other hand." But one of the difficulties I announced arises from this: the said alternation (that, out of concern for clarity, I will be obliged to harden into an *opposition* through the rhetoric of an "on the one hand, on the other hand") will be only the phenomenon or the form of presentation, the logico-rhetorical scheme, of this law—I will even say of the relation to the law in general. It would be necessary to go beyond the form of this schema and interrogate in its possibility that which thus sets limits on a complete binary formalization. No doubt I will only be able to sketch this movement with these examples and within the dimensions of an article. But I insist on showing the examples and on marking this necessity, even as I refer to other work, past or yet to come.

Let us say, then, "on the one hand . . . on the other hand," and what is more "on the one hand . . . on the other hand" on both hands. On both hands, both sides it would be necessary to pursue further the overdetermining division.

On the one hand, the *massive, immediate and dominant* effect of all these texts is that of a *relatively* coherent ideological ensemble which, *most often and in a preponderant fashion,* conforms to official rhetoric, that of the occupation forces or of the milieux that, in Belgium, had accepted the defeat and, if not state and governmental collaboration as in France, then at least the perspective of a European unity under German hegemony. A rigorous description of the conditions in which is inscribed what I am *massively* calling here the *massive* effect would suppose taking into account the extraordinary tangle of the political, religious, and linguistic history of Belgium, at least at that critical turning point of the constitutional monarchy when Henri de Man, after having been a socialist minister, decides, as the government is going into exile, to stay with the king whose adviser he will remain until November 1941, the date at which he in turn leaves Belgium. I cannot undertake this description here, but I believe it will be indispensable, in the future, for any serious interpretation of these texts.

But *on the other hand* and within this frame, de Man's discourse is constantly split, disjointed, engaged in incessant conflicts. Whether in a calculated or a forced fashion, and no doubt beyond this distinction between calculation and passivity, all the propositions carry within themselves a counterproposition: sometimes virtual, sometimes very explicit, always readable, this counterproposition signals what I will call, in a regular and contradictory manner, a *double edge* and a *double bind,* the singular artefact of a blade and a knot. As a result, paradoxically, these articles and the attitude that seems to sustain them are not without a certain conformity to the editorial of the *Cahiers* that wanted to avoid "dangerously simplifying."

That is why, in the *three series of examples* with which my hypothesis will be put to the test, I will follow precisely the themes put into perspective by the *Cahiers* editorial: the destiny of the West, Europe and its outside, the nation, democracy and the individual. *And literature*: if it occupies more than just one place among others in this network, the reason is not only that, as in the *Cahiers,* de Man had the responsibility, both official and statutory, to treat of literature in a privileged way.

1. *On the one hand . . . on the other hand,* then
   (*first series of examples*).

On the one hand, everything takes place as if, the German victory leaving no doubt and no exit, it was more imperative than ever to pose the question of Europe's destiny by analyzing the past, the present, and especially the future. For that reason, de Man approves of those who attempt a "critical exposé" in order to "deduce the responsibilities for the defeat."[12] One must "orient one's thinking toward the new problems that have arisen" and not give in to clichés (once again the critique of the "commonplace"): "it is not by spreading the belief that we are inept cowards that we will plan for a better future." It is not enough to accuse "the decayed political climate that provoked the defeat since that climate was not much better in 1914." When it is a question of the defeat, a certain Belgian nationalism, sometimes more precisely Flemish nationalism, seems just as obvious, even if the discourse on the nation and nationalisms often remains more cautious than the praise of the Belgian army whose defeat would have been more "glorious" than that of its allies (ibid.). De Man judges this reflection on the war, that many others—but not everyone, and that is the question—might also think was over, to be just as necessary for France. He is already in a

"postwar" period.[13] He praises the French who, by means of the "symptoms of what may be the future" "reveal the fruitful meditation of a people who are attempting to pull themselves together by understanding objectively how [the] blow that has been struck changes its historical destiny."[14] As in the editorial from the *Cahiers,* a big question cuts across all the articles: that of the future of Europe and of a European unity that, from now on, since the German victory seems irreversible and of profound importance, can only be accomplished around Germany.

Even if the form of his discourse is then more *descriptive* than *prescriptive,* even if it seems to call more for a realization and a knowledge than a commitment and an approbation, de Man permits himself no reservations (could he have done so in this newspaper?) when he defines, for example, what might "interest" the "visitors" on the occasion of an exhibition on the "history of Germany." One recognizes here the concern of someone who never ceased pointing to the necessity of posing the national problem, notably the German problem. And who can reproach him for that?

This is the first element that may interest visitors: to have a clearer vision of the very complex history of a people whose importance is fundamental to the destiny of Europe. They will be able to see that the historical evolution of Germany is governed by a fundamental factor: the will to unite the set of regions that have a like racial structure but that adversaries have incessantly endeavored to divide. The periods of weakness always coincide with a territorial parceling up. Each time there has been an attempt to react against a state of inferiority, it has taken the form of seeking to reconquer and assimilate the lost provinces.[15]

This paragraph echoes a concern whose traces may be found throughout the whole history and all the writings of Henri de Man. His nephew goes back to the treaties of Westphalia and Versailles, then he adds:

There is another reason for which Germany's historical destiny both past and future cannot leave us indifferent: we depend on it directly. . . . no one can deny the fundamental importance of Germany for the life of the West as a whole. One must see this obstinacy that resists subjugation as more than a simple proof of national steadfastness. The whole continuity of Western civilization depends on the unity of the people who are its center. (ibid.)

Likewise, although he assumes nothing directly to his own account, although his language is almost always that of a columnist-commentator, de Man does not openly criticize those who, like Jacques Chardonne, dare "to look in the face of the situation born of the German victory" and form "the hope of finding that the victor has projects and intentions capable of reconstructing a Europe with better social and political conditions."[16] There seems to be no doubt in his eyes that Belgium and Europe are in the process of living a "revolution." That is his term. But this word is also borrowed: it is the rallying cry of all those who, notably in France, speak of "national revolution" in order to name the new Pétainist era. Revolution, which is to say, then, a social and national revolution of the right. It is, moreover, also in reference to France (which, as we shall see, he alternately praises and criticizes) that de Man speaks, as does his uncle during his Marxist and "beyond Marxism" phase, of a "political and social revolution." What is more, he diagnoses a fatality rather than assigning a duty and we ought always to pay attention to the mode of his utterances. On the subject of *Notre avant-guerre* by Robert Brasillach:

I can imagine that, for a cultivated Frenchman, *Notre avant-guerre* still evokes a paradise lost. But he will have to resign himself to completing a political and social revolution before he can hope to regain a similar paradise, one that would have more solid and, consequently, less ephemeral foundations.[17]

Thus the present moment is apprehended, in the then dominant code, as that of a "revolution": the "present revolution,"[18] the "maze of the present revolution,"[19] the "current revolution"[20] or the one to come (for Belgium that "has not yet had its revolution").[21] This "maze," who can seriously see its outcome, the topological design, the essential plan? No one or almost no one, in de Man's eyes, the eyes of someone who, knowing he advances blindly through a labyrinth, pricks up his ears:

For what must preoccupy the minds of those who wish to orient a reform or a revolution is not a search for the means of adapting themselves to new conditions. In the spiritual domain as much as in the political one, they find themselves confronted with new lines of conduct to be recast, with institutions to be recreated, with programs of organization to be elaborated. And one may remark that strictly none of the essays published in such great number in France and French-speaking Belgium since the war contain so much as a slight concern for tracing the givens of the different problems.["SjM"]

One can see that de Man is defining a *labyrinthine* task, to be sure, but an altogether new one, that of a revolution in thinking. One has to think the revolution and do something other than "adapt to new conditions." Does he not feel that he alone, at the time, is up to defining or approaching this task? I have that impression. This labyrinthine task would be both theoretical (abstract) and more than theoretical. It resists its own theorization and the massiveness of the schema I have just outlined.

On the other hand . . .

For, *on the other hand,* the same article speaks of the need for an abstract theorization of problems that have not yet been elaborated—in particular on the subject of the "primordial question of European unity." De Man is politically cautious enough to specify that this theoretical elaboration must not be left to "technicians," even if caution can always (this is the double edge) be turned against itself (antitechnicism, demagogic populism—but this is not the dominant accent in the text):

Which does not mean that only technicians can participate in the debate. The postwar period brings with it philosophical and psychological problems of a *purely abstract* nature just as much as it does difficulties having to do with tangible realities. More than that, one may even say that the most important questions are situated on a *purely abstract* plane. Thus, to take just this example, the primordial question of European unity can only be envisioned from a *quasi-theoretical* angle. ["SjM"; my emphasis]

Why is that? We have just gone from the "purely abstract" to the "quasi-theoretical." That is why, immediately afterwards, the "spiritual givens" of the problem, which are taken to be essential, "cannot be treated in a general and theoretical form." In the rather awkward phrase I am going to cite (and where I do not exclude the possibility of a typo having slipped in, since this wartime newspaper contains many such mistakes), it is difficult to know whether language does or does not belong to these "spiritual givens." Language is defined as "material and direct," an interesting notation that probably also concerns national languages and their diversity, but which no doubt should not be overinterpreted retrospectively in the light of what de Man has since said about materiality:

That which unites the European peoples are precisely those factors that escape all materialization: a similar political past, a common philosophical and religious thinking, an economic and social organization that has gone through an analogous evolution in all countries. On the contrary, that which is material and direct (such as language, habits, popular customs) appears as disparate and variable. One may thus see that, in this case, it is a matter of spiritual givens that cannot be treated in a general and theoretical form. ["SjM"][22]

What is still more interesting, through the convolution of this remark, is its final aim within the article. The article is about a book by Montherlant. As far as I can judge at this point, the list of books, in particular of French books, reviewed by de Man can seem to speak loudly all by itself (Jouvenel, Fabre-Luce, Benoist-Méchin, Chardonne, Drieu La Rochelle, Giono, and so on). By what it retains as well as by what it excludes, the filter seems to correspond to that of the legitimation machine (thus the censorship machine) of the official Pétainist ideology. Is de Man letting these choices be imposed totally from without? Is he responding on his own to a demand? Does he assume responsibility for it? Up to what point? Does he consider that these books, having just appeared (and being authorized to appear with authorized publishers—an enormous French history that I have to leave aside here), were part of the current events about which it is the chronicler's duty to speak, even if, on the other hand, he has already indicated his interest in so many other authors, from Joyce to Kafka, from Gide to Hemingway, and so forth? As for me, I do not have the means to answer these questions. But what I can say, from reading this article on Montherlant, for example, and taking responsibility for this reading, is that the argument I mentioned a moment ago around "theory" seems destined, through de Man's clever and not particularly docile strategy, to discredit Montherlant's political discourse at the point at which it proposes "a general view." How does this text operate when we look at it closely?

It begins by quoting, as if in epigraph and in order to authorize itself, a remark by Montherlant. Then it turns it against him with an irony whose pitiless lucidity, alas (too much lucidity, not enough lucidity, blindly lucid), spares no one, not even de Man almost a half century later. Writing by profession on current affairs, he deals with a current affair in this domain and he announces the oblivion promised those who devote their *literature* to current affairs. Do not these lines, that name "the worst," become unforgettable from then on? It is frightening to think that de Man might have handled so coldly the double-edged blade, while perhaps expecting "the worst":

In this collection of essays by Montherlant, there is a phrase that all those who have followed literary publication since August 1940 will approve of. It is the passage that says: "To the writers who have given too much to current affairs for the last few months, I predict, for that part of their work, the most complete oblivion. When I open the newspapers and journals of today, I hear the indifference of the future rolling over them, just as one hears the sound of the sea when one holds certain seashells up to the ear." One could not have put it any better. And this just and severe sentence applies to all the books and essays in which writers offer us their reflections on war and its consequences, including *Solstice de juin* itself [the title of the book by Montherlant de Man is reviewing]. It is an odd distortion, belonging to our age, to demand from artists and writers, in

particular, directives and judgments on political and historical circumstances. Because writers are capable of expressing commonplaces in an elegant way, they are made into oracles and one takes their words to be providential messages. And the credit they enjoy in this domain is considerable. Gide's quarrels with communism exercised more influence over people's minds than would have numerous documented and serious works treating the same question. And yet there is no reason whatsoever to grant men of letters such authority in an area of human behavior which, manifestly, lies outside their competence. It is surprising to discover the naiveté and nullity of some of their sentences once they have been stripped of the brilliant varnish that a careful style confers on them. A whole side of the question—the economic, social, technical side—is totally alien to them, so that when they venture onto this terrain, in that offhand way that only the ignorant are capable of, one may expect the worst. ["SjM"]

After that, one does not have to wait long for a condemnation of the individual and the individualist Montherlant "who likes to give lessons": his "meditations" are "conventional" and "insipid," "uninteresting" and "ineffective." By "practicing the political essay," Montherlant can only "echo official declarations" and "swell the ranks of those who talk to no useful purpose."

An analogous gesture, although more discreet, as regards Chardonne. After having quoted him, ("Only Germany can organize the continent and that country provides us with the opportunity of an internal rebuilding that was necessary and that it is up to us to accomplish . . ."), de Man adds: "After such sentences, one may perhaps *debate* Chardonne's ideas, but one certainly cannot reproach them for a lack of sharpness [*netteté*]" ["VfC"]. A double-edged sentence—on sharpness, precisely, and on the cutting edge itself. One may suppose, without being sure, that de Man judges these ideas to be very debatable.

Likewise, although de Man often insists, and rightly so, on the riches of German culture, on the complexity of the national problem in Germany, on the fundamental role that it always plays and ought still to play in the destiny of Europe, at no point, to my knowledge, does he name Nazism, *a fortiori* in order to praise it. In all the texts I have been able to read and about which the least one can say is that they were turned in the direction of politics and current affairs, the word "Nazi," "Nazi party" appears only once or twice, if I am not mistaken, and then it does so in a neutral or informative mode. What is more, on one occasion it provides another opportunity to criticize one of the French writers that was then one of the most "authorized" by collaborationist France: Brasillach and his "lack of political sense"!

Brasillach's reaction faced with a spectacle like that of the Nazi Party Congress in Nuremberg, when he manifests a certain terror before the "strange" nature of this demonstration, is that of someone for whom the sudden importance of the political in the life of a people is an inexplicable phenomenon. ["NaB"]

However overdeterminable this remark may be, it indicates not just a distance, but a very critical step back when it comes to writers or ideologues as marked as Montherlant, Chardonne, or Brasillach. As for what remains neutral or suspended in his approach, one must, it seems to me, find a supplementary explanation, and here again it will be a question of "responsibility." In an article titled "Sur les possibilités de la critique" (which will greatly interest those who would hasten toward a recognition of prefigurations in these "early writings"), de Man defines a certain autonomy of literature, but also of literary history. To be sure, there is a responsibility to evaluate the literary object, but it is a specific responsibility. It is not to be confused, he says, with that of a moral and political judgment of the moral or political responsibilities of the writer.

Literature is an independent domain having a life, laws, and obligations belonging only to it and which in no way depend on the philosophical or ethical contingencies stirring at its side. The least one can say is that the artistic values governing the world of letters do not merge with those of the Truth and the Good, and that whoever borrows his criteria from this region of human consciousness will be systematically mistaken in his judgments. . . . One does not have the right to condemn Gide as a novelist because his moral life was debatable. . . . A writer can be attacked for the inadequacies of his style, for sins against the laws of the genre he practices, but never for weaknesses or lacks in his moral personality. The most beautiful pages in the world's literatures are often those that express a failure, a renunciation, a capitulation. And the worst platitudes have been written to exalt the most noble sentiments. All of this is quite obvious and it would be pointless to repeat it if we did not have to listen to reassertions of criticism's duty to "derive from a set of deductions, joined to a philosophy of broad humanism or better yet to a moral responsibility linked to the supernatural fidelity of man."[23]

This is not the place for a substantive debate about all these formulations and about literature as an "independent domain"—which, moreover, de Man does not remove from history, any more than he ever did. This is very clear in the rest of the same article which even speaks of a "philosophy of literary history that is no less fruitful than the philosophy of history as such." It is also "quite obvious" that literary criticism, if it is *critical*, that is, if it is a judgment, an evaluation, an assignment of responsibility, could not be, insofar as it is *literary* criticism of *works*, a moral or political criticism of authors. That being the case, what does de Man do here?

1. If the responsibility of the *criticized* works can be acute in literary terms without that meaning it is a moral or political responsibility, then this is also true for criticism, for *criticizing* criticism of works. Some will be able say, out of malevolence in my opinion, that de Man wants to subtract his critical activity from any future moral and political trial, even though some "capitulation" was readable there.

2. More significant seems to me to be the example of Gide, the "accursed" author of the period. De Man disputes the validity of any moral and political trial that one might bring against Gide's literary work. He even formulates general principles invalidating such a judgment. He puts forth reasons for a radical resistance to the organization of such verdicts. He does it at a moment when moral and political trials, often carried out in the name of, precisely, "humanism," were common and had serious consequences. This seems to me to be a remarkable gesture. For if literature remains neutral in de Man's eyes or at least independent of morality and politics, it is not neutral, it is even an offensive and courageous gesture to recall this axiom and to resist the moralizing orthodoxy at a moment of great repression during which so many writers are being condemned for their moral or political opinions (present or past).

3. The logic of this argument anticipates, up to a certain point, that of Jean Paulhan (whom de Man was rediscovering during the last years of his life, no doubt in reference to other themes, but it is still not insignificant). Writing after the Liberation in *De la paille et du grain* (On the wheat and the chaff), this writer-resistant disputed the right of his "friends" on the National Committee of Writers to conduct, as writers, political trials of other writers known to have collaborated with the enemy. If there were grounds for such a trial, then it was the province of other tribunals competent to judge political acts: there ought to be no literary "épuration" [purge], no writers' tribunals to judge the politics or morals of other writers *as writers*. Nor should there be "voluntary policemen," or "that supplementary force of gendarmes that Charles Maurras cried out for—and that you have invented."[24] My own thinking as regards Paulhan's discourse cannot be summed up in a few lines. Yet, it is remarkable in any case that an analogous logic was put to work several years earlier by de Man *and this time in an opposite context,* so to speak, when it was a matter of protesting against tri-

bunals and purges on *the other side*. Thus, once again do not "dangerously simplify the question"!

In a like manner, finally, although he grants the maximum attention to the role that Germany or "German genius" has played or ought to play in the destiny of Europe, although he recalls constantly the necessity of understanding thoroughly the history of the German nation in order to understand Hitlerism, although he is vigilantly opposed to the commonplace and the "lazy and widespread solution" that comes down to "supposing an integral dualism between Germany, on the one hand, and Hitlerism on the other . . . the latter considered to be a strange phenomenon, having no relation to the historical evolution of the German people, but rather born of a momentary aberration and destined to disappear like a morbid symptom that would have merely upset the normal life of the nation for a little while" ("VfC"), although his analysis leads him to judge German "hegemony" in Europe to be ineluctable, this diagnosis seems rather cold and rather far removed from exhortation. And when, in the same text, he describes the "innovations of totalitarian regimes" and the "obligations" or "duties" taking the place of "anarchy," he underscores that the "style that will result from this process is far from being definitively consecrated. It may appear crude and somewhat rudimentary" because of the "rigid and relatively narrow mold that is the war." Then he concludes by noting that enriching these possibilities may run the risk of "dangerous temptations" ("VfC"). The week before, in an article that was also, let us never forget, a commentary on Daniel Halévy, de Man recognized, admittedly, that in France "immediate collaboration" seemed compelling to "any objective mind," but he warned against an attitude that would be content to "strike out against the nearest guilty parties" or "to adopt the mystical beliefs from which the victors have drawn their strength and power."[25] Here once again, there is an appeal to historical, even the historian's, analysis of the past so as to rediscover the strengths and the patrimony of the nation, but also so as to draw "the lesson from events by means of theoretical considerations" (ibid.).

2. *On the one hand . . . on the other hand* (*second series of examples*)

On the one hand, the question of nations dominates all these texts. It is approached in all its *theoretical* aspects (ethnic, historical, political, linguistic, religious, aesthetic, literary). Nothing could be more legitimate, one might say, especially at that moment, and I will add: still today. But this interest is not only theoretical. In certain of its forms, it resembles nationalist

commitment: Belgian, sometimes Flemish. And there seems to be evidence of a great respect, in a privileged fashion, with regard to German nationalism. Most utterances of a "comparatist" style are made to the benefit of Germany and to the detriment of conquered France. This interest for the nation seems to dominate in two ways: it outweighs interest for the State, notably in its democratic form, and outweighs still more interest for the individual, who constitutes the target of numerous critiques.

We have already seen how this interest was resonating in a muffled way in the editorial from the *Cahiers*. De Man, translator and commentator of A.E. Brinckmann's *Geist der Nationen, Italiener-Franzosen-Deutsche* (1938), speaks in this regard of "national grandeur." His commentary describes "a sober faith, a practical means to defend Western culture against a decomposition from the inside out or a surprise attack by neighboring civilizations."[26] Looked on more or less favorably by the Nazis, Brinckmann's book is concerned especially with the arts. But de Man recalls that it applies to all domains: "what is true in the domain of the history of art holds true for all domains. Europe can only be strong, peaceful, and flourishing if it is governed by a state of mind which is deeply conscious of its national grandeur, but which keeps its eyes open for all experiments and problems that touch our continent" ("AM"). This Western nationalism must adapt itself to the "contemporary revolutions" we spoke of earlier. De Man emphasizes that the aims of the book he is reviewing are not only theoretical. They have value as practical engagement. Does he subscribe to them in his name? It seems that he does, but he does not say so:

The aim of a work like this is not only to analyze the artistic activity from an aesthetic point of view, or to give an explanation of a practical nature. It originated out of an attempt to ensure the future of Western civilisation in all its aspects. As such it contains a lesson, which is indispensable for all those who, in the contemporary revolutions, try to find a firm guidance according to which they can direct their action and their thoughts. ["AM"]

The comparisons between the German and French cultures, notably as regards their literary manifestations, the one dominated by myth, metaphor or symbol, the other by psychological analysis, the predilection for moderation, limit and definition, thus for the finite (one thinks of many of Nietzsche's statements on this subject), seem often to be made to the benefit of the former. Does de Man assume to his own account what he says in commenting on Sieburg? It seems that he does, but he does not say so.

Instead of an artificial and forced denationalization that leads to a considerable impoverishment—such as we have seen happen in Flanders and Walloon Belgium as a result of France's force of attraction—a free contact among peoples who know themselves to be different and who hold onto this difference, but who esteem each other reciprocally guarantees political peace and cultural stability. It is no doubt in this domain that France must perform the most serious turnaround, or risk disappearing forever from the political scene.

As for the spiritual domain [*le domaine de l'esprit*], the forces that seem to have taken over the conduct of history are not very much in accordance with France's specific soul. To realize this, it suffices to examine the opposition pointed out by Sieburg between a certain form of French reason that everywhere seeks to fix limits and to establish the right measure, and the sense of grandeur and of the infinite that indeed seems to characterize present tendencies. We are entering a mystical age [let us not forget that elsewhere de Man speaks of his mistrust as regards the victor's mysticism], a period of faith and belief, along with everything that supposes in the way of suffering, exaltation, and intoxication.["PfS"]

The Flemish nationalism is clearer, notably in "Le Destin de la Flandre," whose pretext was the "Germano-Flemish Cultural Convention." Paul de Man was born in Antwerp, and his family is Flemish. He recalls several times the "Flemish genius" and the struggle against "French influences that, through the intermediary of the complicitous Belgian State, were spreading rapidly." He supports a solution that would guarantee Flanders a certain autonomy in relation to Walloon Belgium and Germany, whether it is a matter of defense or of national, and first of all linguistic, patrimony: "that is to say, of the language before all else and of that form of freedom that permits creators to work in accordance with their impulses and not as imitators of a neighbor whose spirit is dissimilar."[27] This attention to national language appears throughout these first texts which also form a short treatise on translation. Literature is often examined from the point of view of the problems of translation by someone who was also a polyglot, a very active translator (especially in his youth) and an original interpreter of Benjamin's "The Task of the Translator." Resistance to translation is how one recognizes national roots and the idiomatic character of a literary work. From this point of view, one should read the column devoted to "Romans allemands" [German novels]. It begins thus:

There exists an excellent means that permits one to discover if a literary work either does or does not send its roots down into the depths of national feelings: it is to see whether it resists translation. When a novel or a poem carries within itself these somewhat myste-

rious and undefinable virtues that make up the particular genius of a people, the most careful translation will never succeed in rendering the original.[28]

This problematic of translation is, moreover, in accordance with the "comparatism" and the hierarchies (which, by the way, are very unstable) that we were evoking a moment ago. Notably, and in what is all the same the most traditional fashion, between the Germanic spirit and the Latin spirit. If "the most conscientious and most faithful translation cannot render the accent of the original work," it is in particular because of

the divergence between the rational and constructive French spirit and the German tendency toward the visionary, that does not stop at an objective consideration [of the sort de Man does not fail to call for elsewhere!], but penetrates regions where the laws of reason no longer hold. Thus, the virtues of clarity and harmony are lost. The novel [*Léonore Griebel,* by Hermann Stehr] is much less finished and less even than the work of Flaubert. But one gains depth. . . . With the Latin, intelligence and rational reasoning prevail; with the Germanic, it is a stirring poetic intuition. ["Ra"]

Although it has to efface itself before the original text, the translation ought not, therefore, to efface the fact that it is still a translation. One ought to "feel that it is a translation." Hence the reproach addressed to Betz, the translator of Rilke whom de Man already knew and appreciated, when he translated Jünger (another of de Man's favorites) "too well," to the point of making one forget that the original was written in German, "which, especially when he recounts the story of a German invading France, has something amazingly shocking about it."[29]

Between Germany and France, between these two "cultural blocs," Flemish nationalism should endeavor to save "that core that has given humanity admirable products of an independent genius. The political status of Flanders ought to be established in the new Europe in accordance with this destiny" ("F"). Despite obvious affinities, this independent genius cannot be reduced to the German genius, and it is sharply opposed to those ultra-French things that are "abstraction" and "cerebralness" (remember this latter word: it occurs frequently and in a moment we will see it applied to the Jew, not the Frenchman). Flemish genius manifests itself particularly in realist picturality, which does not mean only painting but colorful plasticity, even in literature, and shows less interest in "abstract content." This is the "principal opposition between French and Flemish art." But the "attachment to external forms rather than to cerebral analysis" has nothing "superficial" about it. That is what Hegel says in his own way in the *Aesthetics.* De Man will later study that text closely, perhaps he already knows it when he writes, in the service of Flemish genius—or any genius as it is traditionally called: "This mentality has nothing superficial about it since the external envelope of beings and objects, when it is seen by the careful eye of genius that discovers all its resources, can reveal their deep meaning" ("F").

But *on the other hand,* already clearly enveloped, as we have indicated, by the cautious modality (more descriptive than prescriptive) of the utterances, this nationalist demand is complicated, multiplied, inverted in several ways. First of all, because, through the practice of an abyssal logic of exemplarity, the national affirmation *in general* is caught up in the paradoxical necessity of respecting *the idiom in general,* thus *all* idioms, all national differences. Next, because Flemish nationalism must resist both the French influence and the German influence. Finally, because this young Fleming is also writing in French. If he is a nationalist, his language, his training, and his literary preferences make of him as much a nationalist of French culture as a Flemish nationalist. This war and its fronts thus divide all the so-called "early writings."

Because de Man *also* praises French individualism: it is "more analyst than organizer" and it "survives even if it no longer intends to play an organizing role." It "remains a precious national character."[30] And in the very text that speaks of the necessity for France to open itself to "foreign influences" and to abandon "provincialism [*l'esprit de clocher*]" (which are in themselves and out of context excellent recommendations), praise of the "Latin spirit" compensates for and eloquently overcodes the strategy of motifs that we quoted earlier, like the play of forces that this strategy could serve. But let no one accuse me of "dangerously simplifying": it is true that things can be reversed again, a certain extreme right in France can also play the card of Latinity. Always the double edge. De Man has just spoken of "the lesson of a long humanist past that guards against any obscurantism" and he then continues, out of a concern, once again, not to "conform to the spirit of the day" and "the general orientation":

It is on this last point that one sees the considerable role French genius may still be able to play. It cannot for a moment be a question of wanting to destroy or overlook, on the grounds that they do not conform to the spirit of the day, the virtues of clarity, logic, harmony that the great artistic and philosophic tradition of this country reflects. Maintaining the continuity of the French spirit is an inherent condition of Europe's grandeur. Particularly when the general orientation goes in the direction of profound, obscure, natural forces, the French mission, that consists in moderating ex-

cesses, maintaining indispensable links with the past, evening out erratic surges, is recognized to be of the utmost necessity. That is why it would be disastrous and stupid to destroy, by seeking to modify them by force, the constants of the Latin spirit. And it is also why we would be committing an unforgivable mistake if we cut our ties with the manifestations of this culture. ["PfS"]

Likewise, there are abundant warnings against narrow nationalism and jealous regionalism.[31] Will one say that these warnings can also serve German hegemony? Yet, in opposition to the latter de Man defines a concept of an autonomous Flanders that will let itself be neither assimilated nor annexed by Germany as it was occasionally a question of doing. A moderate discourse, a differentiated position that rejects the "anti-Belgian spirit" of certain Flemish and sees the allegation of an "artificial and forced denationalization" of Flanders as a relic and a "myth." Once again from "The Destiny of Flanders":

But the revisionist situation born of the present war causes various questions to bounce back again, questions that had been more or less skillfully settled before the conflict. And since the organizing force emanates from Germany, Flanders, for whom that country constitutes an eternal point of support, finds itself placed in a peculiar situation. The memory of activism, when Germany supported the Flemish in their legitimate claims, is still too much alive not to provoke certain stirrings in an analogous direction. Nevertheless, it should be pointed out that on this side as well the danger of assimilation exists and all the more clearly because affinities link the two races. As a result, the temptation is even stronger for the Flemish to let themselves dissolve into a Germanic community which risks effacing everything that constitutes their profound originality. It is for this reason that Mr. Elias, burgomaster of Ghent, felt he had to react "against those who wanted to extend the idea of the Germanic State to the reabsorption of the Low Countries (Nederlanden) in an artificial German community." ["F"]

It is true that the burgomaster's speech seems compelled to remain within a contradiction, if I have understood it correctly, unless it is signaling toward some confederation that, however, it does not name. As for de Man, he merely quotes him:

"Many no doubt fear that this would lead to the disappearance of the Flemish as a people and their leveling out as Germans. I have no hesitation about saying that such a conception could lead, in Flanders, to catastrophic results. . . . We can only be worthy members of a Germanic State as long as the State allows us to be worthy Netherlanders." ["F"]

3. *On the one hand . . . on the other hand*
    (*third series of examples*)

I will gather these examples around the article that appeared to me, as to so many others, to be the most unbearable. I mean the article titled "Les Juifs dans la littérature actuelle" (Jews in Present-day Literature).[32]

Nothing in what I am about to say, analyzing the article as closely as possible, will heal over the wound I right away felt when, my breath taken away, I perceived in it what the newspapers have most frequently singled out as recognized antisemitism, an antisemitism more serious than ever in such a situation, an antisemitism that would have come close to urging exclusions, even the most sinister deportations. Even if, in the texts already quoted, no pro-Nazism was ever declared; even if the disjunctions, the precautions, the complications seemed to protect against any simple allegiance, is not what we have here the most unquestionable manifestation of an antisemitism as violent as it is stereotyped? Does not this antisemitism take over from, so as to sharpen its coherence, the "racique" (rather than the racial) as it is frequently called in other texts? For example: the "historical, *racique,* and so forth, components that allow one to determine whether or not a people has a nationality worthy of being respected" ("F"), the "sensibility . . . intimately linked to the virtues of his race" ("Ra") (that of Hermann Stehr, author of *Léonore Griebel,* that de Man is reviewing here). Does not the lack of vigilance regarding racism induce other articles to speak frequently of human "types," according to a familiar code which was not only that of Jünger (whom de Man admired and whom Heidegger criticized on this point in *Zur Seinsfrage*)? Whether or not he assumes it to his own account in the texts of commentaries, this vocabulary never seems to arouse suspicion when de Man speaks, rather pejoratively, of a "certain type of [French]man who was hearty and enterprising, sufficiently gifted to have been able to approach great problems without, however, being able to tolerate the demands made on true genius, the human type with an affection for friendship, irony" ("NaB"); or when he speaks, rather approvingly, of a "certain human type" or of a "personality-type" formed by "great renewals"; or of the "creation of a new set of individual ideals" ("VfC"); or still again, paraphrasing Drieu La Rochelle, of "the creation of a radically new human type."[33] Even when he criticizes the individualist (French) conception of this "new type, human individual," de Man does not seem to distrust this constant reference to "type." Likewise, is not the logic of "The Jews in Present-day Literature," its praise for the "good health" and the "vitality" of a European literature that would keep its "intact originality" despite any "semitic interference" ("Jla"), coherent with the very frequent valorization of "vitality" ("NpD"), of the "healthy" ("NaB"), of the "uncorrupted" ("Ra") as well as sometimes with the critique of abstraction and "cerebralness" here associated with Judaism? Is it not coherent with so many warnings against "outside influences" ("Ra")?

But let us now look more closely at an article that it will be better to quote *in extenso.*

On the one hand, it indeed seems to confirm the logic that we have just reconstituted. In fact, it describes the traits of what, according to some, are "degenerate and decadent, because *enjuivés* ["enjewished"]" cultural phenomena, or yet again an "enjuivé" novel; it mentions the "important role" that the Jews have played in "the phony and disordered existence of Europe since 1920." He has recourse, following a well-known tradition, to the stereotypical description of the "Jewish spirit": "cerebralness," "capacity for assimilating doctrines while maintaining a certain coldness in the face of them." He notes that "Jewish writers have always remained in the second rank and, to speak only of France, the André Maurois's, the Francis de Croissets, the Henri Duvernois's, the Henri Bernsteins, Tristan Bernards, Julien Bendas, and so forth, are not among the most important figures, they are especially not those who have had any guiding influence on the literary genres." And then, in a terrifying conclusion, the allusion to "a solution to the Jewish problem":

The observation is, moreover, comforting for Western intellectuals. That they have been able to safeguard themselves from Jewish influence in a domain as representative of culture as literature proves their vitality. If our civilization had let itself be invaded by a foreign force, then we would have to give up much hope for its future. By keeping, in spite of semitic interference in all aspects of European life, an originality and character intact, it has shown that its basic nature is healthy. What is more, one sees that a solution of the Jewish problem that would aim at the creation of a Jewish colony isolated from Europe would not entail, for the literary life of the West, deplorable consequences. The latter would lose, in all, a few personalities of mediocre value and would continue, as in the past, to develop according to its great evolutive laws. ["Jla"]

Will I dare to say "on the other hand" in the face of the *unpardonable* violence and confusion of these sentences? What could possibly attenuate the fault? And whatever may be the reasons or the complications of a text, whatever may be going on in the mind of its author, how can one deny that the effect of these conclusions went in the sense and the direction of the worst? In the *dominant* context in which they were read in 1941, did not their *dominant* effect go unquestionably in the direction of the worst? Of what we now know to have been the worst?

But one must have the courage to answer injustice with justice. And although one has to condemn these sentences, which I have just done, one ought not do it without examining everything that remains readable in a text one can judge to be disastrous. It is also necessary, when evaluating *this* act, *this* text (notice I do not say the life and work of its signatory which will never be reduced to this act, this text) to maintain a "certain coldness" and to take the trouble of that "work of lucid analysis" de Man associates with this "coldness" even as he attributes it, *in this very text,* to the Jews. As these traits are rules of intellectual responsibility rather than natural characteristics reserved to Jews and Frenchmen, does not the "work of analysis" have to be tirelessly pursued with "a certain coldness"? Therefore, I will dare to say, this time as before, "on the other hand."

Yes, *on the other hand* and *first of all,* the *whole* article is organized as an indictment of "vulgar antisemitism." It is, let us not forget, directed against that antisemitism, against its "lapidary judgment," against the "myth" it feeds or feeds on. In the first two paragraphs, which I am going to cite, de Man proceeds unquestionably toward a demystification, not without certain risks, of this vulgarity, of its "myth," of an "error" and a "very widespread opinion." Once again, as in the *Cahiers* and as he will always do, he takes on the "commonplace." Immediately after this critique, he continues with a "But . . ." ("But the reality is different"). This will then lead us to ask ourselves which reality interests him especially—and we will have to talk once again about literature. Here then is the uncompromising critique of "vulgar antisemitism" and of the contradiction, even of the boomerang effect to which the latter is exposed or which perhaps it already translates. I have just used the word "boomerang"; I could have said that de Man also designates the double edges of the said "vulgar antisemitism." These are the first two paragraphs, in which I hear some mockery:

Vulgar antisemitism readily takes pleasure in considering postwar cultural phenomena (after the war of '14–18) as degenerate and decadent because they are *enjuivés.* Literature has not escaped this lapidary judgment: it has sufficed to discover a few Jewish writers behind Latinized pseudonyms for all of contemporary production to be considered polluted and harmful. This conception entails rather dangerous consequences. First of all, it condemns *a priori* a whole literature that in no way deserves this fate. What is more, from the moment one agrees that the literature of our day has some merit, it would be a rather unflattering appreciation of Western

writers to reduce them to being mere imitators of a Jewish culture that is foreign to them.

The Jews themselves have contributed to spreading this myth. Often, they have glorified themselves as the leaders of literary movements that characterize our age. But the error has, in fact, a deeper cause. At the origin of the thesis of a Jewish takeover is the very widespread belief according to which the modern novel and modern poetry are nothing but a kind of monstrous outgrowth of the world war. Since the Jews have, in fact, played an important role in the phony and disordered existence of Europe since 1920, a novel born in this atmosphere would deserve, up to a certain point, the qualification of *enjuivé.* ["Jla"]

Things are very serious. Rather than going too quickly, it would be better to run the risk of paraphrase and redundancy. What does this article say? It is indeed a matter of criticizing vulgar antisemitism. That is the primary, declared, and underscored intention. But to scoff at vulgar antisemitism, is that also to scoff at or mock the vulgarity of antisemitism? This latter syntactic modulation leaves the door open to two interpretations. To condemn vulgar antisemitism may leave one to understand that there is a distinguished antisemitism in whose name the vulgar variety is put down. De Man never says such a thing, even though one may condemn his silence. But the phrase can also mean something else, and this reading can always contaminate the other in a clandestine fashion: to condemn "vulgar antisemitism," *especially if one makes no mention of the other kind,* is to condemn antisemitism *itself inasmuch as* it is vulgar, always and essentially vulgar. De Man does not say that either. If that is what he thought, a possibility I will never exclude, he could not say so clearly in this context. One will say at this point: his fault was to have accepted the context. Certainly, but what is that, to accept a context? And what would one say if he claimed not to have fully accepted it, and to have preferred to play the role there of the nonconformist smuggler, as so many others did in so many different ways, in France and in Belgium, at this or that moment, inside or outside the Resistance? And I repeat, what is that, to *fully* accept a context? Because this article, in any case, is nonconformist, as Paul de Man, as also his uncle, always was. It is not particularly conformist to denounce antisemitism, an antisemitism, whichever it may be, at that moment, in that place, and to attribute to vulgar antisemitism the recognizable and then widespread vocabulary of *all* antisemitism: "enjuivé," "degenerate," "decadent," "polluted," "harmful." At the very least, it is rather anticonformist to add in the same breath, in the same sentences, that this is a "lapidary judgment," that this antisemitism may have "dangerous consequences," that what we have here is a "myth," an "error," that these judgments turn back against the literature of those who pronounce them and who from then on would give themselves away by talking, finally, only about themselves. Already, in the second paragraph, the argument that would consist in making the Jews coresponsible for this antisemitic "myth" and this "error" is right away discredited. It was evoked merely as a rhetorical ploy: "But the error has, in fact, a deeper cause."

The logic of these first two paragraphs controls everything that follows: it is a matter of condemning antisemitism *to the extent that it is vulgar* (I leave this expression all its ambiguity, which is the ambiguity of the article) and of condemning this antisemitism *as regards literature*: its history, its own laws, its relations to history in general. It is as regards literature that de Man wants to say something and obviously thinks he has something original to say. He especially wants to talk about literature, here as elsewhere, and it is moreover literature that is his domain at the newspaper. This is one of the early articles in *Le Soir,* where he began writing about two months previously. I have yet to find any allusion to the Jewish problem or any declaration of antisemitism in any of the other articles. Left to formulate hypotheses, I can imagine that, for a page devoted to Judaism, he was asked to treat the subject from a literary point of view. What one can read on the same page surrounding this article seems to me to support this hypothesis. One then notices that, if de Man's article is necessarily contaminated by the forms of vulgar antisemitism that frame it, *these coincide in a literal fashion, in their vocabulary and logic, with the very thing that de Man accuses,* as if his article were denouncing the neighboring articles, pointing to the "myth" and the "errors," the "lapidary judgments," and the "very widespread belief" that can be read just to one side, in another article on the same page ("Freudism"—and not Freud—as the product of a "particularly keen Jewish intelligence," well-received in "the intellectual and artistic milieux of a decadent and *enjuivée* society"), as well as the declaration no doubt falsely attributed to Benjamin Franklin: "A leopard cannot change its spots. Jews are Asiatics; they are a threat to the country that admits them and they should be excluded by the Constitution."

De Man wants especially to propose a thesis on literature that visibly interests him more here than either antisemitism or the Jews. But before getting to that, a few points about vulgarity. It is a word and a major motif in all the articles. An *ideology* dominated by a disdain for vulgarity can be evaluated in diverse and contradictory ways. We know these programs very well, so I may be spared further development. But one must be aware that de Man rejects all kinds of conformism of the period

as so much "vulgarity" (the word was also a favorite of his uncle).[34] Once again the double edge. In his view, there can be no salvation for any "vulgarity." Read his "Propos sur la vulgarité artistique" (Remarks on artistic vulgarity). Behind the word vulgarity, and on almost every line, it is "our age" that is condemned, always in a fashion that cuts both ways: what "the radio, the cinema, publishing," even "the press" "undertake to unload on us," and then there are "fake artists," "mechanized formulas that guarantee success with the masses," the "falseness of tone." That these are signs of aristocratism and aestheticism is not at all in doubt, especially since de Man says so himself. Still one must be specific: this aristocratism is more aesthetic than social, it is social *on the basis of* the aesthetic, an aesthetic determined *on the basis of* literature, even if music and painting play a considerable role. Although it intends "French letters" in particular, the conclusion of this article is eloquent in its every word: "Henri Pourrat represents something very pure and very precious within French letters: that regionalism of a noble attachment to the native soil which is the index of an authentic literary aristocracy."[35]

If his focus is on literature, what does de Man want to say about it? Why does he reproach vulgar antisemitism for its mistake *as regards literature*? Why does he write "But the reality is different?" The following four paragraphs, which form the center and the thesis of the article, no longer contain the slightest allusion to Jews or to antisemitism. They speak only of literature, of its original historicity, and of the "very powerful laws" that govern "aesthetic evolutions." There is a history of art and of literature. It is essential and irreducible, but it maintains its originality. It does not merge with sociopolitical history either in its rhythms or in its causal determinations. Historicism, and especially "vulgar" historicism, would consist in mapping one history onto the other, in ignoring the powerful structural constraints, the logics, forms. genres, methods, and especially the temporality proper to literary history, the duration of the waves within its depths that one must know how to listen for over and above the swirls and agitation of the immediate, to listen for the sounds coming from the "artistic life" there where it is "little swayed" by the waves of the present. Literary duration enfolds and unfolds itself otherwise, in a way that differs from the phenomena of sociopolitical history in the brief sequences of their events: it precedes them, sometimes succeeds them, in any case it exceeds them. This notion compromises all the ideologies of literature, even the opinions or the propaganda on the subject of literature whenever they would attempt to enclose themselves in a strictly determined context ("current affairs"). Whether they are revolutionary or not, on the left or the right, these ideological discourses speak of everything except literature itself. Sometimes, from "within" literature itself, manifest discourses of certain literary movements ("surrealism" or "futurism") are, precisely in the form of their "manifestos," ideological or doxical in this sense. They also mistake the historicity proper to literature, the ample rhythms of its tradition, the discreet convolutions of its "evolutions": in sum, a "vulgar" approach to literature.[36]

There would be much to say in a closely argued discussion around this question: literature, history, and politics. Here I must restrict myself to *three points*.

1. Debatable or not, this interesting and consistent thesis concerns, then, first of all the historicity proper to literature and the arts. Forming the central body of the article which has no relation with any "Jewish question" whatsoever, it develops as a theoretical demonstration in three moments: a) general propositions on art; b) illustration using the privileged example of the novel; c) "analogous demonstration" with the example of poetry.

2. In 1941, under the German occupation, and first of all in the context of this newspaper, the *presentation* of such a thesis (for precisely the reasons that some today would judge it to be "formalist" or "aestheticist" or in any case too concerned about protecting "literarity," if not from all history, as we saw that is not the case, then at least from a sociopolitical history and against ideology) goes rather against the current. One can at least read it as an anticonformist attack. Its insolence can take aim at and strike all those who were then, in an active and properly punitive fashion, undertaking to judge literature and its history, indeed to administer, control, censor them in function of the dominant ideology of the war or, as de Man puts it, of a "profound upheaval in the political and economic world."

3. The examples chosen (Gide, Kafka, Lawrence, Hemingway, surrealism, futurism) are troubling in this context. They are visibly invoked as great canonic examples on the basis of which, beyond any possible question, one ought to be able to say what literature *is,* what writers and literary movements *do.* We know from many other signs, his articles in the *Cahiers* for example, that these writers were already important references for de Man. The examples chosen are already curious and insolent because there are no others, because there is no German example, because the French example is Gide, the American Hemingway, the English Lawrence, and because Kafka is Jewish, but especially because they represent everything that Nazism or the right wing revolutions would have liked to extirpate from history and the great tradition. Now, what does de Man say? That these writers and these movements were already can-

onical: they belong to tradition, they have "orthodox ancestors," whether one likes it or not, whether they recognize it themselves or not. Taking the risk of a certain traditionalism (always the double edge), de Manian genealogy reinscribes all of these "accursed ones" in the then protective legitimacy of the canon and in the great literary family. It lifts them out of repression's way and it does so in an exemplary fashion since, he says, "the list could be extended indefinitely." I have said why I will cite this article *in extenso.* Here are the four central paragraphs, where I have underlined the "buts," "But the reality," "in reality":

But the reality is different. It seems that aesthetic evolutions obey very powerful laws that continue their action even when humanity is shaken by considerable events. The world war has brought about a profound upheaval in the political and economic world. *But* artistic life has been swayed relatively little, and the forms that we know at present are the logical and normal successors to what there had been before.

This is particularly clear as concerns the novel. Stendhal's definition, according to which "the novel is a mirror carried along a highway," contains within it the law that still today rules this literary genre. There was first the obligation to respect reality scrupulously. *But* by digging deeper, the novel has gotten around to exploring psychological reality. Stendhal's mirror no longer remains immobile the length of the road: it undertakes to search even the most secret corners of the souls of characters. And this domain has shown itself to be so fruitful in surprises and riches that it still constitutes the one and only terrain of investigation of the novelist.

Gide, Kafka, Hemingway, Lawrence—the list could be extended indefinitely—all do nothing but attempt to penetrate, according to methods proper to their personality, into the secrets of interior life. Through this characteristic, they show themselves to be, not innovators who have broken with all past traditions, *but* mere continuers who are only pursuing further the realist aesthetic that is more than a century old.

An analogous demonstration could be made in the domain of poetry. The forms that seem to us most revolutionary, such as surrealism or futurism, *in reality* have orthodox ancestors from which they cannot be detached. ["Jla"]

Now let us look closely at what happens in the last paragraph of this central demonstration, that is in the conclusion of a sort of syllogism. No more than the central body of the article (the four paragraphs just quoted), the *general* scope of the conclusion, I mean conclusion in its general and theoretical form, is not concerned with the Jews. It does not name them in this general formulation. This conclusion concerns—and contests—an "absurd" *general* theorem regarding current literature, an absurdity that is denounced, precisely, as the axiom of antisemitism inasmuch as it is vulgar. And this conclusion announces by means of a "Therefore . . ." what must be deduced from the preceding demonstration: "Therefore, one may see that to consider present-day literature as an isolated phenomenon created by the particular mentality of the 20s is absurd."

And so we arrive at the last paragraph of the article, the most serious and in fact the only one that can be suspected of antisemitism. There, the return to the question of "Jews in present-day literature" corresponds to the rhetoric of a supplementary or analogical example. It comes to the aid of a general thesis or antithesis opposed to vulgar antisemitism. The demonstration that matters is considered established. De Man adds: "Likewise, the Jews. . . ." Next, and still without wanting to attenuate the violence of this paragraph that for me remains disastrous, let us remark this: even as he reminds us of the limits of "Jewish influence," of "semitic interference," even as, however, he seems to turn the discourse over to "Western intellectuals" by reconstituting their anxieties and then reassuring them, the manner in which he describes the "Jewish spirit" remains unquestionably positive. Even in its stereotyped, and therefore equivocal form, it is presented as a statement that no one is supposed to be able to question: a classical technique of contraband. For who, at that time, could dispense in public with *disputing* such praise? Who could publicly subscribe to it? Well, de Man does not dispute it, on the contrary, he assumes it. Even better, he himself underscores a *contradiction* that cannot go unnoticed and has to leave some trace in the consciousness or the unconscious of the reader:

one might have expected that, given the specific characteristics of the Jewish spirit, the latter would have played a more brilliant role in this artistic production. Their cerebralness, their capacity to assimilate doctrines while maintaining a certain coldness in the face of them, would seem to be very precious qualities for the work of lucid analysis that the novel demands.

One can hardly believe one's eyes: would this mean that what he prefers in the novel, "the work of lucid analysis," and in theory, a "certain coldness" of intelligence, correspond precisely to the qualities of the "Jewish spirit"? And that the "precious qualities" of the latter are indispensable to literature and theory? What is coiled up and resonating deep within this sentence? Did one hear that correctly? In any case, de Man does not say the contrary. And he clearly describes what were in his eyes "precious qualities." (Was he then recognizing the qualities of the enemy or those in which he would have liked to recognize

himself? Later, these were the qualities his American enemies always attributed to him.)

The last lines, the most terrible, begin with another "But in spite of that. . . ." They are attacking once again, let us not forget, the antisemitic obsession that always needs, that has a compulsive and significant need, to *overevaluate* the Jewish influence on literature. Here is the final paragraph:

Therefore, one may see that to consider present-day literature as an isolated phenomenon created by the particular mentality of the 20s is absurd. Likewise, the Jews cannot claim to have been its creators, nor even to have exercised a preponderant influence over its development. On any somewhat close examination, this influence appears even to have extraordinarily little importance since one might have expected that, given the specific characteristics of the Jewish spirit, the latter would have played a more brilliant role in this artistic production. Their cerebralness, their capacity to assimilate doctrines while keeping a certain coldness in the face of them, seemed to be very precious qualities for the work of lucid analysis that the novel demands. But in spite of that, Jewish writers have always remained in the second rank and, to speak only of France, the André Maurois's, the Francis de Croissets, the Henri Duvernois's, the Henri Bernsteins, Tristan Bernards, Julien Bendas, and so forth, are not among the most important figures, they are especially not those who have had any guiding influence on the literary genres. The observation is, moreover, comforting for Western intellectuals. That they have been able to safeguard themselves from Jewish influence in a domain as representative of culture as literature proves their vitality. If our civilization had let itself be invaded by a foreign force, then we would have to give up much hope for its future. By keeping, in spite of semitic interference in all aspects of European life, an intact originality and character, that civilization has shown that its basic nature is healthy. What is more, one sees that a solution of the Jewish problem that would aim at the creation of a Jewish colony isolated from Europe would not entail, for the literary life of the West, deplorable consequences. The latter would lose, in all, a few personalities of mediocre value and would continue, as in the past, to develop according to its great evolutive laws. ["Jla"]

Through the indelible wound, one must still analyze and seek to understand. Any concession would betray, besides a complacent indulgence and a lack of rigor, an infinitely culpable thoughtlessness with regard to past, present, or future victims of discourses that at least resembled this one. I have said why I am not speaking here as a judge, witness, prosecutor, or defender in some *trial of Paul de Man*. One will say: but you are constantly delivering judgments, you are evaluating, you just did so now. Indeed, and therefore I did not say that I would not do so at all. I said that in analyzing, judging, evaluating this or that discourse, this or that effect of these old fragments, I refused to extend these gestures to a general judgment, with no possibility of appeal, of Paul de Man, of the totality of what he was, thought, wrote, taught, and so forth. I continue thus to ask myself questions. If I persist in wondering how, in what conditions he wrote this, it is because even in the sum total of the articles from that period that I have been able to read, I have found no remark analogous or identical to this one. I did not even find any allusion to the Jews or to some "Jewish problem." Or rather, yes: in May 1941, some remarkable and emphatic praise for Péguy the Dreyfusard.[37] How is one to explain this discordance? Who will ever know how, some months earlier, "Les Juifs dans la littérature actuelle" was written and published? Who can exclude what happens so often in newspapers, and especially during that period and in those conditions, when editors can always intervene at the last moment? If that was the case, Paul de Man is no longer here to testify to it. But at that point one can say: supposing this to have been the case, there was still a way of protesting which would have been to end his association with the newspaper. Yes, but he would have had to be certain that this rupture was better than his ambiguous and sometimes anticonformist continuation on the job. He would also have had to evaluate the gravity of the last lines of this article as we are doing today. Now, in order to evaluate them correctly, we must understand what this allusion to "a Jewish colony isolated from Europe" meant at that moment. I admit that, in the present state of my information, I do not understand it. To which "solution," to which hypothesis that was perhaps current at the time was he making allusion? I do not know; perhaps to what was called the "Madagascar solution." As of that date (4 March 1941), the word "solution" could not be associated with what we now know to have been the project of the "final solution": the latter was conceived and put into effect later. At the end of 1942, Paul de Man stops contributing to the newspaper *Le Soir* (to my knowledge, he publishes nothing else during the war and he explains this in a letter that I will cite later). The same year, Henri de Man had left Belgium and given up all public responsibility.

Last September, then, this first reading and this first series of questions led me to an interpretation that is itself divided by what I have called "double bind," "disjunction," and especially "double edge," each term of this division never coming to rest in a monadic identity. The experience of the double edge can be an ironic ruse on one side, a painful suffering on the other, and finally one and the other at every moment. But in what I have

read of these texts, as in what I had learned to know earlier of Paul de Man and which it was difficult for me to abstract, nothing ever authorized me to translate this division into a hypocritical, cynical, or opportunistic duplicity. First of all, because this kind of duplicity was, to a degree and with a clarity that I have rarely encountered in my life, alien to Paul de Man. His irony and his anticonformist burst of laughter took instead the form of insolent provocation—one which was, precisely, cutting. One feels something of that in these "early writings." Second, because cynical opportunism is another form of acquiescence; it is profoundly conformist and comfortable, the opposite of the double edge. Finally, because all of that would have continued after 1942. And this was not the case; the rupture was unquestionably a cut. I have the sense that de Man, in whom a certain analytical coldness always cohabited with passion, fervor, and enthusiasm, must have, like his uncle, obeyed his convictions—which were also those of his uncle: complicated, independent, mobile, in a situation that he thought, incorrectly as did many others, offered no other way out after what seemed, up until 1942, like the end of the war.

So I will continue my story. For my own part, I was quickly convinced at the end of August that what had just been discovered could not and should not be kept secret. As quickly and as radically as possible, it was necessary to make these texts accessible to everyone. The necessary conditions had to be created so that everyone could read them and interpret them in total freedom. No limit should be set on the discussion. Everyone should be in a position to take his or her responsibilities. For one could imagine in advance the effect that these "revelations" were going to produce, at least in the American university. One did not have to have second sight to foresee even the whole specter of reactions to come. For the most part, they have been programmed for a long time—and the program is simple enough to leave little room for surprises. I was also conscious of the fact that the serious interpretation of these texts and their context would take a lot of time. All the more reason not to delay. I discuss it, once again in Paris, with Sam Weber. I suggest that we take advantage of a colloquium that is supposed to take place a few weeks later at the University of Alabama in Tuscaloosa in order to discuss the matter with about twenty colleagues. It is appropriately a colloquium dealing with academic institutions and politics ("Our Academic Contract: The Conflict of the Faculties in America") and bringing together, *among others,* some former students and colleagues of Paul de Man. Sam Weber agrees, as does Ortwin de Graef from whom I request authorization to distribute to all these colleagues photocopies of the articles I have just described. Richard Rand, the organizer of the colloquium, also agrees and makes the necessary arrangements. On 10 October, all the colloquium's participants having read these texts, we had a discussion that lasted more than three hours and touched on both the substance of things and the decisions to be made. I cannot summarize the discussion, all of which was tape-recorded.

Whatever may have been the remarks of the various people, no one, it seems to me, questioned the necessity of making these texts widely accessible and to do everything to permit a serious, minute, patient, honest study of them, as well as an open discussion. What remained to be decided was the best technical conditions in which to accomplish this. In the weeks that followed, broad exchanges led us to confide to Werner Hamacher, Neil Hertz, and Thomas Keenan the task of completing the collection of articles, of preparing their publication, as well as that of a volume in which as many as possible of those who wished to do so could communicate their reflections, whatever may have been their relation to Paul de Man and his work. A letter of invitation was addressed to this effect to numerous colleagues, known for their competence or for the interest they might have in the problem and, let me underscore this point, whatever may have been the extent, the form, or the premises of their agreement or their disagreement with the person or the work of de Man. These two volumes will appear soon. Even though they constitute merely the beginning of work that will have to be long-term and opened to still more people, no one will doubt, I hope, the wish of those who took the initiative for it: to allow everyone to take his or her responsibilities in the clearest possible conditions. Nevertheless, as one could also foresee and as Werner Hamacher has since written to me, those who took this initiative have found themselves faced with a double accusation that is both typical and contradictory: on the one hand, of betraying Paul de Man, on the other hand, of protecting him; on the one hand, of exposing him in great haste to the violence of the most expeditious lapidary judgments, even to a symbolic lapidation and, on the other hand, of wanting to save his work and, at the same time, defend all those for whom, in one way or another, it is important. I can understand this double accusation and the indications it alleges in support. But it seems to me perverse and inevitably unjust. First of all because one cannot do both of these things at once. You could not succeed in doing both of them even if you tried. Second, because those who launch one or the other of these accusations are themselves, necessarily, doing one or the other by obeying one or the other of these motivations. So as to explain how, as I see it, neither one nor the other of these intentions should enter into things, I

will quote now, in its literal and integral transcription, what I tried to say at the outset of the discussion in Tuscaloosa. After an account that corresponds, for the facts although not for the reading of the texts, to the one I have just given, I added this in French (which, because it is part of the archive, I think I have to include in my narrative):

I insist on improvising. For the last two months, I have not stopped thinking in a quasi-obsessional fashion about this, but I preferred not to prepare what I am going to say. I think it is necessary this evening that everyone tell us, speaking personally and after a first analysis, what he or she thinks of these things. On the other hand, I wanted to tell you what my own feeling is. I have known Paul de Man since 1966. You know of the friendship that we shared since then. I knew that he had lived through some difficult times when he left Belgium for the United States. We never spoke of what happened during the war. We were very close, from a certain point of view, but because our friendship remained very discreet, I never felt indiscreet enough to ask him about what had happened then, even though, like many others, I knew that this had been a [singular?; inaudible word] moment in his personal, private but also public (professional, et cetera) history. But I want to begin there: never in the course of these fifteen or sixteen years did I read anything of his nor hear anything from him that leaves the least suspicion in my memory as to any persistence of, let us say—how to name it?—a certain ideology, readable for me in the texts I read with you, in the texts published in French, the only ones I have been able to read directly. On the contrary, everything I can remember of the texts he published afterwards and of conversations I had with him, of all the evaluations of different sorts (social, political, et cetera) leave me with the certainty that he had in any case broken in a radical, internal, rigorous way with anything whatsoever that one might suspect in the ideology of the texts we are going to talk about. I wanted thus to begin by setting temporal limits on the things we are going to talk about. I wanted to set out that everything indicates, in any case for me, that along with what there may be that is shocking in these texts (and I do not hide that), he had broken radically with all that and there was no trace to my knowledge either in his life or in his remarks or in his texts that allows one to think the opposite. He broke with what happened when he was between twenty-one and twenty-three years old. I realize that we will now be able to read all his published texts, everyone will do so, us in particular, the texts we already know, while trying, some will do it with malevolence, with an unhealthy jubilation, others will do it otherwise, to find in the published texts signs referring back to that period.

Even as I improvise and in a somewhat confused way, I would like to say the following: I think there is a continuity and I would like to be specific. Paul de Man is someone who had that experience, who asked himself the questions that are asked in those texts, and who at twenty-one or twenty-three years old, brought to them the answers that are in these texts. He thus went through this experience which is not just any experience, he read the texts you know about, he wrote what you now know.

It is out of the question to imagine that the rupture means all of that is erased. All of it is part of his experience. In my opinion, he must have drawn a certain number of lessons from it: historical, political, rhetorical, of all sorts; and besides the rupture, this lesson must in effect be readable in his texts. It is one thing to read it as a lesson; it would be another to amalgamate everything, as some, I imagine, will perhaps be tempted to do, calling it a continuity, in which nothing happens without leaving traces, from these texts to those that followed. Our responsibility, in any case mine, would be to analyze all these texts, those from Le Soir. We do not have them all and some of them are much more convoluted, complicated, others are simple and unfortunately readable, but others are convoluted, complicated. Those who are seriously interested in the question will have to take the time to work on, analyze those texts, then the texts published in the U.S., with the greatest rigor and attention to detail. I have decided to improvise because I have taken as a rule to ally urgency with patience. It is urgent that we (perhaps I am forcing things by saying we, please excuse me), that some of us hasten to take their responsibilities as regards these texts, to be the first to show that there is no question of dissimulating them or of participating in any kind of camouflage operation. It is urgent that, in one mode or another, no doubt the mode of improvisation, we make the thing public but it is also urgent that, while doing this, we call upon ourselves and those who are interested in the thing, the well-intentioned and the ill-intentioned, to look at them closely, to undertake a reflection on the substance of what made this possible, for Paul de Man and for others, and of what the rupture with that means for someone like Paul de Man, only a part of whose work (or life) we know. We have a lot of work before us if we are to know what actually happened, not only in the political, ideological fabric of Belgium at the time, but also in the life of Paul de Man.

Two more things, perhaps three. Rethinking about all of this in an obsessional way and with much, how to say, worry, consternation, the feeling that wins out over all the others in my bereaved friendship, bereaved once again, is, I have to say, first of all a feeling of immense compassion. Through these texts and through other things [inaudible] of what must have been Paul de Man's life during the 10 years from 1940–50, through the ruptures, exile, the radical reconversion, what I begin to see clearly is, I imagine and I don't think I am wrong, an enormous suffering, an agony, that we cannot yet know the extent of. And I must say after having read these pages written by a young man of twenty-one or twenty-two (I do not mention his age in order to clear him or attenuate anything: at twenty-one or twenty-two, one takes responsibilities and, notably in that situation, people have pointed out, and they are right, that certain young men of twenty or twenty-one took adult responsibilities, in the Resistance, for example, or elsewhere. Thus, when I mention his age, it is not so as to

say "he was a child.") Nevertheless, what appears clearly is that, in a situation that we will have to describe, that of occupied Europe from which hope seemed banished except for a few, through a reflection on what might be the spirit [inaudible] we were talking about earlier[38] and under the influence of his uncle (about whom we will certainly have much to say, perhaps not tonight but later), a young man with clearly an immense culture, gifted, brilliant, exceptional, became involved in all that, we'll talk about this some more, and then found that he had to break with it and turn everything almost upside down, through problems that were also personal problems, indissociable from this whole story. This man must have lived a real agony and I believe that what he wrote later, what he taught, what he lived through in the United States obviously carry the traces of this suffering. I want to say that whatever may be—how to say—the wound that these texts are for me, they have changed nothing in my friendship and admiration for Paul de Man.

One more thing: some of us might think that, having broken with what he said and did under his signature at that time, Paul de Man tried, in the United States at any rate, to hide the thing. The fact is that we did not speak about it and that to my knowledge he did not speak about it very much. Perhaps he spoke to some people we do not know, but in any case most of those here never spoke with Paul about these things. If he did, then people will be able to say so.

But we do know, and Tom Keenan can confirm this in a moment, that in 1955 while de Man was at Harvard, there was an anonymous denunciation concerning his activity in Belgium during the war. And de Man explained himself at that moment, in a letter of which we have at least the draft, to the Head of the Society of Fellows.[39] This is a public act with which he explained himself on these matters. It is a long letter from which we can extract at least this: in effect during the German Occupation, in 1940–42, he maintained a literary column, but when the pressure of German censorship became too much—Tom will read this in a moment—he ceased writing and did what decency demanded that he do. Naturally, we are not obliged to give credence to this presentation of the thing, his version of the facts, in this letter. I don't know. We are, for those who are interested in it, at the beginning of a long movement of approach. But whatever the case may be, whether or not this letter speaks the whole truth about what happened then, about the reasons for which he wrote and then stopped writing, about these texts, what they are or are not, that is less important for the moment and for what I want to say, than the fact in any case (1) that he did explain himself publicly; (2) that he indicated what his evaluation of the thing was, that is, that he wished in 1955 never to have done anything that could be suspected of nazism, or collaboration. He explains himself, he broke with that and there can be no doubt about the kind of look he himself casts at that time at least on the period in question and on the ideological implications that one may read in these texts. He explained himself publicly and in my opinion that is a reason, whatever we might do from now on, not to organize today a trial of Paul de Man. I would consider it absolutely out-of-place, ridiculous, strictly ridiculous, to do something (I am not saying this for us but for others) that would look like a trial, after the death of Paul de Man, for texts, whatever they may be (we will come back to this) that he wrote when was between twenty-one and twenty-three years old, in conditions with which he absolutely and radically broke afterward. I think that anything that would look like such a trial would be absolutely indecent and the jubilation with which some may hasten to play that game ought to be denounced. In any case, personally, I plan to denounce it in the most uncompromising manner.

These are the preliminary things that I wanted to say to you. On the texts you read, there will be much, very much to say, but I do not want to keep the floor any longer. I will take it again when the time comes on the subject of the texts. I already have an extremely complicated relation to these texts. There are things that are massively obvious to me and that seem to me to call for a denunciation whose protocols are rather clear. But these things are woven into a very complex fabric, one that deserves, not only this evening, but beyond this evening the most serious and careful analyses.

Before going to the end of my story, I want to be more specific about certain points touched on in this improvisation. First, about Paul de Man's silence. Although, as I mentioned, it was not absolute, although it was publicly broken on at least one occasion and thus cannot be understood in the sense of a dissimulation, although I have since learned that it was also broken on other occasions, in private, with certain colleagues and friends, I am left to meditate, endlessly, on all the reasons that induced him not to speak of it more, for example to *all* his friends. What could the ordeal of this mutism have been, for him? I can only imagine it. Having explained himself once publicly and believing he had demonstrated the absurdity of certain accusations in the Harvard letter, why would he himself have incited, spontaneously, a public debate on this subject?

Several reasons could both dissuade and discourage him from doing so. He was aware of having never collaborated or called for collaboration with a Nazism that he never even named in his texts, of having never engaged in any criminal activity or even any organized political activity, in the strict sense of the term, I mean in a public organization or in a political administration. Therefore, to provoke spontaneously an explanation on this subject was no longer an obligation. It would have been, moreover, an all the more distressing, pointlessly painful theatricalization in that he had not only broken with the political context of 1940–42, but he had distanced himself from it with all his might, in his language, his country, his profession, his private life. His international notoriety having spread only

during the last years of his life, to exhibit earlier such a distant past so as to call the public as a witness—would that not have been a pretentious, ridiculous, and infinitely complicated gesture? All of these articles, whose disconcerting structure we have glimpsed, would have had to be taken up again and analyzed under a microscope. He would have had himself to convoke the whole world to a great philologico-political symposium on his own "early writings," even though he was only recognized by a small university elite. I would understand that he might have found this to be indiscreet and indecent. And this modesty is more like him than a deliberate will to hide or to falsify. I even imagine him in the process of analyzing with an implacable irony the simulacrum of "confession" to which certain people would like to invite him after the fact, after his death, and the auto-justification and auto-accusation quivering with pleasure which form the abyssal program of such a self-exhibition. He has said the essential on this subject and I invite those who wonder about his silence to read, among other texts, "Excuses (*Confessions*)" in *Allegories of Reading*. The first sentence announces what "political and autobiographical texts have in common"[40] and the conclusion explains again the relations between irony and allegory so as to render an account (without ever being able to account for it sufficiently) of this: "Just as the text can never stop apologizing for the suppression of a guilt that it performs, there is never enough knowledge available to account for the delusion of knowing" (*A*, p.300). In the interval, between the first and last sentences, at the heart of this text which is also the last word of *Allegories of Reading,* everything is said. Or at least almost everything one can say about the reasons for which a totalization is impossible: ironically, allegorically, and *en abyme*. Since I cannot quote everything, I will limit myself to recalling this citation of Rousseau, in a note. The note is to a phrase that names the "nameless avengers." Nameless? Minus the crime, (almost) everything is there, the count is there and it is almost correct, I mean the exact number of years: "If this crime can be redeemed, as I hope it may, it must be by the many misfortunes that have darkened the latter part of my life, by forty years of upright and honorable behavior under difficult circumstances" (*A*, p.288).

Even if sometimes a murmur of protest stirs in me, I prefer, upon reflection, that he chose not to take it on himself to provoke, during his life, this spectacular and painful discussion. It would have taken his time and energy. He did not have very much and that would have deprived us of a part of his work. Since it is at the moment of his greatest notoriety that this "demonstration" would have had some legitimacy, we do not know what price he would have had to pay for it. We do not know to what extent it would have weakened him or distracted him from his last works, which are among the most remarkable, when he was already ill. So he did the right thing, I say to myself, by leaving us also with this heavy and obscure part of the legacy. We owe it to him and we will owe him still more since what he leaves us is also the gift of an ordeal, the summons to a work of reading, historical interpretation, ethico-political reflection, an interminable analysis. Well beyond the sequence 1940–42. In the future and for the future, I mean also the future of philosophico-political reflection, this will not do anybody any harm. Especially not those who, if they want still to accuse or take revenge, will finally have to read de Man, from A to Z. Had they done so? Would they have done so otherwise? It is now unavoidable. You will have understood that I am speaking of transference and prosopopeia, of that which goes and returns only to the other, without any possible reappropriation, for anyone, of his own voice or his own face.

Permit me an ellipsis here since I do not have much more time or space. Transference and prosopopeia, like the experience of the undecidable, seem to make a responsibility impossible. It is for that very reason that they require it and perhaps subtract it from the calculable program: they give it a chance. Or, inversely: responsibility, if there is any, requires the experience of the undecidable as well as that irreducibility of the other, some of whose names are transference, prosopopeia, allegory. There are many others. And the double edge and the double bind, which are other phenomena of the undecidable. Before answering, responding for oneself, and *for* that purpose, in order to do so, one must respond, answer to the other, about the other, *for* the other, not in his place but as if in the place of another "proper self," but *for* him. My ellipsis here, my economical aphorism, is a thought for all these "fors" that make responsibility *undeniable: there is some, one cannot deny it, one cannot/can only deny it* [on ne peut (que) la dénier] *precisely because it is impossible.*

Yes, to read him, that is the task. How shall one do that from now on? Everyone will go about it in his or her own way, many paths have been opened, the work is spreading and becoming more and more differentiated, and no one has any advice to give anyone. Therefore, at the moment of beginning to read or to reread Paul de Man, I will mention only a few of the rules that impose themselves on me today.

First of all, of course, to take account of what we have just discovered, to try to reconstitute this whole part of the corpus (I have mentioned only a few articles) without overlooking any of the "internal" or "contextual" overdeterminations ("public" and "private" situation, if possible—without forgetting what

de Man has said about this distinction), in the direction, for example, of "Belgium during the war" and everything that can be transferred onto the uncle. But taking the 1940–42 articles into account does not mean giving them a disproportionate importance while minimizing the immensity of the rest, in a landscape that would, like those geographical maps of the Middle Ages or the territorial representations organized around a local, immediate, distorting perception. (I am thinking of those projections by Saul Steinberg where a New York street looks larger than the United States, not to mention the rest of the world). How can one forget de Man's world, and first of all the United States? And the map of all his great voyages? The texts of 1940–42 can also be represented there as a minuscule point.

Next, without ever forgetting or overlooking these first articles (how could I?), I would try to *articulate* them with the work to come while avoiding, if possible, two more or less symmetrical errors.

One would consist in interpreting the rupture between the two moments of de Man's history and work as an interruption of any passage, an interdiction against any contamination, analogy, translation. In that case, one would be saying: no relation, sealed frontier between the two, absolute heterogeneity. One would also be saying: even if there were two moments, they do not belong to history, to the same history, to the history of the "work." There would have been a prehistory, some politico-journalistic accidents, then history and the work. This attitude would be giving in to defensive denegation, it would deprive itself of interpretive resources, including the political dimension of the work. Most important, by annulling the so-called prehistory, it would compound its own political frivolity by an injustice toward Paul de Man: what he lived through then was serious, probably decisive and traumatic in his life, and I will never feel I have the right, on the pretext of protecting him from those who would like to abuse it, of treating the experience of the war as a minor episode.

I would also try to avoid the opposite error: confusing everything while playing at being an authorized prosecutor or clever inquisitor. We know from experience that these compulsive and confusionist practices—amalgam, continuism, analogism, teleologism, hasty totalization, reduction, and derivation—are not limited to a few hurried journalists.

So I would make every effort to avoid giving in to the typical temptation of a discourse that seeks to shore up this shaky certainty: everything is already there in the "early writings," everything derives from them or comes down to them, the rest was nothing but their pacifying and diplomatic translation (the pursuit of the same war by other means). As if there were no longer any difference of level, no displacement, *a fortiori* no fundamental rupture during these 40 years of exile, reflection, teaching, reading, or writing! The crudeness of an enterprise guided by such a principle (that, precisely, of the worst totalitarian police) can seek to hide behind more or less honest tricks and take purely formal precautions on the subject of the too-obvious differences. But it cannot fool anyone for long. It is not even necessary here to recall de Man's own warnings against such foolishness or such trickery, against the models of a certain historicism, or against the forms of causality, derivation, or narration that still crowd these dogmatic slumbers. When one is seeking, at all costs, to reconstruct in an artificial way genealogical continuities or totalities, then one has to interpret discontinuity as a conscious or unconscious ruse meant to hide a persistence or a subsistence, the stubborn repetition of an originary project (what this is is good old existential psychoanalysis of the immediate postwar period!). Why is this totalitarian logic essentially triumphant? Triumphalist? And made strong by its very weakness? Why is it recognizable by its tone and its affect? Because it authorizes itself to interpret everything that resists it in every line, in Paul de Man's work or elsewhere, and resists it to the point of disqualifying or ridiculing it, as the organization of a defensive resistance, precisely, in the face of its own inquisition. For example, when de Man demonstrates theoretically (and more than just theoretically, beyond constative or cognitive logic, precisely) that a historical totalization is impossible and that a certain fragmentation is inevitable, even in the presentation of his works, the detective or the chief prosecutor would see there a maneuver to avoid assuming the totalizing anamnesis of a shameful story. With a clever wink and while poking you each time with his elbow, he would find damning evidence everywhere. He would draw your attention to sentences as revealing, from this point of view, as the following, among many others: "This apparent coherence within each essay is not matched by a corresponding coherence between them. Laid out diachronically in a roughly chronological sequence, they do not evolve in a manner that easily allows for dialectical progression or, ultimately, for historical totalization."[41] This modest statement is relayed, everywhere else, by a critical or deconstructive discourse with regard to historical totalization in general. It would thus suffice to extend the scope of these sentences through analogy to all de Man's writings and to conclude confidently that this preface confesses what it hides while declaring it inaccessible. The trap would be sprung, the amateur analyst could rub his hands together and conclude: "de Man does not want to sum up or assume the totality of his history and his writings. He declares that it is impossible in princi-

ple in order to discourage in advance all the policemen, and to evade the necessary confession." Now, one could find examples like this on every page. Before leaving this example, I will quote only the end of this preface to *The Rhetoric of Romanticism*: "The only place where I come close to facing some of these questions about history and fragmentation is in the essay on Shelley's *The Triumph of Life*. How and where one goes on from there is far from clear, but certainly no longer simply a matter of syntax and diction" (*R*, p. ix).

And from there, I would invite whoever wants to talk seriously about de Man to read him, to read this essay on Shelley to its end or its final interruption (*R*, pp. 121, 123). I do not have the room to quote the pages where it is a question of "what we have done with the dead Shelley and with all the other dead bodies . . . ," of the "suspicion that the negation is a *Verneinung*, an intended exorcism," of what "always again demands to be read," of "recuperative and nihilistic allegories of historicism" (*R*, pp. 121–22). Here is how the essay ends:

Reading as disfiguration, to the very extent that it resists historicism, turns out to be historically more reliable than the products of historical archeology. To monumentalize this observation into a *method* of reading would be to regress from the rigor exhibited by Shelley which is exemplary precisely because it refuses to be generalized into a system. [*R*, p. 123]

If I give up playing the policeman's petty game, is it only because the exercise is too easy? No, it is because its dogmatic naïveté will always fail to render an account of this unquestionable fact: a statement can never be taken as a presumption of guilt or evidence in a trial, even less as proof, as long as one has not demonstrated that it has only an idiomatic value and that no one else, besides Paul de Man or a Paul de Man signatory of the 1940–42 texts, could have either produced the statement or subscribed to it. Or inversely, that all similar statements—their number is not finite and their contexts are highly diverse—could not be signed and approved by authors who shared nothing of Paul de Man's history or political experiences.

Even though I give up on this petty and mediocre game, I have at the disposal of those who would like to play it a whole cartography of false leads, beginning with what de Man wrote and gave us to think on the theme of memory, mourning, and autobiography. I have myself tried to meditate on this theme in *Mémoires*. Since Paul de Man speaks so much of memory and of mourning, since he extends the textual space of autobiography to this point, why not reapply his categories to his own texts? Why not read all these as autobiographical figures in which fiction and truth are indiscernible? And, as de Man himself shows, is not this latter problematic political through and through? Did I not underscore that myself in *Mémoires,* in a *certain way?* Yes, but in what way? Can one, ought one to take the reading possibilities that de Man himself offers us and manipulate them as arms, as a suspicion or an accusation against him in a "décision de justice," as we say in French, in a final judgment, authorizing oneself this time to decide in the absence of proof or knowledge? What would be the rule, if there is one, for avoiding abuse, injustice, the kind of violence that is sometimes merely stupidity? Before going any further into this question, here is the beginning of a list of themes that could become weapons in the arsenal of the investigators. The list is, by definition, incomplete, and, one may say it *a priori,* it links up with the "whole" de Manian text in a mode that never excludes "disjunction."

There is "Autobiography as De-Facement," an "autobiography [which] is not a genre or a mode, but a figure of reading or of understanding that occurs, to some degree, in all texts" (*R,* p.70); then there is the autobiographical aspect, *that is, also the fictional* aspect of any text, even if one cannot remain within this undecidability ("the distinction between fiction and autobiography is not an either/or polarity but . . . it is undecidable" [*R,* p.70]); or else, speaking of Lejeune's *Le Pacte autobiographique*: "From specular figure of the author, the reader becomes the judge, the policing power in charge of verifying the *authenticity* of the signature and the consistency of the signer's behavior, the extent to which he respects or fails to honor the contractual agreement he has signed" (*R,* pp.71–72); or else, that about which I myself said it "precludes any anamnesic totalization of self" (*M,* p.23):

The specular moment that is part of all understanding reveals the tropological structure that underlies all cognitions, including knowledge of self. The interest of autobiography, then, is not that it reveals reliable self-knowledge—it does not—but that it demonstrates in a striking way the impossibility of closure and of totalization (that is, the impossibility of coming into being) of all textual systems made up of tropological substitutions. (*R,* p.71)

Or yet again, the insistence on rhetoric and the irreducibility of the tropological substitutions can always be interpreted, by "the reader" as "judge" or "policing power," as a theoretical machine of the ruse meant to lead him or her astray in advance and turn aside the police inquiry; especially the insistence on the hallucinatory prosopopeia, about which I said four years ago that it was "the sovereign, secret, discreet, and ideal signature—and the most giving, the one which *knows how to efface itself*" (*M,* p.26). Is it not de Man who speaks to us "beyond the grave" and

from the flames of cremation? "The dominant figure of the epitaphic or autobiographical discourse is, as we saw, the prosopopeia, the fiction of the voice-from-beyond-the-grave; an unlettered stone would leave the sun suspended in nothingness" (*R,* p.77); and yet again, the motif of "true mourning" and of the nostalgic resistance to the "materiality of actual history"; and then there is the major motif of disjunction, as well as what I called "an uncontrollable necessity, a *nonsubjectivizable* law of thought beyond interiorization" (*M,* p.37), the motif of thinking memory (*Gedächtnis*) beyond interiorizing memory (*Erinnerung*); and then the structure of allegory, even of memory itself, if not as amnesia, then at least as relation to an "unreachable anteriority,"[42] a memory, in sum, without a past in the standard sense of the term. Ah ha! someone will say, is that not a maneuver meant to deny or dissimulate, even to repress say the cleverest ones, an intolerable past? The problem is that the maneuver being suspected, in other words, this *thought* of memory, can be, has been, and will be once again, in this form or in a nearby form, assumed by persons whose past has no relation with de Man's. To the accusers falls the obligation of proving the contrary. I wish them patience and courage.

So many false leads, then, for hurried detectives. The list is incomplete, as I said, the "whole" de Manian text is available as a boobytrapped resource for symptomatologists in training. The latter could even begin by suspecting or denouncing the titles of "all" de Man's books! If they do not understand what I mean, they should write to me and I will point out a few tricks. Besides the pleasure (everyone gets it where he or she can), this exercise for late beginners may even procure a professional benefit for some. Especially if they take advantage of the opportunity to extend the trial, through contiguity or confusion, allusion, insinuation, or vociferation, to all those who are interested in de Man, to supposed groups or schools against whom it is advisable to wage war. I will come back to this in a moment.

As will have become clear, I see these two opposed errors as both intellectual and ethico-political errors, that is, both errors and falsifications. What would I do in the future so as to avoid them, if that is possible? Since it is a matter of nothing less than reading and rereading de Man without simplifying anything about the questions (general and particular, theoretical and exemplified) of the context, I cannot show here, in an article, what I would do at every step of a reading that ought to remain as open and as differentiated as possible. But I can try to advance a few hypotheses and, for the formation of these hypotheses themselves, one or two rules. Even if the hypotheses remain hypotheses, I assume as of now responsibility for the rules.

First rule: respect for the other, that is, for his right to difference, in his relation to others but also in his relation to himself. What are all these grand words saying here? Not only respect for the right to error, even to an aberration which, moreover, de Man never tired speaking of in a highly educated and educating manner; not only respect for the right to a history, a transformation of oneself and one's thought that can never be totalized or reduced to something homogeneous (and those who practice this reduction give a very grave ethico-political example for the future); it is also respect of that which, in *any* text, remains heterogeneous and can even, as is the case here, explain itself on the subject of this open heterogeneity while helping us to understand it. We are also the heirs and guardians of this heterogeneous text even if, precisely for this reason, we ought to maintain a differentiated, vigilant, and sometimes critical relation to it. Even those who would like to reject or burn de Man's work very well know, and will have to resign themselves to the fact, that from now it is inscribed, at work, and radiating in the body or the corpus of our tradition. Not work but *works*: numerous, difficult, mobile, still obscure. Even in the hypothesis of the fiercest discussion, I would avoid the totalizing process and trial [*procès*]: of the work and the man. And the least sign of respect or fidelity will be this: to begin, precisely, by listening, to try to hear what he said to us, him, de Man, *already,* along with a few others, about totalizing violence, thus, to lend an ear, and an ear finely tuned enough to perceive, between the Atlantic and the Pacific, something other than monotonous noise and the rumbling [*rumeur*] of the waves.

The *second rule* is still more demanding, as inaccessible as what is called a "regulating ideal." But it is no less important to me and has been for a long time. Since we are talking at this moment about discourse that is totalitarian, fascist, Nazi, racist, antisemitic, and so forth, about all the gestures, either discursive or not, that could be suspected of complicity with it, I would like to do, and naturally I invite others to do, whatever possible to avoid reproducing, if only virtually, the *logic* of the discourse thus incriminated.

Do we have access to a complete formalization of this logic and an absolute exteriority with regard to its ensemble? Is there a systematic set of themes, concepts, philosophemes, forms of utterance, axioms, evaluations, hierarchies which, forming a closed and identifiable coherence of what we call totalitarianism, fascism, nazism, racism, antisemitism, never appear outside these formations and especially never on the opposite side? And is there a systematic coherence proper to each of them, since one must not confuse them too quickly with each other? Is there some property so closed and so pure that one may not find any element of these systems in discourses that are commonly opposed to them? To say that I do not believe that there is, not absolutely, means at least two things: (1) Such a formalizing, saturating totalization seems to me to be precisely the essential character of this logic whose project, at least, and whose ethico-political consequence can be terrifying. One of my rules is never to accept this project and consequence, whatever that may cost. (2) For this very reason, one must analyze as far as possible this process of formalization and its program so as to uncover the statements, the philosophical, ideological, or political behaviors that derive from it, wherever they may be found. The task seems to me to be both urgent and interminable. It has occurred to me on occasion to call this deconstruction; I will come back to that word in a moment.

I will give some concrete illustrations of these two abstractly formulated rules. In many of the discourses I have read or heard in the last few months (and I was expecting them in a very precise way), whether they attack or defend de Man, it was easy to recognize axioms and forms of behavior that confirm the logic one claims to have rid oneself of: purification, purge, totalization, reappropriation, homogenization, rapid objectification, good conscience, stereotyping and nonreading, *immediate* politicization or depoliticization (the two always go together), *immediate* historicization or dehistoricization (it is always the same thing), immediate ideologizing moralization (immorality itself) of all the texts and all the problems, expedited trial, condemnations, or acquittals, summary executions or sublimations. This is what must be deconstructed, these are a few points of reference (that is all I can do here) in the field open to this research and these responsibilities that have been called, for two decades, deconstructions (in the plural). I would not have pronounced this word here if all the newspaper articles and all the rumors that have reached me as of this day had not, in a way that is both so surprising and so unsurprising, associated deconstruction (in the singular) to this whole affair. By touching quickly on this problem, I will no doubt be able to go *from the rule to the hypothesis* and differentiate a little what I have meant since the beginning of this article by the word "rupture."

In spite of its discouraging effect, I have begun to get used to journalistic presentations of deconstruction and to the even more discouraging fact that the responsibility for them belongs most often not with professional journalists, but with professors whose training ought to require at least some attempt at reading. This time, finding as always its foothold in aggressivity, simplism has produced the most unbelievably stupid statements.[43] Some might smile with disabused indulgence at the highly transparent gesticulations of those who leap at the chance to exploit without delay an opportunity they think is propitious: at last, still without reading the texts, to take some cheap revenge on a "theory" that is all the more threatening to institutions and individuals because, visibly, they do not understand anything about it. One may also wonder, with the same smiling indulgence: but, after all, what does deconstruction (in the singular) have to do with what was written in 1940–42 by a very young man in a Belgian newspaper? Is it not ridiculous and dishonest to extend to a "theory," that has itself been simplified and homogenized, as well as to all those who are interested in it and develop it, the trial one would like to conduct of a man for texts written in Belgian newspapers forty-five years ago and that moreover, once again, one has not really read? Yes, this deserves perhaps hardly more than a smile and most often I manage to shrug it off.

But not always. Today I will speak of my indignation and my worry. First, because the gestures of simplification and the expeditious verdicts have, yes, *in fact,* a relation to what happened around 1940–42, earlier or later, in Europe and elsewhere. When someone asking "not to be identified" sees himself quoted by an unscrupulous professor-journalist,[44] when he says he is "shocked" by the fact that certain people are gathering, if only in order to *discuss* these problems (he would thus like to forbid the right to assembly and discussion? What does that remind you of?), and when he says he is "shocked" in the name of a "moral perspective," you can see why I am indignant and worried; and why it is necessary to remain vigilant; and why more than ever one must guard against reproducing the logic one claims to condemn. Precisely from a "moral perspective." Be on your guard for morality and thus the well-known immorality of so many moralisms.

Second, because, paradoxically, I think deconstructions *do have a relation,* but an altogether other relation, to the substance of the problems we are talking about here. To put it in a word, they have always represented, as I see it, the at least necessary condition for identifying and combating the totalitarian risk in all the forms already mentioned.

Not only can one not accuse deconstruction (in the singular) in the expeditious trial some are dreaming about today, but without deconstructive procedures, a vigilant political practice could not even get very far in the analysis of all these political discourses, philosophemes, ideologemes, events, or structures, in the reelaboration of all these questions on literature, history, politics, culture and the university. I am not saying that, *inversely,* one must organize trials in the name of (singular) deconstruction! But rather that what I have practiced under that name has always seemed to me favorable, indeed destined (it is

no doubt my principal motivation) to the analysis of the conditions of totalitarianism in all its forms, which cannot always be reduced to names of regimes. And this in order to free oneself of totalitarianism as far as possible, because it is not enough to untie a knot through analysis (there is more than one knot and the twisted structure of the knot remains very resistant) or to uproot what is finally, perhaps, only the terrifying desire for roots and common roots. One does not free oneself of it effectively at a single blow by easy adherences to the dominant consensus, or by rather low-risk proclamations of the sort I could, after all, give in to without any risk, since it is what is called the objective truth: "as for me, you know, no one can suspect me of anything: I am Jewish, I was persecuted as a child during the war, I have always been known for my leftist opinions, I fight as best I can, for example against racism (for instance, in France or in the United States where they are still rampant, would anyone like to forget that?), against *apartheid* or for the recognition of the rights of Palestinians. I have gotten myself arrested, interrogated, and imprisoned by totalitarian police, not long ago, so I know how they ask and resolve questions, and so forth." No, such declarations are insufficient. There can still be, and in spite of them, residual adherences to the discourse one is claiming to combat. And deconstruction is, in particular, the tireless analysis (both theoretical and practical) of these adherences. Now, today, from what I have read in newspapers and heard in conversation, I would say that these adherences are more numerous and more serious on the part of those who accuse de Man than in the latter's books or teaching. And this leads me to complicate or to differentiate still more (I warned that it would be long and difficult) what I have said so far about the "rupture."

By saying several times and repeating it again that de Man had radically *broken* with his past of 1940–42, I intend clearly an activity, convictions, direct or indirect relations with everything that then determined the context of his articles. In short, a deep and deliberate uprooting. But after this decisive rupture, even as he never ceased reflecting on and interpreting this past, notably through his work and a historico-political experience that was ongoing, he must have proceeded with other *ruptures, divergences, displacements.* My hypothesis is that there were many of them. And that, with every step, it was indirectly at least a question of wondering: how was this possible and how can one guard oneself against it? What is it, in the ideologies of the right or the left, in this or that concept of literature, of history or of politics, in a particular protocol of reading, or a particular rhetorical trap that still contains, beneath one figure or another, the possibility of this return? And it is the "same man" who did that for 40 years. My hypothesis is that this trajectory is in principle readable in what de Man was, in what he said, taught, published in the United States. The chain of consequences of these ruptures is even what is most interesting, in my view, in these texts, and whose lesson will be useful for everyone in the future, in particular for his enemies who would be well inspired to study it.

Those who would like to exploit the recent "revelations" against deconstruction (in the singular) ought to reflect on this fact. It is rather massive. "Deconstruction" took the forms in which it is now recognized more than twenty years after the war. Its relation to all its premises, notably Heideggerian premises, was from the start itself both critical and deconstructive, and has become so more and more. It was more than twenty years after the war that de Man discovered deconstruction. And when he began to talk about it, in the essays of *Blindness and Insight,* it was *first of all in a rather critical manner,* although complicated, as always. Many traits in this book show that the theoretical or ideologico-philosophical consequences of the "rupture" were not yet drawn out. I have tried to show elsewhere (see *Mémoires,* pp.120 and passim.), what happens in his work when the word "deconstruction" appears (very late) and when, in *Allegories of Reading,* he elaborates what remains his original relation to deconstruction. Is it really necessary to recall once again so many differences, and to point out that this singular relation, however interesting it may seem to me, is not exactly mine? That matters little here. But since it is repeated everywhere, and for a long time now, that de Man is not interested in history and in politics, we can better take the measure today of the inanity of this belief. I am thinking in particular of the irony with which he one day responded, on the question of "ideology" and "politics": "I don't think I ever was away from these problems, they were always uppermost in my mind."[45] It is necessary to read the rest. Yes, they were "in [his] mind" and no doubt more than in the mind of those who, in the United States or in England, accused him of distraction in this regard. He had several reasons for that, experience had prepared him for it. He must have thought that well-tuned ears knew how to hear him, and that he did not even need to confide to anyone about the war in this regard. In fact, that is all he talked about. That is all he wrote about. At moments I say to myself: he supposed perhaps that I knew, if only from reading him, everything he never spoke to me about. And perhaps, in fact, I did know it in an obscure way. I heard it mutedly. "Like the sound of the sea. . . ." Today, thinking about him, about him himself, I say to myself two things, among others.

1. He must have lived this war, in himself, according to two temporalities or two histories that were at the same time dis-

joined and inextricably associated. On the one hand, youth and the years of occupation appeared there as a sort of prehistoric prelude: more and more distant, derealized, abstract, foreign. The "true" history, the effective and fruitful history, was constituted slowly, laboriously, painfully after this rupture that was also a second birth. But, on the other hand and inversely, the "true" events (public and private), the grave, traumatic events, the effective and indelible history had already taken place, over there, during those terrible years. What happened next in America, for the one whom a French writer friend, he told me, had nicknamed in one of his texts "Hölderlin in America," would have been nothing more than a posthistoric afterlife, lighter, less serious: a day after with which one can play more easily, more ironically, without owing any explanations. These two lives, these two "histories" (prehistory and posthistory) are not totalizable. In that infinitely rapid oscillation he often spoke of in reference to irony and allegory, the one is as absolute, as "absolved," as the other. Naturally these two nontotalizable dimensions are also equally true or illusory, equally aberrant, but the true and the false also do not go together. His "living present," as someone might put it, was the crossroads of these two incompatible and disjunctive temporalities, temporalities that nevertheless went together, articulated in history, in what was *his history,* the only one.

2. After the period of sadness and hurt, I believe that what has happened *to us* was doubly necessary. First as a fated happening: it had to happen one day or another and precisely because of the deserved and growing influence of a thinker who is enigmatic enough that people always want to learn more— from him and about him. Second, it had to happen as a salutary ordeal. It will oblige all of us, some more than others, to reread, to understand better, to analyze the traps and the stakes—past, present, and especially future. Paul de Man's legacy is not poisoned, or in any case no more than the best legacies are if there is no such thing as a legacy without some venom. I think of our meeting, of the friendship and the confidence he showed me as a stroke of luck in my life. I am almost certain that the same is true for many, for those who can and will know how to make it known, and for many others, who perhaps do not even realize it or will never say so. I know that I am going to reread him and that there is still a future and a promise that await us there. He will always interest me more than those who are in a hurry to judge, thinking they know, and who, with the naïve assurance of good or bad conscience, have concluded in advance. Because one has in effect concluded when one already thinks of staging a trial by distributing the roles: judge, prosecutor, defense lawyer, witnesses, and, waiting in the wings, the instruments of ex-

ecution. As for the accused himself, he is dead. He is in ashes, he has neither the grounds, nor the means, still less the choice or the desire to respond. We are alone with ourselves. We carry his memory and his name in us. We especially carry ethico-political responsibilities for the future. Our actions with regard to what remains to us of de Man will also have the value of an example, whether we like it or not. To judge, to condemn the work or the man on the basis of what was a brief episode, to call for closing, that is to say, at least figuratively, for censuring or burning his books is to reproduce the exterminating gesture against which one accuses de Man of not having armed himself sooner with the necessary vigilance. It is to not even draw a lesson that he, de Man, learned to draw from the war.

Having just reread my text, I imagine that for some it will seem I have tried, when all is said and done and despite all the protests or precautions, to protect, save, justify what does not deserve to be saved. To these readers, if they still have some concern for justice and rigor, I ask them to take the time to reread, as closely as possible.

The story I promised is more or less finished for the moment. As an epilogue, three more telephone calls, in December. The first is from Neil Hertz. He passes along the account of a certain Mr. Goriely, former Belgian resistant. He knew de Man well; they were friends during those dark years. Throughout the whole period of his clandestine activity, Mr. Goriely communicated in total confidence with de Man. He gives the same testimony to *Le Soir,* in an article dated 3 December 1987: according to this "university professor," de Man was "ideologically neither antisemitic nor even pro-Nazi. . . . I have proof that de Man was not a fanatic from the fact that I saw him frequently during the war and he knew I was a *clandestin,* mixed up with the Resistance. I never feared a denunciation." The same professor has no memory of an antisemitic article, of that article that *Le Soir* claims it cannot find in its archives![46] And he adds: "What is more, I believe I know that our man also gave texts to a Resistance publication: *Les Voix du silence* [The voices of silence]!" Intrigued by this latter testimony and by the Malraux title, Werner Hamacher calls me and asks me to try to learn more from Georges Lambrichs, a Belgian writer who for a long time was the director of the new NRF for Gallimard, and who, while in the Resistance, would have had some part in this episode. De Man had told me they knew each other well. I call him. His response is very firm, without the least hesitation: One must take into account the history and the authority of the uncle. Even though de Man did not belong to an organization of the Resistance, he was anything but a collaborator. Yes, he

helped French resistants publish and distribute in Belgium a journal that had been banned in France (with texts by Eluard, Aragon, and so forth). The title of the journal was not *Les Voix du silence* but *Exercice du silence* (to be continued).

Although my ear is glued to the telephone, I am not sure I have heard him clearly. Lambrichs repeats: "*Exercice du silence.*"

January 1988
Ecole des Hautes Etudes en Sciences Sociales

NOTES

1. See Marcia Graham Synnott, *The Half-Opened Door: Discrimination and Admissions at Harvard, Yale, and Princeton,* 1900–1970 (Westport, Conn.: Greenwood Press, 1979), and Nitza Rosovsky, *The Jewish Experience at Harvard and Radcliffe* (Cambridge, Mass.: Harvard University Press, 1986). I recall the indignation with which certain student newspapers at Yale, while I was teaching there, manifested surprise at the antisemitism that had reigned in their university. I do not recall that there was any echo of this in the major press or among the majority of our colleagues.

2. Derrida, *Mémoires: for Paul de Man,* trans. Cecile Lindsay, Jonathan Culler, Eduardo Cadava (New York: Columbia University Press [The Wellek Library Lectures], 1986), p.150; hereafter abbreviated *M.*

3. The four articles in *Het Vlaamsche Land* translated by Ortwin de Graef are: "Art as Mirror of the Essence of Nations: Considerations on Geist der Nationen, by A.E. Brinckmann," 29–30 March 1942; "Content of the European Idea," 31-May-1 June 1942; "Criticism and Literary History," 7–8 June 1942; "Literature and Sociology," 27–28 September 1942; hereafter abbreviated by title followed by *HVL.*

4. Ortwin de Graef, "Paul de Man's Proleptic 'Nachlass': Bio-bibliographical Additions and Translations," unpublished ms.

5. De Graef, letter to the author, 21 August 1987.

6. *De l'esprit: Heidegger et la question* (Paris: Galilée, 1987); forthcoming in a translation by Geoffrey Bennington and Rachel Bowlby (University of Chicago Press).

7. "Editorial," *Les Cahiers du Libre Examen* 4:5 (February 1940), p.1

8. *Les Cahiers du Libre Examen* 1:2 (April 1937), as cited by de Graef in his introduction.

9. *L'Ordre nouveau* was the title of a journal founded in 1933 by Robert Aron and Arnaud Dandieu. From the first, it proclaimed a broad sympathy with the National Socialist regime in Germany and

was considered a principal forum of extreme right wing thought. Subsequently the phrase "ordre nouveau" became a favored means for certain political discourse in the occupied countries to indicate sympathy for the goal of a unified Europe under German rule without, however, naming Nazism. (Trans.)

10. In an article about the story as reported in the *New York Times* ("Yale Scholar's Articles Found in Pro-Nazi Paper," 1 December 1987), *Le Soir* recalls that de Man was "neither arrested nor tried in Belgium" and then adds:

It should be noted that, as regards Le Soir, *the* New York Times *article is far from a model of journalistic rigor.* Le Soir *is described as "an anti-Semitic Belgian newspaper that collaborated with the Nazis." What our American colleague obviously does not know is that* Le Soir *was stolen and controlled by the occupiers, the directors and editorial board of our newspaper having, on the contrary, decided not to collaborate. Likewise the* New York Times *is completely wrong when it states that Paul de Man's uncle, Henri, was "a minister in the collaborationist Belgian government that tried to protect Belgian autonomy against Nazi domination." Need one recall that, except for the Vichy government in France, there was no collaborationist government in occupied Europe?*

Le Soir is certainly correct to remind another newspaper of "journalistic rigor." But then what must be said of its own rigor when it blindly reproduces the nonsense published in certain American newspapers that are getting their information, in every case, from university professors? I won't bother to comment. Here's what one may read in the same article:

Considered at Yale to be one of the most brilliant lights of the university, says the New York Times, *he was the author of a controversial theory about language, some seeing in him one of the greatest thinkers of the age. This theory, 'deconstructionism,' sees in language an integrally false means of expression which always reflects the prejudices of the user.*

It is true that after reading such stupidities over and over again, one might end up believing them. (F.U., "Indignation aux Etats-Unis: un professeur (belge) de Yale avait été un *collaborateur*," and Michel Bailly, "L'ahurissante équipée d'un *brillant* opportuniste" [Indignation in the United States: A (Belgian) professor at Yale had been a collaborator. The astounding adventure of a brilliant opportunist], *Le Soir,* 3 December 1987, p.4.)

11. The influence of Henri de Man, Paul's uncle and godfather, was no doubt powerful and determining. One must approach this extraordinary European figure in order to understand anything of these dramatic events. During a half century, his reputation radiated through his actions and his writings. Among the latter, all of which are more or less autobiographical, two titles provide brief

self-portraits, but also a prefiguration of Paul: *Cavalier seul* [Lone horseman] and *Gegen den Strom* (Against the current). Here, in a telegraphic style, are a few significant traits, for which I have relied on: Henri de Man's *Au delà du marxisme* (French translation of *Zur Psychologie des Sozialismus,* [Jena: Diederichs, 1926]; reissued by Seuil in 1974 with a very useful preface by Michel Brelaz and Ivo Rens, the foreword to the first French edition [Paris: Alcan, 1926], and a preface by the author denouncing the "nationalist imbecility" and the "prestige of race or nationality"); *A Documentary Study of Hendrik de Man, Socialist Critic of Marxism,* comp., ed. and largely trans. Peter Dodge (Princeton, N.J.: Princeton University Press, 1979); Dodge, *Beyond Marxism: The Faith and Works of Hendrik de Man* (The Hague: M. Nijhoff, 1966); and Jules Gérard-Libois and José Gotovitch, *L'An 40: La Belgique occupée* (Brussels: Centre de Recherche et d'Information Socio-politiques, 1971).

Freemason father, tolerant anticlerical: "one of the purest incarnations of stoic morality," says his son of him. Henri was born in 1885, the year that the POB (Belgian Labor Party) was founded, of which he will become vice-president in 1933. 1905: expelled from the Ghent Polytechnic Institute for having demonstrated in support of the Russian revolutionaries of 1905. Moves to Germany, "the native and the chosen land of Marxism." Meets Bebel, Kautsky, Liebknecht, Rosa Luxemburg. Intense militant and theoretical activity in Germany. First Secretary of the Socialist Youth International. Dissertation on the woolen industry in Ghent in the Middle Ages. In London in 1910, joins the Social Democratic Federation (radical Marxist group). Returns to Belgium in 1911, provokes a crisis in the POB by criticizing its reformism.

First doubts about Marxism as the war begins, after having served as translator in talks between Jaurès and the future chancellor of the Weimar Republic to preserve the peace. Official mission to Russia after the Revolution in 1917. Publishes "La Révolution aux armées" in Emile Vandervelde's *Trois aspects de la révolution russe,* 7 mai-25 juin 1917. In "La Grande désillusion" (1919; The Great Disillusion): "It is not for this reason, it is not so that the Europe of tomorrow will resemble the Europe of yesterday that we fought. It is not for the destruction of the German and Russian nations, it was for the independence of all nations and in order to free Europe of militarism." Plans to emigrate to the U.S., two trips there (1918–1920). Founds a system of worker education in Seattle. Professor of Social Psychology at University of Washington. Dismissed from his position after intervening in a local election campaign in favor of the Farmer-Labor Party. 1919: *The Remaking of a Mind: A Soldier's Thoughts on War and Reconstruction.* 1922–26: lives in Darmstadt and teaches at the Akademie der Arbeit in Frankfurt. 1926: publishes his best-known work, *The Psychology of Socialism* (trans. Eden and Cedar Paul, New York: Allen and Unwin, 1928). 1929–33: lives and teaches in Frankfurt (newly created chair in social psychology). 1933: publishes *Die sozialistische Idee,* confiscated by the Nazis. Director of the Office of Social Studies of the POB (1932) which issues the famous "Plan du travail" (Labor Plan) and the doctrine of planism (socialization of financial capital, credit, monopolies, and large landed property). Minister of Public Works and of Unemployment Reduction (1935), Finance Minister in 1936 in tripartite governments that reduce unemployment and fight back rexism (the extreme right). Appointed by the king to secret missions to preserve peace in 1938. Minister without portfolio for several months. Appointed to a post in the queen's service during the war, in the final days before the defeat perhaps advises the king, who was already inclined in that direction, to share the fate of the army rather than to follow the government into exile. Like many others, believes the war is over. President of the POB, considers the political role of the party to be finished and that the war "has led to the debacle of the parliamentary regime and of the capitalist plutocracy in the so-called democracies. For the working classes and for socialism, this collapse of a decrepit world is, far from a disaster, a deliverance" ("The Manifesto," in *Hendrik de Man, Socialist Critic of Marxism,* p.326). Dissolves the POB, creates a single central labor union in 1940. His relations with the occupiers go downhill quickly. From June 1941, considers the pressures untenable, goes into exile in November 1941 in Savoie (France). Already in July 1940, his program had been considered by the German command, "because of its spirit and its origins" and despite elements that are "formally 'pseudo-fascist,'" to be incapable of ever "being really integrated into a European order, such as Germany conceives it" (quoted in Brelaz and Rens, *Au delà du marxisme,* p.16). Writes his memoirs (*Après coup*). His *Réflexions sur la paix* (Reflections on Peace) banned in Belgium in 1942. Maintains relations with Belgian "collaborationists," unorthodox Germans as well as French Resistants (Robert Lacoste). Informed of the conspiracy and the failed plot against Hitler. 1944: escapes to Switzerland where he is taken in by a Swiss socialist leader who helps him to win political asylum. At the time of the Liberation, severely condemned by a military tribunal "for having, while in the military, maliciously served the policy and the designs of the enemy." Third marriage. *Au-delà du nationalisme* (1946). *Cavalier seul: Quarante-cinq années de socialisme européen* and *Gegen den Strom: Memoiren eines europäischen Sozialisten* are two reworked versions of his 1941 autobiography. *Vermassung und Kulturverfall: Eine Diagnosen unserer Zeit* (1951). On 20 June 1953, his car stops "for unknown reasons" on the railroad tracks at an unguarded crossing near his home. He dies with his wife when the train arrives. It was, they say, slightly behind schedule. (Suicide and allegories of reading: some day we will have to talk about suicide in this history.)

In 1973, in an article whose lucidity seems to me after the fact to be even more admirable and striking, Richard Klein was to my knowledge the first to take the figure of the uncle seriously into consideration. Paul de Man having pointed out to him that he, (that is, Richard Klein!) had taken Henri de Man to be the former's father, Klein's postscript closes with the best possible question: "what, after all, is an uncle?" The rereading of this article, "The Blindness of Hyperboles, the Ellipses of Insight" (*Diacritics* 3 [Summer 1973], pp.33–44), seems to me urgent for whoever is interested in these questions.

12. "Les livres sur la campagne de Belgique," *Le Soir,* 25 February 1941.

13. "Le *Solstice de juin,* par Henri de Montherlant," *Le Soir,* 11 November 1941; hereafter abbreviated "SjM."

14. "Témoignages sur la guerre en France," *Le Soir,* 25 March 1941.

15. "L'exposition 'Histoire de l'Allemagne' au Cinquantenaire," *Le Soir,* 16 March 1942.

16. "*Voir la figure,* de Jacques Chardonne," *Le Soir,* 28 October 1941; hereafter abbreviated "VfC."

17. "*Notre avant-guerre,* de Robert Brasillach," *Le Soir,* 12 August 1941; hereafter abbreviated "NaB."

18. "Content of the European Idea," *HVL.*

19. "*Sur les falaises de marbre,* de Ernst Jünger: deux ouvrages d'actualité," *Le Soir,* 31 March 1942.

20. "Le Problème français: *Dieu est-il français?,* de F. Sieburg," *Le Soir,* 28 April 1942; hereafter abbreviated "PfS."

21. "La littérature française devant les événements," *Le Soir,* 20 January 1942.

22. On "matter" in de Man, see *Mémoires,* chap.2. On the lexicon of "spirit," that is so manifest in these texts of 1941–42, as in the writings of so many others in the period between the wars, see my *De l'esprit: Heidegger et la question.* I wish to make it clear, however, that the number and nature of differences between Heidegger and de Man would render any analogism more confused than ever.

23. "Sur les possibilités de la critique," *Le Soir,* 2 December 1941.

24. Jean Paulhan, *De la Paille et du grain,* (Paris: Gallimard, 1948), p.55. [The principal ideologue and organizing force of the Action Française, Maurras was a prolific and much-admired writer. (Trans.)]

25. "*Trois épreuves,* par Daniel Halévy," *Le Soir,* 14 October 1941.

26. "Art as Mirror of the Essence of Nations" *HVL*; hereafter abbreviated "AM."

27. "Le Destin de la Flandre," *Le Soir*, 1 September 1941; hereafter abbreviated "F."

28. "Romans allemands," *Le Soir*, 10 February 1942; hereafter abbreviated "Ra."

29. "*Jardins et routes*, par Ernst Jünger," *Le Soir*, 23 June 1942.

30. "La littérature française devant les événements," *Le Soir*, 20 January 1942.

31. "Art as Mirror" rejects "sentimental patriotism" and "narrow-minded regionalism."

32. "Les Juifs dans la littérature actuelle," *Le Soir*, 4 March 1941; hereafter abbreviated "Jla."

33. "*Notes pour comprendre le siècle*, par Drieu La Rochelle," *Le Soir*, 2 December 1941; hereafter abbreviated "NpD."

34. Henri de Man speaks, for example, of "pure Marxism and vulgar Marxism" in *The Psychology of Socialism*. The first is a "dead truth," the second is a "living error." Elsewhere, he writes:

I despise all forms of vulgarization, of truth put within reach of those who prefer ersatz goods, radio and phonograph music, champagne for democratic banquets. . . . This confession might sound strange coming from the pen of a socialist, especially a former director of worker education programs. But socialism is not demagogy; and educating the people is not bringing science down to their level, but raising them to the level of science. Truths exist only for those who seek them.

(Foreword to first French edition, *Au delà du marxisme* [Paris, 1926].)

35. "Propos sur la vulgarité artistique," *Le Soir*, 6 Jan. 1942.

36. This is a remarkably constant de Manian concern up until the final articles, and notably the article titled "Continuité de la poésie française: A propos de la revue *Messages*" (Continuity of French poetry: On the journal *Messages*), *Le Soir*, 14 July 1942. The journal *Messages*, which was banned off and on in France, was published and made known in Belgium with Paul de Man's help. See below concerning *Exercice du Silence*, which was the title of the fourth issue of this journal for 1942 (February 1988).

37. "Charles Péguy," *Le Soir*, 6 May 1941. The unmitigated praise for this "genius" who was "notoriously independent and undisciplined" is organized completely around the Dreyfus affair. In the portrait of Péguy the Dreyfusard, and in the history of (Péguy's)

Cahiers, one cannot fail to remark all the quasi-autobiographical traits that de Man seems to take pleasure in proliferating (February 1988).

38. This is an allusion to the lecture I had given the same afternoon on Heidegger (questions of spirit, of Nazism, of nationalism, of language, of the destiny of Europe, and so forth).

39. Letter to Renato Poggioli, Director of the Harvard Society of Fellows, dated 25 January 1955 (from a handwritten draft). Here is an extract from this draft that no doubt will be published: "In 1940 and 1941, I wrote some literary articles in the newspaper 'Le Soir' and I, like most of the other contributors, stopped doing so when nazi thought-control did no longer allow freedom of statement. During the rest of the occupation I did what was the duty of any decent person." According to Charles Dosogne (letter to Neil Hertz, dated 11 January 1988), a contemporary and friend of de Man, "beginning at the end of September 1940, preliminary censorship by the Propaganda Abteilung was limited to important political articles. Literary columns were thus exempted from this, at least until August 1942—date at which censorship was reestablished. It was at this time that Paul de Man's activities as a journalist ceased." It seems, however, that they continued a few months longer.

40. *Allegories of Reading: Figural Language in Rousseau, Nietzsche, Rilke, and Proust* (New Haven, Conn.: Yale University Press, 1979), p. 278; hereafter abbreviated *A*.

41. *The Rhetoric of Romanticism*, (New York: Columbia University Press, 1984), p. viii; hereafter abbreviated *R*.

42. *Blindness and Insight: Essays in the Rhetoric of Contemporary Criticism*, 2nd ed. (Minneapolis: University of Minnesota Press, 1983), p. 222.

43. I will have neither the room nor the patience nor the cruelty to cite them all. I merely recall that they often appear in university campus newspapers and are generally passed along to the journalists by professors.

44. Quoted in Jon Wiener "Deconstructing de Man," *The Nation*, 9 January 1988, p.24. From its title to its final sentence, this spiteful and error-ridden article gathers within its pages more or less all the reading mistakes I have evoked up until now. One shudders to think that its author teaches history at a university. Attempting to transfer onto deconstruction and its "politics" (such as he imagines them) a stream of calumny or defamatory insinuation, he has the nerve to speak of de Man as an "academic Waldheim," practices dogmatic summary without the least hesitation, attributes to me, for example, the foundation of deconstruction even as he also de-

scribes me as attributing its paternity to the "progenitor" Heidegger, about whom it would have been shown that his "commitment to Nazism was much stronger than has previously been realized." Now draw your own conclusion. Having explained myself at length elsewhere, again recently but for a long time already, on all these questions (notably on what the deconstruction that interests me receives from but also deconstructs of Heidegger, on Heidegger and Nazism, and so on), I can here only refer the interested reader to these numerous publications.

For Wiener and others like him, it is once again a matter of grabbing a long-awaited, in fact, an unhoped-for opportunity. There is no more resisting the temptation to exploit *at all costs* a windfall. The dream goes something like this: "What if this very singular sequence in the life of a young man allowed us to rid ourselves today at a single blow of Deconstruction [in the singular] and put a final end to its worrisome proliferation? Are we going to let this chance go by?"

The answer is "no," of course, even though the path followed might appear rather extravagant. It will seem incredible for those who have not yet been witness to the spectacle. The logic of the compulsion produces a quasi-somnambulistic acting out. The rush into action is all the greater in that, this time, people think they can finally point to "facts" as a justification for doing what they have always done: taking shortcuts around reading, analysis, or interpretation. It is as if people said to themselves: "We have never understood anything about deconstruction, moreover everyone says it is too complicated; we will never read it; so quick, here are some 'facts' that are going to save us the trouble. They do not even need to be interpreted, so we can skip the analysis; so what if the above-mentioned 'facts' are part of an individual experience and if they took place during the war, 25 years before this damned deconstruction even began complicating things, putting twists in everything, poisoning the waters of our certainties and our good conscience."

To achieve this liquidation at all costs (that is, at the cost of the most amazing inductions, of crude manipulations and denegations), they are not even afraid of ridicule, they think they can count on finding accomplices everywhere (and in this they are not wrong). It is true that the anger of these prosecutors feeds on and exasperates itself. Endlessly, of course, because it necessarily produces—one had to be very naïve not to have foreseen this—effects that are just the opposite of those counted on. Look at the example of Heidegger in France. Only yesterday there were those who advised, very loudly, that we ought no longer to take any interest in him. The result? Students are more interested in him than ever and there have been seven books devoted to Heidegger this year in this country alone. The confusions I have just mentioned were never

taken seriously, if I may use that euphemism, by those who are really working. The signs of this work are, fortunately, proliferating, even if they do not benefit from the immediate visibility of the media and pass unnoticed on certain screens. This will all be borne out in time. The same will be true, I am convinced of it, for Paul de Man. As for work of the deconstructive type which some would like to reduce quite simply to Heidegger (to "Heideggerianism"! or to "Heideggerians"!) or to de Man or else to their direct filiation ("orthodox" filiation in the terms of those for whom thinking can be divided from now on into two camps: the "orthodox" and the "dissidents"), not only must we recognize that this work is more than ever developing in a diverse and differentiated fashion, in directions and according to styles that often have no relation to the places within which the same inquisitors would like to contain it (academic deconstruction, "Heideggerian" reading). Do we have to recall (I would find it too distasteful to do so), by citing authors' names and titles, that most of the so-called "Heideggerians" are doing many other things—against or without Heidegger, in places and forms that have nothing to do with Heidegger? But people would rather not be told of these many other things; they try to efface them from memory or to render them inaudible by chanting endlessly, magically "Heidegger, Heidegger," etc. Actually, it is in desperate opposition to this very development that so many worried and reactive discourses have arisen.

All of this acquires meaning in a very determined theoretical, historical, and political situation. One may say without exaggeration that it is the situation of all of Western European culture, I mean from Japan to West Berlin passing by way of the two shores of the U.S.A. There is thus nothing surprising in the fact that Jon Wiener's article has provided a model. The author of this article is, however, famous for his mistakes in *The Nation*: on more than one occasion, this journal has had to publish strongly-worded and overwhelming rectifications after the contributions of this collaborator, who has thus proved to be something of a liability [*malencontreux*]. Yet, no matter, his latest exploit immediately inspired, or one should say programmed, other such articles in the United States or in Europe, notably in Germany. Some of these journalists have been content merely to borrow hurriedly his errors, confusions, defamatory insinuations. Others have added their own. That is the case of Mr. Frank Schirrmacher in two articles in the *Frankfurter Allgemeine Zeitung* (10 and 24 February 1988). Like Mr. Manfred Frank (who, for his part, worries that young Germans have fallen "into French hands" (sic), and extends the suspicion of fascism or of "neo-darwinian" "pre-fascism" to the whole "French International," to the "neufranzösische Kritik am 'Logozentrismus'" of "Derrida, Deleuze, and Lyotard" (sic!) in *Frankfurter Rundschau*, 5 March 1988), Mr. Schirrmacher intimates that deconstruction (about which it is clear, in every line, he too knows nothing) has affinities with fascism and other such things, nothing less than that. Then, he takes the reply from Werner Hamacher (which he began by shortening so as to have more room for his own reply, without worrying about the political significance of such a practice in a newspaper for which, I am told, he is in charge of the cultural section) as a pretext to repeat his offense while pretending to retract his insult. Claiming to be interested in the "meaning" [*Bedeutung*] of the "de Man case" "for a theory that has extraordinary influence in the domains of aesthetics and politics," he has the nerve to write the following: "Deconstructionism is too diverse [*vielfältig*] to be destroyed by the Paul de Man case [another way of admitting that this ought to be the question, more precisely the barely disguised desire]. We would have been misunderstood if it was thought that we had qualified deconstructionism as 'fascist.' Deconstructionism undeniably represents a valuable analytic method for a modern comprehension of literature and a modern comprehension of oneself. But this school already finds itself today confronted with the equation: 'deconstructionism is fascism' and it must therefore come up with a response."

Who is dreaming here? And why should a "school" have to respond to these stupidities and to this defamatory equation, one which, apparently, no one can or wants to answer for, not even Mr. Schirrmacher? (Not even Mr. Frank anymore, if I can be allowed a reference to a private letter.) Should one have to defend oneself against this senseless accusation because Mr. Schirrmacher, or other Schirrmachers, found it necessary to invent it and then to let it resonate while pretending to retract it or to attribute it to others? And what would Mr. Schirrmacher do if someone said to him, after having called him a fascist: "Things are more complicated than that. I did not say you are a fascist, I did not even say your methods are fascist, despite appearances, I never said that, certainly not me, and to think that is what I said would be to misunderstand me; but now this accusation has been launched, it is in the air, you have to respond to it"?

Polemics will not suffice. Whenever one can overcome one's repugnance in face of bad faith, resentment, obscurantist confusion or ignorance, even arrogance—which is often difficult to do—then, to be sure, one must reply. But one will have to go much further than that, without limiting oneself to the American or German contexts, to the "cases" (as one now says in the language of psychiatry or criminality) of Heidegger or of Paul de Man. If it is impossible and unjustified to assimilate them to each other or to reduce to their "simplest expression" the work of Heidegger or of Paul de Man, and *a fortiori* all the work of those who read them, interpret them, often to disagree with them, why, all the same, does this homogenizing totalization take place? How does what appears impossible and unjustified get produced? Why, in any case, does it emit so many signs of its existence—signs whose abundance and recurrence are too typical to be fortuitous? For these signs cannot be explained only by the individual mediocrity of the readers, however obvious it may be. Why is there today the attempt to exploit these "cases"? Why the attempt to discredit hurriedly, by means of amalgamation, *current* questions, analyses, problematics which, on the other hand, one knows very well are being employed (and not by limiting themselves to appeals to right thinking, good conscience, or demagogic consensus) precisely to deconstruct the foundations of obscurantism, of totalitarianism or of nazism, of racisms and authoritarian hierarchies in general? (And since on this point people refer to the French context, must I once again recall, for example, the work of Lacoue-Labarthe or Nancy on this subject? May I permit myself to cite also my own work?) Why do people overlook the fact that the exercise of (theoretical and ethico-political) responsibility prescribes that nothing be *a priori* exempted from the deconstructive questions? Because, in my view, deconstruction consists in nothing less than putting this responsibility to work, especially when it analyzes traditional or dogmatic axioms concerning the concept of responsibility. Why do people pretend not to see that deconstruction is anything but a nihilism or a skepticism? Why can one still read this claim despite so many texts that *explicitly, thematically and for more than twenty years* have been demonstrating the opposite? Why the charge of irrationalism as soon as anyone asks a question about reason, its forms, its history, its mutations? Or the charge of antihumanism, with the first question put to the essence of man and the construction of its concept? I could go on citing examples of this sort, the same thing occurs whether it is a matter of language, literature, philosophy, technicity, democracy, of all institutions in general, and so forth. In short, what are people afraid of? Whom do they want to make afraid? Which homogeneity are they trying to protect behind this barrier? Whom do they want to silence in the name of consensus, or in any case its "rallying cry" [*mot d'ordre*]? To what order, precisely, are we being recalled by these sinister disciplinary counsels with their gravely intoned litanies? Is it merely to the order of boredom? No, I fear it is more serious than that.

No doubt I will come back to these questions elsewhere, of course—and once again, because I have done so often. But I want at least to note, here and now, the most general trait of this philosophico-political conjuncture. There is a kind of law here, an invariant whose necessity has to be pondered. It is *always* in the name of ethics—a supposedly democratic ethics of discussion—it is always in the name of transparent communication and of "consensus" that the most brutal disregard of the elementary rules of discussion is produced (by these elementary rules, I mean differentiated reading or listening to the other, proof, argumentation, analysis, and quotation). It is *always* the moralistic discourse of consensus—at least the discourse that pretends to appeal sincerely to consensus—that produces in fact the indecent transgression of the classical norms of reason and democracy. To say nothing of elementary philology. Why? What is this a sign of today, in the actual state of our political, academic, or mediatistic institutions?

The most visible example of this—and no doubt the most influential, particularly in Germany and France—is Habermas. If one wants an indication of this (but I could cite many such indications, in France as well; I deal with this elsewhere ["Toward an Ethic of Discussion," in the expanded edition of *Limited Inc.,* to be published by Northwestern University Press]), look at one of the two chapters that are devoted to me in the latest book by this theoretician of communication (*The Philosophical Discourse of Modernity,* trans. Frederick Lawrence, Cambridge, Mass.: MIT Press, 1987 [*Der Philosophische Diskurs der Moderne,* Frankfurt-am-Main: Suhrkamp Verlag, 1985]). A whole fabric of counter-truths is stretched over twenty-five pages (pp.161–184) *without a single reference to any of my texts* although I am designated by name, from one end to the other, almost in every sentence, as the author of the theses supposedly being discussed. Here is how Habermas justifies his procedure: "Since Derrida does not belong to those philosophers who like to argue, it is expedient to take a closer look at his disciples in literary criticism within the Anglo-Saxon climate of argument in order to see whether this thesis [which is claimed to be mine] really can be held" [*Da Derrida nicht zu den argumentationsfreudigen Philosophen gehört, ist es ratsam, seinen im angelsächsischen Argumentationsklima aufgewachsenen literaturkritischen Schülern zu folgen, um zu sehen, ob sich diese These wirklich halten lässt*] (p.193 [p.228]). Such, then, is the effective practice of a great professor and a famous advocate of communication, one who, however, reproaches me for my "performative contradiction" (p.185 [p. 219]). Is there a more serious, flagrant, significant "performative contradiction" than the one that consists in claiming to refute in the name of reason but without citing the least proof and first of all without even reading or quoting the other? Habermas makes a very casual use of the notion of contradiction and especially of "performative contradiction." It is with something of a smile that I place myself for a moment within such a self-assured logic in order to point out the "performative contradictions" of someone who defends discussion and promises communication, but without respecting the elementary rules of such practices: to begin by reading or listening to the other. However, I think I have shown, a long time ago and again in *Mémoires* (especially in chapter 3), why a performative is never pure, never works well or only works, so to speak, on contradiction. A certain contradiction. Which one? How? In which case? Those are, in my view, more serious questions. What is called deconstruction

is the taking up of these questions. It is also, it seems to me, a strategy—as formalized as possible (but absolute formalization is impossible and this impossibility recognized as such, hence the "contradiction")—for assuming the necessity in which any discourse finds itself to take account of the rules and of the *determined* forms of *this or that* rationality which it is in the process of criticizing or, especially, of deconstructing. Without *this* "performative contradiction," one might even say that (among other consequences) there would no longer be critique, discussion, communication, progress of knowledge, history of reason, nor perhaps any history at all. It does not suffice to denounce this, formally and loudly, in order to escape it. Purely formal denunciation is doubtless the most sterile repetition or confirmation of the said contradiction. So, I would not reproach Habermas for having neglected to quote or even to read me if his objections still had some pertinence. For, of course, it is not enough to quote in order to prove that one has understood or even in order to prove anything at all. No more than writing the word "argumentation" in every sentence suffices to produce in fact a convincing argumentation: the other chapter that Habermas devotes to me does include, in fact, several references, but it seems to me to proceed from the same non-reading and from an equivalent non-argumentation. To say nothing of the foreword (by C. Bouchindhomme and R. Rochlitz) to the French translation [*Le discours philosophique de la modernité,* Paris: Gallimard, 1988]. The latter goes even further and ends up giving an example of the most grotesque, as well as the most violent, forms of dogmatic assurance and philosophical simplism. Since examples of this kind are proliferating, and precisely for the reasons I have just mentioned, we risk seeing readers taken in by them or getting accustomed to them. (25 May 1988. Completed after the publication of this text in *Critical Inquiry,* April 1988, this note remains naturally interminable. I offer my apologies to all the authors of texts analogous to the ones I criticize here; space and time are lacking, as well as my taste for such things.) (July 1988: All the same, one exception, in a more Parisian context and in order to recall again something well-known: edifying discourse is often a comedy of morals. Tzvetan Todorov has multiplied, over several years, venomous but always moralizing attacks against those whom he thinks he can identify, in the greatest confusion, under the name of deconstruction. Now, he has just published in the *Times Literary Supplement* [17–23 June 1988] and in *La Lettre Internationale* ["Correspondance," Summer 1988] an article, against de Man—and some others —, of which one could fairly show that the mistakes, lies, and falsifications number about three out of every four allegations. [Cynthia Chase, at the end of her rectification (*TLS,* 8–14 July 1988), emphasizes rightly, I would say rather charitably, that "these distortions are unworthy of the critic Todorov once was."] With less charity, one could charge to his account still more counter-truths, manipulated with assurance and good conscience by someone who goes so far as to state, for example, that de Man was "an influential propagator of Heideggerean philosophy." Now Todorov, co-founder and co-director of the journal *Poétique,* of which Paul de Man was a member of the editorial committee up to his death, ought at least to know that de Man was always critical with regard to Heidegger's thought. And that, having written about this topic only in a limited and indirect way, he was certainly not an "influential propagator" of it. And "propagator," what a word! Make no mistake—the fact is that it often smacks of the code of censorship, even to that of the police and of denunciation. Earlier, and more than once, we could just as well have recalled that the accusation of "nihilism," often directly helter-skelter against de Man or against deconstruction in general, not only testifies both to the non-reading of texts and to a massive lack of sensitivity to the great question—still open and still redoubtable—of nihilism and of metaphysics. This accusation bespeaks either political amnesia or a lack of political culture. Those who toss around the word nihilism so gravely or so lightly should, however, be aware of what they're doing: under the occupation, the "propagators" of dangerous ideas were often denounced by accusing them of "nihilism," sometimes in violently antisemitic tracts, and always in the name of a new order, moral and right-thinking ["nihilist acid-bath. . . ," "literary, spiritual, human nihilism!"—see, for example, Pascal Fouché, *L'édition française sous l'Occupation,* Paris: Bibliothèque de Littérature française contemporaine de l'Université Paris 7, 1987, vol. I, p.92].)

45. Stefano Rosso, "An Interview with Paul de Man," *The Resistance to Theory* (Minneapolis: University of Minnesota Press, 1986), p.121.

46. I had already been intrigued by *Le Soir*'s remark in the article of 3 December (see note 10) that it could not find in its archives what was perhaps a separately printed special issue, and by the claim of the person (later identified as Mr. Goriely) interviewed—who "knew de Man well and saw him frequently at that time"—to have no memory of such an article. The same surprise is marked by Charles Dosogne in his letter to Neil Hertz (see note 39). Dosogne, who was the first director of the *Cahiers du Libre Examen* (whose contributors included "a certain number of Israelites"), recalls first of all that Paul de Man

found himself at twenty years old, with a young wife and a baby, without a university degree, during a period of governmental disorganization, all of which did not permit him to aspire to a paying job. All he had going for him was his vast culture and his great intelligence, which he was able to take advantage of by accepting what some connections of his proposed to him: an association with Le Soir *and the* Vlaamsche Land.

Then, drawing from the experience of his long friendship (1938–1947), Charles Dosogne adds this:

I can confirm that never, neither before nor after the war, did Paul de Man's remarks or attitudes permit one to suspect an antisemitic opinion—which, let me say in passing, would have ended our relations. Racism was in fundamental contradiction with his profoundly human nature and the universal character of his mind. That is why I remain deeply skeptical concerning the remarks "with antisemitic resonances" cited by the New York Times *that could be imputed to him. Is there not room to ask certain questions concerning a document that does not figure among* Le Soir's *own collection, and, on the copy to be found at the Bibliothèque Albertine, is marked by three asterisks? Why??*

(July 1988:) While all these phenomena remain puzzling, the authenticity of this exceptional article has in the meantime unfortunately been verified. But the numerous testimonies which have come to confirm the rest of what Charles Dosogne said about Paul de Man must also be emphasized. Many of them are included in the present volume, others in the proceedings of a conference which was held recently (24–25 June 1988) in Antwerp, Paul de Man's birthplace. Jean Stengers, historian, and Georges Goriely, both professors emeriti at the Université Libre de Bruxelles, judged the published accusations of antisemitism and collaborationism levelled against de Man to be simply ridiculous. Goriely insisted on emphasizing that he did so with all the more vigilance in that he spoke both as a Jew and a resistant. In the same line, one of the most impressive testimonies, in my eyes, thanks to the richness of its information and the precision of its details, remains today that of M. Edouard Colinet [included in this volume], who was the last president of the "Cercle du Libre examen" and fought in the Resistance (in France) throughout the war. Henri Thomas, who knew Paul de Man in the United States, from 1958–1960, tells me that the image he keeps of his friend "will never be that of a *collabo.*"

To Read Paul de Man

ARIS FIORETOS

Translated from Swedish by Birgit Baldwin

. . . . Paul de Man's past as a literary columnist was treated in
the Swedish newspaper, *Dagens Nyheter,* on February 17, 1988,
by Bengt Holmqvist, a critic who always has shown both sensitivity and a decisive respect for sources. Unfortunately, the title
of Holmqvist's contribution is insinuating and less well-chosen:
"The Godfather's Possibility of Excusing Every Guilt." The next
day in *Expressen,* Gabi Gleichmann reiterated at times almost
verbatim the same information as Holmqvist, under the troubling title "A Waldheim Behind Postmodernism." The headings
share two features. First, both assume that de Man's role within
modern literary theory was that of the patriarch and the authority. That is to say, this role belonged to a man with imperial
power. Second, the titles underscore the highly dubious nature
of this authority. Either the story is about a gangster, with the
implication that he belongs to a "family," united by blood
bonds and oaths of faith that cannot be broken except in death.
Or else it deals with a head of state with such a dubious past
that he, by means of repeated lies masked as patriotism, tries to
save face. In both cases, it is a question of associating authority
with alliances that exercise terror. Holmqvist and Gleichmann
do not, of course, necessarily have to be burdened with the
choice of titles. But, on the other hand, the text in *Dagens Nyheter,* for which Holmqvist indeed has to be considered responsible, states that de Man "was considered to be the godfather of
the hermeneutical school, *capo di tutti capi,* and the principal figure among 'deconstructors.'" The heading thus hardly lacks
support in the article. Besides the fact the quotation here is indirect (it is attributed to no one, but stems from Frank Lentricchia's *After the New Criticism* [1980]), one might ask whether de
Man was ever considered the leader of "the hermeneutical
school." Instead, it would be safer to say that de Man's interest
in rhetoric could not unproblematically be reconciled with hermeneutical study in the German philosophical sense. Luckily
enough, the text in *Expressen* meanwhile lacks the nouns that
figure in its title. Neither Waldheim nor postmodernism are
named by Gleichmann, which naturally is to be welcomed,
since de Man probably would have had a good deal to say concerning both phenomena.

Both Holmqvist and Gleichmann base themselves on two
articles from the American press: the scantily informed text in
the *New York Times* and a misinformed report by David Lehman
in *Newsweek.* In distinction to Gleichmann, Holmqvist names
his secondary sources. For those acquainted with these American products, it is quite clear that they do not distinguish themselves by means of journalistic astuteness. Not only do they
seem to have no knowledge about de Man's Belgian journalism,
a lack that is as telling as it is aggravating, but they have also in-

augurated an ideologically loaded attack on de Man and what his name is considered to stand for. The criticism is by now extensive and thus decidedly more serious. Yet its final goals still remain unclear. The attacks are not, in any event, limited to the journalistic achievements of the twenty-year-old de Man. On the contrary, the contributions to the debate can be seen as maneuvers, with the support of de Man's early journalism, to cast suspicion on the intellectual honesty of deconstruction. The arguments are more often than not poorly anchored in the texts and in history. Those responsible for unquestionably the most glaring attempts at defaming de Man until now are Jon Wiener in *The Nation,* Frank Schirrmacher in *Frankfurter Allgemeine Zeitung,* and Walter Kendrick in the *Village Voice*. These contributions to contemporary psychology would be of no relevant interest (Schirrmacher mentions a "psychotic process of change" and a "schizoid" character), if it were not for the fact that de Man's later works of literary theory are here also being read as a "*product* of a guilt, silenced by death."

Such attempts to conjure forth the basis of de Man's late texts from the young man's journalism are scarcely admirable. They moreover ignore that de Man is no longer present and hence cannot speak for himself. The thinly veiled thesis is as banal as it is vulgarly simplifying: "once a Fascist, always a Fascist." When Gleichmann in his article refers to "malicious adversaries" who compare the deconstructive current with the thousand year Reich, he is referring to a fatal inability to read. And yet the comparison is seriously misleading because of the silent agreement implied by Gleichmann's "adversaries." That deconstruction would be a latter-day parallel to Nazism is a qualified absurdity. This dogmatic naiveté tellingly reveals how one until now carefully has been able to avoid reading de Man. One hastens to draw conclusions by means of a line of argument that is dangerously close to repeating the ideologically burdened logic of which de Man stands accused. More than ever before, it is important to read what he wrote. One should in this context remember that de Man perhaps was the one who most untiringly called attention to the *necessity* of reading. It is therefore not unnecessary to study carefully the texts in question and to clarify the situation, no matter what else one might be led to think, if one has only read Holmqvist's and Gleichmann's insertions.

* * *

On March 4, 1941 the article which has been cited so often in this debate, "The Jews in Contemporary Literature," was printed. One can of course speculate about why de Man wrote the text. But disregarding the fact that it seems to have been written under pressure, that he during several weeks attempted to get out of the assignment, and moreover had Jewish friends, the words remain. These are what must be read. When Holmqvist thinks that de Man "excelled in anti-Semitic attacks," he nevertheless removes himself from what is written. As Geoffrey H. Hartman points out in a clear-sighted essay, de Man's article is "not vulgar anti-Semitic writing." And yet, the text implies dubious views when it in albeit cautious phrases identifies Jewishness with a foreign and unhealthy presence in European cultural life.

De Man argues for the thesis that the Jews have not contributed in any significant way to contemporary literature. They have, he believes, themselves spread the myth of their influence. The ability of Western literature to protect itself against Jewish influence, within such a representative part of intellectual life as literature, is a sign of its greatness. As Hartman maintains, though, de Man remains unclear on whether this sign of resistance is comforting because Jewishness itself is unhealthy, or because any influence of foreign culture on Western intellectual life would have an injurious effect on its vitality. Strangely, however, de Man selects, as his examples of superior writers, Gide, Kafka, Hemingway and Lawrence. This collection, which hardly is particularly representative of the spirit cherished by Nazism and Fascism, could in itself only with difficulty be more subversive. The names represent almost everything that the extreme Right sought to exclude from its intellectual tradition. And yet de Man insists that precisely these authors—"a list that could continue indefinitely"—are the ones that are continuing to write the tradition. Kafka's name is curiously enough misspelled in the article, but in a text about "The Contemporary English Novel," printed in January 1940 in *Les Cahiers du Libre Examen,* de Man quotes an identical list from Aldous Huxley's *Music at Night* (Huxley adds Proust as the fifth man). The quotation gets spelled correctly and concludes that the five enumerated authors have nothing else in common other than a respect for "the Whole Truth." De Man adds: "The authors have thus been transformed into merciless psychologists, enemies of all simplification that would falsify the truth about human nature."

The article about Jews in contemporary literature ends with the only unforgivable passage:

By preserving, despite the Semitic intrusion into all aspects of European life, an originality and a character that have remained intact, our civilization has shown that it is healthy in its deep nature. Moreover, we can anticipate that a solution of the Jewish problem that would envisage the creation of a Jewish colony isolated from Europe would not result, for the literary life of the West, in regrettable consequences. The latter would lose, all in all, some people of mediocre value, and would continue as in the past to develop according to its own great laws of evolution.

This passage contains the most serious expression of anti-Semitism that has yet appeared. It formulates an indefensible intention, but it is not expressed by "a nearly fanatical adherent of the assailants and their ideology," as Holmqvist seems to want to believe. Nor is it a question of whether de Man "expresses a virulent anti-Semitism," as Gleichmann maintains, following the example of Holmqvist and the American press. At the same time, it is of extreme importance to point out that, in the light of the Wannsee Conference one year later, on January 20, 1942, when German potentates decided on a "final solution," more than a theoretical standpoint is at stake here. Hartman acknowledges this in an article saturated with restrained sorrow, but still expresses a more precise and less hasty judgment. The suggestion of establishing "a Jewish colony isolated from Europe" takes on deeply tragic meaning in light of what was to follow. It seems clear that de Man's article appropriates a silent part of the Nazi ideology. The word "Jew" is, moreover, not merely an example in such a rhetoric. Only a few weeks before de Man's article was published, the first pogroms in neighboring Holland began. As Werner Hamacher points out, "every anti-Semitic utterance in such a situation gives consent to hounding."

What makes de Man's conclusion troublesome is that it is expressed by means of a figure of thought that is as well known as it is disturbing. As such, it relies on disguised biologism and unforgivable analogies. European life is to be preserved in its "intact origin," unmixed, in order thereby to be protected against "the all-encompassing Semitic encroachment." It is a sign of health, de Man's text maintains, that the European body is capable of repelling the foreign Jewish element. Jewishness cannot be assimilated. On the other hand, however, nothing is said about the possible destruction or killing off of this "Semitic intrusion." De Man writes allusively about "a solution to the problem of the Jews," which is enough to condemn him, but his "solution" consists of the creation of a Jewish colony isolated from Europe. In an elaborate and thought-provoking essay published in the April issue of *Critical Inquiry,* Jacques Derrida devotes much care to reading the complicated arguments in de Man's article. He condemns the above-quoted lines, but insists that this cannot be done "without examining everything that remains readable in a text one can judge to be disastrous." Indeed, de Man's article is anything but free of contradictions. It is written *against* what he calls "vulgar anti-Semitism" and the

myths supporting it. His article finally falls back on an attitude that criticizes precisely those contexts in which the vulgar appears.

Derrida importantly points out that this aristocratic attitude returns in de Man's other journalistic writings, thereby formulating an aesthetic rather than a political or social outlook. It is reasonable to assume that de Man was given the assignment of writing articles in his capacity as literary columnist. The text appeared on a special page, and presumably his task was to discuss Jewishness and literature. Compared to the other contributions, de Man's text actually stands out as concealed criticism of the vulgarity of these articles. Derrida calls it "an anti-conformist attack." De Man's foremost concern is, in fact, not the Jews, but rather literature. He calls attention to the historical laws that govern literary creation, the "aesthetic revolution." Whether or not one sees de Man's article as unforgivable or deeply compromising, one has to admit that this decidedly contradictory text strives to distance itself from a vulgarly anti-Semitic way of reasoning. Now, one could of course assert—and rightly so—that de Man's text avoids vulgar anti-Semitism, only instead to make it more invisible and thereby also more persuasive. What is equally paradoxical as disturbing is that the article then devotes itself rather to the history of art and literature. This history seems, in de Man's eyes, to be separated from the history of social circumstances. And it is presumably there, at the extraordinarily privileged position literature is allowed to occupy, that the discussion should be localized.

***

The ideological problematics that speak out of de Man's Belgian journalism are complex and full of internal contradictions. When reading the articles, one constantly has to be aware of the modus of the sentences, what is paraphrase and what is commentary, how the subject can slip around, and what figures of thought articulate the argument. The texts treat and praise—but also try to master—conservative revolutionaries such as Drieu la Rochelle and Henri de Montherlant, Robert Brasillach and Ernst Jünger. They are written by a cultural nationalist who wants to protect his country, his people, and his language. The country is Belgium, but in a stricter sense Flanders, which lost its independence in 1830. De Man seems occasionally to imagine a "new Europe" under German hegemony, in which the Flemish nation could be contained in its own right. He sympathizes with German intellectual life in an articulated attempt to distance himself from the influence of French *esprit* on Flanders and Flemish culture. When he in February of 1941 writes that "it is always and everywhere a matter of establishing respect for

Belgian independence," this can hardly be seen as a manifestation of Nazi propaganda. On the other hand, the declaration could well coincide with the demand for a national spirit and autonomy, which of course are thoughts active in every fascist ideology. And yet, one would commit a grave error to conclude from this that love of country is necessarily always ideologically corrupt. One should instead study carefully those contexts in which patriotism appears, which in this case means a genre of text that can be called journalism. One thereby has to take the historical situation into account as well.

In central places, de Man's articles express strongly nationalistic convictions, as for example in a text on the fate of Flanders from September 1, 1942. The state is supposed to function as a leading principle in the life of individuals, the text claims. The fate of citizens has to be subordinated to the more overriding and inflexible conformities to the law. He formulates a teleological view of the fate of nations, in which nationality is connected with literature, and ideology with aesthetics. The present difficulties have to "be suffered through." Similar arguments occur in other texts. Thoughts like these may become problematic in the context of ideas about national or cultural superiority. One of the most striking features of de Man's criticism, which in many respects excels by means of academic discipline rather than journalistic brevity, is precisely the status he grants the nation, the people and its language. These three categories reverberate around an idea about the *place,* where the reverence for and loyalty towards the homeland is unshakable. What is actualized here in large part touches on the question of how a national identity gets grounded and is legitimized. Descent, race, and origin become critical elements in every such operation.

Historically, the period between the eighteenth and nineteenth centuries offers special access. For example, Fichte in his *Speech to the German Nation,* held during the war of independence against Napoleon in the winter of 1807–08, offers something hitherto impossible within theories of nations. Originally enough, Fichte's declaration grounds national feeling in language. The decisive question about race thereby becomes one of the connection between language and residence, of finding a home in language and making it the most essential manifestation of the homeland. But Fichte is far from being the only source for another and newer form of nationalism. One of the presuppositions for German idealism was Kant. The underlying factors that later are at work in Fichte may in part be traced to Kant. For him, Germany's being a nation appears precisely in the fact that this country has no national character. Thus, it becomes possible for him to claim that Germans in turn are better

than other peoples at learning languages. German is a language of trade, he continues. It is thus, above all others, the language of communication and therefore excellently suited to philosophical reasoning. On the other hand, French is seen as superficially intermediary, a language of conversation—which leads Kant to the view that an idiomatic untranslatability exists between the two languages.

For Kant, Germany has not yet installed itself territorially. The country therefore has the character of a non-nation as well as an example. Instead, the German nation accommodates itself idiomatically, he maintains, in its language. This takes place as the promise of a country in the process of becoming. The Germans ought to return to their country, Kant advises, but through a forward returning. This is where Fichte's speech joins Kant's thought. For him, the promise functions as a sign of a more original idiom submerged in German. The German language, in other words, is a kind of idiom of idioms. Fichte wants to see this sign as a privilege, at the same time as a duty: only by respecting the built-in call of language can Germanness be saved without what he calls "humanity's . . . deep humiliation." German is something lesser than other languages because of its national lack of character. But this quality of "lesser" brings with it at the same time something essentially "more"— by means of the idiom's justified claim to universality. Fichte maintains, finally, how German offers certain fundamental human concepts of a general nature that cannot be understood in any other language than German. Despite this fact, the understanding is nonetheless objective.

In this context, it is worth noting the thread in nationalistic philosophy that tends to consider its own spirit as a question of national education or formation, through an exemplary idiom. In an article published in *Het Vlaamsche Land* on March 28–30, 1942, de Man reviews the Flemish translation of the German art historian A. E. Brinckmann's anything but illustrious study from 1938, *Geist der Nationen.* The article, called "Art as a Mirror of the Essence of Nations," points out that the study is a "systematic analysis" that deals with "the relationship of art to the national character traits of nations." Brinckmann's concept of the "spirit of the nation" is defined by the author of the article as "the dominating artistic tendency of a nation." The review then devotes itself to the unity that distinguishes Western art. De Man claims that "[a]t present, now a great stream of thought has been born, as a consequence of the neighboring nation." He adds:

Let this be understood correctly: nationalities as such have always existed, for they are the result of racial mixings that have not aged much over the centuries. What is proper to our time is the consideration of this national personality as a valuable condition, as a precious possession, which has to be maintained at the cost of all sacrifices. This conception is miles apart from sentimental patriotism. Rather, it concerns a sober faith, a practical means to defend Western culture against a decomposition from the inside out or a surprise attack by neighboring civilizations.

The rhetoric of this passage is characteristic of several of de Man's articles during the crucial war years. He stresses a national and cultural multiplicity, but this multiplicity is always ordered under concepts like "Europe," "Western civilization," or "a great stream of thought." The texts almost always deal with the future of Europe, which has to be protected from decay from within and attacks from without. After German victories, European unity has to be determined in relation to the German empire. Meanwhile, the Nazi movement is never really named as such. Rather it seems that German literature and philosophy are what count for de Man. The closest he gets to Nazism is an oblivious review of Flemish propaganda brochures about the Third Reich (on April 12–14, 1941). He says of one of these texts, that it is "indispensable for an objective judgment" of Nazi Germany's "wide-ranging enterprise." It seems hardly imaginable that the otherwise so educated journalist did not realize the character of scandalous glorification and supportive agitation in these writings.

* * *

The present historical situation constitutes the absolute focal point of de Man's journalistic interest, saturated with questions about the fate of nations and the role of literature in the upheavals. Even if his tone for the most part is descriptive rather than prescriptive, it rarely leaves the reader in much doubt as to what is intended. Derrida stresses this in his essay. But a remainder of ambiguity always seems to be present. De Man's way of writing is extraordinarily double-edged. "Europe can only be strong, peaceful and flourishing," he writes in the review of *Geist der Nationen,* "if it is governed by a state of mind which is deeply conscious of its national grandeur, but which keeps its eyes open for all experiments and problems that touch our continent." It is left to the reader to decide what this "state of mind" is, but the same reader also has to decide in what these "experiments and problems" might consist. De Man underscores that he here is extrapolating from Brinckmann's book. His conclusions, however, are not "the expression of an ideal wish, utopian and remote, but . . . a concrete truth, corroborated by a number of facts":

That this endpoint is remote from the nature of the study itself and leads us, starting out from the history of art, to the terrain of the major cultural and political problems, proves how efficient the method of using works of art as study material for the establishing of general knowledge really is. The aim of a work like this . . . originated out of an attempt to ensure the future of Western civilization in all its aspects. As such it contains a lesson, which is indispensable for all those who, in the contemporary revolutions, try to find a firm guidance according to which they can direct their action and their thoughts.

The contemporary revolutions could only be the attempt of the Right at social and national upheaval. In a review of an exhibition on Germany in Brussels, 1942, written for *Le Soir* on March 16 that year, de Man devotes considerable space to stressing Germany's central and guiding importance. The country's "historical fate" is seen as exemplary and of utmost significance for the West. Indeed, "all of Western civilization's continued existence depends on the unity of the people that is its center." Nazified Germany and the people that speak the language of the country thus stand in the center of the European nations. In an earlier "Look at Flanders," printed on December 30, 1941, de Man devotes himself to differentiating between German and French culture. Compared to the French, Germanic culture is more "völkisch," he believes, while hastening to add that Frenchmen, whose vocabulary lacks this German word, do not practice an inferior, but rather a different art form with its "own grandiose perspective." The difference is not qualitative and "establishes no hierarchy" between the two cultures. Flemish has the word "volksch," de Man adds. Thus, it should be ordered under the German side of the cultural differentiation.

* * *

A pattern can, of course, be discerned here. The young de Man seems to have tried to think through the prevailing situation, in which Belgium's fate was of greatest importance to him. Almost always, he is concerned with a future that has to be safeguarded at the cost of every sacrifice. The word "revolution" returns in several of the *Le Soir* articles as a designation for the situation at the time. In a text from January 20, 1942, he notes that Belgium has "not yet had its revolution," while in France a change is presently taking place. In a short notice for Agence Dechenne two months later, in April of 1942, de Man takes up Alfred Fabre-Luce's *Anthologie de l'Europe nouvelle.* The book consists of a collection of texts by French, German, Italian, and English thinkers and shows, writes the reviewer, "what in their work allows the present revolution to be foreseen." De Man continues:

For it would be wrong to believe that this one [revolution] is a momentary phenomenon, abruptly arisen from the play of passing forces, and only dependent on military powers. On the contrary, the crisis we are living has to be related to a vast, gradually growing intellectual movement, that goes back at least one century.

According to de Man, the current crisis thus comes from a spiritual movement with roots in the beginning of the nineteenth century. The crisis has to do with a set of problems shared by all the thinkers that appear in Fabre-Luce's anthology. De Man enumerates them in a parenthesis: "realism, the respect for power, the European idea, etc." By having chosen appropriate texts, he continues, Fabre-Luce's anthology shows "the Western spirit's characteristic forward striding towards its present fate." De Man's tone is assertive, but as usual, it hovers and falters when dealing with direct references. "The Western spirit," "forward striding," "present fate"? Another fate seems to arch over the future of the nations, a fate that rather effects Europe and Western civilization. It is under the sign of this fate that the place of states and individuals must be considered. The sign is most clearly noticeable in cultural life and above all, in literature. De Man's texts sooner or later always come back to this point—both as a beginning and an end. The future of Europe is inscribed in great literature. And precisely this thought—that the fate of history is most clearly expressed in literature—becomes deeply tragic upon reading de Man's introduction to the review (on November 11, 1941) of Montherlant's book of essays, *Solstice de juin*. "In this collection of essays by Montherlant," he writes,

there is a phrase that all those who have followed literary publication since August 1940 will approve. It is the passage that says: "To the writers who have given too much to current affairs for the last few months, I predict, for that part of their work, the most complete oblivion. When I open the newspapers and journals of today, I hear the indifference of the future rolling over them, just as one hears the sound of the sea when one holds certain seashells up to the ear."

"One could not have put it any better," de Man comments. The black irony that we now, in our kind of future, read into these lines could not easily be more devastating.

In a review of two French literary-historical studies, printed in Flemish on June 7–8, 1942 in *Het Vlaamsche Land* under the title "Criticism and Literary History," de Man speaks of "style,"

as "the product of people with one and the same historical temporal alignment." He continues:

There exists, to a certain extent, an aesthetic determinism of which the artist himself is not conscious, the same determinism that is expressed in the course of history, which, after all, does seem to move around a number of constants.

In this view, nothing can be found that necessarily is to be considered as fascistic. But such an outlook may be related to a certain aesthetization of phenomena that need not be of an aesthetic nature. Half a year earlier, on December 2, 1941, he had underscored that literature is governed neither by philosophical nor ethical motives:

Literature is an independent domain—it has a life, laws and duties that belong to nothing but itself and in no way depend on the philosophical or ethical conditions that move alongside it.

De Man mentions, in the article from June 1942, an "aesthetic determinism" that is found "expressed in the course of history," and of Brinckmann's study he says, in March of the same year, that it shows "how efficient the method of using works of art as study material for establishing general knowledge really is." On the one hand, it thus seems as if the literary domain obeys laws that are not grounded in philosophical or ethical conditions. On the other hand, its aesthetic laws are expressed in the course of history. In order to reach "general knowledge," it is not so much from philosophy as from literature that one should seek counsel, since the aesthetic determinations coincide with the historical ones. They can be read from the work of art as a "lesson."

In his classical essay, "The Work of Art in the Age of Mechanical Reproduction," Walter Benjamin wanted to see the aesthetization of politics as the characteristic of intellectual fascism. He there discusses how for fascist ideology war grants "the artistic gratification of a sense of perception that has been changed by technology." Benjamin considers this conception as "the consummation of '*l'art pour l'art*.'" Now, one does not have to read an aesthetic legitimization of politics into de Man's texts. It seems meanwhile obvious that his way of relating to contemporary problems is based on a fundamental conviction about the genuine significance of literature for human life and social existence. But even if de Man defines a country's spirit as "a nation's dominating artistic tendency," and even if united Europe is high on the agenda, it is equally clear that this nevertheless only can be the case in an essentially free West. "Although at first sight it may sound paradoxical," he writes in the review of Brinckmann's book, a European unity is possible only if national sentiments can freely come to expression and if every nation is fully conscious of its own worth and originality.

When de Man in a late essay, "The Resistance to Theory," defines ideology as "the confusion of linguistic with natural reality, of reference with phenomenalism," he gives modern phrasing to Benjamin's clear-sighted thought. Certain shadows of this insight are found in the Belgian journalism—for example, in an article about Agence Dechenne on January 20, 1942, and in a review of two novels by Robert Poulet on June 16 the same year. And on September 1, 1942, a few weeks after the first deportations of Belgian Jews in Brussels, de Man writes a text entitled "Le Massacre des innocents," which deals with Hubert Dubois' poem of the same name. He wants to consider the poem as "a meditation on that guilt that has followed humanity in the dreadful condition that now rules," and speaks of a "catastrophe."

It is, however, the necessity of spiritual renewal that is underscored here. The German nation plays the decisive role in the singular fate of this Europe. The fact that de Man avoids equating Germany with the Third Reich is at the same time admirable and problematic. One has to ask whether, and hence also how, he took responsibility for this hovering with respect to more immediate references. *Le Soir*'s literary columnist must have well known the context in which his articles figured. Was this hovering designed to undermine an ideology that otherwise supported most of the texts in a newspaper like *Le Soir*? Certain signs would indicate this. For example, it is known that de Man had contact with the resistance and his name appears in a journal like *Poésie* 43, the primary literary forum of the French resistance movement, with Aragon, Tardieu, and Eluard as contributors. Furthermore, on July 14, 1942, the anniversary of the French revolution, de Man published a review of the first two issues of the journal *Messages*. There he praises surrealism as a true development of nineteenth-century symbolism and sees the movement as a step forward for literature. *Messages,* it should be added, published poets that were not only members of the Communist party, but also of the resistance movement. According to Georges Lambrichs, for many years the editor of the *Nouvelle revue française* and a longtime friend of de Man, the young columnist is also supposed to have arranged for the continued publication of *Messages* in Brussels after the censorship in Paris grew stricter. As Hamacher points out, though, this of course does not suffice to make of de Man a resistance fighter. But it is enough to throw serious doubt on those publications that insist on calling him a Nazi and a collaborator. Perhaps this

hovering, that so often occurs in the *Le Soir* articles, was a form of expressing for the young intellectual who saw the greatness of the German and continental philosophical tradition, but did not necessarily want to translate it into the vocabulary of Hitlerism. How was this hovering read then, in 1941–42? How can we read it now, forty-five years later?

* * *

One has to ask, finally, what kind of authority speaks behind the attacks on the late writings of de Man. What motivates the most often surprisingly misinformed assaults? So many of them do not allow the reader to realize that the first and most elementary rule is to read. Certainly Holmqvist is right to say that it is "yet too early to sum up." But one can wonder whether de Man's contradictory past can be summed up in the first place. It is at least clear that his *late* texts far from contain a confirmation and a more subtle further development of a dubious vision of history and an equally disturbing concept of language. All one has to do is read his books to understand that. The one who has done so will have a hard time misusing the insights that speak from these texts. In de Man, the reader finds a radical conception of history and language, that lays the ground for a wide-ranging criticism of the theoretical presuppositions for totalitarianism. Moreover, he or she will encounter an acute consciousness of the political consequences of aesthetic absolutism. Large portions of de Man's later works, ever since the middle of the fifties, are expressly directed towards an analysis and criticism—a deconstruction, if you will—of almost every utterance of the sort of exclusive ideology that governed his Belgian employers. His late work attempts, on the contrary, to pry itself out of every aesthetization of ideology or politics. This "turn from the politics of culture to the language of art," Hartman underlines, "was not an escape into, but an escape out of, aestheticism." One can, as Hartman does, see the movement as an admirable act of conscience. The only thing one need not admire is the relative silence that de Man allowed to surround the early newspaper articles. And yet the silence was never total. It was broken, for example, in a letter to the Society of Fellows at Harvard in 1955.

The often directly hostile resistance with which de Man's writings meet—and which foremost is grounded in an attempt at avoiding reading them—seems to depend less on whether one thinks one can recognize in them the intellectual property of National Socialism. The fact that some nevertheless want to do this underscores the incompetence of the slanderers rather than the ideological unreliability of de Man. Is it not much more the case that the criticism against the literary theorist is directed at his interest in assumed values, that are said to deal with individuality, the sovereignty of the bourgeois I, the authenticity of the subject's linguistic expression, etc.? If the pious status of these values is discussed—which would imply that the forms of utterance are observed—this does not mean that their reality is rejected. Obviously, the referential function of language is not being denied, but its authority, as far as "natural" understanding is concerned, is being put into question. Literature is "the place," de Man stresses in "The Resistance to Theory," "where this negative knowledge about the reliability of linguistic utterance is made available." This gives literature its exemplary position. He continues by emphasizing the fact that its fictive character does not come from denying an attached "reality," but rather from the fact that one cannot a priori be sure that literature is a reliable source of information about anything other than its own language. Ideology consists precisely in an active misunderstanding of this insight. It assumes a confusion of linguistic with natural reality. "Those who reproach literary theory for being oblivious to social and historical (that is to say ideological) reality," de Man writes,

are merely stating their fear at having their own ideological mystifications exposed by the tool they are trying to discredit. They are, in short, very poor readers of Marx's *German Ideology.*

In his article, Holmqvist quotes from one of the Rousseau essays in de Man's *Allegories of Reading,* for the purpose of substantiating his thesis that "it has for a long time been evident that deconstructionist ideas about the uncommitting ties of language to reality *can* be used for dark purposes." In the quote from "Excuses" de Man claims that an experience always exists simultaneously "as fictional discourse and as empirical event," and that deciding which of the alternatives is the right one remains genuinely impossible. Quite aside from the fact that one might wonder for whom Holmqvist thinks it has been "evident" that this "deconstructionist idea" can be misused, one has to ask how he reads de Man's text. An essay by Minae Mizumura, called "Renunciation," might be helpful here. Mizumura takes up the asceticism that is dominant in de Man's works of literary theory. She believes that an *ascesis* constitutes the tension itself in these works. This practice could be considered a way for the literary theorist to circumscribe an origin he cannot utter. To discuss the youthful journalistic activity would be to accept the sort of confession he shows, in the analysis of Rousseau, to constitute the reason for fiction. The confession of the I always prevents what it is trying to formulate from getting expressed. Pious sincerity hides its genuine face. The I's deeds can only negatively be represented in a retrospective rhetoric. The

rigor that characterizes the late writings should therefore rather be considered as the methodic meaning of mourning. Even if one refuses to see de Man's relative silence as a result of the insight, that every excuse only would increase the guilt itself, one should still remember the following line from "Excuses": "No excuse can ever hope to catch up with such a proliferation of guilt."

As always, the circumstances are more complicated than one would like to imagine. De Man of the later years knew a lot about such problematics. To read cause together with effect, guilt together with silence, is not merely difficult, but could even be dubious. Instead of considering de Man's mature works as a "product," one can read them as a highly conscious attempt to articulate those mechanisms that make it so hopelessly difficult to articulate the presuppositions of intellectual reflection. In this sense, de Man's works of literary theory offer the most adequate means for finding out about what he once wrote, in among other places, *Le Soir.* It is probably no coincidence that he quotes Proust in his first book: "C'est perpetuelle erreur, qui est précisément la 'vie.' "

The paradox meanwhile remains intact: it is the texts of the literary theorist that show us what is contradictory about reading the early texts as the reason and presupposition for the late ones. But this implies, at the same time, that this is just what we are doing, if we take him at his word and doubt what is valid in such an operation. Given the context, understanding this paradox is not the least painful thing one has to do. . . .

University of Stockholm and Yale University

Note: The above text is an excerpt from an essay published in Swedish in the journal *Ort & Bild* 96, no. 2, 1988.

Ancestral Voices: De Man and His Defenders

WILLIAM FLESCH

Ces faces moins reluisantes du caractère d'un homme de génie déroutent les admirateurs simplistes qui veulent retrouver dans les aspects familiers de leur idole le reflet de la perfection qui les éblouit.—*Paul de Man, 7* October *1941*

Les idées sont choses cohérentes et rigoureuses, ce que les réactions humaines ne sont pas.—*de Man, 24* June *1941*

Ceci pour dire que cette guerre prit, dans le cours de notre vie individuelle, l'allure d'un remous absolument en dehors de la normale. Pour la plupart, son souvenir n'est plus qu'une hallucination dont on a peine à croire qu'elle fut une réalité, un cauchemar éveillé qui ne cessa que lorsque la vie s'ordonna à nouveau, conformément aux anciennes habitudes.—*de Man, 30* April *1942*

I

De Man's writing in 1940–42 is unforgivable. As a public act it is deeply collaborationist. There is no question that collaborationism can often be defended as the lesser of two evils. Historians frequently and rightly distinguish between collaborators and collaborationists, the former out simply for a share of the Nazi's spoils, the latter seeking an alliance which would spare their countries from the utter destruction reserved for less pliant victims of Nazi aggression. In specific cases the distinction is almost always blurred, and so it seems to be with de Man.

My overwhelming impression, after several readings of the *Le Soir* articles, is that they testify to a kind of wistful or wishful arrogance: the arrogance of someone very young allowed very early to render the last judgments on a number of literary and cultural issues; the wishfulness of someone hoping that his new patrons are in fact decent people. It may be that he construed as decent activities that were in fact unforgivable—both theirs *and his own*. He might have been able to imagine that the occupiers, decent and honorable as he would have wanted to see them, would concede certain cultural judgments that they might disagree with.

He can imagine, that is, that he will be able to preserve the cultural values authentically dear to him. But he can only imagine this because *he has convinced himself* that they're not antithetical to Nazi values. And this means not only that he tends to whitewash the aggressor; he also does a lot of special pleading for a theory of culture able to accommodate Nazi ideology as well as his own deeply held beliefs. And so these beliefs, consonant as they largely come to be with the aims of the occupiers, themselves suffer corruption.

I don't think it right to try to untangle the skein of motivations, since motivation is always overdetermined. I think de Man made a fairly easy compromise with the occupiers, one which allows itself hope of a reasonable future in a Europe dominated by Nazi Germany, a flattering future in which such Belgian voices as de Man's will be taken very seriously. For the tone of Olympian detachment and assurance in his articles seems highly self-regarding. In a new order, he would want to maintain the position he has now, that of a cultural arbiter for Belgium. And to want this means two things. He has the laudable goal of preserving, even under German hegemony, the autonomy of Belgian culture (and of Romance culture in general, and also of Flemish culture, against whose assimilation to Germany he warns). But a more venal motive would coexist, since he would profit (and does profit already) from the situation that has made this opportunity available.

He repeatedly insists on the relative autonomy of the aesthetic sphere. This insistence seems to me overdetermined. On the one hand it aims to preserve the aesthetic movements and traditions that were of real value to de Man; on the other, as I will try to argue, he's willing to trade away a great deal of political capital that the occupiers want. In return he gets their indulgence to his theories of aesthetic autonomy. Indeed, in order to preserve that autonomy he's perfectly content to argue the relative unimportance of the aesthetic, and to do so precisely when it suits the political goals of the Nazis. But he shares these goals only, I think, insofar as they enable his position of cultural authority. And the Germans, especially after they start their anti-Bolshevist propaganda campaign in June of 1941, are for their part perfectly happy (at least for a while) to acquiesce in anything that will look like they regard Belgian culture as something to be protected under the umbrella of Germany's task of safeguarding Western values.

De Man made a Faustian bargain, almost literally. The trade-off meant that he'd do a great deal for the Nazi propaganda machine, as long as the propaganda was inflected in such a way as to convey de Man's own genuinely held aesthetic and cultural convictions. The propaganda, it seems evident, he didn't much care about one way or the other. This means that he would have toed the line as much as was required, but had no interest in seeing that line constricted, and probably some interest in seeing it relaxed. Nevertheless he did very largely toe it, at least as long as it gave him room to argue his own literary and cultural beliefs. That, on his own account, he should have quit when the Nazis did start actively interfering in the cultural pieces in *Le Soir* means that he was not so unprincipled as to agree to aesthetic opinions repugnant to him. The principle perhaps evident here seems to me rather pale after what he did consent to, and shows I think the hierarchy of the values that he lived by. The much discussed letter he wrote to the Chairman of the Society of Fellows at Harvard does very little for his case, since it now must effectively constitute acknowledgement that he did consent to the bargain legible in the pieces he wrote for *Le Soir* through the end of November of 1942.[1]

I want to be very clear that I think de Man's later work constituted, for better or worse, a nearly complete break with his wartime activity. This would mean that these revelations should have very little to say to that later work. The press accounts about this business that have appeared are saturated with judgments that are notoriously inaccurate, judgments whose tenor seems to me ludicrously wrong-headed. De Man's life after 1953 stands on its own, and appears close to irreproachable.

Nevertheless, I think that in his second career, in the United States, he might have made some serious gestures of acknowledgement and direct intellectual reparation. And that has to

mean that he should have made public his complicity in the horrible events of the war. Cynthia Chase was I think the first to argue from de Man's analysis of "Excuses" in *Allegories of Reading* that this would have been precisely an act of self-excusal.[2] But I think that's to confuse public and private. It seems to me that the public fact of self-accusation has a far greater importance, especially if well-timed, than the essentially private and confessional act of self-excusal. Perhaps de Man might indeed have thought it too easy on himself simply to declare his own guilt. But as a public act it would have been more useful than his silence.

Thinking this, I went farther in some earlier claims about de Man;[3] my writing was as prey as anyone else's to the urgency of the situation. I went on to complain about the imperturbable authority that de Man always manifested, in person and in his writing; I objected to the way his own implacable authority in the face of his ideas tended to become as unnerving as his unnerving arguments. This I regarded as proving a continued moral failing in de Man, cognate with his moral failings during the war. I now regard this as an error on my part. Whatever equivocation about his past he engaged in seems to me to have been peripheral to the work that he did, and to his conception of his own work. I cannot agree with Geoffrey Hartman that de Man's work looks like "a belated . . . act of conscience."[4] His past is largely irrelevant to his work. I think that as a public fact de Man's authority in the United States has nothing to do with his wartime authority in Belgium. Once you deplore the fact that he did not tell the truth about the past (and I do deplore this) it seems you've said what has to be said about his post-war behavior. You can complain about his image, complain about the way he cultivated it. But you can't hold him any more guilty of that than anyone else, even if he exemplifies a kind of absolute intellectual authority in his deconstruction of authority.

I should also indicate that I knew de Man, though not very well. My personal and private impression of him, an impression I question but still have, was highly positive. Courtly and kind, he seemed to exemplify an intellectual seriousness that also felt like moral seriousness. De Man stimulated people to skepticism not for its own sake but for the sake of an astonishingly elusive truth. He may have cultivated his charisma, but what was charismatic about him was the way he seemed closer to an impossible cognition of what resisted cognition, and the labor of thought that he took as his own and imposed on his students had certainly the feel of a moral imperative. The avoidance of thought is a great evil. De Man's example resisted that evil.

There is a sense in which de Man's greatest innovation was the absolute and uncompromising *style* of his writing. I dislike this absolutism, which I regard as leading to ethically questionable positions. Finally I think de Man's work is a misprision of Blanchot's. The extreme and the absolute are opposed in Blanchot in a way that de Man's rigor resists. The fetish of rigor—contrasted as it is with the flabbiness of "meaning" or "intention"—obscures what Blanchot calls the unhappiness of the impersonal. Beyond the limit of the human de Man describes a kind of crystalline purity of intentionless, affectless language. This contrasts severely with Blanchot's less absolute, more extreme evocation of non-phenomenal *experience*. What is beyond the boundaries of the human, or the quotidian, is the experience of proximity—proximity of death, or unhappiness, of the necessarily impersonal other, and not the phenomenal experience of presence. De Man's quasi-ethical imperative to read is a sort of denatured version of Blanchot's more clearly ethical imperative to attention, attention to unhappiness.

De Man's power as a writer and thinker comes from the sense he gives of being at the absolute. No one can go beyond him. But this sets a term to the interminable that Blanchot evokes, and the diagnostician of blindness appears, in his work, and in his followers' work, as an example, as the only example, of absolute and pitiless lucidity. I disbelieve in pure intelligence, and I think that its allegory in de Man imputes intentionless and affectless intelligence to an extreme region in which many more, far different things are going on.

Blanchot sometimes describes the imperative to attention in historical terms. The history that he invokes is the history of the camps. He says that what the victims of the Nazis, those who survived, have to tell about their untellable experiences must be heeded with the utmost attention. That experience has to change everything, which is to say it has to change the human relationship which responsibility consists in. No one can respond for those victims, but everyone must nevertheless take on responsibility. I say this only because I think this must lend great weight to a fact that both surprised and did not surprise me. People I've talked to who are survivors are nearly unanimous in their judgments that little as de Man really may be said to have done or felt, what he did would have prevented them from ever speaking to him again.

Here I oscillate between the moral certainty that only these people have the right and moral standing to make a final judgment, that we have no right to dispute that judgment; and the moral certainty that not to contextualize is not to be just, and that in a certain context these essays, which could have been a lot worse, which were perhaps under pressure to be a lot worse, are not all that bad. This kind of oscillation seems to me characteristic of any attempt to come to an honest conclusion about de Man's wartime activities. What this means, I think, is that one ought not to object to the violence of some of the opinions

expressed about this issue. Jon Wiener, David Lehman, and others have taken an extreme, self-righteous, and misinformed stance on the meaning of these revelations. In doing so, their reactions and their writings have tended to become the subject of debate, more than de Man himself. And they have given defenders of de Man's wartime activity a weapon for that defense: his evident personal indifference to, if not distaste for, Nazi ideology.

Again, this seems to me to muddy the issue by confusing public and private activity. What I am going to concern myself with here is the fact that there's a lot of this confusion among some of the more ardent and troubling defenses of de Man. I object to the polemics of current day journalists, ignorant and opportunistic as they are, less than I object to some of the writings of those defenders of de Man who have been led by personal loyalty, as it seems to me, to tease out private scruples and resistances in these texts that are not there. In the pages that follow I'm going to be interested in both the public significance of these articles, and in the distortions that some of de Man's defenders seem led to in their selective and privatizing readings. I want to make it perfectly clear that I think close reading is completely inappropriate as a mode of understanding the *Le Soir* articles. They were not intended for close reading, and *all that counts* is what Derrida will call their massive effect. But the fact that I will engage in some close reading of texts by Derrida and Werner Hamacher means that I am troubled by what look to me like private impulses in their writing, and not only by its public effect. That they should polemicize on this issue disturbs me somewhat more than that Wiener and Lehman should, because I regard myself as being of their intellectual party, and I do not wish to see believed arguments made by this party that I do not myself believe. But that they should object in principle, and in extremely violent terms, to impassioned and polemical reactions, *even when these reactions are petty and ill-informed*, and that they should end up being misled by their own rhetoric into moments of praise for what de Man did in 1940–42—these things seem to me to need stressing because of what they may say about the intellectual authority that even deconstruction seems to need, and that de Man provided.

II

Maybe the legal idea of "standing," which I alluded to a minute ago, does matter here. I don't have the standing to render a final judgment, and neither do most of those who've been engaged in polemics about this issue. What we can do is argue about the context, argue about the facts, argue about the local significance of the facts, and this is all I want to do here.

Derrida's *Critical Inquiry* article, precisely because it is so well-balanced, will provide a good example of a moral stance that disguises what I take to be its own unfair objections to polemicism through a kind of deceptive judiciousness. I will use it as a convenient foil for my argument. I am disturbed by the fact that the moments of contempt that arise in it are reserved almost exclusively not for de Man but for the class of people whom Derrida regards as being unfair to de Man. This no doubt very heterogeneous class Derrida several times lumps together as merely opportunistic, as without exception filled with unseemly self-righteousness about this new discovery. Take one charged sentence:

To judge, to condemn the work or the man on the basis of what was a brief episode, to call for a closing, that is to say, at least figuratively, for censuring or burning his books is to reproduce the exterminating gesture which one accuses de Man of.

But, these things are hardly commensurable, unfortunate as some of the more *outre* denunciations of de Man have been. "Exterminating gesture:" that's a strong phrase. But surely, Derrida is at least acknowledging that de Man, even if only through a gesture, that is figuratively, might be plausibly accused of being implicated in the extermination of the Jews? At least as plausibly as Lehman and Wiener? No, for the sentence doesn't end here, and now I'll quote it in full:

To judge, to condemn the work or the man on the basis of what was a brief episode, to call for a closing, that is to say, at least figuratively, for censuring or burning his books is to reproduce the exterminating gesture which one accuses de Man of *not having armed himself against sooner with the necessary vigilance*.[5]

So, absurdly enough, de Man comes off as a lot less guilty than those who attack him so ruthlessly. Collaborating turns out to mean a failure in that infinitely difficult task of vigilance, whereas a violent and ill-informed repugnance towards collaboration means reproducing the exterminating gestures of the Nazis. Another example of Derrida's stacking the deck: he cites the anonymous critic and friend of de Man's quoted at the end of Jon Wiener's ignorant article in *The Nation* (9 January 1988, p.24):

Today I will speak of my indignation and worry. (1) First, because the gestures of simplification and the expedited verdicts have, yes, *in fact,* a relation to what happened around 1940–42, earlier and later, in Europe and elsewhere. When someone asking "not to be identified" sees himself quoted by an unscrupulous professor-journalist, when he says he is "shocked" by the fact that certain people are gathering, if only in order to *discuss* these problems (he would

thus like to forbid the right to assembly and discussion? What does that remind you of?) and when he is shocked in the name of a "moral perspective," you can see why I am indignant and worried; and why it is necessary to remain vigilant; and why more than ever one must guard against reproducing the logic one claims to condemn. (p.647)

Again, Derrida invokes vigilance, that de Manian attribute which, he is about to imply (in the sentence quoted above), *could* have been associated with de Man in 1940–42, even if he did not arm himself with it as he might have. But is anyone forbidding assembly here? Would anyone like to *forbid* assembly? Being shocked is hardly the same thing as forbidding assembly, or of wanting to forbid assembly.

Derrida is willing to engage in polemics even as he complains about other people's engaging in polemics, even as he goes so far as to tar them with the brush of intellectual fascism. And to do so on the basis of an article whose general inaccuracy he excoriates, with good reason. This risks seeming an unwise and ungenerous self-righteousness given the deep passions that the issue at hand must certainly animate. Derrida too shares those passions, and it seems unfortunate to lament their manifestation in others. Derrida's polemical valorization of "discussion" over polemics seems to me, precisely because it appears unexceptionable, secretly prejudicial.

As I'll try to show, Derrida's not being careful enough about history. Unfortunately, the people who are probably the most qualified to speak about de Man's later work are not likely to be trained as historians, and Derrida's no exception. This also contributes to making this episode so baffling. I myself have no training in history, but it seems evident to me that there are grave errors in the way many people have been understanding the situation, errors due to a simplification of history which amounts to ahistoricism. Not that de Man's defenders don't constantly invoke the complexity of the situation. They do, but complexity keeps threatening to become a polemical term and not the impetus to real exploration. To learn to do history in the charged circumstance of this debate is to learn to do advocacy more than history. I am no doubt as guilty of advocacy as anyone else in the historical considerations that I shall put forth. But as I say, I don't object in principle to polemics. I do think that debate (stronger word than discussion) can help get to the truth, and I have no qualms about the fact that much of what I shall say will be debatable. Nevertheless, what I will say does correspond to my own amateur understanding of the situation during the war.

It seems to me historically naive to treat the pieces that de Man wrote during the war as above all indicative of his inner conflicts or his inner life. But most of the mollifying considerations that Derrida urges tend to take the form of ascriptions of interiority, often anguished interiority. The brute fact of the matter is that de Man's writing in *Le Soir* did very little to indicate to his readers that they ought to exercise any vigilance at all against the occupiers.

All these pieces contribute, as public acts, to the occupier's campaign to normalize the appearance of the situation. Thus de Man will indeed write of the "horrors" of present-day Belgium: "One may justly wonder how people who are cultivated and endowed with refinement succeed in living without revulsion among the horrors which surround us" (18 August 1942). This is written less than a month after the deportation of the Jews started. But, alas, the horrors that de Man refers to here are the aesthetic horrors of modern architecture. Another particularly unfortunate article affects a personal tone: "We all experienced that impression in the course of the days following [the German attack on] May 10, that impression of no longer being ourselves, of being an abandoned wreck, borne by currents and forces of which we were not the masters and which we did not understand. This is what explains so many utterly aberrant acts committed at that moment, to mention only the absurd departures for a refuge more than imaginary by persons who had nothing to fear" (30 April 1942). All these pieces advance the goal of German propaganda, which was to defuse resistance by trying, as Jorgen Haestrup puts it, "to keep a vision alive of a New Europe under the leadership of the Axis Powers, but with vague promises to sympathizing and therefore favored countries and population groups."[6] How frequently de Man pushes this line. As an example, take his review of Pierre Daye's "lettres d'un belge à un ami français" (26 August 1941). Daye, a former deputy for Degrelle's fascist party Rex, complains of Reynaud's calling Leopold's capitulation to the Germans treasonous, and de Man agrees with this complaint:

The brochure seems to be especially intended for France, where it answers a real need for clarification about the present development of our country. Many in fact were the French who imagined that in Belgium the democratic regime still functioned impeccably and that the corruption so endemic in France had no equivalent in this country. Pierre Daye's tragicomic revelations about Parliamentary life will clarify them sufficiently on this question. Besides, it was important and necessary to recall to the French how people reacted to the act of the King and to dissipate definitively the misunderstandings that Reynaud's deceitful campaign might have given rise to. In addition to these two chapters principally intended for an audience abroad, the meditations of Pierre Daye will appear equally pertinent and judicious to a great number of Belgian readers. *And in particular, the paragraphs which demonstrate that the present war, besides being an economic and national struggle, is the beginning of a revolution which aims at organizing European society in a more equitable manner.* [My emphasis]

This is no isolated claim in de Man's articles. Another one may be cited, in which de Man writes of Germany that "The entire continuity of Western civilization depends on the unity of the people that is its center. This is why the facts which determine the course of [this people's] history affect us doubly: as Belgians, because they [the facts] influence the values that we share with it, and as Europeans, since the strength of Europe depends on it" (16 March 1942). Imposed upon Germany is "the necessity of reorganizing Europe more rationally and more equitably" (13 February 1941). Readers of the *Le Soir* texts will have no difficulty multiplying examples of this kind of rhetoric. I quote one more:

The establishment of favorable relations between the peoples and ethnic groups of the New Europe would be impossible without a free and frank understanding between them. This is why the German occupying authority has decided, with the concordance of the professional organizations of Belgian publishers and booksellers, to eliminate all literature whose goal is to harm Germany. . . . Envisaged here are writings which through their tendentious and deceitful character have contributed to the systematic poisoning of public opinion in Belgium against the German people, her neighbor. At issue above all are works whose authors, political emigrants and Jewish writers, abusing here as elsewhere the hospitality that was given them, have led the peoples who were their hosts to a dangerous blindness and guided them to the edge of the abyss.

These works have been, in a very large measure imported from abroad. . . . Belgian anti-German works make up an insignificant proportion.[7]

This is not de Man. It is the preamble to the list of books banned by the Nazis in Belgium. The point, though, is that the rhetoric is the same here as in de Man's pieces. And de Man really does very little that doesn't feed into the Nazi propaganda machine. The fact that this is also on a fairly highbrow level is not saving. Goebbels writes in his diary on 15 February 1942 of France: "Sentiment in Paris is not hostile to us. However, the critical food situation does stand between us and the French people. If we were in a position today to supply sufficient food to the occupied areas, we could win countless moral victories. Cultural propaganda is still the best propaganda in dealing with the French. I shall therefore increase it even more."[8] These words are equally applicable to Belgium, where hunger was widespread. Goebbels had already lamented on 3 July 1941 that

"Something very close to starvation is widespread in France and Belgium."[9] Readers who get their sense of daily life in Belgium during the war from de Man's pieces are apt to be surprised by this, since they do work so powerfully to normalize an extremely abnormal situation, and to minimize the effects of the "revolution" they herald. Like Depression era movies these essays contribute to an ideological campaign of normalization intended to make the poverty experienced daily seem aberrant, local, temporary, and insignificant.

Fouché's recent and important book on French publishers during the German occupation describes the German propaganda machine in France in fascinating detail. Lieutenant Eduard Wintermayer, a German propaganda expert, drafted a memo on 10 March 1942 which is illuminating in this regard. Quoting from it will underscore the justice of Derrida's remark anent de Man that "the *massive, immediate, and dominant* effect of all these texts is that of a *relatively* coherent ideological ensemble which, *most often and in a preponderant fashion,* conforms to official rhetoric, that of the occupation forces or of the milieux that, in Belgium, had accepted the defeat and, if not state and governmental collaboration as in France, then at least the perspective of a European unity under German hegemony." This remark is just. But I fear that his piece as a whole tends to minimize it. He says that he is talking about "what I am *massively* calling here the *massive* effect" (p.607); but the force of moments like this tends to be a quick concession followed by exculpatory details which accumulate to undermine the massive judgments. Who would want to participate in the massiveness that was precisely de Man's "disastrous" error? So Derrida's massive, but true, pronouncements are few and far between. Instead, there's a kind of rush to subtlety in his piece, without much of an account of how de Man not only conforms to official rhetoric but collaborates with it and advances its goals. Like Goebbels, Wintermayer in his memorandum stressed the importance of an intellectual collaboration:

Although a year or so ago the largest share of works useful for literary propaganda depended on the immediate instigation of the German propaganda services, the current French book market presents a growing proportion of works which treat the questions of common Franco-German interests and which arise from purely French initiatives. It is precisely these works which are particularly useful as bridges for influencing still more strongly French opinion in our favor. (Quoted by Fouché, I, 265)

Fouché goes on to cite Wintermayer on the favorable events taking place in France. French literature is now engaged in "a critical examination of the pre-war period," and so producing "works occupied with the philosophical transformation of French opinion" (I, 265). For Wintermayer there's no doubt about the importance of the kind of work that de Man is doing and praising. He says that "It is beyond question that the contents of many books of propaganda literature offer favorable bases of discussion for a penetration of the population by propaganda" (I, 265–66). Fouché lists the rubrics under which Wintermayer classified the different varieties of useful works. Among these rubrics is one called "France," which contains works on the war of 1939–40 which, says Fouché, "criticize pre-war France." Wintermayer's goal is what he calls "a propaganda of depression. The critique of the old France aims at turning the French away from its democratic past." Fouché describes another rubric, "The Restructuring of France," for those books "occupied with finding for the new France 'a valuable content and a new form.'" The goal of these works, according to Wintermayer, is "to influence French opinion in such a way that the restructuring of France occurs in the direction of a possible collaboration with Germany" (I, 267).

Among the books that Wintermayer cites is Drieu la Rochelle's *Notes pour comprendre le Siècle* (I, 267). De Man's review of this book (9 December 1941) is not unambivalent, and it testifies to the cultural independence which I think was his goal that he should have expressed reservations about this and about other officially sanctioned authors, such as Montherlant and Brasillach. Here he expresses reservations about Drieu's know-nothing anti-rationalism. He fears Drieu's desire to make literature the ethical barometer for the new anti-individualist and athletic world that he is building.

As always de Man wants to preserve the autonomy of literature. Nevertheless, his last paragraph probably provides all Wintermayer would want as far as the propaganda of restructuring goes. Though de Man objects to many things that Drieu says he goes on to stress "the importance of the vigor and the conviction with which this writer launches into the struggle to create a radically new human type. This is an undeniable sign of vitality, all the more promising in a country fallen as low as France." Six weeks later, in a piece called "French literature in the face of the events" he writes again in large conformity with Wintermayer's goals. He doesn't quite follow the Wintermayer line: once again he maintains the value of pre-war cultural productions, and once again guards the autonomy of the cultural sphere that he would want to regard as his own unassuming but free demesne, the return for the compromises he's willing to make. These compromises are as compromising as Wintermayer would wish. Of the works of French collaborators, including Brasillach's "captivating" *Notre Avant-Guerre,* Bertrand de Jouvenel's *Après la défaite,* and Alfred Fabre-Luce's *Journal de la France,* all of which will appear on the French-Propaganda department's December 1942 "Gesamtliste des foerdernswerten Schrifttums" (reproduced in Fouché I, 376–381), de Man writes:

What are all these analyses and descriptions of the ultimate convulsions of a decomposing regime if not an attempt to escape entirely from a superceded mentality? It is a curious spectacle, perhaps even a little bit of a solemn one: this generation throwing a last glance on a past life before launching definitively into other struggles and new combats. And the best proof that this recapitulative feeling corresponds to a true and timely necessity—at least for us, inhabitants of a country which has not yet made its revolution and for whom these war years are like a gathering before the future tasks—is the completely particular pleasure that one takes in reading these books in which a part of our own experience is reflected.

Here and there, still timidly, one sees the outlines of more progressive tendencies and the sketches of a moral doctrine. . . .

Paradoxically, at a moment when all energies are directed towards collective realizations, the idea that dominates in the mind of the French littérateurs is the safeguarding of the individual. [Another list of four contemporary writers follows—Montherlant, Jacques Chardonne, Halévy, and Drieu, of whom only Halévy, of Jewish descent, does not appear on the list of writers worth furthering.] Here, therefore, is a group of authors who, all of them, are preoccupied with saving man before saving the world, and who are trying to formulate the rules that each individual ought to respect in order not to be crushed by shockwaves which are beyond his understanding.

This can be read in de Man's favor, as attempting to save a place for the individual. But then one would probably also need to exculpate the collaborators that he's praising here, and few would be willing to do that. (The praise for Halévy hardly counts in de Man's favor, since Halévy had decided three decades earlier that his Dreyfusism was wrong, and had allied himself with the French antisemitic right). Indeed, much capital has been made in the writing of some of de Man's defenders out of the fact that elsewhere these writers come in for criticism, a point I will return to below. At any rate, it soon becomes clear that de Man's praise of these writers' individualism in no way interferes with the propaganda which he's allowing himself to be the vehicle of:

One can see [he continues] in this attitude a persistance of the individualist spirit of the French, more inclined to analysis than to organization, never able to abandon itself without hesitation to the intoxication of common efforts. The only change which has occurred—a primordial one, it is true—none of the writers cited has expressed consciously; but it is evident in the fundamental thought which inspires each of the essays in question. Individualism sur-

vives, but it no longer aims to play a guiding role. It does not aim to impose itself as a sovereign power before which all other necessities must bow. *It has at last been understood that in acting this way, the bases and the coherence of society are undermined. They've finally realized, in France, the necessity of an organizing power, and they recognize implicitly that the future State will have to pass outside of narrowly egoist preoccupations.* The problem they pose is no longer that of knowing what political forms the sacred laws of the individual will dictate to the reigning powers, but of illuminating the much more modest question: how to insert the human person in a strongly centralized and disciplined order. (20 January 1942, my emphasis; see also the article "First reactions of literary France," 18 March 1941)

This last sentence may help, but it still gives far too much away. It does address the fears of those who still revere individual rights, but only to say that the new order will be able to accommodate those rights. De Man's concern is again, as he goes on to say, with providing literature "a clearly limited domain in which it can enjoy a complete liberty" under the new order, and go on with its peaceful development. But at least he's protecting aspects of culture antithetical to the Nazis? That's the trade-off throughout. For example on 28 April 1942 he will write that the "French genius" will be able to complement and moderate German mysticism: "Maintaining the continuity of the French spirit is an inherent condition for the greatness of Europe. Particularly when the general orientation conducts towards profound, obscure, natural [!] forces, the French mission, which consists in moderating excesses, in maintaining indispensible links with the past, in balancing erratic impulses, shows itself of the first importance." As I will argue below, even expressing this noble sentiment, this article is one of the worst. Indeed, how is its rhetoric distinctive from all the other mollifying statements being made at the time by those willing to see in Germany the guardian of their own values? "French thought will be able to continue its blossoming, as well as its civilizing mission of the rapprochement of peoples," says not de Man but the preamble to the list of "Ouvrages Littéraires Français non désirables" (reproduced in Fouché, I, 307), once books by Jews and other interlopers have been removed.

The most infamous of these articles is a case in point, and in it de Man makes the same bargain: the Nazis can have the Jews if they leave literature, especially French literature, alone (4 March 1941).

Again, I do not want to argue that de Man meant only to serve the occupiers, that he applauded the triumphs of French culture deceitfully. What I do say is that he gave up a lot that was not his to give up in order to preserve a domain which he was willing frankly to acknowledge as secondary. This was a very good deal for the Nazis, and a very bad deal for their victims, and de Man, alas, lived up to his side of the bargain until nearly the end of 1942.

But some of de Man's defenders see things entirely differently. Others don't and I should stress that there are many notable and honorable defenses of de Man being made, defenses (especially of the later work) that I agree with. Jonathan Culler's arguments, though I differ over some details, and also over some of the emphases, are both formidable and reasonable and I have no major quarrel with them.[10] The evidence he adduces about de Man's personal integrity, even during the forties, is convincing to me. I believe the important fact that de Man served as a front for Jewish friends. I am fairly convinced that there was no personal antisemitism in de Man. What I've been arguing about are public acts, not private feelings, both in the forties and later. And the claim that many people in this issue will make, that de Man's later work constitutes a powerful critique of totalitarianism, is one I respect.[11]

Nevertheless, some things that look like they might throw a more favorable light on de Man's writing in *Le Soir* may not prove what they're intended to. De Man's praise of Péguy, which at first looks promising, does not yield the unequivocal construction that Culler and Norris put on it. Along with Sorel, Péguy was cited by Mussolini as one of the inspirations for fascism, and in the twenties his son Marcel started a fascist cult around his father.[12] Culler and Norris quote de Man as calling Péguy a "dreyfusard jusqu'au bout." This may not be quite accurate. The sentence in its entirety says: "As for his schoolmates, there is no doubt about the stance that this impassioned man, imbued with ideas of socialism and egalitarian justice, will take: he will be a Dreyfusard till the end" (6 May 1941). But later de Man notes that Péguy has made enemies of the Socialists (primarily Jaurès). I myself have great respect for Péguy, but his later rejection of Dreyfus the man, as being unworthy of the great non-conformist movement that grew up around him, made possible the right-wing appropriation of Dreyfusism after Péguy's death.

The arguments of Culler and Norris seem to me to be straightforward. Derrida's piece in *Critical Inquiry,* though careful, balanced, and anguished, is misleading. His "On-the-one-hand-On-the-other-hand" procedure has an effect like that of vector algebra. He takes a resultant and analyses it into component forces. He treats de Man's activity as though it's the average of several different impulses, some impressive or even courageous, others quite horrifying. This means that he can say "On the one hand" de Man said some really awful things (far more awful, I think, than what he did do). But "On the other hand" he fought against these really awful things. And this lat-

ter often takes the palm, because de Man in fact can't be justly accused of what the first hand tentatively puts down against him. All I want to show is that he can't be praised either for what the second hand tends to enter on the credit ledger.

I'll take a brief but charged example. De Man: "The Jews themselves have contributed to spreading this myth [that contemporary literature is thoroughly judaized]. Often, they have glorified themselves as the leaders of the literary movements which characterize our age. But the error has, in reality, a deeper cause [Mais l'erreur a en réalité une cause plus profonde]" (4 March 1941). "On the one hand" this article is "unbearable," says Derrida, and he suggests through a rhetorical question that "we have here the most unquestionable manifestation of an antisemitism as violent as it is stereotyped" (p.621). In fact, the article's antisemitism is evidently unfelt, not violent, and unbearable only because we would want so much more from de Man. The accusation's overstated. But this enables an overstated defense. For "on the other hand," Derrida finds a saving reading of the sentences of de Man just quoted:

Already, in the second paragraph, the argument that would consist in making Jews coresponsible for this antisemitic "myth" and this "error" is right away discredited. It was evoked merely as a rhetorical ploy: "But the error has, in fact, a deeper cause." (p.625)

Is this really supposed to be an "*antisemitic* 'myth' and . . . 'error' "? Isn't the myth and error, according to de Man, one which risks hurting literature, and not the Jews? And certainly de Man *is* making the Jews "coresponsible" for this myth and error. He's just not making them "completely responsible." That he discredits the argument that would make them uniquely responsible for this canard I am willing to believe. But that is not what Derrida says. He says that de Man is discrediting the myth of Jewish responsibility altogether. But Jews, de Man says, bear some responsibility for the idea of their influence, even if there is *a* deeper cause. He does not say, however, what Derrida would like him to have said: that *the* (single) cause of the error is deeper. In French the distinction is even clearer than it is in English.

This may be a reasonable polemical move in Derrida, and the evidence that he reads he also places before you. In other, more public fora than *Critical Inquiry* his presentation of the facts has been less balanced. Thus in a letter to *La Quinzaine littéraire,* Derrida writes frankly that he is merely correcting some errors which the magazine has passed along (from the article in *The Nation*), and that a complete analysis will require a lot more space. But he proceeds to an account whose acknowledged one-sided presentation is nevertheless convincing enough that it will be the last word for many French readers. Here we get only "the other hand." This is all that Derrida has to say about "Les Juifs dans la Littérature actuelle:"

The article of his that you mention deserves a very prudent reading, both "external" and "internal" (I attempt it elsewhere). But one will nowhere find what you nevertheless cite in quotation marks, probably reproducing without saying so (but why) the truncated citation made by an American magazine. That magazine is easily identifiable. It has made a splash for itself in the recent past in the worst manner possible with regard to this subject and is soon to publish protests and rectifications. The antisemitic utterances manifested in the words you cite are in fact *condemned* by de Man who speaks on this subject, I quote, of a "lapidary judgment", of a "myth", of an "error" with "very dangerous consequences."[13]

Derrida is certainly correct to reprove the claim that de Man thought modern literature thoroughly judaized. Nonetheless, the argument in this letter is disturbingly misleading despite its admitted partiality. To contextualize, for "Lapidary judgment," de Man writes, "*Literature* has not escaped this lapidary judgment;" for "Very dangerous consequences," he writes, "This idea gives rise to very dangerous consequences. In the first place it leads to the a priori condemnation of the entirety of a *literature* which does not deserve this fate" (my emphases). It is the Jews who have spread this "myth," though there is also a deeper cause for this "error." Would that de Man's concern for Jews had been slightly commensurable with his concern for contemporary literature. For it is literature that de Man is protecting.

The campaign to exculpate de Man has seen other disturbing claims. I find these claims more disturbing than the ignorant attacks they respond to because they originate among people who are better informed and who should be more reliable. Werner Hamacher's piece in the *Frankfurter Allgemeine Zeitung* is a case in point.[14] There he writes that "the complicated political strategy, which de Man's book reviews followed, cannot be . . . reduced to collaboration." He goes so far as to write of de Man's *courage* in these articles: "In them the twenty-one and twenty-two year old is courageous [*couragiert*] enough to censure such favorites of French fascism as Drieu, Montherlant, and Brasillach because of their apolitical aestheticism."[15] And it is true that de Man does censure these writers, all favorites of Wintermayer, at various points, especially Montherlant.

I see in this censure part of a competition for most-favored-Francophone status. Take the case of Brasillach. In *Notre Avant-Guerre,* much of it written while he was a prisoner of war in Germany, Brasillach describes the ecstatic visit he made to the Nuremberg Congress in 1937. He waxes pastoral about the pretty shops with their peaceful looks and polite signs: "Les Juifs ne sont pas *souhaités* ici."[16] He describes in the most enthu-

siastic of terms the Nazi party congress and the grand spectacle that he saw. He meets Hitler and sees an "insurmountable agony" in his eyes, because his responsibilities are so vast (p.275). But Hitler has created a new religion, or so it would seem, with the Nazi flag as a fascist eucharist. Brasillach is powerfully moved, and returning to France he writes in *La Revue Universelle* in 1937 of this trip: "When we try to remember these days so charged, when we evoke the nocturnal ceremonies illuminated from the side by the light of torches and floodlights, the German children playing like wolves around their souvenirs of civil war and of sacrifice, the leader lifting, in large waves, with plaintive cries, this subjugated crowd, we say to ourselves, in fact, of this country, so near to us, that it is at all events, in the full sense of the word, prodigiously, and profoundly, a country that is *strange*" (reprinted on p.278).

What does de Man say about this? Reviewing the book quite favorably he nevertheless writes: "Brasillach's reaction before a spectacle like that of the Nazi party at Nuremberg, when he evinces some fear before the 'strange' nature of this manifestation, is that of someone for whom this sudden importance of politics in the life of a people is an inexplicable phenomenon" (12 August 1941). I don't see how this can be read as anything but de Man's taking Brasillach to task for maintaining some slight distance from the new and moving manifestations of political life in the nation, and for thinking a similar festive politics somewhat unseemly for, or at least unavailable to the French. People I have talked to have argued very strongly against this view. Their interpretation is that in fact de Man is castigating Brasillach for imagining that he has anything of any value to say about the political scene. Brasillach's political jejuneries, de Man says, show "how much the members of this generation have lacked political sense. Their sphere of action was elsewhere, in that French artistic life . . . [which] was so rich." And I agree that de Man says that Brasillach's discomfort comes from his lack of political canniness. But de Man is still objecting to that discomfort, and implying that a cannier mind would have seen more clearly and more gladly the deep popular commitment to a new political order at Nuremberg. The thesis that he's competing with the French collaborationists for favored status seems supported by something he's said earlier, when he exculpates Brasillach of something nevertheless quite widespread in France: "that bad conscience which has inspired so many revaluations more or less sincere among the old [anti-German] warmongers become repentant."

I think, consequently, that the attacks on the French collaborators won't yield the nonconformism that Hamacher is hoping for. Hamacher goes on to write of the "unmistakably ambiguous formulations" in which de Man attacks the "'religious nationalism' of the French." He sees "the German version of nationalism" also attacked there. But the formulations in the article he cites are hardly ambiguous. De Man indeed writes in his review of Sieburg's *Is God French?* that France's "political spirit [is] made up of a fierce nationalism that Sieburg has justly called a religious nationalism" (28 April 1942). But de Man goes on to explain himself in the next sentence: "It may seem paradoxical to praise the impossibility of the existence of a nationalism at a time which, precisely, tends to raise the value of nationality. This apparent aberration is perfectly explained if one takes account of *the extremely particular character* of French nationalism" (my emphasis). I see no ambiguity here. The article is an out and out attack on nationalism only so far as its object is France. French nationalists in the Maurrasian tradition had always been intensely Germanophobic, and here de Man is approving the attack on Germany's enemies. He goes on to praise "the new European idea," in which nationalism won't be (as it is for the French) exclusive, but complementary. French and German values will complement each other. With Sieburg he contrasts "a certain form of French rationality, which seeks everywhere to fix limits and establish measures, and that sense of greatness and of the infinite which indeed appears to characterize the present hour. We are entering into a mystic era, into a period of faith and of belief, with all that that implies of suffering, exaltation, and intoxication." France will help to moderate this new tendency, and help "guarantee it against all obscurantism."

De Man's article is perhaps defensible, as an argument for his side of the bargain: Romance cultural autonomy in a new order. And I want to stress again how often he pushes for the autonomy of different national traditions. Nevertheless, this article is itself, not unmistakably, but, at best, ambiguous. It is possible that one of the things motivating this attack on the French Catholic tradition of "religious nationalism" was Cardinal van Roey's March sermon declaring the Church's opposition to the German enemy. The Resistance press published his sermon, and the collaborators found themselves overtly at odds with the Church in Belgium. And this article does suggest (as had Brasillach and Montherlant) that there's a new, secular replacement for religion, and a fortiori the Catholic Church, to be found under German tutelage.

I want to cite two other moments in Hamacher's article that seem to me dubious. His strategy, to some extent like Derrida's, seems to be to concentrate everything appalling that de Man did in as narrow a mass as possible, and then to chip away at that mass. So for him, the only seemingly unrecuperable piece is that of 4 March 1941, "Les Juifs dans la littérature Actuelle." And he concedes its repulsiveness. But his formulation is troubling:

"There is among de Man's articles no other which contains anti-semitic expressions. But this one—even if it was extorted under the threat of dismissal and hence of the work camp, even if it is desperately contradictory, and although he, as his Jewish friends testify, had nothing to do with its sentiments and convictions—this article remains disastrous." Notice the progression in the qualifying parenthesis from pure speculation to attested fact. His Jewish friends did defend de Man, and many still do. The article may indeed be desperately contradictory. And so we may conclude that Hamacher has some warrant for suggesting that de Man did write the article under the threat of a work camp (although Belgians weren't officially being sent to work camps, even in Belgium, until June). And what does Hamacher call this article? "Disastrous." I think that the word is a bit evasive. Everyone knows that this article has been a disaster. I would have much preferred him to have called it immoral, or unforgivable, or shocking. "Disastrous" seems to be a very carefully chosen word among some of de Man's defenders. Thus Derrida writes of the same article that it is "a *text* that one can judge to be disastrous" (p.623), and later only of "the violence of this *paragraph* that for me remains disastrous" (p.629, my emphases).

Finally Hamacher praises de Man for writing a highly positive review of Hubert Dubois' poem "Le Massacre des Innocents" (1 September 1942). Hamacher mistakenly believed that this poem had been published by the journal "Messages." Much has been made of de Man's aid to this journal, which published literary pieces by writers the Germans frowned on, and which apparently had been closed down in Paris. De Man got it published in Brussels, and this is very much to his credit: it shows the seriousness of his campaign to preserve Francophone cultural traditions and to encourage their development. But the journal was hardly violently anti-Nazi; indeed it was hardly political, and clearly enjoyed a legal, if precarious, status wherever it was published. Its writers may have been members of the Resistance, but "Messages" was not itself a Resistance journal.

Hamacher sees hope in the fact that de Man is pushing a poem apparently written by the associate of people who hate the occupiers, just after de Man would have begun hearing about the deportations. Hamacher quotes de Man's description of the "repeated crimes against the human person," of "the terrible situation in which [humanity] finds itself at the present moment," of a "catastrophe." He quotes de Man saying "Everything which is happening now is not the blind and unpitying action of destiny, but the consequence of an accumulation of sins [. . . .] The use of such a trial is to cause *us* to become conscious of this culpability [. . .]." I translate from Hamacher's German and follow his bracketed ellipses; I emphasize the word "us" because Hamacher is making it sound as though de Man wants "us Belgians" to become aware of what the Nazis are doing, and of our own culpability in collaborating. Here's what Hamacher leaves out:

[Rachel's] complaint and lamentation [over her children] *cannot be justified,* even in so pitiable a situation. For everything which is happening now is not the blind and unpitying action of destiny, but the consequence of a sin, of an accumulation of moral sins, committed over the ages. The use of such a trial is to make this culpability sensible [not to *us,* however: rather to the sinners being sold to Babylon], to make the crowds see that they have acted evilly. As a consequence, the harsher the chastisement, the greater the hope of seeing, at last, arise true values which will permit a harmonious way of life, instead of the false facilities which have conducted to catastrophe. [My emphasis; translation from the French]

Hamacher had not read the poem, but de Man's account of it is pretty accurate. The present day horrors, Dubois says, are a divine punishment, like that visited on Israel by Babylon. True, Germany comes out as Babylon, but also as the agent of God. And de Man makes this clear in his summary of the poem: "The man able to make sublime the suffering that daily twists humanity at war, capable of seeing, despite an immense pity, that this sorrow is *salutary* because it causes the *expiation* of the repeated crimes against the human person [the phrase that Hamacher quotes], shows in this the deep superiority of his being, a superiority proper to all veritable artistic talent" (my emphases).

As it turns out, the review "Messages" did not publish this poem; it was published in a series of the same name. And Dubois seems to have been a protege of the absurd collaborator Robert Poulet; at least in 1937 Poulet had written a wildly ecstatic introduction for Dubois' book "Le Blé et la neige." Hamacher didn't know this; I mention it only because it seems important for an understanding of this article.

De Man's activities during the war were disgraceful. It is quite possible that the private doubts, nonconformities, resistances, and anguish that Derrida and Hamacher discover were really there. But to weigh them against the public activities seems to me to be comparing incommensurables. I will reiterate what I think about de Man's personal stakes in what he was doing. In my judgment he had no investment in Nazi ideology, and a great deal of investment in the Western aesthetic tradition. He overvalued the relative importance of this tradition and he overvalued his own relation to this tradition. But what he did he probably did out of his love for literature. That love, like all love for abstractions, was at once selfish and noble, and it doesn't seem to pay to try to separate the two. What I've wanted to do here, on the whole, is describe *what* de Man did;

I'm happy to believe, and I do believe, that his motives were never heinous, either in the forties or later, even when he did not tell the truth. And, as I've indicated, these pieces certainly do aim at preserving as much autonomy as possible for those aspects of Western culture and civilization that de Man puts a premium on. And he was extremely young. People change, and reexamine priorities, as I think de Man did. But I think it regrettable that some people should go so far in their own loyalty to de Man as to put forth what seem to me intentionally misleading claims, at the same time as they celebrate his deconstruction of authority. De Man's work is of great importance, and should not need questionable defenses.

Brandeis University

NOTES

1. In this 1955 letter, a response to anonymous accusations lodged against him, de Man says he stopped writing for *Le Soir* because of "Nazi thought control," probably when the Nazis extended censorship to the cultural pages of the newspaper. Tom Keenan read me its relevant portions over the phone. I believe that those sentences are to be published in this issue. Other people have seen in this letter the public acknowledgement that I am about to ask for, but the letter seems to me evasive and misleading. And hardly public, since it was meant to forestall any publication of the allegations then anonymously being made against de Man. On the other hand, I do have to say that I can hardly blame him for the letter. Once he does not acknowledge the whole truth of his past—and very few people would have had the courage to do so—the letter to the Society of Fellows is about as careful to avoid any further harm as could be desired. Any indictment of his character that this essay may be construed as making would treat this letter only insofar as it casts light on the events of 1940–42, not as it casts light on his infinitely more principled behavior in the United States.

2. "Response to Steven Shaviro and William Flesch," Convention of the Modern Language Association, San Francisco, 28 December 1987.

3. "Impersonal and inhuman in Blanchot and de Man," MLA paper, 28 December 1987, and a badly translated letter in the *Frankfurter Allgemeine Zeitung,* 11 March 1988, p.7.

4. "Blindness and Insight," *The New Republic,* March 7, 1988, p. 31.

5. "Like the Sound of the Sea Deep within a Shell: Paul de Man's War," *Critical Inquiry* 14 (Spring 1988), 590–652, p.651, my emphasis.

6. *European Resistance Movements, 1939–45: A Complete History* (Westport, Connecticut: Meckler, 1981), p.220.

7. "Contre l'excitation à la haine et au désordre," 9 July 1941, quoted by Pascal Fouché in *L'édition française sous l'Occupation* (Paris: Bibliothèque de Littérature française contemporaine de l'Université de Paris 7, 1988), I, 39.

8. *The Goebbels Diaries:* 1942–43, ed. and trans by Louis P. Lochner (New York: Doubleday, 1948), p.89; quoted by Fouché, I, 264.

9. *The Goebbels Diaries:* 1939–41, ed. and trans. by Fred Taylor (New York: Putnam, 1983), p.444. See also the entry for 13 February 1941: "Situation in Belgium: close to famine. Widespread bad feeling against us. England is gaining support. I am damming the tide as best I can. But when people are starving, there is not much one can do" (p.232), and many other similar entries. Of course the exiguity of this situation de Man must have felt threatened by also, as many people have noticed, and this may provide *personal, private* motives for his hurtful and hateful activities.

10. "Paul de Man in the light of the recent disclosures," lecture at Brandeis University, 14 April 1988; see also his letter to the *London Review of Books,* 21 April 1988, p.4, and Christopher Norris' letter on the same page.

11. Indeed, I will add to a small number of what I take to be mitigating factors by citing one article of de Man's that seems genuinely usefully and publicly critical of Hitler. On June 17, 1941 he reviewed Gregorio Maranon's book "Tibère," praising it highly as a portrait of the dictatorial personality. Hitler, then, may be being seen as an avatar of the monstrous Tiberius. He concludes his article with a biographical notice about Maranon, in which he praises his moral qualities: "It was thanks to his beneficial influence, in fact, that the Spanish revolution of 1932 occurred without any bloodshed." De Man, as far as I can tell, is confusing two events that occurred in 1932. Maranon, the republican physician of and advisor to the king, and loyal to the Azana government, had defended the starving peasants who had risen against General Sanjurjo's national guard in the last week of 1931 and killed several guardsmen. In fact, Maranon defended them by comparing them to the sympathetic characters in Lope de Vega's play *Fuenteovejuna,* so that de Man may be underscoring the importance of parallel history. The peasants' acquittal was a major embarrassment to Sanjurjo, who was forced to relinquish some of his power (Gabriel Jackson, *The Spanish Republic and the Civil War:* 1931–1939 [Princeton: Princeton University Press, 1965], pp.69–71). In August of 1932 he led a pronunciamento which failed, because Franco did not join. But he stayed friends with Franco, and later joined him. In 1936 Maranon warned Franco to leave Spain alone, so de Man's praise of Maranon is praise of an enemy of Franco's.

12. Hans A. Schmitt, *Charles Péguy: The Decline of an Idealist* (Baton Rouge: Louisiana State University Press, 1967), p.171. De Man will later interest himself in the French youths obsessed with Péguy: "This cult around a figure once isolated and misunderstood is indeed consonant with a generation which feels that it must break with established traditions, but which has not yet been called upon itself to establish the disciplines which will succeed them" (30 September 1941).

13. Lettres à la Quinzaine, 503 (16–29 February 1988), p.31.

14. "Fortgesetzte Trauerarbeit: Paul de Mans komplizierte Strategie / Eine Erwiderung," 24 February 1988, p.35. Derrida wrote an irate letter to the F.A.Z. claiming that they'd censored Hamacher's article. Tom Keenan tells me that in fact they cut out about half of it, and that they ruined its structure, since Hamacher apparently argued for a repetition in the F.A.Z. and other newspapers of precisely the irresponsible journalism that they were lambasting de Man for. I haven't read the original piece; since my critique is going to be about specific sentences, and not about the whole argument, I am trusting the reliability of those sentences. But I have no absolute assurance that they are reliable, although I think that were they completely off base Keenan and others who have heard my complaints and who are in a position to know what Hamacher wrote would have set me straight.

15. Someone defending Hamacher to me said that "couragiert" really means "keck" (bold or fearless) and not "mutig" (courageous or brave). Not according to the dictionaries I've looked at, and not according to the native German speakers I've consulted either, who say it means "mutig" with the added heft of its classical root, that is "really courageous."

16. *Notre Avant-Guerre* (Paris: Plon, 1941), p.266.

Literature, Ideology

HANS-JOST FREY

Translated by Stuart Barnett

In this essay I will attempt to read some of the texts that Paul de Man wrote in the years 1941 and 1942 for the Brussels newspaper *Le Soir* with regard to both the conception of literature that is put forth in them and the political and ideological stance that can be read out of them. I will not attempt in this context to establish connections to de Man's later writing, even though I consider this important for a later phase.

The essay of December 2, 1941 bears the title *Sur les possibilités de la critique* and is an attempt to secure literary criticism's status as an independent discipline by establishing the task specific to it. In pursuit of this, two theses are distinguished which obstruct the realization of such an ambition. The one seeks the criteria of literary judgment in the realm of morality, and the other sees in the work under consideration only an opportunity to display the critic's own creativity. In the first case, criticism becomes moral instruction; in the other, it is itself art. In both cases it is estranged from the actual task by which it acquires its independence: *définir la valeur d'un ouvrage littéraire*. The evaluation of a work presupposes criteria that cannot be taken from just anywhere. These criteria must, rather, specify that which makes literature art. This leads to the thesis: *Le moins qu'on puisse dire est que les valeurs artistiques qui régissent le monde des lettres ne se confondent pas avec celles du Vrai et du Bien et que celui qui emprunterait ses critères à cette région de la conscience humaine se tromperait systématiquement dans ses jugements.* Aesthetics is separated here from ethics. And the ethical content of a work is explained as bearing no consequence for its aesthetic value.

The next step must lie in the investigation of aesthetic criteria. The difficulty that emerges here is that there are no eternal laws of the beautiful. The rules are, rather, continually in flux. *La difficulté de cette entreprise résulte de l'extrême mobilité des préceptes et des formules esthétiques. Il ne s'agit pas d'une Beauté éternelle et immuable, mais d'une série de mouvements qui se superposent et s'entrecroisent, s'influencent et se combattent et qui, tous, ont leur loi propre.* Aesthetics must then be pursued less systematically than historically. This means, however, that the criteria of aesthetic judgment—and thus this judgment itself—are historical. The evaluation of a work is never final; it depends, rather, on the current state of aesthetic norms. This restricts the importance of judgment and at the same time presents the investigation of the change of criteria as a new field of inquiry for criticism. The comparison of different aesthetic possibilities therefore becomes more important than judgment itself (*les jugements proprement dits n'apparaîtront que comme une opération presque secondaire*) and the task of criticism is no longer merely to judge an individual work, but, rather, to situate it in a development within which it can more or less be effective. In another article (April 8, 1941) de Man sees the task of literary history to lie not in determining the worth of the individual work, but in singling out those works that have had an aesthetic effect: *[. . .] on désirerait écrire une histoire littéraire dans laquelle ne seraient cités que très peu de noms, ceux-ci servant de point de repère pour marquer l'évolution d'une formule ou d'un style.* Thus one could imagine a history of music in which Brahms did not occur. Because in contrast with Debussy—and even though his music is not less valuable than Debussy's—Brahms did not contribute anything to the development of music. Works are now no longer merely judged, but the aesthetic principles that are at work in them are also interrogated as to their conservative or innovative character. What is important here is that the observation of aesthetic change and the comparison of different aesthetic possibilities presuppose a suspension of judgment and, furthermore, a diminution of its meaning.

The text *Sur les possibilités de la critique* appears to put forth two basic postulates. One is the autonomy of the aesthetic as opposed to the ethical. The other advocates, within the aesthetic, the recognition of the mutability of norms and a judgment made on the basis of the realization or non-realization of the principles in the work under consideration and not on the basis of a hypostatized norm. An overview of de Man's essays in the years 1941 and 1942 shows that to a great extent they take into account these two postulates. These essays thereby acquire a consistency and coherence. This can be substantiated with a number of examples, of which I will present only a few.

In the article of November 18, 1941 de Man reviews the Flemish novelist Gerard Walschap. In the course of this review the characteristics of the Flemish and French novel are contrasted with one another. While the French pursue psychological analysis and accompany the narrated action with rational explanations, the Flemish cultivate a direct narration in which the persons become accessible through their actions and not by means of the narrator's deliberations. Walschap is thus criticized because he devalues one of these novel types in relation to the other and represents his own manner of writing as the only right one. His reflections *gardent ce manque d'objectivité inévitable qui se fait jour chaque fois qu'un écrivain se mue en critique. Attaché à ses propres desseins et poursuivant obstinément le but auquel son tempérament l'a prédestiné, il ne pourra jamais parler qu'en son nom propre [. . .].* Because of his fixation on his own work the writer loses that capability that is demanded of the critic: the distance from different, equivalent possibilities that stand next to one another under the suspension of evaluative judgment. *Il ne pourrait être question de déduire un jugement de valeur de cette comparaison et d'en conclure à une supériorité absolue de l'art de Walschap sur celui des romanciers français de la même époque.*

The article *Regard sur l'Allemagne* (August 5, 1941) examines the differences between French (Proust, Gide, Valéry) and German literature (Carossa, Wiechert). On the one side there is *lucide clarté de l'analyse, précision, soucis psychologiques,* and on the other *méditation poétique, formes métaphoriques et symboliques, mobiles éthiques* (the ethical here is not a criterion of critical judgment, but, rather, the subject matter of the novel). The French novel is complex, it deals with extraordinary people and makes great demands on the intelligence; whereas the German novel simply presents ordinary people. Although both possibilities are discussed without any evaluative criticism, their equivalence is not expressly emphasized. This occurs, however, in other texts, such as, for example, in *Regard sur la Flandre* (December 30, 1941) where it is stated: *Grosso modo on peut dire que les nations germaniques pratiquent ainsi un art plus* völkisch *que les nations latines, que la France en particulier. C'est là un caractère inhérent qui n'est pas qualitatif. On aurait tort d'en faire un argument en faveur d'une prétendue supériorité. Il s'agit d'une différence, sans plus, qui fixe à la majorité des artistes ressortissant de ces deux contrées des buts et des intentions différents mais qui n'établit aucune hiérarchie entre eux. Les deux mentalités ouvrent des perspectives grandioses, chacune dans leur domaine.* The Völkische is dismissed here as evaluative criterion and the Latin is set against the Germanic as a possibility of equal value.

An interesting example of the equivalent value of aesthetic tendencies is furnished by the article *Le renouveau du roman* (January 27, 1942) where de Man quotes Sartre's critique of Mauriac from the *Nouvelle Revue Française* of February 1939. There Sartre contrasts the omniscient narrator (which he disapproves of) with narration from many standpoints. The distinction is valuable, but the value judgment is untenable: *Le jugement de valeur qui y est inclus est peu légitime car les doctrines esthétiques n'ont pas de valeur absolue et on ne peut discuter de leur mérite respectif.* This means that Mauriac's novel could be just as good or even better than the sort of novel that Sartre has in mind. Yet what is also at work here is what de Man elsewhere said about the change in aesthetic norms (December 2 and April 8, 1941). Mauriac represents *la norme déclinante.* He is a Brahms of literature, whereas the novelist in Sartre's sense would be its Debussy: *[. . .] la théorie de Sartre rompt avec une tradition solidement établie depuis près d'un siècle, et, d'un point de vue constructif, elle ouvre largement la porte à un développement basé sur d'autres préceptes.* This text, as well as the other examples that have been presented, confirm what is said in *Sur les possi-*

bilités de la critique about the suspension of aesthetic value judgment.

A similarly consistent position is evident in the texts with regard to the postulate of the autonomy of literature as opposed to the realms of ethics, religion and politics. I will indicate here a few passages. In the above-mentioned text, which concerns itself with Sartre's polemic against Mauriac, a novel is reviewed that deals with the crisis of modern youth. In the course of this discussion it is contested that a moral or political theme is constitutive of the novel as an artistic genre: *Seulement, ce sont là des soucis de politicien et de moraliste et ce n'est pas parce que l'auteur les présente sous une forme romancé—d'ailleurs très adroitement agencée—qu'elles entrent dans le domaine de l'art pur ou, moins encore, qu'il pourraient servir comme prototype des disciplines littéraires actuellement regnantes. Cette intrusion du politique et du social dans les lettres est un épiphénomène passager qui n'entrave pas la continuité évolutive des genres.* The effort to separate literary quality from ideological content is unmistakably evident since the first book review: *Une bonne thèse n'excuse pas un mauvais roman* (January 16, 1941). And vice versa, a bad thesis does not prevent a novel from being good: *La thèse de Giono sur la primauté de l'artisanat est donc un admirable thème d'inspiration auquel nous devons ses meilleures pages. Ce qui n'empêche pas que cette thèse est fausse ou, si l'on préfère, vaine* (March 24, 1942). De Man goes so far as to deny the very competency of writers when it comes to political matters. Indeed, when the issue is politics one is wrong even to listen to them: *Et cependent, il n'y a aucune raison de donner aux hommes de lettres une telle autorité dans un secteur du comportement humain qui, manifestement, échappe à leur compétence* (November 11, 1941). De Man does not vary from this view even when he deals with extremely collaborationist texts. The then bestseller *Notre avant-guerre* by Robert Brasillach—who was executed after the war—provides the occasion for the observation that in judging the era between the wars the political and artistic-cultural aspects are to be strictly separated from one another. Of Brasillach it is said that he has expertly depicted the cultural atmosphere of Paris. *Mais lorsqu'il en arrive à des circonstances ayant trait aux bouleversements politiques (échec du Front populaire en France, guerre d'Espagne, triomphe du national-socialisme en Allemagne), on sent qu'il s'égare dans un domaine qui n'est pas le sien* (August 12, 1941). Brasillach appears as an aesthete who lacks a sensibility for politics and who, ultimately, is not adequate to the increasing importance of the political in the age of Fascism. De Man takes as a symptom of this Brasillach's obvious shock with regard to the Nürnberg party congress. Brasillach is not criticized either as an aesthete or a Fascist, but as someone who, by becoming a political writer, left the realm

of his competency. He harms the cause of National Socialism in that as an individualist he lacks all sense for the collective, and in that he, like the French elite in general, is not responsive enough to *des modes de vie moins individualistes*. Brasillach is attacked not because he is a collaborator, but because he is not enough of a collaborator. He remains too much a man of letters. One must therefore take care not to seek a position against Fascism in de Man's critical stance toward collaborationist literature. The issue at stake in this critique is the relation between literature and politics: literary competence is not political competence and vice versa.

The critique of the book *Notes pour comprendre le siècle* by Drieu la Rochelle (December 9, 1941) is to be seen in much the same manner. Drieu polemicizes against rationalism and advocates the reevaluation of the *vertus animales qui existent dans l'homme. Selon Drieu la Rochelle, les vertus sportives qu'on retrouve, sur le plan politique, dans les idéologies fascistes constituent le symptôme bienheureux annonciateur d'une régénérescence prochaine [. . .].* De Man objects to the interpretation of history—and especially literary history—as a series of catastrophes that are based on a philosophical error (the predominance of rationalism). Rationalism is rehabilitated as a necessary phenomenon that cannot be attacked from the point of view of ethics. Rather, the development would be better illuminated by means of sociological considerations: *car si les hommes ont, selon l'expression de Drieu, perdu le sens du corps, la chose est due à des causes sociologiques plus qu'à des causes philosophiques.* Drieu's attempt to interpret the devaluation of the body, as opposed to cerebrality, as a moral decline that Fascist ideology is finally beginning to work against, is criticized in as much as he misuses literature to prove his thesis. *Du moment qu'on ne considère plus la littérature sous l'angle de l'art, mais qu'on cherche à y voir le déroulement d'une évolution éthique, on peut lui faire démontrer* [in the text: *démonter*] *n'importe quoi.* The protest against the instrumentalization of art is confirmed by other texts, such as, for example, *A la recherche d'un nouveau mode d'expression* (March 17, 1942). Literature can indeed have an effect in society. *Il est parfaitement normal de se préoccuper de ce moyen d'influence et de rechercher la formule qui pourra le mieux accomplir cette fonction. Mais ce qui n'est plus légitime c'est de la considérer comme le but ultime de l'art et de juger celui-ci en fonction de l'efficacité qu'il atteint dans ce domaine. [. . .] On peut aller jusqu'à exprimer ses regrets lorsque rien dans le style régnant ne se prête à une tache organisatrice. Mais jamais on ne pourra conclure de ce fait à une infériorité de l'art et condamner celui-ci parce qu'il ne se plie pas aux exigences sociales.*

The refusal to allow literature to become an ideological instrument can also explain why de Man—perhaps not coincidentally on July 14, 1942—reviews the journal *Messages* that was opposed to the regime. Here de Man strongly objects to those who want to make literature the means of propaganda. *L'art— et plus particulièrement la littérature—se trouve transformé en un outil, en un instrument, destiné à combattre par tous les moyens une* Weltanschauung *périmée et à en imposer une autre.* As before, the fact that de Man argues for Eluard and for the poetry of Surrealism that emerged out of Symbolism cannot be interpreted as a political position. The issue here as well concerns the autonomous laws of literary development and the claim that the artistic worth of texts cannot be assessed according to their ideological content.

All these examples attest to the attempt to separate literature and ideology from one another. The attempt, moreover, was renewed again and again and maintained with increasing persistence. This separation is consistently argued for and the insistence upon it is perhaps the most conspicuous common element in the texts that de Man wrote for *Le Soir*. Literary texts can indeed refer to the present in many ways, but the ideological constraints that they allow one to recognize do not decide their literary quality. The de-emphasis of the ideological participates in the suspension of judgment. This is why de Man cautions against choosing between different types of novels, for, accordingly, the decision for or against aesthetic possibilities of equal value is ultimately ideologically determined. The tendency to secure autonomy for literature from the realm of the political and moral is everywhere unmistakable. Yet how this tendency is to be situated in the context within which it manifested itself is a difficult question as long as this context is inadequately explored. One could speculate that de Man is concerned to prevent the incorporation of literature into the propaganda machine of the regime and to maintain it as a free space in which judgment would not be subordinated to the constraints of the political moment. But in order to be able to say something conclusive about the matter, one would have to know not only more about the cultural politics of the time, but also more about the position of the newspaper in which the texts appeared. It must also be taken into account that with the notion of an autonomous literature de Man in no way had to place himself in the opposition. He can, rather, simply appeal to *les sages préceptes* of Baldur von Schirach, whom he quotes: *Le mouvement politique qui conduit l'Allemagne n'a jamais inscrit à son programme la création d'un art imposé afin de servir aux fins du parti. Ce serait contraire à l'idée même qu'il défend. Chaque véritable oeuvre d'art vaut par elle-même et à une mission nationale. Elle témoigne de la vitalité du peuple à qui elle doit sa naissance [. . .]* (March 2, 1942). On the other hand, one must acknowledge that the autonomy of art that is asserted here stands only in a verbal proximity to what de Man advocates and that the conflict would come to a head as soon as one posed the question what National Socialist ideology understood by *une véritable oeuvre d'art*. Certainly not what de Man took to be the mainstream of French poetry issuing from Surrealism and which he protected against the attacks of overzealous ideologues. One can easily imagine that certain of de Man's aesthetic judgments—be they negative about pro-German authors or positive about writers close to the resistance—could have gotten him into difficulties. Yet it is pointless to put forth speculations that do not allow themselves to be confirmed.

Nonetheless, it should be possible to interrogate the texts as to whether they themselves satisfy the demands they place on literary criticism, or whether the judgments—in contrast to the explicitly asserted position in the texts—are ideologically determined. An important aspect must at any rate be bracketed. It is hardly possible to judge responsibly the selection of books that are discussed. To do this one would have to know not only whom they concerned, but also more about the political position of the authors and ideological slant of their writings that can be learned from most of the reviews. It would also be important to know which new publications were not taken into account. In all of this ideological decisions are implied, which the texts themselves can give no information about. This could only be reconstructed to a certain extent by painstaking research. It is clear that pro-German authors are in the preference, for only German writers like Ernst Jünger or Hans Carossa that remained in Germany after 1933 are mentioned. It is also strange that Camus's novel *L'Etranger,* which appeared in July of 1942, is passed over. Yet the question who was responsible for this must remain open.

The situation is less uncertain when the issue is the ideological position that is expressed in the texts. There can be no doubt that de Man was pro-German oriented and that he stood for a politics of collaboration. This is clear in many passages, even when it is not easy to determine whether it is a paraphrastic report of the writings being reviewed or an expression of his own opinions. In the article of October 14, 1941 there is a sentence that clearly refers to the critic: *Et cependent, la nécessité d'action qui se présente sous la forme d'une collaboration immédiate, s'impose à tout esprit objectif.* One may well ask, what this objectivity consists of and why the necessity of collaboration is not so much an acknowledged necessity as one which imposes itself (*s'impose*). A later article (July 21, 1942) is of further assistance in this regard. Here de Man summarizes—and adopts—the argumentation of Alfred Fabre-Luce in his *Journal de la France,* according to which there are eras in history in which the weight of events is so great that their development takes a specific direction independent of the will of a nation. *C'est ce qui se produit en ce cas: la politique de collaboration résulte de la situation présente non comme un idéal désiré par l'ensemble du peuple mais comme une irrésistible nécessité à laquelle nul ne peut échapper, même s'il croit devoir marcher dans une autre direction. L'attentisme est donc condamné, non d'un point de vue moral, mais de celui de l'impérieuse réalité: il est intenable parce que contraire au courant de l'histoire qui continue de couler, sans se soucier de la réticence de quelques individus s'obstinant à ne pas comprendre sa puissance.* De Man says about this argumentation that it bases itself not *sur des considérations idéologiques,* but, rather, is *aux nécessités inscrites dans les faits.* What is interesting above all in this is that de Man attempts to downplay the role of ideology even on the political level. Even here judgments and decisions about proper conduct should be based not on opinions but insights. Collaboration is presented as the position not so much of merely the convinced, but, in fact, of the reasonable. The objectivity hinted-at in the article of October 14, 1941, is thereby referred to. The situation is considered from a distance that makes criteria other than mere partisanship available. It brings into view the inexorable movement of history, against which it would be senseless to resist. Yet precisely here is disclosed what in hindsight is easy to determine: the ideological situation that de Man overlooks. What appears to the apparently objective spirit to be the necessary movement of history is only the hypostatization of German power politics, and what presents itself as ideology-free reason is simply acquiescence to power. The explicitness with which this text—without wanting to—portrays collaboration as the helplessness of the weak, is concealed only by the conviction—that is, the ideological fixation—with which the historical mission of the Germans is believed in. In the article of October 28, 1941, de Man speaks of *l'émancipation définitive d'un peuple qui se trouve, à son tour, appelé à exercer une hégémonie en Europe.* This is propounded with the greatest clarity, and one can well assume that de Man's journalistic activity in these years would not otherwise have been possible.

The question is, however, not only what these texts advocate with regard to politics, but also how their political commitment relates to the conception of an ideology-free literary criticism that is otherwise asserted in them. More precisely, the question is: whether the literary judgments are influenced by the political stance or whether political and literary opinions can exist next to one another without affecting one another. In the majority of cases the separation of the two realms seems to me to be maintained, but there are passages in which the relations at least

are not entirely clear. On June 16, 1942 de Man reviews the active collaborationist novelist Robert Poulet. The concluding section of this review is phrased so that it is impossible to decide whether it should be interpreted as literary or political. The sentence: *Il s'est rendu compte de l'épuisement des formules existantes et s'est risqué hardiment sur la piste raide et abrupte du renouveau* can refer just as well to the renewal under German leadership as to the exploration of new formal possibilities of the novel. When it is stated: *Ils [ces pionniers] doivent user leur énergie dans des tâtonnements et des errements, aller à l'encontre du goût du public dont l'habituelle inertie continue à s'accrocher aux normes passées,* one does not really know whether the political inertia of the public (which is termed *l'attentisme* in the review of Fabre-Luce) or the lack of open-mindedness towards literary experiments is intended. And in what sense should it be understood that *leurs oeuvres, qui semblent être des produits artificiels de laboratoire, permettent les plus belles floraisons de demain?* The perhaps-intended ambivalence of this text blurs the distinction of the realms that de Man otherwise insists upon and makes it uncertain whether the praise is meant for the novel or the political position of the author.

A little later, in *Le problème de l'adolescence* (June 30, 1942), de Man refers to the novelistic tradition that celebrates the youth as *un être sympathique, digne d'estime et d'amour.* The conception of youth is circumscribed by the concept *indécision.* The uncertainty of young people—not only with regard to political and religious matters, but also to themselves—that led to inactivity must, according to de Man, appear to the authors in the atmosphere of the era between the wars as representative of the general mental attitude. The novel *L'orage du matin* of Jean Blanzat is thus praised because it is a novel no longer for, but against, this figure of youth. *[. . .] il faut voir dans ce fait plus qu'un simple artifice esthétique. De même que, pour les auteurs d'avant-guerre, l'intérêt exceptionnel porté à l'analyse et à l'étude de cet âge dénotait le goût de l'instabilité intellectuelle et morale, le revirement opéré par les nouveaux romanciers indique qu'on est actuellement à la recherche d'un type d'homme plus simple peut-être, mais plus énergique, plus productif et plus heureux.* The search for a new type of man can, according to the conception of literature that is otherwise asserted, have nothing to do with the worth of the novel. Nonetheless, it is presented here as an *élément novateur* and *mérites considérables du roman* are ascribed to it. The pages which contain the polemic against the glorification of youth are "more than an aesthetic ploy." This means, however, that they are an aesthetic ploy. The border between aesthetics and ethics dissolves and it is no longer to be clearly discerned whether the quality of the novel is derived from its formal realization or from its politically acceptable message.

Such passages are not only rare; they also cannot be clearly pinpointed. There is, as far as I can see, no single example of a book being praised or condemned as a work of art simply because of its ideological content. In his capacity as literary critic de Man is hardly ever in conflict with the guidelines that he expressly formulates in certain texts. This is the background against which the article *Les juifs dans la littérature actuelle* (March 4, 1942) must be read. This text is, in relation to the others, isolated in two ways. First of all, traces of anti-Semitic expressions are nowhere else to be found, even there where there would have been occasion to make them, as in the article of May 6, 1941 where, in connection with Péguy, the Dreyfus affair is referred to. (The one exception—but, then, how anti-Semitic is it?—is the essay of August 20, 1942 in *Het Vlaamsche Land,* where de Man divides the German writers into those who remained true to the specifically German tradition and those who advocate a cerebral, abstract and unnatural conception of art. Of these it is stated: "Small wonder, then, that it was mainly non-Germans, and in specific Jews, that went in this direction.") Secondly, only in this article is the value judgment about texts brought into relation with the origin of their authors. With this de Man appears to contradict what he elsewhere expressly calls for: that differences which have to do with national specificity (in *Regard sur l'Allemagne* the ethical orientation of the German novel and the psychological orientation of the French novel), have nothing to do with the aesthetic quality of texts. This would have to mean that a text in which something Jewish manifested itself could be a good or bad text independent of the manifestation. Nor is this, moreover, contested. A causal relation between the worth of texts and the Jewish origin of authors is nowhere put forth. Rather, it is merely maintained as a historical finding that Jewish authors play a secondary role in the literature of the era between the wars, even though *les caractères spécifiques de l'esprit juif* allowed one to expect something else. *Leur cérébralité, leur capacité d'assimiler les doctrines en gardant vis-à-vis d'elles une certaine froideur, semblaient des qualités très précieuses pour le travail d'analyse lucide qu'exige le roman.* The reason why these good qualifications did not lead to results lies in the vitality of western civilization. Of the "western intellectuals" it is stated: *Qu'ils ont été capables de se sauvegarder de l'influence juive dans un domaine aussi représentatif de la culture que la littérature, prouve pour leur vitalité.* The vitality of western intellectuals is evidenced in that they did not allow the possibilities present in the Jewish character to come to fruition. Thus it is not evidenced by western intellectuals writ-

ing better novels than the Jews, but, rather, by their dominating the Jews so that the latter could not realize their potential. The secondariness of Jewish authors is placed thereby in an unusual light. They are not secondary because they are Jews, but because they could not bring to fruition their gifts in the all too powerful environment in which they lived. This corresponds to the thesis that this text advocates, according to which it is senseless to speak of literature succumbing to Jewish influence. This thesis requires some further explanation.

Above all, it must be asked to what extent it is true that Jewish authors played an unimportant role in contemporary literature. Of the great representatives of the "realistic aesthetic" that stems from the 19th century in the era between the wars, de Man names: Gide, Kafka, Hemingway, Lawrence. Whether the name Kafka is placed here without any thought or with intention cannot be decided. Yet it is, in any case, revealing that a Jewish author appears here. The idea behind the list of names is obvious. A name should be mentioned from each literature: French, German, American and English. From English other names could have been chosen (Faulkner, Joyce, Virginia Woolf), but it would not have been easy to replace Kafka. There could be no question about Thomas Mann, for he had left Germany. Musil was not known at the time and there were no other novel writers of this stature. Instead of Gide, de Man could have named Proust, whom he refers to frequently and with the greatest reverence. But then there would have been two Jews amongst the four representative authors, which would not have agreed with the thesis of the unimportance of Jewish writers. If, however, the thesis is questionable at the outset and if de Man in fact knew this—as the conscious omission of Proust from the list of French Jewish writers confirms—then it must be asked why it is put forth at all. The question arises also because this manner of perceiving the role of the Jews certainly did not correspond to the expectations that were associated at the time with an anti-Semitic cultural page in a daily newspaper. What de Man terms in the first sentence *l'antisémitisme vulgaire* would have corresponded to what is developed in an essay on Jews in painting that appeared on the same page: there the Jews are responsible for the "subversive and destructive character" of the works of Cubism and Surrealism; only Italian Futurism has remained free of the "morbid symptoms" indicative of "Jewish nihilism." That de Man, in contrast to this, contests the Jewish influence was certainly not in accord with the agenda of anti-Semitic propaganda.

It is likewise evident that de Man could not write in the manner of *antisémitisme vulgaire* when one recalls what is repeatedly said in other texts with the greatest consistency about the autonomy of literature and the criteria of literary judgment. To characterize Jewish art as such as bad would be incompatible with the basic position from which de Man never strays throughout the entire body of texts. This means, moreover, that from the point of view of this basic position, the question of the role of Jews in literature is badly put. It is certainly not a question that the writer of the other texts would have posed. This can be taken as an indication that this text could have been written under pressure. That the question was imposed upon de Man explains most simply why this question—which according to de Man's understanding of literature is not pertinent—becomes an issue here at all. Perhaps the manner in which it is answered will become more understandable when one considers that, for the person who is answering it, it is a bad and unimportant question. It is clear from the extensive context within which the article is placed that for de Man what is important is the quality of the work and not the race of the author. Admittedly de Man does not say—and could not have under the prevailing conditions—that the question of the role of Jews in literature is unimportant. Rather, he says that the role of Jews in literature is unimportant. The unimportance of the Jewish influence on literature stands here for the unimportance of the very question about their influence.

Yet such an interpretation, however illuminating it may be, does not prevent one from taking the text at its word. If one does this then the denial of Jewish influence in literature appears as the answer that could do the least damage. For if the influence is as minimal as is here asserted, then it is not necessary for even convinced anti-Semites to undertake anything against it. The motivation is denied to any measure that might be undertaken. In addition, the assertion that the Jews did not play much of a role in the literary development of the literature of the era between the wars is not in itself an anti-Semitic statement. It only becomes anti-Semitic when it is affirmed and valued as a good sign for the health of western civilization. The concept of health suggests that civilization would be sick if there were a Jewish influence. However, in contrast to the essay of Georges Marlier about art which speaks of *symptômes morbides,* such deprecatory phrases are avoided. Only when the notion *force étrangère* is brought in has the text crossed the boundaries of anti-Semitism.

At first sight, it seems that the conclusion of the text must also be counted as one of the undeniable anti-Semitic statements. It is especially unsettling in that it is superfluous from two points of view. The text could just as well have ended with the sentence: *[. . .] elle [notre civilisation] a montré que sa nature profonde était saine.* Everything necessary for the argument is

thereby said. Yet there, where nothing else was needed, is *En plus, on voit [. . .].* The notion of a Jewish colony outside of Europe did not have to be introduced here; it appears abruptly and without a context. This impression arises not only because it is an unnecessary addition, but also because the notion of the deportation of the Jews does not fit at all the argumentation of the text. If the Jewish influence is so minimal, then it is pointless to consider such a measure. That it is considered here can be explained neither by the external pressure under which the text may have been composed nor by its method of argumentation. One could indeed say again here that the exclusion of *conséquences déplorables* stands for the needlessness of the measures and that this plan is thereby exposed as untenable. In addition to there being no justification for considering such an explanation, there is a sentence in the text to which the superfluous conclusion can be brought into relation: *En gardant,* malgré l'ingérence sémite dans tous les aspects de la vie européenne, *une originalité et un charactère intacts, elle [notre civilisation] a montré que sa nature profonde était saine.* The emphasized phrase suggests the following construal of the context: since the Jewish influence is great in all areas of life, it is necessary to deport the Jews. This would have no consequences for literature, since the latter was the sole realm that was capable of protecting itself from their influence. Such a reading, however, is prevented because the sentence as a whole is conspicuously self-contradictory. The pronoun *elle* refers not to literature, but to *notre civilisation.* The shift from the particular realm of literature to civilization in general has occurred imperceptibly in the preceding sentence, where in the place of *un domaine aussi représentatif de la culture que la littérature* the expression *notre civilisation* appears. How, however, can civilization as a whole have remained "healthy" when "Semitic interference" is noticeable in "all aspects of European life?" Either civilization is "healthy" and the deportation of the Jews is as needless as the conclusion of de Man's text, or it is indeed "sick" and must be healed by removing the Jewish influence. The text, however, does not admit this anti-Semitic alternative and not merely because of the contradictory sentence just analyzed. The most astonishing sentence is this one: *[. . .] une solution du problème juif qui viserait à la création d'une colonie juive isolée de l'Europe, n'entraînerait pas, pour la vie littéraire de l'Occident, de conséquences déplorables.* The creation of such a colony would have as its goal the neutralization of the Jewish influence. This would be all the more necessary, the stronger this influence and the more important Jews were as intellectuals. Yet according to de Man's text their exclusion would have deplorable consequences for civilization (or to put it negatively, in the perspective adopted by the text: since there are few important Jewish writers, literature would remain untouched by this loss). What could be thought of as the healing of civilization is explicitly characterized in the text as a loss for it. This formulation, which was probably slipped in, and went unnoticed by the editorial staff, undermines the apparent anti-Semitism of the text. If there are important Jewish artists, then they and their works are important because they are good. If they were absent, it would not be a healing of culture but a loss. This conception, which is in accord with the basic position of all the other texts, comes through in a passage where—because of the predominant and excessive anti-Semitic content—one would least expect to find it.

A reading, such as the one I offer here, is easily exposed to the accusation of wanting to make light of an apparently clear-cut matter and of furthering an exculpation. The reading itself does not require exculpation from this accusation in as much as the way in which its textual understanding is reached can be reconstructed. That the accusation thrown against reading is particularly vehement where anti-Semitic statements are concerned is regrettable and probably due to the fact that a precise reading always makes apparent the complexity of the text being read. This is not desired where clear-cut judgments are sought. Judgment safeguards itself against that which is judged. There is undoubtedly a fear of anti-semitism and also of being susceptible to it. This fear would like to have the matter resolved in the certainty of judgment. Thus the readiness of non-readers to pass judgment and the refusal of those who would judge to read. Against these judgments one can simply say that, to the extent that they are based on the refusal to read precisely, they are invalid. Unfortunately, however, their impact is not thereby diminished, since nothing else can make its way to the broader public. The need for absolutely irrevocable facts that can be set aside once one has arrived at a position with regard to them, is in general too powerful not to suppress the questionability of these fictional facts. Yet no text—not even a newspaper article—can be classified so easily, no matter how great the desire to do so is. There is much to be said for reading precisely an anti-Semitic article that was written in 1941 in occupied Belgium and situated in such a context as I have attempted to disclose. If the result of such a reading is that the anti-Semitism of this text is less clear-cut than might at first appear and that an inner contradiction is present throughout it, then nothing is thereby excused or made light of. Yet perhaps a situation is thereby forged that renders judgment indeed more difficult but all the less precipitate and irresponsible.

Universität Zürich

Paul de Man's 1940–1942 Articles in Context

THOMAS FRIES

Translated from the German by Judith Geerke and Glenn W. Most

In the current debate concerning the articles written by Paul de Man from 1940 to 1942, it is striking that both historical and journalistic factors affecting these texts, as well as the particular situation of Belgium at the time, have largely been ignored. Astonishingly, indeed, renowned newspapers (like *The New York Times, The Nation, Newsweek, Frankfurter Allgemeine Zeitung*) have passed judgement in frivolous ignorance of these factors and often even of de Man's articles themselves. Discounting all the sloppiness and slander, it must be assumed that for most of the authors—as well as most contemporary readers—occupied Belgium is far away while the Holocaust is, at least emotionally, relatively near. However, our refusal to make compromises with the catastrophe, the most evil of our century, does not authorize groundless condemnations, especially if one wishes to respect both that catastrophe and the principles of one's own criticism.

Having established this, I do not intend to brighten the dark shadow that lies upon these texts. To see the name and articles of the man who has sharpened our sensibility for the effects of metonymy printed next to an anti-Jewish caricature or an address by Léon Degrelle to a meeting of German and Belgian Hitler Youth delegations is unbearable. Unbearable not only for the sake of the person, to whom I am still attached, but also, as we *now* know, because the very possibility for the catastrophe arose exactly from this type of tolerated contiguity. However, this should not bar us from continuing our search for the source of learning—especially, since contiguity of this sort did not simply cease in 1945 and can just as well envelope us now. To name just one example, when Louis Malle signs his film *Au revoir, les enfants* with a personal statement on the persistence of the glance from the past, he transmits to us this intense, yet in the final result (even for him) illegible, link backwards to the Occupation, childhood and destruction. If we do not want simply to dismiss this glance and once again acquiesce in a media scenario,[1] we must patiently investigate the context surrounding the extant texts, we must try to understand what has cast this large shadow upon them, how this came to pass.[2]

Whoever examines Paul de Man's 1940–1942 articles in their original context quickly feels that he is passing through what is in many respects a lost country. When one leafs through *Le Soir,* even the familiar details of everyday occurrences seem strange, especially confronted with well-known historical events: strange in the ruins of devastation (not just of war). And the *names,* even among those French authors reviewed by de Man, many have been almost completely forgotten today. Many were proscribed at the time of the *épuration* (the post-war purge of the intellectuals accused of collaboration), some sentenced to death and executed or pardoned, others again accepted into literary life—but under conditions that only to a certain degree demonstrate a consistent policy. Judgement has long since been passed on them and those on whom this judgement was not directly executed have fallen victim to the general oblivion. (Only in *Robert* do some of them continue inconspicuously to exist.) A few names can no longer be tainted by the dark stain on their biographies, making theirs even more a lost country. This applies similarly to most journalists and politicians who accepted or greeted the *fait allemand* in 1940.

Paul de Man can no longer explain himself. While he was alive, he made it clear that he, too, considered this to be a lost country, that is, not a topic for discussion—and not merely because, as present experience has demonstrated, much of academia and the press could not have been expected to listen closely. And the caesura in his life is unmistakable. If I have not overlooked anything, none of the authors about whom he published book reviews at the time is treated substantially in his later work.[3] As far as historical significance is concerned, Paul de Man's name was hitherto not deemed interesting even as one among many in the standard historical works.[4] By the standards applied then, his would not even have been a case at the time of the *épuration*.[5] (By this, I do not wish to suggest that only legal considerations are relevant. It must, however, be assumed that the authorities then were in a much better position to assess requisite confessions of *politique de présence* and expressed these assessments in terms of their criteria.) Also, the *épuration*'s hasty condemnation of even those better-known names that repeatedly occur in conjunction with Paul de Man's journalistic activities and whose names do appear in historical works (especially Hendrik de Man, Robert Poulet and Raymond de Becker) have long since been replaced by a more differentiated view in which various modes of "collaboration" become apparent. However, this does not alter the fact that the most famous among these, Hendrik de Man, certainly as a result of the *épuration,* does not receive the attention he deserves, particularly in his own field.

Therefore, there are several reasons why it seems risky to lift the interdiction placed on this field. Because of the factors indicated above, we can expect, as far as the general historical picture of that time or Paul de Man's main work are concerned, to learn nothing relevant from such an investigation, while the individual approach cannot fail to confirm the uncertainty of our own position. If we decide to persist in spite of this, we ought to be able to justify ourselves. Our curiosity to find a second (third . . .) identity behind known biographical data or the wish to dispose of a disliked literary theory hardly suffice. I justify my own decision to speak about this on the grounds of my indignation at the irresponsibility of *our own* times, with which de Man has been labelled a Nazi and antisemite, but I exclude his private life from this justification.

In the first article of the current discussion, "Yale Scholar Wrote for Pro-Nazi Newspaper" (December 1, 1987), *The New York Times* applied the labels "pro-Nazi" and "antisemitic" more to the newspaper *Le Soir* than to Paul de Man himself. But the title of the article set the tone of the debate that ensued. Other journals adopted the label more or less sight unseen and directed it against the person of Paul de Man with increasing acrimony; the associations that the two photographs in *Newsweek* (February 15, 1988) elicit are obvious enough. Few noticed that the matter was treated quite differently in Belgium itself (*Le Soir,* December 3 and December 15/16, 1987).[6] The fatal entanglement mentioned above is exemplarily evident in the articles published in the *Frankfurter Allgemeine Zeitung* on February 10 and February 24, 1988. These articles, which set the tone in the German-speaking countries, condemn Paul de Man with particular harshness, but without having verified the reported information at all. In the same issue (February 10), in which Paul de Man was publicly exposed as a "convinced National Socialist" and "extreme antisemite," the front page carried an article entitled "The Hunt Goes On," which contained a crude attack against the unnamed American Jews (referred to as "Waldheim's enemies in America") who were said to have no intention of relinquishing their merciless pursuit of the President of Austria. A little earlier, in the so-called "Historians' Debate," this same newspaper had defended *German* academicians. When it went on so vehemently to attack the *Belgian* literary theorist, it could not have known—in its ignorance of Paul de Man's articles—that in the "French Connection" of this case would also surface the name of Friedrich Sieburg (about whom de Man wrote an article),[7] former director of its own literary supplement starting in 1956. During the war, Sieburg and Friedrich Grimm (about whom de Man also wrote an article on August 19, 1941), were the *éminences grises* who determined cultural policy in Paris through the "Propaganda Abteilung," the "Institut allemand" and the "Antenne Rosenberg" under the aegis of Otto Abetz, the German ambassador.[8] With their notorious promotion and proscription lists ("Otto Lists"), their cultural policy also ultimately determined the selection of French authors reviewed by de Man;[9] and it is precisely these reviews, more than those of the Belgian and German authors, which implicate his articles as collaborationist. Now, if one (legitimately) objects that in order to judge Sieburg fairly, one must place his activities within a larger context so as to ascertain more exactly his "European" or "Franco-German" intentions, one thereby makes clear the character of the fatal entanglement and can hardly deny de Man's case identical treatment.

If we want to treat the activity of the young Paul de Man with some degree of fairness, we must inquire not only into the conception of literature and the political goals directly and indirectly evident in his articles, but also into the political goals which the institutions (or the people leading or supporting those institutions) for which he worked pursued. Since the first question will presumably be very thoroughly discussed in this issue, I would like to concentrate on the second.

The names that appear in conjunction with Paul de Man's work for *Les Cahiers du Libre Examen* (the publication of the student organization, "Le Libre Examen," at the University of Brussels), the newspapers *Le Soir* and *Het Vlaamsche Land* and the publishing house, *Les Editions de la Toison d'Or,* associate the young de Man with a political tendency widespread at that time, which pursued a policy of neutrality following the outbreak of war in 1939 and, after the occupation began in May 1940, one of acceptance of the *fait allemand.* The reasons for this attitude varied greatly, and so, as elsewhere in Europe, right-wingers (like the supporters of Charles Maurras who centered around Robert Poulet) and left-wingers (those who followed the politics of Hendrik de Man) found themselves in the same boat with opportunists and traitors. At the same time a dangerous schism emerged on the Left, especially in the Labor Party (Parti ouvrier belge, POB). The description given by Jacques Willequet of the conflict in "Le Libre Examen" in late autumn 1939 shows the upheaval of political orientation and the ensuing general and personal consequences:

La zizanie [because of the political orientation of the Left] éclata au Cercle "Le Libre Examen," une association estudiantine qui se voulait laboratoire de discussion ouvert à toutes les tendances de gauche. On y avait flambé pour la SDN contre Mussolini, davantage encore au profit des républicains espagnols. Depuis, la guerre avait commencé et la Belgique était neutre. Les communistes aussi, depuis le 23 août. Fallait-il maintenir une solidarité morale avec les deux grands voisins démocratiques, prôner encore un internationalisme socialiste toujours plus illusoire depuis ses échecs évidents, et surtout depuis que l'extrême-gauche s'en était dissociée? Beaucoup étaient séduits par le socialisme national proposé par Spaak et Henri de Man, attirés aussi par un progressisme abandonnant les vieux clivages philosophico-religieux. [. . .] Au "Libre Examen," la question se posa: les communistes qui venaient de se conduire en renégats, étaient-ils encore dignes d'y figurer? Il était difficile, voire un peu comique, de découvrir soudain que leur pensée n'était pas libre, et qu'ils obéissaient comme des automates aux

ordres de Moscou. C'est pourtant la raison qui fut invoquée, alors que l'importante minorité demanienne, la plus hostile sur le plan doctrinal, vota au contraire leur maintien pour ne pas affaiblir le front neutraliste. Plusieurs de ceux-ci allaient ensuite travailler dans la presse censurée, et l'un d'entre eux fut même abattu par un résistant.[10]

Besides fear of a new war and of German military superiority, another factor encouraged the politics of neutrality, namely the widespread malaise about the decline of parliamentary democracy, which had proven unable to solve the enormous economic and social problems of the 1930's and which, because of the fragmentation of democratic forces (from the perspective of Hendrik de Man for example),[11] had already lost the battle against Fascism before the Nazis came to power and before the outbreak of war. To a certain extent, this led to a preference for elitist and authoritarian political theories and to a dangerous illusion: many fancied themselves in a revolutionary epoch, counted on the (young) Germans, or believed that they could use Germany's brutal intervention for their own revolution ("Ordre nouveau"). Hendrik de Man records these connections in his German biography, *Gegen den Strom* ["Against the Current"], with amazing openness.

It seemed evident to me that German's military superiority also had a political grounded foundation. As early as May 20, 1940, I recorded in my war diary my conclusions from a conversation I had had in the dunes of De Panne while observing the air raids on Dunkirk: "This war is in fact a revolution. The old social order, the old political system are collapsing. Hitler represents a kind of elementary or demonic power which is carrying out the job of demolition that has apparently become necessary . . . It is impossible to predict whether Hitler will achieve the unification of Europe; more than likely, he is above all a destroyer who will clear the path of hindrances." What was wrong and what was right with this view has since become so apparent that it requires no further discussion here. [. . .] As a Socialist, I also had other reasons for trying to see positive aspects in the new situation. For years I had, rightly or wrongly, fought militant socialism with the argument that adopting fascism's methods was no way to defend ourselves against its advance. I had been—again rightly or wrongly, but in either case from the bottom of my heart—for "Munich." I had disapproved of Britain's policy with regard to Poland and had considered Britain and France's declaration of war on September 3, 1939 a fatal mistake. Based on these considerations, logic was on my side when I wrote in my June manifesto that the democratic governments of the West had, "acknowledged the legitimacy of the verdict of military force by coupling their fate to a victory won by the use of arms." The conclusion that this dictum was to be interpreted as the well-deserved death sentence of a political system suggested itself even more strongly. At the time, I was by no means the only Socialist of this opinion . . .[12]

In many cases, the hope for an authoritarian state without social or linguistic and ethnical division and a European federation of states without war motivated "collaboration," which often outlasted the hope. Sooner or later, almost everyone reached a stage where both had to be given up.[13]

Traces of this illusionary hope are clearly evident in Paul de Man's articles—which in no way alters the fact that a text like "Inhoud der Europeesche gedachte" [The Content of the Idea of Europe] (*Het Vlaamsche Land,* May 31/June 1, 1942) can even today be read without major modifications as a substantial comment on politics of European unification. Certainly, in many cases the Pan-European idea and pacifism were also excuses for collaboration, especially at the beginning of the occupation. However, as the occupation continued, those who seriously considered these ideas increasingly lost the favor of the Germans (especially of the SD and SS). Hendrik de Man's *Réflexions sur la paix* were immediately prohibited upon publication in June 1942.[14] (In the article from *Het Vlaamsche Land* cited above, which was published at the very same time, Paul de Man advocated arguments very similar to those of his uncle.) On November 20, 1942, Hendrik de Man gave a speech in Paris under the same title.[15] His name appears in the November 21–22, 1942 *Le Soir* issue right next to his nephew's penultimate article. Paul de Man's articles cease immediately following this, and Hendrik de Man, under the pressure of the threat of imprisonment, a fate from which his friends in Paris just barely managed to rescue him,[16] had to relinquish all public activity.[17] A connection with the cessation of Paul de Man's writing for *Le Soir* appears quite likely.

I am not presuming hereby to offer family relationship, about which we know little,[18] as an explanation nor am I trying to shift the responsibility for Paul de Man's articles onto Hendrik de Man. But it would seem unrealistic to me to underestimate the influence of an uncle of Hendrik de Man's stature—one of the most important figures in Belgian politics and European Socialism—upon the young Paul de Man and his generation. Up to 1933 as a member of the Frankfurt School, the eminent theoretician of Socialism, whose adventuresome biography is closely interlinked with the great hopes and catastrophes of our century, had committed himself to forming a broad-based alliance, especially in Germany, to combat Fascism and the economic crisis.[19] After 1933, he tried in vain to attain the same goal in Belgium with his "Plan du travail." Starting in 1935 he held the post of Minister in various governments, in 1939 he became President of the Labor Party (POB) and in May 1940, at the beginning of the German invasion, he became one of the king's closest advisers. Disappointment at the inability of parliamentary democracy to cope in the face of Fascism and economic crisis, together with a certain fascination with German efficiency, led him dangerously close to Nazi ideology (criticism of "plutocratic capitalism" and its parliamentary democracies, the fulfillment of a "new Socialism"), even though he distanced himself clearly from its fundamental goals and reconfirmed his 40-year affiliation with Socialism (as in his speech of February 16, 1941).[20] (Even his direct political opponents, like Paul-Henri Spaak and Ernest Mandel, who rejected his policy at that time, viewed his behavior as due to a tragic error and not to reprehensible personal convictions.)

What Hendrik de Man was later especially reproached for is his "Manifesto" of June 28, 1940 to the socialist cadres,[21] in which he called upon them to recognize the German victory without resistance and to consider the role of the Labor Party (POB) as ended. Instead, he argued, it was time to bring Belgians together into a Party of national unity led by an elite and loyal to the Crown. But since the Germans, who had not given their permission for the publication of the manifesto, were not willing to sign a peace treaty or to replace the German military administration with a Belgian civil government (what later turned out to be advantageous for the Belgians), these suggestions had no real basis, as Hendrik de Man quickly had to concede. However, he was able to preserve a certain degree of autonomy for the Belgian Labor Movement (inter alia by the establishment of a new unified union) and to complete some social improvements. He had a wide network of national and international connections at his disposal and used them to further his political goals and to provide assistance in many individual cases. But his difficulties with the Germans continually increased, and he withdrew from Belgian politics to the Haute-Savoie, provisionally at the end of 1941, definitively at the end of 1942.[22]

In associating Hendrik and Paul de Man, it should not be forgotten that Hendrik de Man's orientation was primarily of a socio-political nature while literature (and music) predominate in the case of his nephew. In his articles, Paul de Man continually emphasizes the autonomy of literature as opposed to political and moral considerations (and, if a verdict is to be passed on him, then one would have to judge him in terms of his own adherence to this autonomy in his evaluation of literary texts). The political situation of the years 1940–1942, which we have depicted thus far, brought Hendrik and Paul de Man together in an area alien to both of them—tactics born out of necessity: Hendrik de Man, because he was forced to play a dangerous and duplicitous game with an archenemy of Socialism, and Paul de Man, viewed from his own self-assessment at the time, because he was forced into a field which his main object explicitly excluded. But the latter's political statements should not merely be taken as a concession; their effect can certainly be viewed as supportive of the political goals shaped especially by his uncle since 1939, goals which at first received a great deal of support from many circles ranging from the Belgian king to the "Libre Examen." His activity for *Le Soir* should be seen in this light.

Le Soir, Belgium's largest daily, was reactivated by the Germans in May 1940 shortly after the flight of its owners (then, as now, the Rossel family)—hence it was called *Le Soir volé*.[23] Even before the war *Le Soir* had adopted a neutralist position and, in the view of the Germans, it was supposed to be "recognized by the Belgians as a newspaper written by their own fellow citizens"[24] (in contrast to openly pro-German newspapers like *La Nation Belge,* which had a very limited readership). *Le Soir* managed to enlist various renowned journalists as contributors[25] and to maintain its large circulation (over 250,000, with a significant advertising revenue). The Germans exerted influence on the newspaper from three sides (each different in its political intentions): via the German embassy (especially through Max Liebe,[26] who also had connections with Otto Abetz), via the Propaganda Department of the military administration (under Eggert Reeder), which was also under the influence of Goebbels's own Propaganda Department, and through the services of the ss ("Germanische Leitstelle") and sd. The newspaper was censored and was sometimes also precensored.[27] On top of that, there were agents and informants of the security services in the editorial offices who informed the sd and ss about the behavior and opinions of journalists.[28]

Before judging the journalists' commitment to the censored press, it should be considered that large segments of the Belgian public encouraged the journalists to work for the newspapers in order to safeguard various "Belgian" interests there. The political basis for this engagement was "neutralism," which the vast majority of Belgians had already supported before the war (in contrast to Fascism, which they never supported). Jacques Willequet comments:

Le roi, le gouvernement, les secrétaires généraux, la hiérarchie religieuse, les responsables de la vie économique, les syndicats, les organismes de bienfaisance . . . On n'en finirait pas d'énumérer les institutions et les personnalités qui doivent être rangées peu ou

prou dans une politique de présence en quelque sorte fonctionnelle. On serait bien en peine, le plus souvent, d'y démêler ce qui relève d'une résistance certaine, ou d'une certaine collaboration.[29]

Another factor was that the first months of occupation were relatively lenient, especially as compared to conditions during World War I. The German military administration acted properly; the people surrounding Max Liebe and Otto Abetz were committed to European cooperation. A peace treaty resulting in the return of prisoners of war did not seem out of the question. Above all, it had to be expected that there would be a long period of German hegemony on the continent. This in turn suggested that working to safeguard Belgian interests (the "politique de présence," which must be clearly distinguished from "collaboration" and "collaborationnisme")[30] was extremely important in order to avoid relinquishing the field to the Germans, to those Belgians favoring annexation of Belgium as a whole or of a part of it or to the powerful separatist tendencies in Flanders and Wallonia (some of whom were supported by the Germans).

This "politique belgiciste," which was at the same time based on Franco-German parity, should always be kept in mind when judging Paul de Man's articles. Only this background can explain for example the (in its linguistic orientation) rather peculiar article about the dialect of Liège (April 22, 1941): "On voit donc qu'il y a là [dans le dialecte liégeois] une véritable interpénétration du germanique et du roman. [. . .] Et, en même temps que le spécifique flamand se mélangeait avec le spécifique wallon, la langue, élément sensible entre tous, a pris l'empreinte de cette fraternité." This orientation determined quite generally the editorial policy of *Le Soir,* until in autumn 1943 Raymond de Becker was deposed as editor-in-chief and imprisoned by the Germans for his resistance to the Rexists (the Walloon Fascists who desired annexation). It is possible that the newspaper felt it necessary to make certain concessions to the Germans because of this. That could perhaps explain why *Le Soir* joined the systematic antisemitic press campaign—with which from October 1940 to April 1941, at the Germans' behest, the groundwork for the discrimination and elimination of the Jews was to be laid— to a degree that the Germans did not necessarily expect.[31] The apparently minimal effect of these inflammatory articles[32] cannot excuse them in any way. Yet with regard to Paul de Man's text of March 4, 1941, which has been cited everywhere, one must consider and examine the testimony of his contemporaries that de Man wrote this text under great pressure and was trying to play with the censors in a very sophisticated manner by quoting German antisemitism without quotation works and references and by suggesting his true position to the initiated reader via the names of Gide, Kafka, Hemingway and Lawrence (and also via the name of Menuhin in his article on music which appeared the next day). This testimony is at least not contradicted by his other articles. One could conclude that the young Paul de Man overestimated his ability to outwit the Germans and greatly underestimated the gravity of the context. Those who do not take into consideration this hypothesis misjudge the real power relations and the resulting constraints upon writing (equivocalness as weapon).[33]

The most important person at *Le Soir* was certainly Raymond de Becker, who came to the newspaper in the summer of 1940 at the bidding of the Germans (they had allegedly given financial support to his earlier journal *L'Ouest* already prior to May 1940).[34] He became editor-in-chief in December 1940. De Becker, who was a generation younger than Hendrik de Man and Robert Poulet, had been active in progressive Catholic circles in the mid-1930s and since that period (Plan du travail) was well-acquainted with Paul-Henri Spaak and Hendrik de Man; his association to the latter was due also to the "Salon" of Lucienne and Edouard Didier. This salon was frequented not only by intellectuals of the most varied affiliations, especially progressive Catholics and Socialists, but also by Otto Abetz and Max Liebe, who had already created an important network of connections here long before the outbreak of war.[35] The exchange of ideas that took place at this salon undoubtedly prepared the stage for the unholy alliance of the first period of the Occupation.[36]

In March 1941 Didier founded *Les Editions de la Toison d'Or,* which published three books by Hendrik de Man and one by de Becker[37] as well as a whole series of books by Belgian authors whom Paul de Man reviewed or whose earlier publications he had reviewed: Charles de Coster, Pierre Daye, Marcel Dehaye (pen name Jean de la Lune), Hubert Dubois, Louis Fonsny, Marie Gevers, Emile Lecerf, Rémy Magermans, Félicien Marceau (pen name Louis Carette), Robert Poulet, G. Serigiers (pen name Neel Doff), Gérard Walschap, and Paul Willems. Paul de Man translated three books published by this house.[38] Besides the authors close to *Le Soir* (de Becker, Daye, Dehaye and Horace van Offel), *Editions de la Toison d'Or* published mainly literary works. The editing program from 1941 to 1944 included other Belgian authors, foreign authors such as Henri de Montherlant, Max Dauthendey (both of whom de Man also reviewed), Antonio Baldini, Elio Vittorini, Anatole France, Louis-Ferdinand Céline, Jean Giraudoux, and a series of French and German classics (Abbé Prévost, Voltaire, Diderot, Stendhal, Gebrüder Grimm, Hauff, Hoffmann, Eichendorff). The

management was in the hands of Daye and de Becker; the latter was responsible for the selection of books published. German money was apparently used to finance the publishing house. After the war, when Didier was tried and sentenced to death,[39] it was said that *Mundus,* a publishing house in Pressburg (today Bratislava), with whom Ribbentrop's Foreign Office tried to compete with the publishing influence of the Ammann group (Goebbels), had a share in *Editions de la Toison d'Or* and had helped it with connections (Hachette and Havas), procurement of paper and protection from the Propaganda Department. Here again, the same picture: Belgian orientation of the publishing house, a qualified selection of authors, everything under the political protection of the Foreign Office, or of its representatives, which permitted this orientation and this selection (even though surely with different intentions and without the knowledge of most of those involved).

Whereas Raymond de Becker (and with him *Le Soir*) remained consistent in his national ("Belgicistic") and international ("European") commitments as well as in his support of a "revolution,"[40] labeled "Socialist" throughout and explicitly differentiated from National Socialism, he undoubtedly crossed the borders to collaborationism in other areas, especially in his temporary support of the Germans' solicitation of Belgian laborers and of soldiers for the Eastern Front.[41] One revealing document is the transcript of the editors' conference that took place on September 3, 1943,[42] in which just before he was deposed by the Germans de Becker gave a surprisingly candid account of *Le Soir*'s activities. Again the same themes: First the "justifications nationales," the prevention of a "presse mercenaire" (p.1), then the "euphoria" of 1940: ". . . nous pensions qu'un monde nouveau allait sortir de cette guerre révolutionnaire. [. . .] Chacun croyait être à l'aube d'un nouveau monde. Et certes, nous ne voulions pas en Belgique un régime national-socialiste allemand. Avant la guerre, nous avions combattu pour autre chose" (p.3). Then he goes on to "ce que nous avons appris depuis 1940," their experiences with the Germans: relatively lenient military administration, few convinced Nazis in high offices, unclear, at times contradictory, intentions and interests—with the exception of the ss: ". . . et toute l'activité de ceux-ci a un sens que nous connaissons bien: l'élimination systematique de toute force nationale" (p.4). The Germans, whose political policy completely lacked psychological sensitivity for others and who "had had the good fortune in 1940 to find in Belgium a generally favorable readiness for collaboration," (p.5) had rejected the most talented people "comme Henri de Man, comme Robert Poulet, [. . .] des personnalités indépendantes et sans équivoque au point de vue national." But, de Becker went on, it was now evident that the Germans had only supported revolutionary ideas in as much as they were in keeping with their own Pan-Germanic goals. "L'unité européenne est en train de se faire, mais contre l'Allemagne" (p.6). Then, in conclusion, the admission of self-incapacitation: ". . . sachez que la collaboration ne dépend pas principalement de vous mais des partenaires" (p.10).

In all of this, one is struck by the apparent ease with which one moves from statements which prostitute themselves to the real power (and thereby to the catastrophe) to insights which should have put all this into question in the first place and which, read by themselves, could just as easily stand today. In this context, one moves with the same exasperating ease from political designs which still deserve respect into the antechambers of the Third Reich. The breach that is thus created, or confirmed by the turn history has taken, often cuts right through the middle of a person's writing. The *épuration* of 1944–1946— perhaps understandable as an immediate settling of accounts, certainly not as a concept—located this breach between two camps in order to exclude the polluted and thereby it established a clarity of orientation retroactively. But, especially at the beginning of the occupation, so clear a distinction had existed only in relatively few cases. It is thus obvious that from this perspective everything that lay or could lie on the wrong side was lost twice over. How can learning, a reasonable dialogue, calm listening be possible when everything (perhaps even for the welfare of the listener) depends on the label that subsequently emerges? Forty years should have been enough to overcome the errors of the *épuration*; however, the discussion of the last few months demonstrate that this is not the case. It is naive, if not hypocritical, on the basis of this discussion to reproach Paul de Man for his failure to confess (confess what? when? how? where? to whom?) his journalistic activities from 1940–1942, even the more so since there are also personal catastrophes which in his silence need to be respected. It is just as naive to look precisely here for the unequivocalness lacking in his work, for exactly what these articles, in their contiguity to the catastrophe, address and leave open at the edge of the (autonomously posited) category of the literary—namely the connections explored here—is anything but unequivocal, hence still open, not done with. The equivocalness at the edge is both the condition of existence of these texts[43] and their scandal. It seems to me that Paul de Man's later work never ceased to focus on this equivocalness—not in an "unpolitical" writing, in the separation out of the literary which made his earlier texts "accessible" (*verfügbar*) to political instrumentalization, but rather in a

search for this equivocalness in the literary itself (which is not restricted to literature).

Zürich, May 28, 1988

NOTES

1. "Pour comprendre ce qui s'est passé dans les pays occupés d'Europe occidentale, il faut considérer comment le caractère de la guerre a évolué au cours des cinq années. On ne saurait assez insister là-dessus. Dans ces pays, beaucoup de gens, sous l'impression d'événements plus récents, ont exercé à ce sujet des facultés d'oubli étonnantes. A l'étranger, on est resté sous l'impression d'une propagande littéraire et cinématographique qui n'a popularisé que certains aspects sensationnels de la dernière phase de la guerre; ici aussi, il s'est formé une image étonnamment fausse des réalités quotidiennes, surtout de la période du début." (Hendrik de Man, *Cavalier seul: 45 années de socialisme européen*, Geneva, 1948, p.249.)

2. "Il est trop facile, quand on connaît la fin de l'aventure, de tout reconstruire en fonction de cet aboutissement. Les acteurs, eux, n'avaient que des craintes ou des espoirs; l'avenir, ils ne le connaissaient pas. [. . .] Et maintenant, essayons de rester serein, de ne pas céder aux sentiments qui nous serrent la gorge. L'horreur pour un désastre irréparable que l'ignorance, justement, nous empêcha d'éviter. La pitié pour ceux—tous ceux—qui en furent les victimes. L'horreur et le mépris. . . ." (Jacques Willequet, *La Belgique sous la botte: résistances et collaborations 1940–1945*, Paris, 1986, p.10.)

3. The only possible exceptions (among about 100 names) are Valéry and Gide.

4. Besides the book by Willequet which I have already mentioned, I refer to the following texts: Jules Gérard-Libois and José Gotovitch, *L'An 40: La Belgique occupée* (Brussels, 1971); Els de Bens, *De Belgische dagbladpers onder Duitse censuur (1940–1944)* (Antwerp/Utrecht, 1973); id., "La presse au temps de l'occupation de la Belgique (1940–1944)," *Revue d'histoire de la deuxième guerre mondiale* 20:80 (1970), 1–28 (abridged French version of her book). Additional sources are listed in all of these works. — For the much more extensive documentation of *collaboration* and *épuration* in France, I will name only : Robert O. Paxton, *Vichy France: Old Guard and New Order, 1940–1944* (New York, 1972); Jean-Pierre Azéma, *La Collaboration 1940–1944* (Paris, 1975); Pascal Ory, *Les Collaborateurs* (Paris, 1976); Bertram M. Gordon, *Collaborationism in France during the Second World War* (New York, 1980); Pierre Assouline, "Les trahisons ordinaires des écrivains français," in F. Bédarida (ed.), *Résistants et collaborateurs: Les Français dans les années*

noires, pp.70–79 (Paris, 1985); id., *Épuration des intellectuels* (Paris, 1986).

5. The criteria upon which verdicts in Belgium and France at the time were based included whether an author
— had betrayed national interests (in the case of Belgium this could have come about through support of annexation endeavors, the deportation of Belgian laborers to Germany or the integration of Belgian soldiers into the German Wehrmacht);
— had slandered the allies, the government in exile in London or other national institutions, also if he had slandered Jews, Free Masons or other persecuted groups;
— was an accessory to a crime in a particular, concrete case;
— had himself participated in the notorious trips to Germany (authors' congresses) and/or had himself conspired with the Germans;
— had continued his commitment until 1944/45.

On the other hand, in the trials against Robert Poulet, Raymond de Becker and others, the fact that they could cite the explicit or implicit support of the king, the Belgian government (in exile) or other influential circles of the Belgian public, played an important (though not officially recognized) role.

The only point for which de Man could have been reproached on these grounds (whether he was interrogated at all is uncertain) is his well-known article in the antisemitic supplement of March 4, 1941. More will be said about this later.

6. The allegation advanced in these articles that the anti-semitic supplement of March 4, 1941 could not be located in the *Le Soir* archives is incorrect; it is the last page of this issue.

7. "Le problème français: *Dieu est-il français?* de F. Sieburg," April 28, 1942. (Since *Le Soir* continued to publish various editions even during the war, the cited dates do not always apply for all editions.)

8. Cf. Assouline, "Les trahisons. . . ," especially pp.74 f. and Ory, op. cit., pp. 11 ff., 56 and 216 ff.

9. Assouline ("Les trahisons. . . ," p.73) gives a selection from the "Gesamtliste des fördernswerten Schrifttums bis 31.12.1942" [Comprehensive List of Authors Worthy of Support], produced by the "Propaganda-Abteilung Frankreich, Gruppe Schrifttum." This list is kept in the archives of the *Centre de documentation juive contemporaine* (document DLIV-60) which kindly provided me with a copy of it. Of the French authors listed in the complete document, de Man reviewed (though not always the book indicated on the list) Jacques Benoist-Méchin, Bertrand de Jouvenel, Maurice Betz, Jacques Chardonne, Pierre Drieu La Rochelle, Abel Bonnard, Alfred Fabre-Luce, Robert Brasillach, Henri de Montherlant and Jean

Giono (and of the German authors, Friedrich Grimm, Ernst Jünger, Goethe, Sieburg, Hermann Stehr, Hans Fallada). As to the general outline of his reviewing policy, it is worth noting that de Man does *not* review any of the inflammatory pro-German books of section I or of the anti-English, anti-American etc. and anti-Jewish books of Section II ("Aktives Schrifttum") of this list (the other sections include France before and after 1940, general history, and literature).

10. Op. cit., pp.46 f. Willequet refers to information provided by Pierre de Ligne, who first worked with Paul de Man in the editorial committee of the *Cahiers* and later was also employed (as editor) at *Le Soir.* — Another name that should be mentioned here is that of the president of "Libre Examen," Franz Derijcke, whose fate as described by Willequet (pp.91–95) should also give one pause.

11. See his work *Sozialismus und National-Fascismus* (Potsdam, 1931), especially p.51 ff.

12. *Gegen den Strom: Memoiren eines europäischen Sozialisten* (Stuttgart, 1953), pp.247 f. Hendrik de Man wrote his memoirs in three versions that overlap in part: *Après Coup* (1941, with a Dutch translation), *Cavalier seul* (1948) and the third, German version.

13. Hendrik de Man apparently lost his illusions quickly: "By the autumn of 1940, I had already drawn my conclusion from my practical experiences with the government of the occupation forces that the time had not yet come for the reorganization of Belgium I desired. I formulated this in one sentence: 'National revolution cannot be incited in an occupied country.'" He describes his position at the time as follows: "I was not a traitor because I tried to represent Belgian interests to the occupation forces to the best of my ability. I was separated from the members of the Resistance only by the fact that I did not want to leave the ground of legality. I was not an 'attentist' [who refused to draw the practical consequences of the German victory] because I did not believe that Germany's defeat would in any way solve or even ease the problems before which we stood. However, I did not share the view of the Belgian National Socialists who wanted to integrate Belgium among Germany's allies" (ibid., pp.251 f.).

14. The confiscation occurred even though the book had passed the censor's review after the removal of several pages. One of the few remaining volumes is located at CREHSGM (Centre de recherches et d'études historiques de la seconde guerre mondiale, Brussels). In 1947, an expanded version was published in Geneva under the title *Au-delà du Nationalisme*.

15. On the same day, an important article on the same topic was published by Robert Poulet in the *Nouveau Journal*. In the spring of

1942, Hendrik de Man had given a speech on a similar topic ("La Belgique devant l'Europe," *Le Soir,* April 23, 1942) in Paris, which had been (also officially) well received at the time. Apparently something else was also at stake then. In *Cavalier seul,* Hendrik de Man reports his meeting with Carlo Mierendorff, the "crown prince" of the German Social Democrats (prior to 1933 and alongside Kurt Schumacher), whom he had known since 1923: "Là [dans le bois de Viroflay], le 23 avril 1942, dans un cadre de feuillage tendre et de pervenches en fleurs, Mierendorff m'initia aux projets du groupe dont il faisait partie avec Goerdeler, Leuschner, von Harnack et quelques autres, projets qui aboutirent à l'attentat du 20 juillet 1944. Nous parlâmes peu de ce que mon ami appelait le 'premier acte', et pour cause; car ce côté de la chose ne concernait que les Allemands. Au contraire, nous discutâmes en détail l'aspect politique de l'entreprise, et surtout de ce que je pourrais faire pour faciliter les contacts avec l'étranger après la disparition du principal obstacle à une paix raisonnable." And he quotes from his notes at the time: "Je trouve excellente l'idée de faire un gouvernement mixte, comprenant des représentants de toutes les classes sociales, mais avec le moins possible d'hommes politiques d'avant-guerre, sauf quelques 'martyres du régime' comme Niemöller et Mierendorff lui-même. [. . .] Goerdeler viendra me voir à Bruxelles (projet non réalisé. . .), je m'engage à les aider à établir de bonnes relations en Belgique. . . ." (loc. cit., pp. 274 ff.)

16. Hendrik de Man had good connections to Otto Abetz. In January 1939, Abetz, representing his superior, Ribbentrop, Hitler's Foreign Minister, received de Man in Berlin. At the time, de Man was there on behalf of the Belgian king and governments of the so-called Oslo countries to explore the possibility of a peace conference. Abetz also involved himself in the interests of Belgium (which led to complaints from officials there). He once, probably at this time (cf. note 17), rescued Hendrik de Man from the clutches of the Gestapo. Hendrik de Man writes of him: "Abetz desired agreement between Germany and France but within the framework of Ribbentrop's politics, and that meant that he had to attempt to serve two masters simultaneously. [. . .] and what I saw of his activities confirmed both my high regard for his character and my doubts about the means he used in pursuing his political goals" (*Gegen den Strom,* p.262).

17. Abetz's name is not directly mentioned in *Gegen den Strom*; the speech held on November 20, 1942 at the "Ambassadors" is not mentioned at all: "A year later [than November 1941], this legal situation came to an abrupt end. During my second visit to Brussels, I discovered that my name was on a list of officers who had not yet been imprisoned but who would be apprehended in the next round-up of hostages. In accordance with this, the Brussels author-

ities for the first time refused to grant me a visa for a journey to Paris, where I had hoped to receive from the embassy papers necessary for the continuation of my journey. I nevertheless managed to get to Paris, but was then stopped by the police in spite of the protection granted me by the embassy and taken to the Gestapo headquarters in the Rue de Saussaies. There I had the good fortune that my case was presented to a high officer who knew me personally and had on occasion granted me favors. He telephoned with Brussels and Berlin until he was able to notify me, late in the night, that I would be allowed to return to the Haute-Savoie for one month; after that, one would have to see what happened. My interpretation, that no one would bother with me if I called no further attention to myself, proved to be correct" (loc. cit., pp.258 f.).— That de Man was still able to publish in Germany after this time (Peter Dodge, *The Faith and Works of Hendrik de Man* [The Hague, 1966], p.263) further emphasizes the variety of interests that were involved on the German side as well.

18. It would seem inappropriate to me to speculate here about personal connections. Concerning Raymond de Becker and the Didier's "Salon," I have been told by Georges Goriely that Paul de Man avoided the first and never visited the latter. That a "connection" nevertheless exists is the problem at issue here.

19. Cf. note 11. His acquaintance with Otto Abetz (who had also been affiliated with Social Democracy) and Carlo Mierendorff stems from this period.

20. "Nous allons vers l'unité européenne et l'ordre socialiste. C'est sous ce jour qu'il faut voir l'avenir de la Belgique. [. . .] Dans le passé nous avons commis la faute d'accoupler le socialisme au parlementarisme. Le socialisme c'est s'attaquer aux puissances d'argent et le parlementarisme n'était pas pour cela l'outil souhaité. Il affaiblissait au contraire et le pouvoir de l'argent augmentait. L'action de l'état sur l'économie était paralysée. Tout cela a fait la force du national-socialisme, une force qui fut d'abord destructive et avec laquelle je ne m'identifie point. Je ne suis pas un national-socialiste allemand, je suis un socialiste belge. Ce qui existe en Allemagne correspond à la mentalité allemande; la mentalité militaire. L'Allemagne est une grande puissance humiliée et c'est pour cela que le national-socialisme allemand contient une mentalité de domination. Ce n'est pas la nôtre. . . ." (Quoted from Gérard-Libois and Gotovitch, *L'An 40*, pp.228 f.; this is based on notes taken by a listener "hostile to de Man.")

21. Published in the *Gazette de Charleroi* on July 3, 1940. Published in English translation in Dodge, op. cit., pp.196–198.

22. Cf. n. 17. In 1944, Hendrik de Man, who managed to antagonize almost everybody, reached Switzerland after an adventurous escape; Hans Oprecht rescued him from extradition to the Nazis. In 1946, he was sentenced in Belgium in absentia to 20 years imprisonment and a high fine. In 1953, he died in an accident at an unsupervised railroad crossing near Murten.—It has not proved easy for historical works to treat his politics between 1939–1942 conclusively. Cf. Gérard-Libois and Gotovitch, pp.216–232 and 262–281; Willequet, pp.95–101.

23. After the Rossel family returned from France in August 1940, proceedings for the transfer of ownership took place; however, no agreement was reached.

24. *Tätigkeitsbericht der deutschen Militärverwaltung* (Reeder), No. 8, August 1940; as quoted by Els de Bens, "La presse au temps. . . ," pp.14 f. Willequet describes the attitude of the public towards *Le Soir* as follows: "Acheter *Le Soir* en fin d'après-midi, c'est un réflexe qui continua de jouer sous l'occupation, d'autant plus que d'autres titres avaient disparu. [. . .] Pour chacun, il y avait à boire et à manger dans ce quotidien. Des informations locales, nationales et internationales, évidemment. Des idées fausses (dont la fausseté intrinsèque ne devait, au fond, apparaître souvent qu'après coup), des prises de position patriotiques viscérales, des idéaux d'ordre social et européen louables mais à tout le moins inopportuns, des commentaires sur un passé proche qui, en effet, ne s'était guère révélé exaltant, un anticommunisme qui, en principe ne devait pas choquer grand monde . . . bref, la vie qui continuait. Le lecteur moyen trouvait utile de confronter les informations de Belgapress avec celles de la radio londonienne, amusant parfois de décoder certains habillages de propagande, indispensable de lire les avis administratifs ou, tout simplement, de consulter les programmes de cinéma. L'entreprise, en tout cas, fit d'excellentes affaires" (op. cit., p.175).

25. According to Willequet (ibid., p.82), about 500 journalists applied for work at the censored press where only 50 were needed. Under such circumstances, the 21-year-old Paul de Man could probably not have obtained his position without outside support.

26. Els de Bens (*De belgische Dagbladpers. . .* , pp.346 f.) cites a letter from Liebe to the German Foreign Office dated June 10, 1940. "They [L. and Dr. Klein] have gathered all of the real journalists remaining in Brussels and managed to have the editorship of *Le Soir* placed in their hands."

27. According to Els de Bens ("La presse. . . ," pp.7 f.), the system of preliminary censorship existed first. After October 10, 1940, along with increasing German intervention, censorship "a posteriori" was instigated (together with simultaneous directions from the Propaganda Department sent via its press agency Belgapress). *Le Soir* was warned, reprimanded, etc. several times mostly because of "belgisistic" articles. After August 12, 1942 the newspapers were again submitted to precensorship.

28. Els de Bens, *De belgische Dagbladpers. . .* , pp.347 f.

29. Op. cit., p.53. As representative of many witnesses, I quote the letter from Graf Capelle, the secretary of Leopold III, to Raymond de Becker on January 9, 1941, as cited by Els de Bens (*De belgische Dagbladpers. . .* , p.336): "J'ai eu l'honneur de remettre au Roi votre message ainsi que l'exemplaire d'honneur du numéro spécial du *Soir* consacré à l'unité belge. [. . .] Il est bon de rappeler aux Belges leur histoire et de leur inculquer le sens de l'esprit national. Nous ne formons qu'un chaînon parmi la succession de ceux qui nous ont précédés et qui nous suivront; notre devoir est d'établir par nos actes et nos paroles, le droit à l'existence de la Patrie dont nous ne sommes que les gardiens passagers. Vis-à-vis des générations futures, nous avons des obligations auxquelles nous n'avons pas le droit de nous soustraire." Concerning the position of the king, cf. Willequet, op. cit., especially pp.55 ff.

30. Cf. Willequet, ibid., p.10 as well Chapters 2 and 4.

31. Id., pp.320 f.: ". . . il est surprenant de constater que le *Soir* (volé) adopta d'emblée des thèses carrément racistes. [. . .] Alors, pourquoi ces outrances, exceptionnelles dans la presse censurée? L'administration militaire n'en exigeait pas tant. . . ." Willequet also mentions (p.318) that Robert Poulet was able at about the same time (*Cassandre,* October 22, 1940) to reject the typification in Veit Harlan's *Jud Süss* with relative explicitness. — On March 5, 1941 (thus just following the publication of the anti-semitic supplement on March 4), the front page of *Le Soir* carried an "avertissement allemand à la population belge" from the (German) *Brüsseler Zeitung*. This warning criticized the "attentist" (cf. note 13) position of many Belgians.

32. "On peut dès lors supposer que bien des articles antisémites ou hostiles à la franc-maçonnerie [. . .] furent des concessions jugées bénignes, en vue de faire admettre des professions de foi nationales dont on savait qu'elles n'étaient pas bien vues. Après tout, on n'a guère l'impression que ces thèmes aient beaucoup passionné le lecteur moyen" (id., p.178).

33. In order to understand the difference between "oblique" and "non-oblique" speech (cf. n. 43), I suggest the reading of the series of lectures on German literature which Lutz Mackensen (then professor at the University of Gent, after the war a well-known author and editor of dictionaries, encyclopedias and other publications in

linguistics, journalism and folk literature) gave in 1941 to Flemish students and which were published the same year (*Die Dichter und das Reich,* Brussels, 1941); see, for example, his remarks on Arthur Schnitzler and Thomas Mann (pp.153–161) or on the subject of the book-burnings and the authors who were its victims (pp.246–250). As in many other cases in Germany, it is impossible to tell whether, and if so, how, the academic community cared about this wartime publication.—Here again, this exemplary reference neither explains nor excuses anything with regard to Paul de Man, but it must be kept in mind to adjust the impact and the proportions of the scandal we are talking about.

34. Willequet, p.49.

35. Edouard Didier founded the club "Jeune Europe," in which Franco-German friendship was to be fostered. He had been acquainted with Abetz since 1933. Cf. Gérard-Libois and Gotovitch, pp.230 ff.

36. "De même on est frappé de constater à quel point il y eut convergence de reactions intellectuelles devant la situation de juin 1940, parmi les hommes qui s'étaient connus au salon Didier et qui souvent continuèrent à le fréquenter après l'été 1940, même quand leurs engagements de guerre les avaient séparés" (ibid., p.46).

37. Hendrik de Man, *Après Coup (Mémoires)* (1941); *Réflexions sur la paix* (1942) (cf. note 14); *Cahiers de ma montagne* (1944). — Raymond de Becker, *Le Livre des vivants et des morts (Mémoires)* (1942).

38. Two novels: Paul Alverdes, *Le Double Visage (Das Zwiegesicht)* and Filip de Pillecyn, *Le Soldat Johan (De soldaat Johan)* (both 1942); and a work of art history: A. E. Brinckmann, *Esprit des Nations (Geist der Nationen)* (1943), translated with Jean-Jacques Etienne.

39. *Le Soir,* November 30, 1946. Cf. Gérard-Libois and Gotovitch, op. cit., p.47. The death sentence was not carried out and Didier was later pardoned.

40. As contrasted to Hendrik de Man (cf. note 13), as well as Robert Poulet who left everything rather vague, Raymond de Becker's support of this "revolution" was much more closely connected to the present and was thus dependent on the Germans' agreement. In his articles Paul de Man repeatedly notes that a revolution is in process. However, he avoids drawing any concrete conclusions from this observation.

41. This was the most important charge that led to the death sentence pronounced against Raymond de Becker on July 24, 1946. However, because of his resistance "against annexationist and separationist tendencies" which had led to his arrest, his appeal was granted and his death sentence was converted into life imprison-

ment on June 14, 1947. (Robert Poulet's sentence was treated similarly.) As was common at the time, his punishment was reduced in 1950 and he was released in 1951 under the condition that he leave Belgium and refrain from further political involvement. Thereafter, de Becker lived in Paris and wrote psychological books. In a drawn-out trial before the European Court of Human Rights at Strasbourg, he appealed the denial of his civil rights by the Belgian government and won a partial victory ("De Becker" case, judgement of 27 March 1962).

42. The transcript, which apparently also fell into the hands of the Résistance, is preserved in the archives of CREHSGM; it was reprinted in *Courrier hebdomadaire du* CRISP on October 30, 1970. Of course, it is possible that de Becker wanted to provoke his own removal with this exposé about whose "confidential" character he had no illusions.

43. "Dialogism can, first of all, simply mean double-talk, the necessary obliqueness of any persecuted speech that cannot, at the risk of survival, openly say what it means to say. . . ." In the same connection ("Dialogue and Dialogism," *Poetics Today* 4:1, 1983, p.100) de Man repeatedly refers to Leo Strauss's *Persecution and the Art of Writing*.

Blindness and Hindsight

CATHERINE GALLAGHER

There are presumably many people in this profession who didn't know Paul de Man and who care very little about either the details of his biography or the vicissitudes of his posthumous reputation. The fact that de Man wrote articles for a collaborationist journal has been generally known since last September, but that news did not seem momentous to many of us on first hearing it. Slowly, however, a set of contested and countervailing narratives about de Man, literary theory, and the state of the humanities has come to command the interest of even the most indifferent among us; each of these stories has claimed that something very important can be learned from the recent disclosures. I'm going to discuss three such narratives in order to ascertain just what we have learned from these months of discussion about the subject of Paul de Man.

First I'll consider the story told in the mass press, of which the February 15 *Newsweek* article is an excellent example. *Newsweek* turned the discovery of de Man's early writings into a sign of the failure of the humanities in general and literary studies in particular. The discovery fit very nicely into a story about literature departments that the medium has been telling for years and that goes like this. Some time in the 1960s, literature departments forgot that their job is to preserve, appreciate, explicate, and provide for the orderly communication of "our cultural heritage." Deconstruction seemed in this story to resemble Marxism, feminism, ethnic studies or anything else that challenged Arnoldian assumptions of value, but deconstruction was also different and especially pernicious because it seemed to make all discussions of value obsolete. "Undecidability" was read as meaninglessness, and meaninglessness translated quickly into nihilism. The end of the story either was upon us or was soon to be: social chaos, cultural disunity, widespread illiteracy, and a general inability to distinguish right from wrong.

The discovery that de Man had written for a collaborationist journal fit beautifully into this story because it provided a perfect symmetry between the beginning and the end. Deconstruction was no longer just the harbinger of outrages against humanity; it actually originated in such outrages. The outcome could no longer be in doubt because it was contained in the origin. All that remained for the *Newsweek* reporter to do was remind us that similar thefts and perversions of our cultural heritage, practiced by "the new militant cultural materialism of the left" yet go unexposed: "There's more than a trace of deconstruction in 'the new historicism'—" the article concludes, "which is one reason traditional humanists hope that it, too, will self-deconstruct in the wake of the de Man disgrace."

Why can the presumed discovery of the Nazi origins of deconstruction so effortlessly segue into an attack on the left? Because everybody knows that a stable literary canon containing a universal and decided set of values is the loadstone of democracy, and any critics prepared to remove such an architectural wonder are necessarily anti-democratic and therefore generally interchangeable.

There was in some quarters an hilarious astonishment when this article appeared which was partly caused by the curious ways in which it conformed to and diverged from the stories that left-wing critics of deconstruction had been spinning around the de Man scandal. By "left-wing" I mean critics whose opposition to de Man or to what they took to be de Man's impact on literary studies arose not from their desire to protect our cultural heritage, but rather from a desire to link literary studies to political or historical projects. From their point of view the de Man story *before* the discovery of the early writings went something like this. De Man had taken a potentially very "subversive" instrument for de-authorizing language—deconstruction—an instrument that in other hands was being used to dissolve the category of the literary, break down disciplinary boundaries, and stimulate new readings of the social text—and he had used it instead to solidify disciplinary boundaries and to empower a new ideology of the essential rhetoricity of the literary. Careful readings of de Man may show these charges to be simplistic, but his arguments were on occasion used to define the true nature of the literary, to delegitimize certain readings as not really "*readings,*" and to disqualify whole categories of inquiry into the sources and functions of texts. In short, de Manian deconstruction came to seem just one more attempt to limit the "proper" objects and methods of literary study.

Hence, many critics on the left came to regard de Manian criticism as a tool to "discipline" deconstruction, to lock up the idea of textuality in a celebration of the hyper-rhetoricity of a set of texts that had an uncanny resemblance to the "great works" that once formed "our cultural heritage." In short, deconstruction had not only been disciplined but was being sent out on border patrols to insure the integrity of the discipline's boundaries.

This was the subtext informing the reception of the discovery of de Man's collaborationist writings among certain left-wing critics; we might call it the subtext of the revolution betrayed. From these quarters, in response to the recent discoveries, we again hear narratives of origins, but rather more complex and nuanced ones than those emerging from *Newsweek*'s Arnoldian hysteria. Frank Lentricchia's (reported in Jon Wiener's *Nation* article of January 9) seems typical:

The man tried very hard to separate himself from his Belgian collaborationist past, to cut that thing out of himself. I think he suffered, he wished he never did it. He didn't start graduate school until 1952, when he was 33. What was he doing before that? Working in a bookstore, working for a publisher—a brilliant man, prepared for a literary career, who does nothing for several years. Why?

Then you come to deconstruction: a philosophy that says you can never trust language to anchor you into anything; that every linguistic act is duplicitous; that every insight you have is beset by blindness you can't predict. In an attempt to undercut politically engaged critics, de Man writes that whatever you thought about political events is not the case. His mature work is not just ahistorical; it is a principled, intentional, passionate antihistoricism. He didn't just say "forget history"; he wanted to paralyze the move to history. And the work is beautifully rigorous. There's not a better example in the world.

There are several noteworthy differences between this account of how de Man's stint as a collaborationist journalist determined the rest of his career and *Newsweek*'s. Here, de Man suffers, is remorseful, paralyzed, silenced by what he has done. He buries himself in obscurity. According to the way Lentricchia is quoted here, deconstruction allows de Man to break this silence by making all linguistic acts somehow equally guilty, equally groping, ignorant, blind and irresponsible. Like *Newsweek*'s, this is a story of how an irresponsible linguistic act is followed by a theory of language's necessary irresponsibility, but in Lentricchia's story the theory is a healing balm to crippling wounds of conscience instead of the mere continuation of earlier nihilistic modes of thought. Another difference is that in Lentricchia's account deconstruction predates de Man's use of it; it isn't created by and for de Man's problem. The simple identity of origins, uses and essences is disrupted here. But antipolitical and antihistorical uses of deconstruction, we should note, are laid squarely at de Man's door. In order to save himself from being paralyzed by his history, Lentricchia implies, he tried to "paralyze the move to history" on the part of other critics. The reactionary use of deconstruction does grow out of de Man's collaboration, not as *Newsweek* would have it simply as a continuation of fascist nihilism, but rather as an insistence on discontinuity that would leave history always as the domain of the unknowable.

Lentricchia's story, which I take to be typical of a certain left-wing reaction, relies on an assumed economy of substitutions. De Man's use of deconstruction is sign and symptom of his guilt because it appears in the place of what should have been his confession. First there was the guilty act, then there was silence, then there was deconstruction instead of confession. Since deconstruction appeared where confession should have appeared it is like confession as a sign of guilt and unlike confession as a screen for guilt. It is the equivalent opposite of confession; hence it is doubly guilty. The fact that de Man didn't confess is the often unaduced evidence for characterizing his use of deconstruction as an alibi. De Manian deconstruction occupies the alibi position, that of a counterlanguage to confession, and hence would be suspect no matter what it said. But conveniently it speaks of the impossibility of confession, a feature of this particular alibi that now seems so self serving to some commentators that it need no longer be attended to seriously.

However, other commentators have used this very fact that deconstruction occupies the confession position as the ultimate proof of de Man's intellectual and moral integrity. For these same writings that take the place of confession unsettle the equivalence of opposition between confession and alibi. Most often cited in this regard is de Man's "Purloined Ribbon" essay; it provides the framework for a heroic narrative, a narrative now told by several of his students, friends and defenders. The principle informing this story is that of de Man's integrity, and its point is that de Man did not fail to confess because he wanted to hide the truth; rather he staunchly resisted the temptation to confess because he knew that confession is just another mode of self-excuse. As the "The Purloined Ribbon" maintains, confession is an alibi through which one constructs a narrative of self-overcoming, of progressive enlightenment, and hence of present innocence; self-accusation is inevitably selfexculpation. Geoffrey Hartman expands on the point in *The New Republic* of March 7: "According to de Man's analysis, enlightenment as such cannot resolve error, and even repeats it, if one is deluded into thinking that the new position stands in a progressive and sounder relation to language, that it has corrected a historical mistake once and for all. Even to say, quite simply, 'I was young, I made a mistake, I've changed my mind' remains blind if it overlooks the narrative shape of this or any confession." Rather than risk the perpetuation of such blindness, Hartman implies, de Man substituted for a confession writings that explicate the very substitution they enact by showing that confessions are themselves mere ideological substitutions of personal or historic pathos for the pathos that was actually there—linguistic pathos. This non-confession turns out to be far more revelatory than any mere confession could have been because it bares, in Hartman's words, "the painful knowledge that he had been trapped by an effect of language, an ideological verbiage that blinded critical reflection."

There are powerfully anti-narrative moments in Hartman's story of the anti-confessional confession, as there would have to be since narrative itself is rendered very problematic in this analysis. For example, he urges us to read the relationship between the collaborationist pieces and the later work in a de Manian way: "De Man's method of reading implies that the relation between late and early is interlinguistic only." The collaborationist essays are to be seen as the "original" text, the failures of which are the failures of textuality in general (confusion of linguistic with natural reality, etc.), and the later works are said to play off of the original without committing the error of referring to it or pretending to be about it. The relationship between early and late is tropic.

Hartman's and Lentricchia's modes of constructing the subject of de Man might be usefully counterposed in terms of the opposition between dance and drama that de Man himself developed in his essay on Kleist in *The Rhetoric of Romanticism*. Hartman has substituted for Lentricchia's drama a kind of dance of de Man. For Lentricchia, the deconstructionist writing was caused by an attempt to suppress and/or excuse the collaborationism, was psychologically and personally motivated, and was legitimately expressive of the drama of a guilty conscience. For Hartman the relationship between the two sets of texts better fits this description from de Man of the relationship between movements in a dance: they are "once and for all cleansed from the pathos of self-consciousness as well as from the disruptions and ironies of imitation . . . There is no risk of [their being determined] by the dynamics of . . . passion or emotion rather than by the formal laws of tropes." De Man explains that, "No two art forms are in this respect more radically opposed than drama and dance." And no two accounts of de Man could be more radically opposed than Lentricchia's guilt-ridden man and Hartman's intertextual matrix.

But de Man is not ultimately privileging dance over drama in his essay, and it would be unfair to Geoffrey Hartman's article to imply that it so thoroughly aestheticizes the subject of de Man as to succumb to its own anti-narrative invitation. Hartman doesn't really have the will to keep de Man dancing; his de Man sacrifices the essay's logical rigor by falling into recurrent spasms of dramatic self-expression. Despite themselves the very tropic moves indicate personal, historical, pathos. The anti-confession, the discourse of confessions itself, can't help but become in Hartman's story, "the fragments of a great confession," which "may constitute an avowal of error, a kind of repudiation in its very methodology." The anti-confession, for Lentricchia a mere alibi, becomes the super confession for Hartman because it avoids the self-delusion and self-exculpation at the heart of all other confessions. Thus to Hartman, de Man's dance "looks like a belated, but still powerful, act of conscience."

This act of conscience, moreover, has a clear political meaning. The collaborationist nature of the early work only makes his later writings appear "more and more as a deepening reflection on the rhetoric of totalitarianism." Thus, not only has de Man's embarrassing past proved his utter intellectual and moral integrity, it has also proved the political purity (the anti-totalitarianism) of deconstruction, which is now readable as "not an escape into, but an escape out of, aestheticism: a disenchantment with that fatal aestheticizing of politics . . . that gave fascism its false brilliance." In a striking inversion of the *Newsweek* article, we are asked to remember that there is a totalitarianism of the left as well as the right and that, "Many on the left also welcomed . . . 'sinister unifying,' and succumbed to xenophobic and anti-Jewish sentiment." Whereas *Newsweek* had aligned deconstruction with the right and the left, Hartman suggests that it is a profound critique of political extremism in general.

The answer to my opening question—What has been learned from the revelations about de Man?—should be clear by now. Everyone learned everything he already knew. Hindsight has revised nothing and confirmed everything. Because de Man was a Nazi, according to *Newsweek,* we'd better be on guard against the left. Because he was a collaborationist trying to make a break with his past, according to Lentricchia, his later work has been exposed as reactionary. Because he was a collaborationist and he didn't confess, according to Hartman, we can now see the heroic dimensions of his intellectual honesty and the antitotalitarianism of his later work. De Man and his writings are either worse than ever or better than ever depending on where you started out. This was a revelation that revealed nothing at all.

We could draw many conclusions from this. We could say that this revelation shares its nonrevelatory nature with all revelations, and that we only learn what we already know. Prior emplotments always prevail. But such a conclusion would be at once grandiose, out of all proportion to the subject at hand, and banal. Alternatively, we might conclude that under current circumstances our narratives about ourselves and our profession are uninterruptable. Nothing right now could impede their flow, probably least of all a revelation that asks us to connect our recent intellectual and professional history to the holocaust. As the founding horror of the post-war world order, the holocaust still occupies a place beyond our rational grasp. Finally, we might conclude that we've learned nothing new because we've been asking the wrong question. Each of the above narratives has sought the inherent politics of deconstruction. Each

has tried to decide this politics by defining the relationship between the later theory and de Man's early writings; deconstruction is political insofar as it continues, denies or atones for fascist collaborationism. But the very variety of these claims may in fact demonstrate that deconstruction both has no necessary or inherent politics and is nevertheless highly politicized. If we look to de Man's career to explain this politicization, our thinking necessarily becomes circular because, as we've just seen, the various versions of de Man's career are current political effects as much as causes. If we could admit that de Man's career will not give us the key to the politics of deconstruction, then perhaps we might find more inclusive and dispassionate ways of exploring its significance. But one thing is certain: we have yet to learn what there is to learn from the subject of Paul de Man.

University of California, Berkeley

Edges of Understanding

RODOLPHE GASCHÉ

Undoubtedly, the discovery of de Man's early journalistic writings represents a formidable legacy for his friends and foes alike. The bequest consists of coming to grips, in an intellectually and ethically responsible fashion, with the shocking fact that during a brief period, the young de Man wrote a literary chronicle for *Le Soir,* a newspaper whose political columns were at that time under strong German control. Responsible examination, however, requires detailed and in-depth documentation of the historical, cultural and political situation of Belgium between 1939 and 1942, so that the truly incriminating facts can be established with the necessary precision, and no confusion remains as to what under the given circumstances can and cannot be laid to de Man's charge. Responsible examination also requires that such inquiry be conducted in the spirit of respect that both friend and foe, as Others, demand. Yet, from the precipitation with which de Man's case has been taken up by the academic community and the newspapers, from the ludicrous and delirious charges leveled against him, as well as from the hatred that is evident in so many of the accounts, it is more than clear that the challenge of determining exactly what de Man's wartime activities amount to and what they mean has not been met. Or rather, since most of the discussions that have taken place have deliberately dismissed the most elementary rules of documentation (in this case, reading for instance, the incriminating material) as well as all other standards of philological honesty and integrity, not to mention the basic ethical guidelines for any debate, the minimal conditions for discussion have simply not been met. On cannot but be deeply terrified by the silliness, stupidity and maliciousness of the accounts in question, especially if one keeps in mind that the primary goal of the rage in question is a settling of accounts with "deconstruction." Indeed, one must assume that such trampling of all rules intellectual and ethical in the rampage against de Man and "deconstruction" is supposed to set future standards for the academic community. Disregard of history, disrespect for textual evidence, wild analogization, subjective elucubration, irrational outburst, are among the stupefying exemplars raised to the status of precepts for the learning community.

If we are then to take account of de Man's war-time writings, and if we may, indeed, be compelled to consider them irresponsible and unpardonable, let us at least establish as precisely as possible what it is that we may have to judge as inadmissible. Intellectual probity and moral integrity require that we do so.

De Man's collaboration with a Nazi-controlled newspaper was obviously utterly irresponsible. But if this is not to be an abstract judgment (and thus a misjudgment) the irresponsibility has to be set into its proper context: the desire on the part of the young de Man to write on literature, perhaps at any price (a desire which becomes understandable if one recalls that his education did not permit him to study literature at any Belgian university), his economic situation, the publication opportunities in Belgium at that time, or the fact that he stopped writing for the literary column of *Le Soir* when that column was censured as well, etc. Fully irresponsible also is one article of the approximately 290 articles and reviews that he wrote between 1939 and 1943—"Les Juifs dans la Littérature Actuelle" (*Le Soir,* March 4, 1941)—that uses undeniably anti-Semitic language, and perhaps two others which are much more ambiguous, as we will see in a moment, and which, respectively, hold Jews responsible for decadence in art and seem to celebrate Hitlerianism as the essence of the German soul. But these two last essays—"A View on Contemporary German Fiction" (*Het Vlaamsche Land,* August 20, 1942) and "*Voir La Figure,* de Jacques Chardonne" (*Le Soir,* October 28, 1941)—definitely fall in a different category from the article on the Jews in literature. As I will argue, these two articles, in different ways, give in, more clearly than the others, to some Nazi stereotypes which they are naive enough to believe that they can circumvent and undo by textual maneuvers. To have given in to making use of these stereotypes, however ambiguously, to have perhaps believed that they could be subverted by other articles de Man wrote at that time, is perhaps a sign not necessarily of irresponsibility, but certainly of naiveté and confusion. But let me come back to "Les Juifs dans la Littérature Actuelle." It is the one truly incriminatory piece. Although the essay is undoubtedly rather complex, and is, as Derrida has pointed out—not in what Richard Bernstein calls "a bravura act of deconstruction," but merely in an act of attentive reading of what this text unmistakably tells us—motivated by a desire to criticize vulgar anti-Semitism (and through it perhaps all anti-Semitism),[1] it also speaks of Jews as foreign, or alien powers, of having meddled in all aspects of European life (except literature), and finally refers in a quite equivocal manner to the possibility of solving the Jewish problem by creating a Jewish colony isolated from Europe. Obviously, these statements are a far cry from the official anti-Semitism of the day, but they are nonetheless objectionable and unpardonable. If one can trust testimony by relatives and close friends (Jewish and non-Jewish) of the young Paul de Man, he had not the least strain of Anti-Semitism. But that in order to be able to write in these journals he gave in to the language of Nazi ideology, that he did not resist anti-Semitic stereotypes on several occasions, these are the facts with which we must charge de Man. They speak to his confusion at the time, to a certain blindness and opportunism on his part. These facts are bad

enough, but, making due allowances, one must also admit that, however awful, they are rather harmless. The *Auditeur Général* who examined Paul de Man after the war decided not to pursue his case—in contrast to other journalists of *Le Soir*. This amounts to clearing de Man of the charge of collaboration and is thus evidence of the political and historical insignificance of his wrongdoings. In short, his wrongdoings must be seen in their proper perspective. To disregard the exact nature of his "crime," as it has been called, is to bear witness to an inexcusable injustice resulting either from stupidity or maliciousness. But it is not only an injustice regarding de Man himself—as when Jon Wiener calls him "something of an academic Waldheim"[2]—it is also more importantly, more atrociously, an inexcusable injustice with respect to the Jewish people. To put Waldheim and de Man on the same plan is to show a staggering lack of historical discrimination which implies a shameless belittling of Nazi atrocities and the suffering of the Jewish people during World War II. Indeed, from many of the articles published on the de Man issue, it is rather obvious that their authors, or some of those quoted for statements, are less concerned with historical accuracy than with the attempt to settle accounts, even if this takes place at the price of all justice and decency. The de Man affair, although it has found its way into major newspapers, is a strictly academic affair. It makes sense only with respect to a debate that divides academics around something called "deconstruction." To score a hit against this spectre of perversion as its critics see it, they are willing, as one could witness over the last several months, to trash all standards of intellectual and ethical integrity. What is thus truly at stake in this debate is, as mentioned above, nothing less than the minimal criteria and rules of professional ethics and intellectual probity.

Naturally one understands the groundless assertions and authoritarian presumptions leveled against de Man, without difficulty. Nothing is easier to fathom than their riskless pretensions that are of the order of irrational outbursts and settling of accounts. In traditional terms, they belong to the immediacy of nature, or what Benjamin calls the "mythical." Riskless, these assertions fall behind as they fail to make the leap without which no thinking gets off the ground. Many may share them, and yet they do not hold, to adapt Kantian terminology, before a tribunal that assures to reason its lawful claims. But, one understands them just as easily for their complete lack of all objectivity and universality.

If, consequently, one article which contains decidedly anti-Semitic statements, two that in spite of their ambiguity still seem to tilt in the direction of anti-Semitic ideology or of an uncritical acception of Hitlerianism, and finally the fact that most of these articles were written for a newspaper that followed (as far as its political content was concerned) a Nazi line, are the incriminating charges to be held against the young journalist as clearly disastrous evidence that allows for no attenuation, what then is the status of the remaining articles—288 to be precise? What happens if we read them?

To read, here, means to attentively seek to understand the sense of the writings in question which also implies situating them in their proper context, a skill normally to be expected from educated persons, but nowadays often associated with deconstruction, especially if the sense of the written does not fit preconceived notions. For anyone who is cognizant of the issues debated by both the left and the right between the wars, as well as of the style of those debates, these are not collaborationist or pro-Nazi writings as they have been labeled on numerous occasions. One cannot even say that they express a clear sympathy for German culture and literature.[3] They certainly do not advocate any of the themes of German cultural politics. Still, since the bulk of these articles is far from being unambiguous, and I more often than not feel quite ill at ease with what I read in them,I choose to approach them through the two articles that I have singled out as being on the borderline between anti-Semitism and the inefficient subversion of its premises. Indeed, all the articles written during the occupation that are not just simple reviews have such a double face, owing to de Man's sometimes successful, sometimes unsuccessful, maneuvers between ideological positions. Sometimes the stakes are high as is the case with the two articles in question—"A View on Contemporary German Fiction," and the Chardonne review—most of the time, the issues debated are of secondary interest. But from the start let us emphasize that such maneuvering is not characteristic of Nazi writings. Although one would have liked to see de Man opt unambiguously for one of the positions in question, and in spite of the fact that these articles convey at times a shocking violence, one must have the honesty to admit that in tone and style they are quite different from any of the collaborationist writings of the period. To show this, let me then focus, first on "A View on Contemporary German Fiction." In this article, de Man, seemingly in conformity with the Nazi defamatory evaluation of modern art, classifies expressionism as "aberrant" and "degenerate." In addition, he claims "that it was mainly non-Germans and specifically Jews that went in this direction." It is undoubtedly difficult to remain aloof when encountering such a statement, in particular, since it echoes the accusation made by the Nazis that this art is "subversive," and "un-German" (*undeutsch*). De Man, indeed, demar-

cates the "strongly cerebral disposition founded upon abstract principles and very remote from all naturalness" of the expressionist group, from another group at work in Germany that "remained true to the proper norms of the country." Nothing, ultimately, will make one's discomfort go away regarding these painful utterances by the young de Man. Yet, such distress does not exempt us from the obligation to examine these quotations in their proper context—the content of the article itself, as well as the whole production over the three years in question. Because I am profoundly upset by what I read I am not acquitted from the responsibility of reading the texts in which these statements occur and of properly situating them. Intellectual probity requires that I acknowledge the following: First, expressionism as a whole is not condemned, but only a certain group that uses "the in themselves very remarkable theses of expressionism" in an aberrant fashion.[4] In no way identical to the Nazi condemnation of expressionism which include those "very remarkable theses" as well, and which made no distinction between groups within this movement, de Man's elaborations are also extremely elusive as to the identity of the group he is talking about. Second, the "good" German literature pitted against this limited group of expressionist writers is not characterized in terms that would emphasize their Germanic qualities (*deutsch,* or *völkisch*) but in terms that stress this literature's "assimilation of foreign norms which are transformed and reduced to a number of specific and constant values in order to become the own spiritual property of the nation." Small wonder, then, if among the writers thus celebrated de Man not only lists Carossa and Stehr whose mysticism and ethical concerns are indeed more specifically German according to de Man's classification, but also, and especially, Jünger and Alverdes whose susceptibility to French sensibility and psychological analysis is underlined as a characteristic of the status of their work as "world literature." This characterization of "good" German literature is not in conformity with the premises of Nazi cultural politics geared toward the elimination of all literature not only of bolshevist but also of cosmopolitan signature.Third, the cerebral quality of expressionism, that sets it over and against the other type of German literature, is an attribute associated throughout all the articles not only with Jewish thinking but with French culture in particular. As we have seen, at least one group of the German writers that de Man celebrates in his essay is influenced by a cerebrality which in their case is even raised "to the realm of crystal clear beauty." And finally, the qualification 'degenerate' is, at least, complicated by the fact that de Man seeks to keep French artistic production clear from such accusations. Taken as a whole, French literature is said to be engaged in experiments that show "aberrations of such strength" that they cannot be classified. Yet, he goes on, it would be "a dangerous artificial simplification" to apply the criterion "degenerate" to French art. In an article from the same journal (dated May 17–18, 1942, entitled "Contemporary Trends in French Literature") he notes that "monstrous hair-splitting" and a "style which has used up all of its vital force" (to be found on English and Dutch rather than on French soil) is not without "indisputable merit" if one thinks of Joyce, Woolf, or Vestdijk. As he points out here, "decadence and inferiority are not necessarily synonymous." Considering this positive valorization of the notion of decadence, a valorization based precisely on some of the dominant features of Nazi characterizations of decadence, one cannot but wonder what this notion can still mean when applied to a group of expressionist writers. The fact remains, of course, that de Man depicts this group as "decadent," and that he writes that "mainly non-Germans and specifically Jews" contributed to the production of the group in question. But after what we have seen, what precisely can the semantic value of the term "decadent" be? From the article, one gathers that this term designates cheap showmanship, artificiality, the "calculation of easy effects," "forced and caricatured representation of reality" (which, by the way, is not, as we will see later, the strength of German literary writing, according to de Man), "cheap success by using imported formulas." "Decadent" thus means nothing less and nothing more than lousy, artless art, perhaps also vulgar art in the sense that de Man gives this term on several occasions. "Decadent" also means the inability to assimilate foreign norms—apparently a strength of German literature—and thus the failure to mediate imported values and the spiritual values of a nation. Such failure turns the imported into cheap effects in art, into artless artifice. The article, as we have seen, associates "mainly non-Germans and specifically Jews" with this failure. It is difficult, if not impossible, to know whom de Man is particularly thinking of here, especially since not all of expressionism is included in this condemnation. Moreover, such characterization of the group in question does not match very well with its "apparently strong cerebral disposition." It harmonizes even less with the brilliant cerebral qualities of the Jewish mind, to which he refers in the article on "Les Juifs dans la Littérature Actuelle." In the same way that the pejorative use of "decadent" merely means "cheap" and "artless," the reference to the Germans, non-Germans, and Jews responsible for decadent art seems to boil down to a reference to third-rate artists. Kafka, undoubtedly, does not fall into this category. In short, then, the distressing fact remains that de Man draws on some themes of Nazi ideology, and that he gives in to the denunciatory gestures

of pointing at alien forces and influences. This fact remains, and in all its bewildering force. But what a more careful reading of a text such as the one just analyzed shows is that the terms and the gestures referred to, when not simply hollowed out as is the case with the notion of "decadence," are complicated to the point of confusion. No deconstruction is necessary to see this, just a simple attentive reading. What such a reading brings to light is the true dimension of what we must continue to be upset about—namely to have given in to drawing on Nazi stereotypes and ideological themes, unaware of the danger that they represented, in the naive hope of containing them through textual manipulation. But once again, this sorry fact, for both historical as well as material reasons, is no excuse for calling de Man's early writings Nazi or collaborationist propaganda. Although the ambiguity of some of these texts remains intact, and although one's discomfort with some of their topics lingers on, one must also remain sensible to the strategies they display. One must, to do justice, patiently follow de Man's moves throughout these texts, in a war of displacements that could not be won.

In an article entitled "Que pensez-vous de la guerre?" (*Jeudi,* January 4, 1940), he writes: "In the same way that one has to eliminate the causes of the war in order to overcome the war, so one must prevent creating a terrain propitious to its development in order to overcome Hitlerianism." With this aim in view, he recommends a total reversal of European interior and exterior politics, a reversal that would serve to overcome the nationalist spirit of the European countries which is at the root of the problems that have led to the war. Although the bulk of the articles written for *Le Soir, Cahiers du Libre Examen,* and *Het Vlaamsche Land,* need a more careful and patient study than I can devote to them here, it can be said that with the German occupation of Belgium, with the German hegemony in Europe having become an indisputable fact, de Man turns away from the internationalism of his writings in *Jeudi,* and takes recourse to the themes of nationalism and cultural patrimony in order to resist German rule. This issue which is a decisive thread throughout most of the articles—the concern with national personality and difference, patriotic feeling, the protection if not creative development of the national patrimony, the insistence on the independence of nationalities—is incongruous with the dominant Nazi ideology. Now, it is certainly true that defense of national autonomy belonged, at first, to the type of opposition permitted (and even encouraged for a brief period) by the occupation forces. De Man's emphasis on nationalism would thus seem to be a part of what was tolerated by the Nazis, and to lack all connotations of resistance. But this initial liberalism on the part of the Nazis came to an end toward the beginning of 1943 when it was no longer permitted to publicly reflect on the destiny of Belgium in the new European order. It was not an abrupt end, however, to the extent that truly energetic defense of national independence had never been to the liking of the occupiers. But to evaluate de Man's stress on nationalism it is, indeed, necessary to realize that independently of the initial climate of tolerance that existed in Belgium, national politics could not, in principle, be compatible with the implicit and explicit aims of Nazi politics. According to Heinrich Himmler's directive for "the new European order," all development of national consciousness and culture was to be foiled, especially, (or let's say, first) in the East. All national cultural and artistic life was to be destroyed, as has been demonstrated in the case of Poland.[5] De Man's continuous emphasis on the independence of nationalities, especially in his writing for the Nazi controlled *Le Soir,* is thus a paradox of sorts that needs to be investigated a little further.

From the outset, let me say that not everything in these articles is entirely consistent. Especially when it comes to evaluating the role of Germany in Europe, what Germany's annexational politics and hegemony mean for Europe as a whole, de Man wavers. In March 1942 ("A la recherche d'un nouveau mode d'expression"), he writes: "For him who like me finds himself immersed in the hurly-burly of facts and actions, it is difficult to acquire a sufficiently synthetic overview of things in order to be able to grasp the meaning and the direction of the evolution that one is going through." Yet, in spite of all these doubts, uncertainties, and ambiguities whose effects (to the extent that they produce occasionally one-sided valorizations) are of course not negligible, a quite coherent picture arises if one reads the totality of the articles. This picture provides, indeed, an answer to the question of how de Man understood the German hegemony in Europe, and what the occasional reference to "immediate collaboration" in his articles could have meant. In a review from October, 1941 of Jacques Chardonne's book, *Voir La Figure*—that is, in the second borderline article—de Man explains that "the future of Europe can only be anticipated within the frame of the possibilities and the needs of the German genius." The war, he notes, is the result of "the definitive emancipation of a people that finds itself, in its turn, called upon to exercise a hegemony in Europe," of a people in which the "Hitlerian soul" fuses with the "German soul" for reasons that lie with "elementary givens, that is, with the historical constants that give the German people its unity and specific character." Now, what this means for de Man, and it is clearly spelled out, is that this war has a "national character." However deceptive this conclusion may seem (and we will come back to this issue

later), one cannot overlook its rather unorthodox implication: if the war is a symptom of Germany's coming into its own proper national identity, then the hegemony that it is supposed to play in Europe must, obviously, come to a halt precisely at the borders of the other national blocks that make up Europe as a whole. As for many other thinkers during the years before the war (but afterward as well: E. R. Curtius, for instance), for de Man "Europe," and "Western culture and civilization," are politico-cultural categories in the name of which all events become evaluated. But what distinguishes de Man's concept of "Europe" from that of a Europe under German rule, or of a Europe as a spiritual unity beyond all nationalities (Curtius), is his insistence on the constituting role of the various nationalities that make up Europe as a geographical unit. De Man's emphasis on a "European thinking" in which "national sentiments can freely come to expression and . . . (in which) every nation is fully conscious of its own worth" (*Het Vlaamsche Land,* 29–30 March 1942), has the practical aim of defending "Western culture against a decomposition from the inside out or a surprise attack by neighboring civilizations"(ib.). It goes without saying that this concern with warding off "the increasingly menacing interferences" that threaten the values of the West (*Le Soir,* March 12, 1942), can lend itself to all forms of xenophobia, anti-Semitism first and foremost. "Les Juifs dans la Littérature Actuelle" is ample proof of this, as many of the present accounts of the de Man affair also exhibit a similar xenophobia of their own. Indeed, any discourse, then and now, that becomes set on defending a state of affairs, or values in the name of the proper, homogeneity, continuity, etc. *can* slip into fascist exorcism of the Other. The debate around the de Man affair and "deconstruction" is just another case in point. But, apart from some occasional ambiguities, de Man's insistence on a nationalism whose conception is "miles apart from sentimental patriotism" (*Het Vlaamsche Land,* March 29–30, 1942), serves to counter nationalistic isolation and hardening, and to keep interference by one nation in the affairs of another in check. Indeed, "the disappearance of one of those original centers [the individual nations, R.G.], as a result of political arbitrariness or economic injustice," has to be avoided at all cost since it would mean "an impoverishment for the whole of Europe," de Man writes (ib.). Paradoxically, the idea of a "European parallelism" (ib.), that is of a nationalism that is "the exact opposite of being exclusive," is said to have been developed primarily in Germany (*Le Soir,* March 31, 1942), thus, by that nation which, at the time de Man is writing, has occupied most of Europe. Of this present nationalism, de Man says that it is "complementary. Its object is to discover the national virtues, to cultivate and to honor them, but also to adapt them to those of neighboring peoples in order to achieve through such summation of the particular gifts, a real unification of Western culture" (*Le Soir,* April 28, 1942). This is the point, then, where the references to the question of collaboration can be discussed. It is raised by de Man precisely in the *Le Soir* article on Chardonne (October 28, 1941) in which he argues that the German hegemony and the ensuing war are profoundly nationalistic in character. Yet he notes that the arguments that plead for immediate collaboration please only those who are already of such an opinion while they fail to convince anyone who is not. Similarly, in an article from October 14, 1941, after having claimed that the need for action under the form of immediate collaboration "is a compelling reality to any objective mind," he claims that it is too early to "become disheartened by the universal incomprehension [regarding this necessity, R.G.] and to withdraw into one's ivory tower," because in any case such "activity cannot take on a direct and material form." The context for these statements is a review of Daniel Halévy's *Trois Epreuves* in which de Man insists that France can only be saved if it returns to its past in order to "discover among the laws, customs, and aspirations that constitute the patrimony of the nation, those that need to be eliminated or favored for the regeneration to take place." From this context, it becomes clear that "immediate collaboration," a necessity that arises from the need of a nation under German rule to choose between death and life, in no way means collaboration with the Nazi oppressor in the sense of denationalization and assimilation into the *Reich.* This is clearly spelled out in "Le destin de la Flandre" (*Le Soir,* September 1, 1941), where such temptation is called catastrophic. "Immediate collaboration" is said to be indirect and non-material because all it can consist of is a furthering of national identity and independence (thus exactly the opposite of what the Germans demanded of the subjected countries). It is thus not a collaboration with the occupier that de Man is advocating here, but collaboration at creating a Europe where "a free contact between peoples that know themselves as different and insist on difference, but also hold each other mutually in high esteem, secures political peace and stability" (*Le Soir,* August 28, 1942). It is a collaboration, thus, that seeks to contain the assimilation threat by working at creating a Europe in which each nation, although it tries at first to be itself, also respects the character of other nations, "and does not dream for one moment to impose its own views"(ib.). The question that remains undecided is whether such European parallelism is to be achieved under German rule ("We can only be dignified members of a German state in so far as that state allows us to be dignified Dutchmen"), or in a Europe in which the German cultural bloc is contained by

an equally powerful French cultural bloc ("'To be dignified Dutchmen' amounts to maintaining between the two cultural blocs that are France and Germany that center [*noyau*] that was able to give humanity admirable products of an independent genius"). This uncertainty traverses all the articles, and in particular "Le destin de la Flandre" (September 1, 1941), from which I drew the preceding citations. Yet the sympathy of the young journalist is clearly with a Europe in which a confederation of nationalities evens out the strengths and weaknesses of any particular nation. This is manifest especially in the decisive role that de Man implores the French to play with respect to German culture within a unitary Europe. The fact that de Man is at times critical of French cerebrality, and has some good things to say about German novels, has led a number of hasty interpreters to conclude that his sympathies were unequivocally with German culture. Nothing could be more wrong, as a patient reading of the articles in their totality reveals. Indeed, de Man's pessimistic account of French thought between the wars, and above all since the armistice, has all the qualities of a call to action. In his eyes, only French genius can in the long run contain German mysticism and obscurantism. Let me develop this point in some greater detail.

In a review of Friedrich Sieburg's "Dieu est-il français?" (*Le Soir,* April 28, 1942), de Man defines the collapse of France as "signifying infinitely more than just another episode in the present war. It is the destruction," he writes, "of a spirit, a system of values, of an entire *Weltanschauung,* which marks a decisive date in the history of civilization." What has made this collapse possible, and forecloses any "optimism as to the future possibilities of French culture," is the French's stubborn entrenchment in a mentality of individualism. It is a mentality, de Man remarks in an article on *Notre Avant-Guerre* by Robert Brasillach (*Le Soir,* August 12, 1941), profoundly unpolitical and involved with aesthetic and poetic pleasure. What de Man terms on several occasions "the present revolution," however, is, he writes, political, and corresponds as an "inevitable necessity" to "the peoples who have a very developed notion of the collective, and who have spontaneously turned to modes of life that are less individualistic." The French, by contrast, lack political sense. Their individualism prevents them from understanding the true causes of the collapse of France. It is interesting to note here that it is especially French writers who are right-wing sympathizers that de Man accuses of lacking this sense of the political. Brasillach is a case in point. As proof of this inability on the part of writers to understand what is happening in Germany, de Man writes—in a sentence whose violence remains astounding in spite of the point that it tries to make: "The reaction of

Brasillach before a spectacle such as that of the Nazi party congress at Nurnberg on the occasion of which he shows terror about the 'strange' nature of that demonstration, is that of someone for whom this sudden importance of the political in the life of a people represents an inexplicable phenomenon." This discovery of the political by the German people not only translates as an effervescence of grandeur and a sense of the infinite, it also takes on an aura of mysticism. "We enter a mystical era, a period of faith and belief. . . ," de Man writes in his review of Sieburg's book. It is an era that resembles in many ways that of the Middle Ages. Yet, in an article on Drieu la Rochelle's *Notes pour comprendre le siècle*" (*Le Soir,* December 9, 1941), de Man shows himself very critical of such an ideal, and the antirationalism associated with it ("theories that show a contempt close to hatred for cerebrality and that turn more toward the animal virtues that exist in man"). In the Sieburg review, however, he seems at first to endorse the ideal in question to the extent that the norms that constitute the present political situation, and that "several authors" have compared to those of the Middle Ages, are said to possess today "the superiority of an extremely perfected technical and political organization" and to be permeated with "the lesson of an entire humanist past that protects against all obscurantism." But de Man does not seem to be too confident as to this last point, since it is on this occasion, precisely, that he appeals to the virtues of clarity, logic, and harmony that characterize French spirit. In the same way as he had already praised rationalism against Drieu la Rochelle, here again de Man takes recourse to "a certain form of French reason that seeks to fix the limits everywhere and to establish moderation." Indeed, the role of French cerebrality is essential to contain the obscurantism that pervades the political as it articulates itself in Germany. De Man writes: "The maintenance of the continuity of the French spirit is an inherent condition of the grandeur of Europe. Especially if the general orientation goes towards the deep, obscure, natural forces, the French mission that consists of moderating excesses, of maintaining the indispensable links with the past, of equilibrating the erratic drives, is of utmost importance." (And when right after this statement he calls upon the French "to freely open themselves to the foreign influences," it is precisely to ask them to play a moderating role by assuming the position of a cultural bloc that would hold at bay the nationalist excesses of Nazi Germany.) But this role of French intellectual culture is not merely limited to serving as a force of restraint vis-à-vis German extremism—such a role would, indeed, characterize French cerebrality as secondary and supplementary compared to German political culture—the French analytical and moderating spirit is ex-

pected to play a role equal to that of German profundity and mystical fervor. This becomes particularly clear in the article on "Le destin de la Flandre."

In this article, nationality is determined as an art that is specific to a people of a geographical area (and not in terms of culture which is defined as transnational), and de Man sets out to determine the irreducibly particular nature of Flemish art, and thus of that which profoundly distinguishes the Flemish nation from any other. Flemish art is subsequently determined according to categories that mark it off from those constitutive of the art and national spirit of other countries, more precisely from the art constitutive of what de Man calls here the two cultural blocs of Germany and France. Flemish art, he claims, is first and foremost, pictorial (even in literary writing) and realist. It is consequently different from French art, which is dominated by its abstract content (psychological analysis); but because it is realist, it is also opposed to German art, which "surrounds everything with a dreamlike mist." Indeed, it "remains realist in the sense that it tries to evoke nature in its rough state (*état brut*) without trying to catch its mystery by means of symbols"—the hallmark of German art. But symbolism which for de Man constitutes the essence of German artistic expression is also Romantic. Yet, in the same way that Flemish art must defend itself against French influences that risk hampering the Flemish creative elan, it must also be on guard against the German paradigm. As de Man puts it, "the romantic periods are not very favorable to the brilliant vitality of the Flemish artistic temperament which is oriented in an opposite direction." What is more, to become dissolved in a Germanic community would lead to the catastrophic state of effacing what constitutes, precisely, the profound originality of the Flemish genius. Under no circumstances must the political forces crush this creative potential, de Man notes, because it is bound to play a decisive role between the two cultural blocs of France and Germany, which are thus staged as independent, equally important nationalities and art styles. De Man's emphasis on the irreducible specificity of the Flemish genius thus seems to promote a plurality of independent nationalities that cohabit in one transnational unit—"Europe"—and in which none imposes its will on the others, although each becomes limited by the others, thus preventing the isolation and hardening of its own specificity. But his stress on the realist character of Flemish aesthetic sense could still have a further implication, namely that of being capable of mediating between the two opposite blocs, France and Germany. Indeed, whereas French genius proceeds to a cerebral analysis of phenomena, German symbolic art "does not teach us anything concrete and does not enrich our knowledge." All it does is to produce "that thrill (*frisson*) that emanates from great art," de Man writes (*Le Soir,* March 1, 1942). The Flemish spirit is thus capable of a mediating role between highly abstract knowledge and a powerful emotional apprehending of things. Since Flemish art (and thinking) "attempts to reproduce reality without hiding any of its aspects even most fleeting and most ignored," its artistic discipline is not only capable of indisputable grandeur, as de Man remarks in the article on Flanders, but perhaps of a knowledge more objective and more balanced than French abstraction and German feeling. De Man's insistence on the role that the Flemish are to play in Europe, "not as imitators of a neighbor whose state of mind is dissimilar," but as creators according to their own impetus, emphasizes the potential of this people for a less prejudiced understanding and realist accounting of what is happening in Europe.

Let me pause here for a moment. After having read as carefully as the present context permits some of the articles written for *Le Soir* and *Het Vlaamsche Land,* it should be evident that in spite of a variety of uncertainties and ambiguities that they contain, these articles cannot be called Nazi writings. They are not even sympathetic to the Nazi cause. They are, primarily, interested in protecting Flanders' independence. It must, however, be said that de Man's analytical vocabulary—his typology of nationalities and artforms, the binary oppositions of the aesthetic and the political, the abstract and the emotional, the spiritual and the social, the individual and the collective, rural and urban values, etc., as well as his emphasis on the spiritual unity of Europe (including Western civilization), and on what the individual nations are to contribute to it—has a strong traditionalist and conservative bent. Yet only someone who is ignorant of the intellectual climate between the wars, both on the left and the right, could mistake this analytical apparatus, and its use in de Man's journalistic writings, for rightist or collaborationist ideology. But to stress the traditionalist origin of de Man's categorial apparatus, as well as of his moves, is also to say that these articles are not very original and in themselves not especially interesting except perhaps for his emphasis on the specific character of the Flemish nation and the idiosyncratic implications of this valorization. Had he not become a well-known scholar at Yale, and were he not seen as a proponent of "deconstruction," these articles would have continued to go unnoticed. Although not particularly original, the articles are, however, intelligent, especially as far as their organization and their argumentative strategies are concerned. De Man's admiration for Valéry (and the rationalist spirit) is clearly expressed in several of the articles. On January 10–11, 1942, he writes: "This continuous need to reverify, to question (*mettre en doute*), to express reservations, is

an inevitable characteristic of any thinking that wishes to be rigorous." And he continues by saying that such "intellectual probity" manifests itself in a concern for exactitude and precision. Although de Man's categorial apparatus is very traditionalist, it is used with an analytical intent, and serves to get a hold on the events of the time by trying to circumscribe their meaning as precisely as possible. De Man's intellectual probity in the bulk of his journalistic writings—a probity, by contrast, blatantly absent from many of the recent articles published on his wartime productions—can be beheld in these essays' constant requestioning and delimiting of all the subjects broached. The typological vocabulary, as well as the set of binary oppositions, here serves to determine with as much accuracy as possible the contemporary situation, political and artistic, and not to polarize and to obscure it as would have been the case if the aim of the essays had been to commend Nazi ideology. This point being made, it must, however, also be acknowledged, that the essays of *Het Vlaamsche Land* and *Le Soir* do not show de Man to have sensed the catastrophic danger that Nazi Germany represented not only with respect to the Jewish people, but to the whole of Europe and the celebrated values of Western civilization as well. This is rather difficult to understand today, after the fact. But if de Man did not come to grips with the horror that was in the offing, it was *among other things* because his analytical apparatus did not provide the means to capture the viciousness and aberration of the Nazi endeavor *on all fronts.* Like so many other contemporary thinkers on the left and the right, the only categories that de Man had at his disposal to conceptualize his inevitable experience of the darker sides of Nazi ideology and the occupation, were those of obscurantism, historical and cultural regression, extremist polarization, etc. In spite of what I believe to have been a truly passionate attempt on de Man's part to understand as precisely as possible the reality he was facing, his intellectual instruments (like those of most of his contemporaries, and of many present intellectuals as well) prevented him from doing so. Faced with what was already visible in 1941 and 42, confronted with the implications of Nazi ideology, and in front of what was to come (the holocaust), humanistic language, traditional modes of thinking, and the type of understanding that it permits, had to fail miserably. It was left to the later de Man to systematically put into question all those blinding schemes, categories and concepts by means of which he had, in his journalistic writings, unsuccessfully tried to gain insight into the political situation in Belgium in the early forties.

Undoubtedly, it is the relation, the absence of relation, or something other than a relation (as I will suggest) between the early journalism and de Man's mature work that represents the most interesting problem in the debate triggered by the discovery of the early texts. All hasty assessments of this relation will necessarily take place at the price of intellectual accuracy and moral honesty. The number and complexity of the questions that have to be resolved before anything can be firmly established about this relation are enormous. The manner in which this relation has been described in several journals is clear evidence of the fact that none of these questions has been addressed, and that the linkage is being made in a prejudiced fashion—no analysis of what is to be related, of the *sort of relation that is possible, in the first place, between the relata,* seems to have been undertaken. In any case, the "critics" knew already in advance what they were going to say. The fact that it is seen as a relation between anti-Semitic and collaborationist texts and deconstructive texts is already testimony of such a prejudice, not to speak of the assessment of the relation between the two as either a covering up or as a secret continuation of the alleged pro-Nazism of the early texts.[7] Do the "critics" in question know what "deconstruction" is, and especially in its complex de Manian version that may—considering de Man's explicit reservations regarding deconstruction—share only the name with this brand of thinking? The answer, obviously, is no. Have they read the texts that they call pro-Nazi writings—read in the minimal sense defined above? Of course not, since that would considerably complicate their agenda. As for the relation that they establish between the two types of texts, anything goes as long as it can serve to deal a blow, preferably a violent one, to what most of these critics know by hearsay only or simply do not understand and that they call "deconstructionism," "deconstructivism," "deconstructionalism," "deconstruction," or the like.

I will not venture presently into a discussion of the complicated relation of de Man's mature work to deconstruction. I will refer only to what I consider the thrust of that later work by de Man, and to what sort of relation, hypothetically, one could perhaps consider worth discussing between that thrust and some of the issues in the earlier work. But in order to do so, I must return to the writings of the journalistic period. Although, in these early articles, de Man claims that literature is "an independent domain that has a life, laws, and obligations that belong to it alone, and that in no way depend on the philosophical and ethical contingencies that take place on its margins" (*Le Soir,* December 2, 1941), the inquiry characteristic of the bulk of all these essays written between 1939 and 1943, is historical, sociological, and pursues issues that are of immediate practical concern. The early de Man shares, indeed, with those "critics" who, at the present moment, want to turn this early

work against his later writings, a similar, if not the same method and aim of interpretation, and to a large extent the same values (humanistic, Western, etc.) with respect to which interpretation of literary works is to occur. This is, of course, one of the ironies of the present debate, and a clear sign of the rush and furor with which it is conducted. But let me do justice here to the early de Man, whose interesting understanding of history and its relation to literature, may become clouded through such a comparison with contemporary advocates of historical and sociological approaches to literature. The de Man of the forties was not a close reader of literary works (another trait he has in common with his enemies). In "Sur les possibilités de la critique" (*Le Soir,* December 2, 1941), he writes that "the analysis of works is not the ultimate aim of it [literary criticism, R.G.], but constitutes only a secondary and sometimes superfluous part of the examination." But although de Man did not consider analysis of individual works the main goal of literary criticism, he had a very clear sense of the specificity of the literary work, of the criteria that govern artistic values and that are not to be confounded with extraliterary values such as Good and Evil. The history that de Man is interested in concerns precisely these criteria that account for the specificity of artistic values. If de Man delves into the laws of genres, into their past origins, he does so not because of some aestheticist ideology that contemporary "critics" like to blame on anyone who respects the specificity of the domain of literature, but precisely for what he also considers the task of literary criticism to be, namely "a guide for the critical investigation of existing conditions" ("Criticism and Literary History," *Het Vlaamsche Land,* June 7–8, 1942). It is on the basis of such an historical investigation into the particular laws of the novel that de Man can refute arguments made on moral prejudices, on extraliterary inclinations—that is, on much the same ground on which the enemies of textual analysis, or of what they view as deconstructive readings, object to contemporary trends —, and which at the time de Man is writing served right-wing thinkers and Nazi ideologues to broadcast their indignation about the development of literature since the end of World War One (and to accuse the Jews of being responsible for this decadence). The historical study of the immanent laws of the genres permits de Man to argue for a necessary continuity between nineteenth century developments in the novel and what takes place in the writings of Proust, D. H. Lawrence, Gide, Kafka, and Hemingway. It represents the basis of his argument against vulgar anti-Semitism (in the article "Les Juifs dans la Littérature Actuelle") which made the Jews responsible for the alleged decadence since the end of the war. De Man's point here is that since the developments in twentieth century literature are the result of a continuous evolution of the realist agenda of the novel as a genre, there is no Jewish problem (at least as far as literature is concerned). Hence deporting the Jews to some colony isolated from Europe would not only have no deplorable consequences for the literary life of the Occident, but nothing would be won since literature would continue to evolve anyway according to its own laws as it always has. De Man's emphasis on history, his claim, in "Sur les possibilités. . . ," that "before being a critic, one must first be the historian of that branch of human activity that is literature," thus has two functions: to secure respect for that domain, and to serve as a tool to "pass judgment on what is happening around us *now*." Then and now, "critics" by resorting to extraliterary criteria have repressed the history proper to genres and modes of thinking. Yet, as de Man notes in "*Notes pour comprendre le siècle,* par Drieu la Rochelle" (*Le Soir,* December 9, 1941), "from the moment that one does not consider literature from the angle of art, but that one seeks to look at it as the unfolding of an ethical evolution, one can make use of it for just anything." Without trying in the least to exonerate the disconcerting aspects of these early texts, one cannot but remark that the "critics" have not been able to avoid the pitfalls pointed out by the young de Man. They have made his texts say just anything whether in the name of good intentions or just out of pure hatred. Ironically, they confirm a law formulated by the later de Man, that the meaning attributed to a text is always the result of a violent and arbitrary imposition.

I have returned to de Man's articles of the forties once again in order for anyone familiar with his later work to realize how different they are in tone and intent. They are sharp, undoubtedly, and yet of a sharpness that traditional forms of literary criticism at times possess.[8] But considering what the later de Man was to develop, the writings during the war cannot be called de Man's mature work, which, by the way, is one of the reasons why all comparison between Heidegger and de Man is impossible. Heidegger's collaboration, a collaboration that is much less equivocal than that blamed on de Man, took place when his thinking had already matured. De Man's early writings, however, are a far cry from what he was later to become involved in, and thus it is no small task to demonstrate any *significant* relations between the two corpuses, that is, relations that are not based on analogical inference, or that are not simply pure inventions. If the later work is called "deconstructive," then there is no relation whatsoever between the early essays and the later work, because the antecedents of deconstruction lie with phenomenology. No trace of phenomenology can be detected in de

Man's wartime publications. The difficulty in making a connection, however, has more profound, even essential reasons.

Although de Man has declared himself not to be a philosopher, his later work, say from *Allegories of Reading* to the project on aesthetics and ideology, indisputedly has a philosophical thrust. Even if it is the case that his later writings are not philosophical in a technical sense, if they make their argument in an unconventional manner, and do not even lead to the kind of tangible insights one would expect from philosophy, they presuppose and operate on a level of thinking comparable to that of philosophy, which demarcates them from other (empirical, regional) discourses such as literary criticism, for instance. Yet since such elevation to thinking does not go without what one variously calls abstraction, reduction, bracketing, or even stepping back, *simple* linkage of what has thus been transcended to the order of thinking, is no longer possible. All coupling, especially if it mobilizes types of relation that are themselves of empirical origin (cause/effect, reflection, metaphor, analogy, etc.), necessarily presupposes a disregard, a lack of awareness of the difference that thinking makes. In short, to decree a relation of thinking (according to models of relation that thinking transgresses) to doxa, ordinary consciousness, the natural attitude, is to do so out of ignorance of the specificity of philosophical thinking. When such connections are not made out of sheer ignorance of the difference of thinking, they are the result of a resentment against thinking.

In other words, if the later work of de Man has an undeniable philosophical bent, then it is impossible to make it derive from the writings of the journalistic period whether such derivation is conceived of either as a direct consequence, covering up, or as analogical reference. To bring the early work to bear on de Man's later work is a sign of disrespect for the realm of thinking to which his later texts have raised themselves. Now, this does not mean that these later texts could not contain explicit or implicit references to the writings of the war years. However, to hunt these references down without attention to their particular status in the thinking enterprise of the later de Man, that is, without taking into account what they serve to perform on the level of philosophical argumentation (a performance that is possible only if what these reference point to has been transformed to a certain level of generality), is an exercise in futility, if not merely an act of revenge.

But to demarcate as radically as I have done here the realm of thinking from that of ordinary experience—a difference that presupposes a bracketing of common modes of thought and concerns in order to achieve the realm of ideality characteristic of thinking as such—does not mean that no trace of what could be said to have been put to death, or actively forgotten, remains within thought itself. But if thinking is what it is, then such a trace to the past, the natural, the empirical, etc., cannot be a singular, concrete event, a particular past. What remains encrypted in the pure ideality of thinking as a trace of the abstraction and idealization process, must also be ideal in some sense. In short, since the universality inherent in thought presupposes that it is intelligible to any one, the trace of what has been bracketed by thinking to reach its specific domain cannot be something individual, singular. To put it differently, if it can be shown that the philosophical discourse mourns what it has put to death, then this must be a mourning that all of us can share and can become involved in to the extent that we are thinking beings. If de Man's later texts are, as I contend, philosophical in thrust, then the trace to a past and the mourning of what has been left behind, cannot ever be simply an autobiographical past or the particular expression of grief by a concrete individual. They must be assumable by others.[9] We must, therefore, out of respect for the order of thought that constitutes de Man's mature work, seek the relations that may exist between it and the writings from the journalistic period on a level appropriate to his thinking.

I mentioned already that by paying attention to the singular thrust of de Man's mature writings one could, perhaps, risk a hypothesis regarding possible links between it and the early writings. If one has already in advance decided on de Man's work as being "deconstructionist," this thrust cannot come into view, however, and one has, even before reading the work, lost the possibility of being challenged by it. To determine the particular verve of de Man's strong thinking I shall focus not on the whole of his work, but only on a particular important thread within it. This thread corresponds to what I have analyzed elsewhere in greater detail, as the attempt to conceive of, and to enact on a level pertinent to thinking, the absolute and irreducibly singular. Before concentrating on this issue, let me emphasize something that must be said of de Man's later work as a whole: it is a consistent and relentless attempt at debunking totalities, totalizing gestures, and ideologies in danger of turning totalitarian (even where his own work is concerned, including its "theoretical" direction). The thinking of irreducible singularity is one aspect of this critical journey. From what we have established with regard to the journalistic articles, it should be clear that de Man's concern with national peculiarity represented for him at that time the major critical tool for resisting the occupation forces and Nazi ideology. A continuity, on the basis of such a concern with singularity, could thus be affirmed between the two corpuses. But such a judgment would

indeed miss the essential, namely the difference between the two types of resistance against totalizing practices and gestures. Indeed, national particularity for de Man in the forties, although clearly braced against the notion of a *Reich,* is conceived of as a part of a whole—the spiritual unity of Europe. In addition, such national peculiarity, as has been seen, is determined in a differential manner (according to criteria such as symbolic, abstract, realist, for instance) which stresses the complementarity and mutual limitation of the various nationalities. Finally, de Man's mobilization of the notion of nationality takes place in the name of property and originality (the national patrimony), and is at the service of ideals such as continuity, unity, permanence, inner bond ("lien profond," says the article on "Le destin de la Flandre"), and so forth. Yet de Man's later work extends its criticism of totalizing gestures to precisely the categories that conditioned his early attempts to conceptualize singularity and its subversive function. Throughout his mature work, de Man consistently points to the totalizing function of categories such as continuity, organicism, bondage, etc. On this basis alone it is already imprudent to establish a continuity between the later and the earlier texts. But the rupture is, indeed, much more incisive if one considers that the interest in singularity has become a *philosophical* issue with the later de Man. With this I do not mean, of course, that his early attempts to grope with this issue are negligible. The later essays, however, have raised it to a level of thought, and to a type of treatment, unparalleled in the earlier reflections on national singularity. But as we will see in a moment that is not yet the whole difference.

First, let me briefly circumscribe what such an endeavor of thinking the absolutely singular involves. The activity of thinking consists, according to Hegel (but Hegel's definition is not particular to Hegel alone since he determines thinking in line with the tradition), of elevating (sublating) all limitation and particular singularity to the level of, and into, the universal. Such elevation by thinking is possible because a singularity, although a pointlike and entirely exterior moment, is never a purpose in itself. *As* a singularity (that is, according to its logical status), it refers not only to other singularities, but to its opposite, its Other, the universal, the whole thing (*die ganze Sache*), as Hegel puts it.[10] Because the singular and the contingent *relate to,* and thus *exit from themselves,* they are determined and destined from within to pass into the universal. Hegel expresses this necessary determination of the singular in a most succinct manner when he notes that the truth of the singular is the universal. To think the absolutely singular thus implies the thinking of a singularity that has no relation to, and thus withstands the dialectic of universalization. Absolved of all relation such a singular escapes thinking as the act through which the universal as such is taken possession of. Ultimately, such a singularity free of all reference (that is of reference to Other, but *to self as well*) does not fit any of the classical philosophical definitions of philosophy. From a standpoint of thinking it is a thoroughly idiosyncratic notion, that resists the universalizing bent of thought. The elaboration of such a notion is a prime thrust of de Man's rhetorical readings. What they seek to articulate by analyzing the literal, *material* properties of language, the *mechanical* rules of grammar, and the *historical* occurrence of linguistic acts, is nothing less than the entirely arbitrary (that is, void of all meaning, because entertaining no relation to), atomistic individualities (of language), each one of which is its own species (if one can still make use of this terminology), stripped of all generality or universality.

I have spoken before of the mourning constitutive of philosophy as universal discourse, of the grief without which no thinking as elevation to the universal can take place, and have insisted on the fact that such grief cannot be the personal, singular grief of a singular individual. It must be a general grief, intelligible to anybody. If de Man's decisive writings are to be philosophical, or to have a philosophical inclination, then they must, in some way or another, take this structure of universalization and mourning into account. De Man's investigation of absolute singularity, as an enterprise of thinking, cannot but pursue this problem in a fashion that yields to the universalist standards of intelligibility, and in doing so mourn, in ways that all of us can assume, that which is forgotten, left behind, put to death by this very operation. Yet, precisely because of what thinking sets out to think in this case—absolute singularity— thinking steps back from the realm of universality, and risks becoming unintelligible, purely idiosyncratic. Indeed, the attempt to conceive of what is entirely without relations is that which cannot be thought, and any attempt to do so sacrifices the claim to universality inherent in thinking. Yet what makes thinking fail as thinking, in this case, is nothing less than thinking itself. In attempting to conceive the absolute limit of the relationless, it encounters its own limit of universalizing. It encounters encrypted in itself the irreducible contingency of itself, the singularity of its universalist claims. To "think" the absolutely contingent and singular, the irreducibly arbitrary, corresponds, indeed, to a mourning of another past that had to be forgotten for thinking to come into its own. And this mourning of the singularity of the universalist gesture of thinking, of the lack of generality of the act that gives rise to thinking, of its solitary happening forever cut loose from the particular philosophy it gives rise to, is a mourning of a past, an absolute past, which is

not simply personal either. We can, *in general,* assume that grief as well. Yet such mournful thinking of an absolute, and hence meaningless past of thinking—an attempt that renounces all claim to universality, and that thus risks its existence as thinking and remains utterly singular—also borders on the unintelligible, on what is so singular that we cannot assume it in general. Beyond the irreducible finitude at the heart of all thinking, a finitude owing to the singularity of its occurrence, de Man's decisive texts also speak (of) something unspeakable, something so utterly contingent and unmotivated, that we cannot share it.

I said before that by calling attention to the singular thrust characteristic of de Man's work, a possible link between the later work and his early writings could perhaps be envisioned. This link is the concern with singularity, and with its disruptive function with regard to totalization, and as we have now seen, universalization. It is a concern with an issue that appears as disruptive of thinking and which forces thinking to abandon all authority and its claims to universality. But with this continuity of de Man's intellectual concerns we also encounter a profound rupture in his writings. Should I venture to say that the sacrifice of universal claims that de Man's later elaborations on the absolutely singular entail, is a sort of atonement or expiation of the earlier claims made? It would be presumptuous to do so. It would, indeed, imply that I have been able to read and understand the purely idiosyncratic in de Man's texts which beyond the finitude at the heart of all thinking hints at another unspeakable past. I do not penetrate its darkness and I must refrain from imposing any meaning on it. To do so would represent a violent imposition and disrespect of the Other, of a thinker in particular, who as Other and as thinker demands that I also assume my inability to understand the unspeakable to which his texts point us. For the same reason I shall abstain from categorizing the link that may exist between the early journalistic work and the thinking enterprise of the later writings. To call this link either a continuation or a covering up of the undeniably unpardonable aspects of some of the earlier texts, is to miss the leap and the rupture that de Man's critical and philosophical writings have undertaken.

Precipitation in labeling this link is evidence of an unconsciousness with respect to what thinking means or simply disdain of thought. But above all, it is a contemptuous dismissal of what in thinking in general remains Other, other to the point of demanding that where thinking enters on its borders, a toll is inevitably taken of understanding.

SUNY—Buffalo

NOTES

1. Jacques Derrida, "Like the Sound of the Sea Deep Within a Shell: Paul de Man's War," *Critical Inquiry*, Vol. 14, Nr. 3(Spring 1988), pp.621 ff.; Richard Bernstein, "Critics Attempt to Reinterpret a Colleague's Disturbing Past," *The New York Times*, July 17, 1988, E6.

2. Jon Wiener, "Deconstructing de Man," *The Nation*, Vol. 246, Nr. 1 (January 9, 1988), pp.22–24.

3. On this point I disagree with Geoffrey Hartman's otherwise lucid article, "Blindness and Insight," *The New Republic*, March 7, 1988, pp. 26–31.

4. On two other occasions at least, de Man speaks positively of German expressionism. In light of what I am developing here regarding "A View on Contemporary German Fiction," from August 20, 1942, it is in particular the article "Un Roman allemand, *Loups parmi les Loups*, de Hans Fallada" (*Le Soir*, September 16, 1941), that must be mentioned. In this article, in which de Man demarcates expressionism as a whole from "the truly German way" of writing (characteristic of writers whom he criticizes rather sharply in other reviews) he justifies expressionism's excesses and deformations, monstrosities and hypertrophies, as resulting, according to "the imperious law of evolution," from the attempt to rejuvenate a concept of reality "around which more than half a century of artistic life was centered." Expressionism, he claims, "illustrates the end of a development that has exhausted its last resources." But although it "constitutes a true theoretization of this decadence," and although its works of art "are more remarkable as phenomena than as artistic achievements properly speaking" (which implies that its artistic "production was not of the first order"), such "degeneracy" is *not* to be considered pejorative. The law according to which it takes place is imperative as seen, and "one has seen masterpieces originating in such moments." And he concludes that "to belong to such a generation cannot serve as a pretext for passing a definite sentence on an artist." But the other text, "André Lhote, *Peinture d'abord*," *Bibliographie Dechenne*, August 1942, p.20, is remarkable as well, and I will quote it almost in its entirety: "He, André Lhote, has made himself the protagonist of a tendency that is fully opposed to the traditions of conventional realism. At the basis of his ideas you find the following condition that 'in order for a painting to reach truth, it can express it only with the help of particular, that is to say, deforming means.' This apparent paradox is constitutive of the whole originality and importance of the expressionists. By bringing this question up again for discussion, a particularly authoritative and intelligent voice has come to express its support in favor of a theory whose present eclipse is perhaps infinitely less advantageous (*heureuse*) than some seem to believe."

5. Hildegard Brenner, *Die Kunstpolitik des Nationalsozialismus*, Hamburg: Rowohlt, 1963, pp.131ff.

6. His interests seem to go rather toward British literature, D. H. Lawrence and Charles Morgan, for instance, to whom, significantly enough, he compares Ernst Jünger at one point, who of the German writers he reviewed, is the only one he admired. (See *Le Soir*, March 1, 1942).

7. See in this respect Jeffrey Mehlman's statement in David Lehman, "Deconstructing de Man's Life," *Newsweek*, February 15, 1988, pp. 63–64.

8. Let me mention here that one of de Man's favorite literary critics is Marcel Raymond (see *Het Vlaamsche Land*, June 7–8, 1942).

9. See Jacques Derrida, *Memoires for Paul de Man*, New York: Columbia University Press, 1986.

10. G. W. F. Hegel, *Grundlinien der Philosophie des Rechts, Werke in Zwanzig Banden*, Frankfurt/Main: Suhrkamp Verlag, 1970, Vol. 7, p. 127.

Regarding the Signatory

ALEXANDER GELLEY

It would be so nice to have it all behind us and get on with our work.[1] There is a widespread wish, both in the scholarly-critical community and outside it, for a quick resolution, a clear judgment. The news media have so accustomed us to summary judgments that a call to express oneself publicly about an individual who has been "in the news" seems automatically to invite a categorical, global judgment. Yet even in more reasoned circles I have the impression of some impatience with this picking over one man's reputation.

But to acquiesce in this kind of impulse is to abandon precisely those criteria—theoretical, political, moral—that are at work, that are constantly being tested and refined, in the best sort of criticism. Paul de Man was one of the foremost teachers to a generation of literary scholars of just this kind of criticism. We can do no less than to abide its lesson in considering his own writings. When this is done (and the task, for the most part, still lies ahead) I venture to say that he will not come off lightly. But, I also think, much in his teaching and in his example will survive.

The impact that the disclosures about de Man's early work has had in recent months is in a sense an index of the impact that de Man himself had in the American scene of the last two decades. He was called on to play a singular role in this scene, one that we should try to understand in terms of the phenomenon as a whole rather than of personal gifts or intentions on the part of de Man or anyone else. Not that the function of an individual is irrelevant, but it is all too tempting to inflate this function and neglect the much harder task of examining a historical scene, our scene, one in which we are still caught up even as we try to articulate its pre-history. What is at stake is less de Man the person than a "de Man effect." I want to frame the issue so that it will be possible to reflect on de Man's place in this effect, but without limiting that effect to his ideas, his personality, his possible culpability.

"We ought, to be true to his spirit, to resist that piety [toward the work or toward the man] as hard as some have resisted his theories." Thus wrote E.S. Burt in the *Yale French Studies* memorial issue for de Man (YFS 69, p.12). One might think that the revelation of the '41–42 articles has facilitated that task, relieved us of interfering piety and allowed us to look more directly at the substance of de Man's work. But for myself any such release from piety only displaces the problem of how to read de Man. For that is what it still comes down to, how to read . . . de Man, Rousseau, Proust, Derrida, many others. But also there is a change. One cannot pretend that the texts remain the same. Something has shifted when we add those early articles to the corpus of de Man's oeuvre, a modulation has come over the name itself as signatory of the texts, and what that modulation consists of becomes my burden as reader, that is, insofar as I want to, need to read those texts and other texts allied to them.

Jacques Derrida, in his recent *Critical Inquiry* essay, pinpoints certain issues in a salutary manner. It is a great merit of his piece to open the debate, in a sense, at a level that is deserving of serious consideration. He has intervened promptly, he has not avoided some of the most troubling features of de Man's early texts, he has brought to bear on them his extraordinary analytic powers. I cannot follow him in many of his conclusions while I admire the forcefulness and the generosity of his effort.

Thus when Derrida writes, "I said that in analyzing, judging, evaluating this or that discourse, this or that effect of these old fragments, I refused to extend these gestures to a general judgment, with no possibility of appeal, of Paul de Man, of the totality of what he was, thought, wrote, taught, and so forth" (LS, p.631), I wonder whether the claim isn't too extravagant. None of us who took, and still take, de Man seriously (and this clearly excludes those who, in the name of journalistic sensationalism or academic polemics, merely adopt de Man as a symbol and target) imagine that evaluating, judging this or that text is equivalent to a judgment "of the totality of what he was, thought, wrote, taught, and so forth."

But for all that, judgment cannot, by its nature, be so clearly circumscribed as Derrida's statement suggests. In another passage Derrida speaks of the necessity of "evaluating *this* act, *this* text" and then adds in a parenthesis: "(notice I do not say the life and work of its signatory which will never be reduced to this act, this text)" (LS, p.623), a formulation that, in distinguishing the person from the signatory (in a way that Derrida himself has accustomed us to), sharpens the question as to who this new signatory is, the author of the texts signed Paul de Man.

Of course, this way of putting the question only displaces the matter at issue, the matter of continuity, of coherence. There is no easy way to bring together the image one has of de Man in his early twenties with the de Man one knew, in person or by reputation, in his maturity, just as there is no easy way of bringing together those early texts and the later ones. For the second alternative, that involving the texts, I possess more reliable analytic instruments and far more complete materials. Yet the first, the question of the person, cannot be thus simply done away with. It will remain, though I may conclude that I shall never have the means to answer it.

As someone who has admired the person Paul de Man, as someone who sees in the thinker Paul de Man a preeminent innovator in the field of criticism, the recent revelations by no means relieve me of the need to analyze, evaluate, judge. Rather, they impel me to be as scrupulous as possible regarding the parameters of a judgment—its object, its criteria, its addressee. Who/What should be judged, on what grounds, for what purposes? I will return to this in a moment.

First I want to take up Derrida's reading of the most notorious of the early de Man articles, "Les Juifs dans la Littérature actuelle." Derrida does not hesitate to voice in general terms his shock and dismay over this piece. But it is with the specifics of Derrida's reading that I must take exception. In that article de Man had written,

Their [the Jews'] cerebralness, their capacity to assimilate doctrines while keeping a certain coldness in the face of them, would seem to be very precious qualities for the work of lucid analysis that the novel demands. (Jla, cited in LS, p.630)

For Derrida this passage offers evidence for one possible reading of the article, namely, as a covert attack on "vulgar antisemitism" (de Man's phrase), possibly even on antisemitism tout court.

Unquestionably, de Man's article strives to separate itself from a "vulgar antisemitism," and certain formulations in it (such as the list of exemplary novelists—Gide, Kafka, Hemingway, Lawrence) might be indicative of an "anticonformist attack" (in Derrida's phrase) against the more blatant type of propaganda that could be found in the pages of *Le Soir* and elsewhere. But that much said, it would go too far to attempt to characterize the article as a calculated, oppositional tactic. Derrida suggests as much when he writes,

To condemn vulgar antisemitism may leave one to understand that there is a distinguished antisemitism in whose name the vulgar variety is put down. De Man never says such a thing, even though one may condemn his silence. But the phrase can also mean something else, and this reading can always contaminate the other in a clandestine fashion: to condemn "vulgar antisemitism," *especially if one makes no mention of the other kind,* is to condemn antisemitism itself *inasmuch as* it is vulgar, always and essentially vulgar. De Man does not say that either. If that is what he thought, a possibility I will never exclude, he could not say so clearly in this context. One will say at this point: his fault was to have accepted the context. Certainly, but what is that, to accept a context? And what would one say if he claimed not to have fully accepted it, and to have preferred to play the role there of the nonconforming smuggler, as so many others did in so many different ways, in France and in Belgium, at this or that moment, inside or outside the Resistance? (LS, p.625)

Indeed, "what is that, to accept a context?" The most sympathetic and subtle reading of de Man's article, even one that might establish certain inner, mental reservations on de Man's part (which Derrida does not claim, but only raises as a possibility), cannot lessen the responsibility of having accepted the context, which is to say, the responsibility for the plain consequences, the impact which this piece of writing—appearing where it did, when it did—was designed to have. "Designed," not, perhaps, in the sense of a personal intention on de Man's part, but precisely in terms of "the context," one to which de Man acceded and about which he could not have been ignorant.

The context, indeed, whatever it is that de Man "accepted," is what we need to recover in order to assess a sentence like, "Their [the Jews'] cerebralness. . . .," and though this may be, in a sense, a very large undertaking, with far-reaching ramifications, we need not shirk it for that reason, nor should we suspend judgment until we have reached its outer limits. Judgment is often required on pragmatic grounds. We need to make certain judgments—provisional ones, certainly, subject to revision—in order to undertake certain acts, to follow a certain kind of behavior, for example, whether to read more of de Man, whether to take seriously, to struggle with certain ideas or methods that we find in his texts, etc.

Will I still scrutinize his essays, take them as exemplary of a certain kind of reading, look for the subtle thread of his meditation once I have concluded that "Their cerebralness . . ." is to be classed with those forms of crude national-racial classification that have long been a staple of antisemitic discourse, whether "vulgar" or not? Yes, I myself will. But the question cannot simply be assumed. It must be addressed. For I will not be reading the same essays. A new dimension will have been added to them, one supplied by the revision of the signatory. To what extent my earlier interest may be "spoiled" I cannot say, but I want to know the worst as I proceed.

Derrida is fully alert to the register of national classifications in the de Man texts:

Comparisons between the German and French cultures, notably as regards their literary manifestations, the one dominated by myth, metaphor, or symbol, the other by psychological analysis, the predilection for moderation, limit, and definition, thus for the finite (one thinks of many of Nietzsche's statements [on] this subject), seem often to be made to the benefit of the former. (LS, p.617)

He reminds us too that there is another nationalism, the Flemish, that de Man defends, that he feels especially called on to defend in the face of both the German and the French traditions. And, finally, Derrida points acutely to the "abyssal logic of exemplarity" regarding any discourse of national affirmation,

namely, that it "is caught up in the paradoxical necessity of respecting *the idiom in general,* thus *all* idioms, all national differences." (LS, p.619)

Well and good. But it is not "*all* idioms, all national differences" that de Man espouses in the articles in question. He presents himself as a mediator among certain national traditions, and especially as a champion of some over others: thus, of the Flemish "genius" against both the French and the German ("Le destin de la Flandre"), or, more than once, of the German against the French.[2] The method at work, if it may be called that, is a rudimentary version of milieu theory, not very supple nor sophisticated, to be sure, but sufficient to generate a terminology of national-racial characteristics that fits all too easily in either an aesthetic or a national framework. While the comparisons relative to German, French, and Flemish matters are not markedly evaluative, where a Jewish element is involved de Man is not so even-handed.

An essay written in Flemish in a Flemish periodical, "A View on Contemporary German Fiction,"[3] develops a contrast between two currents of post-war (World War I) German literature: one described by terms like "cerebral," "abstract," "expressionism," "tricks," "artifice," and associated with "mainly non-Germans, and in specific, jews." The other is "the proper tradition of German art which had always and before everything else clung to a deep spiritual sincerity." The former is "aberrant," the other is "true to the proper norms of the country. . . ."

Here, then, is another element of the context that leads me to think that in writing "Their [the Jews'] cerebralness . . ." de Man was not trying to undermine the aims of the Nazi organ for which he worked by covertly introducing a positive trait regarding the Jews, but, on the contrary, simply pursuing a code that was well-established and that he evokes often enough in these articles. The fact that he applies it only twice (as far as I know) explicitly to Jews in no way mitigates the practice. The code is what he uses, and the code has its own agenda.

As a code it is not, by its nature, wholly transparent. Though we may think that, in its general sense, we understand it, there are nuances that may escape us and such nuances may be sufficiently important to lead to divergent readings. An interview with Maurice Bardèche in Alice Yaeger Kaplan's *Reproductions of Banality*[4] alerts me to some nuances of French antisemitism between the wars. First of all, a distinction between an instinctive (read vulgar) brand, and a "political," "rational" one. Bardèche, as we may imagine, aligns himself with the latter:

There's an anti-Semitism "under the skin," if you like—they can't stand Jews, "those dirty Jews" etc., whatever—what you find in Céline and Rebatet. That kind of furor you find the minute it's a question of Jew, etc. This kind of anti-Semitism was completely foreign to Robert [Brasillach], as well as to me. And then a political anti-Semitism whose roots are in the work of Maurras. Robert very quickly became a sympathizer of the Action Française. . . . An anti-Semitic milieu, consequently—but a rational one. (p.172)

And then, in characterizing the "rational" antisemitism Bardèche goes on (responding to the interviewer's question),

Which means nationalist, if you like. The opinion of the French people who found that the Jews occupied in intellectual and political French life a role disproportionate to their number. And especially that one heard them too much. (ibid.)

Now in the light of this, it is indeed conceivable that de Man's denigration of the Jewish contribution to European culture[5] can be taken as an attempt to deflect a familiar argument of this more sophisticated, "non-vulgar" antisemitism of the period.

What conclusion does this interpretation lead me to? Perhaps that the young de Man was very clever in both satisfying the demands of the Nazi-controlled organ for which he was writing and, at the same time, maintaining a certain distance to its slant, a distance that possibly a few astute contemporary readers might catch. If we need to classify forms of antisemitism, this might be termed an opportunistic brand and ranked a notch above the "rational."

And what have I gained for the larger issue, how to read de Man, how to read the scene that includes him (and me)? That is clearly a harder question, one that I confront with far less confidence. As I indicated earlier, the writings of de Man are probably as a good a place as any to find the criteria with which to read, analyze, judge the (early) work of de Man. Not that those writings are notably self-referential (though it may be that they will seem more so henceforth, with our awareness of the early pieces), but that the mature work of de Man has articulated, as well and as fully as almost any other recent thinker's, what questions matter in our field. I say advisedly, "what questions matter." De Man has not given us ready answers, clear instructions. This is a source of considerable irritation for many. But for others it is an important part of what constitutes his stature.

On the first page of one of de Man's most programmatic essays, "The Resistance to Theory," we find this intimidating assertion,

Overfacile opinion notwithstanding, teaching is not primarily an inter-subjective relationship between people but a cognitive process in which self and other are only tangentially and contiguously in-

volved. The only teaching worthy of the name is scholarly, not personal. . . . (YFS 63, p. 3)

This statement might lead us to think that we have been on the wrong track all along in assuming any possible connection between de Man as teacher, as exemplary critic, and the ideas that he has espoused and that we try to understand. For it is this implicit connection—the individual as authoritative source, as personal guarantor for the ideas he articulates—that underlies all our efforts to understand this man, to bring together the author of the "early" de Man and the "late" de Man. If his "teaching" (whether directly to his students or mediately, to those who read him and respond to the authority of his reputation) is not significantly tied to an "inter-subjective" factor, why all the fuss?

To begin to answer this kind of question is to embark on what is most resistant, most bedeviling, yet still, for many of us, the inescapable challenge of de Man's teaching. Clearly, the individual matters. We cannot read the criticism and ignore the signatory. (I don't say this cannot be done in principle. But I am speaking here of the present context, what I have termed the "de Man effect.") But *how* he matters is what we can never take for granted. In another passage from the same essay de Man broaches the issue from another angle:

In a genuine semiology as well as in other linguistically oriented theories, the referential function of language is not being denied—far from it; what is in question is its authority as a model for natural or phenomenal cognition. Literature is fiction not because it somehow refuses to acknowledge "reality," but because it is not a priori certain that language functions according to principles which are those, or which are like those, of the phenomenal world. It is therefore not a priori certain that literature is a reliable source of information about anything but its own language. (YFS 63, p.11)

If we transpose this statement to the problem that confronts us here; if, for example, instead of applying it to the fictionality of literature we apply it to the authority of a teacher, of an author, the problem remains. We are not told to deny the "referential function," the "reality" coefficient, but we are induced to question it, and to do so in ways specifically appropriate to the claims that it makes on us. (I see here, incidentally, one of the places where de Man's thought significantly engages a political and historical problematic, something which certain of his critics deny him altogether. Exploring this matter is clearly one of the most urgent tasks that our discipline faces at present.) Stated thus abstractly the questioning of the referential is hardly novel or illuminating. It verges on the commonplace. But pursued with any degree of rigor, it becomes the instrument, the unprogrammed and unprogrammable method, of our discipline.

In thinking about the claims raised by this second memorial volume to Paul de Man I came upon these words written in the first:

If the death of a writer makes a difference in the way we read him, one manifestation of such a difference may be the sudden urge we feel toward grasping what we read as having its own history. An end calls for a beginning—and a good story in between.[6]

Minae Mizumura here brings to the surface a natural impulse, and for that reason, an unreflected one. We have a very natural wish for "a good story," but we had better be careful that in wishing for one we do not manufacture it. Her essay is one demonstration, and a brilliant one, of a resistance to that kind of desire, a resistance carried out under the aegis of de Man's analysis of a similar form of desire in certain literary texts. A demonstration of what? Of the desire or the resistance? Of both, and thus of the teaching as well, a teaching that was capable of generating not only a desire—to understand it, to think with it—but also a resistance, the capacity to break loose and think against it.

University of California, Irvine

ABBREVIATIONS

LS Jacques Derrida, "Like the Sound of the Sea Deep within a Shell: Paul de Man's War," *Critical Inquiry* 14 (Spring, 1988), 590–652.

Jla "Les Juifs dans la Littérature actuelle," *Le Soir* 55:54, March 4, 1941, 10.

YFS 63 *The Pedagogical Imperative: Teaching as a Literary Genre, Yale French Studies* 63, 1982.

YFS 69 *The Lesson of Paul de Man, Yale French Studies* 69, 1985.

NOTES

1. I am grateful to Daniel Brewer, Maria Brewer, Mieke Gelley, and James McMichael for reading versions of this essay and helping me clarify a number of points.

2. "Romans allemands" (*Le Soir* 56:34, Feb. 10, 1942) compares Hermann Stehr's *Léonore Gabriel* and Flaubert's *Madame Bovary*. "Regards sur l'Allemagne" (*Le Soir* 55:183, Aug. 5, 1941) deals with a novel by Ernst Wiechert by way of an extended contrast between the "psychological" manner of French fiction and Wiechert's typically Germanic "ethical" preoccupation.

3. In *Het Vlaamsche Land,* Aug. 20, 1942. I cite from Ortwin de Graef's English version, typescript.

4. Minneapolis: University of Minnesota Press, 1986.

5. "Looking at the matter more closely, this influence even seems of extraordinarily little importance, since one would have expected, given the specific characteristics of the Jewish mind [*de l'esprit juif*], that they would have played a more brilliant role in this artistic production." (Jla)

6. Minae Mizumura, "Renunciation," YFS 69, p.81.

Disfiguring de Man: Literature, History, and Collaboration

SANDOR GOODHART

I would never have by myself undertaken the task of establishing such a collection, and, grateful as I am to Bill Germano for his initiative, I confess that I still look back upon it with some misgivings. [RR, viii]—*Paul de Man*

The "collection" to which de Man refers is, of course, *The Rhetoric of Romanticism,* published shortly after his death (containing some of the last texts he wrote—the epigraph, for example, is drawn from the preface), and the "misgivings" he speaks about concern what seems to him the book's embarrassing failure to cohere in any recognizable dialectical form.

Such massive evidence of the failure to make the various individual readings coalesce is a somewhat melancholy spectacle. The fragmentary aspect of the whole is made more obvious still by the hypotactic manner that prevails in each of the essays taken in isolation, by the continued attempt, however ironized, to present a closed and linear argument. This apparent coherence *within* each essay is not matched by a corresponding coherence *between* them. Laid out chronologically in roughly chronological sequence, they do not evolve in a manner that easily allows for dialectical progression, or ultimately, for historical totalization. Rather, it seems that they always start again from scratch and that their conclusions fail to add up to anything. [RR, viii]

De Man's remark is, of course, itself ironic, since, beyond the familiar self-effacement in which prefaces commonly engage (and in which his prefaces engaged increasingly—although pursued here with perhaps a bit more intensity than we might have expected), it replays what we will later come to recognize as his primary concern within the book—namely, the failure, in each instance where we might expect dialectical totalization (within or outside of literature), of precisely such ordering distinctions.

The essay on Shelley's *The Triumph of Life,* for example, at the book's center, seems a case in point.[1] De Man is concerned there to show the way in which the poem already dramatizes in advance as it were the very gestures by which the interpretative labor of critics regarding the poem (or regarding romanticism at large) would complete itself, a series of defragmentizing gestures which the poem is able to thematize as it found such labor already prefigured in the narrator's haunting interlocutor, Rousseau, and his account of his own relation to predecessors. "What is the meaning of *The Triumph of Life,* of Shelley, and of romanticism?" de Man asks somewhat rhetorically, at the outset of the essay, echoing the questions of the narrator to his ghostly companion. [RR, 94]

What shape does it have? How did its course begin and why? Perhaps the difficulty of the answers is prefigured in the asking of the questions. . . . Such questions allow one to conclude that *The Triumph of Life* is a fragment of something whole, or romanticism a fragment, or a moment, in a process that now includes us within its horizon. What relationship do we have to such a text that allows us to call it a fragment that we are then entitled to reconstruct, to identify, and implicitly to complete? This supposes, among other things, that Shelley or romanticism are themselves entities which, like a statue, can be broken into pieces, mutilated, or allegorized. . . . Is the status of a text like the status of a statue? Yeats, one of Shelley's closest readers and disciples, wrote a fine poem about history and form called *The Statues* which it would be rewarding to read in connection with *The Triumph of Life*. But there are more economic ways to approach this text and to question the possibility of establishing a relationship to Shelley and to romanticism in general. After all, the link between the present I and its antecedents is itself dramatized in the poem, most explicitly and at greatest length in the encounter between the narrator and the figure designated by the proper name Rousseau, who has himself much to say about his own predecessors. [RR, 94–95]

De Man's remark in the book's preface, in other words, is another example of the same problem of demonumentalizing that he describes within it—within his essay on Shelley, within Shelley's relationship to his predecessors (for example, Rousseau), and within, in his view, the work of those predecessors themselves, within, that is to say, the full range of the poem's relation to antecedent versions. Shelley's poem already "warns us," de Man claims, of the fragmentary nature of all such hypotactic interpretative moves, "that nothing, whether deed, word, thought, or text, ever happens in relation, positive or negative, to anything that precedes, follows, or exists elsewhere but only as a random event whose power, like the power of death, is due to the randomness of its occurrence," a warning, moreover, which fails to free us from performing them repeatedly since "it also warns us why and how these events then have to be reintegrated in an historical and aesthetic system of recuperation that repeats itself regardless of the exposure of its fallacy" [RR, 122].

But if we allow the proper name in the first sentence of the epigraph to the current essay—which refers to de Man's young editor at Columbia University Press—to drift a little, it is not hard to fantasize that de Man may have been thinking about another "collection" about which he may also feel some "misgivings," a collection, moreover, which may indeed have constituted for the writer an even more "melancholy spectacle" and confer upon his fear that he always "start[s] again from scratch" and that his "conclusions fail to add up to anything," an unexpected resonance (and thus help to explain its odd intensity). For the recent discovery by Ortwin de Graef and others of a cache of papers (290 texts by recent estimates) written by Paul de Man—published in Belgium during the years 1939 through 1943, for the socialist journals *Jeudi* and *Les Cahiers du Libre Examen* at the Université Libre de Bruxelles, then later during the

war for the collaborationist publications *Le Soir* and *Het Vlaamsche Land,* and for the *Bibliographie* of the Agence Dechenne, when he was 19 until he was 23—would seem to suggest that at the outset of his career, these same concerns whose failure he now registers—namely, evolving dialectical progression, historical totalization, and the relation of these to the values of literature and literary analysis—were already his subject matter, although pursued there in strikingly different manner.[2]

So different, in fact, is de Man's position in the earlier essays, that it would be tempting to tell a story in which de Man begins with one position and turns to the other—were such a recuperative allegory not just what he was already warning us against in the later essays. In the course, for example, of an essay entitled "Art as Mirror of the Essence of Nations: Considerations on *Geist der Nationen* by A. E. Brinckmann," which he wrote for *Het Vlaamsche Land* [March 29–30, 1942, p.3], in which he is reflecting upon the values of a "national personality" for promoting the values of "Western culture," de Man identifies an "indispensable" "lesson" [OG, 29].

What is proper to our time is the consideration of this national personality as a valuable condition, as a precious possession, which has to be maintained at the cost of all sacrifices. This conception is miles apart from sentimental patriotism. Rather, it concerns a sober faith, a practical means to defend Western culture against a decomposition from the inside or a surprise attack by neighboring civilizations. . . . The aim of [Brinckmann's] work is not only to analyze the artistic activity from an aesthetic point of view, or to give an explanation of the phenomena of creation. Its effect leads to a different plane, which is also of a practical nature. It originated out of an attempt to ensure the future of Western civilization in all its aspects. As such it contains a lesson, which is indispensable for all those, who, in the contemporary revolutions, try to find firm guidance according to which they can direct their actions and their thoughts. [OG, 27–29]

That here at the outset of his career, the twenty year old journalist endorses a conception of a Europe that "can only be strong, peaceful and flourishing if it is governed by a state of mind which is deeply conscious of its national grandeur," and that the derivation of "this endpoint" "from the history of art . . . proves how efficient the method of using works of art as study material for the obtaining of general knowledge really is" offers us a stark contrast with the older critic who would affirm the radical fragmentariness of history and the radically demonumentalizing nature of great literature, a contrast that would seem readily to lend itself to a narrative or allegory of disillusion [OG, 28–29]. To the positive, substantive, essential value and knowledge of literature (and of the history of criticism which relates that knowledge and value to us), and the progressive, civilizing advance of Western history—no more contrastive position could be found.

And, all other things being equal, were such examples of literary essentialism and historical progressivism all that were uncovered, we would have little difficulty, I suspect, charting that conversion. For we should be able then to identify such a pattern as precisely the blindspot in context of which de Man's persistent warnings about it made sense. But all other things were far from equal. The political and social program of "this national personality" which the writer claims must be "maintained at the cost of all sacrifices," and the precise nature of "the contemporary revolutions" then taking place in Nazi Germany and elsewhere, as well as the precise details of the "practical means to defend Western culture against a decomposition from the inside or a surprise attack by neighboring civilizations"—all these are known only too well. De Man himself further identifies such "decomposition" in another essay on literary trends in contemporary Germany which appeared in the same journal ["A View on (sic) Contemporary German Fiction," 20 August 1942, p.2] in which he also feels "one can legitimately speak of degeneration" [OG, 2].

When we investigate the post-war literary production in Germany, we are immediately struck by the contrast between two groups, which moreover were also materially separated by the events of 1933. The first of these groups celebrates an art with a strongly cerebral disposition, founded upon some abstract principles and very remote from all naturalness. The in themselves very remarkable theses of expressionism were used in this group as tricks, as skillful artifices calculated at [sic] easy effects. The very legitimate basic rule of artistic transformation, inspired by the personal vision of the creator, served here as a pretext for a forced, caricatured representation of reality. Thus, [the artists of this group] came into an open conflict with the proper traditions of German art which had always and before everything else clung to a deep spiritual sincerity. Small wonder, then, that it were mainly non-Germans, and in specific jews [sic] that went in this direction. [OG, 2]

The reference to Jews in relation to talk about "decomposition from the inside" by "foreign force(s)" is not capricious. In a special page of *Le Soir* devoted to anti-semitism and "the Jewish problem" which appeared the previous year [55:42, Tuesday, March 4, 1941, p.10], de Man had pondered the consequences of proposed solutions (vulgar or otherwise) to this concern. "Vulgar anti-semitism," de Man writes, "is readily content to consider cultural phenomena of the post-World War One period as degenerated and decadent in so far as it is Judaized [*enjuivé*]."[3] But, the young journalist counters,

[we] should not formulate a great many hopes for the future of our civilization if it allowed itself to be invaded without resistance by a foreign force. In preserving intact, in spite of semitic interference [*ingérance*] in all aspects of European life, an originality and a character, it has shown that its profound nature is healthy. Moreover, we thus see that a solution to the Jewish problem, which would envisage the creation of a Jewish colony isolated from Europe, would not entail, for the literary life of the West, deplorable consequences. Europe would lose, all in all, a few personalities of mediocre value, and would continue, as in the past, to develop itself according to its own great evolutionary laws.[4]

It is hard to read this language without historical hindsight. We know, for example (as de Man presumably did not) that less than a year after these words appeared orders were given (and preparations began) for the murder of eleven million human beings at Auschwitz and other deathcamps in the East—although the deportations would not begin in Belgium until August of the following year (the same moment as the appearance of the above article in *Het Vlaamsche Land*).[5] We also know— and this knowledge involves less hindsight—that by March of 1941 restrictive orders regarding Jews had already appeared in Flanders (some on the same page of *Le Soir* in which articles of this kind were published). Raul Hilberg notes that "by late summer [of 1942], Jews [in Belgium] went into hiding in large numbers, that nothing had been heard from the deportees, that efforts had been made to find out what was going on and that doubts about the fate of the Jews were rapidly dispelled, certainly in educated circles, before the end of 1942."[6] In light of such macabre details, the distinctions between vulgar and nonvulgar anti-semitism begins to sound academic.

The concern that this discovery has engendered is understandably widespread, for it seems to have implications, not just for the reputation of this particular scholar, but for the intellectual enterprize with which he had become (not without qualification—although finally with acquiescence) increasingly associated, perhaps even for the wider context of humanistic study in this country. Moreover, it is complicated by the fact that a concern with the relation of ethics to critical reading (and with de Man's work as a central figure in that concern) had already begun to make itself felt throughout the humanities before these writings became known. It is as if, not unlike the author of Shelley's poem (whose death, de Man tells us, becomes readable within it), de Man has become through this discovery a figure of his own critical literature, a figure, moreover, "disfigured" in the same manner as the drowned poet, since he speaks to us now from a place where imaginary, symbolic, and real considerations have become fused. "[To] read," de Man writes (in the essay on Shelley), "is to understand, to question, to know, to forget, to erase, to deface, to repeat—that is to say, the endless prosopopeia by which the dead are made to have a face and a voice which tells the allegory of their demise and allows us to apostrophize them in our turn" [RR, 122].

How does the discovery of Paul de Man's wartime journalism affect our reading of his later work? Are the two specifically anti-semitic essays compatible with the rest of this early writing or isolated instances, aberrations, which might be dismissed as demanded by political or personal expediency? To what conclusions are we led as result of this discovery about the man himself or the intellectual movement with which in the seventies and eighties he became increasingly associated, a movement that has come in recent years increasingly to engage the question of ethics (which may be why their discovery today is so controversial)? These questions—and many others that we have not articulated—are likely to concern us for some time to come and it seems hardly possible at this early stage to do more than make a few tentative and preliminary suggestions about a few of these early texts (their very compiling looks as if it will run to four hundred pages), even though it seems equally incumbent upon us to do at least that much.

To begin to take stock, then, of the implications of this discovery (and the allegory or demise they apostrophize), I would like to consider three bodies of material. In the ten essays de Man wrote for *Het Vlaamsche Land* and the one explicitly anti-semitic essay he wrote for *Le Soir,* de Man lays out what might be identified as a unified position. Then in 1966, in "The Literature of Nihilism," which he wrote for the *New York Review of Books,* he articulates what might be thought of as a new position, one which rejects the Nazi enterprize but affirms the tradition of German literature and philosophy as distinguishable from it.[7] And in the essays written in the 1980's, for example, "Shelley Disfigured," he reaches what by dint of his death became his final position, one which was different again from either of the earlier two. Now he sees words and action as intimately bound up with each other in the notion of a performative (the peculiar way in which language is figuration—at once constative and performative) and finds the value to be gleaned from literature about history to concern the fragmentary nature of any historical narrative, and the failure of any allegorical or aesthetic recuperation, in short, the defiguration or de-facement that literature performs.

Read in concert with the later material, these early essays may offer us a new coherence to de Man's life-long project, a new sense of the man behind de Man, so to speak. They may also allow us to raise again some of the questions with which he was most concerned (for example, in *The Rhetoric of Romanti-*

cism), even if those questions now include de Man himself as a stake—to ask, for example, whether from one body of material to another there is anything like dialectical progress, or whether in each case we are compelled to "start again from scratch." Finally, they may enable us to raise some of the larger issues to which their discovery has given rise, questions about the intellectual movements with which he associated himself and whose fortunes some recent commentators have felt to be in jeopardy as a consequence.

* * * * *

I am not given to retrospective self-examination, and mercifully forget what I have written with the same alacrity I forget bad movies—although, as with bad movies, certain scenes return at times to embarrass and haunt me like a guilty conscience. . . . Thus seeing a distant segment of one's past resurrected gives one a slightly uncanny feeling of repetition. [B12, xii]—*Paul de Man*

In "Art as Mirror of the Essence of Nations: Considerations on *Geist der Nationen* by A. E. Brinckmann" [29–30 March 1942, p.3], the first of the ten essays he wrote for *Het Vlaamsche Land* between March and October of 1942, de Man lays out a coherent position [OG, 24–29]. The "ideal" is the "realization of pure science, which could succeed in establishing the eternal movements of nature in general laws." But when applied to "the purely human problem" the goal is "not easy to reach." The enterprize is worth undertaking, the writer feels, "if one could reach the same stage in the study of man [as the physical scientist is able to obtain in his field]." In that case, "some individual reactions could also be foreseen. And if this knowledge were to be expanded from the study of the individual to that of society, then we would in a certain sense be masters of our historical future." Political, social, economic events would no longer seem "adroit improvisations" but "applications of a generally holding system which is irrevocably stable."

Sociology, historical science, or social psychology have not yet been able to achieve such results because of the difficulty of setting up the conditions for "a strictly scientific investigation in this domain."[8] Creative art, on the other hand, offers us "the most fertile domain of research in relation to the knowledge of men and groups of men." The creative artist who is intuitive by nature cannot himself offer us these laws which are "forced upon him via the mysterious way of the gift" ("He obeys the laws of an evolution of style completely unknown to him," de Man asserts). But "a scientific history of art" can achieve that end since it "raises itself above the consideration of individual talents, and tries to explain why creative art does not run its course completely erratically and arbitrarily, but appears to arrange itself around certain forms—styles—which vanish and return in cyclical fashion" and thus is "more than an enumeration of individual particularities."

A. E. Brinckmann's book, *Geist der Nationen,* excels in the writer's view in this regard. He shows that Western art is a unity (distinguishable "from all other spheres of culture in form and in essence") but within this whole "separate circles delineated themselves" corresponding to "the great European states." "Nationalities as such," de Man notes, "have always existed." "What is proper to our time is the consideration of this national personality as a valuable condition, as a precious possession, which has to be maintained at the cost of all sacrifices." "This conception . . . concerns a sober faith, a practical means to defend Western culture against a decomposition from the inside or a surprise attack by neighboring civilizations." Such national peculiarities show up in art as "contrastive forces," as "an opposition, a tension between the different elements that determine a style." Thus "'the spirit of the nation' i.e. the dominating artistic tendency of a nation, is one of the main ingredients which made Western culture possible." These conditions are not "an ideal wish, utopian and remote," de Man affirms, "but . . . a concrete truth corroborated by a number of facts." The fact that we can move "from the history of art, to the terrain of the major cultural and political problems, proves how efficient the method of using works of art as study material for the obtaining of general knowledge really is." It helps to "ensure the future of Western civilization in all its aspects" and "as such . . . contains a lesson . . . for all those who, in the contemporary revolutions, try to find a firm guidance according to which they can direct their action and their thoughts."

Subsequent essays in *Het Vlaamsche Land* expand and refine these ideas. In contrast to national values, which base themselves upon infrastructural "almost personal" elements ("a railway system, a beautiful local folk-dance, a world record in sports"), the European idea (in "Content of the European Idea" [31 May-1 June 1942]) is "superstructural" with "a purely spiritual content" [OG, 30–34]. Thus, an important task falls to "today's intellectual elite": to "establish a synthesis," "to unite the creative forces of all European states." In "Criticism and Literary History" [7–8 June 1942, p.3], de Man specifies the goal of all historical study which grounds such a synthesis: "to pass judgement upon what is happening around us *now*" [OG, 35–39].

What we ask of history is not that it show us the picturesque and peculiar sides of a past civilization. . . . if we continually turn to the past, this is because we intuitively feel that our own personality and the surrounding world are, as it were, determined by this past. And

that consequently we cannot acquire conscious control over our opinions—and, a fortiori, over our actions—if we do not take into account what has happened before us. [OG, 35]

Individual criticisms of art find their justification here only in function of a burgeoning general investigation. Two recent books, each tracing the history of French literature from 1870 to 1940, illustrate this point for the journalist contrastively. René Lalou offers us a simple "enumeration of talents," while Marcel Raymond asserts "il m'a semblé qu'une ligne de force, dont le dessin apparait ici de lieu en lieu, commandait le movement poétique depuis romantisme [it seemed to me that a line of force, the design of which appeared here and there, was governing the development of poetry since romanticism]." "There is a certain homogeneity," de Man writes, "a uniformity of actions and creations:"

every generation of poets has an aesthetic discipline proper to all its members. On the other hand, there is a certain continuity, one generation ensues logically from the preceding one, in the sense that it gives more depth to the formulae of the precursors or, when these are completely exhausted, searches for an innovation and fights or avoids the old rules—which is after all still a means for those rules to exert a decisive influence, be it in a negative sense. In short, modern French poetry appears from this study as a well-rounded whole whose parts match each other, as a creative phenomenon with internal cohesion. [OG, 37]

It is this "impression" de Man writes [and not that left by the book of Lalou] which "corresponds to reality." The development of art

does not depend upon arbitrary, personal decisions, but is connected to forces which perform their relentless operations across the doings of individuals. . . . There exists, to a certain extent, an aesthetic determinism of which the artist himself is not conscious, the same determinism that is expressed in the course of history, which, after all, does seem to move around a number of constants. It follows that we give a wrong impression of things if we do not allow these organizing evolutionary laws[4] to speak clearly. [OG, 38]

"The failure of Lalou," de Man writes, is that his "criticism is . . . not concerned about . . . enduring significance" but "becomes a helpless manifestation of feeling without significance." "History," as a result, "becomes a dead and boring enumeration."

In "Contemporary Trends in French Literature," [17–18 May 1942, p.3] this enduring significance is clarified [1–5]. Art proceeds according to its own evolutionary laws independent of even the most traumatic events (for example, the "current revolutions"). Speaking of French literature, the writer suggests that the "war has exercised no influence on artistic creation. . . . For this war is not the cause of changes, but rather the result of an already existing revolution. . . . a similar phenomenon, in a different domain, of the fermenting we find in the world of literature." And what is the content of that artistic creativity? The "bringing [of] the psychological analysis and the study of man's inner essence to a nearly startling perfection."

And this "similar phenomenon" at work in both the war and literature is specified in another essay. The true artist, he asserts in "German Literature. A Great Writer: Ernst Jünger" [26–27 July 1942, p.2], although destined to express national traits, should be open to other possibilities that alone will promote full development. "A sincere artist can never renounce his proper regional [character], destined by blood and soil, since it is an integrating part of his essence which he has to utter. But he systematically impoverishes himself, he refuses to make use of that which constitutes the vital force of our European culture, if he in order to remain true to his own people, does not want to become acquainted with that which comes into being elsewhere" which "is an exhortation to the full development of the proper personality" [1–4].

In context of even this brief a survey—and there is a great deal more to say about even the few essays we have considered—de Man's position is fairly clear. He attaches himself to an historical progressivism—the perfectibility of man in accordance with natural evolutionary laws through the intermediary agency of science and rational discourse—and to a literary and philosophic essentialism—the value of great literature (as interpreted for the masses by the intellectual elite) as civilizing and reflective tool in this ongoing spiritual advance, this mastery of one's historical destiny.

But it also becomes clear that, far from aberrant, the anti-semitic writings are endemic to that position. In "A View on Contemporary German Fiction" [20 August 1942, p.2] (cited above), for example, he further elaborates a situation in which he feels such Western values are ignored and as a consequence "one can legitimately speak of degeneration" [1–4]. Speaking of "the post-war literary production in Germany" he identifies two groups—the first "cerebral," "abstract," "remote from all naturalness," employing "forced caricatured representations of reality," using "the very remarkable theses of expressionism" as "tricks," which is to say, "skillful artifices calculated at [sic] easy effects" ("small wonder, then," he writes, "that it were mainly non-Germans, and in specific jews [sic], that went in this direction") and another which did not give in to "this aberrant fashion" but respected "the proper traditions of German art which had always and before everything else clung to deep spiritual

sincerity." And he concludes by urging Dutch publishers and translators to "offer their compatriots the possibility to get acquainted with authors who remained true to their natural disposition, despite the seductiveness of scoring cheap successes by using imported formulas." "By not giving in to this temptation these writers have not only succeeded in producing an art of abiding value but they have also secured the artistic future of their country."

Or again in "Les Juifs dans la Littérature actuelle" ["Jews in Contemporary Literature"], the essay from *Le Soir* (published roughly a year before the essays from *Het Vlaamsche Land*) that has aroused so much consternation, he articulates a view which is entirely harmonious with the other essays he has been writing.[9] He scolds vulgar anti-semites for dismissing—through the blindness resulting from their hatred of Jews—the proper German literary and cultural tradition on display in contemporary artistic activity which prizes the inner psychological essence of man and proposes what amounts to a more sophisticated antisemitism.

Vulgar anti-semites, he says, are content to dismiss the whole of contemporary culture as Judaized [*enjuivé*] and therefore polluted and harmful. In doing so, he argues, they in effect give the Jews too much credit since they buy into the notion of a Jewish takeover—a notion that Jews themselves have helped to spread. As a result, they in fact throw out in the process cultural productions which are far from degenerated and thereby lose what is proper and important to the tradition—a result which is ironically as dangerous to German culture proper as the Jews.

Take the case, for example, of literary artists. On the one hand, he says, we regard them as worthy of our praise. On the other, we regard them as imitators of a culture which is Judaized and therefore degenerated and decadent, a culture which in fact is foreign to them. Anyone who has looked deeply into such matters recognizes that aesthetic evolution obeys certain very powerful laws which are not disturbed even by events as otherwise disruptive as a world war. The artistic forms that we see are the continuation of traditions that are at least a century old. Novelists, for example, who pursue the inner psychological essence of man are following the great tradition pursued by Gide and Stendhal, among others, a realist aesthetic that has been with us since the nineteenth century. The same case could be made for modern poetry—for surrealism and futurism.

It is not, in other words, in order to attribute to the Jews an alternative significance to the importance with which vulgar anti-semites would invest them that the young journalist would draw such a distinction between two components of contemporary literary activity but rather to specify their insignificance in that domain, a fact which he adds is actually surprising since the qualities displayed by their writing—cerebrality, coldness— seem ironically appropriate to the kind of precise analysis contemporary literature requires. Jewish writers are uniformly of second rank, in his view, and were they all to be deported outside of Europe the loss would be negligible and European literature would continue according to its own evolutionary patterns. The very fact, moreover, that in a domain of cultural activity as important as literature they would not be missed is a great tribute to that European tradition and a sign of its enduring vitality and health.

Far from aberrant, in other words, the anti-semitic remarks in these essays are critical to the position he has erected (whether or not the twenty-one year old journalist feels conviction about it, which is another matter). They rely upon the same notions of evolutionary laws, the inner psychological essence of man, the value of national characteristics, and the study of literature as a means to insure the future of Western values that the writer develops elsewhere. There is no evidence that we might suspect the writer to be concealing within them another view which would be independent (or even critical) of anti-semitism, unless we are to consider the journalistic activity as a whole as opportunistic. They are of the same fabric as the perspective expressed, for example, in Brinckmann's *Geist der Nationen*.

Nor should that come as a surprise to anyone who studies the milieu in which de Man worked. On the other hand, what may surprise us is the proximity in spirit of the anti-semitic remarks to the writing de Man undertook as late as the mid sixties, a proximity which only becomes readable by virtue of their discovery.

* * * * *

In "The Literature of Nihilism," a review which he wrote for *The New York Review of Books* (June 23, 1966), de Man takes to task two recent commentaries on German literature and philosophy from about 1870 through 1945 (Erich Heller's *The Artist's Journey into the Interior and Other Essays* and Ronald Gray's *The German Tradition in Literature 1871–1945*) which uniformly condemn "German philosophy and literature, from the late eighteenth century on" as "having provided the intellectual basis for Nazism" [16] by suggesting that the two activities—however much we may wish the case were otherwise—had very little to do with each other. Nazism, de Man agrees, was a "mistake," a "catastrophe," the attempted "murder of [a] civilization." But far from the source of that error, the intellectual tradition — which might been sought for counsel—was abandoned by it.

The discrepancy between intellectual values and actual behavior has rarely been so baffling as in this case. No one could claim . . . that the Nazi movement somehow rooted itself in a venerable and mature tradition. It was, if anything, notable for its profound anti-intellectualism and the crude but effective manner in which it played on the most primitive mass instincts. . . . The Nazis received little support from German writers and intellectuals and were not very eager to enlist them in their ranks. . . . If Hitler triumphed in Germany it was in spite of the intellectual tradition of the country, rather than because of it. There was a *trahison des clercs* to the precise extent that literary thought and political action lost contact with each other. The problem is not that a philosophic tradition could be so wrong [as Heller and Gray claim] but that it could have counted for so little when it was most needed. The responsibility does not rest with the tradition but with the manner in which it was used or neglected. . . . It is not in the power of philosophy or literature to prevent the degradation of the human spirit, nor is it its main function to warn us against this degradation. . . . one should be careful about praising or blaming writers for events that took place after they ceased to exist: It is just as absurd to praise Rousseau for the French Revolution as to blame Nietzsche for Hitler. [17]

In context of the writing we have been studying, de Man's position would seem eminently clear. His denunciation of Hitler and of the Nazis, and his defense of the independence of the German intellectual tradition before those who would currently see in it the roots of fascism, contrasts sharply with the sentiments of the journalist of twenty years earlier who welcomed the partisans of just such "contemporary revolutions" with considerable enthusiasm.

Moreover, within the liberal humanist mood of the mid sixties in the American university, the position looks entirely familiar. The intellectuals, who remain the bastion of good sense and rational discourse in a modern industrial democracy, have been betrayed once again. Politics and cultural concerns (like literature and philosophy) are mutually exclusive domains. The former concerns power and the latter knowledge and wisdom. But there can be dialogue between the two. Indeed, it is encouraged that politicians look to the intellectual tradition to inform its decision-making and things are thought to go especially well when such guidance is sought although a continuity between the two is strictly forbidden.

From this perspective, then, Nazi Germany cannot but be regarded as aberrant and degenerate. Far from employing the intellectual tradition, National Socialism decisively shunned it. And the disastrous consequences that accrued cannot but be laid at the doorstep of these decision-makers. It is not the intellectuals who failed—as the title that de Man borrowed from Benda's book had come to imply—but those who failed to heed their advice.

Were such a position, in other words, all we had—and it was for a long time—we should be hard put to distinguish it (at least in general terms) from so many others in the sixties with which it collaborates and whose political posture it conserves. But the more precise the opposition to the earlier writing appears, the more in fact another scenario begins to emerge. For in the earlier writing it was just such a continuity between the political and the cultural that the young writer advocated. Literary study is undertaken as a means of gaining knowledge beyond seemingly erratic and arbitrary individual styles or fashions, and that knowledge serves the larger scientific project of insuring the future of Western civilization by making us masters of our own historical destinies. The fact that we can move, de Man wrote, "from the history of art, to the terrain of the major cultural and political problems, proves how efficient the method of using works of art as study material for the obtaining of general knowledge really is." Indeed, if there were aberrant tendencies into which matters degenerated, or if things decomposed into more primitive forms, such events could be attributed in cultural matters at any rate to non-Germans and "specifically jews [sic]."

We are always, of course, the most critical of others who are now acting the way we did a moment ago and de Man is no exception in this regard. We should hardly be surprised that quite apart from his specific objection to the books of Heller and Gray there is a personal stake in this review that the discovery of the earlier position enables us to read. Moreover, there are other traces of the earlier writing that are of a similar sort. At one point, for example, de Man is taking Heller to task for "a certain oversensitivity to national characteristics" [17]. "National categories applied to literary and philosophic matters always tend to miss the mark" [17].

The aberration that led such a figure as Wagner . . . to adopt nationalistic attitudes can only be understood from a perspective that is no longer national. The confusion stems precisely from the fact that the nation, a perfectly legitimate concept in itself, acts as a substitute for something more fundamental and encompassing. Figures of the recent German past—[such as Walter Benjamin]—had already reacted against this confusion of values. The reaction continues in some of the most influential spokesmen of contemporary Germany—Adorno, Ernst Bloch, Günter Grass, etc. Those critics actively engaged in "demythologizing" national values, have found powerful antecedents among writers who are [in Heller's or Gray's book], implicitly or explicitly, being attacked: Hölderlin, Kleist, and Nietzsche. . . . Critical nationalism, rare in the United States, is a frequent sin among European critics. [17]

The critical nationalism which the journalist of twenty years before had so prized now appears as a "confusion," a "European" sin, and perhaps most interestingly, as a "substitute for something more fundamental and encompassing." Moreover, the "demythologizing" that is taking place regarding this critical nationalism is at work in contemporary Germany in literature as well ("the reaction continues," he writes, "in some of the most influential spokesmen of contemporary Germany"). In his discussion of Rilke, for example, he remarks that "the reasons [for Rilke's withdrawal from the given order of the natural world to the self in its relation to this world] are lengthily and often convincingly stated" [18].

They arise out of an essential awareness of the essential contingency of the human condition, coupled with the realization that many psychological, philosophical, and theological attitudes have no other purpose than to hide this contingency from our insights into ourselves. Rilke's reassertion of the self does not occur as a proud, Promethean (or even Faustian) statement of the power of the mind over nature, but originates in a feeling of loss and bewilderment. The same is true of most of the major poets and thinkers of the period, although the form in which this bewilderment is experienced varies considerably of course from writer to writer. [18]

De Man's formulations remain to some extent "existential" and reminiscent of the vogue for Continental phenomenological thinking in the sixties—and instead of "loss," "bewilderment," or "negativity," he will speak in his later work more of "failure," "ineluctability," and "impossibility." But the challenge to the earlier positive investment in literary knowledge and national spirit has already been broached.

But there are other ways in which traces of the earlier writing remain, considerations that cast a light of a different sort upon this work and that begin to confer upon de Man's reference to concepts that "[act] as a substitute for something more fundamental and encompassing" an unexpected resonance. The rhetorical structure, for example, of the current essay recalls the structure of "Les Juifs." Within the American setting, de Man is explaining to presumably more sympathetic readers the general misunderstandings of his professional colleagues who would somewhat simplistically dismiss all of modern German literature and philosophy as polluted on the basis of the Nazi disaster. Once again the less sophisticated practitioners of his craft—who would style themselves readers of the contemporary literary scene—would dismiss the entirety of a literary and cultural production because of the failure of a few aberrant and degenerate types whose contribution to it remains insignificant (even though this latter group has helped to spread the rumor of its own significance). Once again the tradition that has been obscured in this way remains in the writer's view vital and healthy—proceeding according to its own developmental patterns—despite such nihilist historicizing. And once again the writer can envision the thorough removal of such foreign and primitive elements from the cultural scene with negligible loss to the tradition as a result.

The similarity in argumentative structure is striking and here is probably a clear example of an insight that could not have been discerned apart from the current discoveries. Moreover, the constancy of his use of that rhetorical strategy enables us to observe an unexpected irony regarding the identity of the participants. For a substitution seems to have occurred. It is not just any group who appear where the Jews formerly appeared but those precisely who would be their most heinous adversaries.

Has de Man in the middle of the sixties become philo-semitic? Have Jews now come to enjoy the positive endorsement that the practitioners of the "contemporary revolutions" of the forties received? And is it in terms of this substitution that we should understand his alliance, for example, with Derrida whom he meets at the same moment?

It would be prudent, I would suggest, in responding to these questions, as in considering all matters pertaining to this affair, to be cautious. For there may yet be one more level on which traces of the earlier writing persist, a level perhaps more powerful—even constitutive—of the others, and in context of which the substitution we have observed assumes a new importance. For the tone of his remarks about the Nazis and the substitution they imply is curiously insistent and seems somehow to exceed the text—as if across the distance of those years, and beyond any reversals that might have taken place, it is somehow the same discussion that we are observing.

The possibility of such a continuity remains somewhat obscured by a semantic shift that took place regarding the words "Nazi" and "Hitler" after the war in English and German speaking countries. In the post war American context, in the wake of the disclosures of the Nuremberg trials, and, somewhat later, Hanna Arendt's coverage of the Eichmann trial, these words had come to designate anti-semitism itself, and it is understandable that in this context de Man's anti-Nazism could have appeared to support that posture.

But in fact there is in "The Literature of Nihilism" not one reference to Jews or to anti-semitism. And if the current narrator charges the Nazis with the attempted "murder of [a] civilization" it is German culture (and not Judaism) that he is talking about. Moreover, these passages remain among the most straightforward that we have of de Man. The tentativeness and self-effacement that has become in recent years almost the hallmark of his style—and is already present to some extent in the earlier writing (and is even present in the second half of this essay where he talks more specifically of literature)—is curiously absent in the passages on Nazism. And we would seem left to conclude either that de Man's position really is harmonious with the surrounding intellectual climate—although de Man nowhere makes such a suggestion explicit and in fact such a determination would render this material incompatible with much of what he has written before or since—or there is another context in which that denunciation makes sense, one which we have not as yet uncovered, and that renders its appearance in this context responsive to demands of a different sort.

It is to this second possibility that I would like to turn. For it may be that the substitution we have noted is not an invention of the sixties—for reasons of liberalism or for any other reasons—or of any of the years intervening since the earlier writing but rather a rhetorical strategy which has already been operative from the outset, the remnants of an ongoing dialogue that has simply become a little more overt in the present context.

For if we return for a moment to an essay like "Les Juifs," we note that the same substitution is already at work. Consider, for example, the opening paragraph.

Vulgar anti-semitism readily contents itself to consider cultural phenomena of the post World War One period as degenerate and decadent in so far as it is Judaized [*enjuivé*]. Literature has not escaped this lapidary judgement. It is sufficient that one discover certain writers to be Jewish under the cover of Latinized pseudonyms for the entire production of the contemporary scene to be considered polluted and harmful. This conception leads to consequences which are fairly dangerous. Above all, it causes us to condemn a priori an entire literature which in no way merits this fate. Moreover, it would hardly be a flattering appreciation for Western writers—the moment after we are content to grant them a certain merit—to reduce them to being simply the imitators of a Jewish culture which is foreign to them.

That the writer reflects an anti-semitism that is shared with both the "vulgar anti-semites" with whom he would lodge this argument and the audience to whom he would appeal it goes without saying. The Jews are foreigners to German culture proper and have negligible influence upon it (much as they would like to think otherwise). And it would be a misreading of the weight of the passage to shift attention from that common assumption in order to focus upon the particular bone of contention between the young journalist and his more militant colleagues. The crescendo to which this position leads in the final paragraph—where he asserts that the ability of Europeans to safeguard themselves from Jewish influence proves their vitality, that if European culture had allowed itself to be invaded by such foreign forces it might as well give up any hope for the future, that semitic "interference" has been evident in all aspects of European life, that proposed solutions to "the Jewish problem" in which the Jews would be removed from Europe to a colony outside might proceed without deplorable consequences in his view—since only a few personalities of mediocre value would be lost—all of this language renders the objection that he makes to the vulgar anti-semites of little consequence. Nor is it a great deal of comfort in this context that the phrase "vulgar anti-semites" can also be construed semantically to read as an attack against anti-semitism, a proposition he nowhere else sustains.

At the same time, in view of the turn that his writing does take later in his career it is worth at least noting that much of what he will later say of the Nazis is already present here in germ form. What is viewed as "dangerous" for example in this essay is not in fact the Jews—who are in his view without significant influence—but the consequence of misunderstanding their insignificance, a misunderstanding that his co-revolutionaries display. And it is dangerous in particular for the area of cultural life that de Man has spent so much of his energy defending—the German tradition of literature and philosophy. Moreover, there is an irony attendant to this particular misunderstanding since in assuming the Jews are influential and need to be eradicated from the contemporary scene, and then proceeding to condemn contemporary literature on that basis, the vulgar anti-semites achieve ironically for the Jews the very influence that the Jews themselves have been unable to achieve.

Already at the outset, I would suggest, a displacement has been at work behind more overt concerns and it may be this displacement that explains for us the insistent tone of his remarks in the later essay. Imagine the academic of the sixties reflecting back upon his experience of the last twenty years. Despite his repeated admonitions, the vulgar anti-semites undertook a project that was in significant ways destructive of the goals they both shared. The Nazi censors arrived and he was compelled to resign. Then having taken over the country, they proceeded to lose the war and he was compelled to leave the country.

Twenty years later, he is safely ensconced within the American academic literary critical establishment and along come these two products of post-war liberalism to argue that Naziism had its intellectual basis in the German tradition, the very argument, that is to say, the Nazis were trying to proffer twenty years before and whose failure he has so egregiously witnessed. He is livid and his anger issues into in some of the most forceful prose he has penned to date. It is not the German intellectual tradition that is to blame for fascism but the Nazis. The intellectuals would have urged an entirely different course but their counsel was abandoned. The claim that the German tradition—which the Nazis undertook in fact to destroy—was responsible for Nazism is a "warped" conception of history that can only be attributed to a simplistic response to the complex relationship between thought and action that such events should have taught us.

It is a powerful scenario, attractive for reasons that probably exceed the confines from which they issue. But before acceding too quickly to its appeal, it might be wise to examine its costs. For it binds us to a particularly troublesome consequence: that de Man in the sixties, in continuing the ongoing debate with the vulgar anti-semites (who have now become indiscriminately "the Nazis" and "Hitler"), depends, at least in part, upon the same assumptions that formed the parameters of the earlier discussion—namely, anti-semitism. Is it not, in other words, at least implicitly the case that in continuing to debate, de Man argues for a more enlightened and sophisticated position which would not be incompatible on the one hand with the defense of German culture, but on the other with the exclusions of all foreign elements from it, "and in particular jews [sic]?" In short, is the sixties essay read in this fashion—which is to say, from a position already at stake within its subject matter, a reading strategy that psychoanalytic theorists would identify as repetition, and that de Man himself, from within the deconstructive context of his later writing, would designate a domestication and reenactment—not still, by implication if in no other fashion, anti-semitic?

Once again, it behooves us to be cautious. De Man's anti-semitism at its worst in the forties is a far cry from the demagoguery of a Léon Van Huffel whose essay framed the page on which de Man's most disturbing essay appeared—and whose essays had been appearing regularly in *Le Soir*. And in the sixties de Man is infinitely more concerned with defending the German tradition and with the devastating effect wrought by those who, in the name of defending that tradition against its enemies, achieved their goal than he is in pursuing the exclusionary postulates that they share.

So destructive, in fact, have these co-partisans been that de Man is even receptive to allying himself with their adversaries in the service of the cause that is of primary importance to him. And when he meets in 1966—the same year as the publication of "The Literature of Nihilism"—a young French researcher at the Johns Hopkins University conference on "The Languages of Criticism and the Sciences of Man" who is interested above all in German culture and thought, who had begun his thesis work in France on literature, who has been able to put aside his religious and ethnic origins (and seems equally content to remain at some distance from the fashionable psychoanalytic, anthropological, and marxist currents of the times), and who has just published a series of essays on Rousseau in which he argued the availability in Rousseau of a criticism of the very positions acted out by his critics, their encounter seems destined. If Derrida didn't exist, de Man would have had to invent him.

De Man's 1966 essay, in short, is both more anti-semitic than we might expect and less. It is more because it is not part of the liberal context in which it appears but reflects an anti-Nazism that in one fashion or another de Man has been arguing already for some time and which relies upon their identification of a common adversary. But it is also less since by the sixties de Man is significantly more concerned with defending the German cultural tradition against those who attack it from within in the name of that defense than those who are genuinely foreign to it.

Do we understand better in this context the reticence of the man we knew to speak after the sixties of political matters? No doubt if de Man had been called upon to express himself on Nazism he would have denounced it. But might he then not also have been called upon to articulate the basis for his denunciation and, as his reasons differed from those of others, might he not better have advised himself to eschew all such discussions?

What in any case does seem clear—beyond all such risky motivational speculation—is that far from arbitrarily related to the rest of his corpus, far from harmonious with the writing surrounding it—and all appearances to the contrary—the essay is pivotal to both what preceded and what followed. It makes clear in no uncertain terms that de Man's fundamental concerns remained constant. His advocacy remained the tradition of German literature and philosophy whether he is defending it against foreigners (such as the Jews), the vulgar anti-semites (who in the name of defending it would destroy it), or, in his final two decades, university liberals who would collapse that tradition with its worst enemies—and thereby not only lose the

advantage of its demythologizing force but enact the condemnation levied years before by those who would destroy it. He will do battle with academic humanists who, like Heller and Gray, would distort that Germanic tradition, often in the same breath as their discussion of the Jews ("We do not fight Judaism but *Destruktion*," E. R. Curtius is reputed to have said, "not a race but a negation. . . . Our Jews, it must regretfully be said . . . are self-devoted to skepticism and *Destruktion*").[10]

But by the same token, it also makes clear, against the register of that constancy, de Man's successive strategies. De Man begins believing that he can move freely between politics and culture. But when the traumatic events of the war reveal to him that politics is no guarantee against decomposition from within he retreats to a province safely removed from most social concerns—from politics, psychology, and anthropology (all of which he had previously engaged fairly freely). Within this new province he will become proportionately more energetic in speaking about literary, linguistic, and philosophic matters and from within that position he will launch in fact a profound criticism of precisely the literary essentialism and historical (and political) progressivism in which he himself began. In the battle from the sixties on between the academic humanists and the Continental philosophers, de Man will increasingly align himself with Heideggerian *Destruktion* even if it is disseminated in America (as it was earlier in France) primarily by Jews. It remains one of the minor ironies of this new alliance that it will lead him, once he has thought through the performative and rhetorical aspects of language more fully, to the very opinion about the mutual complicities of language and action in the world that in the sixties essay, in the work of Heller and Gray, and with regard to Nazi Germany, he had so forcefully been denouncing.

* * * * *

[Aristotle] . . . cannot be separated from the "woes and wars" his pupil Alexander the Great inflicted upon the world. Words cannot be isolated from the deeds they perform; the tutor necessarily performs the deeds his pupil derives from his mastery. [RR, 102]—*Paul de Man*

It is not my intention here to trace de Man's relation to Derrida or to deconstruction with which he has been associated (and with which he has associated himself)—interesting and important and ongoing as that engagement is—as much as to register the effects that the thinking of this French Jewish writer has had upon the latest body of de Man's work in so far as those effects suddenly seem related to the writing we have been considering. For if de Man's writing in the sixties seemed at once like and unlike the earlier work, there is one more scene in this ongoing drama whose dimensions remain to be plotted, a scene in many ways more decisive than all the others, and which, after de Man, and for more than one reason, we might entitle the "madness of words."

The phrase itself occurs toward the end of his essay on Shelley's *Triumph of Life* in which de Man is considering the relation of the poem Shelley left us to antecedent versions and concerns the "naive belief" that insight or knowledge about the ways in which we "monumentalize" or construct recuperative allegories about our experience confers upon us no freedom from repeating it. The theme is not unrelated to earlier interests of de Man. Although "The Literature of Nihilism" contains a number of ideas which will gain increasing ascendancy in de Man's work—the demythologizing of national categories, the recognition that the value of literary artists consists not in their promotion of Western values but in their critical investigation of our promotion of them—it also reflects a number of ideas and energies that are continuous with the earliest writing and which the later essays will abandon. "It is just as absurd," he writes in 1966, "to praise Rousseau for the French revolution as to blame Nietzsche for Hitler."

This does not mean that philosophers and poets have no moral or political responsibility even when their work is apolitical. But it means this responsibility should be evaluated within the full philosophical or literary context of their work, not their lives, still less the effect that their work may or may not have on other people. The real and difficult problems that the German tradition formulated during the last two hundred years cannot be dismissed because it is supposed to have led to a national catastrophe. [17]

Words, in this view, have an absolute and complete value to them—like precious possessions—which is separable from political action, and our ability to use these words to convince and persuade is premised upon this value and this distinction. Whether "the Nazis" and "Hitler" refer to anti-semites (as opposed to moralists) or vulgar anti-semites (as opposed to more sophisticated practitioners of anti-semitism) this distinction remains constant.

Such an idea in de Man's work is about to be displaced entirely by another but its removal is somewhat concealed behind more thematic matters. In 1970, de Man publishes at Oxford *Blindness and Insight* in which the demythologizing power of literary texts (over the labor of critics who in the name of reading these literary texts would domesticate and reenact them) is given center stage. There are always only two interpretations of

things, de Man says in this book, those that are blind and those that are aware of their blindness. There are no non-blind positions and insight in this connection must be understood as positions that are more or less aware of the blindnesses in which they (like every other perspective) inevitably participate.

In subsequent essays, some of which were published in *Allegories of Reading* but many of which were circulated privately or in professional journals, de Man fastens upon the notion of a performative which was developed by J. L. Austin but given prominence in this country by John Searle and the debate between Searle and Derrida (which showed up in Derrida's work as "Signature Event Context" and Limited Inc"). Austin's most powerful insight in this connection was probably the recognition of the impossibility of sustaining the distinction between a constative and a performative, that all language was in one way or another a form of action (meaning is the force language exerts in a context) and thereby an exercise of power. The notion served de Man to expand his conception of the critical reading lesson that literature teaches from rhetoric to disfiguration, a critical investigation of the way in which language tropes, which is to say, constitutes at once metaphor and rhetoric, representation and persuasion.

And it is this notion of disfiguration, or de-facement, which the *Rhetoric of Romanticism* above all pursues. As a kind of sequel to *Blindness and Insight,* its concern is no longer simply with the nature of literary insight (the recognition of blindness which is its condition of possibility) but the status of this recognition and in particular what, in another vocabulary, might be called the danger of the idolatry of the law of anti-idolatry or, in still a third vocabulary, the problem of transference: what happens when the fact of monumentalization itself has become a part of our consciousness (when Shelley discovers, for example, the same recognition in Rousseau)? If it is impossible for us to escape recuperative allegories in cultural life (any more than it is to stop breathing), is it possible at least to acknowledge the naiveté or evasive manoeuvering of such a gesture?

It is the naiveté of believing in even this possibility (any more than in the recuperative strategy itself), or that this naive belief will not itself be repeated endlessly in countless new forms of historicization or aestheticization that de Man takes up in this essay, a series of reflections that will enable us to close the circle we have been tracing and offer de Man's clearest perception to date on the position with which he began.

Such monumentalization is by no means necessarily a naive or evasive gesture, and it certainly is not a gesture that anyone can pretend to avoid making. It does not have to be naive, since it does not have to be the repression of a self-threatening knowledge. Like *The Triumph of Life,* it can state the full power of this threat in all its negativity; the poem demonstrates that this rigor does not prevent Shelley from allegorizing his own negative assurance, thus awakening the suspicion that the negation is a *Verneinung,* an intended exorcism. And it is not avoidable, since the failure to exorcise the threat, even in the face of such evidence as the radical blockage that befalls this poem, becomes precisely the challenge to understanding that always again demands to be read. And to read is to understand, to question, to know, to forget, to erase, to deface, to repeat—that is to say, the endless prosopopeia by which the dead are made to have a face and a voice which tells the allegory of their demise and allows us to apostrophize them in our turn. No degree of knowledge can ever stop this madness, for it is the madness of words. What would be naive is to believe that this strategy, which is not our strategy as subjects, since we are its product rather than its agent, can be a source of value and has to be celebrated or denounced accordingly.

Whenever this belief occurs—and it occurs all the time—it leads to a misreading that can and should be discarded, unlike the coercive "forgetting" that Shelley's poem analytically thematizes and that stands beyond good and evil. It would be of little use to enumerate and categorize the various forms and names which this belief takes on in our present critical and literary scene. It functions along monotonously predictable lines by the historicization and the aestheticization of texts, as well as by their use, as in this essay, for the assertion of methodological claims made all the more pious by their denial of piety. Attempts to define, to understand, or to circumscribe romanticism in relation to ourselves and in relation to other literary movements are all part of this naive belief. *The Triumph of Life* warns us that nothing, whether deed, word, thought, or text, ever happens in relation, positive or negative, to anything that precedes, follows, or exists elsewhere but only as a random event whose power, like the power of death, is due to the randomness of its occurrence. It also warns us why and how these events then have to be reintegrated in an historical and aesthetic system of recuperation that repeats itself regardless of the exposure of its fallacy. This process differs entirely from the recuperative and nihilistic allegories of historicism. If it is true and unavoidable that any reading is a monumentalization of sorts, the way in which Rousseau is read and disfigured in *The Triumph of Life* puts Shelley among the few readers who "guessed whose statue those fragments had composed." Reading as disfiguration, to the very extent that it resists historicism, turns out to be historically more reliable than the products of historical archeology. To monumentalize this observation into a method of reading would be to regress from the rigor

exhibited by Shelly which is exemplary precisely because it refuses to be generalized into a system. [RR, 122–123]

Even within the context of the explosive and profuse insights deconstruction has accustomed us to expect, the passage, I would suggest, is dazzling in its range and its power. It is hard to imagine a more comprehensive, more critical, or more self-reflexive position. All that remains, in order for de Man to elaborate a full-blown theory of language (and of its monumentalizing nature), is to relate it to the other-than-human origins from which in his view it springs—an elaboration which he seems to have begun at the moment of his death and which others have taken up since.[11]

At the same time, no less astonishing—in light of the themes we have been pursuing in this essay is the directness with which it confronts the position of the journalist of forty years earlier—the native belief in historical progress and in essential or substantive value. "*The Triumph of Life* warns us," he says to the journalist who believes in the progress of evolutionary laws, "that nothing, whether deed, word, thought, or text, ever happens in relation, positive or negative, to anything that precedes, follows, or exists elsewhere but only as a random event whose power, like the power of death, is due to the randomness of its occurrence." And to the literary essentialist he tells his "demonic" "ghost story," that "to read is to understand, to question, to know, to forget, to erase, to deface, to repeat— that is to say, the endless prosopopeia by which the dead are made to have a face and a voice which tells the allegory of their demise and allows us to apostrophize them in our turn. . . . What would be naive is to believe that this strategy, which is not our strategy as subjects, since we are its product rather than its agent, can be a source of value and has to be celebrated or denounced accordingly."

Words, in short, in this new view, rather than precious possessions (like national categories), are themselves possessed. The "madness of words" is at once our complete freedom to use them and the life they lead independently of us the moment we do so, the thoroughgoing arbitrariness of language at the moment of its deployment and its absolute necessity once it has been exercised, the way in which, in short, the very possibility of understanding rests upon a repetition that could not but occur and yet was undertaken in complete freedom. To monumentalize is to construct an experience as a text, to aestheticize it, or historicize it, in order that we might derive some instruction from it or gain some mastery over it. But in telling the story of our experience in this way, we necessarily belie it since that experience always already contained within it (in so far as it was also an experience of such stories) the seeds of our current behavior, and if the experience was particularly complex—like literature, for example—the more knowledge we think we gain about it, the more we think we read it (the more mastery or instruction we derive from it), the more in fact we only play out or repeat the stories we have read and the more literature is reading us. Moreover, no "degree of knowledge [about this repetition or reenactment that we undertake] can ever stop this madness," this compulsive transferential (or mimetic) behavior, since it "is not our strategy as subjects" (as "we are its product rather than its agent"). "What would be naive is to believe that this strategy [or repetition] . . . can be a source of value and has to be celebrated or denounced accordingly."

On the other hand, what we can do is "dramatize" it in all of its implications and complicities. That is the reading lesson that literature teaches us. Aristotle "cannot be separated from the 'woes and wars' his pupil Alexander the Great inflicted upon the world" not because Aristotle's philosophy is imperialistic but because Alexander's imperialism is also Aristotelian philosophy, a duplication (in a particularly graphic way) of the stories already contained within Aristotle's teaching and precisely to whatever extent Alexander (or Aristotle) felt he had mastered that teaching. "Words cannot be isolated from the deeds they perform; the tutor necessarily performs the deeds his pupil derives from his mastery." Aristotle is not responsible for Alexander's reenactments—Alexander might have done otherwise—but neither are the actions of the two men separable. What Alexander plays out it is always necessarily the dramas upon which Aristotle was already at work. The intellectuals are as implicated in Nazi thinking as the Nazis—whatever the degree to which either chose to act out that thinking in the world. The root of fascism is lodged not in our decision to aestheticize or romanticize our politics but in our decision to politicize our aesthetics. And as Aristotle to Alexander, so, we must assume, de Man would argue, Rousseau to the French Revolution, and Nietzsche (or perhaps more properly Hegel) to Hitler.

Can we be sure that this latest phase of de Man's work is not just a negative imitation of his earliest, a continuation of the old energies if expressed now only in completely negative or critical form? If it is no longer the Jews or the Nazis who are expendable as aberrant or degenerate from within the realm of Western values or within a Platonic conception of literature and philosophy, is it not possible that there is another threat to be guarded against from within the notion of langauge as performative? Is it possible that as he retreated in the mid sixties from what he perceived as the disturbing and degenerate mixture in Nazism between politics and cultural production (in which the Jew was

the enemy, "nihilist allegories" were the order of the day and the true intellectuals were abandoned) to a perspective within the university and intellectualism (from which position political degeneracy could be denounced), so again in the eighties he may only have retreated once more from the vicissitudes of intellectual activism (of the sixties and early seventies) to a notion of language which already contains within it both representation and action and from within which the primitivism of another enemy (old guard humanism in its reaction to deconstruction?) could be denounced? Is there, in short, any guarantee that his position is not just another allegory by which he may retrieve or recuperate the native land from which he feels alienated?

None. In fact, if there were such a guarantee things would be considerably more precarious than they are. But for the first time in the later work it would seem to be the failure of such a narrative that is as much at stake as its success and the limitations of any totalizing gesture as much as their benefits. What we may want to ask about this later view is not whether it is superior to the older perspectives—more insightful, less blind—but rather whether it delivers on its promise to offer us, in addition to the insights by which it establishes itself, a way of acknowledging the blindnesses in which it also inevitably participates and from which in fact those insights inevitably derive. If we understand what de Man is saying then the fact that we demonumentalize is no guarantee that we are free from repeating that monumentalization at another level or of any superior insight about it since it is not recuperative allegories—which we can never escape—which are the enemy but their appropriation within an absolutizing and totalizing framework. In this context, the "naive belief" in such freedom or such insight may in fact constitute the most dangerous and egregious example of such absolutizing.

* * * * *

. . . while digging in the grounds for the new foundations, the broken fragments of a marble statue were unearthed. They were submitted to various antiquaries, who said that, so far as the damaged pieces would allow them to form an opinion, that statue seemed to be that of a mutilated Roman satyr; or, if not, an allegorical figure of Death. Only one or two old inhabitants guessed whose statue those fragments had composed.—*Thomas Hardy, "Barbara of the House of Grebe," quoted by Paul de Man [RR, 93]*

Anti-semitism is a disappointment whenever it shows up. It invariably drags along with it the sickening sense of having been here before, of its having lain dormant for a while but upon encountering the right combination of circumstances having come out of the woodwork. It is particularly disarming when it shows up in the university, which prides itself as an institution upon the free exchange of ideas within the environment of liberal humanist studies, and ironically so when it appears in the career of a scholar or critic who prides him or herself (even builds a career) upon uncovering such prejudicial cecity.

The case of Paul de Man is no exception. The early works are an indelible moral blot upon an otherwise increasingly formidable intellectual presence and we can no longer responsibly read the later works without taking them into account. No amount of biographical, psychological, or historical research can ameliorate or extenuate the damage. The fact that he was under family or political pressure, that there were only one or two explicitly anti-semitic essays (and that his version of anti-semitism was far milder than that of others who also published essays—often in close proximity to his), that the journalist was only twenty-one when he wrote the majority of these texts, or that he may have had a friend in the resistance—all these "explanations" do less to soften the impact of the discovery than to situate it. The fact remains that the writer could have chosen otherwise and did not. Others who had a great deal more to lose than de Man at twenty one chose very differently. To make such a comparison is certainly not to suggest that de Man *should* have chosen another course but to take stock of the course that he did choose. At the very moment that he is writing the words we have been examining from *Le Soir* and *Het Vlaamsche Land,* the Nazis, who by this point have already murdered thousands of human beings, are constructing the procedures for the systematic killing of eleven million more in countries to the East. Long after anyone (except someone guilty of remaining in Hartman's phrase "deliberately ignorant") could see their practical effects, de Man wrote reviews in which he called for the success of the "current revolutions" at the "cost of any sacrifice" and reflected that the removal of the Jewish community to a colony outside of Europe would not have regrettable consequences for European literature, which would remain healthy. The consequences for those who were in fact removed some seventeen months later were less healthy. We all live with the consequences of our decisions—the bad ones perhaps even more than the good.

But in Paul de Man's case, the fact also remains that the burden of his particular past, the ineluctability of his special history, seems to have served—as it did, for example, in his characterization of Rousseau and of Shelley—to spur him on to his best insights about precisely such processes. Now more clearly than ever before it begins to look as if de Man's later work was a prolonged meditation on just such earlier total-itarian complicities or collaborations. Read in context of the earlier writings, the later essays seem almost obsessively concerned with undoing the notions with which he began—notions about the organic or unifying nature of art and its value as a civilizing force, and about the march of history as an advance towards a new spiritual order. His later work is an insistent refusal to grant this particular privilege to literature and this understanding of history, an unending demonstration that there where we believe literature upholds such values, it reveals in fact their collapse (and if we grant the monstrous and demythologizing critical writing we label "literature" any special privilege it derives from this particular revelation), and an incessant demonstration that there where we have so narrativized history socially or personally we have done little more than excuse ourselves before moments that by their radically fragmentary nature have no necessary relation to each other whatsoever, an incessant engagement, in short, with his own particular and peculiar past (and thus a symptom of its presentness and of the impossibility of its being mourned). Only those who refuse to read de Man or who read him poorly could see the earlier texts as a confirmation of his true position in the later since it is precisely against that perception that his later writing continued to work. It is probably not the smallest of ironies in this whole matter—and one that more properly illustrates his point than challenges it—that those critics who have not read the later writings or have not understood their demythologizing force (and think therefore that he has done little but play with words as a front for nihilist agendas) charge him with denying history or promoting rather essentialistically the value of literature.

To what conclusions, then, do these newly unearthed fragments of de Man's work lead us? "Whose statue" do they "compose?" Do we have any better sense in their shadow of the man behind de Man? It should be clear by now that "the difficulty of answering is prefigured in the asking of the question" and that the answer that we give to this question matters less than the way in which we use it. It is not as if we have a choice whether or not to invoke a conversion narrative—we cannot but do so; we do so all the time; we are bound to do so one way or another—but whether the conversion narrative we invoke contains within it—like Shelley's *Triumph of Life*—the possibility of its own reading. To view de Man secretly as a nihilist or an anarchist and to see the recent discoveries as confirmations of what he *really* is (which was before only dimly perceived) is not distinguishable finally from deciding he is *really* an iconoclast. The greatest obstacle to the understanding of his work, I would suggest, is to decide that he is either one or the other on the basis of that discovery rather than exploring with the increased corpus of de Man's writings, in increasingly comprehensive ways, the limitations of such decision-making—its origins, its strategies, and its consequences.

Nor would I suggest that these limitations should in turn be pursued simply for their own sake. De Man's statements about the radical fragmentariness of history or about the radically demonumentalizing nature of literature can themselves be made to appear uniquely valuable only if we essentialize or "freeze-frame" his thinking at any one given moment, even the moment interrupted by his death. We may feel such notions to be part of a prolonged effort to challenge his own initial positions. They have all the earmarks, Hartman writes, "of a belated, but still powerful, act of conscience" [Hartman, 31]. More importantly for scholarship and criticism, perhaps, they seem to us but the first step of an effort to clear the way to a more powerful account of literary and historical understanding, a "deepening reflection on the rhetoric of totalitarianism," whether that rhetoric is observed within aesthetics or more ominously within the appropriation or "fatal aestheticizing" which Hartman suggests is politics itself and "which gave fascism its false brilliance" [31].

But the forte of de Man's work, I have suggested, like the literature he read (and in contrast to the nihilist allegories he denounced and which critics have seen fit to impose upon him), was that it was open-ended. How can we be sure that the latest efforts of de Man were a clearing of the way on the path to a new positive view and not a negative imitation of the older perspectives? We cannot—by virtue, moreover, of the very reading lesson de Man teaches us. There is in fact no way of deciding between the two possibilities since the evidence in either case would look the same. De Man himself may have continued in the direction of his later work, recognizing the dangers of inherent in "the assertion of methodological claims made all the more pious by their denial of piety." On the one hand, he tells us, "reading as disfiguration, to the very extent that it resists historicism, turns out to be historically more reliable than the products of historical archeology" although "to monumentalize this observation into a method of reading would be to regress from the rigor exhibited by Shelly which is exemplary precisely because it refuses to be generalized into a system." On the other hand, he may have succumbed in his own terms to that "reliability" and that "regression." What he left us is only the difference between the two, between an insight that totalizes itself and an insight that takes stock of its own totalizations.

There is, of course, a long history in the West for such theorizing and it would be an extraordinarily ironic turn indeed for de Man, who began as an anti-semite, to have ended as philosemitic. But the temptation to see de Man's final project as

"Jewish" (and his critique of monumentalization as a critique of idolatry, or perhaps, more precisely, of the idolatry of anti-idolatry) may promise more than an ironic allegory of his personal fortunes here. For to identify de Man's "reading lesson" as in some sense Jewish is to name the second step after the ground is cleared: the step which in fact since his death has been so much a part of our discussion (and may even explain why we are so upset when the credentials of the leading philosopher of reading turn out to be questionable) which is that a philosophy of reading is always an ethics; reading is a form of ethical practice.

It would be prudent to be cautious in this domain. De Man himself steadfastly refused an ethical dimension to his work. In his discussion of "ethicity" for example in his analysis of Rousseau in *Allegories of Reading* he resolutely refused to see ethics as interpersonal or subjective in any fashion other than "linguistic."[12] If there is persistence of the earlier work into the later it is probably this refusal to give up the humanistic grounding, the language-centeredness, that World War Two exploded and rather to continue in the shadow of its scandal the possibility of a purely linguistic and rhetorical analysis, even if by "rhetoric" here we include the notion of a performative. The fact that he went further than many others in ferreting out within the literature he read the dangers of an aestheticizing or historicizing domestication or recuperation is no guarantee a priori that he would pursue his project further—to pose, for example, other-than-linguistic relations—notions concerning for example ethical responsibility—as Martin Buber, Gabriel Marcel, and most recently Emmanuel Lévinas among others have done.

But since his death others have taken up that project and who is to say finally he would not have collaborated in this effort as much as he did with liberalism of the sixties, deconstruction in the seventies, or with the romantic essentialism of National Socialism initially ("collaboration" in this sense seems to have been his theme throughout his life). Had these current discoveries come to light during his lifetime, can we really be sure that he would not have confronted them, for example, in the essays on religious and political discourse in Kierkegaard and Marx he intended to write—now that he felt he had the performative apparatus of language under control, so to speak—and whose conclusions he suggested he knew as little about as anyone. "I have always maintained," he told Stefano Rosso in the final interview he gave in 1983, "that one could approach the problems of ideology and by extension the problems of politics only on the basis of critical-linguistic analysis, which had to be done in its own terms, in the medium of language, and I felt I could approach those problems only after having achieved a certain control over those questions" [RT, 121].

I feel now some control of a vocabulary and of a conceptual apparatus that can handle that. It was in working on Rousseau that I felt I was able to progress from purely linguistic analysis to questions which are really already of a political and ideological nature, so that now I feel to [sic] do it a little more openly, though in a different way than what generally passes as "critique of ideology." It is taking me back to Adorno and to attempts that have been made in that direction in Germany, to certain aspects of Heidegger, and I just feel that one has to face therefore the difficulty of certain explicitly political texts. It is also taking me back constantly to problems having to do with theology and with religious discourse and that's why the juxtaposition of Marx with Kierkegaard as the two main readers of Hegel appears to me as the crux, as the problem, one has, in a way to solve. . . . I look forward to seeing what I will produce and know as little about it as anybody else.

So did we. The "melancholy spectacle" that he saw, in the posthumous preface to *Rhetoric of Romanticism,* as his life's achievement on romanticism, is hardly the kind of epistle from Paul (to Jacques and beyond?) we would have desired. And the fact that his life's work should now once again be in danger of being discredited is probably an irony which he would have found sadly familiar. Moreover, unless some new texts turn up, matters are likely to remain roughly where they are and this discussion is likely to occupy the concern of critics of his work for quite some time.

But there may at least be a way of formulating such feelings more concretely. In the middle of an essay in *Het Vlaamsche Land* on Max Dauthendey, he speaks of a writer who he identifies as a kind of literary anthropologist who is able to feel especially well the sensibilities of the natives whose spirit he inhabits.[13]

Not only has he noticed their external, material appearance and life style, but he has also penetrated their temperament so profoundly that he can speak their language, interpret their mind, sense their drives. The achieved result is wonderfully beautiful, we are transported in a world which has nothing in common with ours any longer, not only because it offers an amazing wealth of colour and a changing splendor of landscapes, but most of all because it is governed by a state of mind which is that of the real native. [2]

And in the midst of this essay, he offers a more detailed description of one of Dauthendey's books which is extraordinary in any number of ways—not the least of which is stylistic (since this passage seems to be one of the few—perhaps the only—place(s) in the ten essays where de Man make available to us the plot of a literary work under discussion).

The book is entitled *Raubmenschen* and the plot concerns "the theme of alienation." "The suffering of a European who has been torn out of his own natural environment in order to live in a completely different atmosphere which, to him, is shocking, is depicted" [3].

The hero of the story is transported outside of his own ethical norms in a world where the holiest rules are not respected, where the most somber crimes can take place without anyone forbidding them. He consequently feels surrounded by mysterious, horrifying forces which try to attack him with all means and rob him of everything that is dear to him. An almost unbearable tension is thus achieved: one constantly feels the burden of a threat without being able to localize it, because it is in fact the entire country which attacks the foreign traveller and wants to master him. And here and there through this ever-increasing atmosphere of anxiety shimmers the soft yearning for a distant native country, the sole place on earth where equilibrium and happiness can be found. [3]

The resonances of this passage in the present context are striking. In light of the Holocaust and the deathcamps, does not the description of someone "transported outside of his own ethical norms in a world where the holiest rules are not respected, where the most somber crimes can take place without anyone forbidding them" sound ominously like the experience of the Jews? How are we to understand this "working through" of de Man's, his fascination with this "exotic image?" Has he heard rumors of the camps or of the fate of the deportees during the previous month, and is this an expression of sympathy? Is this a personal expression which comes from his being thrust at twenty odd years into a project about which he has serious anxieties? Or, more ominously than either of these two possibilities, is it a Nazi fantasy, the dream of someone who longs for home and who will in fact construct the camps in order to act out those dreams in all of their complexity in the world—a kind of romanticism with a vengeance?

Again, in light of the subsequent history of a man who has been displaced from the world he knew in the forties and forced to start again from scratch—in the face of the massive evidence of the failure of his earlier conclusions—could this image not also encompass the de Man of the sixties, the seventies, and eighties who experienced "the suffering of a European who has been torn out of his own natural environment in order to live in a completely different atmosphere which, to him, is shocking" [3]?

But in what is no doubt the most ironic possibility, does not the passage resonate the most profoundly from beyond the grave? Is it not tempting to fantasize a de Man who is observing these current discoveries and the handling (or perhaps manhandling) of them by the antiquaries of our profession, a man who may constantly feel himself attacked by forces around him which are mysterious to him and which want to take from him everything that was dear to him, one who "constantly feels the burden of a threat without being able to localize it, because it is in fact the entire country which attacks the foreign traveller and wants to master him."

Does not the passage, in short, come to summarize (in the way images do—by collapsing consecutive sequences into a unique presentation) a life of alienation—of starting again from scratch, of being surrounded by massive evidences of the failure of one's conclusions to amount to anything, and of the haunting return of these forgotten scenes like those from bad movies, repetitions which afflict like a guilty conscience?

The narrative of disillusion is an attractive one. It seems to have attracted another de Man (who knew another Poulet and who also spent time in Switzerland), who also experienced himself as an exile from his native land as the result of political fortunes, and who took up residence in a foreign country after leaving Belgium.

In the end, however, it became everyday clearer that this belief in progress rested on self-deception: however different things may be, they will not be better. One expects that the zone of catastrophe will give birth in suffering to all sorts of wonderful things that cannot be found in everyday life, but the miracle does not come to pass. The real product is only pains—and the regrets of the morning after.

. . . By turning away from reality, that is, from the duties of the life placed before the individual, to the non-existent or the unattainable, the worst service to men that can be performed has been performed: the illusion that they are capable of shaping their own collective fate has led them to construct their own catastrophe. [OG, 6][14]

In such a scenario of the good gone wrong, the "arch-debunker" turns out also to have been a self-deconstructor, a boa-self-deconstructor (to neologize from a name that was once attached to the "contemporary revolutions" with which he associated himself).[15] And the "reading lesson" to be gleaned from this discovery of demonic collaboration turns out to be more about the "allegorical figure of Death" than any of the antiquarians suspected (although Derrida, who was perhaps closer intellectually to de Man than anyone, had already identified in the theme of an impossible mourning a critical path through his work).

But as before there is no more (or better) reason to make this claim than any other. What is clear is simply the difference between the earliest and the latest work and the vastly more comprehensive stature of the latter. The conversion from Paul

to Saul may be an unlikely theme for literary critical biography (and somewhat more than we bargained for). But perhaps today and in this connection especially it confers upon the haunting medieval anti-semitic refrain "until the conversion of the Jews" (which Christians took, even through the end of the Renaissance, to be synonymous with "the end of time") more resonance than we might have expected (or wanted). In the shadow of Hegel (who thought he was witnessing the end of history as he was completing his *Phenomenology,* and with whose totalitarian ideas we continue to struggle—via the story of Oedipus, the memory of the Holocaust, or Otherwise), perhaps a sentence which links the fate of the non-Jew irretrievably with the fate of the Jew is not inappropriate. Paul Adolf de Man begins as far from Jewish thought as possible and there are no signs that he was ever interested in Judaism religiously ("he didn't seem to have a religious bone in his body," Hartman writes, half-facetiously). But in his critique of monumentalism and the "madness of words"—and in his recent talk about the way in which language originates in the otherwise-than-human—it may be that those who would today mount an ethics of reading (Jewish or otherwise) will come to identify in his most mature work—as painful as it might have been for him to speak in these terms—an authentic support.

The challenge we face on the basis of these new discoveries is whether we can continue to read that critique in de Man's writing without defacing it once more, without collaborating again in its misunderstanding (a misunderstanding which the work itself, taken in its entirety, has dramatized), or perhaps, more faithful to de Man, without remaining blind to the collaboration and defacement in which we will inevitably participate. "I feel myself compelled to repeated frustration," de Man writes, in *The Rhetoric of Romanticism,* "in a persistent attempt to write as if a dialectical summation were possible beyond the breaks and interruptions that the readings disclose. . . . Such is the cost of discursive elegance, a small price to pay, perhaps, compared to the burden of constantly falling back to nought" [ix].

Cornell University

ABBREVIATIONS

RR *The Rhetoric of Romanticism* (New York: Columbia University Press, 1984)

AR *Allegories of Reading: Figural Language in Rousseau, Nietzsche, Rilke, and Proust* (New Haven and London: Yale University Press, 1979)

RT   *The Resistance to Theory* (Minneapolis: University of Minnesota Press, 1986)

BI   *Blindness and Insight: Essays in the Rhetoric of Contemporary Criticism* (New York: Oxford, 1971)

BI2   *Blindness and Insight: Essays in the Rhetoric of Contemporary Criticism,* Second Edition, Revised (Minneapolis: University of Minnesota Press, 1983)

OG   "Four Early Texts by Paul de Man," in Ortwin de Graef, "Paul de Man's Proleptic 'Nachlass': Bio-bibliographical Additions and Translations," pp.1–42 (circulated privately)

HVL   *Het Vlaamsche Land*

NOTES

1. "Shelley Disfigured," 93–123.

2. At this writing, these materials have not been published, although a volume, *Paul de Man. Wartime Journalism, 1939–1943,* is forthcoming from the University of Nebraska Press. The essays from *Het Vlaamsche Land* (ten) have been translated from the Dutch by Ortwin de Graef. Four of the ten essays were circulated as part of his essay, "Paul de Man's Proleptic 'Nachlass': Bio-bibliographical Additions and Translations." The other six have been circulated separately. The essays from *Le Soir* (170, from December 1940 through November 1942) and *Les Cahiers du Libre Examen* (three) are in French and where I have cited them in English the translations are my own unless otherwise indicated. There are also seven articles in *Jeudi,* the newspaper of the Cercle du Libre Examen at the Université Libre de Bruxelles, and 100 more texts published by Paul de Man in the *Bibliographie* of the Agence Dechenne from February 1942 through March 1943, although I have not had the opportunity to examine them.

3. "L'anti-sémitisme vulgaire se plait volontiers à considérer les phénomènes culturels de l'après-guerre (d'après la guerre de 14–18) comme dégénerés et décadents, parce qu'enjuivés."

4. "Il ne faudrait pas formuler beaucoup d'espoirs pour l'avenir de notre civilisation si elle s'était laissé envahir sans résistance par une force étrangère. En gardant, malgré l'ingérance sémite dans tous les aspects de la vie européenne, une originalité et un caractère intacts, elle a montré que sa nature profonde était saine. En plus, on voit donc qu'une solution du problème juif viserait à la création d'une colonie juive isolée de l'Europe, n'entraînerait pas, pour la vie littéraire de l'Occident, de conséquences déplorables. Celle-ci perdrait, en tout et pour tout, quelques personalités de mediocre

valeur et continuerait, comme par le passé, à se développer selon ses grandes lois évolutives."

5. On the Wannsee conference, which took place on January 20, 1942, at which the "final solution" to "the Jewish question" was announced, see Raul Hilberg, *The Destruction of the European Jews* (New York: Harper and Row, 1961), 264 ff. For maps of "Jews Marked Out For Death, 20 January, 1942" both within and outside of Nazi rule, see Martin Gilbert, *The Macmillan Atlas of the Holocaust* (New York: Da Capo Press, Inc. 1982), Maps #99 and 100. For a map of "The Jews of Belgium and Luxembourg" who were deported, see Map #134. "The first deportations from Belgium," Gilbert writes, "took place on 4 August 1942. . . . Henceforth, over a period of two years, a total of 26 trains set off to the 'unknown destination' from the internment camp at Dossin, near Malines. The destination was in fact, Auschwitz" [Gilbert, 110].

6. For example, on January 10, 1941, an article about "L'élimination des enterprises juives en France" appeared. On January 23, 1941, a photo appeared entitled "ENTREE INTERDITE AUX JUIFS" with the caption "Certains grands cafés de Bruxelles ont affiché des avis interdisant aux Israélites l'entrée de l'établissement." In September of 1941, an article entitled "Ordonnance portant limitation de la libre circulation des Juifs" appeared (a "communiqué" from L'Agence "Belgapress") with the subtitle "Il leur est interdit de circuler entre 20 heures du soir et 7 heures du matin." On September 8, 1941 there was a notice about the obligation in Germany for Jews to wear "Une étoile jaune à six pointes de la grandeur d'une soucoupe." And so on.

At the same time, essays were appearing in which anti-semitism was made thoroughly explicit. At the head of the same page of *Le Soir* (March 4, 1941), for example, on which de Man published "Les Juifs" (a page entitled "Les Juifs et Nous"), an article, entitled "Les Deux faces du judaisme," and signed by Léon Van Huffel, appeared which began with the following paragraphs:

> *En tête de cette page consacrée à l'étude de quelques aspects de la question juive, il nous parait utile de souligner les éléments essentiel de notre antisémitisme.*
>
> *Nous ne croyons pas qu'il suffit de justifier ce dernier par des raisons d'ordre social. Les Juifs ont commis socialement beaucoup de tort, c'est entendu. Par leur ruse et leur tenacité, ils se sont emparés des leviers de commande de la politique, de l'économie et de la Presse et ils ont profité de leur situation privilégiée pour s'enricher au détriment des peuples qui les accueillaient et pour entraîner ceux ci dans une politique catastrophique dont l'issue ne pouvait être que la guerre.*
>
> *Mais tout n'a pas été dit quand on a stigmatisé la nuisance du Juif. De plus, il serait téméraire de lui endosser toute la responsibilité des excès*

du regime capitaliste dont nous vivons aujourd'hui douloureusement l'écroulement.

Notre antisémitisme est d'order racial. Il voit, dans l'ensemble des Juifs, une vaste communauté d'individus reliés entre eux par un certain nombre de trait physiques et moraux communs.

En gros, les Juifs nous apparaissent comme d'une essence foncièrement étrangere et radicalement opposée à notre sang et à notre mentalité.

Nous croyons à l'existence d'un type juif, d'un génie juif. Nous sommes résolus à nous interdire tout métissage avec eux et à nous affranchir spirituellement de leur influence dissolvante dans le domaine de la pensée, de la littérature et des arts.

"What is especially grievous," Geoffrey Hartman writes, in a recent review of these matters in "Blindness and Insight: Paul de Man, fascism, and deconstruction," *The New Republic* (March 7, 1988), 26; 28–31, "is that de Man continued an association with overtly anti-Semitic and collaborationist newspapers to the end of 1942—well past the time when all but the deliberately ignorant would have known that the persecution of the Belgian Jews, begun before the end of 1940, had taken a drastic turn" [26]. Hilberg's remarks occur in a letter in *The Nation* [April 9, 1988], 482.

7. See "The Literature of Nihilism," *New York Review of Books* (June 23, 1966), 16–20.

8. It is interesting to consider the reasons that de Man cites for the failure of results "in this domain."

One has only got the confused and contradictory experiments which are derived from history at one's disposal. A clear delineation of the operating forces, the first necessity of all scientific work, cannot be accomplished here. Neither can one dispose of a sufficient number of experiments in order to clearly and distinctly perceive the phenomenon one wishes to explain, which is absolutely indispensible for all statistical laws—and those are the majority. [25]

Whatever else it is, Nazism seems to be the systematic breaching of these boundaries. In a sense, the deathcamps were precisely the places where the Germans granted themselves permission for such experiments to be performed. One need no longer be confined just to history. Social Darwinism offered a clear delineation of the operating forces. The numbers for the experiments were available. But to say as much, of course, is to say—as I have elsewhere maintained—that Nazism is not an "aberration" but an extension of the projects—humanist as well as a number of others—of the culture in which it is born. Ingmar Bergman's much maligned film, *The Serpent's Egg*, seems to me to make precisely this point.

9. This essay is widely available both in French and in English. The French text has been circulating since the Fall of 1987 with other essays from *Le Soir*. For the English, see, for example, Jacques Derrida, "Like the Sound of the Sea Deep within a Shell: Paul de Man's War," *Critical Inquiry* 14, no. 3 (Spring 1988), 624; 628–629; 630–631, and this volume, pp.127–164.

10. For the quote from Curtius, see Hartman, 28.

11. See, for example, "'Conclusions': Walter Benjamin's 'The Task of the Translator'" in RT, 73–105 and especially the discussion that followed de Man's delivery of this lecture at Cornell (94–105). The question of the possibility for an ethics of reading in relation to de Man's work has been taken up by Hillis Miller in *The Ethics of Reading* (New York: Columbia University Press, 1987).

12. "Allegories are always ethical, the term ethical designating the structural interference of two distinct value systems. In this sense, ethics has nothing to do with the will (thwarted or free) of a subject, nor *a fortiori,* with a relationship between subjects. The ethical category is imperative (i.e., a category rather than a value) to the extent that it is linguistic and not subjective. Morality is the same language aporia that gave rise to such concepts as "man" or "love" or "self" and not the cause of the consequences of such concepts. The passage to an ethical tonality does not result from a transcendental imperative but is the referential (and therefore unreliable) version of a linguistic confusion. Ethics (or, one should say, ethicity) is a discursive mode among others" [AR, 206].

13. "German Literature. A Great German Lyricist: Max Dauthendey," in HVL, 6–7 September 1942, p.2.

14. De Graef cites another passage from Henri de Man—from *Après coup (Mémoires)*—as the epigraph to his essay.

Certes, j'ai vécu à une époque ou le mouvement auquel je m'étais donné a traversé une phase de régression, de décadence, de décomposition. Qu'importe, puisque la douleur que j'en ai ressentie m'a poussé à repenser toutes mes pensées, au point de me sentir aujourd'hui en contact plus réel avec les faits que quand j'ai commencé à vouloir agir sur eux.

It is interesting that the same words that Paul has used—régression, décadence, décomposition—to identify threats from the outside are employed here to refer to the whole period. Paul himself will, of course, make the same kind of shift in "The Literature of Nihilism."

15. For an interesting discussion between Abrams and de Man, on the occasion of de Man's last public lecture at Cornell, regarding the relation between the understanding of language that de Man is proposing and humanism, see RT, 99–102.

Looking Past the De Man Case

GERALD GRAFF

In the controversy touched off since the existence of Paul de Man's collaborationist writings came to light, much of the attention has been directed at the effect of the discoveries on our view of de Man's mature work. This is not surprising. The politics of de Manian deconstruction—and of deconstruction generally—was already a topic of intense polemics in the literary-theory world before the facts about de Man's early journalism became widely known. Given the political tendency of this early journalism, it obviously has to color subsequent assessments of the later de Man.

Yet it seems important to ask how much illumination such a retrospective reading of the later de Man can give. Doesn't the theoretical value of de Man's mature work have to be judged on its own terms, irrespective of the circumstances and motives that may have led up to it? The question seems no less pertinent even if the effect of de Man's later work is to make treating a text or body of work on "its own terms," with the assumption of textual identity this implies, seem less simple than we thought.

It is true that our knowledge of the early de Man cannot help affecting subsequent interpretations of the later de Man. But to say this is not to settle matters, because we now have sharply conflicting stories of the connection between the two. The most hostile story constructs a later de Man who was impelled to call the concept of history into question because he had to escape or rationalize his collaborationist past. The most generous story constructs a later de Man who repudiated the earlier de Man's glorification of organic national cultures.

These accounts are not as different as they at first seem. It is noteworthy that the features of de Man's work that his supporters adduce to establish de Man's credentials as a subversive demystifier of ideology are often the same ones his enemies adduce in order to characterize de Man as an apolitical aesthetic escapist. For one group it is de Man's questioning of totalizing modes of thought that makes his work politically oppositional, whereas for the other it is this questioning of totalizations that makes it politically irresponsible and impotent. The difficulty is compounded by the ill-defined nature of a concept like "totalization," not to mention the elusiveness of de Man's claims in general, which are couched in a style of argumentation that resists measurement on a calculus of complicity vs. subversiveness.

But whatever account is chosen of how de Man's later work is tied to his earlier politics, the question still remains what relevant bearing it will have on judging the theoretical validity of that later work. If the so-called "genetic fallacy" is still a fallacy (as I think it is), then the truth-value of a theory of language or literature (or the truth-value of any generalized body of ideas) cannot coherently depend on the motives or conditions which generated it. Nor can a theory's truth depend on its political consequences. To put it another way, the "ideological" effect of a theory (or interpretive practice) cannot be inferred from the theory itself, but depends on how the theory is *used* in particular circumstances and contexts, and the same theory can have very different ideological colorations in different contexts.

Terry Eagleton makes this point in an essay on "Ideology and Scholarship" when he says that "ideology is less an immanent quality of particular kinds of language than a question of language's contextual effects."[1] According to this "conjuncturalist" line of reasoning, theories "in themselves," divorced from their contexts of use, are politically *ambidextrous*.[2] The same theory can serve the purposes of the Left, the Right, and other positions on the political spectrum. (Again, the point does not lose all force even if, as de Man might argue, calling something "the same" theory when it is contextualized in different ways begs certain questions.) A theory can be "progressive" in some contexts and "regressive" in others, or progressive at one moment and regressive at a later one. Which is one reason, among others, why disputes over whether deconstruction is "really" radical or reactionary have not always led to very useful discussion, and one reason why it is wrong to treat the de Man case as if it put deconstruction in general on trial.

This is not to deny that all theories are necessarily "political" merely by virtue of being social practices with social consequences. It is simply to say that the particular *way* a theory is political, what its social consequences *are,* is not deducible from the theory itself, but is contingent on how the theory is inserted into specific conjunctures. None of this relieves writers from responsibility for the consequences of their work, for a writer can assess the situation that his work will be entering. At the time he wrote for *Le Soir,* the young de Man certainly knew—or could have known—enough about what was happening to Jews in Belgium and Europe to be fully responsible for the consequences of the reprehensible statements in several of the reviews. But no writer can be aware of all the contexts in which his or her work may be read, nor can any writer foresee the new contexts of reception that will inevitably arise over time. In writing his later works, de Man probably could not have anticipated the way the recent revelations would recast the way those later works would be read.

But doesn't the fact that we distinguish between the "use" and "abuse" of theories (or interpretive practices) imply that there must be some internal connection between a theory and how it is "used"? Wouldn't it seem perverse, for example, if a group of capitalists used *Das Kapital* as a how-to-do-it manual for exploiting the proletariat, or if a group of prison wardens used Foucault's *Discipline and Punish* as a handbook for controlling and normalizing inmates? Or suppose, to take another kind of case, that a white supremacist were to excuse blatantly racist opinions on the grounds that theories in themselves cannot predetermine how they will be used. When a year or two ago a baseball executive, Al Campanis, made statements on television to the effect that blacks lacked the intelligence to qualify for managerial positions in the sport, one did not have to do much contextual analysis to know how such a "theory" was likely to be "used." Had anyone defended Campanis' statements on the ground that no theory is racist in itself but only in certain contexts, such a defense would have seemed specious. Is this then an argument for some limited degree of essentialism? If an idea had no inherent tendency to be used in some ways rather than others, how could we explain its functioning contextually in a predictable and consistent fashion?

Perhaps this problem accounts for the equivocation in Eagleton's formulation. When he says that "ideology is *less* an immanent quality . . . *than* a question of language's contextual effects," Eagleton seems to leave open the possibility that ideology is *to some extent* "an immanent" quality." Citing the example of the statement, "men are superior to women," Eagleton observes that not even such overt sexism "is inherently ideological, since it might always be deployed in an ironic or sardonic context which demystifies rather than deludes."[3] Would this still be the case, however, if the statement were not ironic? The notion of "function within a context" evidently could use further analysis.[4]

But clearly it is one thing to estimate the effects of crude statements like "men are superior to women," and another those of highly sophisticated theories of language. The more complex and qualified a body of work is, the less predictable and calculable the relation figures to be between the work "itself" and its ideological effects. All else being equal, the "ambidextrous" potential of a text increases in proportion to its complexity. De Man's claims do not translate unequivocally into a "theory that denies the possibility of knowing the truth about the past," as a hostile critic, Jon Wiener, has written in *The Nation*.[5] And again, even if de Man's argument could be reduced to such a theory, it is not obvious that some single kind of politics would follow from it. Scepticism toward the possibility of knowing the truth about the past (like more positive theories of knowledge) has been embraced by radicals and conservatives, revolutionaries and fascists, anarchists and apoliticals. Insofar as fascist ideology trafficked in philosophies of knowledge, it was sometimes sceptical and relativist, sometimes absolutist. Either way it had no problem justifying racial superiority and anti-semitism.

I am not suggesting there is no point debating the politics of the later de Man in the light of the earlier de Man, but I am calling attention to factors that make it difficult for the debate to advance beyond its currently deadlocked state. Even if we could agree that the theories of the later de Man had one overriding political tendency, we would still be left with the question of whether those theories are *true*. If and when the smoke clears concerning the politics of the later de Man, we will still have to grapple with the more important question of what to make of his thought as a theoretical and interpretive project. I call this "the more important question," because we would not be troubling ourselves about de Man's early and late politics if major theoretical claims had not been made for de Man as a thinker and reader of texts.

I

I have already mentioned the popular image of deconstruction which reduces it to a form of scepticism about truth and determinate textual meaning. This image has been jointly created by enthusiasts who reduce deconstruction to slogans and by detractors who seize on these slogans and mount their refutations accordingly. (I know how this works: you read a pro-deconstruction tract and you think, "Well, this guy is *for* it—so he must know what he's talking about.) Hostile critics have approached deconstruction primarily with an eye to detecting its fallacies, without also attempting to imagine what in it might be true and useful, refusing to try out an unfamiliar way of thinking and see what happens. (I confess my own past sins in these respects.) As a result, it is the more sensational of the deconstructive themes (the "unreadability" of all texts, etc.) which have attracted the most attention, obscuring more interesting themes, or more interesting constructions that might be put on the more sensational ones.

Consider the fate of Jacques Derrida's maxim, "there is nothing outside the text," which has been widely understood as if what Derrida meant was that reality is nothing but words. Yet if one looks at the work of the scholars who accept this trivializing interpretation of the maxim and attack deconstruction accordingly, one finds that many of them have silently assimilated its actual and more useful import: that all social phenomena can be usefully viewed as "texts," in the sense that we encounter them only through interpretive systems whose choices and exclusions "inscribe" themselves in the results of interpretation. This "textualist" premise has proved immensely useful to Marxists, feminists, new historicists, and other socially-oriented scholars who have been challenging the established conceptions of the disciplines and their boundaries. This is another reason why I don't think deconstruction itself is really on trial in the de Man case—it has already proved its usefulness, even in the work of many who now attack it.

One aspect of the textualist message is that seemingly innocent choices of research strategy, choices we take to be transparently justified by the objects of our investigation, involve exclusions that our standard categories obscure. Consider, for instance, the way seemingly natural departmental demarcations like "English," "philosophy," and "political science" encourage the implication that to raise political or philosophical questions about literature is to venture "outside the field," or at least to take up questions of secondary or "extrinsic" importance. The choice of a context in which to read a text—the decision that literature should be read in a "literary" rather than, say, a feminist context—involves a repression which can be "read" in written and institutional texts. The point (accounting for the overload of scare-quotes in this paragraph) is that what counts as a "literary," "political," or "philosophical" context is open to debate and subject to change over time. The very notion of a specifically literary context of discussion, distinct from the contexts of moral and natural philosophy, is a relatively recent invention.

This challenge to falsely naturalized disciplinary categories and boundaries underlies the ill-understood recent insistence on the indeterminacy and undecidability of textual meanings. In the standard attacks on these indeterminacy theories, it is hardly ever noticed that the key issue is one of how institutions regulate the contexts of discussion. (This explains why the Johnsonian rock-kicking strategy of these attacks seems beside the point to their targets.) When current theorists assert that all meaning is indeterminate, what in many cases they are doing is claiming the right to read texts in contexts other than those circumscribed by the author's intention or by official disciplinary conventions. I say "the right," because the question of the context in which a given text will be read involves matters of institutional power, being a question of who gets to set and delimit the agenda of discussion.

Which is not to say that rationality plays no role in disputes over the proper context of discussion, but that that role occurs in a setting which has already been shaped by institutional power before rational dispute gets under way. In other words, it is perfectly *rational* to raise questions about the non-rational prior constraints in which rational discourse takes place. Literature departments continue to teach received classics not just because good reasons can be given for teaching them (as often they can), but also because, quite apart from any reasons, those texts have been taught in the past and powerful groups want them to keep being taught. When conservatives bitterly complain that the universal values the curriculum is supposed to embody have been eroded by "special interest groups," they conveniently assume that their own interests are exempt from being viewed as "special." What they never acknowledge is that who gets to say which interests will be defined as universal and which as special is a political issue.

One can attack such a view on the ground that insofar as it is used to discredit knowledge and interpretation, it is self-refuting. Freed from this sceptical application, however, the view contains an important truth. Our culture and intellectual disciplines have been extraordinarily oblivious to the social contexts in which knowledge-production and dissemination take place, and if leftist rhetoric often becomes strident and overheated in pointing this out, this is largely because the reasonable core of its message has hardly registered. We still act as if the fact that the epistemic status of knowledge is independent of its social origins or consequences were sufficient to ward off any questions about the political functions knowledge may be performing. And it is still easy to avoid dealing with such questions merely by accusing them of vulgar reductionism.

It is largely thanks to the textualist model that it has become less justifiable to dismiss those questions this way. Wary though deconstructionists are of the concept of "ideology," deconstruction has made possible a reformulation of the terms and methods of ideology-critique. This it has done by conflating psychoanalytic, political, and linguistic categories. Language becomes a site of psychic repression and social exclusion, in a way that is more subtle and useful than the old Freudian leftist equation of political tyranny with psychic taboo. The argument is that the meaning of a text includes what the text does *not* say as well as what it says explicitly, or, more precisely, that a text's exclusions are part of what it "says." In order to say something about any subject, I have to set aside an infinity of other subjects (i.e., define them as not part of the subject). Though some of my exclusions will be more or less rationally justifiable (e.g., I can present good reasons why I am not discussing the price of milk in this essay), they cannot all be. It is always possible to challenge any of my exclusions (even the price of milk, for all I know) from another perspective.

What makes this a potentially fruitful premise for ideological criticism is that by enlarging the "context" of writing and interpretation to include the contexts writers and readers exclude as well as the ones they include, it allows us to see exclusion as a structuring principle of texts and readings instead of a mere "ex-

trinsic" determinant. Fredric Jameson's elaboration of "the political unconscious" as a structure of "containment strategies," or agendas that narratives exclude or repress, is a kind of dialectical transformation of this deconstructive tactic. Equally indebted to deconstruction is the new historicist strategy of treating a seemingly marginal element of a text as the thread that unravels repressed preoccupations of the whole. One could extend the list of these debts much further.

This is not to say that deconstruction is immune to reductionism of its own kind, but then what mode of thought is? Certainly the belief that we can escape the dangers of reductionism by eschewing theory and retreating to empirical facts (or texts) in themselves is one of the fallacies that has been effectively smoked out of the closet by deconstructionists and other textualists. The real quarrel of textualism with empiricism is not, as is often thought, with the assumption that facts exist or that they can be tested, but with the assumption that facts somehow speak for themselves, unaffected by the way knowledge-production is organized. It is this assumption, that the knowledge accumulated by compartmentalized departments adds up to a transparent and self-interpreting whole (otherwise known as the discipline, or the cultural tradition), which obscures the contested nature of knowledge and its social contexts.

One of de Man's most suggestive formulas held that every "insight" is systematically enabled and limited by a certain "blindness."[7] If one thinks of the formula as a statement about institutions as well as other kinds of texts, one can begin to see how de Manian deconstruction need not be another formalism, but can become a model for social and historical analysis as well as literary explication. I stumbled on this realization in writing my recent book, *Professing Literature: An Institutional History*. More precisely, reviewers of the book made me aware of what I had only half-discerned while writing it, that deconstructive motifs of repression and forgetting had structured my narrative of professional history.[8]

As I tell the story, the modern university, though it has claimed to represent a unified humanistic tradition, was founded on the repression of the methodological and ideological conflicts that erupted with the earliest emergence of professionalized academic disciplines. In my account, the concept "literature department" has sustained its shaky coherence by systematically forgetting—and hiding from students—a long succession of potentially disruptive conflicts, which continue today in our controversies over the canon, theory, deconstruction, and the de Man case itself. This structured amnesia is rooted in the organization of disciplines and curricula into fields and courses which, being unconnected, do not have to air their differences in public. As long as potentially troublesome new fields are quietly added to the aggregate without anyone's needing to confront the challenges they pose to entrenched ones, the university becomes a text of increasingly more radical contradictions which are never acknowledged as such and remain mostly invisible to outsiders.

I end up proposing an alternative curriculum which would foreground these contradictions instead of assuming the need for a foundational consensus. Samuel Weber has argued along similar lines in *Institution and Interpretation*. Weber writes of the way "the exclusion of limits from the [academic] field organizes the practice it makes possible," thus effacing the conflicts that ought to be addressed by the curriculum. The critique of academic professionalism that emerges from Weber's "deconstructive pragmatics" seems to me highly compatible with my own.[9]

II

So far I have argued that, unlike the de Man who wrote for *Le Soir,* the later de Man is a complex thinker whose works resist classification on a simple left/right axis. Polemics which, in the light of the early work, characterize the late work as either "reactionary" or "subversive" tell us more about the careless use of these political labels in recent academic discourse than about de Man's later work. But even if such labels did apply, it would still be necessary to evaluate the later de Man by the theoretical cogency of his arguments.

These arguments seem to me flawed, and I want now to turn to the aspects of de Man's later work that continue to trouble me, though my aim here will be to reopen questions rather than to close them. The question that remains the most troublesome for me is whether the textual aporias de Man so persistently unearthed are genuine problems or are forced upon texts by a tendentious theory of language. It is not that I think the linguistic scandals uncovered by de Man are merely bogus, but I wish de Man had elaborated more fully on the sense in which they are (and are not) scandalous.

Take what is probably de Man's most influential contribution to the theory and practice of literary criticism, the argument that the "rhetoric" of an utterance radically suspends its "logic" and "opens up vertiginous possibilities of referential aberration."[10] The context of this particular formulation is the celebrated case of Archie Bunker's bowling shoes, taken up in de Man's essay "Semiology and Rhetoric." Archie is asked by his wife Edith whether his bowling shoes lace over or under.

"What's the difference?" he querulously retorts, only to have his would-be rhetorical question taken with naive literalness by Edith, who patiently explains what the difference is: you see, Archie, lacing over is like this, under is like that . . . (p.128).

"As long as we are talking about bowling shoes," de Man says, "the consequences are relatively trivial" (p.128). But the case exemplifies a fact of great consequence for interpretation, the tension between "grammar" and "rhetoric" that renders meaning undecidable. Archie intended his "What's the difference?" as a discussion-closing rhetorical question, the force of which, in effect, was "I don't give a damn what the difference is" (p.128). But we could imagine the same words being spoken by a Nietzsche or a Derrida, in which case we could "not even tell from his grammar whether he 'really' wants to know 'what' difference is or is merely telling us that we should not even try to find out" (p.129). What makes "What's the difference?" an instance of undecidability, then, is that "the same grammatical pattern engenders two meanings that are mutually exclusive: the literal meaning asks for the concept (difference) whose existence is denied by the figurative meaning" (p.128). "A perfectly clear syntactical paradigm (the question) engenders a sentence that has at least two meanings, one which asserts and the other which denies its own illocutionary mode" (p.129). "The sentence by means of which we ask [the question] may deny the very possibility of asking." We cannot "authoritatively decide whether a question asks or doesn't ask" (p.129).

De Man sums up the point as follows:

The grammatical model of the question becomes rhetorical not when we have, on the one hand, a literal meaning and, on the other hand, a figural meaning, but when it is impossible to decide by grammatical or other linguistic devices which of the two meanings (that can be entirely contradictory) prevails. Rhetoric suspends logic and opens up vertiginous possibilities of referential aberration. (p.129)

In failing to recognize the undecidability of his utterance, Archie becomes the archetypal deconstructionist straight man, "confronted with a structure of linguistic meaning that he cannot control and that holds the discouraging prospect of an infinity of similar confusions, all of them potentially catastrophic in their consequences" (p.129).

But what exactly is the catastrophe? When I first read this essay some years ago, I thought that de Man had simply succumbed to a mistaken notion of grammar and syntax. It is only on the false assumption that grammar and syntax generate "literal" meanings (evidently a residue of the grammaticism of Genette and other structuralists, which de Man opens his essay by attacking) that we could have a situation in which there is a lit-eral meaning that can be undercut by "rhetoric." According to most philosophers of language since Wittgenstein, meaning is determined not by grammar or syntax, but by use in pragmatic situations. By this view, the notion of a literal meaning, inde-pendent of any context, no longer makes sense. For, in itself, the grammatical or syntactical form of an utterance is insuf-ficient to tell an interpreter what kind of speech act is being per-formed. Therefore, whether the expression "What's the dif-ference?" is a question or an assertion is indeed undecidable if the expression is taken by itself, but only because any utterance is undecidable until we infer how it is being used in a specific situation. The "catastrophe" described by de Man would be real, then, only if one arbitrarily refused to play with a full deck linguistically—if one isolated utterances from specific speech-situations and treated them as if they had a "grammatical" or "literal" meaning apart from any use.[11]

Though I still suspect there is something funny about de Man's notion of grammar, syntax, and literal meaning, I no longer think this objection discredits de Man's argument for construing Archie's remark as undecidable. This argument draws its primary force from a more challenging idea, which is that the Wittgensteinian concept of use that I just invoked above opens up as many questions as it settles. It is not just that the same words can be used to perform different speech acts, but that there is no privileged way of determining how lan-guage is being "used" in a given case. In this sense, what is meant by the undecidability of language is its vulnerability to context-switching.

The current rereading of de Man's later work in the context of the revelations about his early journalism is an intriguing in-stance of this very vulnerability. Presumably, de Man no more intended his later work to be read in the context of his early journalism than Archie Bunker intended his remarks to his wife to be read in the context of Nietzsche and Derrida. Yet de Man's later work is being read that way now, and who would say it should not be, or that such a reading is irrelevant to its meaning or out of bounds? To argue that the context of the early de Man is irrelevant to understanding the later de Man would seem an arbitrary exclusion, and not just to deconstructionists.

De Man's point is that there is always a discrepancy between a speaker's interpretation of his meaning (the context in which he would have us understand it) and an interpretation from the standpoint of another context, and that this discrepancy is both a precondition of the existence of communication and some-thing that breaches or fissures it from within. Because our speech acts can never control their range of application, they are displaced from their originating intentions and, according to de Man, thematize this displacement in their structure. What Ar-chie's "What's the difference?" can be used to "do" is not lim-ited by Archie's intention, for someone can do something different with the same words, read those words "against the grain" of their intention, or interpret their intention itself against the grain, which is to say, show that it includes other in-tentions it does not acknowledge. The later de Man cannot ex-clude the earlier de Man as a context that determines what its speech acts perform.

Understood this way, the argument of "Semiology and Rhetoric" becomes considerably more powerful and cannot be dismissed as the product of a mere mistake about grammar. It has close links with Derrida's thesis that repetition always in-volves transformation ("iterability alters") in his dispute with John R. Searle in "Limited Inc."[12] But what is the argument an argument *for* in de Man's case? Granted, when read against the grain, Archie's, de Man's, or anybody's utterances can be used to do something different from what their speakers intend. But what then? At what point and in what sense does this become a problem? If it is not a pertinent objection to de Man (as it isn't) to adopt a rock-kicking demeanor and say, "Come on now, we know perfectly well what Archie's statement means," neither is it a helpful explanation to say that de Man has "put language into question," or has "problematized" the relation between meaning and rhetoric, or has pointed out that we cannot "mas-ter" language, etc. The question is what such expressions are supposed to mean. In other words, *so what*?

I am not, however, suggesting that de Man is just working himself up over a pseudo-problem. In the previous section of this essay, I spoke of specific institutional situations in which control over the contexts of interpretation becomes an impor-tant issue, and before that I spoke of the discontinuity between theories and their political uses. But de Man stops short of iden-tifying specific contexts like these which might clarify the ways in which linguistic decontrol can legitimately be called "cata-strophic." He tends to write as if the catastrophe is absolute, all-pervasive, and metaphysical, just mysteriously *there,* somehow, outside any particular context.

In this respect, the most pertinent question may be the one we are least likely to ask, which is why the catastrophe in ques-tion is "relatively trivial" as long as we are talking about bowl-ing shoes. Why should it matter whether the subject is bowling shoes or ontology? If it is a problem that utterances are divided against their own conditions of use and performance, then it needs to be explained why this problem is less real for commu-nications about bowling shoes than for those in literature or philosophy. For one thing, this distinction itself tends to be blurred by de Man's argument. For another, what is so trivial about an exchange in which a man bullies his wife on a television program viewed by an audience of millions?

To put it another way, if communications about bowling shoes can get on with their business regardless of their state of catastrophic undecidability (as de Man implies), then why can't "higher" forms of discourse do so too? What is it about different kinds of discourse that makes their performative conditions a stumbling-block in some cases but not necessarily in others? What de Man leaves unclear is the relation between undecidability and "getting on" with the business of communication. Where and how does undecidability become an impediment to something speakers and writers are trying to do?

No doubt I am failing to control my own meaning here as egregiously as anyone, but I am trying to suggest that we need a clearer account than de Man provides of the sense in which undecidability and its interference with the effort to control one's discourse become a problem. Perhaps the concept of "control" over one's discourse needs more specificity than de Man gives it. For me anyway, Weber (in *Institution and Interpretation*) makes clearer what can be at stake in the issue of control, because he connects the performative-constative aporia to specific institutional conflicts. Thus he argues that it is necessary to "reveal the strategic nature of apparently constative academic discourse"[13] and then goes on to suggest what kinds of institutional changes this should lead to.

The nearest thing to such a recognizable strategic context in de Man's case is his apparent attempt to protect the status of literature as a special mode of discourse. I am not the only one who wonders if the states of interpretive catastrophe cultivated by de Man are rooted less in some universal need to control our discourse than in de Man's need to associate literature with "vertiginous possibilities of referential aberration." To those of a certain generation, who were taught in college that the upstaging of practical, scientific, constative discourse is the special and privileged business of literature, de Man's theory and practice will not seem so unfamiliar or radical. They are a throwback to the old opposition between literature and "statement," by which literature has long been seen as an alternative to the technocratic way of knowing, a consolation prize for letting others run the world. De Man frequently essentializes literature in this compensatory way, as when in "Semiology and Rhetoric" he does not "hesitate to equate the rhetorical, figural potentiality of language with literature itself" (p. 129–30). The trouble is, to equate literature with disruptive rhetoricity in this way is merely to equate it with features of language that one happens

to *like*—features that one feels need to have their end held up in a utilitarian-commercial culture which has little use for them.

Which brings me to the other difficulty I have with de Man's work: that its insights sometimes seem gained at the cost of a certain blindness to their having possibly been rigged in advance. As many of de Man's critics have noted, there is something too monotonously predictable about the facility with which de Man repeatedly generates the same sorts of textual aporias—again in order to vindicate the preassigned role of literature as an archagent of vertigo.

Consider de Man's analysis of Shelley's *The Triumph of Life,* particularly of the mysterious figure of the "Shape all light" that plays a central role in the poem:

> A Shape all light, which with one hand did fling
> Dew on the earth, as if it were the dawn
> Whose invisible rain forever seemed to sing
>
> A silver music on the mossy lawn
> and *still* before her on the dusky grass
> Iris her many-colored scarf had drawn.

De Man points out that the Shape is introduced as if it is going to explain the question raised by the poem, the meaning of human suffering, but it utterly fails to address this question coherently and finally almost seems to forget it had been asked.[14]

So far so good—it is a tellingly good observation—but de Man does not stop here. He goes on to allegorize the Shape all light as "the figure for the figurality of all signification" (p.62), and therefore (since figurality for de Man is by definition always deconstructive) for the self-undoing nature of signification. The Shape thus becomes an exemplification of the necessity and the impossibility of meaning. The Shape dramatizes the fact that we impose "on the senseless power of positional language the authority of sense and meaning . . . but language cannot posit meaning; it can only reiterate (or reflect) it in its reconfirmed falsehood. Nor does the knowledge of this impossibility make it less impossible" (p.64). The Shape conveys that "the positing power of language is both entirely arbitrary . . . and entirely inexorable in that there is no alternative to it" (pp. 62–63). Like Archie Bunker's remark, the Shape exemplifies the disruptively figural, rhetorical potentiality not only of all literature, but now of all texts. A reading of the poem, de Man says, "establishes that this mutilated textual model exposes the wound of a fracture that lies hidden in all texts" (p.67).

But how does de Man arrive at his allegorization of the Shape all light as "the figure for the figurality of all signification"? The Shape is a figure, and it fails to deliver on a promise to explain something, and according to de Man signifying processes are marked by their failure to deliver on their explanatory promises. But this is a frail justification: it rests, in effect, on an attribution of de Man's theory of language to Shelley. De Man assumes that if something is generally the truth about language, this truth must be part of what is thematized by Shelley or by all poetry. He confuses the truth about signification, as he understands it, with what poetry has to be saying.

As if it buttressed his interpretation (the Shape=the figure for the figurality of signification), de Man adds that "the figure is not naturally given or produced but . . . is posited by an arbitrary act of language" (p.62). But according to de Man, *no* figure of speech is "naturally given or produced." If not being naturally produced makes a figure into a figure for the figurality of signification, then every figure can be construed in this way. And at times one wonders why, given his *modus operandi*, de Man could not read any figure he chose as a figure for the figurality (and thus the futility) of signification. The way seems open for construing any figure anywhere as an allegory of reading. But if it is true categorically that "a wound of a fracture . . . lies hidden in all texts," then the revelation of this "wound" in any particular text becomes inevitable and, arguably, less interesting—even though one can work hard, as de Man does, to make the wound look sufficiently different each time around. What is axiomatically true of all texts goes without saying when applied to any one.

De Man has taken a fact about how meaning is presumably produced and made this fact the theme of what all language—or all literary language—is *about*. If figures of speech are arbitrarily produced, this fact about their condition of production is what those figures mean. Anything that can be said about the operations of the language or the logic of a text, then, is what the text is about. In his essay "Beyond Interpretation," Jonathan Culler argues that this thematic "displacement" has been the "central methodological principle" of the *American* branch of deconstruction, something which, Culler implies, helps account for the widely-alleged mechanization of deconstructive readings on this side of the Atlantic. American deconstructionists assume, according to Culler, that "the text does not just contain or perform a self-deconstruction but is *about* self-deconstruction. . . ."[15] The problem is with a mode of reading that knows what texts are about before it reads them.

True, de Man issues a disclaimer denying that he has a system or a method: to monumentalize his observations "into a *method* of reading," he says, "would be to regress from the rigor exhibited by Shelley which is exemplary precisely because it refuses to be generalized into a system" (p.69). But if de Man has

nothing so grand as a method or system, he does have an *a priori* which "generalizes" textual meanings in a predetermined and highly specific fashion.

Of course such a criticism raises questions about hermeneutic circularity that could be used to challenge any interpretation. But it is not enough to point to the hermeneutic circle and retort, as if it absolved de Man of the charge of a priorism, that after all there are no presuppositionless readings, that all reading depends on interpretive "preunderstanding," that all interpreters "know" something of the meanings they will find before they start reading.[16] It is true that interpreters anticipate the kinds of meanings they find by virtue of their having to come to texts with certain interests in mind, but the meanings they ascribe to texts need not be as specific as those ascribed by de Man. The fact that the questions interpreters are predisposed to ask delimit the range of answers they get does not mean that their answers are specifically predetermined. More needs to be said about the issue, but this should be enough to suggest a problem in de Man's work that needs to be addressed.

Treated on "their own terms," then, the later de Man's theories and interpretive practices seem to me subject to serious difficulties. At the same time, de Man's work has opened up valuable lines of inquiry whose implications have not yet been fully understood and explored. The wisest course is not to reject de Man, but to carry further the debate over the mode of analysis he began. Doing so will be a way of improving on the analysis itself.

Northwestern University

NOTES

1. Terry Eagleton, "Ideology and Scholarship," in *Historical Studies and Literary Criticism,* Jerome J. McGann, ed. (Madison: University of Wisconsin Press, 1985), p.115.

2. On the "ambidextrous" nature of theories, see my essay, "The Pseudo-Politics of Interpretation," *Critical Inquiry* 9, no. 3 (March 1983), p.603; reprinted in *The Politics of Interpretation,* W. J. T. Mitchell, ed. (Chicago: University of Chicago Press, 1983).

In my treatment of these and other issues here, I have profited greatly from discussions with my colleague Jules Law, who read an earlier draft of this paper.

3. Eagleton, "Ideology and Scholarship," p.115.

4. Even the relatively clear-cut Campanis example is complicated by the possibility that Campanis' remarks will have "progressive" ef-

fects, having made it harder to deny the prevalence of racist attitudes in baseball's top management.

5. Jon Wiener, response to letters, *Nation* 246, no. 14 (April 9, 1988), p.502; Wiener is defending his article, "Deconstructing de Man," *Nation* 246, no. 1 (January 9, 1988), pp.22–24.

6. For the most recent attempt by Jacques Derrida to correct this misinterpretation, see the Afterword ("Towards an Ethic of Discussion") in the new publication of *Limited Inc.* (Evanston: Northwestern University Press, 1988), pp.136–137.

7. I pass over the question of whether de Man was as yet technically a "deconstructionist" in 1971, when he published *Blindness and Insight: Essays in the Rhetoric of Contemporary Criticism* (New York: Oxford University Press, 1971).

8. Gerald Graff, *Professing Literature: An Institutional History* (Chicago: University of Chicago Press, 1987). The deconstructive tenor of the book has been pointed out by Paul Jay, in a forthcoming review in *Genre*.

9. Samuel Weber, *Institution and Interpretation* (Minneapolis: University of Minnesota Press, 1987), p.32; see especially, chapters 1, 2, 3, 4, and 9.

10. Paul de Man, "Semiology and Rhetoric," in *Textual Strategies: Perspectives in Post-Structuralist Criticism,* Josué Harari, ed. (Ithaca: Cornell University Press, 1979), p.129; further references to this essay will appear in the text.

    Several of the points made in this section elaborate on my previous criticisms of de Man in *Literature Against Itself,* pp.173–79; and "Come Back to the Raft Agin', Strether Honey!" *Georgia Review* XXXIV, no.2 (Summer, 1980), pp.413–16.

11. This is essentially what James Phelan argues when he observes that deconstruction treats language as if it had no "pragmatic component" ("Thematic Reference, Fictive Character, and Literary Structure: An Examination of Interrelationships," *Semiotica* 49, no.3–4 [1984], pp.345–65).

12. Jacques Derrida, "Limited Inc," *Glyph* 2 (1977), p.200; reprint forthcoming (see note 6 above).

13. Weber, *Institution and Interpretation,* p.32.

14. Paul de Man, "Shelley Disfigured," *Deconstruction and Criticism* (New York: Seabury Press, 1979), p.44; further references to this essay will appear in the text.

15. Jonathan Culler, "Beyond Interpretation," in *The Pursuit of Signs* (Ithaca: Cornell University Press, 1981), p.15.

16. This, in effect, is the only substantive argument Rodolphe Gasché makes in response to my earlier criticisms of de Man's circularity. (". . . Graff's criticism of an in-advance predication also demonstrates his inability to grasp the constitutive function of pre-understanding in the formation of understanding. Is not Graff's accusation of circularity true of his own realistic approach as well?" [Gasché, "Unscrambling Positions: on Gerald Graff's Critique of Deconstruction," *Modern Language Notes,* XCIV (1981), p.1023.]) To Gasché's question I would answer, "No, not to the same degree as de Man, since I do not have a theory differentiating literary language from other forms of language and specifying what all literary language is bound to do."

    The debate over circularity is part of a larger debate over whether deconstruction ought properly to be considered a form of "interpretation." On this issue see Culler's essay (note 15 above) and Christopher Norris' discussion of Gasché's critique in *The Deconstructive Turn: Essays in the Rhetoric of Philosophy* (New York and London: Methuen, Inc., 1984), pp.166–173.

Impositions: A Violent Dawn at *Le Soir*

PEGGY KAMUF

Virtually from the first encounter with Paul de Man's work, but with increasing certainty as his thinking developed after *Blindness and Insight,* I was convinced of its indispensable pertinence for any analysis of the totalitarian impulse insofar as it transmits itself in texts. To take only the most obvious example, the chapter on the *Social Contract* in *Allegories of Reading:* what other engagement with Rousseau's epoch-making text goes so far in *effectively* exposing the devices of a totalizing appeal to national entities, to property, and to versions of collective will? For de Man, "it is impossible to read the *Social Contract* without experiencing the exhilarating feeling inspired by a firm promise." Likewise, it *ought* to be impossible to read this essay, titled "Promises," without registering its import for the historico-political analysis of textuality in general. I quote the memorable last lines of the essay:

We are not merely pointing out an inconsistency, a weakness in the text of the *Social Contract* that could have been avoided by simply omitting sentimental or demagogical passages. . . . The redoubtable efficacy of the text is due to the rhetorical model of which it is a version. This model is a fact of language over which Rousseau himself has no control. Just as any other reader, he is bound to misread his text as a promise of political change. The error is not within the reader; language itself dissociates the cognition from the act. *Die Sprache verspricht (sich)*: to the extent that it is necessarily misleading, language just as necessarily conveys the promise of its own truth. This is also why textual allegories on this level of rhetorical complexity generate history.

It *ought* to be impossible, I said, to read lines such as these otherwise than in the sense of summing up an *effective* analysis of historical acts, acts which are dissociated from cognition by language. The status of act in language is one of the most constant preoccupations not only of this essay but of de Man's thinking in general as reflected in all his later work. That preoccupation has always seemed to me clearly and intensely political. And yet, a chorus of de Man's detractors has attempted to persuade that this appearance is precisely contrary to the truth of his profound disinterest in or even disdain for political, historical reality. Leaving aside what may be distasteful motives for such acts of interpretation, which one senses in the fervor of an attack that has even included personal characterizations, I think it is possible to retrace some of the steps that produce the accusation of "apoliticism"—or worse—without having to look any further than these final lines of "Promises."

For what does de Man say there of the *Social Contract*?
1) That it is a textual allegory of the sort that generates history. The *Social Contract* is a political text, not in the trivial sense that

it speaks of political matters, but in the strong sense of an act that has consequences for a political entity; 2) that the act in question is that of "a promise of political change," a reform of the state in the direction of, for example, greater social justice or greater security; 3) that the actor or the promisor is not Rousseau, but language which "to the extent that it is necessarily misleading . . . just as necessarily conveys the promise of its own truth." The signatory Rousseau would have also been the first misreader of his text, taken in as were others subsequently by "the exhilarating feeling inspired by a firm promise"; 4) that although there is error, it "is not within the reader" because language "dissociates the cognition from the act." And if Rousseau is a reader of his own text, then the error is not "in" Rousseau either. Before there can be anything like a cognition of linguistic meaning, there must be a promise that language means anything at all. If this error is "in" anything, one would have to say that it is in history, that it is the dissociation or gap that generates history as a series of acts intersected by another series of belated cognitions.

Now, what is it about these four points that could be made to seem "apolitical"—or worse—if someone wanted to be able to advance that assessment? 1) De Man implies that the *Social Contract* has generated a history of political consequences, but he never takes these directly into account when reading that text. Rather, he considers the *Social Contract* in isolation from its political, historical circumstances. This is fundamentally the accusation of "formalism," one which has been frequently launched by those eager to argue de Man's disregard of history or politics. It itself disregards, however, the central fact that de Man is challenging with his reading precisely such a formalist/ historicist division. Indeed, this reading act should be understood as exposing the inadequacy and profound ahistoricism of much "historicist" interpretation because the latter is far more likely to treat written works as formal entities that can do little more than reflect or confirm historical, political conditions. Such "historicism," in other words, can account for a text's generation of history only by referring to contingent relations that are finally selected arbitrarily by the interpreter. 2) By deconstructing the promise of political change, de Man encourages abstention from any direct political activity insofar as the latter must rely, to a greater or lesser extent, on some expectation of positive political, social change. This accusation seems to me at once the most unfounded and the most dangerous. Dangerous because it has the odor of the very sort of demagoguery that de Man is concerned to deconstruct in a text like the *Social Contract*. To make such a charge, one must be convinced that one's own political discourse is not demagogic, and yet the energy

devoted to attacking an effective tool for the analysis of political language forms what at times looks like a symptom of denegation. Yet, lucid, committed political activity need not remain within the formalist/historicist opposition and thus stands to benefit from de Manian deconstruction by welcoming in it an ally. And nothing in de Man's texts prohibits such an alliance; it is even a little absurd to try to imagine what form such a prohibition could have taken. But here one touches on another aspect of the charge of "apoliticism." The fact that de Man rigorously avoids advocacy, exhortation, or other explicit modes of discursive persuasion (such as promising), prescription, or coercion is, in a perverse way, partly responsible for the suspicion that his writing encourages this or discourages that. Because, that is, de Manian writing practices a kind of rhetorical ascesis, it is vulnerable to the impatient expectations of readers who wait to receive their readymade instructions, in the form of cookie-cutter formulations, from handbooks of political "correctness." 3) and 4) By affirming that language is the actor and that error is not in the writer, who is a misguided reader of his own text, de Man dissolves the position of the subject of political responsibility. He thereby also absolves all apparent political actors of their acts, even their crimes, providing them with the ready excuse of a language that "dissociates cognition from the act." This charge is in itself irresponsible and, what is more, of rather dubious political value for two principal reasons. First, it appeals essentially to a political thinking still wed to an anthropomorphic subject who fully wills his/her acts. Such thinking is incapable of affirming the necessity for a politics of the "unconscious," either in the Freudian or the de Manian sense, and it thereby must reiterate modes of political discourse that have become largely irrelevant, whereas it leaves unexplored the vast terrain opened up by analyses such as de Man's. Second, the demonstration of the dissociation between act and cognition can in no way be made to serve as anyone's excuse from responsibility of whatever sort. On the contrary. If one always knew exactly what one was doing when one was doing it and what that act was going to mean (for oneself, for others, in particular and in general), if, in other words, act and intention were indeed *inseparable,* then the problem of—taking, assigning, avoiding—responsibility would never even arise. But it is *because* acts and intention (or cognition) *are* detached and detachable from each other that there is responsibility and it must be taken. To suggest otherwise is politically regressive and irresponsible, because any "theory" of responsibility that does not recognize the dissociation of acts and meanings must prove to be ethically, practically useless.

In some version or another, these three or four charges have been taken up again, and with a vengeance, in the present controversy over de Man's earlier writings for the Belgian collaborationist press. Whatever complications have been introduced concern the relation between the wartime journalism and, especially, the most influential later theoretical work. Those who can now read a more complete "complete works" are asking and must ask: what relations become manifest when such distant objects are conjoined by the signature "Paul de Man"? Whether or not this question is explicitly posed, it necessarily informs every approach to these texts and that signature, if only because the earlier writings would have been forgotten by all but a few, along with their signatory, if de Man had ended his career as a literary critic in 1942. Thus, even if one were to attempt to read the journalism *for itself,* dissociated from what came after for the signatory—and one must also make that attempt—it would be pointless to deny that one's reading is framed or informed by a prior reading (or non-reading), by a prior evaluation or interpretation of the only writings by Paul de Man that were generally available until very recently.

In the operation that consists in trying to determine the continuity and/or discontinuity between disparate textual-historical acts, one is apparently set before or against "objects" in the world to which one's only relation is that of "outside reviewer." This is the structure of "objectivity," the same one with which we justify the quasi-totality of scholarly evaluation in the academy. Yet in a sense that is no less if not more justifiable, what one is doing in this situation is indissociable from an "internal" operation that consists in adjusting, sifting, accepting, rejecting pieces of one's own experience. In making a thing fit with another, or in seeing how they do not fit, the "thing" constantly at risk of not coming together is located undecidably between the inner and outer versions of an experience, which, moreover, need not be an experience in the conscious sense. This is to say that the act of reading is not solely or even primarily an objective act, and that we must struggle at every turn to prevent its lapsing into sheer transference, projection, or hallucination. At the same time, however, reading is possible only on the condition of these interiorizing/exteriorizing identifications and thus only on the condition of a certain suspension of all the distinctions that commonly serve to order the space of this encounter (subject/object, reader/text, inside/outside, and so forth). There is a double exigency, then, and reading negotiates with a double bind. All this has been described far more subtly and patiently by others, notably by Paul de Man, for a long time now. I recall the analysis in this minimal fashion because the circumspection it recommends for any act of readerly evaluation is more than

ever required to begin to say how these pieces do or do not fit together.

As for me, I am acutely aware as I write—which is why I began there—that I read the newspaper articles of 1940–42 not only against the background of Nazi-occupied Belgium, but also projected on something like an inner screen, a surface framed by what I have admired in the work of Paul de Man and have tried to assimilate within my own writing and thinking. There is stress in the process because much cannot be made to fit onto that screen, whereas the frame cannot be expanded to encompass those images which frighten or warn of danger rather than call for admiration. There results across the whole field a fracture which is not so much the mark of a division as the gap of a necessary and impossible articulation with an irrevocable past. Terrible events, failures of moral strength, blind enthusiasms, willing ignorance, buried hopes, unspeakable suffering: no frame can take them in; yet they must still be held in focus and not allowed to slip into that false oblivion out of which the future prepares to repeat the past, has indeed already done so. I am not speaking now of how Paul de Man lived with or in an experience of fracture, break, or renunciation, which I do not know. It is not even certain that I am speaking of *his* life, *his* past, or *his* experience. Rather, I can only ask about the fracture installed in me, and no doubt in others, by reading these unframed fragments.

I emphasize the fracture for another reason as well. If Paul de Man began to write again several years after the end of the war, he could only do so as a break from his earlier writings insofar as the latter displayed an acquiescence to the organicism of National Socialist cultural theory. This doctrine, the idea that an artistic tradition (somehow) has roots in the "blood and soil" of a delimitable national people (the Germans, the French, the Flemish), is far from providing a dominant, or even a consistent, theme in de Man's wartime articles. It is more like an echo allowed to resonate within what was then his thinking about literature and the arts. Yet it is an unmistakable echo that, at the very least, is never explicitly disavowed or challenged, even if the numerous assertions about literature's autonomous tradition provide a far more consistent counterpoint to it. To close even this tentative opening to the doctrine that fed German (or French or Flemish) nationalism and racism would have required breaking with the idea of *no break,* no discontinuity between the materiality of a national history (which is not the timeless, or cyclically renewable, substance of either blood or soil) and cultural "expressions" that are not necessarily rooted in that history, growing out of it or regenerating it as the flower does a plant. De Man would have had to break not only with the organicism that rooted culture in nature, but also with the implantation of that notion, so to speak, within his thinking about literature as a domain with its own history detached from that of a nation, or other organization of living substance. Organic metaphors (particularly botanical ones) come easily in these early texts, for example: "The essence [*le propre*] of the work of art is to surpass—whether consciously or not, it little matters—its origin and, beyond the simple play with matter (be it acoustic, plastic, or literary), to rejoin the deep roots of the natural, to become *like a living thing* [comme une chose vivante] that draws from this vitality its emotive force and spiritual content."[1] (These lines appear to be assumed by the writer, something one cannot affirm about a great number of the statements in these texts which are either paraphrase or of more ambiguous attribution.) De Man would later devote some of his first published studies of romantic poetry to the necessary failure of the work to "become like a living thing" or, in Hölderlin's phrase, for words to originate like flowers.[2] But in 1940–42, the rhetoric of romantic organicism was still a vital link to an ideology of nation, race, and culture, which at the same time de Man was undercutting with his far more consistently advanced thesis of the autonomous, or at least non-dependent domain of the arts, especially literature.

There is thus yet another reason to emphasize fracture. If indeed the strain of organicism was countered, as I have said, by a more pronounced strain that resisted (not just in theoretical terms, but also in the explicit terms of political actuality) the attempts to appropriate literature to a cultural, political program, if, then, the writing strains at the incompatibility of a political doctrine with a thesis about literature, then the fracture already passes through these texts and is not merely a division that falls between de Man's earlier and later writings. Now, one could observe that this strain was not in any simple sense *imposed* from the moment de Man accepted to write for *Le Soir*. Why and under what circumstances he did accept this association are questions others have perhaps been able to resolve to some extent. It seems to me, however, after reading the articles, that it could not have been a decision based on an overriding political conviction. Such an observation neither defends nor excuses that decision; it merely places it within a larger range of possible motivation. Doubtless it is difficult, and therefore important, to avoid projecting onto that decision what (one hopes) would have been one's own choice in similar circumstances. Even if one tries to make that effort sympathetically—to put oneself in the other's place—the imagined picture of what that place might have been is indelibly colored for us by the knowledge of the war's final outcome, the defeat (at least militarily) of the

German ambition to unify and rule Europe. Too easily erased from this picture is the fact that yielding to what seemed the inevitable in 1940 (after Dunkirk, after the French armistice, during the period of the Soviet-German non-aggression pact, and a year before the entry of the United States into the war) would have been the first reaction of the greatest majority and that this reaction need not have been accompanied by a conviction about the superiority of the Nazi cause in any terms other than military might, where it was undeniable. Onto the inner screen of identification, wishful hindsight also projects too easily an image of a simple choice between wickedness and heroism. This black or white pattern effaces what is too hard to identify: disconcerting patterns of neither simply one nor the other, choices made and lived in a constant negotiation with uncertainty, blind hope, fear, disgust, and error. What is more, such projections, both negative and positive, were already largely in place as concerns Paul de Man long before the wartime journalism was brought to light. Which is why any attempted analysis of this episode from the comfortable distance of more than forty years, and within the still more comfortable shadow arena called "political debate" in the American university, ought to be extremely cautious. Without such caution, one risks doing little more than exhibiting the embarrassing dimensions of one's own blindness to the fact that, when he lived and wrote, Paul de Man was altogether other than the image projected in some internal theater. But finally and most important, recognizing the force of projection onto otherness, which can and does assume the massive proportions of a state ideology, goes to the very heart of the matter in question.

Given the disconcerting fracture cutting across these articles, a judgment of the choice to write, sign, and publish them will soon discover the difficulty of summing up its assessment in a single sentence. One must condemn the choice as a deplorable lack of lucidity into the consequences of a consolidation of the Nazi victory, consequences that had been unfolding already for some time and that became obvious in Belgium within the first few months of occupation. Would it not have been inexcusably naïve to imagine that one could associate oneself with an instrument of that consolidation (which *Le Soir* undoubtedly was) and remain somehow out of reach of its detestable consequences? That one could use the forum to challenge the too-uncritical ideas that were taking over the debate about the place of literature in the new Europe? Or even to exploit the opportunities for some intellectual subversion? Yes, no doubt. Did de Man realize this error only when he resigned from *Le Soir* in November 1942? Who could answer such a question? What is clear is that if there was a realization before then, it did not prevent the continued appearance in *Le Soir* of articles written and signed by Paul de Man. If he found himself compromised by the editorial policy of that newspaper, should he not have ceased his association? Yes, and, for whatever reason, he did not.

This failure cannot but elicit protest when one reads to its shocking conclusion the article "Jews in Present-day Literature." As others have already pointed out, the argument of this article is far from simple: it quotes the antisemitic thesis regarding a nefarious Jewish influence on literature only in order to refute it, even deride it. It thus inserts a considerable distance between the signatory and that thesis. But the final remarks are not distanced in the same way and one can only attribute them to the signatory: "One sees that a solution of the Jewish problem that would aim at the creation of a Jewish colony isolated from Europe would not entail, for the literary life of the West, deplorable consequences. The latter would lose, in all, a few personalities of mediocre value. . . ." It is perhaps above all the seeming equanimity with which this possibility is envisioned, the calm acquiescence to the idea of a Europe free of Jews, that cannot be excused. And this is because no one can retrieve these lines from more than forty years of oblivion without hearing in them a terrible omen of the equanimity with which most of Europe's population would witness the racial "purification" of its land. It is somewhat unfair to hear the text in this sense, but not altogether. De Man himself ought to have been the first to hear the echo of disaster in his own text, which he did not; rather he signed his name to these ignominious words.

Yet as much and even more than any of the others, this text is fractured, the ground it stands on split by these final lines which seem to form a gratuitous addendum to the argument about literary tradition. What I just called an echo of disaster itself has no echo anywhere else in these articles,[3] whereas de Man returns repeatedly to the literary historical argument in more or less the same terms for the remainder of his stay at *Le Soir*. That the article's conclusion presents itself as an anomaly does not, of course, excuse its yielding ground to antisemitic hysteria. It does, however, demand at least to be remarked as such by whoever would attempt to understand these texts in context, and especially if one is going to claim to have understood where de Man located himself ideologically during the two years his journalistic career lasted. I make no such claim, not only because, more than ever, it seems to me unforgivably presumptuous to do so, but as well because I do not want to deny the fracture which no version of ideological adherence, still less allegiance, could take into account. On the contrary: There is in fact far more reason to believe that Paul de Man as well held himself to

the line of the fracture in a highly precarious position that, forty-five years later, appears thoroughly untenable.

If that is the case, then the narrow thread that served as his tightrope was stretched between the past and the future of literature. How to get from the one to the other appears as the overriding concern of the articles when considered together. The image of the tightrope seems particularly apt to describe the urgent way de Man addressed literature's present position, in 1941–42, from which it could not retreat and beyond which it had yet to advance. For example, he repeatedly protests against the ahistoricism that would snap the thread tying literature to its past. This protest is first lodged in a sustained manner in "The Jews in Present-day Literature," which was one of de Man's earliest longer pieces for *Le Soir* (4 March 1941). Here, those who would cut the thread are vulgar antisemites eager to blame everything they disparage on the Jews. Post World War I literature, by their account, is an aberrant outgrowth of Jewish influence in other, non-literary spheres. Although de Man does not depict the conclusion that follows from such reasoning, it is clearly enough implied there: this decadent, "enjewished" literature should be repudiated and an uncorrupted path forged by writers who are worthy to represent the newly "purified" culture. De Man objects that this thesis is wholly unfounded in literary reality: "But the reality is different. It seems that esthetic evolution obeys very powerful laws that continue their action even when humanity is shaken by considerable events. The world war has brought about a profound upheaval in the political and economic world. But artistic life has been swayed relatively little, and *the forms that we know at present are the logical and normal successors to what there had been before*" (italics added). De Man insists on this continuity three more times in the course of the brief article. The most celebrated "new" novelists (Gide, Kafka, Hemingway, Lawrence are mentioned, who also all happen to be anathema to the new regime in Germany) are not "innovators who have broken with all past traditions, but mere continuers who are only pursuing further the realist esthetic that is more than a century old." Likewise, the poetic forms "that seem to us most revolutionary, such as surrealism or futurism, in reality have orthodox ancestors from which they cannot be detached." Notice that surrealism and futurism are mentioned together, which suggests that the argument being made here does not discriminate between the opposite motives Nazi or fascist ideologues could cite for wishing to detach a poetic "innovation" from what precedes it: whether in order to cut out and discard a corrupt aberration (surrealism) or to proclaim the founding of a new poetic regime (futurism) in accord with a new political order, the severance of the historical link is a vain gesture, absurd. "Therefore, one may see that to consider present-day literature as an isolated phenomenon created by the particular mentality of the 20s is absurd."

Elsewhere and in later articles, it is not necessarily vulgar ideologues who are seen as guilty of this absurdity. De Man deplores the same tendency among writers and poets, for example among the "new generation" of Flemish poets who have performed an about-face "against the tendencies of their elders."[4] These elders, the postwar generation, had adopted enthusiastically the experiments of the surrealists in France and their "dislocated style . . . evokes irresistibly a period of rupture, the first stammered signs of a new esthetic that is still searching for its way." Here, de Man is not concerned to deny that surrealism was a rupture or even that it sometimes went too far; on the contrary, he grants that idea in order to insist that the importation of surrealism "corresponds to a very important phase in the development of Flemish letters. It was the first time they broke with the tradition of clarity and wisdom which had reigned there, in order to set out on an adventure that brought with it the risk of lapses and madness." This version of surrealism as an innovation that provokes rupture sets up the principal argument of the article, which is that the latest generation has impoverished Flemish poetry by turning away from the surrealist adventure.

No doubt, as could be foreseen, this discovery provoked some unruliness and disorder. Rushing into these unexplored fields with all the enthusiasm of neophytes, the poets committed many excesses and took many risks that were more than just debatable. . . . But despite that, it is not without a certain regret that one sees how the newcomers remain ignorant of this crucial experiment and continue to write as if these excessive but intensely alive revolutionaries had never existed [*exigé* is no doubt a misprint here]. For that is precisely what is happening. The elements stirred up by the predecessors are not being decanted so that, in a more refined form, they can serve as a basis for the successors. On the contrary, there is no trace, no appearance of all those unknown lands towards which a first glance had been directed. One realizes this most clearly upon remarking the limpid clarity, the total simplicity of recent poems. . . . And one cannot help, on seeing thus the whole obscure and shadowy side of poetry banished forever, from thinking it is an impoverishment. . . . It is with regret that one sees Flemish art refuse to take up the invitation to annex its domains to a more mysterious and secret world. Is it not paying too dear a price for clarity to acquire it by limiting oneself and distancing oneself from the efforts of a generation whose enthusiasm and overflowing vitality would seem to indicate that it was following a fertile path?

About two months later, de Man takes up the questions of continuity and rupture within poetic tradition in a manner that is surprisingly explicit given the context. In "Continuité de la poésie française: A propos du journal *Messages*" (14 July 1942), he once again protests against the attempt, characterized here as "brutal," to make literature fall into line with a totalitarian revolution. This attempt is castigated in no uncertain terms as "harmful to the greatest degree," as dangerously "thoughtless [*légère*]" and as "rash attacks." More perhaps than at any other point, there converge here many of the concerns distributed among the other articles, just as, in de Man's phrase, "the worries and hopes, enthusiasms and revolts" converge in the work of his contemporaries, the writers and poets. This is not the only place one can sense the urgency of the question de Man attributes to these contemporaries: how to go on from here? But the urgency is here virtually untempered by any camouflaging concession to a totalitarian will that aims to distinguish the acceptable from the unacceptable in present-day literature and to do so in terms that have nothing to do with literature itself. The article deserves, as much or more than any other in the collection, including "Jews in Present-day Literature," to be read in its entirety. I will quote my translation of a significant portion of it.

From the first, de Man assumes the question as his own, or at least as one which the critic, no less than the artist, is asking himself:

Events on the scale of those that we are living through at present pose in a sometimes painfully direct manner the problem of artistic continuity. Confronted by the necessities of an integral upheaval, both the artist and the critic ask themselves whether they should definitively break with the past and discover for themselves completely new norms, values totally independent from those gone by, or whether they have to continue to base what they are doing on the experiences and tendencies that were in circulation when the war broke out.

Even if we suspect, after having read his earlier articles, that de Man will respond once again as he already has—more in the latter than in the former sense, more in the sense of a continuity than a definitive break—it would still be a mistake, I think, to hear this question as an empty one for the critic formulating it. The problem would not return with such regularity if it had been resolved. Rather, precisely because de Man resisted the idea of a definitive break with literature's past, when, as one may well imagine, there were everywhere pressures to consecrate such a break with critical acclaim, the question kept returning, and "in a sometimes painfully direct manner."

As he has done before, de Man approaches the problem by distinguishing "very clearly" between "artistic evolution" and the "current revolution." The ideology of the latter is in "absolute reaction" to ideologies of the past, whereas the former is a continual growth from roots that draw from "essentially different" layers than the temporary conditions of revolution. Yet "on the pretext that this revolution is totalitarian, which means that it aims to modify all aspects of individual and collective life, some have brutally included art among its objectives. . . . In other words, art—and particularly literature—has found itself transformed into a tool, an instrument destined to combat by any and all means an out-of-date 'Weltanschauung' and to impose another one."

Having made this distinction and characterized the brutal annexation of literature to the aims of revolution, de Man proceeds to derive a second distinction from the first: the distinction between two kinds of imposition on and by literature. There is first of all the inevitable "imprint [*empreinte*]" of the "concerns that weigh on humanity in our day," concerns that arise from the "profound modifications" affecting civilization and that cannot leave writers and poets indifferent. "But," de Man continues, "this incursion of current events does not determine the course of literary history properly speaking." The imprint is imposed merely on the surface of that history where the "only effect it can have is to cause certain themes of inspiration to dominate, themes that were unknown at other moments." This thematic surface is a "minor constituent in the development of an artistic genre" and it cannot give rise either to a classification or to a judgment. Instead, both description and evaluation of literature are determined by factors other than "these modifications imposed by the revolutionary climate of the period," factors which impose themselves altogether differently on literary history. De Man names, "as an example," form.

Poetic forms—like plastic and musical forms—are not born arbitrarily from an individual will. They are rather *imposed unconsciously* on each individual, since they live like free organisms having a childhood, maturity, and decadence. Their vital process must unfold in a continuous manner, without allowing themselves to be slowed down or arrested by extra-formal considerations. In the case of French poetry, we find ourselves at the beginning of an ascent and consequently, any systematic influencing would be harmful to the greatest degree.

It would thus be at the very least premature to submit art to revolutionary imperatives linked to temporary conditions because its roots go down to essentially different layers whose action we do not control. (Italics added)

In this understanding of literature as "essentially different" from human endeavor, as unconsciously imposed on the writer rather than as submitting to individual will and extra-literary imperatives, there is no doubt some reason to see a precocious version of what de Man would later elaborate by means of speech-act and rhetorical theory. At the same time, however, any effort to project such a continuity must also acknowledge the break we have already mentioned with the organicism that so clearly provides here the language with which to speak of literary continuity. The full significance of that break is as difficult to measure as it is important to take into account. For one thing, one has to be wary of letting a certain vitalism slip back into the picture through the description of some continuous process that could be mapped onto a biography. Instead, the break with such language leaves us with the task of thinking the relation of "writing" to "living" *differently*—unless, of course, we are willing to accept in full awareness the risk of reviving (?) the effects of ideological imposition that are referred to here. If not, then we have to try and learn from the terrible irony marking this text, from an unmistakable imprint that is finally more than just superficial. Imposed (consciously? unconsciously?) on the very statement that refuses the imposition of the "present revolution" on literary form is, precisely, a *form* whose "roots" lead back to that ideology and to its politics of organic nationalism.

Does this mean de Man's resistance to the totalitarian imposition of its ideology was fatally compromised? Perhaps, although that conclusion ought not to minimize the enormous difference that still separates it from impositions that took far more pernicious and "painfully direct" forms. The concluding paragraphs allude to some such instance of imposition on literary evolution, which may have even prompted this article and de Man's protest. Without specifying any exact circumstances, he speaks of the "dangerous thoughtlessness" with which some "cast stones at those who constitute the veritable initiators" of current French poetry, of the "disturbing impression created by rash attacks against healthy forces, on the mere pretext that they appeared during a despicable period." The Parisian literary journal *Messages* is twice mentioned as one place in which surrealist experimentation is now bearing fruit—an evolving form—after having "wandered in vain in search of a means of expression and exhausted itself with endeavors that were as debatable as they were inefficacious." Eluard is cited as one of the representatives of current poetry "who have only just reached the balance and harmony that are the sign of a certain maturity."[5]

What is remarkable in this description is that de Man allows a certain space for the ideological attack on surrealism even as he dismisses the charge of decadence. He concedes that at its beginnings surrealism wandered in some debatable directions, but that this was for lack of a form adequate to its ambitions to "annex the world of dream and myth and to throw itself into dazzling adventures there." Having now begun, in the poetry of Eluard and others, to come into its form, surrealism, de Man can assert, "from the point of view of form, is at the dawn of its splendor" even though, from another point of view, which is that of history according to the "current revolution," it is a decadent holdover from a no less decadent age. There are thus two chronologies converging around the figure of the new or the nascent: "For one must consider it [current French poetry] not as a decadent manifestation but, on the contrary, as a birth [*naissance*], as the beginnings of a great adventure into which the French artistic soul has thrown itself and which cannot be hindered by the political and military setbacks of the country." Whereas political, ideological history conflates the decadence of a state and the decadence of artistic expression, de Man, as he has done before, sets the two chronologies on different tracks and prevents the one from hindering the other. This separation, however, produces an anachronism in the curious figure of a formal artistic "life" stood on its head, its decadent or "debatable" period preceding its birth and growth into maturity.

Elsewhere, de Man reiterates repeatedly his observation that the "present revolution" has yet to have any significant effect on literature's "evolution." The only effects one can point to are superficial, mere thematic modifications which leave no imprint on the form. Or else they are the effects of repressive prescriptions and proscriptions of the sort one can discern behind the praise of *Messages* (which had been banned in France) and Eluard (who ceased publishing openly in France at about this time). Yet, whether enforced by writers themselves or by a censorship regime, the imposition of extra-literary concerns could not produce the sort of "renovation" of literature demanded and awaited by so many. In an article titled "Le Renouveau du roman" [The renewal of the novel], de Man characterizes this expectation of his fellow literary critics before proceeding to give them a lesson in their job:

The climate of the moment is such that a renewal of formulas and procedures would probably be welcomed with more enthusiasm than ever before. In spite of himself, carried away by the desire of his age, the critic is posted on the alert for whatever appears to consummate the rupture with the past and he is ready to shower his benevolent concern on any attempt made in this direction. The facts have proved that all these theoretical efforts, combined with the most imposing [*imposants*] historical upheavals, are not enough to

influence the normal evolution of styles, nor even to accelerate it very much. What has been modified is the receptive sensibility of certain readers who make other demands of literature and want other emotions from it. The same phenomenon has occurred in the minds of authors who are tempted to turn toward unexplored horizons. But one would be making a gross error in perspective if one supposes that this modification, which manifests itself practically by the introduction of subjects different from those commonly treated in preceding years, marks the end of a period in literary history. This introduction of some untried subjects will appear as only a very temporary and superficial circumstance if it is not accompanied by a profound reform in the tone and the basic disciplines. It may be that this change is in the process of its accomplishment and that an attentive observer will even be able to indicate approximately its unfolding, despite the great difficulty there is in sorting out the real fundamental tendencies from the formless heap served up by current affairs [*l'actualité*]. But this movement is independent of political circumstances, and one must look for its origin in works that are clearly anterior to the war.

The constant reminder that "political circumstances," however imposing they may be, have yet to impose any change of direction on literature's course, that critics are committing gross errors when they fail to discern "real fundamental tendencies from the formless heap" of current writing, that their enthusiasm is misplaced and misguided—the least one can say is that such statements are not designed to curry favor with any totalitarian ideologues of culture. As in the article on *Messages,* de Man seems principally concerned to contest the very capacity of the totalitarian will, precisely, to *will* the renewal of literature in ways that would not be either superficial or repressive.[7] Is this defiance of "the climate of the moment" or simply the arrogance of a young man giving lessons to his elders?

In any case, the argument is sustained in an unremitting fashion throughout his career at *Le Soir.* At his observation post, de Man keeps watch for the "renewal," for the new day dawning which his more enthusiastic fellow critics have promised, but what he remarks instead is in the nature of a mass illusion. Here is another long quote from an article titled "Bilan d'une année" [A year's summary]:

The first thing we notice, if we observe artistic creation in relation to political events, is the extraordinarily minimal influence of the war. The Belgian public may well have thought that something had changed, but this illusion stems from a modification of the tone, not in the work of writers themselves, but in the ruling ideas and principles of criticism. If the latter overall seems to have adopted a more revolutionary attitude and to have attacked and denigrated certain firmly established idols, one must not take this audacity to be a result of the upheavals in values produced by present circumstances.

De Man then points out that well before the first shots were fired in the war, attacks had already been launched on the "idols." (He mentions an article by Sartre that attacks Mauriac.) Notice that this argument has fundamentally the same shape as de Man's defense of surrealism (or elsewhere the realistic psychological novel) against precisely the kind of attack characterized here. Just as surrealism has its patent of nobility in symbolism, just as the realistic novel goes back at least to Stendhal, the attack on these forms must not be seen as "a result of the upheavals in values produced by present circumstances," although that may be a currently popular myth or willed illusion. In fact, they predate the war. All that has changed is that these attacks have come into fashion and been generalized. De Man's sarcasm is barely disguised as he describes this phenomenon:

But at present, now that the fashion is to judge severely the period between the wars, it is normal enough that the offensive be conducted with more fervor and in a more general manner. Suddenly people notice that the writers of the last few years were men far removed from reality, that they were turning in circles within a narrow world, the product of their imagination, and that they were in no way contributing to the solution of the urgent problems that were arising.

De Man here lets it be understood that the tendency to blame writers for the errors of the past (Bertrand de Jouvenel's *Après la défaite* is cited as an example[8]) points to the deluded faith in the power of a "beautiful politics." But he is particularly concerned with exposing the illusion of a sudden break with a "detestable" past, of the dawning of a new age which has changed the rules of writing and criticism. Even as he concedes that there is probably "an authentic need for renewal which is making its appearance and of which this campaign of destruction is one echo among others," de Man sees principally the dangers in this "mentality" that is "no longer directed toward an admiration of the established greats, but ardently demands something new and original. . . . One would be deluding oneself dangerously to believe that, because there are some who wish it, this renewal is going to rise up overnight. Or even to suppose that the war, although it has shaken men's minds down to their foundations, has dug such a profound gulf between the past and the present that, necessarily, any writer worthy of that name will try to regenerate and modify his art."

De Man finds very little new has grown up overnight and

arisen with the German dawn. "The novels and poems of the young generation are, to tell the truth, discouragingly mediocre." A sampling of new poetry from the *Nouvelle Revue Française* is "banal and . . . insignificant." As for the novel, de Man mentions only Giono, as he does frequently in this regard and each time to disparage the artificial and forced "naturalness" of the-feeling-of-nature writing that Giono initiated and others quickly imitated. In other articles, de Man employs various tactics to dismiss "le gionisme." On the one hand, "the-feeling-of-nature" remains what he calls a "theme of inspiration" which Giono and his followers try to impose on the form of the novel. They are "writers whose expression is dictated by an imperious internal demand and they want to impose a thesis."[9] "Giono and Ramuz claim to be obeying more than a simple concern for artistic renewal. Both of them, and especially Giono, believe themselves to be entrusted with an ethical mission: to bring men, who have been deformed and diminished by mechanical civilization, back to a life that is closer to nature, more elementary, healthier."[10] De Man confidently predicts that the "future historian of French literature" will see the enthusiasm Giono inspired as having been "superficial" and not the "basis of a new esthetic." On the other hand, de Man does not fail to get in a reminder that Giono's thesis is not even all that original. He has a predecessor, although one whom the French writer would no doubt be embarrassed to acknowledge: "Twenty years earlier, the Welshman D.H. Lawrence devoted a life of struggle and many volumes, of unequal value, to demonstrating the same thing."[11] De Man concedes that it is too early to judge whether "by continuing Ramuz and Giono a new development will occur," but he is skeptical to say the least: "But nothing is less certain. . . . The great renovators arose, in general, in a more spontaneous manner. To be sure, they reacted against preceding tendencies, but they were less caught up in extra-literary concerns and less careful about cultivating disciples."[12]

Walking the tightrope of literary tradition, this young man adopts a severely conservative stance which had to have stood out against the background of "revolutionary" enthusiasm that largely characterized the collaborationist milieux in Belgium, especially during the early period of the occupation.[13] Whenever it is a question of literature (and it almost always is), de Man can be seen securing the anchor in some past before risking a step forward. This cautious skepticism as concerns literary innovation also clashes somewhat with the more approving tone he adopts when referring explicitly to the future of the political and social "innovations" that were then being promised. As we can read it now with distance and perspective, the contrast points to a *fault* and a fracture, but does not this perspective also block from view what might have been a wholly different configuration of the space in which these articles were first read? Rather than displaying a fracture, the contrast could have on the contrary allowed a troubling and persistent dissonance to slip behind the lines of a discourse about literature and cultural production under the "new order." The configuration would have been that of camouflage, a coloration or intonation taken on to disarm aggressors, or what Jacques Derrida, in "The Sound of the Sea Deep within a Shell: Paul de Man's War," has suggested we could understand as a form of contraband smuggling. Nothing learned so far about the circumstances of de Man's association with *Le Soir,* and nothing one can read in these articles, exclude that the young man made some such calculation and accepted to *impose* an ideological cover on his journalistic enterprise, that he accepted, as again Derrida puts it, to grasp the "double edge" placed in his hands.

And there is the fracture or the fault, which is not confined to the dimensions of just a miscalculation or misstep. The imposition de Man allowed to position his writing cannot, finally, be disentangled from the totalitarian imposition of a political program on literature which he repeatedly denounces. But it is also in that very resistance that the fault lies dissimulated as the thesis of a break between the laws of a literary tradition and the exigencies of political, social change. What looks like an arm against ideological imposition may just as well be laying down arms before the force imposing itself within the thesis of literature's independence from political change. The risk, as de Man also saw, was that of a certain confusion between "external" and "internal" imposition. "The property of great talents to become conscious, in the depths of their being, of the determinant spiritual currents of an age and to exteriorize them in brilliant works *risks being confused with* the simple imposed program that the most mediocre talent can illustrate. . . . The artist obeys internal imperatives that most often escape his reasoning."[14] One is tempted to speak of the blindness and insight of critical discourse which are not in a contingent or merely contiguous relation, but implicated with each other, the one inextricably imposed on the other.

De Man did not, it seems to me, in any simple sense renounce the insight that had been forged at such a cost, even though he eventually cut all ties with the anchoring concepts and figures that had held it in place. The tightrope of literary tradition had to be abandoned for lack of support in some version of organic development and, along with it, any elevated position from which to view the clash of events while remaining above the fray. In the aftermath of that fall, how to continue to write on literature? The answers de Man brought to that question transformed the ground on which it was posed. Principally, they removed the barriers separating so-called literary writing from other modes—political, philosophical, critical, autobiographical—within the field of general textuality. If he nevertheless continued to speak, and in a privileged fashion, of "literature," if he also continued to resist the imposition of referential certainty on fictional discourse, that privilege and that resistance are conditioned by the necessity of acknowledging the fictional or allegorical nature of all writing—fictions or allegories which, on a certain level of complexity, generate history. The articulation between writing and material history defines the task of the literary theorist, a task which de Man accepted with what we now know must have been an acute awareness of the price to be paid for closing the gap between them too quickly. It is, in any case, with such an awareness that we can now reread de Man's texts—mindful of the violence of imposed meaning, careful of the meanings we nevertheless impose.[15] "The positing power of language is both entirely arbitrary, in having a strength that cannot be reduced to necessity, and entirely inexorable in that there is no alternative to it," writes de Man in "Shelley Disfigured."[16] Such a rereading would have to approach what de Man writes there as well about "metaphor as a violent—and not a dark—light, a deadly Apollo." It is the violence of an "*imposition* (l.20), the emphatic mode of positing," which is erased when "a positional speech act is represented as what it resembles least of all, a sunrise."[17] The reference is to the opening sunrise of "The Triumph of Life" and to the imposition of "the Sun their father," a figure of the totalizing will:

> And, in succession due, did continent,
>
> Isle, ocean, and all things that in them wear
> The form and character of mortal mould,
> Rise as the Sun their father rose, to bear
>
> Their portion of the toil, which he of old
> Took as his own, and then imposed on them.

Beware the violent figure of a new day dawning.

The obstacles de Man placed in the path of the immediate moral, pedagogical, or political appropriation of literary criticism and theory were formidable and provoked regular attacks from the direction of just such appropriating maneuvers. The fact that, at the end of his life, the most virulent attacks were launched from a certain left must now be seen beside the other fact that de Man first formulated essentially similar obstacles in resistance to a certain right. That conjunction not only should not be dismissed, but is perhaps the most important thing to re-

tain from this affair—and to study. Of this political and historical lesson, we might say: *cela s'impose*. It is necessary, it is
essential, but also it imposes itself like an unwanted demand
that leaves one no alternative but to respond. Will we know
which imposition cannot be avoided and which should be refused? Will we be able to tell the difference in time?

University of Southern California

NOTES

1. "Les mérites de la spontanéité," *Le Soir,* 5 May 1942.

2. "The Intentional Structure of the Romantic Image" in *The Rhetoric of Romanticism* (New York, Columbia U.P.: 1983).

3. Perhaps another echo might be the quotation of a title as the
bold-faced headline of de Man's column for 1 Sept. 1942: "Le Massacre des Innocents." As Tom Keenan and others have pointed out,
this column appeared soon after the convoys began to leave Malines for Auschwitz (the first convoy: 4 August 1942: 5992 Jews deported from Belgium during the month of August). That de Man
chose at least on occasion the titles of his articles with some care is
confirmed by an earlier article on poetry, "Les Mérites de la poésie
pure" (31 March 1942) which begins: "By inscribing the expression
'pure poetry' in the title of this article on Théo Léger, we wanted to
emphasize the fundamental character of his manner."

4. "Une génération à la recherche d'un style: *Anthologie de poètes flamands (1920 à 1942),*" par René J. Seghers," *Le Soir,* 19 May 1942.

5. Eluard published seven poems in the second issue of *Messages*.
These were also collected in *Poésie et vérité 1942*, of which Eluard
wrote in 1944: "the sense [of the poems] can hardly leave any doubt
about the goal pursued: to regain freedom of expression, so as to
harm the occupier." *Oeuvres complètes* I (Paris: Pléiade, 1968), p.1606.

6. "Le Renouveau du roman," *Le Soir,* 27 Jan. 1942.

7. One might thus see an irony in "Le Renouveau du roman"
which, after this opening paragraph, discusses a novel by Jacques
Perrin that, in the estimation of the critic, could well indicate a new
fundamental tendency in the genre. The title of the novel is *Que
votre Volonté soit faite. . .*—may your will be done.

8. See as well "Premières réactions de la France littéraire," *Le Soir,* 18
Mar. 1941 for an explicit critique of Jouvenel. "It is obvious," writes
de Man, "that to speak of the culpability of writers is a politician's
heresy."

9. "*Le Triomphe de la vie,* par Jean Giono," *Le Soir,* 24 Mar. 1942.

10. "Le Roman français et le sentiment de la nature," *Le Soir,* 22
Apr. 1941.

11. Ibid.

12. Ibid.

13. A pertinent example of this enthusiasm is provided by the
"memoirs" of Raymond de Becker, published in 1942 when he was
thirty years old. *Le Livre des vivants et des morts* (Brussels: Editions
de la Toison d'Or) is the account of how a young Catholic militant
came to embrace the collaborationist cause, and it concludes with a
fervent exhortation to the reader to "consecrate yourself to your
country's vocation, one which can, at the same time, serve Europe
so magnificently." De Becker was editor-in-chief of *Le Soir* between
1940 and 1943.

14. "Les mérites de la poésie pure," italics added.

15. It is in these terms that one would have to refuse the violent imposition of meaning on the events of a man's life or the texts signed
during that life. That journalists and academics have seen in de
Man's "case" a convenient pretext for denouncing political violence
even as they impose interpretations upon such events is thus a most
disturbing indicator of the state of political reflection in these milieux.

16. *The Rhetoric of Romanticism,* p.116.

17. Ibid., p.117–18.

Paul de Man, *Le Soir,* and the Francophone Collaboration (1940–1942)

ALICE YAEGER KAPLAN

De Man started writing for *Le Soir* in December of 1940. It is fairly certain that he got the job through his uncle, Henri de Man, who had been up until the German invasion the head of the Belgian Workers Party. In a Manifesto to the party members on July 2, 1940, Henri de Man announced his support for collaboration in the interests of social justice and dissolved the party.[1] Paul de Man was at the time 21 years old, too young, in ordinary times, to qualify for the job as literary columnist in the biggest Brussels daily. His work at *Le Soir,* which had an obvious propaganda value from the German point of view, may well have saved Paul de Man from the fate of many young Belgian men and women—so-called "voluntary" deportation to one of the German labor camps.

"Tu n'étais qu'un enfant"—"You were but a child," the Belgian liberation government official is reported to have said to Paul de Man in May 1945 when he was called in for investigation,[2] after the most violent purges had taken place. Even agreeing, from a judicial point of view, that Paul de Man was but a child, I think it would be a mistake not to read de Man's wartime writings closely, today, on the grounds that their content is mere juvenilia. The literary column that the twenty-one year old Paul de Man published in *Le Soir* gives us an intense account of a young intellectual celebrating, obfuscating, and then, toward the end of his stint at the paper, quarreling with the circumstances that allow him to write in the first place.

In order to locate both his common and individual position within the collaboration, I am going to work around de Man's reviews. I will be quoting the books that he writes about, comparing other reviews of the same books, mapping authors on a political spectrum, reading pages on which articles appear. Sometimes this means going four or five layers out before getting back to de Man, but it is research that has to be done if de Man is to be understood as part of a community of readers and writers. This community is not the static "background" of de Man's writings, it is the environment, the paper air he breathes, the possible world of positions that he can take within the constraints of censorship imposed by the New Order. The staff at *Le Soir,* the collaborationist colleagues at *Le Nouveau Journal,* a German propagandist, a French fascist role model: these provide the overview, the bigger page on which I will read de Man's own language.

The enabling condition for the publication of De Man's reviews in *Le Soir* was the takeover of the newspaper by a pro-German staff. Much like the French daily *Paris-Soir,* which reappeared in a pro-German version in 1940 against the will of its owners, *Le Soir* was started up in Brussels after the Occupation under new pro-German management. Anne Somerhausen, a former journalist who kept a diary of her life in Brussels from 1940–1945, wrote in July 1940:

My mother-in-law has sworn she won't buy a single newspaper as long as the occupation lasts; she will get all her news by listening to the BBC. She may be right: our Belgian newspapers patently exist now by the grace of the Germans and belong to the New Order the Germans want to establish here—a more just social order, they say. Although our papers have kept their familiar old names and makeup, they are pro-German in content, and not even neutral. Their staffs are brand-new; their owners have been expropriated and most former newspapermen kicked out. Yet I read them; and even through their servile pages there comes to me a vision of these tragic summer months.[3]

Many positions were open at the newly managed *Le Soir* in 1940, in part the result of the exodus that had accompanied the fall of Belgium. Intellectuals were in flight: apparently de Man himself had tried to escape Belgium by travelling through France to the Spanish border at the Pyrenees, but turned back in frustration after no certain passage could be assured;[4] Professor Henri Laurent, whose name appears, along with Paul de Man's, on the cover of the February 1940 *Cahiers du libre examen,* was drowned when the boat on which he was trying to escape to England was bombed off Ostend.[5] The demographic changes in Belgium were dramatic. The Germans promised to release the Belgian prisoners of war quickly but according to some accounts freed the Dutch-speaking Flemish, whom they considered "racially German," before the "Latin" French speaking Walloons. Belgian men who weren't already POW's were being sent to work in German labor camps in large number. In October of 1940, according to one source, 13% of the active masculine population was absent.[6]

And Brussels lived in fear of the British bombing raids. There were strafing planes on Belgian roads, bombs, shell splinters; the Germans advised people to line their floors with sandbags, they fired shots into houses whose windows weren't covered in black paper shades, then fined their occupants. People who needed to walk at night carried pocket flashlights smeared with black ink—the street lamps could not be lit.

I can't insist enough on the problem of perspective that is inevitable in reading de Man's wartime writing. It is entirely misleading to think that because he was to become a unique and original critic, his wartime activities were themselves a unique phenomenon. Intellectuals on the right and on the left reconciled themselves to publishing in Nazi-occupied Europe in magazines and newspapers under German direction. Collaboration, the decision to throw in one's lot with the "new order"

was far from rare. In France, Alfred Fabre-Luce published in 1941 an anthology of articles whose purpose was to assist a high brow reading public in adjusting to the new order. His *Anthologie de la nouvelle Europe* is a pretentious collage of writings in the socialist and nationalist traditions: racial theorists Hitler and Alfred Rosenberg (who was in charge of the racial propaganda for the Reich), socialist utopians like Sorel, political theorists and philosophers Bergson, Nietzsche, Proudhon, Carlyle.[7] The categories of the new European thought represented in the anthology were, in order of appearance: realism,[8] respect of force and *aristocratisme,* biological politics, critique of democracy, a new religion, anti-Marxist socialism, national revolution, the war of 1914 and its consequences, the "collaboration" of 1940, and Europe. Many of these themes appear in Paul de Man's prose.

A number of the books that de Man reviewed favorably can also be found on a "global list of literature to be promoted as of December 31, 1942" which was compiled during the war by Bernhard Payr, a German propaganda office staff member in charge of French affairs.[9] Perhaps these titles were given to de Man to review by an editor at *Le Soir* who had ties to the German propaganda ministry. De Man does indeed promote, to varying degrees, these writers on Payr's list: Chardonne, Fabre-Luce, Sieberg, Benoist-Méchin; he criticizes Brasillach and Montherlant—but only for not going far enough in their political thinking; he admires Drieu's critique of cerebral abstraction but finds it too abstractly presented. Morand is the only one that Payr recommends who comes off less favorably in de Man's column: the French writer is too much a dilettante.

De Man's criticism in *Le Soir,* at least until July of 1942, is deeply marked by support of the collaboration, a support he articulates in a left nationalist vein. His logic is in the hard-nosed realist mode: he begs his reader to understand the times and make the most of them. Among the most recognizable of the clichés are these: on April 14, 1941, de Man writes of "the intense effort of reconstruction" and "the most revolutionary reforms"; on June 8, 1941, of a "regroupment of forces." On June 11, 1941, he refers to the lack of discipline and civic spirit among democratic soldiers; Belgium and France will need to reeducate themselves if they are to play a role in the New Europe. On July 8, 1941, he makes one of many references to "revolutionary periods like the one in which we are living"; on 16–17 August 1941, he maintains that Flemish "liberation" will be aided by the collaboration; on October 28, 1941, de Man surmises that the New Europe is more important than anyone's resentment over German sovereignty; he evokes a new collective society, predicts the death of anarchy and individualism of the French variety. "The future of Europe can only be perceived in the framework of the possibilities and needs of the distinctive German mentality [*génie*]."[10] On April 28, 1942, de Man refers to the mystical era, the new nationalism brought about by Germany. On June 30, 1942 he surmises that if French literature between the war years showed an unusual admiration for adolescence, it was a projection of its "taste for intellectual and moral instability." The human type emerging from the new novelists will be "simpler, but more energetic, more productive, and happier."

De Man's work in *Le Soir* is at once a brilliant and banal example of all the clichés of fascist nationalism: brilliant for the way he argues his position, for the logic he brings to bear, and banal because a thousand other intellectuals claimed the same high ground, reached the same conclusions, had essentially, the same effect. Both a right wing and a left wing rhetoric are available to him: he will use both. He will urge his readers to understand the revolutionary potential of the upheaval of Belgium, to profit from their temporary isolation from their southern neighbor in order to shake off French influence and find their own national cultural models. He will become a literary promoter of the war experience by sponsoring a competition for the public to write stories about it. He will malign an individualistic French mentality and laud a collective German one. But he'll also defend surrealism, which many of his fellow collaborators understood as the ultimate sign of French decadence. De Man argues in his column—the argument is a respectable one of which variants occur in most genre criticism—that literary history follows laws that have little or no direct relationship to local historical or political events. This separation of politics and art is a polemical stance developed throughout de Man's work, but it doesn't prevent him from reviewing books whose subjects are historical and political.

The immediate community that comes through in his writing is the Brussels group of collaborationist writers—Daye, Colin, Robert Poulet. Among German Nazi intellectuals, de Man singles out one particular thinker, Frederic Grimm, who proselytizes the Nazi cause among the French. Reaching south to France, de Man reviews the young Robert Brasillach, the well known collaborationist intellectual around whom so many opinions shape themselves and turn. The anti-semitic pamphleteers and so-called "racial theorists" form a community separate but contiguous to de Man's; they will bring into focus his contribution to the page of *Le Soir* entitled "The Jews and Us: The Cultural Aspects." In relation to these two networks of writers—collaborators and racists—the individual slant in de Man's own writing emerges. Tracing this slant allows me to make a hypothesis about his withdrawal from the paper in the fall of 1942, and to reconsider the post-war de Man and my own intellectual context.

THE AVAILABLE ARGUMENTS

In 1941, de Man reviews enthusiastically books written by the fine flower of Belgian collaboration: Pierre Daye, former parliamentary representative of the Belgian fascist "Rex" Party; Paul Colin, the dean of collaborationist journalists and head of the Belgian association of French-speaking journalists; and Robert Poulet, literary and political columnist with roots in the Belgian Action Française movement, as well as a novelist of an experimentalist bent.[11] All three of these men were writing at the time for *Le Nouveau Journal,* a collaborationist daily founded by Colin after the occupation.[12] De Man refers to the "scientific discipline" of Colin's book on the Dukes of Burgundy: The Burgundian empire in its struggles with France can furnish Belgium with a powerful historical model for a national identity, unimpeded by either German or French forces. He calls Pierre Daye's reflections on the revolutionary possibilities offered by the collaboration "pertinent and judicious": Daye's book produces de Man's first extended endorsement of collaboration in a Belgian context.[13]

Here's a brief summary of the book. Daye's *Guerre et révolution* draws a sardonic portrait of Belgian parliamentary decadence of the 1930s. Daye proposes that the European public think of the period in which they were living not as wartime, but rather as the enactment of a social revolution. Daye evokes the German "regeneration" of Europe, which he contrasts with the damage done to Europe by the French revolution. He likens fascist national-socialism to a new kind of Islam sweeping over Europe, Africa and Asia: "We must understand that there is often more dignity in discipline than in individualism. . . We must rediscover even the sense of ritual that supports the grandeur of a nation and gives to the active individual his equilibrium in society" (76–77).

When de Man reviews Daye's *Guerre et révolution* on August 26, 1941, he takes up Daye's argument in his own statement of revolutionary purpose:

The reflections of Pierre Daye will appear equally pertinent and judicious to a great number of Belgian readers, and particularly the paragraphs which show that the present war is, beyond being a national and economic struggle, the beginning of a revolution that looks to organize European society in a more equitable manner. This is a truth that those who remain blinded by nationalist passions ought to repeat to themselves often. Aside from the questions of supremacy, which are in fact secondary, the situation creates a certain number of practical possibilities in order to put in the place of a political apparatus that had become ill-fated [*néfaste*], an organism that will assure a more just distribution of wealth. For he who believes that such actions [*réalisations*] are possible and necessary, it is his duty not to abstain under the present conditions. For without a doubt he will never find circumstances so favorable for renewal than at this moment when all the institutions are in the process of being replaced. And even if this new program has not yet been precisely worked out, things had come to such a degree of decomposition and degeneration that, above all, the will for modification must exist.

Pierre Daye's "War and Revolution" reminds us in clear and simple terms of such fundamental truths that must govern the action of men of good will.

"Seize the time," is the message; now, when institutions are in chaos, let us make a New Order. The tone of the Daye review is engaged and programmatic: one can sense the writer's impatience with those who refuse to act, his belief that Belgians must act. The writing has a passion that today's reader associates with revolutionary rhetoric; it is difficult for anyone socialized within the myth of the heroic French Resistance to imagine that the collaboration had a revolutionary rhetoric too.

De Man, coming out of a socialist family tradition, is far from sharing with Pierre Daye political ties to the pre-war Catholic fascism promoted by Léon Degrelle and his rexist party. Yet this review indicates that de Man was convinced by the belief promoted by Daye, Poulet, and Colin writing in *Le Nouveau Journal* and *Cassandre*—i.e. that it was time for a coalition between right wing nationalists—Degrelle supporters—, left-wing socialists, Flemish Nationalists, all under the auspices of national socialist ideology. *Le Nouveau Journal* is working toward such a coalition throughout 1941 and I quote below from one of a series of front page letters to young workers on socialism and the New Europe. The rhetoric is materialist and antiintellectual:

A socialist speaks: New Order and Old Disorder. The Junction of Extremes.

In the army, on the front, mixed up with the debacle of his people in exile, the young socialist gained a consciousness of certain national *realities*; having experienced the same adventures, having lived through this misery, having to share it still today, the young nationalist gained the *concrete* notion of certain social realities. This *experience* will be more fruitful than 100,000 volumes meant to demonstrate the possible fusion of the "social" and the "national."[14]

Robert Poulet, a Francophile of the pre-war right, takes essentially the same tack in his page one column entitled, "Colloquium of the right and the left":

What is, notably, fascism? Goal borrowed from the social ideal of the left and means borrowed from the political ideal of the right. . . . That which is most energetic and most intransigent in each camp.[15]

It may, oddly enough, have been easier for collaborationist intellectuals working in Belgium and France to dredge up left wing socialist themes than to work with the nationalist themes already available to them. Charles Maurras and Jacques Bainville, the most influential writers of the dominant right wing Action Française party, had argued that the essence of French nationalism derived from the grandeur of the Latin, Mediterranean tradition. They understood that tradition as radically incompatible with German nationalist goals. Indeed, Germany was perceived by them before the war to be as great an enemy as were their internal political enemies—the Socialists and the Communists of the French Popular Front.

The task for German propaganda as of 1933 was to convince this Mediterranean nationalist French right that there was something for them in a Europe governed by Hitler. In occupied Belgium it was relatively easy to gain support from right wing Flemish nationalists, who thought they had something to gain from the decline of French hegemony. In the French and French-identified Belgian Walloon context, it promised to be an uphill challenge, especially given some of the things that Hitler had had to say about France in *Mein Kampf*: "The inexorable mortal enemy of the German people is and remains France" (619); (. . .) France is "more and more negrified" (624) and

What France, spurred on by her own thirst for vengeance and systematically led by the Jew, is doing in Europe today is a sin against the existence of white humanity and some day will incite against this people all the avenging spirits of a race which has recognized racial pollution as the original sin of humanity (his italics, 624).[16]

Paul de Man, Flemish but Francophone, trained in a French-speaking university, writing for a French language newspaper, was enthusiastic about the contribution of German rule to Flemish nationalism. But he also had to appease the traditionally Francophile—and Germanophobe—Belgian Walloons. He speaks directly to this constituency in his review of Frederic Grimm's *Testament politique de Richelieu*.

Conversion of the Latinate, catholic French right to a pro-Germanic national socialism was Frederic Grimm's intellectual mission.[17] In 1938, Grimm published *Hitler et la France* in which he juxtaposed all the anti-French passages of *Mein Kampf* with conciliatory statements that had been made by Hitler to French journalists since its publication.[18] In *Le Testament politique de Richelieu* (1941) Grimm traced a vengeful French Germanophobia back to the Cardinal de Richelieu (1585–1642), who as minister to Louis XIII had consolidated the power of the king and established French hegemony in Europe. Grimm insists that Richelieu's stand against German unity was a founding moment for French ideology. He draws a genealogy of political theories from those of Richelieu to Barrès and Bainville, he traces political texts from the Westphalia treaty (1648) to the Versailles Treaty (1918) and demonstrates their common belief that Germany must remain in chaos. The defeat of 1940 was, for Grimm, the defeat of Bainville *and* Richelieu. Hitler's gift to Europe, Grimm argued, would be to unite German and Germanic peoples (such as the Austrians) under one nation—because people of a common race should be united—and the French would have a supportive role in the German dominated New Europe. Hitler, he promised, would be clement toward the French, far more clement than the French had been toward the Germans over the centuries. As for *Mein Kampf*, Grimm argued, Hitler's few anti-French statements were grotesquely exaggerated: this exaggeration was in part the work of the English propagandists, who were motivated by their own will to dominance. Grimm ends in elegy: "Adolph Hitler will execute the will of the Germany people and will make his rightful beliefs [*son droit*] triumph. (. .) The war of liberation of the great Germany will conquer the idea of Richelieu, in organizing in Europe a new order, based on justice and reason."[19]

In his August 19, 1941 review of *Le Testament politique de Richelieu,* de Man admires Grimm for his ability to "crystallize" a profound tendency of French ideology in a broadly historical narrative. He criticizes Grimm for exaggerating Bainville's theoretical influence on pre-war France. Not because pre-war France isn't anti-German but because de Man thinks Grimm is granting to French politics a rigor and consistency of position it doesn't have. De Man insists on the theme of parliamentary decadence and characterizes French politics of the 30s as "dilapidated, contradictory, lacking any continuity of intention." The 1938 Munich agreement[20] was one moment where the French seemed to be understanding that they needed to recognize a Germany that had become unified, vigorous and powerful, but, de Man concludes, "contrary influences finished triumphant with the results that we know. There is nothing left for the French to do except to accept, under infinitely less favorable conditions, the collaboration with Germany or to submit passively to England."

Grimm is trying to convert the French to his own way of thinking; de Man is more interested in condemning French political decision-making before the war, and by implication blaming the war on the French. From a Nazi propaganda point of view, de Man's endorsement of Grimm (whose book he calls, in conclusion, "non partisan and scientifically objective") is an endorsement of the German appeal to the recalcitrant French and Belgian nationalist right wing; just as de Man's endorsement of Pierre Daye's notion of the collaboration as a "social revolution" is an endorsement of the German appeal to the French and Belgian left wing: de Man is playing both rhetorical sides of the collaboration, nationalist and socialist.

ROBERT BRASILLACH: THE TEXT OF REFERENCE

Brasillach represents for any young writer of Occupied Europe the "bright young man" of collaborationist literature. What does it mean that de Man is so critical of him? De Man's own tough-minded account of Brasillach's *Notre Avant-Guerre* can be compared to Brasillach's own text, to the reviews that endorse him in 1941, and to the post-war histories that don't.

Robert Brasillach's *Notre Avant-Guerre* (1941) was widely reviewed in 1941 and is still widely discussed in histories of fascism today. Brasillach, as editor of the Parisian fascist weekly *Je Suis Partout,* was perceived as the spokesman for pro-German collaboration with right wing French nationalist roots (he had gotten his start at an extremely young age as critic for the Action Française newspaper.) Today, he has become for the French left a symbol of French intellectual error during the war and for the French right a martyr: he was executed by the French in 1945.

Notre Avant-Guerre, reviewed by de Man in August of 1941, is a memoir that Brasillach wrote at age 32 about Parisian literary and intellectual life of the 1930s. It is written in the first person plural from the perspective of a crowd of friends, high brow students at the Ecole Normale Supérieure. Robert Brasillach's "nous" are esthetes with a passion for cinema and dance. They are also, as he tells it, charmed by the various fascist nationalisms of Germany, Spain, Italy and Belgium, which they encounter primarily as tourists.

De Man's most critical remarks in his review of *Notre Avant-Guerre* are directed at Brasillach's description of a Nazi party rally. In 1937 Brasillach had visited the National Socialist Party Congress in Nuremberg and had published an account of the visit for the *Revue Universelle* (a magazine with strong ties to the Action Française) under the title "Cent Heures chez Hitler" (a hundred hours with Hitler). The essay would become—with minor editorial changes made by Brasillach in 1941—a chapter of the memoirs. Brasillach's attitude toward Hitler in 1937 was somewhere between the cultural suspicion in line with his Action Française past and the pro-collaborationist German stance he would take after the fall of France. The rhetoric of his article was itself ambivalent: "Faced with German National Socialism one remains full of doubt and worry." Germany's Nazi rituals, seen at Nuremberg, seemed to Brasillach strange, even Far Eastern. "Isn't it all too much?" he asked, and went on with a kind of anxious fascination, to describe Hitler's eyes, and the mystical transfusion of energy from the Führer to his people. The "doubt and worry" sentence didn't appear in the 1941 memoirs, but much of the ambivalence did. "We are frightened" [*effrayés*] becomes "we are worried [*inquiets*]; "All this, certainly, is not for us" reads the 1941 text, but also "this is a valuable lesson for us." And Brasillach ends his description of Hitler's Germany by telling his readers how profoundly *foreign* the place is for him.

American historians of Occupied France disagree about the passage. Eugen Weber in his *Action Française* (1962) says that Brasillach "returned from Nuremberg drunk with the romance and *strangeness* of what he described as 'the new religion' of National-Socialism."[21] But Robert Paxton in his *Vichy France* (1972) writes that "Before the war . . . even fascist ideologues like Robert Brasillach found Nazi party rallies foreign and ludicrous."[22] There's a long interpretive distance from the religious to the ludicrous. My own reading of the passage in *Reproductions of Banality* (1986) is an attempt to explain why Paxton and Weber's account of the passage can be so different. I concentrate on Brasillach's ambivalence and his mystification, both of which I associated with boundariless oceanic feelings inspired by the event. Brasillach's syntax in the sentences on the rallies is flowing, swelling; his experience at the Nazi rallies is charged with excitement and fear, which can only be contained by punctuating moments of defensive disdain.[23]

The distance between Weber and Paxton's readings of this text is an important indication of how difficult it is to map out a coherent political reaction to Hitler's Germany in 1937. The rhetorical intensity of Brasillach's writing shows an involvement, an investment, rather than a stance that can be catalogued for or against. The problem in analyzing fascist commitment is that it is often founded, not on a coherent set of theories, but on feeling and belief.

This lack of doctrinal coherence is the basis of de Man's objection to Brasillach. The reading that Paul de Man gives in 1941 to the Nuremberg passage in *Notre Avant-Guerre* is suspicious and *pragmatic,* written very much from the vantage point of a war-time citizen looking back on the innocence of peacetime. De Man is critical of Brasillach for his lack of a sense of reality and his confusion of the political and the esthetic. Unconvinced by any political charge implied by the "nous" of Brasillach's narration, de Man identifies Brasillach as part of a vast, privileged French elite whose energy was absorbed by an exceedingly productive esthetic climate rather than by political questions. Brasillach's description of his pre-war adventures becomes for de Man a demonstration of a whole generation's lack of political sense: the French elite of the 30s was absorbed in individualistic esthetic quests, while the German elite was busily caught up in a collective political quest for world power that made for France's undoing. De Man diagnoses Brasillach's political limits as they surface in the passage on the Nuremberg rally: "The reaction of Brasillach faced with a spectacle like that of the Nazi Party Congress at Nuremberg, when he marks some fright when faced with the 'strange' nature of the demonstration, is that of someone for whom this sudden importance of the political in the life of a people is an inexplicable phenomenon."

De Man concludes his analysis of Brasillach's book with a series of generalizations about the French; generalizations that he calls, with pro-forma politesse, "risky." The French are better suited for the apolitical, esthetic and poetic life that thrived until the mid 30s and will have trouble with political activity that is no longer a game. There is still room for literary activity in today's France, but there must also be room for collective action:

Not to mean at all that artistic creation will be suspended, but rather that literature will not take up the same place in the life of those one calls the intellectuals. A state of mind more appropriate to those peoples having a very developed sense of the collective and who have come spontaneously to the less individualistic ways of life.

Collective spirit, adaptation, political and socialist revolution must compensate for the literary and artistic paradise of the 30s that Brasillach describes.[24] Once again, de Man is choosing a collective German "reality" over a dream-like French esthetic individualism.

The reviews of *Notre Avant-Guerre* published by French journalists are more sympathetic to Brasillach and, of course, pro-French in tone. The *Nouvelle Revue Française,* which, since 1940, had been edited under the direction of fascist intellectual Drieu la Rochelle, prints a review of *Notre Avant-Guerre* signed Fernand Lemoine.[25] It reads like a publicity sheet for the book. Lemoine assumes the "nous" of Brasillach's own narration, he takes no critical distance at all: "we know, we love this period (our adolescence)"; "we read his book in one sitting." He describes a Brasillach "enchanted" by the 1930s but makes no direct reference to the political content of the book. He alludes to the "lively portraits of the people that the author of *Notre Avant-Guerre* has met," but does not mention Hitler. His only reference to the war is in conclusion: "Hélas! This leads us to the [chapter] 'Storms of September' and to this war that comes, to the birth of a new period: it is the end of *Notre Avant-Guerre*. It is good that its history has already been traced." The clearest message of the review is the reviewer's attempt to be completely innocuous.

André Thérive, like de Man, is critical of Brasillach's political style. Writing for *Le Temps,* which had taken refuge in a part of France that was as yet unoccupied, Thérive, unlike Lemoine at the Parisian NRF, makes politics part of his picture. Thérive was one of the few associated with the New Order at the bitter end of the war, and his name appears on the first Liberation blacklist of September 6, 1944. But in 1941 he was still sending the occasional literary column to *Le Temps* from Paris. One of the last reviews he published there was his review of Brasillach's *Notre Avant-Guerre*.[26]

Thérive marks his distance, in *Le Temps,* from Brasillach's lyric passages about the new European fascist man. He calls *Notre Avant-Guerre* a "pamphlet" written by a "party militant"; he quotes Brasillach's definition of the new fascist man and concludes: "Personally the author of *Notre Avant-Guerre* hopes to incarnate the type, he even establishes the equation, for which I leave the responsibility to him, between the Action Française, Belgian rexism, German national socialism, the Spanish Phalanx and the Rumanian iron guard." Thérive ends the review by evoking Brasillach's anarchism, his talent, his poetry, and lauding the lack of seriousness of Brasillach's politics. Brasillach is at bottom a dilettante, writes Thérive:

> The success of nationalism, he [Brasillach] says, came from its power to propose, good or bad, a poetry. Perhaps Georges Sorel would have found this translation of idea-forces and myths somewhat frivolous. He would be wrong, even serious things can be said or thought with a French smile.

So Thérive is somewhat hesitant about the nature of Brasillach's commitment to fascism. There's a patronizing tone (a rivalry?) between the lines of Thérive's review, which makes it difficult to figure out whether Thérive admires Brasillach's frivolity or simply finds it amusing. De Man, much more direct, wants a serious, straightforward commitment to German reality from Brasillach, and proposes a solution—Brasillach should separate his politics from his esthetic concerns.

A Belgian response to Brasillach in addition to de Man's comes from Robert Poulet in *Le Nouveau Journal*.[27] Here was a critic who embodied the "literature-politics" split that de Man wanted Brasillach to adopt: Poulet published a political column on page one of *Le Nouveau Journal* and a literary column on page two. And he wrote novels. Poulet came out of an Action Française, Maurrassien tradition, and he writes about Brasillach as the heir and renovator of the doctrines of Charles Maurras. The title of his review of *Notre Avant-Guerre* is "A New Maurrassien Generation." Poulet understands Brasillach's task at *Je Suis Partout* as one of renewing the youthful, popular energy that Maurras's Action Française group had lost by the 1930s. Poulet's message is directed at the Germanophobe French and Belgian right wing: *Je Suis Partout* and pro-German politics are the wave of the future.

Lemoine's puffed up praise in the *Nouvelle Revue Française,* Thérive's evocation of the fascist "new man," Poulet's right wing community building, all correspond fairly well to what one might expect from collaborationist critics, who in 1941, were setting their sights on the New Order.[28] De Man's impatience with Brasillach's political fantasies, his disdain with a politics that borrows anything at all from literary expression, appears to be all his own. In part his anti-French Belgian patriotism is at play; in part he's impatient with the fuzziness with which creative writers write about politics, the way they lump politics and art together.

THE PAGE ON THE JEWS

There is no trace of explicit anti-Semitism in de Man's articles in *Le Soir* between 1940 and 1942 other than the March 4 article "Les Juifs dans la littérature actuelle," but there is scattered throughout the work an insistence and a reliance upon ethnicity, national proclivities and prototypes, the health or degeneration of the nation. The French are individualistic and psychological; the Germans are collective and mystic; the Flemish are realist and "pictorial," and each group develops its art in those directions. In the spirit of a "New Order" or a "New Europe," de Man also believes in the kind of cross cultural pollination that seems to emanate for him from the novels of Ernst Jünger. His arguments are often grounded in transcendent categories linked to German character—coalition, social justice, national collective pride, and the health of the nation. This transcendent vocabulary dominates much of the collaborationist writing in French-speaking Belgium, with the result that one sees surprisingly little in the way of directly negative racial, anti-Semitic language. There is none at all in Daye's *Guerre et révolution* and very little in Poulet's *Le Nouveau Journal* column.

Anti-Semitism was a specialized sub-genre in the years 1941 and 1942. France and Belgium fallen, the exodus come and gone, the New Order underway, 1941 was a year of jockeying for position, of making lists, clamoring for prestige, provocation and effect. The anti-Semitic industry had inherited from before the war a healthy stable of authors, a market, and a network of publishers and distributors who dealt in everything from the most modest mimeographed brochures to the deluxe illustrated versions of Céline produced by Robert Denoël. Céline and Rebatet were the best known names in French anti-Semitic diatribe: Céline's *Les Beaux Draps* came out in February of 1941; his 1937 *Bagatelles pour un massacre* was reissued in a new illustrated edition in November. Rebatet's *Les Décombres,* appeared in the fall of 1942 and became very quickly a literary sensation and a bestseller in France—*the* literary and political event of 1942–1944, according to one historian. Perhaps on the strength of the success of *Les Décombres,* editor Denoël reissued Céline's 1938 *L'Ecole des cadavres* soon after it.[29] A reviewer would have to choose deliberately not to review any of these books; "Les Juifs dans la littérature actuelle" can be read as de Man's way of saying he doesn't take the anti-Semitic genre seriously.[30]

What de Man says needs to be put in relief, not only with respect to the language of a Rebatet or a Céline, but with the articles on race in *Le Soir* that come before, after, and alongside his. Two articles appear in *Le Soir* during the first trimester of 1941, both signed by Léon van Huffel, the newspaper's staff anti-semite. Van Huffel's first article of 1941 is dated January 29 and is entitled, "For a racial anti-Semitism." Van Huffel argues here for a "scientific" anti-Semitism and against a "reactionary social anti-Semitism." "Social" anti-Semitism is content merely with accusing Jews of short-term social ills, controlling the economy or the arts, for example. Scientific anti-Semitism, he argues, must be based on a study of milieu, climate, heredity and historical period. Van Huffel brings the usual philosophical formulae to bear, arguing against the principles of the French revolution that man doesn't live for abstractions such as liberty, equality and fraternity but that he carries in his blood the concrete mark of previous generations. Liberal, individualistic and atomistic philosophies must be countered with a "collective and organic conception of societies." The same argument against abstraction and for organic collectivity appears without any explicit racism in de Man's reviews of Chardonne, Brasillach, Daye.

A second van Huffel article dated February 11, 1941, is entitled "Y-a-t-il une race juive?" [Is there a Jewish race?]. Here Van Huffel uses Georges Montandon, the racist anthropologist and author of the 1940 pamphlet, "How to recognize a Jew," as an authority to advance a theory of a Jewish *type* or *ethnicity.*[31] "Type" or "ethnicity" is, according to Montandon, a more inclusive and more challenging category than race, more difficult to define "scientifically" because it is composed of racial, psychological, and intellectual elements.

Van Huffel asserts, on 11 February: "[the Jew] constitutes, biologically and psychologically, a foreign being whose blood does not mix with impunity with ours" and "The nature of Judaism [*le génie propre du judaïsme*] is totally inassimilable and fundamentally opposed to our western conceptions."

It is Van Huffel who organizes the March 4 page of *Le Soir,* which he calls: "The Jews and Us: The Cultural Aspects." He writes an epigraph in italics across the top of the page, reiterating his line about a "racial" anti-Semitism as opposed to a "social" one. Georges Marlier writes the art column, and underneath him, De Man writes the literary column; there is also an article about Freud and the Jews.

The first argument de Man makes in "Les Juifs dans la littérature actuelle" is not anti-Semitic; it is against the vulgar anti-Semites. "Les Juifs dans la littérature actuelle" appears initially more motivated by elitism than racial thinking and thumbs its nose in an obstreperous sort of way at the "vulgar" claims of Jewish takeover of culture and finance articulated by Georges Marlier in the article above his.

De Man alludes in his March 4 article to "vulgar anti-Semites"; he may well have been thinking of Céline, whose third anti-Semitic pamphlet, *Les Beaux Draps,* had just come out. Robert Poulet's review of *Les Beaux Draps* in *Le Nouveau Journal* the week of March 20 is a useful point of comparison with de Man's review, because Poulet also dislikes vulgar racism, and because he extends the general lines of de Man's attack using Céline as a specific target. Poulet vaunts the richness of Céline's imagination but ridicules his violently populist brand of anti-Semitism; he thinks it gives serious anti-Semitism a bad name:

> The biggest service one can render to Jewish imperialism is to systematically exaggerate the complaints that the Western order, white civilization, precious human equilibrium rightfully harbor against it.

Poulet chides Céline, who, he says, in his role as racist, is little more than a low-life loud mouth. Poulet advises him to go back to what he's good at, writing novels.[32] Poulet shares de Man's disdain for the "conspiracy theories" of vulgar anti-Semitism but he departs from de Man when he implies that white civilization is being threatened by a Jewish imperialism. In this sense

Poulet resembles Van Huffel, who wants to substitute one kind of anti-Semitism (thoughtful and scientific) for another (short-term social). These are micro-polemics among anti-Semites, polemics that divide anti-Semitic texts along class lines or "taste" lines. In France something very similar happens as Brasillach defines his own "rational" anti-Semitism against the "irrational" anti-Semitism of Céline. Bernhard Payr, in composing for the German propaganda staff in France a list of books to be promoted, excludes from his list Céline's pamphlets for their "negligent French," their "hysterical language" which, he argues, "reduce the author's intentions—certainly good ones—to nothingness."³³

De Man would seem to offer his own intellectual contribution to the debate among anti-semites by taking even higher ground: he proposes that the Jews won't, can't, haven't, infiltrated Western literature—French literature in particular—simply because they are mediocre. The rhetorical gesture is witty, it's patriotic (our European tradition is basically uncorrupt, he is proclaiming), and it is deeply reassuring: with the Jews gone, nothing will be lost. . .

The basic stance is not incompatible with the so-called "extremist" one. When you compare de Man's article with the "irrational" anti-Semitism of a Céline, you find that claims of Jewish mediocrity and insignificance are also there, alongside claims about a Jewish takeover of culture. The Jew portrayed in Céline's *Bagatelles pour un massacre* is a "robot" of literary standardization who destroys and perverts natural national style; he is above all an imitator, no country or style of his own:

The immense ruse of the Jews consists in taking away from the masses and standardizing all taste for the authentic, and then taking away from the indigenous artists all possibility of expressing, of communicating their sensibility to their racial brothers, all possibility of awakening in them any authentic emotion.³⁴

Rebatet in his 1942 *Les Décombres,* has a lot of trouble making the same argument, because he keeps coming up with exceptions: all Jews should be banned from music, but he wouldn't mind keeping Horowitz and Menuhin around to play for the Aryans. There are no Jews with any talent in the plastic arts, except, oh yes, Pissarro, "the only great painter that Israel, this incredibly anti-plastic race, has produced." There are no great thinkers across the centuries in literature, and philosophy, "except for one or two accidents, such as that of Spinoza." And so he goes, passing through the canon until he can conclude that the losses incurred by banishing Jewish "spirit and works" hardly count compared to the gains.³⁵

In addition to the claim about the mediocrity of current Jewish writers, two points in De Man's article have been the subject of much speculation since the discovery of the *Le Soir* texts this past fall: the allusion to Kafka and the proposal of a Jewish colony.

De Man refers approvingly to Kafka, as one of four novelists who, even in their most innovative aspects, remain profoundly tied to an age old realist esthetic.³⁶ What is one to make of the fact that de Man mentions "Kafka," a writer officially forbidden by the German censor because of his Jewish origins? A mistake, an oversight on the part of whatever censor went over that day's *Le Soir*?³⁷ A willful playfulness, to see if the censor will catch on? De Man mentions Kafka in the company of Gide, Hemingway, Lawrence: a Frenchman, an American, a British writer—the list is provocatively non-Germanic. And in the next paragraph, de Man couples surrealism—frowned upon in Nazi doctrine, with futurism. Futurism is, of course, formally quite similar to surrealism but in a local political sense it is surrealism's opposite: the surrealists aligned themselves with communism, the futurists with Italian fascism. Surrealism and futurism, de Man asserts, are part of a history of forms that extends far back in time. Is he being willful, is he willfully . . . willfully doing what?

De Man alludes in the conclusion of "Les Juifs dans la littérature actuelle," to a specific solution to the "Jewish problem":

What is more, we see then that a solution of the Jewish problem that would envisage the creation of a Jewish colony isolated from Europe would not entail deplorable consequences for the literary life of the West. It would lose, all in all, a few personalities of mediocre value and would continue, as in the past, to develop according to its great evolutive laws.

The press of the 1930s and 1940s refers with some frequency to such a solution. Large populations of Jewish immigrants were leaving Germany and Austria following Hitler's anti-Jewish legislation. In diplomatic circles in England, France, Poland and the United States something called "The Madagascar Plan" was discussed as a way to ease the Jewish refugee burden.³⁸ Madagascar was at the time a French colony, and there were echoes of the "Madagascar affair" in the French press of the 1930s and in Nazi propaganda. In 1937, the Nazi funded anti-Semitic information bulletin called the *Welt Dienst,* or in its French translation, *Le Service Mondial,* discussed the relative merits of deporting the European Jews to Palestine or to Africa. After arguing that the Arabs would never agree to have their country invaded by Jews, *Le Service Mondial* notes:

However, the solution of Madagascar has also found partisans in France; we would like to quote as proof this phrase that has been seen written by us a number of times in French newspapers: "Madagassez les Juifs" [Mada-gas the Jews].[39]

The reference is obviously to the World War I "gassing" of soldiers, rather than to gas chambers—it is nonetheless, as a figure, horribly proleptic.

Lucien Rebatet, in his 1942 *Les Décombres,* calls specifically for a ghetto to be created for world Jewry in one of the vast British or Russian colonial spaces in Siberia or Africa; Céline, far less programmatic, evokes Jewish deportation to Africa at the same time as he "Africanizes" the Jews:

the Jews in Jerusalem, a little lower on the Niger, they don't bother me! they don't bother me at all! . . . I'll give them all their Congo! all their Africa! . . .[40]

De Man's allusion to an isolated Jewish colony is very different in tone from either Rebatet's or Céline's calls for sending the Jews to Africa, and this is because de Man does not angrily demand the expulsion of the Jews from Europe, but rather refers to it in passing, as a likely development for the near future. He reassures the public that should it happen—the assumption being that it may well happen—the disappearance of the Jews wouldn't be bad for Western literature. This is collaborationist "realism" at its worst. And de Man, like Rebatet, like Céline, and in the tradition of anti-semitic list mania, makes lists: André Maurois, Francis de Croisset, Henri Duvernois, Henri Bernstein, Tristan Bernard, Julien Benda. The great evolutionary laws of Western Literature will go on without these Jews . . . literature as usual.

Van Huffel's April 9, 1941 "Vers une solution européenne du problème juif" [Toward a European solution to the Jewish problem] can be read as a practical response to de Man's realist speculations of March 4. Van Huffel seems to have written the article after attending a conference in Germany which was to inaugurate an "Institute for the study of Jewish problems."[41] He reports, as though he were writing a press release, the "results" of the conference debate: the Jews would have to leave Europe. They would probably have to go somewhere in Asia or Africa because, the participants of the conference had decided, the Arabs could not tolerate them in Palestine.

In a more pedagogical vein, *Le Soir* published on May 14, 1941 an article by Van Huffel's favorite scholar, Georges Montandon, entitled "Les Tâches de l'anthropologie moderne" [The tasks of modern anthropology]. Montandon blames the fall of France on the insufficient understanding of racial doctrines by the now familiar right wing straw men—French nationalists Charles Maurras, Jacques Bainville and their Action Française

movement. The German race is clearly Nordic, Montandon explains; the Italian race is pure Mediterranean, but the French race presents certain problems for analysis because it is mixed, part Alpine, part Mediterranean. "Characteristics other than racial ones are the markings of French ethnicity: linguistic, cultural and mental characteristics." Georges Montandon figured out how to put his theories about French ethnicity to practical use: he became the official racial theorist on the staff of Darquier de Pellepoix's "Commissariat général aux questions juives," and he made large sums of money by giving "racial examinations" to people threatened with deportation.[42]

The variety of anti-Semitic positions outlined above bring the whole page that *Le Soir* devotes to anti-Semitism on March 4, 1941 into sharp focus. That is, the March 4 articles, read as a whole, are doctrinally confusing: Van Huffel's epigraph; Georges Marlier's "social" anti-Semitic analysis of Jewish painting; de Man's article, with its favorable mention of surrealism, André Gide, D. H. Lawrence—Marlier, for one, would have hated that avant-gardism. Yet when you read these articles even in the slightly larger context of other anti-Semitic pieces I've just analyzed—the Van Huffel articles that come before and after, the Poulet review of *Les Beaux Draps* in *Le Nouveau Journal,* the May essay by Montandon—you see, not so much the slight disjunctions between positions, as a number of approaches to the anti-Semitic genre—cultural, racial, historical—which in their very disagreements, give the appearance of respectable "debate." What is more, all of them draw in some way on a critique of an "incorrect" form of racist thinking that is beneath their dignity, and which is exemplified, for Poulet, by the pamphlets of Céline. As it turns out, Céline is useful to make everyone else sound better. All the positions converge because of the existence of something more vulgar: de Man's article participates in this convergence, and in the legitimation of anti-Semitism.

ART AND POLITICS

De Man's parting reference in "Les Juifs dans la littérature actuelle" to the "grandes lois évolutives," the great evolutionary laws of literary form, is crucial for understanding the evolution of his career as a reviewer. His view of literature above and beyond individual or contextual situation could take him in one of two conflicting directions. It could take him toward a formalist study of the evolution of literature, where the field of study is narrowed to those works considered "literary" with barely a regard to their history, apart from their history within the development of a pre-defined genre or artistic form. Or it could take him toward a transcendent, monumental view of history that says: art *is* tied up in the fate of the nation, yet in a transcendent rather than an obvious, immediate way. De Man tries both paths, and his move from the transcendent nationalist to the more disengaged position lends coherence to his last months as a columnist.

There is a single article in the *Le Soir* corpus where the autonomy of literary forms doesn't conflict with transcendent Nazi doctrines of race and spirit. It occurs rather late in de Man's career at *Le Soir,* on March 2, 1942, and is given the lead space on page one. This is de Man's review of the German book fair held in Brussels, "En marge de l'Exposition du livre allemand. Introduction à la littérature allemande contemporaine." De Man's argument is directed against a crude social realism and against the imposition of political constraints on art. "The national value of a contemporary painting," he argues, "can not be evaluated according to the number of s.a. represented in it . . ." De Man ends his article by quoting at length a Nazi official, the Reichsleiter Baldur von Schirach, who condemns small-minded censorship as a travesty of the true artistic nationalism:

He who accuses Goethe of being a freemason or calls the Magic Flute a freemason opera is not taken seriously by our people. [. . .] the nation is not only the current and the immediate, but the eternal community of language and of blood that maintains itself beyond the evolutions of taste and variable conceptions. This is why there is no art that belongs to one particular period.

De Man's concluding line makes a pitch for Germany: "It's because German literature has lived according to these wise precepts that she has been able to realize her goals and prepare the path for future grandeur."[43] Yet the precepts he refers to are quite different: one guarantees the right to read freemason books and go to freemason operas (as long as they are classics); the other promotes a community of language and blood. It's only by referring to an unusually sophisticated Nazi ideologue that de Man can make these two precepts coalesce.[44]

De Man's writing in *Le Soir* had, from very early on, distinguished itself ever so slightly from the collaborationist idiom by an elitist avant-gardism that's hard to label politically, but that could be said to anticipate de Man's subsequent positions of the 1960s and 1970s. The article of March 1942 appears to be the rhetorical apogee of de Man's collaborationist writing, the place where he is best able to reconcile his artistic standards with an official metaphysics of style and soil. After that, his literary vision falls away from the state.

The cubist use of African primitivist themes and the surrealists' support of communism made both groups targets of Nazi attacks against avant-garde movements. In the crudest pamphlets, like those of Céline, surrealists were considered "jewified" and "negrified." Among de Man's fellow collaborationist critics in Brussels, even the fairly demure Robert Poulet describes the surrealism of Breton, Eluard, Artaud as "the mass suicide of a powerful and despairing race."[45] Georges Marlier makes a similar argument about avant-garde painters on the famous anti-Semitic page: "It is the Jews who have given [to modern art] its violently subversive and destructive character, which had to lead, finally, to the most total anarchy."

Paul De Man defends surrealism in *Le Soir,* not only as crucial literary experimentation but as part of a continuity in French letters that could be traced back to symbolist and romanticist movements before it. One already senses de Man's affection for surrealism in his August 1941 review of Brasillach's *Notre Avant-Guerre.* He defends surrealist art in much more explicit opposition to the collaborationist line on July 14, 1942, in his review of the new French poetry journal *Messages. Messages,* founded by Jean Lescure, was, according to Loiseaux's literary history of the Occupation, the only journal legally published in Paris that openly derided collaborationist writers.[46] De Man lauds the "pure and limpid" poetry of Eluard and speculates that surrealism might finally have come into its own: he is praising the artistic content of a journal openly hostile to collaboration and—consciously or not—singling out a leading poet of the French Resistance.[47] De Man's favorable review of *Messages,* though founded on his belief in the irrelevance of political and historical events to artistic ones, is as close as he will come in *Le Soir* to a negative assessment of the cultural politics of the new Europe; as such it represents a dramatic turn around from the March 1942 article praising the book fair. De Man now attributes to the Nazi regime not an understanding of the transcendent nature of art production but a misguided desire to interfere with art:

under the pretext that this revolution is totalitarian, that is to say it intends to modify all the aspects of individual and collective life, some have brutally placed art among its objectives. (. .) In other words, art—and more specifically, literature—finds itself transformed into a tool, an instrument, destined to combat by all its means a defective "Weltanschanung" [sic]* and impose another one.

[*sic for *Weltanschauung,* ideology or world view: in quotation marks in German in the original French text.]

"Far be it for me to want to pose as admirer of pre-war extravagances," he apologizes in the last paragraph of the *Messages* review, in a superficial concession to the official argument. De Man's sympathies, at least where surrealist poetry is concerned, seem to lie elsewhere.

The same critical tension carries over to de Man's July 20, 1942 review of Robert Poulet's latest experimental novel, *L'Ange et les Dieux*. De Man doesn't like the book for strictly formal reasons, and he explains these at length. He nonetheless refers disapprovingly to those who were criticizing Poulet for writing an "apolitical novel," and he defends Poulet's need and right to separate his artistic from his political activities. On August 4, de Man is extremely critical of Georges Marlier's *Vingt années de peinture et de sculpture en Belgique* which, in its desire to promote "the current atmosphere," has condemned certain pre-war art movements and thereby, according to de Man, distorted history. If Marlier had wanted to renounce the claims to historical accuracy that are implicit in the title of his book, he should have written a manifesto or a pamphlet instead:

Out of fear of having to recognize that French surrealism and German expressionism are not incompatible with certain successes, he [Marlier] goes as far as not to give a group of painters of the first order the place that they deserve.

It is my guess that there's a fight going on behind the scenes here pitting Poulet—the experimentalist—against Marlier—the blood and soil anti-hermeticist. De Man seems ready to defend even a messy experimentalism over a rigid party line.

Soon after, de Man appears caught between his institutional role and his function as a critic. *Le Soir,* with de Man as judge, organized a contest to pick the "best book on the war or on circumstances provoked by the war" written by a Belgian. The initial announcement of the contest appeared June 26, 1941; the entries were to be sent to Paul de Man by March 1 and the deadline was then extended to May 1, 1942. The jury was announced on July 8: it included Pierre Daye, from *Le Nouveau Journal*. The results were finally announced on September 19.

On September 22, three days after the contest ended, de Man devoted a very strange article to his disappointment in the submissions to the contest. He complained that the writers who submitted manuscripts were unduly influenced by journalistic style, as though they felt obliged to imitate the writing style of their sponsor, a newspaper. The writers were too caught up in the immediate, they were reporting, not writing, there was no quest in the manuscripts he read for new forms of expression, and new forms of expression should be the deepest concern of Belgian writers. The submissions didn't live up to his goals.

De Man stopped writing for *Le Soir* in November, a landmark time in World War II chronology, the month of the Battle of Stalingrad, and the defeat of Rommel at El-Alamein. The American troops land in North Africa the night of November 7. On November 8, Anne Somerhausen wrote in her diary:

This is victory, this is the end! What now deters the Germans from making a peace offer? It is clear that they no longer hold the initiative. They are on the defensive now. They are doomed.

It is hard to imagine reading this, that the Occupation of Belgium would drag on for another two years.

The departure of de Man from the staff of *Le Soir* sometime around the end of November, 1942, would seem to come on the heels not only of his statements against political interference in art, his disappointment in his own role as an organizer of a literary event, but also of what many, writing in 1942 and afterwards, consider the very turning point of the war in the direction of an allied military victory. The writer who argues for the evolution of art disconnected from political events is consistent with the de Man of the post-war years; the de Man who gets out of *Le Soir* just as collaboration begins to lose its appeal is pragmatic and politically astute, someone with a very clear sense of events and their consequences. The two de Man's meet in the literary contest—the socially-conscious organizer, building up the literary community by means of a contest, and the avant-gardist who doesn't like the consequences of his own pragmatism, a pile of manuscripts in banal, journalistic style. The de Man who doesn't believe in a connection between art and politics is also the de Man who refuses to review vulgar political pamphlets like Céline's *Les Beaux Draps,* who reviews many of the books on Payr's list of "writings to be promoted" but only one book on the sub-section of the list entitled "anti-Jewish writings"[48]; this is also the de Man who criticized Brasillach's mystified reaction to Hitler but oddly had nothing to say about Brasillach's long description of a fascist movement in Belgium.[49] The "art only" de Man makes no mention of the RAF bombings of the city in which he writes, no reference to the immediate daily context—work deportation, blackouts, food rationing—beyond the code word "reality." The "art only" de Man makes no mention of the obligatory yellow stars for Jews, which appear in great number on June 12, 1942, nor does he mention the fact that the yellows stars vanished from sight after the Gestapo raids several weeks later. Yet he does appear to become disenchanted and he does leave *Le Soir* in time—in time to avoid assassination, trial or condemnation, in time to save himself for the career that we write about today.[50]

For all my emphasis on context, I need to say something about my own context, too, about the post-war de Man who chaired the department at Yale, where from 1978–1981, I wrote a dissertation on French fascist intellectuals of the 1930s and 40s, never imagining that he knew anything about their books.

De Man taught me how to read for polarities and to look at "presence" as a rhetorical ploy. In his seminars, I sharpened my sense of the way that fascism recycled clichés of right and left wing rhetoric in an emotionally powerful populism; I began to think about the way fascist leaders used the media to foster illusions of their own presence.

Partly out of respect for the de Man who taught me ways to read clichés, partly out of my own need to establish boundaries with the material, I was aiming in this article for an emotional deadpan. I was more concerned here with doing the work of placing de Man's writing in a field than with an ultimate "assessment," a "right or wrong," "good or evil"—I didn't want to distract from the complexity of the analysis by my own immediate emotional charge. I especially wanted to give the reader of de Man's wartime work something of a sense of the distance that separates 1988 and 1940, and that makes assessment of his actions so difficult. I wanted the reader to wonder "who the hell are we, writing today, to think we know what it was like to write under a sky riddled with bombs, to face being sent to a labor camp," and also to imagine the yellow stars on the streets, the Gestapo raids, the disappearances.

Reading de Man's texts within the collaborationist field puts into relief their fascist and anti-semitic effects, but I say effects, not intentions, since these I cannot gauge. Because de Man's position evolves, one can't talk about a single political or cultural stance that he maintained, even from 1941 to 1942, much less throughout his intellectual life.

I don't see in de Man's career as a theorist of deconstruction any easy continuity with his fascist positions of the 40s. But I do understand de Man's theoretical career as motivated, to an extent we can't measure, by a need to isolate himself from the kinds of political choices that European intellectuals were forced to make between 1940 and 1945 and that de Man most likely believed he had made badly.

The most insidious statements in de Man's column are, to my mind, made in the name of rigor and a search for higher ground. He declared himself more rigorous in his view of Germany than mystified Brasillach; more sophisticated and witty in dismissing Jewish writers than "vulgar" anti-Semites. I'm struck by the same general strategies in academic writing, by how comforting it is to compare one's own position to a more vulgar one. He depended on disdain then, and we still do now.

My training in graduate school began with the "vulgar reading," the tactless psychologizing which would have to be taken apart, transcended. I remember de Man's essay on "The Resis-

tance to Theory"—it's an emotional memory—not as much for its intellectual argument as for the delicate moment where de Man lets me know what is interesting and what is dull, where he evokes, "the impersonal consistency that theory requires" (6) and equates psychological readings with such horrors as "New Critical Moral Earnestness." I remember a sentence from the end of the article. I look it up and see that it was intended as a critique of pragmatism. But I had remembered it for the way it set up a choice: I could end up in the right or in the wrong, a resister or an embracer of theory:

The equation of rhetoric with psychology rather than with epistemology opens up dreary prospects of pragmatic banality, all the drearier if compared to the brilliance of the performative analysis.[51]

After I left graduate school, I threw myself into research on non-canonical texts: I was drawn to the most insignificant of texts—newspapers, almanacs, advertisements—everything that wasn't literature. I now recognize this as a reaction to my training, a defense of the banal as a way to get at a level of cultural knowledge, a base I felt I had been denied. In my work on fascism, I discovered that it was crucial not to dismiss fascist writers as "stupid" or "banal": if you do so, you can't get close enough to them to understand their own desires, their effect.

My task when I started reading *Le Soir* was to connect de Man's writing to the rest of my work on fascism, but the very first connections I made were to the de Man I remember in the classroom. When I saw that de Man reviewed Jacques Chardonne's 1941 *Voir la figure,* a book that argues, in the collaborationist mode, that the French should "look things straight in the face" and adapt to a German-controlled reality, I thought about figures of rhetoric, about the de Man who insisted that language itself was never adequate to "looking things straight in the face," and I tried to imagine the reading he might have given, in the 1980s, of his 1941 column. I tried to imagine de Man "confessing" and my fantasy was interrupted by my memory of jokes he used to make about a figure of speech, a magazine title, he found particularly oxymoronic—"true confessions."

Reading the early de Man late, too late to interview him, too late to challenge him, I remember the de Man suspicious of the early-late distinction in Nietzsche criticism.

I recognized the de Man I had as a teacher when I read the texts in *Le Soir.* It wasn't because of anything he said, it was his strategies, his process—so familiar—that I recognized across the frontier of 1976 and 1940. The signals were the same: the command of literary history, the vast cultural knowledge he was giving away, because that wasn't what was really important. Then a second paragraph, with a quotation and its logical inconsistency revealed. The same emphasis on rigor, the disdain for vulgarity, indulgence. Except for the endings—and it's a big exception—where, instead of the abyss, the deconstructive finale that I am used to, de Man ends with a kind of proto-fascist community building statement, a slogan: "a necessary condition for the revival of the nation" [6/7/41]; "a serious effort of re-education imposes itself, if these countries want to play a constructive role in the future Europe" [6/11/41]; "a political and social revolution . . . based on more solid, yet less ephemeral foundations" [8/12/41]; ". . . such fundamental truths must govern the actions of men of good will" [8/26/41]; "urgent tasks to accomplish for the well being of all" [8/18/42].

Nothing could be more divorced from the programmatic way de Man ended these polemics, than the way he used to end class, the way his most stunning deconstructionist pieces end: with meaning pulled out from under the reader, with the figurative abyss:

The loftier the aims and the better the methods of literary theory, the less possible it becomes. Yet literary theory is not in danger of going under; it cannot help but flourish, and the more it is resisted, the more it flourishes, since the language it speaks is the language of self-resistance. What remains impossible to decide is whether this flourishing is a triumph or a fall.[52]

He worked against his early work, that much is clear to me. With a dramatic flair and an authority that the young reviewer at *Le Soir* would doubtless have envied. At the same time, of course, he repeated himself, the way we all repeat ourselves; it is the same man, the same emotional structures in 1942 and 1981. He didn't repeat himself in the slogans, but in the skepticism, the elitism, the demands for rigor. And in the ambivalence about his own power: I recognize in his disappointment at the entries to a literature contest he sponsored, the same response he displayed in his introduction to his own students' work in *Studies in Romanticism*.[53] The introduction was so ironic in its references to the effects of his own teaching that the students who were trying to learn what de Man taught felt criticized, even ridiculed.

One of the things that has struck me most about the American reaction to the articles in *Le Soir* is the general shock and surprise that an intellectual be directly involved in an historical event and the rush to construct analogies between academic deconstruction and political fascism: in a sense our own seemingly isolated intellectual structures would encourage us to buy into de Man's own belief in the relative autonomy of art from local political contexts. We—I'm writing now, reluctantly, as a member of that community—view any political involvement with art as exotic and aberrant. European critics—even when arguing for the autonomy of art—have traditionally had a declared political identity linked to their intellectual one. The American university has its own professional politics, but American intellectuals participate in a sphere that is relatively isolated from national ideological and political questions. De Man himself noted this in his 1983 interview with Stefano Rosso, and it was perhaps, given his early experience, one of the comforting aspects of writing criticism in an American scene.[54]

Not confessing, not indulging in his own experience, working for a theory of literature "supremely impersonal" (even unteachable) was, as we know, an important part of de Man's professional stance. Early in his career as an American university teacher, in 1964, when the stance was closer to personal opinion than to theoretical articulation, de Man reviewed Sartre's *Les Mots* and mocked its author for airing his personal laundry in public: "*The Words* is an ideological essay, but it is also an act of self-therapy which, as such, does not belong to literature."[55] I find written in my notes to Paul de Man's introductory seminar in critical theory, fall 1975, a similar caveat to future critics: "Don't confuse this [theory] with your lives!" Advice to young minds, to us, graduate students, who, in our twenties, were the same age as he. . . , the same age as Brasillach when he made poetry of the rallies at Nuremberg. It's advice of a kind that is impossible to extricate from a life, advice that's impossible to follow.

Duke University

NOTES

1. An English translation of the manifesto appears in Peter Dodge, ed., *A Documentary Study of Hendrik de Man, Socialist Critic of Marxism* (Princeton: Princeton University Press, 1979). Henri de Man is often compared to Marcel Déat and Jacques Doriot, two French collaborators of left wing origin. Déat, an Ecole Normale educated intellectual and a renegade from Léon Blum's socialist party, believed that Hitler's plan for Europe was the best plan for Europe's workers. See his newspaper, *L'Oeuvre,* for examples of a left collaborationist line; a number of his articles are reprinted in *Le Soir.* Jacques Doriot was an ex-member of the French communist party who founded the Parti Populaire Français and took to holding rallies in the style of Hitler. Theirs was a far more active form than collaboration took in the case of Henri de Man, the Belgian socialist theorist. In June of 1940, after the fall, de Man issued his manifesto advising Belgian workers to accept German victory in Belgium and to work for socialism within the constraints of occu-

pation. But by November 1941, he had dissociated himself from German policy, though it is not at all clear from the sources I have consulted whether he did so out of disappointed idealism, moral outrage or for completely idiosyncratic reasons. De Launay and Offergeld write that de Man refused to give the German occupants his official support for Hitler's invasion of Russia in November 1941 and subsequently joined the resistance (Jacques De Launay et Jacques Offergeld, *La Vie quotidienne des Belges sous l'occupation (1940–1945)*. Brussels: Paul Legrain, 1983.) Zeev Sternhell (*Ni droite ni gauche: l'idéologie fasciste en France*. Paris: Seuil, 1983) sees de Man's theories as a fundamental nutrient for European fascism. Sternhell argues that de Man's enthusiasm for the occupation was perfectly consistent with his political writings of the 1930s and points out that even after he had left Belgium, de Man continued to contribute articles to occupied French papers as Marcel Déat's *L'Oeuvre*. If De Man wasn't as active as Marcel Déat in the collaboration, in Sternhell's view, it's not by reason of ideological divergence. An unpublished text attributed to Raymond de Becker, the editor of *Le Soir,* also implies that de Man's retirement from collaborationist politics was a matter of temperament as much as politics: "the collaborationist movement did not find in him the guide that certain had hoped for, not only because de Man's ideas became rapidly opposed to those of the Germans, but also because he did not posses a leader's temperament; he was only a man of doctrine and, perhaps, an educator. ["La Collaboration en Belgique (1940–1944) ou Une Révolution avortée." Inédit attribué à Raymond De Becker (extraits). Centre de Recherche et d'information socio-politiques. C.H. No 497–498, 56.] Though his larger project appears to be one of reinstating Henri de Man in the socialist canon, historian Peter Dodge concurs to some extent with Sternhell in arguing that De Man's denigration of procedural democracy, his call for "the recognition of authority, nationality, and order" might have permitted him to mistake Nazism for a socialism. Dodge, however, emphasizes de Man's disillusionment in 1941, his recognition that an autonomous socialist policy could never be carried out in occupied Belgium [Peter Dodge, *op. cit.*].

2. Personal communication from Neil Hertz, based on an interview with Anaïde Baraghian, February 14, 1988.

3. Much of the daily life detail in this essay comes from Anne Somerhausen, *Written in Darkness: A Belgian Woman's Record of the Occupation, 1940–1945* (New York: Knopf, 1946).

4. Personal communication from Neil Hertz, based on an interview with Anaïde Baraghian, February 14, 1988.

5. Somerhausen, 17.

6. Jacques de Launay et Jacques Offergeld, *La vie quotidienne des belges sous l'occupation (1940–1945)* (Bruxelles: Paul Legrain, éditeur, 1982). De Launay and Offergeld disagree with Somerhausen on many details—they refer to the claim that the Germans liberated Flemish prisoners of war before Walloons as "anti-Flemish propaganda."

7. Alfred Fabre-Luce, ed. *Anthologie de la nouvelle Europe* (Paris: Plon, 1942).

8. Much was made by Sartre of the "realist" arguments in collaborationist literature in his essay "Qu'est-ce qu'un collaborateur?" in *Situations III* (Paris: Gallimard, 1949), 43–61, first published in New York, August 1945 in *La République Française*. The "realist" or "historicist" position dictates that because an event has taken place you have to acquiesce to it morally and even go as far as to consider it as progress; a collaborator is, according to Sartre, someone who agrees with the Occupation mostly because it has happened, who invests the need to adjust with idealism.

   Few writers who remained in occupied countries emerged from four years of a foreign occupation completely pure of any hint of having acquiesced or "adjusted." Sartre himself published a review of Giono's translation of *Moby Dick* in *Comoedia,* a Parisian weekly devoted to the arts that, without engaging in any direct political propaganda, was useful to the Nazi cause in promoting Parisian "culture as usual" under German rule. *Comoedia* published a "European page," where the cultural events taking place in the Reich were lauded and books recently translated from the German were presented to the French reading public. Germany was at the helm of the new political Europe; Germany would also be the prime inspiration of the new European mind: this message was transmitted in *Comoedia* by implication, rather than by slogan. Valéry and Cocteau published there alongside official collaborators like Brasillach and Jacques Chardonne. A detailed history of the magazine would make an excellent case study of the political ambiguities of cultural collaboration. See Pierre Assouline, *Gaston Gallimard: un demi-siècle d'édition française* (Paris: Balland, 1984), 342, and Pascal Ory, *Les Collaborateurs 1940–1945* (Paris: Seuil, 1976), 206.

9. The list is published as in Gerard Loiseaux, *La Littérature de la défaite et de la collaboration d'après Phönix oder Asche? (Phénix ou Cendres?) de Bernhard Payr* (Paris: Publications de la Sorbonne, 1984), appendix, 89. Loiseaux's study includes his translation of *Phönix oder Asche,* a detailed exegesis by Bernhard Payr of books deemed helpful or harmful to the German cause.

10. These and subsequent translations from the French are my own. The translations are in no way definitive: they are meant to serve as a convenience for non-Francophone readers.

A note on the word "génie", which appears frequently in fascist and collaborationist polemics and is very difficult to translate. Like "élan" and "esprit" in French or "geist" in German, it is often used to assign intrinsically energetic qualities to the nation. Although it can carry in French the sense of "genius", of extraordinary intellectual power, it also rings closer to its etymological cousins, to "gender," "engender" and "genre"; it denotes an innate disposition or a mentality.

11. De Man reviews work by Daye on August 26, 1941 and on February 3, 1942; Daye is a member of the jury headed by de Man to judge *Le Soir*'s literary contest of 1942. De Man reviews Colin on April 15, 1941 and November 22, 1942; he reviews Poulet on December 2, 1941, June 16, 1942, and July 20, 1942.

12. Colin, as president of the French section of the Association of Belgian Journalists, presides over a June 1942 meeting to commemorate the second anniversary since the reappearance (i.e. the takeover) of *Le Soir*. He is quoted in *Le Soir* in a June 17 account of the anniversary party as reminding his colleagues of the "difficult task of detoxification to which the editorial staff of the *Soir* has attached itself." Anne Somerhausen calls Colin the "cleverest, meanest, most unscrupulous, and most influential of the quisling newspapermen in Belgium": "Paul Colin was pro-German before the war. He was probably cashing propaganda checks from Goebbels long before Belgium was invaded. . . . He has done more than any other man to divide Belgian public opinion against itself. His diabolically clever pen became a veritable machine-gun after the invasion, mowing down intellectuals, lawyers, and politicians against whom he bore a grudge or who would not fall into line with New Order principles. A man of unclean private life; a man who grew rich by graft and embezzlement" (*Written in Darkness,* 205). De Becker, editor of the occupied *Le Soir,* concurs with Somerhausen's assessment of Colin's personality in his post war report on the failure of the Belgian collaboration ("La Collaboration en Belgique (1940–1944) ou Une Révolution avortée." Inédit attribué à Raymond De Becker [extraits]").

13. Pierre Daye, *Guerre et révolution: lettres d'un belgeà un ami français* (Paris; Grasset, 1941). A reporter for *Le Soir* in the 1930s, Pierre Daye became an ardent supporter of the Belgian fascist "Rex Party" led by Léon Degrelle and was president of the rexist group in the Belgian house of representatives. He left the rexist party in 1939, disenchanted with parliamentary politics altogether. Meanwhile he had become the French correspondent for *Je Suis Partout,* the French fascist newspaper whose brightest literary light was Robert Brasillach; he would remain throughout the war closely tied to French fascist intellectual circles. In Belgium Daye wrote for Paul

Colin's *Cassandre*; under the occupation, he became political reporter for *Le Nouveau Journal,* the daily started by Colin. Daye became commissioner of sports in 1943. He was condemned to death in absentia by the liberation government and died in 1960 in Buenos-Aires. [For more information on Daye, see *Je Suis Partout 1930–1944: Les Maurrassiens devant la tentation fasciste* (Paris: La Table Ronde, 1973, 445).] Daye published *Guerre et révolution* in Grasset's collaborationist series "in search of France" which included books by Jacques Doriot (*Je suis un homme du maréchal* [*I am one of Pétain's men*]), Pierre Drieu la Rochelle, and Georges Suarez (*Pétain ou la démocratie? Il faut choisir* [*Pétain or democracy? We have to choose*]).

14. Mil Zankin, "Un socialiste parle: Ordre nouveau et désordre ancien. La jonction des extrêmes," *Le Nouveau Journal,* January 9, 1941.

15. Robert Poulet, "Colloque de la droite et de la gauche," *Le Nouveau Journal,* March 23, 1941, 1.

16. Adolf Hitler, *Mein Kampf,* trans. Ralph Manheim (Boston: Houghton Mifflin, 1971).

17. Grimm was a professor of international law at the University of Münster and official propagandist in the Franco-German cause. In 1938 Hitler named Grimm general counsel in Bern in charge of surveying the French press and its effects on neutral countries. After the fall of France in 1940, Grimm broadcast on Radio Stuttgart to convince French audiences of the validity of Hitler's thesis. His theory was that Bainville's doctrines were the biggest obstacle to penetration of Nazism in France. In Germany, Grimm even managed to convince Hitler to have Bainville translated into German to educate Germans about what they were up against with respect to the French Catholic right.

18. Frédéric Grimm, *Hitler et la France* (Paris: Plon, 1938), cited in Loiseaux, 69–70.

19. Frédéric Grimm. *Le Testament politique de Richelieu,* préface de Fernand de Brinon, ambassadeur de France (Paris: Flammarion, 1941), 200.

20. The Munich agreement took place in 1938. Delegations from France, Great Britain, Italy and Germany met and gave permission to Hitler to reoccupy the Sudetenland.

21. Eugen Weber, *Action Française: Royalism and Reaction in Twentieth-Century France* (Stanford: Stanford University Press, 1962), 503.

22. Robert O. Paxton, *Vichy France: Old Guard and New Order (1940–1944)* (New York: Norton, 1972), 230.

23. Alice Yaeger Kaplan, *Reproductions of Banality: Fascism, Literature, and French Intellectual Life* (Minneapolis: University of Minnesota Press, 1986), 15–18.

24. From a very different historical perspective, cf. Hannah Arendt's argument about the 1930s French elite's lack of a sense of reality in *The Origins of Totalitarianism* (New York: Harcourt Brace, 1966), 326–340; Arendt uses as an example André Gide's admiration for Céline's *Bagatelles pour un massacre* in a 1938 review (André Gide, "Les Juifs, Céline et Maritain," *Nouvelle Revue Française,* April 1, 1938, 630–636). Arendt's position on avant-garde intellectuals and fascism is discussed in my *Reproductions of Banality,* chapter 2.

25. *Nouvelle Revue Française,* August 1, 1941, 253–254.

26. See *Le Temps,* November 5, 1941, 3. Thérive had been the literary critic for *Le Temps* before the war; he wrote no columns for the paper after 1941. *Le Temps* was a politically moderate daily, comparable in size and scope to *Le Soir.* When France fell, it moved to Lyon, in the unoccupied zone. Thérive remained in Paris and became increasingly identified with hard-line collaborators—he contributed to *Je Suis Partout, Nouveaux Temps, Petit Parisien, Pariser Zeitung.* In 1942 Thérive went with a group of French journalists to Germany, on one of several trips organized by the Nazi propaganda ministry: Thérive and his French colleagues were much photographed for propaganda purposes. By 1944, at the bitter end, Thérive was writing for the *Chronique de Paris,* a monthly "high collaborationist" review that emerged after Drieu folded the *Nouvelle Revue Française.*

27. Poulet was sentenced for collaboration after the war. He emerged in France in the 50s as the literary columnist for the right wing magazine *Rivarol;* he was in charge of the posthumous edition of the second part of the manuscript of Céline's *Guignol's band,* to which he gave the title *Le Pont de Londres.* His *Entretiens familiers avec L.-F. Céline* (Paris: Plon, 1958) republished as *Mon Ami Bardamu* (Paris: Plon, 1971) is an important source of information on Céline; the interviews played a role in the recuperation of Céline in the 1960s by formalist critics. Robert Poulet's half-brother, Georges, is the well-known critic of the Geneva School. Georges broke with Robert over political issues in the 1930s. A reconciliation was attempted by Gabriel Marcel in the 1960s without success. Between Robert and Georges, there is an interesting and rare example of a connection between de Man's pre-war and post-war career. See de Man's reviews of Robert Poulet in *Le Soir* (December 2, 1941: "Sur les possibilités de la critique"; June 16, 1942: "Mérites et défauts d'une expérience: à propos de *Handji* et de *Le Trottoir,* de Robert Poulet"; July 20, 1942, "Apport à un débat délicat. *L'Ange et les Dieux* par Robert Poulet") and "The Literary Self as Origin: The Work of Georges Poulet" in *Blindness and Insight* (New York: Oxford Press, 1971), 79–101.

28. Cf. reviews of *Notre Avant-Guerre* in *La Gerbe,* June 5, 1941 (unsigned) and in *Comoedia,* August 23 1941 (signed Marcel Arland)—both papers were published in occupied Paris. See also, from the point of view of the German propaganda staff, Bernhard Payr's résumé of *Notre Avant-Guerre* in "Phénix ou Cendres?," ed. Loiseaux, 151: "When the young fascist who held the closest relationships with Spanish nationalist militants and who had his own idea about the Spanish War, had in 1937 an opportunity to attend the Nuremberg Party Congress and thus to make the acquaintance of Germany, it's doubtless then that he recognized the force of the faith expressed there, without, for all that, finding himself an access to this world which appeared to him as exotic and even stranger than the Far East. . . . And it is not without regret that in seeing this proud German youth and its festivities he thinks about what democracy has done to France. A book of great documentary importance."

29. The Céline and Rebatet texts were all published by Robert Denoël. Denoël tells a reporter in 1941 that *Les Beaux Draps* sold 28,000 during the first three months after it came out (Assouline, 315); see also Assouline, 350–352, on the success of *Les Décombres.*

30. De Man does contribute the following short review of *Les Décombres* to the *Bibliographie Dechenne* XIV, September 1942, where he concentrates on Rebatet's critique of pre-war French decadence:

Lucien Rebatet, like Robert Brasillach, is one of those young French intellectuals who, during the years between the two [world] wars, worked with all their might to combat a politics whose catastrophic and ill-fated orientation they had understood. The entire sum of bitterness and indignation accumulated over the course of those years of vain combat finally overflows in this thick volume, an immense pamphlet of brilliant verve and vigor. One by one, all the guilty parties of the current French decay, whatever the milieu or party to which they belong, are looked over and shot down in a few lapidary and definitive sentences. But this great work of destruction also contains constructive elements: in walking among the ruins [les décombres] of a fallen period. Lucien Rebatet also dreams of reconstruction; and this is why without a doubt his ferocious book ends in words of hope.

31. Georges Montandon, *Comment reconnaître le Juif? Suivi d'un Portrait moral du Juif selon les livres de L.-F. Céline* (Paris: Nouvelles éditions françaises, 1940). The Montandon archives are housed at the Centre de Documentation Juive in Paris. For the connection between Montandon and Céline, see my *Relevé des sources et citations dans "Bagatelles pour un massacre"* (Tusson: du Lérot, 1987), 21, 67–69. Céline mentions Montandon in his 1938 pamphlet *L'Ecole des ca-*

davres in a list of "Judeologues" worthy of study. Montandon's *Comment reconnaître le juif?* is on Bernhard Payr's official list of "Literature to be promoted as of December 31, 1942" under the category "Anti-Jewish writings." Céline's pamphlets, which Payr considered vulgar, are not included on the list.

32. Céline's last novel to that date, *Mort à crédit,* had been published in 1936 and had received very bad reviews; his career as a polemicist started with *Mea culpa,* published later that same year. Poulet, in his post-war role as literary columnist for *Rivarol,* became a great champion of Céline the novelist.

33. Payr, ed. Loiseaux, 167.

34. Louis-Ferdinand Céline, *Bagatelles pour un massacre* (Paris: Denoël, 1937), 187.

35. Lucien Rebatet, *Les Décombres* (Paris: Denoël, 1942), 570. For details of its publication history, see Assouline, 350–352.

36. Paragraph 5 of the review: "Gide, Kafka, Hemingway, Lawrence—the list could be extended indefinitely—they all penetrate the secrets of an interior life according to methods appropriate to their own personalities. In this characteristic, they show that they are not so much innovators who have broken with all the traditions of the past, but simple sustainers who are deepening even further a realist esthetic more than a century old."

37. Readers of the period would have recognized Kafka as a Jewish writer. Works by Kafka had been withdrawn from sale in France and Germany and acquired a large underground following. In France, Gerhard Heller censored the chapter on Kafka in Camus' *Mythe de Sisyphe.* See Loiseaux, 476 and Assouline, 368, 451.

38. For a résumé of diplomatic discussion of the issue, see Michael R. Marrus and Robert O. Paxton, *Vichy France and the Jews* (New York: Schocken Books, 1983), 60–62.

39. *Le Service Mondial,* no. iv/3, February 1, 1937, 3–4; cited in my *Relevé des sources et citations dans "Bagatelles pour un massacre,"* 259.

40. *Bagatelles pour un massacre,* 317–318.

41. Probably created under the auspices of Nazi racial theorist Alfred Rosenberg, who also controlled the *Welt Dienst* or *Service Mondial,* an anti-Semitic news bulletin.

42. Marrus and Paxton, *Vichy France and the Jews,* 300–301. One of Montandon's racial examinations is fictionalized in the 1970s Joseph Losey film, *Monsieur Klein.* The real Montandon was assassinated in 1944.

43. Cf. Céline, *Les Beaux Draps,* on a more vulgar register:

Art knows no country! what stupidity! what a lie! what heresy! what a Jewish dictum!

Art is nothing but Race and Country! This is the rock on which it is constructed! Rock and clouds, in fact, landscape of the soil. . . . (177)

44. Baldur von Schirach (1907–1974) headed the Hitler Youth from 1931–1940 and became one of the most influential propagandists in Hitler's entourage. As a result of political maneuvers by Martin Bormann, von Schirach was relieved of his post in 1940 and made Governor of Vienna. His Viennese cultural policy was liberal: he revived the Vienna Opera, supported the museums, and gave extravagant receptions and banquets for artists. He gradually lost favor with Hitler, who mistrusted him for encouraging Austrian cultural autonomy. In an attempt to appease Hitler and Bormann in September of 1942, von Schirach made a stringent public statement demanding the deportation of the Austrian Jews to an eastern ghetto; the gesture did not restore his influence in Berlin. For a history of von Schirach's career in Vienna, see Radomir Luza, *Austro-German Relations in the Anschluss Era* (Princeton: Princeton University Press, 1975), and for a capsule biography, see Robert Wistrich, *Who's Who in Nazi Germany* (New York: MacMillan, 1982). Several of von Schirach's articles from the Hitler Youth period are reprinted in George L. Mosse, *Nazi Culture: Intellectual, Cultural and Social Life in the Third Reich* (New York: Grosset & Dunlap, 1966).

45. "L'Avenir de la littérature," *Le Nouveau Journal,* January 2, 1941.

46. Loiseaux, 502. *Messages* no. 1 (March 15, 1942), for example, reprints this collaborationist diatribe against the Parisian avant-garde for comic effect: "Thirty years of literary, spiritual, human nihilism! . . . Gide-Corydon, Breton salesman of ectoplasms, Aragon the archbishop of *Ce Soir,* Eluard the rotten fruit [. . .]" etc., etc. (The text originally appeared in *Au Pilori* in 1940. It is cited in Assouline, 300, and in Pierre Seghers, *La Résistance et ses poètes. France 1940–1945* [Paris: Edition Seghers, 1974], 75.)

The two issues of *Messages* reviewed by de Man in his July 1942 article were published in the occupied zone in 1942; *Messages* was later banned and published outside of France.

47. On Paul Eluard's role in the Resistance, see Pierre Seghers, op. cit.

48. De Man reviews Lucien Rebatet's *Les Décombres* in September 1942, not in *Le Soir* but in the Dechenne bibliography (see note 30, above). De Man's review concentrates on Rebatet as a

critic of the Third Republic, and makes no mention of the anti-Semitic portions of the book.

49. *Notre Avant-Guerre,* in *Une Génération dans l'orage* (Paris: Plon, 1955), 207–214.

50. Louis Fonsny, who had been President of the socialist students at the University of Brussels before the war, and who wrote the literary column in *Le Soir* after de Man left, was assassinated on the streets of Brussels on January 28, 1943, at the age of 26. Paul Colin was assassinated on April 15, 1943 by a nineteen-year old student named Arnaud Fraiteur, who would be hanged for it. "With Paul Colin gone," wrote Anne Somerhausen in 1943, "quisling propaganda throughout French-speaking Belgium is practically beheaded. There is none to replace this dangerously brilliant polemicist" (*Written in Darkness,* 205). François Gallez, who wrote literary columns in *Le Soir* after Fonsny was killed, was arrested by Liberation authorities on September 22, 1944; Robert Poulet was found hiding under a false name and arrested on November 2 the same year. According to *Le Soir* of November, 1944 (a *Le Soir* whose prewar management was back in place), five thousand arrests had taken place in Brussels as of November 1, 1944.

51. Paul de Man, *The Resistance to Theory* (Minneapolis: University of Minnesota Press, 1986), 19.

52. *The Resistance to Theory,* 19–20.

53. "Introduction" [to a special issue titled "The Rhetoric of Romanticism"], *Studies in Romanticism* 18:4, Winter 1979, 495–99. See, for example, 498: "Tropes are taken apart with such casual elegance that the exegeses can traverse the entire field of tropological reversals and displacements with a virtuosity that borders on parody."

54. Stefano Rosso, "An Interview with Paul de Man" in *The Resistance to Theory,* 116: "In Europe one is of course much closer to ideological and political questions, while, on the contrary, in the States, one is much closer to professional questions."

55. "Sartre's Confessions" [review of Jean-Paul Sartre, *The Words*], *The New York Review of Books* 3:6, 5 November 1964, 10–13.

DeMan's Resistances: A Contribution to the Future Science of DeManology[1]

RICHARD KLEIN

Le diabolique est intelligent. Il s'infiltre où il veut. Pour le refuser, il faut d'abord le réfuter. Il faut un effort intellectuel pour le reconnaître. Qui peut s'en vanter? Que voulez-vous, le diabolique donne à penser.—*Emmanuel Levinas (*Nouvel Observateur, *January 7, 1988.)*

Whatever DeMan may have thought he was doing, or said he was doing, publishing regular articles in that newspaper, *Le Soir,* at that time in Brussels can only be taken as a discursive act of collaboration. In order to judge the, perhaps criminal, responsibility he bears, it might seem enough to register the context of those articles and to remark his silence regarding them.[2] One does not need to read a word of the hundreds of articles he wrote during that brief period, one need only hold them up for inspection, in order to observe the illocutionary performance which their heinous setting determines. The editors, in addition to everything, have made available the whole cruel page of the newspaper on which appears DeMan's most egregious act of complicity with the racist policies of the Occupant, his article entitled "Les Juifs dans la Littérature actuelle;" one can observe there the immediate context of his work, surrounded by graphic and written material full of scurrilous claims, vicious stereotypes, and perverse lies. In fact, reading DeMan's journalism may already constitute a gesture mitigating his political responsibility in so far as it embarks on the slippery slope that runs from decipherment to interpretation.[3]

If reading, without fail, cannot help but veil the abyss of DeMan's moral responsibility, then perhaps one ought not to read these articles at all. Just say No! to collaboration. One ought to refuse to lend oneself to the business of finding motives and arguments to explain the evidence of this act of conscious cooperation in the enactment of malicious evil, this public performance of sympathy for the Devil. Only observe, do not read. Indeed, there is some question whether undertaking to read closely would not in itself betray, at best, some moral shabbiness, at least a relaxed insensitivity to the questions at issue, and to the fate of lives. Or whether treating them as texts requiring interpretation would not risk, at worst, seeming to insult the memory of those who did truly struggle and die to resist the Occupant. Suppose one read these articles as if they were enigmatic objects of hermeneutical interest, concealing latent thoughts or double meanings, as if conceived and written under the scrutiny of a censor, with a signal or message for those who could read not just the lines but between them. Even to glance at them for consideration like that (as if they weren't already material evidence enough of DeMan's complicity) might smack of a form of Revisionism, analogous to the mendacious arguments of those, like Faurisson, who deny the existence of gas chambers, or to the disculpating powers of positive forgetting with which Waldheim confronts his accusers. A "reader" might "read" the unequivocal evidence, with interest, in order profitably to find there no evidence of a crime or that the crime is collective—for the sake, say, of saving the text of the Master from ignominy: of saving the Master, and hence the Master internalized, thus also oneself. Do common sense and elementary decency command us not to read?

But suppose for a moment, what is almost certainly not the case, that DeMan were the Devil. A common perception of DeMan by adversary critics of different hue as a somehow insidious, malicious influence on literary studies might find confirmation in the vision of his collaboration, a practice that depends on a kind of perverse, devilish subtlety and connivance that invests evil with intelligence. Then, it would be more necessary than ever to read him, to hasten to invent a science of DeManology. It would be urgently necessary to get to know the *diabolique*. Intelligent, the diabolical infiltrates where it wills, pervades everything everywhere, puts intelligence at the service of whatever Order is the strongest, collaborates in many forms of oppression, some the worst. It would not suffice to turn one's back, refusing its work, one would have first to refute it. And refuting would not be easy; before any arguments could be counterposed, it would require a preliminary intellectual effort just to recognize in what the Demanic consists. Recognizing the diabolical is the condition of refuting it in order finally, perhaps, to refuse it, without its taking its revenge, for that is the price of just saying, No. That kind of resistance, without the repetition of argument, without speaking on the terms of the enemy, guarantees that the repressed will return with a vengeance. Re-fuse, re-fute, re-cognize: the sign of iteration, of turning (one's) back on a circle, *re-*, signals the formidable effort of reflective memory fed upon by remorse and ressentiment that would be required to refute the Devil, if DeMan were the Devil, which he probably isn't.

But how does one recognize the diabolical—in order to be able to refute it. It requires an intellectual effort, to see it and to see that it is what it is, to give it its name. And suppose, in the case of the diabolical, what makes it what it is (fiendishly inventive, like a malicious ruse or puzzle) is that it is irrefutable, in the DeManic sense, in the way DeMan in one of his last essays says, that "Technically correct rhetorical readings may be boring, monotonous, predictable and unpleasant, but they are irrefutable" (*The Resistance to Theory*, 1986, 19).[4] To refuse one must first refute, but refute requires that one recognize that the diabolical, however boring and unpleasant, is "irrefutable." Who can boast of having made the intellectual effort to understand it? Who knows or understands what is the power that resists refutation, that refuses to apologize, that indulges no false hopes, but goes about its business, with difficulty, confounding such arguments as wish, in memory of martyred resistance, to judge responsibility, rationally, on this side of good and evil? Believe

me, it isn't easy. So, what else is new? What can I tell you, the Devil gives rise to thought (*donne à penser, gibt denken*).

If DeMan were the Devil, one would have to make the effort to read him, in order, first, to discover in the later work, beneath the political silence, persistence of arguments and recurrence of moves belonging to the early period. If one were to read the work of the literary columnist in *Le Soir,* it would be in order to uncover, in this collection of disparate reflections, the features, perhaps the outline, of the political and literary ideology that authorized or necessitated this performance of collaboration, an ideology whose terms and aims —although disguised by a different context—remains intact. If DeMan, a youth, merely erred, then one could dispense with reading the early writings, for the reason that it would be possible to consider them, with their performative corollaries, as mere traces of an aberration, cut off from any contaminating relation to the later work (reading only perhaps the parts that adumbrate the later writing). If one were to read, it would be in order to decide the extent to which we can discover some continuity or some disjunction between the early positions and the later ones.

Recent discussions of the itinerary of DeMan's work fall roughly into two categories. There are those like Christopher Norris and Geoffrey Hartman who insist on the break, the sharp discontinuity between the early and late DeMan. Their aim is not only to detach DeMan's late work from the worst political and racist implications of the early discursive acts, but to consider those implications as the very dialectical object of the full force of his late critique. DeMan is seen as practicing his deconstructions against precisely the forms of totalitarian thinking which his early work exhibits most repulsively—against, for example, the seduction of organicist metaphors that underlie nationalist claims on culture, on literature in particular, advanced under the signs of blood and soil with whose formulas DeMan's early work is at ease. The discontinuity, in this account of DeMan's itinerary, is also a dialectical reversal, and it permits one to tell a finally happy story of conversion. The agent of that conversion is the passage from Europe to America. In America, DeMan is supposed to have found a culture that no longer sought to determine its projects in a pious relation to some reinterpreted version of the past, which *ipso facto* served to determine the goal of society. Rather he discovered a culture that took its orientation from the "Occidental" movement towards the furthest future horizon of possibilities for freedom—a future for being forgetful and indifferent to spiritual, political claims from the past, and derisive towards their organicist principles of continuity. He also encountered close reading, it is said; DeMan himself, in an uncharacteristic auto-biographical moment, tells the story of his encounter, at Harvard, with the work of Reuben Brower, whose attention to the idiosyncratic specificity and to the totalizing movements of literary texts, especially short poems, detached them from discussions of their historical or psychological significance, their ideological or critical purposes. That gesture of detachment, the formalist moment in New Criticism, was decisive for the development of his own more rigorous, one might say scientific examination of literature's critical resistance to ideological appropriation, its capacity to give us to read the false consciousness that ideology proposes.

One of the difficulties with this happy story is the trouble one has imagining that DeMan was ever a dupe of organicist metaphors. In one of his earliest post-war publications ("La structure intentionelle de l'image romantique," 1960) DeMan already sketches a vast historical perspective in which Romanticism is conceived as representing a giant error in Western culture, an organicist mis-reading and a mis-interpretation of temporal insights whose most authentic moments were still available for expression in the pre-Romantic work of Rousseau. DeMan diagnoses the tendency, visible even in figures as enlightened as Hölderlin, to wish to lend to language, and to whatever is structured like a language, the characteristic mode of unitary being belonging to the dialectical self-unfolding of organic becoming: self-coincidence through metamorphosis (ie. wishing words to originate like flowers: *Worte wie Blumen enstehn*). DeMan in 1941 must have read Nietzsche or Heidegger, at least Bergson, whose critique of organic metaphors of time was a cliché of French philosophical education. It is difficult to believe that at the age of 23, DeMan, that ferocious thinker of negativities, was without irony towards organicist metaphors, was gaily seduced into believing that words, like flowers, spring up from blood and soil.[5] Furthermore, despite appearances to the contrary, the war-time journalism provides some evidence of an already highly developed skepticism towards the categories of vulgar culture nationalism, as we will see.

If it is so difficult to believe in the narrative of some break with the past or some dialectical conversion, one nevertheless feels uncomfortable about the way critics have tended to postulate the continuity of his work. One such view is put forth by critics on the Left, like Frank Lentricchia, who long has felt in DeMan's theory of literature the pressure of some resistance to politics, masking conservative intellectual politics, that, at worst, may reach down into the darkest regions of amoral reaction. In Lentricchia's mythology, DeMan was a mafia don, the chief of a family of interests whose ruthless detachment and gang-land organization evoke shades of proto-Nazi tactics. For critics such as Lentricchia, the current revelations come as no surprise, but rather serve to confirm their worst suspicions. For them, there is the conviction that no aberrant relation links the author of the abstract, philological reflections of the late work to the discursive performance of, say, "Les juifs dans la littérature actuelle." The risk to which this view succumbs is its failure to account for what is powerfully critical in the late work, precisely in order to save its own totalizing gestures and mimetic assumptions against DeMan's resistance, what Geoffrey Hartman calls, DeMan's "powerful act of conscience," his "critique of every tendency to totalize literature or language, to see unity where there is no unity" ("Blindness and Insight," 1988).[6]

It would seem, on the surface, difficult to choose between disjunction or continuity. Either DeMan's late work is substantially free of traces of the early, or it is continuous with it in many of its most decisive moments. If disjunctive, then DeMan may continue to be read for the profit of those who believe, now more than ever, in the necessity and value of directing critical arguments against the often invisible, oppressive hierarchies lying behind our most flattering, utopian cultural productions. If continuous, DeMan's convictions remain, down to his last publications, in certain of its deepest strata, unchanged, perhaps unrepentant, about theoretical positions whose methods and assumptions, whose correlative performance were not in any critical relation of resistance, but in a collaborative one, to the racist Occupant.[7]

There remains a third possibility, more diabolical in its complexity, perhaps not even coherent, which would insist at the same time on the continuation in the late work of positions which made possible his collaboration in the Forties, but which are themselves inextricably implicated in the forms of resistance to ideological constructs that his subsequent work embodies. If there is "resistance to totalitarianism" in the later work it is not unconnected with a conception of literature that, for DeMan, made it possible to collaborate in *Le Soir* and continues, in a late formulation, to make "technically correct rhetorical readings" "totalizing (perhaps totalitarian)." But if there is resistance in the late work, one must, by the same argument, envisage the possibility of its presence early, perhaps from the beginning.

The word "resistance" may be seen to function in DeMan's work as one of those words that Freud in "Fragment of an Analysis of a Case of Hysteria" (1905) calls "switch words": "ambiguous words" that "act like points at a [railroad] junction. If the points are switched across from the position in which they appear to lie in the dream, then we find ourselves on another set of rails; and along this second track run the thoughts which we are in search of and which still lie concealed behind the dream" (in *Dora, An Analysis of a case of Hysteria,* New York: Collier Books, 1963, 82).

The possibility that DeMan may have been in the Belgian resistance was first raised publicly by Jon Wiener, a professor at Irvine, in an article in the *Nation* ("Deconstructing de Man," 1988). He reports that in 1953, after having been denounced as a collaborator, "anonymously, perhaps by his first wife," DeMan told Harvard, where he was a Fellow, and a few close friends, that "he had in fact been a member of the Belgian resistance." Wiener goes on: "The friends, who have asked not to be identified, accepted his response; today at least one them describes that response as a lie" (22). Wiener evokes the possibility of resistance in order, with anonymous sources speculatively named and others named anonymous—in the shadowy language of rumor—to dismiss it and further discredit DeMan: not only a former collaborator, a recent liar.

But, perhaps none of this is true, neither the denunciation, nor the testimony, nor the "friend" who now says that what De-Man had said to Harvard, if he did say it, was a lie. Perhaps this is a rumor, based in no actual fact, or a lie about the lie invented by the professor for the sake of the scandal. When will we know for sure whether DeMan said he was in the Belgian resistance? And how will we know whether, were he to have said it, it was true?

What proof after all is there? And what would count as proof, to give the lie to his response to Harvard? Wiener also reports, for example, that DeMan, when asked by a student what he did during the war, replied: "I went to England and worked as a translator." If that proved to be true, would its confirmation strengthen the plausibility of his having been in the resistance—what he is supposed to have formally responded to Harvard. But suppose that no further evidence comes forth, that the truth, like that of much resistance, may never be known; then only rumors are left and these articles, which if we were to read them, perhaps interpret them, might lead us into reading only our wishes and not any truth. But suppose, as it is the case for the moment, that these articles were all there was. We may never have more decisive evidence of what he did and thought during those years in Brussels during the war than the dozens of articles he wrote and published for a wide audience. And what kind of evidence are they, and how should they be read? Does not the mere existence of these articles lead common sense to say that DeMan could not have both been a member of the Resistance and the author of these regular articles in a collaborationist newspaper punctuated by remarks that Geoffrey Hartman calls "ugly and prejudiced," though deemed "infrequent" (26)? How much is enough reading to convince oneself that what he had written is utterly incompatible with what he swore to Harvard, and his friends, if he did? Yet if one were a friend of DeMan, how could one avoid being an *advocatus diaboli,* trying to read (in the absence of any corroborating proof that he lied) signs of his resistance?

Is it inconceivable, for example, that he might have used his position as a literary and musical reviewer for *Le Soir* as a cover for his resistance? Is the content of what he wrote in those articles so supine, so complacent in its acceptance of defeat and cooperative with the aims of the invader, that it precludes all possibility of his having told the truth? And does the fact of De-Man's public silence, except for what he told Harvard and a few friends, assuming any of this is true, guarantee that he could not have played a role in the struggle against the Nazis? Is it somehow more plausible to think that if he had played a role under cover of being a literary reviewer he would later have announced the fact in his writing or in some public forum? On what occasion could he have revealed his true role, and how could one imagine the form of his explanation of the role he played under the guise of reviewing for *Le Soir*?

How could he have explained, for example, the existence of an article like "Les Juifs dans la Littérature actuelle?" To be sure it is the only one, among hundreds, that is devoted to the Jewish question and that reiterates Nazi "conceptions." If he had been in the resistance could he have avoided suspicion if he had refused to write an article required of the regular reviewer of *Le Soir* for publication in the journal's special page on the Jews? And what weight of resistance should we give, for example, to the fact that the whole argumentative thrust of the article is directed, from its initial sentence to the end, in a rhetoric of alarm, against certain claims advanced by what it characterizes in the first line as the conceptions of "vulgar anti-semitism?" Consider the first few lines of the article:

"Vulgar antisemitism," it begins, "likes to consider cultural phenomena in the post-War period [after 1918] to be degenerate and decadent because *enjuivés.* Literature has not escaped this lapidary judgment: it has sufficed that some Jewish writers have been discovered under Latinized pseudonyms for all contemporary production to be considered polluted and harmful (*néfaste*). This [vulgar anti-semitic] conception entails rather dangerous consequences. First of all, it causes a whole literature to be condemned *a priori* which in no way merits that fate. . ." ("Les Juifs dans la Littérature actuelle," *Le Soir,* 4 mars 1941, my translation; hereafter *J.*)[8]

If we may speak of resistance in these lines, it is only in the attenuated sense in which the argument DeMan advances opposes the judgment of a certain vulgar antisemitism that is resisted as being "lapidary," at least where literature is concerned. In the hardness of its formulation, it proceeds too quickly to the conclusion that literature shares the fate of other cultural phenomena arising in the "decadent" period after the First World War; a more supple, less abrupt judgment considers that view "absurd," and denies the vulgar claim that contemporary literature is "created by the particular mentality of the Twenties," taking care gently to insist on literature's principled indifference to the prevailing cultural and social conditions. In a free indirect style that creates ambiguity about the identity of the speaker, and promotes the indeterminacy of discursive agency, DeMan ventriloquizes the views of vulgar anti-semites, who consider Post War [I] literature polluted and harmful, a conception, writes DeMan, which entails "rather dangerous consequences." [Rather dangerous, indeed, for Jews, as the events in Belgium in 1941 were beginning to demonstrate unmistakably.]

At first glance, it might seem courageous to have affirmed in a newspaper in Brussels in 1941 that the conceptions of vulgar anti-semites were absurd and entailed dangerous consequences. But, of course, his anti-anti-semitism here protests on behalf of Literature, not Jews; it is only Literature that is explicitly being defended by the literary reviewer of *Le Soir,* under the eye of the censor, against the consequences of certain anti-semitic conceptions: "A whole literature [*not* a whole people] is condemned," he writes, "*a priori,*" "qui ne mérite nullement ce sort" ("which [*not* who] in no way merits this fate"). The *a priori* condemnation of a whole people, who in no way merits this fate, is *not* what DeMan patently, explicitly laments, but the fate of Literature.

Yet, if one wished to believe, if only for a moment, that DeMan were in the resistance and that this were a cover for other activities, one would find some plausibility in the strategy he adopts in this article—opposing vulgar anti-semitism in terms which allow him to write sentences that, taken in isolation, may sound like formulas of political resistance, but that in context protest only on behalf of Literature.

Consider, for example, the sentence in the article which is the most startling in its equivocation and ringing in its evocation of the recent history of heroic resistance to the invader (on the condition that its patent meaning, in the context of DeMan's explicit argument, be suspended):

Il ne faudrait pas formuler beaucoup d'espoirs pour l'avenir de notre civilisation si elle s'était laissé envahir sans résistance par une force étrangère. (*J.*) [One should not have much hope for our civilization if it had allowed itself to be invaded without resistance by a foreign force.]

If one allows oneself the hypothesis, only for an instant, that DeMan were in the Belgian resistance, as he may have sworn to Harvard, and to his friends, then imagine the pleasure he must have taken in writing this sentence and making it appear, under the nose of the Nazi censor, at the heart of an excruciating article—the only one of its kind among hundreds—he was forced to write for the anti-semitic page of *Le Soir.* Taken out of context and reset in that other, clandestine one, the sentence may be heard to say, "The fact that there had been [and continues to be] resistance to the invader is what gives hope for the future of Belgian culture." But—let there be no mistake—the sentence says just the opposite of what it might mean if DeMan were in the resistance. The invading "foreign force" refers not to Nazi armies but to the influence of what he elsewhere in the article calls "l'esprit juif." The sentence occurs in the final paragraph of the article where he comforts Western intellectuals against the disparagement of vulgar anti-semites, who are pleased to believe that contemporary literature is polluted and contaminated by Jewish influences. Not at all, says Deman: that Western intellectuals have been able to "safeguard themselves from Jewish influence in a domain as representative as literature proves their vitality. One ought not have much hope for the future of our civilization if it had allowed itself to be invaded without resistance by a foreign force." It should be comforting to Western intellectuals, he asserts, that literature has been able to maintain "its originality and its character intact" despite the "semitic intrusion" (*ingérance sémite*: pushy Jews).

Or, finally, consider the peculiar turn of argument by which he dismisses the claim that Jews were the "creators" of contemporary literature or had a preponderant influence on its evolution. He writes:

Looked at a little more closely, this influence even appears extraordinarily unimportant [*peu importante*], for one might have expected, given the specific characteristics of the Jewish mind [*esprit juif*] that they would have played a more brilliant role in this artistic production. Their cerebrality, their capacity to assimilate doctrines while maintaining a certain coolness towards them, seemed like precious qualities for the work of lucid analysis that the novel demands. But in spite of that, Jewish writers have always remained in the second rank. (*J.*)

The argument is bizarre; it attributes to Jews, in essence, "very precious qualities" which ought to have led them to the forefront of contemporary literature. It is as if they possess naturally, more purely as it were, by virtue of their Jewish mind, qualities which could have allowed them to produce brilliant forms of Western literature of the sort that would be more purely itself, that is free of "foreign," i.e Jewish influences. In order to meet the highest demands of the novel, a writer would have to aspire to the qualities of lucid analysis which belong, as a birthwrite, to the Jew; to be in the forefront, an Aryan novelist, say, might have to aspire to become *enjuivé*. Jewish writers, themselves, however, have always been second rate, says De-Man, even when they hide their identity under "Latinized pseudonyms," although earlier in the article he includes in his short list of the most important figures in the contemporary novel, Gide, Hemingway, Lawrence and . . . Kafka. For the censor he appears to deprecate Jewish writers, for the resistance he may have slipped in the name of Kafka, but viewed from the standpoint of what he calls Western Literature, Kafka, once included in its Pantheon, is no longer the name of a Jew.[9]

The distinction is rather like the one Foucault makes between Nazi anti-semitism and the Spanish Inquisition. In Spain, a Jew could stop being persecuted by becoming a convert to Christian theology and ritual; being Jewish was identified with a certain prescribed or proscribed collection of discursive acts. For the Nazis, being Jewish was a matter of some essential attribute that infused the totality of the Jew's sensibility and expressed itself unmistakably in every gesture and in every act. (Cf. *Histoire de la sexualité, 59–60.*) Having attained to Literature, Kafka can be defended against the vulgar anti-semitic claim; in so far as his work is literature it is uncontaminated by the Jewish spirit, free of any stain of racial or ethnic specificity. Literature is not in allegiance to any entity belonging to the referent, its truth is a negative truth, manifested in fiction, about the capacity of language to propose (unreliable) models for representing reality.

Reading this article, we must be prepared to recognize that the position the narrator implicitly adopts may be distinguished, at least in theory, from the discursive acts that accompany its enunciation. DeMan's explicit rhetorical stance here addresses an interlocutor, who is supposed to share his resistance to vulgar anti-semitic conceptions not from any philo-semitic perspective but from the standpoint of what might be called the Higher Anti-semitism, one which understands the dangerous consequences for literature that the vulgar view entails. High Anti-semitism is the position from which DeMan, in this article, is able to criticize the cultural politics of vulgar anti-semitism, without appearing to give comfort to the enemies of the Occupant; it is synonymous with the standpoint of Literature.

Jews, writes DeMan, do not contaminate literature. To the censor that assertion would appear to mean that it is only the domain of literature, the most representative domain, which is not polluted or contaminated by the "esprit juif." To the Resistance, that argument intimates that Jews do not contaminate.[10] But from the standpoint of Literature, of the Higher Anti-semitism, it means that Literature is not ultimately the expression or the reflection, the imitation or the outgrowth of any particular cultural formation—hence the one cannot contaminate the other. This position may be seen as resistance to the Nazis and to the Resistance. It is not vulgar-anti-semitism, it resists that, but it is not Resistance, rather High-Anti-Semitism. Resisting Resistance and Nazis, Literature, or what he later calls "literariness" (the rhetorical function of language that Literature and Theory display), is "to some extent" a-historical, or rather, allo-historical; it obeys another history: "the forms that we know at present are logical and normal consequences of what there was before" (*J.*). It is a position which aims to be scientific; it examines the persistence of laws of literary genres, long existing principles in the Western institution of literature and its commentary. These laws or principles are "very powerful and continue their action even when humanity is shaken by considerable events" (*J.*). They supervene all manner of historical disruptions of cultural life, revolutions, wars, inflation, crash. Theory, constantly resisted by mimetic theories of the relation of literature to the referent (although not either the dupe of aesthetic formalisms), Theory is the science of a negative truth whose principles stand opposed to the literary premises of both vulgar-antisemitism and the Resistance, which denies the Nazi racist claims. The narrator in this article himself never denies the truth of what vulgar-antisemites say about Jews, only what they say about the relation of literature to the Jewish problem. Literature has no Jewish problem, says DeMan, from the position of the High Anti-Semitism, which is Literature. This discursive position, Literature, resists the vulgar Nazi appropriation of it, even while it collaborates on the pages of *Le Soir*. "Literariness" speaks in history from the standpoint of another history that makes it *a priori* unreliable, unpredictable and irresponsible in its political choices. Baudelaire, it could be recalled, in 1848, between February and June, twice joined the Insurrection and twice edited Reactionary newspapers that denounced it. Like him, the narrator of "Les juifs dans la Littérature actuelle," has a position of permanent "internal resistance,"[11] which is neither identifiable with nor inassimilable with Collaboration and its Resistance, and like him this narrator might have enacted, in life, in the political, social, cultural

History of those terrible years, contradictory discursive performances simultaneously.

One of the interesting differences between vulgar Nazi anti-semitism and the Higher, Literature, or Theory, is that people who embrace the former want to do things to Jews, like sending them off to Jewish "colonies, isolated from Europe" (*J.*). Such a solution of the Jewish problem, says DeMan, "would not entail, for the literary life of the West, deplorable consequences" (*J.*). For Literature, it would mean nothing more than the loss, "*en tout et pour tout*" of "a few mediocre personalities" (*J.*). The censor hears that argument to mean that there is no reason not to create Jewish colonies. The Resistance may assume that it is only for Literature that there are no "deplorable consequences"; Jews and others will have reason to weep. From the standpoint of the High Anti-semitism, of Western Literature, it means that no social, economic, or political step, will in itself inhibit the serene development of Literature, proceeding "according to its great evolutive laws."

Real Jews could take only little comfort from DeMan's resistance to vulgar-anti-semitism; it is not in their name that he is resisting, but against the view that wants to condemn a whole period of Western literature for being the expression or the reflection of what that vulgar anti-semitic view considers to be a degenerate and decadent historical moment, submitted to the "*mainmise*" of Jews. He is against the "rather unflattering" [*peu flatteuse*] characterization of post-War literature [perhaps unflattering to those who make it?], which seeks to reduce contemporary authors to being "simple imitators of a Jewish culture which is foreign to them." DeMan call this an "error," namely, the "[vulgar anti-semitic] opinion according to which the modern novel and poetry might be only a monstrous outgrowth (*excroissance*) of the world war. . . ." To the censor, this means that Literature is *Judenrein*; to the Resistance it refutes the "myth" of a Jewish cultural conspiracy; from the perspective of the Higher Anti-semitism, of Literature, it means that Literature is never the "simple" imitation of any cultural referent, hence cannot be polluted, nor decadent, neither degenerate, nor *enjuivé*—hence, neither dangerous nor to be condemned. Literature is inoculated against all contamination, because it has an other history than the social, economic history which give rise to conditions of cultural decadence. This is the conclusion to which the article's tortuous argument wishes to lead. The Literature of the Post-War period is not enjuivé because literature obeys evolutive laws that determine its productions independent of even the most cataclysmic events in the economic and political sphere. DeMan writes:

As Jews have, in fact, played an important role in the factitious (*factice*) and disorderly existence of Europe since 1920, the novel born from this atmosphere might merit (*mériterait*) up to a certain point, being called *enjuivé*.

But the reality is different. It seems that aesthetic evolutions obey very powerful laws which continue their action even as humanity is shaken by events of considerable magnitude. The [First] World War provoked a profound upheaval in the political and economic world. But artistic life was relatively little moved, and the forms which we recognize at present are the logical and normal consequences of what had been before. (*J.*)

Literature is not historical, in the sense of being an epi-phenomenon, a sign or a symptom, a cause or an effect, the reflection or the expression of developments in the post-War period. It is a-historical, or rather allo-historical, in so far as it obeys its own laws, the laws of genre, whose movements and transformations obey dynamic processes interior to literature itself, not historical but evolutionary, according to the slow unfolding of something one might quickly assume to be its essence or destiny.

Christopher Norris would no doubt seize upon the notion of evolutive laws of literature, enunciated here, as evidence for his claim that DeMan on leaving Europe turned his back on organicist theories of culture. But DeMan's critique here of the vulgar anti-semitic position is one that would precisely disrupt any natural relation between literature and culture, between even vast political and economic events of the post-war period and the production of literature. When DeMan uses the notion of evolutionary laws, he is, one suspects, borrowing a Darwinian expression as a shorthand in order to evoke the allo-historical unfolding of something like a subject or spirit which, faithful to its own inherent laws of development, remains independent of historical "accidents," even cataclysmic ones.

Gide, Kafka, Hemingway, Lawrence—one could indefinitely prolong the list—are exclusively engaged in the attempt to penetrate, according to methods fitting their personality, into the secrets of interiority (*la vie intérieure*]. By this characteristic, they show themselves to be, not innovators having broken with all the traditions of the past, but as simple continuers, who are only engaged in exploring more deeply the realist aesthetic, now more than a century old. (*J.*)

It is characteristic of DeMan to want to identify the most authentic tendencies of these "modern" authors with a literary problematic that goes back to the origins of Romanticism. One knows the persistence in DeMan of the move which shows how the premises of realism becomes undermined, transcended and preserved, when it turns inward to reflect subjectivity. In the "secrets of interior life," what elsewhere in the article he calls, "les recoins les plus secrets de l'âme des personnages," the familiar premises of realism find themselves radically undermined by enigmatic negativities linked in the early DeMan to the structure of temporality and later to linguistic, rhetorical motifs which the self in its self-exploration or reflection uncovers. Norris fails to take into account a certain persistence in the later work of the standpoint DeMan adopts in this article. To be sure, he will no longer employ the vocabulary of evolution, a fact that needs to be remarked. At the same time the ahistorical terms in which he situates what he later calls "literariness" or "literature" continue to bear the same relative autonomy from even the most profound political and economic upheavals.

In *J.*, he writes:

The definition of Stendhal according to which the novel is a mirror walking along a highway bears in itself the law which still to this day governs this literary genre. At first, in it was seen the obligation scrupulously to respect exterior reality. But in digging deeper, one came upon the necessity of exploiting psychological reality. The mirror of Stendhal no longer remains immobile on the highway; it undertakes investigations into the most secret corners of the souls of characters. And this domain revealed itself to be so fertile in surprises and riches that it still today constitutes the novelist's sole and unique field of investigation.

The scrupulousness with which the novel respects the law of its genre guarantees that realism itself is transformed, as it turns inward to reflect the deepest secrets of interiority, just as Stendhal's mirror, changing from a passive reflector to active illuminator, uncovers the riches of subjectivity in the progressive, surprising discovery of its impossibility.

The move here has its analogue in "Resistance to Theory" at the moment DeMan resists "the most current objection to contemporary literary theory," the one which says that Literature as it is defined by Theory can be considered "a pure verbalism, . . . a denial of the reality principle in the name of absolute fictions, and for reasons that are said to be ethically and politically shameful." DeMan replies to this objection, which comes to him from more recent partisans of mimetic realism: By allowing for the necessity of a non-phenomenal linguistics, one frees the discourse on literature from naive oppositions between fiction and reality, which are themselves an offspring of an uncritically mimetic conception of art. . . . Literature is fiction not because it somehow refuses to acknowledge 'Reality' but because it is not *a priori* certain that language functions according to principles which are those, or which are *like* those of the phenomenal world. It is therefore not *a priori* certain that literature is a reliable source of information about anything but its own language" ("The Resistance to Theory," 11).

Note first the fact that here principles have replaced laws. Literature functions according to principles that make it an unreliable reflection or expression of phenomenal, historical reality.[12] The vulgar anti-semite, and those who currently object to literary theory, judge literature only in so far as it is a mimetic reflection or an ideal expression of the political, social, and economic conditions of a particular historical moment. Literature, of course, particularly genres like the novel, reflect that History—"*in part*," "*up to a point*." But what gives Literature its specificity, unlike other cultural phenomena, as a product and production of a precise Western institution, belongs to its capacity to provide unreliable models of the unreliable relation of language to the world.

In the middle of an oft-cited passage in "Resistance to Theory," that we encountered earlier, DeMan writes:

Technically correct rhetorical reading may be boring, monotonous, predictable and unpleasant, but they are irrefutable. They are also totalizing (and potentially totalitarian) for since the structures and functions they expose do not lead to the knowledge of an entity (such as language) but are an unreliable process of knowledge production that prevents all entities, including linguistic entities, from coming into discourse as such, they are indeed universals, consistently defective models of language's impossibility to be a model language. They are, always in theory, the most elastic theoretical and dialectical model to end all models and they can rightly claim to contain within their own defective selves all the other defective models of reading-avoidance, referential, semiological, grammatical, performative, logical, or whatever. They are theory and not theory at the same time, the universal theory of the impossibility of theory. To the extent however that they are theory, that is to say teachable, generalizable and highly responsive to systematization, rhetorical readings, like the other kinds, still avoid and resist the reading they advocate. Nothing can overcome the resistance to theory since theory is itself this resistance. (19)

What DeMan calls the "totalizing (and potentially totalitarian)" character of theory is linked to its capacity to illustrate the autonomy of language from referential restraint, the fictionality of literature. "Whenever this autonomous potential of literature can be revealed by analysis, we are dealing with literariness and, in fact, with literature as the place where this negative knowledge about the reliability of linguistic utterance is made available" (10). Literariness is thus both in literature and in theory, in the canon and its philology, the discourse that displays the rhetorical structures and functions of literary language. The institution of Literature in so far as it arose sometime in the Seventeenth century in Europe constituted itself out of the reflection on this capacity of language to free itself from referential restraint and to codify and legalize and archivize, to gloss and interpret rigorously, that discourse of literariness. Western Literature, as an institution, is inseparable from its commentary and its history.

Theory then is totalizing, perhaps totalitarian, says DeMan. Literature, that institution created in Europe and specific to Western culture, finds its chance in the possibility of displaying the autonomous capacity of language, the indifference language shows to the fate of the earth, not to mention to the Jewish problem. Literature, in its high calling, is High Anti-semitic, a realm that is *Judenrein,* one in which the Jewish problem has always already found a final solution, in the name of a totalizing, perhaps totalitarian, irrefutable theory, that exposes structures and functions that "do not lead to the knowledge of any entity (such as language) but are an unreliable process of knowledge production that prevents *all* (my italics) entities . . . from coming into discourse as such." No entity, no real thing, let alone any ethnic specificity can enter into the totalitarian realm of this negative knowledge, whose a-temporal or allo-temporal condition belongs to the historical institution of literariness in Western culture, Literature.

Theory is irrefutable only in so far as it produces this negative knowledge. Other critical readings of literature may resist this irrefutable reading by mistaking the illusions of fiction for some referential truth about reality—social or subjective, exterior or interior reality. But the risk taken by technically correct rhetorical readings, "to the extent however that they are theory"—their heroism one might say—resides in their willingness and their capacity rigorously, cruelly to "reveal by analysis" "this autonomous potential of language," to produce this negative knowledge in an ever more radical fashion. The negativity is not given, but is permanently subject to discovery, and reformulation. The aim of theory is not to repeat old negativities, the same old ones, but to exacerbate them—resisting the temptation, with the fierceness of a logician before a paradox, to mitigate or domesticate the virulence of the negativity which the anecdote may perhaps be made to reveal. A technically correct rhetorical reading of a literary text is not the only way of reading it; it is a chance which the history of Western Literature has made available for demonstration.

The blank "High Antisemitism" of literature and literariness is not precisely "anti-"semitic, it is, rather, Jew-less, we have said; it is also, for example, Oriental-less and White. It may include Jews, Orientals, and Blacks among its practitioners; it may treat race as its explicit theme; in so far as it is Western literary fiction, in some part, after some point, it cuts itself off from all cognitively reliable or ethically responsible reflection or expression. The institution of literature, which began, say, sometime in the 17th century, which comes to us under the aegis of German Romanticism, is an Occidental interpretation of fiction; derived from Latinity, giving itself origins in Greece, it is the archive and the canon of the Occident. It is that culture which, through the invention of philology, has given rise to and made possible the critical power of Theory, a discourse that is neither a reliable source or medium of knowledge about the world nor only an aesthetic harmony of form and content, but that irrefutably illustrates the negativities that arise from the difference between linguistical and phenomenal representation (and the unreliability of that difference). This discourse, DeMan says, is the condition of all critiques of ideology, beginning, for example, with Marx's *German Ideology*.

DeMan writes:

This does not mean that fictional narratives are not part of the world and of reality; their impact on the world may be all too strong for comfort. What we call ideology is precisely the confusion of linguistic with natural reality, of reference with phenomenalism. What we call ideology is precisely the confusion of linguistic with natural reality, of reference with phenomenalism. It follows that more than any other mode of inquiry, including economics, the linguistics of literariness is a powerful and indispensable tool in the unmasking of ideological aberrations, as well as a determining factor in accounting for their occurrence. Those who reproach literary theory for being oblivious to social and historical (that is to say ideological) reality are merely stating their fear at having their own ideological mystifications exposed by the tool they are trying to discredit. They are, in short, very poor readers of Marx's *German Ideology*. (11)

To discover the linguistic construction of seemingly phenomenal identities is the fundamental gesture behind any iconoclastic project, any critique of ideology. It is an essentially materialist gesture that replaces the illusion of what, lying, claims to be nature with irrefutable evidence of historical contingency, of some class interested, motivated conception. Our material reality is all too really, materially organized by forms of utopian fiction with which dominant classes impose and regulate constricting social roles and desperate economic dependance. The critique of ideology is the critique of representations of reality that create the illusion of being intuited, phenomenal images of reality with the immediacy and seeming transparency of perception, but that actually are in the service of specific classes to mask and to foster the mechanisms of economic and political oppression. The critique of ideology always has as the first condition of its practice the demonstration of the difference between the pretention to phenomenality of a particular piece of ideology and its actual linguistical construction. The first step in a critique locates what Roland Barthes, in "Le mythe, aujourd'hui," calls the "turn-stile" (*le tourniquet,* 209), the troping mechanism by which a sign becomes the signifier of another signified.

It is probably true that Occidental culture is the only one which has given rise to an interpretation and an institution of literature, of literariness, which permits the systematic, the rigorous theoretical exasperation of the question of the fictionality of literature, the implications of the fact that what we call literature may be, in its possibility, without a real referent, as the condition of its being able to manifest reference. The suspension of the referent, and the display of reference, can occur, must occur in literatures everywhere. But Western Literature as a historical institution has made that an irrefutable possibility. In 68, Cohn-Bendit, in the streets of Paris cried, "Nous sommes tous des Juifs allemands." Literary critics, in so far as they are partisans of Literature, are all High Antisemites—like DeMan early and late—giving voice to the negativities of literariness. The defense of theory against resistance is itself a resistance to theory, says DeMan, a form of ethical self-justification.

It may well be, however, that the development of literary theory is itself overdetermined by complications inherent in its very project and unsettling with regard to its status as a scientific discipline. Resistance may be a built-in constituent of its discourse, in a manner that would be inconceivable in the natural sciences and unmentionable in the social sciences. . . . Rather than asking why literary theory is threatening, we should perhaps ask why it has such difficulty going about its business and why it lapses so readily either into the language of self-justification and self-defense or else into the overcompensation of a programmatically euphoric utopianism. Such insecurity about its own project calls for self-analysis, if one is to understand the frustrations that attend upon its practitioners, even when they seem to dwell in serene methodological self-assurance. And if these difficulties are indeed an integral part of the problem, then they will have to be, to some extent, a-historical in the temporal sense of the term. (12)

Resistance is built into theory, into the perspective of Literature. It itself resists itself, for despite its methodological assurance, it is afflicted with permanent anxiety—anxiety against which it constantly seeks to protect itself, either by deluding itself with the mimetic premises of guilty self-justifications or with the scientific illusions of utopian realists: endlessly inoculating itself against the shame of its ethical and political irresponsibility, with guilty protests of resistance, or conversely, overcompensating its modest resistance to on-going collaboration by trumpeting euphoric promises of utopian solutions. The High Anti-Semitism, Literature or Theory, whatever one's personal sympathies or attitudes, ought simply to go about its business with no regret and no promises, permanently frustrated, hence permanently resisting the temptation to put literary work in relation to any ethical claims or political program or vision of mankind's happiness. "Why does theory have so much trouble going about its business?" asks DeMan. Why is theory or Literature constantly resisting its own high detachment, unless theory is nothing else but that resistance? "Nothing can overcome the resistance to theory since theory *is* itself this resistance" (19). Instead of going on, it is in the business of perpetually going out of business —like all business. Behind the mask of serene methodological self-assurance lies an almost pathological insecurity, requiring self-analysis, that arises from the frustrations of its rigorous but modest detachment.

The power of Western literature resides in its capacity to give us to understand the unreliability of linguistic artifacts that are passed off by the dominant ideology as truthful representations of the world, both exterior and interior. It is only by exacerbating the diabolically complicated paradoxes or negativities, which literature gives us to think, that one becomes alert to the ingenuity with which capitalism for example, or socialism, control populations. To fail to teach the fictionality of literature is to deprive our students of the possibility of learning to think critically about culture. The tragedy resides for the critic in the fact, that in order to have access to the critique of ideology one must adopt the standpoint of literature. One must study literature in order to criticize culture, but in our culture, literature, in its institutional perspective, is High Anti-Semitism. The critique of institutional racism depends on an institutionally racist standpoint—subtler, more insidious forms and protocols of totalitarian discourse, that are unpleasant and irrefutable.

A certain amount of the gleeful, polemical, journalistic reaction is a sign of the release people feel who find they now have a pretext for not reading those diabolical late texts by DeMan, deeply difficult, frequently exasperating, challenging always. Some of it is the predictable allergic reaction with which the media responds to any theoretical discourse that raises significant questions about the reliability of mimetic representations of reality; deconstruction has always had a bad press in *News-*

week. But DeMan will not go away. Perhaps his work is dangerous, as many commentators aver, and perhaps it requires the greatest vigilance and suspicion. Nevertheless, it is unavoidable. Perhaps he is the avatar of the Devil for the Nineties. A demonic being whose first and greatest ruse in Modernity, as Baudelaire said, is to make us believe that he doesn't exist (that he can be easily dismissed). The Devil is that about which one does not know what to think, or how, whose existence turns out to be a mystery about which the most contradictory things can be said, whose work, for a critic, is the most interesting, the most difficult and dangerous thing to think. We are perhaps only just beginning to think it. If one wants to refuse him, one first has to refute him. And who can even recognize where the DeManic lies? Who can boast of that? Que voulez-vous, le diabolique donne à penser.

Cornell University

WORKS CITED

Barthes, Roland. "Le mythe, aujourd'hui, *Mythologies,* Paris: Editions du Seuil, 1957.

DeMan, Paul. "The Resistance to Theory," in *The Resistance to Theory,* Minneapolis: University of Minnesota Press, 1986.

———— "La structure intentionelle de l'image romantique (1960)," in *The Rhetoric of Romanticism,* New York, Columbia University Press, 1984.

———— "Les Juifs dans la Littérature actuelle," Brussels: *Le Soir,* March 4, 1941.

Derrida, Jacques. *De l'esprit,* Paris: Galilée, 1987.

———— "Le dernier mot du racisme," *Psyché,* Paris: Galilée, 1987.

Foucault, Michel. *Histoire de la Sexualité,* Paris: Gallimard, 1976.

Hartman, Geoffrey. "Blindness and Insight," *The New Republic,* March 7, 1988.

Klein, Richard. "The Blindness of Hyperboles::Ellipses of Insight," *Diacritics,* Vol. 3, iii, Summer, 1973.

Kramarz, Joachim. *Stauffenberg,* tr. R.H. Barry, New York: The Macmillan Company, 1967.

Norris, Christopher. "Paul De Man's Past," *London Review of Books,* February 4, 1988.

Wiener, Jon. "Deconstructing DeMan," *The Nation,* January 9, 1988.

NOTES

1. This piece owes much to Derrida's recent book, on Heidegger and Nazism, entitled *De l'esprit* (1987). He should not, of course, altogether, be held responsible for the uses I make of him. I am grateful to the participants in my seminar in Contemporary French Thought for their criticisms and contributions, to Sandor Goodhart, and Philip Lewis, for their collegial assistance.

2. If the United States Immigration Service had known that DeMan was the author of those articles in *Le Soir,* would they have had any more reason to give him a visa than they had to deny one to Grandmaster Alekhine, who was accused of having written and signed newspaper articles on "Jewish" chess. He publicly, vehemently denied the charge during his lifetime. After his death, manuscripts were found among his papers. He lie.

In April of this year, the Supreme Court refused to hear an appeal by a former Yale University professor from a Federal appellate decision to strip him of his United States citizenship. Vladimir Sokolov, 75, emigrated to the United States in 1951 and became a naturalized citizen in 1957. He taught Russian literature at Yale from 1959 to 1976. The Government contends he gained citizenship illegally by stating falsely that he had not "assisted the enemy in persecuting civil populations."

"Mr. Sokolov said at his 1986 trial that he wrote articles only to oppose Communism and make a living and that anti-Semitic slurs were ordered inserted by his Nazi censors. He could face deportation (Sokolov v. United States, No. 87–323)" (NY Times, 4–12–88).

3. Reading can probably never avoid interpreting what it construes. Interpretation means coincident correspondences between material textual facts (as they may be deciphered and construed, independent of what one might wish to believe or seek to conceal, like a discursive act of collaboration) and values, things which are said to be equivalent in worth to those facts, that reflect or express them—like the illusions of youth, some biographical compulsion, the spirit of the age, frequently me myself. The inseparability of deciphering and interpretation makes possible the existence of transferal objects like the *I Ching,* whose oracular authority derives from the instant simultaneity with which one reads the ancient judgments and images and interprets their relation to elements of conscious and unconscious life.

To make a connection, any interpretation, requires perspective, the standpoint of a junction or switch, which permits one to pass from one narrative dimension to another, from one rail to the next—a double point from which one thing may be seen to be worth another. Perspectives by virtue of the unity of their idiosyncratic horizon, tend to be totalizing; they are obliged to represent their narrow standpoint as a position of perfect understanding; the allure of understanding, of interpretive insight, is to dissolve moral agency which amounts in effect to forgiveness.

4. In the next sentence he adds "They are also totalizing (and potentially totalitarian). . . ." More later about that.

5. One need only read the early DeMan on the topic of Flemish art to find what, in the poverty of its formulations and its sentimentality, could be a parody of the idea of literature's identity with Blood and Soil. It also signals to the serious question of the nature of national literary identity, if such an idea can be still be seriously maintained, as many critics, in other forms, would argue: up to what point, in what part, is literature determined by its milieu? Such is the question to which he returns.

6. These are the terms with which DeMan himself addresses his critics on the Left, adding that he finds them, in their criticism of literary theory, to be poor readers of Marx. He writes, in "Resistance to Theory": "Those who reproach literary theory for being oblivious to social and historical (that is to say ideological) reality are merely stating their fear at having their own ideological mystifications exposed by the tool they are trying to discredit. They are, in short, very poor readers of Marx's *German Ideology*" (11).

7. In an article published in 1973, entitled, "The Blindness of Hyperboles: Ellipses of Insight (*Diacritics*, 1973), I observed the seductive askesis of DeMan's vaulting ambition (elliptical self-effacement/hyperbolic insight), what Nietzsche might have called a triumph of "modesty overcome": "The charm of insight would be small if there were not so much modesty to overcome on the way" (*Beyond Good and Evil*). Of DeMan I wrote: "DeMan's power as a critic, the force of his exceptional insight, cannot be separated from the deeply modest nature of his work. There are very few modern critics who possess his extraordinary patience and tenacity in the face of literary and philosophical texts, who are able to efface themselves so totally in front of a text in order to pursue and decisively resume the diabolically intricate argument of a critic, say, like Blanchot" (34). There are those who might see some intuited historical necessity in my having linked together Blanchot and DeMan in a diabolical dialogue without at the time being able to be aware of their War-time, anti-semitic episodes. But in fact I made a different sort of case for the continuity of DeMan's work with his past. Unaware of course of what has only now been revealed, I noted in his book, *Blindness and Insight,* traces of a biographical, historical persona, the impersonal figure of an author/narrator, who for all his impassivity and theoretical askesis, was the will or agent behind certain reiterated lapses or inflections in his otherwise serenely, rigorously articulated argument that pointed to unacknowledged personal fears and desires. I wrote for example: "and yet his own work has remained for a long time, in many of its deepest strata, inescapably inscribed within the metaphysical tradition it aims to deconstruct. . . . That weakness to put it brutally—is linked to a serious misunderstanding of his own categories, something simpler and something other than a constitutive blindness. It is closer to what in psychoanalytic terms is called repression, a blindness that is more contingent than what DeMan has in mind, one implicated in a certain historical or biographical situation" (36). I quarrelled with the way DeMan in his book systematically dismissed what he tended to call "the personal version" in accounting for an author's production—"his own radical devaluation of the psychological in favor of the ontological self." Traces of the absence of any trace of Freud or Marx in DeMan's book allowed me to "dream the shape of a psycho-critical narrative" which told a certain (largely erroneous) story of his relation to his notorious Uncle Henri DeMan. It seemed to me that in the pattern of silences of DeMan's work there were signs of Oedipal resistance to the avuncular author of *The Psychology of Marxism* and *The Joy of Work*: "The first serious Marxist thinker to apply explicitly Freudian categories to the analysis of alienation, and in a gesture recalling Fourier [and Marcuse], to the question of pleasurable work" (42). I was struck by what seemed to me the irony of DeMan's resistance to an Uncle whose work on Freud and Marx did not save him from collaboration; the nephew, without ever mentioning the uncle's authors [or topics], devotes a career to attacking the oppressive hierarchies with which the Uncle was criminally complicitous. The truth, it now appears, is elsewhere, both simpler and more complex. I was right to view with some wariness "the bracing and demanding pleasures of a distinguished philosophical mind disinterestedly, patiently, seriously, at work" (Ibid.). And right to understand the silences in deMan's work as evidence of the repression of what he later will call insecurities and frustrations—resistances— arising from the fact that the critic who aims to speak from the standpoint of Literary History is fatally caught up in the political, cultural history of his time. "It is as if in this passage DeMan wanted it both ways, as if, all the while he is trying to establish a certain inherent philosophical necessity, he cannot quite relinquish the ethical realm: the truth is not merely that one cannot speak the truth; anyone who speaks the truth is a fool or a martyr" (19).

8. The reader will forgive the reluctance to translate a word which like *apartheid* has no precise equivalent term in ordinary American. Cf. Derrida, "Le dernier mot du racisme" in *Psyché* (1987). The word *enjuivé* is perhaps the most insulting moment in this article, in so far as it presupposes an essence of the Jewish spirit so unitary and pervasive, so intrusive, that it can be spiritually communicated and adjectively attributed to anything Jews touch or, as they say, contam-

inate. In both cases when DeMan uses the word, it is assigned, in a free indirect style, to the language of vulgar anti-semitic pretensions, against which the article remonstrates.

9. Despite the fact that Jews ought to be great novelists, the greatest are not Jews. DeMan seems to know that someone is Jewish, in the first place by the name. The name of course can be counterfeited, which is why DeMan begins this article on the Jews in Contemporary Literature with a curious reflection on the name. He writes: "Il a suffi qu'on découvre quelques écrivains juifs sous des pseudonymes latinisés pour que toute la production contemporaine soit considérée comme polluée et néfaste" (*J*.). [It sufficed to find a few Jewish writers under Latinized pseudonyms [i.e. André Maurois, Francis de Croisset, Tristan Bernard] for all contemporary [literary] production to be considered [by vulgar anti-semites] to be polluted and harmful.] Anti-semitism depends on names not only to indicate but to guarantee, to countersign, as Derrida says, the racial identity of the Jew. But names, of course, can conceal as well as reveal a biological identity. The name may conceal a secret, but not by being a pseudonym; a name appears to be false, a Pseudo-nym, only when it ceases to be a name at all, anyone's real name. For anti-semites, the trouble with pseudonyms (and hence with naming, in general) is that until they appear false they may serve as well as real names to guarantee identities. DeMan lists the names of several well-known writers, who are Jewish and "mediocre", he says, "not among the more important, nor especially among those who in some way have given direction (*dirigé*) [like in *führen*] to literary genres" (*J*.). Earlier, DeMan had named Kafka but not Proust; he spoke about the importance of Surrealism, but did not mention Breton. Despite their aptitude, Jews do not figure among the names of the leaders of literature in the West in the contemporary period. There should have been more of them, given their talents and precious qualities, but "*malgré cela*", they are not among the most important. That should be comforting to Western intellectuals, whose "vitality" is proven by the degree to which they have been able to remain "free of Jewish influences" just as literature has "preserved its originality and its character intact," and has demonstrated that its "profound nature was healthy" (*J*.). If literature were polluted, by the presence of Jewish writers among the leaders of the genre, it is unclear in what the resulting pollution would consist, or how it would appear, since it is Jews who are supposed to possess most perfectly the qualities which literature finds most precious and requires most urgently. It is as if the moment a Jew, like Kafka, becomes a leader of Western literature his influence ceases to be Jewish; or conversely, the more strictly Jewish is the influence at the summit the less healthy Literature may be said to be. Perhaps DeMan means to differentiate between "mediocre" Jewish

writers, who, even if they are called important, are only Jewish, and leaders, who, once they become great writers, lose their heinous specificity in the sublimation of their talents by another history, which is not racial or determined by what we normally call the history of current events. Jewish "influence" is both the most foreign and the most essential breath, the duplicitous double other of Western literature's inspiration.

10. In the metaphors of vulgar anti-semitism, the Jews are a foreign element that enters the fabric of Western culture like a stain, that contaminates its current with polluting impurities; the metaphors bespeak the intrusion of something radically heterogeneous into the very interior of the culture, which, becoming all but indistinguishable from the thing itself, destroys it from within—turning it against itself, in a duplicitous, mimetic parody of itself during historical moments of degeneracy and decadence. The Western spirit gets infected with its parodic double, Jewish spirit, which is all but indistinguishable from it, however fatal.

In the case of the Jews, the specificity of their ethnic identity is linked to their lack of specificity, their universal "foreignness" which is a menace to the extent it is deemed irredeemably metrocosmopolitan, constantly circulating, inassimilable because universal, what can never be defined by a frontier, nor compose with a determined identity.

11. My colleague Jeffrey Waite reminded me that DeMan's project on first coming to Harvard in the Fifties was connected to the study of Stefan George and his elite aesthetic circle. One of the disciples was Baron Claus von Stauffenberg, of Hitler's General Staff, who, in July 1944, placed the bomb-filled briefcase next to Hitler in the bunker where he almost died. George's poem, "Geheimes Deutschland" gave its name to von Stauffenberg's "resistance movement." (Cf. Joachim Kramarz, *Stauffenberg*, 29.)

12. The unreliability of Literature as a source of truth about the referent requires, of course, that Literature be not always unreliable. It may not be reliably unreliable if it wants to be permanently unreliable; sometimes it has to tell the truth. Simply, one has no right, *a priori,* says DeMan, to expect a literary fiction to tell reliable truths about the referent. DeMan's argument does not deny that there can be reliable forms of discourse: one has a different expectation concerning a recipe, say, whether one finds it in a novel or a cookbook, although the former may turn out to be more reliable than the latter, and the latter more allegorical or artistic than the former.

Opting to Know: On the Wartime Journalism of Paul de Man

S. HEIDI KRUEGER

I

Certainly de Man is the fiercest of the Yale deconstructors, with a rigour not easily explained unless in ethical terms.[1]

The single quality most associated with the later writings of Paul de Man is arguably epistemological rigor. It is epistemological rigor, applied to language, which leads to, and characterizes, his particular kind of deconstruction;[2] epistemological rigor which governs his translation of ethics and pathos alike into logical and linguistic terms;[3] and epistemological rigor which strikes on the limits of rigor itself— thereby at once confirming the authority of "epistemologically rigorous methods as the only possible means to reflect on the limitations of those methods" (AR, p.115), and demanding that we renounce confidence in the ability of "the analytical rigor of the exegetic procedure" to guarantee the "epistemological authority of the ensuing results" (BI, p.289).

These consequences of de Man's election of rigor have angered some and disturbed many—some for the seeming (but only seeming) denial of the essentially human importance of ethics and pathos, some for the recognition of "epistemic failure," which, for writers like Frank Lentricchia, seems (but only seems) to "snuff out" the possibility of future action.[4] Most controversially for the present debates about the relationship between de Man's wartime journalism and his late work, the election of epistemological rigor seems to have authorized a rejection of the options of self-justification and confession, although in different ways at different moments in his career. Thus in a 1966 essay on Rousseau and de Staël, the choice is between self-justification and the renunciation which self-knowledge demands:

To move from self-justification to self-knowledge, the reflection must be able to renounce, not only the hope of overcoming the sorrow, but also the hope of justifying oneself by means of this sorrow. . . .[5]

In *Allegories of Reading,* however, it is the renunciation of epistemological triumph itself which undercuts confession. For there de Man implies that what we want from confession is not so much relief from guilt as the security of knowing that telling the truth is enough, that we reside in an element where truth triumphs, even over considerations of guilt and innocence:

To confess is to overcome guilt and shame in the name of truth: it is an epistemological use of language in which ethical values of good and evil are superseded by values of truth and falsehood. . . . (AR, p.279)

And yet in *Allegories of Reading,* this dream of the triumph of truth, of the orders of epistemology and cognition, is immediately set back into question as the gap opens between confession and excuse, between statement and performance, between, finally, incompatible versions of truth: "The truth in whose name the excuse has to be stated . . . is not structured like the truth principle that governs the confession" (AR, p.280). Considerations of truth and falsehood do not supersede the ethical values of good and evil in de Man's late work, any more than considerations of good and evil supersede considerations of truth and falsehood; and de Man's version of the "ethical" names "the structural interference" of precisely these "two distinct value systems":

But in the allegory of unreadability, the imperatives of truth and falsehood oppose the narrative syntax and manifest themselves at its expense. The concatenation of the categories of truth and falsehood with the values of right and wrong is disrupted, affecting the economy of the narration in decisive ways. We can call this shift in economy ethical, since it indeed involves a displacement from pathos to ethos. Allegories are always ethical, the term ethical designating the structural interference of two distinct value systems. (AR, p.206)

I will return below to the question of the relationship between ethics and deconstruction in de Man's late work. What concerns me here is the fact that de Man's election of epistemological rigor follows *after* the early writings, and that it appears as a choice from among a far broader repertory of values. Rigor, lucidity, and intellectual clarity find mention throughout the articles from these years, and certain passages ring with absolute familiarity to readers of the later de Man. Most striking are passages in his January 1942 article on Valéry, in which de Man writes of the "continual necessity to re-verify, to put into question, to articulate reservations" as "an inevitable characteristic of any body of thought which wishes to consider itself rigorous" (*Le Soir,* 10–11 Jan. 1942). One could argue further that even when de Man praises irrational values in these writings, his own critical disposition is toward lucidity. Thus he writes in July 1942 of the Symbolists' and Surrealists' advances "beyond the bonds of reason," praising instead "the natural force of myth, of the dream"; but his own article supports these assertions with quotations from Breton which demonstrate this "with absolute clarity" (HVL, 6–7 July 1942).

Further, we find throughout the early articles a valorization of intellectual complexity and a rejection of all "false" or "facile" simplifications of the truth. As early as January 1940 he praises Proust, Lawrence, Gide, Kafka, and Hemingway as "enemies of all simplification which might falsify the truth concerning hu-

man nature."[6] And in his September 1942 review of Hubert Dubois' "Massacre of the Innocents," he extends this recognition of complexity to moral issues as well, counterposing the difficult demands of "true values" to the "false facility" (*fausses facilités*) which has led to historical catastrophe (*Le Soir,* 1 Sept. 1942).

Nonetheless, articles like the Valéry essay stand in relative isolation. Moral concern, mentioned frequently in these articles, is often presented as a counter-value to intellectual inquiry, and the disposition to rational analysis—identified throughout the early articles as a typically "French," and sometimes "Jewish," characteristic—is most often the foil for the "German" values of intuition, emotional force, and mythic intensity. Thus in discussing, among others, the work of Ernst Wiechert, a writer who had already spent time at Buchenwald in 1938 for his outspoken opposition to the Nazis, de Man writes that the German mind "prefers poetic meditation to the lucid clarity of analysis," and "metaphorical and symbolic forms" to "expository precision" (*Le Soir,* 5 Aug. 1941). The German novel, he says, "addresses a completely different part of our sensibility than that which is touched by a Proust or a Gide or a Valéry"; for instead of contenting itself with objective psychological analysis, it concerns itself above all with "ethical motives." The French novel is interested in "ethical factors" only as "elements which take their place among others in the complete panorama of the human person." This demands not only "an exceptional capacity for introspection," however, but also "faculties of pure intelligence, capacities for abstract analysis" which, de Man observes, are no longer "current" in a world where the individual is "not clearly aware of the mechanisms which move his inner being." Hence the appeal of Wiechert's novel, which presents

not a psychological drama, but rather a conflict between good and evil . . . a battle between pure and noble forces, on the one hand, and the basest and most vile instincts, on the other. All is sublimated into this symbolic vision of things, which raises the intrigue beyond reality to convey it to spheres where psychological laws no longer apply. (*Le Soir,* 5 Aug. 1941)

De Man uses this French-German typology repeatedly in his writings of these months. In February 1942 he counterposes the typically "French" emphasis on "intelligence and rational reasoning" to German "poetic intuition" with its capacity to move us (*Le Soir,* 10 Feb. 1942); and in his review of the German book exhibition in March he writes of how German authors, confronted with French influence, are pressed to achieve "the difficult synthesis between the cold rationalism of psychological analysis and the more impassioned mentality which characterizes the German mind" (*Le Soir,* 2 Mar. 1942). Here the emphasis also returns to the Germans' peculiarly "moral" disposition; the Germans are said to be "a moralizing people par excellence," and their writers' strong suit their "constant moral care."

While in all these instances, the "French" values of rational analysis and lucidity stand as more or less neutral foil to German moral and poetic qualities, however, the extreme statement of the contradiction between rational and irrational qualities comes several weeks later in de Man's review of Ernst Jünger's *Auf den Marmorklippen* (*Le Soir*, 31 Mar. 1942). What the young de Man extols in Jünger is his "mythic" approach. In contrast to the French psychological novel which aims at "explication," "intelligence," "comprehension," "clarity," and "logic," Jünger chooses "to transport us into plain myth . . . where everything is defined by forces as secret as they are inexpugnable." Jünger rejects the "schematizations" of "rigorous cerebral development"; his novel has no "explicative function," nor does it attempt to "resolve an enigma" or answer "philosophical questions." Its motives are rather "purely evocative," and the result is a vision of the world to be taken "not as a field of investigation for a curious mind, but as the meeting ground of the eternal antagonistic forces of Good and Evil." Such mythic literature, he writes,

will never teach us anything concrete and it will not enrich our knowledge. But it can make pass over us that shiver of excitement which emanates from authentic art [*de l'art véritable*], that thrill of terror or bliss which rises from its violence or its sweetness—and which proves that something fundamental has been stirred in us. French literature since the Symbolists has deprived us of such an emotion, since it has conceived everything under an objective angle of comprehension and judgment. This is why we rediscover [such emotion] with joy in the German Jünger. . . . (*Le Soir*, 31 Mar. 1942)

Several things must strike us as disquieting about this review. One is the extremity of the implied opposition of epistemological value—the possibility of knowledge or cognition—to the thrill of terror or pleasure which is proof of aesthetic authenticity. The opposition is of course as old as Longinus; and yet here, the effects of the sublime are linked with a peculiarly dangerous form of obscurantism, a denial of rational inquiry at the same time that hypostatized values of Good and Evil are being evoked in all their "inexpugnable" force.

Second, while de Man had found the "battle of good and evil" to be typical of German letters already in the reviews cited above, what is new in Jünger's "mythic" literature is that the emphasis on good and evil is no longer coupled with an interest in moral consequence:

The work of Jünger is that of a poet and not of a director of conscience. The conflict is of interest not for its ethical consequences, but as a theme of inspiration, as a motif which his imagination can translate into a series of images of the sun, of fire and blood.

Whereas in the essay on Wiechert, "French" rationality and objectivity were said to lack the moral and ethical preoccupation of the Germans, Jünger's mythic method is presented as at once amoral and anti-epistemological, even anti-rational, eschewing the "structure" that might give his figures "human consistency" (and might support an "enlightened" humanism) in favor of symbols of "irresistible forces and aspirations."

As disturbing as the Jünger review's affinities with fascist ideology, however, may be the fact that it combines these with an appeal to basic and legitimate elements in our experience of art: the power of emotional affect, the transcendence of rational limits, the acceptance of qualities of beauty, mystery, and evocation. For mixed with the earmarks of fascist mystification at the time we also find clear echoes of Mallarmé: in the commitment to a "purely evocative" function of literature, and in the preservation of mysteries unresolved. These, coupled with emotional intensity, are elements that the young author of this review clearly hungered for; and yet they are at the same time bound up in an entire set of anti-epistemological, anti-rational, and finally anti-intellectual values, which de Man would soon, and rightly, reject. Unfortunately, the legitimate affective elements, too, will disappear from de Man's writings. All pathos will become suspect, with consequences for de Man's writings all the way to the end.

Two notes must be added here. First, de Man's rejection of ethical considerations in accounting for the force of Jünger's novel is not, finally, indicative of his overall position in these years on the moral (and political) engagement of literature. The review indeed represents one extension of his defense of artistic values against political or moral coercion in essays like "On the Possibilities of Criticism," where he argues that "the artistic values which govern the world of letters do not merge with those of the True and the Good" (*Le Soir*, 2 Dec. 1941). But the young de Man is also scornful of the pre-war generation that was able to indulge in an "apolitical life, oriented around aesthetic and poetic pleasures" (*Le Soir*, 12 Aug. 1941). He has high praise for the moral emphasis in many of the German novels he cites (not least Goethe's *Wahlverwandtschaften*), and he praises the Belgian novelist Louis Carette for the "political idea" in his novel.[7] De Man's own disposition to moral criticism, moreover, is apparent in instances like his review of Dubois' "Massacre of the Innocents" (*Le Soir*, 1 Sept. 1942):

One could readily call this "Massacre of the Innocents" a meditation on the culpability which has led humanity to the frightful state in which it finds itself at the moment. Complaint and lamentation cannot be justified, even in such a pitiable situation. For what is happening now is not the blind and pitiless action of fate, but rather the consequence of a fault, of an accumulation of moral faults committed through the ages. The usefulness of an attempt of this kind is to raise awareness of this culpability, to make the masses see that they have acted badly. In consequence, the harder the punishment, the greater the hope of seeing, in the end, the rise of true values which shall permit us to live harmoniously, in place of the false facilities [*des fausses facilités*] which have led to catastrophe.

One sees, this is a topic for a moralist. . . . (*Le Soir,* 1 Sept. 1942)

And the authenticity of Dubois' poetic talent is attested to by his combination of formal perfection with "moral and intellectual superiority":

The man capable of sublimating the suffering which daily afflicts humanity in wartime; capable of seeing, despite an immense pity, that this distress is salutary, because it promotes the expiation of crimes repeated against the human person, demonstrates by this the fundamental superiority of his being which is the distinguishing characteristic of all genuine artistic talent [*tout talent artistique véritable*]. (*Le Soir,* 1 Sept.1942)

I would go so far as to argue that the rejection of ethical criteria in the Jünger review derives, at least in part, from another source altogether: from the fact that it is a response, or even coda, to the review of the German book exhibition de Man had published three weeks earlier (*Le Soir,* 2 Mar. 1942), and it is worth taking a moment to look at this earlier piece. Entitled an "Introduction" to contemporary German literature, the article calls upon the French-German typology already identified. This article is trickier than some of the earlier reviews, however, for it bears the telling marks of a struggle with the censor, or at least, of a struggle to maintain some minimal independence of judgment in the face of increasing pressure. On the one hand there are concessions of position and rhetoric: the article declares that this "lovely exhibition" shows Belgians the "true face of contemporary German literature," with every understanding that "true" (*véritable*) here means "acceptable to the Nazi occupiers." German "moral concern" is praised for keeping contact with its "primitive roots," thus providing a "beautiful example of patriotic loyalty." Still, French readers are urged to consider ("one can only insist on the fact") that there is "no fundamental incompatibility between the spirit of German letters and that of the other European literatures."

On the other hand, de Man is explicit in his assertion that "this so sensible attitude has not yet led to any true masterpieces [*véritables chefs-d'oeuvre*]." He argues that

True artistic nationalism [*le véritable nationalisme artistique*] is never synonymous with pettiness or narrow-mindedness. . . . It is only when this nationalism turns into a tyrannical obligation, subordinated to purely political ends, that its influence becomes detrimental, and even deadly.

And he then concludes with a long, two-paragraph pronouncement by Reichsleiter Baldur von Schirach, which seeks to assure us that

'the political movement which leads Germany has never put into its agenda the creation of an art forced to serve the ends of the party. That would be contrary to the very idea it defends. Every true work of art [*chaque véritable oeuvre d'art*] is valuable in itself and has a national mission. It testifies to the vitality of the people to whom it owes its birth. It is there, if you will, that it shows its political leanings.'

Goethe and Mozart, whom the Reichsleiter is quick to exonerate from charges of Freemasonry, of course survive, expressing as they do not only individual temperament and national traits but also that "eternal community of language and blood which preserves itself beyond the evolutions of taste or variable conceptions."

The question is how we are meant to read this final endorsement from the Reichsleiter. De Man had used quotation strategically before, most conspicuously in his interview with Abel Bonnard (*Le Soir,* 7–8 June 1941), where he lets Bonnard damn himself and his project of anti-intellectual elitism with his own words, appending only a perfunctory closing sentence at the end. Even the title of the Bonnard interview is given in quotation. Here, while ostensibly quoting the Reichsleiter in support of his own contentions that literary criteria ought to be independent of political coercion, de Man in fact writes the unseen censor into his text, while at the same time equipping his readers to see through it. As in the Bonnard review, he follows the long quotation with a single sentence:

It is because German literature has lived in conformation with these sage precepts that it has been able to realize its goals and prepare the way for future greatness.

But de Man has already pointed out that no true masterpieces have been produced; if the German goals have been met, these were other than literary excellence. The title of the article may be ironic in its own right, since de Man had been "introducing" contemporary German literature in his column for the past twelve months. The implication would be that the reader is now being introduced to the official position on German literature, and ought to be prepared to compare this to de Man's earlier, more independent reviews.

But it is de Man's manipulation of the word *véritable* which demands our attention, for the essay is in fact structured as a battle for possession of the term. De Man introduces it in its politically controlled sense, as a mark of the Nazis' "cleansing" of the canon. He takes back possession of the word, however, when he writes that the official German attitude has not yet produced any "veritable" masterpieces: the criterion here is not ideological correctness, but literary quality, which de Man asserts the right to assess; and he goes on to use the word in an even more confrontational way when he defines "veritable" artistic nationalism as a rejection of the "tyranny" of political control. Finally, de Man sets the first politically narrowed use of the term back into flat contradiction with the use of the term to designate something having to do with "real" artistic integrity by giving us the Reichsleiter's promise that there will always be room in Germany for "veritable" literature. Does *véritable* here mean "officially sanctioned" or "artistically authentic"? The Reichsleiter of course urges us to believe that the two are one and the same; and yet de Man's article is written in such a way that we cannot miss the ironic clash of these opposing interpretations in the Reichsleiter's citation of the "authentic" artists Goethe and Mozart who have been officially certified as uncontaminated by association with Freemasonry or other undesirable ideologies.

I would suggest that it is this battle for the definition of authenticity, for possession of the designation *véritable,* which is continued in the review of Jünger's *Auf den Marmorklippen* three weeks later. Whereas de Man could observe on March 2 that Germany's "moral" (and officially sanctioned) literary project had not yet produced any "veritable" masterpieces, he presents Jünger's novel as just that. This masterpiece, however, is at once a vindication of German (as opposed to French) inclinations and a clear step beyond official German "moral concern." Here, de Man declares, is authentic art (*l'art véritable*), triumphant in its own power:

[Mythic literature] will never teach us anything concrete and it will not enrich our knowledge. But it can make pass over us that shiver of excitement which emanates from authentic art [*de l'art véritable*]. . . . (*Le Soir,* 31 Mar. 1942)

Further, the implication that de Man was rejecting the pressures of German moral orthodoxy, rather than the relevance of moral

criteria to literature at all, is reinforced by his identification of genuine artistic talent (*tout talent artistique véritable*) with "moral and intellectual superiority" in the review of Dubois' "Massacre" five months later (*Le Soir,* 1 Sept. 1942).

A second note concerns Jünger and *Auf den Marmorklippen.* The Jünger review is disquieting at best, but whether this builds a case against Jünger's novel or the literary values de Man finds there is a separate question altogether. Jünger's relationship with fascism is a highly ambiguous one. Although he outlined his own project of nationalistic, socialistic, and militaristic totalitarianism in works like *Der Arbeiter* (1932) and initially endorsed the rise of the Nazis, he refused party membership when the Nazis came to power, refused the seat in parliament they offered him, refused membership in the newly "cleansed" Academy of Poets, and protested the serialization of his work in *Völkischer Beobachter.*[8] To add to the complications, *Auf den Marmorklippen,* already banned in Germany at the time of de Man's review, is widely considered an anti-Nazi allegory; Gerhard Loose counts it "among the significant literary contributions of the so-called *Innere Emigration*—of those writers who opposed the Hitler regime but chose to remain in Germany."[9] It is unclear whether de Man recognized *Auf den Marmorklippen* as an anti-Nazi allegory or knew it was banned in Germany at the time of his review, and while de Man will eventually drop Jünger, it is sobering to recall that he praises *Der Arbeiter* as late as September 1942.[10]

What matters for our present purposes, however, is the particular configuration of values de Man identifies in Jünger in these years. In the summer of 1942, de Man will seek and find attempts at a synthesis of the "French" and "German" values of rational lucidity and mythic intensity, of psychological analysis and moral concern, in a variety of authors, among them Goethe, Rilke, and the Surrealists. Most successful, interestingly enough, is his mediation between the two sets of values in his essay on Novalis, where, however, he manages to describe Novalis' "efficacy of expression" without explicit recourse to the crude national typology (*Le Soir,* 9 June 1942). More telling for our present purposes, however, are de Man's attempts to find this synthesis in both Jünger and Valéry, each of whom had formerly represented one of the opposed poles, Jünger the mythic, Valéry the cerebral. In Valéry, he writes in July 1942, "one encounters a special, subtle and ultimately unharmonious compromise between the irrational, romantic inclinations of his master [Mallarmé] and the demands of the classical tradition" (HVL, 6–7 July 1942). Valéry's still unharmonious compromise falls short of the Surrealists' goal "to penetrate the point where all external antagonisms melt together into one single, sublime unity" (HVL, 6–7 July 1942), and Valéry's work is finally rather foreign to the "exciting spectacle" of the Surrealists' battle "to renew poetry by means of an amalgamation of the irrational with the national, rational tradition" (HVL, 6–7 July 1942)—a description which, in another context, might define fascism as adequately as it does Surrealism. Moreover, in the writings of these years, it is finally Jünger who is said to achieve the "fusion of German mythical romanticism and French rational humanism" (HVL, 26–27 July 1942).

Yet in the end it is Valéry's "unharmonious compromise" that wins out over "fusion"; "intellectual probity" over the "proof" of emotional force. Exactly half of de Man's repertory of values from these years will be dropped, without residue, and certainly not the half to which the young de Man had any lesser attraction. What drops out is the "German" half—the mythical, irrational, emotional, and, at least in its coercive forms, the morally orthodox. What remains is the earlier portrait of Valéry, and the qualities de Man would eventually take as his own:

This continual necessity to re-verify, to put into question, to articulate reservations, is an inevitable characteristic of any body of thought which wishes to consider itself rigorous. And this manifests itself in the case of Valéry in an extreme concern for exactitude and a constant preoccupation, perceptible in his work and in his speech, with sharpening and circumscribing the sense of the words he uses. This is not a true concern of the fastidious aesthete, but rather a need inhering in all intellectual probity. (*Le Soir*, 11 January 1942)

Already here "intellectual probity" takes the form of setting into question; and already here this is applied to language. In a telling passage, de Man reports Valéry's confession of the desire to present "a complete vision of the possibilities of knowledge." To which Valéry adds, in de Man's report: "But the means at our disposal—namely language—are not adequate to that end" (*Le Soir*, 10–11 January 1942).

II

Why did de Man elect the "French" (and by his account, "Jewish") values of lucidity, knowledge, and intellectual rigor as the values which would authorize his later discourse, and suspend the others, which is to say, keep them on the margins of his discourse?

We must dismiss, from the outset, the explanation that he was simply dissociating himself from things "German," or from things that might imply continued association with "bad" Germans. His reading takes him not only to Hölderlin and Rilke but to Heidegger and Nietzsche, and while in an ideal world, no intellectual should need fear accusations of guilt by association, certainly publishing on Heidegger would have been an ill-calculated strategy for anyone attempting to cover up a pro-Nazi past. It looks far more like the mark of continued inquiry, regardless of appearances.

In this latter respect, we should note, too, that de Man does not by any means stop concerning himself with intuitive, poetic, or non-rational properties of literature or thought; his chosen literary field, after all, would be Romanticism, and in his 1955 essay on Heidegger and Hölderlin, he still outlines two distinct forms of literary analysis:

Any exegetical method will ultimately have to come to grips with the same problem: how to elaborate a language capable of dealing with the tension between the ineffable and the mediate. The ineffable demands the direct adherence and the blind and violent passion with which Heidegger treats his texts. Mediation, on the other hand, implies a reflection that tends toward a critical language as systematic and rigorous as possible. . . . (BI, p. 263)

But de Man would write and reason, above all, about the reason in Romanticism, and while his deeply personal response to literature (and his encouragement of such response in his students) can have escaped no one who knew him,[11] we also find him, already in 1955, reading Hölderlin toward the very criteria of rigor he praised in Valéry:

But we are far from knowing this great poet, for he presents the major difficulty of being precise above all. The abundance and the beauty of the images, the richness and the diversity of the rhymes entrance us, but this ebullience is always accompanied by a thought and an expression that are always in search of the extreme rigor and meticulousness. (BI, p.247)

De Man's choice of lucidity, of knowledge, responds instead first, I think, to the dangers of obscurantism brought out in the review of *Auf den Marmorklippen* in March 1942. The issue of obscurantism is named already in his review of Sieburg four weeks later:

We are entering into a mystical era, into a period of faith and belief, with all the suffering, exaltation, and intoxication this entails. Even the concept of happiness has been modified and approximates the norms which many authors have thought comparable to those of the Middle Ages. With, however, the advantage of a vastly perfected technical and political organization. With, by the same token, the lesson of a whole humanist past which guarantees against all obscurantism.

It is on this last point that one sees the considerable role which the French genius may always be able to play. . . . Particularly when the general orientation tends toward deep, obscure, natural forces, the French mission, which consists in moderating excess, maintaining indispensible ties with the past, evening out errative drives, turns out to be of the utmost necessity. (*Le Soir,* 28 Apr. 1942)

The review remains critical of French chauvinism, and here still presumes (or urges) that Germany's own humanist past is guarantee enough against obscurantism. Yet the emphasis on the French values of "clarity, logic, and harmony" as necessary counterforce is unmistakable. One thinks of de Man's advice, already in 1941, that the Belgians not adopt the "mystiques" of their German conquerors (*Le Soir,* 14 Oct. 1941); one thinks also of his assertion in his article on Valéry that "one cannot, without dire consequences, lose all respect for certain forms of human intelligence which can only be exercised in calm and serenity" (*Le Soir,* 10–11 Jan. 1942). In July, de Man will in fact modify his account of Jünger, crediting him now with a "profound humanism" which derives from having "correctly understood the mentality of the rational analysts" (HVL, 26–27 July 1942). The qualification is only partial; Jünger's "care for psychological human questions" is still "fused together with other elements of a purely mythic nature," and in September de Man will still praise Jünger's *Der Arbeiter* for its combination of rational and intuitive inquiry.[12] But in fact, a subtle shift has taken place from the earlier association of the French analytical tradition with ethical indifference (and the valorization of German "moral concern") to the relocation of humanist values on the side of rationality.

One also finds, in the summer of 1942, a shift away from the strict linkage of rational and irrational traits to French and German national characteristics. In May (HVL, 17–18 May 1942), de Man locates the mythic-cerebral split within French literature, contrasting the analytical "perfection" of Gide, Valéry, Proust, and Claudel to the "mythical," "primal," "passionate," and "violent" elements in writers like Montherlant, Céline, and Giono. And while here the "mythic" values remain on the side of writers associated with fascism, in "Contemporary Trends in French Poetry" (HVL, 6–7 July 1942), de Man attempts to distinguish non-rational poetic qualities in their own right, turning not to Montherlant or Céline but to Baudelaire and Mallarmé.

Despite these signs of a disposition to separate out the poetic uses of the irrational from political and ideological mystification, however, de Man does not finally take the route of dissociating irrational literary qualities from their questionable political resonances and thereby "purifying" them for purely

formal or literary use. He absents them, rather, from the center of his literary discourse; and while throughout his career, writers like Mallarmé remain touchstones of literary authenticity, the irrational qualities de Man describes in these years are, when treated at all, subjected to sharp scrutiny. To this must be added the distrust of pathos evident throughout his later work, the abiding suspicion of what he will call "unreflected affectivity" (BI, p. 272). This distrust seems, in light of the early writings, to have political origins, and de Man will remain critical throughout his writings of the "pathos of ideology or belief."[13] But the distrust of pathos will continue with regard to literature as well; thirty-two years after the review of *Auf den Marmorklippen,* we still feel the recoil from that review's embrace of the "proof" of emotional affect and its association of emotional power with anti-epistemological obscurantism; and once again it is epistemological rigor which is called upon to mitigate against the dangers of that conjunction:

But no theory of poetry is possible without a truly epistemological moment when the literary text is considered from the perspective of its truth or falsehood rather than from a love-hate point of view. The presence of such a moment offers no guarantee of truth, but it serves to alert our understanding to distortions brought about by desire. (BI, 272)

And yet the dangers raised in the review of Jünger's *Auf den Marmorklippen* do not finally account for the force of renunciation we find in the later work, for the turn not only to knowledge but to self-knowledge, or, as pointedly, for the direction of suspicion not only against pathos but against rhetoric itself. Here, I think, we must look to the question which has rightly caused the most concern about these writings, namely, the issue of anti-Semitism. Two articles concern us here, one of which, I would suggest, has become notorious for the wrong reasons, and the other of which, while having largely eluded the spotlight, is finally far more damaging. The first is "The Jews in Contemporary Literature" (*Le Soir,* 4 March 1941); the second is "A View on Contemporary German Fiction" (HVL, 20 August 1942).

"The Jews in Contemporary Literature" is indeed a key essay for evaluating de Man's wartime activity, the nature of his collaboration, and his relationship to anti-Semitism, and it is both an enlightening and disturbing index to his concerns—and lack of concern—in these years. It has also been grossly misrepresented and, in the great majority of instances, not read, in the most elementary (non-Demanian) senses of the term. For to say, as Tzvetan Todorov does in TLS, that "de Man really did advocate deportation as a 'solution to the Jewish problem,'"[14] is not only to choose to misread a conditional as an indicative (a choice perplexing enough from a grammarian); it is to suggest that the emotions raised by the moral gravity of certain issues entitles us to abandon the most basic considerations of reading: including attention to context of utterance, strategies of indirection, and most pertinently here, irony. It is as if to say that Swift "really did advocate" the eating of Irish babies in "A Modest Proposal":

I do therefore humbly offer it to publick Consideration, that of the Hundred and Twenty Thousand Children, already computed, Twenty Thousand may be reserved for Breed; . . . That the remaining Hundred Thousand may, at a Year old, be offered in Sale to Persons of Quality and Fortune, through the Kingdom; always advising the Mother to let them suck plentifully in the last Month, so as to render them plump, and fat for a good Taste.[15]

"The Jews in Contemporary Literature" is not Swift's "Modest Proposal." Although its net result is, if anything, to argue that the Jews pose no threat, and that there is therefore is no need to bother about the Jews at all (a conclusion disturbing in its own right), there is also no question that its publication contributed to a campaign of anti-Semitic propaganda. But we miss both the thrust of what is wrong with this article, and the nature of what it was that de Man might have had cause to regret about the writings of these 23 months, by ascribing to it positions it does not support.

I would submit that what is wrong with "The Jews in Contemporary Literature" is not that it is, in the first instance, anti-Semitic, but rather that if we read it in isolation, it is almost impossible to tell where it stands with regard to the situation of the Jews. This frustration of the reader's ability to pin down a position is, moreover, the dominant characteristic of the essay, one hard not to see as the result of design.

This quality of rhetorical evasiveness makes the article particularly susceptible to shifts in the context in which it appears, and we should not discount the fact that it first circulated on a photocopy which left it framed by a flagrantly anti-Semitic image, on one side, and an equally pernicious quotation (ascribed falsely to Benjamin Franklin) on the other. The shock of finding de Man in such company at all tended to leave the reader overwhelmed by the association, unable or disinclined to resist letting "The Jews in Contemporary Literature" be pulled into the orbit of the other two, far less equivocal documents.

When we read the full page on which "The Jews in Contemporary Literature" appears, however, we get a very different picture. "The Jews in Contemporary Literature" not only differs vastly from the other articles in terms of tone, argument, and sheer caliber; it also presents itself as a critique of the positions represented in the other pieces. The repudiation of "vulgar anti-Semitism" with which it begins, that is, loses all abstraction in the company of the anti-Semitic, anti-intellectual, and lie-ridden pieces of propaganda which precede it.

The article's strategies, moreover, include not only condescension but also provocation, and it is as provocation, I think, that we are asked to read de Man's capping suggestion that the removal of the Jews to an colony isolated from Europe would have no "deplorable" consequences so far as the (thereby "comforted") guardians of "occidental" literature were concerned. We know now that the suggestion about deportation was in fact not outlandish enough, and we respond with shock rather than dismissive alienation when we read it.[16] But although one can argue that the irony of "The Jews in Contemporary Literature" misfires, it is difficult, reading the article as a whole and in the context of the articles with which it appears, to read it as other than a calculated (and parodistic) fore-grounding of the premises and applications of "vulgar anti-Semitism" evidenced in the other essays on the page. The tone, moreover, is one of detached mockery throughout the sections dealing with the Jews, and the object of the mockery is clearly not the Jews but rather the anti-Semites. Even the attribution of the view that the Jews have had disproportionate influence on "occidental" literature to the Jews themselves reads, in this context, less as the all too familiar strategy of blaming the victim, than as tweaking the nose of the "vulgar anti-Semites," showing them that their own most vehemently pronounced positions are those of the scapegoats they wish to expel.

And yet one senses—and unfortunately not in the sense that would exonerate its author from blame—that the effort is not quite serious; that this is neither the kind of organized satire of Swift's "Modest Proposal" nor an evasion of the project of supplying an entry to the page of anti-Semitic propaganda pieces systematic enough to distance its author effectively from the page's main propositions. Moreover, it is clear that de Man's attention is elsewhere, that there are other issues he cares more about: establishing his distance not only from anti-Semitism but from vulgarity; defending the integrity of literature, its unadulteration and unadulterability, not so much by Jews (he names Kafka as one of his four great writers) as by any "outside" forces or criteria—including those of a page of articles which attacks Picasso and modern art; staking and protecting his own chosen territory; and finally, demonstrating his own intellectual superiority and independence. One senses that he is here performing a tour de force, presenting—as if in his first significant debut in *Le Soir,* or at least the first occasion on which he can differentiate himself from his colleagues—the intellectual entity that would go with the byline "Paul de Man." Representing himself; and yet, when one looks for the integrity of the position represented by the piece as a whole, for its position on the "Jews" of the title, not just "Contemporary Literature," one also gets the sense of an author answering to Gertrude Stein's description of Oakland: "There is no there there." We have less the "Mann ohne Eigenschaften" than the "Eigenschaften," the attributes, without the man. On the specific question of the Jews, the piece is all voice, as if the irony had no other function than to imply that there must be an author who controlled the irony by "intending" something else. But it smacks of the illusionist's trick; for if we try to find that author (that is, find the article's intention so that we may attribute it to an author), we are left empty-handed. This tour de force might in itself be seen as a successful evasion of political censorship; and yet it is only evasion, not an effective political response. We are thrown back into context yet again, reminded that despite the fact that our simplest definition of rhetorical irony proceeds from intention ("meaning" the opposite of what it says), the measure of irony is never the author's intention; it depends utterly on the context into which it enters (just as it is up to Swift's audience to justify the wagered indecency of his modest proposal by understanding it as satire). And while one can imagine a private "intended audience" (if only of one) which would have appreciated the joke, or at least the prowess, of "The Jews in Contemporary Literature," there is finally no context available here which can mitigate the recklessness, the ruthlessness—in the old sense of the word "ruth" as caring or concern—of this piece. Read in the context of the page on which it appears, it indeed puts the other pieces to shame, exposes the mediocrity and ignorance on which they, and the whole page of anti-Semitic pieces, is based. And yet there are other juxtapositions to be made. I think, for instance, of a short, three-sentence notice which appears on the same page as de Man's article "The Destiny of Flanders," which reports that the Jews in occupied France may no longer own radios, this measure having been "rendered necessary" by the "fact" that the Jews had been spreading "false news" (*les fausses nouvelles*) among the public (*Le Soir*, 1 Sept. 1941).[17] This is a juxtaposition and contextualization of another kind; and if the first tells us more than we know in isolation about what its author cared about (a demonstration of cultural and intellectual superiority), this second tells us what he was prepared to be careless about (the situation of the Jews).

There is yet another, no less urgent, context in which "The Jews in Contemporary Literature" must be read. "The Jews in

Contemporary Literature" stands at one extreme of the articles in *Le Soir*, written at a point in time, and with a cockiness, that suggests that the young de Man still thought he would be able to get by the censors by his wits. He in fact resorts to a wide range of strategies in the months that follow, sometimes maintaining a clear measure of independence, sometimes, as in the "Introduction" to German literature above, struggling for a balance of compromise. But the strategies of compromise grow increasingly unsatisfactory as the summer of 1942 progresses. De Man's review of the journal "Messages," for instance, which contains a bold defense of the Surrealists, ends with a straight disclaimer:

Far be it from me to pose as an admirer of the extravagances of the years between the wars. But when we are speaking of a movement like Surrealism, it is necessary, even as we specify that we have gone beyond it, that we distinguish that which is of enduring value from that which is false and aberrant. (*Le Soir*, 14 July, 1942)

And in "A View on Contemporary German Fiction" (HVL, 20 Aug. 1942), we find complete capitulation: on matters of the canon, where de Man had shown resistance six months earlier; on matters of authenticity itself; and on the question of the Jews. Here de Man promotes the new "cleansed" version of German literary history which excludes the work of artists "of a strongly cerebral disposition, founded upon some abstract principles and very remote from all naturalism," and instead substitutes the work of "another group . . . which did not give in to this aberrant fashion" (HVL, 20 August 1942). The first group is comprised of expressionists, "mainly non-Germans, and in specific Jews."

"A View on Contemporary German Fiction" is more significant and more damaging than "The Jews in Contemporary Literature" for two reasons. One is the date on which it appears: for while it might have been possible—if scarcely admirable—to have miscalculated the seriousness of the threat to the Jews posed by anti-Semitic propaganda pieces like those in *Le Soir* in March, 1941; possible even to have found rumors of the Madagascar plan too outrageous to be taken seriously; there was no question of the gravity of the situation in August 1942. Whole neighborhoods were rounded up in July, and the deportation of all Jews who were not Belgian citizens began in August. This is hardly to say that anti-Semitism was justified in March 1941, and actions against the Jews had begun already in 1940; but the measures of persecution reached new levels of not only brutality but visibility in these months, and it would appear from de Man's own recourse to strategies of self-protection in his articles that he was well aware that threats by the Germans and the Belgian members of the SS were in earnest.[18]

Second, "A View on Contemporary German Fiction" shows no signs of irony; there is no mitigating distance here, not even a margin created for doubt. Instead we find only capitulation to the party line; and even if the phrase about the Jews was added or demanded by the censors, the article is compromised throughout. Barring the possibility that the censors attached de Man's name to an article he did not write (which does not seem likely), the responsibility he must bear for this article is grave indeed; and although de Man would write three more articles for *Het Vlaamsche Land,* this one alone ought to have been—and may have been—signal enough that a threshold had been crossed, that it was impossible to negotiate in these waters without loss of integrity. Or at least, that he was failing to do so.

I have asked myself what the author of these pieces (which is not to say the later de Man) was likely to have been ashamed of in them. In the case of "The Jews in Contemporary Literature," the answer is telling. Not of the voice without a person; the tour de force was, after all, successful. Not, for the same reason, of a mode of irony lacking in rigor—that would come later. Not of a passionately held anti-Semitism, because there is no passion or commitment there. Of the human consequences of the enterprise to which his articles contributed: one hopes yes, but there is no evidence in this article. Of being proved wrong about the desirable future of Europe or the relative value of certain authors: more likely. And yet the one thing that seems very likely indeed is the simplest and most obvious: of having been vulgar, and more particularly, of having been intellectually vulgar. This struck me as I read all the pieces, but it struck me even more forcefully as I reread Sartre's long essay on anti-Semitism, and particularly, his reproach of anti-Semitism as anti-intellectualism:

. . . there is a passionate pride among the mediocre, and anti-Semitism is an attempt to give value to mediocrity as such, to create an elite of the ordinary. To the anti-Semite, intelligence is Jewish; he can thus disdain it in all tranquillity. . . .[19]

Sartre does not write this until after the war, and I make no case for influence here. My point is simply that while it is likely that the author of "The Jews in Contemporary Literature" would have endorsed the scorn for mediocrity and anti-intellectualism, perhaps even have been able to resist seeing that his own essay was not sufficiently distanced to quarantine him from the very positions he condemned, the article of 20 August 1942 leaves no such room for self-delusion. Either the young de Man is writing

something he does not believe, or he is susceptible to all the reproaches of anti-Semitism, including vulgarity and anti-intellectualism. Or, and perhaps this the crux of the matter, both. I make no case here that de Man read Sartre's essay in 1946 or in any other year, or that he reacted to it in a particular way. But thinking not only of the pretensions and intellectual ambitions of the young man who wrote the articles we now have from 1940 to 1942, but also of the kind of work de Man would go on to do, I find much that would have stung in Sartre's reproaches, not least of the anti-Semite's substitution of a passion for reason ("How can one choose to reason falsely?"):

The rational man groans as he gropes for the truth; he knows that his reasoning is no more than tentative, that other considerations may supervene to cast doubt upon it. He never sees very clearly where he is going; he is 'open'; he may even appear to be hesitant. But there are people who are attracted by the durability of a stone. . . .

We have here [in the case of anti-Semites] a basic fear of oneself and of truth. What frightens them is not the content of truth, of which they have no conception, but the form itself of truth, that thing of indefinite approximation. It is as if their own existence were in continual suspension. But they wish to exist all at once and right away. . . .[20]

While this has everything to do with the later de Man—it is in fact for his insistence that the truth always takes the form of "indefinite approximation" and that the self is in "continual suspension" that he is often attacked—it stands as a reproach to the author of "The Jews in Contemporary Literature" and "A View on Contemporary German Fiction" in precisely the terms he valued most. For here is a young author who valorizes intellectual difficulty, complexity, and authenticity; who scorns "false facility"; who poses as a moralist of a particularly complex kind. And yet perhaps nothing is more "false" than the moral facility—which is abetted by the rhetorical facility—of "The Jews in Contemporary Literature." And in "A View on Contemporary German Fiction," even rhetorical distance is lacking.

There is a final aspect of self-betrayal which should be registered here. De Man allies himself in these years with the "enemies of all simplification which might falsify the truth."[21] He is critical of the "falsity of tone" in "vulgar" art, of the "false" theses of Giono, and the "false and insipid" imitations of Giono.[22] He criticizes narrative strategies which "falsify" reality, and praises translations which do not "falsify" their originals.[23] And his rejection of "false facility" extends the association of authenticity to moral and aesthetic discipline alike.[24]

And yet "false" is a word as subject to political occupation as "veritable" and "aberrant," one which under the Nazis becomes a travesty of the criterion of truth. One recalls, for example, that the Germans' excuse for confiscating radios from the Jews was that they were spreading "false news" (*les fausses nouvelles*).[25] When, therefore, in the "Messages" review, de Man dissociates himself from literary qualities which are "false and aberrant" (*Le Soir*, 14 July 1942), more is at stake than a literary retraction, for he is also choosing to speak the language the Nazis had made their own. The earlier struggle for words like *véritable* is given up. And while the strategic reasons for de Man's disclaimer at the end of the "Messages" review are obvious enough, the infiltration of his language by this debased vocabulary also unsettles it to its very foundation. De Man's rejection of *fausses facilités* takes place *after* the "Messages" review and "A View on Contemporary German Fiction," and it is not impossible to find there a measure of response to the demoralization of those earlier pieces. And yet the rejection of "false facility" itself takes place in a language which can no longer vouch for the truth, or "non-falsity," of its own utterances.

I am not suggesting that anti-Semitism can be reduced to anti-intellectualism or explained away as rhetorical slippage; nor, certainly, am I suggesting that de Man would have repudiated anti-Semitism only to the degree that it was evidence of anti-intellectualism. I am concerned, rather, with de Man's choice of *rational* remediation, of *intellectual probity as response,* and with the questions this raises about what it was that de Man was putting behind him, what it was he did not confess. It is imaginable that an anti-Semite who changed his mind might confess that conversion. It would have been a formative act. But what if the issue was not conversion but recognition: of the pernicious effects of "false facility" and its peculiar carelessness, of having chosen not to notice the victims, of having committed two acts in writing which were anti-Semitic in their effects when this was in fact contrary to his own sentiments? I do not pretend to have the question right; but I am looking for the question that is responded to, if not answered, by the choice of interrogation, of vigilance, of suspicion; by sharpness of attention to what is meant, and what is said, and what is done by the saying of it. I am thinking of a man who would write, in 1960, that "to be present to one's time begins in total inwardness, certainly not out of indifference towards history, but because the urgency of one's concern demands a lucid self-insight. . . ."[26] And I am thinking of the "critical moralist of rhetorical suspicion" (AR, p.206) which de Man, no less than Rousseau, would become.

III

this mixture of rigor, pathos, and suspicion which ought to guide whoever takes the chance of a genuine act of reading.[27]

Words like "false" and "true" and "aberrant" have an afterlife in de Man's writings. His preoccupation with "the truth" and with "language's uncanny power to refuse the truth that nonetheless it never stops demanding" (LPD, p.51) informs nearly all his later work, and it is his recognition of language's demand-refusal of the truth which prompts him to name pathos, albeit in the protective custody of rigor and suspicion, as an attribute of reading. But one could also spend an entire essay on the word "aberrant" and the radically opposite use to which it is put in de Man's late, as opposed to his early, work. In "A View on Contemporary German Fiction," one recalls, writers of "aberrant fashion," "mainly non-Germans, and in specific Jews," were replaced by writers said to uphold "the proper traditions of German art which had always and before everything else clung to a deep spiritual sincerity" (HVL, 20 Aug. 1942). Words like "proper," "spiritual," and "sincerity" are equally debased here. And yet it is the word "aberrant" which is systematically redefined in de Man's later work, converted from a weapon for the most cynical forms of exclusion to a word which, in the later writings, makes exclusion itself impossible. Deconstructed, "aberrancy" comes to name a common predicament; and deconstruction itself can be understood as the systematic undermining of aberrancy's capacity to function as a concept of exclusion, or rather, of any concept's capacity to exclude its "other." Moreover, while de Man's late work deconstructs the term as it was used in his earlier writings, we should not fail to see what juxtaposition with the early writings does to our reading of the later work: for while in one sense, the word "aberrant" is depoliticized in de Man's later writings, retrieved from the Nazi lexicon, in another sense, it is repoliticized for us as well, reminding us that the "repetition of . . . aberration" which ends *Allegories of Reading,* for example, signals less the loss of fixed values (or "nihilism" or "martyrdom") than a radical disempowering of the rhetoric of deviance.

In de Man's mature work, such deconstruction follows as a logical consequence of epistemological rigor, applied both to language and to the truth which language "never stops demanding." Deconstruction in this most basic form, moreover, remains a powerful tool for the critique of all privileged hierarchies, whether based on race, gender, class, or any other criterion of difference.

And yet we may do well to consider, in the present context, that de Man's own identification of an "ethical" moment comes not in considering the practical applications of deconstruction but rather in considering elements for which deconstruction does not, finally, account. Ethics becomes a consideration not only in the form of "a rigor not easily explained unless in ethical terms,"[28] but also, and more specifically, at the moment when rigor itself encounters its "other": when ethical and epistemological terms fail to be reconciled.

In the chapter called "Allegory" in *Allegories of Reading,* de Man outlines a passage "from figural deconstruction, first to the theoretical and then to the practical ethical dimension of allegory" (AR, p.209), and it is to the "theoretical ethical" that de Man refers when he writes, in the passage quoted at the beginning of this essay, that "allegories are always ethical, the term ethical designating the structural interference of two distinct value systems" (AR, p.206).

And yet this "structural interference of two distinct value systems" also continues to characterize the relationship between the two versions of the ethical which de Man goes on to polarize: the theoretical ethical and the practical ethical; that of Rousseau the "critical moralist of rhetorical suspicion" (AR, p.206) and that of Rousseau the "man of practical wisdom." More pointedly for our purposes, this "ethical" interference continues to define the relationship between "an austere analytical rigor that pursues its labors regardless of the consequences" (AR, p.207), "a mental attitude that is highly self-reflective, persistently aware of the discrepancies between the formal and semantic properties of language" (AR, p.207), and, on the other hand, the position of a Rousseau who "also speaks naively about his desire to be useful," who writes that "'in order to make what one wishes to say useful, one must first of all be intelligible to those who have to make use of it'" (AR, p.207).

What is interesting about de Man's description of this contradiction is that he does not proceed immediately to a second deconstruction. He lingers, rather, on the fact that Rousseau's pieces of practical advice "*have to be* uttered, despite the structural discrepancy between their intellectual simplicity and the complexity of the considerations on which they are predicated" (AR, p.207). "The ethical language of persuasion," he says, "has to act upon a world that it no longer considers structured like a linguistic system, but that consists of a system of *needs*" (AR, pp.208–9). Under such conditions, allegory "speaks out with the referential efficacy of a *praxis*" (AR, p.208); allegory becomes a narrative to the second power for which "the undoing of signification has taken on ethical dimensions" (AR, p.208).

The question becomes what to do with this second interference between "an austere analytical rigor that pursues its labors regardless of the consequences" and considerations of "a world . . . that consists of a system of needs." In the chapter we have been considering, de Man goes on to pursue the epistemological implications of the choice before us:

The co-presence of thematic, exhortative discourse with critical analytic language points to an inherent characteristic of all allegorical modes. The resulting discourse of praxis is however not only devoid of authority (since it is the consequence of an epistemological abdication), but it occurs again in the form of a text. (AR, p.209)

For de Man this leads, not surprisingly, back into deconstruction: "With the reintroduction of needs, the relapse into the seductions of metaphor is inevitable and the cycle repeats itself. . ." (AR, p.210).

Some readers of de Man have chosen to stop here: to recuperate the deconstructive cycle under the thematics of "unreadability," and this is in fact one function which de Man's allegories of reading—which is to say, allegories of unreadability—serve. While such a thematic reading has the virtue of intelligibility, however, it also has the drawback of all thematic readings based on pathos, namely, that it substitutes its own pathos for the absence of what it mourns (in this case, "readability"). This is the structure de Man identified earlier in Rousseau, where "the presence of desire" for control over language replaces the absence of such assurance, thus allowing the text to become "the representation of its own pathos":

Pathos is hypostatized as a blind power or mere 'puissance de vouloir,' but it stabilizes the semantics of the figure by making it 'mean' the pathos of its undoing. (AR, p.199)

Such readings are doubly seductive, restoring pathos and legibility at once; and with a writer as difficult as de Man, it has been comforting to be able to sum him up under any theme, "unreadability" included.[29] Moreover, de Man himself clearly anticipates the necessity of such thematic interpretations, however "illegitimate" they may be:

Reading is a praxis that thematizes its own thesis about the impossibility of thematization and this makes it unavoidable, though hardly legitimate, for allegories to be interpreted in thematic terms. (AR, p.209)

And yet de Man is very explicit in locating the specifically ethical moment of allegory *elsewhere*: "We can call this shift in economy ethical, since it indeed involves a displacement from pathos to ethos" (AR, p.206). There is a vast difference, finally, between the "ethical" moment of allegory which holds in suspension "the structural interference of two distinct value systems" and the thematic recuperation of this interference as the story of illegibility. Allegories of reading serve in both capacities; but the specifically ethical moment remains a moment of contradiction.

In fact, the "ethics" which names "the structural interference between two distinct value systems" is another name for irony —irony not, however, as the trope by which one says the opposite of what one means, but irony in the tradition of Friedrich Schlegel or the late Goethe or Baudelaire, for whom irony entails "deux êtres en présence" (RT, p.212), or as de Man puts it, the "co-presence" of contradictory options.[30] And the recognition of "ethicity" here requires an ironic double vision, one which in the first instance confronts the interference of the value systems of epistemology and ethics itself (which leads first to the "theoretical ethical"), but one which also goes on to confront the interference between the conclusions reached by "an austere analytical rigor" and the contingencies of "a world . . . that consists of a system of needs."

Under such circumstances we become aware of a number of possible responses to the interference of the values of rigorous reading and practical efficacy. We can follow the repetitions of the cycle of deconstruction; we can thematize these as the story of unreadability; but we can also choose to pursue the moment where rigorous reading "has to act upon a world that it no longer considers structured like a linguistic system but that consists of a system of needs" (AR, pp.208–9). I think here of the recent work of Barbara Johnson, or of the 1986 interview in which she speaks of having "gone as far as I want to go with opening up ambiguities. I need to attach that kind of consideration to questions whose answer cannot simply be, 'It's undecidable.'"[31] Ethics does not consist here in giving up rigorous reading, but rather in choosing to sustain the double vision that such an "attachment" or "placing alongside" requires:

What you would have to figure out is how to ask questions that would take the impossibility of answering a question like [Zora Neale Hurston's 'How it Feels to be Colored Me'], alongside the social system that acts as if there is an answer, and then analyze the relation between those two.[32]

Or, coming back to the specific issue of anti-Semitism, I think of Derrida's distinction between knowledge and acknowledgement in a passage from "Violence and Metaphysics":

Not only is the thought of Being not ethical violence, but it seems that no ethics—in Levinas' sense—can be opened without it. [The thought of Being] . . . conditions the respect for the other as what it is: other. Without this *acknowledgment, which is not a knowledge,* or let us say without this 'letting-be' of an existent (Other) as some-

thing outside me in the essence of what it is (first in its alterity), no ethics would be possible.[33]

It is acknowledgment of the existent other which is so utterly lacking in "The Jews in Contemporary Literature"; and the ethical irony of *Allegories of Reading* stands in sharp contrast to that earlier, evasive irony which was finally no more than a play of voice. The "practical ethical" irony of de Man's later work in fact begins, one could argue, with the doubled knowledge and acknowledgment of the structural interference between the two distinct value systems of rigorous knowledge and acknowledged need. But we should also remember that this conjunction appears, in de Man's writings, on the far side of rigor, not as a retreat from it; or that it is in the first instance rigor which counters the "false facility" of "The Jews in Contemporary Literature," and which puts a halt to the unexamined slippage of language and values in the writings of 1941–2.

Many have cause to remember the later de Man as a master of this ironic double vision, as a man whose writings, however relentlessly a "knowledge," came from a life full of "acknowledgment of the other"; and left now with only the writings, the "knowledge" looms increasingly large. He insisted so relentlessly that we not abuse the trope of the "human," that we not purchase our pathos too cheaply, that we are far more likely to remember his assertions that "Benjamin's language of pathos . . . really describes events which are by no means human" (RT, p.96) than the less frequently articulated use of this rigor which, in his case, seems to have cleared a space for the lived life:

So what [Benjamin] calls the pains of the original become structural deficiencies which are best analyzed in terms of the inhuman, dehumanized language of linguistics, rather than into the language of imagery, or tropes, of pathos, or drama, which he chooses to use in a very peculiar way. To the extent that this text is human, all too human in the appeal it makes to you, and its messianic overtones to name something which is essentially nonhuman, it displaces our sense of what is human, both in ourselves and in our relationship to other humans. (RT, p.96)

I have suggested that in de Man, the rigorous reading which eventually takes the form of deconstruction has its origins, in part, in the rejection of the "dehumanized," mythic language of pathos we find in such writings as de Man's 1942 review of Jünger's *Auf den Marmorklippen*; and in fact we can still hear the rejection, or recoil from the recognized danger, of that earlier essay in these comments on Benjamin 40 years later. I would go further to suggest, however, that despite the current tendency to polarize deconstruction and humanism, the rejection of pathos in passages like these is still being made on essentially human, and humanist, grounds.

In his 1964 review of Sartre's *The Words,* de Man observed that

many autobiographies have been written in which the author narrates a conversion, a change of mind that makes him change his ways. But *The Words,* for all its semi-religious overtones, does not quite fit this pattern. No effort is made to recapture the quality of an inner crisis. If the Sartre who considers literature to be a 'critical mirror' of the self were to write his autobiography, it would be a very different kind of book.[34]

If Sartre's autobiography provides no account of inner crisis or conversion, we have even less of a "confession" from Paul de Man. Where we might look for the retrospective collection of the life into an act of autobiographical writing, marking out a plot to explain the continuities and contradictions, we find instead the work of a man who opted to move forward, problem by problem, reading by reading.[35] And where we might look for a confession of conversion, we find instead the choice to reason, to know, and above all, to read.

Some have interpreted the absence of confession as itself incriminating, choosing to see de Man's career as a passage from committed culpability to self-exoneration in the name of a lesser commitment. This makes assumptions about both the early and the later writings which are in many cases premature and often open to debate. But I have also suggested that we find an opposite movement: not from committed culpability to an evasion of responsibility, but rather from a peculiar kind of irresponsibility, in the earlier writings, to a radical circumscription of room for error. De Man would finally put our ability to circumscribe error into question as well. But I would argue that far from being a sign of evasion, this appears as further testimony to that initial choice of rigor, to the "continual need to re-verify, to put into question" which he found in Valéry. And while some have chosen to see de Man's career as an attempt to escape from his past, I would argue that, to the contrary, we in fact find a balance very much carried forward.

Eugene Lang College
New School For Social Research

ABBREVIATIONS

AR   *Allegories of Reading* (New Haven and London: Yale Univ. Press, 1979)

BI   *Blindness and Insight* (1971), Second revised edition (Minneapolis: Univ. of Minnesota Press, 1983)

HVL *Het Vlaamsche Land,* translated by Ortwin de Graef.

LPD *The Lesson of Paul de Man,* ed. P. Brooks, S. Felman, J. H. Miller. *Yale French Studies* 69 (1985)

RT   *The Resistance to Theory* (Minneapolis: Univ. of Minn. Press, 1986)

NOTES

1. Christopher Norris, *Deconstruction: Theory and Practice* (London and New York: Methuen, 1982), p.104.

2. See further in Norris: "If Hartman represents deconstruction in its ludic or libertarian vein, Paul de Man exemplifies the opposite qualities of hard-pressed argument and high conceptual rigor" (p.99); "De Man's readings draw out the innermost logic of the text, showing how figurative tensions develop to a point where that logic is implicitly confounded by its own implications" (p.100); "De Man pursues these figurative detours with a rigour of argument none the less 'logical' for its end result in paradox and aporia" (p.101). See also Barbara Johnson on "Rigorous Unreliability" in LPD, pp. 73–80.

3. "In this sense, ethics has nothing to do with the will (thwarted or free) of a subject, nor *a fortiori,* with a relationship between subjects. . . . Ethics (or, one should say, ethicity) is a discursive mode among others" (AR, p.206). "The reasons for this pathos, for this *Wehen,* for this suffering, are specifically linguistic" (RT, p.86).

4. Frank Lentricchia, *Criticism and Social Change* (Chicago and London: Univ. of Chicago Press, 1983), p.42; see also p.41: "the most privileged epistemic term in his vocabulary . . . is 'lucidity,' and the consequences of his meditation on this term for the life of praxis are corrosive."

5. "Madame de Staël et Jean-Jacques Rousseau" (1966), trans. Minae Mizumura in "Renunciation," LPD, p.85.

6. *Les Cahiers du Libre Examen* 4:4 (January 1940), p.17.

7. *Le Soir,* 10 Mar. 1942; the Goethe review appears in *Le Soir,* 26 May 1942.

8. On *Auf den Marmorklippen* and the censors see Gerhard Loose, *Ernst Jünger* (NY: Twayne, 1974), pp.62 ff. and J.P. Stern, *Ernst Jünger* (New Haven: Yale Univ. Press, 1953), p.14. On *Der Arbeiter* and the ambiguity of Jünger's politics see Loose, pp. 30–41 and *Ernst Jünger in Selbstzeugnissen und Bilddokumenten,* ed. K. O. Paetel (Hamburg: Rowohlt, 1962), pp.43–73. Roger Woods also takes up the question in *Ernst Jünger and the Nature of Political Commitment* (Stuttgart: Akademischer Verlag Hans-Dieter Heinz, 1982).

9. Loose, p.63.

10. Just when de Man loses enthusiasm for Jünger is impossible to say, although it is worth considering the limitations de Man would have struck upon had his pursuit of Jünger continued. Interesting in light of de Man's own later work is Roger Woods' summary of Jünger's relationship to Nietzsche. Jünger, Woods writes,

rejects freedom in favor of absolute commitment, and intellectual inquiry in favor of mental ease. And if obliged to state in a single sentence how Jünger differed from Nietzsche, we would look for the difference here. When Jünger reinterprets Nietzsche's ideas he is essentially trying to put an end to that ruthless self-questioning at which Nietzsche so excelled. (Roger Woods, *Ernst Jünger and the Nature of Political Commitment* (Stuttgart: Akademischer Verlag Hans-Dieter Heinz, 1982) p.295)

If, in the writings of 1941–42, the young de Man betrays some interest in "absolute commitment," it is also clear that he would already then have been alarmed to find this associated with "mental ease": not only the reality, but also the posture, of the early articles privileges intellectual difficulty. And certainly the later de Man seeks out Nietzsche precisely for the qualities which Jünger, in Woods' account, seeks to lay to rest: the "ruthless self-questioning" above all.

11. See, for example, the eloquent testimony of Yves Bonnefoy in LPD, pp.18–19 and pp.328–329.

12. HVL, 27–28 Sept. 1942. The fact that we find de Man praising *Der Arbeiter* for its "excellent outcomes in practice" as well as theory as late as September 1942 must remind us how little we are entitled to speak of any conversion in these years.

13. De Man, "Heidegger Reconsidered," *New York Review of Books* 2:4 (2 April 1964), p.15.

14. TLS, June 17–23, 1988, p.676.

15. *The Writings of Jonathan Swift,* ed. R. Greenbey and W. B. Piper (NY: Norton, 1973), p.504. The example is perhaps too obvious, but given recent publications in the *New York Times* and elsewhere it is useful to remind ourselves that it does not require deconstruc-

tion—never mind a "bravura act of deconstruction" (*New York Times,* July 17, 1988)—to see that Swift does not "really mean" that Irish babies should be eaten by wealthy Englishmen. Pleased as some might be to find that deconstruction has become the name for all competent acts of reading, it is not, in fact, deconstructive to read satire as intentionally ironic, or to credit a text with ambiguity, or to argue that an article that begins by attacking vulgar anti-Semitism might in fact be an attack on vulgar anti-Semitism (a deconstructive reading would be more likely to undermine so obvious an assertion).

16. It is one of the bitterer (and I assume unintended) ironies of this article that it was published just as the "Madagascar proposal" (the proposed deportation of the Jews to the island of Madagascar) was being abandoned by Hitler in favor of extermination. See Raul Hilberg, *The Destruction of the European Jews* (NY: Harper and Row, 1961), pp.259–61. According to Hilberg, "the killing phase" began on March 13, 1941; "The Jews in Contemporary Literature" was published on March 4.

17. Radios had been confiscated from Belgium's Jews already in June of the same year; see Anne Somerhausen, *Written in Darkness: A Belgian Woman's Record of the Occupation* 1940–1945 (NY: Alfred A. Knopf, 1946), p.77.

18. On August 5, 1942, Somerhausen reports that Gestapo raids had started a few weeks previously, and writes of rumors, eventually confirmed, of the surrounding of whole neighborhoods, men, women and children "shoved into moving vans, shut in, and driven to barracks at Malines, thence to be deported to the East in cattle cars." (p.145)

The question of who knew what when elicits the contradictory answers one might expect. Paul Struye, in his *L'Evolution du Sentiment Public en Belgique sous l'Occupation Allemande* (Brussels: Les Editions Lumière, 1945), does not report separately on the Jews, and in his introduction (p.12) warns the reader that nothing is said in his book about atrocities discovered later at Breendonck and other camps. Somerhausen, on the other hand, not only writes of Breendonck in April 1942 but uses it to speculate about what is happening in the concentration camps in the East:

How those so-called Communists will suffer in concentration camps behind the Russian front is readily imagined by every Belgian; we know so well what is going on in our one Nazi concentration camp at Breendonck. Men are hounded to death there by privation, beating, and torture. Men are shot and hanged there under slight pretexts. (125–6)

Still, Somerhausen's account attests to the tendency to rely on the improbability of measures we now accept as horribly true. She writes in July 1941 that she had long noted but simply dismissed anti-Semitic propaganda in the "quisling press"—to which de Man's "The Jews in Contemporary Literature" contributed—but that she "had not given ['the 'Jewish problem'] much thought" until she took in a Viennese Jewish tenant (p.74). From then on, she follows the anti-Jewish measures closely; eventually she will save a Jewish colleague and her family by bureaucratic manipulation which keeps them at the holding camp at Malines until the liberation. Yet even as informed a citizen as Somerhausen finds preposterous the "gruesome tale of Jews shipped in hermetically sealed cars to Berlin, killed with poison gas on the way, and thrown into a canal on arrival" told by the man who comes to take her Jewish tenant into hiding.

It is a ridiculous story, of course. Who would believe these fantastic tales about gassing people? I thundered at the man for telling this outrageous nonsense to a frightened woman like Mlle. V. It took a long time to quiet her. She talked incessantly about death, death. (p.147)

This is written on August 8, 1942.

19. Jean-Paul Sartre, *Anti-Semite and Jew,* trans. G. Becker (NY: Schocken Books, 1948), p.23.

20. Sartre, pp.18–19.

21. *Cahiers* 4:4, January 1940, p.17.

22. *Le Soir,* 6 Jan. 1942; *Le Soir,* 24 Mar. 1942; *Le Soir,* 30 Sept. 1941.

23. *Le Soir,* 10 Mar. 1942; *Le Soir,* 10 Feb. 1942.

24. Dubois, he says, "detests all facility, holding to the most difficult form" (*Le Soir,* 1 Sept. 1942); so too de Man admires the "new discipline" of the Modernists which enabled them to tell the "Whole Truth" (*Cahiers* 4:4, January 1940, p.17).

25. Abel Bonnard dismisses the only "false" great men who must be replaced by a young (fascist) elite (*Le Soir,* 7–8 June 1941). De Man applies the term himself to less than favorable accounts of the fall of Belgium (*Le Soir* 25 Feb. 1941), and, with the same politically motivated charge of "not corresponding to reality", to French politics before the war (*Le Soir,* 31 Mar. 1942).

26. De Man, *Mallarmé, Yeats, and the Post-Romantic Predicament* (Harvard University Diss., May 1960), pp.54, 84. Cited in Lentricchia, p. 41.

27. De Man cited by Shoshana Felman in LPD, p.51.

28. Norris, p.104.

29. The tendency to reduce de Man to a thematics of pathos (whether of blindness, epistemic failure, or unreadability) is especially evident in Lentricchia and, more recently, Tobin Siebers, *The Ethics of Criticism* (Ithaca and London: Cornell Univ. Press, 1988), pp.98–123. On the other side, although J. Hillis Miller writes unreadability into the register of ethos rather than pathos in *The Ethics of Reading* (NY: Columbia Univ. Press, 1987), he too invests heavily in the thematics of unreadability.

30. On Goethe's irony, and the relationship between the ironies of Goethe and Friedrich Schlegel, see Ehrhard Bahr, *Die Ironie im Spätwerk Goethes,* (Berlin: Erich Schmidt Verlag, 1972), especially pp.173–6.

31. Interview with Imre Salusinszky in *Criticism in Society* (New York and London: Methuen, 1987), p.170.

32. *Criticism in Society,* p.170.

33. Jacques Derrida, "Violence and Metaphysics: an Essay on the Thought of Emmanuel Levinas," *Writing and Difference,* trans. Alan Bass (London and Chicago: Univ. of Chicago Press, 1978), pp.137–8; emphasis added.

34. "Sartre's Confessions," *New York Review of Books* 3:6 (5 November 1964), p.13.

35. De Man himself was acutely aware of how much his readings "always start again from scratch," and how little he had gathered his readings into a retrospective plot. See his introduction to *The Rhetoric of Romanticism* (NY: Columbia Univ. Press, 1984), p. viii, and, in a more positive light, the last entry of his 1983 interview with Stefano Rosso in RT, p.121.

From the Authority of Appropriate (De)form(ation) to—:

Toward De Man's Totalitarian Acts

JEFFREY S. LIBRETT

Not having been a personal friend or direct student of Paul de Man, I am not principally concerned with the at once difficult, ghastly, and somewhat ludicrous question of whether or not as a person he should posthumously lose his face as a result of arguments concerning the ethical status of his intention in maintaining all but utter silence, while in America, about his Belgian past. Nor will I indulge—beyond this refusal of indulgence—in a histrionics of horrified indignation which could only amount by its very inauthenticity to disrespect for past and present suffering and death under military dictatorships and genocidal regimes. Instead, I am principally concerned here with the texts De Man published since 1953, especially from *Blindness and Insight* on. My question is quite simply: in what way do the ideological beliefs present in the articles from 1941–2 affect the work after De Man's emigration? I pursue first the question of what these beliefs were while postponing the question of how "ideology" is to be defined until the second part of the following three-part argument:

(I) De Man's journalistic engagement during the period of the occupation in the early 40's will have been a totalitarian act, a parasitic collaboration with totalitarianism having as the central necessary condition of both its conformity with and its deviations from the fascist project the belief in the attainability of organically appropriate form. (II) In the work from roughly *Blindness and Insight* on, De Man's traversal of phenomenology, existentialism, new criticism, and (post)structuralism struggles to distance itself from this ideology of the possibility and necessity of appropriate form which guided his parasitic collaboration. (III) In the practice of critical deformation expressly affirmed in the last essays, a certain parasitic collaboration with or performance of post-fascist forms of metaphysical totalitarianism remains openly legible. Although different in ethically necessary and proper ways from the collaboration with fascism, this collaboration remains both explicitly uncertain about its own distance from the authority it had left behind, and unfit to assure either its own collaborators or its opponents that their distance from what both parties fear and detest about fascism is as securely established as either might wish.

I

In the articles of the early 40's, De Man thrives parasitically on the "revolution" in which he finds himself a participant and, in accordance with his parasitic position, seems at times to wound or weaken the doctrines on which this "revolution" was by 1940 obviously based. At the risk of seeming to reduce politics to literary critical games, and drawing on a remark De Man made some 40 years later—that only quotations have performative power[1]—one can view his parasitic participation in the fascist movements as a citational "performance" of fascism. For his quotations of the fascist idiom—drawing on the vocabulary of nationalism, anti-semitism, vitalism, post-individualism, mythic authenticity, and elitist leadership of the masses—both at times simply affirm this idiom and at times, attempting to turn this idiom in a direction which was not its own, speak in its name for what it is not and thus seem merely to pretend to affirm it. It is often difficult to decide on the basis of De Man's journalism whether there is, behind the duplicity of De Man's totalitarian acts, in fact a consciously subversive intent or rather simply a naïve confusion as to what the fascists were prepared to tolerate. In all likelihood there was some combination of these two moments. And in all likelihood, the two moments contributed to each other such that the occupying Nazis' tolerance of the humanist plea for a certain liberal toleration legible in some of De Man's articles led De Man to be less hostile to the Nazis than he otherwise might have been. In this interplay between non-compliance (merely acting like a fascist) and compliance (being a fascist) are to be situated both what appears today as the difficulty of reading De Man's fascist performance and the uncertainty with which one can imagine the De Man of the early 40's to have found himself confronted as to whether or not he was in fact a 'good' fascist. Of course, it remains that De Man could have chosen to act otherwise, for example as a member of the resistance—at greater risk to his life and with the effect that his commitment to the other of the Nazis' brand of fascism would have seemed then and now more clear. And so in this section I attempt to explain his attraction to the fascist alternative as a consequence of his investment in the ideology of organic form which the nationalist program so effectively exploited.

The texts from *Le Soir* and *Het Vlaamsche Land* are pervaded by a paranoid, reactionary, and above all vain concern to preserve the spiritual values of European culture against any influences which might be considered foreign to the European racial and national essences.[2] This concern with the spiritual values of Europe seems at times quite close to the project of German fascism and at other times to militate against it.

As for the proximity, despite his insistence on the importance of individual nationalities, De Man attributes to Germany, as the privileged geographico-spiritual center of Europe, the phantasmatic role of saving Europe from communists, Russians, Jews, and other Asian principles of disintegration that threaten to overwhelm it.[3] There is indeed little trace in these early texts of any acknowledgement that the European totality could be the non-central fragment of a whole larger than itself. And thus De Man must conceive the European totality as a har-

monious balance of tendencies. According to this conception, each national culture is comprised, in its health, of a material substratum—*Blut und Boden*[4]—that brings forth and is at one with its appropriate form. In construing the balance of tendencies that comprises the European spirit, De Man opposes Germany and France in predictable yet telling ways that allow both phantasmatically and imprecisely for a homology between the structure of Europe and the structure of its individual nations. The spirit of the French is characterized as analytic, abstract, "cérébrale,"[5] psychologically egocentric, and superficially clear. In an all too familiar contrast, German culture epitomizes the synthetic, concrete, physical/intuitive, mythical, creatively primitive, universal, and the romantically obscure and deep.[6] The synthesis of French and German culture, which European culture in general and Belgian culture in particular would manifest, and which is nonetheless exemplarily portrayed by Germany, seems thus to amount to an imprecisely, irrationally conceived synthesis of form and matter. One can begin to describe this irrationality by pointing out that the synthesis appears—as Belgian realism and German depth—on the side of matter and on the side of the synthesis, but not on the side of the French. For although De Man argues in "Le destin de la flandre" that Flemish culture is threatened by absorption not only into French culture but also into a pan-germanic state, he sees the latter threat as the threat of absorption into what remains similar to Flemish culture, while French culture is utterly "dissemblable". And thus, on De Man's phantasmatic map of European culture, "cerebral" France represents a more radical threat to Flemish culture than Germany. Where radical formalism and cerebrality stand for the difference and disarticulation of forms themselves, the difference between form and matter is internal to form but not to matter. For this reason Germany is good: its matter is contained by no form, i.e. it is not divided from itself, has excluded from itself all internal division. For this reason too however the site of the synthesis of form and matter—Belgian culture—is particularly threatened with becoming form, becoming French, becoming pure difference. And thus, it must imitate Germany's non-imitation, its achieved self-sameness or unity of form and matter, so as to exclude all form from itself on the model of European unity, Europe's ultimate exclusion of form as difference (of form and matter). What will be the vehicle by means of which this difference will be carried off from Europe? One privileged vehicle, however seldom and complexly mentioned by De Man, is the Jews. For the Jews clearly represent the ultimate scandal to a nationalism that affirms the organic tie between literal earth/race and national-cultural superstructure because their culture is at once national and a-national, their nation one without any but the deferred ground of an unearthly promise. Their form is thus, for this phantasmatics of national form-matter unity, radically form without matter. It is in all likelihood for this reason that De Man would be content—as he states in "Les juifs dans la littérature actuelle"[7]—to see them situated on some particular site, where they would then come to confirm the principle and value of nationalism as he understands it.

In "Les juifs dans la littérature actuelle", De Man writes that the Jews cannot pretend, although they do so, and despite their "cerebrality," to have influenced strongly post-firstworld-war European literature:

A examen quelque peu proche, cette influence apparait même comme extraordinairement peu importante, car on aurait pu s'attendre que, vu les caractères spécifiques de l'esprit juif, ceux-ci auraient joué un rôle plus brillant dans cette production artistique. Leur cérébralité, leur capacité d'assimiler les doctrines en gardant vis-à-vis d'elles une certaine froideur, semblaient des qualités très précieuses pour le travail d'analyse lucide qu'exige le roman. Mais malgré cela, les écrivains juifs sont toujours restés au second plan. . .

Therefore, European literature can do without the Jews. To quote the already well-known passage yet again—for it should be read:

En gardant, malgré l'ingérance sémite dans tous les aspects de la vie européenne, une originalité et un caractère intacts, [notre civilisation] a montré que sa nature profonde était saine. En plus, on voit donc qu'une solution du problème juif qui viserait à la création d'une colonie juive isolée de l'Europe, n'entraînerait pas, pour la vie littéraire de l'Occident, de conséquences déplorables. Celle-ci perdrait, en tout et pour tout, quelques personnalités de médiocre valeur et continuerait, comme par le passé, a se développer selon ses grandes lois évolutives.

The establishment of the (European) unity between thought and phenomenon, abstraction and act, division and unity, can be attained then at the apparently small cost of displacing this internal division onto the border between European and non-European, here Jewish, culture, and naming that border "Jewish."

* * *

On the other hand, to the extent that De Man insists on the compatibility of intra-European unity with the preservation and peaceful coexistence of the individual national unities that comprise it, his collaboration with the occupying forces must attempt however confusedly or ambivalently to subvert the National Socialist insistence on the exclusive priority of the German national revolution. As a result De Man proposes a liberalized and "humanized" version of the national "idea." Where not only the German and Italian but also the French, Belgian and other national identities are to be affirmed,[8] the German national identity would have to be limited to its proper sphere. Since moreover De Man insists on the legitimate existence of particular cultures other than the German, even in the "decadent" state of their "catastrophic" defeat, he makes clear that for him the national "idea" does not concern principally political power, that the nation is a cultural-linguistic entity[9] which includes in its realization the peaceful interpenetration with the cultures that surround it.

Beyond this belief in the saving power of national wholes integrated into a harmonious European totality, De Man exhibits in these early works a belief in the saving power of the individual who, although he belongs to and expresses his national identity, develops within himself a harmonious balance between physical and spiritual characteristics. De Man praises the Italian fascists for developing a system of education that leads to a "harmonieux équilibre" between intellectual and physical development, an equilibrium not unlike that equilibrium Schiller had earlier formulated under the name of aesthetic "grace" and that De Man would take apart in its last essays under the name of aesthetic "ideology."

On the other hand, even in the early 40's, De Man seems to waver on the question of the desirability of the ideology of this equilibrium. For example, he reduces Drieu la Rochelle's hatred of cerebrality—his arguments in "Notes pour comprendre ce siècle" for a synthesis of spiritual and physical values—to a mere "profession de foi." And De Man claims with what seems a certain irony, despite the praise of "élan" and the—given the context—appalling affirmation of the creation of a new humanity, that La Rochelle's work is interesting only as the spectacle of a lively but chaotic intelligence:

qui n'hésite pas à englober dans un même système des vertus aussi disparates que celles des chrétiens, des mystiques, des héros et des sportifs. Bien plus que *toutes les tentatives assez vaines faites pour démontrer l'inévitable et le mérite d'une telle attitude,* importent l'élan et la conviction avec lesquels cet écrivain se lance à l'assaut de la création d'un type humain radicalement nouveau.[10]

De Man's derisively superior attitude here toward La Rochelle's affirmation of spiritual-physical unity may well, then,express his doubts as to the value of the fascist projects for such unity. In De Man's report, one month later, of a meeting with Valéry these doubts become more explicit. For here, De Man mentions with a certain awed respect precisely the seriousness of Valéry's attempt to defend "les valeurs de l'esprit" and his concern with the cultivation of form[11] in a state of "calme et sérénité." To be sure, here too the principle that this form must be adequate to a particular content, that it must provide the material container appropriate to a proper spirit, remains in force. But nonetheless, the article marks De Man's distance from the irrationalist cult of animal and mechanical dynamism—that is, from a particularly brutal, fascist version of the ideology of the form-content, matter-spirit synthesis—and it also affirms spirituality or thought[12] itself, despite the dangers of excessive analysis to which De Man elsewhere responds with advocation of flight into the mythical, the obscure, the romantic, the deep, the German.

Finally, the principle of novelistic representation and aesthetic representation in general, including modern "psychological" fiction, is that of a Stendhalian—and also quintessentially Flemish—"realism." As is well known, De Man later came to speak of this principle only in the most aggressively critical terms.[13] It is what his later work characterizes as the principle of the aesthetic itself as of the representational agreement between discourse and its referent.—In turn, the methodological principle of De Man's notion of literary history in the 40's is that of a realist history of empirical genres within national traditions. The progress of the aesthetic through time is to be guided by the "grandes lois évolutives" that can be represented in a well-ordered realist narrative[14] along with the products of artistic genius that embody these laws. The unity of form and essence as the value of the work is repeated across an eternalized history as historical forms and eternal essence unite in the lawful evolution of a change that is none. This principle is in some cases reconcilable with elements of the Nazi program, and indeed De Man invokes it in the context of his argument for the acceptability of isolating the Jews from Europe. On the other hand, its associated imperative of conformity to the norms dictated by a historically situated genre remains in force in the context of De Man's discussion of Hubert Dubois' "Le massacre des innocents,"[15] an essay which protests with rare indiscretion at once the genocidal and the aesthetic programs of the Nazis. The strictly "political" neutrality of this principle does not prevent it however from remaining one of the versions of the ideology of naturally motivated form.

* * *

Thus, on the levels of Europe, the nation, the individual, the literary work, and literary history, De Man's totalitarian act has as one of its necessary conditions the commitment to the mutual and natural appropriateness of form and content. It is to the authority of this mitigated formalism (as opposed to the "French" hyperformalism he feared) that his early work most fundamentally responds, both in its more simply affirmative acting out of fascism, and in those moments when it gestures toward a liberalizing and humanizing resistance. But in the writing that follows upon his emigration from Belgium, De Man pursues tirelessly the implications of the insight into the insufficiency of precisely this authority of appropriate, motivated form. The paradoxical question within which his thought does not cease to move can be stated as follows: what is the appropriate form or expression of the thought that form is never adequate to its thought, that a signifier cannot be in an immediate (non)relation to its signified, that appropriate form has no authority? Clearly, a mere formlessness or pure deformation—the radically irrationalist abandonment of the attempt to say what one believes oneself to mean—would only be appropriate to the content of non-authority and thus authoritarian in its turn, a new avatar of the immediate fallacy.—But rather than pursue my own (de)form(ation)s of these questions, I would introduce two sites on which De Man develops his "own" discourse of this authority of (de)form(ation): in the demystification of demystification and in the naming of ideology as name.

II

The distance between the nationalist historicism that De Man proposes in the articles of the 40's and the anti-nationalist anti-historicism of his texts from the 50's and beyond is the distance between simple mystification—the ideological imperative of a harmonious form-content or signifier-signified agreement—and the demystification of the demystification of this mystification. In "Criticism and Crisis" (1967), he argues that the "concept of literature [or criticism] as demystification" is "the most dangerous myth of all":[16]

demystifying critics are in fact asserting the privileged status of literature as an authentic language, but withdrawing from the implications by cutting themselves off from the source from which they receive their insight.

For the statement about language, that sign and meaning can never coincide, is what is precisely taken for granted in the kind of language we call literary. Literature, unlike everyday language, begins on the far side of this knowledge; it is the only form of language free from the fallacy of unmediated expression. All of us know this, although we know it in the misleading way of a wishful assertion of the opposite.[17]

I wish, then, to take these signs to mean: the negation of the desire to exclude difference from the form-content relation belongs to this desire. Of course, this is not quite to say that there is no difference between a mystified consciousness that adheres to the authority of this desire of the same and the demystification of demystification or the awareness of the dialectical character of demystification. Rather, this awareness is the awareness that it repeats what it nonetheless denounces, the illusion of appropriate form, whereas a first-order demystification, which would announce as the truth of literature the incapacity of literature to attain its truth, both depends on the mystification it denounces and simply repeats this mystification in assuming itself to have attained both the truth of literature and its own truth. To say then that "literature . . . is the only form of language free from the fallacy of unmediated expression" is to situate "literature" in its impropriety between the mystified text and its demystification. Literature is thus no longer—as it was in De Man's articles from the 40's—an empirical thing or a constatable event or place; indeed literature is not but (re)moves itself between itself and its critical undoing. For to say that literature is free from the fallacy of immediacy, as De Man does, (necessarily) misspeaking himself, would be to attribute to it a transcendent status that amounts to the repetition of this fallacy. Whatever would be free of this fallacy would be adequate to its own truth, yet the possibility of such adequation is precisely what literature is to denounce as a delusion. The (in a double sense) literary criticism of De Man, then, at this point in his career authorizes the freedom from the fallacy of unmediated expression, in the place of the humanist[17] freedom from mediation he had sought in the 40's, as the goal of the henceforth not quite human humanities. But the place has "substantially" shifted, since the unattainable goal is at this point articulated as unattainable, as the unattainable, ateleological telos of the proper articulation of the impropriety of articulation.

This account of demystification is incompatible with the value of organic form asserted in De Man's criticism of the 40's on the level of the European, national, individual, aesthetic, and literary historiographical unities. At the risk of arguing for the obvious, I shall nonetheless illustrate this incompatibility with respect to De Man's engagement for European unity concerning the issue of anti-semitism, before I turn to the repetition, in the explicitly rhetorical and ideology-critical "terminology" of his last essays, of the "nothing" De Man states in "Criticism and Crisis" with such élan.

How then can one apply this view of demystification to the political-moral outrage or disappointment of De Man's apparent acceptance of the "isolation" of Jews from Europe? In "Criticism and Crisis," on the way to pointing out the self-inconsistency of Husserl's Eurocentric defense of a philosophy of self-reflexion, De Man writes as follows, of the psychoanalytical and political analogies of the necessary undecidability between subject and object, criticism and literature, in any hermeneutic relation:

In the case of a genuine analysis of the psyche, it . . . would no longer be clear who is analyzing and who is being analyzed; consequently the highly embarrassing question arises, who should be paying whom. And on a political level, the equally distressing question as to who should be exploiting whom, is bound to arise (10).

Whether or not one is repulsed by the "inappropriateness" of De Man's good humor here, one ought not fail to see that this comment marks a great distance from the articles of the 40's. The uncertainty as to who should be exploiting whom here arises because the reader of another political group can never know whether or not he is in fact only reading himself, only reading his reading. De Man's acknowledgment of this uncertainty indicates his recognition that, in his earlier approval of the potentially genocidal "isolation" of Jewish culture from European culture, he was in fact attempting to cast out that "cerebral" distance—between assimilated doctrines and intention, between linguistic universality and private Meinung, between "French" abstraction and "German" intuition, between rationality and its own tendency to produce a chaos of fragmentation—that comprised his proper impropriety. To say that the difference or heterogeneity embodied by the non-European in De Man's early anti-semitism and anti-communism was in fact his own difference is to demystify, to negate, the mystification of that phantasm of embodiment. But to reflect one step further on this difference, to realize that it means his difference from himself, is to demystify the demystification: what was to be cast out sacrificially was not anything properly belonging to the self but the impossibility of identifying what might properly belong to the self, the impossibility of identification or of self-hood itself. The politics of this recognition that the difference between self and other is a difference within (the one and the other of) the self is a politics for which difference, heterogeneity is not indifferent but nonetheless neither here nor there. It is to this extent productive of and compatible with a certain tendency toward non-violence that is dictated by the authority of deformation, by the knowledge of the non-knowledge of the borders of same and other.

The impossibility of self-identification which results here from a certain demystification of demystification proceeds upon and so does not evade the attribution of responsibility for mystification: De Man's attempt to exclude his own internal difference was his own attempt. Beyond this demystification, however, a second-order demystification takes the sequence of attributions of responsibility one step further and in so doing more or less knowingly repeats the mistake of this attribution in identifying the source of the guilt of attribution as the undecidability of identity. A quarter of a century after the publication of "Criticism and Crisis," at the far end of a terminological displacement which he seems to have found valuable, De Man has renamed this impossible identification "anthropomorphism," and associated the latter with the "ideology" of value itself. Since the term, "ideology" carries more explicitly "political" connotations than "demystification," and since "ideology" appears in connection with De Man's last attempts to address precisely the political, this shift must be taken into account if one would gauge De Man's progress, in his mature work, beyond the mystification of his journalistic engagement of the 40's.

In "Anthropomorphism and Trope in the Lyric," De Man argues—by reference to Nietzsche's famous line, "Was ist also Wahrheit? Ein bewegliches Heer von Metaphern, Metonymien, Anthropomorphismen. . ."[18]—against the possibility of saving "controlled discourse" by means of the reduction, through an economy of equal exchange, of concept to figure. That is, he argues against precisely that aestheticizing certainty he is so frequently accused of attempting to establish: namely, that rhetoric as an order of figures or forms could render the contents of conceptual discourse void by reducing conceptuality without remainder to itself. De Man argues in his reading of Nietzsche that one cannot establish a controlled certainty of uncertainty in a pure, homogeneous figurality. For figurality is not merely plural but heterogeneous, internally broken into a) a "tropological" discourse of predication, in which predicates remain mediate and non-essential with respect to their subjects; and b) an "anthropomorphic" discourse of naming in which predicates substitute themselves for their subjects, becoming by virtue of a forgetfulness of their status the immediately present essences of the subjects with which they are thus seen as fused. This incompatibility of the discourse of mediation with the discourse of immediacy does not, however, for De Man prevent their inevitable intertwinement. Characterizing this intertwinement in the improperly temporal, narrative terms of "becoming," and renaming "name" as "norm," "value," and "ideology," De Man writes: "Truth is a trope; a trope generates a norm or value; this value (or ideology) is no longer true" (242). A name, norm, value or ideology is "no longer true" because it is assumed to allow access to a subject-predicate unity that could thus be identified, sought as found, and appropriated. "It is true that tropes are the producers of ideologies that are no longer true" (242).

And so in the case of Nietzsche's critical reduction of conceptual to figural discourse, it would be ideological to read an identification of anthropomorphism with the tropes with which it is implicitly identified. For such a reading would amount to turning "trope" into a name that covers fully its extensive field,

into a predicate that achieves its subject. The inclusion nonetheless of "anthropomorphism" in the list of tropes criticizes thus the critical reduction of concepts to tropes, disrupts the tropological certainty of this reduction to a homogeneity. In turn, the criticism of criticism is here not exempt from the "distortion" it introduces into or effects on what it criticizes. For to define anthropomorphism as the ideological form of tropes is to name it, to value the discovery, on any given occasion, that a trope is being addressed.

If "ideology" is thus the name[19] for the becoming-name of trope, or for the reading of a trope as a name, then wherein does the power of ideology for De Man consist and on what is it exercised? Elucidating Nietzsche's metaphorical name for truth as "army" of tropes, De Man insists that the power to which "army" alludes is not a power which would be exercised by tropes simply against that which would be external to them.[20] Rather, it is the violence they inflict at once upon themselves and upon their proper otherness in functioning at once as inessential predications secure in their non-securing action and as essentializing enablers of address. "Violence" becomes thus a name for the incomprehensibility, inaccessibility, uncontrollability of the passage from trope to anthropomorphism that occurs as the opaque 'origin' of subjectivity 'out' of the figures it always already addresses; "violence" is a name for the imposition of the imperative of appropriate form, an imposition uttered by the non-voice of an inaccessible authority of deformation. "Violence" dictates the attribution of responsibility or ground to what neither is nor has one.[21]

III

To point out the incomprehensibility and originlessness of this imperative is not to escape the latter, but only to respond to it by naming its groundlessness as responsible party. Indeed, De Man acknowledged the failure of this escape, asserting in what he knew to be one of his final public testimonies that he cannot be taken to have found the appropriate form for the inadequacy of form to content, an inadequacy that his reading of Nietzsche illustrates in the disjunction, within form or figurative language, of trope and anthropomorphism, trope and its becoming-name. In the "Preface" to *The Rhetoric of Romanticism*,[22] he writes that his essays collected there do not amount to a totality, that the "apparent coherence within each essay is not matched by a corresponding coherence between them" (viii). At once praising and damning himself for having remained faithful to a hypotactic mode, he suggests that the:

apparent resignation [in such writers as Adorno and Auerbach] to aphorism and parataxis is often an attempt to recuperate on the level of style what is lost on the level of history. By stating the inevitability of fragmentation in a mode that is itself fragmented, one restores the aesthetic unity of manner and substance that may well be what is in question in the historical study of romanticism (ix).

Of course, the clever refusal to have found the form appropriate to the mutual inappropriateness of form and content itself can be taken to imply that, in the failure of De Man's candidly insistent attempt to establish hierarchical order, he has in fact found the appropriate form of an inappropriate relation between a hypotactic style and a paratactic message. However, even in this aggressively and obliquely claimed appropriateness, the failure to fail to respond to the imperative of appropriate form would remain apparent. To this extent, De Man bequeaths his work precisely to those who would not simply imitate its manner or passively accept its message. It is as if he would remind his readers that "ideology," as well as all the other concepts or figures he finds or puts into play in his texts, are not names and are not to be addressed as such.

In "The Resistance to Theory," he characterizes the status of his "own" method of rhetorical reading in terms which provide further evidence of this reminder. For when he claims total authority for rhetorical readings, total authority for appropriate deformation, he inscribes himself in what he has characterized earlier in the same essay as the anxious resistance to theory.

It is a recurrent strategy of any anxiety to defuse what it considers threatening by magnification or minimization, by attributing to it claims to power of which it is bound to fall short. If a cat is called a tiger it can easily be dismissed as a paper tiger; the question remains however why one was so scared of the cat in the first place. The same tactic works in reverse: calling the cat a mouse and then deriding it for its pretense to be mighty (5).

Although De Man attempts having made this assertion to "call the cat a cat and to document, however briefly, the contemporary version of the resistance to theory in this country" (5), he nonetheless ends this essay by calling rhetorical readings infinitely powerful in their very powerlessness, and thus akin to real tigers made out of paper:

Technically correct rhetorical readings may be boring, monotonous, predictable, and unpleasant, but they are irrefutable. They are also totalizing (and potentially totalitarian) for since the structures and functions they expose do not lead to the knowledge of an entity (such as language) but are an unreliable process of knowledge production that prevents all entities, including linguistic entities, from

coming into discourse as such, they are indeed universals, consistently defective models of language's impossibility to be a model language. They are, always in theory, the most elastic theoretical and dialectical model to end all models and they can rightly claim to contain within their own defective selves all the other defective models of reading-avoidance, referential, semiological, grammatical, performative, logical, or whatever. They are theory and not theory at the same time, the universal theory of the impossibility of theory. To the extent however that they are theory, that is to say teachable, generalizable and highly responsive to systematization, rhetorical readings, like the other kinds, still avoid and resist the reading they advocate. Nothing can overcome the resistance to theory since theory *is* itself this resistance (19).

The hyperbolizing anxiety De Man exhibits here with respect to his "own" theory exemplarily performs the resistance he metaphorically identifies with (this) theory. But since this performance is not merely a model for but also a mere example of such resistance, what it claims cannot be taken as authoritative. The totalitarian potential that resides in rhetorical readings and in the "concepts" and "terminology" with which they are inadequately taken to operate, i.e. their "self-resistance," arises from their capacity to be addressed as names, norms, values, or ideologies, applied as if they were universals which were not defective. De Man ironizes his success, points out precisely this totalitarian potential, by obliquely alluding, in the "resistance" to theory, not so much to Freud as to the "resistance" to the fascism with which theory is nonetheless not to be identified.

The passage then from De Man's totalitarian acts in the 40's to his totalitarian acts from the 50's to the 80's cannot be adequately described as a passage from one empirical position to another, from evil or stupidity or ugliness to its negation by good or intelligence or beauty. It can and should be—however "inadequately"—described as the passage from a nationalist aestheticism which has as necessary condition the firm belief in the *value* of natural and adequate form—i.e in the value of value—to an anti-nationalist anti-aestheticism which incessantly restates the implausibility of any belief in (this) value while acknowledging its own incapacity to cease precisely *addressing* the problem of value. The notion of a "passage" from "early" to "late" in De Man's work remains impure because the narrative form of its however "lived" representation tends to efface the impossibility for example of the "late" either to return to the immediacy of the "early" or to return to its present as to its proper "belatedness." These impossibilities do not entail that a subject will not at each moment have carried the burden of responsibilities. Rather, precisely *because* there is no immediate relation to either presence or pastness, the burden of non-assured, impure, political intervention in the contexts of delegitimation that offer themselves "here" and "now" cannot be evaded. De Man's "passage" from adherence to the authority of form to adherence to the authority of (de)form(ation) names, then, neither an excuse nor a condemnation but the task to figure and act out political transformation at all times in terms other than those that promote the installation of any naturalized propriety of the desirable. The extension and interrogation of De Man's readings in contexts—such as the psychoanalytic, marxist, feminist, and juridical—which he addressed only obliquely is in the process of responding to this task. The "passage" of De Man discussed above reminds "us" to attempt not to treat his legacy as the terminology or grammar it emphatically is not.

Loyola University of Chicago

NOTES

1. "Hegel on the Sublime," in *Displacement: Derrida and After,* ed. Mark Krupnick (Bloomington: Indiana Univ. Press, 1983), p.139–153.

2. See, for example, "Art as Mirror of the Essence of Nations: Considerations on 'Geist der Nationen,' by A. E. Brinckmann"; "Content of the European Idea"; from *Het Vlaamsche Land,* 29–30 March: 3 and 31 May-1 June: 3, respectively. All articles from *Het Vlaamsche Land* cited here have been read in the unpublished English translations of Ortwin de Graef.

3. See "Art as Mirror of the Essence of Nations: Considerations on 'Geist der Nationen' by A. E. Brinckmann," *Het Vlaamsche Land,* 29–30 March 1942: 3. De Man writes there of the "national personality" as "valuable condition, as a precious possession, which has to be maintained at the cost of all sacrifices . . . It concerns a sober faith, a practical means to defend Western culture against a decomposition from the inside out or a surprise attack by neighboring civilizations." And see further "L'exposition Histoire d'Allemagne au cinquantenaire," *Le Soir,* 16 March 1942: 2. According to De Man, the visitors to this exhibit, staged in Brussels by one Major Gehardus, Chief of the Section on Propaganda for Belgium, could benefit from learning that Germany's evolution is "régie par un facteur fondamental: la volonté d'unifier un ensemble de régions qui ont une même structure raciale, mais que les adversaires s'efforcent sans cesse de diviser. . . . Même les coups les plus durs—tel le Traité de Versailles—ne suffirent pas à annihiler l'élan d'une population qui veut affirmer sa cohésion et, partant, sa force. . . . nul ne peut nier la signification fondamentale de l'Allemagne pour la vie de l'Occident

tout entier. Il faut voir, dans cette obstination à ne pas vouloir se laisser subjuguer, plus qu'une simple preuve de constance nationale. Toute la continuité de la civilisation occidentale dépend de l'unité du peuple qui en est le centre."

4. The phrase appears in its Flemish equivalent in "German Literature. A Great Writer: Ernst Jünger," *Het Vlaamsche Land,* 26–7 July 1942: 2.

5. In "Le destin de la flandre: après les journées cuturelles germano-flamandes," *Le Soir,* 1 Sept. 1941: 1, this "analyse cérébrale" of the French is opposed to the Flemish attachment to "exterior forms", to "pictorial" and "realist" dimensions of aesthetic experience. The German "force organisatrice" is responsible for liberating Flemish art—and as this article argues, the very touchstone of a nationality is the specificity of its art—from the servile imitation of the French "voisin dont l'état d'esprit est dissemblable." Again, contrasting Jünger's work to the style of the French ("Chronique littéraire: 'Sur les Falaises de marbre' par Ernst Jünger," *Le Soir,* 31 March 1942: 2), De Man praises Jünger's mythical novels because they avoid the "cerebral": "De même, les scènes ne sont pas là pour constituer le schema d'une évolution cérébrale rigoureuse" . The word "cérébrale" is also used to characterize and lightly to chastise the tendency of the works of Aldous Huxley who, straying from the English psychological novel, tends to reduce his characters to the ideas they embrace, that is, to allegories ("Le roman anglais contemporain," *Cahiers du Libre Examen* 4:4, January 1940).

6. See in particular the characterization of Ernst Jünger in "Literature and Sociology," *Het Vlaamsche Land,* 27–8 Sept. 1942: 2, and, in "Chronique Littéraire, 'Jardins et routes' par Ernst Jünger," *Le Soir,* 23 June 1942: 2.

7. *Le Soir,* 4 March 1941: 10. It may at first seem possible to read De Man's minimalization of the role of Jews in either perverting or enhancing the development of European artistic and literary life as a strategy meant to exonerate them, despite the censorship under which De Man was writing, from the accusations that led to non-German complicity in the Nazis' genocidal project. But the moral of the story with which the article closes makes this interpretation seem excessively generous.

8. See for example the assertion that "l'on trouvera les mêmes dispositifs acoustiques dans toutes les contrées" in the context of a discussion of the value of the historical study of musical instruments for determining "la personnalité propre d'un groupe ethnique" from "L'histoire de l'instrument est aussi l'histoire du peuple," *Le Soir,* 28 Jan. 1941: 10, and the insistence on the value of French and

Belgian literary and musical traditions in the many articles on these themes.

9. See the apparently liberalizing argument in "En marge du dialecte liègois," *Le Soir,* 22 April 1941: 10, that historians have discovered interpenetrations and transfers of words between Flemish and Wallon dialects, and that therefore there is reason to affirm a Belgian unity. Does this not also imply that the Aryan phantasm and its phantasmatic other might also not need be "toujours considérés comme des étrangers ou . . . comme des ennemis" but might come to consider themselves as in a "grande solidarité" with their scapegoated others on the model of the solidarity of Flemish and Wallon for which De Man here argues?

10. *Le Soir,* 9 Dec. 1941: 2. Italics mine, J. S. L.

11. "Paul Valéry et la poésie symboliste," *Le Soir,* 10–11 January 1942: 3.

12. Cf. De Man's defense of the poetry of the pre-fascist "pessimists" in his two articles on Italian poetry: "La vogue de la tristesse et du désespoir montaliens ne prouve qu'une chose: que le régime fasciste laisse entière liberté au poète pour chercher sa source d'inspiration où il veut, même dans le domaine qui semble le plus opposé à l'état d'esprit civil et guerrier cher aux éducateurs du peuple," in "La troisième conférence du professeur Donini," *Le Soir,* 18 Feb. 1941: 2. This praise of Italian fascism functions obviously as a demand that censorship of "decadent" forms not be practiced. Its naïveté consists only in its implicit hope that such demands could be tolerated for long by the fascists for whom De Man's intervention on behalf of the surrealists from July 1942 on would ultimately, it appears, become his German overseers' reason for letting him go. Cf. Jacques Derrida, "Like the Sound of the Sea Deep Within a Shell," *Critical Inquiry* 14 (Spring 1988): 591–652; Werner Hamacher, "Fortgesetzte Trauerarbeit: Paul de Mans komplizierte Strategie/ Eine Erwiderung," *Frankfurter Allgemeine Zeitung,* 24 Feb. 1988: 35.

13. For example in "Lyric and Modernity," *Blindness and Insight: Essays in the Rhetoric of Contemporary Criticism* (Minneapolis: Univ. of Minnesota Press, 1983), p.166–186.

14. See "Sur les possibilités de la critique," *Le Soir,* 2 Dec. 1941: 2 and "Criticism and Literary History," *Het Vlaamsche Land,* 7–8 June 1942: 3.

15. *Le Soir,* 1 Sept. 1942: 2.

16. *Blindness and Insight: Essays in the Rhetoric of Contemporary Criticism,* Second Edition, Revised (Minneapolis: Univ. of Minnesota Press, 1983), 14.

17. He praises Jünger in 1942 for his "profound humanism" in "German Literature. A Great Writer: Ernst Jünger," *Het Vlaamsche Land,* 26–7 July 1942: 2. And in a moment of clear protest against the militarization of the spirit of renewal, he praises Rudolf Kassner and Jünger together two months later ("Aspects de la pensée allemande: 'Le livre du souvenir' de R. Kassner," *Le Soir* 125 Sept. 1942: 2) for having made clear a non-Nietzschean but nonetheless fully German "attitude morale" characterized by a peaceful and self-limiting visionary imagination.

18. I omit the discussion of Baudelaire whereby De Man illustrates this argument with respect to "lyric." It is however perhaps not superfluous in this context to remark the non-nationalist gesture by means of which De Man points out the "same" disruption, which concerns anything but national character, in German and French texts, whereas in his reading of Baudelaire in 1942, he was interested in Baudelaire's "Correspondances" as "a practical poetic representation of the mysterious alliance of nature with man's inner essence and experiences," and in Baudelaire's break with rationalism as a break with the French spirit: "It seems to us that this new orientation—which corresponds very precisely to that of German romanticism—contains something which is irreconcilable with the French spirit." Indeed, De Man's partisanship for surrealist poetry, which nonetheless ended up distancing him from the cultural programs of the fascist occupying forces, takes the explicit and apparently ingenuous form of a defense of the surrealists' attempt to find an appropriate form for the irrational substance of things: ". . . how deeply serious the intention of the surrealists was, who strove to obtain nothing less than the "Golden Age" of total harmony which Novalis has sung about so beautifully. It is not reason which can lead them in this, but the natural force of myth, of the dream. Consequently, these become the proper content of poetry," "Contemporary Trends in French Poetry," *Het Vlaamsche Land,* 6–7 June 1942: 3.

19. It is also in the late De Man the name for the mistaking of a referential function of "language" for a neat fit between concept or signifier and concrete, intuitive referent: "What we call ideology is precisely the confusion of linguistic with natural reality, of reference with phenomenalism." "The Resistance to Theory," *The Resistance to Theory* (Minneapolis: Univ. of Minnesota Press, 1986), p.11.

20. To "say that truth is an army (of tropes) . . . can certainly not imply, in *On Truth and Lie* that truth is a kind of commander who enlists tropes in the battle against error. No such dichotomy exists in any critical philosophy, let alone Nietzsche's, in which truth is always at the very least dialectical, the negative knowledge of error" (242). Having read the relationship of "Correspondances" to "Ob-

session" as the passage from "analogy into apostrophe" or from "trope into anthropomorphism," and characterized the comprehension of this passage as "a hermeneutic, fallacious lyrical reading of the unintelligible," De Man asserts: "The power that takes one from one text to the other is not just a power of displacement, be it understood as recollection or interiorization or any other 'transport,' but the sheer blind violence that Nietzsche, concerned with the same enigma, domesticated by calling it, metaphorically, an army of tropes" (261–2).

21. The ideology of appropriate form, the imperative that form match up with and be justified by what it forms, is itself another form of the principle of sufficient reason, a principle which both requires that we pose the question of its reason and requires that we do not—for what installs it cannot be subject to its law. "Violence" is indeed one name for the aporia of this double requirement. Cf. Martin Heidegger, *Der Satz vom Grund* (Pfullingen: Verlag Günther Neske, 1957).

22. Paul de Man, *The Rhetoric of Romanticism* (New York: Columbia Univ. Press, 1984).

Perspectives: on De Man and *Le Soir*

JEFFREY MEHLMAN

Some years ago, in a text of homage to Derrida, Emmanuel Levinas, without malice but with a touch of the unwitting resentment that only the deconstructed perhaps harbor, proposed the oddest of analogies. The historical sequence he was invariably reminded of upon reading Derrida, he wrote, was the "exodus" of 1940: "A retreating military unit arrives in a town as yet unaware of anything, in which the cafés are open, ladies are shopping in ladies' shops, haircutters cutting hair, bakers baking, viscounts meeting other viscounts in order to exchange anecdotes about viscounts, and in which everything is deconstructed (*déconstruit*) and desolate an hour later."[1] Such would be the *frisson nouveau* introduced by Derrida: a traumatic rendering of the traditional sites of thought so "uninhabitable" that the principal shock it evokes out of Levinas' memory is the evacuation of town after town in anticipation of Hitler's surge westward. Ortwin de Graef's discovery of the numerous articles published by Paul de Man in *Le Soir* during the first half of World War II is perhaps first of all an invitation to imagine Levinas' improbable metaphor as metonymy, his analogy as sequence. For de Man, it now appears, served, in the course of his life, as champion of two radical cultural movements from abroad: as partisan of the Nazi "revolution" among the Walloons in the 1940's and as advocate of "deconstruction" among the Americans in the 1970's. Hitler's jolt to European sensibilities—too devastatingly rapid, as de Man repeatedly suggests in *Le Soir,* to have registered in psychological terms—and Derrida's, that is, are less the stuff of grotesque analogy (Levinas) than nodes of a complex continuum one name of which may be the "life of Paul de Man."[2]

Metonymy is the trope of contamination, which is one source of its appeal to deconstruction in its efforts to dismantle what de Man, on Proust, has called "the totalizing stability of metaphorical processes."[3] But the intertextual contamination deconstruction all but *demands* between de Man's two "revolutions" (of the 1940's and the 1970's) is open to a restricted—or remetaphorized—reading we should do well to confront at the outset. For those who have always warmed to the liberatory aspect of deconstruction's destabilizing tendencies, the revelation of de Man's enthusiastic endorsement of a Nazi Europe might be contained by claiming that deconstruction was plainly the remedy—acknowledged or not—for the ill of collaboration. *Ecclesia super cloacam*: the church remains no less splendid for being built over the sewer of European history. That such a proposition repeats in its structure the triumphalist interpretation of Proust that de Man rejected should give us pause: to "save" deconstruction by subsuming the relation between de Man's "deconstruction" and his "collaboration" with the Nazis to that between "art" and the "life" it would redeem is to affirm a dialectical configuration pre-eminently vulnerable to deconstruction. Nevertheless, Geoffrey Hartman, in a piece in the *New Republic,* concludes on precisely that note: "In the light of what we now know, however, his work appears more and more as a deepening reflection on the rhetoric of totalitarianism. . . . De Man's critique of every tendency to totalize literature or language . . . looks like a belated, but still powerful, act of conscience."[4] Might it be that in order to "save" deconstruction one is reduced to resorting to language that ought to make any deconstructor blush?

* * *

How serious a collaborator with the Nazi regime was Paul de Man? A reading of the sum total of de Man's articles in *Le Soir* reveals that political issues were far from a daily obsession for the young journalist. Still there can be no doubt of de Man's avid support for the New Order. On March 25, 1941, five months after the *Militärbefehlshaber* of Belgium issued the first anti-Jewish decrees, de Man could speak shamelessly of "the impeccable behavior of a highly civilized invader."[5] On November 14 of that year, in an article on Daniel Halévy's *Trois épreuves,* de Gaulle's resistance movement in London was dismissed as a "parody"; moreover, immediate collaboration with the occupier was said to be an "imperative obvious to any objective observer." Lest de Man's reading of the situation be interpreted as a response to geo-political (rather than ideological) realities, note should be taken that two weeks later (October 28), in an article on Jacques Chardonne, one of the stars of the Collaboration in Paris, de Man rejected as inadequate any effort to distinguish between Nazism and Germany; on the contrary, "the war will have but united more intimately the two quite kindred realities which the Hitlerian soul and the German soul were from the beginning, fusing them into a single unique force. This is a significant phenomenon, since it means that the Hitlerian dimension cannot be judged without simultaneously judging the German dimension and that Europe's future can be anticipated only within the framework of the possibilities and exigencies of German genius." The time had come for Germany's "definitive emancipation," but such emancipation, for de Man, meant German "hegemony" within Europe, and within such a context no distinction was to be made between Germany itself and Hitler. On January 20, 1942, in a review of French apologists of the Collaboration (Brasillach, Drieu la Rochelle, Chardonne, Montherlant, Fabre-Luce), Belgium is referred to as "a country which has not yet made its revolution and for which these war years are like a meditative pause in the face of future tasks." The

prospect is of the "intoxication" of great collective efforts in the New Europe; in the interim, Belgians, we read, will have "rarely felt closer to the French" than in the "anguished and quivering (*frémissant*)" reflections of the *gratin* of the Collaboration whose reading de Man recommends. By March 31, 1942, the future revolution has already become "the current revolution," and a significant contribution to it is said to be made by Alfred Fabre-Luce's *Anthologie de la nouvelle Europe,* admired for its attempt to "defend Western values against increasingly threatening intrusions." With the final solution (unmentioned) well under way, the article offers a rare display of indignation by the (already) aloof de Man—against "the criminal errors of the past." (Such language should be read, I believe, as implicitly endorsing the prosecution of Léon Blum and other pre-War anti-Nazi leaders in show trials.)[6] On April 20, 1942, de Man weighed in with a strong endorsement of Paul Alverdes' journal *Das innere Reich,* which was created in order to counter the impression of a massive flight of the German intelligentsia from Hitler's Germany.[7] De Man was just then translating Alverdes's novel *Das Zweigesicht,* a book here described as participatory in the "virile" outlook of the journal. It is in fact Alverdes' success in evoking "virile, patriotic, and exalting" materials in a work of art of "quasifeminine finesse" that de Man most admires in the author. Wherein he appears to be toying with Nazi ideology in its more jaded manifestations.

Of all the articles cited as evidence of de Man's sympathy with the New Order, his contribution on March 4, 1941 to a special section on "cultural aspects" of the Jewish question has been most frequently referred to. "Les Juifs dans la littérature actuelle" is a very curious piece. For it grafts the question of the Jews onto a second issue, which is in fact a far more insistent concern in his articles for *Le Soir*: the subject of literature's ultimate autonomy in relation to the impure world of politics, history, etc. Against the "vulgar" anti-Semites de Man would take his distance from, the author maintains that modern literature—*unlike the modern world*—has not been contaminated (or "polluted") by Jewish influence. On the one hand, "the Jews have in fact played an important role in the factitious and chaotic existence of Europe," so much so that a novel emergent from such a world might indeed be qualified as *enjuivé*. On the other hand, however, it is the specificity of literature to maintain its own autonomy relative to the world: "It seems that esthetic developments (*les évolutions esthétiques*) obey quite powerful laws whose action persists even while humanity is racked by formidable events." In all its crudity, the analogy informing the article is between literature and history (or "reality"), on the one hand, and Europe and the Jews on the other. The argument, moreover, is clinched by a demonstration. In the case of France, "Jewish writers have always been of the second rank"; figures such as "André Maurois, Francis de Croisset, Henri Duvernois, Henri Bernstein, Tristan Bernard, Julien Benda, etc. are not among the most important, and certainly not among those who have oriented in any way the genres of literature." On these grounds, de Man congratulates the West on its ability to fend off "Jewish influence" (or "Semitic infiltration") and signs on to an embryonic form of the "final solution," mass deportation: "In addition, it will be seen that a solution to the Jewish problem intent on the creation of a Jewish colony isolated from Europe would not entail any deplorable consequences for the literary life of the West."

De Man's analogy—whereby art, in its purity, need be protected from a reality whose degradation is tantamount to a Judaization—is bizarre, but not unique. Surprisingly enough, the only figure of stature to have embraced such an ideology, at times unwittingly, was Marcel Proust. The most succinct expression of the reverie—or fairy tale—on which Proust's position was based is a sequence in *Le côté de Guermantes*.[8] The scene is a restaurant in Balbec divided by the slimmest of partitions. On the one side, the "Hebrews"; on the other, "young aristocrats." Marcel enters, makes for the side of the restaurant reserved for nobility, but is ignominiously shunted into the other room; his humiliation (and physical discomfort) are all but total until Saint-Loup enters and sweeps Marcel blissfully into the warmth of the aristocratic section. That division between (Jewish) suffering and (French) salvation, I have demonstrated elsewhere, is a motif that is affirmed throughout Proust's writings.[9] It is cognate both with the opposition between life and art in *Contre Sainte-Beuve* and with the scenario of salvation-through-art in *La Recherche*.[10] It begins, in the novel, when all of life's ills are placed, in the good night kiss scene, under the sign of Abraham, Isaac and Sarah, continues in the protracted metaphor assimilating Jews and homosexuals as the world's "cursed races," and is perhaps most revealing in a later text in praise of Léon Daudet, in which Proust ponders the cruel imperative that has a Dreyfusard such as himself choosing *Action Française* as his sole newspaper, despite the injustices it espouses, out of sheer love of Daudet's vintage prose: "In what other newspaper is the portico decorated by Saint-Simon himself, that is, by Léon Daudet. . ."[11] "Art", in brief, in its opposition to "life" is as (French) style in its opposition to (Jewish) suffering, and the triumph of the former lay in its utter imperviousness to the latter.

But is not Proust's position, thus construed, almost identical to de Man's in the article under consideration? Between the fu-

ture novelist Marcel's rescue from the "Hebrews" of Balbec and de Man's affirmation of literature's salutary autonomy in relation to a desperately Judaized (*enjuivé*) world the similarity is patent. Indeed one might almost imagine de Man quoting Proust in support of his position. But, of course, he didn't. Not only is Proust not quoted, but in the list of exemplary French Jewish authors he is not even mentioned. For the mere mention of his name would have shattered de Man's argument that such writers were invariably second rate. This bit of dishonesty, I believe, is the most egregious moment in the article. For de Man was not unaware of Proust's stature; he is referred to as a major figure in several other pieces.[12] Yet in order to make his anti-Jewish point stick, he suppressed the principal item of evidence on the subject.

De Man's fling with anti-Semitism, that is, was not a good-faith error, but an indulgence in deception. His subsequent reputation for probity—exercised over the years in the discrimination between the first- and second-rate in American academia—no doubt deserves to suffer as a consequence. The relation to deconstruction, however, is another matter. Consider that the one figure of stature, Proust, who might have been quoted to bolster de Man's argument about literature's autonomy from a Judaized world was the one figure the mere mention of whose name would have destroyed de Man's argument. And that irreconcilable tension between the constative worth of Proust's testimony and the performative vice of its provenance is, I take it, as convincing a demonstration of a certain validity of deconstruction as one might hope to encounter. Deconstruction, that is—but the term is beginning to fray—provides as illuminating a reading of the shoddiness of de Man's text as one might want, and I see no reason to be anything other than grateful for it.

Might it be, however, that de Man's indifference to the Jews during the War was actually a function of his indifference to the "Jewish question" itself? The presupposition of "Les Juifs dans la littérature actuelle," the autonomy of literature in relation to political reality, paradoxically resurfaces in other articles in *Le Soir* in the form of admonitions to literary collaborators with the Nazis to return to their literature. Thus, an article (August 12, 1941) on Brasillach's *Notre Avant-guerre* begins, like the essay on the Jews, by establishing a water-tight distinction between (flourishing) art and (decadent) politics in French life, and warns that the eminently "sympathique" Brasillach, a leader of the Collaboration in Paris, was plainly out of his element when treating such matters as the triumph of national-socialism in Germany, the failure of the Popular Front in France, and the Spanish Civil War. Similarly, on November 11, 1941, we find de Man upbraiding Montherlant for *Solstice de juin,* the book that earned him an accusation as a collaborator after the war, with the following generalization: "there is no reason to grant men of letters such authority in an area of human behavior which manifestly escapes their competence. One is astonished by the naiveté and insignificance of certain of their judgments once they are stripped of the brilliant veneer they derive from their carefully elaborated form." Better, de Man suggests, leave such matters as the "spiritual" grounds of European unity to "specialists." Taken together, the three articles on Brasillach, Montherlant, and the Jews lead one to suspect that de Man's commitment was to the proposition that art was autonomous in relation to political life, and not to any view on the Jewish question. Of course, the fact that de Man was sufficiently opportunistic to tack his specious argument about the Jews onto the more fundamental proposition is not precisely a recommendation. . .

* * *

There is an odd sense in which the more insistent target of de Man's collaborationist articles is not at all the Jews, but the French. For what gives so many of the pieces for *Le Soir* a recognizably de Manian tone is a certain disabused skepticism as to the abilities of the majority of his audience to rise to the occasion they celebrate. On August 12, 1941, writing of Brasillach, de Man characteristically ponders whether the "French elite will be able to perform the about-face demanded by circumstances and adapt to disciplines entirely opposed to their traditional virtues." A month later (September 30), the new French literary generation is said to be "hopelessly mediocre." On October 14, observing the "incoherent convulsions" rocking France since the armistice, a skeptical de Man "can but formulate pessimistic views as to future possibilities." Perhaps the most explicit article to this effect is a review of a re-edition of Sieberg's *Dieu est-il français?* on April 28, 1942. De Man manifests "very little optimism as to the future possibilities of French culture." Given the "mystical age" Europe was about to enter, an era of "suffering, exaltation, and intoxication," France would plainly have to modify its secular cult of reason to survive. Worse yet, France in its chauvinism suffered from what de Man, following Sieberg, calls "un nationalisme religieux," a spirit the new Europe would not tolerate. The reference to "religious nationalism," the vice (of intolerance) anti-Semitism has traditionally found intolerable in the Jews, all but clinches the shift: de Man's obsession during the War was less the evil of the Jews than the inadequacies of the French: not Zionism, but what he calls "Gionism," the cult of the writings of the regionalist novelist Giono, is characterized as "detestable" (April 22, September 30, 1941).

The fact that the articles seem on the whole more consistently anti-French than anti-Jewish (the day after the piece on the irrelevance of the Jews de Man was capable of invoking Yehudi Menuhin as exemplary violinist) is worth recording not simply to set the record right. Rather it establishes an odd continuity between the earlier and the later writings. For in both his writings in French on behalf of the Nazi "revolution" among the Walloons in the 1940's and his writings in English on behalf of "deconstruction" among the Americans in the 1970's, the idiosyncratic discursive feature binding the two endeavors, each in furtherance of a radical cultural movement from abroad, is a pronounced pessimism regarding the abilities of his broader audience (the French in the 1940's, American academia in the 1970's) to muster the wherewithal needed to respond to the demands each movement was putting on them. Consider an admirable piece, such as "The Return to Philology" (1982), in this light. It concerns a deluded "resistance" to an invasion from abroad: "the final catastrophe of the post-structural era, the invasion of departments of English by French influences that advocate a nihilistic view of literature, of human communication, and of life itself."[13] This invasion is, in fact, part of a movement that is "revolutionary," for which reason local "resistance" to the occupation from abroad has been quick to organize. De Man asks: "Why, then, the cries of doom and the appeals to mobilization against a common enemy?"[14] And the first answer he comes up with is the havoc the "common enemy" is wreaking on a traditional investment in ethics: "the attribution of a reliable, or even exemplary cognitive, and by extension, ethical function to literature indeed becomes much more difficult." The new "return to philology," an apparently "revolutionary" restoration led from abroad, will, however, in all probability, know failure: "The institutional resistances to such a move, however, are probably insurmountable."[15] The new skepticism is so far-reaching as to spare not even itself: "One sees easily enough why such changes are not likely to occur." What remains is an unswerving commitment to an ideal whose glory, in defeat, will no longer be able to be denied even by its adversaries: "Yet, with the critical cat so far out of the bag that one can no longer ignore its existence, those who refuse the crime of theoretical ruthlessness can no longer hope to gain a good conscience."

Many who read "The Return to Philology" in the *Times Literary Supplement* in 1982 cannot but have been moved by its libertarian gesture of countering on their own traditional—philological, but also Harvardian—grounds those who would shut a younger generation of scholars out of tenure. Yet within the echo chamber excavated by Ortwin de Graef, the piece sounds almost like an unwitting parody of the position repeatedly voiced by de Man forty years earlier in *Le Soir*. Specifically:

1. The idiosyncratic phrase "crime of [theoretical] ruthlessness," used to characterize the "revolution" from abroad, however ironically pitched in 1982, takes on a sinister aptness in light of the *Le Soir* articles. It is one thing, that is, for Geoffrey Hartman, in *The New Republic*, to fault de Man for "underestimating the ruthlessness of the Nazi regime."[16] It is another, far stranger one for de Man himself to conjure up "ruthlessness" as the characteristic par excellence of the movement he was championing in 1982.

2. The skepticism as to the prospects of "deconstruction" in American academia is very much of a piece with the skepticism regarding the French—the broader audience a French-language critic of literature could not but be addressing—in Hitler's new Europe. It will be perceived that what binds "The Return to Philology" and its attendant texts to the articles of the 1940's is a chiasmus. In 1941–2, we have seen, a deluded resistance to the salutary revolution from abroad was the vice of the French; in 1982, "resistance" (to theory) was an American shortcoming in the face of a "revolution" coming *from* France. In each case, moreover, there was an enlightened enclave among the benighted recipients of the good news in whom de Man placed exceptional faith. On September 30, 1941, the future of Francophone culture lay for de Man with the Walloons: "I do not believe it a lack of objectivity to claim that the young are closer to this goal in Belgium than in France. . ." And again: "these books [by Belgians writing in French] are more attuned to the desired revolution than those presently being written by Frenchmen of the same age." At some level, one imagines, the Yale graduate students were cast in the role of the Walloons of the 1970's.

3. The traditional investment in literature's "ethical function," threatened by the new (theoretical) "ruthlessness" of the 1970's, serves as a reminder that de Man's articles for *Le Soir* were shot through with statements about ethics. Specifically, the repository of ethical wisdom in the West was the German novel: works of a Germany, it will be recalled, whose soul was essentially "Hitlerian." Whereas the French novel, we are told on August 5, 1941, is essentially "psychological," the Germans introduce us to a dimension that is ethical: "not a psychological drama, but a conflict between Good and Evil." By March 2, 1942, the Germans are said to be "un peuple moraliste par excellence," and their perennial investment in intervening in the "struggle between good and evil" has issued in the current "fine example of patriotic fidelity" on the part of German authors. No sooner, however, does de Man confront a German work of

apparently anti-Hitlerian tenor, Jünger's *Auf den Marmorklippen* (March 31, 1942), than he begins retreating from the centrality of the ethical dimension in German literature. True, the book is about the struggle between "Good and Evil," but it must not be confused with a "pale moralizing sermon." Moreover, "the conflict does not interest him [Jünger] for its ethical consequences, but as an inspiring pretext (*thème d'inspiration*), as a motif his imagination can translate into a sequence of images of sun, fire, and blood." Hitlerian Germany, that is, is essentially "ethical" until the issue of Hitler s evil is confronted, however indirectly, at which point the ethical is deflected into ultimate irrelevance. But that deflection of the ethical, at the hands of a new "ruthlessness," is precisely what is reaffirmed forty years later, in the face of a new resistance, in "The Return to Philology."

* * *

The superimposition of the 1982 text and the articles of the 1940's—however intriguing the chiasmus it enables (or is enabled by), however uncanny the return of the motifs of "ruthlessness," "skepticism" and "ethics"—remains, it will be objected, a mere formal exercise. Deconstruction, of course, is ill-suited to object to considerations of "mere form" (in the name of "substance"?), and at its most forceful will in fact be inclined to think matters of difference (say between the writings of the young and the mature Paul de Man) in terms of repetition. . . As a style of reading, that is, deconstruction is singularly ill-equipped to contain contamination by the articles in *Le Soir*. A generation that has thrilled to the intertextual oscillation, in Derrida's *Glas*, between the philosophy of Hegel and the erotics of Jean Genet, cannot, I believe, in good faith, claim that between the writings of de Man's youth and his maturity there is, in Hillis Miller's words to *The Nation*, "no connection."[17] Ultimately, the effort to spare "deconstruction" any contamination by de Man's collaborationist texts is dependent on reviving, on the whole without acknowledgment, the quaint notion of a *coupure épistémologique*. Thus Christopher Norris, in an attempt to demonstrate the "utter remoteness" of the early from the later de Man, falls back on the notion of the later work as an "ideological critique" of "organic" values and metaphors.[18] If dividing line there must be, of course, the critique of the organic is as good a theme as any around which to elaborate it. But not only is the notion of a *coupure épistémologique*—Althusser's dubious marriage, within the text of Marx, of a motif from Bachelard with Lacan's reading of Freud's "castration"—deconstructively problematic, it also fails to acknowledge the striking continuities: a scorn for the values of liberal—or individualist—humanism (see de Man's contempt, on January 20, 1942, for the French dream of "saving man"); the investment in dismantling binary oppositions (*Ni droite ni gauche,* it will be recalled, is the title of Sternhell's masterly study of Fascist ideology in France). . .[19]

The question of deconstruction-and-fascism, if there be one, however, is sufficiently idiosyncratic as not to be available to resolution in terms of thematic continuity or discontinuity. I refer to a phenomenon so glaring and so unacknowledged as to loom as something of a purloined letter over the entire debate: the fact that no fewer than three of the most sterling careers flanking deconstruction (that is, Derrida's own career) were profoundly compromised by an engagement with fascism. Indeed, my first fantasy upon hearing of De Man's writings during the war was of a caricature entitled the Passion of Deconstruction with Derrida on the cross flanked by Blanchot, crucified under the sign *Combat* on the one side, and de Man, suffering similarly beneath the rubric *Le Soir,* on the other. As for the Father-who-has-forsaken-him, the cruelest moment of the fantasy would have Heidegger, from whom Derrida received the word "deconstruction," flashing from above the Nazi membership card he did not relinquish until after the war. . .[20] Blanchot (in France), de Man (in the United States), and Heidegger (in Germany) are arguably the three most important contemporaries to figure in the international enterprise we have come to recognize in Derrida's work, the subject, in fact, of three recent books he has authored: *Parages* (1986) on Blanchot; *Mémoires: for Paul de Man* (1986); and *De l'esprit: Heidegger et la question* (1987).[21] My point is that "deconstruction" is centrally the thought of Derrida, that de Man's "deconstruction" was in many ways born of his relation with Derrida, and that the question of deconstruction-and-fascism (in de Man or elsewhere) is perhaps best broached in the works of Derrida, specifically on those thinkers, central to his writing, who had at one time or another invested in the ideology of fascism.

Now almost more striking than the fascist careers of our trinity (Blanchot until 1938, de Man until at least 1942, Heidegger throughout the war) is the role that dimension plays in the books Derrida has devoted to them:

1. Maurice Blanchot's writings for *Combat,* apologies for acts of terrorism against the "degenerate" government of Léon Blum, receive no mention in *Parages.*[22] Surely, in a writer as intent on assessing the radical heterogeneity of writing, the omission of such texts (which were known to Derrida) from a discussion of his work is troubling. More specifically, I have shown elsewhere, Derrida's failure to bring Blanchot's *Combat* pieces into play in a long reading of *L'arrêt de mort* (whose ac-

tion transpires in October 1938) has led to a failure to perceive the structuring role of the myth of Iphigenia in that novel and, consequently, to a misreading of it. . .[23] But for the moment, what is of interest is simply the omission of the fascist articles of the 1930's from the Blanchot texts discussed by Derrida in his book.

2. *Mémoires: for Paul de Man* is a moving work, written on the death of Derrida's friend, partially, perhaps, out of identification with Blanchot himself, whose *L'Amitié* was conceived in memory of Blanchot's departed friend, Georges Bataille. For its subject is, in part, "the unique, the incomparable friendship that ours was for me."[24] The book was written, of course, before the revelation of the articles for *Le Soir,* and thus makes no reference to them. Thus we are confronted with yet another book bypassing a politically nefarious past. And one wonders: was there no room in that "incomparable" friendship—or its record, *Mémoires*—for revealing writings of such importance? As if in unwitting mockery, Derrida's book (on the writings of a man who, one suspects, spent considerable energy forgetting his assent to a Nazi Europe) responds: "that he [de Man] existed himself in memory of an affirmation and of a vow: yes, yes."[25] Surely, to have gotten the configuration so *precisely* wrong is a feat worth pondering.

3. It is the third of Derrida's three recent books, however, *De l'esprit: Heidegger et la question,* which is most central to the question of deconstruction and fascism, since it confronts the issue of Heidegger's collaboration with the Nazis *dans le texte.* To what end? The book, it should be noted, is one of the most surprisingly and intricately conceived of all Derrida's works. For those who have lamented a certain predictability in the author's recent work, a reading of *De l'esprit* will serve as a reminder—indeed much more than a reminder—of the glory days of deconstruction.

Perhaps the book's import is best broached through a consideration of structure. We are presented with the discovery of a particularly liberating problematic, its subsequent repression, and a later (sublime) return of the repressed. The discovery—of an authentic interrogation of the being of *Dasein*—comes in 1927. Crucial to its consolidation is a relegation of mind (*Geist, esprit*) to the category of those (all too Cartesian) words that Heidegger would have one use only "in quotation marks." The repression comes in 1933 with the celebration of *Geist* or Mind—without quotation marks—as the motivating theme of the Fribourg Rector's Speech, traditionally regarded as the principal document of Heidegger's career as a Nazi. (What were "repressed," that is, were the quotation marks.) The sublime return of the repressed comes in 1953, in a discussion of Trakl's poetry, wherein *Geist* makes its reappearance no longer as a derivative of the Platonic *geistig,* but of the sacral, if un-Christian, adjective *geistlich. Geist,* in 1953, comes into its old-Germanic own as *fire: l'esprit,* in a phrase rife with Derridean indeterminacy, *en-flamme.*

Now concerning this scenario, the most surprising development is the reading of Heidegger's Nazism as a humanism. The appeal to mind, the forgetting of Being, or rather: the repression of the quotation marks, of the question of *écriture,* is read as an effort to save Nazism from its own biologism, to "spiritualize Nazism." And between the collaboration with Nazism and the lapse into humanist metaphysics, Derrida seems hard pressed to decide which is worse: Heidegger "capitalizes the worst: to wit, the two evils at once, the support accorded to Nazism and the still metaphysical gesture."[26] Simultaneously, in two long footnotes, Derrida is particularly severe on the great humanists of pre-Nazi Europe, Valéry and Husserl. The latter, in particular, is taken to task for a "sinister" passage in which "Indians, Eskimos, and Gypsies" are excluded from the realm of European spirituality.[27] The implication is plain: if Heidegger, to the extent he was a Nazi was a humanist, the humanists Husserl and Valéry, to the extent they were humanists, were racists. In strict logic, between Nazis and anti-Nazis, we are given little to choose. For which reason Derrida and his readers can only be relieved at the passing of the Nazi interlude—which is perhaps best characterized, within the logic of *De l'esprit,* as the Nazi-anti-Nazi interlude—and the reemergence of the original problematic (of 1927), in even more extreme form: it is within the splendidly and eminently *written esprit-en-flamme* of the 1953 meditation on Trakl that Derrida's Heidegger, one feels, and Derrida himself, come into their deconstructive "own." The Nazi-anti-Nazi interlude, within the logic of the book, was a misreading of 1927, comically beside the point, a ludicrous performance: "Here Comes the Rector!," one all but hears as Derrida hoists the curtain for his reading of Heidegger's *Rektoratsrede.*

Concerning *De l'esprit,* I should like to make two points, the first of which concerns an article of my own. In 1985, in "Writing and Deference: The Politics of Literary Adulation," I speculated that one unacknowledged ancestor of deconstruction might be Jean Paulhan.[28] Paulhan, a particularly adroit delver into the conundra of language, a former leader of the Resistance, became after the war a champion of the cause of amnesty for collaboration with the Nazis. His position was based on a—questionable—chiasmus. The crux of recent French history, he maintained, was that the majority of the wartime Resisters in France had long been trumpeting, prior to the war, their eagerness to *collaborate*—with the Russians; and simultaneously the majority of the Collaborators had long been preparing a resistance, in the name of French national values, against the Russians. Given that configuration, Paulhan claimed there could be no basis for moral outrage after the war against either group. His only regret, wrote Paulhan, was not being a Jew so that he might forgive France for not having defended him better. In my article, I suggested that the advent of deconstruction might be read speculatively as a fulfillment of Paulhan's dream of amnesty, retaining the irreducible form of the chiasmus, but voiding the political crux in which it was grounded. (That conclusion was somewhat misrepresented in a truncated quotation in the *Newsweek* article on Paul de Man.)[29] The reaction of deconstructors near and wide, I have been told, was less than enthusiastic.[30] In retrospect, however, *De l'esprit* strikes me as confirmation of my point. Between Paulhan, on the one hand, claiming his collaborators were originally resisters and his resisters collaborators, and Derrida, on the other, that Heidegger was a Nazi only to the extent he was a humanist and Husserl and Valéry humanists only to the extent they were (Eurocentric) racists, the continuity seems to be so substantial as to be conclusive.

My second point concerns the return of a radicalized *Geist* in 1953 as irreducibly metaphorical fire. For if the Nazi-anti-Nazi interlude was a misreading (of 1927), a deluded literalization of what is fundamentally figural or written (in quotation marks), then one is left with the sense that a literalization of the metaphorics of *das Flammende* (p.132) would similarly be beside the point. But note that for Derrida, the interpretation of old German *Geist* as more originary than Latin *spiritus* or Greek *pneuma,* is part of a "brutal foreclosure or exclusion" (p.165): of the primordial Hebrew *ruach.* In addition, Derrida goes to pains to modify the received translation of *entsetzt* in the Trakl essay: mind aflame does not merely *displace,* it *deports* (*déporte*) (p.158). Nazism, fire, exclusion of the Jews, deportation: does not the whole of Derrida's text, with its implied warning against any literalization of what is irreducibly figural (Heidegger's comic error in 1933), move toward a "deconstruction" of what has, after all, served as transcendental signified par excellence for two generations: the Holocaust? To read Derrida seriously is, I fear, to arrive at no other conclusion.[31]

* * *

To take Paul de Man seriously is to imagine him perennially vexed by his implication in the Nazi order, a wound, one hopes, that did not heal easily. What better balm for it than the philosophy that was to reach a brilliant culmination after his death in *De l'esprit*? For that, not *Mémoires,* is the volume, one suspects after the fact, which might best have been subtitled *For Paul de Man*. With its inability to find an anti-Nazi stance not always already contaminated by the rot of metaphysics (or racism: *la mythologie blanche*), its implied "deconstruction" of the Holocaust, *De l'esprit,* or the thought from which it emerged, was *the* solution to the ethical quandary one imagines de Man struggling with throughout his life.

One of the mythical moments of contemporary criticism, related by both de Man and Derrida, centers on their first encounter in Baltimore.[32] What brought them together was a shared interest in Rousseau's *Essai sur l'origine des langues*. But if ever there was a misencounter around a text it was this, for the two were manifestly working at cross purposes. This is clearest in de Man's misreading of both Derrida and Rousseau on the subject of music. For whereas the point of departure for Rousseau (and Derrida) is a denigration of harmony (resembling in its intervalic or differential essence writing) in relation to melody (as voice, plenitude, imitation), de Man gets things precisely backwards, maintaining that discontinuity—or writing—is on the side of melody ("a succession of discontinuous moments. . . chronology is the structural correlative of the necessarily figural nature of literary language"[33]). Once that position is consolidated, there is indeed little ground for any true dialogue on the text. All of which is to suggest that the mythical meeting of minds over Rousseau was perhaps steeped more deeply in myth than has been acknowledged. And that suggestion in turn, combined with our knowledge of the articles for *Le Soir,* leads one to speculate that the true meeting of minds, which of necessity never took place, was the one all but staged within the intricacies of Derrida's *De l'esprit*.

* * *

The popular press has seized on the similarities between the cases of de Man and Waldheim, and—from the failure to acknowledge past complicity with the Nazis to the exalted post-War eminence—such analogies are surely there to be drawn. Yet in retrospect the most instructive aspect of the link between the two cases is a fundamental disparity. For the election of Waldheim to the presidency of Austria, a country that provided three-fourths of extermination-camp commanders during World War II and committed 40 per-cent of all war crimes, was in important ways enabled by that sorry history: in electing Waldheim, Austria was in effect normalizing (if not exalting) its own Nazi past.[34] For the relatively small group of American critics affected by the de Man revelations, the situation has led to anything but a normalization. To the contrary: a generation raised in the belief that Nazism was evil—or *otherness*—itself

has suddenly been forced to negotiate the spectre of Nazism as it has surfaced, after the fact, from within their own identification with de Man. For many, it is not simply that the "great man" turned out to have collaborated with the Nazis, but that the individual they had, at some level, been bent on *being* (through an act of identification with either his person or the force of his signature on the letters of recommendation to which they owed their careers) turned out to have done so. And if he had, what of them? "Certain historic destinies place individuals before quite exceptional circumstances. . . ," wrote de Man in an article of June 17, 1941. We now know that de Man himself had such a fate. But how many of his adepts now feel secure that under identical (exceptional) circumstances they would not have acted similarly? That such a question should now be consigned to the realm of the "undecidable" is perhaps the final lesson of Paul de Man.

Unless, of course, the current polarization around the de Man case is further exacerbated. For there is a sense in which the present configuration resembles nothing so much as the final chapters of *Madame Bovary*: after the death of his beloved, Charles indulges in an orgy of sentimental grief, only to stumble one day on Emma's cache of adulterous love letters. A spell of "howling" and "sobbing" subsides into "somber fury," and then, as Charles puts the whole episode behind him, into a particularly degraded mode of the "dismal lifelessness" which has characterized him from the beginning. "It is the fault of Fate," is his final abject comment (in de Man's revised translation of the book) on the whole abortive episode. One can already hear, after the sentimentalities of the *Yale French Studies* tribute, the posthumous discovery of the pro-Nazi articles, and the "howling" that ensued, the academic equivalent of Charles Bovary's *mot*: So he was a Nazi. . . . That is: so what! That what has been called the "relativization" of Nazism, already well under way in academic Germany, might end up being an item on the agenda of American "deconstruction" is a particularly grim prospect. The fact that the opposition, momentarily riding high, is for the most part peopled by the academic counterparts of Monsieur Homais should, needless to say, be of no consolation at all.

Boston University

NOTES

1. Emmanuel Levinas, "Jacques Derrida/Tout autrement" in *Noms propres* (Paris: Fata Morgana, 1976), p.66. Levinas' essay originally appeared in an issue of *L'arc* (no. 54, 1973) dedicated to Derrida.

2. Concerning the havoc wreaked on psychological understanding per se by Hitler's *Blitzkrieg,* see, for example, de Man's article of December 23, 1941: "There was thus at no phase of the present conflict that installation in suffering . . . which gave the 1914 war its quite peculiar psychological aspect." Similar remarks on the "shock" of sudden defeat can be found on April 30, 1942.

3. Paul de Man, *Allegories of Reading* (New Haven: Yale University Press, 1979), p.63.

4. Geoffrey Hartman, "Blindness and Insight," *The New Republic,* March 7, 1988, p.31.

5. On the Belgian anti-Jewish decrees, see Raul Hilberg, *The Destruction of the European Jews* (New York: New Viewpoints, 1973), p.384.

6. The Riom trial of Léon Blum, which was going disastrously for the Collaborators, began on February 19, 1942, and was still in session when de Man's article appeared. See Jean Lacouture, *Léon Blum* (Paris: Seuil, 1977), pp.469–481.

7. On *Das innere Reich,* see Victor Farias, *Heidegger et le nazisme* (Paris: Verdier, 1987), pp.250–251.

8. The sequence is well discussed in J. Recanati, *Profils juifs de Marcel Proust* (Paris: Buchet/Chastel, 1979), pp.54–56.

9. See my *A Structural Study of Autobiography* (Ithaca: Cornell, 1974), pp.200–64, and my "Literature and Collaboration: Benoist-Méchin's Return to Proust," *MLN,* Comparative Literature Issue, 1983, pp. 968–982.

10. For a provocative reading of anti-Semitism as fundamentally a mode of estheticism, see Philippe Lacoue-Labarthe, *La Fiction du politique* (Paris: Christian Bourgois, 1987), pp.92–113.

11. Marcel Proust, "Léon Daudet" in *Contre Sainte-Beuve* (Paris: Gallimard, 1954), pp.439–440.

12. On May 17–18, 1942, for example, in *Het Vlaamsche Land,* "Contemporary Trends in French Literature," de Man wrote of Gide, Valéry, Claudel, and Proust as "the major figures, the leaders of the entire European world." In *Le Soir* itself, on June 9, 1942, Proust and Joyce are listed together as major innovators.

13. Paul de Man, "The Return to Philology," *The Resistance to Theory* (Minneapolis: University of Minnesota Press, 1986), p.22. The article originally appeared in *Times Literary Supplement,* December 10, 1982.

14. Ibid., p.25.

15. Ibid., p.26.

16. Geoffrey Hartman, op. cit., p.31.

17. Miller is thus quoted in Jon Wiener, "Deconstructing de Man," *The Nation,* January 9, 1988, p.23.

18. Christopher Norris, "Paul de Man's Past," *London Review of Books,* 4 February 1988, p.7.

19. Through a bizarre irony, deconstruction, at its most politically repugnant, has resorted to pairing off its "left-wing" and "right-wing" adversaries as equally deluded. I refer to Hillis Miller's vitriolic—and silly—presidential address to the MLA in 1986, well analyzed by Walter Kendrick in "De Man That Got Away," *The Village Voice, Voice Literary Supplement,* April 1988, p.7.

20. The most extensive available compilation on Heidegger's Nazism is Farias, op. cit. Of Lacoue-Labarthe's rather hostile critique of the book, the most important sentence appears to me to be: "as far as its documentary complexity is concerned, Farias cannot be reproached: the facts cited are, to my knowledge, incontestable." In *La Fiction du politique,* p.180.

21. *Parages* and *De l'esprit* were published in Paris by Editions Galilée, *Mémoires* in New York by Columbia University Press.

22. For a discussion of Blanchot's role among fascist intellectuals of his generation, see my *Legacies: Of Anti-Semitism in France* (Minneapolis: University of Minnesota Press, 1983), Chapter I, as well as Zeev Sternhell, *Ni droite ni gauche: l'idéologie fasciste en France* (Paris: Seuil, 1982), pp.241–242.

23. See my "Deconstruction, Literature, History: The Case of *L'Arrêt de mort," Proceedings of the Northeastern University Center for Literary Studies,* vol. 2, 1984, pp.33–53. Derrida's analysis of *L'arrêt de mort,* "Living On," first appeared in translation by James Hulbert in the collective volume *Deconstruction and Criticism* (New York: Seabury Press, 1979), pp.75–176.

24. Jacques Derrida, *Mémoires: For Paul de Man,* p.19.

25. Ibid., p.21. It is perhaps worthwhile in this context to quote the fundamental affirmation of the proto-Nazi "Kridwiss circle" in Thomas Mann's "Nietzsche novel," *Doctor Faustus,* trans. H.T. Lowe-Porter (New York: Random House, 1948), p.371: "It is coming, it is coming, and when it is here it will find us on the crest of the moment. It is interesting, it is even good, simply by virtue of being what is inevitably going to be, and to recognize it is sufficient of an achievement and satisfaction."

26. Jacques Derrida, *De l'esprit: Heidegger et la question* (Paris: Galilée, 1987), p.66.

27. Quoted in Ibid., p.95.

28. "Writing and Deference: The Politics of Literary Adulation," *Representations* 15, pp.1–14.

29. David Lehman, "Deconstructing de Man's Life," *Newsweek,* February 15, 1988, p.64.

30. See, for instance, Ann Smock's comments (along with my response) in *Representations* 18 (Spring 1987), pp.158–164. By virtue of having published my article, the editors of *Representations* themselves were consigned by Hillis Miller, in his 1986 presidential address to the MLA, to the benighted ranks of the "left-wing" adversaries of deconstruction.

31. That "deconstruction" or dispersion may already be at work in a moving page of Derrida's *Schibboleth: pour Paul Celan* (Paris: Galilée, 1986), p.83: "There is to be sure the known date of the Holocaust, that inferno of our memory; but there is a holocaust for every date. Every hour counts its holocaust."

32. See de Man, "An Interview" (with Stefano Rosso), *The Resistance to Theory,* p.117, and Derrida, "In Memoriam," *The Lesson of Paul de Man, Yale French Studies,* No. 69, p.14.

33. Paul de Man, "The Rhetoric of Blindness: Jacques Derrida's Reading of Rousseau," *Blindness and Insight: Essays in the Rhetoric of Contemporary Criticism* (New York: Oxford University Press, 1971), pp.131, 133.

34. Benno Weiser Varon, "Waldheim—A Post Mortem," *Midstream,* November 1986, p.18.

An Open Letter to Professor Jon Wiener

J. HILLIS MILLER

Department of English and Comparative Literature
University of California, Irvine, CA 92717
March 20, 1988

Professor Jon Wiener
Department of History
University of California, Irvine

Professor Jon Wiener,

I have been reluctant to write to you, since I think controversy among colleagues is likely to generate more heat than light, but both of us have responsibilities to the larger academic community and to wider communities as well. I wanted to wait, as I had recommended you should do too, until it was possible to see the full set of de Man's articles in *Les Cahiers du Libre Examen, Le Soir,* and *Het Vlaamsche Land* before writing. I also had waited to see if you would retract your article and try to correct its errors and unjustified insinuations. I know some at least of these have been pointed out to you by others.

I think your de Man piece is one of the most misinformed, distorted, and irresponsible of all the journalistic essays I have seen on this subject, and that is saying quite a bit. You will say that you allowed both "sides" to speak in your essay and gave your readers the opportunity to judge for themselves, but the "evidence" you give leaves no doubt what conclusions you would draw and would expect your readers to draw both about de Man and about so-called "deconstruction." What you have allowed to be published has done great damage to the possibilities of rational and informed discussion of de Man's writings and of the issues they raise, damage both in this country and in Europe, where your errors have, as you must know, been reprinted, picked up and compounded. Thousands and thousands of readers both in this country and in Europe will have read your article and the ones that copied it as an accurate reporting of the facts. If de Man must be held responsible for what he wrote and for the effects of what he wrote, as I believe he must, I believe also that you bear a great responsibility for the effects of what you have written. You will say that you wear two hats, one as a journalist and one as a historian, but surely your primary obligation is, or ought to be, the one common to both professions: the obligation to state the facts, responsibly and correctly. Your article has carried special weight and authority because it was written by a professor of history. Of course you are free, like everyone else, to pass judgment on de Man and his writings, and on "deconstruction" too, but surely this judgment should be based on an accurate identification of the facts to be judged and on a careful reading of the documents, particularly in a case of such gravity.

You quoted me correctly, as well as I can remember what I said. (It is amazing to me that you can think, as your recent letter to me suggests, that this is all I could find to quarrel with in your article.) You did not, however, heed my most important recommendation, namely that you should take the time to inform yourself about all de Man's wartime writings and about "deconstruction" before writing about it. You said when we talked on the phone, as I remember, that you had an urgent deadline and had to work fast. That may, sometimes, be an excuse for a journalist, who has time constraints, has no need to have expert knowledge about the subject on which he writes, and can work with opinions quickly gathered by phone, but it is not an excuse a historian can afford to make with anything he writes.

Your article is so full of errors, defamatory insinuations, and distortions that I hardly know where to begin in listing them. This includes what you say about "deconstruction," where almost everything you say is in error. It will be a tedious business to go through them all, but I shall try to do so. Since the errors of your essay have been so widely repeated and since the falsifications of so-called "deconstruction" in your article are exemplary of the characterizations that have appeared almost everywhere in the international media, it has a more than local importance to try to get things straight.

1) De Man died in 1983, not 1984, at age 64, not 65.

2) David Carroll has written you a letter about the "academic Waldheim" slur. It is an example of the ugly rhetoric of your essay throughout. What de Man wrote and published is so different from what Waldheim is said to have done that any analogy between them can only be said to be defamatory. In de Man's case it is a question of writing, publishing, and of the probable political effects of that.

3) The two articles—"in one of the articles . . . , in another"—in *Le Soir* on the 'Jewish question' you refer to are in fact one article. How could you have made that mistake? Had you really read the article in question? Your paraphrase of it is woefully inadequate and misleading.

I am not saying that elements of fascist ideologies (primarily a dangerous belief in intrinsic national and racial characteristics and a view of history as developing "organically") and support for collaboration with the German occupant are not present in what de Man wrote for *Le Soir* and *Het Vlaamsche Land*. They are. Nor am I saying that de Man should not be held to account for what he wrote and its probable effects. He should. I am saying only that much more than that is present in those writings

and that you present a distressingly inadequate report of what he actually said even in the group of writings available to you, I presume, even when you wrote your article—not to speak of the full set of writings. Did you really read them, or did you depend, as is clearly the case with de Man's later writings and with "deconstruction" generally, on what someone else told you they said?

4) It is simply foolish to insinuate that, because Hans Robert Jauss taught as a visiting professor at Yale, he and de Man were a couple of old Nazis conspiring together. Since Jauss has been invited to lecture all over the place in the U.S., including UCI, I believe, the guilt you ascribe to de Man would be pretty widespread. A look at de Man's essay on Jauss in *The Resistance to Theory,* rather than the few paragraphs on him in *Blindness and Insight* which you mention, would have sufficed to clear up the "matter of [their] relationship." The essay is by no means a eulogy. In fact it is quite critical of Jauss.

5) Kristeva's study of Céline is not anti-Semitic, but the reverse. Reading it—or even glancing at it in a hurry—might have saved you from making that mistake. De Man's praise of it has exactly the opposite meaning from the one you ascribe to it. He praises Kristeva's book for exposing the mechanisms of anti-Semitism.

6) You say, "Nevertheless, one can assume that the young journalist who urged isolating Europe's Jews on an island did not find the deportations of 1942 objectionable." Let's be serious—journalistically and academically—and read what it says. He did not "urge," nor did he "propose," anything. The sentence in "Les Juifs dans la littéraire actuelle" says, "En plus, on voit qu'une solution du problème juif qui viserait à la création d'une colonie juive isolée de l'Europe, n'entraînerait pas, pour la vie littéraire de l'Occident, de conséquences déplorables [In addition, one sees that a solution to the Jewish problem that would aim at creation of a Jewish colony isolated from Europe would not result, for the literary life of the West, in deplorable consequences]." That is a terrible thing to say, and it is terrifying to think of the way it may have given support to the deportations of Jews from Belgium that began over a year later. But you should explain what it says, not make things up. The article is restricted to what its title names, namely "contemporary literature," and comments only on "literary life." Rather than "urging" the isolation of anyone, de Man unequivocally condemns what he calls "vulgar anti-Semitism" and vigorously criticizes the "myth" of a Jewish "pollution" of European literature. And he lists Franz Kafka among the four most important authors of modern literature. It is in fact an implicit condemnation of the other articles adjacent to de Man's in this special

page of *Le Soir* on "the Jewish question." These other articles, a hideous one on "Les deux faces du judaïsme," an attack on Freud, and a vilification of "la peinture juive," represent just that "vulgar anti-Semitism" which de Man vigorously rejects in his own article.

In addition, there *is* another article which raises, from a rather different angle, similar "questions." I gather you were not able to read this one, given your deadline, for had you read it you could not have failed to take notice of it. This one reviews a book on Charles Peguy, and begins with a fairly extensive recounting of Peguy's role in the Dreyfus Afffair. De Man praises Peguy for his wholehearted defense of Dreyfus and his commitment to egalitarian socialism. He was a "Dreyfusard *jusqu'à bout,*" writes de Man, with evident approval. Historians would surely understand the significance of the appellation "Dreyfusard" in that time and place. How about a little respect for history, and some attention to the documents?

7) You quote Jeffrey Mehlman, whom you call "a practitioner of deconstruction" (!), as saying that de Man's articles in *Le Soir* "plugged the Nazi hit parade." The reality is far more complex. Did you give a journalistic glance, or cast a historian's gaze, at these articles, so as to verify the interpretation of your source? Did you look at de Man's articles on Montherlant's *Le Solstice de juin* (11 November 1941), on Brasillach's *Notre Avant-Guerre* (12 August 1941), or on Drieu's *Notes pour comprendre le siècle* (9 December 1941)? Even a brief inspection would have revealed, for example, that de Man is extremely critical of the political views expressed in Montherlant's book and insolently attacks his qualifications as a political and historical commentator. The other two are just as unkind. How did you miss them?

Your account of de Man's political position in those articles is a one-sided distortion of a complex matter. To say, as you do, that "out of a sense of malaise, of having been defeated by history," "the young de Man became a Fascist," lock, stock, and barrel, is simply wrong, not to mention unhistorical, and could not be based on a reading of the articles in question—which is, after all, what we are talking about. And it is your account that has been repeated all around the United States and in Europe by journalists who have taken your word for it. Perhaps because you are a professor of history as well as a journalist, and therefore speak with authority, these other journalists have made no attempt to read de Man's writings themselves or to verify the accuracy of your report.

8) If you had been truly interested in exploring the question of whether "Paul de Man became a Fascist," or in actually reporting on his political convictions, there were other options open to you beyond the time-consuming reading of all those articles. Sometimes journalists interview witnesses. Surely relevant here is the testimony of two people who knew de Man during the war, Charles Dosogne, the first editor-in-chief of *Les Cahiers du Libre Examen,* of which de Man, as you know, was editor in 1940, before the Occupation, and Georges Lambrichs, a Belgian writer who was a close friend of Paul de Man in his early years and who after the war became an editor at Minuit and Gallimard in Paris. Two or three telephone calls and you could have quoted the former affirming that he never heard de Man, neither before nor during the war express a single anti-Semitic opinion or attitude. Or the second asserting that de Man was "anything but a collaborator," and that he had assisted French resistants in publishing and circulating a publication prohibited by the Germans in Paris (with texts by Eluard, Bataille, etc.), called *Exercice du silence*.

Sometimes journalists read other newspapers. A short walk to the library and you could have read in Belgium's biggest newspaper (the present-day *Le Soir,* 3 December 1987, p.4) the words of an anonymous third person who knew de Man during the war (later identified as a certain Georges Goriely) and who, he said, had been at that time "*clandestin,* mêlé à la Résistance." "According to our source," wrote the newspaper, de Man was "idéologiquement, ni antisémite, ni même pro-nazi." Goriely told the Belgian reporter that he never (*jamais*) feared at all that de Man, who knew he was linked to the Resistance, would denounce him.

All of this information was not difficult to come by, surely not for the contributing editor of a journal with a reputation for breaking tough stories. Certainly not for a journalist with a sharp eye for "revelations" that would "shock and dismay." Not to mention for a historian. That is just the point I am making: in a matter of this gravity a historian has a responsibility to get as many of the facts as possible and to get them right, even to wait a little when it is known that important additional documents will soon be available, to make a few extra telephone calls, to be prepared to be patient, to take the time to read and to think before passing judgment. [Note added August 11, 1988: In the months since this letter was written a great deal more testimony has come in from those who knew Paul de Man in Belgium during the war. This new information confirms the fact that if de Man was not a member of the Resistance he nevertheless cooperated in their work. It now appears, for example, that de Man probably lost his job with the publishing agency Dechenne in the spring of 1943 precisely because he had helped arrange the publication there of the Eluard, Bataille, et al. volume *Exercice du silence*.]

9) Then there is the topic of the supposed "hero worship" of

de Man by students and colleagues in the sentences you quote from Frank Lentricchia. You will say that you did not say this, that you were just quoting your sources accurately, but surely even a journalist has a responsibility not to pass on errors and defamatory insinuations. What you quote Lentricchia as saying is a condescending slur on all those students and colleagues who studied with de Man, read his work, and found it indispensable for their own work. You, with Lentricchia's help, imply that they were hypnotized by some kind of charismatic personality, as Mario was by the magician in Thomas Mann's allegory of the rise of Italian fascism, "Mario and the Magician." The facts are far otherwise. Charismatic teachers are abundant at the universities in which de Man taught. It takes more than that to attract the sustained attention of all those brilliant students and colleagues of such diverse orientation in literary study. The fact is that it was, and is, de Man's learning, rigor, and original insight into major works by Proust, Rousseau, Kant, Hegel, Wordsworth, Baudelaire, Yeats, and many others, into literary history, into the working of language generally, literary and otherwise, into the relation of literature and history, into literary history as such, and into literary theory that attracted students and colleagues to read his essays and attend his seminars. These features of his work will continue to draw serious students of literature to read his work.

Whatever de Man wrote in 1941–42, there is nothing whatever fascist, anti-Semite, or politically reactionary in what he wrote and published after 1953. Quite the reverse is the case. In fact I should say, now that I have had time to read those "early writings" and think about their relation to the later work of de Man, not that there is no connection between the two sets of writings, as it appeared to me when we talked by phone last January, but that the relation is one of reversal or putting in question. The special targets of his radical questioning of received opinions about particular authors, about literary history, and about the relation of literature to history in his later work were just those ideas about these topics that recur in the articles he wrote for *Le Soir*: notions about specific national and racial character and about the uniqueness of each national literature, notions about the independent and autonomous development of literature according to its own intrinsic laws and according to a model of organic development, that is, according to what he called in his latest essays "aesthetic ideology." Now having access to those "early writings," I have a better understanding of the urgency with which de Man advised me, the first time we met, in 1966, not to read the later Heidegger but to go back to *Sein und Zeit* if I wanted to read Heidegger, or the equal urgency with which he vigorously put in question, at a conference

that took place in Zürich about 1969, some ideas I proposed in a paper about the organic development of the novel toward greater and greater sophistication and complexity. I was prepared to believe that those ideas were in error, but reading these newly discovered "early writings" has given me a new understanding of what is potentially at stake politically in what might appear to be merely "academic" questions.

But already the articles in *Le Soir* present evidence of a transformation under way or of an intellectual battle within de Man's mind, for example in the difference between "Les Juifs dans la littérature actuelle" and the article on Charles Peguy published only two months later. One might in fact apply to his own case what he says of such changes in a review of a novel by one Herman de Man, *Maria et son charpentier*. Speaking of the implausibly rapid transformation from evil to good of the protagonist of this novel de Man says: "Presque toujours, le changement dans l'âme du personnage est présenté d'une manière trop brusque et trop rapide, alors qu'elle traînera en réalité sur longues périodes de transition durant lesquelles des forces contraires se disputent dans le coeur du héros" (4 March 1941). Nor is it the case that de Man's writings after 1953 are all of a piece, any more than the writings of 1941–42, though, as I have said, there is no trace remaining of the nationalist and organicist ideas of the "early writings" in the writings after 1953, except when they are identified as ever-present temptations in literary studies that must be vigorously contested. De Man's work was continually passing beyond positions previously held, and for a period of a decade or more after 1953 his work was within a region that might be called "phenomenological," in which the important categories were consciousness, intentionality, and temporality, though already with anticipations of the interest in figurative language that marked his work after the mid-sixties. The major essay, "The Rhetoric of Temporality," presented at Johns Hopkins in 1967, marks a turning point to a new phase. Thereafter the key terms in de Man's work tended to be linguistic ones: allegory, metaphor, prosopopoeia, rhetoric, irony, the distinction between constative and performative uses of language. Attention to history, politics, and to what he called "aesthetic ideology" becomes more explicit in his latest work, though it was present all along, especially in his constant concern to put in question the validity of period terms and the global generalizations they codify. "Romanticism" and "modernism" were his special concerns in this research.

Whatever de Man wrote in 1941–42, these later writings make him one of the most important literary critics and theorists of his time, indispensable reading for *our* time too, for reasons I shall try to specify later. Testimony to his importance is the fact that Mehlman, Lentricchia, and others of his hostile critics have been and remain fascinated by his work, obsessed with it, full of envy of it and resentment toward it. It is *their* fascination that is an inverse hero worship, not the sober reading, assessment, and practical use of his work by students and teachers all across the country, for example by the authors of the essays in *Reading de Man Reading* (edited by Lindsay Waters and Wlad Godzich, forthcoming from the University of Minnesota Press), or in the recent balanced essays by Geoffrey Hartman (in *The New Republic*), Jacques Derrida (in *Critical Inquiry*), and Jonathan Culler (forthcoming).

10) Then there is what you say about "damage control" and the publication of the "early writings" in French. I was present at that meeting in Tuscaloosa. The collective decision was to acquire good copies of all of de Man's writings of 1941–42, to distribute them in photocopy to anyone interested, and to publish them with all possible speed so they would be widely available. You speak as if you think doing that was a way of hiding them—by publishing the original documents, in facsimile, in their original language. Think about that—it is an outrageous suggestion, and a strange thing for a historian to say. Surely you know that waiting to translate 400 pages of material would have taken a very long time. Now the articles—all the articles [including some discovered as recently as June (11 August 88)] —will be available this fall, providing a reliable basis for a reasonable discussion, and a translation, of all those pages. Our decision was for the utmost possible speed in making all the writings widely available. Does that sound like "damage control"? What sort of historian calls complete republication of original documents "damage control"? Is it "damage control" to try to correct and persuade you to retract the errors and defamatory insinuations of your article?

11) The number of articles by de Man in *Le Soir* is of course not 92, as your incomplete information in January led you to say, but 170, as well as a careful search has been able to determine. These will all be included in the forthcoming University of Nebraska Press volume, along the ten articles published in *Het Vlaamsche Land* and the three earlier texts from *Les Cahiers du Libre Examen* [as well as the even more recently discovered articles in the *Bibliographie Dechenne* and in the prewar socialist student newspaper *Jeudi* (11 Aug. 88)].

12) Moving on now to what is the real center of your article, and of all the others around the world that have repeated your falsehoods, namely an attempt to discredit and obliterate so-called "deconstruction" by making it continuous with de Man's supposed total commitment to fascism:

First, what you say about so-called "deconstruction" and

Heidegger. You speak of Jacques Derrida, absurdly, as the "founder" of "deconstruction," as though it were a bank or a "school," in any case some kind of identifiable "it," and then go on to say two more utterly erroneous things. First, you say that "Heidegger's commitment to Nazism was much stronger than has previously been realized." In fact, as the serious European reviews and comments have shown, Farias' book has added little new to what has already been known for decades. Second, but much more heinous, especially in its context, is your false assertion that Heidegger is "the German philosopher acknowledged by Derrida as the intellectual progenitor of deconstruction." The facts are far otherwise. Both de Man and Derrida have been consistently, carefully, patiently critical of what Heidegger says. Heidegger has been one of the major targets of so-called "deconstruction," not its progenitor. De Man's "Tentation de la permanence," an essay of 1955 (well before he knew any work by Derrida, by the way) is a major essay exposing Heidegger's submission to a mystified aesthetic ideology. Another de Man essay rejecting Heidegger's belief that poetic language, as exemplified in Hölderlin, could speak "Being" directly, is "Heidegger's Exegeses of Hölderlin" (also 1955). Moreover, Derrida's *De l'esprit: Heidegger et la question* (1987) had been published when you wrote your article, not to speak of many earlier essays by Derrida on Heidegger, so you had had an opportunity to read them, if you had cared to learn something about the topic on which you were writing. *De l'esprit* is the best book I know that shows through careful reading of Heidegger how a certain fascist nationalism enters deeply into Heidegger's late philosophical works, not just into the *Rektoratsrede*. It is an instructive book. You should read it if you are interested in Heidegger and fascism.

13) What is worst, most defamatory, about what you say about Heidegger and so-called "deconstruction" is that it is part of the assertions about "deconstruction" that are in fact the essential message of your article. The sequence of implied arguments or enthymemes goes like this, in a crescendo of errors: De Man was a fascist through and through in his "early writings." In his later writings he was a "deconstructionist." His "deconstructionist" writings are all of a piece with his "early writings." Therefore all deconstructionists, including Derrida and me (I as "the leading deconstructionist in the United States and a friend of de Man," Derrida as the "founder" of "deconstruction"), are fascists. Moreover, Derrida has admitted that Heidegger, a fascist philosopher, is the "progenitor" of deconstruction. Therefore we come back again to the conclusion that all deconstructionists are fascists, including the two "leaders" mentioned. After you have published this, do you really expect

me to sit down with you and have a friendly little chat about your article, as one of your notes to me suggests we should do. Let's be serious!

14) The sequence of false argumentation that leads to that terrible implied accusation against me, Derrida, and all others who have worked in this mode of literary and philosophical study, goes by way of and depends absolutely on the account you give of so-called "deconstruction," with the help of Said, Mehlman, and Lentricchia. It is erroneous throughout. Everything you say about so-called "deconstruction" and about de Man's later writings is false, except your quotations from Esch, Hertz, and Graff. You will say that this is not your fault, that you informed yourself as best you could (mostly by way of phoning some self-proclaimed opponents of so-called "deconstruction"), but of course you had an obligation, particularly in view of the gravity of the charges you were bringing against "deconstruction," to get it right, to learn enough about the topic to know what you were talking about. And you do speak for yourself in your description of "deconstruction" at the bottom of third column, p.22, and top of first column, p.23, of your article. There you repeat the most erroneous clichés of previous journalistic accounts. Let me try to identify these.

a) With all respect for my good friend Edward Said, I do not recognize the work of de Man, Derrida, or myself in what you quote from him. Are you sure you quoted him correctly? In any case, in de Man's work or Derrida's, "rhetoric" and "stated content" are not separated in the way you quote Said as saying, nor is it true that the "deconstructed meaning" (whatever *that* means) "locates itself" "in the range of decidable meanings." Said may have given a valiant try at a capsule definition, but, assuming you quoted him correctly, I would have to say he did not get very far toward a correct or coherent definition, though I do not suppose he intended to be other than helpful. To say of the so-called "deconstructionists," as you say Said said, that "their whole point is that their positions are not paraphrasable" is ridiculous. It would be as difficult to "paraphrase" in a sentence or two Said's argument in his admirable *Beginnings* as it would be to paraphrase in a sentence or two de Man's *Allegories of Reading* or Derrida's *Of Grammatology* or his recent *De l'esprit*. There is nothing whatsoever scandalous or unique to "deconstruction" in recognizing the difficulty and inherent dangers of oversimplification and outright falsification in attempting to paraphrase a complex intellectual position.

b) The next paragraph, where you are more on your own, is much worse. You show no understanding of what is at stake in saying a war is a text. One of de Man's main points in his later work was that words have a terrible power to bring about what

he called "the materiality of history." The effect of journalism, both of de Man's wartime writings and of what you and other journalists have written now about de Man, is a good example of that. As a good Marxist historian, as I am told you pretend to be, you surely do not believe that all those civilians in Nicaragua have been getting killed because the Contras and Sandinistas have been out having a little target practice? Or that we were in Vietnam for reasons that had nothing to do with words and the ideology expressed in "texts." Those wars, like all wars and revolutions, are "textual" through and through.

So-called "deconstruction" does not by any means "presuppose" that "literature is not part of knowable social and political reality," or that "one must be resigned to the impossibility of truth." Quite the reverse is the case. "Deconstruction" is in all its many forms a contribution to knowledge by being a contribution to good and accurate reading of "social and political reality" as well as of literary and philosophical texts and of the relation between the former and the latter. You must have picked up your ideas from an earlier article in *Newsweek* or some such source. You could never have learned them from a careful reading of even one work by de Man or Derrida.

Nor is "deconstruction" "nihilistic." Again, just the reverse is the case. I have written about the charge that "deconstruction" is "nihilistic" in my essay in *Deconstruction and Criticism*. "Nihilism," if it means anything precise, rather than being just a polemical name for something we do not like and want to call by a harsh word, is the name of a moment intrinsic to Western metaphysics when the highest values are devalued by the vanishing of what had seemed their necessary transcendent ground. Nothing could be further from that than the commitment of de Man, Derrida, or myself to a rigorous truth-telling about the nature of language, about the meaning of major texts in the Western tradition, about the relations of literature or philosophy to history.

Nor is "deconstruction" in any way "implicitly authoritarian," as you charge. Again the exact opposite is the case. Deconstruction works to free people from ideological mystifications and aberrancies, for example deeply ingrained notions about the organic development of literature as a separate "aesthetic" realm, or, on the other hand, the notion that a work of literature is entirely determined and can be entirely explained by its historical context. Far from being "authoritarian," "deconstruction" functions in manifold ways to free us from totalizing and totalitarian thinking, thinking, for example, that makes "deconstruction" one single, homogeneous, monolithic thing.

c) Your next paragraph repeats two of the most common and

most erroneous clichés about deconstruction, namely that it makes criticism "the creative activity of the period" and that it says "the critic [can] create meaning." This is your version of the false notion that deconstruction is an extreme form of "reader response" criticism and that it holds texts mean nothing in themselves, so the critic is free to make them mean anything he or she likes. Again, the exact opposite is the case. In his "Foreword" to Carol Jacobs' *The Dissimulating Harmony,* de Man, citing Hölderlin, gives full authority to the text to determine what happens in any act of reading that text:

What makes a reading more or less true is simply the predictability, the necessity of its occurrence, regardless of the reader or of the author's wishes. "Es ereignet sich aber das Wahre" (not *die Wahrheit*) says Hölderlin, which can be freely translated, "What is true is what is bound to take place." And in the case of the reading of a text, what takes place is a necessary understanding. What marks the truth of such an understanding is not some abstract universal but the fact that it has to occur regardless of other considerations. . . . Reading . . . has to go against the grain of what one would want to happen in the name of what has to happen; this is the same as saying that understanding is an epistemological event prior to being an ethical or aesthetic value. (p. xi)

d) Your account of "Excuses," de Man's essay on Rousseau's *Confessions,* is erroneous throughout, as is your account of what de Man means by "allegory." De Manian allegory has nothing to do with hidden autobiographical elements in a text. As for "Excuses," even if one were to read this essay as a disguised autobiographical confession, an extremely dubious, unauthorized, and unauthorizable procedure, however tempting it may be as a way to avoid reading what de Man really said, the meaning of the essay would still be the exact opposite of what you make it mean. The essay would give no comfort whatsoever to de Man himself or to anyone else who might hope to use a speech act to exonerate himself from some prior act. "Excuses" focuses on the disjunction between performative and cognitive dimensions of language. It says that, for Rousseau at least and perhaps in other cases too, an excuse is a performative use of language that never works. Far from functioning to free the excuser from a prior guilt, the excuse repeats the crime or even commits the crime from which it would free the excuser. "Excuses generate the very guilt they exonerate," says de Man, "though always in excess or by default," and "No excuse can hope to catch up with such a proliferation of guilt" (*Allegories of Reading,* p.209).

e) I turn, finally, to what you say, with the help of Frank Lentricchia, about the way de Man supposedly cuts off literature and literary study from history. Once more, what you say is the exact contrary of the truth. Far from being "antihistorical," de Man was in all his work, early and late, passionately concerned with the relation of literature to what he came to call "the materiality of history." De Man explored with great insight the ways in which literature makes history rather than just reflecting it, and he had a deep sense of the way apparently innocuous errors in conceptions about literary history and about the relation of literature to history as such (what he called "aesthetic ideology") can have disastrous political effects. One of his last and as yet unpublished essays, on Schiller, is extremely explicit about this, but the concern for history is manifest everywhere in what he wrote, for example in "The Resistance to Theory," when he says: "This does not mean that fictional narratives are not part of the world and of reality; their impact upon the world may be all too strong for comfort," or when, in an interview a few months before his death, he says, in response to Stefano Rosso's observation that the terms "ideology" and "politics" are now appearing frequently in his writing and lectures: "I don't think I ever was away from these problems, they were always uppermost in my mind. I have always maintained that one could approach the problems of ideology and by extension the problems of politics only on the basis of critical-linguistic analysis, which had to be done in its own terms, in the medium of language, and I felt I could approach those problems only after having achieved a certain control over those questions" (*The Resistance to Theory,* pp.11, 121). Those who affirm that de Man has no concern for history are really objecting to a vision of history that differs sharply from their own and that threatens their assumptions about the relations of literature and history.

This brings me to the concluding section of what I have to say. Why is it, exactly, that so-called "deconstruction" in particular and literary theory generally have been so violently attacked and so falsely described in your article and in the other journalistic ones? Why is it that the falsehoods have taken just the form they have taken, the claim, for example, that so-called "deconstruction" is anti-historical, nihilistic, and says works may be made to mean anything the interpreter wants them to mean, when in fact exactly the opposite is the case? Why is it that the discovery of these "early writings" by de Man has produced a violent outpouring of these clichés, a somnambulistic repetition of just these received opinions, as in the case of your article, written as if by a ventriloquist's dummy through whom a programmed procedure of thought control is speaking? Just why is that so many supposedly responsible newspapers and weeklies leaped to condemn de Man without waiting to read what they were writing about—not to mention making a careful review of the evidence—and why is it that all made the move to condemn so-called "deconstruction" as something that would follow logically from the condemnation of de Man, again without waiting to read and reflect, to sift the evidence, as if one could say now, "Ah ha, we knew it all along, but now we have the proof: deconstruction is fascist"? Why is it that though *The Nation* is supposedly liberal or on the "left," so many newspapers and weeklies on the "right," even the extreme right, have leaped eagerly to repeat the falsehoods in your article? Why is it that the authors of so many of these attacks are, like you, professors as well as journalists, professor-journalists who use the prestige of their university positions to promulgate these falsehoods? Just what is at stake that would lead to the wholesale suspension of the ordinary rules of academic and journalistic responsibility?

No doubt this outpouring of falsehood is "overdetermined." It has many and perhaps contradictory "causes" and concomitant conditions, including, no doubt, plain stupidity and ignorance, though these would not account for just the form the errors have taken. But the essential reasons I think can be identified. As de Man himself put it one of the last times I saw him, a few days before his death, "the stakes are enormous." He was speaking, first and most immediately, of a deplorably ignorant and malicious essay by René Wellek in *The New Criterion* accusing de Man and others of "Destroying Literary Studies." A copy was on de Man's bedside table with a friendly inscription from Wellek. It attacks not only de Man, but also Derrida and me, and so-called "deconstruction" generally, more or less in the same terms as you do and repeating more or less the same falsehoods, gathered as far as I can see from the mass media and from academic gossip. It certainly could not be based on a careful reading of what we have written. You might want to reflect on what it means that a so-called Marxist historian like you finds himself allied with a conservative like Wellek who publishes in a place like *The New Criterion* against what seems to you both a common enemy. I shall have a bit more to say about that later.

But de Man's reference when he said "the stakes are enormous" was also to the wider context of the perpetual war on behalf of good reading (that is, rhetorical reading, or, to give it another of its more recent names, so-called "deconstructive" reading) as a major defense of literary studies and of other precious aspects of our culture against the ever-present danger of various sorts of totalizing or totalitarian thinking. Make no mistake about it. The real target of your article and of the other journalistic ones that preceded it and followed it, in the *New York Times,* in *La Quinzaine littéraire,* in the *Frankfurter Allgemeine Zeitung,* in various university newspapers, etc. is,

whether consciously or "unconsciously," explicitly or implicitly, deliberately or by a somnambulistic happenstance, not de Man's early writings or his personality, but the kind of work with which his name is associated, that is, so-called "deconstruction," and, beyond that, literary theory generally—as the extension of the attack, in the *Newsweek* piece, from so-called "deconstruction" to the so-called "new historicists," what that piece, quoting Frederick Crews, calls "the new militant cultural materialism of the left," and as a recent attack, in *The Wall Street Journal,* on the Duke English Department for destroying canonical literary studies, unmistakably demonstrates.

In the name of what standards, implicit or explicit, does this league of the so-called left with the so-called right in American and European journalism take place? The clear aim of the writing on both political "sides" is to discredit and obliterate, as far as possible, de Man's work as a whole and that of his associates, to prevent it from being taught and students or anyone else from reading it. From that it is an easy step to a wholesale condemnation of literary theory generally. You will say that your article ends by saying no more than that "a revaluation of the politics of deconstruction and the writings of de Man is now at the top of the agenda of both the deconstructionists and their critics," but that, in its context, does not imply a rereading of de Man's work, only an acceptance of the juridical procedure of condemnation you have outlined in your article. Insofar as you are a Marxist theorist, as I am told you are, you were shooting yourself in the foot, as they say, by writing and publishing your article against de Man and "deconstruction," since you were participating, whether deliberately or inadvertently, in the current attempts to suppress theoretical reflection generally about literature and about the relation of literature to society. De Man's work is an invaluable part of that reflection, necessary reading, for example, for those young Marxists and Foucauldians, some of whom I named in my MLA Presidential address; necessary reading, for example, for those who want to understand what might be meant by the "material base" in its relation to ideology. Once again, it is a question of reading and of the taking of responsibility. And once again, it is de Man himself, in this case in one of his most powerful essays on the relations of literature, theory, history, and ideology, "The Resistance to Theory," who has in his later work said something essential on this topic, as on so many others in this region of thought and action:

. . . what is it about literary theory that is so threatening that it provokes such strong resistances and attacks? It upsets rooted ideologies by revealing the mechanics of their workings; it goes against a powerful philosophical tradition of which aesthetics is a prominent part; it upsets the established canon of literary works and blurs the borderlines between literary and non-literary discourse. By implication, it may also reveal the links between ideologies and philosophy. (*The Resistance to Theory,* p.11)

De Man's formulations here help us to understand the violence of the outpouring of denunciations of de Man and of "deconstruction" based on errors of the sort I have identified in your essay. The violence is a reaction to the genuine threat posed by de Man's work and by that of the so-called deconstructionists generally to a powerful tradition of ideological assumptions about literature, about history, and about the relation of literature to human life. Fear of this power in "deconstruction" and in contemporary theory generally, in all its diversity, accounts better than any other explanation for the unreasoning hostility, the abandoning of the canons of journalistic and academic responsibility, in articles like yours and the many other subsequent attacks on de Man, on "deconstruction," and on critical theory as such. Insofar as the received opinions deconstruction challenges are "aberrations" and "mystifications," and they are that, they are exceedingly dangerous, politically and ethically, as all falsehood is. Insofar as literary study is politically, socially, and ethically useful, deconstruction as a form of such study performs a fundamental work of what might be called the "critique of ideology." It is not surprising that the resistance to it should be so strong, but it is also the case that the health of our culture depends on the presence of the lessons of deconstruction within what is most vital and productive in literary and cultural study today.

J. Hillis Miller

Resisting, Responding

KEVIN NEWMARK

Je ne pouvais savoir s'il s'agissait d'une question ou seulement d'un ordre, d'un encouragement. Comme j'avais l'impression que ces mots ne s'adressaient pas précisément à moi, je ressentais à leur égard une certaine liberté, celle de pouvoir, le cas échéant, y répondre légèrement, moi aussi . . . c'est une effrayante épreuve . . . à qui n'a rien, elle demande; celui qui répond à sa demande ne le sait pas et, à cause de cela, ne répond pas . . . l'appel a toujours lieu, il n'a pas besoin qu'on réponde, il n'a jamais réellement lieu, c'est pourquoi il n'est pas possible de lui répondre. Mais celui qui ne répond pas, plus que tout autre, est enfermé dans sa réponse.--*Maurice Blanchot*

Ordinarily, that is, under so-called normal circumstances, we understand the role of the respondent to be one of informing and interpreting; because of a privilege that is certainly temporal but also perhaps one of perspective or point of view, the respondent occupies a place of mediation between an event, often textual, and the potential meaning of such an event.[1] The respondent's job is first to bring to light and then possibly to reflect on those elements of an event, or a text, that can most effectively be used to initiate the process of its future interpretation or understanding. To respond in this sense requires certain skills and a certain amount of instruction or learning so that the process by which the event actually takes place can then be communicated in an accurate and intelligible way by the respondent to those for whom he is speaking or writing. But it can also happen that somewhere along the way, due to unforeseen circumstances, things change, and that therefore the respondent is no longer to be understood in this way as a mere reporter or interpreter. It can happen that the respondent has not so much been invited to speak to a neutral and disinterested audience of fellow hermeneuts as summoned or even subpoenaed to answer or testify in a court of law composed of a judge and jury; let us not forget that only a slight change of context is needed to make a respondent over into a defendant. And this can happen even when your name is not literally printed in the docket.

This, of course, is the strange story—which is also, at least to some extent and in a certain way, the impossibility or collapse of all story-telling—that befalls the anonymous narrator in Blanchot's *La Folie du jour* (*The Madness of the Day*).[2] Written in 1948, the text deals with someone who discovers to his surprise that he is not, or is no longer dealing directly with the light, with the light of day, *le jour,* conceived at once as daylight and the light of understanding. The narrator, responding to a solicitation that remains unspecified in the first pages of the text, begins to tell a kind of autobiographical story whose possibility is predicated on the light: "I am not blind, I see the world and that is my extraordinary good fortune. I see it, this day outside of which there is nothing. Who can take that away from me?" (20) This day, outside of which we are at first told there is nothing, is equally capable of illuminating the formative "paths of youth" as it is of descending and penetrating at a different stage the depths of library books and the "somber spirit" of their meanings. And whatever the initiative to which he is responding, the narrator seems at first perfectly capable of using the day retrospectively to bring these facts to light in his own text and then to reflect on them: "Those I have loved, I have also lost . . . I was, however, and almost all the time, extremely happy. That gave me something to reflect on" (20). The surprise is that this pattern of informing and interpreting, of bringing to light and reflecting on, is radically interrupted when the story comes to an episode in which the light itself becomes eclipsed by the question of the day, and when the text slips from being a simple autobiography to becoming the official transcript of a police interrogation. But what can it mean to refer to the "question of the day" in this way? In this text it seems to suggest both the fundamental question posed *by* the light as such, the principle and source of all luminosity whether physical or intelligible, *as well as* the purely idiomatic, topical question that finds itself at this particular moment in the light, or in the air. The "light," which allows the story to be told, is put into question in the course of the story, though we should not assume too quickly that we know whether this occurs because the text's principle of articulation has become for the first time a genuine source of critical reflection or because it has merely been blotted out in the precritical confusion of immediacy and ideology.

How, then, is the light of day put into question in this text? On the thematic level, it seems to happen as the result of an unsettling *collision*. The light, the day, the truth of the day, "having stumbled against a *true event*," was rushing toward its end (24). Something takes place here, an actual event, an event so cataclysmic and threatening that the light of day itself can no longer support itself against this event. This, according to the narrator, is the beginning of the end, the end of the light, *la folie du jour,* and it also coincides here with the institutionalization of the narrator; that is, it coincides with his confinement within a medico-penal as well as a linguistic institution, for the law prescribes not only that he be incarcerated, but also that he tell with clarity the story of how it came to be that he has now been deprived of his light and freedom. What kind of "true event" could possibly have produced such a situation? Does the narrator eventually tell the story in such a way that it would allow us to identify this event?

In an essay on Blanchot that claims merely to be following the commentary of Levinas, Jeffrey Mehlman answers these questions by identifying the "originality" of the story with "its articulation of an (anti) metaphysical figure with a political and historical meditation."[3] According to Mehlman, then, the metaphysical figure here would be that of the sun, whose "madness" consists of a subversion of phenomenology from within its own system, while the historico-political reality that reflects this philosophical madness would consist primarily, though not exclusively, of the representation in the text of a Nazi concentration camp, and thus of the holocaust. On a purely formal, thematic level, the identification of the holocaust as the historically "true event" that would somehow correspond to the meta-

physical disruption of the turning of the sun, its occidental movement through history, and the solar light of cognition, is provocative and deserving of reflection. However, part of the difficulty connected with the reading of Blanchot's text is that it is precisely these formal links between the categories of the "metaphysical" and the "historico-political" that are being put into question and subjected to reformulation by the narrative. By claiming that *La Folie du jour* provides a simple "*articulation*" of the (anti-) metaphysical ("the knell of philosophy") and the empirical ("the glass in the eye"), Mehlman's own narrative makes a theoretical delirium and a social insanity back into an unquestioned metaphorical figure in which each half blindly mirrors the other. The essential question raised in Blanchot's text by the "collision" and eventual undoing of the specular relationship between the metaphysical (light, clarity, reason, theory) and the empirical (a true event) is itself erased in Mehlman's attempt to reattach them in a metaphorical genealogy that would account for a certain form of "French literary modernity" by turning it into the direct and easily recognizable offspring of "French fascism in the 1930's" (817).[4]

The question of the holocaust, precisely because of its seriousness, is not simply assumed in this text, either to liquidate it or to monumentalize it on the basis of an unexamined metaphorical model of experience and consciousness. It would be more accurate to say that this text attempts to deal with the holocaust in such a way that it would not simply disappear (and for this same reason possibly reappear) under a specular, metaphorical, and ultimately fictional logic of denial and affirmation. This, at any rate, is what Blanchot actually does say about the holocaust in a series of fragments to be found in another text, *L'Ecriture du désastre* (*The Writing of the Disaster*). The first question to be asked seems to approach the holocaust as obliquely and problematically as *La Folie du jour,* addressing itself at the same time to Mehlman's reading of the earlier text:

> *Why is it that all misfortunes, finite, infinite, personal, impersonal, those of right now as well as of all times, have had as substratum (pour sous-entendu), recalling it incessantly, the historically dated, yet undatable misfortune of a country already so reduced that it seemed almost effaced from the map, and whose history extended beyond world history? (débordait l'histoire du monde?) Why?*[5]

Without yet responding, "the holocaust," this fragment already points to the system, the constellation of terms, in which such a name by necessity functions, though perhaps not without disrupting its internal coherence. The system that is composed by these terms is History, a system of dates and maps whose principle of articulation is the question: Why? This question asks about the meaning, the "whys and wherefores" of what is not, or not yet (fully) *understood,* that is, it asks about an event that underlies and participates in the meaning of all else, but is itself only *sous-entendu,* incompletely registered or understood. The question questions the status in History of this one event that seems to exceed the dates, the maps, and even the history of meaning that it makes possible. And in so doing, the question of this event finally questions the question itself, questions History as a meaningful system of question and response: *Why why?*

The question, then, asks about the one event that is presupposed, implied, and recalled by every other event in history, without in its turn being explained or understood by any of them. By responding, "the holocaust," to this question, however, nothing has been responded, and the question returns elsewhere:

The unknown name, outside nameability:
The holocaust, history's absolute *event, historically dated, this all-burn in which all history was set ablaze, in which the movement of Sense was engulfed (s'est abîmé), in which the gift, without pardon, without consent, (où le don, sans pardon, sans consentement), was ruined without giving way to anything that could be affirmed, or denied, gift of passivity itself, gift of that which cannot give itself. How to watch over it (comment le garder), even in thought, how to make of thought that which would watch over the holocaust in which all was lost, including watchful thought (y compris la pensée gardienne)?* (80)

It would be more than just a mere error to understand this to mean that because all the events of history somehow presuppose the holocaust, because it is history's "absolute" event, the holocaust itself, dated and mapped out with all possible historical precision, was inevitable and therefore in some sense excusable. The holocaust was neither inevitable nor excusable, nor was anything that contributed to it inevitable or excusable: such an event, in Blanchot's terms, is quite clearly *sans pardon, sans consentement.*

And yet, and yet, to read Blanchot more closely is to be made unavoidably aware that the discourse that refuses to grant pardon or consent is itself only part of the question, a part that, no matter how necessary, is still necessarily preliminary and incomplete: that is, such a refusal still does not refuse enough. For if the "excuse" would sidestep the grievousness of the event on the basis of a retrospective logic of "inevitability," then the "*sans pardon*" would be required by the same token to mediate the "absoluteness" of the event in a logic of "free choice" that could somehow be re-established in a temporality *prior to* the event itself and that would be seen to lead up to it. But it is precisely the oppositional logic of affirmation and denial that rules such distinctions between "inevitability" and "freedom" that is disrupted by the absolute event of the holocaust: *The holocaust, history's* absolute *event in which the movement of Sense was engulfed, in which the gift was ruined without giving way to anything that could be affirmed or denied.* What is irretrievably engulfed or undermined (*abîmé*) is the movement of Sense or meaning as oppositional logic of sense and non-sense, what is ruined (*ruiné*) is the *don,* the possibility of determining between the opposition "free" and "unfree." The logic of the "excuse" and the *sans pardon* requires a hermeneutics of something like the gift: that is, it works within a movement of Sense that would be free to slip behind the holocaust *as such* in order to reconstruct the coherence of a logic and a story that would finally permit a determination of "inevitability" or "freedom" for the relationship between the holocaust and any given sensible or non-sensical event. To some extent, then, such a hermeneutics always requires the freedom to make the actual holocaust into a "hypothetical," even "fictional" rather than "absolute" event: for the sake of the excuse or the *sans pardon,* recourse has to be made to the familiar procedures of Sense and the free/non-free oppositions of the *don* that were implicated and undone by the absolute event of the holocaust. But to take the holocaust seriously is to take into account its actual occurrence: because it actually did occur it is now too late for such "fictions," and so we are no longer free to return to the same kind of "sensible" historical discourse ("the movement of Sense") that *may have been* possible before the holocaust, though even this possibility becomes unverifiable after such an event. In order not simply to remain at this stage of the "hypothetical" and to dispose in this way of the radicality of the event that is the holocaust—which would also be another way of remaining too much *within* it—it becomes a question of moving beyond the logic of affirmation and denial, of sense and non-sense, and of developing another kind of discourse, one that articulates the difference the holocaust actually makes to both "sense" and the "gift." To come back to the question of "sense" and the "gift," but by way of the holocaust, requires a different kind of "thought," one which, according to Blanchot, "would be able to watch over the holocaust in which all was lost, including watchful thought."

We are getting closer to the question of the question, the response, and the kind of responsibility engaged by all these questions. For if the question is always a question of meaning (*Why?*), then, as we have seen, the responsibility to the holocaust would require, also in part, questioning this question—*why why?*—by *not* responding to it within the same logic of question/response, a logic that is no longer wholly legitimate since it is always predicated, at least in part, on a movement of sense which is itself no longer to be left unquestioned. "Can the disaster be interrogated? Where to find the language in which response, question, affirmation, negation, intervene perhaps, but are without effect?" (43–44) How to respond to the absolute disaster of the holocaust, then, without merely responding, and without therefore confirming the system of sense that was to be questioned, that was in fact questioned by the absolute event of the holocaust? Such would be what Blanchot also refers to, "abusively, impossibly," as the "other" responsibility, or as the responsibility of the "other" philosophy:

Not to respond or to accept a response, such is the rule: which is not enough to prevent the questions. But when the response is the absence of response, the question in its turn becomes the absence of question (the question mortified), the word passes, comes back to a past that has never spoken, past of every word. (54)

"When the response is the absence of response, the question becomes in its turn the absence of question": such is not a call to some form of facile irrationality (47), nor is it an abdication of any relationship to meaning whatsoever (86), nor is it the passivity of quietism (31), but it is rather the formula for a thought and a responsibility: for that alone which watches over, *garde* or *veille,* the specificity of a past which has never spoken the language of question and response, the past which passes into every word, but as its absent sense, its ruined sense, its asemic sense, its disaster. To say, as Blanchot never tires of saying, that the *passivité* (passivity) that watches over this *passé* (past) is *writing* is to say something infinitely more and infinitely less than an absence of response, at least until one has taken the trouble to respond, as Blanchot himself is constantly doing, by reading writing.

"Reading writing," how is that to be read? A first and indispensable reading of such a proposition is straightforward: *One cannot respond until one has read that which has been written.* Or: *Only by reading what has been written does one respond.* Such a reading is indispensable, for without it, without connecting the predicate "reading" to both the subject "responding" and the objective complement "writing" in order to produce a grammatically correct and coherent proposition, the most aberrant and wilful misunderstandings can take place, and in any number of directions.[6] But even when such reading has taken place, it is still not enough, for in its very project of forming a meaningful statement it does not take into account the unformed or absent sense of the disaster which Blanchot situates *in* writing: "To write, to 'form' in what refuses form an absent sense (*'former' dans l'informel un sens absent*) . . . To write is perhaps to

bring to the surface something like absent sense, to make way for the passive push (*accueillir la poussée passive*) that is not yet thought, being the disaster of thought" (71). A reading that would not take account of such a "disaster," or "absent sense," in writing always stops short of the question of the holocaust, even when it seems to be writing about nothing else. So it is necessary to read writing differently, necessary to allow the absent sense to come to the surface, necessary to leave a space in reading writing for the abyss that is thought's disaster. Such a space unsettles the connections and coherency of grammatical units and produces a reading that could no longer be conceived in passive opposition to writing, as though we knew already what kind of activities both "reading" and "writing" were, as though we knew what the "abyss" were.

"Reading writing for the abyss," then, can no longer name a reading that is able, actively or passively, and on the basis of a simple *desire* or *understanding,* to jump over the asemic abyss of the disaster that is inscribed in writing. It would begin instead to name a kind of reading whose own passivity is not opposed or receptive to any other activity. Such a reading responds to the abyss of writing by not (just) responding to it, in other words, it responds to the "other" passivity of writing with an "other" passivity of its own. What would such a reading writing be?

There is an active reading, productive—producing text and reader, it carries us beyond (*elle nous transporte*). Then the passive reading that betrays the text, by appearing to submit to it, by giving the illusion that the text exists objectively, fully, supremely: wholly. Finally, the reading no longer passive, but of passivity, without pleasure or joy, would elude both comprehension and desire: it is like nocturnal watchfulness, 'inspiring' insomnia in which the 'Saying' beyond the all is said (*le 'Dire' au-delà du tout est dit*) would be heard and in which the testimony of the last witness would be pronounced. (157–58)

Reading does not actively produce a writing that was not yet there, nor does it passively submit itself to a writing that pre-existed it fully and objectively. According to this fragment, reading eludes both comprehension and desire, and in so doing becomes a kind of witness to the "saying" that does not stop when all seems to be said and done: reading is a "saying" that extends writing beyond all that has been said. Reading allows writing to be heard by allowing the abyss that is written beyond all that is said in comprehension and desire to be heard. It is, in fact, the testimony of the last witness to this absent sense, and this is a very grave thing to say in a text that is called *l'écriture du désastre* and that speaks of the holocaust. It may mean that late in the night, after all the other witnesses have spoken or written, then something like reading will also have to be heard and that it, reading, is the last in terms of importance and urgency. But it may also mean that it is already very late and that there is no longer any witnessing whatsoever outside of reading, that all other witnessing—saying, writing—must now go by way of reading.

"Reading writing," then, is a witnessing of the abyss, but how precisely does it testify to this? For Blanchot, and for all those who come after the holocaust, that is, for us, reading writing cannot simply disclose this abyss as a "something" (sense) or a "nothing" (absence, non-sense) that could ever be read passively in order at some later time to respond to it (actively and perhaps by writing). Reading writing is itself the *passivité* that witnesses or watches over the "absent sense" that passes into every written word now read: *l'écriture du désastre*. And the way that reading writing witnesses or watches over the words' absent sense, says Blanchot, is in a *cry* of silence: "*How to watch over [the holocaust] . . . how to make of thought that which would watch over the holocaust in which all was lost, including watchful thought? In the mortal intensity, the elusive silence of the limitless cry*" (80). How to read: A writing and a crying whose absent sense is excessive with respect to all language: "The cry, like writing, tends to exceed all language . . . the patience of the cry, that which does not stop with non-sense, while remaining nonetheless outside of sense, a sense infinitely suspended" (86). For those who read writing after the holocaust, the ruin of infinitely suspended meaning passes into the silence of writing's limitless cry: *le sens absent passe dans le silence du cri innombrable de l'écriture*. Such is the risk of our responsibility. It is a risk because the suspended sense it speaks of threatens in a very real way to make of the most serious of questions the most frivolous and perversely meaningless. It is not the limited threat posed to sense by non-sense, which can always be recovered retrospectively by a calculated return to sense. The risk here would be the far more threatening possibility that there would no longer be a vantage point from which to tell sense and non-sense apart, that their suspension as an opposition would be excessive, infinite. And this is *our* responsibility because it is only on the condition of such a risk that it is possible to watch over the absolute suspension of sense threatened by the holocaust. For it follows that a kind of discourse that (mistakenly) believes itself to be once and for all sheltered from such a risk of meaning's perversion, rather than its mere destruction, believes itself by the same token (and just as mistakenly) to be absolutely sheltered from the perversion of meaning that was the holocaust. Such infinite shelter, were it attainable, would preclude the possibility of witnessing and watching over that from which it would be sheltered.

L'écriture du désastre/le silence du cri: the silence of the cry in which, Blanchot tells us, the holocaust can be watched over, becomes readable in the writing of disaster. And this absent or suspended sense of the holocaust becomes readable there beyond any calculable logic of affirmation or denial, beyond any calculable procedure of comprehension or desire. It becomes readable in the undermining and perversion of sense and in the ruin of the gift, of the freedom to decide between free and non-free. It becomes readable in the *cri* that lies silently at the heart of *écriture*. Such is the risk of reading writing. For how would it ever be possible to calculate with certainty the overdetermining effect of these seemingly random and gratuitous letters *c-r-i* within the deadly and intensely serious logic of Blanchot's text? To respond adequately to this question it would be necessary, in this one text that names and discusses the holocaust, to decide and reflect on: 1) whether the crucial relationship that links *écriture* and *cri* to the watching over of the holocaust is freely motivated by a privileging of the concept "wailing" over the concept "writing," or vice-versa; 2) whether the play of the letter, which is discussed in this text with respect to the configuration "passivité/passion/pas," is purely idiosyncratic and senseless in this particular case, and thus is not intended to play a semantic role here. It would be necessary to decide, in short, whether *c-r-i* are mere letters that have not yet begun to function as meaningful language, or whether they are already the words of a kind of language that always and everywhere signifies a "wailing" over its disaster. Such a decision is not simply possible, we have no language in which to speak of the conditions of language, to speak meaningfully of the moment in which meaningless letters become meaningful words, in which inarticulate cries become meaningful writing: "The cry, like writing (*le cri, comme l'écriture*: the cry which is like writing, but also, perhaps, the cry conceived *as* writing), tends to exceed all language, even if it can be recovered as an effect of language" (86). For a mere "effect" of language could never be used to account for that language's very possibility.

And yet, whatever we think of it, however we try to dispose of it, this "collision" in Blanchot's text of a "reflection" on the holocaust with an absolutely random "event" of the letters *c-r-i* is *true*, it actually does take place, even *at the risk* of turning the absolutely essential question of the holocaust into mere wordplay, into the most horrible degradation of the absolute event it would watch over. But contrary to a facile kind of thinking and an outmoded kind of logic, the question of responsibility cannot even be broached in connection with the holocaust short of facing up to the occurrence of such an absolute threat to meaning. Or rather, short of this threat, that the most essential question become the most perversely meaningless and futile of exercises, the concept of responsibility can only represent a hypothetical and therefore deluded return to a thinking and a logic made forever inadequate by the holocaust. To take the risk of an actual responsibility by reading writing, though, is not to decide its outcome in advance, is not to respond by assuming that it is possible to know in advance whether *l'écriture du désastre*—the writing about the holocaust as well as the writing the holocaust will have become for us—will itself turn out to be a meaningful question or a futile exercise. To raise the question of reading writing, of the *cri* in *écri*ture, for instance, is not the same as celebrating it or denouncing it. It is to respond to it by not resisting it, or to resist responding to it by answering for it, as though all actually were said and done and could as a consequence be duly celebrated or denounced. For this reason, it is a responsibility oriented toward the *future,* a responsibility that suspends the response to reading writing into the space of a future that resists anticipation, predictability, calculation. Such a responsibility is therefore also a kind of promise.

It is not a promise in the sense that it promises *something*; such promises belong to the outdated logic of programmability and totalization that makes any "future" theoretically superfluous because knowable in advance. The claim to mastery implicit in such systems of thought is also implicitly totalitarian in its pretension to saturate and account for all unpredictable factors, and in its refusal to tolerate the openness of a promise that does not yet know what it is promising. We already know the outcome of such totalizing promises, and they do indeed deliver exactly what they promise: they make the future theoretically superfluous by making it empirically intolerable. The responsibility of reading writing, on the other hand, is promising only to the extent that, and as long as, it can make no promises whatsoever about its own future as promise. In Blanchot's terms, it is a form of language that eludes both comprehension and desire, and for this reason it remains unpredictably open to the openness of its future.

To take a risk, to give one's word, to speak of responsibility, to point toward the future, to promise: what kind of response is that? And especially when one has been asked only to recount and reflect on the facts of the past, to tell a story. Is it possible to make a story out of such "events"? These are some of the questions asked during the course of *La Folie du jour,* or rather, some of the questions of the day to which the text, *La Folie du jour,* responds. The narrator of the text gives two versions of response. One version seems to be the story of his life and the events he

has been a party to, and this includes or is subsumed by his recounting to the medical and legal authorities of how he watched as the day went mad, how the light of day was interrupted and was on the verge of going out. The other version, which is more or less disruptive with respect to medico-penal surveillance, speaks of a different kind of response, when silence entered into the words and they began to speak by themselves. Perhaps also when they began to watch over and to promise, without knowing what it was they were promising precisely because they were promising only that which had never been heard or seen: "no . . . never again."

Yale University

NOTES

1. An earlier version of this paper was delivered as a "Response" to a special session on Blanchot and de Man at the MLA in San Francisco, December, 1987.

2. Maurice Blanchot, *The Madness of the Day/La Folie du jour,* bilingual edition. (Barrytown, New York: Station Hill Press, 1981). Page references will be in the text, translations are my own.

3. See Emmanuel Levinas, "Exercices sur *La Folie du jour*" in *Sur Maurice Blanchot* (Paris: Fata Morgana, 1975) and Mehlman, "Blanchot at *Combat*: Of Literature and Terror," *MLN* 95, p.822.

4. Mehlman is perhaps excessively modest in subsuming his commentary on *La Folie du jour* under Levinas'. Not only does Levinas nowhere claim a simple articulation in Blanchot between the metaphysical and the empirical, he goes out of his way to caution against such a straightforward collapse: "*La Folie du jour* pourrait donc être dit libre de toute limitation temporelle au sens courant du terme, si la non-liberté—mais la non-liberté moins libre que tout déterminisme et que toute tragédie—une non-liberté infernale—n'était pas le propos de ce texte" (59). The question of the "non-free freedom" of Blanchot's writing from referential codes based on metaphor is treated at length by Levinas in the first section of the essay, "De poésie à prose." The question of the non-free freedom of writing is treated by Blanchot, among other places, in *Celui qui ne m'accompagnait pas* (Paris: NRF/Gallimard, 1953).

5. *L'Ecriture du désastre* (Paris: NRF/Gallimard, 1980), p.64, Blanchot's emphasis.

6. One of the very first misunderstandings comes about with respect to the question of the holocaust and language. "Reading, writing the holocaust": is it not derisively irresponsible to link the holocaust in this way with the question of language? "After all, it is

all a question of language." Is such a thoughtless cliché not the height of arrogance and lunacy? But is there an alternative to making such a cliché into a thought and a responsibility? If there is any access to the experience of the holocaust can it be conceivable independently of the question of language? As communication, as memory? "Mais le danger (ici) des mots dans leur insignifiance théorique, c'est peut-être de prétendre évoquer l'anéantissement où tout sombre toujours, sans entendre le 'taisez-vous' adressé à ceux qui n'ont connu que *de loin ou partiellement* l'interruption de l'histoire. Cependant, *veiller* sur l'absence démesurée, il le faut, il le faut sans cesse, parce que ce qui a recommencé à partir de cette fin (Israël, nous tous), est *marqué* de cette fin avec laquelle nous n'en finissons pas de nous *réveiller*" (134). Whose acquaintance with the holocaust—here, now—would not be at a distance, partial? Coming to terms with the "marks" of this distance—and the specificity of *all* the ways such "marks" can occur, can be registered—such would be the responsibility of a watchfulness and a waking.

Rigor Vitae

RICHARD RAND

I

*   Over the past eight months, these questions have come to mind: was Paul de Man, in his wartime writings, pro-Nazi? Was he pro-fascist? Was he pro-German? Was he anti-Semitic? anti-French? pro-Belgian? a propagandist? a collaborator? a *résistant*? an opportunist? a boy? a nephew? a man?

*   These questions, which will not, and must not, relent, are bound to go nowhere if they do not touch, from the very first, a place of serious import. Some of us cannot, in the first place, lay any *immediate* claim to the issues or the stakes of Paul de Man's wartime scene; to ignore this fact is to invent a fantastic solidarity with colleagues and friends whose *donné,* perhaps, starts elsewhere; it is to ideologize. We owe this quickly forgotten (if obvious) insight to Paul de Man himself, who, in his essay on the poetry of John Keats, observes that "Romantic literature, at its highest moments, encompasses the greatest degree of generality in an experience that *never loses contact* with the individual self in which it originates" (emphasis added).

*   When Jacques Derrida calls the last paragraph of "Jews in Present-day Literature" an "indelible wound," he also issues an utterance, a silent appeal, from a place of serious import: "do not delete, do not obscure, do not defuse this word—this delible word 'indelible'—or the notable thing it becomes (the name for the wound I have received)." At first I discounted this phrase and took, as it were, the side of de Man's "youthful errors": "How," went the thinking, "could Derrida *take offense* at the crude moves of a foolish and driven young man? To what *standards* does he hold de Man?" Such a response imagines that Derrida "took offense," though he never, in fact, did any such thing (he received an indelible wound), and it also forgets that the wound is not one but *two*: the wound of the insult is wounded by the wound of de Man's "mutism." We should also add that the "standards" in play are not, in reality, "standards": they are the Law of unconditional Friendship, authorizing us to share the story of our misdeeds as a guard against harm to the alliance itself. Not to have done so argues in de Man an utterly intransigent *decision*—not to be moved or touched by the understanding and trust of a singular colleague.

*   Granted that an alliance can be undone when one of its parties omits to *die in advance* for the other (see the essay by Derrida on *Romeo and Juliet*), how was Derrida to reconcile, after the revelation last August of de Man's wartime writings, the Law of Friendship with the alliance thus transgressed? By announcing the event of an "indelible wound", by owning and signing that wound, Derrida made it a lever, a springboard, a *mochlos* for launching the Law of Friendship itself on its multitudinous paths through the non-Law.

* De Man also obeyed the Law. To the spirited letter of the Law he was absolutely, even madly, faithful—as the essays of the past thirty-five years so tenaciously demonstrate. A singular statement of such devotion is the study from *Blindness and Insight* entitled "Ludwig Binswanger and the Sublimation of the Self": in the space of a few paragraphs, we read the narrative of a trial, complete with courtroom, judge, jury, charge, verdict, sentence, and the faithful execution of that sentence, fulfilling the observance of the Law. It is unavoidable to discern the figure of de Man himself between the lines of this account; he stands there convinced and convicted, a figure of conviction set off by the bars of his own *Sprachgitter*.

* In the article on Binswanger, where we shall tarry for a short while, de Man phenomenologizes a classical (and a metaphysical) opposition between the *vita activa* and the *vita contemplativa*; he does so in terms of a horizontal and vertical "spacing" that recalls de Quincey's account of "the literature of knowledge and the literature of power." It also reads like a letter from jail by Boethius or John Bunyan. The pertinent points are these:

1.) *The Crime (horizontal)*: "It is possible to lose oneself in the distance, to be waylaid in the world of action to the point of criminal transgression." Though the concept here of "loss" allows for any transgression, de Man includes, among the possibilities of the "transgressive," the "world of action" itself as the most general possibility: the "world of action" is itself a Great Crime *in potentia*. A mark of its criminality is the possible irresponsibility of all "action"—its undecidable culpability, as indicated, in the sentence cited above, by the uncertain syntax of the phrase "to be waylaid" (who is the agent of this hold-up? is it the person who "loses his way"? the "world of action" itself? some unthinkable third party?). As a scene where ethical agency declines to be fixed, the "world of action" is always already convicted—of precluding univocal conviction. It precludes the strict observance of that most sacred of Laws, *Ratio quique Reddenda* ("Each man must give an accounting").

2.) *The sentence*: The mere knowledge of this predicament, the recognition of "action-as-crime," becomes itself the sentence-for-life *of* the crime. It is marked by a mood which "combines an idea of being locked up in too narrow a space, with the temporal ordeal of being steadily urged on," a "mood of harassment and oppression that oppresses a self imprisoned within its own facticity."

3.) *Doing time (vertical)*: de Man points out that this "prison" becomes, for those who have it in them to decide (the prisoner serving as judge, jury and warden), the occasion of its own effectual change, of its own release-without-escape; for the prisoner "aspires" upward, and his aspiration takes the unremittingly ascetic and negative form of intellectual labor, the labor of "constituting the self" in its verbal realization. At the minimum, the artist abstracts himself from the world of "action," to pursue a kind of work that is pure "act": in de Man's words, "The work is a hyperbole in the Mallarméan sense, demanding that the subject forget itself in a projective *act* that can never coincide with its own desire. . . . (The thinker) *acts* like an adventurer in entering a domain that he knows to lie beyond his own reach" (emphasis added—to mark the abyss dividing an "act" from "action"; We are someday to be schooled in a theory of "speech acts").

4.) *The death penalty*: Paul de Man's entire post-war oeuvre is composed under the threat of death—under a penalty of death which imposes itself at the moment when the labor of the negative "act" ceases, or pauses, or suffers its sense of purpose to relax. Throughout his essay on Binswanger (to which I have done, be it mentioned in passing, an impardonable *violence* in the drive for point and for brevity; these comments are not to be read as responsible paraphrase), de Man makes a repeated, an obsessive issue of the hazards attached to the literary enterprise: it "requires a difficult and constant effort of interpretative vigilance;" it calls for sacrifice, in which "family, place of birth, psychological and sociological conditions, all (have) to fade before the project of a future literary work"; it never recuperates its losses, for "the sacrifices and renunciations that are demanded from the writer are not to be understood as a kind of bargain in which false values are being traded for safe ones"; it intends a radical economy of ends and means, called, by de Man, a "reduction": "(it is) the intent of the constitutive self to reduce itself to its own immanence," and "to clear itself"—not of its crimes, for these are its grounds and its premises—but "of whatever, in consciousness, is not entirely immanent to it . . . resist(ing) any temptation of being distracted from its own self" (emphasis added).

To this *distraction*—which is, in fact, his very "penalty of death"—de Man gives, in keeping with the *vertical* orientation of this enterprise, the names of "lapse," "relapse," and "fall": "we fall prey," he remarks, "to an almost irresistible tendency to relapse unwittingly into the concerns of the self as they exist in the empirical world;" or again, "the kind of knowledge contained in art is specifically the knowledge of this fall, the transformation of the experience of falling" into "an act of knowl-edge;" elsewhere (drawing on the phenomenology of travel), he says that "the comings and goings of the wanderer or the sea-farer are voluntary and controlled actions, but the possibility of falling, which is forced upon the mountain climber by an out-side force, exists only in vertical space. The same is true of expe-riences that are closely related to falling, such as dizziness or relapses."

5.) *Mutism*: One peculiar kind of lapse takes the form, not of falling *down,* but of falling *up,* of "ascending beyond (one's) own limits into a place from which (one) can no longer de-scend" (a condition Binswanger calls "*Verstiegenheit*"). Con-cerning this lapse, de Man makes the following remark: "The man who, by his own vision, climbed above the limits of his own self and who is unable to return to earth without the assis-tance of others may well end up falling to his own destruction." The interest of the example lies in its status as a form of *triple* jeopardy: having reached this state by *falling upward* (*first* death penalty), one may either "end up falling back to earth" (*second* death penalty), or one may "return to earth" with "the assis-tance of others." Concerning this third possibility, de Man of-fers only the severest, the most uncompromising indictment: it is to "*fall back upon* a normative precept favoring a harmonious relationship between extension and depth as a necessary condi-tion for a well-balanced personality" (*third* fall, *third* lapse, *third* penalty of death).

De Man was above all determined to avoid this third course—in effect, a passage from "act" to "action," the most seductive and the most insidious temptation from the rigors of the Law-against-Distraction. To share, for example, with a friend—someone singular, compassionate, comprehending, resourceful and patient—the facts of one's youthful "actions," is to jeopard-ize, even to forfeit, the future promise of "acts" yet to come. Such sharing is the courting of intellectual suicide—the sort of gesture to which de Man gave, on occasion, the curious desig-nation of "going under"—appropriate, perhaps, to the "wan-derers and seafarers" of "direct action" (and who can forget that de Man himself "wandered" to the United States by steamship, or that his mother and his uncle alike died of suicide?) but not to the "mountain climbers" of the Absolute Act. Suicide, for Paul de Man, was the ultimate crime against the Law.

*   Jacques Derrida and Paul de Man—two laws, two incom-mensurable lines of life and of thought: how can we ever start to read their transactions? At the distance (maximal/minimal) which lets them *appear*—to intersect crosswise, parting and de-parting against an indeterminate background, upon their im-pertinent-pertinent pathways (*kreuzweise Durchstreichung*).

II

"Hartman uses every trick of the trade to shift attention away from a fact he wishes would go away: that his teacher, colleague, and friend hated Jews and was a Nazi. . . . To deconstructionism, things are what you say they are. So up is down and black is white and east is west and somehow this disreputable and disgusting Nazi, de Man, has been turned into a man of conscience, no less. . . . No Jew can admire Hartman for writing this way about a vicious anti-Semite and Nazi collaborator." Jacob Neusner, "Anti-Semitism: No Ifs or Buts;" *The Jewish Advocate,* vol.179, no.13, 31 March 1988.

Was Paul de Man ever an anti-Semite, "vicious" or otherwise? I do not agree that he was, and I say so here and now—mindful though I am that Jacob Neusner, elsewhere in his article, asserts that "deconstructionism forms a comfortable match with Naz-ism." My argument turns on the premise that anti-Semitism must positively *identify* "the Jew"; to omit this essential (and es-sentializing) step is to trivialize the habit from its onset; in this one decisive respect, de Man's article on "Jews and Present-day Literature" (4 March '41) is a demonstrably incoherent gesture towards an anti-Semitism that it does not, and cannot, attain. And though this fact—if it is indeed a fact—does nothing to minimize the ugliness or the collaborative culpability of the ar-ticle, it nonetheless *counts,* in a legalistically fine way, for anyone wishing to read the redoubtable dossier of the wartime years. (If I have read this essay in error, then I certainly stand accused, as Jacob Neusner would have it, of arranging that "things [shall be] what you say they are".)

At issue is the schema itself of the essay: de Man, as we may re-call, draws one line of demarcation between the sphere of "liter-ature" and the politico-economic scene, and draws another, within the "artistic" sphere itself, between, on the one hand, the great, continuous, "evolving" traditions of literature, and, on the other, the marginal influence of the "Jewish spirit." The ar-gument indeed takes a turn toward anti-Semitism at this point, and one which Derrida's patient analysis has thoroughly ex-posed: to secure itself as anti-Semitic—to merit the strictures visited upon it by Jacob Neusner—the article has merely to dis-tinguish the *non-Jewish* character of the intellectual mainstream from the "Jewish spirit" as positively determined. Such is the move which de Man fails to make: for having argued, as he does in the central passage of the essay, that contemporary writing sustains its continuity throughout the ruptures and the disarray of the *entre-deux-guerres*; and having argued that this continuity is clearly evident in the career of the European novel—evolving from a mode of "exterior" realism (the legacy of the nineteenth century) to a mode of "interior" psychologism (the definitive practice of the twentieth)—de Man provides his curious list of contemporary examples: *Gide, Kafka, Hemingway, Lawrence— on pourrait allonger indéfiniment la liste* . . .

The incoherence lies in the application of the list to the story: for though one may perhaps describe, as de Man proposes, the work of these authors in "psychological" terms, only one of them (André Gide) can be seen as a remarkable, or an *original* exponent, of this particular trend. Either de Man is re-inventing literary history, or his schema "remembers" someone else whose name is omitted for prudential reasons, and the inclusion of whose name is indispensable to the logic of his "history."

"On pourrait allonger indéfiniment la liste": if one did so, whose names could one possibly cite? On 27 May '41, de Man himself provides another list. He does so by way of an almost *imperial* disquisition on the English novel. It seems that English writers, D.H. Lawrence among them, have put themselves to school in France:

Very little connects the novels of Huxley, Joyce or Lawrence to those of the preceding English generation, whereas their link to French models is evident. It is fair, in this sense, to recognize the superior originality of contemporary French literature: the spiritual forbears of the English novel go by the names of Gide and Proust, not Galsworthy or Hardy.

In later essays, and in the same laudatory style, de Man multiplies his references to Proust (17 June '41; 16 Dec. '41; 24 Feb. '42; 19 March '42). In all logical consistency, then, we are obliged to summarize as follows: the modern novel is at the center of contemporary European literature; Proust is a principal source of the modern novel; contemporary literature is, therefore, in its most original tendencies, a "Jewish," as well as a "non-Jewish," literature. (More precisely, it may be neither of these: de Man does not address the "Jewish" qualities of Marcel Proust.) The ellipsis of 4 March—*"on pourrait allonger indéfiniment la liste"*—is less an abbreviation (the mere mention of "Proust" would be briefer by five words than the elliptical phrase itself) than a witting, a *legible* accommodation, hesitation, or collaboration. (It may, for that matter, have been de Man's decision to substitute "Kafka" for "Proust"—the name of "Kafka" being suitably obscure at the time.)

Did de Man direct, I wonder, his elliptical phrase as a mitigating wink to those in the know? If such was his intent, it certainly failed, and the more witting the essay seems, the more craven its composition becomes. And lest we forget Jacob Neusner, let us admit that we may have performed here the very fallacy of "filling the blank" that de Man describes in his famous essay on "Excuses" (1979). Closer to hand, and in the redoubtable dossier itself, de Man evinces an almost superstitious regard for the integrity of the proper name and the signature: "Attached to his own plans (*ses propres desseins*) and in obstinate quest for the ends to which his temperament predestines him, he will only be able to speak in his proper name—just as his work will only 'write, uniquely and singly, about himself'." (18 Nov. '41; see, also, 1 Nov. '42.) By his own standards, de Man is most certainly accountable for anything he signed—including, if such it is, the omission, the culpable omission, of the proper name of "Marcel Proust."

III

As others have done for other ends, I now turn to the slander attempted by *The Nation* of 9 January 1988. We would do best to read the work as two essays rather than one: There is, on the one hand, a farrago of *gaffes* against historiography and mere reason, seasoned with errors of fact and quotation (twenty-one errors at last count)—the output, as it were, of one professor's reckless *cuisinart*. Lurking within this essay, however, is another and different work, a model of argumentative clarity and sure tone, performed in unison by any number of able voices. Reaching beyond the charges of "anti-Semitism" and "Nazism" against de Man, this other essay proclaims some truly remarkable crimes, of which, as it seems, there are three to be counted as *cardinal*:

1.) de Man lied to his friends: he betrayed his nearest and dearest when he ought to have told the truth (he "told a few friends . . . that the charge was false . . . one of them describes that response as 'a lie' . . . ");

2.) de Man had a terrible way with his students: he poisoned, as it were, their very thinking (" 'The real problem of the de Manians is hero worship . . . it's very bad to communicate this hero worship to students. It's politically ugly . . . ' ");

3.) de Man bears a nearly direct responsibility for the murderous deeds of the Germans against the Belgian Jews—and particularly against the youngest victims of those deeds (" 'Paul must have known the Jews of Belgium were being carted away.

We are discussing the butchery of the Belgian Jewish community, down to the babies . . .'").

These charges are dispersed throughout the essay; They are unevenly developed (or not even developed unevenly); and they are put in the mouths of many people with few names. And yet they are certainly linked—and in two distinct and rhetorically reinforcing directions: in the first place, the charges are logically circular (lies are poisonous, poison is infanticidal, infanticide is betrayal, betrayal is lying), and in the second, these charges belong—in their circular configuration as a *trio,* and in their topical, and their traditionally topical, specificity—to a grand and familiar tradition of calumny. The three charges, in their logic, their linkage, and their aggression, echo the great libels operated by the major anti-Semitisms of the past eight hundred years: they are the slander of "Judas," the slander of "well-poisoning," and the slander of "Herod" ("O cursed folk of Herodes al newe"—Chaucer, *The Prioress's Tale*). In its ruminations on Paul de Man, *The Nation* has furnished this nation—as well as Germany, France, England and Switzerland—with a very neat, a very up-to-date piece of old-time "anti-Semitism." But the truly instructive thing about the exercise lies less in the perennial retail value of its bloodlust, than in the undeniable validity of its insight, and in the visionary correctness of its charge: for are not, indeed, Paul de Man and his deconstruction somehow overwhelmingly Jewish—as Jewish as anyone, perhaps, in our multi-national 1980's, can be? That Paul de Man, biographically speaking, was not himself Jewish, is nothing to the point: From the sixteenth century onward, American anti-Semitism, among other varieties, has been a discourse of bigotry *displaced*—targeting, over and through its ancient and programmatic codes, Native Americans and their more recent surrogates in the Far East, as well as continental Europeans of the Old World—often, though not invariably, Europeans of the Roman Catholic faith (Melville's Amasa Delano, commenting on Benito Cereno: "was the Spaniard less hardened than the Jew, who refrained not from supping at the board of him whom the same night he meant to betray?").

What is the "Jewish" threat, at last, of Paul de Man's writings? Is it prescriptive, in the manner of Moses? Is it historical, in the manner of Esther? Is it prophetic, in the manner of Jeremiah? Is it all of these at once? How did de Man's work become such a threat, as it had not yet become in the wartime writings of his Belgian years? We know, for example, that Paul de Man, at the close of the Second World War, translated, into Flemish, that most Judaic of American novels, *Moby Dick*: are we licensed to construe his own life as a translation in turn of that transla-

tion—as a version, for instance, of Jonah's career, as it is related to us in Father Mapple's sermon? These questions, ecstatically speculative as they may seem, are unavoidable—prompted, and indeed aroused, by our nations' ideological foreplay.

IV

I should like to close on a note of *caution,* the thing that Paul de Man did not have—or did not sufficiently have—at the setting forth of his passionate career, and which he was to develop so obsessively later on, though in ways that were to cause real pain to his friends during the past winter. Did he himself suffer pain at his own silence? I, for one, am prepared to suppose that he did, and I further suppose that he would, were he brought back from the dead at this moment, be heart-struck at the noisy sequel to his quiet lifetime. So saying, of course, I merely allegorize the unreadable figure and pathos of "*Caution*" itself; and because I do so less forcefully than others have done, I take this occasion to cite from yet another allegory, John Bunyan's *Pilgrim's Progress,* to which I was first introduced by Paul de Man himself exactly thirty years ago.

Two men, Christian and Hopeful—having languished for a spell in the dungeon of Doubting Castle, and having emerged and travelled for another spell—suffer the shock of a retrospective vision from an elevated place, a "vertical" setting supplied, as it seems, by certain "Shepherds." In this vision, Christian and Hopeful see still *other* travellers, who, having passed through the same torments, wander around in a "horizontal" setting of far less promise. As is characteristic of strong allegory, this scene is as obscure as it is overdetermined; it is a passage almost impossible to read:

Then I saw that they had them to the top of another Mountain, and the name of that is *Caution*; and bid them look a far off: Which when they did, they perceived, as they thought, several men walking up and down among the Tombs that were there. And they perceived that the men were blind, because they stumbled sometimes upon the Tombs, and because they could not get out from among them. Then said *Christian, What means this?*

The Shepherds then answered, Did you not see a little below these Mountains a *Stile* that led into a Meadow on the left hand of this way? They answered, Yes. Then said the Shepherds, From that *Stile* there goes a path that leads directly to *Doubting-Castle,* which is kept by *Giant Despair*; and these men (pointing to them among the Tombs) came once on Pilgrimage, as you do now, even till they came to that same *Stile.* And because the right way was rough in that place, they chose to go out of it into that Meadow, and there were taken by Giant *Despair,* and cast into *Doubting-Castle*; where, after they had a while been kept in the Dungeon, he at last did put out their eyes, and led them among those Tombs, where he has left them to wander to this very day, that the saying of the wise Man night be fulfilled, *He that wandereth out of the way of understanding, shall remain in the Congregation of the dead.* (Prov. 21. 16.) Then *Christian* and *Hopeful* looked one upon another, with tears gushing out; but yet said nothing to the Shepherds.

University of Alabama

De Man Ce Soir

HERMAN RAPAPORT

Roberte, her skirt still raised, with one hand seems to be adjusting her girdle or her stockings while with the other, holding them between the tips of her fingers, she tenders Victor a pair of keys which he touches without ever taking: for the two of them seem hanging in suspense in their respective positions.
—*Pierre Klossowski,* Roberte Ce Soir

This essay divides into two parts, the first describing some features of Paul de Man's rhetoric of collaboration during the early 1940s, and the second establishing stylistic and ideological 'weak' links between these early pieces and the later work on Hegel's *Aesthetics* written during the 1980s. Although I expect readers to draw their own moral conclusions, I want to say from the outset that, as one might anticipate, de Man's early writings are enormously complex and profoundly ambiguous. The main trajectory of my argument is that precisely where one might expect to find a close identification with Nazism in the young de Man's collaborative writings of the early 1940s, one finds instead numerous and subtle resistances which are working in the service of contradicting Nazi ideology and politics. Whereas, in his reflections on Hegel in the 1980s one discovers that in the place where one would expect fascism to be of no consequence, de Man makes certain muted, fragmentary links to this ideology even as he enacts features of a collaborationist style reminiscent of the writings he had developed some forty years earlier. That the relations between the later and earlier work are fragmentary and are to be found in the infrastructures of the writing means that only a very crude or reductive reading would claim that de Man's critical writings of his major phase stem from an objectionable political ideology. Yet, only by turning a deaf ear to some of what is said in de Man's late work can one believe that nothing from a disquieting political past survived.

I

Drab, distantly anonymous, and muted, the war time writings of Paul de Man appear to be a collection of uninspired articles evoking ideologies of occupation. It is true that at times the vague ideological rhetoric of the young Paul de Man becomes quite pointed, yet one senses it is rarely the kind of rhetoric that is supposed to move people into action. Rather, it is a lethargic rhetoric fatigued by burdensome thoughts, as if assigned by some outside agency, making reflection difficult. Sometimes even the most basic observations require laborious examination and overly cautious judgments, giving the impression of an analytical scrupulousness that, in fact, is not merited or even wanted in such situations. Sometimes little of significance appears to be said in what looks like intellectual space fillers written for the sake of preserving the appearance of a normal cultural climate. And yet, something is stirring in these articles. Their apparent vacuity upon closer inspection strikes one as by no means unintelligent, and hardly mediocre, as if one were up against a subtle writerly camouflage, perhaps even intellectual subterfuge.

Not atypical is a passage written by the young de Man in 1941 on Pierre Drieu la Rochelle.

Selon Drieu la Rochelle, les vertus sportives qu'on retrouve sur le plan politique, dans les idéologies fascistes constituent le symptôme bienheureux annonciateur d'une régénérescence prochaine, car elles sont les premières à promettre une fusion du corps et de l'âme dans une unité harmonieuse.[1]

Infused with ideological tautology, this does not immediately appear to be a striking passage. And yet it is not simplistic, either. In fact, one wonders why such an apparently empty statement has been achieved at the cost of so many carefully assembled verbal elements. Is the passage simply drawn out to cover the pages of a collaborationist newspaper, or is something less dull occurring? For example, an ironic detracting from the Nazis that intricately constitutes itself as only apparently banal? One wonders. What does de Man's passage mean when it says, "car elle sont les premières à promettre une fusion"? Is it implying that Nazism has failed to harmoniously unify body and soul, the material and the spiritual? Does the passage say that Drieu La Rochelle's work is succeeding where German fascism has not? If so, the passage could be suggesting several things. 1) That the spiritual aims of fascism, so far a debacle, see their fruition only in the work of collaborators whose fascist ideology, rooted in French fascism of the 1930s, is superior to Hitlerism. 2) That it is not in politics, but in aesthetics that the unification of spirit and matter can be sighted. 3) That the violence and disruption of Nazi politics is not part of a harmonious social vision such as that proposed by fascist intellectuals in the occupied countries. From this, furthermore, some surprising inferences follow. One of them is that Nazism must await its fulfillment as a philosophy in the occupied zones; and it remains, then, to be asked whether this fulfillment is one that decides in favor of Hitler or not. Perhaps the ambiguities are, in fact, quite enormous, something that does not immediately suggest itself to those who are taken in by the passive tonalities of a labored style.

Matters become more complicated the moment one considers de Man's judgment of Drieu la Rochelle's reading of literature in "Notes Pour Comprendre le Siècle": "Du moment qu'on ne considère plus la littérature sous l'angle de l'art, mais qu'on cherche à y voir le déroulement d'une évolution éthique, on peut lui faire démonter n'importe quoi." And, attacking Drieu, de Man writes, "En comparant les notions littéraires, comme romantisme, symbolisme, naturalisme avec des notions morales comme mysticisme et christianisme, on doit nécessaire-

ment s'exposer à des errements puisqu'on met sur le même plan des concepts essentiellement différents. C'est cependant ce que fait Drieu la Rochelle . . ." De Man's argument, which is consistent with many of his other pieces during this period, clearly falls on the side of reading literature aesthetically rather than morally. An Anglo/American reader may well surmise a new critical spirit in de Man's remarks, something that complements his interests elsewhere in the literature of figures like Henry James, James Joyce, D.H. Lawrence, Aldous Huxley, and Virginia Woolf. Has de Man's strong interest in English writers included an interest in what were then the more recent English trends in criticism? Does his Anglophilia extend so far? When de Man says that Drieu's arbitrary interpretations never have any demonstrative value, one's suspicions are raised.[2] Aside from the inclinations de Man expresses for the type of rigorous reading that he himself will undertake in unforeseen ways decades after the Second World War, this passage expresses a distance taking from Drieu La Rochelle, if not from a politics of literary interpretation, generally. Again, many inferences are unresolved. Is de Man invoking a purer literary aesthetics where soul and body harmoniously come together in what is beyond the merely ethical or political? Or is de Man dismissing Drieu la Rochelle's metaphysical vision and, in fact, tacitly reinstating German politics? On what side of these issues is de Man standing? Throughout many of the young de Man's articles the appeal to both a literary aesthetics and a metaphysical discourse sometimes functions less as a vehicle for fascist ideology than as a reserve of abstract terms which makes unquestioned generalizations seem possible, even though they may contain inferences which are problematic. For example, in "Le Roman Anglais Contemporain," of January 1940, de Man invokes the term "style."[3] The term is used in a most general if not shop worn manner to note the difference between *Ulysses* and the *Forsythe Saga*; *Démon du Midi* and *Du côté de chez Swann*; or *Buddenbrooks* and *Der Schloss*. De Man points out that writing *qua* writing in these works dominates the nineteenth century notion of character to which writing was once subordinated as speech. De Man calls this a liberation of writing from character and terms it "style." Far from anticipating anything like Barthes' "writing degree zero," de Man considers style only as part of an elaborate psychological portrayal of the human condition which is not impeded by the schemas of familiar character types.

It is curious that de Man alludes to Joyce's Leopold Bloom in this connection, because the inference is that the Jewish condition in modern European society may not be definable in terms of the crude character typing so familiar to the Nazi experience. Rather, what the liberation of style allows is the opening up of literary schemas by freeing language from the duty of imitating everyday speech and the vulgar social portraits that are held in common by members of society. This liberation is marked, moreover, by the establishment of much more difficult literary styles than had been previously developed. De Man is turning to English (and Irish) literature, in particular, which ambiguously manifests both the values of those fascisms which arose in the occupied countries before the German invasion as well as values that go against a National Socialist conception of literature strongly rooted in a theory of the character type. In this instance, comparative literary examination is being used for the sake of turning European fascisms contrary to one another without announcing the fact that this is being undertaken in a daily newspaper under German eyes. De Man's interest in literary aesthetics, which is discussed in many of his articles, is used, then, as a tactic by means of which one can incrementally unalign forces that should be perfectly synchronized.

In "Le Destin de la Flandre" [*Le Soir,* September 1, 1941], de Man again raises the topic of aesthetics even as he turns away from the traditions of other countries in order to make a case for Belgian cultural nationalism. Indeed, "nationalism" itself is an instance of an ideological term that is used so platitudinously and hence abstractly that it begins to become rather amorphous. De Man's carefully downplayed assumption is that the Nazi occupation should not be seen in terms of an antagonism between the Belgian and the German peoples. Rather, everyone should understand that the Germans have occupied Belgium in order to liberate it from the moribund political conditions of the 1930s. Hence the Belgian people should begin to start thinking about the nationalization of Belgian cultural heritages. But if de Man is invoking political contradictions sanctioned by National Socialism, he is also suggesting that the Belgians must resist a German aim which is to annex Flemish peoples and culture as part of the "German State."

This position as well as the rhetorical downplaying or tonal banalization of terms like nationalism is, in fact, politically ambitious in the sense that de Man is implicitly criticizing what Pascal Ory calls "Les Flamands du Führer." Spearheaded by Jean-Maire Gantois, Het Vlaamsch National Verbond de Belgique (started in 1933), became a collaborationist organization with close ties to the National Socialists. In 1940, Gantois addressed Hitler in the name of the "Flamands de la France du Nord" and said, "Nous sommes des bas-Allemands, et nous voulons faire retour au Reich."[4] Furthermore, Gantois in addressing Hitler, wrote:

Führer,

Nous, Flamands de la France du Nord, qui avons pu suivre, de loin seulement, mais avec sympathie, la lutte du Reich allemand pour son unité raciale, nous Flamands de la France du Nord auxquels l'histoire, jusqu'à présent, n'a réservé qu'un *destin tragique,* qui avons mené, sans détour et sans défaillance, aux avant-postes de la Germanie, une lutte paraissant presque sans issue contre l'emprise française, nous avons depuis longtemps le sentiment et la conviction que vous, Adolphe Hitler, êtes devenu, par votre action et votre combat, en cette période décisive de l'histoire mondiale, le Führer de tous les Germains.[5]

De Man, quite to the contrary, resists a nationalistic identification with Germany in "Le Destin" and generally subdues the word nationalism by strategically bogging it down in vague cultural contexts that are without striking qualities.

Perhaps de Man was aware that the National Socialist "revolution" had a cultural agenda for Europe which included a political reconfiguration of national boundaries, cultural identities, and racial distributions. "Le Destin de la Flandre" may have appealed to literary aesthetics in order to show that cultural productions manifest not merely "la trace strictement individuelle de l'auteur" but certain traits which belong "à des collectivités entières." To have the same common ancestors, to live in the same country and cultural climate, and to have the same enemies, all of this contributes to a collective identity, one that affects the deepest levels of one's personality. Artistic sensibility directly reflects a national temperament that is embodied in an identifiable style. These points, of course, delicately align themselves with the kind of nationalist sentiments inherent in Gantois' rhetoric while deflecting its political aims from an alliance with the Germans to a consideration of "the deepest levels" of individuality.

Even when more broadly considering society, de Man employs two rather inconspicuous aesthetic terms, the pictorial and the realistic, in order to characterize how Flanders reflects its collective artistic styles. Here de Man is not only considering Belgians, but the Flemish of Northern France. His point is that unlike French artistic practices, the Flemish pay more attention to the surfaces or plasticity of things. De Man implies that in those regions culturally divided between Flemish and French speaking peoples, one must come to terms with Flemish aesthetics as a means of keeping both Flemish and French speaking peoples together. Hence one must view Flemish culture as dialectically associated with French culture. A denationalization of Flemish speaking peoples by the Germans would, de Man says, be catastrophic. "Je n'hésite pas à proclamer qu'une telle conception pourrait mener, en Flandre, à des états catastrophiques." In "Le Destin de la Flandre," then, nationalism is ambiguously being used both as a term siding with National Socialism even as it resists a German denationalization and reconfiguration of Belgian culture. Again, as in the essay on English literature, de Man uses aesthetics, in part, as a means to turn both towards and against the Germans.

An essay that has received much recent attention is "Les Juifs dans la Littérature Actuelle" [*Le Soir*, March 4, 1941]. Toward the very end of the article de Man writes, "En plus, on voit donc qu'une solution du problème juif qui viserait à la création d'une colonie juive isolée de l'Europe n'entraînerait pas, pour la vie littéraire de l'Occident, de conséquences déplorables." That these words were published at a time when Jews were being sent to concentration camps puts de Man in the unenviable position of having been a public accomplice to Jewish persecution. And yet, these remarks are peculiarly elusive. As in the articles cited above, de Man relies on shop worn right wing platitudes—for example, that the Jews are cultural imitators rather than innovators—and develops them by way of a certain indirection. For contrast, notice Jean Troupeau-Housay, a French collaborationist echoing Hitler. Speaking of the penultimate act of the drama that is World War II, he writes, "Le grand capital est anéanti. Le pur et vrai socialisme est instauré de l'Oural à Gibraltar . . . A tout jamais Israël est mis dans l'impossibilité de perpétrer ses crimes: *tous les Juifs sont stérilisés*."[6] De Man's remarks, however objectionable, maintain a distance from this kind of rhetoric. In fact, de Man's rhetoric is suggesting that Jews are so culturally nugatory that if they were expelled literary culture wouldn't know the difference. Certainly, this is not a compliment, and mention of a "solution du problème Juif" directly implicates de Man in the holocaust. Yet de Man's text is also taking distance from Nazi anti-Semitism in that it is saying the Jews are innocuous. They are not, as so many others insisted, criminals who culturally threaten the life blood of the state. It is striking that de Man downplays the Jewish cultural role in establishing modernist traditions. Whereas Hitler accused the Jews of having criminally perverted culture through developing what we would today call a modernist aesthetic, de Man takes the view that, in fact, the Jews are not responsible for significant aesthetic movements in the arts. In staging his point anti-Semitically, de Man manages to say something not wholly congruent with National Socialism. In short, his remarks, highly objectionable as they may be, are somewhat asymmetrical with those of the Germans and with many of those in the Belgian and French collaboration with Germany.

To consider de Man's asymmetries or asynchronicities a bit

further, it is helpful to read "Les Juifs" in relation to two essays previously discussed, "Le Roman" and "Le Destin." In "Les Juifs" the argument of "Le Roman" is contradicted. Not only Kafka, who was positively valorized only a year earlier in "Le Roman," but Gide, Hemingway, and Lawrence are condemned as rear guard writers whose styles merely conceal a nineteenth century habit of literary composition. Apparently, the political climate had changed so much by 1941 that even de Man—who was inclined to prefer Anglo/American and even Jewish literature to, say, the literary works of the Belgian folk—was required to change directions. Yet, "Les Juifs" preserves an ideological style behind which there is a characterless and virtually anonymous writer who inhabits an interstitial position between different national cultural fronts: English, German, French, and Flemish. Even if "Les Juifs" turns against earlier aesthetic positions, it is still as a piece of writing very much aligned with what de Man was earlier calling "style," as if still allying itself with writers not unlike Kafka who had moved beyond Nineteenth Century conceptions of writing.

"Les Juifs" also maintains strange accords with "Le Destin de la Flandre," which was written some six months later. What does it mean for the Jews, who are elected by Hitler as phase one of European cultural and demographic reconfiguration, to be extradited? Provided that the Jews are considered a threat to national identity generally and to Belgium's already divided culture in particular, de Man may be suggesting that they ought to undergo denationalization in place of the Flemish peoples. "Les Juifs" does not fail to suggest in relation to "Le Destin" that if viewed by the collaborators as cultural parasites (de Man calls them imitators), the Jews could be a threat to Belgian resistance, and in forsaking them, Belgium could at once appease its occupiers and better resist them at the same time. Yet, as already noted, "Les Juifs" doesn't unilaterally characterize the Jews as entirely threatening, since their "influence" has been minuscule, even if it has some nationalist repercussions. But if this is maintained, the case for denationalization and deportation is inherently undermined, upholding the view in "Le destin" that German denationalization of occupied peoples is undesirable. Here, as elsewhere in de Man's essays, the positions are somewhat less decided than one might at first suppose, since they are inherently fissured even though they borrow from a strong ideological vocabulary.

II

Having pursued some of the asymmetries in the early articles by de Man, I wish at this point to turn to de Man's writings on

Hegel published near the end of his life. For it is here that de Man returned to a recognition of the aesthetic and the political in ways both rhetorically and ideologically reminiscent of the earlier work. I am thinking in particular of "Hegel on the Sublime," one of the last essays de Man composed. Not unlike the essays we have been discussing, "Hegel on the Sublime" allows for unsynchronized positions to resonate in textual fissures and subterranean fragments that both approach and reject, or collaborate with certain aspects of what the Yale School has called deconstruction. Certainly, "Hegel on the Sublime" is one of de Man's most difficult essays, and it continues an argument developed in "Sign and Symbol in Hegel's *Aesthetics*" which juxtaposed dominant to subdominant terms: symbol/sign; aesthetic/art; *Erinnerung*/*Gedächtnis*; the symbolic/the allegorical, etc.[7] In part, de Man explains that contrary to what most Hegel scholars have thought, the aesthetic of Hegel is highly semiotic and already anticipates Derridean deconstruction by radically counterpointing and inverting a dominant terminology of ontological identity with a subordinate terminology of ontological difference. Although Hegel's *Aesthetics* might be the last place to expect a thorough destabilizing of aesthetic categories, it is precisely here that a very radical theory of language profoundly breaks with the reflective philosophical tradition. Of course, de Man's immediate political aims in this essay are twofold: 1) to demonstrate that Derridean deconstruction is grammatologically developed to a high degree in Hegel's *Aesthetics* and that Derrida is far more derivative or imitative than has been acknowledged, and 2) that de Man's own allegorical project of reading, fully developed by the late 1970s, is more directly indebted to a Hegelian rather than Derridean rhetoric of deconstruction. These are implications of great importance, because they show that even in paying homage to Derrida, de Man takes his distance and suggests that for him not the Jewish Derrida, but the German Hegel is of more immediate significance. As in the early writings, the rhetoric of affiliation is not entirely synchronized. In fact, it is littered with fragmentary undercurrents, some of which are easily overlooked and which in retrospect are quite troubling.

In "Hegel on the Sublime" the implications of "Sign and Symbol in Hegel's *Aesthetics*" become more pronounced in the subtle but repeated rejection of Jewish thought. In part, the project in "Hegel on the Sublime" is to investigate how Hegel's understanding of the beautiful and the sublime went beyond Kant's already dialectical understanding of these terms in *The Critique of Judgment*. Problematic for de Man is the Kantian understanding that the sublime is key to the beautiful in the same way that, in "Sign and Symbol in Hegel's *Aesthetics*," art is key

to the aesthetic. What de Man demonstrates in "Hegel on the Sublime" is that, contrary to one's expectations, such a symmetry in Hegel does not hold and that the sublime is hardly a category that will withstand dialectical integrity or recovery through an *Aufhebung*. One of the passages that establishes the radical difference between Hegel and Kant specifically names the Jews.

More revealing, perhaps, though still merely formal, is the place Hegel allots to the sublime in the dialectical continuum of the various art forms. "We find the sublime first and in its original form primarily in the Hebraic state of mind and in the sacred texts of the Jews."[8]

De Man points out that this identification of the sublime with the Jews refers to a Kantian sublime which has been trivialized if not contaminated by semitic thought. Kant, de Man says, has been treated "shabbily" by Hegel, though ironically it is this shabby treatment de Man clearly supports. Indeed, de Man's whole project is aimed to take distance from a Jewish or "monotheistic" conception of the sublime. De Man explains that the Hegelian conception of the sublime is no proper concept at all, but is rather an iterated series of textual or linguistic resistances to symbolicity which has the effect of disarticulating "the order of discourse and the order of the sacred" as well as deconstituting a self-identical notion of "the One, of Being, of Allah, or Jawhe, or I. . . ."[9] For de Man the sublime is a nihilistic moment that is not subsequently recovered or raised up into some still higher idea or spirit, but a violence that bears semiotic traces. In this sense, de Man is much closer to René Girard's notion of a sacrificial violence indebted to an undecidable destabilizing of differences than one might ordinarily expect, a point to bear in mind given Girard's interest in the scapegoat.

In a long and tortuous analysis of a "performative" statement from Genesis and a "constative" statement from Psalms, de Man uses the Hegelian sublime to thoroughly lay waste the conceptual structure of Jewish monotheism by demonstrating that the discourse of the Bible is rhetorically asymmetrical with itself and not recoverable in any synthetic way. In short, the Bible cannot be read intelligently in terms of a transcendental subject. In connecting this demonstration with Hegelian aesthetics and politics, de Man writes, "The political in Hegel originates in the critical undoing of belief, the end of the current theodicy, the banishment of the earliest defenders of faith from the affairs of the state, and the transformation of theology into the critical philosophy of right."[10] Although de Man is speaking in very general terms, the target of these remarks is evident to anyone sensitive to the issues and undercurrents of the essay. In short, we are to learn from Hegel's aesthetics a political lesson through which we understand that one of the aims of Hegelian deconstruction is the banishment of the defenders of the faith from the affairs of the state, these defenders being, given de Man's contexts, the Jews. What Hegel's *Aesthetics* teach us, then, is that one cannot understand art without coming to understand the politics of being *Judenfrei,* something that extends even to the study of Kant.

This position, however, is buried beneath an extraordinarily evasive move wherein de Man switches referents, hence allowing fragments of anti-Semitism to resonate while specifically naming language the animus of Hegelian politics. Hence de Man demolishes what is now identified as a Kantian notion of language by showing that the sublime as undecidable difference violently inheres as an asymmetry between sign and meaning which debilitates our capacity to conceptualize the Hegelian differences outlined in de Man's previous piece, "Sign and Symbol in Hegel's *Aesthetics,*" namely, the difference between symbol and sign, which, not incidentally, is the assumed crux upon which Jewish monotheism and Kantian aesthetics rests. The sublime, then, opens before us a sacrificial moment, in Girard's sense, wherein the language of Hegelian aesthetics undergoes destruction at that moment the sublime invades dialectics with its indeterminacies. This *Anschluss* or annexation of the aesthetic by the sublime comes at the expense not of its own conceptual or even political incompatibilities but, rather, at the expense of sacrificing Kant and, more broadly, his Jewish mentors. That this is itself an allegory of reading that reflects the dynamics of a certain difficult collaboration I will leave to one side.

Indeed, all this might not be so engaging were it not for the last few sentences of "Hegel on the Sublime."

Hegel's *Aesthetics,* an essentially prosaic discourse on art is a discourse of the slave because it is a discourse of the figure rather than of genre, of trope rather than of representation. As a result, it is also politically legitimate and effective as the undoer of usurped authority. The enslaved place and condition of the section on the sublime in the *Aesthetics,* and the enslaved place of the *Aesthetics* within the corpus of Hegel's complete works, are the symptoms of their strength. Poets, philosophers, and their readers lose their political impact only if they become, in turn, usurpers of mastery. One way of doing this is by avoiding, for whatever reason, the critical thrust of aesthetic judgment.[11]

That this prosaic and enslaved place of the aesthetic is what de Man specifically calls the "banal" ["The *Aesthetics* seem to provide only banal and empirical answers . . ."][12] is already a disquieting identification for those familiar with de Man's early

writings, especially since this banal writing takes the place of what is called "usurped authority," the authority of Kant, certainly, but also of the Jews. That this alliance of Kant with the Jews is not just a Hegelian notion, but is reestablished in the twentieth century in terms of the neo-Kantianism of Ernst Cassirer, who was Jewish and who was also persecuted by the Germans, already makes the identification in Hegel piquant when it is reiterated in de Man. In fact, if de Man is subtly invoking a Hegelian antipathy to the Jews through allusion to *The Aesthetics* (and less conspicuously, *The Early Theological Writings*), he cannot do so as if to forget those fascist cultural identifications of the Jews that followed in the wake of 19th century German anti-Semitism, identifications reiterated by de Man himself in "Les Juifs dans la littérature actuelle" of 1941 wherein certain intellectuals who usurp mastery are subject to a Hegelian turn whereby as "masters" (usurping Jews) they are vanquished by the "slaves" (oppressed Aryans). Or, as Hegel puts it, "but just as lordship [*Herrschaft*] showed that its essential nature is the reverse of what it wants to be [*ihr Wesen das Verkehrte dessen ist, was sie sein will*], so too servitude [*Knechtschaft*] in its consummation will really turn into the opposite of what it immediately is."[13]

It is unsettling, therefore, that the close of "Hegel on the Sublime" suggests that to avoid a "usurped mastery" associated with the Jews, one must demolish in the name of Hegelianism the "critical thrust of aesthetic judgment" by means of resorting to a peculiarly violent if not sacrificial interpretation of Hegel's sublime: such an interpretation not only disarticulating the Kantian aesthetic grounds for interpretation but banishing certain defenders of the faith from the State. That "Hegel on the Sublime" contains such disturbing suggestions is most peculiar, since during the Second World War it was precisely these inferences de Man was muting and diffusing. One wonders why, during the 1980s, de Man was developing fragments of an argument whose ideology he had somewhat resisted during the war. My suspicion, given my two points made about "Sign and Symbol in Hegel's *Aesthetics,*" is that the understructure of "Hegel on the Sublime" is meant to obliquely take distance from Derridean deconstruction, from what "Sign and Symbol in Hegel's *Aesthetics*" considers a philosophy based on false mastery, the usurpation of Hegel by Derrida, and perhaps de Man by Derrida. If this psychological intuition is correct, we would be witnessing a most interesting phenomenon wherein at the moment de Man wrote his most ambitious philosophical project in the service of dismantling the mimetic legacy of monotheism, he was still psychologically working in the service of an ego which found it necessary to draw on the events and ideas of its youth, as if to seek a more authentic ground beneath that which had been usurped by the false cultural formations established after the fascist debacle.

University of Iowa

NOTES

1. *Le Soir,* December 2, 1941.

2. Also see "Sur les possibilités de la critique" in *Le Soir,* 2 Dec. 1941. "Un écrivain peut être attaqué pour des insuffisances de son style, pour des péchés contre les lois du genre qu'il pratique, mais jamais pour les faiblesses ou les manquements de sa personnalité morale. Les plus belles pages des littératures mondiales sont souvent celles qui expriment un échec, un abandon, une capitulation. Et on a écrit les pires platitudes pour exalter les plus nobles sentiments." Later in the same article, de Man refers to the Arnoldian "touch stone" or "pierre de touche," a reference that suggests, once more, an interest in English literary criticism. And he ameliorates stylistic integrity with the notion of "esprit." This text is characteristically ambivalent. It is, of course, an alibi for fascist immorality, but it also cuts another way by suggesting that the relationship between authors and texts is immaterial. This has interesting consequences for de Man's anti-Semitic position which I discuss later, because it suggests by way of implication that Jewish literary works can't be taken to task on intentionalist grounds. Style, spirit, genre and aesthetics become part of a vocabulary of anti-intentionalism (one is reminded of the New Criticism) that radically breaks with aesthetic positions taken by figures such as Hitler, even as this vocabulary supports fascism in the arts. The anti-intentionalist conviction is interesting, too, in that it institutes a style that resists the identification of the subject (i.e. the author) with its content. That this should be fundamental to a rhetoric of collaboration goes without saying.

3. *Les Cahiers de Libre Examen* 4:4, January 1940, pp.15–19.

4. Pascal Ory, *Les Collaborateurs 1940–1945* (Paris: Editions du Seuil, 1976), p.172.

5. *La France Allemande,* ed. Pascal Ory (Paris: Gallimard, 1977), p.130. Italics mine.

6. *La France Allemande,* p.180.

7. "Sign and Symbol in Hegel's *Aesthetics,*" *Critical Inquiry,* Vol. 8, No. 4, 1982, pp.761–776.

8. *Displacement,* ed. M. Krupnick (Bloomington, Indiana University Press, 1983), p.143.

9. *Displacement,* pp.144–145. I realize that de Man is invoking metaphysics, generally, in this remark. Not only the Jews, but the Ancient Greeks, Islam, and those who belong to a Cartesian tradition are invoked. However, "Hegel on the Sublime" focuses on the context of a Judaic legacy, and hence it is the invocation of the Jews in this passage that stands out most strongly. That the invocation of Islam, Ancient Greek thought, or Cartesianism is meant to deflect attention from a specific target is rather self-evident, given the contexts of de Man's discussions.

10. *Displacement,* p.149.

11. *Displacement,* p.153.

12. *Displacement,* p.142.

13. *The Phenomenology of Spirit,* trans. A.V. Miller (London: Oxford, 1977), p.117.

Mourning Becomes Paul de Man

TOBIN SIEBERS

Mourning always implies a fusion of identities and, necessarily, a confusion over identity. What happens in the event of a double mourning? Given the fusion of identity characteristic of mourning, can such a thing as a double mourning take place? What would it mean to have one's mourning interrupted by mourning?

A process of mourning has now interrupted another mourning. The victims of the holocaust are now mourned in the same place as some mourn for Paul de Man. De Man's youthful anti-Semitism has created a structural interference between his own death and the death of six million Jews. The effect is a loss of mourning, a loss of the loss, that is baffling, embarrassing, and pernicious. It is baffling because the figure of de Man risks becoming an antisymbol for his own mourning as well as for the mourning of the Jews. It is embarrassing because the discovery of de Man's collaborationist writings proves a scandal to every critic who has at one time or another admired his work; and this scandal will be the basis of attacks on critical theory itself. It is pernicious, potentially, because the confusion of identities in mourning may now transform de Man into a martyr figure whose insistence makes it more difficult to concentrate on the Jewish victims of the holocaust. In this last scenario, one expects to hear an implicit defense of de Man, suggesting that the theory, the man, or the career are the victims of a youthful anti-Semitism. While many people will refuse to defend de Man, quite a few will feel sorry for him. This form of regret represents de Man as his own victim and obstructs our view of the real victims. We mourn de Man instead of the Jews.

Paul de Man died in 1983, but the mourning for him has not ceased. His name continues to appear in various dedications and expressions of regret. The special issue of *Yale French Studies* on "The Lesson of Paul de Man" reads like an elegy.[1] The opening funeral orations chart each speaker's first or most personal experience with Paul de Man, and they tell, inevitably, of death; or, rather, they tell of Paul de Man engaged in an act of reading inseparable from the act of mourning. Each scene pictures de Man reading a text about death: Peter Brooks shows de Man reading Yeats's "At Algeciras—A Meditation on Death"; Geoffrey Hartman cites de Man's fascination with the "cold mortality" of Shelley; and Jacques Derrida repeats de Man's reading of Mallarmé's "Tombeau de Verlaine" and exposes his own feelings of "la mort dans l'âme." Surely, the occasion of the orations has something to do with these memories. People look for talk of death in the event of death. But I want to explore the possibility that the funeral orations were true to de Man's method of reading: reading in de Man's definition always exposes a rhetoric of mourning. What are the consequences of reading for de Man's relation to the victims of the holocaust? How do these consequences figure in the mourning of Paul de Man.

There can be only a personal response to these questions. For, inevitably, the questions lead to an argument ad hominem. By ad hominem, I do not mean, necessarily, that we must interrogate the person of Paul de Man to understand his method of reading. This will occur, no doubt, but the facts are simply too clear in what is most important to bear a "reading" in the de Manian sense. There exists an early essay entitled "Les Juifs dans la littérature actuelle," in which de Man makes his anti-Semitism evident for all to see.[2] At this level, the immediate and popular response—*The New York Times* response—is correct and truthful. Any attempt to invalidate this response, to turn it aside as too popular, will reproduce an elitism as virulent as de Man's youthful prejudice. The popular response is more important than ever because its very existence stands in such cases as a challenge to elitism. This is not to say, however, that we must remain uncritical of the responses current in the popular press. We need to enter into dialogue with them.[3]

Rather, by "ad hominem," I refer to the process of introjection or incorporation found in mourning. In mourning, a body is incorporated in the mourner, so that the figure of the absent one becomes a constant trope within the mourner's attempts to read the world. The reaction to Paul de Man's death produced this kind of iconography, and present holocaust studies continue to grapple with the problem of mourning in similar terms, returning again and again to the iconography of the death camps to stage inhuman memories.

Mourning insists on giving body to the language of the dead. De Man's theory of reading, of course, claims that a structural interference exists between anthropomorphism and trope. When we read tropes, according to his theory, we always read anthropomorphically, thereby misreading language. De Man's originality consists in his rigorous attempts to read against the grain of anthropomorphism in order to discover language as such; but by the logic of his own argument, his reading must necessarily collapse into human terms. Here is a double movement, in which each phase is indicative of mourning. Mourning tries to incorporate into human terms a figure colored by death and de Man's attempt to read "inhumanly," to paraphrase his description of language, strives to undo mourning's originary impulse in order to be done with mourning before its activity accomplishes its own end.[4]

If it seems that I am overemphasizing the relation between reading and mourning in de Man's work, we might recall that one of his last essays, "Anthropomorphism and Trope in the Lyric," defines reading specifically in the context of mourning.[5] This is not a limited context but one that applies to all reading. De Man claims that a kind of double textuality, a competition between two senses, exists in every reading. This double textuality can be briefly summarized in the relation between Baudelaire's two poems "Correspondances" and "Obsession": "There always are at least two texts, regardless of whether they are actually written out or not; the relationship between the two sonnets . . . is an inherent characteristic of any text" (pp. 260–61). The relationship between the two sonnets consists of the play between a nonhuman, purely linguistic world of enumeration and a psychological obsession with reading this world in anthropological terms, the paradox of de Man's theory being that the obsessive reading is not the product of a human psychology but its creation in language. The essay ends by trying to capture true mourning in a description of pure reading, so that true mourning and rhetorical reading merge into a single act: "If mourning is called a 'chambre d'éternel deuil où vibrent de vieux râles,' then this pathos of terror states in fact the desired consciousness of eternity and of temporal harmony as voice and as song. True 'mourning' is less deluded. The most *it* can do is to allow for non-comprehension and enumerate non-anthropomorphic, non-elegiac, non-celebratory, non-lyrical, non-poetic, that is to say, prosaic, or, better, *historical* modes of language power" (p. 262; de Man's emphases). "True mourning" is emphatically an "it" because it does not stabilize itself around the figure of a human being, thereby creating an aesthetic or ethical object. In other words, it reads its history purely as language power. But this effect is in fact closer to melancholy than to mourning. For melancholy is the activity of mourning for an object that cannot be either objectified or incorporated at a conscious level. In other words, when de Man attempts to purify mourning of its object, he finds not true mourning but true melancholy.

I have always felt that de Man's writings evoked a sense of melancholy. Some critics have accused him of nihilism, but they have confused the nothingness of nihilism with the repression of the object found in melancholy. The discovery of de Man's collaborationist writings finally provides a motivation for his melancholic refusal of the object of mourning. Melancholy allows the mourning of the loss of a loss; and politically, in terms of de Man's past, it describes an activity of mourning in which the object of mourning, the Jews, cannot be named.

This effect becomes strongest and most apparent with the death of de Man himself because the response of his disciples both amplifies and exposes it. De Man's theory of reading asks us to interpret without constituting a human object, and a whole generation of his students reads in this manner. Yet when they confront the death of Paul de Man, their reading breaks down, as he predicted reading always must, because their interpretations fix on the figure of the smiling mentor. But this imperative to mourn for de Man gains extra purchase, when we realize that a subtext exists in which he is already performing a reading that wills to mourn without an object but fails because it always turns back on itself, egotistically, to constitute the reader—in this case, Paul de Man—as the object of mourning. To name the objects, de Man's reading tries not to mourn for the Jews in his past, but it turns necessarily into a mourning for his own past. Here one would have to trace how "history" in de Man's theory works specifically as a metaphor for the violent history of World War II. One would also have to expose de Man's use of a rhetoric of marginality as well as his talent for appropriating the victimary status of authors such as Rousseau, Hölderlin, Shelley, Keats, Baudelaire, Nietzsche, and Rilke.[6] The surprise is that de Man's disciples cannot imitate his reading because a true reading in this style would always name the reader as the mourned object, but his students turn to discipleship instead, that is, they name de Man in place of themselves.

It would take considerably more space than I have here to justify this hypothesis, but let me turn briefly to two cases. The first is de Man's relation to Freud. De Man's relationship to Freud has been difficult for critics to pin down. He seems to use a Freudian discourse at times, but he never names Freud. Richard Klein has tried to trace the association, and he expresses amazement at the fact that de Man manages to maneuver without ever referring to Freud. Yet Klein does not resituate Freud in de Man's text. More recently, Cynthia Chase has written about de Man's relation to Freud in terms of the idea of resistance, but she does so without naming the most obvious point of attachment.[7] De Man's "The Resistance to Theory" echoes Freud's "The Resistances to Psycho-Analysis" on many fronts, the most interesting one in this context being a parallel between Freud's solitary stand against anti-Semitism and de Man's solitary stand against the MLA. Of course, de Man also repeats Freud's argument that resistance to psychoanalysis demonstrates the truth of psychoanalysis, concluding that the resistance to theory is theory itself. But, for Chase, resistance is not really a Freudian concept; it becomes de Man's word. I cannot help thinking in this context of the article on "Une Doctrine juive: Le Freudisme" printed next to de Man's text of anti-Semitism in *Le Soir*. Here is a true phantom text, close to de Man's, bordering on it: and yet not the same text. Its author contends that Freud's own disciples made his theory more Jewish than it was, giving it additional force in a "société décadente et en-

juivée." Similarly, de Man's "Les Juifs dans la littérature actuelle" strives to save modern literary phenomena from an apparent decadence, "parce que enjuivés," by describing their ability to purify themselves of Jewish influences. The irony, according to de Man, remains that "vulgar anti-Semitism" views modern literature as decadent because it fails to comprehend the essentially anti-Semitic nature of modern forms! In the specific case of Freud, then, we try to name Freud as Jew in de Man's text, but we end by naming instead a textuality that will not permit his Jewishness to emerge. We discover, in short, a textuality whose essence is a Jewish refusal of Jewishness, a textuality whose force resembles all too clearly the theories of Paul de Man.

The second case is de Man's relation to Derrida. I want to suggest, half seriously, that Derrida has become de Man's disciple. There have always been those who have tried to name de Man as a disciple of Derrida, but the label has not held. Others have tried to purify Derrida of the "vulgar Americanism" of de Manian deconstruction, but Derrida has himself rendered the attempt ineffective by turning to de Man for guidance. The initial encounter between Derrida and de Man occurs in "The Rhetoric of Blindness," where de Man outmaneuvers Derrida at his own game by giving away the game to Rousseau. Derrida is the master of the game, "Whoever loses wins," but de Man underbids Derrida in a kind of intellectual equivalent to golf by coming in with a lower score.[8] Derrida deconstructs Rousseau, but de Man names Rousseau as the exemplary case of self-indictment on which the text of modern philosophy is founded. Rousseau deconstructs himself, de Man argues, and Derrida is guilty of trying to win, simply because he takes Rousseau as an object. Reading without this object, de Man transforms all textuality into that of "Rousseau." By losing himself to Rousseau, de Man wins the right to be "Rousseau."

Derrida is still reeling from his initial encounter with de Man. He dedicates books to de Man, as if he were the disciple. He returns to the scene to replay the debate. Whether Derrida's gesture bespeaks true admiration or only makes the attempt to underbid the master in order to make him "win" is probably unimportant. For both gestures belong to the same game. The point is moot in the end because de Man died prematurely, making it difficult to underbid him. Derrida then turned to the lecture circuit, reading his private correspondence with de Man on stage. He wrote *Mémoires* for de Man, while simultaneously trying to write his own life story.[9]

Mémoires is, above all, a work of mourning, but it is less obvious that it also imitates de Man's method of reading. Derrida creates two powerful and personal analogies that rely ultimately on de Man's technique in "The Rhetoric of Blindness." First, he accepts de Man's description of Hölderlin's "sacred singularity" and then gives that position to de Man, the "Hölderlin in America." Second, Derrida repeats de Man's reading of Rousseau for de Man: "always already, as Paul de Man says, there is deconstruction at work in the work of Rousseau . . . always already, there is deconstruction at work in the work of Paul de Man . . . " (p.124). *Mémoires* shows that Derrida has learned the proper humility from de Man. He will not attempt an act of mastery this time. He will win only by giving in to loss. Indeed, *Mémoires* plays out a strange transference, in which Derrida appropriates de Man's funereal marginality by giving everything away to him. The book situates de Man amid the constellation of the great mad thinkers of Western modernity but remains oddly silent about its author. De Man, not Derrida, is responsible for "deconstruction in America." De Man, not Derrida, is the object of attacks. Derrida does not speak in his own name. Il donne au nom de l'autre.

To give to the name of the other, or to give in the name of the other, serves the work of mourning. But it also plays the game between reading and mourning discovered by Paul de Man. This game secretly guides the relationship between Derrida and de Man for many years, but it can no longer be contained when de Man dies. When Derrida speaks at de Man's funeral of "la mort dans l'âme," he finally presents the problem of mourning as introjection in explicit terms, although it has been there implicitly for a long time. In short, Derrida encounters de Man's melancholy, his relentless desire to read without an object other than himself, and like the good student, like de Man himself (for de Man is his own best student), he turns it into mourning by naming the master as object.

How de Man's disciples will react to the present controversy will be interesting, to say the least. For now de Man has really lost the game. His situation is closest to that of the mature Nietzsche, another master of the game of wining by losing. After a life time of trying to find a position of marginality and uniqueness, Nietzsche attained the position posthumously when his sister gave him away to the Nazis, thus transforming him into a convenient icon for everything that the West has now rejected. The future of de Man's theories depends on whether the present "loss" can be construed as a "win" and on whether his followers can continue to name their master as an object. If they are able to name de Man in their texts, the work of mourning and anthropomorphism will continue. If they cannot name de Man, if they refuse the object, their writings risk turning melancholic. In both cases, however, whether they name or repress de Man, their readings may well continue to repeat a melancholy subtext that refuses to name the true object of mourning.

If reading and mourning are indeed parallel structures, as de Man's theory suggests, then there is no way out of this dilemma: and we are destined to remember or to repress the figure of de Man in the space that he left absent for that purpose. But if this parallel is merely an effect of de Man's personal history, then we should be aware of the ideological and egotistical intent lurking in any theory that would confuse mourning and reading. De Man's essay on "Les Juifs" concludes with an unmournful solution. He argues that the loss of the Jews will not affect the future of literature: "En plus, on voit donc qu'une solution du problème juif qui viserait à la création d'une colonie juive isolée de l'Europe, n'entraînerait pas, pour la vie littéraire de l'Occident, de conséquences déplorables. Celle-ci perdrait, en tout et pour tout, quelques personnalités de médiocre valeur et continuerait, comme par le passé, à se développer selon ses grandes lois évolutives." No doubt, de Man spent the rest of his life mourning this solution, but he never named the true object of mourning. If the inevitable outcome of mourning is the incorporation of a figure, let us be sure to remember the right one. The number is six million; their name in history is the Jews.

University of Michigan, Ann Arbor

NOTES

1. *Yale French Studies* 69 (1985).

2. "Les Juifs dans la littérature actuelle," *Le Soir* 55:54, March 4, 1941, 10.

3. Geoffrey Hartman's "Blindness and Insight: Paul de Man, Fascism, and Deconstruction," in *The New Republic,* March 7, 1988, 26–33, is the best assessment to appear in the popular press so far. But the essay by Jon Wiener in *The Nation* and the one by David Lehman in *Newsweek* are riddled with error. The latter is especially disturbing because its layout, which juxtaposes pictures of de Man and Nazi soldiers on the march, bears a remarkable similarity to the original page of *Le Soir* where de Man's essay first appeared. See Jon Wiener, "Deconstructing de Man," *The Nation,* January 9, 1988, 22–24, and David Lehman, "Deconstructing de Man's Life," *Newsweek,* February 15, 1988, 63.

4. The term "inhuman" arises in a discussion of de Man's "Task of the Translator," in *The Resistance to Theory* (Minneapolis, Mn: University of Minnesota Press, 1986), pp.94–99.

5. "Anthropomorphism and Trope in the Lyric," in *The Rhetoric of Romanticism* (New York: Columbia University Press, 1984), pp.239–62.

6. See my "Paul de Man and the Triumph of Falling," in *The Ethics of Criticism* (Ithaca: Cornell University Press, 1988), chap.5.

7. Cf. Richard Klein, "The Blindness of Hyperboles: The Ellipses of Insight," *Diacritics* 3, no. 2 (1973), 33–44, and Cynthia Chase, "The Witty Butcher's Wife: Freud, Lacan, and the Conversion of Resistance to Theory," *MLN* 102, no. 5 (1987), 989–1013.

8. Derrida locks on to the phrase "Whoever loses wins," in *Margins of Philosophy,* trans.Alan Bass (Chicago: University of Chicago Press, 1982), p.20.

9. Jacques Derrida, *Mémoires: For Paul de Man,* trans. Cecile Lindsay, Jonathan Culler, and Eduardo Cadava (New York: Columbia University Press, 1986), 12.

Observations on Occupation

S. DAVID SPERLING

As a member of the Tuscaloosa symposium on "Our Academic Contract," I was privileged to be among the first group of scholars to examine the early writings of Paul de Man, including some with identifiable anti-Semitic elements. As the lone outsider—a philologist who works in ancient Semitic languages, Old Testament and early Judaism—among a gathering of distinguished literary theorists and philosophers, I felt obligated to offer my own observations. While I cannot claim expertise in the work under consideration, I hope at least to provide an additional perspective.

Paul de Man, by virtue of his Belgian nationality, embodies in himself some of the conflicts which have been a force in Jewish literature from its beginnings. The questions of national identity, and the attitudes of Jews towards foreign powers, occupiers and oppressors have never been resolved fully in Jewish history. At the same time, they are in many ways, the driving forces of Jewish creativity.

Reactions to occupation by foreign powers are documented in the Hebrew Bible as early as the eighth century B.C.(Isaiah 1:7). The related sense of being an alien in countries where one's ancestors have lived for generations is already witnessed in the Aramaic papyri written by the Jews of Elephantine in Egypt of the fifth century B.C.and continues unabated thereafter. Several of de Man's early pieces recall a spirit markedly similar to these ancient Jewish texts.

The review, "L'exposition 'Histoire d'Allemagne' au Cinquantenaire, " dated March 16, 1942, presents a rather favorable view of the Germans. One might argue that the description of the Germans as "un peuple dont l'importance est fondamentale pour le destin de l'Europe" is an unenthusiastic statement of resignation to almost two years of German rule. Such a charitable reading, however, would ignore the positive lessons that, according to de Man in the same piece, Belgians could learn from "une source vivante de notre civilisation."

I call to the reader's attention an anecdote found in the Babylonian Talmud (Shabbat 33b). The story is set in the second century A.D.in the Roman province of Syria-Palestine, formerly, Judea:

Rabbi Judah, Rabbi Jose and Rabbi Simeon were sitting together. Judah, son of proselytes, was sitting with them. Rabbi Judah began the discussion by saying: 'How good are the deeds of this nation (the Romans)! They have set up markets, bridges and bathhouses.' Rabbi Jose remained silent but Rabbi Simeon spoke up and said: 'Everything they have set up, has only been for their own needs. They set up markets to seat prostitutes, bathhouses for their own indulgence, and bridges for the collection of tolls.' Judah, son of proselytes, related the discussions, which came to the attention of the ruling powers,who decreed: '(Rabbi) Judah who alibied shall be elevated (Hebrew pun: *yehudah she-'illah yit 'aleh*); Jose who was silent shall be exiled to Sepphoris; Simeon who defamed shall be executed.'

De Man's appreciation of the Germans seems to be akin to Rabbi Judah' s evaluation of the Romans. It is collaboration with people "dont l'importance est fondamentale," justified by the citation of their visible achievements.

But at least one piece, the now-notorious "Les Juifs dans la littérature actuelle," points in a different direction. First, one wonders why a fascist by conviction would have taken the trouble to deny the significance of the Jews in contemporary literature. It was far easier and more common to affirm negative Jewish influence and to join in the Nazi effort towards its extirpation. Second, in the seemingly off-handed favorable reference to the Jewish writer Kafka, de Man includes him in the same literary tradition as Gide. This is particularly striking, given that in 1914 Gide had written: "the virtues of the Jewish race are not French virtues . . . the contribution of Jewish qualities to literature is less likely to provide new elements (that is, an enrichment) than it is to interrupt the slow explanation of a race and to *falsify seriously, intolerably even, its meaning*" (emphasis added. See *Journals of André Gide,* trans. J. O'Brien, 2 [1948], 4). In other words, De Man's essay contains the seeds of its own negation.

In this connection I was reminded of the Jewish "Prayer for the Government." Allegedly based on the advice given by Jeremiah (29:7) to the Babylonian exiles of the sixth century B.C. to pray for the peace of the foreign cities in which they dwelt, the prayer as shaped in the Middle Ages served as a protestation of Jewish loyalty to often hostile powers. The standard form of the prayer begins:

May the one who gives salvation to kings and dominion to princes, whose kingdom is an everlasting kingdom, who delivers his servant David from the destructive sword, bless, preserve, guard, assist, exalt and aggrandize the sovereign [royal name and titles] . . . May the king of kings incline the sovereign to deal kindly with us and with all Israel.

The prayer concludes with two quotations. The first (Jeremiah 23:6) reads: "In his day Judah will be redeemed and Israel will dwell in security." The second reads: "A redeemer shall come to Zion (Isaiah 59:20)." Both of these verses belong to Jewish messianic tradition, which looks to the restoration of Jewish sovereignty in the land of Israel and the end of the Diaspora, where Jews are subject to foreigners. By ending in this fashion the prayer negated its stated purpose of asking for the blessing and preservation of the gentile sovereign.

The irony that an occupied people employs to vent its frustrations and hopes is, by necessity, subtle. Indeed Jewish rabbinic sources abound in irony. Belgium, in many ways, shared aspects of the Jewish experience of uncertain identity and subjugation, elements that would have been most pronounced during the Nazi occupation. Perhaps the parallels from Jewish sources cited here will aid in the understanding of Paul de Man and his work.

Hebrew Union College
Jewish Institute of Religion

Determinations: Paul de Man's Wartime Journalism

MICHAEL SPRINKER

Like many of the contributors to the present volume, I came to know and admire Paul de Man personally. Long before I saw or met him, I had been impressed by the intellectual rigor and the passion for the truth exhibited in essays like "The Rhetoric of Temporality" and those collected in *Blindness and Insight*. I well remember my first encounter with the person behind the words. I was greatly taken aback by the charm and urbanity of his manner, and above all at the gentle amusement he showed in discussing the sexual overtones in Locke's theory of metaphor. This tension between the severity of de Man's writing, and the disarming wit and humor of the person, is not easily resolved, as the testimony of former students and colleagues attests. In my experience of him, de Man could be by turns tough and unyielding, or tender and encouraging. Not an easy man to figure out, I often thought. But it never surprised me that he could inspire in equal measure adulation and mistrust or fear. What did sometimes surprise me was that his friends were scarcely ever wary of him, since he could be quite as bitingly sarcastic with them, as ruthless in exposing the weakness in their speech and thought, as with any opponent.

In the spirit of de Man's own critical practice, we are called upon to exercise our most severe judgment in examining the writings of our friends. This is not to say that one should rush to join the chorus of detractors who now feel licensed to lodge the most outrageous charges against de Man's later writings and against deconstruction in general. The links between de Man's youthful journalism—and it was just that; he was not yet twenty-three when he resigned from *Le Soir* in November 1942—and his mature theoretical work are, in the present state of scholarship and criticism, tentative at best. It may be possible to construct a plausible itinerary leading from his wartime writings to the essays written during the 1960s and ultimately to the final chapters of *Allegories of Reading*. But the long interpretive labor required for such an undertaking has to date never been performed—least of all by de Man's leading critics. My task here is a more humble and limited one: to wit, to assess the political determinations that formed the immediate context of de Man's wartime writings and to interpret the significance of these latter in the light of the historical situation that produced them. My contribution to this debate is therefore less concerned with the moral indictment or exculpation of Paul de Man than with understanding the political configuration of which he was at this period one symptom. The emphasis in what follows falls more on the forces and circumstances that produced Paul de Man than on what he himself wrote or thought. To speak in a jargon for which de Man had at most grudging (although near the end of his life, growing) respect, the central question addressed here will be: what structures did Paul de Man bear that led him to write texts that could arguably be called collaborationist, and, in a few instances, in the voice of a sometime anti-semite?

In addition, I shall in conclusion take up a question that the debate over de Man's early career has raised with increasing urgency. It concerns the pertinence of journalistic presentations of academic theory to the political valence which theory can be said to exhibit, that is, the so-called politics of theory. De Man's own career poses this question most starkly, since it is precisely the relationship between the later theoretical work and the earlier journalistic writings that is at stake in the public debate over de Man. The division between de Man's defenders and detractors tends, in many cases, to split neatly along the theory/journalism fault line, which is not to say that the writings of theoreticians remain exogenous to journalistic discourse. I leave it to readers of this piece to judge on which side of the divide my own contribution falls.

* * * * *

The principal motifs of de Man's wartime texts will be familiar by now. They include at least the following: Europe and its historico-political destiny; the fate of the Flemish (or occasionally the Belgian) nation in the wake of occupation; the cultural specificity of France versus that of Germany; the nature of literature and its autonomy from political and ideological determination. The most striking—and at the same time most puzzling—thing about these articles is their attempt to mediate between literary production, declared again and again to be a distinct and separable sphere of human activity, and politics, history, and society. On the face of it, the texts seem to propose two contradictory claims. 1) Literature is a particular kind of thing, with properties distinguishing it from political or ideological discourse; correlatively, literary history evolves solely according to laws intrinsic to literature itself. 2) In literature one can read the signs of a nation's or an entire civilization's evolutionary trajectory; literature allows ready access to the laws of development governing the history of cultures and societies.

My initial question about these texts is the following: what is at stake in the attempt to negotiate or perhaps simply to comprehend this apparent contradiction? Or, to return to our way of formulating the general problem of de Man's writings, more fundamentally: what determined the production of a series of texts that simultaneously embrace the two opposed discourses of what we might call formalism and historicism? If we but mention the names of Shklovsky, Eichenbaum, Tynianov, Jakobson, Mukařovský, Bakhtin, and even Sartre, one sees imme-

diately that the problem exceeds the scope of the person Paul de Man and the writings we are now discussing. *A fortiori,* its full significance cannot be grasped by appeal to simple categories like collaboration or resistance, much less anti-semitism. These punctual facts of the period certainly inflected the theoretical problems mobilized in de Man's texts; they did not, however, determine them in any univocal way. To invoke once more a terminology for which an older Paul de Man had scant sympathy, what is most notable about the articles in *Le Soir* and *Het Vlaamsche Land* is just their complex overdetermination, precisely their manifest contradiction.

What were the material determinations of these wartime writings? We may isolate four principal factors, schematized according to a method of demarcation that by now ought to be familiar to an anglophone audience. They are the economic, the political, the ideological, and the theoretical. If we provisionally denote de Man's texts as theoretical, this is not to suggest that they remain entirely exterior to the other instances or levels just enumerated. It should not be necessary here to indicate the ways in which they participated in or resisted—it is far from settled which it may have been—certain ideological forms dominant in that period and that place. Neither is it difficult to see in their very ideological functioning certain political effects, although once again the precise nature of those effects is yet to be measured. Their impact upon economic practice is more obscure, difficult even to imagine. But their *determination by the economy* is scarcely in doubt. De Man's marginal position in occupied Belgium, his lack of any profession or immediate means of material livelihood, is well-known. He would not have been the first or the last intellectual who turned to journalism when the prospects for an academic career vanished. One could say more, were space available, about the peculiar constraints that operated upon bourgeois intellectuals in the occupied nations of Europe after their economies were integrated into the German state's war effort, but it would be a diversion from our main purpose here. Let the matter rest thus: he wrote, and he did so for money.

Our second determining instance, the political, presents a more complicated case. It has long been known that de Man's relationship to his uncle Henri was an important factor in his early formation. It now appears that this same uncle was at least in part responsible for the nephew's being granted the extraordinary opportunity to write a regular column on literature and culture for the principal daily newspaper in Brussels. Could we then conclude that the political horizon of these writings was generally the line followed by Henri de Man during the first years of occupation? I shall in any event hazard the view that this is so, but it remains to give an account, however preliminary and inadequate, of the uncle's political itinerary during this period and in the years leading up to it.

The salient facts are undisputed and can therefore be rehearsed briefly. Born into a prosperous Flemish bourgeois family in Antwerp, Henri de Man became involved in socialist politics as a young man, taught for many years in workers' educational institutions, became disillusioned with orthodox Second International marxism in the aftermath of World War I, pursued an academic career in Germany and the United States during the 1920s, participated in Belgian politics—including service in several governments as minister of public works and later finance—helped formulate the policy of Belgian capitulation to the Nazis pursued by Leopold III, continued to work within the existing political institutions during the first years of Nazi occupation, and fled to an Alpine refuge after the German invasion of the Soviet Union. Probably the most notorious fact known of him is that he was convicted *in absentia* of collaboration.

Henri de Man claimed life-long allegiance to socialism, although his conception of what the term signified and his understanding of the means for realizing it in the developed capitalist world would alter radically in the more than forty years of his political and intellectual career. Espousing something like Sorelian anarchism in his youth, he would ultimately embrace a forbiddingly pessimistic view of politics and the prospects for socialist transformation closely resembling the post-war position of Horkheimer and Adorno, in whose immediate milieu he had taught and written in the twilight of the Weimar Republic. The decisive issue here, however, involves his decision to counsel capitulation and to maintain active involvement in the political affairs of occupied Belgium, thereby lending a measure of legitimacy to the Nazi occupiers. What factors could have led to this apparent *volte face* in de Man's political thinking and actions?

Let us hypothesize four, in no particular order of temporal or causal importance: 1) the betrayal of Belgium at the Treaty of Versailles; 2) disillusionment with the achievements of revolutionary socialism (in particular, a marked anti-Bolshevism that ante-dated its Stalinist *dénouement*); 3) distaste for the obstacles placed in the path towards socialism by parliamentary politics; 4) a certain *haut bourgeois* disdain for working-class life and culture, what one might call a native elitism not unfamiliar in class traitors whose politics were less open to censure (Adorno comes to mind again, but so for that matter does Lukács). The last three are of course ideological vectors that inflected Henri de Man's political trajectory, but it is only possible to gauge the

significance his political judgments and actions in terms of these ideological determinations. One can say with some confidence that a gradual loss of faith in the prospects for revolutionary socialism, combined with his long-standing rejection of capitalist democracy, left Henri de Man without any viable or coherent political alternative to capitulation, and pushed him, temporarily to be sure, into an uneasy alliance with Nazism. Unlike more spirited and committed ideologues of fascism or nationalism (say, Gustave de Clercq or Léon Degrelle), de Man collaborated *faute de mieux,* a decision he would ultimately come to regret.

Where does this leave the case of the nephew? It is not possible in the current state of the scholarly record to know how closely Paul de Man followed in the political footsteps of his uncle. Nonetheless, one recognizes the lineaments of the latter's position in the actions and in the words of the former. Cooperation with the occupiers was for both a means of survival: for the uncle it held out the hope for an independent Belgium preserved from the worst ravages of military conquest; for the nephew it was a necessary (although perhaps not the only available) means to pursue an intellectual career. Something of the uncle's hope is apparent in the nephew's articles. The uncle's recognition of his error was followed within a year by the nephew's abandonment of his position at *Le Soir.* The costs of working under the Nazis became clear to both in the end; the immediate causes of their common realization remain obscure.

We have already mentioned some of the ideological forces that determined Paul de Man's wartime writings, but only from the angle of his uncle's political itinerary. Of the principal motifs already noted in these articles, Eurocentrism and pro-Germanism leap out, if only because they are of most immediate moment for the two charges that have been brought against de Man: anti-semitism and collaboration. There can be no doubt that anti-semitism thrived in an environment where German nationalism and the discourse of "Europe's destiny" coincided. To the degree that de Man's writings participated in anti-semitism, they did so in just this way, precisely excising Jewish writers from "the great tradition" of European thought, at the same time extolling the virtues of German literature. One might argue that pro-German sentiments were the price one had to pay for writing at all in occupied Belgium at this period, but it is impossible to ignore the note of conviction in de Man's prose when he writes about the authentic destiny of European civilization and the signal importance of German culture in realizing it. That the matter is more complicated than this, that de Man's discourse also contests the very chauvinism (interestingly, a word that appears in one of the articles on Jünger, only to be corrected to "classicism" in a subsequent *erratum* note) it exhibits, is beyond doubt. But to say so does not reduce the force of this discourse's pull on de Man's theoretical position. As it is the latter that most concerns us here, we may turn to it now.

It was suggested earlier that the salient contradiction structuring these texts consists in the opposition between formalism and historicism. One must insist on the term "contradiction" being taken in its strongest sense, that is, as the cohabitation in a single text or series of texts of incompatible motifs, ideologemes, or theoretical programs. What remains most theoretically noteworthy about de Man's wartime writings is their stubborn refusal to sacrifice either pole of the formalism/historicism dyad, their continuing enterprise of trying to square the circle of this problematic. The desire for deliverance has a name, and de Man invokes it often: literature. The incapacity to escape the force of contradiction has a name as well, and de Man cites it nearly as frequently: history. It would not be entirely wrong, therefore, to say that these texts stand convicted, not of collaboration (although one could say that too), but of isolation, or if one prefers, of defeat. To the extent that they hypostasize the autonomy of literature in relation to politics, history, and ideology, they reproduce the political and ideological program of capitulation. To the extent that they also maintain the unavoidable historical determination of aesthetic practice by socio-historical forces, they resist the very ideology they proclaim. Whether this resistance was itself but a subtler form of collaboration with the then dominant ideology of culture can only be decided by more careful treatment of the texts themselves in relation to the full range of discursive positions available at the time. It is far from certain at this juncture what the terms "collaboration" and "resistance" can be said to encompass. If de Man's texts and his actions can be said to veer in one direction or the other at different moments between 1940 and 1942 (or after), this does not signify the abandonment of his problematic, the overcoming of the contradiction. The rigor of theoretical practice does not admit such easy resolutions.

* * * * *

For nearly two full years, Paul de Man was a journalist engaged to write on literature and the arts. On the evidence available to me at the time of writing, he seems to have abandoned his position under the pressure of increasing censorship, although he did not cease entirely his associations with various publication organs under Nazi control. Until the liberation, de Man continued to work in the interstices of the existing cultural apparatus, as, if you will, a journalist still. After the war, he emigrated to the United States, did graduate work in comparative literature

at Harvard and ultimately secured full-time academic employment in American and European universities.

If one examines the archive of de Man's published writings (as it has been reconstructed up to this point), surely its most puzzling feature is the imbalance between the prolific output of his youth and the comparatively sparse production of the two decades after the war. Even once de Man began again to publish regularly from the mid-1960s, the scale of production remained modest by comparison with that in his early years. One can imagine any number of reasons for this: the necessity to compose quickly when one's livelihood is tied directly to the quantity one writes, compared with the relative security conferred by an academic salary; the protocols of scholarly writing which require time-consuming research as opposed to the less stringent demands of writing for non-scholarly publications; the commitment of time to teaching and administration of which every academic complains (not without reason), and from which journalists are blissfully free. Doubtless some combination of these differences between the working conditions of journalists and those of university professors obtained for the mature Paul de Man and prevented his attaining the same level of productivity he had reached in his early twenties.

I wish to suggest, however, that another, and arguably more coercive, factor was at work in de Man's later career, limiting his published work by imposing on it a discipline that did not operate with the same force in his wartime writings. One regularly encounters in these latter the broad outlines of a program of research that could only be carried out over a long period, certain claims about literature and culture that require infinitely more empirical substantiation than can be presented in the space of a one or two-page article. One can discern, in short, the lineaments of a theory grossly underdetermined by the evidence adduced for it. We have already given a schematic account of the theoretical problematic of these writings. But this problematic remained, one feels, largely *impensé* in the writings themselves. This is to say that de Man's journalism failed precisely to register the contradictions which produced it, however lucid it may have been about some of the conditions to which it was responding. We might even say that de Man was guilty here of a certain naivete, particularly if, as is surely possible, he thought that by writing for the occupation press he was engaged in a form of resistance. In any event, the record as we have it will not support the view that his writings were a consistent prosecution of resistance by other means. De Man's rupture with his past came later and in a form that did not simply repudiate all that he had previously written.

What de Man did give up was the mode of writing and inquiry that had produced those most culpable pieces (notably "Les Juifs dans la Littérature actuelle"). He had been a literary journalist; he would become a theoretician of literature. I remarked earlier that to be engaged in theoretical work by profession does not exclude one from the domain of journalistic discourse. Nor is journalism itself exempt from theoretical responsibility. And yet one must insist that these two modes of intellectual inquiry and intervention remain distinct in their relation to politics and ideology. The relative autonomy of theory is a consequence of the cognitive autonomy of science, which imposes a discipline on its practitioners that journalism only rarely honors or observes.

De Man's break with his past, the signs of which are already present in the contradictory unity of his wartime writings, consisted not in any facile change of political allegiance, but in a life-long commitment to the labor of sustained theoretical reflection. Any consequent determination of the relationship between his youthful writings and the theoretical position he occupied in the final two decades of his life will have to take into account the different levels of inquiry on which each proceeded. That itself is a theoretical point, but one that journalists, to the degree that they are concerned with establishing the truth of matters, ought perhaps to heed. They decline to do so on pain of reproducing the same type of distortion of which they, not without warrant, accuse the journalist Paul de Man. Theoretical vigilance has its place in journalism, too. Greater respect for the demands it makes on thinking and writing would act as a brake on the in-built tendencies of journalism to generalize too hastily about and simplify the complexities of history. If one doubts this, I recommend examining a later set of journalistic texts by the then professor and theoretician Paul de Man. His reviews of contemporary European literature and thought published in the *New York Review of Books* during the 1960s are a model of mature speculation, compressed by scholarly standards, but no less precise or perspicacious for that. Read against the background of de Man's wartime writings, these texts exemplify the higher standard to which literary journalism can demonstrably aspire—higher, that is, than either the youthful Paul de Man or his contemporary detractors achieved.

SUNY-Stony Brook

De Man and Guilt

ALLAN STOEKL

I am not given to retrospective self-examination and mercifully forget what I have written with the same alacrity I forget bad movies—although, as with bad movies, certain scenes or phrases return at times to embarrass and haunt me like a guilty conscience.—*de Man, "Foreword to Revised, Second Edition of Blindness and Insight."*

So it was the fact that Sartre wrote essays like *L'Imaginaire, L'Etre et le néant,* which were technical philosophical books, while at the same time being a literary critic, at the same time being somebody who expressed strong opinions on political matters—that somewhat bicephalic dissent of the philosopher—had a very strong attraction; I don't think anybody of my generation ever got over that. We all somehow would like to be like that: it takes about a whole life to get over this notion [. . .]—*de Man, "Interview with Stefano Rosso," in* The Resistance to Theory

The knowledge of radical innocence also performs the harshest mutilations.—*de Man, chapter 12* ("Excuses"), Allegories of Reading

There are two types of readings of Paul de Man's *Le Soir* articles that should be, I think, avoided. The first is what I would call a naive Sartrian reading, which attempts to present all of de Man's later work as inherently "reactionary" because, at the age of 21 and 22, he wrote newspaper articles, in a German funded and controlled paper, that were clearly sympathetic to the changes taking place in the "revolutionary epoch" (as he calls it)[1] in which he was living. In this sure to be played out scenario, Sartre gets his revenge on de Man; the really important de Manian writings will not be read, but, as so often happens, de Man's "life decision" will be examined, his personal "choice" will be evaluated, and no doubt condemned. That the kind of analysis elaborated in *Allegories of Reading* does not lend itself easily (or at all) to use by ethicists, estheticians, hermeneuts or formalists will be attributed to the fact that de Man all along was only "a fascist." Above all, the argument will be put forward that his apparent elimination, for example at the end of *Allegories of Reading,* of the possibility of a morally responsible subjectivity is proof, at best, of "moral idiocy," and, at worst, a simple refusal to come to terms with his own guilt.[2] The complexities of the text will be ignored, while biographical evidence will be sifted; moral evaluation will be issued, both of de Man "himself," and of "deconstruction." One need only read Sartre's biography of Baudelaire (or Genet, Mallarmé, Flaubert) to see where this kind of approach leads. The second tactic, equally misguided, and carried out with an equally clear conscience, will attempt "rhetorical readings" of certain of the 1941–42 articles, no doubt to show that they too can be "deconstructed," that de Man is not writing about the decadence of French culture, the role of the Jews in post-WW I literature,[3] the "necessity" of the replacement of prewar individualism with the recognition of the tasks to be carried out in a German-occupied "postwar" Europe—he is "really" writing only about language itself, and the problems of rhetoric that go along with it. This kind of approach—which many critics affirm when it is used by de Man himself in an analysis of, say, Rousseau's *Social Contract*—seems insufficient when we are talking about a writing practice that was, one could argue, inseparable from a larger policy of the intellectual "pacification" of a conquered, but (from the Nazi point of view) not entirely trustworthy, people.[4]

Are we, as readers of de Man, to be caught between these two poles, torn between a simplistic moral or political judgment of the young de Man and an uncritical acceptance of the later de Man's theory? How, in other words, can one talk about the seemingly inevitable political and social responsibility of the engaged intellectual (for this is what de Man was in 1941–42, and what he fervently resisted later), or of the thinker in general, while at the same time affirming, or at least taking seriously, an approach that seems to leave no possibility whatsoever for any kind of moral responsibility, individual conscience, or free subjectivity? If we can pose this question—the real "cassetête" of contemporary theory—it will only be because we have recognized, first, that no simple dividing line can be drawn between de Man's *Le Soir* articles and (for example) *Allegories of Reading*. Many of the Belgian articles pose problems that are still being grappled with forty years later—and, even near the end of his life, de Man was positing a textual "machine" whose method of accounting for the production and excusing of guilt will suddenly be seen as a necessary (and also highly suspect) strategy when one recognizes the gravity of the implications of the writings that were kept secret for so long. My purpose in this article is not to put forward any moral evaluation or condemnation, but rather to follow, if only very briefly, the inscription of guilt in de Man's text—guilt as a theme, but also guilt as the very practice of writing itself—and the various binds that this inscription entails. I will not attempt to resolve the aporia (if one chooses to call it that) between ethical judgment and rhetorical reading, but to stress the necessity and impossibility of the collaboration between these two options, in de Man's text itself. As we will see, both at a very early stage of de Man's career, and at a very late one, de Man rigorously excludes a guilty responsibility—the gesture of political and moral interpretation and commitment (in an early article from 1942), the interpretation which itself imputes guilt (in a chapter from *Allegories of Reading*)—which, in the end, only forces him ever further into collusion with the very gesture he would refuse.

I want to examine first an article that appeared in *Le Soir* on 31 March 1942, a book review of the French translation of Ernst Jünger's *On the Marble Cliffs*.[5] Through this article, one can see quite clearly the problem de Man faced in writing a necessarily political article on a book that he maintained was rigorously apolitical.

De Man starts by presenting a theme that recurs often in his reviews: the French novelistic tradition, going back at least to Stendhal, was decadent; it promoted individualism, dry psychological and moral analysis, and it tended to display its own passionless, mechanical functioning. This decline is clearly associated with that of the French nation as a whole—a state of affairs that made the German conquest inevitable.[6] "Since Stendhal, the French novel is an explanatory work, a work of the intellect. It necessarily turns around a case, a problem, and its principle concern is to show, cog after cog, the complex mechanism that is made to function before our eyes."

The antidote to this decadence—de Man rather unconvin-

ingly (given what he says elsewhere about the weakness of France before the war) says that he is presenting it without the least desire to judge the French tradition—is, not surprisingly, German. For if the French approach is presented often as leading to, or inseparable from, weakness, the German is usually seen by de Man as one of strength, affirmation, synthesis, collectivity, in and through literary style.[7] And if French fiction and criticism entails dry analysis based on concerns alien to the specific strength of literature—de Man strongly criticizes literary analysis that judges works of art on psychological or moral grounds[8]—then German works will stress esthetic form at the expense of "extraneous" concerns; "poetic meditation," and the search for "metaphoric and symbolic forms" will be preferred to the "lucid clarity of analysis" and "precision in expression." This distrust of a literature or criticism that would perform the tasks of psychological, ethical, religious or political argumentation is ratified by Jünger's *On the Marble Cliffs*—or at least it is upheld by de Man's presentation of that novel. For, according to de Man, this is not an intellectual work; there is no message, only the depiction of characters who are "symbols," carried along by "forces and irresistible aspirations." "[O]ne must not confuse this conception of the world, field of battle between vice and virtue, of grandeur and baseness, with an insipid moralizing lesson. The work of Jünger is that of a poet and not a spiritual adviser." Indeed the novel, it would seem, is only a pretext for an "inspirational theme," a series of images of "sun, fire and blood."

De Man, then, closely associates imagination, inspiration and artistic form with an esthetic fusion that is represented in the novel by images of violent conflict and death. Despite all the talk of "mythical" experience, however, and of the "frisson that comes from true art," one can see that de Man is also pulled in another direction: "form" here is nothing other than "pure narration." Narration, in other words, about narration itself—for what else could the elements in the novel "symbolize," if they do not "objectively" refer to anything, and if they, unlike the contents of the French novel, have nothing to do with "comprehension and judgment"?

It might seem that the young de Man is still in fairly safe territory here, arguing for an esthetic self-reflexivity that the later de Man was to single out as just another "ideology."[9] But de Man's reading cannot remain purely esthetic, and in that way it risks falling from a neat specularity into a most treacherous vicious circle. For *On the Marble Cliffs* is not "inherently" esthetic and apolitical; de Man's is a highly tendentious interpretation, and one that is also profoundly political. In fact the conflict between the "forces of Good and Evil" in Jünger's novel practically force on the reader an allegorical interpretation of the crudest kind: the "Old Woodsman" ("Evil") is, one is led to conclude, none other than Hitler himself; the two brothers who are working in their mountain retreat ("Good") are easily interpreted as the elitist but impotent German intellectual opposition of the late 1920s and early 1930s. The novel is certainly suggestive as a roman à thèse—so much so, in fact, that the Nazis prohibited its reprinting in the early 1940s. To argue that the novel is not political—and to suggest that Jünger is therefore innocent of carrying out a subversive political gesture—is itself already political.[10] De Man's refusal of the "extra-literary" is inseparable, at this early stage, from the profoundly political gesture of affirming an esthetic quietude in the face of the Nazi "revolution"—all the more so since Jünger's novel virtually forces itself on the reader as an allegory of precisely that kind of withdrawal and its consequences.[11]

De Man is caught in a paradoxical position: he affirms a severing of art and criticism from morality and politics, but his very affirmation is necessarily political. He can only reassert this depoliticization by discrediting his own (political) affirmation of it. Like the serpent biting its own tail, the more he denounces the "engagement" of the writer and critic, the more "engagé" he finds himself, and thus all the more vulnerable to his own denunciation. To quote the later de Man himself, he "has to reaffirm, at the end of his argument, the priority of the category against which his argument has been consistently directed" (AR, 245).[12] That category, in the case of the article on Jünger at least, is a belief in the metaphorical analogy between the esthetic object (the self-reflexive literary work and the criticism that affirms it) and the realm of political and moral judgment.[13] (Indeed immediately after his discussion of Jünger's novel, de Man goes on to present, in a favorable light, two openly political books, one of which, *Agonie de la paix,* by Georges Suarez and Guy Laborde [1942], is a frank apology for the Nazi foreign policy immediately before and after the Munich crisis—the real culprits responsible for the war, according to the rather suspect narrative of Suarez and Laborde, were the French themselves, who, along with their Czech accomplices, from the Versailles treaty on unjustly attempted to weaken and contain the Germans.)

Put another way, the more innocent of writing a subversive thesis novel Jünger is, the more guilty of collaborating with the Nazis his writing becomes; in the same way, the more de Man asserts (via his proxy, Jünger) the innocence of his own writing in relation to any "extrinsic" morality or politics, the more guilty it too becomes. In this way de Man's criticism, rewriting Jünger's novel, becomes an allegory of the confrontation not so much of a mythical "Good and Evil," but of the "pure narration" of the force of an incessantly reaffirmed innocence which is always betrayed at the moment of its positing, in and through its positing, but whose betrayal always necessitates its reaffirmation and reelaboration.

We can ask, then, if the Jünger novel, as presented by de Man, is a purely self-referential esthetic object after all. Its "pure narrative," its "battle between Good and Evil" that is conveyed by symbols, must in fact be seen as an allegory not only of its own form, or of a certain political or social conjunction, but of the bind in which de Man's own critical text finds itself. In its very innocence it affirms its guilt and vice versa; this procedure would seem to entail not a definitive representational closure, but an open-ended repetition. De Man's writing can continue to excuse itself (as it does throughout these early articles) by arguing for an exclusively esthetic role for the novel and criticism;[14] the gesture after a while becomes both guilty and purely automatic—like the "cogs" of the French fiction to which de Man so strongly objects, but with which we can now see that his writing is in complicity. And here we are faced with a question which, as any reader of the later de Man knows, comes to have an overwhelming importance: does the guilt—the moral category and the responsible subjectivity it implies—"cause" the author to excuse himself by repetitiously valorizing a nonmoral (or extramoral) writing? Or is the guilt a mere after-effect of the exclusively mechanical positing of innocence? In other words, does the esthetic writing that refers only to writing present an "inner" conflict between "Good" and "Evil"—between moral terms, in other words, like guilt or innocence—or does it present a kind of incongruous juxtaposition (which perhaps can only be represented through images of violence, of heated conflict, of mechanical operation or mutilation) of a purely automatic process of excuse making and the inevitably moral or psychological representation and judgment which interprets— and misinterprets—it? Given de Man's orientation even in his early writings, we would be forced to opt for the latter position—but then, if the novel is fully divorced from questions of morality, as he argues, why would it present a struggle between eminently moral, pre-Nietzschean categories such as "Good" and "Evil"? Those very terms, and this conflict, must be read as allegories of something else—of the "pure narrative" that is the mechanism of the text, and that is the point of conjunction and rupture between the repetitive, mechanical excuse making and the guilt that is inevitably produced by it, and that serves only as a device through which the process can be known, and can continue.

Is this kind of argument, in the context of these early writngs, objectionable? Most of us, de Manians or not, would probably say so; it is impossible to read these pieces without forming a negative moral evaluation of the young de Man's conduct. He certainly knew what he was doing, there was nothing mechanical or blind about it—he was evidently a highly intelligent and well-read reviewer, and his contributions could only lend prestige and credibility to a collaborationist paper. They were a small part of the German strategy to undermine opposition by funding or in other ways backing relatively sophisticated and reputable newspapers like *Le Soir,* or highly prestigious reviews like the *Nouvelle Revue Française*. But then the question returns: how can we come to any conclusion about de Man's responsibility, his "engagement," how can we evaluate him from a political and moral standpoint, while at least respecting the methods of analysis he has left us?[15] The answer, which will probably be troubling for many, is that de Man's later writings precisely preclude the possibility of any moral or political critique or analysis of his early work. One certainly has the uncanny feeling when rereading them that certain pieces—such as the last two chapters of *Allegories of Reading*—were written in the shadow of the early articles (even with the expectation that those articles would one day be discovered), as extremely elaborate devices whose net effect is to defuse the very question of de Man's responsibility or guilt. The last chapter in particular can be read as an allegory of de Man's relation to his own responsibility: Rousseau's autobiography, in other words, can be read not only as an allegory of reading, but as an allegory of de Man's own reading of his own autobiography. But how can we see the last chapter of *Allegories of Reading* as autobiographical? Is there really any justification for this argument in de Man's text itself? Or is his text written in such a way that it precisely forestalls such an argument?

De Man first considers the stolen ribbon episode from the *Confessions* from the point of view of a reading oriented toward a critique or interpretation of desire. Such a reading, no doubt compatible with methods taken from psychoanalysis, is also suggested to anyone who has read the passages in the *Confessions* in which Rousseau indulges in his exhibitionistic tendencies. It is impossible not to associate the perverse pleasure Rousseau takes in his own exhibitionism (with Mlle Lambercier, for example) with the dialectic of desire implicit in the very writing of the *Confessions*. In other words, Rousseau himself, *in* his autobiography, suggests a method that will "uncover" his desire—and which he will inevitably affirm just as much as he affirms his "exposure" (in the act of exposing himself) by the various authority figures he presents in his text. Discussing this kind of approach early in his chapter, de Man notes the "true" shame of Rousseau's destruction of Marion: Rousseau carries it out "in order to provide him[self] with a stage on which to parade his disgrace or, what amounts to the same thing, to furnish him[self] with a good ending for Book II of the *Confessions*" (AR, 286). This "self perpetuating" structure entails a true "mise-en-abîme" in which "each new stage in the unveiling suggests a deeper shame, a greater impossibility to reveal, and a greater satisfaction in outwitting this impossibility."

The operative mode here is concealment; excuse making is always belated, occurring after the crime: "the excuse consists in recapitulating the exposure in the guise of concealment." Interpretation will involve a hermeneutics, a process by which the truth or the true meaning of the original guilt is revealed, freed from the many overlying strata of excuses. This logic is already implied by Rousseau himself in this episode; he says that he "accused Marion of doing what he wanted her to do"; in this way he exposes himself, or at least he exposes his own underlying (guilty) desire. De Man writes: "What seemed at first like irrational behavior bordering on insanity has, by the end of the [stolen ribbon] passage, become comprehensible enough to be incorporated within a general economy of human affectivity, in a theory of desire, repression, and self-analyzing discourses in which excuse and knowledge converge" (AR, 287).

This ethical model is also the model the reader cannot escape if he or she suddenly finds in this chapter a de Manian autobiographical resonance, a veiled confession not only of his "guilt," but of the structure of that guilt. After all, the very writing of a chapter—the final one of the book—in which the strategies of excuse making and the guilt that accompanies it are analyzed must seem, in the light of the *Le Soir* articles, to be the same kind of self-lacerating movement that reveals in the act of creating an "impossibility to reveal," and that revels in the shame of "outwitting this impossibility." And, by this logic, the more de Man seems to be writing about a textual guilt, one that is an after-effect of the automatic repetition of the speech act, the more he is simply covering his own guilt, the better to reveal it.

Of course de Man's main argument goes precisely against the possibility of such an uncovering, and works to discredit it. But it must also be understood how de Man in effect shifts the guilt from the excuse making author onto the reading that would interrogate the responsibility of the producer of excuses. De Man's argument rests on a quote from Rousseau's *Fourth Rêverie*, which he interprets in this way: "Fiction has nothing to do with representation, but is the absence of any link between utterance and a referent" (AR, 292). Rousseau's affirmation of the harmless "pure fiction"—which is not a lie since it "fails to concern justice in any way"—is associated by de Man with Rousseau's lie, in the *Confessions,* that Marion had stolen the ribbon. De Man thus links the notion of a "harmless" fiction with Rousseau's "unmotivated lie," when he accuses Marion only because she is the "premier objet qui s'offrit." For de Man now quotes Rousseau against himself, noting a point in Rousseau's text when the latter does *not* claim to be acting because of hidden motives or desires, but rather only out of sheer impulse. Against the method of hermeneuts and psychoanalysts, and against Rousseau himself, then, de Man in this instance takes Rousseau's claim entirely seriously: there are unmotivated fictions, Rousseau's accusation of Marion was strictly a matter of random selection. One cannot delve into a "psyche" to uncover ever deeper and more thoroughly concealed motives, urges, and causes.

This kind of argument raises a problem that de Man readily recognizes, but for which he has an ingenious response. The inevitable objection is that the first kind of fiction, mentioned in the *Rêverie,* is "harmless," has nothing to do with moral or legal evaluation, while the whole point of the stolen ribbon episode is that Rousseau faced a kind of impromptu legal tribunal, lied, and thereby permanently injured his victim. The second kind of "fiction," while still perhaps unmotivated, is hardly harmless. De Man's response is simple: in the case where someone is injured by a fiction, the fault lies not with the "author" of the fiction—if such a term can even be used—but with the *misreading* of the lie, its interpretation along ethical or legal lines. Indeed if Rousseau's judges had understood the lie correctly, they would not have been forced to choose between Rousseau's and Marion's versions of the theft. Judgment, the potentially dangerous ascription of innocence or guilt to a subject (or to the subject's "fiction"), is intimately tied to a misguided affirmation of the primacy of "referential meaning."

If the essential non-signification of the statement had been properly interpreted [. . .] they would have understood [Rousseau's] lack of guilt, as well as Marion's innocence. [. . .] *Not the fiction itself is to blame for the consequences, but its falsely referential reading.* As a fiction, the statement is innocuous and the error harmless; it is the misguided reading of the error as theft or slander, the refusal to admit that fiction is fiction, the stubborn resistance to the "fact," obvious by itself, that language is entirely free with regard to referential meaning and can posit whatever its grammar allows it to say, which leads to the transformation of random error into injustice. (AR, 292–93; emphasis added)

This does not mean, of course, that "pure fiction" can ever be simply separated from a "misguided reading" that is "resistance," that adds a referential (mis)interpretation, and which therefore imputes guilt: the moment of non-referential fiction, in other words, can never be isolated. ("It seems to be impossible to isolate the moment in which the fiction stands free of any signification; in the very moment at which it is posited, as well as in the context it generates, it gets at once misinterpreted into a determination which is, *ipso facto,* overdetermined" [AR, 293].) De Man notes that "empirical experience" also shows that "fictional discourse" and the "empirical event" always are caught in a kind of mutual interference: one can never decide between them, and thus one can "excuse the bleakest of crimes because, as a fiction, it escapes from the constraints of guilt and innocence," but, at the same time, one can "accuse" fiction, "the most innocent of activities," of "being the most cruel" (AR, 293).

It becomes clear already, at this stage of the argument, that the recognition of the "guilt" of the excuse (pure fiction is "the most cruel" of activities) is for de Man of a different status than its radical fictionality (its "lack of guilt," in other words, is not necessarily the equivalent, or the symmetrical opposite, of a moral category like innocence). For the awareness of the "guilt" of the excuse is only the "empirical" experience of an "empirical" event (de Man uses the word twice), but the very category of the "empirical" is itself associated with reference, truth-value, and all the terms that are compatible only with a "falsely referential reading." The reading of the fiction as "guilty," even while unavoidable, will, from de Man's perspective, never be anything other than "false," a "misguided" reading. Indeed it is that very reading, according to de Man, that "is to blame"—that is guilty.

This is borne out by the rest of the chapter; the misinterpretation of the text—the excuse-making process that generates distortion and the necessary but deluded application of terms like "guilt"—is first shown by de Man to be represented in Rousseau's text (again in the *Fourth Rêverie*) by the figure of bodily and textual mutilation. But mutilation implies a natural metaphor, the body as subject of mutilation (as well as a phenomenological approach on the part of the reader), and so the "threat remains sheltered behind its metaphoricity" (AR, 297). Mutilation and headlessness imply nothing more than the recognition of the undecidability of authorship, which "remains ensconced within the figural delusion that separates knowing from doing." Beyond this cognitive and self referential model—the same one that would, finally, mandate a reading of a text and the author "responsible" for it as "guilty" or "innocent"—there is another: the machine. "The text as body, with all its implications of substitutive tropes ultimately always re-traceable to metaphor, is displaced by the text as machine, and, in the process, it suffers the loss of the illusion of meaning" (AR, 298).

The possibility of meaning really is illusion, then; the excuse is generated not through a process of desire, which seeks to reveal by covering up—in other words, through metaphor and a system of tropes—but through a purely automatic process of positing, through the speech act: the performative and not the constative. This performative aspect of language is "anti-grav" (one imagines a word processor on autopilot drifting off into the void of space),[16] operating like a grammar, with no necessary links to "human" purpose or intention, but also "entirely ruthless in its inability to modify its own structural design for nonstructural reasons" (AR, 294).

The "resistance"—of theory—comes when the "machine's" effects are inevitably misinterpreted, as an after-effect of the unavoidable imposition of the referential or cognitive moment. Guilt is an after-effect of the inhuman process of excuse making: "It is no longer certain that language, as excuse, exists because of a prior guilt but just as possible that since language, as a machine, performs anyway, we have to produce guilt (and all its train of psychic consequences) in order to make the excuse meaningful. Excuses generate the very guilt they exonerate, though always in excess or by default" (AR, 299). There may be an excess or shortage of guilt, but it is clear that guilt, and the cognition that it implies, is both made possible ("any speech act produces an excess of cognition" [AR, 300]) and is precluded by the performative. In order for a text to "come into being" (an interesting turn of phrase, in which one can perhaps note de Man's "earlier" Heideggerian orientation), "the referential function had to be radically suspended"—otherwise "there would have been nothing to excuse since everything could have been explained away by the cognitive logic of understanding" (AR, 298). We can say, then, that the impossible moment of the performative "machine" always has a kind of absolute priority, though it can never be "known" without the referential function of language, which itself "can never hope to know the process of its own production" (AR, 300)—but which nevertheless paradoxically and impossibly does so, in de Man's theory itself. The result is a "disjunction" between performative and cognitive, the "anacoluthon" or "parabasis" that implies "the sudden revelation of the discontinuity between two rhetorical codes" (AR, 300).

This presentation of de Man's argument in the last chapter of *Allegories of Reading* has been necessary, I think, because only if we have some grasp of these arguments can we see how de

Man himself in his later work handles the problem of a "personal" guilt that follows from an earlier act. In fact, if we are as faithful as possible to de Man's reasoning on this point, we cannot justify even asking about the motives, desires, and responsibility of the (un)committed intellectual.

Our earlier impulse, to read the chapter on excuses in autobiography from *Allegories of Reading* as an elaborate autobiographical excuse for the *Le Soir* articles (an excuse in the Rousseauian sense, where the compulsion and pleasure of revelation is inseparable from the labyrinthine game of repeated concealment), is checked by the argument in the closing section of the chapter itself. Indeed de Man is demonstrating there the fallacy of interpreting a text to uncover the originary guilt complex that underlies it. How can one even imagine an "autobiography" based on the revelation of a "guilt" that is only a function of a mechanical movement of positing (and not at all a "compulsion")? Under no circumstances are we justified in reading the chapter "Excuses" as autobiographical. There can be no consideration of an originary consciousness, subjectivity, or the recognition of a "personal" responsibility in de Man's model. Guilt is only a residue of the inevitable misinterpretation of the mechanized excuse making process, a function of a misreading.

Yet it is difficult not to read this text as an autobiography, above all when de Man shows why this approach is "misguided." For what better excuse for the early articles can there be than the fact that the performative "code" eliminates the possibility of a responsible subjectivity on the part of the author, as well as a coherent ethical stand on the part of the reader, and that the tendency to judge is based on a (moreover unavoidable) misunderstanding of the operation of the textual machine? The author purchases his non-guilt, in effect, at the rather modest cost of proclaiming himself a necessarily misinterpreted mechanism. The more this kind of approach is presented, the more suspect it becomes (and it is implicit in all of de Man's later work, where poetics is given priority over hermeneutics); when we realize what de Man is excusing himself of (through his proxy, Rousseau), we do not want to accept his version of things quite so easily. Was "Marion" really just an arbitrary signifier, "the first word" that came into Rousseau's head? Does she really have no cause for complaint? Are there other victims in this story? Will they remain as silent as Marion, who is of importance only because she furnished a pretext for excuse making? Does what de Man says about Rousseau's (and Marion's) situation also apply to his own—that "the disproportion between the crime that is to be confessed and the crime performed by the lie adds a delirious element to the situation" (AR, 294)?

We are caught in a vicious circle. The more we recognize and affirm the power of de Man's arguments against an autobiographical subjectivity, and a personal responsibility, the more we recognize their significance for a (re)writing of his own biography, or autobiography. He has come up with the one excuse that really "works," that really gets him off the hook, precisely by no longer worrying about the point at which the excuse would intersect with the "cognitive level of understanding." And, following his logic, as soon as we consider de Man's own biography, and in any way try to "judge" him, it is our reading that is guilty, that inevitably ascribes guilt to a purely aleatory act, and sees de Man's larger argument, so rigorous, so irrefutable, as just another excuse. Our ascription of guilt is, however, necessary to the functioning of de Man's system, just as the glance of the outraged spectator or reader is necessary to any of Rousseau's gestures of shameful or embarrassing sexual or textual self-exposure. As soon as we accuse de Man of unjustifiably excusing himself, we are caught in his game, we are just another cog in his machine; now we are the ones who automatically provide the unavoidable "resistance to theory," ours is the bad reading that produces the guilt that always will be produced (and that projects it onto him). Ours is the cognitive, theoretical moment, the inevitable misinterpretation that is guilty when we misread de Man's text as guilty: it is the "falsely referential reading" that is "to blame for the consequences" (AR, 293). Of course it is not a question here of a "personal" guilt on our part—one that somehow adequately characterizes our subjectivity. Instead it is our reading that bears the burden of the culpability of the affirmation of the primacy of personification (the attribution of a responsible consciousness and intention), judgment, reference, knowledge, and truth.

It might be objected that such misreadings are inevitable, that this kind of resistance is inherent to the process. The sheer performative "fiction" can never exist in isolation; there will always be a referential moment, a cognitive rhetoric, that interferes with it. While that may be true, it is clear that for de Man some readings are more misguided than others; his own text enjoys a greater level of self-reflexivity even when, and because, it "knows" that "there is never enough knowledge available to account for the delusion of knowing" (AR, 300). In other words, de Man's reading itself knows the futility of trying to know, to perform a reading that would "know" anything resembling a subject's true responsibility. In that way it is not as responsible—at least in the same way—as those misguided readings that would try to "uncover" and thereby know hidden causes or

originary meanings and which, in that way, only produce more guilt. De Man's text is innocent of that delusion, at least. It knows about it.

We can see the progress de Man has made over the earlier bind he faced in his review of Jünger's novel. There, the more de Man asserted the innocence of writing—a removal from political "engagement," the affirmation of "pure narration"—the more guilty of political collaboration his text became. The continuous, automatic reassertion in different reviews of a lack of engagement through a higher estheticism was itself a commitment.[17] De Man's defense of a seemingly guilty (in the eyes of the Nazis, for writing a compromising thesis novel) but really "innocent" Jünger became the unavoidable, repetitious inculpation of his own text. If we read this early article, then, we realize that de Man's inescapable guilt, such as it is, is never distinguishable from a repetitive, always rewritten and reposited, will to innocence. In his chapter on Rousseau's *Confessions,* this model is inverted; de Man is now able effectively to affirm an innocence in practice, if not in principle (since he would reject the priority of an ethical vocabulary), by recognizing the inescapability of guilt. The "anti-grav" linguistic machine is beyond good and evil, to be sure, but at the same time its commitment/culpability is only an inevitable misinterpretation, a theoretical, referential, "resistance." Pure esthetic withdrawal, pure narration (affirmed in the Jünger article), although already implicitly supplanted in the early articles by an unreflective, mechanical repetition, is now openly replaced by sheer fiction, by the inhuman process of an arbitrary positing and repositing of meaning.[18] Now any attempt to "blame" de Man, or to judge him, will fly back in the accuser's face; the reader-theorist's text is to blame when it attempts to establish a coherent, moral grounding for the determining of the innocence or guilt of the author or the autobiographical subject. The more we question the other's innocence, belatedly attempting to establish the criteria for determining an autobiographical innocence—in other words, the harder we work to establish the conditions of possibility for our own innocence—the guiltier our own reading becomes, and the more guilt our anthropomorphizing reading generates in order to "make the excuse meaningful" (AR, 299), and to assign a truth value to a fundamentally arbitrary speech act/judgment. We suddenly realize that the ethical text is now simply repeating the bind in which de Man found himself in the early articles, when he too could only attempt to affirm his own and others' innocence through the guilty complicity of his writing.

But it is only through our paradigm of guilt—in which our own position doubles his guilt from the early articles—that we are able to perceive a guilt in de Man's later work: when we see his later texts, in other words, as doubling the guilt of the early ones by attempting to excuse them—and succeeding. In this larger view, the more de Man proves not so much his innocence as the absence of any possibility of subjective responsibility, the more suspect his arguments become. . . but, by the same token, from the de Manian perspective, the more suspect ours become as well. The guilt of his later writing is then simply a double of the earlier bind he found himself in, one in which we too now find ourselves.

The only guilt that de Man's text can recognize is its own, when it affirms the guilt of the resistant reading. As we know from the essay "The Resistance to Theory," when the rhetorical reading knows itself *as* theory, when it is at its most referentially accurate, codifiable and teachable, it is then that it most resists itself *as* a theory of reading. "Nothing can overcome the resistance to theory since theory *is* itself this resistance."[19] In the same way, the text's certainty of the guilt of another reading (the inevitable statement that it is the *other* reading, the "falsely referential one"—and what theory, including de Man's, is not in the end "falsely referential"?—that must "take the blame"), the unavoidable prosopopoeia[20] by which de Man's text determines another text's responsibility, can only be a recognition of its own guilt, its own responsibility (since it too is now in the business of issuing judgments); it is the moment of rhetorical reading's strongest truth, its greatest self-knowledge and self-certainty as theory, the most definitive attribution of guilt to the other theory, but for that reason it is also the moment of its greatest "self-resistance," as de Man calls it—and self-betrayal.

This is perhaps the impossible final point in de Man's centerless labyrinth. De Man's text—but not de Man "himself"—will have to take the blame for determining the guilt of other (mis)readings that would ascribe guilt to subjectivities "responsible for" false writings, lies, ideology, propaganda, and so on—readings that would, in other words, ascribe guilt to de Man the subject, the "person," who determines that only texts, misreadings, can be guilty, and not subjects. De Man's writing as self-betrayal, as the always repeated resistance to theory, is thus in profound complicity with all the "weak" (or "inattentive," etc.) readings that would strive for theoretical certainty and ascribe guilt, and that are also—but on a lower level—resistances to theory. De Man's theory knows more than they do, to be sure—as de Man says, "technically correct rhetorical readings [. . .] are irrefutable" (RT, 19)—but in its very certainty, in its more advanced knowledge, in its more accurate attribution of guilt, it is a more profound resistance, and it is thus in an ever deeper complicity with all the other resistances. In its resistance to resistance, it is the most advanced resistance-movement. Its

affirmation in practice of the priority of accurate judgment, truth-value, reference—which allows it to argue in theory for the priority of the performative, with the generation of truth (and the determination of guilt and innocence) as an after-effect, an inevitable misinterpretation, of the "fiction" of the speech-act—establishes de Man's text as a double of those (mis)readings that, perhaps naively, perhaps cynically, argue for the priority in principle of accurate judgment, truth-value, and cognition. The stable, full (self)knowledge of de Man's text is the moment of its greatest deviation from the rigor of its project of reading, the moment in which it doubles all other theories. It is the necessary moment of self-awareness that the knowledge of the theory of rhetorical reading is not different in kind from all the other knowledges. That de Manian knowledge, in other words, at the moment of truth in which it would most rigorously exclude, even purge, other methods—such as psychoanalysis, Marxism, and feminism,[21] all of which depend on the priority of reference and an affirmation of the self-certainty and responsibility of individual (or collective) subjectivity—becomes indistinguishable from them, indeed automatically repeats them, in their essential feature, their total resistance to a radically heterogeneous practice, to a method of reading that alone—impossibly—does "justice" to an unknowable and inhuman force: the performative, grammar, etc.

Rhetorical reading's most codifiable and truthful affirmation of an innocence that is not the symmetrical opposite of guilt is also the moment at which, inevitably, it will enter into collaboration with those methods that would accuse it, and the "author" "behind" it (and who is, in any case, today nothing more or less than a collection of texts) of guilty responsibility. The more de Man's writing "knows" its difference from other theories, the more it is certain of itself and its truth (it is "the universal theory of the impossibility of theory" [RT, 19])—the more strongly it works, in other words, to expel them, and the more thoroughly it recognizes that they are "to blame" for the inevitable misreadings and ascriptions of guilt—the greater is its complicity with other guilty, truthful theories (which themselves always cast the blame on the other), and the greater is its self-betrayal as well. If there is to be a "unification" of the different approaches in literary theory, then, it will take place not under the sign of a dialectical synthesis or a harmonious eclecticism, but in and through culpability, betrayal, and self-resistance: "[. . .] literary theory is not in danger of going under [. . .] because the language it speaks is the language of self-resistance" (RT, 19–20).[22]

Yale University

NOTES

1. See, for example, the opening paragraph of de Man's review of Drieu la Rochelle's *Notes pour comprendre le siècle,* in *Le Soir,* 2 December 1941.

2. I am referring to the by now famous *Newsweek* article, "Deconstructing de Man's Life" (15 February 1988, p.63), where the phrase "moral idiocy" is used. At least those who decry de Man's gesture in *Allegories of Reading* should face the fact that they are opting for a return to a moral notion of subjectivity; rather than simply slinging accusations, they are then obliged, it would seem, to come to terms with the problems of such a formulation, which is by no means self-evident. Whose or what notion of subjectivity are they affirming? Sartre's? Someone else's? Upon which texts are they basing their arguments? How can we read those texts? Responsible subjectivity or consciousness is not a concept that we can all agree on simply because the authority of *Newsweek* is behind it, nor is it, at this late date, a term that we can straightforwardly affirm as a given, without argument and with a clear conscience.

3. See "Les Juifs dans la littérature actuelle," *Le Soir,* 4 March 1941.

4. If one refrains at this point from hastily judging or morally evaluating de Man's actions, or at least resists as much as possible the tendency to do so, one should nevertheless try to grasp the larger political implications of his writings of 1941–42. This is not such an easy task. It should first be noted that the Nazis, at least in Belgium and France, took intellectuals very seriously, and valued their cooperation above all. In the eyes of the Germans, any writer who published with Gallimard, for example, was collaborating, even if the contents of his book did not in any way celebrate the Occupation. (Many French authors of the period, however—including Sartre, Camus, Simone de Beauvoir, Blanchot, Bataille, Ponge, Paulhan, Brice Parain, and others—managed to convince themselves that, while publishing in the *NRF* was unacceptable because the editor [Drieu La Rochelle] openly excluded Jews, publishing a book with Gallimard, the publisher of the review, was still all right. The Germans, however, never recognized this fastidious distinction; they in fact took the opposite view, that publishing with Gallimard was *equivalent* to being in the review.) The author who published his work from June 1940 to August 1944 was demonstrating that intellectual life was continuing under the Nazis, that it was possible to cooperate with them at least to the extent that one dealt with a firm that necessarily excluded Jews and Communists, and so on. Gallimard—and most other publishers of the period—were bringing their books out with the official approval of the censor, they were able to obtain precious paper, and so on. They could never have operated if the Germans had seen their books as being in any way in-imical to the Occupation. See, on this topic, the biography *Gaston Gallimard,* by Pierre Assouline (Paris: Balland, 1984), especially chapter six, "Sixième époque, 1939–44," pp.263–362, and *Paris allemand,* by Henri Michel (Paris: Albin Michel, 1981), pp. 334–39.

The same clearly applied to the press—journalism and book publishing—in Belgium. De Man was one of the literary and cultural critics of the most influential French-language Belgian newspaper, and he reviewed, and hence promoted, the books that the Nazi-approved houses were publishing. It is no coincidence that many of the books he reviewed were French translations of German works; one of the policies of the authorities—which publishers like Gallimard were happy to go along with—was to finance the translation and diffusion of "apolitical" but respectable German literature, including modern authors (such as Jünger) and the classics, as a way of burnishing the somewhat tarnished image of German culture. An important part of de Man's job at *Le Soir,* then, was to argue for, and exemplify, a Francophone opening of French culture to German influences; see, in this context, the end of the review of F. Sieburg's *Dieu est-il français?* (28 April 1942). (De Man, of course, was also during this period a French translator of German authors, such as Paul Alverdes and A. E. Brinckmann; Brinckmann's book, *Esprit des nations: France-Italie-Allemagne*[Bruxelles: La Toison d'or, 1943] itself is a call for cultural collaboration between European "peoples"—German "spirituality" is presented in this work as a higher synthesis that justifies and saves, through negation, the lesser tendencies of French "rationalism" and Italian "sensualism.") On the importance of *Le Soir* as a collaborationist paper, see *Contribution à l'histoire de la résistance Belge,* by George K. Tanham (Bruxelles: Presses Universitaires de Bruxelles, 1971). p.118, and pp.157–59.

With all this said, it should be stressed that de Man's "collaboration," such as it was, should be sharply distinguished from that of the Brasillach or Céline variety. Although, at least for a while, he clearly supported the "revolution," or at least saw it as a fait accompli that had to be accepted, in a number of instances his notion of "collaboration" amounts to little more that a non-xenophobic communication between cultures; see, for example, his Flemish review of Ernst Jünger's work ("A Great Writer: Ernst Jünger," *Het Vlaamsche Land,* 26–27 July 1942). De Man writes in this article: "[A writer] systematically impoverishes himself, he refuses to make use of that which constitutes the vital force of our European culture, if he, allegedly in order to remain true to his own people, does not want to become acquainted with that which comes into being elsewhere." We should also note that de Man gave favorable reviews to two literary publications that were known, under the Occupation, to be forums for dissent and even resistance: *Messages,* a French-Belgian review that published surrealists such as Eluard and other writers, including Sartre and Bataille (*Le Soir,* 14 July 1942); and *Das*

Innere Reich, a German literary review with a conservative Christian orientation, many of whose contributors had been executed by the end of the war (*Le Soir,* 20 April 1942).

5. A coincidence: the translation is by Henri Thomas, the French novelist and author of the roman à clef that, rumor has it, recounts de Man's early experiences in the US, *Le Parjure* (Paris: Gallimard, 1964).

6. The reader can compare the favorable image that de Man presents of German literary practice (as in the article "Regards sur l'Allemagne" [3 August 1941]) with the negative one he usually has of French authors, even right-wing ones. See, in the latter case, the review of Brasillach's *Notre avant-guerre* (12 August 1941); Drieu's *Notes pour comprendre le siècle* (2 December 1941); Montherlant's *Le Solstice de juin* (11 November 1941), and so on. These reactionary French authors are guilty, in de Man's view, of many of the sins of French literature in general: elitism, "cérébralité," Parisian stylishness, individualism (see "La Littérature française devant les événements" [20 January 1942]), the preaching of morality, and (related to the often abstract or mechanical didacticism) the attempt to hold forth on topics beyond the competence of the writer. (This latter accusation has been a staple of right-wing attacks on intellectuals at least since the Dreyfus affair.) The few French authors who escape these tendencies (such as Giono) are seen as exceptions that confirm the rule.

7. See de Man's other review of a work by Jünger, "Jardins et routes" (23 June 1942). It is interesting to note that when de Man wrote on Jünger for a French-speaking audience, he made a sharp distinction between the cold and analytic French tradition and the mythic and vital German one, whereas, when he wrote on the same book for a Flemish audience ("A Great Writer: Ernst Jünger," *Het Vlaamsche Land,* 26–27 July 1942) he explicitly modifies the position he took in the *Le Soir* article on *On the Marble Cliffs*: in an argument reminiscent of those to be found in A. E. Brinckmann's *Esprit des nations,* de Man argues that Jünger's novel is a kind of higher synthesis between French "rational humanism" and German "mythical romanticism." Why the change? Perhaps de Man decided that the French audience needed to have its own tradition demystified before it could see the literary value of Jünger's somewhat obscure novel; on the other hand, the Flemish, who would only be too happy to reject the French tradition, would benefit from the eclecticism implied in a view of Jünger's work as an affirmation of what was best in the French tradition. Of course at this late date it is pointless to speculate about what de Man "really" believed; throughout his writings of this period, he affirmed both the valorization of German "myth" over French "reason," *and* a synthesis of those "conflicting" traditions. In any case, as we see in Brinckmann's book (see footnote 4, above), these two positions themselves are not necessarily mutually exclusive; in pseudo-Hegelian fashion, one can argue that the "higher" German synthesis (in this case Jünger) both negates a manifestly inferior French tradition, and, in transcending it, nevertheless incorporates it.

8. De Man's strongest early statement on this topic is in the article "Sur les possibilités de la critique" (2 December 1941). In fact on this point he never wavered; near the end of his life, in "The Return to Philology," he was still maintaining, as the most basic gesture of his approach, the refusal of a criticism that would play an ethical, moral, or "religious" role.

9. See, for example, de Man's critique of H. R. Jauss' use of this approach in the article "Reading and History" (in *The Resistance to Theory* [Minneapolis: The University of Minnesota Press, 1986], p.69).

10. Maurice Blanchot, in the essay "Une Oeuvre d'Ernst Jünger," in *Faux pas* (Paris: Gallimard, 1943), pp.287–92, makes a point very similar to de Man's: Jünger's novel should not be seen as a thesis novel. No doubt Jünger himself, perhaps for very practical reasons, maintained the same thing. Such fervent arguing that the novel should not be read in a political light only underscores the fact that it so easily lends itself to such a reading; it also incites one to question the motives behind the flat refusal of a political interpretation.

11. Jünger's novel, however, much like the Scorsese film *Taxi Driver,* has an ironically "happy" ending, which can be interpreted naively, but is all the more disturbing when read as a "fairy tale" that cannot begin to keep its promise, and knows it. . .

12. This quote is taken from *Allegories of Reading* (New Haven: Yale University Press, 1979), hereafter AR.

13. This is precisely why de Man, in the early articles, criticizes authors like Montherlant or Drieu, who stray beyond their competence and assume that there is some referential or analogical connection between the literary text and political reality.

14. When he does argue in favor of a history, it is one of esthetic forms and solutions. Here his influence was probably Marcel Raymond (see the article "Criticism and Literary History" [*Het Vlaamsche Land,* 7–8 June 1942] for a discussion of Raymond's *De Baudelaire au surréalisme*).

15. I am thinking here not so much of the blind respect of the disciple as of the respect of any careful reader who would necessarily take the arguments of the text he or she is analyzing seriously, and

follow them as far as they will go. Not to do so inevitably leads to much of the simple-minded commentary that has proliferated in our most highly respected magazines and newspapers since the de Man "scandal" broke: cheap accusations, guilt by association, etc.

16. De Man's problematizing of the "humanity" of the grammatical machine here no doubt owes much to a Foucauldian dehumanization of the Lévi-Straussian structuralist-mathematical model of a differential language (in, for example, *Les Mots et les choses*). Beyond this, however, there is an echo here of Heidegger's discussion of the machine, and its defamiliarization, in *Being and Time*.

17. Even when de Man posits a "synthesis" between committed writing and a pure estheticism—as in his article "Paul Alverdes et sa revue 'Das innere Reich'" (20 April 1942)—it is clear that the two sides only come together in order to remain completely separate: "And as, in addition, expression is a form whose beauty consists in an eternal value, *independent of the contingencies of the hour,* one can imagine the merit that this creation assumes" (emphasis added).

18. Of course we can discern a "middle period" in de Man's work where this repetitive positing was already evident; one thinks of articles such as "Intentional Structure of the Romantic Image" and the last page of the book review of Hillis Miller's *The Disappearance of God* in *Partisan Review* (Fall 1964). At this point what would later be presented as a result of the mechanical functioning of the machine-grammar is still presented in a Heideggerian terminology of "temporality."

19. This essay appears in the collection *The Resistance to Theory* (Minneapolis: The University of Minnesota Press, 1986), hereafter RT; this quote is on p.19.

20. On prosopopoeia in de Man, see chapter 4 of Cynthia Chase's *Decomposing Figures: Rhetorical Readings in the Romantic Tradition* (Baltimore: The Johns Hopkins University Press, 1986), "Giving a Face to a Name: De Man's Figures."

21. There is a moment in the chapter on "Excuses" when a feminist reading suggests itself—and which de Man explicitly avoids; we are clearly not to interpret Rousseau's singling out of Marion as his victim as having anything to do with the fact that she is a woman. "In the spirit of the text, one should resist all temptation to give any significance whatsoever to the sound 'Marion' [. . .]" (AR, 289). Clearly, the last chapter of *Allegories of Reading* is directed against the possibility of a psychoanalytic reading, just as the second to last, on Rousseau's *Social Contract,* is directed against the possibility of a historicist or Marxist one. No matter what some of his followers might say, for de Man there was never any possibility that any of these methods could be "coordinated" with his own. Instead, his method definitively excludes them.

22. While de Man asserts, in "The Resistance to Theory," that his theory subsumes other, weaker or less complete ones (grammar, semiology, reference, reading-avoidance, etc.) (RT, 19), it is clear that certain ones—Marxism, psychoanalysis, feminism—are explicitly eliminated; this is made clear in the last two chapters of *Allegories of Reading*. One can argue that de Man's method can only constitute itself through this rigorous exclusion-expulsion.

Terrible Reading (preceded by "Epigraphs")

ANDRZEJ WARMINSKI

Aux écrivains qui ont trop donné, depuis quelques mois, à l'actualité, je prédis, pour cette partie de leur oeuvre, l'oubli le plus total. Les journaux, les revues d'aujourd'hui, quand je les ouvre, j'entends rouler sur eux l'indifférence de l'avenir, comme on entend le bruit de la mer quand on porte à l'oreille certains coquillages.

[To writers who have given too much these last months to recent events, I predict, for that part of their work, total oblivion. When I open the newspapers, the journals of today, I can hear rolling over them the indifference of the future, as one hears the sound of the sea upon lifting certain seashells to one's ear.]—
Henri de Montherlant, Le Solstice de juin *[translation by Jeffrey Mehlman[1]]*

EPIGRAPHS

The above sentences from Montherlant's *Solstice de juin* —"the volume that earned Montherlant his accusation as a collaborator"[2]—are quoted by Paul de Man at the beginning of his article on Montherlant in the November 4, 1941 issue of *Le Soir*. "One could not say it better," says de Man and adds that this "just and severe sentence" applies to all the books and essays in which writers have offered us their reflections on the war and its consequences—including the *Solstice de juin* itself. There is more than one irony in these reflections—and, as always in the case of irony, more than one reflection in these ironies. Not the least of them—reflections, ironies—is de Man's turning Montherlant's words back upon themselves: that is, the very words Montherlant uses to consign to oblivion the writing of his contemporaries are the "same" words that in turn would consign Montherlant's writing to oblivion. Another obvious enough irony and reflection in de Man's use of these words is their turning back upon de Man's own wartime writing—back upon the 169 plus articles in *Le Soir* and *Het Vlaamsche Land* in which he "gave too much" to recent events, to *l'actualité*. A certain self-immolating self-reflection—a self-ironization—takes place here, as both Montherlant's words about his contemporaries and de Man's about Montherlant say one thing and mean another. But the ironies do not end here—indeed, irony, once it begins (and it has always already begun), never just ends, at least not just here. No matter how self-immolating it may be, the act of self-reflection always leaves remainders, traces, ashes—a *reste* or a *restance du texte,* as Derrida might put it, that resists the totalization of any oblivion, that insures a certain memory for every forgetting, even "the most total." And if there is a remainder to the ironies, it is not just because we can go to the library and find (or "discover") the writings of Montherlant's or de Man's "forgotten" (or "hidden") past, the books and articles that they consigned to a future of oblivion for having given too much to the present. No, the *Solstice de juin* and the 169 articles in *Le Soir* are *not* what remains, they are *not* the remainder (or the "remaindering"?) of the text, *la restance du texte,* no matter how many times we pick them up and try to listen to them like shells upon the shore. The only memory possible for *those* remainders is the same journalistic "memory" of the present, the one that "remembers" only the present and hence has neither past nor future (and hence does not happen, is not an event, is not historical)—or only *the* past and *the* future of total oblivion. The part that remains is, ironically enough (but with an irony other than that of mere self-reflection), precisely the part of these writings that did *not* give too much to the present, the part that predicts total oblivion for others and for itself. What does not get forgotten, ironically, is the prediction that all will be forgotten. This reminder is what remains—and remains to be read. And it remains to be *read* in the text (and *as* the text) of Montherlant and de Man as the mark of the heterogeneity of these texts *as* texts, a certain self-division of these texts against themselves, which is nevertheless *not* a self-division that can be accounted for by the economy of (binary) oppositions and its undivided line between sides and positions, good and bad, collaborators and resistance fighters, etc. The history of the Montherlant quotation bears this out, for that history is longer, more divided, than its passage from Montherlant to de Man to Derrida.[3] In an essay on Montherlant entitled "De l'insolence considerée comme l'un des Beaux-Arts" (in *Journal des Débats,* January 6, 1942), Maurice Blanchot ends his essay by citing the same lines from *Solstice de juin,* with approval and with an at least implied application to Montherlant's own wartime writing. Blanchot then takes this essay up again and uses it as the last text in his collection *Faux pas* (1943). Jeffrey Mehlman takes the meaning of this gesture to be plain: "Plainly, this concluding 'retraction' is Blanchot bidding farewell to his political career as . . . a propagandist for terrorism."[4] How plain is it? The "same" words, the "same" citation, used again and again as a figure to mean one thing and its opposite, or, better, to mean one thing *and* an other that need not be an other *of* the same. The same words to divide the texts—of Montherlant, of de Man, of Blanchot, of Mehlman, of Derrida—differently. What's the point? The point is, again, not just the irony that the words that would consign to oblivion (the writing of others and their own writing) are precisely the words destined to be remembered like no other. The point is their different, other, remembering, the mode of their remaining to be read. They remain to be read, to remind us of the necessity of reading (these words and any other words, *all* words as other words), because they make, better, *mark* a difference. These words remain to mark a difference—the "indifference of the future" does not roll over them—because they have not given too much to the present, they were already differentiated, already marked, already "in quotation marks," in the text of Montherlant. As the difference or heterogeneity of Montherlant's text to itself, these words open up the possibility of a future, a different future, a future different from the present. They are the mark of the promise of a future inscribed in all texts *as* written. All it takes—all it takes to preserve the possibility of a future—is to be able to read them.

The marks of this heterogeneity, the marks of the text, are already readable in the seashell. On the one hand, the seashell is inscribed in a clear figural logic: when one holds it to one's ear, one hears the sound of the sea which, as a figure for the indif-

ference of the future, is what Montherlant hears when he opens the newspapers and journals of the day. But, on the other hand, this logic is less clear as soon as we start reading it. For the sound of the sea is *not* what we hear when we pick up a shell; that is already a figural reading for the sound we *do* hear: the echo of the noise inside our own heads. And we hear this echo thanks to the instrument of the shell: a cleaved, hollowed-out replica of the ear that allows the noise in our heads to be repeated, quoted, marked, written—suspended in quotation marks, as it were. In short, the shell is a writing instrument that on the one hand makes it possible for us to hear the noise inside our heads, to create a phenomenal figure for it which can then enter a tropological system of exchange in which it can stand for anything and everything—for instance, the noise can be taken as a figure for the sound of the sea which can be taken as a figure for the indifference of the future which, by way of some mediations, can be taken as a figure for Montherlant's or de Man's bad conscience or Blanchot's remorse . . . etc. But, on the other hand, even though it can figure or represent all kinds of things, what the sound of the shell actually means, the only thing it says over and over, is the material fact of its (re)production—a stutter that says nothing but "marking," "writing," "written." And this stutter, as marking or writing, is not something we can hear, it is not phenomenal, it is not a figure, it is not aesthetically pleasing. A mark as mark, writing as writing, is not something to be heard or seen, it is something to be *read*. (Just as we can hear [b] and [p], but the *difference* between them that constitutes one as [b] and the other as [p] is not something we can hear—it is a marking that makes it possible for us to [think we] "hear" [b] and [p].) As that which can and has to be read, this inaudible and invisible stutter is nevertheless that which opens up a future—an other future, a future open to . . . the other.[5] Hence its possibility—the possibility of the necessity of reading—needs to be preserved, maintained, as Wordsworth's Arabian Knight well knows: he wants to save the shell that prophesies, pre-figures, apocalypse (in which one hears an ode in passion uttered that foretells destruction to the children of the earth) from the literalization of that apocalypse (the "deluge now at hand").[6] And what needs to be resisted, fought, mocked, ironized, is anything or anyone that would suspend the necessity of reading, that would suspend the suspension of the quotation marks, and claim to be able to calculate, to decide, to judge—to know and judge that this statement can be aligned with that (good or bad) political position and no other. The suspension of the necessity of reading needs to be resisted because it closes down the possibility of a future. (In doing so, it is inevitably totalitarian, whereas reading, in suspending, is not *inevitably* totalitarian, which does not mean that it is inevitably democratic either—reading is not inevitably anything, that's why it holds out the promise of a future.) In his text on Paul de Man's War, Derrida resists better than anyone:

Since we are talking at this moment about discourse that is total-itarian, fascist, Nazi, racist, antisemitic, and so forth, about all the gestures, either discursive or not, that could be suspected of com-plicity with it, I would like to do, and naturally I invite others to do, whatever possible to avoid reproducing, if only virtually, the *logic* of the discourse thus incriminated.

Do we have access to a complete formalization of this logic and an absolute exteriority with regard to its ensemble? Is there a sys-tematic set of themes, concepts, philosophemes, forms of utterance, axioms, evaluations, hierarchies which, forming a closed and identi-fiable coherence of what we call totalitarianism, fascism, nazism, racism, antisemitism, never appear outside these formations and es-pecially never on the opposite side? And is there a systematic coher-ence proper to each of them, since one must not confuse them too quickly with each other? Is there some property so closed and so pure that one may not find any element of these systems in dis-courses that are commonly opposed to them? To say that I do not believe that there is, not absolutely, means at least two things: 1) Such a formalizing, saturating totalization seems to me to be pre-cisely the essential character of this logic whose project, at least, and whose ethico-political consequence can be terrifying. One of my rules is never to accept this project and consequence, whatever that may cost. 2) For this very reason, one must analyze as far as possible this process of formalization and its program so as to uncover the statements, the philosophical, ideological, or political behaviors that derive from it and wherever they may be found. The task seems to me to be both urgent and interminable. It has occurred to me on occasion to call this deconstruction.[7]

The point, as always, is the necessity of reading. As such, it is obvious enough. That the "de Man case" in its complexities, self-divisions, heterogeneity, is a *text* in need of being read (in its heterogeneity)—rather than a case in a court of law where it is a question of trying, judging, sentencing, and executing—is even more obvious. Its obviousness can be stated summarily in three "theses" pertaining to: 1) the man and his actions, 2) his writings of 1941–42, 3) the relation between these writings (1941–42) and the later writings (1953–83).

1) It is obvious that the man and his actions before, during, and after the war were ambiguous enough, contradictory enough, divided enough, in ways or according to an economy that makes *any* judgment hasty, premature, uninformed, inde-cent, stupid. What do you know about the man, his circum-stances, the place, the time? Who are you to draw a line between good man and bad man, resistance and collaboration?

All the lines of division in the "de Man case" are divided lines that make it impossible ever to say anything like "Up to this point, up to this line, he was a collaborator, but past it he was something else. . ." They are lines that render his case a text—as always, to be read. If you are stupid enough to judge him, you judge at your peril, for that judgment, like the sound inside a seashell, judges only you. This is especially the case of all the ac-ademic journalists who have been clamoring for a "confession": "Why didn't he confess?" "Why did he keep it a secret?" etc. What do they want de Man to have done? To have sent out a press release, held a news conference? "In 1941 and 1942 I was a bad man, I didn't know any better, but today I am a better man, I'm better than that de Man then, I know better, I have drawn a line under my past, etc. . ." Only the trivially guilt-ridden pa-thology of bitter academics who have always resented de Man's intellectual, i.e., critical, power would want de Man to have in-scribed himself in a conversion narrative![8] Better than anyone, he knew and analyzed the self-mystifications and self-delusions that wanting a good conscience produces. He knew better than to delude himself into thinking that he knew better.

2) It is obvious that the writings of 1941–42 cannot be inter-preted according to an economy of binary oppositions like good/evil, politically correct/politically incorrect, etc. Just like the man, they need to be read rather than judged. Derrida has already marked out the structure of the economy that renders these texts (*as* texts) heterogeneous, and he has done it so well that it is hard to imagine how anyone could say anything about these texts that would not be in some sense already pre-written, pre-scribed, by Derrida's text. One may do more research, un-cover more facts, know more, but it is unlikely that anyone will read these texts' heterogeneity any better. (And the reason is not just Derrida's intrinsic "ability" [or courage or honesty] but the fact that he was "ready" to read these structures, since he has been dealing with precisely the same structures in his long-run-ning seminar on "nationalisme philosophique.") In any case, even more obvious is the fact that it is not these writings per se that are the issue. Except perhaps for historians of the Belgian occupation or the de Man family, the 1941–42 writings are of lit-tle interest. Had Paul de Man become, say, a stock broker, no one would be bothering with them. No, these writings are (and should be) an issue only on account of the *later* writings (1953–83, say), only because de Man became the literary critic and teacher that he became. De Man's having written, and our read-ing, the 1941–42 articles is an issue only because the work of 1953–83 has made *the writing and the reading* of the 1941–42 arti-cles an issue. In short, at issue is neither the 1941–42 nor the 1953–83 writings but the "relation" between them: how to read

them "together," according to what economy of exchange or substitution, according to what principle of articulation?

3) It is obvious that this "relation" (between the writings of 1941–42 and those of 1953–83) cannot be read according to any *simple* economy of exchange. The only thing more foolish than to draw a simple continuous line from the wartime writings to the later writings is to draw a simple, undivided line between them according to a principle of simple (i.e., ultimately always determinate) negation. It is foolish, for instance, to see the later writings as some kind of "flight" from or "repression" of "history" and "politics" due to de Man's imputed experience of "disillusionment." Aside from their primitive (pre-critical, anti-theoretical, anti-intellectual) psychologism or historicism, such non-readings are worse than foolish. For not only do they exhibit a dismaying ignorance about even the thematic content of de Man's texts, they are in fact part of a strategy of containment that has marked the reception of de Man's (and Derrida's) work in the American academy from the beginning. That is, the "discovery" of the 1941–42 writings is being used to perpetuate the old myths about so-called "deconstruction"—that "it" is anti-historical, that "it" is apolitical, that "it" is just a continuation of the New Criticism, that "it" is just a technique or method of close reading, that "it" limits its "deconstruction" only to "texts" and does not extend it to the social, etc. "Deconstruction" is this . . . "deconstruction" is only . . . "deconstruction" is just . . . The same old stupidities are trotted out again and again to tell us (*who*, us?) what "deconstruction" is, to identify "it," circumscribe "it," mark "its" borders, contain "it," put "it" into "context," etc. But today—after the "revelation" of de Man's 1941–42 writings —there is a difference in the *tone* of these stupidities. Today that tone is shrill, strident, violent, (male) hysterical. Who is it, finally, that needs so badly to know, to be told over and over again, what "deconstruction" is? Who is it that needs so badly to identify "deconstruction" and thereby mark its borders and limits (for instance, as a phenomenon that is of no interest outside the ivory tower)? Who or what is being threatened by the possibility that "deconstruction" may not be one, identifiable, calculable, decidable, in the terms of any (dialectizable) economy of oppositions like pro and con, inside and outside, humanist and nihilist, "text" and "real world," etc.? Why the hysteria and the frenzy of hatred over a dead man who was not really known outside the scene of academic literary criticism and whose "influence," at least as far as the "trends" or "fashions" on that scene are concerned, was already on the wane? The typical *ressentiment* of academics—whose primary commitment is to the institution and institutional values and criteria—towards anyone with intellectual values (which, by the mere fact of *being* intellectual values always represent a po-

tential threat to the institution and its creatures) does not quite explain the anti-intellectual hysteria of the reaction to the "revelations." What could make so many of these creatures crawl out from under the rocks of their pathologies?[9]

Here is a (very direct) hypothesis: precisely at a time when de Man was safely buried, when his work was no longer an *issue*, when presumably entire generations of students in literature and theory could "come of age" without feeling that they have to read de Man . . . precisely at that moment de Man returns, comes back—that's already plenty annoying! And he comes back not only to become an issue, not only as someone whose work has to be read and discussed (not again!), not only as someone you now *have* to take sides on . . . No, it's much worse than that (for the business of academic business as usual). It's that he comes back *in a way that* makes it forever impossible — for "supporters" and "enemies" alike—to mouth the old stupidities about his work (and about "deconstruction") and be believed by anybody for very long. De Man's work as "anti-historical" or "apolitical"! Oh, come on, grow up! It is nothing but a sustained, relentless, meditation on history and the political. In other words, the "revelations" of the 1941–42 writings make it impossible for even the most recalcitrant nonreaders (whether supporters or attackers) of de Man's work to pretend otherwise. Those writings force a re-reading of his later work— a re-reading that now necessarily has to deal with the questions of history and the political—which may discover that de Man's texts do not say what "we" thought, that they say something else, something different from the usual attempts to contain them.[10] Again, de Man comes back in a way that broaches, divides, the line between the academy and its "outside," that makes it impossible to take his "case" or his work as a question internal to ivory tower trends and fashions. Hence the hysteria, hence the frenzy. For the more you keep repeating that de Man and "deconstruction" are over and done with, are unimportant, an academic game, a matter of opportunism, politically suspect, morally reprehensible, nihilistic, etc., the more interest in de Man's work you create, the more of a real issue it becomes, the more (re-)readers it wins . . . etc. The mechanism is a familiar one—a resistance that promotes the cause of that which it resists—and it propelled the fortunes of "deconstruction" on the American scene in the 1970's. But it is working even better today, thanks to the "revelation" of de Man's 1941–42 writings. For these writings have made the old lines of defense against "deconstruction" untenable, self-contradictory, foolishness, a mockery. (One of my favorite examples of hysterical self-contradiction among recent attempts to re-bury de Man: a nationally known academic philosopher, Richard Rorty, who in the course of a lecture [and the discussion after it] on Derrida and de Man was able to say that de Man both 1) had "seduced a whole generation of students" and 2) was "too boring" and "too predictable" to read. I don't know about Professor Rorty, but I would say that whatever seduction may be, it is not boring —especially if it's as successful as he claims.[11]) So, the threat is obvious: it's the necessity of reading and re-reading—a necessity that, again thanks to the 1941–42 writings, can no longer be ignored, circumvented, or reduced to the old stupidities. It happened, it's an event, it's history—no amount of pretense or self-mystification will allow one (supporters or attackers) to go back, to ignore the breach made by something that, among other names, goes under the name of "deconstruction," or, better, deconstruction*s*. And *as* an event, *as* what happened, *as* history, the threat of the necessity of (re)reading is not just a threat. It is also a promise—the promise of a future, the promise of an other future—for, among other things, something that had been *mis*read or *un*read under the name "deconstruction." In other (harsher) words, we have de Man's 1941–42 writings to thank for the future—*our* future (not the future of "de Man" or "Derrida," for *their* future was assured long ago)—or at least that "part" of these writings ("the part of the text," call it) differentiated from itself enough, marked enough, written enough, like the sound inside a seashell. And it is not too much to say that the later (1953–83) writings *are* that "part" of the wartime (1941–42) journalism: the part that, in predicting the oblivion and the indifference of the future, marks the present and thereby promises the memory and the difference of the future. The reading of this "part" remains, is yet to come—from the future. It is the chance (*chance, Glück*) of "de Man" and "deconstruction in America." "O wie wir *glücklich* sind, wir Erkennenden, vorausgesetzt, dass wir lange genug zu schweigen wissen! . . ." (Nietzsche, *Zur Genealogie der Moral*).

TERRIBLE READING

[The following remarks were delivered at a special session on de Man and Blanchot at the December 1987 MLA convention in San Francisco. The quotation from Montherlant was their epigraph. The paper seemed appropriate for the occasion, and, as a call for *reading* rather than *judging,* it is, unfortunately, still appropriate today.]

"Time constraints being what they are—namely, what one could call "journalistic"—I will confine myself to speaking in short-hand, as it were, and tell three quick stories: three parables, three fables, three allegories. The first takes the form of an anecdote. After a discussion of the content and the implications of the December 1st *New York Times* article about the "revela-

tion" of Paul de Man's newspaper articles in the 1941 and 1942 *Le Soir,* a student remarked on the photo of "Professor Paul de Man in 1975" accompanying it. "You know," said the student, "on the dust-jacket of *Allegories of Reading* he always seemed rather kindly and gentle. Here [in the *New York Times*] he seems threatening and somewhat menacing." A curious observation, thought I, for indeed the photo was exactly the same as that which had graced the dust-jacket that clothed the book. It is true that the one in the *Times* was a bit smaller than the one in the book—and quite a bit smaller than the larger-than-life monumentalizing version of the same photo on the cover of the *Yale French Studies* devoted to de Man. Still, despite the more modest size of the photo, the face of the dead man—at least on the surface—remains the same. Clearly enough, what makes the difference and seems to authorize the substitution of one de Man for another, as it were, is not the face or the facial expression in the pictures but the text accompanying them. Although the *Times* article praises de Man as he has never been praised before—calling him "one of the most brilliant intellectuals of his generation" and "the originator of a controversial theory of language some say may place him among the great thinkers of his age"—its report also makes it possible to blame him as he has never been blamed (at least publicly) as a collaborator with Nazi occupation authorities and the author of at least one anti-Semitic newspaper article. In other words, the difference between the two de Man's—the one apparently a kindly great man, the other apparently threatening—is not due to anything one can *see* but, as always, to what one can, and has to, *read.* And the reading that makes all the difference in this case is quite clearly an instance of *allegorical* reading—which, by a pure act of the mind, converts that which one can see, the phenomenal appearance before one's eyes, into an allegorical sign for an abstract meaning that has nothing to do with that sign's phenomenal appearance and whatever empirical reality it may represent. In short, the allegorical reading turns the phenomenal appearance into a conventional, written sign, into an inscription, that may look like all kinds of things but that means something else. For instance, Giotto's Charity—heart in hand—may look like a cook handing a cork-screw out a basement kitchen window; or, in another vein, it could perhaps be taken as, say, the representation of a woman cannibal offering a heart. Fortunately, Giotto has supplied the inscription KARITAS to pre-empt such possibilities and pre-empty the picture.

Now Paul de Man would no doubt have been at least a little amused by the student's unwitting allegorical reading of de Man BEFORE and de Man AFTER. Perhaps he would have smiled the much fabled smile of the picture (which, as anybody who has ever understood anything written by de Man knows, was not ambiguous but truly undecidable). For, as we know, he knew something about allegory and had a great deal to say about it—from the beginning and to the end. And from the beginning what he said about it took the form of a distinction, a disjunction, which, expressed in very general terms, is a disjunction between, on the one hand, phenomenalizing, representational types of signification and, on the other hand, nonphenomenal, non-representational, arbitrary signification. But text-bound terms formulate the disjunction more precisely here. For instance, in the case of de Man's reading of Yeats in his dissertation (which dates back to the late 1950's) the distinction and disjunction is put in terms of "image" and "emblem." As the two terms already suggest, "image" here refers to a more "natural" form of signification in which the primacy of the sensory object and a mode of linguistic representation consistent with sensory perception remains unquestioned; whereas "emblem" refers to an arbitrary, more "artificial" form of signification in which the sensory image is pressed into service for the ends of a meaning whose key or guarantee lies not in the sensory world and empirical experience but rather in the mechanical application of a conventional code—for instance, a code-book of emblems. Already recognizable in the juxtaposition of image and emblem are later, similar formulations of the same disjunction: most clearly symbol and allegory, of course, but also, later, rhetoric and grammar, say, or Apollinian and Dionysian, symbol and sign, or even, more problematically, phenomenal and material, trope and inscription, trope and anthropomorphism, etc. But what remains consistent in this list of terms is not just the disjunction between them but the nature of that disjunction: that is, the mutual intrication of the paired terms in a particular text. That intrication is one in which the latter term inevitably undoes, disrupts, dis-articulates, the mode of signification and the meaning produced by the former. What happens to the pair image/emblem in the reading of Yeats and the pair Apollinian/Dionysian in the reading of *The Birth of Tragedy* provides good examples. The reading of Yeats arrives at a conception of his poetry as a poetry of the image-hyphen-emblem, the image-emblem—in which the seductiveness of the natural image is put into question as soon as the image is read emblematically (i.e., allegorically): that is, the emblematic meaning undermines the authority of the imaged meaning and gives it the lie. (One of the implications being that therefore there never was any such thing—in the case of Yeats or any other poet—as a poetry of the pure image *or* a poetry of the pure emblem, for both are always mutually, and mutually destructively, intricated in any given image which hence is always already an image-emblem, or a symbol-allegory . . . Another implication being that therefore the story of Yeats' progression from a poetry of the image

through a poetry of the emblem to a poetry of the image-emblem is not a history but an allegory—an emblematic allegory—for the very first image and all its sensory seductiveness were always already undermined by its inevitably having an emblematic, allegorical function . . .) So in the case of de Man's reading of *The Birth of Tragedy,* the disjunction is not the trivial and clichéd distinction bequeathed to us by intellectual history—i.e., between the Apollinian serenity of the surface and the Dionysian existential horror underneath—but rather the disjunction proper to the Apollinian itself: that is, between its representational function and its radically semiotic, indeed allegorical, function. De Man formulates it as follows: "the actual *meaning* of the Apollinian appearance is not the empirical reality it *represents* but the Dionysian insight into the illusory quality of this reality"[12]—a formulation in which the disjunction between what the Apollinian appearance *represents* and what it *means* is nicely visible, nicely readable. The Apollinian representation of tragedy may *represent* all kinds of things in the empirical world—the sufferings of Oedipus and his family problems, say—but what it actually *means* is the destruction of what it represents. In short, there is no Dionysus (as a deeper substratum, reality, or *Ding an sich*)—only an Apollo who is divided against himself as what he represents and as what he means, and what he *means* is the destruction of what he represents. (One could call that meaning "Dionysian" but it is "Dionysian" in a new, re-inscribed sense: one that has nothing to do with the existential pathos of human suffering and everything to do with the non-tragic, prosaically toneless, functioning of not-so-human language.)

But time—or the times (as in *New York Times*)—constrains. The point in all these examples is the nature of the disjunction: how the allegorical function interferes with, disrupts, disarticulates, the meaning that the phenomenal non-reading (a reading modelled on *seeing*) produces. But the disjunction "itself" is not something that you can hold in your hand. (As de Man put it on one occasion: "Unreadability is not something you have in your hand.") Because it is not something you can *see* but rather have to read, the allegorical function, call it (for short-hand), has many ruses and snares. For instance, in the case of our one, double portrait of de Man—BEFORE and AFTER—the "allegorical" reading of the picture as threatening is, of course, no reading at all. For it is an understanding pressed into the service of the phenomenal, the empirical, the psychological—into the service of that which we can all see and understand. That is, to take *this* picture as threatening is to interpret it according to a *con*junction (rather than a *dis*junction) between text and phenomenal appearance: this man, this de Man, reports the newspaper, was a collaborator with the Nazis, an anti-Semite *sans* *doute,* and now that we know that, we've got him, we've got him in hand, we can put our (accusing and judging) fingers on him—despite the irony of that smile and the difficulty of those readings. And now that we've got our man, we find that he is not so threatening after all, for, after all, look at how easily he too can be re-inscribed in the familiar systems where phenomenal appearance and its meaning bear a referential relationship to one another, where picture and text, seeing and reading, fit together like the two halves of a symbol. And that this system is of systematic non-reading is not at all surprising, for, after all, we are talking about *newspapers,* which necessarily have a referential moment built into them and, as such, suspend the necessity of reading. If there's one thing that doesn't need to be read, it's the newspaper! How reassuring, then, to have this de Man—that uncompromising purist and fanatic of reading—inscribed in the newspaper for us, and doubly at that: once in 1941 and 1942 and now in *The New York Times.* Finally, at last, we have a de Man we don't have to read. Thanks to the newspapers, we can know him and judge him—in a system where no disjunction between knowing and judging (or, say, between cognitive and performative) is possible. What could be more reassuring? It turns out, then, that the new de Man of the *New York Times* is not all that different from the old "revered," "venerated," monumentalized de Man. Whether we judge him as a great man or as a collaborator (or worse) makes no difference, for both judgments are part and parcel of the same system of non-reading: both are only attempts to deflect attention away from, or even to suppress, the necessity of reading the texts.

Of course, everything changes as soon as we begin reading the texts—that is, begin reading *as* text—even the newspapers. For as soon as we begin to do so, we lose the possibility of using the referential moment inscribed in the newspapers as a reliable model for a cognition on the basis of which we could take action—for instance, like the act of judging de Man as either guilty or innocent. Reading suspends: it suspends knowledge and it suspends judgment, and it suspends, above all, the possibility of ever knowing whether we are doing one or the other. Reading suspends the decision between the thematic, referential meaning and the rhetorical, allegorical function that turns upon it. This is why reading is truly threatening and truly terrible—not because it suspends you between two meanings but because it suspends you between meaning and the material, linguistic conditions of meaning (that always dis-articulate it radically as they make it possible). In the case of our portraits, then, there is no doubt about *which* picture is threatening. It is certainly not the picture of the collaborator (or worse) in the *New York Times* (nor is it the picture of the monumental, giant master-teacher [under the title "The Lesson of Paul de Man"]

on the cover of *Yale French Studies*). No, *that* picture is un-threatening and reassuring because what it says is: "I am a newspaper: you don't have to read me." The threatening, terrible, terrifying picture is of course the one on *Allegories of Reading.* And it is terrible not on account of anything one can *see* there but on account of what *it* says. For it says that the "actual meaning" of the picture is utterly indifferent to the picture's representing *either* a great man *or* a collaborator. It says that this "actual meaning" is also utterly indifferent to our judging the picture as threatening or as kindly, utterly indifferent to our accusations and our excuses and our worries and our fears and our hand-wringing: it is a text and it doesn't care. It says: "I am a text and you can't read me." This is also why the smile—as textual smile, as smile of reading, as it were—is truly terrifying: *not* because it may be either kindly or threatening. Both of these possibilities are reassuring; both have only anecdotal value. No, the smile is terrifying because its "actual meaning" has nothing to do with what we take it to represent: that is, it has nothing to do with the phenomenal, empirical, psychological existence of a human being. Rather it is ironic, terribly ironic, because its irony is the irony of language, not that of a person.

This structure—the juxtaposition of and the disjunction between a seeing that does not read and a reading that does not see—and the two terrors proper to it—one being a phenomenal, empirical, psychological terror, the other a material, philosophical, epistemological terror—is the structure of what de Man in his late essays calls "aesthetic ideology." What is aesthetic ideology? In the case of the second term—ideology—we get a relatively direct definition in "The Resistance to Theory": "What we call ideology is precisely the confusion of linguistic with natural reality, of reference with phenomenalism." *Aesthetic* ideology would be the particular version of this confusion that manifests itself in a certain misreading of the category of the aesthetic in truly critical philosophical reflections on aesthetic theory (for instance, those of Kant and Hegel). For despite their explicit thematics and their substantial ideological investment in the aesthetic—as the articulation of pure reason and practical reason, epistemology and ethics, in Kant, and as the "sensory appearance of the Idea" (*das sinnliche Scheinen der Idee*) in Hegel—the aesthetic in both Kant and Hegel, once read, marks a radically linguistic "moment" that threatens to dis-articulate their respective systems. One such "moment"—in both Kant's *Third Critique* and Hegel's *Aesthetics*—is their interpretations of the sublime. As de Man puts it, summarizing his reading of the sublime in Kant: "The critique of the aesthetic ends up, in Kant, in a formal materialism that runs counter to all values and characteristics associated with aesthetic experience, including the aesthetic experience of the beautiful and of the sublime as described by Kant and Hegel themselves."[13] The "formal materialism" of the vision of the sublime in Kant is purely material since it is "devoid of any reflexive or intellectual complication," as de Man puts it, and purely formal since it is "devoid of any semantic depth and reducible to the formal mathematizations or geometrizations of pure optics." As such, it is the "formal materialism" of the inscription, of written letters. "The bottom line in Kant as well as in Hegel," writes de Man, "is the prosaic materiality of the letter and no degree of obfuscation or ideology can transform this materiality into the phenomenal cognition of aesthetic judgment." The tradition of Kant and Hegel interpretation, however,—even though it has not been able to transform materiality into phenomenality—has nevertheless entirely overlooked this "material aspect" of their theories and has instead seen only their figural, "romantic" aspect: that is, it has turned their truly critical thought into ideology by, for instance, re-phenomenalizing the radical (linguistic, inscriptional) materiality of the sublime. The inaugural and paradigmatic figure in this tradition of ideologizing misreading (or non-reading) would be of course Schiller, in particular his misreading of Kant on the sublime. Although it would take some doing and too much time to retrace de Man's reading of "Kant and Schiller"[14] what happens, what takes place, between Kant and Schiller (according to de Man) can be stated in straightforward terms. Or rather because what Schiller does is to regress from the radicality of Kant's insights and the materialism that is their bottom line, precisely *nothing* happens, *nothing* takes place, in Schiller's reception of Kant. As de Man puts it, this regression is not historical because it takes place in a temporal mode and as such is not history. (De Man writes: "One could say for example that in the reception of Kant, in the way Kant has been read, since the Third Critique [and that was an occurrence, something happened there, something occurred] that in the whole reception of Kant from then on, nothing happened, only regression, nothing has happened at all. Which is another way of saying . . . that reception is not historical, that between reception and history there is an absolute separation and that to take reception as a model for historical event is in error . . .") In any case, precisely because *nothing happens* in Schiller's regression from Kant—despite the fact that, as de Man admonishes, in all our thinking about art, literature, and the teaching of literature as art, "We are all Schillerians; no one is Kantian anymore"—it can be stated summarily: Schiller (in the early essay "Vom Erhabenen") turns that which in Kant is a critical, transcendental questioning of the structure and the limits of the imagination, of knowing, into a pragmatic, empirical, psychological question—into something that we can all see and understand and confirm in our experience. How does he do

this? Schiller does it by re-naming and re-characterizing Kant's sublime: what Kant calls the "mathematical" and the "dynamic" sublime, Schiller calls the "theoretical" and the "practical" sublime, and values the latter over the former: that is, the practical over the theoretical sublime. Why? "The practical sublime is distinguished from the theoretical sublime in that it stands in opposition to the demands of our existence, whereas the theoretical stands in opposition only to the demands of knowledge." In other words, this re-naming, re-characterization, and re-valuation completely overturns the Kant. Whereas in Kant the danger and the terror occurs as a failure of representation and is thus of interest to Kant because it tells us something about the structure of the imagination, in Schiller it occurs as a threat to our desire for self-preservation, in the practical sublime the ultimate ground of all the manifestations of our cognitive powers, namely existence itself, is under attack. No wonder, then, that much more is at stake in the practical than in the theoretical sublime. "So," summarizes de Man, "the practical sublime has much more at stake, since our entire existence is being threatened, whereas the only thing that was threatened by the theoretical sublime was just our ability to represent, our ability to know. Who cares about knowing when the tempest is beating at his door, that's not the moment that you want to know. You want to be self-preserved, and you want to survive, psychologically, the assault to which you are submitted. Much more is at stake, your whole existence; whereas a little loss of knowledge can always be made up the next day . . . hmm?" Schiller's is a familiar misreading or non-reading—and it empties out in familiar ironies. For one, precisely on account of his valuation of the practical, empirical, and psychological Schiller's version of the sublime ends up in total idealism, in an utter separation between mind and senses—in the notion of a pure intellect that can separate itself entirely from the body in order to preserve itself in the face of sublime terror. Whereas Kant's "idealism"—despite, or precisely *on account of,* its emphasis on the theoretical, critical, and transcendental —instead ends up with a genuine materialism—in a pure material vision devoid of intellect, devoid of semantic depth or tropological substitution (i.e., it is neither literal nor figurative). I won't follow out this (predictable) itinerary —the denouement of the story of aesthetic ideology (which also happens to be the story of what is called our "modernity")—which leads to an aesthetic education in the service of the state (and dismayingly close to conceptions of aesthetic education advocated in more recent readings of Schiller like that in the novel *Michael* by Joseph Goebbels). Instead, I'll tell one last story.

The story is that of Wordsworth's drowned man in Book V of *The Prelude*. Roving up and down along the shores of Esthwaite's Lake, the boy Wordsworth spots a "heap of garments," left as he supposes "by one who there was bathing." He watches for a long time, "but no one owned them." The unclaimed garments having told "a plain tale"—namely, that their owner had drowned—the next day a company goes to drag the lake: "At length, the dead man, 'mid that beauteous scene /Of trees and hills and water, bolt upright /Rose with his ghastly face, a spectre shape—/Of terror even." And yet no "vulgar fear" possesses the young Wordsworth. He is able to preserve himself, his self, against the terror of natural death by recognizing it as a sight that his "inner eye" had seen before "among the shining streams /Of fairyland, the forest of romance"—that is, he can recognize this sight as something he had seen before *in books,* in the fairy tales and romances that have made up his reading. From books, from his reading, comes a spirit that hallows what he sees "With decoration and ideal grace, /A dignity, a smoothness, like the works /Of Grecian art and purest poesy." That's the story. It is very much a story of aesthetic education at work: thanks to reading, the ghastly face of the drowned man is converted into a beautiful art object, as the presumably very stiff corpse of the dead man gets turned into Greek sculpture—the highest art (according to Hegel). And the Schillerian (and Winckelmannian) terms of this aesthetification—"decoration," "ideal grace," "dignity"—almost beg to be read in German: *edle Einfalt und stille Grösse, Anmut und Würde,* etc. Indeed, we have here virtually a text-book Schillerian version of the sublime, as the Reason, Wordsworth's imagination say (which is "highest reason in a soul sublime"), acts on Terror and preserves him from it. No doubt the drowned man would have been pleased, for the notes to *The Prelude* identify the body as that of a local school-teacher who, in this case, continues teaching even after death! Surely it would be perverse (as in "turning the wrong way") to see anything but a phenomenal, phenomenalizing, aesthetic model of art and literature here. This is clearly a story of aesthetic education—and, as we shall see, aesthetic ideology—at work. And that it works on the basis of the possibility of mediating, synthesizing, totalizing *seeing* and *reading* is equally clear, and one could formulate it thus: what the boy Wordsworth *saw* in *reading* allows him to *read* what he *sees*. What he *saw* in *reading* allows him to *read* what he *sees*—a neatly chiasmic mechanism. How does it work?

In linguistic, rhetorical terms, it works as a closed tropological system of metaphor based on the analogy: body is to soul as garments are to body. This is an old analogy, and it generates some common metaphors: for instance, one can call the body the "garment of the soul." Hence it is not surprising that the body can be re-inspirited after the soul has left it—for the (dead) body is only a (dead) body in relation to a (living) soul

just as garments are only garments in relation to the body that can put them on. It is no wonder, then, that, no matter how terrible, the corpse of the drowned man is not all that fearful: *as* the (dead) corpse *of* a (living) spirit it is only awaiting re-inspiriting, awaiting being put on again by its owner (whether now or at the last judgment . . . amen). This is all well and good and as it should be—but only as long as we keep turning to the corpse—and *from* the corpse to the books understood on an incarnational body is to soul model. The real threat and the real terror in this passage is not the *corpse* of the drowned man but rather the *garments* of the corpse. The garments are the real threat because they are *not* the dead covering of a living cover*ed, not* the dead garments of a living body, but rather the dead covering of a dead covered, the dead garments of a dead corpse. They are, in short, the garment of a garment (or "the corpse of a corpse"). In other words, once the corpse is introduced into the slot of the analogy occupied by the body—in garments are to body as body is to soul, which *now* reads garments are to *corpse* as *corpse* is to soul—the tropological system of metaphor is opened up radically and necessarily produces weird figures that will not be returned to it. For in the analogy garments are to corpse as corpse is to soul, the dead *corpse* is now in the slot formerly occupied by the living body (in relation to the garments) and hence becomes the figure for a dead spirit; and, symmetrically, the living soul or spirit, in occupying the analogous slot (in relation to the corpse), then becomes the figure for a living corpse or the living dead. And there is no halt to this regular production of dead souls, dead spirits, zombies, living corpses, or the living dead—as soon as we turn to the garments, that is, to the garments *as* the garments of a corpse. (The moral being that there is nothing to fear from naked corpses; it's only a corpse with clothes that will get you.) But that's not very dignified, decorative, or particularly graceful. The story of the unsightly, abandoned garments is indeed a "plain tale" that isn't very pretty. It's not a pretty sight. Much better to turn to the corpse and its beautifiable, re-inspiritable ghastly face.

So what is the point? I'll try not to belabor it. The point is that the turn to the corpse, and from the corpse to books, is not at all a turn from seeing to reading. Because the linguistic and textual model of the book here is an incarnational, phenomenalizing, indeed phenomenological, model, the turn is rather merely a turn *from,* say, a seeing with the external, sensuous eye *to* a seeing with the inner, intellectual (or imaginative) eye. In short, it is a turn to a reading still modelled on seeing. As such, this (non-)reading is not at all threatening or terrible. It can recover from the negativity of any terror, including the terror of natural death—in the worst case, by aesthetifying it, phenomenalizing it, taking that which is dead as the figure for a living spirit, etc. . . . But the turn to the garments would be a turn *from* seeing *to* reading: that is, to a non-phenomenal, dis-incarnate reading based on a truly linguistic, radically rhetorical model. The garments are the *real* books here. The garments—*as* the garments of a corpse—are dead all right, but that "dead" is anything but natural: it is, for lack of a better word, a "linguistic" death, a death proper to language. As such, the garments are threatening and terrible because their terror cannot be recovered for phenomenalizing, phenomenological, incarnational, aesthetic models of language and the text. But since this terror is not a threat to human life, there is no human pathos about it. Rather than threatening your life, it only threatens to suspend you in a certain "after-life" without death, say, or in a death without an anterior life, it only threatens to turn you into a dead spirit, a dead soul, or a living corpse, one of the living dead, a zombie, ghost of no body, *revenant jamais venu,* etc. No, all the terror of reading threatens is the possibility of representation, knowledge, meaning, and so on. Better not to read, then, for what's a little loss of reading? It can always be made up tomorrow, next time, next year. There is always another day, another time, another MLA . . . there is always time for reading. Just now, though, we need to know and judge, no? I'm afraid I'm out of time."[15]

Northwestern University

NOTES

1. Jeffrey Mehlman quotes and translates this passage in his *Legacies of Anti-Semitism in France* (Minneapolis: University of Minnesota Press, 1983), p.12.

2. Mehlman, p.12.

3. See Jacques Derrida's text, "Like the Sound of the Sea Deep within a Shell: Paul de Man's War," *Critical Inquiry* Vol. 14, No. 3 (Spring 1988).

4. See Maurice Blanchot, *Faux pas* (Paris: Gallimard, 1943), p.352 and Mehlman, *Legacies,* p.13.

5. On the "other," see Derrida's recent work, especially *De l'esprit* (Paris: Galilée, 1988) and *Psyché* (Paris: Galilée, 1987).

6. See the "Dream of the Arab" in Wordsworth's *Prelude,* Book V. I have begun a reading of it in "Missed Crossing: Wordsworth's Apocalypses," *MLN* 99 (December 1984), 982–1006.

7. Jacques Derrida, "Like the Sound of the Sea Deep within a Shell: Paul de Man's War," 645–46.

8. One of the striking aspects of the reaction to the "de Man affair" is the attribution of fantastic institutional power to de Man. This is quite clearly a (defensive) displacement for the only power de Man ever had: namely, intellectual power. Because de Man had *that* power, he was also smart enough to know how to (try to) translate it into institutional power—sometimes successfully—but never in as direct or unmediated a way as the academic journalists imagine. Indeed, de Man knew all too well that any direct attempt to use the only power he did have (i.e., intellectual) was bound to backfire on the institutional scene. Equally striking is the concomitant myth of the fabled institutional success of something called "deconstruction" and those who allegedly practice it. Anyone a little experienced in these matters—especially at close range (for instance, anyone who knows a little about the fate of "deconstruction at Yale") —will only smile at the naiveté of those propagating this myth. For an article that retails both of these myths—and in which there is not the slightest hint that de Man's (or "deconstruction's") fabled "success" could have had anything to do with *intellectual* power— see Walter Kendrick, "Paul de Man: Friend or Fascist" in the *Village Voice Literary Supplement* (April 12, 1988). This article explicitly names "resentment" as the motivation of the reaction to the "de Man affair."

9. Anyone who thinks that the reptilian figure here is exaggerated or merely ill-humored should read some of the slime that has passed for "journalism" these last months. For instance, the articles by Jon Wiener in *The Nation* (January 9, 1988), David Lehman in *Newsweek* (February 15, 1988), and Walter Kendrick in the *VLS* (April 12, 1988).

10. Among other things, a re-reading may discover: the fact that nearly all of de Man's work, rather than being "for" self or auto-referentiality or "denying" the referential function of language, stresses throughout what could be called the "irreducibility of reference"; or the fact that the work has been throughout a critique of "aesthetic ideology" and the notion of literature as "play" or the "liberation of the signifier."

11. The case of Rorty is not to be confused with that of the other academic journalists. He quite rightly does not think that de Man's 1941–42 writings are a good reason to discredit "deconstruction." (See his article on Heidegger's politics in *The New Republic* [April 11, 1988].) Nevertheless, the fact that he can bother to spend half a lecture ("Two Versions of Logocentrism: Derrida and de Man," delivered at Northwestern, May 6, 1988) making fun of quotations from de Man—while having read very few (if any) of de Man's texts (or Derrida's, for that matter) aside from quotations in Lentricchia (!)—makes one wonder about the complicity or naiveté that allows him to do it *now,* i.e., *after* the "revelation" of the 1941–42 writings.

Again, why bother denouncing the poor fellow's work if it is too boring for you to read it?

12. Paul de Man, *Allegories of Reading* (New Haven: Yale University Press, 1979), p.92.

13. Paul de Man, "Phenomenality and Materiality in Kant," in Gary Shapiro, ed. *Hermeneutics* (Amherst: The University of Massachusetts Press, 1984).

14. Paul de Man, "Kant and Schiller," forthcoming in *Aesthetic Ideology* (Minneapolis: The University of Minnesota Press, 1989). This was one of the Messenger lectures de Man delivered at Cornell in the spring of 1983.

15. A more elaborate reading of the drowned man's garments is my "Facing Language: Wordsworth's First Poetic Spirits," *Diacritics* (Winter 1987).

Paul de Man: A Sketch of Two Generations

LINDSAY WATERS

"The hour of truth, like the hour of death, never arrives on time."

"Words cannot be isolated from the deeds they perform."—*Paul de Man*

We have much to account for, those of us who have admired Paul de Man. It will not do, I think, to attack journalism for its distortions of the truth. De Man dared to be a journalist in the 40s for *Le Soir* and again in the 60s for *The New York Review of Books* and would have done so again if the occasion arose. For him it was part of the intellectual's job to try to convey complex ideas to as general an audience as would receive them, despite the risks of distortion, the need to make deadline. The undistorted truth about his activities in 1941 and 1942 is unpleasant. De Man lent his considerable intellect to the service of a bad cause when he was a young man, and later chose not to make his activities then or his attitudes to them afterwards a matter of public record. It is true, we have learned, that he was exonerated by a military tribunal in Belgium in 1945, and he seems to have told a number of key people along his career path about his past. But he left all the rest of us in ignorance. We feel called upon now to use language of moral judgment—a form of discourse that we will, alas, not learn from his writings. The considerable power evident in them is devoted to making other sorts of distinctions, and he made it a point of his polemic against conventional criticism that literature and morality must be kept separate. In its place, given the right targets, that polemic of his has much to recommend it. Today it is not what seems most helpful. Before we can fully come to terms with what he did, we must find for ourselves a school in moral language of the sort that Primo Levi conducts in his books so that we can understand and articulate how saddened and more that we are because he wrote what he did when he did and then decided that it need not be any more public than the microfilm collection of a major research library. Until we find that school and develop that language we are confronted with our own failure to understand him. One's sense of being let down is due in no small part to one's expectations of the man. He was not my "doctor father"—I was his publisher—but I certainly idealized him and I suspect that many others did as well. It seems today as if people are compelled to vilify him to the exact same degree that they once exalted him, but surely neither response is an appropriate one. In this small essay I want to try to get at one of the roots of the idealization to speculate why it might have occurred at all, because I think the interest in de Man was not shameful in the way that I cannot but feel today his concealment of his past was. But the irony that this paper asks you to consider consists in my guess that without the past he had de Man would not have been half as valuable to many of us as he has proven to be over the last twenty years or so.

Those critical of de Man have for the last few years argued in different ways and to varying degrees that de Man and the "deconstructionists" turned their backs on politics.[1] We now have, thanks to the emergence of the articles of 1941 to 1943, information that will allow us to develop a more exact understanding of de Man's changing attitudes toward politics. The writings that have newly surfaced make painfully clear, however, that a formative political experience as a writer lies in de Man's past. He had taken the challenge to become an engaged writer some years *before* Sartre articulated his demand for engagement in the second half of the 40s. And if de Man objected to Sartre's notions of what political engagement means for the writer in his essays "The Inward Generation" (1955) and the review of Sartre's *The Words* (1966) as well as elsewhere, it is now clear that his rationale was more complicated than we had previously thought, and that clearly it owes something to his sense of the dangers of engagement, commitment, the putting of literature to the service of state and party, and to his desire to understand the relation of letters to politics in a way that differed not just from Sartre but from his former self, given the absolute necessity of rejecting anything that might lead to a position like the one that he had started from.

A formative political experience stands, then, behind de Man's work. In recent years when he and Jacques Derrida were accused of being apolitical and ahistorical, he asserted that a politics did inform his work and he worked with urgency on the large-scale analysis of what he called the "aesthetic ideology" that was the major project he left unfinished at his death.[2] But his assertions are themselves less significant than what may be apparent now. A concern for the categories of history, agency, and politics runs through his texts, from those in the 50s that directly reflect on the experience of his generation in the wake of World War II, such as "The Inward Generation," on to complex rhetorical analyses and performances like "Shelley Disfigured."[3] We are only now, and in large part because of these revelations, prepared to see what was already in these essays. Even as he rejected the thinkers and writers from Sartre to Jünger whose practice influenced his own at the earliest stage of his writing career, he put himself in their debt. Samuel Weber writes: "In the celebrated second book of *The Genealogy of Morals,* Nietzsche describes the emergence of the sentiment of *guilt* from *debt* that each generation incurs with regard to its predecessors, a debt that increases with the power and performance of the indebted successors."[4] We can now, I think, see the nature of the guilt, of more than one sort, that might have kept de Man tied to the previous generation against whose practice, especially after the war, he decided to forge his own.

The politics that marked him was a low one, no matter how highminded his own allegiance to it. But in coming to terms with de Man's activities early in the war we do well to bear in mind the words of Gottfried Benn quoted by Fritz Stern: "We were not all opportunists."[5] De Man, following his uncle, may well have been an idealist. It is hard at a distance to be certain of what one would have done if one had been there. As Sartre said, speaking for those who were there, "The irreversibility of our age belonged only to us."[6] It must be recognized, however, as Stern writes, "that National Socialism could be a great temptation, that a certain kind of idealist could succumb to the movement as a means of identifying with the nation, of restoring a sense of belonging that had ceased to exist . . . and not for reasons of petty careerism."[7]

The writings of 1941 and 1942 reveal a person who believed he existed in the midst of revolutionary change. Nazi rhetoric was filled with enthusiastic talk of a spiritual revolution. De Man seems to have bought a fair amount of this talk. His commitment was always to literature, however, so he both succumbs to and resists the party line. At one moment he was willing to criticize the French novel for being cerebral, analytic, and psychological and praise the German novel for portraying the battle between good and evil in clear-cut symbolic terms. (It's interesting that the critique of the French novel he employed was largely the one already developed by the French themselves in the 30s. Sartre criticized Proust in the same terms de Man used to question the French novel in order to praise by contrast the German novel.) At other times he defends the French novel as the most advanced form of the genre precisely for its emphasis on psychology, praises Valéry despite his obviously "cerebral" nature. All the ideas presented in the essays do not cohere. Another important conflict in the mind of the person who wrote the essays reveals itself in the appeals that nationalism and cosmopolitanism variously exert upon him. De Man is torn between the German ideology of particularism and the French (ultimately Napoleonic) ideology of internationalism, torn between the idea that nation is the highest form of association and the idea that humankind as a whole stands above the nations and legitimately limits their aspirations. Nonetheless we can see in his essays a commitment to revolutionary change. The young Paul de Man anticipated the radical transformation of European society. He believed the "events" were going to sweep away a decadent and plutocratic society (see *Le Soir,* 25 March 1941). And he foresaw a society in which art would be the determining political force. For him the nation *was* its art, and in believing this he adhered to a version of aesthetic nationalism that went back to Herder and differed perhaps in a key way from the national socialists for whom the nation was the blood group that constituted its people. The article "Les juifs dans la littérature actuelle," as utterly objectionable as it is, is curious in its refusal to identify nation with race in proper Nazi fashion. It argues that art is impervious to race and that therefore the presence or absence of Jews within Europe is a matter of no consequence for the spiritual life of Europe. If Europe has been decaying until this revolution erupted, it is not because of any possible racial contamination but because art is in a subordinate position within a capitalist, democratic schema. The antisemitism of this essay is deplorable, but much more pervasive in all the essays is the aesthetic nationalism. The attitude he expressed there was tied in with the politics of cultural despair, the antidemocratic, elitist aestheticism of a group like the Stefan George circle.

Hard as it may be to accept the idea at first, 1941 was as revolutionary a moment for de Man as 1789. Much of what he said suggests he thought that "bliss was it in that dawn to be alive." It was, he said, "un événement historique sans pareil" (*Le Soir*, 23 Dec. 41). He saw youth coming to power, privilege swept away, and an aesthetic culture assuming power. "Nous sommes actuellement, au point de vue littéraire également, dans une période de crise. . . . Comme conséquence de ceci, on voit quel rôle considérable les jeunes ont à jouer. . ." (*Le Soir*, 18 February 1941). He came to realize this dream was a delusion, Nazi reality a disaster. The occupiers could tolerate such idealism only so far, especially an idealism that was directed more toward a Flemish and pan-European revival than toward a German militarist, totalitarian domination of Europe.

After the war he rejected, he wrote off this earliest step in his intellectual itinerary for reasons he states in the 1955 essay "The Inward Generation." Between 1943 and 1955 many factors and many writers had come to play some role in his formation—the French Hegel of Kojève and Hyppolite, Bataille, Blanchot, the French Heidegger not of Sartre but of the resistance journal *Fontaine*. His notion of how one should engage in politics changed. Commitment to myths of radical transformation were rejected. As he says in the 1953 essay on Montaigne, no doubt reflecting on his own experience, "The wretched myths that surround us are no sooner born than they degenerate into sclerotic bureaucracies. They must appeal to the most factitious loyalties—those to race and nation—in order to gain any vitality at all." He now identified himself with Montaigne and what he said about Montaigne may have represented his own frame of mind as he came to distance himself from the politics of the German occupiers of Belgium. He had been interested in what the Germans had to offer Europe because it seemed to represent youth wiping out the atrophied institutions of a decadent Europe. He says of Montaigne's "conservatism": "If the prevailing orthodoxy hardens, crystallizes into sharp points, becoming

massive and opaque, wounding anyone who comes up against it; if it has no concern but to perpetuate itself as an institution and if its ritual becomes police regulation, Montaigne will be the first to detest it, and it remains for us to imagine what rebellions he is capable of."[8] De Man came to detest the Nazis and their wretched myths. It remains for us to understand the rebellion he was capable of and how he pursued it in the years to come. In his Montaigne essay de Man attempted in some way to come to terms with his past. Here he signaled his judgment against those whom he had in however complicated a way identified with. Is it just wishful thinking on my part to say so? I do not think so. I believe this is the case because to think otherwise does not jibe with the person I knew. To think otherwise means considering that his failure to acknowledge later what he had written in 1941 and 1942 makes him a part of the situation described by Primo Levi in *The Drowned and the Saved*: "the entire history of the brief 'millennial Reich' can be reread as a war against memory, an Orwellian falsification of memory."[9]

De Man's generation, both left and right, has a name. Daniel Bell called it the twice-born generation: "Ours, a 'twice-born' generation, finds its wisdom in pessimism, evil, tragedy, and despair. So we are both old and young 'before our time.'" Between 18 and 21 when the revolutionary hopes of the late 30s and early 40s were projected, such young people became radicals, hoping to live heroic lives, wanting to live at an extreme, criticizing the ordinary person for failing to live at the level of grandeur. The idealist who became an ideologist believed that there was a genuine possibility that the next moment in history could actually be a "transforming moment when salvation or revolution or genuine passion could be achieved." But they came in time to believe that "such chiliastic moments are illusions."[10]

Milosz has written of the "captive mind" of the intellectuals in Eastern Europe who put their minds in service of the state. De Man may have become such a captive mind in a Europe dominated for a decade by Hitler, but we have no reason to be certain about this, given his resignation from *Le Soir*, testimony about his efforts to aid resistance publishing, the example of his uncle's refusal to continue to play a role in occupied Belgium. But it is certain that by the end of the war he rejected the aesthetic nationalism, the decisionism of a Carl Schmitt, and the rest. All of the components of that intellectual position would become problematic after he took the "inward" turn under the influence of Hegel, Husserl, and the philosophy of reflection. He also aligned himself with the, as it were, renegade left— Bataille and others—and not Sartre, Merleau-Ponty, and Camus. De Man rejected thesis-art. He agreed with Adorno that the office of art is not to spotlight alternatives but to resist by its form alone the course of the world, which permanently puts a pistol to men's heads. "Far from being anti-historical, the poetical act (in the general sense that includes all the arts) is the quintessential historical act" (see "The Temptation of Permanence," 1955). The job of art is to dismantle appearance, whereas the notion of a message in art, even when politically radical in the cause of either left or right, already contains an accommodation to the world. He came to share the conviction Kenneth Burke articulated in his *Counter-Statement* that: "An art may be of value purely through preventing a society from becoming too assertively, too hopelessly, itself." The commitment to understand the links that bind poetry to politics remained strong in his work—see the essay on Mallarmé, "Poetic Nothingness" (1955)—but he rejected the notion that art and politics could be identical in the way he seemed in the essays of 1941 and 1942 to indicate at times that he partially believed. To understand his new views in the period when he was at pains to distance himself from the thinker he was, one must consider what he says critically about Malraux in "The Inward Generation" or about Malraux and Heidegger in "The Temptation of Permanence." One should also read for context Nicola Chiaromonte's "Malraux and the Demon of Action" (in *The Paradox of History*).[11]

De Man came to be suspicious of the idea of revolutionary change, so that in the late 60s he was skeptical about the intellectual revolution proclaimed by the structuralists. His comments on Foucault's and Barthes's claims to have revolutionized the human sciences were not favorable. He pursued through the sixties his set of problems, and they were the problems of how to act and think and write given a previous commitment to revolutionary beliefs, and particularly beliefs that aesthetics could guide politics into a millennium. His texts were suffused with the sort of political sensibility he ascribed in a 1966 essay, "Wordsworth and Hölderlin," to Wordsworth:

. . . this consciousness can be had only by one who has very extensively partaken of the danger and failure. Act and interpretation are thus connected in a complex and often contradictory manner. . . . The future is present in history only as the remembering of a failed project that has become a menace. For Wordsworth there is no historical eschatology, but rather only a never-ending reflection upon an eschatological moment that has failed through an excess of interiority.[12]

We owe thanks to Ortwin de Graef for bringing to light the material from Paul de Man's past that will help us understand better his present and future value to us. This "never-ending reflection" of de Man's, always repeating, always changing, always concerned with this failure caused by "the excess of interiority,"

which nonetheless makes de Man aware that his primary task must be to understand the dynamics of interiority and then to move beyond it, this effort of his is precisely what made him acutely important for a set of young people who were also struggling to understand what the future might be for them given the failure of chiliastic hopes in the recent past and the present.

There was a particular sort of dead end into which many of us wandered after the "glorious dawn" of 1968 and the initial political successes of the mobilization against racial segregation in the United States and the war in Viet Nam. This dead end was in effect due to an excess of interiority. Our categories worked against us. Some of us presumed that the evils of the world formed a single closely integrated system, one which might be readily overthrown by the courage and virtue of insurgent youth. "The easy internationalism which identified a unitary capitalism as the cause of global harm and proposed a unitary and almost wholly unanalyzed socialism as its due remedy" was not equipped for the rigors of political struggle.[13] As the revolution manifestly failed to take place, fantasies of revolution grew bolder in the minds of some. For others the force simply dissipated. After Kent State and the Cambodian "Incursion" the New Left collapsed.[14] This led to frustration and disillusionment. One was faced with a failure to understand and a failure to figure out how to proceed. I speak here now of that number of literarily minded individuals who were interested in carrying on the cause of radicalism in however sublimated a form. I speak of a certain cohort of young people who were perhaps on the road to becoming unpolitical people except that the events of the 60s politicized them. To some extent that memory has been forgotten, but the news of Paul de Man's suddenly revealed political past causes a mirror to be thrown up that reveals that we have political pasts too, pasts that we (luckier than he) have no reason to forget and a duty to try to understand. His foundering should enable us to see some of the difficulties that plagued us in the 60s and that plague us still. The privileging of art and aesthetics, as if a revolution in taste would transform politics, was a mistake, but a mistake of a sort we failed to understand. The categories into which too many of the rebellious young divided the world too quickly became a set of binaries that soon betrayed itself as a rigid dualism of good versus evil, revolution versus system.

The paths that seemed to stretch before us in the early 70s were limited unfortunately to two: On the one hand there was the option of eternal resistance, the resistance of the underground person who rejects system because it is system and all systems are corrupt. When some contemporaries took this notion literally as the people in the Weather Underground did, one could not but understand that there were paths that could have led someone to yank that particular abstraction into life, no matter how disastrous such a life was. On the other hand there was the option of learning to identify with the system, the market mechanism; and many of the young people who propelled the Reagan Revolution were—many of them—class of '68 types who took a route that seemed a sensible thing to do given the abyss that seemed to yawn before one if one chose not to embrace the system. The intellectual backing, such as it was, of the Reagan regime was largely built up in the early 70s. Those were the days of Milton Friedman's *Free to Choose*.

It is, of course, a particular form of intellectual and political poverty to imagine a world in which there are only two courses of action, and courses that are so diametrically opposed to each other as that, but many people lived lives of such impoverishment in the early to mid 70s after the failure of the (for some, Miltonic) dream of instituting a *novus ordo seclorum* on earth.

My suggestion in this essay is that Paul de Man offered many people a way out of this poverty. Cornel West has suggested that de Man did something of this sort because of his manifest sense of vocation. "Vocation" puts the matter too much in a religious light for me. I think it was precisely his own political experience as we can now begin to understand it that made him of such importance. Not because he was a Herbert Marcuse, but precisely because he showed a way beyond the idealism and utopianism of a Marcuse. He had had to rescue and rechannel his own revolutionary impulse. He had had to struggle to reorganize his thoughts in the way Daniel Bell described. He had a wisdom, a wisdom that seems on the surface to be couched in terms of pessimism, tragedy, and despair but that actually carried a very positive charge. Where we had to resituate and remotivate a left literary politics, recognizing the dangers of identifying literature with politics, he had moved from a right literary politics to a position of the sort of complex left literary politics represented by a Bataille or the Blanchot of the early 50s. His transformation was more complex and involved his rejection of the antidemocratic literary elitism of the high-toned Nazi sympathizers like those of the George circle and his adoption of that most notorious democrat of the modern world, Rousseau, as one of his major points of self reorientation. Perhaps because his transformation was so complex, the frame of mind he exemplified proved all the more valuable for us—in much the same way that Montaigne's mind was valuable for him. For a set of young people struggling to reorient themselves after the collapse of the student movement and the New Left to a changed world, the world of Kissinger and Nixon as

well as Giscard d'Estaing, he undermined the notion that productive work could be successful in a world thought of in terms of binary oppositions between a sacred "we" and a profane "system." He showed the possibilities for action within a world in which systems can no longer be considered to have a totalitarian grip on actuality. This is the first step to take for any transformative politics. De Man showed that there is no archimedean point outside the "system" from which one judges politics, academic institutions, poetry, or anything else. He showed, in Roberto Unger's words, that to "live in history means, among other things, to be an active and conscious participant in the conflict over the terms of collective life, with the knowledge that this conflict continues in the midst of the technical and the everyday. . . . [N]o ideal form of conduct or form of insight counts until it has penetrated the specialized fields of conduct and thought."[15] But if this is the case, then there is a great deal of very useful work to set about doing and it is this that de Man enabled a set of students, some directly, many indirectly, to do.

De Man's "never-ending reflection upon an eschatological moment that has failed" led him to rethink the categories of thought and action, literature and politics, and this may have instructed a diverse group of people to figure out how to move beyond the problems caused by an "excess of interiority" back into the conflict that continues, as Unger says, in the midst of the technical and the everyday. In this sense the parallel between the generations may have allowed de Man to become the powerful pedagogue he was. I don't mean to underestimate, however, the differences between the two moments—1941 and 1968. It is ironic and instructive that one could think in 1941 that one was serving a revolution of the youth for the sake of spiritual renewal when what one was doing was taking one's place in the rising tide of reaction against the egalitarian, democratic thrust of the American and French revolutions, a tide that had begun to rise in Europe right after the French Revolution. De Man's taking up Rousseau, something that is well represented in *Allegories of Reading* but goes back to his teaching in the 50s at Harvard, shows his need (I would guess) to declare new allegiances. Daniel Bell and his colleagues were interested in the mid 30s in a revolution on the left; so were the members of the student movement in the 60s. In the late 30s, however, the right overpowered the left in dramatic fashion. De Man in 1941 was interested in a revolution on the right. This difference is basic. Beyond this the student movement and its allies in the 60s were interested in some very specific goals that distinguish it in basic ways from the changes thrust on Europe in the 30s and 40s. The New Left sought an acknowledgment of the limits to power and sought to institute these limits by a reemphasis on democratic principles. This is the lesson that the government acknowledged when it ended, slowly and painfully, the war in Viet Nam. The New Left sought as well to have cultural diversity respected. This was the lesson the Civil Rights Movement, slowly and painfully, instructed us all to understand. It had implications for treatment of all sorts of other cultural differences. Beyond this the New Left sought an appreciation of the symbolic economy as against the material economy. The "revolutions" of 1941 and 1968 were diametrically opposed with regard to the questions of democracy and cultural diversity, but certainly a young thinker like de Man in 1941 was striving to assert the power of the symbolic over the economic just as many young people were trying to do in the 60s. The way de Man and others in the 40s resolved the problem, in the form of aesthetic nationalism, was not acceptable. The attempted solutions of the 60s were not adequate either. We still live with this problem because we have no overall theory of how the symbolic and the economic work together. An account now prevalent of how these realms might be articulated is the notion of the Right of cultural decline and spiritual malaise. This talk is as dangerous now as it was in the 1920s and 1930s when it last became the predominant form of discourse on the question of the role of the arts. It was this discourse, articulated by intellectuals like Carl Schmitt and many many others, that led to the politics of cultural despair that was the necessary prelude to the politics of revolutionary revival that de Man at least in part subscribed to in 1941 and 1942. (In this context the words of Jacques Derrida in his essay on "Paul de Man's War" are appropriate: "As soon as anyone talks about 'decadence of Western civilization,' I am on my guard. . . . An insistent reference to the West and to 'Western civilization' [is] a theme or lexicon whose careless manipulation has often slid over into rather undemocratic theses."[16]) It is the persistence of such problems in the debates about Allan Bloom, E. D. Hirsch, and now—in a different way—about Paul de Man that suggests that much more needs to be done to clarify these problems and to think them through in a way that did not happen in the 30s and 40s, nor in the 60s, and has not occurred yet. This suggests why the stakes are so high in coming to terms with *our* Paul de Man problem.

But it is no accident, then, that many of de Man's students were former activists from the 1960s; and they were not wrong—we can now appreciate—to see his thought as a meditation on, around, and about literature and politics. It predicted the need they would come to appreciate to abandon certain revolutionary hopes even as it also provided more constructive (because deconstructive) ways of figuring out how to reharness that idealism for transformative ends. For this there is much to

be grateful. I have certainly left many t's uncrossed and i's undotted in this quick essay, but I may have suggested how hope (however delusory) in the future may emerge from failure in the past and present.

July 1988
Harvard University Press

NOTES

1. A fair amount of the work that lies behind this essay was done in preparation for an introduction I have written for Paul de Man, *Critical Writings, 1953–1978* (Minneapolis: University of Minnesota Press, 1988 [in press]). Many of the references to unfamiliar essays by de Man in my essay are to essays in that volume.

2. In a letter to me dated 11 August 1983, de Man projected a volume to be entitled *Aesthetics, Rhetoric, Ideology* that would have included the following chapters: Epistemology of Metaphor, Pascal's Allegory of Persuasion, Diderot's Battle of the Faculties, Phenomenality and Materiality in Kant, Sign and Symbol in Hegel's *Aesthetics,* Hegel on the Sublime, Aestheticism: Schiller and Friedrich Schlegel's Misreading of Kant and Fichte, Critique of Religion and Political Ideology in Kierkegaard and Marx, and Rhetoric/Ideology.

3. It's impossible to trace out these concerns in detail in this essay. I'll just point to a few interesting passages. In his analysis of Mallarmé's "Une dentelle s'abolit," de Man writes: "The poet's action. . . is the annihilating action of all consciousness, but it might leave a trace, the work's memory suspended in an ideal space and revealing the fact that an action has occurred. . . . This final struggle expresses the central concern of Mallarméan poetics: the conception of the poetic as a privileged action, the only one by which the possibility of a new innocence and of a possible future, beyond negation, can still be conceived." (See "Poetic Nothingness: On a Hermetic Sonnet by Mallarmé," in Paul de Man, *Critical Writings, 1953–1978,* ed. by Lindsay Waters.) In "Shelley Disfigured" he writes, "Words cannot be isolated from the deeds they perform" (*RR* 102, but see *RR* 101–103).

4. Samuel Weber, *Institution and Interpretation,* Theory and History of Literature series, vol. 31 (Minneapolis: University of Minnesota Press, 1987), p.38. What Weber writes on pp.38–39 about the "debt of criticism" seems well worth reflection in connection with the case of de Man.

5. Fritz Stern, *Dreams and Delusions: The Drama of German History* (New York: Alfred A. Knopf, 1987), p.151.

6. Jean-Paul Sartre, *What Is Literature?*, trans. by Bernard Frecht-man (New York: Washington Square Press, 1966; paperback edition of 1949 edition of Philosophical Library), p.156. The Harvard University Press will reprint *"What Is Literature?"* in *"What as Literature?" and Other Essays,* intro. by Steven Ungar, in 1988.

7. Stern, *Dreams and Delusions,* p.151.

8. "Montaigne and Transcendence," trans. by Richard Howard, in Paul de Man, *Critical Writings,* 1953–1978, ed. by Lindsay Waters.

9. Primo Levi, *The Drowned and the Saved,* trans. by Raymond Rosenthal (New York: Summit Books, 1988), p.31.

10. Daniel Bell, *The End of Ideology: On the Exhaustion of Political Ideas in the Fifties* (Cambridge, Mass.: Harvard University Press, 1988; reprint of 1962 Free Press ed.), pp.300–302.

11. Nicola Chiaromonte, *The Paradox of History* (Philadelphia: University of Pennsylvania Press, 1985: reprint of 1970 Weidenfeld and Nicolson ed.).

12. *RR,* 58–59.

13. John Dunn, "Disruptive Values," *TLS,* 15–21 April 1988, p.414. An interesting literary document from this moment is *TriQuarterly,* no. 23/24 (Winter/Spring 1972), entitled "Literature in Revolution."

14. James Miller, *"Democracy Is in the Streets": From Port Huron to the Siege of Chicago* (New York: Simon & Schuster, 1987), pp.309–311.

15. Roberto Mangabeira Unger, *The Critical Legal Studies Movement* (Cambridge, Mass.: Harvard University Press, 1986), p.113. Also see in connection with these several questions Joshua Cohen and Joel Rogers, *On Democracy: Toward a Transformation of American Society* (New York: Penguin Books, 1983).

16. Jacques Derrida, trans. by Peggy Kamuf, "'Like the Sound of the Sea Deep within a Shell': Paul de Man's War," *Critical Inquiry* 14 (1988): 590–652, p.601.

The Monument Disfigured

SAMUEL WEBER

If it is true and unavoidable that any reading is a monumentaliz-ation of sorts. . .—*Paul de Man, "Shelley Disfigured"*

I. *Coming to the Point*

What are we talking about? What have we been talking about? What are we going to talk about? Does it make any sense to begin with such questions? Can one begin without them? Can we assume that 'we' know *who* is talking, and 'about' what? And what does it mean to talk or to write *about* something: for instance, about texts written almost fifty years ago by one Paul de Man, but also about many other texts, written before and since, yet to be written, yet to be read?

Perhaps the difficulty of the answers is prefigured in the asking of the questions. The status of all these where's and what's and how's and why's is at stake, as well as the system that links these interroga-tive pronouns, on the one hand, to questions of definition and of temporal situation and, on the other hand, to questions of shape and of figure.[1]

What exactly are we talking about? What does it mean to talk, to ask 'about'. . . ? For instance, about the "character" of an in-dividual man? About a practice of language, of reading and re-writing, known as 'deconstruction'? About a war fought some half a century ago? About Nazism? Fascism? Collaboration? About academic institutions and academic intellectuals? What about the word 'about,' that relates the question to its object? To talk 'about' something is to position ourselves in its vicinity, to be sure, and yet nevertheless: outside it, alongside perhaps, but still at a certain remove from what we are talking about.

There are those for whom such distance is intolerable. They are impatient to come to the point. Their impatience is gener-ally in direct proportion to the violence of their moral convic-tions. Writing about the first serious, dignified, probing discussion of de Man's wartime writings to appear in English: Geoffrey Hartman's article in the *New Republic,*[2] Roger Kimball accuses Hartman, and through him, "deconstruction," of "in-tellectualized mendacity," of "intellectualizing reality," of "a deviousness that willingly forsakes the most basic moral distinc-tions." What are these distinctions? That, for instance,—it is Kimball's instance—between "intelligibility" and "character." "Note," he lectures his readers,

Professor Hartman's conjecture that "the biographical disclosure may hurt de Man's intelligibility," when what is at stake is not his "intelligibility" (which remains untouched by the disclosure of his early writings) but his character. It is symptomatic of the real blind-ness of deconstruction that it should fail to have any insight what-soever into this fundamental distinction.[3]

In its "real blindness," deconstruction is unable to see the difference between "intelligibility"—the intelligibility of texts, presumably—and "character"; for those endowed with the insight that knows no such "blindness," it is blindingly clear that "character" and "intelligibility" are fundamentally distinct, as distinct as "the real world" is from language. To question this "fundamental distinction," as the various kinds of deconstruction do—but not only they—is to be guilty of "intellectualizing mendacity." The question which alone is "at stake" for Kimball is thus not limited to an individual, Paul de Man, or Geoffrey Hartman; it is the character of deconstruction as a whole that he would like to put on trial.

Here, as in other such essays and reviews, violent indignation serves as a pretext for ignoring, caricaturing or defaming the work of three decades, and not just of an individual, however essential the writings of Paul de Man undoubtedly have been and will continue to be in this respect. The real target, however, is not the work of one man, as Kimball's text makes clear, but rather the 'deviousness' of deconstruction in all of its forms and incarnations, its "intellectualizing mendacity." It is this deviation that is to be hunted down, put on trial, sentenced, and, if possible: *silenced*. The silence of de Man will thus be requited by another silencing, as the cultural editor *in spe* of the *Frankfurter Allgemeine Zeitung,* Frank Schirrmacher, makes abundantly clear in an article significantly entitled: "*Totgeschwiegene Schuld*"—literally: "Guilt Silenced to Death." What the headline suggests, the tone of the article confirms: At stake in this "case" is nothing less than murder and the complicity of those who would silence it. And yet, curiously enough, the conspiracy of silence is also condemned, this time for seeking to bring things out into the open:

The debate in America has only just begun. [. . .] But already "deconstructivists" are lining up to analyze "deconstructively" de Man's shameful texts: ahistorically, as texts among texts, untranslated, in order to preserve "the quality of the original." [. . .] The university apparatus is striving to extend the academic taboo to events that themselves broke with all taboos. It's all the same: the corpus delicti and its commentaries. A friend of Paul de Man's, invited to participate, gave the correct answer to such pointedly skewed detachment (*pünktliche Abgeklärtheit*): "I am shocked that there will be such a symposium. [. . .] We are talking about the slaughter of Belgian Jews including babies. To treat this as the object of a symposium is monstrous. These people must have lost every moral perspective."[4]

To hold a symposium is "monstrous"; to make the incriminated texts available is to "extend the academic taboo"; to interpret

them is "damage control" by "the university apparatus." What are Schirrmacher and his unnamed "friend of Paul de Man's" talking about? Or rather: *against*? The project of making available what Schirrmacher refers to as the "corpus delicti" of "shameful texts," becomes itself a shameful maneuver. The as yet unwritten deconstructive analyses are dispensed with sight unseen: "ahistorical . . . untranslated." Nothing must be allowed to interrupt the wave of self-righteous indignation directed at the "academic taboo" it fears most, and rightly so: *reading*. In its uncontrolled violence, Schirrmacher's diatribe lets the cat out of the bag: what he too is really talking about is the devious deviation of reading, of writing, of "texts among texts."

We are talking, then, about the ineluctable detour, the deviancy of reading and writing. This is the concern, the obsessive fear, the "academic taboo" that the journalist of the *Frankfurter Allgemeine* shares with his fellow editor Walter Kendrick, of the *Village Voice Literary Supplement,* author of the following memorable conjecture:

If Yale had required its Jewish students to wear a yellow star, no doubt Professor de Man would have gone on writing his dense and difficult essays.[5]

What is Walter Kendrick talking about here? The 'argument' that this statement concludes with a flourish, concerns—how could it be otherwise?—"responsibility":

The de Man of 1941 sought to exempt poets and novelists from responsibility for the doings of the nonliterary world. By implication, the same immunity would apply to literary critics—de Man himself, for example. The de Man of the 1980s did exactly the same thing: if Yale etc.

Again, the fateful formula that levels all difference and distinction for the greater joy of recognition: "The de Man of the 1980s did *exactly the same thing*" as the de Man of 1941. Unreconstructed deconstructionists, their heads buried in their texts, lack this fine sense of history. They fail to see what is apparently so obvious: de Man "exempting" poets, novelists and literary critics from responsibility for the nonliterary world, in the 1940s "exactly" as in the 1980s. But in what precisely is this "same thing" supposed to consist? In maintaining that the "laws" of literary history, while related to those of political and social history, were not simply identical to them? In insisting that the political upheavals of the time, however powerful and far-reaching their consequences, could not serve as a pretext for disqualifying an entire literary tradition, that of Symbolism, Surrealism and Expressionism, "under the sole pretext that they manifested

themselves during a detestable period"?[6] To defend "the continuity of French poetry" in this sense against those "who, with a
dangerous lightheadedness, find it necessary to throw stones at
the initiators of French poetry" (7.14.42), becomes, for the editor of the *Voice Literary Supplement,* "exactly the same thing" as
"exempting" writers from "the doings of the nonliterary
world." Those who, in Belgium of the 1940s, advocated the
"non-exemption" that de Man rejected and that Walter Kendrick seems to endorse, who declared the primacy of the "real
world" of German military power over the gyrations of opportunistic intellectuals and deviant artists, were those with whom
de Man is now said to have "collaborated." This might, and indeed should, give some pause to reflect on this apparently so
simple term. Who were the champions of the primacy of politics and 'history' (in the singular) over literature? And what
does it mean that a critique of this position could be mounted
in a newspaper that 'collaborated' in Nazi-occupied Belgium? Is
'collaboration' as simple and monolithic a notion as the op-
probrium attached to it would have us believe? Articles such as
those we are discussing, in their very efforts to anesthetize their
readers to the necessity of posing and pursuing these questions,
provide ample material for such reflection. All one has to do is
to read and reread, patiently, without hurrying to reach (fore-
gone) conclusions.

To assert with even a modicum of responsibility that "the de
Man of the 1980s did exactly the same thing" as the de Man of
the 40s, one would have first to have read at the very least, *and
with considerable care,* a major portion both of the 180 some articles published under de Man's name during the years 1941–42, as
well as the books and essays published since. This would, of
course, be hardly enough, but it remains the bare minimum. It
is clear that the author of "De Man That Got Away" did neither. What then is he talking about when he makes such a statement? Despite the apparent concreteness of the chronological
reference—"the de Man of the 80s"—Walter Kendrick is not
talking about a historical fact: as the slightest *serious* acquaintance with de Man's later writings (those of "the 80s") would
show, in the years referred to he was intensely concerned with
analyzing precisely how much the kinds of dichotomies so evident in Kendrick's distinction of the "literary" from the "non-
literary world" themselves depend upon "aesthetic ideology,"
i.e. the very stance Walter Kendrick projectively attributes to
him in order to justify his verdict. The kinds of questions raised
and pursued by the "de Man of the 80s" can be gleaned from
the following passage, made in the context of a reading of
Kleist's essay on the *Marionettentheater,* concerning the consequences of "formalization" in aesthetics and education:

Formalization inevitably produces aesthetic effects; on the other
hand, it just as compulsively engenders pedagogical discourse. It
produces education, but can this education still be called *aesthetic*
education? It produces a special kind of grace, but can this elegance
be taught? Is there such a thing as a graceful teacher or, rather, is a
teacher who manages to be graceful still a teacher? And if he is not,
what then will he *do* to those who, perhaps under false pretenses,
have been put in the position of being his pupils? The problem is
not entirely trivial or self-centered, for the political power of the
aesthetic, the measure of its impact on reality, necessarily travels by
ways of its didactic manifestations. The politics of the aesthetic
state are the politics of education.[7]

What, then, is Walter Kendrick really talking about, when he
conjures up the image of Yale requiring "its Jewish students to
wear a yellow star. . ." in order then to assert that "Professor de
Man would have gone on writing his dense and difficult essays"? Is Walter Kendrick talking about the Holocaust? About
antisemitism? About opportunism and careerism? Is he talking
about heroism, resistance, martyrdom? What he writes, in any
case, is something very different: in the scenario offered to his
readers, "Professor de Man" is shown doing something heinous, abject, ignominious—and perhaps, indeed, for Walter
Kendrick, he did. He went on "writing his dense and difficult
essays." *This* is what Walter Kendrick cannot tolerate: that one
might persist in the writing of such essays, *no matter what*: no
matter whether the political forces in power like it or not, no
matter whether the majority of educated readers acclaims it or
not, no matter whether it is opportune or not. And as any successful and self-consciously *American*[8] writer cannot but know
(even one less concerned with "professionalism," "opportunism" and career than this article shows Kendrick to be), in a
universe of discourse where "clarity" and "directness" of expression are regarded as the unquestioned norms of style, and
where leading journals and newspapers publish articles with titles such as "De Man That Got Away," or "The (de) Man Who
Put the Con in Deconstruction,"[9] "dense and difficult" writing
is less conducive to professional success than glib quips and
quick fixes. Which is not to say that such persistence is therefore
heroic or even particularly praiseworthy: those who pursue this
kind of writing seldom feel that they have a 'choice' in the matter. No more than those who condemn them are free to appre-
hend the world as anything but a simple and straightforward
place. Far easier, in the short term at least, to hold those who
insist on pointing out complexity to be responsible for its consequences. And all the more so, when those complexities, and
the distinctions and discriminations they demand, turn out to

be truly *formidable* in their implications. For instance, when "collaboration" and "resistance" can no longer *purely and simply* be *opposed* to one another, as though they were mutually exclusive positions or attitudes. Not the least of the difficulties in those "dense and difficult essays" that Paul de Man went on writing—if we may return, for a moment, to something like 'actual history'—resides in the way they challenge and disrupt the logic of binary opposition upon which not only the most familiar moral values are based, but also the purificatory fantasies of Nazism, in which the logic of the 'pure and simple' is carried to its paranoid extreme. That such a 'logic' has remained the indispensable mainstay of virtually all political and moral discourses until today is what renders the complexity of the problem not just formidable, but frightening.[10]

It is precisely such *fright* that moral indignation seeks to suppress, by *representing* it as an *object* or as an *image* whose horror need only speak for itself to *silence* effectively all those seeking to write in a different way: "If Yale had required its Jewish students to wear a yellow star. . ."; "The sufferings of real people" (Kimball); "The slaughter of Belgian Jews including babies" (Schirrmacher's anonymous interlocutor). A hardly veiled complicity links the violence of these images to the violence of the moralism that invokes them in order to condemn: symposia, publications, "intellectualizing." To "intellectualize," for Roger Kimball, is to question the conviction that "the real world"— history and human suffering, for instance—and "language" are *mutually exclusive* domains which *in principle* have nothing to do with one another and which therefore *should* be kept scrupulously separate. Geoffrey Hartman draws his wrath by suggesting that a direct avowal or confession made by de Man could not have been simple in its effects; that it might, as de Man himself argues in his reading of Rousseau, involve a "narrative shape" which, by imposing a meaningful, purposeful trajectory, would necessarily imply some degree of self-exculpation. The very suggestion, in short, that the apparently straightforward gesture of avowing one's guilt before a large audience might not be straightforward at all—that the ostensibly 'simple' might in fact turn out to be terribly, indeed terrifyingly, complex, elicits the already quoted charge of "intellectualized mendacity." What is Roger Kimball talking about? What has Geoffrey Hartman done to provoke Kimball to this accusation, unforgettable in its crudity? "By his second or third page Professor Hartman has transformed the entire discussion into a debate about language" (p.42). One could hardly be clearer, but Kimball manages to become so, as he elucidates the notion of responsibility that informs his moral judgment:

The idea being—what? That since [. . .] language is reputedly not under our control, we are not therefore responsible for the blunders and evil we perpetrate in the realm of "natural experience"? Does it mean that we are henceforth relieved of the obligation to speak and write straightforwardly about such blunders? (p.42)

To be "responsible" is thus equated with "the obligation to speak and write straightforwardly. . . ." From this vantage-point, to insist on the inexorability of linguistic deviation can only lead to 'deviousness' and to irresponsibility. But, for better or worse, even as convinced a defender of "fundamental distinctions" as Roger Kimball must confront that fact that, whatever else we are talking about, whatever else he would like to be talking about, the major, if not only pieces of evidence in the trial he seeks to conduct (prosecutor and judge in one) are *texts* (newspaper articles, written in the early 40s, but also the writings signed by Paul de Man since): that is, things that have to be *read*. However "fundamental" the distinction of "character" and "intelligibility" may be, to talk about "blunders and evil that we"—who, *we*?—"perpetrate in 'natural experience'" is only possible by virtue of a determinate reading of determinate texts. As we approach the point of no return, then, we are still talking about texts and about reading. The question, of course, is: of what kind?

Here, again, Roger Kimball provides us with an illuminating instance. It is hardly a straightforward one, though, since it involves at the very least four different texts: Husserl's lecture on "Philosophy and the Crisis of European Man," de Man's discussion of it in the essay "Criticism and Crisis" (reprinted in *Blindness and Insight*), Hartman's brief mention of it in his *New Republic* article, and Kimball's own rejoinder. As we shall soon see, there are one or two more texts waiting in the wings to join the fray. For Kimball, what is at stake here is the claim of deconstruction to be

superior to other modes of interpretation because it provides especially 'close readings' of texts, readings that reveal nasty things like the 'totalizing' impulses of authors, i.e. their desire for unity and sense. (p. 41)

Let us remember the sarcastic use of 'nasty' here, to designate the clearly innocent "desire for unity and sense": we will have occasion shortly to return to it. But first let us pursue for a moment what Roger Kimball means by responsibility, and above all, how he practices it in reading. He begins by raising the question of why Hartman bothers to cite de Man's reading of Husserl: "Surely one reason is that it gives him the opportunity to speak of 'blindly privileging Western civilization,' a charge that is as common [. . .] among fashionable academics these days as the diction is deplorable." Had Roger Kimball been interested in doing more than "deploring" Hartman's diction, he might have reflected upon the significance of another such nominalization of a verb, one that is currently even more in fashion than 'privileging' ever was: 'critiquing.' Had he done so, it might have alerted him to the fact that the primary 'reason' Hartman alludes to de Man's discussion of Husserl is not to attack Western European ethnocentrism, but to raise the question of the status of *criticism*, upon which Husserl so insists. De Man's 'point,' to which Hartman is hardly insensible but to which Kimball seems entirely impervious, is that the notion of self-criticism, with reference to which Husserl seeks to define the specificity of Western philosophy, itself depends upon a highly contradictory set of assumptions which themselves may well comprise the enabling limit of 'criticism' itself (and which hence would have to remain uncriticized and uncriticizable). These assumptions have to do with Husserl's use of the term 'European' to define and determine the philosophical attitude of self-criticism he is engaged in defending against the crisis that has befallen it.

In the perspective of this argument—de Man's and Hartman's—to state, as does Roger Kimball, that "the main point of the lecture in question was to criticize the 'mistaken rationalism' or 'objectivism' that in Husserl's view had precipitated a major crisis in Western values" may be correct (if we accept the rather considerable and dubious assumption that "the main point" of a lecture or text is identical with its declarations of intention), but it is also entirely beside the point. The questions raised by de Man and Hartman (who here directs them in part at de Man himself) address the problematic premises upon which Husserl's notion of 'criticism'—what Kimball calls: "Husserl's view"—is based. Thus, the question raised by de Man with respect to Husserl (in both senses of that phrase)[11] involves the status of *criticism* itself, and concomitantly, the problem of judgment, that is, of proceeding from the particular (European man) to the general (the universal validity of the self-critical attitude of philosophical thought). What is at stake in this problem is the relation of thinking to alterity, to the others: here, the non-European. The question de Man is raising is that of self-limitation, of *demarcation*. It is to this problem that he points in remarking that, "why this geographical expansion [of philosophical reflection] should have chosen to stop, once and forever, at the Atlantic Ocean and the Caucasus, Husserl does not say." To this Kimball has a ready response:

But Husserl does not say for the simple reason that he never sug-

gests that the spirit of scientific rationality [. . .] *is* bounded "once and forever" by the Atlantic Ocean and the Caucasus. Quite the contrary. Near the beginning of the lecture, he notes that in invoking the spiritual image of Europe he "does not mean Europe geographically, as it appears on maps, as though European man were to be in this way confined to the circle of those who live in this territory. In the spiritual sense it is clear that to Europe belong the English dominions, United States, etc., but not, however, the Eskimos or Indians of the country fairs, or the Gypsies. . . ." It is a small point, to be sure, but it gives one a good indication of the kind of "close reading" one can expect from our premier deconstructionists. (p. 41)

"A small point," indeed, but one that also gives us a good indication of what reading means for those who would disqualify deconstruction in the name of 'straightforward,' plain talking and writing. European man—and one should remember, in Husserl's favor, that 'man' here translates the German *Menschentum* which, overtly at least, is not gender-specific—remains 'European' even, and especially, when he is defined 'spiritually,' beyond the geographical boundaries of his native habitat: for instance in the English dominions, or in its former colonies (the United States). Except—and here is the point addressed by de Man—that the 'spiritual' generalization of European humanity in order to define a norm of thought valid beyond the limits of the European continent, requires necessarily the exclusion and *subordination* of other cultures.[12] Closer to home, Husserl equally excludes "the Eskimos, the Indians of the country fairs, or the Gypsies. . ." from the European spirit. "A small point," Kimball remarks, but perhaps not quite small enough to hide what it supplants. The *points* that follow the word "Gypsies" in Kimball's citation replace the conclusion of Husserl's sentence, which Kimball carefully omits, replace it with his four 'small points.' Strange, that such an impassioned advocate of straightforward speaking and writing, a so uncompromising prosecutor of "intellectualizing mendacity," should have dropped the short phrase with which Husserl finishes his sentence: ". . . or the Gypsies, who persist in tramping all about Europe" ("*oder die Zigeuner, die dauernd in Europa herumvagabundieren*" [p.319]). Perhaps something in this remark about the Gypsies sounds a bit "nasty" after all, reminiscent of a way of thinking that, in the name of a new European Order—although one very different from that envisaged by Husserl—nevertheless put an end to such "herumvagabundieren," at least between 1933 and 1945. Had Kimball allowed Husserl to complete his sentence, its unpleasant resonances might have recalled that "nasty things like the 'totalizing' impulses of authors" are not simply the inventions of irresponsible 'deconstructionists.' And also, that speaking "straightforwardly" may be neither as simple, nor as "responsible," as some might think.

"Will you finally get to the point?" But haven't I been talking about it all the time? About the difficulty of getting to a *single* point, which presupposes that there is one to get to, a point which would be unique and self-identical, capable of closing a sentence, once and for all. Period. But what if, as in Kimball's citation, there were always more than one point, what if *that* were the point? That a point is always more or less beside the point, that it never closes one sentence without at the same time opening another? To come to the point, to write 'about' the point would be to reinscribe its de-limiting traits in all their twists and turns, all their ambiguous and ambivalent trajectories, both joining and separating, stopping and starting, stopping and startling, but never 'simply' coming to a full-stop, never at least without being stopped by something else.[13] What is "nasty" is not that four points should replace a sinister phrase, but that the latter should be subsumed under, and as, "a small point." Assuming that, in its smallness, it was read at all. But this is precisely the 'point': why bother about Eskimos and Indians and especially Gypsies when they are only "there" as a backdrop against which the 'universality' of 'European Humanity' can stand out. Why bother about them when they have no proper place in that Humanity, or when their place is so small as to be insignificant. As insignificant as an igloo. Or as "traveling circuses" (a better translation for Husserl's *Jahrmarktsmenagerien*'). Or even worse, when they have no place of their own at all, when they are purely and simply vagrants and vagabonds, "tramping all about Europe" (*herumvagabundieren*) without fixed place of domicile,[14] without proper identity papers, without proper respect for national frontiers and private property. Why bother to include them in a citation? They have no place in *The New Criterion*. On the contrary, they can only spoil the point.

Is it because those who pursue the ways of deconstruction are somewhat akin to such spoilers, that Derrida, in his recent study of Heidegger, *De l'esprit,* is drawn to cite the same passage from Husserl, this time however in its entirety, deeming it to be as "comic" as it is "sinister"? And to the question, "why recall such a passage and cite it today?" Derrida replies, in part:

Using the example of a discourse that in general is not suspected of [harboring] the worst, it is good to recall that referring to the *spirit,* to *freedom* of the spirit and to the spirit as *European,* could and still can be allied with a politics to which one would like to oppose it.[15]

And, as Derrida suggests towards the end of *De l'esprit,* if it is urgent to retrace the trajectories of such complicities in all of their complexities, it is not primarily to assign blame or praise, but to explore the consequences

of a program and of a combinatorics whose power remains abyssal, unfathomable. In its rigor it vindicates no discourse [. . .] Nor does it leave any clear place for an instance of arbitration. Nazism was not born in the desert. As well known as this may be, it must continually be recalled. And even if, far from any desert, it had sprung up like a mushroom in the silence of a European forest, it would have done so in the shadow of great trees, sheltered by their silence or their indifference, but in the same soil. Of these trees, which in Europe populate an immense black forest, I will not attempt to give a survey or to count the species. For essential reasons, their presentation defies the space of a table (*tableau*). In their dense taxonomy, they would bear the names of religions, philosophies, political regimes, economic structures, religious or academic institutions. In short, what is called, with equal imprecision (*aussi confusément*), the culture or the world of the spirit. (p.179)

Husserl, in describing the spiritual essence of this "world" or "culture," inevitably was compelled to cut out certain *other* groups, if only so that they might provide the indispensable background against which the form of the "European" could stand out in silhouette. In traveling fairs and circuses, such backdrops often serve as targets, testing our aim and our accuracy. Generally, they are fixed in one place, or, if they move, their emergence, however sudden, is predictable. We know where they are likely to pop up, and this fore-knowledge guides us as we take aim and prepare to shoot. It is this kind of fore-knowledge that deconstructive readings bring out into the open. The result is that figure and ground, target and marksman are no longer as clearly delineated as they may have seemed. That, too, is one of the things that we have been, and will be, talking about.

II. *The Unanimous Cycle*

No straightforward confession, then, no pure and simple avowal, nothing pure and simple; rather,

the gift of an ordeal (*épreuve*), the summons to a work of reading, of historical interpretation, of ethical-political reflection—an interminable analysis. Well beyond the sequence 1940–42. In the future and for the future. . .[16]

Derrida has suggested four rules to be considered in the labor of reading that imposes itself. I take the liberty of summarizing and paraphrasing them:

1. Reconstitute as much of the corpus, 'Belgium during the war,' as possible, including 'internal' as well as 'contextual' overdeterminations; avoid giving the articles in question a disproportionate importance by minimizing the rest.

2. Articulate the wartime writings with the work to come while avoiding two symmetrical errors: that of asserting no relation, absolute heterogeneity, and that of asserting complete identity, as though discontinuity, and history, were a mere ruse or epiphenomenon.

3. Respect the other's right to difference, to error, to aberration, and above all, to a history, in the sense of a transformation of the self in a non-totalizable, heterogeneous manner. One sign of such respect: to begin by listening. . .

4. Avoid as much as possible reproducing the logic of the discourses being attacked: Nazi, fascist, antisemitic, totalitarian [to which I would add: collaborationist—S.W.]. Such avoidance will only be possible to the extent one is able to formalize not just the similarities of such discourses, but also and above all: their differences. (pp.640–45)

Let us begin, then, by *listening*. March 25, 1941, "Accounts of the War":

From September to May [1940], the vicissitudes of the conflict were inexistent; then, they erupted in such an overwhelming manner that at no time did anyone have the impression of having the situation under control or of being able to adapt to a particular mode of life, as had been the case in the previous war. Not that there was any lack of adventure for those caught up in the operations in any way. Whether as soldier or as refugee, everyone thought they had gone through a unique experience under extraordinary conditions. But once back home, the tales that emerged were all similar and one realized that what had seemed sensational was quite ordinary [. . .] In the space of a few days, every reasonable person went though a considerable mental evolution. Eyes were opened on a hard reality: the reassuring speeches of governments which were customarily taken at their word turned out to be the worst sort of brainwashing, the force of the democracies believed to be intact appeared in the true light of day, the conventional image of a barbarous and malevolent enemy, created by systematic propaganda, collapsed before the impeccable conduct of a highly civilized invader. From these new givens, everyone drew their own conclusions—conclusions which seemed revolutionary compared to yesterday's convictions. But whereas each individual thought himself alone in discovering this new truth, one soon noticed [. . .] that everyone was saying the same thing. The lesson of these events had been so clear and so limpid that common sense had only been able to interpret it in one single manner.

The self-perception of the university in the United States as well as the social relations and organization informed by it, are, even today, largely directed by an ideal of the *locus amoenus,* not unrelated to the medieval cloister, where a "community" of "scholars" pursues, more or less serenely, the acquisition of "scholarship," at a safe distance from the turbulence and conflicts of the profane world. The unexpected discovery of articles written almost a half century ago, in which Paul de Man appeared to endorse, at least in part, what was arguably the most destructive, brutal and effective political-military force of the modern era, demonstrated, with a shock and an intensity in direct proportion to the influence of his work and to the respect inspired by his person, just how uncertain that "distance" had become, or rather, had always been. The initial shock wave having somewhat subsided, although certainly not without leaving many profound traces, the question remains—and it is not, in the banal sense, merely "rhetorical": How could it have happened? What was it all about? What was *going on,* in and around the articles published in *Le Soir* in 1941 and 1942? And what *is* going on when "we"—but who is this "we" and can 'we' take its unity for granted?—read them today?

Let us talk then for a moment about this "we." Difficult for those of us who have not known such times—and how many of 'us' have?—to imagine just how traumatic the events of May and June 1940 must have been for those who lived through them. Over ten years had passed since the crash of 1929 marked the onset of a world-wide depression that, for most of the liberal economies, only the war was to overcome. The decade of the thirties had witnessed the apparently irresistible political, military *and economic* rise of fascism and Nazism in Europe and in Asia, the defeat of the Spanish Republic, the conquest of Ethiopia, the appeasement politics of the European liberal democracies, the Stalinist purges in the Soviet Union, the annexation of Austria and the Sudetenland and finally, the Hitler-Stalin pact opening the way to the subjugation and dismemberment of Poland and the annexation of the Baltic states. And then, in the space of six weeks, the conquest of Western Europe by the Nazi *Wehrmacht*. Belgium capitulates in eighteen days. Millions of refugees clog the routes of France, fleeing the German advance. Difficult for us to imagine, but no less so for those concerned, whose expectations of military action were formed of memories of the bloody stalemates of World War I. In the Nazi practice of the *Blitzkrieg*, the distinctively modern emphasis on speed and communications received its military-political consecration: "Whoever lived through those days knows perfectly that at that moment we understood nothing of what was happening to us and that, seized by the throats by events, we had not an instant to restore order in ourselves." "The effect produced had the aspect of a shock, because it was both too brief and too intense to become anything else" (4.30.42).

And yet, one—and perhaps even, the chief—function of thought is precisely to limit the effects of shock, by giving them shape, form or meaning, by transforming them for instance into a "limpid lesson":

When one finds oneself placed at the very center of historical upheavals, it is generally difficult to grasp their profound meaning. [. . .] And yet history knows no brutal breaks in continuity. [. . .] The present war is, aside from an economic and national struggle, the beginning of a revolution aiming at organizing European society in a more equitable manner [. . .] In addition to questions of supremacy, which are in fact secondary, the situation creates a certain number of practical possibilities of replacing a political apparatus grown nefarious, with an institutional arrangement (*un organisme*) that would assure a distribution of goods more in conformity with justice. Anyone who believed that such achievements are possible and necessary has the duty of not abstaining under present conditions. For without a doubt, there will never again be circumstances as favorable for a renewal as in this moment, when all institutions are in the process of being replaced. And even if this new program is not yet fixed in all its details, things had arrived at such a degree of decomposition and of degeneration that, above all else, the will to change them should exist. (8.19.41)

The "limpid lesson" that the 21-year old Paul de Man draws here from the collapse of the allies before the German onslaught echoes what was undoubtedly the general sentiment of those in French-speaking Europe. In his study of *Vichy France, Old Guard and New Order, 1940–1944*, Robert O. Paxton provides ample documentation of just how widespread the conviction was that the French collapse marked not just a military defeat but an irreversible historical turning-point, the end of one epoch and the beginning of another. One instance here may stand for many. In his Journal of July 10, André Gide gives his reaction to Marshall Pétain's call for discipline and sacrifice:

It seems to me that I would have a fairly easy time adapting to constraints, and I would accept a dictatorship which alone, I fear, could save us from decomposition. Let me add hastily that I am speaking here only of a *French dictatorship*.

And, two weeks later:

If tomorrow, as may be feared, the freedom of thought, or at least that of expressing this thought is refused us, I will try to convince myself that art, and even thought, will lose less than through excessive liberty.

As late as March 7, 1943, Gide noted:

Long before the war, the stench of defeat in France was overpowering. The country was unravelling on its own, to the point that what might save it, perhaps, was—is, perhaps, this very disaster in which its energies may be restored. Is it chimerical to hope that France will emerge from this nightmare strengthened?[17]

The sense, then, that the defeat of the allies, and France in particular, however surprising its rapidity, had an element of necessity to it, was thus widely held. But de Man's remarks do more than just proclaim that sense of inevitability—they demonstrate the need to which that "sense"—and perhaps *sense* in general—responds: the need to *make sense of the shock*.

In this respect, de Man's response to the German victory of May-June, 1940, provides a striking illustration of a problem that will orient him increasingly in his writings on literature and aesthetics. It is also, not accidentally, an instantiation of the kind of situation that Kant, in the Introduction to the *Critique of Judgment* describes as the condition of "aesthetical judgment": that is, a situation in which the "faculty of judging" is unable to make a true, objectively valid (what Kant calls a "determining") judgment, but instead is compelled to withdraw and "reflect" upon its own operations. Such a situation obtains, Kant argues, when one finds oneself confronted by a situation, object or event that cannot be subsumed under available knowledge: that is, under the concepts, laws, rules or principles that consciousness has at its disposal. Cognitively disarmed before the other, as it were, judgment resorts to a series of pronouncements which seem to bear upon its object—propositions, for instance, such as: "Nature takes the shortest way . . . yet it makes no leap,"[18] which, in de Man's article, is given a somewhat more secular, temporal form: "History knows no brutal breaks in continuity." What Kant, however, is at pains to emphasize, and what will emerge in de Man's later work as a recurrent motif, is the fact that such 'judgments' do not, despite their language, relate to objects at all, to "nature" or to "history," but only to the practice of "judging" itself; they constitute "maxims" which indicate "how we ought to judge" (p.22) in order not to get lost in "the labyrinth" (p.402) of infinite possibilities. Whereas Kant, however, stresses the unbridgeable gap that separates such "reflective judgments" from judgments in the proper sense, the de Man of 1941 confuses the need for intelligibility with what he calls *history*. It is out of this confusion that what de Man will later call "aesthetic ideology" arises.[19]

To be sure, the Kantian distinction of an objectively valid 'determining' judgment from a statement that presents itself *as though* it were a judgment but in fact is only a "maxim," *reflecting* upon what the "power" or "faculty" of judgment "ought" or "should" do in order to *be* judgment—this extremely volatile distinction is present, if at all, in de Man's early texts, in the distinctly ambivalent tone that marks the occasional calls to action, which, half-resigned, half-exhortatory, emphasize the *necessity* of collaboration at least as much as its desirability. Of these, I will cite two instances, the first, in a review of a book by Daniel Halévy, from October, 1941; the second, nine months later, in July, 1942, in a discussion of the second volume of Fabre-Luce's *French Journal* (*Journal de la France*):

We find ourselves confronted by problems of peace in an atmosphere of war. Hence [. . .] the discouraged sense that overcomes Halévy, one feels, towards the end of his essay [*Trois Epreuves—Three Trials*], and which amounts to an avowal of impotence faced with the inertia of the masses. We will have to wait for the end of the war to see if this pessimism is justified. While waiting, one asks oneself, with a certain anxiety, if this stage of inaction is salutary. It creates a troubled climate where the best is mixed with the worst, where the most noble devotion rubs shoulders with the worst careerism. And yet the necessity of action which presents itself in the guise of immediate collaboration imposes itself upon every objective mind. [. . .] It is premature to lower one's arms before universal incomprehension and to withdraw into one's ivory tower. (10.14.41)

At certain moments, the weight of events becomes such that it impels nations in a certain direction, even when their will seemed to oppose this. That is precisely what has happened here: the politics of collaboration results from the present situation not as an ideal desired by the whole people but as an irresistible necessity from which nobody can escape, even if they believe themselves obliged to go in another direction. The wait-and-see attitude is thus condemned, not from a moral point of view but from that of imperious reality: it is untenable because opposed to the flow of history, which continues to flow without worrying about the reticence of certain individuals who insist upon not comprehending its power. Those rare perspicacious spirits who have recognized this appear at present to be isolated, alone in their struggle against the inertia and the hostility of the masses. Later they will turn out to have been the precursors of the will of all. (7.21.42)

The traumatic shock of the German invasion, rapid conquest and occupation of Western Europe is, a year after the fact, reinscribed as the result of a longstanding, indeed teleological development of European history, the continuity of which depends upon Germany. "Naively the Germans were thought to have been definitively defeated after Versailles. Now it becomes increasingly clear that this defeat is only an accident in a historical evolution that clearly points towards ever-increasing domination" (3.18.41). "The basic significance of Germany for the life of the West as a whole" is that "the entire continuity of Western civilization depends on the unity of the people which is its center" (3.17.42).

A few months after writing this, however, it is the "Continuity of French Poetry" that must be defended against certain enthusiasts of the New Order. Writing about—or more precisely, in defense of—the poetry review *Messages* (see note 6), de Man begins by stating his concern at the way "current events raise the problem of artistic continuity, often in a distressingly direct manner," and therefore render it indispensable to distinguish "very clearly artistic evolution from what is rightly qualified as the present revolution." For, de Man argues:

The danger of a revolution is that in its inevitably destructive work, it risks eliminating the eternal values which it itself cannot do without. This is the worrisome impression left by the unreflected attacks against sound forces, under the sole pretext that they manifested themselves during a detestable period. (7.14.42)

The "sound forces" in question here are, above all, the poetic tradition of French symbolism and surrealism:

A first distinction consists in separating very clearly artistic evolution from what is justifiably qualified as the present revolution. Under the pretext that this revolution is totalitarian, i.e that it intends to modify all aspects of individual and collective life, some have brutally included art among its objectives. [. . .] In other words, art—and more particularly, literature—is thus to be transformed into a tool, an instrument destined to combat by all means an outdated 'Weltanschauung' and to impose another in its place.

To be sure, it is beyond all doubt that the profound modifications accomplished as part of the general movement of our civilization cannot leave writers and poets indifferent. Their work will bear the imprint of the concerns that weigh on humanity in these days. [. . .] But this interference of current events does not determine the course of literary history in the proper sense. The sole effect that it can have is to impose certain themes hitherto ignored [. . .] and this is only a minor constituent in the development of an artistic genre, an almost secondary aspect of its growth permitting neither classification nor judgment. (7.14.42)

If the choice of "themes" is subject to conscious volition, and hence subject to political influence, the development of 'form' is quite another matter:

Poetic forms do not develop arbitrarily out of an individual will. Rather, they are imposed upon each individual unconsciously, for they live like free organisms. . . . their vital processes develop in a continuous manner, without being slowed or stopped by extra-formal considerations. (7.14.42)

The specificity of literature is thus defended against its subsumption under the politically dominant forces in power by invoking the relative independence of literary history as a history of *forms*; political power can thus influence the choice of subject-matter, of theme, but it cannot determine the artistic viability of their formal articulation. Nevertheless, the appeal to a relative autonomy of literary history as a history of form is made in the context of a defense against a far more totalizing claim: that of a totalitarian 'revolution' claiming the right to control and determine *all* aspects of social life. It is against such claims that "the de Man of the 40s" seeks to "exempt" poets, writers and, yes, critics. No doubt that the de Man of the 80s "did exactly the same thing," only with far greater awareness and far more effectively. For by then he had discovered and analyzed the complicity between the aesthetic valorization of form and totalitarian claims to hegemony, a complicity that resides in the shared axiom of *immanence*—the consequences of which, in the early 40s, he was experiencing more in the mode of action, or perhaps acting-out, than in that of 'reflection.'

In 1941, to be sure, the 21-year old literary editor of *Le Soir* was in a very different situation. It was through a conception of history as immanent, continuous and teleological that he justified his engagement in a collaborationist newspaper; but it was also in the name of such a history that he clearly and combatively took his distances from the totalitarian demands of Nazi ideology. In short: he *collaborated*, but he did not *capitulate*. The difference is, perhaps, not entirely trivial. It might even be worth exploring.

In this context, two articles devoted to problems of literary historiography are of particular interest: the first, in *Le Soir* of April 8, 1941, on René Lalou's *History of Contemporary French Literature*; the second, in *Het Vlaamsche Land* of June 7–8, 1942, on "Criticism and Literary History," also on Lalou but this time comparing his work with Marcel Raymond's *From Baudelaire to Surrealism*. In his judgment of Lalou, and in particular of the second of his two volumes, dealing with the contemporary period (1920–1940), we come upon the metaphor already encountered in Kant: "In a labyrinth of unthinkable complexity one

searches in vain for a guiding principle." "The chaotic world of Lalou is not only a shocking sight for the mind, it is a false interpretation of reality."[20] This is precisely the gesture that the Kantian notion of 'reflective judgment' will describe as epistemologically problematic while at the same time determining it to be the indispensable origin of aesthetic judgment. Faced with the "shocking sight" of a "labyrinth of unthinkable complexity"—which, as Kant argues, consists in the irreducible "heterogeneity" of an unlimitable "particularity" and "diversity"—the "power to judge" (*Urteilskraft*) responds by treating those "particulars" *as though* they were already subsumed under general laws, i.e. "purposive." By thus 'overcoming' the "shock" of an unfathomable heterogeneity, a "pleasure" is generated which, Kant suggests, inheres in all "recognition," insofar, at least, as judgment thereby feels itself to be in "in tune" with its surroundings. It is this pleasure of recognition which makes 'aesthetic judgment' the most authentically *reflective* pleasure of reflective judgment, but also the least judgmental, since it alone does not—or more precisely, *ought not*—confuse its apprehension of 'beautiful forms' with their 'content,' concept or anything else that might constitute an object of cognition.

De Man's criticism of the literary historiography of Lalou is based precisely on the confusion of 'reflective' with 'determining' (or cognitive) judgment. Lalou presents his readers with the "shocking sight" of a "labyrinth," lacking all "guiding principle," whereas Marcel Raymond's *From Baudelaire to Surrealism* contains

no muddle, then, but a line, a direction around which a certain arrangement takes place. The subtle play of mutual influences [. . .] appears to obey certain laws. There is a certain homogeneity, a uniformity of actions and creations: [. . .] there is a certain continuity, one generation ensues logically from the preceding one [. . .] it gives more depth to the formulae of the precursors. [. . .] In short, modern French poetry emerges from this study as a well-rounded whole whose parts match each other, as a creative phenomenon with internal coherence. [. . .] The chaotic world of Lalou is not only a shocking sight for the mind; it is a false interpretation of reality. The tendency towards unity of Marcel Raymond not only satisfies our natural urge for logical consistency; it is the faithful reproduction of what is recognized as reality. (June 7–8, 1942)

Forty years later, this conception of history, as a "continuity," in which "one generation ensues logically from the preceding one" will be described by de Man, reading Shelley's "Triumph of Life," to be an attitude "that repeats itself regardless of the exposure of its fallacy"; it repeats it, however, as a mirror-image reflects its model, by symmetrically reversing it:

The Triumph of Life warns us that nothing, whether deed, word, thought, or text, ever happens in relation, positive or negative, to anything that precedes, follows, or exists elsewhere, but only as a random event whose power, like the power of death, is due to the randomness of its occurrence. It also warns us why and how these events then have to be reintegrated in a historical and aesthetic system of recuperation that repeats itself regardless of the exposure of its fallacy. ("Shelley Disfigured," p.122)

The two interpretations of history manifest in these two texts—the critique of René Lalou and the reading of Shelley's poem—are separated by a practice of reading which is both informed by a theory of language and which transforms it in turn. The "reintegration" of the "random event" into "a historical and aesthetic system of recuperation" is described as inevitable, but also as susceptible of different possible implementations. Thus, "recuperation" is necessarily at work in the "monumentalization" which all "reading" entails, inasmuch as it inexorably imposes meaning upon intrinsically "random sequences." But such imposition can be more or less "naive," depending upon the power of the reading to resist "repression of a self-threatening knowledge": the knowledge, that is, of a randomness which is incompatible with the coherence required of a 'self.' The power to sustain "self-threatening knowledge" is what de Man delineates in *The Triumph of Life* and what he calls there, and elsewhere: *disfigurement*. Reading as "monumental disfigurement" or as the disfiguring of monuments: that is *also* one of the things we are talking *about* as we reread these two texts and as we retrace in them the necessity of a certain disfigurement, of a certain 'defacing.'

Writing in 1941, Paul de Man is, to be sure, far from such thoughts; and yet, one of the things that bothers him most in René Lalou's *History of Contemporary French Literature* is the author's all too obtrusive concern with providing "portraits":

All these studies of great authors, whether of Péguy, Claudel, Gide or Valéry, are detailed enumerations of personal characteristics, efforts to show how this author is not the same as that one. It is as though each writer created his own artistic law, which is born with him and which dies with him and in accordance with which he is to be judged. In what respects was Gide always faithful to Gide, how did Romains manage never to betray Romains, asks René Lalou, and when he has thus been able to trace the complete portrait of an artist [. . .] he is completely satisfied.[21]

Lalou's aim is to give his history a human face, by providing a series of faces that express the unique self-identity of each individual author, in his specific difference from all others. This concern with individual portraiture causes Lalou to neglect what, for the young Paul de Man, constitutes

the principle goal of [. . .] a critical exposé: an image of the spirit, a synthesis of the thought of an age [. . .], that panorama of synthetic views which, by its very definition, a work of history ought to provide. (4.8.41)

The individual 'face' is criticized, but in the name of another kind of "image": that which would synthesize the "spirit," the "thought of an age." "What interests us in every special case is that by which it integrates itself into a unanimous cycle (*un cycle unanime*)." This "unanimous" cycle, which would have a single soul, speak as with one voice, would also be an almost *anonymous* one: "Individualities are of little importance and it would be desirable to write a literary history in which very few names were cited, serving only as a point of reference to mark the evolution of a formula or of a style." Here is yet another instance of the attitude described by Derrida: "Even when he criticizes the individualist (French conception) [. . .] de Man does not seem to distrust the constant reference to type" (p. 622). Indeed, his critique is made in the *name* of such generalizations: of a 'people,' a 'race,' or the 'spirit of an age.' Derrida has conjectured that ultimately, the temptation of totalitarianism might be a product of nothing more or less than "the terrifying desire for roots" (p. 648)—"terrifying," precisely by virtue of its banal ubiquity. Much the same might be said of racism, which could be described as the result of a no less ubiquitous, no less banal *desire of recognition,* operating at the same time as a defense against the *other* (of) *recognition* known as the "uncanny." The racist temptation could thus be described as the incapacity to accept the reflexivity of "reflective" judgments, and consequently, the compulsion of treating them as though they were *determining*.[22] The reference to Kant suggests why 'aesthetic' categories should play such a prominent and persistent role in racist attitudes: not just conceptual stereotypes, but stereotypical *images, caricatures,* for instance, which in their own way claim to give "an image of the spirit," "a panorama of synthetic views." In order to deny the difference separating reflective from determining judgment, aesthetic judgments must be credited with a cognitive authority to which, in the Kantian perspective increasingly embraced by de Man in later years, they can have no legitimate claim. This cognitive investment of the aesthetic, of the "image," would thus find a particular provocation in the mosaic prohibition of "graven images." Related to the valorization of the *image* is that assigned to the *proper name.* In order to put the other in its place, racism assigns it a name that is held to be proper and generic at once. The "Indians" are named and placed, once and for all, in "traveling circuses"; the "Gypsies" are assigned the parasitic site of an aimless and predatory vagrancy. At its most brutal, however, racist appellation will deny the heterogeneous diversity of the other precisely by *singularizing* the name and applying it to a collective: *the* Jew, *the* Black, *the* Arab.

In his later work, de Man will reflect on the way "anthropomorphism freezes the infinite chain of tropological transformations and propositions into one single assertion or essence which, as such, excludes all others," precisely through "the singleness of a proper name."[23] But he will also argue that this "freezing" of trope into name "is built into the very notion of trope" (p.242) itself, the transformational turns and substitutive exchanges of which are necessarily informed by a telos of infinite totalization. It is the question of this telos that opens the way to a reading of what is arguably the one truly deplorable article signed by Paul de Man, of the more than the 180 he published in those two years, not to mention all those since.

III. *Mirror on the Move: "The Jews in Contemporary Literature"*

"The Jews in Contemporary Literature"—Jacques Derrida has written movingly and incisively about this text, about the "wound," the shock, the hurt inflicted on all those whose lives have been changed by Paul de Man, by his writings, his teaching, his friendship, his acquaintance. To that change now belong, indelibly, the scars left behind by this article, whatever the mitigating conditions may have been under which it was written, and there are many: the fear of material insecurity, belief in the irreversibility of the German victory and in the necessity of seeking an accommodation with the occupant, and perhaps above all, the absence of any other explicit reference to the Jews in the hundreds of pages of text written and published during those years, much less thereafter—with one exception,[24] to which I shall return shortly.

This being said, the shock, hurt and their aftermath should not be allowed to become an alibi for the abdication of thought. The question that remains, that indeed imposes itself with new intensity, is that with which I began: *How was it possible? What* exactly was it, that *was* possible, that *happened,* that does not cease to happen, and not just in the one text signed by Paul de Man? How does that text relate to de Man's subsequent work, or rather, inversely: how does that work relate to what happened in, and as, "The Jews in Contemporary Literature"? Obviously, all that can be done here is to begin to address these questions, or rather, to continue the insightful and promising

beginning already made by Hartman and by Derrida, a familiarity with whose writings on the subject, as well as with the article itself, is here assumed.

Before turning to that text, it may be useful to summarize an argument which has emerged from the foregoing discussion: namely, that it was the conception of history that informed the thought of Paul de Man in the early 40s, and that he increasingly criticized in his later years, that *both* justified his collaboration—his decision to write for *Le Soir*—*and also* allowed or even constrained him to demarcate himself in those writings from essential aspects of official Nazi ideology: above all, from the notion of "race" as a *biological invariant* decisively determining all aspects of social life, including science and art no less than politics and economics.

This "demarcation" from a biologistic racism does not mean that the terminology of racism was never employed by de Man in the writings of the time, but rather that on the relatively few occasions when it was, it was inevitably used to designate not biological traits but "cultural" and "historical" particularities, having more to do with language and customs than with "blood and soil." Even on the (to my knowledge) unique occasion where this phrase itself can be found, among the hundreds of pages published by de Man in 1941–42, it is to challenge the Nazi ideal of racial purity by arguing, as he does elsewhere, for the artistic necessity of "mixings and exchanges" between different cultures, and by asserting that "there is by no means a contradiction between the demands of originality and those of cultural receptivity."[25] The following instance, where de Man draws lessons for Flemish writers from the "fusion," in the work of Ernst Jünger, "of Germanic mythical romanticism and French rational humanism" ("however dangerous such schematic concepts may be"), is exemplary of this attempt to subvert the tenets of racism through the calculated use of its own vocabulary:

For Flemings there is a lesson to be learned from Jünger's aesthetic tendency that cannot be repeated often enough: I mean the usefulness for a writer to be open to all expressions of Western civilizations, not to confine himself in local traditions. A sincere artist can never renounce his proper regional [character], destined by blood and soil, since it is an integrating part of his essence, which he has to utter. But he systematically impoverishes himself, he refuses to make use of that which constitutes the vital force of our European culture, if he, allegedly in order to remain true to his own people, does not want to become acquainted with that which comes into being elsewhere. In that case, the use of local color is merely an easy pretext in order to replace an absent wealth with superficial regionalism.[26]

"True artists," like Jünger, recognize the necessity of acknowledging not only "kindred, but in some aspects opposed artistic values" in order to reach their "full development." Jünger's "synthesis" of the French and the Germanic—"however dangerous such schematic concepts may be"—holds "the formula of the future of European literature." In another article in the same Flemish journal, de Man cites the names of Joyce and Virginia Woolf "in order to point out that decadence and inferiority are not necessarily synonymous" (May 17–18, 1942).

The reference to "race," then, is not racist, not at least in the sense of designating a biologically determined norm, to be kept pure of external influence; rather, it designates a principle of cultural individuation that requires open exchange with other cultures in order to avoid succumbing to mediocrity and provincialism. The emphasis is constantly on the need for diversity in order to avoid the nefarious consequences of inbreeding, as in the following remark from a review of Brinckmann's *Geist der Nationen (Spirit of Nations)* which de Man helped translate:

[Brinckmann's] historical exposition presents the life process of European art as an endless capacity for renovation, based upon the fact that a number of contrasting forces are simultaneously present in it. There is always an opposition, a tension between the different elements that determine a style. To this tension we owe the persistent revival and the immortal dynamism of our culture [. . .] its incomparable diversity.[27]

The culture thus characterized by this "incomparable diversity" is not just European, it is *national,* i.e. "the result of racial mixings that have not aged much over the centuries." National culture is "racial," but only in the sense of the "mixing" of different particular groups. Nevertheless, the "incomparable diversity" has, inevitably, its limits:

What is proper to our time is the consideration of this national personality as a valuable condition, a precious possession which has to be maintained at the cost of all sacrifices. This conception is miles apart from sentimental patriotism. Rather, it concerns a sober faith, a practical means to defend Western culture against a decomposition from the inside out or a surprise attack by neighboring civilizations. (March 29–30, 1942)

What is "proper to our time," then, is not simply the valorization of the national or of nationalism, but rather the sense of these values being threatened: by internal "decomposition" or by "surprise attack." What is "proper to our time," in short, is

the sense of danger from without and from within, and the heightened sense of the "precious possession" that is *ours*. What is "ours," not "theirs," is "incomparably diverse," but only *by comparison with* what is not ours, but 'theirs.' It is not enough to define the identity of Europe internally, as it were, in terms of the "mutual exchanges" of the different national groups that inhabit the European continent. That identity must also be *set off* and *apart from* what it is not, from the non-European, the foreign. That is, from the Other. Pure immanence, in short, is not enough. Totality is never whole. The contour can only delineate a figure by simultaneously describing a ground, or rather, by relegating everything it excludes to the function of background. The other of the European, whether local, regional or National, is, first and foremost: the Jew. It is the Jews who intrude, deranging the "continuity" and immanence of Western History: in this case, that of German Literature, thus causing it to deviate from its proper, predestined course. From an article on "Contemporary German Fiction" (*Het Vlaamsche Land,* August 20, 1942):

When we investigate the post-war literary production in Germany, we are immediately struck by the contrast between two groups, which moreover were also materially separated by the events of 1933. The first of these groups celebrates an art with a strongly cerebral[28] disposition, founded upon some abstract principles and very remote from all naturalness. The in themselves very remarkable theses of expressionism were used in this group as tricks, as skilful artifices calculated for easy effects. The very legitimate basic rule of artistic transformation, inspired by the personal vision of the creator, served here as a pretext for a forced, caricatured representation of reality. Thus [the artists of this group] came into open conflict with the proper traditions of German art which had always and before everything else clung to a deep spiritual sincerity. Small wonder, then, that it was mainly non-Germans, and in particular Jews, that went in this direction.

The Jews, here designated as "non-Germans," allow what is properly German to emerge all the more clearly: "deep spiritual sincerity," *as distinct from* "tricks"; the "in themselves remarkable theses of Expressionism," *as opposed to* "skilful artifices" designed to produce "effects"; "the basic rule of artistic transformation" *in contrast to* "forced, caricatured representations of reality." The Jews, in short, introduce an element of disruption into the flow of European (here: Germanic) literary history, they help divert it from its proper course. Such diversions exceed the "incomparable diversity" of European literature and thereby trace its limits.

The place of "the Jews," then, is precisely located in this discourse through the priority assigned to the internal over the external, to continuity over discontinuity, to self-identity over difference, to the "natural" over "artifice," "tricks" or "intellectuality." The place assigned the Jews is that of the "non-": the non-German, the in-sincere, the unnatural, the devious. But art too, as the de Man of 1941 well knew, is itself nonnatural, artificial, devious. In the passage quoted above referring to the Jews, it is expressly stated that "artistic transformation" is a "legitimate basic rule," i.e. that art must necessarily *denaturalize*. But there are better and worse denaturalizations. And although de Man here refers to the "personal vision of the creator" as the *source* of such transformations, their aesthetic value depends ultimately not upon personal or individual factors, but upon an historical development conceived of as being essentially continuous and "evolutionary." It should, however, be noted that in this same article (but also elsewhere) de Man distinguishes the "strong artistic continuity" that marks German literary history from the situation in France, where

one sees [. . .] experiments which, taken separately, do come to pass very logically and rationally, but which, taken as a whole, show aberrations of such strength that it is difficult to reduce them to a unitary type. (August 20, 1942)

The Jews, then, in their otherness, constitute an aberrant diversion of the continuous flow of German literary history; at the same time, in their non-natural deviousness, they cannot entirely be separated from art itself, which depends upon devices and techniques, if not upon "tricks." A year and a half earlier, de Man had already described the consequences of this situation in "The Jews in Contemporary Literature." In the course of the essay, this title takes on something of an antiphrastic turn. For the Jews, de Man argues, are not really "in" contemporary literature at all. Nor even in contemporary culture. To argue the contrary is the error of "vulgar antisemitism," which the article starts out by criticizing. Such an attitude itself turns out to be almost the opposite of what it seems and wants: it does the Jews too much honor and the West too little. Moreover, "this conception" is not merely erroneous, it can involve "rather dangerous consequences." Its tendency is to condemn "all of contemporary literature (*toute la production contemporaine*)" and, correlatively, to regard Western writers as nothing more than "mere imitators of a Jewish culture that is alien to" them.

Thus begins the article, which, as Derrida has argued, in his two-handed reading ("On the One Hand. . . on the Other Hand" [pp.621–631]), follows an abysmally equivocal strategy. I want to try to negotiate a few of its tortuous turns by focusing upon what I will call its *strategy of denigration*. The article be-

gins with what is manifestly a critique of "vulgar antisemitism," of its blanket, totalizing condemnation of contemporary literature and culture *in general* as "judaized." Since the notion of "vulgarity" here is obviously overdetermined, it is worth emphasizing that at least *one* of its meanings, by no means the least trivial, is not the most obvious one, i.e. that determined by the *opposition* of vulgar to non-vulgar, popular to refined, common to sophisticated, but rather, far more palpably, by the degree of *violence* involved. In its totalizing lack of discrimination, "vulgar antisemitism" implies not merely the segregation, exclusion or confinement of the other, but its removal and ultimate elimination, since its mere existence and survival are apprehended as a mortal *threat*. This, of course, was the attitude and ultimate policy of Nazi antisemitism. What de Man's strategy in this article demonstrates is what antisemitism of this sort, like racism in general, is unable to admit: the extent to which its fear and hate implies *recognition* of the other in at least two different senses. First, it implies *identification of* the other (and hence, to a certain extent, *with the other*).[29] And second, it implies 'recognition' of the other's *power*: to *threaten,* potentially if not actually. Without this recognition of the power of the other, antisemitism loses its *raison d'être*: the virulence to which all forms of racism tend, and which otherwise would appear to be both gratuitous and unnecessary. It is this recognition which the strategy of belittlement practiced by de Man in this article, seeks to undercut, first by demarcating itself from "vulgar antisemitism." And yet, the logic of this demarcation works relentlessly to rearm the very "vulgar antisemitism" that the strategy of denigration seeks to neutralize. The strategy proceeds by the following steps:

1. In response to the blanket condemnation of contemporary Western Literature for its having been taken over by a foreign element, the Jews, the strategy responds that this does the Jews too much honor and Europe too little. Such antisemitism, far from defending the values of Western Civilization, betrays and contributes to the latter's demoralization.

2. It is not enough to describe the error of vulgar antisemitism; its causes must also be understood. To these may be counted, first of all, the tendency of the Jews themselves to self-aggrandizement: they have presented themselves as a determining factor in the development of modern art and culture, and they have been believed. Second, they have been believed because they in fact "played an important role in the factitious and disorganized existence of Europe since 1920," and because the literature of this period is widely regarded as "a sort of monstrous outgrowth of the [First] World War."

3. "The reality, however, is different." The error of vulgar

antisemitism resides in its erroneous conception of literary history, or more precisely, in its inability or unwillingness—there is, after all, de Man's language suggests, both *will* and *pleasure* involved[30]—to admit a difference between History, considered in the socio-political-economic sense, and the history of art and/or literature. Proceeding from the obvious fact that the War caused a "profound upheaval in the political and economic world," vulgar antisemitism extends this perception to the world of art, thus ignoring the specificity of its history:

It seems that aesthetic evolutions obey very powerful laws which continue their action even when humanity is shaken by considerable events. The world war provoked a profound upheaval in the political and economic world. But artistic life remained relatively impervious to the shock (*relativement peu remuée*) and the forms we know today are the logical and normal consequences of what was there before.

For the novel, the result of these "powerful laws" is best expressed in the Stendhalian formula of a "mirror walking along a great highway," reflecting the reality of the world about it. "But Stendhal's mirror," de Man continues, "does not stand still on the highway." It begins to move, and with it, so does the strategy of denigration. The mirror extends its reflection to the innermost corners of the psyche.

4. The aesthetic value of the novel, then, depends on the novelists' ability "to penetrate, in accordance with the methods appropriate to their personalities, the secrets of the inner life." A list of exemplary names follows: "Gide, Kafka, Hemingway, Lawrence." The writers named are "simple continuators" of a century-old aesthetics of psychological realism, they are not "innovators" who have "broken with the traditions of the past." As Hartman and Derrida have already observed, not only is one of the writers cited Jewish, but the three others can hardly be considered as conforming to Nazi or fascist literary tastes.[31] This emphasis on the immanent continuity of the history of literary forms excludes the widespread attitude, also adopted by "vulgar antisemitism," that contemporary literature can be considered in "isolation" from its past, i.e. as susceptible of being affected directly by the "mentality of the 1920s." Since the cultural influence of the Jews has already been determined as a function of their role in this postwar atmosphere, it is excluded, a priori as it were, by the laws that determine the development of literary history, that contemporary literature might in any way be subject to Jewish influence.

5. This conclusion, based on a priori principles, is confirmed by empirical evidence: another enumeration of proper names serves to demonstrate that Jewish French writers "have always

been of secondary importance" and have never been "among those who have in any way determined literary genres." The absence here of any reference to Marcel Proust, in a discussion of the novel as psychological analysis, is too glaring to be overlooked by any literate reader, in 1941 no less than today. In de Man's other articles of this period, Proust is mentioned regularly as *the* exemplary instance of the psychological novel in contemporary French literature (see, for instance, the articles published February 11, June 17, and December 16, 1941). To be sure, in accordance with the conception of literary history at work in these articles, the presence or absence of a proper name is of secondary importance, since, considered from the point of view of aesthetics, those names are not 'proper' but rather 'generic': they designate not individuals, but 'schools' or styles. But this is precisely how the name *Proust* is used in the texts referred to. The immanent logic of literary evolution goes its own way independently of individuals. To be sure, here and elsewhere de Man appears to reserve a considerable place for what he calls "personality." But if the latter is said to be the source of the particular artistic "method," it does not determine the general direction that method must take. If there is a principle of individuation discernible in the development of the "powerful laws" of literary history, its locus is not the individual's "personality," but rather the character of the group: local, regional, but above all, national.

6. What, then, of the group under discussion? At this point the argument takes a turn that leaves at least one reader rubbing his eyes.[32] The strategy of denigration pulls, as it were, its trump card: Yes, there *is* a "Jewish spirit." Yes, it has "specific characteristics." And what's more, these characteristics *should* have allowed it to "exercise a preponderant influence on the evolution" of the psychological novel. *And yet*: this influence seems "of extraordinarily little importance," especially given what one has every right to expect. In short, the fear of "vulgar antisemitism"—the negative recognition it accords the Jews—turns out to be not as unfounded as one might have concluded from the previous discussion. What are these characteristics?

Their intellectualism (*cérébralité*), their capacity to assimilate theories while retaining a certain coolness towards them, would seem to be very precious qualities for the labor of lucid analysis demanded by the novel. But despite this, Jewish writers have always been of secondary importance (*au second plan*).

Vulgar antisemitism is thus correct in its estimation of the *qualities* and potential power of the Jews; it is however incorrect—and this, we must suppose, is the essential point of the strategy of denigration—in *underestimating* the powers of resistance of

"Western," that is: non-Jewish, "intellectuals." Which is why these intellectuals, and others, can "take comfort" in the fact that *despite* the qualities of the Jews, they—"we?"—have been able to protect them—*our?*—selves "from Jewish influence in a domain as representative as literature." This fact, precisely *because* of the analytical predisposition of the Jewish spirit, bears witness to the "vitality" of Western Culture, of European Literature. The paranoic fear of "vulgar antisemitism" thus turns out to be not only unfounded, but more "anti-European" and "anti-Western" than the enemy it fears: in exaggerating the danger of the latter, it denigrates itself. The strategy of denigration purports to turn this around, almost dialectically, by concluding that "despite the Semitic intervention in all aspects of European life," the latter has been able to keep its "originality and character intact." Indeed, the "soundness" of this character can be measured by its success in resisting alien penetration. This is all the more remarkable in the case at hand, where the "alien" group appears as almost a mirror-image, an uncanny double of that from which it is supposedly alienated: the literary "spirit" brought forth by the intrinsic development of Western literature, in the form of the psychological novel.

7. Having reached this conclusion, why go on? Why does the text find it necessary to go on, when the argument has in essence shown the fears of "vulgar antisemitism" to be as groundless as its "consequences" are "dangerous"? Having ostensibly achieved its aims, why does the strategy of denigration not stop? Has something been *forgotten*? Something that had not yet happened? Some "dangerous consequence"? A *problem*, still awaiting solution?

"*Kolonie liebt, und tapfer Vergessen der Geist.*"[33]

Something *more* remains to be said:

Moreover (*En plus*) it is clear, therefore, that a solution of the Jewish problem which would aim at the creation of a Jewish colony isolated from Europe would not involve, for the literary life of the West, deplorable consequences.

The Jews, who have no place "in" contemporary literature, if it is not that of a mirror of a moving mirror, must themselves be removed, placed in a colony, without reason, and yet inevitably. The alien group that has failed to make any difference whatsoever in the development of "the literary life of the West," must *nevertheless,* if only in an exercise of thought, in a *Gedankenspiel* that by all rights is, or should be, entirely gratuitous, be *removed* from the body it has failed to penetrate. It must be *isolated* from the "*literary life of the West,*" which, because *it* is not isolated, because *it* is embedded in a tradition and a history, has

remained as unaffected by the presence of the parasite as it would be by its absence. All such a removal would cost are merely "a few personalities of mediocre value," and as has been demonstrated, the history of literature does not depend upon personalities. The removal of the Jews to a "colony isolated from Europe" would not affect the continued self-development of "the literary life of the West" any more than the removal of certain names from a list, or of certain books from circulation. Nothing can, nothing must be allowed to interrupt the continuity of that development, least of all, the "cold" reflections of mirrors on the move.

Mirrors reflecting mirrors: the rhetorical gesture, 'removing' the Jews to a colony "isolated from Europe," reflects, as in a mirror—that is, in reverse—the non-isolation of contemporary literature: "Henceforth, it is clear that it is absurd to consider contemporary literature as an isolated phenomenon." Isolated from what? From a history determined by "great evolutionary laws," a history that knows no breaks and interruptions, no leaps and bounds, no confusing reverberations or glaring reflections. And yet, if it is reflection itself that must thus be protected, the strategy of denigration can never rest assured, for there will always be a mirror-image returning to threaten the demarcation upon which it depends. The "unanimous cycle," its single spirit, is haunted by *names,* mentioned and unmentionable, and by *images* which turn out to be its mirror-image: the same, but backwards. The "colony" will never be remote enough, never sufficiently isolated to solve the problem.

> *Glaube, wer es geprüft! nämlich zu Haus ist der Geist*
> *Nicht im Anfang, nicht an der Quell. Ihn zehret die Heimat,*
> *Kolonie liebt, und tapfer Vergessen der Geist.*
> *Unsere Blumen erfreun und die Schatten unserer Wälder*
> *Den Verschmachteten. Fast wär der Beseeler verbrannt.*[34]

IV. *Starting Again From Scratch*

To what extent the strategy of denigration, or elements of it, returned to play a role in the later writings of Paul de Man is a question I cannot address here. It is indisputable, however, that the notion of history, and in particular, of literary history, which is at work in these early articles, became an increasingly urgent subject of critical reflection for him. And yet, already in 1941, such reflection is legible, significantly enough not where historical matters are addressed in *general,* as in the article on Lalou, but rather where they are analyzed in particular, and especially, where the practice of poetic language enters the picture.

The article I have in mind is that devoted to Charles Péguy,[35] in which, as Derrida remarks, de Man "seems to take pleasure in proliferating" a series of "quasi-autobiographical traits" (p.631, note 43). No doubt that for the 21-year old de Man, Péguy represents something of an idealized self-image: "Imbued with socialist ideas of egalitarian justice," he "will be a Dreyfusard to the bitter end"; but at the same time, his independence of mind and "his notorious indiscipline" will cause him to fall out with all his superiors and with many of his former socialist comrades, without thereby becoming more acceptable to his enemies on the right. "Caught between these two enmities, Péguy will continue to walk head high, defending his work," until, "leading his men in an attack," during the battle of the Marne, he is cut down by a burst of machine-gun fire.

Péguy, as de Man describes him, is something of an isolated case: separated by his convictions from the left and the right, estranged from his superiors, almost alone, and yet not quite:

Not quite without friends, however, for he will be able to surround himself with several faithful followers and inform them about the project he is considering. He wants to start a journal, no longer indebted to a party, but which would be published freely (*librement*), still defending socialistic ideas, but without being censured by anyone. The title? *Notebooks* (*Les Cahiers*), in memory, Halévy says, of his school notebooks, so clean, so well kept.

In memory, too, of those *Cahiers du libre examen* in which de Man published and which he briefly edited in the months immediately preceding the German invasion. But also, perhaps, "in memory" of a future yet to come, in which schools and notebooks will have their part to play.

But de Man's affinity for Péguy is by no means limited to this image of the poet's life, which takes up over two-thirds of the article. It is followed by a discussion of Péguy's poetry, and here a rather different aspect of that affinity emerges. And strangely enough, what fascinates de Man are traits he has elsewhere condemned: *enumeration* and a certain *artificiality*. For the latter, as we have read, the Jews are criticized and separated from the literary mainstream, at least in Germany; for the former, René Lalou has been severely taken to task a scant month earlier. Here, de Man defends Péguy on both counts, against literary criticism. "Some have seen in his continual enumerations (there are in *Eve* one hundred and twenty-two verses beginning with 'You no longer knew') a quasi-artificial procedure." However severely de Man himself has taken Lalou to task for his penchant to "dead enumerations," here he is categorical in affirming the value of Péguy's repetitions. "Rather" than condemning them as artificial, he continues,

we should see in them the very rhythm of Péguy's thought, which proceeds by jolts (*par à-coups*), backtracking each time, adding several centimeters to the way traversed. Gide has magnificently defined this style as "similar to pebbles in the desert, following and resembling one another, each like the other, just a little bit different." Halévy will say "that he advances in the manner of a tide," pushing his thought by "long waves, each one covering up the preceding one and exceeding it by a line."

The insistence of Péguy is thus not just limited to his person; it also makes him "the French writer of recent times bearing most clearly the mark of genius," a genius that is inseparable from a "rhythm" of "enumerative repetition" that de Man will rediscover, towards the end of his life, to be the hallmark of "prosaic, or better, *historical* modes of language power" ("Anthropomorphism," p.241). To be sure, the description of Péguy's repetition is suspended between a progressive, forward movement and a recurrence, a 'backtracking' in which each individual element turns out to be "just a little bit different." But what is remarkable is that this rhythm, although constant, is anything but continuous, a value that the de Man of this period otherwise regards as indispensable. Rather, Péguy's poetry proceeds by "à-coups," by fits and starts, by jolts and interruptions, falling back again and again, *almost* to its point of departure. It is a rhythm that de Man will describe four decades later, in the Preface to *The Rhetoric of Romanticism*, as that of his own essays, which carry "the burden of constantly falling back to nought" (p. ix), hence, of "always" having to "start again from scratch," and which lead to "conclusions" that "fail to add up to anything." The condition of this "fall," of this constant relapse, is the very totalizing tendency that was so determining in the writings of 1941–42:

I feel myself compelled to repeated frustration in a persistent attempt to write as if a dialectical summation were possible beyond the breaks and interruptions that the readings disclose. (p. ix)

What the later readings document, however, is what certain of the early writings, such as the article on Péguy, demonstrate: that "falling back to nought" is not the same as turning in a circle, that having to "always start again from scratch" does not necessarily mean returning to one's identical point of departure. For "nought" here, as de Man demonstrates in his reading of Pascal, is not the same as "non-being,"[36] any more than a "scratch" is the same as a tabula rasa. The *scratch* is what is left when one has "gotten the point," when point meets surface, whether as incision, inscription or both. The point scratches, tears, punctures the cohesion, interrupts the sequence, but at the same time it permits that which it separates not to remain *isolated,* allows it to *relate,* however allegorically: that is, with an "(ironic) pseudo-knowledge [. . .] which pretends to order sequentially, in a narrative, what is actually the destruction of all sequence" ("Pascal," p.23). The scratch which separates, hurts and leaves scars, makes *reading* possible, not only as "monumentalization," but also as *disfigurement.* The scratch from which de Man is forced again and again to "start," brings him, bring us back to what all figuration seeks to hide, and what his readings seek to bring into the open, if only for an instant. As in his discussion of Kleist's reference, in the essay on the *Marionettentheater,* to the statue of a young boy, extracting a splinter from his foot, a figure whose equivocal grace both conceals and also suggests what

> may be a ruse to hide the flaw that marred aesthetic perfection from the start or, in a more perverse reading, to enjoy, under the cover of aesthetic distance, pleasures that have to do with the inflicting of wounds rather than with gracefulness. ("Aesthetic Formalization," p.280)

Reading from scratch is disfigurement, but one which never ceases "falling back to nought" in its attempt to *point out* the scratch, to give the nought a name:

> The continuous universe held together by the double wings of the two infinities [the infinitely large and the infinitely small—S.W.] is interrupted, disrupted *at all points* by a principle of radical heterogeneity without which it cannot come into being. Moreover, this rupture of the infinitesimal and the homogeneous does not occur on the transcendental level, but on the level of language, in the inability of a theory of language as sign or as name (nominal definition) to ground this homogeneity without having recourse to the signifying function, the real definition, that makes the zero of signification the necessary condition for grounded knowledge. ("Pascal," p.10)

In short, it is precisely *because* language is *referential,* "because it always refers but never to the right referent,"[37] that "the zero of signification" becomes the *real* and *impossible* condition of meaning; for the same reason, this zero must give rise to its "systematic effacement [. . .] and its reconversion into a name" ("Pascal," p.11). Disfigurement is thus both the distortion of the figure and the dissimulation of this distortion, the scratch and the repeated effacement of the scratch, remembrance *and,* and *as,* forgetting. The "and" of these impossible couples itself receives a name in de Man's later work: power. This impossible, implausible name takes us back almost to our point of departure: the overpowering events of May, 1940, and their aftermath. An aftermath which, needless to say, continues to this day.

V. *The Power of Reading*

In one of the first articles he writes for *Le Soir,* reviewing "Books on the Belgian Campaign," de Man asserts that the sole and major difference between 1914–17 and 1940 was "the skill and power with which the Germans were able to exploit their success and impose victory" (2.2.41). His decision to write for *Le Soir* in 1941 grows out of an interpretation of this difference in *power*: the difference between the Germans' ability "to exploit their success and impose victory" in May, 1940, as compared with the First World War. It is an interpretation in terms of *intelligible forces*: of implacable laws; of historical necessity determining irrevocable shifts in hegemony; of the exhaustion of economic, social and political forms of organization (identified with those of 'liberal, parliamentary democracy'); of the supplanting of one mode of social organization by another ("individualism" by "totalitarian" collectivism). Some forty years later, de Man will once again turn to another highly mobile army, not of troops this time but of tropes, inscribed in "Nietzsche's perhaps better known than understood definition of truth as tropological displacement: '*Was ist also Wahrheit? Ein bewegliches Heer von Metaphern, Metonymien, Anthropomorphismen. . . .*'" ("Anthropomorphism," p.239). This definition leads de Man to the following remarks:

> Truth, says Nietzsche, is a mobile *army* of tropes. Mobility is coextensive with any trope, but the connotations introduced by "army" are not so obvious, for to say that truth is an army (of tropes) is again to say something odd and possibly misleading. [. . .] To call them an army is [. . .] to imply that their effect and their effectiveness is not a matter of judgment but of power. What characterizes a good army, as distinct for instance from a good cause, is that its success has little to do with immanent justice and a great deal with the proper economic use of its power. (p.242)

Despite the difference between troops and tropes, it might seem that "the de Man of the 80s" and the de Man of the 40s had similar, if not identical views regarding power: for the latter, "the skill and power to impose (*forcer*) victory," reflected general and intelligible historical tendencies. For the reader of Nietzsche in 1980, the factors involved in the "proper economic use" of power are, however, quite different. The "economy" of the "mobile army of tropes" does not depend simply upon technical organization, not at least understood as the application of means to ends, nor upon any other such *cognitive* judgment.

The "mobile army of tropes" derives its power not from "judgment" but from factors which "exist independently of epistemological determinations." Truth, the indispensable criterion of knowledge, cannot itself, without being guilty of a *petitio principii,* be defined by what it in turn makes possible: epistemology. Something else is required. Of that enigmatic something else, the name, "power," is the enigmatic, catachrestic cipher. If the events of May, 1940 can be seen as the "scratch" which gave Paul de Man a "start," it is towards that startling breakdown of schemes of intelligibility which returns in his later work to epitomize the advent of history, language and power:

From the moment that words such as 'power' and 'battle' and so on emerge on the scene, there is history. [. . .] there is occurrence, there is event. History is therefore not temporal, it has nothing to do with temporality, but [with] the emergence of a language of power out of a language of cognition.[38]

In the as yet unpublished lecture on "Kant and Schiller," from which this passage is taken, the notion of "power" has several determinations. *First,* as we have just read, it "emerges" from a *breakdown* of cognition and of the tropological *system* upon which knowledge depends. *Second,* and correlatively, it is, rigorously speaking, *unnameable.* As such, however, it necessarily gives rise to the tropological system of exchanges that will name it, figuratively, thus "reinscribing" it into a system of meaning, erasing its radical heterogeneity by giving it an intelligible face (prosopopoeia). The exemplary instance to which de Man refers in this context is the abrupt shift he observes in Kant's Analytics of the Sublime, from the "mathematical" to the "dynamical" sublime, "the blank between section 27 and section 28." In the former, Kant "push[es] the notion of trope to the extreme, trying to saturate the whole field of language," but only revealing, by this very effort and the rigor with which it is pursued, that "certain linguistic elements will remain which the concept of trope cannot reach, and which then can be [called] performative." *Third and last,* although the recuperative process of reinscription—aesthetization, monumentalization, figuralization—is prescribed by the advent of power itself, the historical event as such, in its radical alterity, remains *irreversible.* "It goes in that direction and you cannot get back from that one to the one before." What Schiller does in his reading of Kant is to "recuperate" the irruptive event of 'power,' so to speak, "by a kind of reinscription of the performative in a tropological system of cognition [. . .] That relapse, however, is not the same as a reversal. Because this is [. . .] open to critical discourse. . . ."

The function of critical reading is thus to move in that opening, retracing, not retracting, the historical event that consists in the rigorous self-exhaustion of the prevailing cognitive system of language, its break*down* and the concomitant break*out* of a language of power, which is hardly language any more: "blank," "zero," "enumeration," "stutter," and which, already in being named as such, not least of all by the 'retracing' of critical reading itself, is already on its way back into a new cognitive-tropological system. Critical discourse is thus "balanced," "poised between the two modes of discourse," tropological and performative, and in its "poise" it reveals the power, and the impotence, of a radical heterogeneity that is always *about* to obliterate itself.

In his reading of Kant's Third Critique, de Man locates this moment in the figure of the "*Augenschein,*" in the following passage, where Kant is seeking to describe the *a-cognitive* glance required of an authentically aesthetic judgment, that is, one which would have freed itself of all epistemological and teleological determinations:

If, then, we call the sight of the starry heaven *sublime,* we must not place at the foundation of judgment concepts of worlds inhabited by rational beings and regard the bright points, with which we see the space above us filled, as their suns moving in circles purposively fixed with reference to them; but we must regard it, just as we see it [*wie man ihn sieht*], as a distant, all-embracing vault [*ein weites Gewölbe*]. Only under such a representation can we range that sublimity that a pure aesthetic judgment ascribes to this object. And in the same way, if we are to call the sight of the ocean sublime, we must not think of it as we ordinarily do, as implying all kinds of knowledge (that are not contained in immediate intuition). For example, we sometimes think of the ocean as a vast kingdom of aquatic creatures, or as the great source of those vapors that fill the air with clouds for the benefit of the land, or again as an element that, though dividing continents from each other, yet promotes the greatest communication between them; all these produce merely teleological judgments. To find the ocean nevertheless sublime we must regard it as poets do [*wie die Dichter es tun*], merely by what the eye reveals [*was der Augenschein zeigt*]—if it is at rest, as a clear mirror of water only bounded by the heavens; if it is stormy, as an abyss threatening to overwhelm everything.[39]

Such a glance is, to be sure, strictly inconceivable, it can only be thought *against thought,* as it were. This "against," however, would itself be conceived in too cognitive a manner, were it construed dialectically, as the absence or negation of knowledge. This is why de Man associates it with the moment of *breakdown,* in which for an instant something like pure reflection can be glimpsed, a *mirror* reflecting only the eye itself, in turn seeing only the mirror:

The "mirror" of the sea surface is a mirror without depth, least of all the mirror in which the constellation would be reflected. In this mode of seeing, the eye is its own agent and not the specular echo of the sun. The sea is called a mirror, not because it is supposed to reflect anything, but to stress a flatness devoid of any suggestion of depth. In the same way and to the same extent that this vision is purely material, devoid of any reflexive or intellectual complication, it is also purely formal, devoid of any semantic depth [. . .] The critique of the aesthetic ends up, in Kant, in a formal materialism that runs counter to all values and characteristics associated with aesthetic experience [. . .]. (p.16)

The "mirror" that took the high road in 1941, has returned, but in a very different guise. For what it reflects, now, is nothing but the eye itself, the "light of the eye," and precisely in its "flatness," that light strikes us—with a power that is next to powerless, that "prosaic" sobriety which de Man, in a tradition that includes Benjamin and that goes back at least to Hölderlin, makes his own. It is an *impossible* vision, and all the more haunting in its impossibility. Therein resides the "power" of de Man's texts: the readings they articulate are so precise, so striking, so implausible and yet so self-evident, that they force us to backtrack, to reflect, to reread, and to remember, even as we forget, that there is no going back.

University of Massachusetts, Amherst

NOTES

1. Paul de Man, "Shelley Disfigured," *The Rhetoric of Romanticism*, New York: Columbia University Press, 1984, p.94.

2. March 7, 1988, pp.26–31.

3. Roger Kimball, "Professor Hartman reconstructs Paul de Man," *The New Criterion*, May 1988, p.43.

4. *FAZ*, February 10, 1988, Nr. 34.

5. Walter Kendrick, "De Man That Got Away, Deconstructors on the Barricades," *The Village Voice Literary Supplement*, April 1988, p.7.

6. Paul de Man, "The Continuity of French Poetry," *Le Soir*, July 14, 1942. This article is a review—and above all, a *defense*—of the poetry journal *Messages*, published in Paris, later in Brussels and then in Geneva, and conceived as an alternative to the *Nouvelle Revue Française*, which had been placed under the editorship of Drieu la Rochelle at the end of 1940. Paul de Man's articles from *Le Soir* will generally be noted in the text by their date of publication, here 7.14.42.

7. "Aesthetic Formalization: Kleist's *Über das Marionettentheater*," *The Rhetoric of Romanticism*, p.273.

8. I note in passing the chauvinist overtones of an article which would derive "de Man's formidable stature as a thinker [. . .] in large measure" from "his unassimilated Europeanness," from his "foreignness," "arcane vocabulary and a Germanic density of style," while regretting that "kowtowing Americans love to perform at the feet of Continental imports." De Man is placed "in the ill-assorted company of Kurt Waldheim and Martin Heidegger—an appropriately European crew." And "literary Academe" is described as a place "where the currriculum is mostly European," the "peddlers" of which "suffer, with reason, from a chronic shortage of self-esteem." Kendrick here echoes the "argument" of Jeffrey Mehlman, who, in "Writing and Deference," compares the "literary adulation [of] the Americans for Derrida" with that of the German censor in Nazi-occupied France, Gerhard Heller, for Jean Paulhan (*Representations* 15, 1986, p.11).

9. The title of an article by David Lehman in the book review section of the *Los Angeles Times*, March 13, 1988.

10. That 'deconstructionists' should dare to question the unlimited validity of the "left/right" dichotomy as *the* determining parameter of political discourse draws Walter Kendrick's special wrath: "If deconstruction transcends vulgar politics—all that chatter about *left* and *right*—it does so by leaving the status quo alone and profiting from it when the chance comes along." As though calling the authority of "left" and "right" into question were a particularly effective means for profiting from the status quo. To be sure, it can be this, but no more or less than can the unquestioning endorsement of those received ideas. What counts, here as elsewhere, is the particular ways such established oppositions are questioned or assumed. But such discriminations are precisely what the blanket accusation of "opportunism" (spiced with that of "obnoxiousness") is here designed to preempt: it serves as a constant alibi for refusing to question simplistic paradigms, however consecrated they may be by the "status quo." Such an alibi, needless to say, is always opportune.

11. De Man treats Husserl with a "respect" that is more than mere politeness; it acknowledges his own indebtedness, since if he questions Husserl, it is only by extending Husserl's conception of critical self-reflection to the philosopher's determination of self-criticism as "the historical privilege of European man" (de Man), in

order to argue that the very project of attributing universal validity to a localized phenomenon reveals that the notion of self-criticism itself reposes upon an uncriticized, and perhaps uncriticizable, presumption of "self." Or, as Heidegger might have said, that the essence of criticism cannot itself be critical. (Cf. "Criticism and Crisis," *Blindness and Insight,* 2nd revised edition, Minneapolis: University of Minnesota Press, 1983, pp.14–16.)

12. Husserl explicitly excludes Indian, Babylonian, and Chinese culture from any participation in European "philosophy," to which however he accords universal validity. "Es ist eine Sinnesverfälschung, wenn man, in den von Griechenland geschaffenen und neuzeitlich fortgebildeten wissenschaftlichen Denkweisen erzogen, schon von indischer und chinesischer Philosophie und Wissenschaft (Astronomie, Mathematik) spricht, also Indien, Babylonien, China europäisch interpretiert." Non "Western," i.e. non-European, philosophy and science is characterized throughout this text as "mythical-practical," as distinct from truly "theoretical," and hence, truly philosophical. See Edmund Husserl, *Gesammelte Werke,* The Hague: Martinus Nijhof, 1962, vol. VI, p.331.

13. On the difficulty of getting to the point(s) in time, see Jacques Derrida, "Ousia et Grammè, Note sur une note de *Sein und Zeit,*" *Marges de la philosophie,* Paris: Minuit, 1972, pp.63 ff.

14. "Unbestimmter Wohnsitz" ("No fixed residence") replies Odradek to the question of the "Housefather"—and then laughs, "a laugh that sounds roughly like the rustling of fallen leaves." *Sorge des Hausvaters* [*Cares of a Family Man*], in Franz Kafka, *Sämtliche Erzählungen,* Frankfurt: S. Fischer, 1981, p.157.

15. Jacques Derrida, *De l'esprit,* Paris: Galilée, 1987, p.95, note.

16. Jacques Derrida, "Like the Sound of the Sea Deep within a Shell: Paul de Man's War," translated by Peggy Kamuf, *Critical Inquiry* 14 (Spring 1988), p.639.

17. Cited in *La France de Vichy,* Paris, 1973, pp.43–44. (I cite the French translation of Paxton's study, the only version available to me at the time of writing this essay.)

18. I. Kant, *Critique of Judgment,* tr. Werner Pluhar, Indianapolis, 1987, Introduction, V, p.21. Future references to this work given in text in parentheses.

19. "How can a positional act, which relates to nothing that comes before or after, become inscribed in a sequential narrative? How does a speech act become a trope, a catachresis which then engenders in its turn the narrative sequence of an allegory? It can only be because we impose, in our turn, on the senseless power of positional language the authority of sense and of meaning. But this is

radically inconsistent: language posits and language means [. . .] but language cannot posit meaning. [. . .] This impossible position is precisely the figure, the trope, metaphor as a violent [. . .] light, a deadly Apollo" ("Shelley Disfigured," pp.117–18). The disjunction between, here, "language" and the "imposition of meaning" is revealed to be the site of a *violence,* that "art" and aesthetics" will strive to conceal, in part successfully, but always only in part.

20. "Criticism and Literary History," *Het Vlaamsche Land,* June 7–8, 1942. Citations from this journal refer to the English translations of Ortwin de Graef, and will generally be noted in the text by date of publication, here June 7–8, 1942.

21. "Une Histoire de la Littérature Française contemporaine," *Le Soir,* April 8, 1941, p.6.

22. A similar line of argument can be found in Adorno and Horkheimer's reflections on antisemitism as the "limit of enlightenment": "What is pathological in antisemitism is not the activity of projection as such, but the absence of reflection. Insofar as the subject is no longer capable of giving back to the object what is has received from it, it itself is not enriched but impoverished. Reflection is lost in both directions: since the subject no longer reflects the object, it no longer reflects upon itself and thus loses the ability to differentiate (*die Fähigkeit zur Differenz*)." *Dialektik der Aufklärung,* Amsterdam: Querido Verlag, 1947, p. 223.

23. "Anthropomorphism and Trope in the Lyric," *The Rhetoric of Romanticism,* p.241.

24. Like Geoffrey Hartman, I have found only one other reference to the Jews in de Man's wartime writings: in an article entitled, in the English translation of Ortwin de Graef, "A View on Contemporary German Fiction," and published in August, 1942, in the Flemish journal, *Het Vlaamsche Land.*

25. "Contemporary Trends in French Literature," *Het Vlaamsche Land,* May 17–18, 1942, p.3.

26. "German Literature. A Great Writer: Ernst Jünger," *Het Vlaamsche Land,* July 26–27, 1942.

27. "Art as Mirror of the Essence of Nations: Considerations on *Geist der Nationen* by A.E. Brinckmann," *Het Vlaamsche Land,* March 29–30, 1942.

28. Another, more idiomatic translation for "cerebral" here would, of course, be "intellectual". . . .

29. Cf. the brilliant and still unsurpassed discussion of antisemitism as "the limit of the Enlightenment" in Adorno and Horkheimer's *Dialectics of Enlightenment,* pp.199–244. Their analysis of the func-

tion of *mimesis* and mimicry anticipates in certain respects the critique of "mimetology" developed more recently by Philippe Lacoue-Labarthe in regard to the political aspects of Heidegger's thought and its relation to Nazism (cf. Philippe Lacoue-Labarthe, *La fiction du politique,* Paris: Christian Bourgois, 1987, chapters 7 and 8 ["National-esthétisme" and "Mimétologie"]; "La transcendance finit dans la politique," *L'imitation des modernes,* Paris: Galilée, 1986).

30. In a literal translation, the beginning of the essay might read: "Vulgar antisemitism takes pleasure in willfully (*se plait volontairement*) considering the cultural phenomena of the postwar period [. . .] as being degenerate and decadent, because judaized."

31. This list repeats, with one name missing, an enumeration of Aldous Huxley (*Music at Night*) which de Man had cited one year earlier in an article on "The Contemporary English Novel"; the missing name, to be sure, is: *Proust.* ("Le roman anglais contemporain," *Les Cahiers du Libre Examen,* January, 1940.)

32. "One can hardly believe one's eyes. . . ," J. Derrida, p.630.

33. "Colonies love the spirit, and courageous forgetting." Hölderlin, "*Brot und Wein,*" *Werke und Briefe,* Friedrich Beissner, ed., Frankfurt am Main: Insel, 1969, vol. I, p.119.

34. Hölderlin, "*Brot und Wein.*"

35. "Charles Péguy," *Le Soir,* May 6, 1941.

36. "The verbal, predicative form *néant,* with its gerundive ending, indicates not the zero, but rather the one, as the *limit* of the infinitely small, the almost zero that is the one." "Pascal's Allegory of Persuasion," in Stephen J. Greenblatt, ed., *Allegory and Representation,* Baltimore and London: Johns Hopkins University Press, 1981, p.11 et passim.

37. "Aesthetic Formalization. . . ," p.285; de Man prefaces this phrase with the remark: "Such is language: it always thrusts but never scores."

38. "Kant and Schiller," to be published in Paul de Man, *Aesthetic Ideology,* ed. Andrzej Warminski, Minneapolis: University of Minnesota Press, 1990, forthcoming.

39. Kant, *Critique of Judgment,* cited in de Man, "Phenomenality and Materiality in Kant," in *Hermeneutics,* Gary Shapiro and Alan Sica, eds., Amherst: University of Massachusetts Press, 1984, p.13.

Paul de Man and the Cercle du Libre Examen

EDOUARD COLINET

As a student at the Université Libre de Bruxelles, from 1937 through 1941, Paul de Man was involved in the political and literary activities of the Cercle du Libre Examen. He wrote for the group's newspaper *Jeudi* and its monthly journal *Les Cahiers du Libre Examen*. In the course of our correspondence with some of his pre-war and wartime acquaintances, we received from Edouard Colinet the following letter, a brief history of the group associated with the *Cahiers,* which he had prepared with the help of a number of his, and Paul de Man's, contemporaries. We print it here and, with his permission, have added in endnotes supplementary material gathered from published sources and from others who knew Paul de Man during the 1930s and 1940s.—Eds.

Brussels, 17 May 1988

Dear Professor Hertz:

[. . .]

When Belgium entered the war on May 10, 1940, I was serving as President of the Cercle du Libre Examen. In that position I was one of those responsible for the publication of *Les Cahiers du Libre Examen* and was a close friend of the members of its editorial board as well as of a number of its contributors, including Paul de Man. I am shocked by the attempt to impeach Paul's honor on the part of people who either do not take into account all the facts concerning the period 1940–1944 or have never even known them.

I shall first try to describe the situation in the Cercle du Libre Examen in the years 1936–1940, then try to comment on what I learned about the period 1940–1945 immediately after my return to Belgium in February 1945. I lived in Southwest France during the war years and was involved, part-time, in underground activities directed against the Germans and Italians. At first, in 1941, I worked with Italian antifascists under the leadership of Silvio Trentin; later I joined the armed group Corps Franc Pomies, a group staffed by officers of the French Army. Being a foreigner, I did not think it fit to be involved in actions that were a mixture of acts against the invaders and French internal politics. The mayor of the little town where I lived— L'Isle-Jourdain (Gers)—was Joseph Barthelemy, a professor of international law at the Université Catholique de Paris and later Garde des Sceaux in a couple of French governments led by Maréchal Pétain.

Through these connections I became aware of the ambiguities of real politics and learned by experience that in politics things are never clear; what is right and what is wrong depends on how you look at the situation and on your background. I hope it will be understood that while I cannot be considered a "collaborator" of the Germans or of their friends, neither could I be considered an unconditional follower of ideas promoted by officially labelled "Resistance" political parties.

In Belgium, although I was raised in a French-speaking family, I was never anti-Flemish. Indeed, during my student years I was a member of the Flemish Students' Association at the ULB known as "Geen taal, geen vrijheid" ("No Language, No Freedom"), even though I was myself unable to deliver a speech in that language. In sum, I think that I may be held an unbiased witness of human behavior during those years.

First, a word about Paul de Man's background. Paul's uncle, Henri de Man, was a high-grade political philosopher and successful Belgian politician during the 1930s. In the late 20s and early 30s, Henri de Man studied in Germany and after that became the "thinker" of the Belgian Workers' Party (POB). To understand the political climate of this period, it is necessary to read his books—*Au-delà du Marxisme** (1929), *La joie au travail* (1930), *L'Idée socialiste** (1935), *L'exécution du Plan de Travail* (1935), *Masses et Chefs* (1937)—as well as those he published after 1940: *Après Coup* (1941), *Cahiers de ma montagne* (1944), *Au-delà du nationalisme* (1946), and *L'Ere des masses et le déclin de la civilisation** (1951–52) (*books originally written in German). Henri de Man was a member of the Belgian parliament and a minister under Leopold III. With Paul-Henri Spaak and Camille Gutt, he was one of the most influential politicians before the war and during the following months.

Paul's father, Robert (Bob) de Man, was a businessman, manufacturing and selling medical instruments and x-ray equipment in Antwerp. Paul's elder brother died in an accident and, after that, his mother committed suicide: Paul had the bad luck of being the first to find her hanged—he was about 15 years old at the time. Paul's father was so disturbed by these two violent deaths that for a time Paul had to be taken care of by his uncle Henri.

I first met Paul de Man at the Cercle du Libre Examen in 1937, if I remember correctly. In those years—1935–1940—the Cercle du Libre Examen was the meeting place of the intellectually active students at the ULB, outside their academic duties, of those bright young men and women whose interests were broader than merely learning what they were supposed to learn. Ilya Prigogine, for example, who won the Nobel Prize for Chemistry in 1983, was one of them.

In those days, the political allegiances of the students were, most of the time, of affective origin: if the most important thing for you was "Freedom," you were a member of the Liberal Students; if the most important thing was "Social Justice" then you were a member of the Socialist or Communist students, the latter divided into Stalinists and Trotskyists. In 1939, out of a total of 3500 students at the ULB, only 39 were members of the (Stalinist) Communist Students; a dozen or two were Trotskyists; a few hundred were members of the Socialist or Liberal students' associations. It must be noted that before 1937 socialist and communist students were grouped under the denomination Etudiants Socialistes Unifiés. The parting of the two groups was a consequence of the Moscow trials of 1936–38, which had a very deeply disturbing effect on young intellectuals of Marxist faith.

The Etudiants Socialistes were also divided between two divergent tendencies, a consequence of Henri de Man's ideas: an "old faction," direct scion of the old Marxist-oriented leaders such as Emile Vandervelde and Louis de Brouckere, and a new way of thinking whose leaders were Paul-Henri Spaak and Henri de Man. Spaak was a pragmatist and de Man a theoretician.

World War I had demonstrated the inefficiency of Internationalism even within the "proletariat." Henri de Man's book *Au-delà du marxisme* had had a profound effect during the early 30s. De Man's slogan, "socialisme national," brought to the Socialist Party many young men dissatisfied with the Liberal Party, and all the more as everything there was blocked by old hands such as Paul Hymans and Albert Devèze. De Man's "socialisme national" was only apparently related to Hitler's National Socialism, but as Henri de Man was an advocate of German culture and German philosophy, his enemies, even before the war, used this possible confusion against him.

Late in 1939—in November, I think—the Cercle du Libre Examen expelled those of its members who belonged to the (Stalinist) Communist Students on the grounds of the incompatibility between allegiance to the Communist Party and membership in the Cercle du Libre Examen. In fact, this problem had been the subject of endless controversy, and the final decision could not have been reached before the conclusion of the Russo-German agreement in September 1939.[1]

As for the extremists on the right or the conservative side, they numbered only a dozen or two and apparently had no genuine organization within the ULB. They belonged to outside organizations and didn't mix with the common crowd.

It must be noted that the Université Libre de Bruxelles (ULB) had been established in 1834–35 by Theodor Verhaegen, a Protestant and a Liberal, with the objective of counterbalancing the political influence of the Université Catholique de Louvain. The philosophical basis of the ULB was the "principe du libre examen," freedom of thought concerning any human activity. In political practice, the ULB was always against the Catholic Party. Liberal, Protestant or Jewish families sent their children to the ULB, while Catholics sent theirs to Louvain. This trend was still very much alive during the period under consideration, slightly less so now. However, as the ULB provided the best available training in medicine in Belgium, many Catholics who would normally study at Louvain came to Brussels. There they were grouped in a Cercle Saint Luc under the leadership of a priest whose name I do not remember. They had practically no influence outside the School of Medicine.

Who were the leaders of the Cercle du Libre Examen and of *Les Cahiers du Libre Examen* during 1937–1940?

The leadership was shared between Jean Burgers and Charles Dosogne—both were more of the "man-of-action" type than the others. Burgers was labeled a socialist, Dosogne a *socialiste révolutionaire* (more or less related to Trotsky); Burgers was unconditionally anti-nazi and against all other "fascists";

Dosogne was as "anti-fascist" as he, but had a more neutralist position.

Marcel Sluszny, the most gifted speaker of that generation, was a socialist, as were Adella Englert and Youra Livschitz. I do not recall Jacques Kupissonoff's allegiance—he was mostly interested in art, particularly in cinema. Gilbert Jaeger and Paul de Man were also labelled socialist; both of them had a more logically structured belief than the majority of us. As for the three pre-war presidents of the Cercle, two were liberals—Christian Lepoivre and myself—and one, Pierre de Ligne, was a socialist of the "demanist" variety.

I didn't feel, during those few years, a very marked evolution of the *basic* way of thinking in the group of men and women I lived with, even if our immediate interests were focussed on the question of the moment. There was, it must be noted, a progressive shift away from the belief in the rightness of the Russian Marxist experiment. Within the framework of our individual political beliefs, we were all "antifascist" or, maybe more precisely, "anti-totalitarian"; those two concepts were felt to be more or less synonymous. We considered "fascist" the tenets of Mussolini's regime, of Hitler's, of Horthy's in Hungary, Salazar's in Portugal, Batista's in Cuba—later, of Franco's in Spain and, finally, of Stalin's in the USSR.

After the Moscow trials (1936–38) another incitation to our changing our way of thinking was the Spanish Civil War of 1936–38 and the spectacle of the impotence of "democratic" governments in helping the Spanish government in its fight against the "rebel" Franco. We were generally unwilling to imagine, at that time, that this obvious impotence could have been the consequence of a secret decision to stop the establishment of a communist government in Spain. We also became, very slowly and reluctantly, aware of the fact that the fight between communists and anarchists, which was raging in Spain in the government-controlled areas, killed more people than military activities. Trotskyists also were physically eliminated by Stalin's adepts (the POUM affair).

In 1938, after a Brussels street demonstration in favor of the Spanish government asking for military assistance—that is, weapons—to be sent to the democratic forces, I was one of the students who were admitted to an interview with P.-H. Spaak, the Minister of Foreign Affairs: we were told that any help was impossible due to the non-intervention position taken by the League of Nations, although this agreement was not being respected by the Germans and Italians. This position looked to us like a denial of justice—P.-H. Spaak was a Socialist leader (as was Léon Blum, his French counterpart, who adopted the same position)!! This experience helped us to become aware of the fact that in politics ideals were not the leading forces, and that other, often "non-public," factors were more powerful.

With respect to international problems, we became more and more consciously aware that the hopes of solving international conflicts through negotiation—hopes born with the establishment of the League of Nations, impelled by President Woodrow Wilson—were dying out and that Western Europe was heading towards an armed clash.

In the fall of 1935 the Italians concluded their conquest of Ethiopia, the first violent international aggression by a fascist government and, along with the reoccupation of the Rhineland by the Germans in 1936, a bitter failure of the League. Those failures were to be followed by the impotence to stop Italian and German interference in the Spanish Civil War and, later, to stop Hitler from occupying Austria (the Anschluss). On the international level, it seemed that the "Gangster's Law" was the only valid rule. This was confirmed by the Sino-Japanese conflict, which had started in 1933. All these developments culminated with the annexation of Czechoslovakia by the Germans after the conclusion of the Munich Agreement on 29 September 1938.

In their feelings about the impending war, Belgians were divided into more or less four factions:

(1) those who were unconditionally on the side of the Franco-British alliance.

(2) those who were "neutralists," but still somewhat in favor of the Franco-British, and who were ready to join the first group in the event of a German aggression.

(3) those who were "absolute neutralists."

(4) those who were, secretly or not, in favor of the Germans. Of these, there were two main subgroups:

— the Communists who became favorable to the Germans after the conclusion of the Russo-German agreement, 23 August 1939.

— those who were persuaded of the collapse of the European democratic systems and who were ready to use the Germans to establish a "new order." Later developments, after 1940, showed that the larger part of these had not fully understood the intrinsic dangers of Nazism. In fact, practically nobody had, at that time, fully understood the bases or the implications of the Nazi "philosophy," in particular their complete break with Christian thinking.

At the Cercle du Libre Examen we were practically all classified in the first two groups. As time went on the first group increased in numbers. Everybody, with the exception of the Communists, was on the side of the Finns after the USSR's aggression against them in the winter of 1939.

Our "childish" beliefs in Justice, in Freedom, in Democracy—that is, in parliamentary democracy—were badly damaged and finally crushed by what we were witnessing. Our governments did not behave as they said they would; they were weak; mediocrity was the only qualification that could be attached to most of our political leaders. On the other hand, the "fascist" governments were booking all the successes and seemed to be more apt to lead countries efficiently through bad weather: we had a tendency to forget that in a gangsters' world the first to break the rules wins, as had been demonstrated a century and a half earlier by Napoleon Bonaparte.

What were our hopes in case of a real armed clash between France, England, Belgium and the Netherlands on the one hand and, on the other, the Germans and Italians? We hoped that developments would be more or less similar to those of 1914–1918, including the participation of the USA.[2]

After May 10, 1940

May 10, 1940 was not a surprise, nor was the advance of the German Army. What *was* unexpected for the majority of us was the rapid collapse of the French Army and the crushing material superiority of the Germans.

After the retreat of the British forces to their islands, the surrender of the isolated Belgian Army on the 28th of May, and, less than two weeks later, of the French Army, what was also a surprise was the decent behavior of the German Army. We had been brought up with the idea that Germans were barbarians, whose army would behave like terrorists against civilians: as a consequence, in May 1940 the civilian population fled as far as it could. In fact, as soon as the military operation was finished the Germans behaved as politely as was possible in time of war. When rumor of this spread most of those who had fled returned to their homes as soon as possible, including the Jews.

Nevertheless the summer of 1940 was really a very bad moment for all of us: the prospect of a free Europe had died. The probable victory of the Germans seemed to be an unavoidable logical conclusion. All our youthful illusions were lost; all the democratic governments had failed; America was far away and apparently disinterested.

Then, four months later, for some of us a faint hope was brought by the victorious resistance of the British under the leadership of an old bull: Winston Churchill. And also, to a lesser extent, by the rebellion of a young French general, Charles de Gaulle. In any case, however, we could not be free again except at the end of a very long haul, perhaps never. The odds did not improve before the end of 1941 or the beginning of 1942: then, when the German Army had not succeeded in defeating the Soviet Army, a German defeat could logically be expected.

What happened to our group of *Les Cahiers du Libre Examen*? To understand the different behavior of each of us, one should remember the mood that prevailed at the time and the problems that had to be solved by each one of us.

It is easy, when you are not occupied by a foreign army, to tell how you should have behaved in those circumstances or, if you know the end of the story, to lay out a possible long-term policy. This was not our situation: we had to solve the practical, on-the-spot problem—how do we survive? how will we find food and how will we make the money needed to buy food, to rent shelter and to survive? The migration of the whole community was not feasible; there was no question of stopping one's economic activities because that would be a death sentence.

During the summer and fall of 1940 the whole of continental Western Europe had to face these problems and solve them. Whether you liked it or not, you had to resume economic activities in collaboration with the occupying forces—no possible escape! Only one choice remained: do I work just to survive and help my fellow citizens to survive, or do I collaborate with the occupying forces to help them reach a final victory, acquiring by my zeal political influence for myself and building, at the same time, a fortune? To write such a sentence is easy, but in day-to-day life it is not so simple to draw a borderline between the two. Any judgment *post factum* is easily biased and unfair. Extreme caution is necessary in judging precisely those cases that weren't at the extremes.

How did we react? Two extremes:

— Jean Burgers. A man of action and a born conspirator. He became the organizer and the leader of the "Group G"—*action et sabotage*. The group lost many members killed in action or put to death by the Germans. The group survived the war but Jean Burgers was arrested by the Gestapo, deported to the concentration camp of Buchenwald, and had his head cut off with an ax in 1945.

— Pierre de Ligne. An ambitious young man with a penchant for politics. Originally a Liberal, he was converted to socialism by Henri de Man and was sincerely attached to the idea of Belgium. Under the influence of Raymond de Becker, a convinced believer in the "new order," he became Administrative Director of *Le Soir*. De Becker and de Ligne thought that collaboration with the Germans was the price that had to be paid to guarantee that, after the war, some freedom would be left to a Belgian state under German rule. De Becker and de Ligne maintained their collaboration with *Le Soir* until [October] 1943, when they were expelled from their position by the Germans because they insisted on a proposal disapproving the policy of the Rexist leader, Léon Degrelle, a policy favoring the straightforward annexation of Belgium by the German Reich. After the war, in 1945–46, de Ligne was sentenced by a Belgian court-martial to 10 years in prison and the loss of his civil and political rights.(He has since been reinstated in his rights).[3]

As regards the others:

— Christian Lepoivre and Youra Livchitz[4] were active resistants: only the first survived.

— Edouard Colinet stayed in the southern part of France, participated in armed resistance to the Germans and survived.

— Adella Englert[5], Jacques Kupissonoff[6] and Marcel Sluszny[7], being Jews, had to hide, and had the luck to survive.

— Charles Dosogne[8] and Gilbert Jaeger[9] engaged in no conspicuous political activities and survived.

Paul de Man

I had a relatively close friendship with Paul de Man from 1937 until May 1940. I saw him practically every day and we spent at least an evening together each week. He was a profound, intelligent man, versed in art, literature, music and politics. Hypersensitive, normally self-controlled, he could have—rarely—short outbursts of anger and passion; sometimes he could be obstinate in his opinions. I would also say that he had a much greater human maturity than most of us, and that he could express himself in writings of great depth and sensitivity.

In spite of the possible influence of his uncle's ideas, he was neither Henri de Man's representative, nor the leader of the "demanist" faction in the association of socialist students at the ULB. He never occupied any of those positions, although he was, in 1944, falsely accused of having done so, and violently attacked in the periodical of the Fédération Bruxelloise des Etudiants Socialistes Unifiés.[10] Neither position would have fitted his psychological type.

Although Paul de Man had been raised in French, he was deeply rooted in Flemish culture, as were his uncle Henri and his cousin Jan, Henri's son. Paul felt particularly at ease with men educated in a germanic cultural frame. His main centers of interest in literature were in French, English and Flemish and, to a lesser extent, in German.

I should note that I was out of touch with Paul after I left Belgium in May of 1940. My information about his life during the war was collected—both after my return to Belgium in 1945 and recently—from mutual friends who had remained behind.

When the war began Paul was about twenty years old; he had not yet acquired any diploma on which he could base a professional career. The war had had disastrous effects on his father's business and he could not expect any significant material assistance from that side. He had to face everyone's problem: how to survive—and he had a wife and a young baby to care for. The only way to make some money that was open to him was to write a column (as a critic of music and literature) for a newspaper. There were only two newspapers written in French that were being published in Belgium at the time[11]—*Le Soir* and *Le Nouveau Journal,* both controlled by the Germans (as were all newspapers, periodicals and any printed matter). The latter was labelled "new-order" under the leadership of Robert Poulet; the former had a more "Belgian" reputation. I think that this is the reason that Paul chose to send his articles to *Le Soir*—but he was never a regular member of the editorial staff, as some have accused him of being. Probably two other factors—the influence of his uncle (who was advocating a more or less independent Belgian state in a Europe dominated by the "Deutsche Reich") and Paul's deep admiration for German culture—combined to inhibit any possible feelings of guilt for this "collaboration." On the other hand, Paul was convinced—as were the majority of Belgians at that time—that the Germans had won the war; it was unthinkable to destroy all economic life and not to resume cultural activities. We have also to keep in mind that the ULB (like the Université Catholique de Louvain) reopened its doors in the fall of 1940, accepting German supervision; eventually the ULB had to close a year later when the German censorship became unacceptable.

Paul de Man's collaboration with *Le Soir* had consequences: he could not refuse to write an article on the influence of Jewish authors on present-day French literature, an article published March 4, 1941 in the afternoon edition. All witnesses agree that he did it reluctantly, fearing to lose his livelihood.

I think one should sketch here the feelings vis-à-vis Jews in our country before and after May 1940. We have to be very cautious about the meaning of the words we shall use, as our readers should be when interpreting them. In Belgium antisemitism was never a violent feeling, nor a very common one. We would never support any action against Jews—such as excluding them from any social activity or concentrating them in ghettos, let alone sending them to concentration camps or to some territories outside our borders. To kill them because they were Jews would have been always, for us, an abomination. Even before Hitler's time, there was constant immigration into Belgium of Jews coming from East Germany, from Poland and a few from Russia. The feelings vis-à-vis Jews were different from place to place. In Brussels most of the established Jews were of the "assimilated" type. In Antwerp the situation was markedly different because, in addition to the established assimilated Jews, there existed (and still exists) a large colony of orthodox Jews who of their own free will agglomerated in a kind of "free ghetto" in the blocks surrounding Pelican Street: they speak Yiddish and wear orthodox clothing. We may sum up the diversity of feelings vis-à-vis Jews in Belgium by stating that there has never been in our country any antisemitic resentment matching the antisemitic feelings in Central Europe or even in France. Only in the vicinity of the large Jewish communities did there exist some feelings of rejection based on the fear of economic competition (remnants of the Great Depression) and based, psychologically, on the Christian myth that they were the people who had killed God. But even those feelings were never of a violent nature.

At the ULB antisemitic feelings were very unpopular and were resented as quasi-inhuman; it would not be fashionable to express them. Of the twelve members of the last *comité de rédaction* of the *Cahiers du Libre Examen,* four were Jews and one of them [Youra Livschitz] would be killed by the Germans because he was a Jew.

During the German occupation of Belgium, when we became aware that the Nazis arrested and deported Jews in large crowds, a quasi-general feeling of complicity developed in our country in favor of the Jews; many tried to help them to hide, even though we were aware of the serious danger involved in disobeying German regulations (if caught, you and your family could have been deported). Nevertheless, we didn't know at that time the monstrous and systematic extension of the Holocaust.

Even if, at the time, Belgian citizens indulged in denouncing people to the Germans, this was generally not based on antisemitic feelings, and the denunciations were not at all limited to Jews. Such behavior was a consequence of the deep moral degradation, at all levels, which develops in time of war and which, progressively, comes to "justify" individual violence.

Back to Paul de Man. In his article of March 4, 1941, Paul de Man adopted the thesis that, if contemporary French Jewish authors had not existed, the consequences for French literature would have been practically unnoticeable. This is the most severe of Paul's sins during those years, a sin that was more the consequence of a slight cowardice due to his fear of losing his livelihood than it was of any hostile feelings versus the Jews, feelings that nobody had ever noticed. We have to remember that during the same period Paul de Man was hiding Jewish friends in his home. One of them, whom I met recently, told me that she could not believe that Paul had any antisemitic feelings.[12]

Paul de Man put an end to his collaboration with *Le Soir* in 1942, mainly for financial reasons: he wished to secure a more stable and better-paid job. I think that many complementary factors may have been at work to produce that decision: a narrowing of the degree of freedom left to a columnist, even on artistic subjects; the concomitant warning of the Belgian government in London, that any collaboration with the Germans would be punished at the end of the war; finally, the departure of his uncle, who had ended his collaboration with the Germans, either for opportunistic reasons, or because he recognized that his fight in favor of a free Belgian state in a Europe dominated by the Germans was useless, or else because he realized that the Germans would in the end lose the war.

Whatever his reasons, Paul started work with the Messageries Dechenne—a distribution agency of printed matter (under German control)—and with the Editions de la Toison d'Or. Like all other publishers at the time, this one was officially under German supervision—there was no other choice. Paul occupied a third- or fourth-rank situation there, and was certainly not involved in any politically meaningful decisions on the part of the management.[13]

One other fact that has been held against Paul de Man is connected with another attempt to increase his earnings: the publication of his translations of two books by the Editions de la Toison d'Or—*Le soldat Johan* by Filip de Pillecijn and *Le double visage* by Paul Alverdes.[14] Both books have no explicit political flavor, but the two authors were known to be favorably inclined towards collaboration; de Pillecijn was head of the Flemish cultural council under the occupation, and Alverdes continued to publish in Germany throughout the war.

In the end Paul de Man left his employers to start his own publishing business—Editions Hermès—specializing in books on art, and, as he was a very poor businessman, he failed.

People who have not lived in Belgium or France during the days and months that followed the "libération" cannot imagine the unbelievable wave of hatred and revenge that broke over those countries. People like Pierre de Ligne and even the venial sinner Paul de Man could have been sentenced to death and executed. Some of their friends, as well as others who had followed similar paths, have been. It is important to notice that, even in those difficult circumstances, Paul de Man was never sent before any court of justice, although he was violently attacked in newspapers or periodicals during the last months of 1944. There is no publically available file concerning him at the Attorney General's office, as far as I could ascertain.

Paul de Man's psychology was such that I do not think he would have been ashamed of his collaboration with *Le Soir.*

This activity could not be recognized in his mind as a fault, even if it was a political mistake, an opinion to which he apparently adhered in 1944.

A number of reasons may be given for Paul de Man's decision to leave Belgium in 1948:
— on the material level, it would have been difficult for Paul to secure a decently paid job during those times of "patriotic" fervor and hatred, even if his "collaboration" had been too venial to bring him before a court-martial. In addition, because of the war, he had no university degree enabling him to start a career; and finally he was marked with the label "bankrupt" after the financial failure of his business, Editions Hermès. In Antwerp, especially among the commercial bourgeoisie, this qualification would have cut off any possibility of starting a new commercial venture.

These reasons could justify Paul in leaving Belgium and in trying to start anew somewhere else. But they are much too weak to explain Paul's complete flight from his past and from all his friends. In trying to develop a second line of reasons with deeper emotional implications, I came to the conclusion that they could have been the following:
— a profound disenchantment with the "archetypal" value of the German culture he had loved so much and which had symbolically failed in Treblinka and all the other extermination actions of the Nazis and their collaborators.
— a deep sadness about the fate of his uncle Henri de Man, the brilliant socialist thinker who alone had endeavored to develop a socialist theory freed of the errors of Marx, but who had committed the political mistake, during the first years of the German occupation, of honestly trying to save what was possible to save of the Belgian state, and who later had been judged the worst of all renegades by his former political friends, when they felt that the Germans were losing the war.
— a heartbreaking feeling when he was violently attacked (in the publication of the FBESU, 6 September 1944)[15] for his behavior from December 1940 to early 1943 by those of the orthodox Marxist-Leninist creed who, from August 1939 to June 1941, had unconditionally supported the Germans.
— a deep disenchantment upon observing the fact that the USSR's having been a powerful wartime ally was apparently sufficient to obliterate the memory of its pre-war sins—the Moscow trials, the Stalinists' slaughters in Russia and Spain, the shameless opportunism of the Russo-German agreement.
— a feeling of disgust as a consequence of the unscrupulous opportunism of those of his fellow-countrymen who had agreed to a mild collaboration with the Germans and who later rushed, as soon as they thought the Germans had lost the game, to take up a violently repressive attitude towards those who had been venial sinners, as well as towards those who had behaved criminally.

Joined together and amplified by Paul's acute sensitivity as well as by some family problems, these elements created a situation where life looked unbearable for him in Antwerp and he fled his past as completely as he could.

I think that the value of a work—scientific, literary, musical or artistic—has to be judged independently of the personality of the author, and any attempt at destroying it with ad hominem arguments is immoral, shameful and invalid. Anyway, I do not think that anybody has the right to try to destroy the good name of a renowned professor on the basis of a forty-year-old story about two venial charges:
— to have written criticism of works of literature, music or the plastic arts in *Le Soir* during the German occupation.
— to have published *once* an article with a slight antisemitic flavor, about the possible influence of Jewish authors on contemporary French literature—a misdeed that was largely made up for by the risks he took in hiding Jewish friends.

Unfortunately a well-intentioned researcher, working on a doctoral thesis about Paul de Man, has, through his inquiries, started up rumors about Paul's youthful activities during the war. Once these rumors had begun circulating, it became possible to ring the "antisemite" bell, and that "argument" has now been used to try to ruin Paul de Man's intellectual achievements. An *incomplete* description of the conditions in which these misdeeds were committed had, as a consequence, a more or less intentional overemphasizing of their implications: much ado about nothing.

I have tried, by describing Paul de Man's background and situation as unemotionally as possible, to put the facts in the correct perspective and to facilitate a more just evaluation of his actions.

[. . .]

Sincerely yours,
Edouard Colinet

Editors' Notes

(1) According to the historian Jacques Willequet, "discord erupted in the Cercle 'Le Libre Examen,' a student association which aimed at providing a forum for discussion open to all left-wing tendencies. They had agitated [*flambé*] for the SDN

against Mussolini, even more in support of the Spanish Republicans. Since then, the war in Europe had started and Belgium was neutral. So were the communists, after 23 August. Was it necessary to maintain our moral solidarity with Belgium's two great democratic neighbors, and advocate a socialist internationalism all the more illusory after its obvious failures, especially since the extreme-left had dissociated itself from it? Many were seduced by the *socialisme national* proposed by [Paul-Henri] Spaak and [Henri] de Man, attracted also by a progressivism which abandoned the old philosophico-religious divisions. The circle of marxist students [Etudiants Socialistes Unifiés], unified up until then, split: on the one hand, those socialists left hostage to the communists; and on the other hand, a new, resolutely demanian, socialist circle. At the 'Libre Examen,' the question went like this: did the communists, who had behaved like renegades, still deserve to be members? It was difficult, that is, a little comical, to discover that their thought was no longer *libre,* and that they obeyed Moscow's orders like robots. Nevertheless, this was the reason that was invoked for expelling them, even though the important demanian minority, the most hostile to the communists on doctrinal grounds, voted, on the contrary, to keep them in the circle, so as not to weaken the neutralist front. A number of them went on to work for the censored press, and one of them [Louis Fonsny] was even assassinated by the resistance." (*La Belgique sous la botte: Résistances et collaborations, 1940–1945*, Paris: Editions Universitaires, 1986, 46–47. For a somewhat different version of these events, see the articles quoted in note 10 below. According to Pierre de Ligne [conversation with Edouard Colinet, September 1988], the Stalinists were *not* supported by the "de Mannists" in the Libre Examen vote on their expulsion.)

(2) In a letter of 23 May 1988, to the Director of the Centre de Recherches et d'Etudes Historiques de la Second Guerre Mondiale, Edouard Colinet adds that "the activity of the Cercle continued unabated through March 1940. During the winter of 1939–40, numerous demonstrations in favor of Finland and against the USSR took place (marches in the street, organization of film screenings and soirées, etc.). We were even able to collect the sums necessary to send a light ambulance to Finland (at a cost of 75,000 Belgian francs, a considerable amount for us at that time). This anti-Hitler and anti-Soviet agitation was such that Rector Frans van den Dungen found it necessary to reprimand us for it."

Colinet recalls that he succeeded Pierre de Ligne, "at that time a member of the Etudiants Socialistes," as president of the Cercle in "October 1939 (de Ligne, called up for military service,

was obliged to resign), and I remained in charge until the elections of April 1940." He also recalls that of the 3500 students at the ULB, some 1400–1600 were members of the Cercle du Libre Examen at that time, of whom around 100 took voting parts in the group's general assemblies.

(3) In a letter of 28 July 1988, Pierre de Ligne writes: "In fact, it was my wife and Anaïde who were friends first. As of July 1939 I was called up for military service, and I resigned the presidency of the Cercle du Libre-Examen and lost contact with the group during the period when positions were being taken in the student milieu for or against the politics of independence (with regard to the great powers) of H.M. King Leopold III, supported by his minister Spaak.

"[. . .]

"We knew Paul at the cercle du L.E. and we spent evenings, from time to time, with Paul, Anaïde, her first husband Gilbert Jaeger, and other friends. Given our wives' friendship, our relationship continued after May 1940.

"I never met Paul at *Le Soir,* and I was even surprised to find his signature there, which suggests to me that he was rather secretive.

"I do not know if it was Paul who proposed this literary column to Raymond de Becker, the editor-in-chief, or if it was he who solicited Paul. His work at the Editions de la Toison d'Or is explained by the fact that it was the same de Becker who directed it.

"The criteria 'resistant' or 'collaborator' did not enter into, as far as I can tell, Paul's choices of social or intellectual relationships. He was of a nature opposed to political militancy and engagement. That said, he was certainly not a 'resistant,' and in the ignorance—as we all were—of what was happening in the concentration camps, he did not have an 'allergic reaction' to the Germans or to a certain collaboration, such as that promoted by his uncle Henri de Man.

"Paul's work for *Le Soir* was absolutely exterior, 'free-lance'; he was completely unknown to the editors.

"Actually, if Paul was interrogated by the military court—not by the *auditeur* handling the case of *Le Soir*—and not charged, that, given the severity of the repression of intellectual collaboration in Belgium, seems to me to prove the non-political character of his writings, of his professional activities, and of his behavior in the years 40–44."

(4) Youra Livschitz (1917–1944), whose articles appear in both *Jeudi* and the *Cahiers du Libre Examen,* completed his medical studies at the ULB just before the war. On 19 April 1943 he and two other members of the resistance stopped a train

headed for Auschwitz (the twentieth such convoy); in the ensuing fire fight, a number of deportees escaped. Livschitz was arrested shortly thereafter, held at the S.S.concentration camp at Breendonck, north of Brussels, and executed there 17 February 1944. (See Maxime Steinberg, *Le Dossier Bruxelles-Auschwitz* [Brussels: Comité Belge de Soutien . . . , 1980], 151–152 and 159, and Marcel Liebman, *Né Juif* [Paris-Gembloux: Duculot, 1977], 95–99.)

(5) In a letter to Peggy Kamuf (July 1988), Adella (Englert) Kay writes: "Paul de Man and I were part of a small group of friends who met frequently, at one or another's houses, during the 'drôle de guerre.' But at a certain moment (it seems to me, although my memories are a bit vague, that it was the situation I found in September 1940, upon my return from the 'exodus'), the composition of the group had changed and Paul de Man was no longer part of it. For us he had become a collaborator, and we had crossed him out. We were very young and intransigent and it must be said that the situation hardly lent itself to nuances." Mme.Kay also recalled a visit, in November 1940, to the house where Gilbert Jaeger, Anaïde Baraghian and Paul de Man were living: Anaïde came to the door and told her to leave quickly because the Gestapo was there. It was a "perquisition." She and others of the group were at high risk and indeed some were arrested. She had no contact with Paul de Man after 1940.

Colinet adds (in a letter of 10 August 1988) that "all the students who had engaged in 'political' activity during the years preceding May 1940 were subjected to questioning by the Gestapo. Even Pierre de Ligne was questioned, in spite of the fact that he was, at the time, one of the managers of *Le Soir*; the Gestapo seemed to be unaware of the fact. After questioning, a few were held in custody for some days or weeks."

(6) Jacques Kupissonoff wrote essays on film in *Jeudi* and the *Cahiers du Libre Examen*. In 1945, the Antwerp publishing house Helicon published a book prefaced by him called *Les plus belles images du cinéma,* a collection of still photographs from European and American films (a Flemish version titled *Filmbeelden Uit Heden En Verleden* was published in 1946). The title page identifies its author as Georges Lambrichs. But, according to Lambrichs (conversation with Peggy Kamuf, 1 July 1988, Paris), he had had nothing to do with the book—his name had simply been placed on it by Paul de Man, who ran a small publishing firm in Antwerp immediately after the war, which Lambrichs recalled as the one which published *Les plus belles images*. In 1945, Helicon also published a Flemish translation of Herman Melville's *Moby Dick*. Paul de Man later spoke of having translated *Moby Dick,* and although the Helicon volume does not in-clude the name of its translator, a number of Paul de Man's friends—including Walter Van Glabbeek of Antwerp (telephone conversation, July 1988)—recall that this edition was de Man's work. The printer of the Helicon books is identified as "J.-E. Buschmann, Antwerpen," Paul's uncle Jan Buschmann with whom he later founded Editions Hermès.

(7) Marcel Sluszny, after finishing his studies at the ULB, became a lawyer in 1941 and practiced law in Brussels throughout the occupation. In a conversation (Brussels, 23 June 1988), he explained that this was possible because only one of his parents was Jewish: half-Jews (if they were Belgian citizens, and if they did not practice their religion, and if they were not married to a Jew) were not officially classed as Jews. He added that he nevertheless "lived a very retired life" during most of the war. In January 1941, however, when students at the ULB boycotted the lectures of a professor who had been brought in to teach from Cologne, a number of former student activists were arrested by the Gestapo. Sluszny was among them, and remained in jail for three months. That, he added, was no doubt why he had not read Paul de Man's article about the Jews when it appeared in March of 1941. He finds it, now, "very astonishing," because it did not correspond to anything he observed in his personal relations with de Man, whom he thought of as a "liberal, open person, *un brave garçon*" who had never concealed his friendships during the war.

(8) Charles Dosogne, who had met Paul de Man in 1938–39, selected him as *directeur* of the *Cahiers du Libre Examen* when Dosogne left that position in January 1940. Dosogne writes, in a letter of 11 January 1988, that "the group of friends who made up the editorial board and actually produced the *Cahiers* included a certain number of Israelites. Still, in our day-to-day relations, there was never a question of antisemitism, to which we were all opposed."

On the question of Paul de Man's political sympathies, Dosogne writes: "It is necessary first of all to exclude, where Paul de Man is concerned, the hypothesis of a formal adherence to National Socialism: that would have been in profound contradiction with his personality, which was made up of complex and highly nuanced tendencies. That said, it must be recalled that Paul de Man was Flemish and that, despite the breadth of his culture, he felt himself to be, in his words, 'very Germanic,' and so, found himself relatively at ease in a milieu where the Germanic influence was, under the occupation, preponderant."

After describing the "ideological context" in which Paul de Man began to write for *Le Soir* and *Het Vlaamsche Land*, Dosogne adds that, "beginning at the end of September 1940, preliminary censorship by the Propaganda Abteilung was limited to important political articles. Literary columns were thus exempted from this, at least until August 1942—date at which censorship was reestablished. It was about this time that Paul de Man's activities as a journalist ceased." (Paul de Man's last article in *Le Soir* appeared in November 1942.)

Dosogne insists that "the personal situation of Paul de Man influenced his decision. He found himself at twenty years old, with a young wife and a baby, without a university degree, during a period of governmental disorganization, all of which did not permit him to aspire to a paying job. All he had going for him was his vast culture and his great intelligence, which he was able to take advantage of by accepting what some of his connections proposed: an association with *Le Soir* and the *Vlaamsche Land*."

Friends with de Man "from 1938 to 1947," he continued to see him throughout the war, when de Man and his family would visit Dosogne and his wife, Frida Vandervelden, for stays, "sometimes of several weeks, in our country house." On the basis of this intimacy, "I can affirm that never, neither before nor during the war, did either the words or the attitudes of Paul de Man permit one to suspect him of antisemitic opinions—opinions, let it be said in passing, which would have put an end to our relations. Racism was in fundamental contradiction with his profoundly human nature and the universal character of his mind. That is why I remain deeply skeptical concerning the remarks 'with antisemitic resonances' cited by the *New York Times* that could be imputed to him. Is there not room to ask certain questions concerning a document that does not figure among *Le Soir*'s own collection, and, on the copy to be found at the Bibliothèque Albertine, is marked by three asterisks? Why??"

(Some of these questions have been answered by the discovery that *Le Soir*'s original claim (in an article on 3 December 1987) that it could not find this article in its archives has turned out to be mistaken. The article, and the full page on which it appeared, were indeed published, on 4 March 1941. The three asterisks there refer only to the particular edition of that day's paper, not to the article's authorship.)

(9) Gilbert Jaeger, first husband of Anaïde Baraghian and a fellow student at the ULB, who shared an apartment with Paul de Man in 1940, writes (letter of 9 January 1988) "Paul de Man's taking a job at *Le Soir* ought to be attributed, I think, to his need to earn a living, and not at all to any ideological preoccupations or orientations." Of the article on "The Jews in Contemporary Literature," he writes, "I seem to recall that this was an article that Paul de Man was asked to write. For him, it was

an exercise—probably a very disagreeable one—in what you call 'skating on thin ice.' I have no reason to believe that Paul de Man was antisemitic."

(10) This was in the first legal issue of *Debout* (organ of the Fédération Bruxelloise des Etudiants Socialistes Unifiés) which was published in Brussels on 6 September 1944, within days of the liberation of the city. Under the title "Et voici, l'élite' de l'ULB." (p.3), this article denounces, among others

PAUL DE MAN—nephew of Henri. Leader of the demannists (obviously) at the University. Introduced by his very dear uncle to the self-proclaimed 'Soir' of Schraenen-de Becker, he dissects novels and essays in literary *chroniques* as unreadable as those he wrote in the *Cahiers du Libre Examen*. After a while, he senses that things are taking a bad turn and he beats a very prudent retreat. His name no longer appears in the columns of the self-proclaimed 'Soir.' The poor little carcass of this little man, blond and frail, with his lock of hair à la Hitler, deserts the Place de Louvain. But in compensation Henri's nephew receives from his fascist friends the position of editor at Belgapress. [*Le Soir*'s offices were at the Place de Louvain; "Belgapress" seems to be an error for the Agence Dechenne.]

A similar denunciation had earlier appeared in *L'Etudiant* 3, the wartime clandestine journal of the same Etudiants Socialistes Unifiés at the ULB, in September 1941, soon after Germany's invasion of Russia had realigned Belgian Communists with the anti-Nazi resistance. Entitled "Guignol à l'ULB" (p.4), it attacked four of that same "élite," and reads, in part:

Out of 2800 students, there are four! Four who slavishly lick the Germans' boots. . . .

Four! out of 2800, who have such a magnificent opinion of themselves that they find themselves writing that wisdom seems to bring the youth of the university to these just and grandiose conceptions of reality on the march.

Four! [Pierre] de Ligne, [Paul] de Man, [Louis] Fonsny, [Jean] Barthélemy. . . .

De Man (Paul), feverish, restless, his look more haggard than ever, sought out his uncle the day after the war and emerged from the meeting with a political position [*opinion*], which to believe it eternal would be to predict presumptuously the constancy of De Man (Henri).

. . . But for us Etudiants Socialistes Unifiés, the sad nomenclature listed above [i.e.the four names] is not without political significance—remember that these four marionettes were among the fierce protagonists of the campaign waged against our group and our members. Remember that Fonsny and De Man were both members of the *comité de direction* of the already ex-group of *Etu-*

diants Socialistes which formed the base for the schism of the socialist forces at the university; that De Ligne was president of the [Cercle du] Libre Examen when a large part of our comrades were excluded from said group; and Barthélemy would only work with the Libre Examen on the condition of our being expelled.

Paul de Man was also denounced, along with 43 other journalists of *Le Soir (volé),* in a pamphlet published in the fall of 1943 by the resistance newspaper *L'Insoumis* entitled "*Galerie des Traitres,* 1ère série, Dans l'antre du *Soir-Erzatz*." Next to a photograph of him taken from *Le Soir* of 8 July 1942, the text reads:

DEMAN, Paul, living at Rue du Musée, 10, in Bruxelles. Correspondant for de Becker's *Le Soir*. Nephew and godson of Henri Deman. This individual knows who to stick with. Was placed at *Le Soir* by his godfather and thanks to his energetic propaganda succeeded in staying there.

Note that the address given is that of the Editions de la Toison d'Or, and that de Man had ceased writing for *Le Soir* in November of the previous year.

(11) Raymond Rifflet, a contemporary of Paul de Man at the ULB, writes (letter of 10 February 1988) of the widespread feeling that the Germans had definitively won the war: "I myself joined the university resistance at about this time, and from then on was well-placed to know that there were very few of us who believed in any other outcome, right up to the moment that the United States itself entered the war. To my knowledge, Paul de Man never 'collaborated,' but it is likely that the defeatist atmosphere of the time and the attitude of his illustrious uncle, combined with the fact that he was himself very young, could have caused in him confusion sufficient to explain certain regrettable acts, even if I don't myself think of them as serious. He no doubt felt marvellously relieved, like many others, when the first of Hitler's defeats renewed a reasonable hope."

(12) These sentences refer to, among others, Esther and Nahum Sluszny. In a telephone conversation (27 June 1988, Brussels), Esther Sluszny recalled the episode: Sometime in 1942 or 1943, she and her husband found themselves accidentally locked out of the apartment where they had been hiding, and on the streets of Brussels long after the curfew. They took refuge with Anaïde Baraghian and Paul de Man, who sheltered them for several days, until they could get back into their apartment. "I can guarantee you," she added, "that he was not anti-semitic."

Another Jewish friend, Georges Goriely, writes (letter of 18 November 1987): "I had relations that I would characterize as friendly, and in any case, fairly continuous, with Paul de Man between 1938 and 1947, in Brussels at first and in Antwerp between 1945 and 1947.

[. . .]

"I insist on being fair with regard to his collaboration: he had no ideological sympathies with the *Ordre nouveau*. He knew about my life and my clandestine activities and I never had any hesitations [*inquiétudes*] about expressing my views to him, which, in addition, he never contested.

"In fact, his was not a political mind [*esprit*]. It was simply that an occasion presented itself for a young man of about twenty to become the literary critic for a newspaper with a large circulation and which certainly paid its contributors well. The few texts which emanated from his pen and which went in the direction of the *Ordre nouveau* expressed primarily his opportunism [. . .] and his profound lack of moral conscience rather than any ideological choice.

"His relations with his uncle, Henri de Man, who had moreover left Belgium by the beginning of 1942, were correct. Paul knew the writings of his illustrious relative very well (we often discussed them together), but he was influenced very little by them."

(13) Georges Lambrichs (conversation with Peggy Kamuf, 1 July 1988, Paris) reports that Paul de Man found him a job at the Agence Dechenne in 1942, which he held until his dismissal in 1943 for his role in the publication of an issue of the journal *Messages,* called *Exercice du silence*.

According to Georges Goriely (conversation, 23 June 1988, Brussels), de Man's position as *lecteur* at the Editions de la Toison d'Or enabled him to hire as translators people who needed work but could not legally obtain it, including Goriely himself. Goriely also reports that his friend Hilda Rosner was one of those hired by de Man. Her name, anagrammatically transposed as "H. Rensor," appears as the translator of Max Dauthendey's *Le jardin sans saisons* (Brussels: Toison d'Or, 1943). Mme. Rosner confirmed (conversation with Moshe Ron, July 1988, Kibbutz Givat Haim, Israel) that she was in fact responsible for this translation and that de Man was aware that she was Jewish. It is also probable that de Man commissioned the French translation of Filip de Pillecijn's *Hans von Malmédy* (Brussels: Toison d'Or, 1943) by Georges Lambrichs and Marie-José Hervijns.

(14) The original editions of these books were: Paul Alverdes, *Das Zwiegesicht* (München: Langen und Müller, 1937), and Filip de Pillecijn, *De Soldaat Johan* (Amsterdam: Van Kampen, 1941).

Paul de Man also translated, with Jean-Jacques Etienne, the German art historian A.E. Brinckmann's *Esprit des Nations* (Brussels: Toison d'Or, 1943). This book was originally published as *Geist der Nationen: Italiener-Franzosen-Deutsche* (Hamburg: Hoffman und Campe, 1938), in the series "Europa-Bibliothek" edited by Erich Brandenburg, Erich Rothacker, Friedrich Stieve, and I. Tönnies.

According to Boris Rousseeuw, in his *Van hier tot Peking: Over Willem Elsschot* (Antwerp: Dedalus, 1983), de Man also translated the Flemish author Gerard Walschap's *Genezing door aspirine*. This book was published in 1943 by Snoeck-Ducaju, Ghent, both in Flemish and in a French version, *Cure d'Aspirine,* with illustrations by René de Pauw. The French translation, which says "traduit par Willem Elsschot," was in fact done by de Man, writes Rousseeuw, after the noted Flemish writer Elsschot's version was not accepted. "Het Frans van Elsschot kon er echt niet mee door, vond men. Paul de Man, toen student, moest dan maar een nieuwe vertaling make maar om Elsschot niet te kwetsen zette men toch zijn naam er onder" (p.25).

(15) FBESU is the acronym of the Fédération Bruxelloise des Etudiants Socialistes Unifiés, which published *L'Etudiant* and *Debout*. See note 10 above.

Journals, Politics

Notes on Paul de Man's Wartime Journalism

WERNER HAMACHER

And thanks to Tom

November 12, 1987

These early newspaper articles of de Man cannot be read without considering their uses, both then and now. The articles themselves were composed for immediate consumption, daily commodities with relatively small ideological mobility. Utterly political. Despite the control they exercise over it, the vocabulary of the time is virtually never scrutinized or redefined. Their stereotypes, along with the models of thought they propagate, belong among the most appalling products of the century. A cultivated wasteland in which *anything* can happen. Frightening.

These articles enter their second phase of use, now. Without further ado, the signature they bear will be taken as that of de Man's later texts, and they will be turned to use against everything he later wrote. But we ought to ask whether this use does not indicate a *need*—and what is it, today, this need for horror as a polemical tool?

December 12, 1987

The journal is not a form of the fragmentary. Comparable in this only to the aphorism, it is the form of literary perfection under the threat of fragmentation. It registers the completeness of one, and yet another, and still another day gone by, a day that for this individual diarist might find no repetition and renewal in a next day. The diarist is in the situation of the skeptic who is no longer absolutely sure that the sun will rise again in the morning; and the habit of expecting it to do so has become just as doubtful to him as the certainty that the truths of today will still be valid tomorrow. The entry of one day stands for no other. Each is written from the perspective of the absolute disaster—that it cannot be continued, revised, renewed, or outdone. The diarist's every word could be his last. Thus in the form of the diary—and in every related form, from the aphorism to the newspaper article—the absolute skepticism about the durability of the written word and its meaning is intertwined with an astonishing optimism that demonstrates itself more in the compactness and conciseness of its linguistic expression than in its contents: since each entry could be the last, everything that comes together in it must appear under the aspect of its perfection, that is, of closure and finality. The world and language of the journal are finished. Its words are no longer intended for someone else, not even for the writer—thus the diary's appearance of empty interiority, thus the newspaper's merely formal, abstract public aspect, thus the pathos of the obsessively detailed realism of both. The diarist and the journalist write less as clerks of their own interior life, or of political history and its ideological overlay, than as clerks of the last word that can be pronounced on their experiences and their world. Where they appear as psychologists, anecdote collectors, critics or propagandists, they do so in order to signal an extreme danger—the danger of their own end. Journalists and diarists are prophets of their deadline. Their *métier* is catastrophes—preferably those affecting their audience and themselves. They are the realists of the last days, notorious prophets of the apocalypse. Their criticism promises: we are at a critical point in our history, at a zero-meridian (the diarist Ernst Jünger's phrase), we write and act along the border between two ages. They are without exception the diagnosticians of crisis who propagate the politics of decision. "Souverän ist, wer über den Ausnahmezustand entscheidet."—"That person is sovereign who decides on the state of emergency." This formula from Carl Schmitt, the friend of Ernst Jünger, proves itself first of all, even if not otherwise, in the manner in which it is presented. With the definition, aperçu, aphorism, the theorist of the state sets himself up as the linguistic sovereign over the parliamentary confusion of words. Schmitt's formula defines first of all itself. Which is how and why it fascinates. But it also defines the gesture that characterizes the war diaries of Jünger, as well as the rhetoric of decision in war- and catastrophe-journalism, in propaganda. For this journalism as well always speaks of itself as if it were the last word, speaks of itself as the deciding, judging and executing word by which the newspaper becomes an appearance of the Day of Judgment. Schmitt's formula is the formula of the journal: prior to whatever cognitive content it claims to have, whatever political effect it actually has, it is first of all a defensive formula. In every case, the danger to which the sovereign decision responds is undecidability. Only with this decision does the realm of decidability open. The journalist, in his function as critic, or the diarist, who notes the last word on the occurrences of the day, defines the danger, wards off the threat of indefinite events, and installs himself and his word as the last sovereign of his short epoch.

January 4, 1988

In 1943, under the title "Responsabilité des Ecrivains," Roger Caillois has 'Philippe' and 'Ariste' carry on a dialogue in the pseudo-classical style. It was published in 1946, together with some other short pieces on contemporary history, in the volume *Circonstantielles*. The dialogue concerns the issue of literary collaboration, for which the names Chardonne and Montherlant are introduced elsewhere as examples.

—*Nous avons, Philippe, des écrivains à Paris qui collaborent avec l'ennemi, aident à sa propagande, répandent ses arguments, diffusent sa doctrine. Il faudra les punir. (. . . .) Sincères ou non, ils nuisent tout autant. Au reste, je ne peux pas le savoir et peu importe. Ils trahissent. Cela suffit. Aussi doivent-ils payer comme les autres.*

—*Je connais ce langage. C'est celui des nazi contre Thomas Mann, contre Einstein, contre Ernst Erich Noth, contre tant d'autres qu'ils accusèrent semblablement de trahir la communauté nationale allemande parce qu'ils ne pensaient pas comme eux. Ne parliez-vous pas alors de crimes, de barbarie, de péchés contre l'esprit? (. . . .) Vous n'aviez pas assez de mots pour condamner les mesures que vous demandez aujourd'hui qu'on prenne. Vraiment il ne vous manque plus, pour parfaire la ressemblance, que de découvrir que ces traîtres sont en outre juifs ou albinos ou hémophiles.*

—*Vous vous moquez, Philippe. Vous savez assez ce que je pense.*

—*Mais je découvre comment vous le pensez.* (83–84)

The mode of thought that Philippe discovers in Ariste is that of loyalty to and betrayal of the *communauté nationale*. Ariste has to invoke this national community in order to assert the demand to punish the collaborators, but by doing so he simultaneously invokes the principle of national community followed by the Nazis. The logic of both communities' thought is the logic of nationality. It can appear as logic, as a consistent mode of thought, because it makes the claim that the nation, the national community, is itself a homogeneous and substantial form not only of that which has been thought, but of thought itself. Therefore nationalism is a substantialism—a substantialism of community conceived of as nature. But while, as substantialism, it must claim universal validity, as social naturalism it bears a merely mimetic relationship to every other nationalism. That is why Philippe can speak of *semblablement* and *ressemblance*. Thus the pretended substantialism in the mode of thought of the *communauté nationale* is an effect of mimesis, in which the identity of the one nation always already defines itself in accordance with the form of the other, only to challenge simultaneously its singularity in a fight to the death. Nationalism is an agonism. It draws its life not from the natural community of a nation, but rather from the will to destroy the other, in whose image it is at the same time supposed to be created. The logic of nationalism is the logic of homicidal, suicidal identification.

One of the most glaring cases in which the logic of national identity is executed is that of the collaborator who, while in one nation, takes sides with the other: he must be "punished," that is "removed," in order to reconstitute the integrity of the social body. But this logic of nationality is only confirmed in the case of the collaborator because it has not succeeded with him: in him the *communauté nationale* turns against itself as that which is foreign. This is the Nazi mode of thought 'Philippe' discovers in the opponent of the Nazis. He emphasizes that what is done to the collaborators could also, by the same "logic," be done to "Jews, albinos and hemophiliacs"—even if it is executed by anti-fascists—because all of them are said not to conform to the law of the national, natural and normal community.

Caillois does not succumb to the temptation of stylizing the collaborator as the martyr and hero of an "other" society. His goal is to free anti-fascism from the mimetic paroxysm into which it falls in the face of fascism. "Je suis leur ennemi pour différer d'eux, non pour leur ressembler" (86).

But his own recommendation for dealing with collaborators also remains obedient to the principle of mimesis: "Je veux qu'ils soient punis par où ils ont péché" (87). Thus the cynical grimace of his own—but already no longer his own—language in quoting the Nazi list, "Jews, albinos and hemophiliacs."

December 17, 1987

At issue in all of what I can note down here is the question of what it was in the historical situation of Belgium and in the ideological situation of the Belgian intelligentsia in the years 1939–1944 that made possible articles like those de Man wrote for *Le Soir* and *Het Vlaamsche Land*—especially the one on "Jews in Contemporary Literature" and the one on Chardonne. What was it that—I do not say, 'motivated,' such articles as these and others, not 'motivated,' for this constellation, like any other, could have also motivated entirely different, less disastrous, and counter-disastrous articles, but rather, I ask—what was it that *did not prevent* such articles? Only when it is asked in this way is the question not already a question about a hidden determinism to which the intellectuals of that time would have fallen victim; and only when asked in this way does the question give the answer a chance to isolate factors in the situation of intellectuals that would still, even today, not prevent a comparable commitment to a no less disastrous politics.

So what were, in detail, those political (social-, language-and literature-political) motifs of thought that did not prevent his commitment to a series of fascist ideologemes and their practical realization?

These motifs, it seems to me, cannot be regarded as genuinely totalitarian when considered independently of their respective historical and ideological contexts. They are all ideologemes that develop their totalitarian potential only when they enter into a close association with related ideologemes. This is the case with the evolutionary model of history de Man

promulgated in those years; it is the case with the idea of European unity that even socialists who felt not the slightest sympathy for a pan-Germanic dictatorship advocated between the world wars; it is also the case with the decision-compulsion of journalistic discourse, which is not necessarily incompatible with relatively liberal positions; and it is even the case with the emphatic nationalism that de Man supports in his articles. In all of these ideologemes a pronounced tendency to the hierarchization and monopolization of certain social and political forces is virulent. But these ideologemes do not become a real danger until the historical moment when they are fused and put into the service of a political power held to be uncontrollable, or of an historical development sanctioned as necessary. As long as they have not yet joined together like words in a syntactic formation, they can still be turned against their own totalitarian tendencies and even, from case to case, against a fascist system's claim to power. This ambidexterity of ideologemes—which has still not ceased to be a social and political problem of the first order, since we are far from having put the fascisms behind us and since nothing is more necessary than analyzing, with the greatest vigilance, their elements on all levels and in all their varieties—this ambidexterity of ideologemes can perhaps best be studied with regard to the subject of nationalism as it is thematized and used in de Man's articles. It is the ideologeme he employs most pervasively, the one that, manifestly or latently, as a background-ideologeme or as an explicit theme, accompanies his entire career as a journalist with *Le Soir* and *Het Vlaamsche Land*. And since it is so extremely loaded, both politically and aesthetically, we need to clarify the particular Belgian situation in which de Man wrote and determine the extent of his collaboration with the Nazi ideology. In determining that extent we will also be able to tell where de Man, in his complicity with the occupant, set a limit to it.

July 15, 1988

A number of articles were recently discovered that de Man contributed in November 1939 and January 1940 to *Jeudi,* a short-lived newspaper published by the "Cercle du Libre Examen," a socialist, but after the Hitler-Stalin pact decidedly anti-Stalinist, student organization at the Université Libre de Bruxelles. Two of these pieces give a fairly clear picture of de Man's political convictions in the period before the Nazi invasion of Belgium. Both represent a defense of the Belgian policy of neutrality and both at the same time leave no doubt that German politics, which he calls "imperialist," represent an acute threat to Belgium. After de Man has made clear *que la responsabilité de la guerre incombe à l'Allemagne,* and that there is agreement on standing up *pour la cause des démocraties, contre les dictatures,* he discusses the possibilities of Belgian politics between the power blocs of Nazi Germany and the Allies. Although he ascertains *qu'on craint, à juste titre, une tentative d'invasion par les troupes allemandes,* he opts for the neutralist policy of the Belgian government, because an alliance with England and France would hardly increase the weight carried by the Western powers and would not contribute to the withdrawal of Nazi troops, now protected by the pact with Stalin, from the East and particularly from Poland. What in his view also speaks against an alliance with England and France is that the two great Western democracies have flagrantly neglected their international obligations in the collapse of planned sanctions against fascist Italy and through non-intervention in Spain (a fact that de Man, with great reserve, calls *bien entendu, profondément regrettable*), and that, in the case of a Nazi invasion of Belgium, further neglect of their democratic obligations is to be expected from these relatively stable democracies. He rejects the communist demand, *dès qu'on est anti-hitlérien il faut necessairement entrer en guerre,* with the pacifist argument that for Belgium—*un petit peuple indépendent*—certainly a defensive war, but no *guerre idéologique,* is legitimate; but it is clear that de Man claims for himself as well the supposition, *qu'on est anti-hitlérien.* While the Belgian perspective is decisive in this "Défense de la Neutralité"—the title of the article of November 9, 1939, i.e., two months after the allied Western powers' declaration of war on Nazi Germany—the article of January 4, 1940, written four months before the invasion of Holland and Belgium and carrying the title "Que pensez-vous de la guerre?," concentrates on the tasks that would follow upon an Allied victory over Germany; the possibility of a Nazi victory is *not* brought into consideration. De Man justifies the Allies' declaration of war thus: *On se trouvait bel et bien devant une volonté de colonisation intra-européenne, qui était une forme des plus caractéristiques d'impérialisme naissant, et qui d'ailleurs ne se cachait pas. (. . .) D'un point de vue purement anti-impérialiste, ce serait une grave erreur de tactique d'admettre une paix immédiate, laissant à Hitler un immense bénéfice moral et matériel. Entre deux impérialismes il faut choisir le moindre, et bien l'anglais, ne fut-ce que parce qu'il est le plus facile à combattre.* But after he has approvingly quoted the English battle cry, "*we must crush hitlerisme,*" de Man adds that a merely military victory will not suffice; in order to win the war against national-socialist imperialism, he argues, the *grounds* for this war have to be removed. He explains that the inability of the democratic states to eliminate unemployment and satisfy basic needs is to be blamed for the attraction of the *mystiques total-*

itaires; as long as a fundamental reorganization of the economy has not been accomplished, poverty will prevail, which has repeatedly favored fascist movements and thus threatens to render war a "periodic phenomenon." Even if the conditions of 1930 were restored after a victory over Nazi Germany, those conditions would thus be restored in which Mussolini could say, *l'état de guerre est l'état normal et usuel.* Besides the necessity of economically reorganizing the democratic states—which in this context is also probably meant to indicate capitalist states—de Man emphasizes another necessity: that of a practical critique of the *esprit nationaliste.* He writes: *Le problème* (by which he means the problem of international relations) *est insoluble si on le considère dans un état d'esprit nationaliste aussi longtemps qu'on reste persuadé qu'un pays doit mépriser ses voisins, s'isoler économiquement, s'agrandir au dépens des faibles et réaliser une domination mondiale.* Thus, going by the political position de Man defends at the beginning of 1940, probably in agreement with his socialist friends from the "Cercle du Libre Examen," the war against Nazi Germany only makes sense if the military battle is continued and extended in a *revirement total dans la politique extérieure et intérieure de tous les pays européens*—which we can translate as meaning: a pan-European anti-imperialist and anticapitalist revolution is the only way to crush hitlerism. In this process the standpoint of nationalism need not be surrendered, but must be changed in the sense that no nation can any longer claim a prerogative over another. Only then would Europe—thus I continue to translate—be a free confederation of socialist nations and the Western European war beginning now, in 1940, not be a *carnage épouvantable et stérile.*

December 17, 1987

In the September 1, 1941 article in *Le Soir,* entitled "Le destin de la Flandre," de Man gave one of the most programmatic descriptions of his political-aesthetic theory of nationality. It represents his response to the 'journées culturelles germano-flamandes' organized in Ghent (Gand) by De Vlag—the collaborationist *Deutsche-Flämische Arbeitsgemeinschaft*—on which he had given a short report in *Le Soir* of August 16–17. According to that first report, *De Vlag*'s event was intended to present as complete a picture of Flemish cultural life as possible to the so-called (and thus clearly euphemized) German 'guests' (*invités allemands*), to demonstrate the need for an economic reorganization of the Flemish regions, and to make clear that Flanders' regionalist fight for independence (to use the words of Elias, Ghent's mayor and V.N.V. representative, which are reported without commentary) now places all hopes of victory in the *collaboration avec le Reich allemand*.

In "Le destin de la Flandre," there is no longer any talk of such *collaboration*. De Man's article is concerned with the definition of 'nation'—here particularly the Flemish nation —in terms of aesthetic theory, and with the political requirements following from it in the current historical situation. For in de Man's definition, a nation is an art-nation. Only that population of a country is entitled to be called a nation that has produced its own culture and, more precisely, an art that is characteristic of it alone. While the title of 'culture' is bestowed on the abstract generality of knowledge and thus without differentiation on the entire civilized world, only art, which arises out of the *émotion subjective* and is focussed *directement à (la) sensibilité*, demonstrates the *personnalité* of an entire collective and thus, as an *empreinte nationale*, makes a people worthy of being respected as a nation (*nationalité digne d'être respectée*). A nation does not so much find its expression in art; rather, only through its art does it receive the stamp that makes it a nation. If, as de Man would have us believe, the essence of a nation lies in its art, if a nation is thus in the strictest sense an art-essence, then all ethical and political legal entitlements that are expressed in talk about respect and cultural autonomy are grounded in those *propriétés originales* that present themselves in national art, in the nation (that is) art.

This essentialist definition of the nation as art has at least three significant consequences. First, art—as national-art—is to be understood in the strictest connection with the social and historical reality of a people, for outside of their art the *habitants de la contrée* have no permanence. That which is called art, called nation, allows for no radical differentiation between formal characteristics and historical experiences. The form and the history, the art and the political status of a region are of a kind; and if they are not, then according to the imperative of autonomy de Man puts forward, they should become so. De Man's theory of national-art is anything but apolitical aestheticism. It is the theory of a politics whose substance is art. Second, the definition of nation through art leads to the conviction that each individual nation has a specificity all its own. For de Man nations are, in the tradition of romantic aesthetics, art-individuals, each with its own particular, irreplaceable and inimitable form, each gifted with a characteristic *génie* and an *âme particulière*. In de Man's article, concepts come together that reveal the mythical nucleus of the notion of art-individuals: *origine, couches fondamentales, propriétés originales, race, familier, appartient, chez lui*. Third, the irreducible plurality of art-nations follows from the theorem of their original individuality—the

plurality of incompatible "values" that, precisely because they can claim to be equally original, are exposed to artistic-political life-and-death conflicts.

The moment in which the young de Man presents this national-political aesthetics—by which I mean not only September 1, 1941, but the entire two years in which he works for *Le Soir* and *Het Vlaamsche Land*—is determined in "Le destin de la Flandre" as a moment of such conflict, a conflict that threatens to eliminate Flemish art and with it the individuality, the nationality of the Belgian nation. (I will have to return to the problem of the relationship between the Flemish and Walloon parts of Belgium and to de Man's "Belgicist" position.) Flemish art, and with it what is specific to the Belgian nation, is threatened, and not for the first time in history, by two imperialist art-nations: France and Germany. While Flemish art has distinguished itself by its pictoriality, its directness and its realism (realism in every sense being for the de Man of these newspaper articles a key word), French art concentrates on psychological analysis, authorial distance, intellectual coldness and "cerebrality," and the German art-nation and its relationship to the Flemish is characterized with clearly negative and threatening attributes: *Des constituants de l'imagination qui déforment le réel* (that is, the genuine object of Flemish art), *telle la vision poétique qui entoure toute matière d'une brume de rêve et qu'on trouve fréquemment chez les Allemands, sont étrangers à la sensibilité picturale*. As the defender of Belgian autonomy demanding *garanties de défense*, de Man opposes these two art-imperialisms, which threaten on the one hand to shatter Flemish reality and on the other to obscure Flemish *matière*, with the argument that Flemish art—that is, the Flemish nation—constitutes in its works of indisputable greatness (for example, Flemish painting) *une valeur, une possibilité de développement qui ne doit être en aucun cas détruite*. After Flanders has already once won *une telle lutte défensive contre les influences françaises* and the fight against a *dénationalisation artificielle*, it must now concentrate its vigilance on the German influence. For from this side as well, de Man continues and thus comes to the decisive point of his reflections on the *destin de la Flandre*, which he unambiguously characterizes as a *destin politique*—from the German side as well, *le danger d'assimilation* threatens Flemish interests. This danger threatens all the more obviously as *des affinités relient les deux races* (the German and the Flemish). *La tentation n'en est que plus forte pour les Flamands de se laisser dissoudre dans une communauté germanique qui risque d'effacer tout ce qui constitue leur originalité profonde*.

De Man shares this anti-assimilatory, anti-integrationist program with Hendrik Elias, whose warning against a *résorbtion des*

Pays-Bas (Nederlanden) dans une communauté germanique arti-ficielle, against the *disparition des Flamands* that goes along with it and against their *nivellement comme Allemands* de Man quotes in great detail. He also quotes Elias' sentence, *"Nous ne pouvons devenir les dignes membres d'un Etat germanique qu'en tant que cet Etat nous permette d'être de digne Néederlandais."* De Man does not comment explicitly on the indications in this sentence of Elias' anti-assimilatory but nonetheless obviously pro-Germanic politics; but immediately following this quotation is the closing paragraph of his article, which points up its enormously important political stakes: de Man insists on the central goal of maintaining the Flemish *génie indépendent between* the cultural and power blocs of France and Germany—*between* them, *not* integrated into one or the other—and closes his article with the conclusion: *C'est conformément à ce dessein que le statut politique de la Flandre doit être établi dans l'Europe nouvelle.* De Man writes *dans l'Europe nouvelle,* but not *dans un Etat germanique.*

I recapitulate: on September 1, 1941 Paul de Man develops a relatively systematic theory of the national specificity of art, which, as a theory of the originality, autonomy and essence of a nation, demonstrates unmistakable affinities with the national-aesthetic myths of origin propagated in fascist Germany at the same time. There can be no doubt about the proto-fascist substance of this theory. But—with it de Man makes himself the defender of the art-nation Flanders against the cultural and political imperialisms of the neighboring nations and above all against the pan-Germanic annexation policy of the National Socialist regime. De Man turns the national-aesthetic ideolo-geme—which not only suited the occupation powers and their organized Belgian supporters, but was even borrowed from their own ideological resources—against the Nazis' integration plans, which were based on economic and power politics, and uses it as an argument not only for the cultural autonomy but also for the political independence of Belgium: *génie indépen-dent . . . conformément . . . statut politique.*

If one wanted to speak of collaboration with regard to this article, as well as all those for which it can stand as an example, then one would have to say it is the document of a collaboration *with* a piece of Nazi ideology turned *against* the actual politics of the Nazis.

It is, evidently, a complicated affair. And it does not get any less complicated when one takes into account the goals—and the illusions—of the different, sometimes aggressively competitive political organizations in occupied Belgium. In addition, one would have to consider the policy of damage limitation favored in Leopold III's circle as the continuation of the earlier policy of neutrality; one would have to consider the Belgicist politics of the liberal *ministre d'Etat* Count Maurice Lippens, the politics of state regeneration and an anti-capitalist alliance with National Socialism pursued by Hendrik de Man, and the politics of the extreme right-wing groups Rex, V.N.V., and De Vlag, which were financially and ideologically supported by the Nazis. And furthermore, in order to outline the political-ideological spectrum within which Paul de Man's journalistic work took place, it would be necessary to clarify the political line followed by the editor-in-chief of *Le Soir,* Raymond de Becker. I will restrict myself to a single point of view—that of anti-annexationism and the guarantees demanded by de Man for the independence of Belgium—and to short notes about the politics of two people who were of importance for de Man's article of September 1, 1941: Hendrik Elias and Raymond de Becker.

Hendrik Elias, who had been a Flemish representative since 1932, became in May 1940 a member of the leadership of the V.N.V. (*Vlaamsch Nationaal Verbond*), which was founded on October 3, 1933 by Staf de Clercq. At the end of 1940, Elias became mayor of Ghent, and in October 1942, after the death of de Clercq, succeeded him as leader of the V.N.V. As the quotations from de Man's article already indicate, Elias was intermittently an active supporter of the Nazi regime's pan-Germanic policy of integration. At the same time, he expected this to lead to the recognition of Flanders as a relatively independent or at least linguistically and culturally autonomous province in a Germanic state. Thus he campaigned energetically for the establishment of the V.N.V. as the Flemish-nationalist unity party; thus he also opposed the Nazis' annexation policy, which, in accordance with Hitler's plans, was being conducted in a particularly drastic manner by the S.S. and had been transparent to all political authorities at least since August 1941. While Elias then emphatically advocated political and military collaboration with Nazi Germany and the entry of Flanders *dans le complexe des peuples germaniques,* after he took over the leadership of the V.N.V. (against the resistance of the S.S.) he worked at carrying out an intensified anti-annexation policy. I quote from Els de Bens' "La Presse au Temps de l'Occupation de la Belgique (1940–1944)" (*Revue d'histoire de la deuxième guerre mondiale* 80 [October 1970], pp.1–28): *(. . .) le discours de Elias à la diète V.N.V., de Gand le 14 avril 1943, dans lequel il s'insurgea en tant que Flamand contre les aspirations annexionistes de l'Allemagne et rompit une lance en faveur de l'idée de la plus grande Hollande. Aprés son discours, Elias fut convoqué chez Reeder, chef de la Militärverwaltung. (. . .) En 1943 H. Elias (. . .) refusera d'ailleurs de recruter, parmi les membres du V.N.V. de nouveaux soldats pour le front de l'Est* (p.24). Not until very late does the V.N.V. see itself disappointed in all its hopes of autonomy and then arrange a demonstrative break with the Nazi authorities: *Au cours d'un entretien (27 février 1944) avec Himmler, en présence de J. Van de Wiele, Elias exigea que les Flamands soient considérés comme peuple autonome, et que De Vlag se limite dorénavant à son rôle culturel primitif.* (Since the middle of 1942, at the latest, De Vlag had formed a unified front with the S.S., the proclaimed political goal of which was the "Anschluss" of Flanders to the Third Reich; Van de Wiele was the leader of De Vlag.) In their *L'An 40: La Belgique occupée* (Brussels: CRISP, 1971), Gérard-Libois and Gotovitch give the following portrayal of the conversation between Elias and Himmler: *Himmler lui-même ne laissera d'ailleurs aucune illusion à H. Elias en février 1944, lors d'une rencontre à Salzburg: la Flandre, devait déclarer le chef de la S.S., serait purement et simplement annexée au Reich. H. Elias, réfugié en Allemagne, refusera fin 1944 d'entrer dans un gouvernement de Flandre (Vlaamsche Landsleiding) voulu et créé par la S.S. et dont Jef Van de Wiele était la tête de file. Ce refus lui vaudra de terminer la guerre à Hirschegg, en résidence surveillée* (p.305).

So much for an outline of some of the positions and movements of the radical right-wing Flemish nationalist politics of collaboration. Its fundamentally separatist orientation was a chip of the highest value for the Nazi regime—not only because it once again practiced the banal rule of thumb, *divide et impera,* but also because it increased the chances of success for their policy of ethnic realignment. From the beginning the policy of the division of Belgium served the goal of the annexation of Flanders to the greater Germanic Reich. Hitler's orders had been: *The Führer has not reached a definite decision concerning the future of the Belgian state. For the time being, he wishes all possible consideration for the Flemish, incl. the return of the Flemish prisoners of war to their homeland. No favor should be accorded to the Walloons* (reported in letter of OKW chief Keitel, July 14, 1940; *L'An 40*, pp.200–201). Already in December 1939 we find in the papers of Ernst von Weizsäcker the following remarks on the "pax germanica": *Belgium and Holland, along with their colonies, could be bound more tightly and subjected to us. Thus England would be held, from the sea and from the air, under permanent German threat. One would probably have to understand the pax germanica in this way and no other. A peace of this kind would be a permanent state of war, without any shots being fired* (*Das dritte Reich: Weltmachtanspruch und nationaler Zusammenbruch 1939–1945*, ed. W. Michalka [Munich: dtv, 1985], p.119). In the May and June, 1940 notebooks of the envoy Braun von Stumm we read under the titles "Border Questions in the West" and "Ethnographic Points of View": *Apart from German Alsace and Lorraine as well as the Grand Duchy of Luxembourg it is the Belgian regions around Arlon (Arel) and Limburg (west of Eupen) that, ac-*

cording to the principle of national traditions, are to be annexed immediately to the bordering regions of the Reich. He continues: *No less than in Alsace, German Lorraine and Luxembourg may we miss our cue to attach once again the North German homeland in French Flanders to its phylogenic core. (. . .) in the interest of organic realignment the administrative annexation of the French-Flemish areas around Dunkirk to the Flanders of Ghent and Brugge is to be undertaken as soon as possible, in order to have the psychological moment of reconstruction come not in the context of the French environment, but rather already under the new national conditions* (ibid, pp.129–131). In a memorandum dated June 1, 1940, ambassador Ritter of the Foreign Office remarks succinctly on a broad economic area ruled by Germany: *1. Greater Germany (including Bohemia, Moravia and Poland) is the economic and political center of this area. 2. To be annexed to it, in a political-economic form yet to be determined, are Holland, Belgium, Luxembourg, Denmark, Norway* (ibid, p.133). And Ribbentrop, Ritter's superior, decrees on April 5, 1943: *For the time being it is still out of the question to discuss the political structure of the future Europe. If one wanted to announce principles for that future structure, these principles, in order to be attractive, would have to be in line with the wishes of the peoples for as separate and independent a statehood as possible, and in this respect would have to contain promises, even though it is already certain now that safeguarding the future Europe against threats from outside will demand precisely the opposite—limitations of independence and sacrifices by each individual country* (ibid, p.151).

In short, the National Socialist plans for the "new ordering" of Europe—which were founded on speculations concerning power politics, economic politics and, moreover, racial mythology—needed the idea of a confederation of states with equal rights as a propagandistic subterfuge. *From all of that the Führer*—thus he himself boasts on May 8, 1943—*has come to the obvious conclusion that the jumble of small states that still exists in Europe must be liquidated as quickly as possible* (ibid, p.154). The Belgian separatist groups actually worked toward this "liquidation" at the hands of the greater German Reich and a "broad economic area" ruled by Germany, even though their ideology of the autonomous nation was supposed to have protected them against precisely this "liquidation."

This, it seems to me, is a decisive ideologico-political point: to be able, in a given historical moment, to estimate precisely how far the resistance and how far the exploitability of a particular ideologeme reaches. Apparently, Flemish nationalism was easily exploitable because it did not take care to protect itself against the political intentions of the occupant through a supplementary program for Belgian unity. Correspondingly,

Hendrik de Man had, as we read in *L'An 40, aucune sympathie pour le V.N.V., qu'il considérait comme un parti séparatiste* (p.299).

His nephew Paul distances himself as well from the *esprit antibelge qui continue d'avoir cours dans certains milieux* as a *mythe* without real political force. In an article printed in *Le Soir* on April 22, 1941 under the title "En marge du dialecte liègeois," he adopts a pronounced anti-separatist position: with historical-linguistic arguments he attempts to convince his readers that precisely in the border region between Flanders and Wallonia, between Liége and Limburg, a *véritable interpénétration du germanique et du roman* has occured, where the *âme populaire* and the *dialecte vulgaire* testify to *une grande solidarité* and *fraternité* between the two populations—*en même temps que le spécifique flamand se mélangeait avec le spécifique wallon, la langue, élément sensible entre tous, a pris l'empreinte de cette fraternité*. Thus the cultural-political axiom of the radical boundary between Flanders and Wallonia, propagated by those de Man contemptuously calls *éléments séparatistes,* is dismissed. And thus the foundation is laid for a Belgicist—that is, for an in principle anti-annexationist—politics. As far as I can see right now, those were the politics of the cultural journalist Paul de Man during his two years at *Le Soir.*

But that is not all.

December 18, 1987

The political line followed by Raymond de Becker belongs among the institutional conditions of Paul de Man's journalistic work, even if it was not strictly determining. De Becker became editor-in-chief of *Le Soir* on December 5, 1940; de Man's first article dates from the 24th of the same month. Coming from a milieu of Catholic socialists with a pronounced authoritarian tendency, de Becker was an advocate of a strong state and a royalist, an energetic opponent of Belgian subservience to France and, prior to the invasion, a supporter of an ultra-neutralist politics. He maintained close ties both to Hendrik de Man and to Max Liebe, the head of the German embassy's "press office" in Brussels, from which *Le Soir* received part of its financial support. Until August of 1941 de Becker was a leading member of a "Bureau politique" founded by the extreme right-wing Rexist, Pierre Daye, which aimed at establishing a single Walloon political party and creating a new, federal Belgian state under the occupation. National unity and the kingdom were to be preserved; democratic institutions, on the other hand, were to be replaced by a "State Party." The line taken by de Becker in collaborating with the occupant is less difficult to determine than that of de Man. For example, the minister of justice, Jan-

son (who had fled to Vichy), wrote to Daye in a letter dated July 25, 1940, that he would do a *service signalé au pays* by working for *Le Soir* as long as he could contribute to preserving for it *un caractère aussi belge que possible* (*L'An 40*, p.317). And in a letter of January 9, 1941 to de Becker, Leopold III's secretary, Count Robert Capelle, expressed the king's thanks for a special issue of *Le Soir* on the unity of Belgium: *Il est bon de rappeler aux Belges leur histoire et de leur inculquer le sens de l'esprit national. (. . .) notre devoir est d'établir par nos actes et nos paroles, le droit à l'existence de la Patrie dont nous ne sommes que les gardiens passagers* (Els de Bens, *De Belgische dagbladpers onder Duitse censuur (1940–1944),* [Antwerp/Utrecht: Nederlandsche Boekhandel, 1973], p.336). De Becker's politics become clearer when one compares "Un avertissement allemand à la population belge," printed in *Le Soir* on March 5, 1941, with de Becker's response in the same edition, which appeared under the title "La Belgique et le Pacte des Trois Puissances." The *avertissement* from the Nazi-controlled *Brüsseler Zeitung* invites Belgium, in the tone of open threat, to act according to the example of Rumania and Bulgaria and join the Axis powers; quoting Goebbels' dictum, one is either against us or for us, it closes with an invitation to work, to collaboration *avant qu'il ne soit trop tard*. De Becker, on the other hand, refers in his commentary to the words of his king, "*se remettre au travaille*" and, reminding his readers of the tasks of a *collaboration européenne* in the hope of *un avenir libre,* he continues: *Mais (. . .): on ne pourra demander au peuple belge une adhésion totale et sans réserves à la politique de l'Axe que le jour où cette adhésion pourra librement se manifester*. For de Becker, the prerequisite for such a 'free collaboration' is not fulfilled as long as there is no Belgian government and as long as "the masses" cannot follow the directions of their *chefs naturels*. But there was no such government and the most natural of the *chefs naturels,* the king, was and remained a prisoner of the Nazis.

De Becker—statist, elitist, royalist—collaborated with the Nazis in the hope of achieving 'free collaboration' until it became clear to him (very late) that the Nazis were conducting a systematic policy of denationalization, the goal of which was the annexation of Belgium to the "Reich." On August 16, 1943, he sums up his experience by concluding in a letter to the *Oberfeldkommandantur* that collaboration with Germany is possible for him only on a strictly national basis, but that Germany has ceased to respect this basis since the beginning of the year. De Becker was relieved of his duties as editor-in-chief of *Le Soir* in September 1943 and was taken into German custody (*résidence surveillée*), first in Genapp and later in the Bavarian Alps (cf. *L'An 40*, pp. 314–315). On July 24, 1946 he was sentenced to death by a Belgian court; the chief reason given by the court for the sentence, which was not unusually harsh at the time, was the fact that although de Becker had supported a politics of national independence and restitution of the state—which the court acknowledged—he had betrayed the contents of that politics by linking it to the idea of a "new Europe" under German hegemony and by repeatedly taking a position in favor of recruiting Belgians for the German army and for "labor service" in Germany. A year later, on the basis of de Becker's resistance to the separatist and annexationist intentions of the occupant, the death sentence was commuted to life in prison. He was released in 1951.

While Raymond de Becker agreed for some time to work under political censorship (which especially affected the explicitly political part of the paper) and thus made massive concessions to the *Propaganda Abteilung,* Paul de Man—who did not belong to the regular editorial staff, but rather was a freelance contributor—was able to write his articles without the pressure of preventive censorship. Not long after the reintroduction of preventive censorship on August 12, 1942, de Man quit working for *Le Soir.* The conditions during the period of "a posteriori" censorship lead Els de Bens to address, three times in the course of her short study of "La Presse au temps de l'occupation de la Belgique," the continuous and sometimes extreme tensions between the controlling German authorities and the Belgian newspapers. These tensions and the reprisals that followed them were triggered by extensive debates about the future of Belgium, what type of state it would be, the status of Flanders and Wallonia within that state, and the status of Belgium in a "new Europe" or in the Third Reich. The occupation powers were afraid these debates would weaken their prestige and strengthen Belgian efforts for autonomy (cf. de Bens, "La Presse," pp.6, 8, 27; *L'An 40*, pp.308–309). De Man, who as far as I can see at the moment supported a distinctly Belgicist politics in almost all of his articles, wrote in a letter of January 26, 1955 to Renato Poggioli, then Director of the Harvard Society of Fellows, in which he responded to anonymous accusations, that censorship was the reason for ending his work at *Le Soir.* He writes (and we know now that the dates he gives are inaccurate): *In 1940 and 1941, I wrote some literary articles in the newspaper 'le Soir' and, like most of the other contributors, I stopped doing so when nazi thought control did no longer allow freedom of statement.*

Early July 1988

After the liberation of Belgium, de Man was interrogated by the *Auditeur général* in Antwerp concerning his journalistic activity,

but, unlike de Becker and most of the editors of *Le Soir,* he was not charged, much less found guilty or sentenced. A letter to the director of the *Centre de Recherche et d'Etudes Historique de la Seconde Guerre mondiale,* dated June 23, 1988 and signed by a representative of the *Auditeur général,* notes that, although the records of this interrogation have not yet been found, *un fait est cependant incontestable: Paul de Man n'a pas fait l'objet de poursuites devant le Conseil de guerre pour son attitude ou son activité pendant la guerre.*

The fact that Paul de Man was not charged with collaboration can hardly be attributed to 'personal connections,' for at about the time of the trials of *Le Soir's* editorial staff his uncle Hendrik de Man was sentenced *in absentia* to twenty years in prison. Nor can the absence of any indictment against Paul de Man be attributed to the court's underestimation of the propagandistic effect of cultural journalism. The *exposé des faits* in the *Le Soir* case reveals that two editors in the paper's cultural section, Paul Brohée and Georges Marlier, were charged with collaboration because they were involved in cultural propaganda for Germany and for National Socialist artistic doctrines. In the case of Marlier one of these doctrines is specified: *que l'art d'avant guerre était décadent parce que fruit d'une époque décadente et que mai 1940 amenait en Belgique un art plus noble et plus digne, correspondant à la grande révolution qui se faisait.* Furthermore, the *Auditeur général's* resumé of the case against Marlier establishes that *les Allemands attachaient énormément de prix à la propagande dans le domaine culturel en faveur de la pénétration culturelle allemande en Belgique. C'était un des buts de l'action de la P.A. (rapport du Kommandeur, août 1941, pièce 2 et 30, déposition Nabokoff pièce 34 b.).* Since one can assume that de Man's articles were subjected to just as thorough a juridical examination as those of the other *Le Soir* journalists (whose articles the *auditeur* frequently cites by title and date), the only probable explanation for the fact that de Man was not charged would be the estimation that he was involved neither in pro-German propaganda nor in the organized betrayal of Belgian interests.

It is remarkable that this *exposé des faits* in the *Le Soir* case never refers to the anti-semitic propaganda that was carried on by many of the editors and freelance writers. In the discussion of de Becker, in particular, there is no mention whatsoever of his systematic anti-semitic activities.

May 23, 1988

After reading the article published by one Lothar Baier this weekend in the *Frankfurter Rundschau,* I see that my response in the *FAZ* to Schirrmacher's "Totgeschwiegene Schuld" allowed for malicious misunderstanding by some interested parties. I had written: *The complicated political strategy pursued in de Man's book reviews cannot, as Wiener and Schirrmacher suggest, be reduced to the common denominator of collaboration* [*Die komplizierte politische Strategie, der de Mans Buchrezensionen folgen, lässt sich nicht, wie Wiener und Schirrmacher suggieren, auf den Nenner der Kollaboration bringen*]. Without my consent, the editors of the "Geisteswissenschaften" page accentuated this sentence by the addition of a subtitle—the title, subtitles, and intertitles were all written or inserted by the *FAZ* editors, none by me. After Gumbrecht's reproach of "whitewashing" (a commentator starts by accepting the projections of another), the misunderstanding caused by this highlighting was almost inevitable. Simplifications and their repetitions tend to produce meanings, whether they happen to correspond to the actual texts at hand or not. In this case as well. My wording, which emphasizes *complication* and the *single* common denominator, of course includes the fact that there are collaborationist elements in de Man's articles. When one is talking about strategy, and moreover a complicated strategy, then only a simpleton could think that one is not also speaking of collaboration, as the comment about the *fascistoid typology of nationalities* was meant to underscore. Like so many of my remarks (for example, the reference to Sieburg, the defender of Nazi interests in Paris who nevertheless later became the "Feuilleton" editor at the *Frankfurter Allgemeine Zeitung*!), this comment of mine was studiously ignored for the sake of simplicity, and in order to conform to Wiener's model of "here an accuser, there a defender." Once again: nothing in de Man's articles can be defended, everything is to be analyzed.

One more word about Baier's article, which, beyond this, I won't bother to characterize. This Baier quotes, in the context of a cynical mock apology for de Man, Hitler's differentiation between the *"anti-semitism of passion"* and the *"anti-semitism of reason."* And he does not notice that he thus repeats Hitler's suggestion that reason could be capable of anti-semitism! *"Anti-semitism of reason,"* this cultural critic writes, and is not ashamed to take up Hitler's horrendous expression and pass it on to his readers as a serious concept.

December 1987

One Theodor Lüddecke writes in his book, *Die Tageszeitung als Mittel der Staatsführung*, which appeared in Hamburg in 1933:

The written word will once again return to its original purpose—that is, to trigger actions and to prepare them. The organized masses will constitute the new state; thus, this state will not stop where the official bureaucracy stops. Every citizen will be, in one form or another, an agent of the state. (. . .)

In a technical respect, a dictatorship is, among other things, a rationalization of political work. It reduces both the time needed for devising constructive plans and the channels through which they are carried out. For this technical reason alone, an absolute claim to power is imperative for every government that wishes to get the job done.

(. . .)

(. . .) The entire German national economy is a large business, and the entire nation is its work force. In a business only one opinion may reign if its production goal is to be achieved.

In this business, the newspaper must be consciously fashioned into a means of issuing slogans [Paroleausgabe] (pp.172–173).

According to Joseph Wulf, from whose collection of documents this text is quoted (*Presse und Rundfunk im Dritten Reich* [Gütersloh: Mohn, 1964], p.65), Lüddecke was the director of the Press Institute at the University of Halle.

June 8, 1988

In Sartre's excellent analysis, "Qu'est-ce qu'un collaborateur?," there are a number of sentences which also apply to an important aspect of the positions de Man articulated while working in Belgian collaborationist institutions. Before quoting them, however, I should stress that Sartre's characterizations are intended to designate a *type*: "the" collaborator. The irreducible particularity of individual authors, politicians, and agents in specific situations disappears into the generality of this type, along with whatever traits cannot be subsumed under the concept of "collaboration."

Sartre writes, among other things: *(. . .) Si les collaborateurs ont conclu de la victoire allemande à la nécessité de se soumettre à l'authorité du Reich c'est qu'il y avait chez eux une décision profonde et originelle qui constituait le fond de leur personnalité: celle de se plier au fait accompli, quel qu'il fût. Cette tendance première qu'ils décoraient eux-mêmes du nom de "réalisme" a des racines profondes dans l'idéologie de notre temps. Le collaborateur est atteint de cette maladie intellectuelle qu'on peut appeler l'historicisme. (. . .)*

(. . .) Par sa docilité aux faits—ou plutôt à ce fait unique: la défaite française—le collaborateur "réaliste" fait une morale renversée: au lieu de juger le fait à la lumière du droit, il fonde le droit sur le fait; sa métaphysique implicite identifie l'être et le devoir-être. (. . .)

(. . .) Le collaborateur, qu'il ait ou non l'occasion de se manifester comme tel, est un ennemi que les sociétés démocratiques portent perpétuellement en leur sein. (. . .) (Sartre's text was first published

in August 1945 in New York. In 1949 it was incorporated into *Situations III*; I have quoted from the latter, pp.51–60.)

There is much to say about Sartre's analysis—its metaphorics of pathology, its concept of the enemy—but here I will limit myself to the following. The existential-psychological supposition of a *décision profonde et originelle* (which, incidentally, lies in the same field as the isolation of a *type,* a *personnalité*) itself actually performs the same reduction for which it reproaches "the" collaborator: both reduce history and the historical possibilities of another, and again another, decision. If one is concerned with these other possibilities and thereby the possibility of history in general, one may not think the *décision* of which Sartre writes as either *profonde* or *originelle,* and least of all as definitive. There is no decision that does not continually have to be made anew, and accordingly no decision exists that could establish a certain *type* for all time. The decision itself cannot be typified. The relative openness of the decision, splintering it into an heterogeneous multiplicity of decisions, is connected with the irreducibility of *ought* to *is,* of obligation (*le devoir-être*) to being (*l'être*) (what Sartre here calls *l'être*). Their relation must not be thought as symmetrical if one wishes to avoid the reduction of obligation to a *fait accompli,* and thus to a further "reality." Sartre's critique of "realism" is itself in many respects still a "realistic" critique. We should, of course, take care not to label Sartre a collaborator of "the" collaborator. (Actually, Sartre, like Valéry, Cocteau and Paulhan, also contributed at least one piece to the Parisian collaborationist paper *Comoedia*; of all things, Sartre's article reviewed Jean Giono's French translation of *Moby Dick,* a novel which in the mid-forties was translated into Flemish by, of all people, Paul de Man.)

As little as I care for its existential-analytic phrasing, Sartre's insight seems to me nonetheless important: the ideology of realism, identified as a central element of collaboration, is itself a danger to democratically organized societies. The pragmatism, positivism, and historicism which have long been a part of the ideological profile of democracies can hardly be regarded as anything other than variants of that realism which finds the final guarantee of reality in the power of so-called facts. This reality is actually first generated by all sorts of societal—and not only societal—institutions and all sorts of techniques—among them techniques of language—creating an unhomogeneous, contradictory, and fragile formation in which the most diverse interests and illusions can stabilize, intensify, and come into conflict with each other. The ideology of realism—and pragmatism—has long been growing into the dominant ideology of the democracies. It is in realism that Sartre marks the point of complicity between democratic and fascist systems. Putting this

realism into question is an eminently political act, even if it is not articulated in explicitly political terms, but rather in linguistic and philological ones (as, for example, in de Man's later writings). No one with a critical mind will be startled that the institutions of this ideological realism try to denounce any such questioning as an attack on the basic foundations of "Western values." It would cause just as little astonishment if they were unable to recognize in de Man's *Le Soir* articles on realism in politics and in literature exactly those ideologemes to which they hold so fast today.

January 30, 1988

Seeking an answer to the question of what it was in de Man's attitudes, convictions and inclinations that did not *prevent* him from writing an article such as the one on "Jews in Contemporary Literature," one must at some point take into account his explicit statements on the issue of collaboration. I will briefly discuss four passages in which he addresses this issue.

The first of these passages is found in his discussion of *"Le testament politique de Richelieu* par Frédéric Grimm" (*Le Soir,* August 19, 1941), where he writes: *Il ne reste plus aux Français d'accepter, dans des conditions infiniment moins favorables* (that is, under the conditions of a partial occupation of France), *la collaboration avec l'Allemagne ou de se soumettre passivement à l'Angleterre.* At least two things in this sentence are noteworthy. First, it speaks of collaboration in a descriptive mode, portraying it as one of two possibilities available in the face of the present relation of forces; ideological motives for such a collaboration are not mentioned. Second, it mentions submission to the politics of England as the alternative to collaboration—an alternative that was virtually nonexistent at that time and that, given the term "submission," is presented as unacceptable. But this suggests at the same time that collaboration with the Germans, however involuntary it might be, would not be an act of submission, but rather one of relative freedom and political good sense. What this sentence contains is thus a guarded invitation to collaboration. The motive it cites for this is the present power situation; the motive it suggests is the remnant of freedom that could be exercised within the context of collaboration.

The second passage expressly referring to the problem of collaboration can be found in the review of *"Trois épreuves* par Daniel Halévy" (*Le Soir,* October 14, 1941). The passage is complicated and should therefore be quoted at length: following the debacle of France, de Man writes, everyone has been in a state of deepest uncertainty, discouragement, and passivity, and he continues: *Et cependant, la nécessité d'action qui se présente sous la forme d'une collaboration immédiate, s'impose à tout esprit objectif. Même si cette activité ne peut prendre une allure directe et matérielle, que les loisirs forcés de cette époque de transition servent au moins à certaines méditations fécondes et à certaines mises au points indispensables. Il est prématuré de baisser les bras devant l'incompréhension universelle et de se retirer dans sa tour d'ivoire. Mais certaines révisions doctrinales et certaines tentatives de tirer la leçon des événements par des considérations théoriques s'imposent.* At the center of these thoughts on collaboration lies *action*: it is the remedy de Man recommends against *inaction forcée* and the pessimism that results. But this action that imposes itself (*s'impose*) on every "objective mind" in the form of *collaboration immédiate*, even if it cannot be "direct and material," should at least assume the form of certain revisions in traditional theories of social and political life. These are also said to impose themselves (*s'imposent*). Immediate collaboration with the Germans is thus one of the two available alternatives. Of the other, de Man speaks only in the very vaguest of terms. He himself gives the reason in an earlier passage: *(. . .) les actes qui peuvent sauver la France ne sont pas de ceux qu'on peut exposer dans des livres, sous la forme de programmes théoriques.* A reader of this article can say of this theoretical activity only that it opens the perspective of a politics that would *not* be one of collaboration, not even of ideological collaboration: an earlier passage from the same text states explicitly that *il suffit pas de frapper les coupables immédiats, ni d'adopter les mystiques dans lesquelles les vainqueurs ont puisé leur force et leur puissance.* In each case—and de Man recommends both collaboration and active non-collaboration as salutary—it is a matter of necessary reactions to a condition brought about by force (he speaks of *désastre, débâcle, grands chocs*), of reactions that also impose themselves with compelling force and thus without ideological predetermination. It is therefore clear that in this way collaboration is legitimized as a response to the power of facts and is thus legitimized by force. Its alternative is unclear.

The third passage on collaboration comes from the article on "*Voir la figure* de Jacques Chardonne" (*Le Soir*, October 28, 1941), which I consider to be, along with "The Jews in Contemporary Literature," the worst of de Man's articles. Without any hesitation, it repeats unspeakable stupidities like those concerning *l'âme hitlérienne* and *l'âme allemand* along with national-Bolshevist slogans like collectivity and *personnalité-type*; this is, moreover, as far as I can see, the only text that fails to insist on the principle of Belgian autonomy: it portrays National Socialism as the *émancipation définitive d'un peuple qui se trouve, à son tour, appelé à exercer une hégémonie en Europe.* One can read de

Man's statements on collaboration in this article as the scornful revenge for this self-subjugation. With the same dry realism with which he earlier pointed out the necessity of collaboration, he now establishes the absoluteness of its limits. I quote: *Il est en effet assez vain de se consacrer uniquement à la répétition des arguments qui plaident pour une collaboration immédiate. La chose fait sans doute plaisir à ceux qui sont déjà de cette avis et qui se sentent heureux de voir leur rangs grossis d'une nouvelle adhésion. Mais quant à convaincre les autres, c'est une entreprise qui en bien des cas s'avèrera impossible.* Whatever can be mustered as an "argument" for collaboration appears here as mere opinion, and the reference to the collaborators, who are gratified by the swelling of their ranks, may be a sarcastic dig, but this entire passage also suggests that collaboration is a phantom problem that would be dissolved by the realities of the new collectivism. Thus the implicit slogan here is: *against* the jargon of collaborationism, *for* the reality of collaboration. The awareness that even this slogan might itself be jargon is demonstrated by a great many comments in the text, comments that, although they are not to be taken lightly (for example, on the personality-type: *Il peut encore paraître fruste et un peu élémentaire*), do not interfere with the general gesture of impatient realistic affirmation.

What all three passages share, namely the 'realistic' acceptance of the force of 'facts,' finds its programmatic formulation almost one year later in the review of "*Journal de la France* par Alfred Fabre-Luce" (*Le Soir*, July 21, 1942). There one reads: *la politique de collaboration résulte de la situation présente non comme un idéal désiré par l'ensemble du peuple mais comme une irrésistible nécessité à laquelle nul ne peut échapper, même s'il croit marcher dans une autre direction. L'attentisme est donc condamné, non d'un point de vue moral, mais de celui de l'impérieuse réalité: il est intenable parce que contraire au courant de l'histoire qui continue de couler, sans se soucier de la réticence de quelques individus s'obstinant à ne pas comprendre sa puissance.* Although these sentences represent a paraphrase of Fabre-Luce's thoughts, they can be understood as a programmatic outline of de Man's own position—or at least as one of the determinants of his position. One does not decide to collaborate on the basis of moral principles or even ideological sympathies with the occupant; it is, rather, a simple consequence of what is seen as an unavoidable "necessity," so to speak the cognitive-political result of the "present situation." As de Man portrays it here, collaboration is the policy of that realism that sees no reason to defy an "imperious reality" (*impérieuse réalité*), because for him the final ground for all political decisions seems to be exclusively this reality itself. The alliance he establishes between present reality and necessity (an *alliance* because every reality that imposes itself with irresistible *force* is already, for precisely that reason, declared a necessity) allows him to transfigure both into an *historical* necessity: what exists, he thinks, is for precisely that reason also necessary, and the disinterested power of history (*courant de l'histoire qui continue de couler*) is the final authority instituting this necessity. This blurring of the concepts of "reality," "necessity," and "history" hides the fact that the quality of *power* supposedly common to all three belongs not to them at all, but rather to the strength of the German army. Admitting this fact would open the political possibility of fighting against it, on the basis of the moral perspective (*idéal désiré, point de vue moral*) which de Man explicitly disqualifies. In this article "reality" is an ideologeme: it suggests that the force of the German war machinery *is* the power of history. Consequently it allows for no other history than that of force and the "realistic" submission to it. The "realistic" rejection of ideological—namely, moral—arguments in this case functions itself as ideology. One can hardly imagine a more persuasive, a more convincing rhetoric than one that insists that it speaks (entirely un-ideologically) "only" in the name of the force of facts, of the *nécessités inscrites dans les faits,* for thus it presents itself as one of these necessities. This rhetoric must have been especially convincing to the Belgians, whom de Man never tires of describing as a people of realists.

Paul de Man did not always invite his readers to mistake Nazi Germany's military superiority for the power of history. In a *Le Soir* article of February 25, 1941 on "Les livres sur la campagne de Belgique", he writes: *Ce n'est pas tant le climat politique pourri qui provoqua la défaite, car celui-ci ne valait guère mieux en 1914. Mais ce qui a joué un rôle définitif a été l'habilité et la puissance avec lesquelles les Allemands ont pu exploiter leurs succès et forcer la victoire.* And in order to strengthen Belgian self-confidence he continues with this plea against defeatism: *Il était utile de le signaler ici car ce n'est pas en répandant la croyance que nous sommes des lâches et des incapables que nous préparerons un meilleur avenir.* Here the Belgians are addressed as autonomous subjects who can determine their own future, as long as they are not taken in by the suggestion that they are the powerless victims of historical and natural circumstances. I read the same sense of an autonomous determination of one's own future in the short announcement of a book about *Le Prince Eugène de Ligne* (February 12, 1941) that praises his efforts on behalf of Belgian independence as exemplary, hence as a model for the conduct of Belgians. We read about him: *dans l'exercice de ses devoirs, il parvient toujours et partout à faire respecter l'indépendance belge. Il est utile pour nous, de nous documenter sur cet homme d'Etat, dont la mentalité constitue un exemple pour tous.* (Added June 9, 1988: Writing my response to Schirrmacher I made a mistake in trans-

lating the first of these sentences as saying "What always and everywhere matters is establishing respect for Belgian independence." Of course it should have read: "he always and everywhere succeeded at establishing respect for Belgian independence." The difference seems to me rather insignificant, since in fact the descriptive sentence about de Ligne is given a prescriptive sense, in that his conduct is presented as *exemplary*: just as he supports the cause of Belgian independence, so should everyone.) Here, again, it is an historical reality (the Belgian fight for independence) to which de Man refers, but this time in order to move his readers to continue their politics of autonomy, *not* in order to make them succumb to the "reality" of defeat.

These statements by de Man on collaboration do not outline the only political position he supports in his articles, nor by any means the exemplary one. Considering that the majority of his contributions to *Le Soir* concern the literary culture of Belgium—its specificity and future—and considering that de Man leaves no doubt that the cultural autonomy of Belgium, in order to remain secure, requires a corresponding political form, we might then speculate (if a generalization may be allowed here) that he is appointing himself the advocate of collaboration *with a view toward* this Belgian autonomy in a "new Europe"—in a Europe that, precisely because of the repeatedly emphasized national independence of its states, would hardly have anything to do with the Nazi idea of a 'greater German Reich.' On the other hand, his statements—whatever political direction they may point to in the final analysis—can indeed be seen as programmatic for one thing, namely for de Man's concept of "reality" and "realism." It is, I think, this "realism" that, sometimes implicitly, but far more often explicitly, stands at the center of his statements on problems of literature, politics, history and social change. This concept of "realism" and the ideology of the *impérieuse réalité* can explain his dual political commitment—to the cause of the Belgians and to that of the Nazis—as well as his literary-political commitment to literary realism and to its transformation into surrealism. And, finally, this "realism" is the dominant ideology of a certain type of journalism to which de Man apparently felt committed. If one wants to understand what takes place in de Man's articles, what made them possible and what did not prevent them, then one will, above all, have to analyze the determinants and functions of the ideology of realism. It is, by and large, the ideology of journalism—and not only of journalism—still today, in what we call the democracies as well.

May 21, 1988

Of de Man's articles in *Le Soir,* more than seventy deal with Belgian books and Belgian culture, approximately thirty concern French literature, and less than twenty treat German literature (including Goethe and Novalis, Jünger and Fallada, Wiechert, Carossa, Stehr). He admires Goethe, Novalis and Jünger; he reviews the books of the French writers, with few exceptions, in a tone of tense distrust; and he treats the Belgian authors with demonstrative sympathy. De Man maintains some distance in almost every case.

There can be no doubt that de Man is following his personal (distinctly nationalistic) inclinations when he repeatedly gives preference to Belgian, and especially Flemish, literature. He openly admits it himself in one of his reviews. And he attempts to justify his preference both systematically and historically. As I have already noted, both (the systematic and historical justification as well as the pronounced sympathy) have rather ambidextrous political implications, given the situation of Belgium between 1940 and 1944, and must be read as forms of a (doubtlessly conscious) political involvement. On July 8, 1941, in an article entitled "Productions de la nouvelle génération, en Belgique," de Man declares: *ma préférence va, en générale, à ceux qui se bornent à raconter* directement *un de ces petits événements (. . . .) J'aime moins ceux qui s'aventurent sur le terrain de la méditation intérieure ou de la symbolisation* (my emphasis; W.H.). De Man himself explains the preference he gives to the directness of narration over the mediatedness of the symbol and over psychological analysis. He attributes it to the direct emotional bond between reader and story and to the *affinités entre le lecteur et l'auteur,* which become possible through the elimination of the narrator, that *grand maître omnipotent* by means of which the novelist since Flaubert had positioned himself (by analyzing, psychologizing, and rationalizing) between immediate sensory experience and its re-presentation. While, as de Man writes, novels since Flaubert tell us nothing about *la personne même* who writes them, the individuality of the young Belgian authors, such as Magermans and Libert, becomes *la source unique de leur inspiration.* What they describe *est ce qu'ils portent en eux de plus personnel.* He continues: *Cette tournure d'esprit est aussi subjective et* directe *que l'autre était cérébrale et préméditée* (my emphasis; W.H.). This turn from mediated to immediate narration, from the abstract rationality of analysis to the sensory description of that which is individual, from cold distance to proximity and affinity—this turn is of course not an indifferent one for de Man, but rather a turn from the reader's indifference to his immediate affective engagement. It is a turn from the characteristically French to the characteristically Belgian. And it is a turn to *directe participation à l'action.* Not only to participation in the action that is being narrated, but also to direct participation in the course of literary "evolution." For de Man leaves no doubt that to him it represents a "logical" step forward in literary-historical development when a literature becomes capable *d'exprimer* directement *une expérience profonde et vécue* (my emphasis; W.H.).

In the article of June 17, 1941 he praises the Belgian neo-surrealist Marcel Lecomte's art of *minutieuse description,* which he calls pictorial description in order to distinguish it from Marcel Proust's analytical and explicative description; he then integrates this (for him) specifically Flemish and Belgian characteristic into the great movement of literary history since the 19th century: *Il fallait, à Victor Hugo, la bataille de Waterloo pour alimenter son inspiration. L'histoire d'une famille suffit à Zola, celle d'une abstraite crise morale à Gide, d'une banale journée de premier venu à James Joyce, d'un homme assis dans un café, enfin, à Marcel Lecomte.* This literary history of ever greater refinement of realism, which started with the French panorama and continued in the Anglo-Saxon mythography of everyday life, thus reaches its finale in the Belgian miniature. De Man insists that the book he discusses here marks the end of a particular aesthetic development, the possibilities of which now appear to be exhausted. But this entire development moves toward what is in de Man's view a typically Belgian culmination, a maximum of pictorial directness, *capable de provoquer ce tressaillement intérieur qu'est l'émotion artistique.* De Man rejects the possible objection that this art is a phenomenon of *décadence* as one of the *préjugés de l'heure* (presumably a prejudice of National Socialist artistic doctrine), and emphasizes that it represents the result of a *continuation logique* of the realist tradition.

The historical path of European literature, a path marked by the cultivation and exhaustion of the possibilities of realism, is treated by de Man as a path toward the immediate, into the closest affective and geographical proximity: for de Man, at this time, it is literature's path to Belgium. The history of literature is, for him at this time, the history of its Belgianization. In his review of "*Mariage sans enfants*: un roman flamand" on June 10, 1941, he writes: *Le naturalisme a si profondément marqué les romanciers flamands que, alors qu'il est depuis longtemps dépassé dans d'autres pays, il continue à imposer ses lois en Flandre. (. . .) C'est une espèce de dette de reconnaissance que payent les auteurs de nos jours, quand ils respectent une esthétique qui permit le renouveau littéraire de leur pays. Ou bien, la chose provient d'une caractéristique innée du tempérament artistique flamand, plus pictural qu'analytique et, indubitablement, plus à l'aise dans le domaine de la description que de la réflexion abstraite. Quoi qu'il en soit, le réalisme et le naturalisme trouvèrent dans ce pays un terrain particulièrement propice à leur croissance.* Whether out of respect for its own history or out of a natural—national—disposition, Belgium is the privileged, the authentic, ground of realism, the site of its growth and preservation and the literary-historical site where realism ceases to be a merely historically determined aesthetic form and, literally, *realizes* itself. After de Man has spoken of an *impression quasi-photographique de réalité,* he continues by praising the Flemish style: *Tout cela est si extraordinairement vrai, jusque dans les moindres détails, qu'on en oublie qu'il s'agit d'une fiction. (. . .) C'est la réalité toute nue qui nous est offerte.* Literary realism in Flanders thus erases its own aesthetic, fictional character; it eliminates all barriers between reality and the work, and directly presents reality. Realism realizes itself in Flanders as reality—as the characteristic, natural, national reality of Flanders.

This fundamental claim, for which J. Hendriks' *roman flamand* serves only as an example, is not weakened by the qualification which follows— *Le roman purement réaliste est sans doute un genre assez limité*—because against the background of a general evolutionary model of European literary history, this claim systematically (but also provisionally, as will become apparent) privileges three instances and brings them into an essential relationship to one another: the pictorial *realism* of minute and direct description as the most highly developed form of European aesthetics; *Belgium,* and especially Flanders, as the nation in which realism has its natural ground; and *reality* as unmediated everyday life which speaks to the senses and the imagination and engages all experiential faculties. Realism is thus that aesthetic form in which the Belgian nation becomes immediate reality. And Belgium is real only in realism, the style of art that is no longer artificial, no longer aesthetically distanced, no longer a medium of fiction, but rather a medium of immediacy, of directness, of actual experience. Thus—in this historical moment (1941, 1942, 1943) in which Belgium exists neither as a state nor as an autonomous nation—Belgium's realism should make Belgium *itself,* Belgium as *reality* itself, into a reality. Realism is the Belgian artform *par excellence*—namely, the one in which Belgium should present itself in its political reality, a reality undistorted and unhindered by all foreign influences.

The maxim of the Belgian realism of this time is not 'culture as usual,' but rather 'national Realpolitik.' And de Man's cultural journalism during the occupation was for the most part a contribution not so much to the distraction and diversion of the educated public, but rather to the discussion of national art,

to the preservation of its integrity and to the creation of its political reality. (For as much as de Man insists on the *descriptive* character of Belgian realism, it still has for him a *prescriptive* function: as its aesthetic form is substantially 'realistic,' so the political form of the nation *ought* to become real, as an autonomous state.)

In order to make de Man's Belgicist art-politics clear, one would have to comment in great detail on the following four programmatic texts from the *Bibliographie* of the Agence/Agentschap Dechenne: "Ontwikkeling der Zuid-Nederlandsche Letterkunde," February 1942 (*Vlaamsche volkskarakter zijn eigenaardigheid en zijn persoonlijkheid, konstanten van het volkskarakter, onzer kunstziel, eeuwige Vlaamsche natuur,* etc.), "L'Apogée d'un Chef-d'oeuvre" of April 1942 (on de Coster's *La Légende d'Ulenspiegel*), "Noorden Zuid-Nederlandsche Letterkunde van heden," July 1942, and "Condition actuelle de la littérature d'expression française" of February 1943 (*il existe un spécifique des lettres belges qui reste maintenu, en ce moment plus que jamais (. . .); la place très honorable de la poésie belge dans l'ensemble de la littérature française du moment*). And of course one would also have to subject all of the reviews devoted to Belgian books to a thorough political reading. Instead, I will at this point quote only one of de Man's short reviews for Dechenne from May, 1942. De Man comments, in two languages, on a German series of "Flämische Schriften" in which *Das Flämische Kampfgedicht* appeared: *Car elles contribuent à cette tâche considérable que les conditions politiques présentes imposent à tout esprit clairvoyant: prendre clairement conscience des origines, des affinités, des possibilités de son peuple, afin que la prochaine reconstruction de l'Europe puisse se faire d'une manière harmonieuse et conforme aux aptitudes de chacun des constituants. (. . . .) Et, dans le cas de la Flandre, rien ne peut plus justement et plus efficacement servir sa cause* [the Flemish version is more graphic: *verdedigen van zijn rechten (the defending of its rights)*] *que ces vues sur ce qui constitue son patrimoine culturel et artistique. Il en ressort clairement l'existence d'une grandeur et d'un "spécifique" flamand [oorspronkelijkheid (originality)] qui force le respect pour ce peuple et garantit ses considérables possibilités d'avenir.*

In short, de Man's articles on Belgian literature and art understand themselves as the cultural-journalistic equivalent to that *politique de présence* supported by Paul's uncle Hendrik de Man and practiced by the Belgian king. This politics of presence, of national realism and of the current reality of the nation, is a politics of defending Belgium's national identity (de Man speaks of *verdedigen van zijn rechten*) and of securing its future in a reorganized Europe, the principles of which would not be those of power politics but of aesthetics (*harmonieuse*) and morals (*respect*). Such a *Realpolitik* presupposes recognition of the *status quo* (*les conditions politiques présentes*) in order to derive from that recognition the tasks for the future (*cette tâche considérable*). For de Man, reality, here as at many points in his newspaper articles, is not only what presents itself as the present situation but also what this situation contains in the way of possibilities and—in moral terms—tasks for the future. But he sees the future, like the past, only in the "objective" image of a present that *needs* that past and this future in order to be able to enter into a lawful order. De Man's artistic, historical and political convictions are based on a realism of the order of presence.

May 21, 1988

For better or worse, a journalist is always a presentist—attempting, according to certain notions of order, to create a comprehensible picture from the prevailing artistic, social and political situation. But the presentism of the press does not explain all aspects of de Man's position, and it "excuses" nothing at all. For notions of order and their habitual or institutional fixation on the 'present' can, and could at that time as well, take on decidedly different forms than de Man's articles did. But if one wants to understand what political functions and what possibilities the ideology of the realism of presence had at the time, as well as what constraints, both external and internal, it had to submit to, then one should not divert one's attention from this realism too quickly. Interrupting this analysis usually harbors the danger of assessing all too euphemistically the other possibilities for relating to the present. If yet another opportunity to analyze the structure of National Socialist ideologies is not to be wasted, they must not be treated as a monolithic block and thus as an invariable *res*; otherwise, one would merely be walking into the trap of another "realism." Nothing can guarantee that this other "realism" would be more immune to totalitarian consequences than the one that forms the basis of de Man's early *engagement*.

Already earlier (December 12) and again today, but with a different emphasis, I have attempted to explain that de Man's theory of National Realism, as closely as it may be related to certain fascist ideologies of art, served as a defense of Belgian claims to autonomy against Nazi imperialism. In an April 1942 review of the book *La Révolution du XXe Siècle* in the *Bibliographie Dechenne*, he provides the most economical formula for this procedure. By focussing on the term 'National Socialism' and ascertaining that it unites two hitherto opposed concepts, de Man can claim that *cette révolution*—by which he means the radical change in all elements of individual and social life since the beginning of the war—*sera différente dans chaque pays, puisqu'elle comporte également un élément national qui varie selon la contrée*. After thus emphasizing the national character of the 'National Socialist revolution' and therefore its plurality (contrary to the Germans' claim to hegemony), he goes on to derive an obligation for the Belgians: *C'est ce qui nous oblige à chercher le mode qui convient le mieux à notre tempérament propre*. The politics implicit in this statement has nothing in common with the massive collaborationism of, for example, the Rexists and De Vlag; it is, rather, very close to the politics of presence and the state-socialist ideas of Hendrik de Man. As the fate of Hendrik de Man, Elias, and even de Becker, shows, such a politics of national autonomy cannot have pleased the Nazis in the long term. They tolerated it temporarily and on a strictly ideological level, but suppressed it wherever it threatened to have concrete political consequences.

The second tendency of the realism of presence promulgated by Paul de Man during the war years is what one could call its political positivism, which I also discussed earlier (January 30). What counts as real is the 'fait accompli,' the 'positive fact,' the 'objective situation'—which is, in the political as in every other respect, also a situation brought about by force. De Man's realism turns into a justification of the actual power situation in Belgium and in France (and in Germany as well) wherever he ceases to differentiate between the sphere of justice and that of facts. Even if it occurs only rarely in de Man's texts, this blurring of facticity and legitimacy obviously comes quite easily to him. The reason for this is that justice and reality appear to him to be on the same level of positive existence. As a result, justice can become for him a form of force, while force can become a source of historical and political justice. Force is what makes justice a fact and justifies the fact; the realism de Man embraces is thus, also, a realism of force, for in his view nothing but force bestows reality on the real and on justice. The thought that right, justice and, *a fortiori,* ethical relations could belong to a sphere that is incommensurable with actual power relations does not occur to him. (In contrast, de Man's late texts, at the very least since *Allegories of Reading,* make a point of dealing attentively, scrupulously—and in a manner infinitely distanced from the early positions—with the problems of ethics, imperative, *imposition,* force and event; I have offered some reflections on these problems in my essay "LECTIO—de Man's imperative" three years ago. What his latest texts address under the problem of materiality, which he attempts to separate strictly from that of phenomenality and which is obviously closely connected to the complex of imperative and *imposition,* can be read as an elaboration of the early theme of realism.)

Just as the young de Man's realism could lead him to a politics of defending Belgian autonomy, so it could thus also lead him to collaborate with the Nazis. This collaboration, as a meticulous reading of the texts attests, was *not* founded on pro-Nazi sympathies, but rather on a realism to which force appears as an authority that produces facts and justice. Regardless of the form this force takes, the realist accepts it, for he hopes that it will lead to an ordered, secured, "harmonious" reality. Many people must have missed such a reality during the turbulence of the war years. That is why there were, among intellectuals as well, so many 'realists.' De Man was one of them.

That 'reality' is not simply a *factum* but could also be an ideological construct, a fiction or *fictum,* suggesting its own irrevocable self-sufficiency in order to lift the burden of freedom inherent in its mutability—this thought first occurs in de Man's work more than a decade later in "Tentation de la Permanence" (1955). The epistemological analysis of what 'reality' is and how it de-constitutes itself in the tensions of language has been at the center of de Man's work ever since.

Besides the two already mentioned, there is a third tendency of de Man's realism, one that neither exhausts itself in a politics of defense nor amounts to complicity with the occupation. This tendency is connected with the transformation of realism into surrealism.

May 24, 1988

Tout est réel ici—de Man quotes this "categorical affirmation" from the title of a novel by the Flemish novelist Paul Willems, and comments: *c'est-à-dire même les visions les plus fantasques et les hallucinations les plus extravagantes du moment qu'elles jaillissent des profondeurs de la vie subconsciente* (*Le Soir,* July 15, 1941). The reality in question is further specified as a *réalité humaine* which lies inside and outside the borders posited by consciousness. The fantastic novels of Flemish authors that de Man continually recommends to his readers with great critical sympathy, are, in his opinion, supposed to present the "extra-rational" regions of human experience, the *surnaturel* or *supra-réel,* which German romanticism (de Man names Novalis) explored as the sphere of dreams and French surrealism explores as the sphere of the unconscious. While the interior monologue (de Man points to Joyce) still investigates the outermost borders of the conscious in the tradition of the psychological novel, it is in de Man's view the privilege of the surrealists to take the necessary next step in the investigation of human reality; they must pass beyond the "first reality" and step onto the ground of a second. The fantastic realism of the Belgians, especially the Flemish authors

Willems, Hellens, and Gevers, follows the same tendency of literary evolution. Their art is neither the art of the rational analysis of consciousness, nor the art of the symbol, which, de Man claims, only substitutes an image for the concrete situation and therefore cannot claim any independent material reality. Flemish supra-realism is the historical extension of Flemish pictorial realism, in that even everything to which consciousness would deny reality is presented there as material reality. The unreal is not an image of another, higher or more distant reality: it is itself materially real in this literature.

It is difficult to follow de Man's deliberations, but leaving aside the question of their phenomenological appropriateness, their intentions should be clear. The characterization of Belgian supra-realism concerns, first of all, the further determination of the specificity of present Belgian art; secondly, its literary-historical legitimation in terms of the development of realism; and thirdly, the securing of its position between German romanticism and French surrealism. All three functions have clear political implications: according to the formula (expressed in "Le destin de la Flandre," September 1, 1941, but, as far as I can see, valid for all of these articles) which identifies art as the essence of the nation, and according to the supplementary formula which calls for a correspondance between political and cultural autonomy (*génie indépendant . . . conformément . . . statut politique*), the point is to emphasize the national character of Belgian fantastic realism, to legitimize it as the historically most advanced form of the realist novel, and to assign it a relatively autonomous zone between literary production in Germany and in France. Relative autonomy means: fantastic realism, the suprarealism of the Belgians, participates in both the romantic literature of the Germans and the surrealist poetry of the French (this is why Novalis is quoted on the one hand and the surrealists on the other) and yet is distinct from both of them. Belgian literature is nothing less than the autonomous site of the synthesis of the continental European literatures. The "new Europe" announces itself in Belgium. Certainly neither 'pan-Germanic' nor 'French-rationalist,' it is a Europe in which the most advanced forms of both of the neighboring nations would permeate each other and create a new form. Belgium, the autonomous center of western Europe, would be the model for Europe. But what in the antagonistic art-nations ought to join together to create this Belgian unity must itself already have the character of the European synthesis: de Man praises Goethe's combination of a *sensibilité latine* and a *sensibilité germanique, la synthèse de ces deux tempéraments nationaux*; and he lauds Ernst Jünger, the only other German author for whom he shows unrestrained admiration, for his combination of myth and reality. A certain logic is evidently at work when an article that deals with the possibilities of developing new realities in Belgian modernism not only speaks of an *instinctive défense contre l'assimilation* but also lacks any trace of that vocabulary of race which de Man employed repeatedly in earlier articles in order to lend biological credence to the idea of national autonomy. Instead, it reads: *Un mélange hétéroclite de Flamands et de Wallons se trouva confronté avec cette tâche délicate*: inventer *une littérature sans qu'il y eut même—comme en Flandre—un exemple établi (. . .)* ("Sur les caractéristiques du roman belge d'expression française," *Le Soir*, February 24, 1942; my emphasis, W.H.; compare also "Noorden Zuid-Nederlandsche Letterkunde van heden," *Bibliographie Dechenne*, July 1942: *uit het niet*, out of nothing). Belgian literature must thus be *invented*, it must give itself a reality that it possesses neither in the myth of race nor in the political rationality of the present time, so that Belgium gains, in its literature, its material reality.

The self-generation of literature as political reality: de Man's concept of the supra-realist and surrealist Belgian literature follows this program of a political aesthetics of an art-nation. The art-nation can be considered, and not without good reason, as a political hallucination. The concept of hallucination plays in fact a striking role in these articles (it also appears again later in an important passage from "Hypogram and Inscription" [1981] in connection with Hugo and Riffaterre), yet what is interesting here is not the reality value of this *nationalité artistique* (February 24, 1942) but the political function of its program. Here it is a question of the autonomy of what, for the time being, has reality only in literature and ought to present a *political* reality *sui generis*. This is not aesthetic disengagement—rather, art is here genuinely and effectively political.

Nowhere did de Man proclaim this autonomy of art as *Politikum* so forcefully as in his article "A propos de la revue *Messages*" (July 7, 1942). He does not defend Belgian, but rather—and this may carry even greater political weight—French, surrealism. More precisely, he defends the neo-surrealism of the group gathered around Jean Lescure and the review *Messages* against the repressive ideological demands of the *révolution présente*, which in this case is to be understood as that of National Socialism. He writes: *Sous prétexte que cette révolution est totalitaire, c'est-à-dire qu'elle entend modifier tous les aspects de la vie individuelle et collective, d'aucuns ont rangé brutalement l'art parmi ses objectifs. (. . .) En d'autres termes, l'art—et plus particulièrement la littérature—se trouve transformé en un outil, en un instrument, destiné à combattre par tous les moyens une "Weltanschauung" périmée et à en imposer une autre.* De Man protests against the instrumentalization of literature into propaganda with an argument which also preempts any criticism of his own position: literary history, he writes, moves according to laws over which individuals have just as little power as daily political events. The organicist ideas about the course of literary history, the ideas of its necessity, uncontrollability and unconsciousness, could only be welcomed by the National Socialists among his readers. But de Man twists all of these ideologemes, including that of the "eternal values" of literature, in such a way that they conform to a poetic praxis which the Nazis and their followers banned as destructive and demoralizing [*zersetzend*]. He reproaches them for the *dangereuse légèreté* with which they conduct their *attaques inconsidérées contre des forces saines*: certainly a courageous critique, but also one which employs the jargon of the pathological diagnosis of sickness and health, degeneracy and vigorous growth, a jargon fascists of all times and places masterfully employ for their propaganda.

So what does de Man do in this article? With the terminology of the Nazis (and not only the Nazis), he produces propaganda—against the instrumentalization of literature into Nazi propaganda. De Man exploits the heterogeneity of the dominant ideology, using those elements that he wishes to make his own in order to discredit other elements as dangerous: the "eternal value" of literature cannot be reconciled with its historically specific propagandistic function; the organic laws of the life of art render the struggle against its regressive forms superfluous; the autonomy of literary evolution cannot be restricted to the autonomy of a single national literature. Moreover, de Man inverts the hierarchy of these ideologemes as established by the Nazis in such a way that its points are turned against the interests of German imperialism. His plea for the surrealists is a defense of the members of the "révolution surréaliste." It is printed on July 14, not the date of the "revolution présente" but that of the French Revolution.

No doubt de Man's gesture of splitting and inverting German ideology remains mimetically bound to it. No doubt either that de Man and his commitment to the surrealists and neo-surrealists remained within the confines of 'legality.' For although *Messages* published almost exclusively pieces by authors with ties to the *résistance* (I shall mention here only Ponge, whose "14 Juillet" was published in the second issue of *Messages*, Paul Eluard, and Jean Lescure; Jean Cayrol, who would later write *Nuit et brouillard*, was one of the "correspondents" of the journal), it was only after three issues, at the end of 1942, that it could no longer be published in Paris—apparently because its paper supply was cut off. Gérard Loiseaux writes in *La Littérature de la Défaite et de la Collaboration*: Messages, *la revue créée à Paris par Jean Lescure, occupe une place unique dans la littérature de Refus.*

Ce fut la seule revue publiée "légalement" à Paris et qui brocardait avec brio les écrivains collaborateurs (Paris: Publications de la Sorbonne, 1984, p. 503). According to the accounts of Jean Lescure and of Georges Lambrichs, the Brussels *correspondant* for *Messages* and a friend of Paul de Man from the 1930s to the time of his death, it was Paul de Man who made it possible for this issue of *Messages,* which could no longer appear in Paris, to be printed and distributed in Brussels. *Exercice du Silence,* contained, among other pieces, texts by Eluard ("Basse-Terre"), Bachelard, Queneau, Adamov, Leiris, Sartre ("La Mort dans l'âme") and Bataille ("Le rire de Nietzsche"). 1200 copies were printed, and the volume's colophon identifies the publication date as December 10, 1942.

At this point de Man had stopped writing for *Le Soir* and *Het Vlaamsche Land* and would publish only a few more short reviews and one further essay in the *Bibliographie Dechenne*. His sympathy for the surrealists— presumably not only a sympathy with their literary production—remained unchanged. His article on *Messages* from July 14, 1942 singles out Paul Eluard and insists that *les seules manifestations poétiques dignes de ce nom dérivent en droite ligne du mouvement surréaliste et ne font qu'en continuer les principes,* and in February 1943, he writes: *le surréalisme a ouvert des voies qui mènent dans des régions encore totalement inexplorées. Entièrement en marge d'un public qui ne comprend en rien la signification de l'essai entrepris, un groupe fervent continue la grande aventure dans laquelle la poésie française s'est lancée et entretient l'espoir que le jour où les formules expérimentées auront pu se stabiliser et se fixer, naîtra une poésie d'une profondeur et d'un éclat incomparable.* ("Condition actuelle de la littérature d'expression française," *Bibliographie Dechenne.* In this text de Man names Saint-Exupéry alongside Chardonne, and Aragon alongside Jouhandeau, as the most important authors of the last two years; de Man had already cited Aragon's definition of surrealism in *Le Soir* on September 16, 1941). All this remains part of a dubious rhetoric of surveillance and control, of justification and of cheap celebration; yet de Man's emphatic interest in and public commitment to the cause of French and Belgian surrealism is a *parti pris* for the literature and the literary politics least compatible with the Nazi cause. We do not know exactly why de Man gave up his work at *Le Soir* in November 1942. It is not improbable that he did not wish to give in to the pressure of the recently reinstituted censorship; it is possible that he was not enough of a propagandist for the editorial board. We know just as little why his contributions to the *Bibliographie Dechenne* end in March 1943. According to Georges Lambrichs, de Man's efforts to make possible the publication of *Exercice du Silence* are probably behind his departure. In any

case, Lambrichs, who himself had contributed to the *Bibliographie* for several months, was fired from his job at about the same time. Tom Keenan has discovered, in another *journal de refus* (*Poésie 43,* no. 14, May/June 1943), this postscript following a report by Pierre Seghers on the literary situation in Belgium at that moment: *BRUXELLES.—Une révolution de palais a évincé de la direction de certaines éditions Georges Lambrichs et Paul de Man qui défendaient la jeune littérature française* (p.95).

De Man had collided with the collaboration's political authorities. It was the collision between the *parti pris* for surrealism and a reality which could not tolerate surrealism's claim to freedom. With de Man's firing, a reality had asserted itself which ruled out interpretations, because each interpretation carried the threat of the subversion of that reality.

The reality of language, the tension between reality and language, the collusion and collision between one language and another, one reality and another, the discrepancies, fissures, breaks, heterogeneities which burst open the system of the one, entire, totalitarian "reality" called "language": this remained almost obsessively—but who does not suffer from this obsession?—the subject of de Man's critical work since the 1950s. Fascism was, among other things, the complete *collapse* of language and reality, of meaning and act, intention and fulfillment, one and all—the system of the elimination of the other, of the denial of *other* realities, of the denunciation of language's otherness. As long as de Man wrote for the collaborationist press, he contributed to this collapse, if for the most part cautiously, and tried, rarely energetically enough, to turn the heterogeneity of totalitarian ideology against the hegemonic claims made by its representatives. The later works of the literary theorist, which address vigilantly the totalizing tendencies in literature, literary criticism, and corresponding ideologies, are practical contributions to their dissolution. To the dissolution of language's *res*; of its, of our, *res*-ism.

August 17, 1988

Cassandre—its extreme right-wing editor Paul Colin was shot by a young member of the *résistance* in April 1943—published a violent attack on *Exercice du Silence* and its editor Jean Lescure on January 24, 1943. The end of the article summarizes the situation: *on "résiste" comme on peut.* . . .

Georges Lambrichs, who remembers this article and another one published the previous week, recalls that they were the catalyst for his, and probably Paul de Man's, removal from the Agence Dechenne.

Early January, 1988

Many years ago—it might already be twenty—Max Horkheimer recommended a little experiment during a television interview. He suggested reading newspapers a few weeks or
months after their publication. With this he bent over to pick
up a stack of rather gray papers that lay next to his chair.

I cannot recall his comments on this piece of advice. But one
can imagine that the effect he had in mind was supposed to be
both philosophical and political. Indeed, the effect of this small
postponement on the reader, on his perception of time and on
his attitude to news and published opinion, should be considerable. The reader of these old papers will notice that the imperatives, attractions and threats heralded in them reveal themselves
as such only to the degree that they no longer directly affect
him. The judgments that the newspapers imposed on him at another time can now be dismissed as hectic presumptions. In the
future he will no longer so easily obey the regulations of the
newspapers and their time. Horkheimer's advice may owe
much to the glance cast on life by the aging, by someone whose
experiences mean something else to him now than they did
when he first had them. But it differs completely from resignation. Horkheimer's is a piece of political advice that looks forward to the suspension of coercion and to its transformation for
another way of life.

Try to imagine what would happen if daily papers printed
news and commentary of three and a half months ago today, if
others printed that of fifteen years ago and still others that of
1941, of 1922. The effect would not be to blur past and present,
but rather to make them more pronounced. After all, one of the
dangerous effects of the chronological order in which newspapers appear is the numbing of the sense of what history and
what the present could be.

April 16, 1988

The notion of "historical understanding of the text" obviously
involves some peculiar problems—all the more so when it takes
place in a journal. Not only in the US, where Jon Wiener, a professor of American history, has mastered it in stunning fashion,
but also in West Germany, where Hans Ulrich Gumbrecht has
demonstrated his talent for it in a "feuilleton" article in the
Frankfurter Allgemeine Zeitung of April 7. Gumbrecht, a literary
critic, begins his "Die Kultur im Kriege" by commenting on the
hermeneutic premises of his reading of de Man's *Le Soir* articles:
*My reading respects the hermeneutic truism that understanding a
text historically* [historisches Textverständnis] *and applying the
results to the present time are phases of the reading process which,
while related to each other, must also be separated.* Gumbrecht's
grasp of the "historical understanding of a text" becomes apparent in his inability, even—and I quote—*with the best of intentions,* to discover the "unmistakably ambiguous wordings"
which I had pointed out in de Man's Sieburg review of April 28,
1942. *The best of intentions,* in fact, are not enough to understand
a newspaper article; it also demands the rudimentary philological ability to recognize connections and the probity to acknowledge them. Such as: de Man, using the jargon of nationalism,
attests to the *fort courant spirituel* of the *génie germanique* and
reproaches, along with Sieburg, the *génie français* for its *nationalisme religieux, exclusif et prétentieux.* He then asserts, mis-
leadingly and with dreadful naïveté, that *Le nationalisme
actuel*—that is, the type of nationalism propagated by the Nazis
in their "new European idea"—*est tout le contraire d'exclusif: il
est complémentaire.* He laments France's policy of denationalization in Flanders and Wallonia and offers the optimistic prog-
nosis that in the new Europe, the individual nations will live
together in "free contact" and with "mutual respect" for their
differences: *qui se savent différents et qui tiennent à cette différence
mais qui s'estiment réciproquement (. . .).* In this mutual respect
de Man sees the guarantee of "political peace and cultural stability." So much for these reflections, which can be read both as
propaganda *for* the Nazis and as demands made *on* them. What
follows, however, is "unmistakably ambiguous": a clear critique
of German nationalism, formulated with the concept of reli-
giosity which he had just associated with the *nationalisme religieux* of the French. So here are the formulations that *the best of
intentions* of an "historical understanding of the text" could neither discover nor quote: *Nous entrons dans une ère mystique, dans
une période de foi et de croyance, avec tout ce que cela suppose de
souffrance, d'exaltation et d'ivresse. La notion même du bonheur en
a été modifiée et se rapproche de normes que plusieurs auteurs ont cru
pouvoir comparer à celles du Moyen-Age.* (Mysticism is de Man's
standard criticism of Nazi Germany; cf. the article of October
14, 1941, in which he writes that it does not suffice *d'adopter les
mystiques dans lesquel les vainqueurs ont puisé leur force et puissance.*) In the face of the threat coming from Nazi Germany, the
tradition of the *génie français* has to intervene—the *génie français* which, with its *vertus de clarté, de logique, d'harmonie* and its
passé humaniste, garantit contre tout obscurantisme (evidently that
of the victors) *(. . .) Particulièrement lorsque l'orientation générale* (i.e., that induced by National Socialism) *conduit vers les
forces profondes, obscures, naturelles, la mission française qui consiste
à modérer les excès* (i.e., the German), *à maintenir les liens indispensables avec le passé, à équilibrer les poussées erratiques* (again the

German) *s'avère de première necessité*. What began as caustic criticism of France flows into severe criticism of Nazi cultural imperialism, their mysticism of violence, their obscurantism. Is it justified then, as Gumbrecht finds opportune, to speak about "de Man's joy over the military defeat of France"? Can one maintain, as Gumbrecht does, that de Man was "obviously fascinated by the national humiliation of France" after reading the following passage?—*il serait néfaste et inepte de détruire, en voulant les modifier par la force, les constantes de l'esprit latin*. And de Man continues: *Et c'est également pourquoi nous* (i.e. the Belgians) *commettrions une erreur impardonnable en rompant les liens avec les manifestations de cette culture*. Why does Gumbrecht find it opportune to "redeem" (Gumbrecht's word) de Man's article from its "literal wording"? Would he consider probity apologetic? And why? One cannot but wonder.

Gumbrecht cites, from "Le destin de la Flandre" (September 1, 1941), de Man's warnings against cultural assimilation and political annexation into the *communauté germanique*. He quotes a sentence by Hendrik Elias quoted by de Man and explicitly marked with quotation marks. But what does Gumbrecht write? *Subsequently, de Man seems to be quoting the mayor of Ghent (here too one cannot determine unambiguously the border between indirect discourse and direct quotation) (. . .)* (my emphasis; W.H.). This border could not be more unambiguous: not only because Elias' statements are surrounded by clear, legible quotation marks, but also because Elias' political position departs from de Man's line of argument in one very decisive point. While Elias supports the politics of "a Germanic state," de Man insists—and he does so as emphatically as Elias will do only much later—on Belgium's cultural and political independence from both France and Germany: *à maintenir, entre les deux blocs culturels que sont la France et l'Allemagne ce noyau (. . .) d'un génie* indépendant. *C'est conformément à ce dessein que le statut politique de la Flandre doit être établi dans* l'Europe *nouvelle* (my emphasis; W.H.). Instead of recognizing these obvious political differences, and discussing their political and ideological dimension, between complicity and opposition, Gumbrecht chooses, in this context, to speak of psychology: of *joy, fear, desire* and *concerns*. . . ! And since his familiarity with the historical background of Belgian politics under the occupation is apparently not what it might be, he takes refuge in the proven demagogic method of insinuation. . . . But I will forego any further commentary on this practice of an "historical understanding of texts," which is neither historical nor understanding. I have already made some notes on Belgian political history and Paul de Man's engagement (for example, on December 17).

I come to the second section of Gumbrecht's "hermeneutic

truism," the "application" of "results" of "an historical understanding of texts" to "the present time." Gumbrecht ventures to speak of a tendency to "trivialization [*Bagatellisierung*]" of de Man's position, and he dares to use the slogan "whitewashing." Is it a "trivialization" of de Man's anti-semitic text to call it, as I did, *disastrous* and *inexcusable*? Wasting no words on either ethics or politics, Gumbrecht for his part presents this text—in which de Man most blatantly failed, both morally and politically—in the vocabulary of a psychologist: the *tenor* of the article, he writes, reflects de Man's *concerns* in the face of the *perspective of cultural homogenization*! That cannot be? It can. Read the sentences, noteworthy in every respect, Gumbrecht devotes to de Man's article: *On the other hand the perspective of cultural homogenization* [Gleichschaltung] *gave de Man some concern. To these concerns corresponds* (!) *the tenor* (!) *of the abominable article on "The Jews in Contemporary Literature" in* (!) *its unmistakable desire to compensate for his inferiority complexes vis-à-vis Jewish intellectuals, which is connected with an all too noble dissociation from "vulgar anti-semitism."* . . . . *Concerns* about cultural homogenization as the *tenor* of a piece of anti-semitic propaganda. . . . A more than dubious hermeneutics of psychologizing and empathizing allows Gumbrecht secretly to deny the moral and political catastrophe of de Man's article and give it a highly suspect psychological "intelligibility"—for who, it is suggested, would not sympathize with *concerns* about cultural homogenization. . . ? Using the vocabulary of psycho-pathology—*inferiority complexes* and their *compensation*—only camouflages the real, the ethical problem of both the article and its reading, in the interests of a representational schema oppressively reminiscent of the "sick versus healthy" schema which grounds de Man's tract. The continuity between de Man's and Gumbrecht's articles, in this respect, is irritating, to say the very least. Certainly no one would be seriously inclined to confuse the political implications of this rhetoric with Gumbrecht's own political convictions. The ideological resources, though, from which de Man's article draws its energies have, evidently, not yet been exhausted; their tenacity is indebted to, among other things, a type of "hermeneutics" which replaces historical analysis with blurring ignorance and political reflections with pathologization. This means that Gumbrecht—and he is just one of many representatives of the new German, and not only German, ideology—need not even "apply" the "results" of his "historical understanding" to the "present time," because the "past" still dictates the rules of his "present" discourse.

We do not just write "after Auschwitz." There is no historical or experiential "after" to an absolute trauma. The historical continuum being disrupted, any attempt to restore it would be a vain act of denegation. The "history" of Auschwitz, of what made it possible, supported it, and still supports it in all its denials and displacements—this "history" cannot enter into any history of development or progress of enlightenment, knowledge, reflection, or meaning. This "history" cannot enter into history. It deranges all dates and destroys the ways to understand them. "Historical understanding" demands, at the very least: to understand that historical understanding, that history, in a strict sense, is impossible *and* most urgently necessary— and that here, in this disaster of a history, something other than history is about to happen, monstrously. Whoever avoids exposing himself to this disaster is bound to end in cynicism—in the cynicism of the historicist, of good conscience, or of the beautiful soul.

March 12, 1988

An instructive historical and political question that should be asked while reading de Man's early journalism: which of the convictions and theories advocated in these articles could be translated into the present and still published in today's newspapers; which of them have become obsolete; and which radically untranslatable?

If one wanted to answer this question honestly, one would have to admit with a certain bitterness that much of what de Man wrote during the war could indeed have been written between the 1950s and 80s—not by de Man, to be sure. For instance, this passage from "Sur les possibilités de la critique," a text published by de Man on December 2, 1941, could easily be found today in an article by any number of literary historians who attempt to grasp the formal characteristics of literature through their historical changes. I translate: *This investigation cannot be undertaken on the basis of preconceived beliefs, but demands, on the contrary, a liberation from all prejudices and all extraliterary inclinations. Literature is an independent domain which has a life, laws and obligations belonging only to it, and which are in no way dependent upon the philosophical and ethical contingencies which assert themselves along its borders. (. . .) It is thus necessary to verify constantly one's methods of evaluation and adapt them to the modalities of the time. And this can only be accomplished by applying methods which derive directly from the domain of history. That is to say, one must consider the set of experiences and symptoms furnished by the examination of the past. (. . .) M. Davignon's assertion, that the critic is not an historian, is only true to a certain extent. For before he can be a critic, he must be an historian of that branch of human activity which is literature. (. . .) What matters above all is to investigate, in the tendency of a work or a writer, the way in which it integrates itself into the greater trends of the period, and the contribution its production makes to subsequent developments.*

Is it not conceivable that a friendly and approving critique of Sartre, like the one de Man published on January 27, 1942, under the title "Le renouveau du roman"—quoting in some detail the criticism of the auctorial narrative perspective from Sartre's "M. François Mauriac et la liberté" (⋯, February 1939)—could be published in many places today? (It is obvious, by the way, that a considerable number of the arguments de Man used in his *Le Soir* articles derive from this Sartre text. In his interview with Stefano Rosso, de Man himself called attention to his early reading of Sartre.) For de Man, Sartre's lesson is that *Le romancier n'est point Dieu.* I translate: *Revolutionary language, if that is the case.* (Let me emphasize that it is *Sartre's* language which de Man calls revolutionary here. One must assume that de Man regarded positions like Sartre's as part of a general European revolution, a concept which appears frequently in de Man's writings of the time and which should not be hastily identified with that of the Nazis.) *Revolutionary language, if that is the case. The implied value judgment is not entirely legitimate, for aesthetic doctrines do not have absolute value, and it is impossible to debate their respective merits. But it is normal that, once one of them has had its moment and is preparing to give up its place to another, one notices a certain bad humor in the judgments made against the declining norm. That is a characteristic index of the turbulences which disturb the atmosphere. And, in fact, Sartre's theory breaks with a tradition which has been firmly established for almost a century, and, from a constructive point of view, it opens the door to a development based on other precepts.*

And what about the following comments on the influence of modern French literature on English novels? Couldn't they be written today by a conservative comparatist? I translate: *Very little connects the novels of Huxley, Joyce, or Lawrence to those of the preceding generation in England, while their filiation with French models is obvious. In this sense, it is justified to recognize the superiority of current French literature as far as originality is concerned: the spiritual parents of the English novel are named Gide and Proust, not Galsworthy or Hardy. By making contact with the other side of the Channel, an entire group of writers freed themselves from the constraints imposed by a school which had already reached the heights of its perfection. The new breeze they felt in "A la recherche du temps perdu" or "Les Faux Monnayeurs" was an irresistible appeal to them* ("Le Coeur Intraitable: Une traduction de l'anglais," *Le Soir*, May 27, 1941).

The contemporary defenders of subjectivity, immediateness and the personal voice in the novel, and the enemies of "desubjectivization," "formalism," "structuralism," and so forth—couldn't they have written sentences similar to those by de Man in his *Le Soir* article of July 8, 1941? I translate (here too, incidentally, de Man follows an argument of Sartre): These *modern novels tell us absolutely nothing about the person who created them. We know nothing more about Roger Martin du Gard after reading the Thibaults, nor about Jules Romains after the "Hommes de bonne volonté." No aspect of their inner life, of their tastes, or of their way of life, has passed into their work. Things are completely different with Magermans and Libert. We are offered, on the contrary, a distinctly personal experience and emotion. It is not a matter of practicing subtle speculations, but of directly expressing a deep, lived, experience. (. . .) We come into direct contact with the characters of these writers, since what they describe is what is most personal in them. Instead of concealing their individuality behind a detached, impersonal attitude, it becomes the unique source of their inspiration.*

All of these statements, as old as they are, and as problematic as their original ideological context is, could presumably still have been published, with only minor modifications, in a good many journals and newspapers of the last few years. And yet they are part of an ideological tradition which was able to ally itself—if only at certain times and at certain points—with Nazi ideology, an ideological tradition which did not prevent the composition of articles like the one on Chardonne and "The Jews in Contemporary Literature."

The question we are left with is simply: What thinking, and what in thinking, would be capable of rendering impossible the disastrous political engagement of this tradition?

Early April 1988

Whenever one wants to give the appearance of a scholarly discussion, one argues, as they used to do, in the debates over Formalism (which de Man attacked sharply time and again), and then again in those over Structuralism, and yet again in those concerning what they call Post-structuralism: one speaks, that is—reproachfully and in the rhetoric of the defense of established 'values'—of an attack on the responsible subject, on history, and on the world in general. All of them, it is said, are being dissolved in the "acid bath of language" (!), referents disintegrating, realities vaporizing. . . . One speaks of the fetishization of language and thinks that, with this word from Sartre, one has dismissed Heidegger's apophthegm "Die Sprache spricht." Heidegger aside, one can only turn this argument against de Man if one has conveniently forgotten that de Man himself, for instance at the beginning of "Self (*Pygmalion*)" in *Allegories of Reading,* accepts Heidegger's proposition that we

are the property of language only to accept its *converse* as well. Only from the impossibility of deciding on the truth-value of *both* propositions does he draw the conclusion *that all discourse* has to be *referential but can never signify its actual referent.* This can be understood to mean that for language there is no present reality to which it could refer *as* present—and that there is *in* language only a 'reality' to which it cannot but must refer, which remains inaccessible for its own mode of signification. All discourse, then, would be the experience of the indeterminable other of discourse.

In April of 1986 Andrzej Warminski told me a little story from de Man's seminar that goes well here: The seminar was trying to clarify what a referent is, and the question seemed easily answered—someone said, this table here, for example, is a referent. No, countered de Man, this is not a referent, this —and here he knocked on it—is a table.

In the story, at least, the table is no longer a table. . . .

November 18, 1987

. . . . *the question of reading as the necessity to decide between signified and referent, between violence on the stage and violence in the streets.* . . . .

("Aesthetic Formalization in Kleist," p.280)

February 1988

This sentence by Paul de Man, along with some worse ones, appeared on March 4, 1941: *Gide, Kafka, Hemingway, Lawrence—on pourrait allonger indéfiniment la liste—ne font tous que tenter de pénétrer, selon des méthodes propres à leur personnalité, dans les secrets de la vie intérieure.* De Man's list of authors comes from the chapter on "Tragedy and the Whole Truth" in Aldous Huxley's *Music at Night* (Garden City, N.Y.: Doubleday Doran, 1931). In his *Le Soir* article de Man shortens the list by one significant name that stands at the head of Huxley's list, a name that de Man repeatedly mentions with the greatest respect in many other articles: Proust. One has to assume either that de Man did not have the courage here, in the context of a special anti-semitic newspaper page, meant to serve as propaganda for the pogroms, to associate the name of a well-known Jewish author with the great realist tradition of the novel, *or* that Proust's name, if it was included, was deleted by the editors (this is the only one of de Man's *Le Soir* articles that does not fill all the available space). The name Kafka, however, is not missing. In Huxley's 1931 essay, from which de Man had already quoted the full list in "Le Roman Anglais Contemporain" (*Les Cahiers du Libre Examen,* January 1940), we read: *Proust, D. H. Lawrence, André Gide, Kafka, Hemingway—here are five obviously significant and important contemporary writers. Five authors as remarkably unlike one another as they could well be. They are at one only in this: that none of them has written a pure tragedy, that all are concerned with the Whole Truth* (p.16). When he published the abbreviated Huxley list a year later, there is no doubt that de Man was not concerned with the Whole Truth: he betrayed it with his article. But he names Kafka. He had also named him in the article of January 1940 when he referred to *Das Schloss* as a counterpart to *Buddenbrooks.* In the essay "On Grace" (*Music at Night,* pp.80–81) Huxley provides a short characterization of *Das Schloss* without mentioning Kafka's relationship to Judaism. Since, as far as I can tell, de Man does not refer to Kafka's work anywhere else, either earlier or later, it seems reasonable to suppose that he did not associate Kafka's name with a sense of opposition, because it simply was not clear to him whom he was citing. This is conceivable, but it is not probable. For de Man could hardly *not* know that *none* of the authors on Huxley's list was compatible with the notions of literature that the Nazi administrators promulgated in Belgium: the list consisted, that is, of a 'decadent' psychologist, a militant anti-fascist, and an author who not only appealed constantly to psychoanalysis but who was notorious even among liberal contemporaries as a pornographer. And Kafka. Translations of *Die Verwandlung* and *Das Schloss* had been published by Gallimard in May and November of 1938. In 1942 Gerhard Heller—who together with Otto Abetz, Karl Epting and Friedrich Sieburg worked at mitigating French "Germanophobia" and "purifying" French literature of all "undesirable elements"—made sure that Albert Camus' *Le Mythe de Sysyphe* appeared without the section on "L'Absurde dans l'oeuvre de Franz Kafka," even though in his text Camus had established no connection between Kafka and Judaism. (Cf. Loiseaux, *La Littérature de la Défaite. . . ,* p.476, and Albert Camus, *Essais* [Paris: Pléiade, 1965], pp.200, 1414–1416). Gerhard Heller, this "Allemand à Paris," certainly knew why he suppressed Camus' Kafka essay; it is improbable that the extraordinarily well-read Paul de Man did not know what he was doing when, in an anti-semitic article, he placed Kafka in the ranks of the great realist novelists of Europe. It is, however, not certain. And that is the problem —not merely hermeneutic, but rather political and ethical—with the citation of this name.

At issue here is not a detail that decides the meaning of the entire text from March 4, 1941, and certainly not a detail that decides the position of this text's author or its effect on his readers then and now. But this detail, the name *Kafka, could* have and

should have decided all of that. It could have and should have been cited—plainly, clearly, unambiguously—as the name of resistance against racist terror; instead it functions, at best, as an anti-anti-semitic allusion. In the ideological-political context of the time, the name *Kafka* could have and should have been a protest against the division of the world and of literature into the Jewish and the non-Jewish. Only when used decisively—as the name of a decision, clear and discernible to anyone—could the name have opposed that division. Accordingly, in the Belgium of 1941 the name should have been not *Kafka,* but *Proust.* And that means the *entire* article would have had to be written such that it would have been *un*acceptable to the editors of *Le Soir* and their German authorities, and thus *un*printable. Only then would justice have been done to the names Kafka and Proust in this historical situation: they would have prevented an injurious and, indeed, a terrorist article. They were, objectively, names against the politics of black-listing and denunciation of names, through names; but in de Man's article they are *not.* He participates in this politics by leaving the significance of the name *Kafka* unclear and by going so far as to include in his text a second, clearly denunciatory list with names from Maurois to Benda. *Proust* and *Kafka* were names of the ethical—they stood against the terror of naming and of classification, and for the indivisible community of that which is human. For de Man, the ethical dimension of names—that they call for the affirmation of the indeterminable—remained unrealized.

And with this only the *very* least has been said.

May 28, 1988

About de Man's article of March 4, 1941, "Les Juifs dans da Littérature actuelle," I do not have much to add to what I said in the *Frankfurter Allgemeine Zeitung* of February 24th: *this one article—even if it was extracted from de Man by the threat of dismissal from his job and hence a labor camp, even if it is desperately contradictory, and although, as the Jewish friends of the young de Man have confirmed, it did not reflect de Man's feelings or convictions— this article remains disastrous. It was written, of course, almost a year prior to the murderous decisions of the Wannsee-Konferenz and the "solution to the Jewish question" accepted by de Man cannot be directly associated with the "final solution" as we know it. But a few weeks before de Man wrote this article the first pogroms and deportations had begun in neighboring Holland. In this situation, any anti-semitic remark was an approval of manhunts.*

That de Man was pressured into writing this article cannot excuse him. The threat of dismissal and forced labor may have been real, as de Man's first wife asserts, or at least perceived to be real (according to statistics in *L'an 40*, pp.155–158, the number of unemployed people "volunteering" to serve the German economy had already exceeded 90,000 in December 1940, and by July 1941 had reached 190,000)—still, it would have required only a minimum of civil courage not to write the article. The reports from de Man's friends of the time are clear and unambiguous: none of them had observed anti-semitic sentiments, much less convictions, either before or after he wrote this text. But he did write it. The article is, without a doubt, contradictory, as Jacques Derrida has demonstrated in great detail in "Paul de Man's War." And it should not have been contradictory; it should have unambiguously, and without compromise, opposed the racist madness and the manhunt.

What in the structure of de Man's arguments made this infamous approval of deportation possible; what, at least, did not forbid it? What allowed de Man to argue about a matter when the mere existence of the discussion was shameless?

De Man makes use of the argument of "reality" to reject as absurd the anti-semitic thesis of the *mainmise juive*. He writes: *Mais la réalité est différente.* The "reality" referred to here is that of the "law" of aesthetic evolution: *Il semble que les évolutions esthétiques obéissent à des lois très puissantes qui continuent leur action même que l'humanité est secouée par des événements considérables.* The continuum of literary history, which over the last century and a half has been a history of realism (of the *réalité extérieur* and the *réalité psychologique*), is supposed to be so completely determined by the "reality" of these general evolutionary laws that current historical events—wars, mass unemployment, major political changes—are incapable of breaking this continuum. The law—"reality"—is the law of aesthetic autonomy, against which the empirical reality of historical events or individual intentions is powerless. These are placed either at the level of the law—in which case they deserve the title of originality, of "reality"—or else they remain, like "les Juifs" whom de Man characterizes by their ability to assimilate and hence to imitate—on a *second plan* where they are unable to interfere with the law, with "reality," with originality, and where they are, therefore, considered dispensable in terms of "reality," the law of literature and its history. Jewish writers thus have no place in the "reality" which in this article, and so many others, is the only one which counts for de Man. They are foreigners to it, he says, a *force étrangère* opposed to *notre civilisation,* foreigners to a "reality" which is called "ours." As imitators they are exiled from "reality," from the law, unreal even before they have been driven out of Europe, and thus—such is the logical consequence de Man draws from the alleged law of aesthetic autonomy—considered deportable without *conséquences déplor-*

ables. De Man's "realism" makes the Jews deportable because "reality," the "reality" of literature and of history, has no need for their "imitation."

The logic of "reality" and of the *esthétique réaliste* which de Man pursues here, without restraint, is a logic that makes it possible to deny Jewish writers their reality. While this logic seems, at the beginning of the article, determined to reject "vulgar anti-semitism," it becomes clear, at the end of the article at the very latest, that it is the logic of a *structural anti-semitism,* which in principle abandons to unreality all those who do not obey de Man's proclaimed law of historical "reality." The "reality" of which he speaks here is hypostatized as an historical self-determination of the "proper" culture in order to be able to exclude *la culture juive* as "foreign." The "foreign" is not respected as a possibility alongside the "proper," but is subordinated to the "proper" as one of its epigonal, mimetic forms. The determination as "foreign" already destines it for exile.

The system adopted by de Man in his article rules out the possibility of respecting the "other" because it knows nothing of the respect for the otherness of the other. Again and again in these early articles de Man demanded respect for the independence of Belgium and attempted to give force to this demand through the determination of the specific differences between Belgian literature and the literatures of France and Germany. His Belgicism was, in principle, anti-hegemonic. In spite of its defensive traits, the "realism" which de Man supports in "Les Juifs dans la Littérature" is strictly hegemonic: his hypostasis of the law, of "reality," rules out regard for the difference of other histories and for the realities of other human beings. The "reality" which he talks about here was in fact a murderous myth; even if it referred to aesthetic evolution, it served sheer societal violence; every other reality which was not determined according to its measures had to disappear before it. And thus the elementary law of morality—respect for the other in its freedom and virtual indeterminability—disappeared before the ideological "law of reality."

The ideology of "realism"—one of those that led to Auschwitz.

May 29, 1988

The disturbing but symptomatic reaction of journalism to de Man's early newspaper articles has consisted of homogenization and condemnation. Often without even the most rudimentary knowledge of the texts and the dates, all of the articles have been homogenized with that one; de Man's changing, often confused, but for the most part distanced Belgicist positions have been homogenized with collaboration *tout court*; his early ideological positions have been homogenized with his later critique of ideology; and finally this confused mass was somehow homogenized with the views of an imaginary collective called his "school." This 'uniformation' of texts, times, countries, languages, and persons was pursued with such force that one has good reason to see it as a version, however unwitting, of *Gleichschaltung*. The most surprising aspect of these presentations is perhaps that their authors, who, having hastily established a consensus, have presented themselves as caretakers of history, have been the least willing to allow for the possibility that someone can change, that someone can distance himself from earlier viewpoints by experience and reflection, that someone can have a history. In the background of this denial of history, one can sense the old idea of the continuum of historical development, which provided the basis for de Man's anti-semitic article: it is the idea of *one* history which tolerates no other, of a hegemonic line of development undisturbed by any change, determining everyone and eliminating everything which, in those changes, points to an *other* history. "History," this vague abstraction, seems then and now to function as a powerful means of homogenizing and making a taboo out of history—namely *that* history which exists only concretely, singularly, idiosyncratically, painfully. To judge history on the basis of its empty generality is to deny the past its particularities, and to run the risk of repeating it in its worst traits.

March 1988

The question of why de Man did not admit to his "errors" publicly, why he did not confess and why not apologize, keeps being repeated. But the question itself gives one more to think about than does the lack of an answer.

The question presumes that de Man's articles, and especially the anti-semitic one, are something that could be called an error, a failure, a moral mistake, which it would have been possible to confess. But although the article on "The Jews in Contemporary Literature" contains indisputable inconsistencies and undeniable oppositional tendencies, it remains, even where it rejects "vulgar anti-semitism" as "dangerous," *lapidaire*, contradictory and "absurd," it remains intimately linked to the ideologies that are promulgated by nearly all of the other articles: the ideologies of reality, race, value, evolution according to fixed laws, certainty in judgment, and the determining power of names. These articles form a loose, open system in which almost anything is possible and every ideology can enter, according to the rule of journalism: "everything is worth dis-

cussing." Its logic of terror—all too obvious in the one article, more refined and thus concealed in the others—lies in the readiness to admit the appalling into the realm of practical possibilities and to accept it as a tool of political or social planning. If this one article and the others connected with it are "errors," then they are systematic errors. And this system, essentially a system of judgments, decisions, and determinations of the other, is not only still possible today, it is still dominant. To speak of an "error" and a "mistake" does not protect de Man— de Man is dead—but it does protect those who are speaking in these terms. It is one of the ways to obstruct the necessary dissolution of the whole system of ideological practices implied in de Man's articles, and to prevent the emergence of different forms of speech not based on judging and condemning. Any avowal, any confession, de Man *could* have made would have been *in*sufficient, in that it would not have begun to undo the ideological premises underlying nearly all his articles. (This does not explain why de Man failed to confess, nor does it, as the moralists like to put it, "excuse" him. Who could ever, in the strict sense of the word, ex-cuse someone? But then again, moralists have always been most effective in cultivating a lax concept of morality.)

The question of why de Man did not publicly admit his "error" teaches, I think, something else. The vocabulary of the question and the position from which it is asked are those of the police who have seen a spectacular case slip out of their hands. The missed trial is made up for now, *après coup*. The representatives of the "public"—the journalists—first present themselves as the prosecution; then, again as representatives of the "public," they declare themselves judges; and finally, still representing the "public," they carry out the sentence—public ignominy—which was already contained in the indictment. This "public" supposedly *represented* here is, however, in fact *constituted* by the journalists in the first place, and constituted as a public that unites all three juridical functions in itself: plaintiff, judge, and executioner. The principle of the separation of powers, one of the basic institutions of non-totalitarian societies, is suspended in the sphere of the so-called media, the public sphere *par excellence* of our techno-democracies. The only thing, in this techno-public sphere, which still allows for differences and differentiations, and for a semblance of the separation of powers, is the division of the press. But it too has proven in this case relatively ineffective: apparently *The Nation, Newsweek, La Quinzaine littéraire,* the *FAZ,* and the *Manchester Guardian* form an ideology cartel which cuts across all, sometimes enormous, political differences. In this respect the scandal could not be more normal. But the press, a notorious metaphor machine, attempts to follow out its image of the trial—accusation, conviction, and the missing confession—and, accordingly, it needs public defenders. Since no one has "defended" de Man's articles, those who have corrected distorted, abbreviated, or invented information are transformed by journalistic verdict into the "defenders" of the texts they discuss; and in place of the deceased defendant, *they* now are put on the stand and sentenced. This is how the "public" has reacted to the lack of a "public confession." In the question of why de Man never confessed one should hear the threat of just this reaction. The "public," *this* "public" of demo-technocracy, here defines itself by the collapse of all juridical instances to a single one: the executing word. With it the language of technology has reached the point where it turns into mythic slogan [*Parole*].

Why did de Man not refer publicly to his early activities as a journalist, particularly to his anti-semitic article? The question has to be taken seriously, even if it can hardly be answered. I add another one which should be taken just as seriously. It concerns Thomas Mann, the energetic, clear-sighted spokesman for the exiled German authors and one of the sharpest and most effective critics of Nazi barbarism. The following passage comes from Mann's *Leiden an Deutschland—Tagebuchblätter aus den Jahren 1933 und 1934*, one of the most cutting attacks on the beginning of the Nazi dictatorship: *Exorcism of the middle class-humane spirit, which clothes principally in the robes of anti-semitism, and reduction to the national-racial* [Völkisch-Nationale] *with unprecedented thoroughness and force. Suppression of the control the Jewish spirit has exercised over the German is ruinous* (GW XII [Frankfurt: S. Fischer, 1974], p.700). This passage, like all the other journal entries which Mann combined and published in 1945, is a revised version of the 1933 and 1934 journals. The second sentence of the passage just quoted reads, in its original form, as follows: *The revolt against Jewishness would have my sympathy* [Verständnis], *so to speak, if the suppression of the control the Jewish spirit exercises over the German were not so problematic for the German, and if Germandom were not so dumb as to throw someone of my type into the same pot and drive me into exile* (*Tagebücher 1933–34* [Frankfurt: S. Fischer, 1977], p.54). A bad remark, and not the only one of its kind. In the same journal, in an entry dated "Monday 10.IV.33 Lugano," Mann writes: *But nevertheless, are significant and great revolutionary things happening in Germany? The Jews. . . . That Kerr's arrogant and poisonous Jewish-accented Nietzsche interpretations* [Nietzsche-Vermauschelung] *are no longer possible is ultimately no disaster; likewise the dejewification* [Entjudung] *of justice.—Secret, stormy, strained thoughts. Hostile, malevolent, low and un-German things in the higher sense will continue to exist in any case. But I am beginning to suspect that the process is, nevertheless, one of those which has two sides . . .* (p. 46). "Ultimately no disaster"—is this not exactly that gruesome sanctioning of forced exile which Paul de Man pronounces with the words "pas de conséquences déplorables"? But Thomas Mann goes further than de Man and relates what he calls "dejewification" to "significant and great revolutionary things," evidently the Nazi revolution. The "poisoning" which Mann talks about is precisely what de Man rejected as absurd. And while there is sufficient reason to suspect that de Man was pressured into writing his anti-semitic article, the same cannot be said of Thomas Mann's private diary entry: he not only made these statements, he meant them. Why did Thomas Mann never distance himself, clearly and unambiguously, from the anti-semitic diary entries, though he clearly knew that they would be published unabridged after his death? Why did he not seize the opportunity in 1945, with the publication of *Leiden an Deutschland*, to denounce and analyze the other *Leiden* which befell not merely "Germany" but also himself: anti-semitism. And on the same occasion, he could have said something about his "Blood of the Walsungs." Not a word; although he should have known that in the case of a writer of international reknown even the most private feelings can have widespread public effects. And "Blood of the Walsungs" was not merely an entry in a journal or an article in a daily newspaper.

It seems to me that the question of de Man's silence is necessary. And even more imperative than finding an answer is thinking about the question and the assumptions connected with it. We should also think about the fact that questions like this are not always asked when they should be. The selection made by the agents of "public opinion" allows for the suspicion that they are not really interested in these questions, but rather in preventing the emergence of others. . . .

These other questions would concern the *public*, as it is constituted by a discursive technology in which language and history, reduced to the state of "news," not only serve as commodities but as 'proof of reality' for whatever and whoever is involved in the general movement of its utterances. They would investigate the technical production of social reality, and expose the public matter, the matter of the public, the *res publica* to what it is supposed to be: to debate, investigating the historical destiny of public discourse, of our discourse, especially about guilt, conscience, and related things (—and perhaps more specifically than Freud, for whom guilt was the very foundation of society). It would be within this framework that the debate about fascism and guilt, about Schmitt, Heidegger, Jünger, Benn, Blanchot, Pound, Lewis, de Man and all the others, comparable and incomparable, would have to be conducted in order to prepare the dismantling of a public realism—or a *res publicanism*—that tends, in fact, to suppress or at least to instrumentalize the discourse of guilt, moral conscience, and mourning. The alternative would be our fixation in the techno-mythic sphere.

June 11, 1988

From a letter of June 7:

"(. . .)

(. . .) The reason for the contradictory argumentation and sudden turns which characterize almost all of de Man's longer articles is not to be found in a concealed systematics which might resolve the contradictions, but probably lies in de Man's ambivalent relation to the occupation forces. On the one hand, de Man like his uncle expected the dissolution of a capitalist society, in the disguise of liberal parliamentarism, and the opening of a way toward a national socialism; he feared, on the other hand, that the occupation forces would destroy Belgian national autonomy and thereby make a genuinely new social order impossible. This split in his position corresponded to that of a public which included censors and German sympathizers as well as skeptical, distanced, and critical readers. De Man's articles are, it seems to me, a continual compromise with the expectations and demands of these two groups, a compromise between complicity and criticism. This compromise generally takes the form of 'on the one hand, on the other hand'; often it takes that of a juxtaposition of elements of criticism with elements of open conformism; occasionally de Man distances himself from the dominant ideology by expressing his admiration of authors and tendencies that were incompatible with the doctrine and the mentality of the Nazis. This includes not only the counter-doctrinal assertion that the continuity of literary evolution—particularly in Belgium—was not interrupted by the victory of national socialism, but also the energetic engagement for the surrealists and an article like the one on Charles Péguy (May 6, 1941), where you will find, for example, this sentence: *ce passionné, imbu d'idées socialistes et du justice égalitaire: il sera dreyfusard jusqu'au bout.* De Man attributes this belief to Péguy's friends, but the entire article is a hymn to Péguy, leaving no doubt that de Man counts himself among these friends and shares their ideas and hopes. Belgians at the time were probably aware of Péguy's support for Dreyfus, and de Man's remark was easily legible as a plea against the anti-semitism he had given voice to just two months before. This article could hardly have been written by an anti-semite or a convinced Nazi. Understanding this presupposes, however, a minimum knowledge of

history and the ability to read between the lines and see what single words, phrases, and names connote. I am sure you will agree with me that the veiled discourse [*Sklavensprache*] here is not articulated with an especially loud voice.

Things are not very different with the article '*Le Massacre des Innocents.*' (Incidentally, the series 'Messages' in which the Dubois poem was published has nothing to do with Lescure's neo-surrealist journal of the same name; my comment in the *FAZ* that such a connection existed was a mistake.) Of course one could read it as an interpretation whose immanent consistency stems from its closeness to the Dubois text. But book reviews in a newspaper are neither read nor written that way. What counts is what is in the article, what it accents and which contemporary events it connotes. The article, as you know, was published on September 1, 1942; between August 4 and mid-September 1942, 10,000 Jews were deported from Belgium to Auschwitz (cf. Nora Levin, *The Holocaust* [New York: Schocken 1973], p.421). I cannot believe that an otherwise well-informed journalist with many Jewish friends would have known nothing about the deportations. Along with its date, the emphatic title of the review connotes a specific reference which I believe I do not need to elucidate for you. Read the sentences I have quoted in this historical context, and any immanent reading collapses in a pile of banalities. Here, where I have more space than in a newspaper, I shall quote in greater detail: *On pourrait volontiers appeler ce* Massacre des Innocents *une méditation sur la culpabilité qui a conduit l'humanité à l'état affreux dans lequel elle se trouve à l'instant.* (Fascists do not usually talk about the guilt of humanity—which would implicate them as well—but rather about the guilt of others.) *La plainte et la lamentation ne peuvent se justifier, même dans une si pitoyable situation. Car tout ce qui arrive maintenant n'est pas l'aveugle et impitoyable action de la destinée, mais la conséquence d'une faute, d'une accumulation de fautes morales commises au cours des âges.* (Certainly this is a rather large gesture, but it says 'nostra culpa' once again.) *L'utilité d'une telle épreuve est de faire prendre conscience de cette culpabilité, de faire voir aux foules qu'elles ont mal agi.* Unlike you, I do not find it astonishing that de Man puts his hopes in the sober consciousness of the guilt of 'mankind' and in the possibility that 'the masses' will become aware of their mistakes so that they finally contemplate the 'true values.' It is entirely consistent with journalistic moralism, as practiced over the last hundred years of bourgeois criticism, to call for a transformation of the dominant conditions of social life in the vocabulary of a morality of values which has since become obsolete. If you read this passage in the context of its dates, you cannot help but overhear not merely a protest against the prevailing state of things, but *also* a *nostra culpa* in face of the deportations. If you do not do that, you are reading it without its date, and thus reading only half of it.

My last comment concerns another procedure frequently at work in de Man's articles; namely, turning National Socialist ideologemes against the practical politics of the occupant. At a time when public discussion of the future of the Belgian state was disliked, but not yet forbidden, by the Nazis, on March 17, 1941, de Man writes about a lecture on the Italian 'Risorgimento' which had emphasized the 'strictly national character' of the 'national revolution' in Italy: *On voit donc bien que ce n'est pas dans une servile imitation d'une expérience étrangère que l'Italie a puisé ses forces pour réaliser sa nouvelle grandeur. (. . .) Et la leçon est importante pour les Belges qui désirent voir leur pays se reconstruire: ils verront comment il faut trouver ses forces régénératrices, non pas en regardant au delà des frontières, mais en tirant parti de qualités spécifiques qui s'étaient tout au long de l'histoire du pays.* The argument follows the paradoxical logic of national specificity: Italy's 'national revolution' is exemplary in that it follows no example. The national reconstruction and regeneration of Belgium must, accordingly, develop independently of events 'beyond the borders'—independently also of events in Germany.

You will also find similar remarks in his other articles. They do not rule out the prospect of a Belgian fascism, but they do refuse to recognize a hegemonic power (except in the article about Chardonne). In this regard, it seems to me, one can distinguish de Man's position relatively clearly from the views of, for example, Drieu La Rochelle, who proclaimed already on November 14, 1940 in *La Gerbe*: *Point de fédération sans hégémonie. L'égalité n'existe pas. Une hégémonie déclarée vaut mieux qu'une hégémonie dissimulée* (quoted in Pascal Ory, *Les Collaborateurs 1940–1945*; Paris: Seuil 1976; p.212–213). And yet, de Man remains caught in the paradox of being able to wish for a 'national revolution' only on the example of the National Socialist and the fascist 'revolutions,' whose example, according to the imperative of singularity, should not be imitated. (You will notice here another version of the mimetological problem his article about "the Jews" raised: treated as figures of imitation, "the Jews" are abandoned by the European reality of history and society; the Belgians would be exposed to a similar fate if they were to subject themselves to the model of the imperialist nations, a model nevertheless oppressively present.)

All these maneuvers by which de Man tries to preserve his autonomy and the independence of his 'nation' remain within the framework of nationalist and socialist ideologies. You will agree with me that these maneuvers do not count for much. But they do count as nuances which should not be retouched—not for the sake of historical and philological precision, but because

one can learn nothing about and nothing against fascism without paying attention to such nuances. By emphasizing them one takes a step in the direction of the disintegration or dissolution [*Zersetzung*] which all fascisms, national socialisms, and totalitarianisms had to combat. De Man did not leave their domain during the 1940s, for all the ideologemes he sought to mobilize against the dominant ideology constituted the essential medium of this ideology itself: national identity, continuity of development, autonomy, individuality, immediateness, realism and reality. They have been dissolving ever since, but they still define, in altered configurations, important parts of today's ideological and political realm. They must be exposed to the ongoing critical labor of, as you say, 'Zersetzung,' if we want to think, to practice, singularity and society, democracy and technics, and first of all, in them all, language differently.
    (. . . .)"

March 19, 1988

On the technique of a literature which would undercut the techno-political destruction of literature, Brecht writes in "Über reimlose Lyrik mit unregelmäßigen Rhythmen" (March 1939): *It was a question of transmitting single sentences to distant, artificially dispersed audiences. The sentences had to be put into the most concise form, and one had to make allowances for disruptions (by jamming stations).* (*GW* 19, Frankfurt: Suhrkamp, 1971, p.403)

July 23, 1988

These notes not only seek to respond to some of de Man's articles, they also try to question, to specify, to multiply this response: giving not just *one* response, but assembling a chorus of responses, establishing a sort of 'internal' but unhomogenous 'public' of responses, and at different times to different problems in different tones; including not only responses to de Man's texts but responses to the responses of others as well.

They are the attempt to give not just a *response*: not only to *react* to the impudence of these newspaper articles but to find in an open polylogue the space for reflections not defined by their logic of evaluation and dismissal. Mere reactions are powerless, especially when dealing with the discourse of totalitarianism. The moralistic reaction draws its ability to fascinate from this powerlessness: it is itself merely fascinated by its *vis-à-vis* and, entranced, follows its dictate. Hence the distressing theatrics of its gesticulations, hence its tendency to demonize, hence the blindness of its diagnoses. This *moralism* has long since laid down the weapons of criticism because, for it, it is enough to rely on the vague consensus of good will. But good will never was reliable. While good will is confident of its own goodness and takes fascism to be already transparent, it is one of the elementary demands of morality—and not only intellectual morality—to understand totalitarian discourse in detail, *not* to presume that this understanding is already secured and that its form is *entirely* different from that of its object. Elements of totalitarian ideologies live on—and most stubbornly in those who proclaim their own immunity. To break with these ideologies effectively, it is not enough to pass final judgment on them after a short trial. *Frontal* opposition is not enough—the politics of fascism was a front-politics. Moralistic consensus is not enough—it shares its most crucial premises with the consensus of the *Volksgemeinschaften*. Responses to totalitarian discourse can be *effective* and *responsible* only if they resist vague homogenization, if they break with totalitarian logic in all its traits, multiply the fronts and analytic procedures. And join the use of their weapons with the criticism of them.

It is thus not only a matter of *giving* a response, but of *disrupting* the *one* response (it always hypostasizes itself as a model) with the diversity of responses. And yet, beyond the disruption, to continue speaking with other responses from other times, earlier or later. The assembly of these responses should not neutralize any of them, but give each of them its particularity. It serves the heightening, not the reduction, of attention. Mutually refracted in this way, these responses seem to be best suited to contribute to the dismantling of a discourse whose power may have been most brutal "then," but still can strike every one of us now. For this discourse is not only a matter of the power of this or that person, or group, or society, but of the socializing power of language. It can be homicidal.

To assume responsibility is always to assume it before the possibility that we cannot assume responsibility: I talked about this problem in "But 4" the day before I read the first of these newspaper articles. We are, that is, more than responsible—responsible even for our inability to respond. That makes for always awkward, sometimes monstrous, and never quite 'correct' responses. We have no others.

August 13, 1988

On May 26, 1942 de Man writes—under the title "Universalisme de Goethe," a discussion of Goethe's *Wahlverwandtschaften*—several sentences which are not written by an ideologue, a tactician in a politico-literary battle, or an accomplice of the collaborationist press, but by a *reader*. The other sentences must not be forgotten; these should be remembered as well. They concern the "strange interlude" in the middle of the novel, in the early chapters of the second section, during which "absolutely nothing happens which would advance the development of the drama." I translate de Man's comments: "There has been a great deal of discusssion about the appropriateness of these pages, which seem unbearably long to some. And yet, they constitute one of the most alluring and original parts of the whole work. (. . .) It seems, though, that their principal *raison d'être* is the introduction into the novel of the factor time, of the *duration* of events. Reality never presents itself as an uninterrupted movement towards a dénouement: it marks the stopping times (*temps d'arrêt*) during which, under the empire of inertia or human automatism, entirely eventless periods unroll their monotonous uniformity. A narrative which aims to produce the real rhythm of existence must insert such epochs. Several recent authors have done this quite well: think of André Gide in *L'Immoraliste*, Charles Morgan in *The Fountain*, E. Hemingway in *A Farewell to Arms*. But the interlude in the *Wahlverwandtschaften* is certainly one of the most successful attempts of this kind."

The interlude in the *Wahlverwandtschaften* is about the dead.

The Johns Hopkins University

Translated by Susan Bernstein,
Peter Burgard, Jonathan Hess,
Eva Geulen and Timothy Walters.

Documents: Public Criticisms

THOMAS KEENAN

Ce vice impuni, la lecture . . .
(Paul de Man, *Le Soir*, 22–7–41)

The advance reviews of this volume were not altogether favorable.

The publication of de Man's pro-Nazi articles [. . .] will be accompanied by comments from critics; fifty have been invited to contribute, including both those who have previously supported his work and those who have criticized it. Some have refused to contribute; one critic who was very close to de Man but asked not to be identified, commented, "I am shocked that there is a symposium. Paul must have known the Jews of Belgium were being carted away. We are discussing the butchery of the Belgian Jewish community, down to the babies. To treat this as one more item about which to have a symposium is outrageous. The people who are organizing this have lost all moral perspective; they are so much under the sway of the man they cannot bear to consider what they are doing." (Jon Wiener, *The Nation*, 9–1–88)

What is, exactly, this outrage about responses? About public, signed responses?

Paul de Man's writing in *Le Soir* and elsewhere during the German occupation of Belgium was a public act, signed with his name and exposed to the public scrutiny of reading, then and now. Some of *it* was outrageous, some of it truly *terrible*. The unidentified critic warns against the traps of this public sphere, wisely: de Man's wartime journalism cannot be engaged merely as one more item for discussion, as one more commodity for academic or journalistic consumption. To do so would be to risk reproducing precisely its reduction of public space and time to the present of a market in which selected possibilities have been fixed as necessities, where it remains only to choose from the available "solutions" to a "problem." But neither can we treat it as a pretext for an individual agony of conscience or a private friendship which asks not to be identified, in the name of a "moral perspective." We cannot hide from *this* anxiety of influence or of political contamination. Public acts demand public responses, something the well-known anonymous critic knew well, of course: the refusal to contribute to one forum is offset by the very public appearance in another, another of a highly spectacular and stereotyped kind, where even anonymity is a signature. The question is a strategic one; publication happens, even and perhaps especially to shocked refusal, and the responsibility of the one who discusses is to negotiate with that public sphere as it is presently constituted while exposing it to what it seeks to exclude, to what the shock-seeking and problem-solving newsymposium cannot dissolve. And hence to open it onto another public, a future public. Although public discussion guarantees nothing, the attempt to restrict it in the name of morality or pseudo-psychology, and to censure in advance the attempt to open some other time and place for discussion, does not aid the process of coming to terms with a past still all too close for comfort.

One of the aims of this project has been to make available for public examination, for reading and discussion, the record of Paul de Man's wartime journalism. All of the texts he is known to have published during that period have been reprinted in *Paul de Man: Wartime Journalism, 1939–1943* (Nebraska, 1988). Collected here are a number of additional, mostly public, documents of that engagement. They are arranged in a kind of chronological order, along with a few notes for background information. They are reprinted here in order to make available some of the other textual traces of the critical public in which Paul de Man wrote.

* * *

The last issue of the *Cahiers du Libre Examen* published before the German invasion, in April 1940, was titled "Etudes sur le *Totalitarisme,*" and edited by Paul de Man. Although de Man did not write anything in the issue, the table of contents was his responsibility (in the copy of this issue held at the Bibliothèque Royale Albert I in Brussels, the italicized words are added in pencil to the right margin):

Sommaire

L'état totalitaire.	B. Weinberg.	*juif*
L'état totalitaire et l'économie.	B. Gourary.	"
Totalitarisme.	A. Abel.	"
La dictature du prolétariat.	A. Legrève.	

Notes

L'économie de guerre.	P. Hiernaux.	
Livres ignorés, livres méconnus.	Y. Livchitz.	*idem*
Politique extérieure.	G. Jaeger.	*idem*
Evolution du cinéma américain.	J. Kupissonoff.	*idem*

* * *

In the September 1941 issue of *L'Etudiant* (no. 3), a four-page, mimeographed, clandestine "organe des Etudiants Socialistes Unifiés" (probably in Brussels), the following unsigned article appeared on the back page.

Guignol à l'U.L.B.

Sur 2.800 étudiants, ils sont quatre! Quatre qui larbineusement lèchent les bottes fridolines: "Vous seuls êtes la lumière, vous seuls sauverez nos âmes, vous seuls apportez de progrès—Jadis nous étions jeunes, aveuglés, trompés intoxiqués; aujourd'hui disciples de Rosenberg et du grand Céline nous nous détachons superbement de la puante bassesse galeuse des lâches charoguards d'une Université de youtres et de métèques."

Quatre! sur 2.800 qui ont si magnifique opinion d'eux-même qu'il leur arrive d'écrire que la sagesse semble ramener la jeunesse universitaire à des conceptions justes et grandioses des réalités en marche.

Quatre! De Ligne, De Man, Fonsny, Barthélemy.

The four are treated in order, with particular reference to prewar political struggles in the Cercle du Libre Examen and ESU at the ULB. After de Ligne, the paragraph about Paul de Man reads:

De Man (Paul) fébrile, inquiet, l'oeil plus haggard que jamais, chercha au lendemain de la guerre son oncle, et ramena de l'entrevue une opinion politique, la croire éternelle serait augurer présomptueusement de la constance de De Man (Henri).

After treating Fonsny and Barthélemy, the article concludes:

Mais pour nous Etudiants Socialistes Unifiés, la triste nomenclature faite ci-dessus n'est pas vide de sens politique—Rappelons nous que les quatre pantins furent parmi les farouches protagonistes des campagnes menées jadis contre notre cercle et contre nos membres. Rappelons que Fonsny et De man furent tous deux membres du Comité de direction du déjà ex cercle des étudiants socialistes base de la scission des forces socialistes de l'Université; que De Ligne était président du Libre-Examen lorsqu'une grande partie de nos camarades fut exclue dudit cercle et que Barthélemy ne travailla au Libre Examen qu'à la condition de notre expulsion.

Rappelons aussi que ses campagnes se déclenchérent sur la thème de notre sympathie (?) pour les états totalitaires et [two words unreadable] . . . . . .

This article was echoed three years later, just after the liberation of Brussels, by another article in *Debout,* the journal of the "unified socialist students" (communists) at the Université Libre de Bruxelles (reprinted below). Edouard Colinet's contribution to the present volume clarifies helpfully some of the stakes of these articles.

* * *

In March of 1942, the poet, critic, and already longtime resistant Jean Lescure founded, or more precisely re-activated, the review *Messages* in Paris. It was intended as an alternative to the *Nouvelle Revue Française,* the primary literary review in Paris which since December 1940 had been in the control of Drieu la Rochelle and hence in the service of the occupant. Because the

German authorities had not yet imposed censorship rules in the occupied (northern) zone of France, *Messages* was initially free to publish those who could not, or did not want to, publish in the *NRF*. (The only restriction was the degree of risk the editors and writers were willing to run.) Gerhard Heller, the German lieutenant responsible for literary propaganda in Paris, called *Messages* "une sorte d'anti-*NRF*" (*Un Allemand à Paris 1940–1944* [Paris: Seuil, 1981], 99). Gérard Loiseaux writes that *Messages*—"dont l'audace et la qualité sont bien méconnus aujourd'hui"—"la revue créée à Paris par Jean Lescure, occupe une place unique dans la littérature du Refus. Ce fut la seule revue publiée 'légalement' à Paris et qui brocardait avec brio les écrivains collaborateurs" (*La Littérature de la Défaite et de la Collaboration* [Paris: Publications de la Sorbonne, 1984], pp.115, 503; see also: Wolfgang Babilas, "Der literarische Widerstand," in Karl Kohut, ed., *Literatur der Résistance und Kollaboration in Frankreich* [Wiesbaden: Akademische Verlagsgesellschaft Athenaion, 1982], 73 and n. 368, and Jean Lescure, *Un Eté avec Bachelard* [Paris: Luneau-Ascot, 1983], 19–29, 251, 276–279). Some details of the contents of *Messages*' first issues can be found in the present volume's Chronology.

On 27 April 1942 the German authorities instituted a requirement that publications be submitted to the Propaganda Abteilung in advance, on the pretext of paper shortages; *Messages* was able to print its second and third issues on available paper stocks and with false dates. This could not be done forever, though, and apparently the issues were already attracting the attention of the occupant in Paris. Paul de Man reviewed the first two issues in *Le Soir* (14–7–42), and remarked of them, as representing "l'actuelle poésie française," that "nous ne pourrons que regretter que quelques-uns, avec une dangereuse légèreté, ont cru nécessaire de jeter la pierre à ceux qui en constituent les véritables initiateurs." As a result of the "attaques inconsidérées contre des forces saines" by the authorities of the "révolution totalitaire" in Paris, as de Man put it, the fourth issue could not be printed in Paris; Jean Lescure says it was "interdit" because it was "nettement résistant." According to Georges Lambrichs, who was both a very close friend of Paul de Man from the Université Libre de Bruxelles and the Belgian *correspondant* for Lescure's journal, the next issue was able to appear at the end of 1942 thanks to de Man:

Il m'a en effet aidé à publier—il dirigeait une agence de distribution du livre, à l'époque—et moi j'avais la possibilité de reprendre un numéro spécial de *Messages,* sous le titre de "L'exercice du Silence." *Messages* était dirigé à Paris par mon ami Jean Lescure. Ce numéro n'avait pas reçu l'autorisation de la censure allemande. Je me suis chargé de le faire publier à Bruxelles. C'est le point précis où Paul de Man m'a aidé avec amitié et désintéressement. [Letter to Neil Hertz, 28–3–88]

Lambrichs brought the issue from Lescure to Brussels, and asked de Man if he would publish it through the Agence Dechenne. According to Lambrichs, de Man immediately agreed. The issue, titled *Exercice du silence,* was published in Brussels by "Librarie du Centre, Jean Annotiau, éditeur," bearing the date 10 December 1942. It was very well received, as contemporary articles in the so-called "littérature de refus" attest:

Quand une revue ne peut plus s'appeler revue on dit d'elle: 'un témoignage collectif.' Il nous vient de Bruxelles et non plus de Paris, ce témoignage qui est un autre 'Message,' intitule 'Exercice du silence.' Très peu d'exemplaires sont entrés en France, et de cette rareté il faut parler: elle témoigne de l'opiniâtreté dans l'espoir et dans le travail de notre camarade Jean Lescure. Louons ici le courage et la ténacité. Mais aussi la qualité du recueil. [. . .].

(Pierre Seghers, "Revue des revues: *Messages,*" *Poésie* 43 [Villeneuve-lès-Avignon] 13, March-April 1943, 99–100; see also other contemporary reactions in: Auguste Angles, "Les Cahiers de Messages," *Confluences* [Lyon] 26, November 1943, 652–655, and Jean Tortel, "Revue des revues," *Cahiers du Sud* [Marseille] 256, May 1943, 403–407.)

Two groups, however, disagreed, for very different reasons. The few surrealists remaining in Paris, a group loyal to Breton and of Trotskyist orientation called "La Main à Plume," had earlier tried to join forces with *Messages* but given up the idea after a dispute over the eclectic, non-doctrinaire character of the journal. On 1 May 1943, La Main à Plume published an incendiary tract titled *Nom de Dieu!,* excoriating Lescure and *Exercice du silence,* which had included work by the group's former member Raoul Ubac and by Breton's legendary opponent Georges Bataille, for its quasi-religiosity (*Messages* becomes *La Messe à tous les âges*) and abandonment of surrealism, in strongly political terms. Because *Nom de Dieu!* has been reprinted elsewhere, here is simply an exemplary passage:

[. . .] *Messages* veut remplacer le surréalisme. Voilà. Bien entendu, tout en retenant-du-surréalisme-ce-qu'il-a-de-valable, et patati et patata . . . Ce projet n'est pas quelque chose de bien grave, nous en tombons d'accord. Autant vouloir remplacer l'amour: le surréalisme—qui a changé, change et changera—est dorénavant lié à l'aventure humaine, à l'entreprise humaine. D'ailleurs à voir *Messages,* le surréalisme ne nous semble remplaçable que par de vieilles lunes, la vieille lune idéaliste par exemple.

Mais il y a confusion. Il n'a pas de confusion pour nous: nos signatures ci-bas en font foi. [. . .] La pire des confusions sur lesquelles *Messages* repose est celle-ci: *Messages* ne doit rien aux circonstances, *Messages* aurait été *Messages* en tous temps, *Messages* sera *Messages* après la guerre; [. . .]. Il faut principalement dénoncer cet abus des circonstances, cet abus tactique. *Messages* compte sur les circonstances pour prendre pied, telle est la seule tactique à laquelle il se livre. Le reste provient de l'esprit de son clergé, et non d'une stratégie qui, tout en étant peu dangereuse, serait condamnable. (L'activité de la Main à Plume suffit à renverser l'argument d'Ubac selon laquelle "l'esprit volontairement éclectique dont témoigne *Messages* est le seul souhaitable actuellement.")

(For full details of this battle, and *Nom de Dieu!*, as well as for the best available treatment of the Paris literary avant-garde under the occupation, see: Michel Fauré, *Histoire du surréalisme sous l'Occupation* [Paris: Table Ronde, 1982], 107–108, 132–134, 193–243, 296, 308–310, esp. pp.196 and 224–225. See also: José Pierre, *Tracts Surréalistes et Déclarations Collectives 1922–1969*, t.2: 1940–1969 [Paris: Le terrain vague, 1982], xi-xv, 9–10, 299–306.)

The issue was also not well received among the extreme right-wing literary journalists of Brussels at the weekly newspaper *Cassandre*. Although the earlier issues of *Messages* had been positively reviewed (12 July and 16 August 1942), *Exercice du silence* was attacked there in perhaps even more explicitly political terms than those of the surrealists, just a month after its printing date, in two short articles signed pseudonymously and typical (according to its contributor Robert Poulet) of "le genre *Cassandre*." They were probably written, says Poulet, by Gaston Derycke, at the request of Paul Colin.

ICI, IL Y A DES PIEGES A LOUP . . .
Petite chronique du travail du chapeau

Il vient de paraître à Bruxelles une nouvelle revue, une revue surréaliste—car il paraît que le temps n'est encore passé de ces jeux. Elle s'intitule *Exercice de silence*. Ne vous y fiez pas! Car le bavardage le plus déliquescent se donne libre cours tout au long de ces cent pages bien tassées.

Voici en quels termes un M. J.L. présente la nouvelle revue:

"Les révolutions se sont accumulées sur les révolutions, pour que, dérisoirement, l'homme, accumulant au plus profond de soi les monstres de sa honte, ne survive qu'il ne s'affuble des masques divers de ses fonctions. Une énorme avidité de se rasseoir sur ses biens l'enferme dans les positions qui lui paraissent les plus imprenables—défendues qu'elles sont par une société policée—le pétrifie en des statues qu'il imagine toujours plus insécables. . ."

Vous voyez bien de quoi il s'agit? Oui? Vous avez bien de la chance. . .

"Il faut rallumer le cerceau de feu et la rumeur du silence" dit en-

core M. J.L., qui n'en s'en fait fichtre pas faute . . . Car il y en a ainsi pendant des pages et des pages et l'on ne peut évidemment songer à tout citer.

Côté poésie, ce n'est pas mal non plus. Exemple (signé Georges Lambrichs):

"J'aimais le lit en elle dans la mesure où nous sommes attachés vertueusement au règne du morceau de bois, du quarteron de papier, de l'enveloppe de soie ou de chair, au règne des musées, des bibliothèques, des édicules" (sic).

Mais laissons nos poètes à leur curieux "exercice du silence," et au "règne des edicules." Chacun prend son plaisir où il peut, comme disait l'autre. . .

LE BRACONNIER DE SERVICE

This appeared in *Cassandre*, 17 January 1943, p.4. The second article followed a week later:

Quand le silence n'est plus d'or. . .

Alors que le papier se fait de plus en plus rare, on en trouve encore pour éditer des revues surréalistes . . . C'est comme on a l'honneur de vous le dire: il vient d'en paraître une nouvelle, à Bruxelles, sous le titre qu'on voudrait humoristique d'*Exercice du silence* (cent pages, vingt noms au sommaire, parmi lesquels ceux de . . . Baudelaire et de Jean-Paul Sartre, dont on se demande vraiment ce qu'ils viennent faire dans ce bachot).

Admettons. Il y a peut-être des gens que ces jeux amusent encore. On leur recommande tout particulièrement la préface de cet ensemble de poèmes et de proses également illisibles, signée J.L., et dont le "Braconnier de service" de *Cassandre* citait, il y a huit jours, quelques passages spécialement joyeux.

Mais la dite préface, pour qui sait lire entre les lignes et ne se laisse pas rebuter dès l'abord par ce jargon de primaire en délire, contient aussi certaines allusions et insinuations assez transparentes. Invoquant Pascal (!), son auteur parle à mots couverts (oh combien!) d'"Inquisition," de la nécessité de parler malgré les "persécutions" (?), de la Société, "fléau de la vérité," etc., etc. On a compris.

"Jamais les saints ne se sont tus" dit fièrement, après l'auteur des *Provinciales* (Pascal surréaliste, vous vous rendez compte!), le préfacier plus ou moins anonyme d'*Exercice du silence*. Après quoi ses collaborateurs y vont de leur petite logomachie absconse.

On "résiste" comme on peut. . .

REMUS

(In the "Carnet littéraire," *Cassandre*, 24 January 1943, p.5.)

These public attacks—in a newspaper known for its talent at political denunciation, and in terms as damaging as "resistance"—had an impact almost immediately, according to Lambrichs: he was fired from the Agence Dechenne, without being told why, but he understood that it was because of his role in publishing *Exercice du silence*. And soon after that Paul de Man lost his job there as well, for the same reason.

Lambrichs' recollection finds its confirmation in a surprisingly public place. In the spring of 1943, the French poet and editor Pierre Seghers, publisher of *Poésie 40* etc. and spiritual father of the "poètes de la résistance," visited Brussels to see his literary friends there. He wrote about the trip in the next issue of *Poésie 43*, in a long article of which the relevant parts are as follows:

Signaux de Belgique

[. . .] A Bruxelles, comme à Paris, les nuits de black-out ont un goût d'aventure. Les tramways belges, célèbres dans le monde entier, glissent rapides et silencieux: une lumière bleu apparaît, s'avance, grossit, et nous partons. 'Nous allons retouver la Toison d'Or!' dit Marcel Lecomte. La Toison d'Or, le café le plus littéraire de Bruxelles, qu'il ne faut pas confondre avec la maison d'éditions du même nom. Paul Colinet, Ed. Vandercammen, Roger Verheyen, d'autres amis nous attendent. [. . .] Pour nos amis, par manque d'information, la poésie française contemporaine s'arrête à Patrice de la Tour du Pin et aux Elégies de Pierre Emmanuel. Cela remont à 1939. Je parle à tous du 'Crève-Cœur' d'Aragon; 'les Yeux d'Elsa,' 'Brocéliande' n'ont pas été distribués en Belgique. Je parle de Poésie et Vérité 1943, de Paul Eluard, également non-diffusés. [. . .] J'affirme que la France existe. [. . .] C'est Georges Lambrichs qui me montrera le prochain sommaire du No. 5 de 'Messages,' sommaire à vous faire pâlir d'envie. [. . .].

After the signature (P.S.) is found this post-scriptum:

BRUXELLES.—Une révolution de palais a évincé de la direction de certaines éditions Georges Lambrichs et Paul de Man qui défendaient la jeune littérature française.

(*Poésie 43* [Villeneuve-lès-Avignon] 14, May-June 1943, 93–95; see also Pierre Seghers, *La Résistance et ces poètes* [Paris: Seghers, 1974], 260.)

* * *

Perhaps the café of which Seghers speaks is the one in which the Flemish author Paul Willems thinks he met Paul de Man. What follows are some excerpts from a long letter, dated 28 June 1988, in which Paul Willems reflects on Paul de Man's activities under the occupation:

[. . .] Je ne connais pas ces écrits, mais je serais étonné qu'on y trouve "de quoi fouetter un chat," au point de vue politique, et je serais tout aussi étonné d'apprendre qu'il ait été coupable d'actes as-sez graves pour qu'au nom de ces actes, on condamne *aujourd'hui* ses écrits d'après guerre. Je l'ai vu souvent en 1941 et 1942, moins souvent après (sans qu'il y ait de raisons à ceci). Ma femme et moi allions passer la soirée chez lui, il venait chez nous, à Bruxelles. Ces soirées n'avaient rien de réunions littéraires. Nous nous rencontrons pour le plaisir de la conversation. Il était à cette époque très jeune (je n'ai jamais su son âge) et parraissait plus jeune encore qu'il ne l'était réellement. Il avait tout de l'adolescent super-doué et cette jeunesse lui donnait un attrait irrésistible. Sa femme Anne assistait à ces réunions. (Vous n'ignorez pas qu'elle lui avait donné trois fils. Elle est partie avec ces trois enfants en Amérique du Sud, en même temps—je crois—que Paul de Man aux Etats-Unis.) Sauf elle et ma femme, personne d'autre n'assistait je crois, à ces réunions. Quoiqu'il en soit, ma femme et moi n'en avons pas le souvenir. Tout cela se passait, n'oubliez pas, il y a plus de quarante ans. [. . .]

Paul était donc très brilliant, très intelligent, très jeune, et comme tous les "adolescents prolongés," il aimait le risque total des idées et se penchait sur les gouffres métaphysiques en riant. Il me faisait penser à ce danseur de corde fameuse qui a frondu les chutes de Niagara sur un filin d'acier tendu entre les deux rives. Il y avait en lui cette qualité—dangereuse—des hommes très jeunes: *l'inconscience-innocence*. Au cours de nos conversations il n'a jamais abordé les questions, pourtant vitales, de l'attitude à prendre sous l'occupation, il n'a jamais rien dit, même allusivement, en faveur de la collaboration. Cela lui semblait impensable probablement, bête, médiocre. Quant à la "pensée" nazie, je suis sûr que pour lui elle *n'existait pas*.

Il faut, pour pouvoir comprendre cette attitude, ou plutôt ce comportement, se souvenir de la situation en 1940, et particulièrement de la situation de la Belgique. Vous connaissez sans doute les grandes lignes de l'histoire de ce pays. Depuis des siècles, la Belgique a été le champ de bataille des grands puissances, et les victoires ou les défaites qui ont eu lieu sur son territoire ont été les défaites ou les victoires des autres. Nous avons appartenu tour à tour à l'Espagne, l'Autriche, la France, les Pays-Bas. Deux fois depuis 1830, date de notre indépendance, nous avons été occupés par les Allemands et, à chaque fois, nous avons vécu pendant 4 ans sans gouvernement, c'est-à-dire sans référence politique. (Notre gouvernement était exilé en France lors de la guerre de 14, et en Angleterre lors de la dernière guerre.) La population belge s'est repliée sur elle-même. Chacun a du trouver en lui-même, seul, où était son devoir. Dans l'ensemble le comportement des Belges a été digne. La "collaboration" a été même moins importante que dans d'autres pays occupés. Le roi des Belges Leopold III, ne s'est pas exilé, voulant, a-t-il dit, partager le sort de la population. Le fait de sa présence en Belgique a évité une prise de pouvoir politique nazie. L'occupation allemande est restée militaire. Nous n'avons pas eu chez nous l'horreur d'une "Zivilverwaltung." (Toutefois cela n'a pas empeché l'inhumaine déportation des Juifs.)

Imaginez à présent le désarroi profond, total de toute la population dès l'juillet 1940. Imaginez spécialement le désarroi d'un jeune intellectuel comme Paul de Man qui se trouve soudain devant la question "Que faire?" Comme presque tous les Belges il a pris une position de retrait—non pas "attentiste"—mais de retrait devant le vide politique du pays. De la Belgique il ne restait qu'un chaos: l'armée belge défaite en 18 jours, nos gouvernants en fuite et divisés, la France vaincue, les Anglais se rembarquant à Dunkirke et se retirant dans leur île, les Etats-Unis ne prenant pas encore position. Déjà, en 1939, il y avait eu la première grande désillusion: l'U.R.S.S. pactisait avec les Nazis! J'ai vécu ce bouleversement. Il est peut-être difficile pour un Américain, citoyen d'un grand pays qui *fait lui-même son destin* et dont chaque citoyen se sent engagé de comprendre la mentalité des citoyens d'un petit pays comme la Belgique dont la destinée est décidée par ses grands voisins. Je crois qu'un citoyen Belge n'a pas—ou rarement—l'impression d'avoir un drapeau à défendre. Ses attachements sont ailleurs. Il a un amour très individualiste de la liberté, et cette liberté il la défend lui-même comme il peut. Je crois que Paul de Man a agi de même. Il a resté fidèle à ce qu'il aimait: la littérature, et la philosophie. Fidèle aussi à une certaine pensée, une certain conception de l'homme. Et cette pensée n'était certainement pas la "pensée" nazie qui était brutale et bête. Je n'ai pas lu les articles que Paul de Man a écrit pendant la guerre, mais je mettrais mon main au feu que je n'y trouverais rien de condamnable. Et s'il en était autrement j'en serais fort triste. Et sauf qu'il a écrit des choses criminelles comme des dénonciations ou des attaques contre les Juifs—ce qui me parait impossible—si j'étais membre d'un jury je l'acquitterais, vu la situation de la Belgique sous l'occupation. Croyez-vous qu'il est juste de condamner un homme et une oeuvre pour une erreur (éventuelle) de jeunesse?

[. . .] Tout ceci n'est pas une réponse à vos questions, mais je n'ai pu m'empêcher de donner un témoignage moral pour un homme que j'ai connu et apprecié. Je suis profondement persuadé que tout jugement concernant l'attitude d'un homme en un temps d'exception doit tenir compte du contexte social et politique dans lequel il a vécu.

[. . .] Comment ai-je connu Paul de Man? Je ne me souviens pas. Peut-être l'ai-je rencontré dans un café de la Porte Louise à Bruxelles où se rencontraient parfois—de façon occasionnelle—des écrivains comme Georges Lambrichs, Colinet, Lecomte, et peut-être André Souris et Goemans. Je sais que Paul de Man voyait beaucoup Lambrichs. Ils travaillaient d'ailleurs tous deux à l'Agence Dechenne, mais je ne sais pas ce qu'ils y faisaient.

Avant la guerre la vie littéraire n'était pas fort active à Bruxelles, sauf le groupe surréaliste. L'activité était fort centrée sur Paris. Les bons écrivains y étaient édités. Il n'y avait donc pas de vie littéraire très structurée, et ce qu'il y avait a éclaté en 40. La jeune génération s'est groupée par affinité. [. . .] Il me semble que Paul de Man et Lambrichs voyaient le groupe dont je parle ci-dessus et qu'ils étaient plus au moins interessés par le néo-surréalisme. Leur dieu était Paulhan (N.R.F. Gallimard, à Paris).

[. . .] Je ne sais pas pourquoi il a cessé d'écrire et je n'en ai jamais discuté avec lui. Je crois qu'il considérait ces travaux comme purement alimentaires. En dehors de ces travaux-là je crois qu'il lisait énormément la littérature et la philosophie, mais uniquement les tendances qu'il aimait ou qui l'interessaient. [. . .] Je crois la publication d'*Exercice du silence* de Lambrichs a été encouragée et rendu possible par Paul de Man. [. . .] Si P. d. Man a défendu la jeune littérature française c'est *certainement* la littérature qu'il aimait et celle que défendait Lambrichs: la littérature soutenue et encouragée notamment par Paulhan.

[. . .]
Croyez moi bien cordialement votre,

Paul Willems

* * *

L'Insoumis was a clandestine resistance newspaper, founded in March 1941 at Braine-le-Comte. According to the dossier in the Fonds Union Nationale de la Presse Clandestine, at CREHSGM in Brussels, about 600–700 issues were mimeographed monthly from March 1941 through March 1943; starting in May 1943, issues were printed, in quantities of several thousand. After October 1943, the group transformed itself into a "mouvement d'action et résistance," and took on other projects such as sabotage, intelligence gathering, aid to downed fliers and Jews in hiding, as well as "stigmatisation des traîtres et collaborateurs (publication de la 'Galerie des traitres du "Soir" volé')."

This latter publication—titled "*Galerie des Traitres*, 1ère série, Dans l'antre du SOIR-ERZATZ," and "Edité par L'INSOUMIS à destination de tous les vrais Belges"—was probably published in the fall of 1943, although it bears no date. It is a thirty-two page, pocket-sized booklet, printed on glossy paper, devoted entirely to the denunciation of forty-four editors and writers for *Le Soir (volé),* including Paul de Man. It includes photographs of most of the 44 people named and brief commentaries on all of them, generally with birth date and address. Its preface reads:

L'Insoumis qui s'est imposé la mission de dénoncer et de pourchasser les traîtres, est parvenu à pénétrer dans le repaire des kollaborateurs du Soir-ersatz.

C'est avec joie que nous offrons à nos lecteurs la bobine de tous ces tristes individus, qui pour quelques deniers, se sont sciemment mis au service de l'ennemi.

Amis lecteurs, regardez ces têtes! Le vice ce lit sur la face de ces tarés. . .

Tout commentaire nous paraît superflu.

Le crime de ces gens est connu et prouvé.

Le châtîment que nous réclamerons pour eux sera impitoyable!

Sous peu, nous ferons paraître notre second recueil, qui contiendra les photos d'autres traîtres attachés à la presse asservie et à la Gestapo.

————

In-fine:

"Un jour viendra qui tout paiera."

The entry for Paul de Man is found on the nineteenth page, next to the photograph of him that had been published on the front page of *Le Soir* (8–7–42) in an article about the "concours littéraire" he was then conducting for the newspaper. The public "stigmatisation" reads:

DEMAN, Paul. Domicilié à Bruxelles, rue du Musée, 10. Correspondant du SOIR de De Becker. Neveu et filleul de Henri Deman. Cet individu sait de qui tenir. A été placé au SOIR par son parrain et grâce à sa propagande effrénée est parvenu à y rester.

Note that the address given is that of Editions de la Toison d'Or (see Chronology), and that de Man is described as a "correspondant," not a "redacteur," the title applied to almost all the others listed. He had stopped writing for *Le Soir* the previous year. The entry for Louis Fonsny, another former libre-examenist and literary-political critic for *Le Soir,* who had been shot and killed at a Brussels tram stop by resistant Jean Coppens in January 1943, ends with the declaration: "Abbatu! Justice est faite!"

* * *

Three days after the liberation of Brussels, on 6 September 1944, the first legal issue of the bi-monthly *Debout,* "Organe de la Fédération Bruxelloise des Etudiants Socialistes Unifiés" at the ULB, carried the following unsigned article on the third of its four pages. It echoes the September 1941 text in the ESU's *L'Etudiant.*

Et voici, l'"élite" de l'U.L.B.

Vous ne connaissez pas l'élite des étudiants de l'U.L.B.? Vous ne connaissez pas les purs défenseurs du Libre-Examen? Ils l'ont défendu pendant l'occupation, eux. Et pas pour rire. Pas à moitié comme vous et nous. Eux, leur canard n'était pas un pauvre format de papier jauni, mal ronéotypé, qui se vendait sous le manteau.

Eux, ils ont défendu le libre-examen de concert avec le Gestapo, avec la petite torture caline pour ceux qui ne pensaient pas fasciste, de concert avec Rex, avec le V.N.V., avec De Vlag. . . Pour eux, le paradis c'était six billets (grand format) par mois et un ravitaillement inépuisable. Oh, vous pouvez être sur qu'ils ont fui ou qu'ils se sont terré. Mais nous saurons les retrouver où qu'ils aillent et quoiqu'ils fassent!

Mais sans doute désirez-vous qu'on vous parle un peu de ces messieurs. Une ultime fois. Avant de laisser leur noms tomber dans l'oubli méprisant. Notre organe national *L'Etudiant* a en son temps, déjà publié une biographie de ces tristes sires qui ont pu échapper aux patriotes grâce à la protection allemand. Ils ne perdent rien pour attendre.

Short "biographies" follow of Pierre de Ligne, Paul de Man, Jean Barthelemy, Emile Lecerf, Yvan Dailly, Lucien Rama, and "feu Louis Fonsny." Paul de Man's reads as follows:

PAUL DE MAN—neveu d'Henri. Chef des de Mannistes (évidemment) de l'Université. Introduit par son très cher oncle au soi-disant *Soir* de Schranen-de Becker, il dissèque les romans et essais en de chroniques littéraires aussi peu lisibles que celles qu'il écrivait dans les Cahiers du Libre Examen. Au bout d'un moment, il sent que cela tourne mal et il fait un retraite très prudente. Son nom ne paraît plus dans les colonnes du soi-disant *Soir.* Sa pauvre petite carcasse de petit homme blond et malingre, à la mèche à Hitler, déserte la place de Louvain. Mais en compensation, le neveu d'Henri reçoit de ses amis fascists un poste de rédacteur à la "Belgapresse."

The article concludes:

Camarades, comparez avec l'attitude d'un Mardulyn, d'un Clérin, d'un Fraiteur, d'un Leten, d'un Brunfaut et nous en passons tous arrêtés ou tués par les nazis, de nos camarades engagés dans le F.I. et les Partisans, enrôlés dans l'armée belge de Londres. Comparez. . . il vaut mieux se taire pour étouffer son indignation.

Notes: according to friends, PDM was not the "chef des de Mannists" at the ULB; *Le Soir*'s offices are at the Place de Louvain in Brussels; and "Belgapresse" seems to be a mistake for the Agence Dechenne.

* * *

According to those who knew him at the time, including his first wife Anne Baraghian Ipsen, in May 1945 Paul de Man was called in for questioning about his activities during the occupation. He appeared for one day before representatives of the *Auditeur général,* the Belgian state prosecutor charged with investigating and trying cases of collaboration, at the Palais de

Justice in Antwerp, and was not charged with any crime for his behavior during the war. In Brussels, some months later, twenty-eight editors and correspondants for *Le Soir (volé)* were charged by the Auditeur there with criminal behavior as a result of their journalistic activities. According to the office of the Auditorat Général in Brussels, a search of the files has not yet revealed any record of Paul de Man's interrogation.

> Auditorat Général, près la Cour Militaire
> 2e Bureau A
> Réf.: DIV. 2/88
> 1000 Bruxelles, le 23 juin 1988
> Palais de Justice

M. le Directeur,

Me référant à votre lettre du 20 juin 1988 [. . .], j'ai l'honneur de vous faire savoir qu'il est possible, et même certain, que Paul De Man a été interrogé en 1945 à Anvers où il habitait à l'époque, au sujet de son activité journalistique, puisqu'il collabora au "Soir volé" et au journal "Het Vlaamsche Land," pendant un court lapse de temps.

Il est tout à fait normal que mon office n'est pas était informé des dizaines de milliers d'interrogatoires auxquels fut procedé en 1945 et 1946.

Un fait est cependant incontestable: Paul De Man n'a pas fait l'objet de poursuites devant le Conseil de guerre pour son attitude ou son activité pendant la guerre.

Veuillez agregé, monsieur le Directeur, l'assurance de ma consideration très distingueé.

> [signed]
> L'Auditeur général

à M. J. Vanwelkenhuyzen, Directeur du Centre de Recherches et d'Etudes Historiques de la Seconde Guerre Mondiale,
Place de Louvain 4, boîte 19,
1000 Bruxelles

* * *

Paul de Man came to Boston in the fall of 1951 to teach languages at the Berlitz school there, after holding a post as Instructor in French for the previous two years at Bard College in Annandale-on-Hudson, N.Y. He saw members of the Comparative Literature department informally that year and was admitted to the graduate program the following fall. He completed two years of graduate study in Comparative Literature and received his M.A. in 1954, and in September of that year he was appointed a Junior Fellow in Harvard's Society of Fellows.

In Janaury 1955, planning to go abroad to begin research for his dissertation, de Man sought a new Belgian passport. Apparently as a result, information about his wartime writing for *Le Soir* and his postwar work at Editions Hermès, as well as other matters, was communicated to the Society of Fellows, and de Man was asked to explain himself. As far as I have been able to determine, this is the only *public* document dating from after his arrival in the United States in which Paul de Man discussed his activities during the occupation. Although it deals with other matters as well, and raises some further questions, it is printed in full here, without commentary, to conclude this collection of documents.

Harvard University   Boston, January 26th 1955
Cambridge, Massachusetts   30 McLean Street

Dear Professor Poggioli:

I understand that, following my application for a passport to go abroad, the Society of Fellows has received information of a highly derogatory nature regarding my past history. I gladly take the opportunity which is given me to clarify and to explain my situation. The matters that have arisen seem to fall under the following headings:

(1) modalities of my admission at Harvard and of my election to the Society

(2) conditions under which I entered this country and my present status with the Department of Immigration

(3) my political past, particularly under the German occupation

(4) legal charges brought against me as a result of the liquidation of a publishing-firm to which I was attached.

I will deal with these matters in this order.

(1) I was admitted to the Graduate School of Arts and Sciences Department of Comparative Literature by Professor Poggioli in September 1952. During the previous year, I had had informal contacts with Professor Levin and during the Spring I decided, on my own initiative, to apply for admission. My admission was based on the following data:

(a) an undergraduate degree in Chemical Science from the University of Brussels from 1940

(b) references from colleagues at Bard College, where I taught for two years previously to coming to Boston, in particular from Mr. Ted Weiss and Joseph Summers, now at the University of Connecticut

(c) a literary paper which I had given to Prof. Levin and which he had passed on to Prof. Poggioli, a first draft, in fact, of the very project on which I am working now.

In my application, I pointed out that there had been a change in my academic career from science to the humanities, and I stated my continuous interest in literary problems, as it appeared from writing I had done, from the courses I taught at Bard, etc. I never invoked any other titles or documents; I did not claim any graduate credits and did not apply for the scholarship that I sorely needed, estimating that, since nobody at Harvard knew me well, I first had to prove myself. The financial strain of having to pay tuition and support my family without any outside help was extremely hard. Throughout my two years as a graduate student, I earned a living by teaching languages at the Berlitz School, by translations, readings for a publisher, etc. In my second year, a teaching fellowship eased the financial burden somewhat, though not that of overwork.

Professor Poggioli admitted me "on trial," precisely because there had been a shift in my field of study and also because my application came in quite late. That term, I could only afford to take two courses and the Graduate School does not allow students admitted on trial to take less than a full load. I pointed this out to Professor Poggioli, who was kind enough to remove this stipulation.

The rest of my career in the Graduate School and my admission to the Society is a matter of record known to the Senior Fellows.

In connection with this, I hear that I have been charged with misrepresentation by calling myself "professeur." I did indeed use this term under the heading "profession" on my passport application, for absolutely no other reason than that it seemed the simplest way to describe my situation. In that context, the word "professeur" does not mean at all that I would hold this rank in a university, but simply that I earn a living by teaching. I had nothing to gain by calling myself that way and no confusion was possible, since on the same blank I a so stated myself as being a Junior Fellow in the Society of Fellows.

(2) I entered the United States on a Belgian passport LA 68916/11516 with an American visa given at Antwerp. This was in May 1948. My status was that of a visitor. Being married to an American citizen, I was allowed to remain here and started naturalization proceedings, going through the normal series of hearings and investigations. When I was interviewed as a candidate for the Society, I was asked when I expected a decision and I stated my belief that it would be in 1954. On September 28th 1954, I was informed by the Department of Immigration that, in order to obtain a permanent status, I would have to exit from the U.S. and re-enter under the sponsorship of my wife. The legal term used is "voluntary departure." I wish to point out that, in order to obtain this permission which is considered a privilege, one has to establish good moral character. This means that my entire history, here and abroad, was investigated by the Immigration Service and found to be satisfactory. I foresee no difficulties in accomplishing the formalities leading to my reentry and subsequent naturalization.

(3) My father, Hendrik de Man, former Belgian Minister and Chairman of the social-democrat party, is a highly controversial political figure. Because of his attitude under the German occupation, he was sentenced in absentia after the war and died in exile in Switzerland last year. He remains an extremely debatable case and, for reasons that go to the roots of internal Belgian political problems, his name arouses extremely strong feelings at least in some Belgians, apparently still to-day.

I certainly am in no position to pass judgment on him, but I know that his mistakes were made out of a lack of machiavellism and not out of lack of devotion to his ideals. He did what he thought best for his country and his beliefs, and the final evaluation of his acts is a matter of history. One can find his own justification stated in the last two chapters of his autobiography, published last year in Germany under the title *Gegen den Strom*.

I hear now that I myself am being accused of collaboration. In 1940 and 1941 I wrote some literary articles in the newspaper "le Soir" and, like most of the other contributors, I stopped doing so when nazi thought-control did no longer allow freedom of statement. During the rest of the occupation, I did what was the duty of any decent person. After the war, everyone was subjected to a very severe examination of his political behavior, and my name was not a favorable recommendation. In order to obtain a passport, one had not merely to produce a certificate of good conduct, but also a so-called "certificat de civisme," which stated that one was cleared of any collaboration. I could not possibly have come to this country two times, with proper passport and visa, if there had been the slightest reproach against me. To accuse me now, behind my back, of collaboration, and this to persons of a different nation who can not possibly verify and appreciate the facts, is a slanderous attack which leaves me helpless.

(4) In 1945, after the war, I became co-founder, with three partners, of a publishing firm called Hermes, which specialized in the publication of art-books. I visited this country for the first time in 1947 on behalf of this firm. I left the firm in 1948, when I decided to return to the U.S., but retained the title of manager which I shared with the three others, in order to assist with whatever contacts I had made in this country. Since 1950 or 51, I have not heard from the firm. This made me assume that things were not going well but, since I had other things on my mind, I did not give it much thought. I now hear, altogether indirectly, that charges are made against me of mismanagement, forgery, etc. I have two statements to make in answer to this:

a. I have never received any notification of charges against me, although my address has always been known in France and in Belgium, where I have not ceased to correspond with several people and even to publish articles. Up to the moment when I was notified that there were restrictions against granting me a regular passport, I never knew that anything was wrong. Up to this very day, and although apparently more has been told to others than to myself, I ignore entirely of what I am accused.

b. I know, in my own conscience, that as long as I was directly connected with the firm, nothing dishonest was done by either myself or my partners. I am not only confident but eager to answer any questions I may be asked about my responsibilities in this matter; as I stated before, this is my main purpose in returning to Belgium immediately. As long as I have not done so, I can offer only this statement to the Society and ask to be given an opportunity to prove it.

I would like to conclude with two general remarks. I think that the way in which this information has been communicated to the Society was calculated, wilfully or not, to cause me a maximum of harm. It made it appear as if I was holding back information about myself which, in fact, I did not possess. It happened entirely without my knowledge, in spite of several personal conversations with the Consul, one, two weeks ago, of nearly an hour which was altogether social and friendly. Also, the content of this information is slanted such as to cause as much damage as possible. The fact that this attitude was certainly not caused by viciousness, but merely by the connotations of my name is hardly a consolation to me.

I have no illusions about the extent of the damage all this has caused me, regardless of what rebuttal I can and will offer. This sudden reflux of a past presented in such a light, when I had devoted the last seven years of my life to building an existence entirely separated from former painful experiences, leaves me weary and exhausted. The only incentive I have to face up to all this, aside of my family, is the strong desire to continue and finish my work. I am certainly in no position to ask the Society of Fellows for anything but a chance to prove the truth of what I have stated in this letter—which means, in very practical terms, the possibility to serve to the end of my first year as a Junior Fellow, letting the future depend on what will happen in Belgium.

I am very grateful for the consideration I have received and the opportunity I was given to justify myself.

Sincerely yours,

[signed]

Paul de Man

* * *

Thanks to Allan Stoekl for unearthing the story of *Nom de Dieu!*; to Georges Lambrichs for remembering the *Cassandre* articles, Andrzej Warminski for finding them, and Alain Dantoing for communicating with Georges Poulet; to Georges Lambrichs and Jean Lescure for their help with *Exercice du silence,* and Peggy Kamuf for talking with them; to Paul Willems for writing; to Myriam Abramowitz for *Galerie des Traitres*; to Frida Vandervelden and Ortwin de Graef for *Debout*; to Anne Ipsen and the others who recalled Paul de Man's appearance before the Auditeur Genéral; and especially to Pat de Man for the letter to Harvard and Chantal Kesteloot of the Centre de Recherches et d'Etudes Historiques de la Seconde Guerre Mondiale [CREHSGM] in Brussels for copies of *L'Etudiant, Galerie des Traitres,* and the Auditeur Général's letter.

Princeton University